The Law of Receivers and Administrators of Companies

AUSTRALIA
LBC Information Services
Sydney

CANADA and USA
Carswell
Toronto—Ontario

NEW ZEALAND
Brooker's
Auckland

SINGAPORE and MALAYSIA
Sweet & Maxwell Asia
Singapore and Kuala Lumpur

The Law of Receivers and Administrators of Companies

By

Sir Gavin Lightman

LL.M. (University of Michigan), LL.B. (Lond.)
*One of her Majesty's Justices and
a Bencher of Lincoln's Inn*

And

Gabriel Moss

Q.C., M.A. B.C.L. (Oxon.)
of Lincoln's Inn, barrister
Sometime Eldon Scholar in the University of Oxford

With

Richard Snowden

M.A., (Cantab.), LL.M. (Harvard)
of Lincoln's Inn, barrister

LONDON
SWEET & MAXWELL
2000

First edition 1986
Second edition 1994

Published in 2000 by
Sweet & Maxwell Limited of
100 Avenue Road, London NW3 3PF
(http://www.sweetandmaxwell.co.uk)
Typeset by Dataword Services Limited, Chilcompton
Printed in Great Britain by
MPG Books Ltd, Bodmin, Cornwall

A CIP catalogue record for this book is available from the
British Library

ISBN 0421 673702

No natural forests were destroyed to make this product,
only farmed timber was used and re-planted.

To Naomi and Judith and Kirsti

To Naomi and Judith and Kirsti

PREFACE TO THIRD EDITION

It was not long after the publication of the second edition of this work that the publisher began raising with us the question of a third. The law in the fields of receivership and administration of companies is a growth area and the task of reconsidering as well as updating the many topics covered was forbidding. In order to make this enterprise manageable, the authors decided to invite Mr Richard Snowden who had assisted them in the preparation of the second edition to become a joint editor with them of the third edition.

In this edition we have included one additional chapter on the new European Union Regulation on Insolvency and the UNCITRAL Model Law. We are heavily indebted to Professor Ian Fletcher and Mr Nick Segal as the contributors to this chapter. To make room for this addition and some elaboration of other topics, we have omitted the extracts from the Insolvency Act 1986 and the Insolvency Rules 1986, both of which are readily available elsewhere. We have made every effort to produce a complete and authoritative work, and for this purpose we have secured the contributions (large and small) from those whose expertise in the topics covered would lend weight and substance to the contents of this work. These contributions have been fully and willingly provided. Whilst it is invidious to refer to particular contributors in this respect, we are bound to acknowledge our special debts to Professor Robin Morse in respect of the chapter on Conflict of Laws and to Mr Hamish Anderson in respect of the chapter on Administration. All contributions we gratefully acknowledge in the list of contributors which follows where (so far as practicable) we indicate the chapters benefiting from their contributions. We as editors accept responsibility for any errors.

We again thank our wives Naomi, Judith and Kirsti (to whom this edition is dedicated) for patiently putting up with us when we have been detained and distracted by our work on this edition.

We have attempted to state the law as at July 28, 2000.

Sir Gavin Lightman
Gabriel Moss Q.C.
Richard Snowden

CONTRIBUTORS TO THE PREPARATION OF THE THIRD EDITION

Specific Chapters:

Chapter 2	Daniel Lightman, Barrister, Serle Court, Lincoln's Inn.
Chapters 3 & 5	Richard Nolan, Barrister, St. John's College, Cambridge and Erskine Chambers, Lincoln's Inn.
Chapter 6	Antony Zacaroli, Barrister, 3/4 South Square, Gray's Inn.
Chapter 7	Daniel Lightman, Barrister, Serle Court, Lincoln's Inn.
Chapter 9	Michael Woollard and Mark Simpson, Solicitors of Hammond Suddards Edge.
Chapter 10	David Marks, Barrister, 3/4 South Square, Gray's Inn.
Chapter 11	Lloyd Tamlyn, Barrister, 3/4 South Square, Gray's Inn.
Chapter 12	Adam Goodison, Barrister, 3/4 South Square, Gray's Inn.
Chapter 13	Philip Ridgway, Barrister of Deloitte & Touche and David Goldberg Q.C., Gray's Inn Chambers, Gray's Inn.
Chapter 14	Hilary Stonefrost, Barrister, 3/4 South Square, Gray's Inn.
Chapter 15	Sue Prevezer Q.C., Essex Court Chambers, and Paul Morgan Q.C., Falcon Chambers.
Chapter 17	Lloyd Tamlyn, Barrister, 3/4 South Square, Gray's Inn.
Chapter 18	Richard Davis, Solicitor, consultant at Masons.
Chapter 19	John Bowers Q.C., Littleton Chambers, Temple.
Chapter 20	Antony Zacaroli, Barrister, 3/4 South Square, Gray's Inn.
Chapter 21	Felicity Toube, Barrister, 3/4 South Square, Gray's Inn.
Chapter 23	Hamish Anderson, Solicitor of Norton Rose.
Chapter 24	Robin Ellison, Solicitor of Eversheds and Paul Newman, Barrister, Wilberforce Chambers, Lincoln's Inn.
Chapter 25	Professor Robin Morse, King's College, London.
Chapter 26	Professor Ian Fletcher, Queen Mary & Westfield College, University of London and 3/4 South Square, Gray's Inn and Nick Segal, Solicitor of Allen & Overy.
Generally	Richard Nolan (as above) and Daniel Bayfield, Barrister, 3/4 South Square, Gray's Inn.

CONTENTS

TABLE OF CASES

TABLE OF STATUTES

TABLE OF STATUTES
OUTSIDE THE UNITED KINGDOM

AUSTRALIA

HONG KONG

IRELAND, REPUBLIC OF

NEW ZEALAND

SINGAPORE

UNITED STATES OF AMERICA

TABLE OF STATUTORY INSTRUMENTS

TABLE OF INTERNATIONAL TREATIES AND CONVENTIONS

CHAPTER 1

RECEIVERS, ADMINISTRATIVE RECEIVERS AND ADMINISTRATORS

1. THE RECEIVER AND MANAGER

The power of the Court of Chancery to appoint a receiver to safeguard **1–001** equitable interests is centuries old.[1] By comparison, the right of a mortgagee to appoint a receiver out of court under the terms of the contract with the mortgagor is of more recent origin. Prior to the development of the concept of a floating charge in the latter part of the nineteenth century, security for a loan or other indebtedness took the form of a fixed mortgage of specific items of property. If the mortgagee went into possession of the charged property he was subject to a strict liability to account to the mortgagor both for what he had received and for what he ought to have received from the property. In order to overcome this disadvantage, mortgagees began to insist on the insertion of a provision in the mortgage giving the mortgagee the right to call upon the mortgagor to appoint a receiver of the charged property with the task of receiving any income (such as rent) produced by the assets, to apply such income to the payment of interest on the secured debt and to pay any surplus to the mortgagor. The important feature of the private appointment of receivers in this way was that they acted as agents for the mortgagor, who was solely responsible for their acts and omissions. In time the contractual powers given to receivers were extended and they were given powers to preserve, manage and sell the charged assets in the event of default by the mortgagor.[2]

This method of securing credit had two limitations. First, the fixed **1–002** charge froze and barred dealings with the property and accordingly could not be attached to assets such as stock in trade with which the borrower required to deal in the ordinary course of his business. Secondly, in the case of a charge by a business-owner, the sale of the charged assets piecemeal was likely to achieve less than a sale of the business as a going concern, for a charge over specific assets did not empower the mortgagee to sell the business as a going concern or to manage it as an interim measure pending sale.[3]

---

[1] See, *e.g. Hopkins v. Worcester & Birmingham Canal Proprietors* (1868) L.R. 6 Eq. 437 at 447, *per* Giffard V.-C. For receivers appointed by the Court see below, Chap. 22.

[2] See, *e.g.* the historical account of the development of the law and practice in relation to the appointment of receivers out of court in *Gaskell v. Gosling* [1896] 1 Q.B. 669 at 691, *per* Rigby L.J., referred to in *Medforth v. Blake* [2000] Ch. 86.

[3] A mortgage of land can confer on a mortgagee the power to carry on business on the land without charging the existing business carried on there by the mortgagor, but in this case the mortgagee cannot sell the assets of the mortgagor's business or prevent the

1–003 The concept of the floating charge was a late nineteenth century creation of equity which overcame these limitations, and reconciled the requirements of the borrower for freedom to carry on his business and of the lender to have the most ample form of security in the event of jeopardy to his repayment.[4]

> "The floating charge was invented by Victorian lawyers to enable manufacturing and trading companies to raise loan capital on debentures, offering a charge over the company's whole undertaking, without inhibiting its ability to trade."[5]

1–004 The floating charge is a form of charge over one or more classes of assets of a company which gives the company freedom to deal with the assets during the ordinary course of its business until a specified event occurs which causes the charge to "crystallise" and become a fixed charge, preventing any further dealing by the company with the charged assets. Traditionally the company granted fixed charges over assets with which it did not require to deal, and a floating charge over the remainder.[6] Such a floating charge would normally include the whole (or substantially the whole) undertaking of a company. In a case where a floating charge is granted over the undertaking, the mortgagee is given the right to carry on and sell the business of the company as a going concern. To facilitate the exercise of this right, the floating charge ordinarily gives the mortgagee the powers to appoint a receiver to receive the income and preserve the assets pending sale, and to appoint the receiver or another person as manager of the subject-matter of the floating charge, whose responsibility it is to carry on the business and sell it and the other assets charged in order to repay the mortgagee. These powers enable the mortgagee to take the management of the company's property out of the hands of the directors and entrust it to a person or persons[7] of his

---

mortgagor closing, or selling the assets and goodwill of, the business: *Atkins v. Mercantile Credit Ltd* (1985) 10 A.C.L.R. 153. A valuer in making a valuation for mortgage purposes must take this into account: *Corisand Investment Ltd v. Druce & Co.* (1978) 248 E.G. 315 at 407, 504, Gibson J.

[4] Equity had also created the concept of the floating trust in the law of mutual wills which arose on the death of the first to die and crystallised on the death of the survivor: see *Birmingham v. Renfrew* (1937) 57 C.L.R. 666 H Ct. of Australia, cited in *Re Cleaver* [1981] 1 W.L.R. 939 at 946.

[5] *Re Brightlife* [1987] Ch. 200 at 214–215, *per* Hoffmann J. Subsequent legislation meant that property subject to a floating charge was no longer regarded as belonging wholly to the debenture-holder: *Re Barleycorn* [1970] Ch. 465 at 474D, *per* Lord Denning M.R..

[6] In recent times, in spite of the fact that chargor companies naturally wish to collect in and utilise the proceeds of their book debts to finance the conduct of their business, lenders have invariably insisted that companies grant what purport to be fixed charges over their book debts in an attempt to give the lenders security which will rank in priority to the claims of preferential creditors in a liquidation. The issue of whether and if so to what extent this can validly be achieved has given rise to considerable litigation over the last 20 years: see below, Chap. 3.

[7] In the exercise of his powers, the mortgagee may appoint: (i) a receiver alone; (ii) a manager alone; (iii) different persons as receiver and manager; (iv) a single person as

choice.[8] To enable the mortgagee to avoid responsibility for the receiver's management of the undertaking, the floating charge declares the receiver to be the agent of the company, which accordingly is solely liable for his acts and defaults.[9] An appointee with the dual role of receiver and manager accordingly becomes the new managing agent of the company.[10]

Although the concept of a receiver and manager was well established **1–005** prior to 1986, the law relating to his powers and liabilities was often obscure and unsatisfactory. One of the primary aims of the Insolvency Act 1986 was to update and rationalise this area of the law. Another aim was to fill the gap in cases in which there was no person who could appoint, or who was willing to appoint, a receiver and manager to a company so as to enable its business to be sold as a going concern rather than simply being put into liquidation. These aims resulted in the creation by the 1986 Act of the new offices of the "administrative receiver" and the "administrator".

2. THE ADMINISTRATIVE RECEIVER

The most important innovation of the 1986 Act in relation to receiver- **1–006** ship was to create and to invest with a special status a particular category of receivers or managers called "administrative receivers".

According to section 29(2) of the Insolvency Act 1986 an administrative receiver is:

"(a) a receiver or manager of the whole (or substantially the whole) of a company's property appointed by or on behalf of the holders of any debentures of the company secured by a charge which, as created, was a floating charge, or by such a charge and one or more other securities; or

(b) a person who would be such a receiver or manager but for the appointment of some other person as the receiver of part of the company's property."

---

receiver and manager; or (v) a receiver with power to employ a manager. In case (v), the receiver is treated as a receiver and manager if he exercises the power of appointment, for the manager is his agent, responsible to him: see *Parsons v. Mather & Platt* (unreported, No. 392A of CA Transcripts of 1974). In practice the mortgagee normally appoints the same person as receiver and manager.

[8] *Shamji v. Johnson Matthey Bankers Ltd* [1986] F.T.L.R. 329 at 330, *per* Oliver L.J. CA.

[9] It has been suggested that "The so-called 'agency' of the receiver is not a true agency, but merely a formula for making the company, rather than the debenture-holders, liable for his acts": *per* Peter Millett Q.C. in "The Conveyancing Powers of Receivers After Liquidation" (1977) 41 Conv. (N.S.) 83 at 88. But "this agency of the receivers is a real one, even though it has some peculiar incidents": *per* Nicholls L.J. in *Re Offshore Ventilation* (1989) 5 B.C.C. 160 at 166A–66B CA; see also *Ratford v. Northavon R.D.C.* [1987] Q.B. 357, CA and *Astor Chemicals Ltd v. Synthetic Technology Ltd* [1990] B.C.L.C. 1 at 11, *per* Vinelott J.

[10] *Re Mack Trucks (Britain) Ltd* [1967] 1 All E.R. 977 at 982.

1-007 Under the first alternative in section 29(a), the requirements for classification as an administrative receiver are accordingly:

(a) the appointment as "a receiver or manager": either position is sufficient;

(b) "of the whole or substantially the whole of a company's property": this provision reflects the fact that a certain proportion of the company's property may be excluded[11] or released[12] from the charge created by the debenture or from the appointment. It is thought that the criterion of whether the subject of the receivership is of substantially the whole of a company's property is primarily value to the company[13] and that the judgment is to be made as at the date of the appointment so that the character of the office held is not altered by subsequent events, *e.g.* the disposal by the company of the excluded property or the release by the debenture-holder of charged property from the debenture.[14] Where a charge covers all of the assets of the company, present and future, and is not in form exclusively a fixed charge, the fact that the company does not have any assets, or any assets which are not the subject of a fixed charge, at the time of creation of the charge does not prevent such a charge from falling within section 29(2).[15] "Company" in this context includes corporations incorporated abroad which can be wound up as an unregistered company under Part V of the Insolvency Act 1986[16];

(c) "appointed by or on behalf of the holders of any debentures[17] of the company". Accordingly, receivers or managers appointed by the court are excluded;

(d) "secured by a charge which, as created, was a floating charge or by such a charge and one or more other securities": at least one of the charges under which the appointment is made must at the date of its creation have been a floating as opposed to a fixed charge, but the length of the period before crystallisation would seem to be irrelevant. On a literal reading of the words of the provision it might be suggested that as long as the

---

[11] Property held by the company as trustee for third parties will be excluded from the ambit of every floating charge.

[12] *e.g.* causes of action against the debenture-holder or receiver or onerous leases. But see *Scottish & Newcastle plc, Petitioners* [1993] B.C.C. 634 (Ct of Session) where the release was so extensive that the appointees were held receivers, and not administrative receivers.

[13] This would appear to be necessary if (for the purpose of the judgment to be made) like is to be compared with like.

[14] Each office has distinct legal responsibilities and privileges from inception until vacation.

[15] *Re Croftbell Ltd* [1990] B.C.L.C. 844.

[16] *Re International Bulk Commodities* [1993] Ch. 77. The reasoning in that case was questioned in *Re Devon and Somerset Farmers Ltd* [1993] B.C.C. 410 but it is suggested that it is correct. See also below, Chap. 25.

[17] A mortgage, charge or other security issued by a company is called a debenture: *Downsview Ltd v. First City Corporation* [1993] A.C. 295 at 311D–E, PC.

debenture under which the appointment is made is secured by a floating charge and one or more fixed charges, then an appointee under one or more fixed charges not appointed under the floating charge could still be an administrative receiver. This was clearly not what was intended by the legislature. The central concept of an administrative receiver involves a receiver who is appointed under a floating charge.[18] The words "or by such a charge and one or more other securities" simply provide for the usual modern situation where the debenture contains fixed as well as floating charges. It has been held that a receiver who could have been but was not appointed under a subsisting floating charge in a debenture but was appointed only under a fixed charge in the debenture could not be an administrative receiver and did not need to be qualified as such.[19]

Under the second alternative in section 29(2), an administrative receiver **1–008** will be "a person who would be such a receiver or manager but for the appointment of some other person as receiver of part of the company's property". This provision contemplates the appointment as receiver or manager of a person who would qualify under alternative (a) in section 29(2), but for the prior appointment of a receiver or receivers of a part or parts of the company's property where the part or parts in question are such that the remainder cannot fairly be regarded as substantially the whole of the company's property.

3. DISTINCTIONS BETWEEN ADMINISTRATIVE RECEIVERS AND OTHER RECEIVERS

Whether an appointee is or is not an administrative receiver is a **1–009** question of law, and neither his description in the appointment nor the parties' intention is necessarily relevant. A receiver or manager who does not fulfil the statutory conditions (*e.g.* because he is appointed over specific assets only) will fulfil the role of receiver or manager largely unaffected by the Insolvency Act 1986. To a degree, such a receiver and manager might fairly be described as a lower form of receiver or manager, for, unlike an administrative receiver:

(a) his appointment does not preclude the appointment of an administrator[20];

---

[18] *A Revised Framework of Insolvency Law*, Cmnd. 9175, p. 19; *Cork Report on Insolvency Law and Practice*, Cmnd. 8558, paras 495–498, 504, 508, 520.

[19] *Meadrealm Ltd v. Transcontinental Golf Construction Ltd* (unreported, Vinelott J., November 29, 1991). The necessary qualifications for an administrative receiver are dealt with below, Chap. 4.

[20] See below, Chap. 23.

(b) he is not, and does not enjoy the privileges and investigatory powers of, an office-holder[21];

(c) his powers are strictly limited to those conferred by the debenture and are not deemed to be extended unless the contrary intent appears[22];

(d) a person dealing with him (but not with an administrative receiver), even if acting in good faith and for value, is concerned to inquire whether the receiver is acting within his powers[23] and whether there has been any defect in his appointment, nomination or qualifications[24];

(e) he is strictly liable to third parties if he seizes or disposes of their property, notwithstanding the absence of negligence and the existence of reasonable grounds for believing (as well as actual belief) that he is entitled to seize or dispose of the property[25];

(f) the court may, on application by an administrative receiver, order that a sale be made of property free of any charge, the charge instead being made to attach to the proceeds of sale[26];

(g) there is no statutory bar on the removal and replacement of an ordinary receiver or manager by his appointor at any time[27];

(h) such receiver or manager need not be qualified to act as an insolvency practitioner in relation to the company.[28]

THE ADMINISTRATOR

1–010 Before 1986 there was no procedure by which a company in financial difficulty could obtain a temporary breathing space from its creditors to see if it could be rehabilitated or to reach a compromise or arrangement with its creditors. Further, if no person was entitled to, or was willing to, appoint a receiver and manager of the undertaking of the company, there was no mechanism by which the business and assets of the company could be realised as a going concern for the benefit of creditors. The Cork Committee[29] recommended that this gap be filled by the power of the court to appoint a judicial manager of an insolvent company and this proposal was given effect in Part II of the Insolvency Act 1986 which introduced a new concept, the administrator.

1–011 An administrator is an insolvency practitioner appointed by the court for a limited period to manage the affairs of an insolvent company, with

---

[21] See below, Chap. 5.

[22] As to the extensions of the powers of administrative receivers, see s. 42(1) and Sched. 1 to the Insolvency Act 1986.

[23] *cf.* s. 42(3) of the Insolvency Act 1986.

[24] *cf. ibid.*, s. 232.

[25] *cf. ibid.*, s. 234(3) and (4) and *Welsh Development Agency v. Export Finance Co. Ltd* [1992] B.C.C. 11, CA.

[26] Insolvency Act 1986, s. 43(1) and (7).

[27] As to the bar on the removal of an administrative receiver, see below, para. 21–002.

[28] Insolvency Act 1986, s. 388(1).

[29] Cmnd. 8558.

the benefit of a limited statutory moratorium on adverse acts by creditors and with the objective of restoring the company or part of its business to good health, facilitating a compromise or arrangement with its creditors, or achieving a more advantageous realisation of its assets than would be achieved in a winding up.[30]

As envisaged by the Cork Committee, the appointment of an admin- **1–012** istrator is an alternative to the appointment of an administrative receiver or a liquidator. Notice of the presentation of the petition for an administration order must be given to any person who has appointed or may be entitled to appoint an administrative receiver,[31] and an administrator cannot be appointed if an administrative receiver has been appointed unless the court is satisfied either that the appointor has consented or that, if the administration order were made, the charge or security by virtue of which the receiver was appointed would be liable to be released or discharged under sections 238 to 240 or would be avoided under section 245 of the Act.[32] An administrator cannot be appointed after the company has gone into liquidation.[33]

In many ways the administrator is similar to the administrative **1–013** receiver. An administrator is an office-holder and has many of the same rights and privileges given to an administrative receiver under the Insolvency Act 1986[34] together with some additional powers.[35] In common with an administrative receiver, the administrator acts as the agent of the company.[36] His appointment also displaces the powers of the company's directors to the extent that they might interfere with the proper exercise of his powers.[37]

There is, nevertheless, an important conceptual difference between **1–014** administrators and administrative receivers. An administrator is an officer of the court who has additional privileges and responsibilities accordingly. In particular he is responsible for managing the company under his control for the benefit of all those interested in the insolvent estate, and must hold the balance fairly between all those parties. The administrative receiver, by contrast, owes his primary duties to the person who appointed him, and where the interests of the debenture-holder conflict with those of the other creditors of the company, he is entitled to put the interests of his appointor first.[38]

---

[30] See below, paras 2–029 to 2–034 and Chap. 23.

[31] Insolvency Act 1986, s. 9(2).

[32] *ibid.*, s. 9(3).

[33] *ibid.*, s. 8(4).

[34] *e.g.* the powers in Sched. 1 of the 1986 Act (s. 14(1)), the power to deal with charged property (s. 15).

[35] Such as the power to remove directors: see s. 14(2).

[36] s. 14(5). The consequences of this agency are not identical: see, *e.g.* the different approaches to adoption of contracts in ss. 19(5) and 44 of the Act and the decision of the House of Lords in *Re Paramount Airways Ltd, Powdrill v. Watson* [1995] 2 A.C. 394.

[37] Again, the comparison between an administrator and an administrative receiver in this respect is not exact: see below, paras 2–022 to 2–025 and 2–033 below.

[38] *Medforth v. Blake* [2000] Ch. 86.

CHAPTER 2

THE COMPANY IN FINANCIAL TROUBLE: AN OVERVIEW

2–001 When a company falls into financial difficulties, control of the company and its undertaking may pass from the board of directors to a receiver, an administrator or a liquidator, and indeed successively from one to another. During the period of a receivership or administration, control may be shared between the receiver or administrator and the board of directors, though in this case the board will have a limited role and be very much the junior partner. There may be concurrently receivership and liquidation,[1] and in this case, though the liquidator has certain distinct functions, the receiver has the predominant role in preserving and realising assets. In view of the overlapping functions and responsibilities of the board of directors, receivers, administrators and liquidators, an overview of their respective roles and legal duties in the context of insolvency is called for.

1. THE RESPONSIBILITIES OF MANAGEMENT AT A TIME OF FINANCIAL DIFFICULTY

2–002 Directors do not have a duty to ensure that the company does not trade at a loss, but they are at risk of personal liability or subsequent disqualification from acting as a director if they allow the company to trade when insolvent.[2] Continuing to trade without due consideration for the consequences involves the risk of challenge, if the company does not survive, on the grounds of fraudulent or wrongful trading or in disqualification proceedings brought by the Secretary of State or the Official Receiver.

(a) Duties of directors to the company
2–003 In general, a company owes no duty of care in the conduct of its business to present or future creditors, and its directors likewise owe no duties to the present or future creditors of their company.[3] But if the company is insolvent, the directors owe a duty *to the company* to take care to protect the interests of its creditors.[4] This duty will be enforceable in the name

---

[1] An administration cannot exist at the same time as either an administrative receivership or a liquidation: see above, para 1–012.
[2] *Re CS Holidays Ltd* [1997] B.C.C. 172 at 178.
[3] *Per* Dillon L.J. in *Multinational Gas and Petrochemical Co. v. Multinational Gas and Petrochemical Services Ltd* [1983] Ch 258 at 290.
[4] See *per* Dillon L.J. in *Liquidator of West Mercia Safetywear v. Dodd* (1988) 4 B.C.C. 30, CA, referring with approval to *Kinsela v. Russell Kinsela Pty Ltd* (1986) 4 N.S.W.L.R. 722, Court of Appeal of New South Wales; and *Yukong Line Ltd of Korea v. Rendsburg Investments Corp. of Liberia* [1998] 1 W.L.R. 294 at 312. See also *Nicholson v. Permakraft*

of the company by a liquidator, administrator or administrative receiver. The time at which the directors' duties require them to have primary regard to the interests of creditors rather than the interests of share-holders is difficult to define with any precision. It may be that as a company's financial situation worsens, the directors will be under a duty to pay greater attention to the interests of its creditors, and that duty will be reinforced if a potential transaction or proposed course of action carries a high level of risk and therefore of potential prejudice to creditors if it goes wrong.[5]

(b) Fraudulent trading

If in the course of the winding-up of a company it appears that any **2–004** business of the company has been carried on with intent to defraud creditors[6] of the company or creditors of any other person, or for any fraudulent purpose, the court may on the application of the liquidator of the company declare that any persons who were knowingly parties to the carrying on of the business in such manner are to be liable to make such contribution (if any) to the company's assets as the court thinks proper.[7]

For the purpose of this section, the authorities establish the following propositions:

    (a) for a person to be held liable for fraudulent trading, it must be established that he was personally dishonest, and the more improbable such personal dishonesty, the more compelling must be the evidence needed to satisfy the court on the balance of probability.[8] Dishonesty is an essential element. The required intent to defraud is essentially subjective, not objective, and it is accordingly necessary to show that there was either an intent to defraud or a reckless indifference whether or not the creditors were defrauded[9];

    (b) the carrying out of one transaction alone may be sufficient, for example the acceptance of a deposit or the purchase price for

---

(NZ) Ltd [1985] 1 N.Z.L.R. 242, Court of Appeal of New Zealand. It is suggested that the *obiter dictum* of Lord Templeman in *Winkworth v. Edward Baron Development Co. Ltd* [1986] 1 W.L.R. 1512 at 1516, H.L., which suggests that the duty is owed to creditors as well as to the company, does not accurately represent English law. Such a direct duty has, nevertheless, been held to exist in Ireland: see *Jones v. Gunn* [1997] 3 I.R. 1 (High Court of Ireland).

[5] See *per* Street C.J. in *Kinsela v. Russell Kinsela Pty Ltd* (1986) 4 N.S.W.L.R. 722, N.S.W. CA.

[6] The term "creditor" denotes one to whom money is owed, whether or not the debt is presently recoverable; in the context of the section the term includes both existing contingents and future creditors: see *R. v. Smith* [1996] 2 B.C.L.C. 109 at 122; and see *Cannane v. J. Cannane* [1998] 192 C.L.R. 557 at 566.

[7] Insolvency Act 1986, s. 213. This section and s. 214 (below) may be applicable to foreign companies operating in the U.K.: consider *Re A Company* [1988] Ch.210.

[8] *Aktieselskabet Dansk Skibsfinansiering v. Brothers* [2000] 1 H.K.L.R.D. 568, Court of Final Appeal of Hong Kong; *per* Lord Hoffmann; *Re H (Minors)* [1996] A.C. 563 at 586–7; *per* Lord Nicholls.

[9] *Hardie v. Hanson* (1960) 105 C.L.R. 451 (H Ct. of Australia) and see also *Cannane v. J. Cannane* [1998] 192 C.L.R. 557.

goods in advance knowing that the goods cannot be supplied and the deposit or price will not be repaid[10];

(c) the mere giving or receipt of a preference over other creditors will not necessarily constitute fraudulent trading[11];

(d) to be a "party" to the impugned trading, there must be shown: (a) to have been fraud on the part of the company in the conduct of its business[12]; and (b) that the individual concerned took some active step to promote such business on the part of the company. It is not sufficient that he failed to warn or advise against it or indeed failed to prevent it[13];

(e) it is not necessary that the individual should have had any power of management or control over or have assisted in the carrying on of the company's business. It is sufficient that he has knowingly taken advantage of such trading, for example by accepting repayment of his debts from moneys he knew to have been obtained by the company carrying on business in this way for the purpose of making the repayment[14];

(f) there is a sufficient intent to defraud if credit is obtained at a time when the person knows that there is no good reason for thinking that funds will become available to pay the debt when it becomes due or shortly thereafter. It is unnecessary to establish knowledge that funds will never become available.[15]

2–005 The real problem for management under this section is how far and how long they can continue to incur credit when they realise that the outcome of future trading is uncertain and that there is a real risk that things may not improve so that creditors may not be paid. It may help them to ask whether the risk is one which an honest and reasonable director would be prepared to take, but at the end of the day the directors will not be able to escape liability by saying that, even though others would have regarded their conduct as dishonest, they saw nothing wrong with it. Further, although the hypothetical honest and reasonable director might provide an objective base standard for the concept of dishonesty, the court ought to guard against testing the honesty or dishonesty of the

---

[10] *Re Gerald Cooper* [1978]1 Ch. 262; (followed by the Court of Appeal in *R. v. Lockwood* [1986] Crim.L.R. 244). ". . . [A] man who warms himself with the fire of fraud cannot complain if he is singed". ([1978] 1 Ch. at 268 F–G, *per* Templeman J.). Query whether the provision requires that the party should be an accessory before, and not merely after, the fact, and therefore to have given some encouragement to the trading in question before it takes place.

[11] *Re Sarflax* [1979] Ch. 592; *R. v. Grantham* [1984] Q.B. 675.

[12] *Re Augustus Barnett* [1986] B.C.L.C. 170.

[13] *Re Maidstone Builders* [1971] 1 W.L.R. 1085.

[14] *Re Gerald Cooper* [1978] Ch. 262.

[15] *R. v. Grantham* [1984] Q.B. 675. "A company incurs a debt when by its choice it does or omits to do something which, as a matter of substance and commercial reality, renders it liable for a debt for which it otherwise would not have been liable": *Standard Chartered Bank of Australia Ltd v. Antico* (1995) 18 A.C.S.R. 1 at 57. In this respect, the fraud of the company is the same as that of any customer for goods or services who obtains credit on the basis of an express or implied representation that he can and will pay in due course: see *D.P.P. v. Ray* [1974] A.C. 370.

particular directors concerned by reference to such a standard. At the end of the day, dishonesty is a subjective question of fact.[16]

(c) Wrongful trading[17]

In any case where directors[18] have been responsible for wrongful trading **2–006** by the company which, by depleting its assets, has occasioned loss, section 214 of the Insolvency Act 1986 empowers the court to impose on those directors liability to contribute to the assets of the company for the benefit of its creditors . Two conditions have to be satisfied before that power can be exercised:

   (a) the company must have gone into insolvent liquidation (meaning liquidation at a time when its assets are insufficient for the payment of its debts and other liabilities and the expenses of winding up); and

   (b) at some time before the commencement of the winding-up of the company the person to be held liable was a director and either knew or ought to have concluded that there was no reasonable prospect that the company would avoid going into insolvent liquidation.[19]

In any case, when these conditions are satisfied, the court may, on the application of the liquidator (and no-one else), declare that such person is liable to make such contribution to the company's assets as the court thinks proper unless it is satisfied that after the date of such actual or constructive knowledge the person took every step with a view to minimising the potential loss to the company's creditors as he ought to have taken (assuming him to have known that there was no reasonable prospect that the company would avoid going into insolvent liquidation).[20] Accordingly, the burden of proof of "due diligence" is squarely placed on the director.

---

[16] See the observations of Lord Hoffmann in *Aktieselskabet Dansk Skibsfinansiering v. Wheelock Marden* [2000] 1 H.K.L.R.D. 568, Court of Final Appeal of Hong Kong, referring to the exposition of the concept of dishonesty in *Royal Brunei Airlines v. Tan* [1995] 2 A.C. 378, PC.

[17] See *Re A Company* [1988] Ch. 210; *Re A Company* (1988) 4 B.C.C. 424; *Re Produce Marketing Ltd* (1989) 5 B.C.C. 569; *Re DRG Contractors Ltd* (1990) B.C.C. 903;

[18] The term "director" for this purpose includes (1) a *de jure* director; (2) a *de facto* director (*i.e.* a person who assumes the status and functions of a director although never or never validly appointed); (3) a "shadow director", *i.e.* a person (not claiming or purporting to be a director) in accordance with whose directions or instructions (but not on whose advice in a professional capacity) the directors are accustomed to act: Insolvency Act 1986, ss. 214(7) and 251. It is sufficient that the shadow director has a real influence and it is unnecessary that the directors adopt a subservient role: see *Secretary of State v. Deverell* [2000] 2 W.L.R. 907 (CA). For a valuable analysis, see In *Re Kaytech International Plc* [1999] 2 B.C.L.C. 351, CA. In that case, the Court of Appeal did not agree with the notion that the two concepts of a *de facto* director and a shadow director did not overlap, a view which had been espoused by Millett J. in *Re Hydrodan (Corby) Ltd* [1994] B.C.C. 161.

[19] Insolvency Act 1986, s. 214(2)(b), (c). So long as he had the required knowledge whilst a director, it is not essential that he remained a director when the acts or omissions constituting wrongful trading took place.

[20] Insolvency Act 1986, s. 214(3).

2–007   For the purpose of determining the extent of his constructive knowledge and for the purpose of determining the propriety and sufficiency of the action taken, the standard is taken to be that of a reasonably diligent person having both:

> "(a) the general knowledge, skill and experience that may reasonably be expected of a person carrying out the same functions as are carried out by or entrusted to that director in relation to the company; and
>
> (b) the general knowledge, skill and experience that that director has."[21]

2–008 The following distinctions between fraudulent and wrongful trading stand out:

(a) liability for fraudulent trading can attach to anyone, whatever his role in or relationship to the company: in the case of wrongful trading, liability can extend only to directors (including *de facto* and shadow directors);[22]

(b) liability in the case of fraudulent trading depends on some positive act, whilst liability for wrongful trading can attach in respect of an omission to act;

(c) in the case of fraudulent trading, the burden of proving fraud lies squarely on the complainant; but in the case of wrongful trading, once the two conditions for establishing liability are satisfied, the burden is upon the director to prove that he was diligent in attempting to avoid loss to the creditors;

(d) fraudulent trading involves primarily[23] a failure to have proper regard to the interests of future creditors (*i.e.* those giving credit to the company); wrongful trading involves a failure to have regard to the interests of creditors as a class;

(e) for the purpose of fraudulent trading actual knowledge must usually be established of the company's actual or prospective inability to pay debts as they fall due; for the purpose of wrongful trading there need only be shown that the director ought to have known of the inevitability of insolvent liquidation.

(d) Disqualification of directors for trading whilst insolvent

2–009 In cases under the Company Directors Disqualification Act 1986, a ground of unfitness often relied upon is that the director concerned was responsible for the company trading whilst insolvent and that in so doing he took "unwarranted risks with creditors' money". In *Re CU Fittings Ltd*[24] Hoffmann J. summarised the position as follows:

---

[21] Insolvency Act 1986, s. 214(4) and (5), *cf. DHSS v. Evans* [1984] I.C.R. 317.

[22] In *Re A Company (No. 005009 of 1987)* (1988) 4 B.C.C. 424.

[23] It is possible (though relatively rare) that a company's business is carried on with intent to defraud existing creditors.

[24] (1989) 5 B.C.C. 210 at 213.

". . . directors immersed in the day-to-day task or trying to keep their business afloat cannot be expected to have wholly dispassionate minds. They tend to cling to hope. Obviously there comes a point at which an honest businessman recognises that he is only gambling at the expense of creditors on the possibility that something may turn up . . ."

In *Secretary of State v. Laing*,[25] Evans-Lombe J. referred to the **2–010** importance in all such cases of the directors maintaining accurate financial records and management accounts in order to know the position of their company with a reasonable degree of accuracy at any particular time and stated,

". . . where it can be demonstrated that a company has continued trading for a substantial period of time while it was insolvent and as a result has put the claims of existing creditors at unwarrantable risk and has incurred fresh creditors at the unjustifiable risk of not being able to pay them, it is not open to a director of the company to avoid responsibility by contending that he did not know at the material time that such was taking place. It is the duty of all directors to ensure that they have from time to time a reasonably clear picture of the financial state and trading profitability of their companies."

In light of the above, once the directors appreciate that to continue **2–011** trading will involve incurring further credit with no reasonable prospect of payment, they should not cause the company to trade at the risk of future creditors. Neither the directors nor the court can sanction further trading at the expense of future creditors. This would seem to be so even if a cesser of trading will damage the company and its current creditors, in particular by precluding a beneficial sale of the undertaking as a going concern. Continued trading is only legitimate if it is in the interests of creditors generally and either (a) the future creditors are warned and agree to accept the risk of non-payment or (b) further credit obtained is underwritten by somebody of sufficient substance.

If neither of these conditions is satisfied, closure of the business is **2–012** probably inevitable unless:

   (a) there is a voluntary arrangement under sections 1-7 of the Insolvency Act 1986 or a scheme of arrangement under section 425 of the Companies Act 1985; or

   (b) a debenture-holder appoints an administrative receiver (as he may be invited to do by the company); or

   (c) an administrator or interim manager is appointed by the court; or

---

[25] [1996] 2 B.C.L.C. 324 at 342.

(d) on presentation of a petition for winding up a provisional liquidator is appointed and is authorised to continue the company's business; or

(e) on a compulsory winding-up the liquidator is authorised to continue trading with a view to a beneficial realisation[26] or on a voluntary liquidation the liquidator decides to take this course.

2. COMPANY VOLUNTARY ARRANGEMENT AND SCHEMES OF ARRANGEMENT

2–013 In 1982 the Cork Committee proposed that the existing procedures for company voluntary arrangements were entirely unsuitable and suggested a new form of voluntary arrangement for companies which could be concluded without an order of the court but which would still be binding as between the company and its creditors.[27] Part I of the Insolvency Act 1986 gave effect to that proposal. The principal feature of the legislation is that any voluntary arrangement to be voted upon by creditors will have been reviewed and endorsed and will be administered by an insolvency practitioner. The voluntary arrangement cannot affect the rights of secured creditors without their consent.[28]

2–014 The voluntary arrangement may be proposed independently of, or pursuant to, an administration order[29] or in a liquidation. A proposal is formulated by the directors if the company is not in administration or liquidation, or by the administrator or liquidator if it is, and is voted upon by meetings of the company and its creditors. If accepted at the respective meetings, the arrangement will become binding upon all persons who in accordance with the rules had notice of, and were entitled to vote at, the meeting as if they were parties to the voluntary arrangement.[30] This has been described as giving rise to a statutory hypothesis that the creditor was a party to the arrangement as if he had consented to it.[31] A person entitled to vote at the meeting is entitled to challenge a decision made at the creditors' meeting by application made to the court within 28 days of the outcome of the meetings being reported to the court, and the court has the power to revoke or suspend the approvals and/or give a direction for the summoning of further meetings.[32]

2–015 If approved, the voluntary arrangement is thereafter administered by a supervisor who must be a qualified insolvency practitioner. The supervisor is not an officer of the company and has no power to act in the name of the company unless given authority to do so pursuant to the

---

[26] *Re General Service Co-operative Stores* (1891) 64 L.T. 228.

[27] Cmnd 8558 paras 419 *et seq.*

[28] *March Estates plc v. Gunmark Ltd* [1996] 2 B.C.L.C. 1; *Razzaq v. Pala* [1998] B.C.C. 66.

[29] s.8(3)(b) of the 1986 Act.

[30] s.5(2) of the 1986 Act.

[31] *Johnson v. Davies* [1999] Ch. 117; *Raja v. Rubin* [1999] 1 B.C.L.C. 621.

[32] s.6 of the 1986 Act.

terms of the voluntary arrangement. The supervisor is subject to the supervisory control of the court, and both he and creditors who are dissatisfied with any act, decision or omission of his can apply to the court for directions.[33] It has been held in relation to the analogous case of an individual voluntary arrangement that a supervisor is not susceptible to an action for damages for breach of statutory duty or tort in relation to his supervision of the voluntary arrangement.[34]

The Insolvency Act 1986 contains no provision enabling a voluntary **2–016** arrangement to be amended or varied, whether by vote of creditors,[35] or on an application to the court for directions.[36] It is therefore usually desirable to include a provision permitting amendments to be made in the scheme itself.[37] The voluntary arrangement will end upon the making of a winding up order on a petition by the supervisor,[38] but not on the making of an order on the petition of a creditor who is not bound by the voluntary arrangement.[39]

As an alternative to a company voluntary arrangement, it may be possible for a scheme of arrangement to be promoted and sanctioned under sections 425–427 of the Companies Act 1985. Section 425 provides that if a compromise or arrangement is proposed between a company and its members or creditors,[40] or any class of them, is approved by a majority in number representing 75 per cent in value of those present in person or by proxy at meetings of each class of member or creditor, and is subsequently sanctioned by the court, it shall be binding upon all members or creditors, or upon the class of members or creditors, and upon the company. Where a scheme involves a reduction of capital, the statutory provisions in that regard must also be complied with.[41]

The concept of a compromise or arrangement is a wide one.[42] Whilst the court will be slow to differ from the views of the statutory majorities of members or creditors, the role of the court in deciding whether to exercise its discretion to sanction a scheme is not simply to "rubber-stamp" the decisions of the relevant meetings.[43] Not only will the court decide whether the relevant class meetings have been held[44] and the

---

[33] s.7 of the 1986 Act.

[34] *King v. Anthony* [1998] 2 B.C.L.C. 517, CA.

[35] *Raja v. Rubin* [1999] 1 B.C.L.C. 621 (a case on individual voluntary arrangements).

[36] *Re Alpha Lighting* [1997] B.P.I.R. 341.

[37] *Horrocks v. Broome* [1999] B.P.I.R. 66.

[38] *Re Arthur Rathbone Kitchens Ltd* [1997] 2 B.C.L.C. 280.

[39] *Re Excalibur Airways Ltd* [1998] 1 B.C.L.C. 436.

[40] Every person who has a pecuniary claim against the company, whether actual or contingent, is a creditor within the Act. This will, for example, include a lessor of property to the company.

[41] *Re White Pass Ry. Co.* [1918] W.N. 323.

[42] See *e.g. Re NFU Development Trust Ltd* [1972] 1 W.L.R. 1548.

[43] See *e.g. Re English, Scottish and Australian Chartered Bank* [1893] 3 Ch. 385 at 398 and 409, CA; *Re National Bank Ltd* [1966] 1 W.L.R. 819 at 829; and *Re BTR plc* [2000] 1 B.C.L.C. 740 at 744, CA.

[44] The approach of the Court to the composition of classes was set out by Bowen LJ in *Sovereign Life Assurance Co. v. Dodd* [1892] 2 Q.B. 573 at 583: "It seems plain that we must give such a meaning to the term 'class' as will prevent the section being worked so as to result in confiscation and injustice, and that it must be confined to those persons whose

procedures properly followed[45] and check that full and accurate information has been given to members and creditors,[46] but it will also decide "whether the proposal is such that an intelligent and honest man, a member of the class concerned and acting in respect of his interest, might reasonably approve".[47] This is an obvious difference to the court's role in relation to a company voluntary arrangement, which, in the absence of challenge from dissident creditors, is far more administrative in nature.

3. THE APPOINTMENT OF A RECEIVER

2–017   There is in most cases a world of difference between the value of a company's undertaking as a going concern and its scrap value. It is for this reason that creditors seek floating charges on the undertaking as well as specific charges on certain assets of the debtor company. A debenture in the ordinary case provides for the appointment by the secured creditor, on the occasion of any default by the debtor or the occurrence of specified events, of a receiver with power to carry on the company's business. The appointment takes the management of the company's property out of the hands of the directors and places it in the hands of the receiver.[48] This power may be exercised either with a view to reviving the company or with a view to the beneficial sale of the undertaking as a going concern. The power to carry on the business of the company through an administrative receiver is deemed to be granted by the debenture except in so far as the existence of such power is inconsistent with any provision of the debenture.[49] The power to present or defend (and presumably by implication to support or not oppose) a petition to wind up the company is likewise deemed to be granted,[50] and if properly exercised must preclude any representation of the company at

---

rights are not so dissimilar as to make it impossible for them to consult together with a view to acting in their common interest." The question of whether classes have been correctly constituted will depend upon the facts of each case: see *Re Osiris Insurance* Ltd [1999] 1 B.C.L.C. 182; *Re BTR plc* [1999] 2 B.C.L.C. 675 (Ch. D), [2000] 1 B.C.L.C. 740, CA; and *Re Anglo-American Insurance Company Ltd* (unreported, Neuberger J., April 12, 2000). The focus is on the effect of any differences in the creditors' *rights* against the company rather than differences in their individual *interests*: see *Re BTR plc* (*supra*).

[45] See Practice Note [1934] W.N. 142.
[46] See *Re Minster Assets plc* [1985] B.C.L.C. 200.
[47] See *per* Maugham J. in *Re Dorman, Long & Co. Ltd* [1934] 1 Ch. 635 at 657. See also *Re National Bank Ltd* [1966] 1 W.L.R. 819 at p. 829A–E; *Re Hellenic and General Trust Ltd* [1976] 1 W.L.R. 123; *Re Osiris Insurance Ltd* [1999] 1 B.C.L.C. 182 at 188g–189g; *Re BTR plc* [1999] 2 B.C.L.C. 675 at 680b–g, [2000] 1 B.C.L.C. 740, CA.
[48] *Re Joshua Shaw & Sons* (1989) 5 B.C.C. 188 at 190. The appointment does not terminate the office of director: *Re Barton Manufacturing Co. Ltd* [1998] B.C.C. 827 at 828; but the loss of control means that directors are unlikely to be able to act to safeguard the interests of creditors and therefore will not be held to be in breach of such duties to the company.
[49] Insolvency Act 1986, s. 42(1) and Sched. I, para. 14, formerly the Insolvency Act 1985, s. 48(1) and Sched. III, para. 14.
[50] *ibid.*, para. 21.

the instance of the directors.[51] A non-administrative receiver will only have such powers if conferred by the debenture.[52] The appointment of a receiver in no way precludes other creditors petitioning for winding up, and indeed unsecured creditors may be well advised to petition to protect their position in case a surplus exists after completion of the receivership and in order to preserve the "relation back" period for any challenge to the grant of the debenture to the secured creditor under sections 238 (preferences) and 245 (avoidance of floating charges) of the Insolvency Act 1986. The appointment does not prevent time running for purposes of limitation[53] and the liquidator may exercise some supervision and restraining influence on the receiver.[54]

In the case of such a floating charge, the creditor has the choice **2–018** whether to make the appointment.[55] Once the appointment is made, it is then for the receiver to decide whether to carry on the business with the objective of a rescue in the long term or of a beneficial sale as a going concern in the short term or to close the business and sell up. There is no general duty on the creditor or the receiver to carry on business on the mortgaged premises in order to safeguard the company's goodwill or attempt to procure the most beneficial realisation.[56]

If the receiver does continue the company's business, five limitations **2–019** on his freedom of action come into operation. First, the receiver will ordinarily be granted power and authority to carry on the company's business as agent of the company.[57] But though the power to carry on the business survives liquidation, the agency does not. Thereafter the receiver can only trade as principal or (with his debenture-holder's consent) as agent for his debenture-holder.

Secondly, the provisions of section 213 of the Insolvency Act 1986 will **2–020** apply to the receiver in respect of the period of his carrying on business as agent for the company prior to liquidation, and accordingly if he is a party to fraudulent trading, he may be subject to a claim in a subsequent liquidation.[58] The wrongful trading provisions of section 214 of the

---

[51] *Bank of New Zealand v. Essington Developments* (1991) 9 A.C.L.C. 1039. The only course available to the directors if they oppose such action by the receiver will be an application to the court for a contrary direction to be given to the receiver, but such direction can only be expected if it can be shown that the receiver's proposed course of action would be unconscionable. *cf. Edwards v. Singh* (1990) 5 N.Z.C.L.C. 97–426.

[52] In the case of such a receivership, if the power is not so conferred, the directors can authorise the company's defence to the petition: see *Re Reprographic* (1978) 122 Sol. J. 400.

[53] *Re Cases of Taff's Well Ltd* (1991) B.C.C. 582.

[54] *Re Northern Developments (Holdings) Ltd* (unreported, Templeman J., June 16, 1976, affirmed by the Court of Appeal, unreported, on March 1, 1977). Although not its usual practice, the Companies Court has the power to adjourn a winding-up petition for long periods if the interests of unsecured creditors so require (*ibid.*).

[55] See below, Chap. 7.

[56] See *Medforth v. Blake* [2000] Ch. 86 at 102 and below, Chaps 7 and 8.

[57] In the case of the administrative receiver the power and authority are deemed to be granted by the debenture in the absence of some inconsistent provision in the debenture: Insolvency Act 1986, s. 42(1) and Sched. I, para. 14. In the case of non-administrative receivers, they must be conferred by the debenture.

[58] See *Re Leyland DAF Ltd* [1994] 2 B.C.L.C. 760 at 771–772 and para. 7.

Insolvency Act 1986 may also apply to him if he exercises real influence over the affairs of trading subsidiaries so that the directors of those companies become accustomed to act on his directions or instructions.[59]

2-021   Thirdly, in respect of certain aspects of his conduct he owes duties to the company and may be held liable in negligence or for acts which damage the company. [60] All his powers (statutory and otherwise) are exercisable only for the purposes for which he is appointed, *i.e.* the preservation, recovery and realisation of the assets subject to the charge in order to bring about a situation in which interest on the secured debt can be paid and the debt itself paid.[61]

2-022   Fourthly, the directors' powers of management of the undertaking are placed in suspense during the period of his appointment in so far as their exercise would be inconsistent with the exercise by the receiver of powers conferred on the debenture-holder under his debenture.[62] There is no kind of diarchy over the company's assets: the board has no power over assets in the possession or control of the receiver. The directors remain in office[63] and their powers remain exercisable so far as they are not incompatible with the right of the receiver to exercise the powers conferred on him.[64]

2-023   The law is unsettled as to the extent to which, independently of the receiver, the directors have the right in the name of the company to bring proceedings on causes of action of the company. In *Newhart v. Co-op Commercial Bank*,[65] Shaw L.J. stated that the appointment of the receiver:

> "does not divest the directors of the company of their power, as the governing body of the company, of instituting proceedings in a situation where so doing does not in any way impinge prejudicially upon the position of the debenture-holders by threatening or imperilling the assets which are subject to the charge . . . . If in the

---

[59] See *Secretary of State for Trade & Industry v. Deverell* [2000] 2 W.L.R. 907, CA in relation to the meaning of "shadow director".

[60] See below, Chaps 7 and 8.

[61] *Bank of New Zealand v. Essington* (1991) 9 A.C.L.C. 1039 and *Medforth v. Blake* [2000] Ch. 86 at 102G.

[62] See Brightman J. in *Re Emmadart* [1979] Ch. 540 at 544. "The receiver replaces the board as the person having the authority to exercise the company's powers", *per* Lord Hoffmann in *Village Cay Marina Ltd v. Acland* [1998] 2 B.C.L.C. 327 at 333.

[63] *Independent Pension Trustee Ltd v. L.A.W. Construction Co. Ltd* [1996] O.P.L.R. 259, Outer House of the Court of Session.

[64] Their statutory duties to keep accounts under the Companies Act 1985, ss. 221–223 continue (notwithstanding that the effect of the appointment of the receiver is to deprive them of access to the funds required to pay for the discharge of them), and they have a continuing right to require the receiver to provide information for this purpose: see para. 7–068. See *Gomba Holdings v. Homan* [1986] 1 W.L.R. 1301 (the directors have no right to information from the receiver in order to prosecute an action where the provision of such information would be contrary to the interests of the debenture-holder); and *Re Geneva Finance Ltd* [1992] 10 A.C.L.C. 668.

[65] [1978] Q.B. 814 at 819, followed in *Shanks v. Central Regional Council* [1987] S.L.T. 410, which differed from the view expressed in *Imperial Hotels (Aberdeen) Ltd v. Vaux* [1978] S.L.T. 113. See also Brightman J. in *Re Emmadart* [1979] Ch. 540 at 544. But contrast the language of Danckwerts L.J. in *Lawson v. Hosemaster* [1966] 1 W.L.R. 1300 at 1315. As an alternative the court may appoint a receiver *ad litem*: see below, Chap. 22.

exercise of his discretion [the receiver] chooses to ignore some asset such as a right of action, or decides that it would be unprofitable from the point of view of the debenture-holders to pursue it, there is nothing in any authority which has been cited to us which suggests that it is not then open to the directors of the company to pursue that right of action if they think it would be in the interests of the company. Indeed, in my view, it would be incumbent upon them to do so . . ."

In line with this approach, the directors have been allowed in the name of the company to institute proceedings challenging the validity of the debenture or the appointment of the receiver, and, acting as monitors of the stewardship of the company's affairs by the receiver, to challenge his actions in the court[66] and to seek to enforce independent causes of action against the appointing debenture-holder. Indeed Shaw L.J. questioned whether the receiver can enforce claims against the debenture-holder, for such a step and any negotiations for compromise would involve such conflicts of interest on his part as to make it desirable that enforcement is left to the directors.[67] Protection of the assets charged and the interests of the debenture-holders may require provision of an indemnity to the company against any liability for costs.[68]

In *Tudor Grange Holdings Ltd v. Citibank N.A.*,[69] Sir Nicolas Browne-   **2–024**
Wilkinson V.-C. expressed substantial doubts whether the decision of the Court of Appeal in *Newhart v. Co-op Commercial Bank* was correct, though he accepted that the decision bound him. He was of the view that the reasoning based on the embarrassment of the receiver deciding to sue his appointor could be met by an application by the receiver under section 35 of the Insolvency Act 1986 to the court for directions as to the course to be taken, a point apparently not drawn to the attention of the Court of Appeal; and that the decision ignored the difficulty which arose if two different sets of people, the directors and the receiver, who may have widely differing views and interests, both have power to bring proceedings on the same cause of action. He raised the question, in the situation where the directors bring proceedings and there is a counterclaim directly attacking the property of the company, as to who is to have the conduct of the counterclaim. Browne-Wilkinson V.-C. insisted that in any event any action at the instance of the directors must be struck out until the company provides a complete indemnity in respect of any liability for costs.[70]

---

[66] *Hawkesbury Development v. Landmark Finance* (1970) 92 W.N. (NSW) 199 at 210 and see *Watts v. Midland Bank* [1986] B.C.L.C. 15 where Gibson J. held that the mortgagor company was entitled to sue the receiver in respect of an improper exercise of his powers.
[67] See above, n. 28.
[68] See *Tudor Grange Holdings Ltd v. Citibank NA.* [1992] Ch. 53; *Newhart v. Co-op. Commercial Bank* [1978] Q.B. 814 at 819. And consider *Fairholme and Palliser v. Kennedy* (1890) 24 L.R. Ir. 498 (receiver permitted to sue in name of personal representatives on giving indemnity).
[69] [1992] Ch. 53.
[70] For a "reconciliation" placing critical importance on the availability of the indemnity as to costs, see *L. Lascomme Ltd v. UDT* [1994] I.L.R.M. 227, Keane J.

2–025   It is suggested that two different situations require to be considered:

> (a) where both the receiver and the directors have power to represent the company, *e.g.*, on a petition to wind up the company, if the receiver properly exercises his power, the power of the directors is suspended and is not exercisable. The exercise of such power by the receiver must be bona fide. On this ground a receiver's purported discontinuance of proceedings commenced by the directors in the name of the company for a declaration that the debenture was invalid as already cancelled and that the appointment of the receiver accordingly was invalid, was held capable of challenge[71];
> (b) where the company's cause of action is included in the debenture, it is thereby assigned to the mortgagee.

It is suggested that the solution to this quandary lies in the recognition that the relevant relationship is not between the directors and the company and the receiver and the company, but between the rights of the company and the debenture-holder respectively or mortgagor and mortgagee of the relevant chose in action. After the assignment has been effected by the charge, the assignee alone can seek to enforce the assigned right. Accordingly in respect of any cause of action charged to the debenture-holder, only the debenture-holder can sue. The only qualification is that in practice the receiver, without objection, sues in the name of the company, though technically the claimant should be the mortgagee.[72] The company itself by its directors can only sue (i) in respect of causes of action not assigned to the mortgagee or released by the mortgagee from the charge[73]; or (ii) in respect of causes of action so assigned after redemption or perhaps with the consent of the debenture-holder.

2–026   Fifthly, as soon as the debenture-holder and preferential creditors and all receivership costs, liabilities and expenses are or can be paid off, the receiver must in the absence of any provision to the contrary in the debenture cease to act and hand back to the directors the powers of management.[74]

2–027   Occasionally, but comparatively rarely, the court will appoint a receiver and manager of a company. Usually this is done on the application of a debenture-holder when the debenture for some reason does not enable him to make an appointment out of court or does not give the powers required to ensure a beneficial realisation of the company's undertaking in the interests of all to the company's creditors. An appointment may also be made if the validity of the debenture or of the appointment of a receiver out of court is challenged. A court-

---

[71] *Edwards v. Singh* (1990) 5 N.Z.C.L.C. 96, 426.
[72] *cf.* below, Chap. 16.
[73] All that is required for a release is a unilateral consent to the release: *Scottish & Newcastle plc* [1993] B.C.C. 634.
[74] See below, Chap. 21.

appointed receiver is an officer of the court and does not act as agent for the company or anyone else, but in so far as he carries on business he contracts and incurs liabilities personally. Such appointments are invariably short-lived, being designed to achieve an early sale as a going concern.[75]

Whichever the form of the appointment, if the company's fortunes **2–028** improve, the receivership will give way to a resumption of management by the directors. If the receivership merely produces sufficient money to pay off the appointing debenture-holder, its conclusion may give rise to a further appointment of a different receiver by a subsequent encumbrancer, the appointment of an administrator or a liquidation.

4. ADMINISTRATOR[76]

The office of administrator is the creation of statute, namely Part II of **2–029** the Insolvency Act 1986, and his role is to secure one or more of the following statutory purposes[77]:

(a) the survival of the company which is presently insolvent or whose insolvency is imminent in respect of its undertaking in whole or in part; or

(b) the approval under section 4(1) of the Insolvency Act 1986 of a composition in satisfaction of the company's debts or a scheme of arrangement of its affairs referred to, in either case, in the 1986 Act as a "voluntary arrangement"[78]; or

(c) the sanctioning under section 425 of the Companies Act 1985 (as amended) of a compromise or arrangement between the company and any of the persons mentioned in that section; or

(d) a more advantageous realisation of its assets than would be effected on a winding-up.

Insolvency for this purpose means not merely inability to pay debts as they accrue due, but also a deficiency of assets in relation to liabilities.[79]

Administration is intended to be "only an interim and temporary **2–030** regime"[80] which is not to remain in force for a long time[81] and which is "designed to revive, and to seek the continued life of the company if at all possible".[82] If the applicant satisfies the court that there is a real

---

[75] See below, Chap. 22.

[76] For full consideration of this topic, see below, Chap. 23; and for consideration of the possibility of making an administration order in respect of a foreign company, see below, para. 25.15.

[77] Insolvency Act 1986 s. 8(3).

[78] Insolvency Act 1986, s. 1(1).

[79] Insolvency Act 1986, s. 123(2).

[80] *Re Atlantic Computer Systems plc* [1992] Ch. 505 at 528, *per* Nicholls LJ.

[81] *Re Arrows (No. 3)* [1992] B.C.C. 131 at 135.

[82] *Re MTI Trading Systems Ltd* [1996] B.C.C. 400 at 403, *per* Saville LJ.

prospect[83] (but not merely a hope[84]) that one or more of the stated purposes may be achieved, the court has a discretion to order a period under the stewardship of the administrator in which to set the affairs of the company in order, to reorganise and repay its debts or dispose of its business or assets for the benefit of creditors.[85] Though it is convenient to describe the breathing space afforded to the company as a moratorium, there is no authorisation to the company to postpone payment of its debts or discharge of its liabilities, but merely a limited immunity granted to the company against the enforcement of a number of legal rights and remedies (including various rights incidental to securities) without the leave of the court or the consent of the administrator. If the court is satisfied that there is a real prospect of an administration order achieving one of the statutory purposes, it may make an administration order despite the opposition of more than half in value of the creditors.[86]

2–031   Whilst the appointment of a receiver (administrative or non-administrative) can co-exist with that of a liquidator, the appointment of an administrator cannot co-exist with the appointment of an administrative receiver or liquidator.[87]

2–032   The court cannot appoint an administrator if there is an administrative receiver in office without the consent of his appointor, unless it is satisfied that the security under which the receiver was appointed could be challenged on specified grounds.[88] Once an administrator is appointed, no administrative receiver can be appointed throughout the administrator's period in office.

2–033   The administrator has extensive statutory powers and has power to continue the company's business as agent for the company.[89] He is given power to appoint and dismiss the directors,[90] and any powers of the directors which might interfere with the exercise by the administrator of his powers are exercisable only with his permission.[91] Once the administrator has fulfilled his role, or his role ceases to be capable of fulfilment, his appointment will be terminated by order of the court, and either the board of directors (as reconstituted) will regain full power or the company will be wound up.

---

[83] Re Harris Simons Construction Ltd [1989] 1 W.L.R. 368 at 371; Re Arrows (No. 3) Ltd [1992] B.C.C. 131 at 134.

[84] Re SCL Building Services Ltd (1989) 5 B.C.C. 746 at 748.

[85] Examples are to be found in cases decided before the Insolvency Act 1986 of companies which went into liquidation but whose insolvency was only "temporary", e.g. Re Rolls Royce [1974] 1 W.L.R. 1584, and for the conversion of an insolvent into a solvent liquidation see Re Islington Metal and Plating Works Ltd [1984] 1 W.L.R. 14.

[86] Structures and Computers Ltd v. Anys Inc [1998] B.C.C. 348.

[87] As to co-existence of administration and non-administrative receivership, see below, Chap. 23.

[88] See below, Chap. 23.

[89] He may pay off in full pre-administratorship order debts out of the company's assets to ensure the survival of the company as a going concern: Re John Slack Ltd [1995] B.C.C. 1116. He should seek the guidance of the court where there is a substantial change in the circumstances which led to the making of the administration order, but should not seek the court's guidance as to the making of commercial decisions: Re C.E. King, unreported, Neuberger J., April 29, 1999.

[90] Insolvency Act 1986, s. 14(2)(a).

[91] ibid., s. 14(4).

There are four substantial limitations on the effectiveness of this **2–034** jurisdiction. First, there is no power to appoint a provisional administrator although an interim manager may be appointed. Secondly, the administrator cannot be appointed against the wishes of a debenture-holder if there is a floating charge under which the debenture-holder has appointed an administrative receiver. Thirdly, the jurisdiction is not exercisable in respect of a company which has already gone into liquidation. Fourthly, the moratorium is of a strictly limited character.

5. PROVISIONAL LIQUIDATOR

At any time after the presentation of a winding-up petition, the court **2–035** may "appoint a liquidator provisionally".[92] A winding-up petition may be presented by, *inter alia*:

    (a) a creditor on the ground that the company[93] is insolvent in that it is unable to pay its debts when due[94] or that it is just and equitable to wind up the company[95]; and/or

    (b) a contributory, but only if there is a probability of surplus assets available to be returned to the contributories[96] (barring exceptional circumstances[97]).

Both conditions or one only may be satisfied at the same time, for a company may have a surplus of assets over liabilities but the assets may not be liquid, being assets which can only be realised over a relatively long time span; or the company's assets may be liquid but there may be a deficiency of assets to longer-term liabilities.

---

[92] Insolvency Act 1986, s. 135. The liquidator so appointed is referred to as a "provisional liquidator".

[93] The jurisdiction is exercisable in respect of a foreign company if (1) there is a sufficient connection with England and Wales; (2) there is a reasonable possibility of benefit to those applying for the winding up; and (3) one or more persons interested in the distribution of the company's assets are subject to the jurisdiction of the court: In *Re Latreefers Inc.*, *The Times*, March 15, 2000, CA.

[94] Insolvency Act 1986 s. 122(1)(f) A petition may be presented and an order made against a substantial company which fails to pay an undisputed debt: *Cornhill Insurance plc v. Improvement Services Ltd* [1986] 1 W.L.R. 114. If however the company has a prospect of success in its defence, it should be given the benefit of the doubt and the petition should be restrained: In *Re A Company* [1992] 1 W.L.R. 351. The existence of a cross-claim not yet established by litigation though substantially over topping the debt is not a ground for restraining the petition, but relevant only to the exercise of discretion at the substantive hearing: In *Re A Company* [1992] B.C.C. 794. See below, para. 2–037.

[95] Insolvency Act 1986, s. 122(1)(g); *Re Dollar Land plc* [1993] B.C.C. 823 (contingent creditor).

[96] *Re Chesterfield Catering Co.* [1977] 1 Ch. 373; *Re Commercial & Industrial Insulation Ltd* [1986] B.C.L.C. 1919. But *cf. Re DJH Consultants Ltd* (unreported, Civil Appeals (No. 164 of 1984)) where the Court of Appeal of Hong Kong in a judgment delivered on November 29, 1984 questioned this rule of practice and its applicability in Hong Kong.

[97] See *Re Newman and Howard Ltd.* [1962] Ch. 257. In the situation where relief is sought against a number of companies, a separate petition ought to be presented in respect of each company, at least when the companies are not included in any group or the subject of a common holding company: *Re A Company* [1984] B.C.L.C. 307.

2–036   Save in exceptional circumstances a winding up petition should be dismissed if it requires the Companies Court to determine a substantial dispute raised on bona fide grounds as to the existence of the creditor's debt or the standing of the petitioner as a contributory.[98] Though it is not an inflexible rule of law, it is a well-established rule of practice that if there is a bona fide and substantial dispute as to whether the petitioner is a creditor (and not merely as to the amount of the debt) or a contributory, the petition should be dismissed whilst the issue is determined in other proceedings.[99] "It is not in general convenient that the very status of the petitioner to proceed with his petition should be fought out on a winding-up petition".[1] Whilst a petition may legitimately be presented against a solvent company which has no defence and merely seeks credit to which it is not entitled,[2] if a solvent company does put forward a defence in good faith which has some prospect of success the court will usually give the company the benefit of the doubt and dismiss its petition.

2–037   For the purposes of determining the petitioner's right to present a winding up petition, a right of set-off is a defence, but a cross-claim not amounting to a right of set-off is not.[3] The existence of such a cross-claim is not a ground for restraining the presentation of the petition, but is relevant to the exercise of the court's discretion whether to make the order for winding up at the substantive hearing of the petition.[4] At the substantive hearing the petition will generally be dismissed or adjourned if the company has a cross-claim which (i) is genuine and serious (ii), the company has been unable to litigate[5] and (iii) is in an amount greater than the petitioning creditor's debt.[6] There is, however, a residual discretion which allows the court to depart from the rule in exceptional cases where, for example, if the petition is struck out, the petitioner is likely to lose his remedy altogether. This situation was held to arise in a case where the petitioner claimed to be a creditor of a foreign company with assets in the jurisdiction.[7]

2–038   The rule of practice is more strictly enforced in the case of a contributory's petition[8] but even in this case the application of the rule

---

[98] *Re A Company (No 006685 of 1996)* [1997] B.C.C. 830.

[99] *Re Claybridge Shipping Co. S.A.* [1997] 1 B.C.L.C. 572; *Mann v. Goldstein* [1968] 1 W.L.R. 1091. *cf. Re Welsh Brick Co.* [1946] 2 All E.R. 197.

[1] *Per* Oliver L.J. in *Re Claybridge Shipping Co. SA* [1997] 1 B.C.L.C. 572.

[2] *Cornhill Insurance plc v. Improvements Services Ltd* [1986] 1 W.L.R. 114.

[3] *Re A Company (No. 0012209 of 1991)* [1992] 1 W.L.R. 351 and see below, para. 16–007. *Cf. Malayan Plant v. Moscow Narodny Bank Ltd* [1980] 2 MLJ 53 at 55, PC.

[4] It is possible that in a case where it is plain at the date of presentation of the petition that the court's discretion could only be exercised in favour of dismissing the petition, the court may anticipate the inevitable and restrain presentation.

[5] In *Re a Debtor (No. 544/5D/98)* [2000] 1 B.C.L.C. 103 at 114F–G (a case in the field of personal insolvency) Robert Walker L.J. held that delay in litigating the cross-claim is merely a factor in evaluating whether it is put forward in good faith.

[6] *Re Bayoil S.A.* [1999] 1 W.L.R. 147, CA; *Re Latreefers Inc* [1999] 1 B.C.L.C. 271 (not appealed on this point).

[7] *Re Claybridge Shipping Co. SA* [1997] 1 B.C.L.C. 572, above at 579. For a consideration of the jurisdiction in respect of foreign companies, see below, paras 25–045 *et seq.*

[8] *Re JN2* [1978] 1 W.L.R. 183.

may be displaced, where, for example, the only interested parties have implicitly agreed that the issue be determined in such proceedings or the relief sought is not a winding-up order[9] or in the absence of the petition the contributory would be left without an effective remedy.[10]

The right of an unpaid creditor to obtain a winding up order is a class **2–039** right to be exercised by the petitioner on behalf of the general body of creditors.[11] The court will ordinarily respect and give effect to the view of the majority in value of the independent creditors unconnected with the company and its directors as to what course of action best promotes their interests.[12] and the existence of a receivership is no bar.[13] The power of the court to adjourn petitions should be exercised with caution, for the effect is to prolong the period during which the company has to trade with the petition hanging over its head and the existence of the petition on the file effectively prevents other creditors presenting a petition.[14]

The company can itself petition at the instance of the directors if they **2–040** are authorised by the articles of association to present a petition in the name of the company, or otherwise pursuant to a resolution of its members in general meeting.[15] The need for such authorisation has been removed in that directors now have locus to present a petition in their own names.[16] As long as the directors as a board have resolved that a petition should be presented, any one or more of their number may present the petition on behalf of all the directors.[17] Prior to the Insolvency Act 1986, a receiver could present a petition in the name of the company only if such a power could be inferred on the true construction of the debenture.[18] Such a power is deemed to be granted to an administrative receiver unless inconsistent with the terms of the debenture.[19]

The presentation of a winding-up petition does not affect the powers **2–041** of the directors or the authority of the company's agents, but section 127 of the 1986 Act retrospectively invalidates dispositions of the company's property after the date of presentation of the petition if a winding up order is made on the petition.[20]

[9] *Re Garage Doors* [1984] 1 W.L.R. 35.
[10] *Alipour v. Ary* [1997] 1 W.L.R. 534.
[11] *Re a Company* [1894] 2 Ch. 349; *Re Crigglestone Coal Co.* [1906] 2 Ch. 327; *Re a Company* (1983) 1 B.C.C. 98,937; *Re Leigh Estates (U.K.) Ltd* [1994] B.C.C. 292; *Bell Group Finance (Pty) Ltd v. Bell Group (UK) Holdings Ltd* [1996] B.C.C. 505 at 513G–514A; *Re Transtec (Campsie) Ltd*, unreported, Jacob J., March 31, 2000.
[12] *Re P & J Macrae Ltd* [1961] 1 W.L.R. 229.
[13] See below, para. 11–007.
[14] *Re Boston Timber Fabrications Ltd* [1984] B.C.L.C. 328 at 333 *per* Oliver J. *cf. Re Northern Development (Holdings) Ltd* (unreported, Templeman J., June 16, 1976 and CA, March 1, 1977).
[15] *Re Emmadart* [1979] Ch. 540. The view of Brightman J. that an article in the terms of art. 80 in Table A is insufficient for this purpose has been rejected in New South Wales: *Spicer v. Mytrent Pty. Ltd* (1984) 8 A.C.L.R. 711.
[16] Insolvency Act 1986, s.124.
[17] *Re Equiticorp International plc* (1989) 5 B.C.C. 599.
[18] *Re Emmadart Ltd* [1979] Ch. 540.
[19] Insolvency Act 1986, s. 42(1) and Sched. 1, para. 21.
[20] See *Coutts & Co. v. Stock* [2000] 1 W.L.R. 906.

2–042   As noted above, the presentation of the petition is a condition precedent to the appointment of a provisional liquidator. At any time after the presentation of an effective petition,[21] the court may on application appoint a provisional liquidator to hold office.[22] The provisional liquidator has traditionally had the role of securing the company's property pending the outcome of the petition, of maintaining the status quo and of preventing any creditor gaining priority.[23] His powers may accordingly be limited by the order appointing him,[24] and he is discharged if the petition does not result in a winding-up order.[25] His position in the past has been similar to that of a receiver of property in dispute appointed pending determination of the dispute, and he has had to display independence and neutrality in areas of potential conflict between the company and its creditors, and between the creditors themselves. Thus, he was not able without the authority of the court (which was most unlikely to be forthcoming) to take proceedings to set aside a debenture (though this might be desirable from the point of view of the unsecured creditors) or bring an end to the proceedings for winding up.[26]

2–043   The rescue culture now prevalent in insolvency has led to provisional liquidation being treated, where appropriate, in ways similar to administration order proceedings. Recent examples of this include the petition in relation to the Bank of Credit and Commerce International S.A., in which provisional liquidators were appointed at once, but themselves took part in negotiating possible schemes and rescues and themselves made representations to the court in respect of adjournments of the petition.[27] In *BCCI* and other substantial recent international insolvency and insurance cases, the powers of the provisional liquidators have been set out in wide terms in the order appointing them.

2–044   The person appointed provisional liquidator in any ordinary case used to be the official receiver,[28] though in exceptional circumstances some other person could be chosen.[29] The "exceptional" cases have become

---

[21] *Re A Company* [1973] 1 W.L.R. 1566; [1974] 1 All E.R. 256.

[22] Insolvency Act 1986, s. 135(1). The court may dispense with notice to other parties and hear the application immediately: *Re W.F. Fearman Ltd.* (1988) B.C.C. 139. The application must be made to the Companies Court judge who may hear the application in private: *Practice Direction (Companies Court: Provisional Liquidator)* [1997] 1 W.L.R. 3.

[23] *Re Dry Docks Corporation of London* [1888] 39 Ch.D. 306.

[24] Insolvency Act 1986, s. 135(5).

[25] If the petition is dismissed, the applicant for the appointment may be ordered to reimburse the company the provisional liquidator's remuneration and expenses: *Graham v. John Tullis* [1991] B.C.C. 398, Ct. of Session. But the Secretary of State for Trade and Industry, when applying without notice for the appointment of a provisional liquidator pending determination of a public interest winding-up petition is not required to give a cross-undertaking in damages.

[26] *Re Chateau Hotels Ltd.* [1977] 1 N.Z.L.R. 381.

[27] See the judgments reported at [1992] B.C.C. 83 and Moss and Phillips: "Provisional Liquidators: New Uses for an Old Remedy" (1992) Insolvency Intelligence. The passage in the text and the article were cited with approval by H.H. Judge Dean Q.C. in *Smith v. UIC Insurance Co. Ltd*, January 19, 1999.

[28] *Re Mercantile Bank of Australia* [1892] 2 Ch. 204.

[29] *Re Croftheath, The Times*, February 18, 1975; *Re W.F. Fearman Ltd* (1988) 4 B.C.C. 139 (joint appointees).

more frequent in recent years in view of the exceptional size, complexity and specialised nature of some recent insolvencies. Private insolvency practitioners are now regularly appointed as provisional liquidators where there is a business or a specialised industry or where complicated investigation is required. The provisional liquidator is bound to carry out such functions as the court may confer on him.[30] In any case where a company has gone into liquidation, or a provisional liquidator has been appointed, the liquidator or provisional liquidator may apply for the appointment of a special manager (such as a director[31]) to manage the business or property of the company with such powers as may be entrusted to him by the court.[32] The provisional receiver or special manager may be directed to carry on the company's business, and indeed the winding-up order itself may authorise or direct that the business be continued thereafter.[33]

An application for the appointment of a provisional liquidator may be **2–045** made by the petitioner, a creditor, a contributory, the company itself, the Secretary of State or any person entitled to present a petition for winding up. The applicant must show sufficient ground.[34] The court has a general discretion whether or not to make an appointment of a provisional liquidator. Two factors have traditionally been taken into account:

(a) the existence of a good prospect that the company will eventually be wound up,[35] at least if no more satisfactory exit, *e.g.* a scheme under section 425 of the Companies Act 1985, becomes available.

(b) the urgent need for relief pending the hearing of the petition, which is normally the safeguarding of assets within the jurisdiction which are in jeopardy, but in exceptional cases may extend to ascertaining the whereabouts and recovery, *e.g.* of a vessel abroad.[36]

The traditional aim and purpose of the appointment was usually to secure the assets of the company so that they may be available for equal distribution to creditors. Accordingly, obvious insolvency and jeopardy to assets are reasons for an appointment, but not the only reasons. Other reasons include the public interest in the protection of the public from

[30] Insolvency Act 1986, s. 135(4).
[31] As in *Re Mawcon* [1969] 1 W.L.R. 78.
[32] Insolvency Act 1986, s. 177(1). In *Re Union Accident Insurance Co. Ltd* [1972] 1 W.L.R. 640, the application was made without notice the day after the provisional liquidator was appointed. As to the status and remuneration of the special manager, see *Re US Ltd* (1983) 127 S.J. 748.
[33] *Re General Service Co-operative Stores* (1891) 64 L.T. 228.
[34] Insolvency Act 1986, s. 135 and Insolvency Rules 1986, r. 4.25. In case of an application by the company the court will require to be satisfied that the directors should not retain control pending the outcome of the petition: *Re Tamaris plc*, November 9, 1999.
[35] In *Re A Company* [1986] 1 W.L.R. 281 at 285, *per* Hoffmann J.
[36] In *Re A Company* [1986] Ch. 210.

the successful frauds of the company[37] and the need for an immediate vigorous investigation by a totally independent officer of the court.[38] The avoidance of a scramble by creditors for assets and the protection of the assets pending the putting forward of a scheme under the Companies Act 1985 have been accepted in recent cases as good reasons for the appointment of provisional liquidators.[39]

2–046   The serious consequences for the company of the appointment of a provisional liquidator require a relatively high standard of proof in cases in which the appointment is not sought by the company itself. The greater the prospect of the eventual order for winding up being made, the lighter the requirement for the urgent grant of relief, and vice versa.[40] If the directors unreasonably cause the company to oppose the application, an order for cost may be made against them personally.[41]

2–047   The offices of liquidator and provisional liquidator are statutory and their powers derive solely from statute: the powers of the directors do not vest in them nor can they exercise powers vested in the board.[42] The order for the appointment operates to divest the directors of powers (and in particular the power of management) by conferring those powers hitherto exercisable by the directors on the provisional liquidator and it likewise operates to revoke the authority of agents appointed to act on behalf of the company by or under the authority of the directors and this includes the agency of a receiver for the company.[43] The gazetting of the appointment constitutes notice that the directors are no longer the company's authorised agents.[44] The displacement of the powers of the directors (unlike the displacement effected on the appointment of an administrator) is not the result of any express statutory provision, but an implication arising from the inconsistency between the statutory role of the provisional liquidator and the continued existence of the directors' powers. Accordingly, the displacement is not total and does not extend to powers which cannot reasonably have been intended to vest in the provisional liquidator. Thus, it does not extend to the power of the board in the name of the company to oppose the winding-up petition, to apply

---

[37] In *Re Highfield Commodities Ltd* [1985] 1 W.L.R. 149.

[38] *Re Pinstripe Farming Co. Ltd* [1996] B.C.C. 913 (where the company was already in voluntary liquidation, but the liquidators were not perceived to be sufficiently independent); *Re Latreefers Inc* [1999] B.C.L.C. 271 (this point is not affected by the appeal); *Integro Fiduciaine SARL v. Denito Ltd* (unreported, Jacob J., March 10, 1997 noted at (1998) II Insolvency Intelligence 69 by F. Toube).

[39] This will almost invariably be the case in relation to insolvent insurance companies, where administration orders are not available, and where knowledge of the potential insolvency of the company may cause a scramble for assets and result in "short-tail" creditors receiving preferential treatment over "long-tail claimants": see *Re Andrew Weir Insurance Company Ltd* (unreported, Harman J., November 12, 1992) and *Re English & American Insurance Co. Ltd* [1994] 1 B.C.L.C. 649 at 650.

[40] *In Re Capital Expansion, The Times*, November 30, 1992.

[41] *Gamelstaden plc v. Bracklands Magazines* [1993] B.C.C. 194.

[42] *Butterell v. Docker Smith* (1997) 41 N.S.W.L.R. 129

[43] *Pacific & General Insurance Co. Ltd v. Home & Overseas Insurance Co.* [1997] B.C.C. 400 not following *KVE Homes Pty Ltd* (1979) 4 A.C.L.R. 47 at 49; [1979] 1 N.S.W.L.R. 181 at 183. The appointment of a provisional liquidator does not automatically crystallise a floating charge: *Re Obie Pty Ltd* (1983) 74 F.L.R. 231 (Sup. Ct. of Queensland).

[44] *Re Mawcon* [1969] 1 W.L.R. 78; [1969] 1 All E.R. 188.

for the discharge of the provisional liquidator or to appeal from the making of a winding-up order.[45]

The provisional liquidator can of course revive the authority of agents **2–048** of the company whose authority lapsed on his appointment.[46] The provisional liquidator is an officer of the court, and in no way the agent of the person who secures his appointment.

On the appointment of a provisional liquidator, as on the making of a **2–049** winding-up order, no action may be proceeded with or commenced against the company except by leave of the court and subject to such terms as the court may impose.[47] The provisional liquidator is bound to take into his custody or under his control all the property and things in action to which the company is or appears to be entitled.[48]

The appointment will leave the contractual relations between a **2–050** company and its employees unaffected if the petition does not result in a winding-up order,[49] and it is submitted that a subsequent winding-up order will not alter the position retrospectively. Dismissal should only occur if the provisional liquidator exercises the power of dismissal or by reason of the winding-up order being made.

If the provisional liquidator or the special manager continues the **2–051** company's business, though he may be given wide powers,[50] he carries on business as agent of the company and incurs no personal liabilities.[51]

The provisional liquidator is not entitled to appear on the hearing of **2–052** the petition[52] but in exceptional cases the court may in fact allow him to appear and to make representations in the interests of creditors.[53]

6. LIQUIDATOR[54]

The liquidator in the case of a winding-up by the court is an officer of **2–053** the court,[55] but this is not so in the case of a voluntary liquidation.[56] This

---

[45] *Re Union Accident Insurance Co. Ltd* [1972] 1 W.L.R. 640. But the directors cannot in the name of the company initiate proceedings.

[46] *Pacific & General Insurance Co. Ltd v. Home & Overseas Insurance Co.* [1997] B.C.C. 400.

[47] Insolvency Act 1986, s. 130(2).

[48] Insolvency Act 1986, s. 144(1). He may, however, be directed by the court not to spend scarce resources where it is not practical or cost-effective to pursue assets, *e.g.* where they are abroad in a jurisdiction which does not recognise the appointment.

[49] Consider *Re Dry Docks Corporation of London* [1888] 39 Ch.D. 306.

[50] Insolvency Act 1986, s. 177.

[51] *Stead Hazel & Co. v. Cooper* [1933] 1 K.B. 840; *Smith v. Lord Advocate* [1978] S.C. 259. Tax liabilities incurred in continuing to trade are to be paid in priority to other expenses incurred in the winding up: In *Re Grey Marlin Ltd* [1999] 4 All E.R. 429.

[52] *Re General International Agency Co.* (1865) 36 Beav. 1.

[53] *Re B.C.C.I.* (1992) B.C.C. 83.

[54] On the making of a winding-up order, the Official Receiver, by virtue of his office, becomes liquidator pending his replacement by an appointee capable of acting. In view of the temporary nature of his tenure of office, prior to the Insolvency Act 1986, he was confusingly called a "provisional liquidator", though he enjoyed the full powers of a liquidator: see *Re A.B.C. Coupler (No. 3)* [1970] 1 W.L.R. 702 at 715. Section 136(2) of the Insolvency Act 1986, now terms the official receiver "liquidator", and the term "provisional liquidator" is accordingly no longer apposite in this context.

[55] *Deloitte & Touche A.G. v. Johnson* [1999] 1 W.L.R. 1605.

[56] *Re T.H. Knitwear (Wholesale) Ltd* [1988] Ch. 275, CA.

difference in status is reflected in the degree of autonomy conferred upon them. The liquidator in the case of a winding-up by the court may, with the sanction of the court or the committee of inspection, carry on the business of the company so far as may be necessary for its beneficial winding-up.[57] No such sanction is required in the case of a voluntary winding-up,[58] and if the voluntary liquidator, after taking all proper advice, honestly and reasonably decides to carry on business he is not liable even if the decision turns out to be ill-fated.[59] It is however, advisable for the liquidator to seek the consent of the court if the wisdom of carrying on business may be questioned later or if the period of such continuation of business will be protracted.

2–054   The court will be very slow to interfere with the exercise by a liquidator of his powers in relation to the realisation of assets, which is essentially regarded as a matter of commercial judgment.[60] So long as the liquidator acts only in the name of the company and discloses that it is in liquidation, all debts and liabilities incurred in the course of the carrying on of such business are liabilities of the company, and not the liquidator personally. Such liabilities rank as costs of the liquidation and in priority to the general debts and liabilities of the company.[61]

2–055   The making of the winding-up order operates by implication[62] to divest the directors of all powers the exercise of which is inconsistent with the powers intended to vest in the liquidator.[63]

2–056   In the case of a voluntary liquidation, on the appointment of the liquidator, statute expressly provides that the powers of the directors shall cease except as (in the case of a member's voluntary liquidation) the members in general meeting or the liquidator and (in the case of a creditors' voluntary liquidation) the committee of inspection or the creditors sanction their continuance.[64] The directors in a voluntary liquidation accordingly retain no residual powers.

2–057   In both cases, the company's directors and employees continue to be under a duty not to disclose confidential information of the company, for this is as much the property of the company as any other asset.[65] The directors also become subject to a duty to comply with section 208(1) of the Insolvency Act 1986 which requires them to cooperate with the

---

[57] Insolvency Act 1986, Sched. 4, Pt. II, para. 5.

[58] Insolvency Act 1986, Sched. 4, Pts. II and III.

[59] Re Great Eastern Electric Co. Ltd [1941] Ch. 241.

[60] Re Buckingham International plc (No. 2) [1998] B.C.C. 943 (CA); Re Edennote Ltd [1996] B.C.C. 718 (CA); Mahomed v. Morris (unreported, CA, February 17, 2000).

[61] Re S. Davis & Co. [1945] Ch. 402.

[62] But see contra (query per incuriam) Shaw L.J. in Newhart v. Co-op. International Bank [1978] Q.B. 814 at 819.

[63] It has been held that the powers retained by the directors extend to instructing solicitors and counsel in the name of the company to appeal against the order: Re Union Accident Insurance Co. Ltd [1972] 1 W.L.R. 640. This exception is perhaps a historical anomaly and has been superseded in Australia by a statutory provision empowering the court to appoint an agent for a company in liquidation authorised to appeal: Rock Bottom Fashion Market Pty Ltd v. HR & CE Griffiths Pty Ltd (1997) 25 A.C.S.R. 467, Queensland CA.

[64] Insolvency Act 1986, s. 91(2) (members) and s. 103 (creditors).

[65] Re Country Traders Distribution Ltd [1974] 2 N.S.W.L.R. 135.

liquidator and pro-actively (rather than reactively) to disclose and deliver to the liquidator the company's property.[66]

Liquidation is in all ordinary cases the end of the road for the **2–058** company,[67] though not necessarily for its undertaking and business. This is reflected in the principle of law enshrined in section 107 of the Insolvency Act 1986 that on the commencement of winding-up the beneficial ownership by the company of its assets is terminated and such assets are thereafter held subject to a form of statutory trust for distribution to creditors and contributories according to their entitlement[68]:

> ". . . on a winding-up . . . the statutory scheme for distribution of a company's assets among its creditors comes into operation . . . once the company has gone into liquidation, the unsecured creditors are in the nature of cestui que trust with beneficial interests extending to all the company's property under that scheme. Realistically in view of [section 127 of the Insolvency Act 1986], the scheme relates back to the commencement of the winding-up."[69]

In the case of a compulsory or voluntary liquidation, the liquidator **2–059** may sell for cash the whole or any part of the company's undertaking.[70] In the case of a members' voluntary liquidation, he may (with the sanction of a special resolution) sell or enter into a transaction whereby the whole or part of the undertaking is transferred to another company in return for benefits in the form of cash, shares, policies or other interests in the transferee company provided either to the transferor company or directly to its members.[71]

Even a winding-up order may be stayed and the company given a fresh **2–060** lease of life if, by reason of some turn of events, it is proved that the company is viable.[72] This jurisdiction is however, to be exercised with the utmost caution and cogent reasons need to be demonstrated.[73] Prior to the Insolvency Act 1986, the discretion to grant this relief could only be exercised if it was shown that:

(a) the creditors would be paid off in full or otherwise satisfied, *e.g.* by means of a scheme pursuant to s.425 of the Companies Act 1985;

---

[66] *R v. McCredie, The Times* October 5, 1999, CA.

[67] In *Re MTI Trading* [1998] B.C.C. 400, CA at 402–403 *per* Saville L.J. said that winding up orders "bring the life of the company to an end". The life of the company can however be revived if the winding up is stayed: see below.

[68] *Ayerst v. C & K (Construction) Ltd* [1976] A.C. 167; *Re Calgary & Edmonton Land Co. Ltd* [1975] 1 W.L.R. 355 at 359.

[69] *R. v. Registrar of Companies, ex p. Central Bank of India* [1986] 1 All E.R. 105 at 112 *per* Dillon L.J. (CA.) citing as authority Lord Brightman in *Victoria Housing Estates Ltd. v. Ashpurton Estates Ltd* [1983] Ch. 110 at 123.

[70] Insolvency Act 1986, s. 167 (compulsory), s. 165 (voluntary) and Sched. 4.

[71] Insolvency Act 1986, ss. 110, 111.

[72] Insolvency Act 1986, s.147(1).

[73] *Re Piccadilly Property Management Ltd* [1999] 2 B.C.L.C. 145.

      (b) the liquidator would be safeguarded; and
      (c) the members consented or payment of at least as much as they would receive on a winding-up was secured.[74]

A similar jurisdiction existed in respect of companies in voluntary liquidation and the same considerations applied.[75]

2–061   As noted above, the Insolvency Act 1986 provides that the liquidator himself may now propose a company voluntary arrangement. The court may stay the winding-up proceedings pending the outcome of the meetings and, if the proposal is duly passed (in the case of a compulsory liquidation) rescind the winding up order and (in the case of a voluntary liquidation) permanently stay the liquidation[76] to facilitate the implementation of the scheme or composition under the supervision of the supervisor.

---

[74] *Re Calgary & Edmonton Land Co. Ltd* [1975] 1 W.L.R. 355.
[75] *Re SS Titian* (1888) 36 W.R. 347. Such an application would now be made under Insolvency Act 1986, s.112.
[76] *Re Dollar Land (Feltham) Ltd* [1995] 2 B.C.L.C. 370.

CHAPTER 3

THE BASIS OF APPOINTMENT OF RECEIVERS: FIXED AND FLOATING CHARGES

1. FIXED AND FLOATING CHARGES

(a) General

Receivers over the property of a company[1] are commonly appointed **3–001** under the terms of a debenture containing a mixture of fixed and floating charges.[2] In *Re Bank of Credit and Commerce International S.A. (No. 8)* Lord Hoffmann described a charge as a proprietary interest granted by way of security, and continued,

> "Proprietary interests confer rights in rem which, subject to questions of registration and the equitable doctrine of purchaser for value without notice, will be binding upon third parties and unaffected by the insolvency of the owner of the property charged. A proprietary interest provided by way of security entitles the holder to resort to the property only for the purposes of satisfying some liability due to him (whether from the person providing the security or a third party) and, whatever the form of the transaction, the owner of the property retains an equity of redemption to have the property restored to him when the liability has been discharged. The method by which the holder of the security will resort to the property will ordinarily involve its sale or, more rarely, the extinction of the equity of redemption by foreclosure. A charge is a security interest created without any transfer of title or possession to the beneficiary. An equitable charge can be created by an informal transaction for value (legal charges may require a deed or registration or both) and over any kind of property (equitable as well as legal) but is subject to the doctrine of purchaser for value without notice applicable to all equitable interests."[3]

---

[1] It has been suggested that an individual cannot create a floating charge unless he has the statutory power to do so: see *e.g.* the Agricultural Credits Act 1928 in relation to farmers. For a discussion of the justice of this discrimination, see J. Weisman, "Floating Charges on Assets of an Individual" (1986) 21 Israel Law Review 129.

[2] Generally speaking, there is no need for the purposes of this work to distinguish between a "charge" and a "mortgage". "The technical difference between a 'mortgage' or 'charge', though in practice the phrases are used interchangeably, is that a mortgage involves a conveyance of property subject to a right of redemption, whereas a charge conveys nothing and merely gives the chargee certain rights over the property as security for the loan . . .", per Slade J. in *Re Bond Worth* [1980] Ch. 228 at 250E. See also per Buckley L.J. in *Swiss Bank Corporation v. Lloyds Bank Limited* [1982] A.C. 584 at 594–595, CA.

[3] [1998] A.C. 214 at 226, HL. See also the classic description of a charge by Atkin L.J. in *National Provincial and Union Bank of England v. Charnley* [1924] 1 K.B. 431 at 449–450

3–002 Strictly speaking, a debenture is merely a writing of a company creating or acknowledging a debt and may be secured by a charge or charges over the assets of the company or may be unsecured.[4] However, it is only a secured debenture which will normally provide for the appointment of a receiver by the holder of the debenture, for the right to appoint is in practice invariably an incident of the charge on property. In theory, an unsecured debenture or other contract could provide for the appointment of a receiver or manager, but this does not occur in practice.[5]

3–003 In the absence of a provision to the contrary, a debenture is freely assignable,[6] but in so far as it is a chose in action, the assignee takes subject to all equities subsisting between the assignor and the company at the date that notice is given to the company, unless the debenture contains a provision that the assignor may transfer free of such equities.[7]

(b) Distinguishing between fixed and floating charges

3–004 In the leading case of *Re Yorkshire Woolcombers Association Ltd, Illingworth v. Houldsworth*, a fixed charge[8] was described as a charge that "without more fastens on ascertained and defined property or property

and the statement of Millett J. in *Re Charge Card Services Limited* [1987] Ch. 150 at 176. There should be a clear conceptual distinction between a charge and a trust: see *Re Associated Alloys Pty Ltd v. ACN 001 452 106 Pty Ltd* (2000) 171 A.L.R. 568 at 571, High Court of Australia; but in *Re Bond Worth Limited* [1980] Ch. 228 at 250 Slade J. held that a debtor can create an equitable charge by declaring himself to be a trustee of property "by way of security" for the payment of a specified debt. See also the differing approaches to this idea in *Re ILG Travel Limited* [1995] 2 B.C.L.C. 128 (Jonathan Parker J.) and *Stephens Travel Service International Pty Ltd v. Qantas Airways Limited* (1988) 13 N.S.W.L.R. 331, N.S.W.C.A.

[4] See, *e.g. Austral Mining Construction Pty. Ltd. v. NZI Capital Corporation Ltd* (1991) 9 A.C.L.C. 651. cf. "A security issued by a company is called a debenture . . ." *per* Lord Templeman in *Downsview Ltd. v. First City Corporation Ltd* [1993] A.C. 295 at 311E, PC. On the other hand a charge may be created where the chargor has no personal liability to make a payment: see *Re Conley* [1938] 2 All E.R. 127. Such a collateral security might take the form of a floating charge. Such a charge, though neither creating or acknowledging a debt would, for practical legal purposes, be treated as a debenture.

[5] A debenture need not be executed as a deed, but it is desirable that it should be for at least two reasons. First, because certain statutory powers are only conferred on a mortgagee where the mortgage is created by deed: *e.g.* powers of sale and to appoint a receiver: s.101 of the Law of Property Act 1925. Secondly, although the common law rule that an agent cannot deliver a deed unless he is appointed under seal has been abolished by section 1(1)(c) of the Law of Property (Miscellaneous Provisions) Act 1989, that statute does not appear to have abolished the common law rule that an agent cannot execute a deed unless his authority to do so has been conferred under seal: see Harpum and Virgo "Breaking the Seal, the New Law on Deeds" [1991] Lloyd's Maritime and Commercial Law Quarterly 209. If a debenture is granted by a company under seal and contains a clause irrevocably appointing any receivers who might be appointed by the mortgagee to be attorneys for the company with power to execute deeds, this will satisfy the common law rule. Thus, receivers who were subsequently appointed only in writing could validly execute a deed: see *Phoenix Proprties Ltd. v. Wimpole Street Nominees Ltd* [1992] B.C.L.C. 737.

[6] See, *e.g. Re Portbase (Clothing) Ltd* [1993] Ch. 388 for a suggestion that the benefit of a fixed charge might be assigned as part of an agreement as to priority between chargeholders.

[7] *Hilger Analytical Ltd v. Rank Precision Industries Ltd* [1984] B.C.L.C. 301. Such clauses are commonly inserted in debentures.

[8] Sometimes referred to as a "specific" charge. In this context, the terms "fixed" and "specific" are interchangeable: see *Re ASRS Establishment Ltd* [2000] I B.C.L.C 272, *per* Park J., whose decision was upheld on appeal, unreported, July 20, 2000, CA.

capable of being ascertained and defined".[9] The fixed charge creates an immediate interest in the chargee, either at once in the case of existing property or, in the case of future property, at the point of acquisition of that property by the company.[10]

In the Court of Appeal in the same case[11] Romer L.J. set out three **3–005** characteristics of a floating charge. As Romer L.J. indicated, if a charge has all these features it will be a floating charge, but they are not an exact definition and need not all be present in a floating charge. In reality the features are helpful tests or indicators to assist the determination whether a charge is a floating charge.[12] The three features mentioned are:

(a) that it is a charge on a class of assets of a company present and future[13];

(b) that the class is one which, in the ordinary course of the business of the company, would be changing from time to time; and

(c) that it is contemplated that, until some future step is taken by the chargee, the company may carry on its ordinary course of business in respect of the class of charged assets.[14]

The last two indicia mentioned by Romer L.J. have generally been **3–006** taken to mean that if the charge is granted by reference to a general class of assets which it is anticipated will be changing in the ordinary course of the company's business, and the charge permits the company to dispose of assets from that class at will and for its own account, then even if other assets are acquired to replace those disposed of, the charge will not be a fixed charge. As Vaughan-Williams L.J. stated in *Re Yorkshire Woolcombers Association Ltd*[15]:

"I do not think that for a 'specific security' you need to have a security of a subject-matter which is then in existence. I mean by 'then' at the time of the execution of the security; but what you do require to make a specific security is that the security whenever it has come into existence, and has been identified or appropriated as a security, shall never thereafter at the wish of the mortgagor cease to be a security. If at the wish of the mortgagor he can dispose of it and prevent it being any longer a security, although something else may be substituted more or less for it, that is not a 'specific security.'"

[9] [1904] A.C. 355 at 358, *per* Lord Macnaughten.

[10] *Tailby v. Official Receiver* (1888) 13 App. Cas. 523.

[11] [1903] 2 Ch. 284 at 295; and see the comments in *Re Bond Worth Ltd* [1980] Ch. 228, *per* Slade J.

[12] See, *e.g. per* Vinelott J. in *Re Atlantic Medical Ltd* [1992] B.C.C. 653 at 658E–658F.

[13] See also *Re Panama, New Zealand and Australia Royal Mail Co.* (1870) L.R. 5 Ch. App. 318.

[14] It is implicit that if the company carries on its business in the ordinary way, it does so for its own account.

[15] [1903] 2 Ch. 284 at 295.

3–007 The passages referred to above were cited in *Re Cosslett (Contractors) Ltd*[16] and Millett L.J. (as he then was) continued,

> "The essence of a floating charge is that it is a charge, not on any particular asset, but on a fluctuating body of assets which remain under the management and control of the chargor, and which the chargor has the right to withdraw from the security despite the existence of the charge. The essence of a fixed charge is that the charge is on a particular asset or class of assets which the chargor cannot deal with free from the charge without the consent of the chargee."

3–008 The exact nature of a floating charge has occasioned considerable academic[17] and judicial[18] debate. It is clear that a floating charge is a present security and not merely an agreement to create a future charge.[19] However, it is unclear whether, and if so to what extent, a floating charge creates a proprietary interest in any assets covered by its terms. The traditional view is that, whilst a floating charge creates a species of immediate equitable interest over the class of charged assets in favour of the chargee, it does not create an immediate proprietary interest in any specific assets.[20] Instead, the interest "floats"[21] over the company's property, leaving the company free to deal with and dispose of the

---

[16] [1998] Ch. 495 at 510c.

[17] See, *e.g.* J.H. Farrar (1980) 1 Company Lawyer 83; Gough, *Company Charges* (2nd ed.) pages 97–101; Goode, *Legal Problems of Credit and Security* (2nd ed.), pp. 47 *et seq.*; E. Ferran, "Floating Charges, The Nature of the Security" [1988] Cambridge Law Journal 213; S. Worthington, "Floating Charges: An Alternative Theory" [1994] Cambridge Law Journal 81.

[18] See, *e.g. Driver v. Broad* [1893] 1 Q.B. 744; *Re Yorkshire Woolcombers' Association Ltd* [1903] 2 Ch. 284; *Illingworth v. Houldsworth* [1904] A.C. 355 at 358; *Evans v. Rival Granite Quarries Ltd* [1910] 2 K.B. 979; *Re Dawson* [1915] 1 Ch. 626; *Re Manurewa Transport Ltd* [1971] N.Z.L.R. 909; *Cretanor Maritime Co. Ltd v. Irish Marine Management Ltd* [1978] 1 W.L.R. 966; *Landall Holdings v. Caratti* [1979] W.A.R. 97; *United Builders Pty Ltd v. Mutual Acceptance Ltd* (1980) 144 C.L.R. 673; *Hamilton v. Hunter* (1982) 7 A.C.L.R. 295; *Re Margart Pty Ltd, Re Hamilton v. Westpac Banking Corp* (1984) 2 A.C.L.C. 709; [1985] B.C.L.C. 314; *Tricontinental Corp Ltd v. Federal Commissioner of Taxation* (1987) 5 A.C.L.C. 555; *R. in Right of British Columbia v. Federal Business Development Bank* (1987) 65 C.B.R. 201; *Re Atlantic Computer Systems plc* [1992] Ch. 505; *Fire Nymph Products Ltd v. The Heating Centre Pty Ltd* (1992) 7 A.C.S.R. 365; *Re Atlantic Medical Ltd* [1992] B.C.C. 653; *Re New Bullas Trading Ltd* [1993] B.C.C. 251; [1994] B.C.C. 36, CA; *Royal Trust Bank v. National Westminster Bank plc* [1996] 2 B.C.L.C. 682, Ch.D. and [1996] B.C.C. 613, CA.

[19] *Evans v. Rival Granite Quarries Ltd* [1910] 2 K.B. 979 at 999 *per* Buckley L.J.; *Re Cimex Tissues Ltd* [1995] 1 B.C.L.C. 409 at 420.

[20] *Evans v. Rival Granite Quarries Ltd* [1910] 2 K.B. 979 at 999 *per* Buckley L.J. See also *Tricontinental Corp Ltd v. Federal Commissioner of Taxation* (1987) 5 A.C.L.C. 555; *Fire Nymph Products Ltd v. The Heating Centre Pty Ltd* (1992) 7 A.C.S.R. 365; *Re Cimex Tissues Ltd* [1995] 1 B.C.L.C. 409. Alternative theories of the nature of a floating charge suggest that the charge does not confer a proprietary interest of any description over property until crystallisation (Gough, *op. cit.*); or that the floating charge does create an immediate equitable interest in the charged property but that such property can be disposed of to third parties in the ordinary course of business who will take free of the debenture-holder's interest (Farrar, *op. cit.*; Ferran, *op. cit.*; Worthington *op. cit.*). Gough's view has received some judicial support in Australia: see *Lyford v. Commonwealth Bank of Australia* (1995) 17 A.C.S.R. 211 at 217–218, and *Wily v. St George Partnership Banking Ltd* (1997) 26 A.C.S.R. 1 at 5–10, which was, however, doubted on appeal, (1999) 30 A.C.S.R. 204 at 209–214.

[21] Knox J. has remarked that "The concept of a floating charge appears to defy judicial definition without the aid of metaphor": see *Re New Bullas Trading Ltd* [1993] B.C.C. 251.

property in the ordinary course of its business.[22] The equitable interest created is, however, capable of binding a third party who acquired property subject to a floating charge other than in the ordinary course of the company's business with actual or constructive notice of the nature of the charge and the circumstances of transfer.[23] Moreover, whilst the charge is still "floating", the debenture-holder may obtain an injunction to restrain the company from dealing with the assets other than in the ordinary course of business[24] or may obtain the appointment by the court of a receiver where the security is in jeopardy.[25]

Under the traditional theory, the floating charge only becomes effective **3–009** to pass equitable title and is only immediately enforceable when it attaches to specific property on the occurrence of a specified event or events, thereby taking on the form of a fixed charge.[26] This process is referred to as "crystallisation" of the floating charge and brings to an end the right of the company to deal with the property which is the subject of the charge for its own benefit in the ordinary course of its business.[27]

It will be apparent that an important element which distinguishes a **3–010** floating charge from a fixed charge is the right of the company to deal with the charged assets "in the ordinary course of business" of the company.[28] It is not possible to define conclusively what may be included

---

[22] *Re Yorkshire Woolcombers' Association Ltd* [1903] 2 Ch. 284, *per* Romer L.J. and *Re Brightlife Ltd* [1987] Ch. 200 at 209, *per* Hoffmann J.

[23] See, *e.g. Hamilton v. Hunter* (1982) 7 A.C.L.R. 295; *Reynolds Bros. (Motors) Pty Ltd v. Esanda Ltd* (1983) 8 A.C.L.R. 422; (1983) 1 A.C.L.C. 1, 333.

[24] *Hubbuck v. Helms* (1887) 56 L.T. 232; *Re Woodroffes (Musical Instruments) Ltd* [1986] 1 Ch. 366 at 378A, *per* Nourse J.; *Atkins v. Mercantile Credit Ltd* (1985) 10 A.C.L.R. 153.

[25] *Edwards v. Standard Rolling Stock Syndicate* [1893] 1 Ch. 574; *Re Victoria Steamboats Ltd* [1897] 1 Ch. 158; *Re London Pressed Hinge Co. Ltd* [1905] 1 Ch. 576. See further below, para. 22–013.

[26] See, *e.g.* Gough, *op cit.,* pp. 135 *et seq.*; E. Ferran [1988] C.L.J. 213; *Driver v. Broad* [1893] 1 Q.B. 744; *Durham Bros v. Robertson* [1898] 1 Q.B. 765 (where the floating charge was likened to an incomplete assignment completed on crystallisation); *Wallace v. Evershed* [1899] 1 Ch. 891 at 894, *per* Cozens-Hardy J.; *Evans v. Rival Granite Quarries Ltd* [1910] 2 K.B. 979 at 994 and 996, *per* Fletcher-Moulton L.J.; *Re Manurewa Transport Ltd* [1971] N.Z.L.R. 909; *Business Computers Ltd v. Anglo-African Leasing Ltd* [1977] 1 W.L.R. 578; *Re Tullow Engineering (Holdings) Ltd* [1990] I.R. 452, *per* Blayney J., H.Ct. (Ireland) (in which the crystallisation of a floating charge over shares was said to constitute an equitable assignment of the shares to the debenture-holder which thus prevented a third party from exercising options to purchase the shares which had been granted after creation of the floating charge). See also *Re ELS Ltd* [1994] B.C.C. 449. However, *cf. Re Margart Pty Ltd, Re Hamilton v. Westpac Banking Corp* [1985] B.C.L.C. 314 (followed by Vinelott J. in *Re French's (Wine Bar) Ltd* [1987] B.C.L.C. 499 and referred to with approval by the same judge in *Re Atlantic Medical Ltd* [1992] B.C.C. 653) in which a disposition of property caught by an uncrystallised floating charge to the chargee was said not to require the approval of the court pursuant to the equivalent of s. 127 of the Insolvency Act 1986 because the effect of the floating charge was to pass an equitable interest in the property to the chargee. These decisions are criticised by Gough, *op. cit.,* at pp. 354 *et seq.*

[27] See, *e.g. per* Gleeson C.J. in *Fire Nymph Products Ltd v. The Heating Centre Pty Ltd* (1992) 7 A.C.S.R. 365 at 373.

[28] See, *e.g.* the discussion in *Willmott v. London Celluloid Co.* (1886) 34 Ch.D. 147; *Hamer v. London City and Midland Bank Ltd* (1918) 118 L.T. 571; *Re Cummins* (1986) 62 A.L.R. 129; *Re GE Tunbridge Ltd* [1995] 1 B.C.L.C. 34; and the *dicta* of Millett L.J. in *Re Cosslett (Contractors) Ltd* [1998] Ch. 495, CA referred to above in para. 3–007. The expression "ordinary course of business" is also used in the New Zealand voidable preference provisions and in that context was considered by the Privy Council in

in this concept, but it is clear that the expression has a wide meaning. The payment of trade debts and the sales of stock-in-trade[29] (including sales on hire purchase[30]) will usually be regarded as being in the ordinary course of business.[31]

3–011   However, it is suggested that it is an essential pre-requisite of any such disposition that it be made with a view to the continuation of the company's business as a going concern.[32] Thus, for example, the transfer by a company of the whole of its stock back to its supplier in circumstances where the company was insolvent and there was no prospect of the company continuing to distribute the products would not be a transaction in the ordinary course of the company's business.[33] Similarly, the sale of assets or a part of the business of a company at an undervalue or on extended terms as to payment at a time when the company is insolvent or facing insolvency is unlikely to be regarded as a sale in the ordinary course of business.[34] Likewise, the transmission of funds by a provisional liquidator to various bank accounts in order to circumvent the freezing of the company's bank accounts is likely to be outside the usual course of the company's business.[35]

3–012   The grant of specific charges over some or all of a company's assets may be regarded as being in the ordinary course of its business,[36] as will the subsequent grant of a floating charge over some part of the same assets, even if it is expressed to rank in priority to the earlier charge.[37] However, the creation of a subsequent floating charge which is expressed to rank *pari passu* with an earlier floating charge over the same assets will apparently be regarded as inconsistent with the bargain with the earlier chargee under which the company was granted the freedom to deal with its assets in the ordinary course of its business.[38]

3–013   It is often critical to determine whether a particular charge over defined assets is fixed or floating. A fixed charge is generally the best

---

Countrywide Banking v. Dean [1998] 1 B.C.L.C. 306. Compare the approach of the Privy Council to the words "in the ordinary course of its [*i.e.* the particular company's] business" in the context of the then Australian law on financial assistance in *Steen v. Law* [1964] A.C. 287, PC.

[29] *Willmott v. London Celluloid Co.* (1886) 34 Ch.D. 147; *Hamer v. London City and Midland Bank Ltd* (1918) 118 L.T. 571; *Re Old Bushmills Distillery Co.* [1897] I.R. 488; *R. in Right of British Columbia v. Federal Business Development Bank* (1987) 65 C.B.R. 201.

[30] *Dempsey v. Traders' Finance Corp Ltd* [1933] N.Z.L.R. 1258.

[31] See also *Mac-Jordan Construction Ltd v. Brookmount Erostin Ltd* [1992] B.C.L.C. 350, in which the Court of Appeal thought that the existence of floating charge would not, until crystallisation, have prevented a property development company from fulfilling its contractual obligations to create a trust fund into which to pay retention moneys due to a builder.

[32] It has been said that a floating charge is founded upon what is taken to be the mutual assumption of the parties that the company's business will continue as a going concern: *per* Sheller J.A. in *Fire Nymph Products Ltd v. The Heating Centre Pty Ltd* (1992) 7 A.C.S.R. 365 at 376.

[33] *Fire Nymph Products Ltd v. The Heating Centre Pty Ltd* (1992) 7 A.C.S.R. 365.

[34] *Torzillu Pty Ltd v. Brynac Pty Ltd* (1983) 8 A.C.L.R. 52.

[35] *Re Bartlett Estates Pty Ltd* (1988) 14 A.C.L.R. 512.

[36] *Cox Moore v. Peruvian Corporation Ltd* [1908] 1 Ch. 604; *Reynolds Bros (Motors) Pty Ltd v. Esanda Ltd* (1983) 8 A.C.L.R. 422; (1983) 1 A.C.L.C. 1 at 1,333.

[37] *Re Automatic Bottle Makers Ltd* [1926] Ch. 412.

[38] *Re Benjamin Cope & Sons Ltd* [1914] 1 Ch. 800.

type of security for the creditor as it gives the chargee priority over preferential creditors and other claims on the company's assets.[39] If a receiver is in any doubt as to the character of the charge, he should investigate any material facts that may not be clear,[40] seek legal advice and, if necessary, seek the directions of the court.[41]

Resolution of the question of whether the charge in a particular case **3–014** is fixed or floating may involve two stages. The first stage (which is only a live question in rare cases) involves consideration of whether, in so far as the debenture purports to create a fixed charge on a particular asset, the provision in the debenture is susceptible of challenge on the grounds that the debenture should be rectified or the specific provision ignored as a sham. To establish a claim to rectification, it must be proved that the parties to the debenture had a prior agreement that the charge in respect of the particular asset should be a floating charge, and that the debenture was intended to but did not give effect to that agreement as a result of a common or, exceptionally, a unilateral mistake by the parties.[42] To establish a sham, it is necessary to show that the parties to the debenture actually agreed or intended at the time of execution that the debenture should not operate according to its terms, *i.e.* that notwithstanding the supposed imposition of a fixed charge, the parties in fact intended that company should be entirely free to deal with the property in question without reference to the terms of the written document.[43]

Once it is accepted that the documents genuinely represent the **3–015** transaction into which the parties have entered, the second stage is the construction of the terms of the charge documentation against the commercial background in order to ascertain the true legal character of the transaction. In the case of a charge, the relevant background will include the terms of the company's memorandum and articles of association, the nature of its business, and the relationship between the company and the chargee.[44] The label "fixed" or "floating" attached to the charge by the parties in the documentation will not of itself be

---

[39] Such as liquidation expenses.

[40] If he is an administrative receiver and it becomes necessary to do so, using his special powers under ss. 235 and 236 of the Insolvency Act 1986; see paras 5–011 to 5–071 below.

[41] Under s. 35 of the Insolvency Act 1986.

[42] For rectification generally, see Snell, *Principles of Equity* (30th ed.), Chap. 43. Rectification will generally not be permitted if it would prejudice a bona fide purchaser for value who has acquired an interest in the property dealt with in the instrument sought to be rectified. The court may refuse rectification of a debenture following liquidation of the company on the grounds that it would prejudice unsecured creditors who acquired an interest in the assets of the company upon winding-up: see *J.J. Leonard Properties Pty Ltd v. Leonard (W.A.) Pty Ltd* (1987) 5 A.C.L.C. 838.

[43] *R. v. Knightsbridge Crown Court, ex p. Marcrest Properties Ltd* [1983] 1 W.L.R. 300 at 308, citing *Snook v. London and West Riding Investments Ltd* [1967] 2 Q.B. 786 at 802. See also the dicta of the Court of Appeal in *Welsh Development Agency v. Export Finance Co. Ltd* [1992] B.C.C. 270 and *Orion Finance v. Crown Financial Management Ltd* [1996] 2 B.C.L.C. 78, CA; [1996] B.C.C. 621, CA.

[44] See, *e.g. United Builders Pty Ltd v. Mutual Acceptance Ltd* (1979) 33 A.L.R. 1; *Boambee Bay Resort Pty Ltd v. Equus Financial Services Ltd* (1991) 6 A.S.C.R. 532; (1992) 10 A.C.L.C. 56, NSW, CA; *Re GE Tunbridge Ltd* [1995] 1 B.C.L.C. 34; *Re Cimex Tissues Ltd* [1995] 1 B.C.L.C. 409; *Re Cosslett (Contractors) Ltd* [1998] Ch. 495, CA.

decisive, but the court will only depart from the expressed intention of the parties if it is apparent that the legal effect of the terms of the charge are inconsistent with that expressed intention.[45]

3–016   Although the concept of a fixed charge fits best where the charged asset is part of the enduring capital structure of the company, rather than where the charged asset is one which will come and go in the normal routine of business operations,[46] as a matter of law the assets which may be the subject of a fixed charge are not limited to any particular category or description.[47] It is, moreover, conceptually possible to create a fixed charge over a specified class of assets, coupled with a limited licence to the chargor to deal with those charged assets.[48]

3–017   Accordingly, in construing the terms of the charge, it will be necessary to identify the nature of the class of charged assets[49] and to ascertain whether the parties have agreed that the charged assets must be retained by the company as the subject of a specific charge, or whether the company is intended to be at liberty to deal with the assets in the ordinary course of its business as a going concern, free from the chargee's security. Any unfettered freedom in the chargor to deal with a fluctuating class of assets in the ordinary course of his business without the consent of the chargee will be inconsistent with the existence of a fixed charge over those assets.[50] Resolution of this issue will therefore

[45] *Evans v. Rival Granite Quarries Ltd* [1910] 2 K.B. 974 at 993; *Siebe Gorman & Co. Ltd v. Barclays Bank* [1979] 2 Lloyd's Rep. 142 at 159, *per* Slade J.; *Re Falcon Sportswear Pty Ltd* (1983) 1 A.C.L.C. 690; *Re Wallyn Industries Pty Ltd* (1983) 7 A.C..L.R. 661; *Re Quarry & Foundry Engineering Pty Ltd* (1984) 2 A.C.L.C. 714; *Norgard v. Deputy Federal Commissioner of Taxation* (1987) 5 A.C.L.C. 527; *Re New Bullas Trading Ltd* [1993] B.C.C. 251 (Knox J.), reversed, [1994] B.C.C. 36, CA.; *Re Cimex Tissues Ltd* [1995] 1 B.C.L.C. 409; *cf. Street v. Mountford* [1985] A.C. 809 at 824 (lease or licence); and *cf. Welsh Development Agency v. Export Finance Co. Ltd* [1992] B.C.C. 270, CA. (sale or charge); *Orion Finance Ltd v. Crown Financial Management Ltd* [1994] 2 B.C.L.C. 607 (assignment or charge), upheld [1996] 2 B.C.L.C. 78 at 85e, CA; *Re Cosslett (Contractors) Ltd* [1998] Ch. 495, CA (right of possession or charge; mere power of sale or charge); *Re Hamlet International plc* [1998] 2 B.C.L.C. 164 affirmed, [2000] B.C.C. 602, CA (lien with power of sale or charge); *Re ASRS Establishment Ltd* [2000] 1 B.C.L.C. 727, affirmed by the Court of Appeal, unreported, July 20, 2000.

[46] See *Re ASRS Establishment Ltd, (supra) per* Park J. at [2000] 1 B.C.L.C. 727 at 732

[47] See, *e.g. State Bank of India v. Lisbellow Ltd* [1989] 2 H.K.L.R. 604, *per* Godfrey J. (holding that a textile "quota" granted by the authorities in Hong Kong was capable of being the subject of a fixed charge). But the contract creating a chose in action may prohibit the assignment or charging of the chose: see *Linden Gardens Trust Ltd v. Lenesta Sludge Disposals Ltd* [1994] 1 A.C. 85. In such a case, the charge would not attach to the non-assignable contractual rights: see *Re Turner Corporation Ltd* (1995) 17 A.C.S.R. 761. A charge may still be created over a purportedly non-assignable right if there had been effective waiver of the prohibition on assignment, or if an estoppel precludes reliance on the prohibition: see *Orion Finance Ltd v. Crown Financial Management Ltd* [1994] 2 B.C.L.C. 607.

[48] A limited liberty to deal with specific assets in a non-fluctuating class was held not to be incompatible with a fixed charge in *Re Cimex Tissues Ltd* [1995] 1 B.C.L.C. 409 at 420–424.

[49] In *Re ASRS Establishment Ltd*, unreported, July 20, 2000, the Court of Appeal left open the question of whether a clause in a debenture which listed a number of different types of assets and purported to subject them all to a fixed charge, had necessarily to be construed on an "all or nothing" basis. At first instance Park J. had favoured the view that this was so: [2000] 1 B.C.L.C. 727.

[50] See *per* Millett L.J. in *Royal Trust Bank v. National Westminster Bank plc* [1996] B.C.C.

require an examination of the nature and extent of the restrictions placed by the charge upon the dealings by the company with the charged assets to see if the chargee has retained control of the assets in question.[51]

The character of a transaction, whether or not a charge and (if a **3–018** charge) whether a fixed or floating charge, is to be determined by reference to the facts as they were or might be foreseen at the date of the transaction.[52] The parties may subsequently vary the character of their agreement[53] but, in the absence of an express agreement to this effect, the courts are likely to be slow to infer that any fundamental change in the nature of the transaction has taken place merely because in commercial practice the parties have occasionally departed from the strict terms of the contract. For example, in *Lloyd's and Scottish Finance Ltd v. Cyril Lord Carpets Sales Ltd*[54] the parties had set up a block discounting arrangement. Although there had been "some inconsistency" with the contractual arrangements and "rough edges" in the way that business had been done, given the flexibility of the block discounting agreement and the large number of transactions involved, the House of

---

613 at 618D, 618H; and also *per* Millett L.J. in *Re Cosslett (Contractors) Ltd* [1998] Ch. 495 at 510C. The courts have in general been unwilling to characterise charges which permit the debtor to deal with a fluctuating class of charged assets in the ordinary course of business as fixed charges with a licence to deal. The courts generally characterise such charges as floating charges. See, *e.g.* the discussion in *R. in Right of British Columbia v. Federal Business Development Bank* (1987) 65 C.B.R. 201, CA British Columbia. For a discussion of this topic from an historical perspective, suggesting that in principle it ought to be possible to have a fixed charge with a licence to deal as an alternative to a floating charge in relation to a fluctuating class of assets, see Gregory & Walton, "Fixed Charges over Changing Assets: The Possession and Control Heresy" [1998] Company, Financial & Insolvency Law Review 68. It is suggested that such historical analysis cannot be reconciled with the approach adopted in cases since *Illingworth v. Houldsworth,* including in particular the approach of Hoffmann J. in *Re Brightlife Ltd* [1987] Ch. 200 and of Millett L.J. in the *Royal Trust Bank* and *Cosslett (Contractors)* cases (*supra*).

[51] See, *e.g. State Bank of India v. Lisbellow Ltd* [1989] 2 H.K.L.R. 604 at 609–610, referring to *Siebe Gorman Co. Ltd v. Barclays Bank* [1979] 2 Lloyd's Rep. 142 and to *Re Brightlife Ltd* [1987] Ch. 200. In *Re New Bullas Ltd* [1993] B.C.C. 251 Knox J. held that the "touchstone" for determining whether a charge was a fixed or floating charge was the extent to which the chargor company was left free to deal with the charged assets. In *William Gaskell Group Ltd v. Highley* [1993] B.C.C. 200, Morritt J. referred to the need for a "sufficient restriction" on dealings and found the requirement satisfied by clauses requiring the proceeds of book debts to be paid into a designated bank account and preventing drawings from that account without the consent of the chargee. See also *Re CCG International Enterprises Ltd* [1993] B.C.C. 580.

[52] See *Re Armagh Shoes Ltd* [1984] B.C.L.C. 405, referred to by Morritt J. in *William Gaskell Group Ltd v. Highley* [1993] B.C.C. 200 at 205C. On the construction of contracts, see generally *Mannai Investments Co. Ltd v. Eagle Star Life Assurance Co.* [1997] A.C. 749, *Investors Compensation Scheme Ltd v. West Bromwich Building Society* [1998] 1 W.L.R. 896 and *Scottish Power plc v. Britoil (Exploration) Ltd, The Times,* December 2, 1997. Moreover, as Knox J. pointed out in *Re New Bullas Trading Ltd* [1993] B.C.C. 251, s. 40 of the Insolvency Act 1986 determines the priority to be given to preferential debts by reference to whether a charge was, "as created", a floating charge.

[53] On possible agreements to convert a fixed into floating charge, see below para. 3–086.

[54] [1992] B.C.L.C. 609 — a decision of House of Lords of March 29, 1979, also noted at (1979) 129 N.L.J. 366 and (1980) 130 N.L.J. 207. "A right is not diminished because for a period its existence or full extent is not appreciated", *per* Lord Morris in *Wickman Machine Tool Sales v. Schuler* [1974] A.C. 235 at 260, cited by Knox J. in *Re A Company (No. 005009 of 1987)* (1988) 4 B.C.C. 424. See also the *Atlantic Computer Systems* case [1992] Ch. 505 at 534 discussed below para. 3–046.

Lords was not prepared to conclude that the parties had abandoned the block discounting agreement as the basis of their relationship.

(c) Particular problems

(i) Book debts

3–019 Many of the recently reported cases concerning the construction of charges relate to charges over book debts and other receivables.[55] In the case of a trading company these may represent a very substantial proportion of the valuable assets of the company, and the issue of the entitlement of the debenture holder to existing and future book debts arising from any continued trading in the receivership may be of principal importance in determining the course of the receivership.

3–020 The expression "book debt" is not a specifically defined legal term, but is commonly thought to mean:

> "a debt arising in the course of a business and due or growing due to the proprietor of that business that . . . would or could in the ordinary course of such a business be entered in well-kept books relating to that business . . . whether it is in fact entered in the books of the business or not".[56]

Moneys standing to the credit of the company at its bank (either on a current "trading" account or a "non-trading" account) are unlikely to fall within the terms of a charge on "book debts and other debts" which is commonly to be found in debentures.[57] The normal business or accountancy treatment of such moneys is "cash at bank".[58] Further, the realisation of charged assets by way of a sale by a receiver will not give rise to a "book debt".[59]

3–021 It would seem to be accepted, at least in England, that there is no objection in principle to a fixed charge being created over book debts, either existing or future. The validity of such a charge was upheld by

---

[55] In *Re ASRS Establishment Ltd* [2000] 1 B.C.L.C. 727, affirmed by the Court of Appeal on July 20, 2000, the court proceeded on the basis that the same approach to construction of charges applied in the case of charges over other receivables as in the case of charges over book debts.

[56] *Per* Buckley L.J. in *Independent Automatic Sales v. Knowles and Foster* [1962] 1 W.L.R. 974; *Re Falcon Sportswear Pty Ltd* (1983) 1 A.C.L.C. 690 at 695; *Coakley v. Argent Credit Corporation plc* (unreported, Rimer J., June 4, 1998).

[57] *Re Brightlife Ltd* [1987] Ch. 200; *Re Permanent Houses (Holdings) Ltd* (1989) 5 B.C.C. 151, *per* Hoffmann J.; *Northern Bank Ltd v. Ross* [1990] B.C.C. 883, CA. (NI). See also the comments of Lord Hoffmann in *Re B.C.C.I. S.A. (No. 8)* [1998] A.C. 214, HL. In the *Permanent Houses* case, Hoffmann J. was at pains to point out that the issue is essentially one of construction of the terms of the debenture.

[58] See Balance Sheet formats at Sched. 4, para. 8 of the Companies Act 1985. It was formerly questioned whether it was conceptually possible for a book debt due to a company to be charged in favour of the debtor itself. In *Re Charge Card Services Ltd* [1987] Ch. 150, Millett J. held that this was not possible, but this was doubted by Dillon L.J. (*obiter*) in *Welsh Development Agency v. Export Finance Co. Ltd* [1992] B.C.C. 270. The possibility of such a "charge back" was accepted by the House of Lords in *Re BCCI SA (No. 8)* [1998] A.C. 214, HL.

[59] See *Re Falcon Sportswear Pty Ltd* (1983) 1 A.C.L.C. 690.

Slade J. in *Siebe Gorman & Co. Ltd v. Barclays Bank*.[60] In order to create a valid fixed charge, it will certainly be essential for the company to be prevented from alienating the uncollected book debts without the consent of the chargee, *e.g.* by factoring, discounting or selling the same. However, in a series of English and Irish decisions it has been held that it is not enough for the charge simply to impose restrictions preventing the company from alienating the book debts before they are paid. These authorities hold that to create a valid fixed charge it will also be necessary for the charge to contain restrictions on the manner in which the company is entitled to receive and deal with the proceeds of the book debts.

The earliest case in question is the decision in *Re Yorkshire Woolcom-* **3–022** *bers Association Ltd, Illingworth v. Houldsworth*[61] In that case, at first instance, Farwell J. said,

> "A charge on all book debts which may now be, or at any time hereafter become charged or assigned, leaving the mortgagor or assignor free to deal with them as he pleases until the mortgagee or assignee intervenes, is not a specific charge, and cannot be. The very essence of a specific charge is that the assignee takes possession, and is the person entitled to receive the book debts at once. So long as he licences the mortgagor to go on receiving the book debts and carry on the business, it is within the exact definition of a floating security."

This *dictum* was approved in the Court of Appeal, where Romer L.J. **3–023** said,

> ". . . in the present case, if I look at the deed which created the charge here, to my mind it is clearly contemplated that until some step is taken by or on behalf of those who are to have the benefit of the charge, the company would be able to receive the debts due to the company in the ordinary course of business, and to deal with them for the ordinary purposes of the business."

In the House of Lords, Lord Halsbury said, **3–024**

> ". . . it seems to me that the whole purport of this instrument is to enable the company to carry on its business in the ordinary way, to receive the book debts that were due to them, to incur new debts, and to carry on their business exactly as if this deed had not been executed at all. That is what we mean by a floating security."

---

[60] [1979] 2 Lloyd's Rep. 142, following the Canadian case of *Evans, Coleman Evans v. Evans Nelson (R.A.) Construction Ltd* (1959) 16 D.L.R. (2d) 123. Followed by the Irish Supreme Court in the case of *Re Keenan Bros.* [1986] B.C.L.C. 242 and by Knox J. in *Re A Company (No. 005009 of 1987)* (1988) 4 B.C.C. 424. Distinguished by Hoffmann J. in *Re Brightlife Ltd* [1987] Ch. 200 and in *Re Armagh Shoes* [1984] B.C.L.C. 405, *per* Hutton J, N.I. See also *Re ASRS Establishment Ltd* [2000] 1 B.C.L.C. 727, affirmed by the Court of Appeal, unreported, July 20, 2000.
[61] [1903] 2 Ch. 284, Ch.D. and [1904] A.C. 355.

3–025 In *re Brightlife Ltd* [62] Hoffmann J. (as he then was) said,

> "In this debenture, the significant feature is that Brightlife was free to collect its debts and pay the proceeds into its bank account. Once in the account they would be outside the charge over debts and at the free disposal of the company. In my judgment a right to deal in this way with the charged assets for its own account is a badge of a floating charge and is inconsistent with a fixed charge."

3–026 This statement was expressly approved by Millett L.J. (as he then was) in *Royal Trust Bank v. National Westminster Bank plc* [63] where he stated,

> ". . . the proper characterisation of a security as 'fixed' or 'floating' depends on the freedom of the chargor to deal with the proceeds of the charged assets in the ordinary course of business free from the security. A contractual right in the chargor to collect the proceeds and pay them into its own bank account for use in the ordinary course of its business is a badge of a floating charge and is inconsistent with the existence of a fixed charge."

3–027   Following this line of reasoning, it has been held to be sufficient to create a valid fixed charge that the company should be obliged by the terms of the charge to pay the proceeds of the book debts into a bank account either with or in the name of or to the order of or in trust for the chargee. [64] Further, if the chargee is a bank, a provision requiring payment of the proceeds of the debts into the company's general account with the bank has been held to be consistent with a fixed charge, for the proceeds are earmarked for payment to the chargee. [65] However, charges which left the company in question free to collect in the proceeds of book debts, to pay them into its normal bank account other than with or for the benefit of the chargee, and thereafter to use the proceeds in the

---

[62] [1987] Ch. 200.

[63] [1996] 2 B.C.L.C. 682; Ch.D. and CA; [1996] B.C.C. 613, CA, noted by S. Worthington, (1997) 113 L.Q.R. 562. In *Re ASRS Establishment Ltd* (unreported, Court of Appeal July 20, 2000) Otton L.J. emphasised that Millet L.J.'s comments were strictly *obiter*. They will fall to be considered by the Privy Council in the appeal from the decision of the Court of Appeal in *Re Brumark Investments Ltd* [2000] 1 B.C.L.C. 353; see further paras. 3–041 to 3–045 below.

[64] *Re Armagh Shoes* [1984] B.C.L.C. 405; *Re Brightlife Ltd* [1987] Ch. 200.

[65] In such a case, it has been suggested that if the debenture confers upon the company the unrestricted right to deal with the proceeds of the book debts so long as the account remains in credit, the charge can probably only subsist as a floating rather than a fixed charge: see *per* Slade J. in *Siebe Gorman & Co. Ltd v. Barclays Bank* [1979] 2 Lloyd's Rep. 142 at 149. See also *William Gaskell Group Ltd v. Highley* [1993] B.C.C. 200, in which Morritt J. upheld a claim to a fixed charge over book debts. The debenture which had been created in favour of a bank contained clauses requiring payment into a special bank account and preventing withdrawals from the bank account without the consent of the bank. After creation, the charge had been assigned to a non-bank which was held to have obtained the right to veto drawings from the special account so that the nature of the charge had not altered on assignment.

ordinary course of its business have been held to be floating charges only.[66]

The practical consequence of the analysis set out above is that **3–028** chargees who are not bankers are generally unable to obtain valid fixed charges over the book debts of their borrowers, who for obvious commercial reasons will not be prepared to agree to pay the proceeds of collection of their book debts into a bank account in the name of the chargee.

As a matter of general law there is a conceptual distinction between a **3–029** book debt and its proceeds. The book debt exists while uncollected, but is extinguished by payment, at which point the company acquires a new asset, namely the moneys paid by the debtor.[67] The case of *Re New Bullas Trading Ltd*[68] represented an ingenious attempt by a non-bank lender to employ this conceptual distinction between an uncollected book debt and its proceeds in the context of company charges, so as to maintain a fixed charge over the former notwithstanding that the company was left free to deal with the latter.

In the *New Bullas* case, the debenture contained what was expressed **3–030** to be a fixed charge over book debts and other debts, and a floating charge over the remainder of the company's property and assets. The debenture also contained clauses:

(a) requiring the company to deal with the debts in accordance with any directions given by the debenture-holder from time to time, but in the absence of such directions, to deal with the debts in the ordinary course of business by getting them in, and not to sell, assign, factor or discount the same;

(b) requiring the company to pay the moneys received from the debts into a separate designated account of the company with a nominated bank and to deal with such moneys in accordance with any directions given from time to time by the debenture-holder; and

(c) providing that in the absence of any directions from the debenture-holder under (b) above, upon payment into the

---

[66] See, *e.g. Re Pearl Maintenance Services Ltd* [1995] B.C.C. 657. It is an interesting question whether a valid *second* fixed charge can be taken over book debts if the charge simply permits the company to pay the proceeds of the book debts into its account with the first chargee, and control over drawings from the account vests solely in the first chargee. It is suggested that although the company does not have an unfettered right to deal with the proceeds because of the control exercised by the first chargee, the lack of control exercised by the second chargee should lead to the conclusion that the second charge is a floating charge only.

[67] When the proceeds of a debt are received, they cannot themselves be described as a "debt": see *Loc-Tex International Pty Ltd v. Bolfox Pty Ltd* (1990) 8 A.C.L.C. 1,146. See also the discussion as to the distinction between a book debt and its proceeds in the context of construction of a reservation of title clause referring to the "receipt of proceeds" in *Associated Alloys Pty Ltd v. ACN 001 452 106 Pty Ltd* (2000) 171 A.L.R. 568, High Ct of Australia.

[68] [1994] B.C.C. 36. See Goode, "Charges over Book Debts: A Missed Opportunity" (1994) 110 L.Q.R. 592 and Berg, "Charges over Book Debts: A Reply" [1995] Journal of Business Law 433.

designated account, the moneys would stand released from the fixed charge on debts and would be subject only to the floating charge over the other property and assets of the company.

No directions had been given by the debenture-holder prior to appointment of administrative receivers.

3–031 At first instance, [69] Knox J. followed the approach in *Re Brightlife Ltd* and held that in the absence of any direction from the debenture-holder, the freedom given to the company to deal with the proceeds of the debts compelled the conclusion that the charge over the debts was a floating charge only.

3–032 In the Court of Appeal, the Inland Revenue, representing the preferential creditors, conceded that there were no considerations of public policy which prevented the company and the debenture-holder making any contract they chose.[70] It was also apparently accepted that there were no terms of the debenture which were inconsistent with the express intention of both parties to treat the uncollected debts as distinct from their proceeds, and to subject the former to a fixed charge and the latter to a floating charge. In light of these concessions, the Court of Appeal stated that the sole question which had to be answered was whether the law permitted such an agreement which drew a distinction between a debt and its proceeds.

3–033 It was submitted on behalf of the preferential creditors, (i) that the distinction between a debt and its proceeds was unrealistic because a debt was worth nothing unless and until it was turned into money, and (ii) that the charge contravened the essential characteristic of a fixed charge, namely that once appropriated, charged assets should not be released from the charge without the consent of the debenture-holder.[71]

3–034 The Court of Appeal rejected these submissions and held that there was no principle of law which prohibited recognition of the intended agreement of the parties. The Court sought to explain how the debenture fitted the essential description of a fixed charge by stating that the debts did not cease to be subject to a fixed charge solely at the will of the company, but only pursuant to an express agreement of the parties that, once the proceeds of the debt had been paid into the designated account, the debt would be released from the fixed charge.[72]

---

[69] [1993] B.C.C. 251.

[70] This view has been accepted by the Court of Appeal in *Re ASRS Establishment Ltd*, unreported, July 20, 2000 *per* Robert Walker L.J. *cf.* the express recognition of questions of policy in *R. in Right of British Columbia v. Federal Business Development Bank* (1987) 65 C.B.R. 201.

[71] Citing the *dictum* of Vaughan-Williams L.J. in *Re Yorkshire Woolcombers Association* referred to above para. 3–006.

[72] [1994] B.C.C. 36 at 41F–G. This reasoning is illogical. If it is accepted that it is possible to distinguish between the uncollected debt and its proceeds, it ought also be apparent that it is the act of payment which destroys the debt and hence takes it out of the scope of the fixed charge. This process does not depend on what is done by the company with the proceeds.

It would seem that the concession by the Revenue that the parties had **3–035** an intention to create a fixed charge on the debts whilst they were uncollected was crucial, and permitted the Court of Appeal to be deflected from dealing with the real issue of whether the liberty to deal with the proceeds of the debts was inconsistent with the expressed intention to create a fixed charge over the uncollected debts.[73]

Whilst as a matter of the general law a conceptual distinction might be **3–036** drawn between an uncollected debt and its proceeds, nevertheless in the context of the grant of a security interest, it may, as Millett L.J. indicated in *Royal Trust Bank v. National Westminster Bank*, be unrealistic to separate an uncollected debt from the proceeds of its realisation.[74]

The essential purpose of the grant of a security interest is to permit **3–037** the chargee to realise money from the charged property with which to discharge the company's debt to him. In the case of a charge over a debt, this can be achieved either (i) by the chargee receiving the proceeds of collection of the debt, or (ii) by the sale of the debt in its uncollected form by or on behalf of the chargee to a third party. But in either case the fixed charge over the uncollected debt must carry with it and confer upon the chargee the right to the proceeds of the debt if the essential purpose of the security, namely repayment of the secured debt, is to be fulfilled.

That is obviously the case if the security over the debt is to be realised **3–038** by collection: the security will be worthless if the holder of the charge does not also have the right to receive the proceeds. But it is also the case if the security is realised by the sale of the debt, because the chargee must be able to sell the right to receive the proceeds in due course, this being the very essence of the economic value of the debt without which the debt would be worthless to any buyer.

It might also be observed that if the drafting technique in *New Bullas* **3–039** is effective, there would seem to be no obvious reason why it could not be deployed in relation to other classes of circulating assets owned by a chargor company, such as raw material or stock in trade, so as to impose fixed charges on such items, with an agreement that they be released from such fixed charge when converted into finished products or sold.[75] Such a result would seem to run quite contrary to the reasons given for the creation of the floating charge in cases such as *Re Yorkshire Woolcombers Association Ltd, Illingworth v. Houldsworth*.[76]

Accordingly, it is suggested that *Re New Bullas Trading Ltd* may have **3–040** been incorrectly decided. It is indeed notable that *New Bullas* has been distinguished rather than applied in subsequent English cases at first

---

[73] See Moss, Fixed Charges on book debts—puzzles and perils (1995) 8 Insolvency Intelligence 25.

[74] [1996] 2 B.C.L.C. 682 at 704g.

[75] This would create interesting issue in relation to goods supplied under retention of title clauses: see below Chap. 12.

[76] See also *per* McCarthy J. in *Re Keenan Bros Ltd* (1986) 2 B.C.C. 98,970 at 98,974 referring the first instance judgment of Keane J.

instance.[77] Moreover, it has also recently been doubted by the Court of Appeal of New Zealand in *Re Brumark Investments Ltd*.[78]

3–041   The *Brumark* case involved a dispute between the New Zealand Commissioner of Inland Revenue, a preferential creditor of Brumark, and the receivers for its secured creditor, Westpac Banking Corporation. There were insufficient funds in the company for both the Bank and the Revenue to be paid in full, so the priority of the Bank's claim was crucial. The charge sought to distinguish between book debts and their realised proceeds. The debts themselves together with their proceeds were purportedly subject to a fixed charge, but there was an exclusion from the fixed charge for the "proceeds of those debts which are received before the first to occur of Westpac requiring such proceeds to be paid into [a specially designated account], and the charge ... crystallising or being enforced ...".

3–042   In the High Court of New Zealand,[79] Fisher J. doubted the reasoning in the *New Bullas* case, but held that a distinction could be drawn between an uncollected book debt and its proceeds and also indicated that he thought that a charge over uncollected book debts "has real commercial value whether or not attaching to the proceeds once collected".[80] The judge held that the restrictions on alienation of book debts in the debenture were sufficient to create a fixed charge over those uncollected debts notwithstanding that the charge over their proceeds was expressed only to be a floating charge until Westpac intervened.

3–043   The Commissioner of Inland Revenue appealed. The Court of Appeal of New Zealand stated that the crucial question was whether the company was free to deal with the charged book debts, but took a novel approach which enabled it to avoid the debate over whether the freedom of the company to deal with the proceeds was inconsistent with a fixed charge over the uncollected debts. The Court simply held that in determining whether the company was free to deal with the uncollected debts, there was no distinction to be drawn between dealing by alienation of the uncollected debts and dealing by collection of the debts. Hence, because the charge did not, as created, restrict the company from collecting in the debts on its own account, it was not a fixed charge over those debts.

---

[77] See, *e.g. Re Pearl Maintenance Services Ltd* [1995] B.C.C. 657, *Re ASRS Establishment Ltd* [2000] 1 B.C.L.C. 727, affirmed by the Court of Appeal, July 20, 2000; and *Re CIL Realisations Ltd* (unreported, Hart J., February 29, 2000). In *Royal Trust Bank v. National Westminster Bank plc* [1996] B.C.C. 613 Millett L.J. did not express any view on the correctness of *New Bullas*, Nourse L.J., who gave the only reasoned judgment in *New Bullas*, decided the case on other grounds, and Swinton Thomas L.J. simply agreed in the result. See Zacaroli, Fixed Charges on Book Debts — "There is nothing further that I wish to add.", (1997) 10 *Insolvency Intelligence* 41.

[78] [2000] 1 B.C.L.C. 353.

[79] (1999) 19 New Zealand Tax Cases 15,159

[80] Fisher J.'s reasoning assumed that if a book debt was collected by the chargor company, the proceeds fall outside the scope of the fixed charge on book debts, but that if the debt was collected or otherwise realised by the chargee, *e.g.* by collection or factoring, the proceeds would fall within the scope of the fixed charge and could be applied in reduction of the secured indebtedness. This approach seems to beg the question at issue.

The Court of Appeal of New Zealand's reasoning is unsatisfactory, as **3–044** the concept of collection of a debt does not relate to an act or freedom of the company at all, but to the act of the debtor in making payment to the company. Further, as the very essence of collection of a debt is the receipt of money, it would seem that the Court's concept of collection of debts "for the company's own account" ought inevitably to have led to an inquiry into the ownership of the proceeds. In particular, the Court did not explain whether and if so how it thought that the company would have been free to collect in the debts for its own account if it had been given a direction by Westpac requiring the proceeds of collection to be paid to an account of the company with Westpac.

An appeal in the *Brumark* case is expected to be heard by the Privy **3–045** Council in October 2000. The confused state of the law in this difficult area awaits a definitive judgment, but the decision in the case will perhaps be of more relevance for English law than for the law of New Zealand, because the distinction between fixed and floating charges will be abolished in New Zealand when the Personal Property Securities Act 1999 (NZ) is brought into force.

The decision of the Court of Appeal in *Re Atlantic Computer Systems* **3–046** *plc*[81] is also relevant to any consideration of the law relating to charges over book debts. The Court of Appeal had to consider the nature of charges taken by the owners of numerous items of computer equipment which had been leased to a company. With the consent of the owners, the equipment had been sub-leased by the company to end-users. In the case of each sub-lease, and as security for the payment of the head-lease rentals relating to that equipment, the company assigned to the owners of the equipment all the benefit of the terms of the sub-lease, including all rental moneys to which the company was or might in the future be entitled under or by virtue of the sub-lease. The charge did not require the sub-lease rentals to be paid direct to the owners of the equipment and, in practice, the sub-lease rentals were paid to the company and were used by it in the ordinary course of its business.

The company went into administration. Following the making of the **3–047** order, the administrators collected in sub-lease rentals and paid them into designated bank accounts. The question arose as to whether the charges created by the assignments were fixed or floating charges. The Court of Appeal held, without reference to any cases such as *Siebe Gorman Co. Ltd v. Barclays Bank* or *Re Brightlife Ltd*, that the charges were fixed charges.

Giving the judgment of the Court, Nicholls L.J. said[82]:   **3–048**

> "The notable feature of the present case is that the charges were not ambulatory. The property assigned by the company was con-fined to rights to which the company was entitled under specific,

---

[81] [1992] Ch. 505. The decision was somewhat surprisingly described as "non controversial" by Otton L.J. in *Re ASRS Establishment Ltd*, unreported, Court of Appeal, July 20, 2000.

[82] [1992] Ch. 505 at 534.

existing contracts. The assignments consisted of the company's rights 'under or by virtue of' subleases each of which was already in existence at the time of the assignments and each of which was specifically identified in the relevant deeds of assignment. In each case the payments due to the company under a specific sublease were charged as security for the payments due by the company under the head lease relating to the same equipment. The company's right to receive future instalments from end users in due course pursuant to the terms of the subleases was as much a present asset of the company . . . as a right to receive payment of a sum which was immediately due . . .

We have in mind that in practice sums payable by the end users under these subleases were paid to the company and utilised by it in the ordinary course of business. In so far as this is relevant, it may well be that this was what the parties intended should happen. The company was to be at liberty to receive and use the instalments until [the chargee] chose to intervene. We are unpersuaded that this results in these charges, on existing and defined property, becoming floating charges. A mortgage of land does not become a floating charge by reason of the mortgagor being permitted to remain in possession and enjoy the fruits of the property charged for the time being . . ."

3–049 The decision in *Atlantic Computer Systems* may be distinguishable from earlier cases on the basis that the earlier cases had been concerned with charges over a class of present and future debts rather than with a charge over specifically identifiable debts pursuant to existing contracts which could be regarded as present debts.

3–050 Other than on this basis, it is difficult to reconcile the approach of the Court of Appeal with the earlier cases which viewed contractual restrictions on dealings with book debts and their proceeds as essential to the existence of a fixed charge. As indicated above, earlier cases had held that if the lack of express restrictions in a charge gave a company the liberty to collect the moneys due under the charged debts and then to use them in the ordinary course of its business, this was inconsistent with the chargee having a fixed charge over those debts.

3–051 In any event, it is submitted that the land and fruits analogy employed in the *Atlantic Computer Systems* case was not a good one. Even assuming, contrary to the views advanced above,[83] that a distinction could validly be drawn for the purposes of characterisation of the charge between the sub-leases and the sub-rental payments, the sub-rental payments were not simply the "fruit" of the charged property but were themselves charged property. As Nicholls L.J. acknowledged in the passage quoted above, the payments due under the sub-leases were themselves charged by the company to the owners. When the company was using the sub-rental payments in its business on its own account, it

[83] See, paras 3–036—3–038.

was not simply enjoying the "fruits" of the charged property, but was actually consuming charged property.[84]

(ii) Fixed and replaceable plant and machinery
In *Re Hi-Fi Equipment (Cabinets) Ltd*,[85] Harman J. considered the ambit **3–052** of the phrase "fixed plant and machinery" which appeared in a debenture as the subject of a fixed charge. Harman J. held that the expression was to be construed as containing a single item and that it connoted plant and machinery which was in some way firmly attached to the company's premises. A similar approach was adopted by Henry J. in the High Court of New Zealand in the case of *National Bank of New Zealand Ltd v. Commissioner of the Inland Revenue*.[86] Henry J. held that a specific charge over "fixed plant and machinery" did not include computer software (source codes) which were accordingly only covered by a floating charge.

As noted above, it may well be that fixed plant and machinery is more **3–053** amenable to being the subject of a fixed charge, but the question will often still arise as to whether any freedom given to the chargor company to replace such machinery, in whole or in part in the ordinary course of business (*e.g.* by renewal or repair) would result in the charge being held to be a floating charge only. The answer to this question would depend on the facts, but that the freedom given to a chargor to dispose of or replace specifically identified manufacturing equipment in the ordinary course of its business would not necessarily be inconsistent with the existence of a fixed charge over that equipment.[87]

(iii) Stock-in-trade
By analogy with book debts, it might be thought legally possible to create **3–054** a fixed charge over stock-in-trade provided that there was a sufficient

---

[84] The decision in *Re Atlantic Computer Systems plc* was applied by Vinelott J. in *Re Atlantic Medical Ltd* [1992] B.C.C. 653 on the basis that the charging clauses were materially similar in the two cases. The learned judge held that it was not crucial that the charge in *Atlantic Medical* purported to be a specific charge not only over the company's right and interest in existing sub-leases (as had been the position in the *Atlantic Computers* case) but also over the rights and interest in any future sub-leases, since all sub-leases would relate to the same, existing chattels. In response to a submission that there was a distinction to be drawn between the nature of the charge over the sub-leases themselves and the charge over the rentals due under them, the learned judge held that such a distinction would be "unreal". However, the distinction between the sub-leases and the rentals arising under them was at the heart of the "land and fruits" analogy employed by the Court of Appeal in *Atlantic Computer Systems plc*.

[85] [1988] B.C.L.C. 65. See also *Re GE Tunbridge Ltd* [1995] 1 B.C.L.C. 34.

[86] [1992] 1 N.Z.L.R. 250. The contrary decision of Jeffries J. in the earlier New Zealand case of *Tudor Heights Ltd v. United Dominion Corporation Finance Ltd* [1977] 1 N.Z.L.R. 532, in which it had been held that the phrase did not connote "fixtures" as that term is used in land law but merely connoted that the items would be expected to be retained by the company in its business, cannot be considered good law.

[87] *Re Cimex Tissues Ltd* [1995] 1 B.C.L.C. 409. The case is very much on the borderline, and turned on the fact that the charge in question concerned specifically identified items of machinery which were agreed to be subject to a fixed charge. The judge indicated that same result might well not follow in relation to charges expressed generically to cover the class of "fixed plant and machinery", where the subject of the charge could well be said to be ambulatory in the full sense of that expression.

restriction on dealing in the debenture. However, in order to operate such a fixed charge, the company would have to seek the consent of the chargee to any disposal of such stock. As this is unlikely to be feasible in practice, subject to the point made above about any extension of the drafting technique deployed in *New Bullas Trading Ltd,* it is suggested that a court is likely to construe any such charge as a floating charge rather than as a fixed charge.[88]

(d) Priorities[89]

(i) As between fixed charges

3–055   A first fixed charge will generally prevail over any subsequent charge.[90] The only major exception is that a prior fixed equitable charge will be defeated by a purchaser of the legal title for value without notice.

3–056   In the absence of a clear contractual restriction imposed by the chargor, it is possible for two chargees to agree between themselves to vary their priority rights without the consent of the chargor.[91] However, care should be taken in drafting any priority agreement. In *Re Portbase (Clothing) Ltd,*[92] a fixed charge-holder had agreed with a subsequent floating charge-holder that, purely as a matter of contract, the fixed charge should be postponed to and should rank after the floating charge. Chadwick J. held that both chargees ranked behind the claims of the liquidator for his liquidation expenses and behind the preferential creditors.[93] The learned judge accepted, however, that it would be possible for two secured creditors to enter into an agreement by which they exchanged their rights under their respective securities, *e.g.* where the fixed charge-holder assigned to the holder of a subsequent floating charge some part or all of his rights to receive payment under the fixed charge.

(ii) As between fixed and floating charges

3–057   As explained earlier, it is a feature of a floating charge that the company is permitted to deal with the charged assets in the ordinary course of its

---

[88] See *R. in Right of British Columbia v. Federal Business Development Bank* (1987) 65 C.B.R. 201, CA (British Columbia); *Re Lin Securities (Pte)* [1988] 2 M.L.J. 137; *Re E.G. Tan & Company (Pte)* (unreported, November 13, 1992, CA (Singapore)).

[89] See, *e.g. Goode, Legal Problems of Credit and Security* (2nd ed.), Chap. 4. The interrelationship between questions of priorities and registration is discussed below, para. 3–135.

[90] In the case of two equitable charges, priority of time prima facie gives the better equity: *Abigail v. Lapin* [1934] A.C. 491 at 503–504, PC, regarding as disapproved the rival formula in *Rice v. Rice* (1854) 2 Drew. 73 at 78, *per* Kindersley V.-C. to the effect that, if the equities are in all other respects equal, priority of time gives the better equity.

[91] *Cheah Theam Swee v. Equiticorp Finance Group Ltd* [1992] 1 A.C. 472, PC; *Re Portbase (Clothing) Ltd* [1993] Ch. 388. See the discussion of the correctness of *Portbase* on a different issue in Chap. 11.

[92] [1993] Ch. 388.

[93] Relying on *Re Camden Brewery Ltd* (1911) 106 L.T. 598; *Re Robert Stephenson & Co. Ltd* [1913] 2 Ch. 201 and the decision of Nicholson J. in the Supreme Court of Victoria in *Waters v. Widdows* [1984] V.R. 503 in relation to the question of the priority to be accorded to the preferential claims; and upon *Re Barleycorn Enterprises Ltd* [1970] Ch. 465 and ss. 115 and 175(2)(b) of the Insolvency Act 1986 in relation to the priority of the liquidation expenses.

business as a going concern. This freedom will permit the subsequent grant of a specific mortgage or charge in the ordinary course of the company's business which will take priority over the earlier (uncrystallised) floating charge even if the subsequent chargee has notice of the earlier charge.[94] However, a specific charge granted outside the ordinary course of the company's business to a chargee with notice of the prior floating charge will be postponed to the floating charge.[95]

The freedom given in a floating charge to the company to deal with its **3–058** assets in the ordinary course of its business as a going concern will not permit the grant of a second floating charge over the same assets without the consent of the holder of the prior floating charge.[96] If the earlier floating charge permits the company to grant further charges over specified assets, the company may create a second floating charge on those assets ranking in priority to the earlier.[97]

(e) Restrictive clauses

As a result of the possibility that charges subsequently granted by a **3–059** company may obtain priority over earlier floating charges, modern debentures very frequently contain restrictions on the company's freedom to charge or deal with (and less frequently to create liens on) the assets covered by the floating charge ("negative pledge" clauses).[98] Such provisions are binding as between the company and the debenture-holder as contractual covenants, but are "mere" or "personal" equities only.[99] The questions thus arise as to whether, and if so in what circumstances, such clauses will be binding upon third parties who subsequently deal with the company.

The short answer is that third parties will be bound by the restrictions **3–060** in a prior charge if they have actual notice of such restrictions.[1] Although registration of a floating charge at the Companies Registry will constitute constructive notice of the particulars required to be registered

---

[94] *Re Hamilton's Windsor Ironworks* (1879) 12 Ch.D. 707; *Re Colonial Trusts Corp* (1879) 15 Ch.D. 465 at 472; *Wheatley v. Silkstone & Haigh Moor Coal Co.* (1885) 29 Ch.D. 715 at 724; *Fire Nymph Products Ltd v. The Heating Centre Pty Ltd* (1992) 7 A.C.S.R. 365 at 377.

[95] *Hamilton v. Hunter* (1982) 7 A.C.L.R. 295.

[96] *Re Benjamin Cope & Sons Ltd* [1914] 1 Ch. 800. In *Griffiths v. Yorkshire Bank plc* [1994] 1 W.L.R. 1427, a later floating charge was crystallised by notice before the earlier floating charge over the same property was crystallised by the appointment of a receiver. The second charge, which was first to crystallise, was held to have priority. This decision has been widely criticised: see, *e.g.* Walters, "Priority of the Floating Charge in Corporate Insolvency" (1995) 16 Company Lawyer 291. The decision in *Griffiths* on other matters (the application of Insolvency Act 1986, s. 40) has been doubted and was not followed in *Re H & K (Medway) Ltd* [1997] B.C.C. 853.

[97] *Re Automatic Bottle Makers Ltd* [1926] Ch. 412.

[98] It would now seem to be too late to argue that such restrictions are inconsistent with the nature of a floating charge and are thus invalid: see Farrar, "Floating Charges and Priorities" (1974) 38 Cony. (N.S.) 315 at 318.

[99] *Latec Investments Ltd v. Hotel Terrigal Pty Ltd* (1965) 113 C.L.R. 265; *Landall Holdings Ltd v. Caratti* [1979] W.A.R. 87; *Fire Nymph Products Ltd v. The Heating Centre Pty Ltd* (1992) 7 A.C.S.R. 365 at 377–378.

[1] *Re Valletort Sanitary Steam Laundry Co. Ltd* [1903] 2 Ch. 654; *Wilson v. Kelland* [1910] 2 Ch. 306 at 313; *Fire Nymph Products Ltd v. The Heating Centre Pty Ltd* (1992) 7 A.C.S.R. 365 at 377. Whilst the rationale for this rule is yet to be finally stated, it is suggested that

and disclosed on the register to those persons who would reasonably be expected to search in the ordinary course of business,[2] notice of the existence of a floating charge does not give the third party constructive notice of a restrictive clause contained in the charge.[3] The present requirements concerning registration of charges under the Companies Act 1985 do not allow for the application of concepts of constructive or implied notice of restrictive clauses so as to bind third parties[4] because the legislation does not require details of any restrictive clauses to be mentioned on the appropriate form. It has been argued that restrictions are now so common in floating charges that, even in the absence of any registration of a restriction or notice of the existence of a floating charge, a person will have what is tantamount to implied notice of a restriction,[5] but this suggestion runs contrary to the statutory scheme.

3–061   The matter is more complex where the debenture-holder gives notice of the restriction on Form 395. It has been suggested that a cautious lender proposing to advance funds ought to search and, as part of the search, inspect the form lodged by the debenture-holder.[6] There is, however, no obligation to search and accordingly, even if a restriction is included on the registered form but no search is made, it is submitted that a subsequent chargee will not be bound.[7] There is, however, no direct authority on point. If the proposed lender sees the restriction on the registered form, he obtains actual notice and is bound by it. If he searches and yet fails to look at the form, it has been suggested that he might be bound by constructive notice,[8] but this surely cannot be the case since this is not a matter required to be registered and to allow it to bind third parties would be an undesirable extension of the application of the doctrine of constructive notice.[9] In any case, it is difficult to see

---

dealing with the company in breach of such prior contractual restraints on the company constitutes a wrongful interference with the contractual relations between the company and the debenture-holder. The rule has been doubted in *Griffiths v. Yorkshire Bank plc* [1994] 1 W.L.R. 1427 at 1435F. It is suggested that the extemporary comments of Morritt J, that the "negative pledge" has no effect on third parties, are *obiter* and probably incorrect: see Walters, "Priority of the Floating Charge in Corporate Insolvency" (1995) 16 Company Lawyer 291.

[2] A person who would not ordinarily be expected to search the register in the ordinary course of business should not be fixed by constructive notice: see Goode, *Legal Problems of Credit and Security* (2nd ed.), pp. 44–45.

[3] *Wilson v. Kelland* [1910] 2 Ch. 306 (notice of a document is not notice of its contents); *Siebe Gorman Co. Ltd v. Barclays Bank* [1979] 2 Lloyd's Rep. 142.

[4] *Siebe Gorman Co. Ltd v. Barclays Bank* [1979] 2 Lloyd's Rep. 142; *Welch v. Bowmaker* [1980] I.R. 251 and see *Swiss Bank Corp v. Lloyds Bank* [1979] Ch. 548 at 575; [1979] 2 All E.R. 853 at 874.

[5] Farrar, "Floating Charges and Priorities" (1974) 38 Conv. N.S. 315 at 319.

[6] Salinger, *Factoring Law and Practice* (1991), p. 156; Lingard, Bank Security Documents (2nd ed.), para. 1.23. These suggestions are not repeated in the most recent editions of these works.

[7] See Goode, *Legal Problems of Credit and Security* (2nd ed.), pp. 43–44.

[8] Reeday, *The Law Relating to Banking* (5th. ed., 1985), p. 148.

[9] See *per* Lindley L.J. in *Manchester Trust v. Furness* [1895] 2 Q.B. 539 at 545: "as regards the extension of the equitable doctrines of constructive notice to commercial transactions, the Courts have always set their faces resolutely against it". See also *Panchaud Frères SA v. Establissements General Grain Co.* [1970] 1 Lloyd's Rep. 53 at 57, *per* Lord Denning M.R.: ". . . our commercial law sets its face resolutely against any

why, if the creditor is under no duty to search, he should be in a worse position because he undertakes a perfunctory or incomplete search than if he makes no search at all.

(f) Crystallisation

(i) General

Floating charges are founded in contract. As such, the circumstances in **3–062** which a charge may cease to "float" and become attached to specific property are also primarily a question of contract.[10] Following this principle, the courts have accepted the validity of "automatic crystallisation" clauses (see below). It would also appear to be possible for the debenture to make express provision for crystallisation to take place with respect to some class of charged assets and not others.[11] In the absence of such a provision the debenture-holder cannot restrict crystallisation to some, and not all, of the charged assets[12] and any action on his part will be ineffective to crystallise his floating charge unless it unequivocally terminates the company's licence to deal with the entire subject-matter of the floating charge.[13]

The events which may or may not cause crystallisation of a floating **3–063** charge can be considered under two headings: crystallisation by intervention (including crystallisation by the giving of notice) and automatic crystallisation.

(ii) Crystallisation by intervention

The conceptual basis of crystallisation by intervention is that the **3–064** company's freedom to deal with the assets which are the subject of the floating charge in the ordinary course of its business is terminated by

doctrine of constructive notice." Examples of the refusal of the courts to extend to doctrines of constructive notice to commercial transactions can be found in *Siebe Gorman Co. Ltd v. Barclays Bank* [1979] 2 Lloyd's Rep. 142, *per* Slade J.; *Official Custodian for Charities v. Parway Estates Developments* [1985] Ch. 151, C.A.; *Re Montagu's Settlement Trusts* [1987] 1 Ch. 264, *per* Megarry V.-C.; *Eagle Trust plc v. SBC Securities Ltd* [1991] B.C.L.C. 438 at 458, *per* Vinelott J.; *Cowan de Groot Properties Ltd v. Eagle Trust plc* [1991] B.C.L.C. 1045 at 1109–1110, *per* Knox J. *cf.* the comments of Peter Gibson J. in *Baden, Delvaux Lecuit v. Société Generale* [1983] B.C.L.C. 325 at 414 that "The courts will not readily import a duty to inquire in the case of a commercial transaction but [it is not correct] that a duty to inquire can never arise in a commercial transaction", which were approved in *Westpac Banking Corp v. Savin* [1985] 2 N.Z.L.R. 41 but have not generally been followed in the more recent cases.

[10] See *per* Hoffmann J. in *Re Brightlife Ltd* [1987] Ch. 200 at 213H–215G; and *per* Gleeson C.J. in *Fire Nymph Products Ltd v. The Heating Centre Pty Ltd* (1992) 7 A.C.S.R. 365 at 371.

[11] *Re Griffin Hotel Co. Ltd* [1941] Ch. 129.

[12] See below, para. 17–004. *Evans v. Rival Granite Quarries Ltd* [1910] 2 K.B. 979.

[13] *R. v. Consolidated Churchill Copper Corp* (1978) 5 W.W.R. 652; (1978) 90 D.L.R. (3d) 357, *per* Berger J. (notice to company to terminate licence to carry on part, but not all, its business held ambiguous and ineffective to bring about crystallisation); *Evans v. Rival Granite Quarries Ltd* [1910] 2 K.B. 979.

some form of external intervention.[14] Clearly, the appointment of a receiver, whether by the debenture-holder or by the court, will crystallise the floating charge.[15] The right to intervene by the appointment of a receiver may be triggered by the happening of any one or more of the events or defaults stipulated in the debenture. Examples of circumstances giving rise to the right to appoint a receiver which are frequently included in debentures include:

(a) if the company defaults in making the payments secured by the debenture;
(b) if an order is made or an effective resolution passed for the winding-up of the company;
(c) if a receiver or administrative receiver is appointed of the undertaking or assets of the company;
(d) if a petition is presented for an administration order;
(e) if a distress or execution is levied or enforced upon the property of the company;
(f) if the company stops payment or ceases or threatens to cease to carry on its business;
(g) if the company becomes unable to pay its debts within the meaning of section 123 of the Insolvency Act 1986; and
(h) if the company makes an unauthorised disposal of charged assets.[16]

3–065 In the case of "eligible" companies, *i.e.* essentially small companies which are not banks or insurance companies, the right to appoint a receiver under a debenture will be restricted if the Insolvency Bill 2000 is enacted in its current form in the event that the directors file for a moratorium with a view to a voluntary arrangement.[17] Under paragraph 42 of Schedule 1 to the Bill, any clause in an instrument will be void if it provides that obtaining a moratorium under the Bill (to facilitate the making of a voluntary arrangement), or anything done with a view to obtaining a moratorium, will constitute grounds for appointing a receiver.

3–066   The commencement of winding-up will cause a floating charge to crystallise[18] (even if the winding-up is merely for the purposes of

---

[14] A mere demand for payment does not constitute an intervention: *Evans v. Rival Granite Quarries Ltd* [1910] 2 K.B. 979; *Chase Manhattan Bank v. Circle Corp* (1986) 37 W.L.R. 160, CA of Eastern Caribbean States.

[15] See, *e.g. Evans v. Rival Granite Quarries Ltd* [1910] 2 K.B. 979 at 1000–1001, *per* Buckley L.J.

[16] In the absence of a specific clause to this effect, default in payment of the secured debt will not be a crystallising event: see *Government Stock and Other Securities Investment Co. Ltd v. Manila Rwy Co. Ltd* [1897] A.C. 81. Also, in the absence of a specific provision in the debenture, the debenture-holder cannot appoint a receiver because he considers that the security is in jeopardy. He must apply to the court: see *Cryne v. Barclays Bank plc* [1987] B.C.L.C. 548 and see below, para. 22–013.

[17] The Bill will provide for a moratorium on the making or enforcement of claims against the company in order to allow a voluntary arrangement to be made.

[18] *Re Florence Land and Public Works Co.* (1878) 10 Ch.D. 530; *Evans v. Rival Granite Quarries Ltd* [1910] 2 K.B. 979 at 1000, *per* Buckley L.J.

reconstruction[19]), for the company in liquidation no longer has the power to carry on its business other than for the purposes of a beneficial winding-up. In the absence of a clause in the debenture, however, the floating charge will not be crystallised by the mere presentation of a winding-up petition[20] or the appointment of a provisional liquidator[21] or the appointment by the court of a receiver at the instance of another creditor.[22]

Floating charges now normally contain a clause enabling a debenture- **3–067** holder to appoint a receiver if a petition is presented for an administration order. The appointment of an administrative receiver will generally block the appointment of an administrator.[23] Absent any such appointment of an administrative receiver, it is an open question whether the appointment of an administrator will cause a floating charge to crystallise.[24] It is submitted that the better view is that the appointment of an administrator does not automatically cause a crystallisation of the floating charge for, unlike a liquidator, an administrator may have the power to carry on the business of the company with a view to its survival as a going concern; and, unlike the appointment of an administrative receiver, the appointment of an administrator is not an act by the debenture-holder, or an event which determines the company's implied licence to deal with the charged assets for its own account. In any event, the practical significance of this issue is substantially reduced by the power given to an administrator by section 15(1) of the Insolvency Act 1986 to deal with assets free of any charge which, as created, was a floating charge.

In *Re Brightlife Ltd*[25] Hoffmann J. held that a floating charge which **3–068** contained a clause enabling the debenture-holder to serve a notice on the company crystallising the floating charge was valid and effective and that there was no public policy reason to refuse to give effect to such a term of the contract between chargee and chargor. Hence, service of the notice constituted intervention by the debenture-holder which caused the crystallisation of the floating charge.[26] Crystallisation by the giving of notice is often referred to as "semi-automatic" crystallisation.

(iii) Automatic crystallisation
There has been much debate over the questions whether it is possible or **3–069** desirable to give effect to a clause in a debenture providing for

---

[19] *Re Crompton & Co. Ltd* [1914] 1 Ch. 954.

[20] *Re Victoria Steamboats Ltd* [1897] 1 Ch. 158.

[21] *Re Obie Pty Ltd* (No. 2) (1983) 8 A.C.L.R. 574.

[22] *Bayhold Financial Corp Ltd v. Clarkson Company Ltd* (1991) 10 C.B.R. (3rd) 159, Sup. Ct. App. Div, Nova Scotia.

[23] Insolvency Act 1986, s. 9(3).

[24] See, *e.g. Gower's Principles of Modern Company Law* (6th ed.), pp. 369–370; Goode, *Legal Problems of Credit and Security* (2nd ed.) at pp. 63–64; and *Palmer's Company Law*, para. 13.129.

[25] [1987] Ch. 200.

[26] See [1987] Ch. 200 at 215F. The point appears to have been conceded in *Re Woodroffes (Musical Instruments) Ltd* [1986] Ch. 366. See also *Re Griffin Hotel Co. Ltd* [1941] Ch. 129. The giving of the notice operates as the determination of the company's licence to deal with its assets in the ordinary course of its business.

automatic crystallisation of a floating charge on the happening of specified events without any intervention by the debenture-holder.[27] However, much of the potential significance of automatic crystallisation has been reduced by the introduction of section 40(1) of the Insolvency Act 1986 which gives preferential creditors priority over the claims of the holders of charges which, as created, were floating charges, irrespective of whether or when such charge crystallised. In relation to "eligible" companies,[28] automatic crystallisation on an attempt to obtain a moratorium with a view to a voluntary arrangement under the current version of the Insolvency Bill 2000,[29] and automatic crystallisation on the occurrence of anything done with a view to obtaining such a moratorium, will be prohibited if paragraph 42 of Schedule 1 to the Insolvency Bill 2000 is enacted in its current form.

3–070   Absent any such express legislative prohibitions, and in spite of the Cork Committee having recommended that automatic crystallisation should be generally prohibited, it would seem to be accepted that there is no public policy reason why the courts should not give effect to a clause providing for automatic crystallisation in the contract which has been made between the company and the debenture-holder.[30] Any such clauses will, however, be narrowly construed and only enforced if there is a well-defined crystallisation event.[31] This will promote commercial certainty and minimise the potential prejudice to third parties who might not have notice of crystallisation.[32]

3–071   The permissible conceptual limits of automatic crystallisation were tested in the Australian case of *Fire Nymph Products Ltd v. The Heating Centre Pty. Ltd.*[33] The clause in question sought to produce the effect that a floating charge automatically crystallised and became fixed "at the moment immediately prior to" any dealing with the charged property other than in the ordinary course of the company's business. The clear intent was to produce the consequence that the extraordinary dealing

---

[27] Academic discussion includes articles by Farrar, (1976) 40 Conv. (N.S.) 397 and (1980) 1 Company Lawyer 83; A. J. Boyle, [1979] J.B.L. 231; R. L. Dean, (1983) Company and Securities Law Journal 185. See also Gough, *op cit.,* Chap. 11; Gough in *Equity and Commercial Relationships* (ed. P. Finn), p. 239; Goode, *Legal Problems of Credit and Security* (2nd ed.), pp. 69 et seq.; *Palmer's Company Law,* paras. 13.129-13.130; and Lingard, *Bank Security Documents* (3rd ed.), paras. 9.25–9.31. See also the comments of the Review Committee on Insolvency Law and Practice (Cmnd. 8558), paras. 1570–1582. Judicial analysis can be found in cases such as *Stein v. Saywell* (1968) 121 C.L.R. 529; *Re Manurewa Transport Ltd* [1971] N.Z.L.R. 909; *R. v. Consolidated Churchill Copper Corp Ltd* (1978) 5 W.W.R. 30; (1978) 90 D.L.R. (3d) 357; *Re Brightlife Ltd* [1987] Ch. 200; *Fire Nymph Products Ltd v. The Heating Centre Pty Ltd* (1992) 7 A.C.S.R. 365. See also *Re Horne & Hellard* (1885) 29 Ch.D. 736; *Re Bond Worth* [1980] Ch. 228 at 260D, *per* Slade J.; and *Re Woodroffes (Musical Instruments) Ltd* [1986] Ch. 366 (where Nourse J. treated crystallisation on cesser of business as a species of automatic crystallisation).

[28] Essentially small companies which are not banks or insurance companies.

[29] The Bill will provide for a moratorium on the making or enforcement of claims against the company in order to allow a voluntary arrangement to be made.

[30] See *Re Brightlife Ltd* [1987] Ch. 200 at 212, *per* Hoffmann J.; *Fire Nymph Products Ltd v. The Heating Centre Pty Ltd* (1992) 7 A.C.S.R. 365 at 371, *per* Gleeson C.J.

[31] *Covacich v. Riordan* [1994] 2 N.Z.L.R. 502.

[32] See the comments at [1987] Ch. 213 and (1992) 7 A.C.S.R. 371.

[33] (1992) 7 A.S.C.R. 365, CA (NSW).

which resulted in crystallisation would not itself escape the consequences of that crystallisation. It was held that the clause could not operate so as to bring about a retrospective crystallisation but that it was possible for automatic crystallisation to occur contemporaneously with the crystallising event such that the assets passed to the disponee subject to a fixed charge. How the third party disponee was affected by this state of affairs would depend upon the nature of the title which he acquired and whether he had notice of the crystallisation of the charge.[34]

(iv) Cesser of business

A question which arose for decision in *Re Woodroffes (Musical Instru-* **3–072** *ments) Ltd*[35] was whether, absent any clause to this effect in a debenture, cessation of business by a company would automatically crystallise a floating charge. In the case, the company in question had created two floating charges in similar terms over its undertaking and assets. The first had been granted to the company's bank; the second (which was created in breach of the restrictive provisions in the first charge and which was expressed to rank after the first) was in favour of one of the company's directors. Each debenture expressly permitted the debenture-holder to convert the floating charge into a fixed charge by giving notice to the company.

The second debenture-holder gave notice to crystallise the second **3–073** floating charge. The significance of this notice appears to have largely escaped the company which continued its business for a short time over a Bank Holiday weekend until the first debenture-holder made a demand under its debenture and appointed a receiver. The question primarily concerned priorities as between the first debenture-holder and the preferential creditors of the company. Priority as between the first debenture-holder and the preferential creditors depended upon whether the first floating charge had crystallised prior to the appointment of the receiver (the case pre-dated section 40(1) of the Insolvency Act 1986).

Nourse J. held that cessation of business, which necessarily put an end **3–074** to the company's capacity to deal with its assets, automatically caused a floating charge to crystallise, but that, on the evidence, such cessation of business was not made out. In reaching this conclusion, Nourse J. based himself upon a line of cases which had "to a greater or lesser extent" ssumed that crystallisation took place on a cessation of business. The learned judge stated that on a cessation of business "That which kept the charge hovering has now been released and the force of gravity causes it to settle and fasten on the subject of the charge . . .".[36] Although such a test may cause great factual uncertainties in ascertaining whether, and if

---

[34] See further below paras. 3–079 *et seq.*
[35] [1986] Ch. 366.
[36] [1986] Ch. 366 at 378B. See also the *dictum* of Gleeson C.J. in the *Fire Nymph* case that: "Part of the original idea of a floating charge was the freedom of a debtor company to carry on its business as a going concern and dispose of its assets in the ordinary course of business notwithstanding the existence of the charge. The corollary was that, if the company suspended trading, it should cease to be free to dispose of its assets".

so when, a company has ceased to carry on its business, the principle of automatic crystallisation on cesser of business would now appear to be established.[37] It should be noted that the decision is not authority for the proposition that a floating charge will automatically crystallise on the company ceasing to trade profitably or upon it becoming insolvent.

(v) The effect of crystallisation of one floating charge upon other floating charges

3–075 On a second issue in *Re Woodroffes (Musical Instruments) Ltd*, Nourse J. held that, in the absence of any express provision in the first debenture, the crystallisation of the second floating charge did not result in the automatic crystallisation of the first floating charge over the same property. Nourse J. held that the contention that crystallisation of the later floating charge operated to crystallise the earlier charge "over the head" of the first charge-holder and "possibly contrary to its own wishes" was inconsistent with the contractual provisions which operated as between the company and the first debenture-holder. The learned judge held that there was neither an express nor an implied term in the bank's floating charge causing automatic crystallisation of that charge upon crystallisation of the later floating charge.

3–076   It is suggested that Nourse J. ought to have held that crystallisation of the second floating charge resulted in crystallisation of the first floating charge.[38] The learned judge appeared to accept that ". . . a fixed charge on the whole undertaking and assets of the company would paralyse it and prevent it from carrying on its business".[39] If this was so, then it is difficult to see why the crystallisation of the second floating charge into a fixed charge over the whole undertaking and assets of the company was not thought to paralyse the company and to prevent it from lawfully carrying on its business, resulting in the automatic crystallisation of the first charge.[40] Such a conclusion would also remedy the problem encountered in *Griffiths v. Yorkshire Bank plc*[41] of a second floating chargee gaining priority over the holder of a first floating charge.

(vi) Problems of automatic crystallisation and the position of third parties

3–077 Apart from the problems of conflict between successive chargees referred to above, difficult questions may also arise as to the

---

[37] See *William Gaskell Group v. Highley* [1993] B.C.C. 200; *BCCI v. BRS Kumar Brothers Ltd* [1994] 1 B.C.L.C. 211, and *Re The Real Meat Co. Ltd* [1996] B.C.C. 254.

[38] Picarda, *The Law Relating to Receivers and Managers* (2nd ed.) pp. 26–38 refers to s. 14(1) and para. 14 of Sched. 1 to the Insolvency Act 1986 and suggests that the appointment of a receiver would not necessarily bring about a cessation of business by the company. But this surely misses the point: the company's licence to carry on business on its own account is determined by the appointment of a receiver.

[39] [1986] Ch. 366 at 377G–378C.

[40] The Cork Committee (Cmnd. 8558) acknowledged that it was uncertain whether a floating charge automatically crystallised on the appointment of a receiver under another charge held by another debenture-holder. It proposed that legislation ought to be enacted to specify that this was so: see paras. 1573 and 1580 of the Report. The suggestion has not been taken up.

[41] [1994] 1 W.L.R. 1427

consequences for the debenture-holder of an unrecognised or unwanted automatic crystallisation. Whilst a debenture-holder may waive a provision for crystallisation before the event occurs, once the provision has been triggered, there may be irreversible consequences[42] and the process itself may be irreversible (see below).

Moreover, if steps are not taken by the chargee to prevent the company from continuing to trade and deal with its assets after crystallisation, there may well be the risk of claims by subsequent chargees that the debenture-holder has waived his right to rely upon the automatic crystallisation clause.[43]   **3–078**

So far as third parties are concerned, an obvious problem with automatic or semi-automatic crystallisation clauses is that there may be no means by which persons dealing with the company can determine with certainty whether crystallisation has occurred. Given the potentially far-reaching nature of some automatic crystallisation clauses, the making of inquiries of each registered debenture-holder or of the company on the occasion of each subsequent transaction can scarcely be practicable, is unlikely to be acceptable to the company and is not guaranteed to produce a reliable answer in any event.   **3–079**

It is suggested, however, that, in the absence of legislative intervention, there is no over-riding reason why automatic crystallisation clauses ought not to be given effect because of concerns about the position of third parties, who can be sufficiently protected under existing legal concepts. In the *Fire Nymph* case Gleeson C.J. stated[44]:   **3–080**

> "It is not sufficient objection to say that [automatic crystallisation clauses] could possibly be unfair to third parties. We are dealing with the operation of a contract, and there is nothing in legal theory that prevents parties from making a contract that might produce results adverse to third parties. In any event, the way in which third parties are affected will depend upon the rules as to priorities, often involving questions of notice, and those rules, generally speaking, operate in a fashion that gives practical effect (albeit in a somewhat formalised way) to considerations of fairness."

As indicated above, it is an essential feature of a floating charge that the company has the power to deal with the charged assets in the ordinary course of its business free of the charge. If the third party has no notice   **3–081**

---

[42] Contractual provisions may be triggered and leases may be rendered subject to forfeiture.

[43] See *Campbell v. Michael Mount PPB* (1995) 16 A.S.C.R. 296. Note also *Dovey Enterprises Ltd v. Guardian Assurance Public Ltd* [1993] 1 N.Z.L.R. 540 at 548–549, and Tan, "Automatic Crystallisation, De-crystallisation and Convertibility of Charges" [1998] Company, Financial & Insolvency Law Review 41 at 47-48. *cf. Re Atlantic Computer Systems plc* [1992] Ch. 505 upholding a claim to a fixed charge, notwithstanding that the company was permitted to deal with charged assets until the chargee chose to intervene. Some of the risks of "overkill" in the drafting of automatic crystallisation clauses are well summarised by Professor Goode, *Legal Problems of Credit and Security* (2nd ed.).

[44] (1992) 7 A.C.L.R. 365 at 373.

that the charge has been crystallised, the third party should be entitled to continue to deal with the company on the basis that the power continues in force.[45] This conclusion can be reached in two ways, depending on whether one takes the view that the company's power stems from authority granted to it by the debenture-holder, or from its own continuing right to dispose of charged assets in the ordinary course of its business.

3–082   If the company's power to dispose of assets free of a floating charge to which they are subject in fact stems from authority given by the debenture-holder to make such disposals, then a third party dealing with the company is entitled to assume that this authority continues, unless and until he knows or is put on notice that it has determined. The debenture-holder originally took a floating charge and so held the company out as having authority to deal with its assets in the ordinary course of its business, free of the charge, unless and until the contrary became known or could reasonably have been ascertained. The third party will thereby obtain rights to the assets in priority to those of the debenture-holder by operation of the doctrine of ostensible authority.[46]

3–083   If the company's power to dispose of assets free of a floating charge to which they are subject stems from the company's own continuing and paramount right as owner of the assets, then a third party who deals with the company after that right has in fact determined may nevertheless gain title to the assets free of the crystallised charge by reason of the law relating to priorities. If a company disposes of its assets after a floating charge has crystallised into a fixed equitable charge, and the disposal appears to be in the ordinary course of the company's business, a purchaser in good faith who acquires legal title to the assets for value without notice of the crystallisation will take the assets free of the crystallised charge. The floating charge, when granted, did not create an immediate property interest in any specific assets which would bind a third party who acquired such assets from the chargor company in the ordinary course of its business.[47] Such an interest only arises on crystallisation, but being an equitable interest, a bona fide purchaser takes free of it if he acquires a legal right in the asset concerned and, at that time, has no notice of the equitable interest. The fact that the purchaser might have notice of the uncrystallised charge is irrelevant. Actual or constructive notice (arising from registration) of the debenture does not constitute the required notice of the terms of the provision for crystallisation,[48] still less that the event has occurred.

---

[45] See, *e.g. Robson v. Smith* [1895] 2 Ch. 118 at 125, where Romer J. upheld the title of the person dealing with the company on the ground that the crystallising event, namely stopping business, had not occurred and that, in any event, the person had no notice of any stoppage. See also *Bower v. Foreign & Colonial Gas Company* [1877] W.N. 222.

[46] See Goode, *Commercial Law* (2nd ed) pp. 738–742.

[47] See above, para. 3–008—3–009.

[48] Constructive notice of a document by reason of registration does not import constructive notice of its contents: *Siebe Gorman & Co. Ltd v. Barclays Bank* [1979] 2 Lloyd's Rep. 142, following *Wilson v. Kelland* [1910] 2 Ch. 306 and *Re Standard Rotary Machine Co.* (1906) 95 L.T. 829.

A third party who seeks to take free of a crystallised charge will find **3–084** an argument based on the law of priorities more difficult if, as a result of a transaction which appears to be in the ordinary course of the company's business, he acquires not a legal title but only an equitable interest in the charged property, either as a result of the disposition which itself caused crystallisation (as in the *Fire Nymph* case) or after automatic crystallisation has occurred. In the case of two competing equities, prima facie the first in time prevails.[49] Consequently, it might appear that a debenture-holder whose charge crystallises before some third party acquires equitable rights in assets subject to the charge will have the prior and better right, whether or not the third party had notice of the crystallising event. However, it is suggested that the principles of estoppel by representation ought to operate so as to ensure that the disponee without notice takes free of the crystallised charge as a matter of priorities. By the taking of a floating charge, the debenture-holder represents to the world that the company has the power to dispose of the charged property in the ordinary course of its business. Unless and until the debenture-holder takes some active step to displace the appearance of continued powers of management and dealing on the part of the company, he should be estopped from challenging the priority of the interest acquired by the third party.[50]

(vii) After-acquired property
When crystallisation has taken place, after-acquired property of the **3–085** company (*e.g.* income generated by trading by the receiver) becomes subject to the fixed charge arising on crystallisation.[51]

(g) De-crystallisation or re-flotation
The question arises: can a fixed charge resulting from a crystallised **3–086** floating charge be re-converted into a floating charge?[52] As illustrated above, the essential distinction between a fixed and floating charge is that in the case of the floating charge the company is given a right to deal with the charged assets in the ordinary course of its business which is terminated upon the happening of stipulated events. It may be that a debenture-holder with a fixed charge can grant the company a licence to deal with the charged assets. However, can a debenture-holder with a

---

[49] In the *Fire Nymph* case, the Court identified, but on the facts did not need to resolve, the "difficult question" of which of the two equities was prior in time when the crystallisation of the floating charge was held to have occurred contemporaneously with the disposal to the third party.

[50] See Gough, *op. cit.*, pp. 255–256 referring, *inter alia*, to the *dictum* of Lord Shand in *Governments Stock and Other Securities Investment Co. v. Manila Rly. Co.* [1897] A.C. 81 at 87–88 to the effect that "active interference" was required by the debenture-holders to make it known that the company's licence to deal had been determined. On the loss of priority through estoppel, see also Meagher, Gummow & Lehane (3rd ed) pp. 230–232.

[51] *Robbie N.W. & Co. v. Witney Warehouse Co.* [1963] 3 All E.R. 613 at 621; *Ferrier v. Bottomer* (1972) 126 C.L.R. 597; *Mineral & Chemical Traders Pty Ltd v. T. Tymczyszyn Ltd* (1994) 15 A.C.S.R. 398.

[52] See Grantham, "Refloating a Floating Charge" [1997] Company, Financial & Insolvency Law Review 53, and Tan, "Automatic Crystallisation, De-crystallisation and Convertibility of Charges" [1998] Company, Financial & Insolvency Law Review 41.

fixed charge reach an agreement with the company to convert his fixed charge into a floating charge and thereby grant a right to the company to deal with the charged assets in the ordinary course of business? This question is one of considerable practical importance, since it is not exceptional for a company's fortunes to revive after crystallisation of a floating charge or for the triggering default to prove a false alarm. The debenture-holder as well as the company may wish that the company be given a second chance.

3–087 It is clear that the debenture-holder and company can agree to replace a charge which has always been a fixed charge with a floating charge. However, such a substitution may have serious consequences for the debenture-holder:

(a) the newly-created floating charge will require registration and may be vulnerable to attack if liquidation follows within the statutory period; or

(b) the newly-created floating charge will be postponed to charges created after the fixed or crystallised floating charge and before its own date.

3–088 In the case of a fixed charge arising from crystallisation of a floating charge, it is in the interests of the debenture-holder that the re-floated charge be treated not as a replacement for, but as a continuation of, the original charge. This possibility will be most likely to be accepted if the debenture contains provisions for "re-flotation" in certain circumstances and, accordingly, the seeds for its own regeneration.

3–089 However, although there might be some commercial advantages by way of flexibility if the concept can be embodied in a coherent legal doctrine, there are undoubtedly very real theoretical difficulties with the notion of a charge that can continue to exist through the processes of crystallisation and re-flotation.[53] Most commentators appear to favour allowing re-flotation to a greater or lesser extent, providing that no liquidator has actually been appointed, but as yet there has been little discussion of the issue and it remains to be seen whether the courts or the legislature (if and when regulations are enacted dealing with the registration of crystallisation are made) will adopt this approach.[54] It should be borne in mind, however, that, even if this approach is adopted,

---

[53] One might, for example, consider the difficulties created by re-flotation of a charge in circumstances where a second floating charge has automatically crystallised. In such a case it would seem that the second debenture holder would have to consent to the re-flotation of the first charge.

[54] See, *e.g. Goode, Legal Problems of Credit and Security* (2nd ed.), pp. 75–76; Picarda, *The Law Relating to Receivers and Managers* (2nd ed.), p. 39; Lingard, *Bank Security Documents* (3rd ed.), para. 9.30. De-crystallisation is statutorily recognised under Scottish law: see s. 62(6) of the Insolvency Act 1986. Goode and Picarda both take the view that re-registration ought not to be required, as the charge is the same security interest as originally created but which has simply first attached and then detached. If regulations are brought into force requiring registration of crystallisation, provision will have to be made to permit notification of re-flotation so as preserve the accuracy of the register.

if a receiver has been appointed, he will have a positive statutory duty to pay preferential creditors out of assets reaching his hands before directly or indirectly making any repayment to the debenture-holder.[55] Also, if he is an administrative receiver, he cannot be removed other than by order of the court.[56]

Careful consideration should also be given to the terms of any **3–090** guarantees and the prior consent obtained (if possible) of any guarantors, for there may be a substantial risk that the release of the fixed charge over assets (involved in the replacement of the fixed by the floating charge) may prejudice the rights of the debenture-holder against guarantors. It is, however, thought that this course cannot give rise to any claim against the debenture-holder by subsequent mortgagees.[57]

2. THE VALIDITY OF CHARGES

Apart from non-registration (as to which see section 3 below), the **3–091** charge under which a receiver is appointed may be invalid or at least its validity may be challenged on a number of grounds. These include:

(a) illegality;
(b) lack of capacity on the part of the company to enter into the charge;
(c) lack of authority on the part of the directors to execute the charge;
(d) abuse of power or conflict of interest by the directors in granting the charge;
(e) defect of form; and
(f) as a result of various statutory provisions taking effect on the liquidation or in the administration of the company.

(a) Illegality
The grant of the charge may be illegal, *e.g.* the provision by a company of **3–092** financial assistance by way of guarantee or security for the purpose of the acquisition of shares in that company or a company of which it is a subsidiary in breach of sections 151–154 of the Companies Act 1985. In such a case, the charge will be void.[58] Note that it may be possible to

---

[55] Insolvency Act 1986, s.40. See *I.R.C. v. Goldblatt* [1972] Ch. 498, *per* Goff J.
[56] *ibid.*, s. 45.
[57] A debenture-holder may release assets from his charge as suits his interest: *Scottish & Newcastle plc, Petitioners* [1993] B.C.C. 634.
[58] *Heald v. O'Connor* [1971] 1 W.L.R. 497. The failure to comply with a substantive (as opposed to a procedural) requirement of the Companies Act 1985 may have a like consequence: see, *e.g. Precision Dippings Ltd v. Precision Dippings Marketing Ltd* [1986] Ch. 447, CA. A charge taken in contempt of an order of the court would also be void for illegality: *Clarke v. Chadburn* [1985] 1 W.L.R. 78 at 81C, *per* Megarry V.-C.; but *cf. Chapman v. Honig* [1963] 2 Q.B. 502, CA (holding valid a notice to quit given in contempt of court in order to victimise a witness). In *BCCI v. BRS Kumar Brothers Ltd* [1994] 1 B.C.L.C. 211, it appeared that the plaintiff and the defendant had colluded in a tax avoidance scheme. This involved the payment to an offshore recipient of monies lent by

sever the lawful part of the transaction from the unlawful part and to enforce the lawful part.[59]

(b) Lack of corporate capacity[60]

3–093   The law relating to corporate capacity (the *ultra vires* doctrine) underwent a major reformation as a result of the passing of the Companies Act 1989. Companies are now permitted to adopt a clause in their memorandum stating that the object of the company is to carry on business as a general commercial company, as a result of which the company will have the power to do all such things as are incidental or conducive to the carrying on of any trade or business by it.[61] Further, whilst directors continue to have a duty to observe any limitations on their powers flowing from the company's memorandum and the members can still apply to the court to restrain the doing of an act which would be beyond the company's capacity, section 35 of the Companies Act 1985 (as substituted by the Companies Act 1989) provides that the validity of an act done by a company shall not be called into question on the ground of lack of capacity by reason of anything in the company's memorandum. In addition, the new section 35B of the Companies Act 1985 provides that a party to a transaction with a company is not bound to enquire as to whether it is permitted by the company's memorandum.

3–094   In practice, these changes mean that a potential chargee will not now need to concern himself over the capacity of the company to grant the charge in his favour. It must be noted, however, that nothing in these provisions will affect the validity or invalidity of any act done by a company prior to February 4, 1991.[62] It would thus appear that the old common law (as modified by what was previously section 35 of the Companies Act 1985[63]) will still govern the validity or invalidity of charges granted prior to that date.

3–095   The pre-1991 law in relation to *ultra vires* was extensively reviewed by the Court of Appeal in *Rolled Steel Products (Holdings) Ltd v. British Steel Corporation plc.*[64] Slade L.J. (with whose judgment Lawton L.J. agreed) summarised the law as follows:

the plaintiff to the defendant. The loan from the plaintiff to the defendant was secured by fixed and floating charges. On an interim application, the court held that the debenture deed was not void for illegality, and so BCCI could appoint a receiver under it. It was held that any illegality did not constitute "an affront to the public conscience", such that the charges were void. From the brief details given at p. 222 of the report, it appears that the parties were *in pari delicto*. See also *Tinsley v. Milligan* [1994] 1 A.C. 340, HL on the issue of the effect of illegality.

[59] *Carney v. Herbert* [1985] A.C. 301, PC. A guarantee of a company's *ultra vires* contract may be effective: see Rowlatt, *Principal and Surety* (5th ed.), p. 131.

[60] See generally Ferran, *Company Law and Corporate Finance* (1999), Chaps 4 and 5.

[61] Companies Act 1985, s. 3A.

[62] Para. 7 of the Companies Act 1989 (Commencement No. 8 and Transitional and Savings Provisions) Order 1990 (S.I. 1990 No. 2569).

[63] Formerly s. 9(1) of the European Communities Act 1972.

[64] [1986] Ch. 246.

"(1) The basic rule is that a company incorporated under the Companies Acts only has the capacity to do those acts which fall within its objects as set out in its memorandum of association or are reasonably incidental to the attainment or pursuit of those objects. Ultimately, therefore, the question whether a particular transaction is within or outside its capacity must depend on the true construction of the memorandum.

(2) Nevertheless, if a particular act . . . is of a category which, on the true construction of the company's memorandum, is capable of being performed as reasonably incidental to the attainment or pursuit of its objects, it will not be rendered *ultra vires* the company merely because in a particular instance its directors, in performing an act in its name, are in truth doing so for purposes other than those set out in the memorandum . . .

(3) . . . the court will not ordinarily construe a statement in a memorandum that a particular power is exercisable 'for the purposes of the company' as a condition limiting the company's corporate capacity to exercise the power; it will regard it as simply imposing a limit on the authority of the directors . . ."[65]

In construing a memorandum, the court will generally have regard to **3–096** well-established rules of construing documents.[66] However, given the nature of a memorandum of association (being a statutory document of the company), the court will not readily permit incorporation of powers by reference to the terms of another document and will not permit a term to be implied from extrinsic evidence of surrounding circumstances.[67]

In addition, there are a number of particular rules of construction **3–097** applicable to objects clauses. The court will give full force, so far as possible, to any "independent objects" clause which may exist, requiring each sub-clause of the memorandum to be construed independently of the other sub-clauses. However, this will not be done if either the object is of its very nature incapable of constituting a substantive object or if the wording of the memorandum indicates expressly or by implication that the sub-clause was intended only to constitute a power ancillary to other objects.[68] For example, in *Re Introductions Ltd*[69] one of the "objects" in the memorandum was the borrowing of money and the issue of debentures. The Court of Appeal held that this could not form an

[65] At 295. Browne-Wilkinson L.J. (who agreed with Slade L.J.) formulated the principles essentially to the same effect: see at p.306.

[66] As to the general rules of construction, see, *e.g. Mannai Investments Co. Ltd v. Eagle Star Life Assurance Co.* [1997] A.C. 749, HL, *Investors Compensation Scheme Ltd v. West Bromwich Building Society* [1998] 1 W.L.R. 896, HL and *Scottish Power plc v. Britoil (Exploration) Ltd, The Times,* December 2, 1997, CA.

[67] *Proprietors of Royal Exchange Buildings, Glasgow* [1911] S.C. 1337; *Bratton Seymour Service Co. Ltd v. Oxborough* [1992] B.C.C. 471, CA.

[68] See *Cotman v. Brougham* [1918] A.C. 514, HL and *Rolled Steel* at 288H–289B *per* Slade L.J.

[69] [1970] Ch. 199.

independent object but was merely an ancillary power, for borrowing was not generally an end in itself but had to be for some purpose.[70]

(c) The authority of corporate representatives[71]

3–098 In addition to reforming the law on *ultra vires*, the Companies Act 1989 also altered the law relating to limitations on the authority of directors and others to bind a company. Again, the changes took effect from February 4, 1991. The relevant provisions so far as transactions with third parties unconnected with the directors of the company are to be found in sections 35A, 35B and 711A of the Companies Act 1985 (as amended).[72] Broadly speaking, these sections aim to protect third parties who deal with companies in good faith from technical objections as to the validity of transactions based upon a lack of authority on the part of the agents of the company. There is a less favourable regime for transactions between the company and its directors and those connected or associated with them. In relation to directors and connected persons, section 35A is to be read subject to the section 322A, under which, subject to certain limitations, such a transaction will be voidable at the instance of the company if the board of directors exceed any limitation on their powers under the company's constitution.[73]

3–099 So far as third parties are concerned, section 35A(1) provides that, in favour of a person dealing with a company in good faith, the power of the board of directors to bind the company, or to authorise others to do so, shall be deemed to be free of any limitations under the company's constitution.[74] Section 35A(2) provides that, for these purposes, a person "deals with" a company if he is a party to any transaction or other act to which the company is a party[75]; a person shall not be regarded as acting in bad faith by reason only of his knowing that an act is beyond the powers of the directors under the company's constitution; and a person shall be deemed to have acted in good faith unless the contrary is

---

[70] In the *Rolled Steel Products* case, the Court of Appeal considered a provision which stated that an "object" of the company was to lend or advance money or give credit to such persons, firms or companies and on such terms as might seem expedient, and in particular to customers of and others having dealings with the company, and to give guarantees or become security for any such persons, firms or companies. The Court held that whilst one could form a company to give guarantees, that would be a most unusual object. Given the nature of the company (reinforced by the reference to "customers"), the provision was to be construed merely as a limited ancillary power, and the expediency provision was to be construed merely as a limited ancillary power, and the expediency referred to meant "as may seem expedient for the furtherance of the objects of the company". See [1986] Ch. 246 at 289C-289F.

[71] See generally Ferran, *Company Law and Corporate Finance* (1999), Chaps 4 and 5.

[72] Section 711A is still not in force.

[73] See s. 35A(6). The scope of the European First Company Law Directive (68/151/EEC) which gave rise to what is now s. 35A was considered in *Coöperative Rabobank v. Minderhoud* [1998] 1 W.L.R. 1025, ECJ. The European Court of Justice held that transactions where there was a conflict of interest so far as the director was concerned were outside the First Directive and remained therefore a matter for national laws.

[74] The reference to limitations deriving from the company's constitution is extended by s. 35A(3) to include limitations deriving from resolutions of the shareholders or from shareholder agreements.

[75] The reference to "other act" is designed to catch gratuitous transactions which had been excluded under the old s. 35.

proved. Additionally, section 35B states that a party to a transaction with a company is not bound to inquire as to any limitation on the powers of the board of directors to bind the company or authorise others to do so.

A further important change will also be made if and when section 711A is brought into force, abolishing the doctrine of constructive notice by providing that a person shall not be taken to have notice of any matter merely because it is disclosed in any document kept by the Registrar of Companies or made available by the company for inspection.

A key component in the statutory test under section 35A is the **3–100** requirement that the third party be acting "in good faith". This concept requires some elaboration. First, whilst the terms of section 35B mean that an allegation of lack of good faith cannot be made *solely* by alleging that inquiries ought to have been made which the section states a person is not bound to make,[76] it does not mean that a failure to inquire cannot be a component part of an allegation of bad faith. Moreover, whilst it may often be that a finding of bad faith will be accompanied by a finding that the third party actually knew that the act in question was beyond the powers of the directors under the company's constitution, and although section 35A(2)(b) makes it clear that a person will not be regarded as being in bad faith by reason *only* that he knew that the transaction was beyond the powers of the directors,[77] it is nowhere suggested that actual knowledge is a necessary prerequisite for a finding of bad faith.

In other words, the section envisages that it is neither necessary nor **3–101** sufficient to establish actual knowledge of a lack of authority. It is suggested that in most cases, if actual knowledge of lack of authority is established, little more will be required. Alternatively, an allegation of bad faith might be justified if the third party consciously chose not to make an inquiry as to whether the execution of a debenture was authorised because he strongly suspected that it was not, and did not want his suspicions confirmed; *a fortiori* if an inquiry *was* made, and a plainly unsatisfactory answer was not pursued by further inquiries.[78]

It is suggested that the means by which the concept of "good **3–102** faith" can best be understood is to recognise that in all cases a finding of bad faith under section 35A is akin to a finding of dishonesty,[79] which is

---

[76] See *TCB v. Gray* [1986] Ch. 621.

[77] See *Barclays Bank v. TOSG* [1984] B.C.L.C. 1 at 18c–g.

[78] This is consistent with the approach to the requirement of "good faith" in s. 9(1) of the European Communities Act 1972, a precursor of, though substantially differently worded to, ss. 35A and 35B of the Companies Act 1985: see *Barclays Bank Ltd v. TOSG Trust Fund Ltd* [1984] B.C.L.C. 1. In that case (at p. 18), Nourse J. indicated that good faith was a subjective concept, but that bad faith might nevertheless be shown where someone did not know of a fact, but ought in the circumstances to have known of it. The *dictum* of Lawson J. in *International Sales and Agencies Ltd v. Marcus* [1982] 3 All E.R. 551 at 559g, that good faith is entirely subjective cannot now be supported (see below).

[79] See, *e.g. Medforth v. Blake* [2000] Ch. 86 at 103D "In my judgment, the breach of a duty of good faith should, in this area as in all others, require some dishonesty or improper motive, some element of bad faith, to be established". It has been recognised that "bad faith" and "dishonesty" are often used interchangeably: see *Three Rivers DC v. Bank of England* [2000] 2 W.L.R. 1220, HL.

essentially a question of fact and which will depend upon the particular facts of each case.[80] The leading case on dishonesty in a commercial setting is *Royal Brunei Airlines v. Tan*[81] in which Lord Nicholls stated,

> "Honesty has a connotation of subjectivity, as distinct from the objectivity of negligence. Honesty, indeed, does have a strong subjective element in that it is a description of a type of conduct assessed in the light of what a person actually knew at the time, as distinct from what a reasonable person would have known or appreciated. Further, honesty and its counterpart dishonesty are mostly concerned with advertent conduct, not inadvertent conduct. Carelessness is not dishonesty. Thus for the most part dishonesty is to be equated with conscious impropriety.
>
> However, these subjective characteristics of honesty do not mean that individuals are free to set their own standards of honesty in particular circumstances. The standard of what constitutes honest conduct is not subjective. Honesty is not an optional scale with higher or lower values according to the moral standards of each individual. If a person knowingly appropriates another's property, he will not escape a finding of dishonesty simply because he sees nothing wrong in such behaviour . . .
>
> . . . [it must be kept in mind] that honesty is an objective standard. The individual is expected to attain the standard which would be observed by an honest person placed in those circumstances. It is impossible to be more specific. Knox J. captured to flavour of this, in a case with a commercial setting, when he referred to a person who is "guilty of commercially unacceptable conduct in the particular context involved": see *Cowan de Groot Properties v. Eagle Trust plc*.[82] Acting in reckless disregard of others' rights or possible rights can be a tell-tale sign of dishonesty. An honest person would have regard to the circumstances known to him, including the nature and importance of the proposed transaction, the nature and importance of his role, the ordinary course of business, the degree of doubt, the practicality of the trustee or the third party proceeding otherwise and the seriousness of the adverse consequences to the beneficiaries. The circumstances will dictate which one or more of the possible courses should be taken by an honest person . . .
>
> Likewise, when called upon to decide whether a person was acting honestly, a court will look at all the circumstances known to the third party at the time. The court will also have regard to personal attributes of the third party, such as his experience and intelligence, and the reason why he acted as he did."

---

[80] *Aktieselskabet Dansk Skibsfinansiering v. Brothers* [2000] 1 H.K.L.R.D. 568, Court of Final Appeal of Hong Kong.
[81] [1995] 2 A.C. 378
[82] [1992] 4 All E.R. 700 at 761.

The extent to which dishonesty is a subjective or an objective concept **3–103** has been the subject of some debate.[83] It is suggested that the various *dicta* in the cases can be reconciled in the following way. A person is to be judged by an *objective* standard of honesty—he cannot set his own standard. But in judging whether someone has attained this objective standard, the Court looks at what he actually knew and intended, *i.e.* his *subjective* state of mind.

Thus, for example, a failure to make enquiries will not amount to **3–104** dishonesty unless it results from a suspicion that there is something wrong, together with an unwillingness to discover the truth. By contrast, a failure to make enquiries because the person concerned was "an honest blunderer or stupid man"[84] does not amount to dishonesty.

Assuming good faith, the provisions of sections 35A and 35B go a long **3–105** way to protecting a third party who intends to take a charge from a company.[85] They do not, however, provide complete protection in all circumstances for third parties, nor are they intended to do so.

For example, whilst the statutory provisions are aimed at removing the **3–106** effect of any constitutional limitations on the powers of the board of directors to bind the company or to authorise others to do so, they are not intended to operate so as to insulate third parties from the effects of dealing with directors who are acting for improper purposes or in breach of their fiduciary duties to the company.[86]

Nor, by deeming the powers of the board to bind the company or **3–107** authorise others to do so to be free of limitations under the company's constitution, do the statutory provisions actually deem such powers to

---

[83] In *Grupo Torras SA v. Al-Sabah* ([1999] C.L.C. 1469), a case, *inter alia*, about dishonest assistance, Mance L.J. regarded dishonesty as essentially objective, yet he acknowledged that test of dishonesty in *Tan* allowed some subjective considerations to be taken into account: "Ingredient (iii) [dishonesty] was considered in *Royal Brunei Airlines Sdn Bhd v. Tan,* where Lord Nicholls gave the advice of the Privy Council. The case establishes that dishonesty in the context of a knowing assistance claim is an objective standard: see at 389B–G. The individual is expected to attain the standard which would be observed by an honest person placed in the circumstances he was: at 390F. But those circumstances include subjective considerations like the defendant's experience and intelligence and what he actually knew at the time: at 389D and 391B". In a public law context involving the tort of misfeasance in public office, the House of Lords put a distinctively subjective interpretation on the concept of dishonesty: see *Three Rivers DC v. Bank of England* [2000] 2 W.L.R. 1220, HL. In *Aktieselskabet Dansk Skibsfinansiering v. Brothers* [2000] 1 H.K.L.R.D. 568, Court of Final Appeal of Hong Kong, Lord Hoffmann stated, in the context of a fraudulent trading case, that "While I quite accept that a defendant cannot be allowed to shelter behind some private standard of honesty not shared by the community, I think that there is a danger in expressing that proposition by invoking the concept of the hypothetical decent honest man. The danger is that because decent honest people also tend to behave reasonably, considerately and so forth, there may be a temptation to treat shortcomings in these respects as a failure to comply with the necessary objective standard".

[84] See *Jones v. Gordon* (1877) 2 App. Cas. 616 at 628–629.

[85] Most debentures are executed pursuant to a board resolution: in these cases, the chargee will normally be protected against subsequent allegations that the board exceeded its authority under the company's constitution. The position will be less clear where the charge is granted without a board resolution, but it is unlikely that many lenders would in practice be content to accept a charge executed in this way.

[86] The requirements not to act for improper purposes or in breach of fiduciary duty are requirements of general law and not "limitations under the company's constitution".

have been exercised as a matter of fact. So, for example, section 35A would not operate to protect a third party who accepted a charge executed by a lone director or by a director and the company secretary, in a situation where the board had not actually purported to authorise the execution by those persons of a debenture at all. In such cases, the third party would be driven to rely upon the common law principles of agency as applied to companies, together with the rule in *Royal British Bank v. Turquand*[87] (see below).

3–108   At common law, a director may bind the company if he has actual authority (express or implied) to do so. Express actual authority needs no explanation. The implied actual authority of a director derives from his appointment and will extend to his being authorised to perform such acts as are reasonably incidental to the proper performance of his duties or which fall within the usual scope of the office to which he has been appointed.[88]

3–109   Alternatively, even if the director has no actual authority to bind the company, the company may be estopped by reason of its conduct from denying that it is bound, on the basis that the director has "ostensible" or "apparent" authority to bind the company. Ostensible or apparent authority may derive either from a person being appointed to, or held out by the company as occupying a particular position, in which case he may be taken to have all the powers which it is usual for a person in that position to have, or it may derive from particular representations made by or on behalf of the company as to the authority of the person. In any case, it is the totality of the conduct of the company which must be examined to see what ostensible authority a person may have had.[89]

3–110   In either case, however, the estoppel can only operate if the holding out or representation was made to the third party and was relied upon by him, so that it will not operate if the third party either knew or ought to have known that the director did not have any authority.[90] The third party also cannot rely upon any representation made by the director himself as to his authority: the holding out must be by the company or by some person authorised to make such representations on its behalf.[91] A

---

[87] (1856) 6 E. & B. 327; (1856) 119 E.R. 886.
[88] See, *e.g. per* Denning M.R. in *Hely-Hutchinson v. Brayhead Ltd* [1968] 1 Q.B. 549 at 583.
[89] *Ebeed v. Soplex Wholesale Supplies Ltd, The Raffaella* [1985] B.C.L.C. 404, CA. *Armagas Ltd v. Mundogas SA* [1986] A.C. 717, HL.
[90] See, *e.g. Freeman and Lockyer (a firm) v. Buckhurst Park Properties (Mangal) Ltd* [1964] 2 Q.B. 480; *Hely-Hutchinson v. Brayhead* [1968] 1 Q.B. 549; *British Bank of the Middle East v. Sun Life Assurance Co. of Canada (U.K.) Ltd* [1983] B.C.L.C. 78, H.L., *Armagas Ltd v. Mundogas SA* [1986] A.C. 717, HL.
[91] *British Bank of the Middle East v. Sun Life Assurance Co. of Canada (U.K.) Ltd* [1983] B.C.L.C. 78, H.L.; *Ebeed v. Soplex Wholesale Supplies Ltd, The Raffaella* [1985] B.C.L.C. 404; *Armagas Ltd v. Mundogas SA* [1986] A.C. 717. See also the rather unusual case of *First Energy (U.K.) Ltd v. Hungarian International Bank* [1993] B.C.C. 533 in which the Court of Appeal held that although a regional bank manager did not have any apparent authority to decide to offer a loan to a third party, he did have apparent authority to communicate to the third party that such a loan had been approved by the bank's head office and to make an offer on that basis which was capable of acceptance.

simple lack of authority can be cured by ratification by the company in
general meeting.[92]

These common law principles of agency are supplemented in the case **3–111**
of companies by the rule in *Turquand's* case, which states that unless
there are facts putting him on inquiry, an "outsider"[93] dealing with the
company will not be affected by irregularities in the internal procedures
of the company.[94] The rule in *Turquand's* case, however, only allows a
third party to overcome any deficiency in the company's normal internal
procedures such as defects in the giving of notice for, or the absence of a
quorum at, a board meeting to authorise the execution of documents. It
does not enable the third party to hold a company to a transaction where
he could not have established that the director or other representative
would have had the requisite authority (actual or ostensible) even if
there had been no failure to comply with matters of internal procedure.[95]
It also does not apply in the case of forged documents.[96]

**(d) Abuse of power or conflict of interest by the directors in granting
the charge**

If directors abuse their powers by causing the company to execute a **3–112**
debenture, the debenture may be invalid, depending on the state of mind
of the counterparty to it (*i.e.* the intended chargee). If the counterparty
was on notice (actual or constructive) of the directors' improper
purposes at the time the debenture was executed, the debenture is not,
and never was, binding on the company: improper purpose goes to the
power of the directors to bind the company. The law in this respect was
summarised by Slade L.J. in the *Rolled Steel Products (Holdings)* case as
follows:[97]

> "(4) At least in default of the unanimous consent of all the
> shareholders . . . the directors of a company will not have actual
> authority from the company to exercise any express or implied
> power other than for the purposes of the company as set out in its
> memorandum of association.

---

[92] *Grant v. United Kingdom Switchback Railways Co.* (1888) 40 Ch.D. 135, CA.

[93] An outsider is (broadly speaking) someone who is not in such a position within the
company to enable him to know whether or not the proper internal procedures have been
followed.

[94] *Royal British Bank v. Turquand* (1856) 6 E. & L.B. 327; (1856) 119 E.R. 886;
Mahoney v. East Holyford Mining Co. (1875) L.R. 7 H.L. 869; *Morris v. Kanssen* [1946] A.C.
459 at 474, *per* Lord Simonds; *Freeman and Lockyer (a firm) v. Buckhurst Park Properties
(Mangal) Ltd* [1964] 2 Q.B. 480; *Hely-Hutchinson v. Brayhead Ltd* [1968] 1 Q.B. 549;
Broadlands Finance Ltd v. Gisborne Aero Club Inc. [1975] 2 N.Z.L.R. 496. See also the
extensive analysis of the indoor management rule in *Northside Developments Pty Ltd v.
Registrar-General* (1990) 170 C.L.R. 146, HCt of (Australia).

[95] See, *e.g. Freeman and Lockyer (a firm) v. Buckhurst Park Properties (Mangal) Ltd*
[1964] 2 Q.B. 480 at 496.

[96] See, *e.g. Ruben v. Great Fingall Consolidated* [1906] A.C. 439; *Northside Developments
Pty Ltd v. Registrar-General* (1990) 170 C.L.R. 146, H. Ct of Australia. See also The Law
Commission, *The Execution of Deeds and Documents by or on behalf of Bodies Corporate*
(Law Com. Report 253 (1998) paras. 5.34–5.37).

[97] [1986] Ch. 246 at 295.

(5) A company holds out its directors as having ostensible authority to bind the company to any transaction which falls within the powers expressly or impliedly conferred on it by its memorandum of association. Unless he is put on notice to the contrary, a person dealing in good faith with a company which is carrying on an intra vires business is entitled to assume that its directors are properly exercising such powers for the purposes of the company as set out in its memorandum . . .

(6) If, however, a person dealing with the company is on notice that the directors are exercising the relevant power for purposes other than the purposes of the company, he cannot rely on the ostensible authority of the directors and, on ordinary principles of agency, cannot hold the company to the transaction."

3–113 In the same case, Browne-Wilkinson L.J. summarised the principles as follows[98]:

"If . . . the transaction (although in excess or abuse of its powers) is within the capacity of the company, the position of the third party depends upon whether or not he had notice that the transaction was in excess or abuse of the powers of the company."

3–114 If the company's property has been disposed of pursuant to an invalid debenture, this amounts to a disposition in breach of trust. The recipient will be accountable as a constructive trustee if he has the requisite knowledge of the breach of trust.[99] The counterparty would not be able to rely on sections 35A and 35B of the Companies Act 1985 to hold the company bound to the alleged debenture, or to justify a disposition of company property, as improper purposes do not amount to a "limitation under the company's constitution" within the meaning and scope of those sections.

3–115 If directors grant a debenture to one of their number, or to a company that is the creature of one of their number,[1] this will amount to self-

---

[98] [1986] Ch. 246 at 304D.

[99] See *Rolled Steel Products (Holdings) Ltd v. British Steel Corporation* [1986] Ch. 246 in relation to these points. The degree of knowledge required for the imposition of liability as a knowing recipient has been considered recently in two decisions of the Court of Appeal, *Houghton v. Fayers* [2000] 1 B.C.L.C. 511 and *BCCI v. Akindele* (unreported, June 14, 2000). In the BCCI case, Nourse L.J. reconsidered the earlier authorities and stated that he had come to the view that there ought to be a single test of knowledge for knowing receipt and that "The recipient's state of knowledge must be such as to make it unconscionable for him to retain the benefit of the receipt." Nourse L.J. thought that such a test, while it could not avoid difficulties of application, ought to avoid the difficulties of definition which have bedevilled other categorisations of knowledge, such as the five point scale proposed by Peter Gibson J. in *Baden, Delvaux Lecuit v. Société Generale* [1983] B.C.L.C. 325. It is very difficult to predict what degree of knowledge of which facts will make it "unconscionable" for the recipient to keep the received asset.

[1] Consider below paras 7–044 to 7–046 and *Silkstone & Haigh Moor Coal Co. Ltd v. Edey* [1900] 1 Ch. 167; *Re Thompson's Settlement* [1985] 2 All ER 720, cases where the separate corporate personality of the company was disregarded for the purposes of the self dealing rules. Even if the recipient company cannot be disregarded, note that there are restriction

dealing, and the transaction will be voidable unless duly authorised in accordance with the company's articles of association,[2] or by the company in general meeting.[3] Similarly, the grant of a debenture to a director or a person connected with him, will be voidable under section 320 of the Companies Act 1985, if the rights acquired by the director or connected person are of sufficient value to bring the transaction within the scope of the section and the transaction did not have the approval of the company in general meeting.[4]

(e) Formalities
The Companies Act 1989 made a number of significant changes to the **3–116** ways in which companies could execute documents under seal.[5] A company may enter into a contract[6] (a) in writing under its common seal, or (b) by its agents acting under its authority.[7] In practice, most debentures are entered into under the common seal of the company. Traditionally, this required the company's seal to be affixed in accordance with its articles. This method of execution is preserved by the provisions of section 36A(2) of the Companies Act 1985. Section 36A(3) of the Companies Act 1985 provides an alternative method of execution of documents under seal by companies. If a document is signed by a director and the secretary of the company or by two directors and is expressed to be executed by the company, then it has the same effect as if executed under the common seal of the company. This provision removes the doubts as to what constituted sealing which existed under the old (pre-1989 Act) law.[8]

At common law, execution under seal was not of itself sufficient to **3–117** constitute a document as a deed: it needed to be executed with that intention and delivered as such.[9] Section 36A(5) of the Companies Act 1985 now provides that a document executed by a company which makes it clear on its face that it is intended to be a deed has effect upon delivery as a deed and it shall be presumed,

---

in equity on transactions involving a company in which a director is interested, or of which he is also a director: see, *e.g. Transvaal Lands Co. v. New Belgium (Transvaal) Land & Development Co.* [1914] 2 Ch. 488

[2] See, *e.g.* articles such as the 1985 Table A regs. 85–86 and 94–98.

[3] See *Hely-Hutchinson v. Brayhead Ltd* [1968] 1 Q.B. 549 as regards a loan and guarantee, albeit unsecured.

[4] In connection with the grant of a debenture, note the extended meaning of the "transfer or acquisition of a non-cash asset" imported by Companies Act 1985, s. 739.

[5] The changes took effect from July 31, 1990. See generally, The Law Commission, The Execution of Deeds and Documents by or on behalf of Bodies Corporate (Law Com. Consultation Paper No. 143 (1996)); Law Com. Report 253 (1998).

[6] The same considerations apply to the execution of a debenture.

[7] Companies Act 1985, s. 36 (as amended).

[8] See, *e.g. Stromdale & Ball v. Burden* [1952] Ch. 223 at 229; *First National Securities v. Jones* [1978] 1 Ch. 109; *TCB Ltd v. Gray* [1986] Ch. 621, *per* Browne-Wilkinson V-C; affirmed on other grounds [1987] Ch. 458n, CA.

[9] As to the common law complexities of delivery and escrows, see, *e.g. Alan Estates Ltd v. W. G. Stores Ltd* [1982] Ch. 511, C.A.; *Venetian Glass Gallery Ltd v. Next Properties Ltd* [1989] 2 E.G.L.R. 42, *per* Harman J.; *Longman v. Viscount Chelsea* [1989] 2 E.G.L.R. 242, CA.

unless a contrary intention is proved, to be delivered upon its being so executed.[10] Moreover, section 36A(6) states that, in favour of a purchaser (an expression which includes a mortgagee), a document shall be deemed to have been duly executed by a company if it purports to be signed by a director and the secretary of the company or by two directors, and, where it makes it clear on its face that it is intended by the persons making it to be a deed, to have been delivered upon its being executed.[11]

3–118   The result is greatly to facilitate the execution and delivery of documents under seal by companies and more easily to permit third parties to rely upon such documents. But the sections are not without their uncertainties. For example, it is not clear whether the provisions of section 36A(6) will assist a purchaser where the document is a forgery.[12]

3–119   Execution as a deed is not a necessary pre-condition for the validity of a debenture. To be enforceable if not under seal, however, the debenture must (like any other contract not under seal) be supported by consideration. It may also be possible for the court to treat signed but unsealed debentures which are supported by consideration as documents amounting to or evidencing an enforceable agreement to issue sealed debentures.[13] It is possible to stipulate for a power to appoint a receiver in a document not under seal.[14]

3–120   Contracts for a disposition of an interest in land (which will include the execution of a debenture containing a charge over land) must now be made in writing, must incorporate all the terms expressly agreed between the parties and must be signed by or on behalf of both parties.[15] There are no such requirements in the case of charges over personality.

(f) Statutory provisions in a winding-up or administration

3–121   Charges granted by a company may be challenged by a liquidator or administrator subsequently appointed of a company and invalidated under a number of provisions of the Insolvency Act 1986.[16]

---

[10] A suitable form of words for a company to use would be "executed as a deed".

[11] These presumptions and protections for purchasers are more extensive than those under s. 74(1) of the Law of Property Act 1925 (which will thus only be of practical significance in relation to corporations aggregate which do not qualify as companies under the Companies Acts).

[12] Earlier case law has held forged documents to be nullities: see, *e.g. Ruben v. Great Fingall Consolidated Ltd* [1906] A.C. 439. See also the Law Commission Report No. 253, (1998) *op. cit.*, paras 5.34–5.37.

[13] *Re Fireproof Doors Ltd* [1916] 2 Ch. 142, considered in *Byblos Bank SAL v. Rushingdale Ltd SA* [1986] 2 B.C.C. 99,509, CA.

[14] *Byblos Bank SAL v. Rushingdale Ltd SA* above; *Halsbury's Laws of England* (4th ed.), Vol. 32, para. 675.

[15] s. 2 of the Law of Property (Miscellaneous Provisions) Act 1989, which came into force on September 27, 1989, replacing s. 40 of the Law of Property Act 1925. Section 40 (which will continue to apply to charges granted before that date) had simply required that there be a note or memorandum in writing signed by or on behalf of the company. See generally Megarry & Wade, *The Law of Real Property*, 6th ed. by C. Harpum, pp. 651–671.

[16] See below, paras 11–09 *et seq.* An example of a challenge to a floating charge using these provisions is *Re Fairway Magazines Ltd* [1992] B.C.C. 924.

3. REGISTRATION OF CHARGES

Most systems of law require a security interest to be perfected by some **3–122** form of public notice or other act to bring the existence of the security to the attention of third parties. English law has operated a public registration system for company charges since the beginning of the century. The current legislation is embodied in sections 395–408 and 410–423 of the Companies Act 1985 (dealing with companies registered in England, Wales and Scotland) and sections 409 and 424 (dealing with charges created by foreign companies). Following criticism of the system, Part IV of the Companies Act 1989 contained provisions designed to amend the law relating to registration of company charges. These will not now be brought into force, but The Department of Trade and Industry is continuing to review the law relating to the registration of company charges.

(a) Registrable charges

The types of charges[17] which must be registered are listed in section **3–123** 396(1) of the Companies Act 1985:

> "(a) a charge for the purpose of securing any issue of debentures,
> (b) a charge on uncalled share capital of the company,
> (c) a charge created or evidenced by an instrument which, if executed by an individual, would require registration as a bill of sale,
> (d) a charge on land[18] (wherever situated) or any interest in it, but not including a charge for any rent or other periodical sum issuing out of land,
> (e) a charge on book debts of the company,
> (f) a floating charge on the company's undertaking or property,
> (g) a charge on calls made but not paid,
> (h) a charge on a ship or aircraft, or any share in a ship,
> (i) a charge on goodwill, on a patent or a licence under a patent, on a trademark or on a copyright or a licence under a copyright."

The court will investigate whether a particular transaction gives rise to a **3–124** registrable charge.[19] The classic indicia of a charge were identified in *Re George Inglefield Ltd.*[20] as being:

---

[17] Which expression includes mortgages: see s. 396(4) of the 1985 Act. There is a critical distinction between trusts (which are not registrable) and charges (which are): see *Associated Alloys Pty Ltd v. ACN* (2000) 117 A.L.R. 568 at 571 (High Ct of Australia).

[18] In addition to registration under the Companies Act, registration may also be required under the provisions of the Land Registration Act 1925 (registered title) or the Land Charges Act 1972 (charges and mortgages over registered title other than a first legal mortgage).

[19] *Lovell Construction Ltd v. Independent Estates plc* [1994] 1 B.C.L.C. 31.

[20] [1933] Ch. 1 at 27, *per* Romer L.J.

(a) the right of the chargor to redeem the charge;
(b) the obligation on the chargee to account to the chargor for any surplus realisations; and
(c) the right of recourse which the chargee has against the chargor for any shortfall in the secured debt following realisation of the security.

In analysing any particular transaction, the court will not be bound by the description which the parties give to their agreement but will be concerned to ascertain the substance of the arrangement. If the parties have consciously chosen not to cast their agreement using the words of charge, the court will not disregard that language simply because the agreement contains provisions which give rise to the same commercial result as would a charge. In each case the question will be whether the legal effect of the transaction is what it purports to be, and unless the terms of the documents taken as a whole compel a different conclusion, the transaction will be characterised in conformity with the intention of the parties as expressed in the documents.[21]

3–125   "Debentures" are defined in section 744 of the Companies Act 1985 to include "debenture stock, bonds and any other securities of a company, whether constituting a charge on the assets of the company or not". A debenture is a document which acknowledges or creates an existing debt or makes provision for repayment of a loan to be made thereafter.[22] The term has been held to include an ordinary mortgage,[23] or a security for payment of the price of shares under a contract the performance of which was postponed.[24] The expression "any issue of debentures" is not defined in the Act but it is thought that it does not connote the issue of a single debenture (for that would render the remainder of the section largely redundant) but is restricted to the aggregate of a number of debentures issued by the company.[25]

3–126   Category (c) arises because companies are not otherwise subject to the Bills of Sale Acts 1878 and 1882.[26] It is to be noted, that not all documents registrable as bills of sale will be registrable under section 395. It is only transactions which constitute a charge to secure the repayment of money which fall within the section.[27] The precise definition of the nature of a registrable bill of sale is very complex.[28] It generally covers all assignments, transfers, declarations of trust without transfer and other assurances of personal chattels, all authorities or

---

[21] *Welsh Development Agency v. Export Finance Co. Ltd* [1992] B.C.C. 270, CA; *Orion Finance v. Crown Financial Management* [1996] B.C.C. 621, CA.

[22] *Handevel v. Comptroller of Stamps* (1985) 62 A.L.R. 204 (H. Ct of Australia).

[23] *Knightsbridge Estates Trust Co. Ltd v. Byrne* [1940] A.C. 613.

[24] *Handevel v. Comptroller of Stamps* (1985) 62 A.L.R. 204 (H. Ct of Australia).

[25] See *Automobile Association (Canterbury) Inc v. Australasian Secured Deposits Ltd* [1973] 1 N.Z.L.R. 425.

[26] *Re Standard Manufacturing Co.* [1891] 1 Ch. 627.

[27] *Stoneleigh Finance Ltd v. Phillips* [1965] 2 Q.B. 537.

[28] In *Welsh Development Agency v. Export Finance Co. Ltd* [1992] B.C.C. 270 at 286E–286F Dillon L.J. stated that "this territory is bedevilled by law that is now very out of date".

licences to take possession of personal chattels as security for a debt and any agreement by which a right in equity to any personal chattel or to any charge or security thereon is conferred. It does not, however, include transfers of goods in the ordinary course of business.[29]

The Bills of Sale Act 1878 only deals with written documents which **3–127** are effective to pass a proprietary interest and thus does not cover possessory securities. As such, a pledge of goods whereby possession of the goods themselves is given to the creditor will not be caught,[30] nor will a "letter of trust" under which the lender hands back documents of title pledged to it to the borrower to facilitate sale of the goods.[31] Other types of security over chattels not amounting to a charge are also not included, *e.g.* a retention of title clause[32] or a contractual lien.[33]

With regard to "book debts" in section 396(1)(e), the classic descrip- **3–128** tion is:

> "a debt arising in the course of a business and due or growing due to the proprietor of that business that . . . would or could in the ordinary course of such a business be entered in well-kept books relating to that business . . . whether it is in fact entered in the books of the business or not."[34]

Charges on future book debts are registrable.[35] However, it is only assignments of book debts which are intended to be by way of security which will require registration and not outright assignments.[36]

A contractual "lien" on subfreight is a registrable charge on book **3–129** debts,[37] but a charge over an insurance policy issued by the Export Credit Guarantee Department (E.C.G.D.) is not a charge over a book debt.[38]

---

[29] Section 4 of the Bills of Sale Act 1878. At first instance in *Welsh Development Agency v. Export Finance Co. Ltd* Browne-Wilkinson V.-C. held that an agreement to sell future goods other than in the ordinary course of business would be registrable as a bill of sale if made by an individual: [1990] B.C.C. 393 at 410–411, Ch.D. The Court of Appeal did not express any view on this point. *cf. Thomas v. Kelly* (1888) 13 App.Cas. 506 at 512 and 519.

[30] *Wrightson v. McArthur and Hutchinsons Ltd* [1921] 2 K.B. 807. For a valid pledge there must be actual or constructive possession by the pledgee: see *Askrigg Pty Ltd v. Student Guild of Curtin University* (1989) 18 N.S.W.L.R. 738.

[31] *Re David Allester Ltd* [1922] 2 Ch. 211.

[32] See below Chap. 12.

[33] *Barker (George) (Transport) Ltd v. Eynon* [1974] 1 W.L.R. 462, CA.

[34] *Per* Buckley J. in *Independent Automatic Sales v. Knowles and Foster* [1962] 1 W.L.R. 974; *Re Falcon Sportswear Pty Ltd* (1983) 1 A.C.L.C. 690 at 695; *Re Brightlife Ltd* [1986] Ch. 200; *Northern Bank Ltd v. Ross* [1990] B.C.C. 883, N.I.C.A.; *Re BCCI S.A. (No. 8)* [1998] A.C. 214, HL; *Coakley v. Argent Credit Corporation plc* (unreported, Rimer J, June 4, 1998).

[35] *Independent Automatic Sales v. Knowles and Foster* [1962] 1 W.L.R. 974; *Siebe Gorman & Co. Ltd v. Barclays Bank Ltd* [1979] 2 Lloyd's Rep. 142; *Re Brightlife Ltd* [1986] Ch. 200.

[36] See, *e.g. Ashby Warner & Co. Ltd v. Simmons* [1936] 2 All ER 697; *Re Kent and Sussex Sawmills Ltd* [1947] Ch. 177; *Re Welsh Irish Ferries Ltd* [1986] 1 Ch. 471; *Re Marwalt Ltd* [1992] B.C.C. 32.

[37] *Re Welsh Irish Ferries Ltd* [1986] 1 Ch. 471; *Annangel Glory Cia Naviera SA v. Golodetz Ltd* (1988) P.C.C. 37.

[38] *Paul & Frank v. Discount Bank (Overseas) Ltd* [1967] Ch. 348.

3–130   Section 396(2) provides that, where a negotiable instrument has been given to secure the payment of any book debts of a company, the deposit of the instrument for the purpose of securing an advance to the company is not, for the purposes of section 395, to be treated as a charge on those book debts. In *Chase Manhattan Asia Ltd v. Official Receiver and Liquidator of First Bangkok City Finance Ltd,*[39] a company which was owed a book debt had obtained a promissory note from the debtor and had assigned part of the book debt, agreeing with the assignee to repurchase the assigned debt at a specified date in the future. As a term of the assignment, the company had agreed to deposit the promissory note with the assignee to secure the repurchase. The company failed to deposit the promissory note, failed to buy back the assigned part of the book debt and was wound up as insolvent. The Privy Council held that the assignment created a charge in equity on the promissory note, the moneys payable thereunder and the book debt owed by the debtor to the company. However, as the promissory note had not been deposited, the Hong Kong equivalent of section 396(2) did not protect the assignee from the consequences of non-registration. It was therefore unable to enforce its equitable charge over the promissory note.

3–131   An important type of security not covered by section 396 is the category of charges which are not "created by a company" but which arise in some other way, such as by operation of law (*e.g.* an unpaid vendor's lien[40] or a separate lien[41]).

(b) The consequences of non-registration

3–132 By virtue of section 395(1) of the Companies Act 1985, unless the prescribed particulars of the charge together with the document (if any) by which the charge is created or evidenced were delivered to or received by the Registrar of Companies for registration within 21 days of creation, most charges under which a receiver is likely to be appointed will be void "as against the liquidator[42] or administrator and any creditor of the company". In addition, the avoidance of the charge for non-registration makes the moneys secured immediately repayable: see section 395(2) of the 1985 Act.

3–133   The concept of an unregistered charge being void "as against the liquidator, administrator and any creditor of the company" has been explored in a number of cases. It is clear that an unregistered charge will

---

[39] [1990] B.C.C. 514, PC.

[40] *London & Cheshire Insurance Co. v. Laplagrene Property Co. Ltd* [1971] Ch. 499.

[41] See *Associated Alloys Pty Ltd v. ACN 001 452 106 Pty Ltd* (2000) 171 A.L.R. 568 at 596 *per* Kirby J. A charge will be registrable if it is contractual in nature: see *ibid* and *Re Wallis & Simmonds (Builders) Limited* [1974] 1 W.L.R. 391, a case on the creation of a charge by deposit of title deeds. Note that since 1991 such a charge cannot be created over land in England by mere deposit of title deeds, because this will not satisfy the requirements for writing in s.2 of the Law of Property (Miscellaneous Provisions) Act 1989: see *United Bank of Kuwait plc v. Sahib* [1997] Ch. 107, CA.

[42] Note that the principle appears to apply whether the liquidation is an insolvent or a solvent liquidation: see *Re Oriel Ltd.* [1984] B.C.L.C. 241. A solicitor may be held liable in negligence for failing to advise (and possibly) procure registration at the instance of a director who guaranteed the debt secured by charge: see *Re Foster* (1985) 129 Sol. Jo. 333.

be void against secured creditors if the issue of priorities arises between them at any time, and it also cannot be asserted against a liquidator or administrator who brings proceedings in his own name to challenge the validity of the charge for the benefit of the other creditors of the company.[43] It is also clear that the section does not make an unregistered charge void as against the company itself, at least whilst the company is a going concern.[44] A chargee can therefore enforce an unregistered charge against the company prior to liquidation or administration by seizing the charged property or receiving payment under charged debts.[45] Likewise, a receiver can be validly appointed prior to liquidation or administration under an unregistered charge and can act unless and until a challenge to the security is made by a person entitled to do so under section 395.[46]

It would also seem that an unregistered charge will not be treated as void against a company which has ceased to be a going concern and is in administration or liquidation. In *Independent Automatic Sales Limited v. Knowles and Foster*[47] Buckley J. held that section 395 did not avoid a charge against a company in liquidation, so that proceedings could not be brought in the name of the company to recover hire-purchase agreements and the monies paid thereunder which were the subject of unregistered charges in favour of the defendant financiers. Buckley J. permitted the liquidator of the company in question to be joined to the proceedings in order to obtain an order for delivery up of the hire-purchase agreements in question and an account of the receipts under the agreements. It is not clear from the report what independent right it was thought that the liquidator had to obtain such an order in his own name rather than in the name of the company.

A similar approach to section 395 gave rise to a very different result in **3–133B** relation to administrations in *Smith (Administrator of Cosslett (Contractors) Ltd) v. Bridgend County Council*.[48] The claimant administrator sued the defendant council for conversion of plant which had been used by a company to carry out reclamation works on the council's land. After the company had gone into administration and defaulted under the contract, the council exercised its contractual rights (i) to employ another contractor to complete the works using the plant, and (ii) to enter into a contract to sell the plant to the new contractor at the end of the works and to apply the proceeds of sale towards the amounts due to the council

---

[43] *Re Ehrmann Bros Ltd* [1906] 2 Ch. 697 at 708, CA; *Re Monolithic Building Co. Ltd* [1915] 1 Ch 643, CA; *Independent Automatic Sales Ltd v. Knowles and Foster* [1962] 1 W.L.R. 974; *Bank of Scotland v. TA Neilson & Co.* [1991] S.L.T. 8. A creditor cannot apply under the Insolvency Act 1986 for a declaration as to the invalidity of the charge against the liquidator or administrator: see *Re Ayala Holdings Ltd* [1993] B.C.L.C. 256 at 261.

[44] *Re Monolithic Building Co.* [1915] 1 Ch. 643 at 667–668, CA.

[45] See *Re Mercantile Bank of India Ltd v. Chartered Bank of India* [1937] 1 All E.R. 231; *NV Slavenburg's Bank v. Intercontinental Natural Resources Ltd* [1980] 1 All E.R. 955 at 967–968; *Re Row Dal Constructions Pty Limited* [1966] V.R. 249.

[46] *Burston Finance v. Speirway* [1974] 1 W.L.R. 1648 at 1657E, *per* Walton J. The receiver's position, however, is a precarious one and, if possible, the debenture-holder should be prevailed upon to seek leave to register the charge out of time under s.404 of the Companies Act 1985.

[47] [1962] 1 W.L.R. 974.

[48] [2000] 1 B.C.L.C. 775.

under its contract with the company. At a first hearing the Court of Appeal held that the council's contractual right to continue in possession of the plant and to sell it after completion of the reclamation works constituted a charge over the plant which was void against the administrator for non-registration.[49] Subsequently a differently constituted Court of Appeal held that even though it had not been registered, the council's contractual power of sale would have been a valid defence had a claim in conversion been brought by the company in administration.[50]

If correct, these decisions have a curious consequence in relation to the recovery of property in the possession of the holder of an unregistered charge. In a usual case, an office-holder will probably be able to recover tangible property using his powers under section 234 of the 1986 Act; but if the decision of the Court of Appeal in *Welsh Development Agency v. Export Finance Co Limited*[51] is correct, and section 234 does not give an office-holder a right to recover intangibles, then the office-holder may have no means of recovering book debts or their proceeds from the holder of an unregistered charge. It is not easy to see how such a result accords with the statutory policy behind section 395 which is to permit the office-holder to deal with charged property for the benefit of other creditors as if it were not subject to the unregistered charge.[52] It is suggested that the purposes of section 395 would be better served if the section was interpreted to mean that the charge was void against a liquidator or administrator in such a way that he could act on such voidness either in his own name or in the name of the company, depending on where the relevant remedy lay.[53]

3–134   It should be noted that section 395 does not require actual registration of the charge but merely the delivery of the prescribed particulars of the charge[54] to the Registrar of Companies. Thus, where the Registrar refuses to register a charge, section 395 is complied with simply by delivery of prescribed particulars.[55] Likewise, if the prescribed particulars

---

[49] *Re Cosslett (Contractors) Limited* [1998] Ch. 495. The right to possession of the plant to complete the works was held not to be void against the company or the administrator, because it did not amount to a charge.

[50] In fact the claim was brought by the administrator in his own name. In the result the Court of Appeal thought that although the administrator would have had a statutory right to delivery up of the plant in specie, which he could have asserted against the council in his own name under section 234 of the Insolvency Act 1986 if he had found the plant in the possession of the council at the completion of the works (the council's power of sale being void against him), neither section 234 nor the administrators's powers to get in the property of the company under section 14 and Schedule 1 to the 1986 Act provided any basis for a damages claim by him in conversion. See also para. 23–034 below.

[51] [1992] B.C.C. 270 at 287–288.

[52] See *Independent Automatic Sales (supra)* at p.981.

[53] In order to be consistent with the legislative scheme and wording, if the company was restored to solvency and the liquidation was stayed or the administration order was discharged, the charge would be fully enforceable against the company thereafter.

[54] The requirement is to deliver the prescribed particulars of the charge, not of the chargor, so that where a chargee made an error in completing the form as to the registered number of the chargor company, this did not result in the charge being invaidated: *Grove v. Advantage Healthcare (T10) Ltd* [2000] 1 B.C.L.C. 661. A third party misled by the absence of the charge on the file of the company at the Companies Registry might have a claim against Registrar or the person submitting the charge for registration.

[55] *N.V. Slavenburg's Bank v. Intercontinental Natural Resources* [1980] 1 W.L.R. 1076 at 1086D, *per* Lloyd J.

are delivered but the Registrar neglects to register the charge, section 395 is complied with.[56] Conversely, a refusal to register a particular class of charges does not excuse such delivery if it is in fact required by the section. In *N.V. Slavenburg's Bank v. Intercontinental Natural Resources Ltd.*[57] it was shown that the Registrar was then in the habit of refusing to register particulars of charges created by foreign companies with an established place of business in England which had failed to register as an overseas company under the predecessor of the Companies Act 1985. Lloyd J. held that, notwithstanding that the Registrar would not have registered the charge in any event, a charge by a foreign company which then had an established place of business in England but had failed to register itself as an overseas company and had not delivered the prescribed particulars, was void as against the liquidator of the company.

(c) Priorities

The rules relating to priorities of charges apart from questions of non- **3–135** registration have been discussed above.[58] Strictly speaking, the requirements of registration relate to perfection of security and not to questions of priorities which will be determined by reference to the common law and equitable principles discussed above. However, registration under section 395 affects the situation in two ways, first, because a subsequent chargee will be deemed to have constructive notice of an earlier registered charge and, secondly, because unregistered charges will be rendered void as against subsequent chargees. It should also be noted that questions of priorities between registered charges depend upon the dates of creation of the respective charges and not on the dates of registration.

(d) Extension of time and rectification

Section 404 of the Companies Act 1985 provides that, if the court is **3–136** satisfied that the omission to register a charge within the time required or that the omission or mis-statement of any required particular was accidental or due to inadvertence or to some other sufficient cause or is not of a nature to prejudice the position of creditors or shareholders of the company or that on other grounds it is just and equitable to grant relief, then the court may, on the application of the company or a person interested, order that the time for registration shall be extended or the omission or mis-statement rectified.

Prior to the company becoming insolvent, unsecured creditors have no **3–137** sufficient interest to oppose the application and no interest which ought

---

[56] *National Provincial and Union Bank of England v. Charnley* [1924] 1 K.B. 431 at 447.
[57] [1980] 1 W.L.R. 1076. See for the meaning of "established place of business in England", *Re Oriel Ltd* [1986] 1 W.L.R. 180, CA.
[58] See paras 3–055 to 3–058.

to be protected if an extension of time is granted.[59] However, once the company has become insolvent, it would appear that such creditors have sufficient *locus standi* to be heard. The application should be made promptly.[60] The court will not look kindly at a chargee who delays in his application for late registration in order to pursue other ways of advancing his position, such as attempting to take a fresh charge.[61] The court can make an order under section 404 at an interlocutory stage if it can be satisfied of the requisite matters.[62] However, if the application is opposed and there is to be cross-examination on the affidavit evidence, then no interlocutory order will be made.[63]

3–138   In considering whether to accede to the application for late registration, the underlying principle is that the court can exercise a wide discretion based upon what is just and equitable.[64] The imminence of liquidation or insolvency of the company is a relevant factor in the exercise of the discretion but, provided that the application is made before liquidation has actually occurred, the court may exercise its discretion in favour of an extension of time.[65] Once liquidation or administration has intervened, an order for an extension of time will only be made in exceptional cases.[66] Where liquidation is imminent, the order extending time should normally include a proviso based upon the decision in *Re L.H. Charles & Co. Ltd*[67] giving liberty to any liquidator subsequently appointed to apply to the court within a specified period (usually 21 days) of liquidation to discharge the order.[68]

3–139   In granting an extension of time, it became common practice to insert a proviso into the order extending time to the effect that the order

---

[59] *R. v. Registrar of Companies, ex p. Central Bank of India* [1986] Q.B. 1114; *Re Chantry House Developments plc* [1990] B.C.C. 646 at 654, *per* Scott J.

[60] *Re Ashpurton Estates Ltd* [1983] Ch. 110 at 131H, *per* Lord Brightman; *Re Fablehill Ltd* [1991] B.C.C. 590.

[61] *Re Telomatic Ltd* [1994] 1 B.C.L.C. 90.

[62] *Re Chantry House Developments plc* [1990] B.C.C. 646 at 654, *per* Scott J.

[63] *Re Heathstar Properties Ltd* [1966] 1 W.L.R. 993; *Re Telomatic Ltd* [1994] 1 B.C.L.C. 90.

[64] *Per* Hoffmann J. in *Re Braemar Investments Ltd* [1989] Ch. 54 referring to the *dictum* of Lord Hanworth in *Re M.I.G. Trust Ltd* [1933] Ch. 542 at 560.

[65] *Re Braemar Investments Ltd* [1989] Ch. 54.

[66] *Re Ashpurton Estates Ltd* [1983] Ch. 110; *Re R.M. Arnold & Co.* [1984] B.C.L.C. 535; *Re Braemar Investments Ltd* [1989] Ch. 54; *Re Barrow Borough Transport Ltd* (1989) 5 B.C.C. 646 (no extension when company in administration). In *Re Fablehill Ltd* [1991] B.C.C. 590 and *Re Chantry House Developments plc* [1990] B.C.C. 646 the financial positions of the respective companies were unsound, but the courts appear to have placed some weight on the fact that no winding-up petitions had actually been presented and no judgments had been entered in favour of creditors which remained unsatisfied. See also *Commercial Banking Co. of Sydney Ltd v. George Hudson Property Ltd* (1973) 131 C.L.R. 605; *Bloodstock v. Roadrunner Equipment* (1985) 10 A.C.L.R. 36 (extension granted despite liquidation as there was no evidence that money had been paid or credit given on the basis that no charge had been registered during the hiatus period of two to three days); *J.J. Leonard Properties Pty Ltd v. Leonard (WA.) Pty Ltd* (1987) 5 A.C.L.C. 838 (no rectification after liquidation had intervened).

[67] [1935] W.N. 15.

[68] *Re Braemar Investments Ltd* [1989] Ch. 54; *Exeter Trust v. Screenways Ltd* [1991] B.C.C. 477, CA. See *Re Chantry House Developments plc* [1990] B.C.C. 646 for a case where such a provision was not employed because it would have served little purpose.

permitting late registration would be without prejudice to the rights of parties acquired prior to the time when the charge was actually registered.[69] In *Watson v. Duff Morgan and Vermont (Holdings) Ltd,*[70] it was explained that this only protected charges created within the period between expiry of the 21 days for registration and the date of actual registration. Subsequently, the courts have generally adopted a form of wording which makes it clear that the protection is to extend to all charges created between the date of creation of the unregistered charge and the date of its actual registration (as extended). In certain cases, however, the courts have been willing to adopt modified versions of the proviso,[71] or to dispense with it altogether, as the justice of the case required.[72]

If such an extension is granted, it would appear to be open to the **3–140** court in any order, if it is just and equitable, to reinstate the contractual date for repayment of the secured debt in place of the accelerated date for repayment which is the statutory consequence of failure to register in time.[73]

It has been held that the power given to the court in section 404 of the **3–141** Act does not permit the whole registration of the charge to be deleted and that the court has no inherent power of rectification outside of the statute.[74]

(e) The Registrar's certificate

The Registrar's certificate of registration given under section 401(2) of **3–142** the Companies Act 1985 is conclusive evidence that the statutory requirements of registration have been complied with as between the company and all persons other than the Crown. The authorities indicate that this even protects charges whose registrations are erroneous or misleading. Thus, for example, in *National Provincial and Union Bank of England v. Charnley,*[75] a debenture charged both land and chattels. The prescribed particulars supplied to the Registrar stated that the property charged was the land: no reference was made to the chattels. Nonetheless, the Court of Appeal held that the Registrar's certificate was conclusive evidence that particulars of the charge on the chattels had been presented to the Registrar and entered on the register. Likewise, in *Re Mechanisations (Eaglescliffe) Ltd*[76] the Court of Appeal held that the Registrar's certificate was conclusive evidence that the prescribed particulars had been presented to the Registrar and that the maximum

---

[69] *Re Joplin Brewery Co. Ltd* [1902] 1 Ch. 79; *Re Ehrmann Bros. Ltd* [1906] 2 Ch. 697; *Re Kris Cruisers Ltd* [1949] Ch. 138.

[70] [1974] 1 W.L.R. 450.

[71] *Re R.M. Arnold & Co. Ltd* [1984] B.C.L.C. 535.

[72] *Re Fablehill Ltd* [1991] B.C.C. 590 (referring, to *Re S. Abrahams & Sons* [1902] 1 Ch. 695).

[73] Companies Act 1985, s. 404(2).

[74] *Re C.L. Nye Ltd* [1971] Ch. 442, CA.; *Exeter Trust v. Screenways Ltd* [1991] B.C.C. 477, C.A.

[75] [1924] 1 K.B. 431.

[76] [1966] Ch. 20.

amount had been secured, when in fact a lower sum had been incorrectly stated in the particulars and on the register.

3–143   Equally, the Registrar's certificate is conclusive as to the date the charge was created, even if in reality the 21-day rule was infringed. *Re Eric Holmes (Property) Ltd*[77] and *Re C.L. Nye Ltd*[78] show that a charge created outside the 21-day limit and left undated which is subsequently dated and registered within 21 days of the date used will be valid. The certificate is also conclusive as to the date of the application for registration. Thus, in *R. v. Registrar of Companies, ex p. Central Bank of India*,[79] the debenture-holder submitted an incomplete application within the 21-day period and a complete application after its expiration. The Registrar's certificate that the complete application was made on the earlier date was held to be conclusive evidence to this effect.

3–144   A case which indicates the unwillingness of the courts to go behind the Registrar's certificate is the decision of the Court of Appeal in *Exeter Trust Ltd v. Screenways Ltd*.[80] In that case, a certificate had been obtained following a late registration which took place on the same morning but just prior to a liquidator being appointed to the company. Even though the liquidator subsequently obtained an order setting aside the grant of the extension of time, the Court of Appeal held that the Registrar's certificate was conclusive both as to the delivery of the required particulars and also as to the fact that the order extending time had itself been obtained.[81]

3–145   It would appear that the statutory provision as to the conclusiveness of the certificate does not bind the Crown, and accordingly the Attorney-General can challenge a certificate by way of judicial review on the grounds of error of law or fact by the Registrar.[82] But no such right of challenge is available to any other person, save possibly if fraud by the registering party is proved.[83] In case of such fraud, alternative remedies may be available in the form of an action against him preventing him taking advantage of the fraudulently obtained certificate and "It may well be that . . . a creditor damaged by the fraud can take proceedings in personam ".[84] Proof of fraud in such situations is, of course, notoriously difficult.

(f) Foreign companies

3–146 By virtue of section 409 of the Companies Act 1985, the system of registrable charges is extended to charges created by corporations registered outside Great Britain but which have an established place of

---

[77] [1965] Ch. 1052.
[78] [1971] Ch. 442.
[79] [1986] Q.B. 1114.
[80] [1991] B.C.C. 477.
[81] The Court followed an Australian decision, *Wilde v. Australian Trade Equipment Co. Pty Ltd* (1981) 145 C.L.R. 590.
[82] *R. v. Registrar of Companies, ex p. Central Bank of India* [1986] Q.B. 1114.
[83] See also *Walton v. Bank of New Zealand* (1997) 8 N.Z.C.L.C. 261,455 referring to *Sun Tai Cheung Credits Limited v. Attorney-General of Hong Kong* [1987] 1 W.L.R. 948.
[84] *R. v. Registrar of Companies, ex p. Central Bank of India* [1986] Q.B. 1114, *per* Slade L.J. at 1177.

business in England and Wales. As indicated above, in *N.V. Slavenburg's Bank v. Intercontinental Natural Resources Ltd*,[85] an unregistered charge was held void as against liquidators even though the foreign corporation granting it had not registered as an oversea company and the Registrar could therefore not register the charge. The consequences of this decision would appear to be that, as a matter of prudence, if there is the slightest suspicion that the company granting the charge has established a place of business here, particulars should be delivered to the Registrar. The same case is also authority for the proposition that section 395 can be relied upon by a foreign liquidator to avoid an unregistered charge, at least if the foreign liquidation is of a type comparable to a winding-up in England.

4. INQUIRY AS TO THE VALIDITY OF THE CHARGE, APPLICATIONS TO THE COURT BY THE RECEIVER FOR DIRECTIONS AND PROTECTION OF THIRD PARTIES IN CASES OF INVALIDITY

A receiver is bound to make due inquiry as to the validity of the charge **3–147** under which he is proposed to be or has been appointed. Not merely may he be criticised or prejudiced if he fails to make due inquiry[86] but, if the charge is invalid, his appointment will be invalid, and he may become liable as a trespasser in respect of his actions as a receiver or as a constructive trustee of the assets of the company in his hands.[87] The exposure to a claim for damages by the company can be immense. Though the Jenkins Report (paragraph 306) recommended that the court be given jurisdiction to grant relief to the would-be receiver in respect of such liability, this recommendation has not been implemented.[88] As it stands, his only protection is his own investigation, such contractual right to an indemnity from the debenture-holder appointor as may exist and the statutory right to apply for an indemnity conferred by section 34 of the Insolvency Act 1986.

Section 34 of the Insolvency Act 1986 confers on the court a **3–148** discretionary jurisdiction to order the "appointor" to indemnify the "appointee" in respect of any liability arising solely by reason of the invalidity of the appointment. Such liability may presumably be to a claim either by the company, (for example for conversion or trespass) or by a person with whom the receiver has dealt, (for example for breach of warranty of authority). The statutory language is not apposite to cover situations where the "receiver" contracted as such but assumed personal

---

[85] [1980] 1 W.L.R. 1076.

[86] A receiver's failure to make such inquiries might form the basis of an allegation that he had not accepted appointment to his office: see *Harris & Lewin Pty Ltd v. Harris and Lewin (Agents)* [1975] A.C.L.C. 28, 279 at 28, 293.

[87] *Rolled Steel Products (Holdings) Ltd v. British Steel Corp* [1986] Ch. 246.

[88] Such a power was conferred in Scotland by s. 23 of the Companies (Floating Charges and Receivers) (Scotland) Act 1972 and re-enacted in s. 479 of the Companies Act 1985. However, this provision was abrogated by s. 63 of the Insolvency Act 1986 which assimilated Scottish and English law in this respect.

liability, in which case the invalidity would merely deprive him of his right to an indemnity out of the company's assets. The liability would not in this case arise solely by reason of the invalidity (the pre-condition to the statutory indemnity), though his loss would.

3–149   Section 35 of the Insolvency Act 1986 authorises a receiver or manager appointed under powers contained in a debenture, and the debenture-holder himself, to apply to the court for directions in relation to any particular matter arising in connection with the performance of the receiver's functions.[89] On a strict construction of this section, it might be doubtful whether a receiver or debenture-holder could apply for directions to the court to determine the validity of the charge under which he was appointed, for the section would appear to stipulate that the applicant should be validly appointed.[90] But there would appear to be no good reason why the court should not determine this issue: it would have to do so if the appointment were challenged and there may be every reason to anticipate the challenge. The receiver would plainly be a person interested for this purpose, in view of his possible liabilities, his right to remuneration and his statutory claim to an indemnity.

3–150   As a condition of accepting the appointment or continuing to act, the receiver may theoretically require the debenture-holder to seek a declaration as to the validity of the charge by action or, if there is a winding-up, by application.[91] The defendants or respondents should, in this case, include the company and any subsequent debenture-holder. The timescale involved in any such proceedings would however, normally preclude this course, since their desire to appoint would ordinarily postulate the need for immediate action by the receiver to protect the interests of the debenture-holder.

3–151   With limited statutory exceptions, a person dealing with an administrative receiver is likewise concerned as to the validity of the charge and the appointment.[92] One exception is a person paying money to a receiver who is not concerned to inquire whether an event has occurred which enables the receiver to act.[93]

3–152   Section 42(3) of the Insolvency Act 1986 provides that a person dealing with the administrative receiver in good faith and for value shall not be concerned to inquire whether the administrative receiver is acting

---

[89] The power to give directions should be interpreted liberally, but directions should not be sought on matters which are properly matters of commercial judgment: *Deputy Commissioner of Taxation v. Best & Less* (1992) 10 A.C.L.C. 520.

[90] Compare *Re Wood and Martin Ltd* [1971] 1 W.L.R. 293; [1971] 1 All ER 732: an invalidly appointed liquidator cannot apply as "liquidator" for an order under s. 651 declaring that the dissolution is void because the word "liquidator" in the section means a liquidator validly appointed before the dissolution. Nonetheless, within the meaning of the section he is a "person interested" and has a sufficient interest to seek the order in view of his potential claim for remuneration and the potential claim against him for intermeddling with property that was *bona vacantia*.

[91] *Re North Wales Produce and Supply Society Ltd* [1922] 2 Ch. 340.

[92] The debenture may include a provision safeguarding a person dealing with the receiver from an invalidity of the appointment, but it is conceived that no such protection can be afforded in respect of the invalidity of the debenture itself.

[93] Law of Property Act 1925, s. 109(4).

within his powers. But this section postulates dealing with a validly appointed receiver, and will be of no assistance if this proves not to be the case. Section 232 of the Insolvency Act 1986[94] validates acts of an administrative receiver notwithstanding defects in his appointment, nomination or qualifications. Section 232 is designed "as machinery to avoid questions being raised as to the validity of transactions where there has been a slip in the appointment"[95] of the receiver, but does not apply "where the term of office . . . has expired", or "where the office has been from the outset usurped without the colour of authority", or where "there has been no genuine attempt to appoint at all".[96] Nor will this provision validate the acts of persons when the appointor had no power to make any appointment; the substantive power to make the appointment must exist.[97] In this situation, the party dealing with the purported receiver must be content (in default of ratification by the company) with a claim against the purported receiver for breach of warranty of authority, and it is suggested that a like claim should be available against the purported appointor as a joint tortfeasor.[98]

5. STATUTORY POWERS OF APPOINTMENT[99]

Receivers appointed under statutory powers are often called "L.P.A. **3–153** receivers", since the principal relevant powers are contained in the Law of Property Act 1925, Part 2. A specific mortgage or charge[1] will often adopt and extend the statutory power in the 1925 Act to appoint a receiver in certain circumstances to enforce the security. Even where no express provision is made, section 101(1)(ii) of the 1925 Act provides for such a power in the case of any mortgage by deed.

The mortgage document will usually set out expressly the circum- **3–154** stances in which the mortgagee's power of sale arises and in which a receiver can be appointed. Those circumstances are usually the same in each case and, unless the mortgage deed provides otherwise, a receiver cannot be appointed unless and until the power of sale arises.[2]

The statutory power of sale does not arise unless: **3–155**

---

[94] The section validates "the acts", not the appointment: *Re Allison, Johnson & Foster Ltd, ex p. Birkenshaw* [1904] 2 K.B. 327.

[95] *Per* Lord Simonds in *Morris v. Kanssen* [1946] A.C. 459 at 472 (considering the ambit of s. 180 of the Companies Act 1948).

[96] *ibid.* at 471.

[97] *Morris v. Kanssen*, [1946] A.C. 459 at 472; *Woollett v. Minister of Agriculture and Fisheries* [1955] 1 Q.B. 103.

[98] But in *Bank of Baroda v. Panessar* [1987] Ch. 335, Walton J. held that if·the purported appointment of the receiver is as agent of the company, and the receiver purports to act as agent for the company, the appointor is not responsible or liable for his acts.

[99] This subject is dealt with fully in *Kerr on Receivers* (17th ed.), Chap. 18.

[1] "Mortgage" and "charge" may be regarded here as interchangeable for present purposes.

[2] Law of Property Act 1925, s. 109(1).

    (a) the principal moneys secured have become due and notice has
        been served on the mortgagor[3] requiring repayment of the
        principal and default has been made for three months; or
    (b) interest is two months in arrears; or
    (c) there has been a breach of a provision in the mortgage deed
        not relating to repayments of principal or interest[4]; or
    (d) the mortgage deed provides (as it does normally provide) for
        the power to arise without any of the foregoing occurring.

In the case of company charges, there is usually a provision permitting a receiver to be appointed as soon as the principal becomes repayable, or if interest is in arrears for a specified period, or if repayment of the principal or interest has been demanded and default made. If the chargee wishes to rely solely on a provision permitting appointment on the grounds of a winding-up, he must obtain the leave of the court.[5]

3–156   The statutory powers of an LPA receiver are very limited and do not extend to running a business as receiver and manager. LPA receivers were therefore in practice only appointed where the charge in question covered land or (more recently) book debts and not a business. However, in some recent property developments the charges have given LPA receivers greatly extended powers, which have enabled them to complete or carry out very substantial construction works and to deal with the selling or letting of the completed property[6]

---

[3] In *Manton v. Parabolic Pty Ltd* [1986] 2 N.S.W.L.R. 361, it was held that: (1) the notice need only be served on the mortgagor, and need not be served on later mortgagees; and (2) if there was default in service of the notice and this was known to the purchaser, any conveyance to him by the mortgagee took effect subject to the mortgagor's equity of redemption, which continued to be enforceable against the purchaser.

[4] Law of Property Act 1925, s. 103.

[5] Law of Property Act 1925, ss. 110 and 205(1)(i).

[6] See *e.g.* the factual situation in *Re Kentish Homes Ltd* [1993] B.C.C. 212 at 219.

CHAPTER 4

THE APPOINTMENT OF THE RECEIVER

1. QUALIFICATIONS

Prior to the changes introduced by the Insolvency Acts of 1985 and 1986, **4–001** there was no qualification required of a prospective appointee as receiver of a company or its property, save that he be of full age. In the case of an appointment out of court the only persons disqualified from appointment were a body corporate[1] or an undischarged bankrupt.[2] In the case of a court-appointed receiver (who traded on his own account and not as agent for the company or a debenture-holder) persons subject to restrictions on trading (such as beneficed clergymen and barristers) were also disqualified, as were persons immune from the ordinary remedies against a receiver, such as a Member of Parliament or a Peer of the Realm or someone resident outside the jurisdiction.[3] There was no requirement of a practical or professional qualification,[4] though there may have been a duty on the part of the appointor to take reasonable care not to appoint an incompetent.[5] There is apparently no objection to the debenture-holder appointing himself as receiver.[6]

The 1986 Act left the law unchanged in respect of receivers who are **4–002** not administrative receivers, but in the case of liquidators (including provisional liquidators), administrators and administrative receivers of a "company",[7] (as well as nominees under a voluntary arrangement under

---

[1] Insolvency Act 1986, s. 30, formerly Companies Act 1985, s. 489 and see *Portman Building Society v. Gallwey* [1955] 1 W.L.R. 96; [1955] 1 All E.R. 227. The position is similar in Australia (Australian Corporations Law, ss. 418(1)(d), 1279(1)), New Zealand (New Zealand Receiverships Act 1993, s. 5(2) and Hong Kong (Hong Kong Companies Ordinance, s. 297).

[2] Insolvency Act 1986, s. 31, formerly Companies Act 1985, s. 490. Similarly, Australian Corporations Law, ss. 418(1)(d), 206B(3), 1282(4); New Zealand Receiverships Act 1993, s. 5(1)(e); Hong Kong Companies Ordinance, s. 297A.

[3] See *Halsbury's Laws of England* (4th ed.) Vol. 39, para. 847. Walton J. (the long-time editor of *Kerr on Receivers*) apparently disregarded this rule when appointing a Member of Parliament a receiver in *Wiggin v. Anderson* (unreported, March 16, 1982). Members of Parliament and Peers are no longer immune from arrest in connection with the winding-up or insolvency of companies: Insolvency Act 1986, s. 427(7).

[4] See *Bagot v. Bagot* (1841) 10 L.J. Ch. 116 at 120; even illiteracy was held to be no bar in *Garland v. Garland* (1793) 2 Ves. 137.

[5] *Shamji v. Johnson Matthey Bankers Co. Ltd* [1991] B.C.L.C. 36 at 42, *per* Oliver L.J., affirming Hoffmann J. at first instance: [1986] B.C.L.C. 278 at 283. See further below Chap. 7.

[6] See *Mace Builders (Glasgow) Ltd v. Lunn* [1987] 1 Ch. 191 at 197, *per* Donaldson M.R.

[7] "Company" for this purpose is defined in s. 388(4) of the Insolvency Act 1986 incorporating the definition in the Companies Act 1985, s. 735 as meaning a company:
    (a) formed and registered under the 1985 and former Company Acts; or
    (b) a company which may be wound up under Pt. V of the Insolvency Act 1986 as an unregistered company (a category which includes foreign corporations).
Accordingly, a person appointed as liquidator, administrator or administrative receiver or

the Insolvency Act 1986) only individuals (*i.e.* natural persons)[8] who are qualified to act as "insolvency practitioners" can now be appointed.[9]

4–003   There are three disqualifications under the 1986 Act[10]:

(a) the individual must not be an undischarged bankrupt;

(b) he must not be subject to a disqualification order made under the Company Directors Disqualification Act 1986[11]; and

(c) he must not be a patient within the meaning of Part VII of the Mental Health Act 1983.

The Secretary of State is given power to make regulations (inter alia) prohibiting persons from acting as insolvency practitioners where a conflict of interest will or may arise.[12] Such a prohibition already exists under the Code of Professional Practice and Ethics (Insolvency Practitioners Association), the Guide to Professional Ethics (Institute of Chartered Accountants) and the Conduct of Solicitor Insolvency Practitioners (Law Society). Thus, the first two bodies prohibit members from accepting office as receivers (or liquidators) of companies of which their firms have acted as auditors, whilst the Law Society prohibits its members from accepting any appointment as a receiver or liquidator of a company with which they have had a close relationship.[13]

the equivalent of a foreign company cannot act as such within the U.K. unless he is a qualified insolvency practitioner.

[8] Insolvency Act 1986, s. 390(1).

[9] *ibid.*, ss. 389 and 230.

[10] *ibid.*, s. 390(4).

[11] *ibid.*, s.390(4)(b). The provisions of the Company Directors Disqualification Act 1986:

(i) give the court a discretion to make orders disqualifying a person from being a director or liquidator of a company or receiver or manager of its property or being concerned in the promotion, formation or management of a company if found guilty of specific offences or of persistent default in relation to specified provisions of the Act. There may be persistent default without any enforcement order ever being made or conviction obtained. Culpability is not an essential element, though relevant to the exercise of the discretion whether to disqualify (*Re Arctic Engineering Ltd* (No. 2) [1986] 1 W.L.R. 686); and

(ii) impose on the court a duty to make a disqualification order against a director or former director of a company which has gone into insolvent liquidation whose conduct as a director of that company (or of that and other companies) makes him unfit to be concerned in the management of a company (see, *e.g. Re Sevenoaks Stationers (Retail) Ltd* [1991] Ch. 164).

[12] Insolvency Act 1986, s. 419(2)(b). The power has not yet been exercised.

[13] *Sheppard & Cooper Ltd v. TSB Bank plc* [1996] B.C.C. 653 was an unusual case in which the court granted an injunction to prevent two insolvency practitioners from the same firm from being appointed as administrative receivers of a company. Their firm had previously been engaged to investigate the financial affairs of the company on terms that, to avoid any conflicts of interest, the firm "would not undertake any responsibility for the management of the company's affairs either now or in the future". The Court of Appeal stated that the receivers "were not appointed individually" but "were appointed jointly". This statement should be read in the context of the issue which was whether they, as partners of the firm for the time being, were bound to abide by the terms of the earlier contract. Whatever the position as a matter of commercial reality, as a matter of law it is only individuals who can be appointed as office-holders under the Insolvency Act 1986, not firms or partnerships: see, *e.g. Re Sankey Furniture Ltd* [1995] 2 B.C.L.C. 594 at 600–601.

To be qualified to act, a person must either be a member of or subject **4–004** to the rules of a recognised professional body[14] and permitted to act as an insolvency practitioner by that body[15] or be authorised so as to act by the Secretary of State or by any body to which he delegates this power.[16] In addition, there must be security which meets the prescribed requirements in relation to the activities of the insolvency practitioner.[17]

Section 393 of the Insolvency Act 1986 specifies the criteria to be **4–005** satisfied by an applicant for authorisation by the competent authority. These are that:

(a) the applicant is a fit and proper person to act as an insolvency practitioner; and
(b) the applicant meets the prescribed requirements with respect to education and practical training and experience.

Section 393(4) prescribes two grounds on which the competent **4–006** authority may withdraw such an authorisation, namely:

(a) if it appears to it that the holder is "no longer" a fit and proper person to act as an insolvency practitioner; or
(b) the holder has failed to comply with the provisions of Part XIII or XV of the Insolvency Act 1986 or any regulations made thereunder or in purported compliance therewith has furnished the competent authority with false, inaccurate or misleading information.

Without prejudice to the generality of section 393, the following **4–007** matters are to be taken into account in determining whether the applicant is a fit and proper person to act as an insolvency practitioner, or whether he is any longer such a person[18]:

(a) whether the applicant has any previous convictions for dishonesty or violence;
(b) whether the applicant has committed any act in contravention of the insolvency legislation of either Great Britain or any other country;
(c) whether the applicant has had any business dealings of a deceitful, oppressive or otherwise unfair or improper nature (whether unlawful or not) or which otherwise cast doubt upon his probity or competence as an insolvency practitioner;

---

[14] The Secretary of State has recognised for this purpose the following professional bodies: The Insolvency Practitioners Association, The Chartered Association of Certified Accountants, The Institute of Chartered Accountants in England & Wales, The Institute of Chartered Accountants in Ireland, The Institute of Chartered Accountants of Scotland, The Law Society, and The Law Society of Scotland. See the Insolvency Act 1986, s. 391 and The Insolvency Practitioners (Recognised Professional Bodies) Order 1986 (S.I. No. 1764).

[15] Insolvency Act 1986, s. 390(2).

[16] *ibid.*, ss. 392 and 419.

[17] *ibid.*, s. 390(3).

[18] Insolvency Practitioners Regulations 1990 (S.I. No. 439), reg. 4.

    (d) the appropriate independence, integrity and professional skill of the applicant.

If the applicant has been engaged in prior insolvency practice, the following additional factors relating to that practice will be relevant:

    (e) the existence and adequacy of the control procedures, records and accounts;

    (f) whether there has been any failure by the applicant to disclose any actual or possible conflicts of interest to such persons as might be affected.

4–008   In general, "fitness" is a question to be decided in the light of circumstances existing at the date of the determination. The primary consideration is the protection of the public.[19] Past misconduct is always relevant, but there may be other considerations, for it may be shown that the individual has mended his ways. But even in this case, the public might think it wrong that a person with such a record should continue to enjoy a certificate, and as such, regard may be had to public confidence in the system.[20] The words "no longer" indicate that some event must have changed the holder from a fit to an unfit person, but it is suggested that a change in the state of knowledge or belief as to the holder's fitness should also justify revocation, especially if the person would not have been authorised initially had the full facts been known.[21]

4–009   If the competent authority proposes to refuse an application or to withdraw an authorisation, it is required to serve on the applicant or holder written notice of its intention, setting out particulars of the grounds on which it proposes to act and of the right of the applicant or holder to make written representations to the relevant authority within 14 days and within 28 days to require the case to be referred to the Insolvency Practitioners Tribunal.[22] If the holder or applicant requires that the case be referred to the Tribunal, the relevant authority is bound so to refer it unless it decides to grant the authorisation or not to withdraw the authorisation. On such a reference, the Tribunal must investigate the case and make a report to the relevant authority stating their opinion as to the appropriate decision in the matter and the reasons for that opinion. It is then the duty of the relevant authority to decide the matter accordingly. In the absence of such a reference the relevant authority (having regard to any representations made) may give written notice of the refusal or withdrawal in accordance with the previous notice.[23] If the Tribunal or relevant authority were to find the

---

[19] Consider *Quek Leng Chye v. AG.* [1985] M.L.J. 270, PC in the context of disqualification of directors.

[20] *R. v. Crown Court at Knightsbridge, ex p. International Club* [1982] 1 Q.B. 304.

[21] Consider *R. v. Chief Registrar of Friendly Societies, ex p. New Cross Building Society* [1984] Q.B. 227 at 261–262, *per* Griffiths L.J.

[22] The Tribunal's constitution, powers and procedures are regulated by the provisions of Sched. 7 to the Insolvency Act 1986.

[23] Insolvency Act 1986, ss. 394–396.

person concerned not a fit and proper person to practice, it would be most exceptional for the authorisation to be granted or not withdrawn.[24]

No appeal lies from the decision of the Tribunal or relevant authority, **4–010** but if there is a material failure to comply with the statutory procedure or requirements of the rules of natural justice, or if the decision is vitiated by a material error of law or irrationality, the decision may be challenged on an application by way of judicial review. This procedure cannot be used to review the wisdom of the authority's or Tribunal's decision or to substitute the judgment of the court for that of the bodies to whom Parliament has committed responsibility for deciding in the public interest whether the individual in question is a fit and proper person.[25]

The significant aspects of the statutory procedure are: **4–011**

(a) the refusal to issue, and the decision to withdraw, authorisation can only be made on the specified grounds; and

(b) there is no summary power of revocation or indeed power to suspend the certificate pending conclusion of the statutory procedures.

If an unqualified person acts as an insolvency practitioner when he **4–012** knows or has reasonable cause to suspect that he is not qualified, he commits a criminal offence punishable on conviction by imprisonment or a fine or both.[26] But his acts as such insolvency practitioner are valid notwithstanding the defect in his qualification or appointment.[27]

2. MULTIPLE AND JOINT APPOINTMENTS

(a) Introduction

This subject has produced much confusion. For clarity it is first essential **4–013** to separate out a number of different factual situations:

(a) a case where more than one receiver has been appointed over the same property, but under different debentures;

(b) a case where more than one receiver has been appointed over the same property under a debenture in favour of a number of lenders as a result of separate appointments by those different lenders; and

(c) a case where more than one receiver has been appointed over the same property at the same time under the same debenture.

In the first case, which is quite common, questions as to the respective powers and duties of the receivers will depend on identifying the assets

---

[24] *ibid.*, ss. 395, 398.

[25] See *R. v. Greenwich L.B.C., ex p. Cedar Transport Group Ltd* [1983] R.A. 173 at 178, *per* Griffiths L.J.

[26] Insolvency Act 1986, s. 389.

[27] *ibid.*, s. 232. In the absence of such a validating provision, the appointment would be a nullity: see *Portman Building Society v. Gallwey* [1955] 1 W.L.R. 96.

over which the respective receivers have been appointed and, where there is an overlap, resolving the relationship between the receivers as a matter of priorities of the charges under which they were appointed.[28] The second situation is likely to be very rare in practice, but arose recently in *Gwembe Valley Development Co. Ltd v. Koshy.*[29]

4–014   The third situation is routine: it is very common for two partners in the same firm (or occasionally different firms) of accountants to be appointed as receivers by a debenture-holder. This situation does, however, give rise to a number of further issues, such as

(a) whether the receivers can only act jointly or whether they can also act severally. This is essentially a question of construction of the debenture, but also involves consideration of the extent to which section 231 of the Insolvency Act 1986 operates in this area;

(b) whether, if acting jointly, the receivers are jointly and severally liable for their acts and defaults and, if acting severally, whether one receiver will be liable for the acts or defaults of the other; and

(c) whether the receivers' tenure in office is joint in the sense that it will terminate on the death or retirement of one of their number.

In considering these matters, it is of prime importance to distinguish whether the question in issue is one relating to the manner of exercise of the power of appointment by the debenture-holder, or to the manner in which the receivers may exercise their powers under the appointment, or to the liability of the receivers so appointed, or as to the tenure of the receivers in office.[30]

(b) Multiple appointments

4–015 It is a matter of construction of the terms of the debenture(s) and any deed of priorities[31] whether there can be more than one receiver appointed by different lenders over the same property at any one time. In *Gwembe Valley Development Co. Ltd v. Koshy,*[32] Rimer J. had to construe an unusual debenture governed by Zambian law which had been granted by a Zambian company to two lenders to secure separate

---

[28] For a case in which the court was asked to resolve a dispute between rival receivers who had been appointed by mortgagees under separate debentures over the same property, see *Bass Breweries Ltd v. Delaney* [1994] B.C.C. 851. A deed of priority had been executed under which the two charges were expressed to rank equally. The court resolved the resultant conflict by appointing the two receivers as court appointed receivers with a mandate to act jointly or to refer disagreements back to the court for directions.

[29] Rimer J., *The Times,* February 8, 2000.

[30] Many of the cases in this area fail to make these distinctions: see the comments to this effect by Gummow and Kirby JJ. in *Kendle v. Melsom* [1998] 193 C.L.R. 46 at 65, referring to the previous edition of this work and see also the observations of Hayne J. in the same case.

[31] See, *e.g. Bass Breweries Ltd v. Delaney* [1994] B.C.C. 851.

[32] Unreported, Rimer J., December 13, 1999.

loans made by them to the company. Rimer J. held that in the event of disagreement between the two lenders, the particular terms of the debenture permitted each lender to appoint a receiver to hold office simultaneously. Rimer J. also held that the first appointment did not preclude the second, so avoiding any unseemly rush by each lender to make the first appointment so as to shut out the other.

In reaching this conclusion, Rimer J. rejected an argument that the **4–016** existence of more than one receiver appointed by different lenders over the same property would be a recipe for conflict and chaos. He asserted that there was nothing unusual about the conduct of a receivership being in the hands of two or more receivers, that the receivers would each be professional men and that it should not be assumed that more than one appointment would lead to difficulties in practice. Rimer J. suggested that if difficulties arose the receivers could seek the directions of the court, and drew a parallel with the notion of adding an additional trustee to an existing body of office-holders under section 36(6) of the Trustee Act 1925 which confers a general power to appoint additional trustees to act in a trust.

It is suggested that whilst appointment of two or more receivers from **4–017** the same firm by the same debenture-holder is routine, the simultaneous appointment of two receivers over the same property by two different lenders who enjoy equal priority is very unusual. Rimer J.'s analogy with trustees is not a good one, for trustees can generally only act jointly and are appointed to administer the same trust with the same duties to the same beneficiaries. In practice, the efficacy of such a course may well depend upon whether the receivers so appointed are authorised to act only jointly or severally. The existence of two receivers empowered to act severally would be most likely to give rise to conflicts, a risk which would be reduced if the receivers were required to act jointly.[33] Even then, it is suggested that placing reliance on the professional status of the appointees and the opportunity to apply to the court for directions as a means of conflict resolution is unlikely to be a satisfactory solution. The two receivers might well disagree on the essentially commercial question of whether, and if so, how best to realise a particular charged asset. Such disputes could be difficult and cumbersome to resolve by application to the court, and a court might well be unwilling, or consider itself ill-equipped, to make a commercial choice between the different options.

It does not appear that either receiver in the *Gwembe Valley* case was **4–018** an administrative receiver under the Insolvency Act 1986.[34] This also leaves open the question whether, had the same issue occurred in respect of a debenture over the assets of an English company, the court would

---

[33] See the concerns to this effect in *Bass Breweries Ltd v. Delaney* [1994] B.C.C. 851 at 856. If the receivers are able to act severally, there will be the possibility that one receiver might, say, contract sell a piece of property which the other wished to retain for receivership trading; or one receiver might institute proceedings on behalf of the company which the other thought were misconceived and agreed with the defendant to compromise.

[34] It is possible for an administrative receiver to be appointed over the assets of a foreign company under section 29 of the Insolvency Act 1986: see *Re International Bulk Commodities Ltd* [1993] Ch. 77.

have been as disposed to reach the same result as a matter of construction and, if so, whether it would only have been the first of the two appointees, or both appointees, who would have qualified as an administrative receiver invested with particular powers and duties under the Insolvency Act.[35]

4–019   As a practical matter, as Rimer J. recognised, the problems encountered in the *Gwembe Valley* case could have been avoided if the debenture had been drafted clearly so as to provide that the power of appointment could only be exercised by the lenders jointly rather than severally. Certainly this would be the preferable approach so as to avoid the potential conflicts in the conduct of the receivership.

4–020   It is a question of construction of the debenture whether any particular power of appointment permits the appointment of more than one person to act as a receiver.[36] In the absence of some indication of a contrary intention, the singular in the debenture should be construed as including the plural[37] and accordingly the power to appoint a receiver should be construed as a power to appoint more than one receiver.[38]

(c) Power to act jointly or severally

4–021   The question whether joint receivers can act severally as well as jointly is one of construction of the power of appointment given in the debenture and of the terms of the appointment itself.[39] Modern debentures may contain express clauses giving the power to appoint a plurality of receivers who can act severally as well as jointly. In the absence of an express term authorising the appointment of multiple receivers with power to act severally, the court will be required to consider whether a term authorising the use of powers severally can be implied. Whilst there is some force in the observation that the strictness of conventional tests for the implication of terms in commercial documents would seem to mitigate against the implication of such a term,[40] in construing

---

[35] See, *e.g.* the suggestion by Oditah at [1991] J.B.L. 49 that there cannot be multiple concurrent administrative receivers.

[36] *Wrights Hardware Pty Ltd v. Evans* (1988) 13 A.C.L.R. 631 at 633; *NEC v. Lockhart* (1991) 9 A.C.L.C. 658 at 665, *per* Kirby P. and at 667, *per* Meagher J.A.; and *Gwembe Valley Development Co. Ltd v. Koshy* (unreported, Rimer J., December 13, 1999).

[37] Law of Property Act 1925, s. 61(c).

[38] *NEC v. Lockhart* (1991) 9 A.C.L.C. 658 at 663, *per* Kirby P., citing, *inter alia*, the first edition of this work. The debenture itself may provide that words importing the singular are to include the plural: see, *e.g. R.J. Wood Pty Ltd v. Sherlock* (unreported, March 18, 1988, *per* Davies J., Fed Ct of Australia). Compare the decision of Rimer J. in *Gwembe Valley Development Co. Ltd v. Koshy* (*The Times,* February 8, 2000), holding that as a matter of construction of a debenture governed by Zambian law, which has no equivalent to s. 61(c) of the Law of Property Act 1925, only single receivers could be appointed.

[39] See, *e.g.* the cases referred to in n.36 above, together with *Kendle v. Melsom* [1998] 193 C.L.R. 46, H Ct. of Australia.

[40] O'Donovan, *Company Receivers and Managers* (2nd Ed.) para. 3.120 suggests that on basic contractual principles there would appear to be no basis for implying a term allowing a debenture holder to appoint receivers with authority to act severally as well as jointly merely from a term giving a power to appoint multiple receivers. Objection is taken that on the basis of the usual tests for implication of contractual terms as summarised by the Privy Council in *BP Refinery (Westernport) Pty Ltd v. Shire of Hastings* (1977) 180 C.L.R. 266 at 282–283, such a term would not fulfil the requirement of business efficacy because

debentures, the courts have in fact shown themselves to be willing to further what they perceive to be the general commercial purpose of the power to make multiple appointments.

In *Gwembe Valley Development Co. Ltd v. Koshy*[41] Rimer J. considered **4–022** the most recent authorities on this issue from Australia and New Zealand[42] and concluded that there was nothing in the debenture in question which pointed to a conclusion that a plurality of receivers could only act jointly, and that a conclusion that receivers might act severally would be a convenient regime under which the duties of the receivership could be divided between them.[43] Rimer J. observed that the appointed persons would ordinarily be professional people and that if differences arose, they could seek directions from the court. This part of Rimer J.'s decision is, of course, to be distinguished from the earlier part where the learned judge relied upon similar reasoning to reach a conclusion that there could be several appointments by different lenders. So far as the potential for conflict and confusion is concerned, there is every difference as a matter of practice between the appointment of a plurality of receivers by different debenture-holders, and the appointment of a plurality of receivers, usually from the same firm, by the same debenture-holder.

Whilst accepting that the issue in any particular case will be one of **4–023** construction, and that the cases do not appear to be entirely consistent with the conventional tests for implication of terms, the trend towards construing appointments as authorising responsible office-holders to exercise their powers severally as well as jointly is to be welcomed as facilitating the efficient conduct of modern receiverships.

If, notwithstanding the apparent approach of the courts outlined **4–024** above, no express or implied provision can be found in the debenture authorising the exercise of powers severally, unanimity will be required for the exercise of powers by joint receivers.[44] Where the debenture authorises only the appointment of receivers who must exercise their powers jointly, but an appointment is made purporting to authorise the receivers to exercise their powers jointly and severally, then the appointment should be construed as a valid appointment but with the receivers being limited to exercising their powers jointly.[45]

the debenture is effective without it. There is some force in this point, because although it may well be much less convenient for receivers to have to act jointly rather than having the power to act severally, it cannot be said that their appointment would be rendered wholly unworkable if they had to act jointly.

[41] Rimer J., (*The Times,* February 8, 2000).

[42] *DFC Financial Services Ltd v. Samuel* [19901 2 N.Z.L.R. 156; *N.E.C. Information System Australia Pty Ltd v. Lockhart* (1991) 9 A.C.L.C. 658; and *Kendle v. Melsom* [1998] 193 C.L.R. 46. These cases distinguished earlier authorities where there was no express reference to more than one receiver being appointed, such as *R.J. Wood Pty Ltd v. Sherlock* (unreported, Fed Ct of Australia, March 18, 1988); *Wrights Hardware v. Evans* (1988) 13 A.C.L.R. 631 and *Kerry Lowe v. Isherwood* (1989) 15 A.C.L.R. 615.

[43] In so doing, Rimer J. agreed with the majority reasoning of Gummow and Kirby J. in *Kendle v. Melsom.*

[44] See, *e.g.* the presumption that an authority given to two or more persons is given jointly: *Bowstead & Reynolds on Agency,* (16th ed.), Article 11(1), referring to cases such as *Re Liverpool Household Stores* (1890) 59 L.J. Ch. 616.

[45] *NEC v. Lockhart* (1991) 9 A.C.L.C. 658; *Kerry Lowe v. Isherwood* (1989) 15 A.C.L.R. 615.

(d) Declarations under section 231(2) of the Insolvency Act 1986

4–025 If more than one administrative receiver is appointed, the appointment must declare whether any act required or authorised under any enactment to be done is to be done by any one or more of the appointees.[46] This is sometimes done by providing that the administrative receivers may act "jointly and severally", a phrase which appears to be used as shorthand for the ability of each receiver to act for the other. Having regard to the different ways in which that expression can be interpreted in this context,[47] and the uncertainties which this may introduce, it is preferable to follow the wording of the statute.

4–026 Section 231, which applies also to other office-holders, appears to have overlooked the fact that, strictly speaking, most of the acts of an administrative receiver (as opposed to those of a liquidator or administrator) are not required or authorised to be done under any enactment, but are required or authorised to be done under the terms of the debenture or the general law.[48] In terms of drafting, it would be best, therefore, if debentures, appointments and declarations made it clear that the ability of one receiver to act for the other or others is not restricted to acts required or authorised under any enactment but applies to all the acts of any receiver or receivers.

4–027 It is also considered that compliance with the terms of section 231 is not intended to be a condition precedent to the validity of an appointment of administrative receivers. Section 231(1) makes it a precondition to the application of the requirement in section 231(2) that there should be an appointment or nomination. Thus, it is the appointment or nomination that is the precondition of the required declaration and not the other way round.

(e) Liability of multiple receivers[49]

4–028 In practice, the issue of whether multiple receivers are jointly, severally, or jointly and severally liable for their acts or omissions rarely causes any difficulties. Multiple appointments usually involve the appointment of partners in the same firm of accountants. Even where they act severally as a matter of fact, such partners often nevertheless purport to contract on behalf of their fellow appointees, and will certainly tend to do so where they wish to take advantage of any exclusion clauses, for example, in contracts for sale of assets. Similarly, proceedings against such persons generally tend to join all the appointees from the same firm without regard to the question of which particular receiver acted in relation to

---

[46] Insolvency Act 1986, s. 231(2).

[47] See, *e.g.* the judgments of the majority in *Kendle v. Melsom* [1998] 193 C.L.R. 46, HCt of Australia.

[48] See, *e.g.* s. 42 of the Insolvency Act 1986 which expressly states that the powers conferred on an administrative receiver "by the debentures by virtue of which he was appointed" are deemed to include the powers in Sched. 1 of the Act. If it had been intended to confer authority on the administrative receiver by statute, the section would simply have provided that the administrative receiver was to have the powers set out in the Schedule.

[49] As to the liabilities of receivers, see generally below, Chap. 7.

the events in question. The point is generally not taken, because in practice any personal liability which one receiver might attract as a consequence of his actions will be a joint and several liability as a consequence of the fact that the receivers are partners in the same firm.

The issue may, however, arise in the future, because it is possible that **4–029** receivers may be appointed to a company from more than one firm of accountants, with the express intention that they might be called upon to act severally in relation to different areas of the receivership. This may occur, for example, in cases where the firm whose partner is most suited to conduct the majority of the receivership is thought to have a potential conflict of interest in relation to a specific aspect of the receivership, or lacks the necessary expertise in a particular area of the business of the company, or where the debenture-holder acts for a syndicate of banks in which there is a divergence of interests with particular banks wishing to ensure that an office holder of their choice is involved in the receivership.[50] The issue may also arise if insolvency practitioners form limited liability partnerships.

If receivers are empowered to act jointly and do so, their liability to **4–030** their appointor or to third parties may be joint or joint and several.[51] Where receivers are appointed and empowered to act severally, and one of their number commits a breach of duty to the company or to his appointor, it is suggested that he will be individually liable for his breach of duty or tort, and his co-receivers will not be jointly or vicariously liable with him unless they participate in the misconduct in question. The co-appointees may become liable to the company or their appointor if it is shown that they knew or were on inquiry as to their co-receiver's misconduct and failed in their own separate duty to take steps to prevent such acts.[52] So far as liability to a third party is concerned, a receiver will only be liable in tort on the basis of an assumption of personal responsibility,[53] so that there is no question of any joint liability arising purely by reason of the fact that the appointment of receivers was a multiple appointment.

(f) Tenure of office in the case of joint appointments

As indicated below, section 33(1) of the Insolvency Act 1986 contains **4–031** provisions dealing with the time from which the appointment of a receiver will be effective. Provided that the receiver accepts his appointment by the end of the next business day following the receipt by him of

---

[50] The appointment of insolvency practitioners from more than one firm of accountants is more widespread in liquidations and administrations where the interests of a wider variety of creditor groups may be involved: see however the comments of Browne-Wilkinson V.-C. in rejecting an application for the appointment of an additional provisional liquidator in *Re BCCI (No. 2)* [1992] B.C.L.C. 579.

[51] See, *e.g.* the dissenting judgment of Brennan CJ and McHugh J. in *Kendle v. Melsom* [1998] 193 C.L.R. 46.

[52] See, by analogy with the law on directors, *Dovey v. Cory* [1901] A.C. 477 and *Re City Equitable Fire Insurance Co.* [1925] Ch. 407 at 452–453 and 459.

[53] See, again by analogy, *Williams v. Natural Life Health Foods Ltd* [1998] 1 W.L.R. 830, HL and para. 7–059 below.

the instrument of appointment, his appointment will take effect from the time of receipt of the instrument of appointment.[54] In the case of joint appointments, section 33(2) and rule 3.1 of the Insolvency Rules 1986 provide that each joint appointee must similarly accept his appointment, and the appointment will only be effective from the time at which the instrument of appointment was received by or on behalf of all the appointees.

4-032   The Insolvency Act and Rules do not deal in any detail with the question of what happens in the event of the death, retirement, removal from office of, or vacation of office by, one of a number of joint receivers. As a matter of principle, the issue must be resolved by an examination of the intention of the parties to the debenture under which the joint receivers were appointed and the terms of the appointment itself. The general presumption is that, even where an appointment to an office is a joint appointment, the death, resignation, etc. of one of the office-holders does not bring an end to the tenure of office of the other appointees, who will be entitled, as survivors, to continue to exercise the powers which are attached to the office in question.[55] This would appear to be the basis upon which the Insolvency Act 1986 is drafted.[56] Most modern debentures put the matter beyond doubt by providing that in the event of the death, retirement, etc. of one of a number of joint appointees, the remaining receivers will continue in office and will be entitled to exercise the powers given to them under the debenture. The debenture-holder will also be given the power of appointment to fill the vacancy which has arisen.[57]

3. DEMAND AS A PREREQUISITE TO APPOINTMENT

4-033 The debenture may enable an appointment of receivers to be made at any time, on the happening of a specified event or on the occasion of a default by the company. The burden is upon the debenture-holder and receiver to prove that the power of appointment has become exercisable: there is no presumption of a right to act.[58] An appointment for the

[54] For the position prior to the 1986 Act, see *R.A. Cripps & Son v. Wickenden* [1973] 1 W.L.R. 944 referring to *Windsor Refrigerator v. Branch Nominees Ltd* [1961] Ch. 375. See also *NZI Securities Australia Ltd v. Poignand* (1994) 14 A.C.S.R. 1.

[55] On the survival of powers annexed to an office, see, *e.g. Crawford v. Forshaw* [1891] 2 Ch. 261 at 266 (executors) and *Re Smith* [1904] 1 Ch. 139 at 144 (trustees).

[56] See, *e.g.* the reference to a "continuing administrative receiver" in s. 46(2) of the Insolvency Act 1986.

[57] See, *e.g.* the power given in the debenture in *Kendle v. Melsom* [1998] 193 C.L.R. 46 at 69 n.70. The court has no power to appoint an administrative receiver to fill a vacancy, even following exercise of its power to remove an administrative receiver from office under s. 45(1) of the Insolvency Act 1986: see *Re A&C Supplies Ltd* [1998] 1 B.C.L.C. 603 at 609e.

[58] *Kasofsky v. Kreegers* [1937] 4 All E.R. 374; *Lochab Bros v. Kenya Furfural* [1985] L.R.C. (Comm) 737. In *Tricontinental Corp v. HDFI Ltd* (1990) 21 N.S.W.L.R. 689 it was said that a strict approach was required to the question of whether conditions precedent to the liability of a surety had been satisfied. In *Pan Foods Company Importers & Distributors v. Australia and New Zealand Banking Group Ltd* (2000) 170 A.L.R. 579, the High Court of

wrong reason will be valid if a correct ground existed at the time of appointment.[59]

The directors of the company ordinarily have power to invite the **4–034** debenture-holder to appoint a receiver and waive any outstanding condition for the making of an appointment.[60] This course may afford an opportunity for a beneficial realisation of the company's undertaking or some viable part of it as a going concern and thus safeguard the interests of creditors and employees.

When, and if so upon what terms, the repayment of a loan can be **4–035** demanded and a receiver appointed in default of repayment will be determined by the terms of the agreement between the parties. Standard form debentures often provide that the debenture-holder must make a demand for payment before the right to appoint a receiver arises.[61] In the absence of any express or implied term to the contrary, an overdraft will be repayable on demand.[62] The right to demand repayment of other types of loans will be a matter of construction of the terms of the facility and the associated security documents.[63] If a loan is made for a fixed term, a provision will not be implied entitling the lender to require earlier repayment or to appoint a receiver for cause on the ground that his security is in jeopardy.[64]

Where the making of a demand is an express or implied condition **4–036** precedent to an appointment, the right to make the appointment must

Australia was faced with the different issue of whether the conditions precedent to the appointment of receivers in a loan agreement had been satisfied. The court held clearly that they had, and Kirby J. took the opportunity to reiterate his dissenting view in the *Tricontinental* case to the effect that commercial agreements should be construed practically so as to give effect to their presumed commercial purpose. Whatever the position in relation to suretyship, the approach of Kirby J. may well be more justifiable in cases dealing with the appointment of receivers. The issue of whether the right to appoint has arisen should be distinguished from the separate issue of whether the appointment has been properly made as a matter of form, as to which there may be a presumption of regularity: see *NZI Securities Australia v. Poignand* (1994) 14 A.C.S.R. 1.

[59] *Byblos Bank SAL v. Al-Khudhairy* [1987] B.C.L.C. 232; *McMahon v. State Bank of NSW* (1990) 8 A.C.L.C. 315; *Retail Equity Pty Ltd v. Custom Credit Corpn Ltd* (1991) 9 A.C.L.C. 404.

[60] See, *e.g. Encyclopaedia of Forms and Precedents*, Vol. 10 form 321, clause 13.1; *Lingard, Bank Security Documents* (3rd ed., 1993), p. 356 (Specimen Debenture, cl. 7.01).

[61] See, *e.g. Encyclopaedia of Forms and Precedents (op. cit)* and Lingard (*op cit*). Contrast the terms of the debenture at issue in *Pan Foods Company Importers & Distributors Pty Ltd v. Australia and New Zealand Banking Group Ltd* (2000) 170 A.L.R. 579 HCt of Australia.

[62] See, *per* Ralph Gibson J. in *Williams and Glyn's Bank Ltd v. Barnes* (1981) Com. L.R. 205. In *Lloyd's Bank plc v. Lampert* [1999] B.C.C. 507 the Court of Appeal held that although a bank and its customer envisaged that an overdraft facility might be in place for some time, it was not inconsistent with that expectation for a bank to retain an express entitlement to "payment on demand".

[63] So a term requiring payment on demand might be held repugnant to the main purpose of an overdraft facility which was expressed to be for a fixed term of 12 months: see *Titford Property Co. Ltd v. Cannon Street Acceptances Ltd* (unreported, Goff J., May 22, 1975).

[64] *Cryne v. Barclays Bank plc* [1987] B.C.L.C. 548 at 556, *per* Kerr L.J., distinguishing a *dictum* of Ralph Gibson J. in *Williams & Glyn's Bank Ltd v. Barnes*, above, on the ground that the facility in the earlier case was granted in the context of a rescue operation accompanied by a moratorium of the creditors. Jeopardy in this situation is, however, a ground for the appointment of a receiver by the court, see below Chap. 22.

have accrued at the date of acceptance of the appointment by the receiver if the appointment is to be valid and effective. If the right accrues later, this will not "feed" the appointment nor validate the acts of the receiver, but merely justify a fresh appointment.[65] If a first invalid appointment is made and acted on, a second valid appointment cannot be made until after the appointor has restored the company to possession of its assets and renewed its demands.[66] If a fresh appointment is made or could at any time have been made, whilst the actions of the first receiver may be unlawful, it may be difficult for the company to prove that any loss has been occasioned by the initial premature appointment.[67]

4–037   As to the form of demand, it is usual for a debenture to require a demand to be in writing and traditionally many debentures also require a demand to be under the common seal of the bank or under the hand of any duly authorised officer of the bank. Consideration should be given to the question whether the terms of the debenture are wide enough to cover modern forms of communication. For example, a demand by telex would not be a demand "under hand".[68]

4–038   As to the quantum of the demand, unless the debenture states otherwise, the demand need not specify the amount due.[69] If the terms of a debenture require that a demand be made for the exact sum due or for example, that a breakdown of the debt be given, then it is unclear whether a demand for a sum which exceeds the actual sum owed, or which fails to provide the specified particulars, will constitute a valid

---

[65] *R. A. Cripps & Son v. Wickenden* [1973] 1 W.L.R. 944 at 956–957; *Jaffe (R.) Ltd v. Jaffe (No. 2)* [1932] N.Z.L.R. 168.

[66] *R.A. Cripps & Son v. Wickenden*, [1973] 1 W.L.R. 944. Compare the position where a Mareva injunction is obtained without notice in breach of the duty to make full disclosure and the order is discharged, so as to ensure that the applicant cannot benefit from his own wrong, before any fresh application is made: *Bank Mellat v. Nikpour* [1985] F.S.R. 87 (CA.). In *Bank of Baroda v. Panessar* [1987] Ch. 335, Walton J. (*obiter* at 351) took the view that this necessary hiatus period between an invalid appointment and a subsequent fresh demand and valid appointment did not preclude the application of the doctrine of estoppel barring the debtor from challenging the validity of the original appointment when the debtor had dealt with the receiver as validly appointed and the debenture-holder had accordingly refrained from serving a fresh demand and making a new appointment.

[67] See *The Mihalis Angelos* [1971] 1 Q.B. 164.

[68] *Re A Company* [1985] B.C.L.C. 37 at 43. To meet this point, a modern form of debenture may well permit a demand to be made by fax. The use of facsimile machines to serve court documents is now well established where the party to be served has indicated his willingness to be served in this way: see CPR Pt. 6.2 and para. 3.1 of the associated Practice Direction. It remains to be seen whether debentures in general use will provide for service of demands by e-mail, and if so, what conditions may be attached to such provisions so as to ensure that delivery of the demand can be verified and comes to the attention of the relevant person: see *e.g.* the additional requirements for service by e-mail in CPR Pt. 6.2 and para. 3.3 of the associated Practice Direction.

[69] *Bank of Baroda v. Panessar* [1987] Ch. 335 ("all moneys due"); *Bunbury Foods v. National Bank of Australasia* (1984) 153 CLR 491 at 504. *Australia and New Zealand Banking Group v. Pan Foods Company Importers and Distributors* [1999] 1 V.R. 29. The word "demand" need not be used: *Re Colonial Finance, Mortgage, Investment and Guarantee Corpn. Ltd* (1905) 6 S.R.N.S.W. 6 at 9, *per* Walker J., approved by the Court of Appeal in *BCCI v. Blattner* (unreported, November 20, 1986). A demand for a sum due will be valid despite being accompanied with an offer to accept payment in instalments: *NRG Vision Ltd v. Churchfield Leasing* [1988] B.C.L.C. 624.

demand.[70] It is suggested that the ordinary principle should be that a demand will be a valid demand even if the sum claimed exceeds the sum in fact due.[71] An analogy might be drawn with the well-established principle that a notice served by a mortgagee prior to exercise of a power of sale is not void merely on the ground that it demands more than is due. There may, however, be a qualification to this principle if the mortgagee expressly or impliedly refuses to accept less than the amount demanded.[72] Moreover, as Walton J. observed in *Bank of Baroda v. Panessar*,[73] with the complexities of modern trade and bank facilities, in many cases it may be difficult for the chargee to ascertain the precise amount of money due at any point in time, especially if this has to be done very quickly.[74] If, as in the vast majority of cases, the company will not be in a position to pay the debt in any event, there would seem to be

[70] Knox J. specifically left open this point in *NRG Vision Ltd v. Churchfield Leasing* [1988] B.C.L.C. 624 at 638. See also the split decision of the Court of Appeal of Victoria in Australia and New Zealand *Banking Group Ltd v. Pan Foods Company Importers and Distributors* [1999] 1 V.R. 29 on the issue of whether a demand was bad for failing to give an accurate breakdown of the amount demanded. The point was not dealt with on appeal, because the High Court of Australia decided that no demand was necessary at all as a pre-condition to the appointment of a receiver: see (2000) 170 A.L.R. 579. The only judge who expressly dealt with the matter in the High Court of Australia (Callinan J.) agreed with Winneke P.'s judgment in the Court of Appeal of Victoria to the effect that it was the substance and not the form of the notice which was important.

[71] *Deverges v. Sandeman, Clark & Co* [1902] 1 Ch. 579 at 597; *per* Cozens-Hardy M.R. (distinguishing *Pigot v. Cubley* (1864) C.B. (N.S.) 701); *Stubbs v. Slater* [1910] 1 Ch. 632 at 647, *per* Buckley L.J.; *Bank of Baroda v. Panessar* [1987] Ch. 335, approving *Bunbury Foods Pty Ltd v. National Bank of Australasia Ltd* (1984) 51 A.L.R. 609, HCt of Australia. See also *per* Malcolm C.J. in *Hassgill v. Newman Air Charter* (1991) 5 A.C.S.R. 321 at 339. Under Canadian law, a demand for payment will nonetheless be effective if the amount of the demand is incorrect: *Bennett on Receiverships*, p. 77 citing, *inter alia, Four-K Western Equip v. CIBC* (1983) 46, C.B.R. (N.S.) 146, BCSC.

[72] See the cases referred to in *Bunbury Foods Pty Ltd v. National Bank of Australasia Ltd* (1984) 51 A.L.R. 609 at 619–620 and in *Hassgill Investments Pty Ltd v. Newman Air Charter Pty Ltd* (1991) 5 A.C.S.R. 321 at 339. Some limited guidance may also be obtained from cases on the effect of overstatement of the amount due in statutory demands served on companies or as a pre-condition to the presentation of a bankruptcy petition. In England, where it is clear that a certain sum is owing, the mere overstatement of the amount in a statutory demand served on a company will not invalidate the demand provided that the company was in a position to know exactly what it ought to pay: see *Cardiff Preserved Coal and Coke Co. v. Norton* (1867) L.R. 2 Ch. App. 405; *Re A Company (No. 003729 of 1982)* [1984] 1 W.L.R. 1090; *Re A Debtor (No. 10 of 1988)* [1989] 1 W.L.R. 405 at 406. Statutory demands in bankruptcy cases are also not liable to be set aside merely by reason of the over-statement of the amount of the debt: see *Re A Debtor (No. 1 of 1987)* [1989] 1 W.L.R. 271; *Re A Debtor (No 490-SD–1991)* [1992] 1 W.L.R. 507. After considerable judicial differences of opinion, in Australia prior to 1992 it would seem that the view was also taken that a mere overstatement did not render a statutory demand served on a company invalid: see *Hassgill v. Newman Air Charter* (1991) 5 A.S.C.R. 321 referring, *inter alia,* to *Re Fabo Pty Ltd* (1988) 14 A.C.L.R. 518. Since 1992 the position in Australia has been dealt with by statute, pursuant to which a defect does not automatically invalidate a demand, but the court is given the power to set aside a statutory demand if the defect has caused substantial injustice, or if for some other reason it ought to be set aside; *see Topfelt Pty Ltd v. State Bank of New South Wales Ltd* (1993) 12 A.C.S.R. 381 and *Chains & Power (Aust) Pty Ltd v. Commonwealth Bank of Australia* (1994) 15 A.C.S.R. 544.

[73] [1987] 1 Ch. 335.

[74] See to similar effect the *dictum* of Winneke P. in the *Australia and New Zealand Banking Group v. Pan Foods Company case,* [1999] 1 V.R. 29 at 40.

little commercial sense in invalidating a demand merely for inadvertent overstatement of the precise amount due.[75]

4-039   Conflicting considerations are relevant to the issue of the period of time which the law ought to allow for repayment of a loan in response to a demand by the debenture-holder before the right to appoint a receiver arises. The company might contend that it ought to be given a reasonable opportunity to find alternative sources of finance and to raise the sum required. Claims might be made for additional time for legal and administrative reasons (such as holding board meetings to authorise the release of funds for repayment or to obtain any necessary third party or regulatory approval to such repayment). On the other hand the holder of the security may need to take immediate and urgent action if his security is to be safeguarded and to avoid the inherent risk of delay (such as the disappearance of charged assets or their seizure by other creditors).[76]

4-040   Different legal systems have adopted differing approaches to this issue. Under English law, a series of first instance decisions have determined that a debenture-holder in respect of an "on demand" facility need not give the company a reasonable time to pay before appointing a receiver.[77] The company is merely to be allowed the necessary time during banking hours to implement the mechanics of payment by collecting or arranging for the transfer of the money from its bank or some other "convenient place".[78] The company is not entitled to time to raise such money either from its bank or other sources[79] unless such a right is expressly conferred or must necessarily be implied to give business efficacy to the loan agreement.[80] The personal circumstances of

---

[75] This problem is often met by inclusion of a provision in the debenture that a statement of the indebtedness in a particular form (usually a certificate) by the creditor is conclusive. A statement pursuant to such a provision will be conclusive unless some lack of good faith in its preparation can be shown: *Bache & Co (London) v. Banque Vernes et Commerciale de Paris* [1973] 2 Lloyd's Rep. 437; *ANZ Banking Group (N.Z.) Ltd v. Gibson* [1981] 2 N.Z.L.R. 513; *Dobbs v. National Bank of Australasia* (1935) 53 C.L.R. 643, HCt. of Australia.

[76] See *ANZ Banking Group (N.Z.) Ltd v. Gibson* [1981] 2 N.Z.L.R. 513 at 519, *per* Holland J.

[77] *Brighty v. Norton* (1862) 3 B. & S. 305 at 312, *per* Blackburn J: "a debtor who is required to pay money on demand . . . must have it ready, and is not entitled to further time in order to look for it." This statement of the law was approved by Goff J. in *Cripps v. Wickenden* [1973] 1 W.L.R. 944 and by Walton J. in *Bank of Baroda v. Panessar* [1987] Ch. 335 in which the appointment of the receiver was upheld despite it taking place only one hour after the demand.

[78] This has come to be known as the "mechanics of payment" test: see, *e.g. Moore v. Shelley* (1883) 8 App. Cas. 285 at 293, PC; *Bank of Baroda v. Panessar* [1987] Ch. 335 at 348B; *Sheppard & Cooper v. TSB Bank plc (No. 2)* [1996] B.C.C. 965 at 967; and *Lloyd's Bank v. Lampert* [1999] B.C.C. 507 at 512. In the Lloyds Bank case the Court of Appeal declined to be drawn into what Kennedy L.J. described as "the interesting academic question" as to whether the mechanics of payment test should now be affirmed or rejected at appellate level, because on the evidence there was no prospect of the company finding the money to make repayment so that, whatever the test, the bank was entitled to appoint the receivers when it did.

[79] *Titford Property Co. Ltd v. Cannon Street Acceptances Ltd* (unreported, Goff J., May 22, 1975).

[80] *Williams & Glyn's Bank Ltd v. Barnes* [1981] Comm. L.R. 205, where the view was expressed by Ralph Gibson J. that under the facility agreement in question, business

the borrower or officers of the company will not be taken into account unless so provided in the debenture.[81] On the other hand, it has been held that notwithstanding the objective nature of the mechanics of payment test, no time at all need be given if the borrower has by a director indicated that it cannot pay.[82]

In Canada a slightly more liberal approach has prevailed, requiring **4–041** lenders to give a borrower a reasonable time to make repayment of a demand loan before enforcing the security. The debtor must be given some notice on which he might reasonably expect to be able to act.[83] The Canadian courts have not generally been willing to extend very lengthy periods of time to debtors to find the money to make repayment. It has been pointed out that the cases which have given rise to the requirement of reasonable notice dealt with notices of an hour or less, and that whilst what constitutes reasonable notice will depend upon the facts of the particular case,[84] it is unlikely to encompass anything more than a few days.[85]

In Australia, the decision of the High Court of Australia in 1984 in **4–042** *Bunbury Foods Pty Ltd v. National Bank of Australasia Ltd*[86] also appeared to adopt a requirement that a debtor who was liable to repay a debt "on demand" must be allowed a reasonable time to meet the demand before the creditor could take steps to appoint a receiver. The High Court stated that what would constitute a reasonable time would vary according to the facts, including the relationship between the parties, the knowledge of the debtor as to the amount due and the information provided by the creditor in the demand.[87] Subsequently, in

---

efficacy required that sufficient notice be given by the bank to permit the company to explore the possibility of actions such as borrowing elsewhere or selling sites or parts of its undertaking. The judge remarked, *obiter,* that he would be very surprised if such period would have exceeded one month.

[81] See *Oakdown v. Bernstein & Co.* [1985] P. & CR. 282 at 293, *per* Scott J. who stated (rejecting a claim to be excused from completion pursuant to a notice to complete a contract for sale of land on the grounds that the tenets of Jewish law prohibited compliance on the date stipulated which was the Festival of Passover): "If parties wish to excuse themselves on religious grounds from discharging on specific days the contractual obligations which would otherwise lie upon them, they must in my judgment expressly so stipulate in their contracts." *Quaere* whether such a stipulation might be implied in the case of a contract between two devout adherents of the same faith, and what might be the effect of assignment upon any such term.

[82] *Sheppard & Cooper (No. 2)* [1996] B.C.C. 965, criticised in *Rowlatt on Principal and Surety* (5th ed., 1999), p. 116 and n.46.

[83] *Ronald Elwyn Lister Ltd v. Dunlop Canada Ltd* (1982) 135 D.L.R. 1, Supreme Court of Canada referring to *Massey v. Sladen* (1868) L.R. 4 Ex. 13 at 19. See also *Royal Bank of Canada v. W. Got & Associates Electric Ltd* (1999) 178 D.L.R. (4th) 385 at 391–392.

[84] Relevant considerations have been said to include (1) the amount of the loan, (2) the risk to the creditor of losing his money or security (3) the length of the relationship between the debtor and the creditor, (4) the character and reputation of the debtor, (5) the potential ability to raise the money demanded in a short period, (6) the circumstances surrounding the making of the demand, and (7) any other relevant factors: see *per* Linden J. in *Mister Broadloom Corp (1968) Ltd v. Bank of Montreal* (1979) 101 D.L.R. (3rd) 713 at 723, referred to with approval in *Royal Bank of Canada v. W. Got & Associates Electric* (1999) 178 D.L.R. (4th) 385 at 391.

[85] See *Whonnock Industries Ltd v. National Bank of Canada* (1987) 42 D.L.R. (4th) 1.

[86] (1984) 51 A.L.R. 609; (1984) 153 C.L.R. 491

[87] *Bunbury Foods v. National Bank of Australasia* (1984) 51 A.L.R. 609 at 618.

Bond v. Hongkong Bank of Australia Ltd[88] the majority of the Court of Appeal of New South Wales indicated a preference for the "mechanics of payment" test as exemplified by Bank of *Baroda v. Panessar*.

4–043   In New Zealand the courts have adopted the "mechanics of payment" test. In *ANZ Banking Group (New Zealand) Ltd v. Gibson*[89] the Court of Appeal rejected the approach in the Canadian cases, preferring to adopt an objective test which did not depend upon any matters personal to the parties so as to promote certainty in commercial matters. Richardson J. suggested that although no-one would expect the borrower to have large cash sums immediately on hand, all that was required was that the debtor be given a reasonable time to convert resources presently available to him into immediate cash or to utilise them within the same time to obtain financial cover with which to make the repayment. Further time to negotiate a loan with a third party was not comprehended within the concept of a reasonable time.[90]

4–044   One point which is made in many of the cases referred to on this topic is that in most situations the question of the precise legal test to be applied will be entirely academic. The factual position will usually be that the company will be unable to make repayment, or prove that it had any realistic prospect of doing so, in the period of time which would be permitted by either test. It is important not to lose sight of the fact that the issues discussed above relate to demand liabilities, and it will be a very rare case indeed in which the debtor company has no warning of the bank's intention to take steps to call in its loan and enforce its security. Most companies in financial trouble are in regular contact with their bankers and have sufficient opportunity to take steps to seek alternative finance long before the final demand is served.

4–045   If the demand for payment specifies a date but not a time for payment, there is no default until midnight.[91]

4–046   To avoid the appointment of the receiver or the exercise of any of the creditor's other rights under the debenture, the company must either tender or pay into court the sum claimed to be due[92] or (if the sum claimed is on the face of the mortgage excessive) the sum actually due.[93]

---

[88] (1991) 25 N.S.W.L.R. 286

[89] [1986] 1 N.Z.L.R. 556.

[90] In *Housing Corporation of New Zealand v. Maori Trustee (No. 2)* [1988] 2 N.Z.L.R. 708 the *ANZ* case was cited with approval, but in rejecting the claim that an unreasonably short period of time had been given, the court curiously referred to the fact that the mortgagor had long been in default, time had been given, and promises made but not kept. These factors would seem to be irrelevant to the objective test of the reasonable time to convert presently available resources into immediate cash with which to make payment.

[91] *Afovos Shipping Co. S.A. v. Pagnan* [1983] 1 W.L.R. 195.

[92] *Macleod v. Jones* (1883) 24 Ch.D. 289, CA. The company cannot unilaterally discharge the security without payment by appropriating a cross claim: see *Samuel Keller v. Martins Bank* [1971] 1 W.L.R. 43 and *Ashley v. Zacharia* [1993] 1 W.L.R. 62 and see below, Chap. 16. On the other hand, if the mortgagee undoubtedly owes moneys to the mortgagor, the mortgagor appears to be able to "redeem" the mortgage by giving notice to the mortgagee to appropriate the debt due to the mortgagor in repayment of the mortgage; *Parker v. Jackson* [1936] 2 All E.R. 281 at 290. See also *National Westminster Bank v. Skelton* [1993] 1 W.L.R. 72, CA. and *Ashley Guarantee Ltd v. Zacaria* [1993] 1 W.L.R. 62, CA. and below, para. 16–04.

[93] *Hickson v. Darlow* (1883) 23 Ch.D. 690.

If the debtor makes or tenders payment, an injunction will be granted restraining the debenture-holder from enforcing his security.[94] The company will be temporarily excused from making any tender or payment as a condition of its right to prevent the debenture-holder enforcing his security if the debenture-holder alone has knowledge of the sum secured and he fails to specify it in his demand.[95]

If the company,[96] with knowledge of the facts which invalidate an appointment of a receiver, acquiesces in the receiver exercising his powers by, for example, continuing to run the company's business, it may be estopped from subsequently challenging the validity of the appointment.[97] It is unnecessary for this purpose that the company should know that these facts give rise to a right to challenge the validity of the appointment.[98] **4–047**

4. METHOD OF APPOINTMENT[99]

If the power to appoint a receiver has become exercisable, the debenture-holder owes no duty of care to the company or to its unsecured creditors or to any guarantor in deciding whether to exercise it, provided he acts in good faith.[1] **4–048**

A receiver must be appointed in accordance with the terms of the debenture. If the debenture merely requires an appointment "by writing" an appointment is sufficient if under hand and need not be under seal.[2] Non-administrative receivers may, but do not need to, be appointed by deed to execute any deed as agent for the company (*e.g.* a conveyance or transfer or lease).[3] In the case of administrative receivers, on the other hand, their implied power to use the company's seal and to execute deeds and other instruments in the name and on behalf of the company is in no way dependent on the form of their appointment.[4] **4–049**

---

[94] *Duke v. Robson* [1973] 1 W.L.R. 267; *Inglis v. Commonwealth Trading Bank of Australia* [1972] 126 C.L.R. 1611, HCt of Australia.

[95] Consider *Albermarle Supply Co. Ltd v. Hind & Co.* [1928] 1 K.B. 307 (a case of lien). A mortgagor is entitled to know how much he is liable to pay and how that sum is arrived at: *Cityland and Property (Holdings) v. Dabrah* [1968] Ch. 166 at 172–173.

[96] Acting for this purpose by its directors.

[97] *Bank of Baroda v. Panessar* [1987] Ch. 335 at 353; *Village Cay Marina Ltd v. Acland* [1998] 2 B.C.L.C. 327 at 333h, PC. In *Australia and New Zealand Banking Group Ltd v. Pan Foods Company Importers and Distributors* [1999] 1 V.R. 29 in the Supreme Court of Victoria, Buchanan J.A. appeared to treat the matter as one of estoppel in the strict sense. He referred to the *Bank of Baroda* case but rejected a claim that the company and its directors were estopped from disputing the validity of the receiver's appointment, because the bank's view as to the validity of the appointment was based upon its construction of the debenture in question as a matter of law, and there was no evidence that such belief had been induced by any conduct or factual representation by the company and its directors.

[98] *Peyman v. Lanjani* [1985] Ch. 457.

[99] For court-appointed receivers, see below Chap. 22.

[1] *Shamji v. Johnson Matthey Bankers Ltd* [1991] B.C.L.C. 36, CA.; *Re Potters Oils Ltd* (No. 2) [1986] 1 W.L.R. 201. See further below Chap. 7.

[2] *Windsor Refrigerator Co. v. Branch Nominees* [1961] Ch. 375; [1961] 1 All E.R. 277; *R. A. Cripps & Son v. Wickenden* [1973] 1 W.L.R. 944 at 953–4.

[3] See *Phoenix Properties Ltd v. Wimpole Street Nominees Ltd* [1992] B.C.L.C. 737.

[4] Insolvency Act 1986, s. 42 and Sched. 1, paras. 8 and 9.

4–050   An instrument of appointment may be executed in anticipation of a default and subsequent use.[5] Section 33 of the Insolvency Act 1986 provides that an appointment of a receiver or manager shall only be effective if it is accepted by the nominee before the end of the business day next following that on which the instrument of appointment is received by him or his behalf. The appointment is then deemed to have been made at the time at which the instrument of appointment was received by the nominee. Section 33 also applies to the appointment of two or more persons as joint receivers or managers of a company's property under powers contained in an instrument, in which case the appointment must be accepted by all the nominees and will be effective from the time at which the instrument of appointment was received by or on behalf of all the appointees.[6]

5. SCOPE OF THE APPOINTMENT

4–051 The appointment will normally extend to the whole of the subject-matter of the charge. But on occasions it may be appropriate to exclude from the appointment valueless[7] or onerous[8] property. It should be considered whether the extent of any property excluded may be such as to prevent the receiver being receiver of substantially the whole of the company's property, in which case he will not qualify as an administrative receiver.[9]

6. VALIDATION OF ACTS WHERE THERE ARE DEFECTS IN APPOINTMENT OR QUALIFICATIONS

4–052 Section 232 of the Insolvency Act 1986 provides that the acts of an office-holder (meaning a liquidator, provisional liquidator, administrator or administrative receiver) shall be valid notwithstanding any defect in his appointment, nomination or qualifications. The defects in question are limited to defects in the form of or procedure for appointment, and do not extend to validating the acts of a person in a case where the appointor had no right or power to make any appointment[10] or where there has been no genuine attempt to appoint at all.[11]

---

[5] *Windsor Refrigerator Co. v. Branch Nominees* [1961] Ch. 375; *R. A. Cripps & Son v. Wickenden* [1973] 1 W.L.R. 944 at 953–954. The appointment is effective as against creditors: *Re Zurich Insurance Co. and Troy Woodworking Ltd* (1984) 45 O.R. (2d) 343; *MacKay and Hughes (1973) Ltd v. Martin Potatoes Inc.* (1984) 9 D.L.R. (4d) 439, CA Ontario.

[6] Insolvency Act 1986, s. 33(2). See Insolvency Rules 1986, r.3.1 (as amended).

[7] *Re Griffin Hotel Co. Ltd* [1941] Ch. 129 (hotel subject to prior charge excluded).

[8] Such as unproductive property exposing the receiver to liability for rates.

[9] See above, paras. 1–006 *et seq.*

[10] A distinction is drawn in the Act between an invalid appointment (s. 34) and a defect in appointment (s. 232). In *Woollett v. Minister of Agriculture and Fisheries* (1955) 1 Q.B. 103 at 121, 128 and 137, the Court of Appeal held that a similarly worded validating provision in the Agriculture Act 1947 validated the decisions of an agricultural lands tribunal where two of its members, who were eligible to sit, were wrongly appointed by the secretary of the Tribunal instead of the Minister.

[11] *Morris v. Kanssen* [1946] A.C. 459.

7. DURATION OF APPOINTMENT

Prior to the Insolvency Act 1985, the appointor could (subject to the **4–053** provisions of the debenture and appointment) remove and replace a receiver and a manager at will. This continues to be the case in relation to non-administrative receivers. Under the Insolvency Act 1986 the appointor has no power to remove or replace the administrative receiver and any provision to this effect in the debenture or appointment will be void. This change in the law is designed to enhance the independence and standing of the administrative receiver, reflecting the professional status of the insolvency practitioner and his official powers and duties as an office-holder.[12]

An administrative receiver will remain in office unless and until: **4–054**

(a) he ceases to be qualified to act as an insolvency practitioner in relation to the company[13];
(b) he is removed by order of the court[14];
(c) he resigns[15]; or
(d) the receivership is concluded.

The removal, resignation, termination and discharge of a receiver are dealt with in detail in Chapter 21.

8. PRACTICAL PRECAUTIONS[16]

Before making or accepting appointment as administrative receiver and **4–055** then acting as such, inquiries ought, in so far as circumstances permit, to be made so that appointor and appointee are satisfied as to the following matters.

(a) Validity of debenture[17]

If the debenture is void *ab initio*, so must be the appointment, and the **4–056** receiver is at risk of being held liable as a trespasser and the appointor as a joint tortfeasor.[18] Further, both the appointor and appointee may be held liable as constructive trustees or to account for property which comes into their hands, given actual or constructive knowledge of the

---

[12] See below, Chap. 5.

[13] Insolvency Act 1986, s. 45(2). The vacation of office is immediate and automatic: consider *Re A.J. Adams (Builders) Ltd* [1991] B.C.C. 62.

[14] Insolvency Act 1986, s. 45(1).

[15] *ibid.*

[16] A good practical guide to the issues which confront any person intending to make or take up an appointment is contained in Chaps 5–9 of Samwell, *Corporate Receiverships; A Practical Approach* (2nd ed., 1988).

[17] See above, paras 3–091 *et seq.*

[18] *Ford & Carter Ltd v. Midland Bank Ltd* (1979) 129 N.L.J. 543, HL. See *also Re Jaffe Ltd* [1932] N.Z.L.R. 195 and *Harold Meggitt Ltd v. Discount and Finance Ltd* (1938) 56 W.N. (N.S.W.) 23.

invalidity.[19] Section 34 of the Insolvency Act 1986 gives the court a discretionary jurisdiction to require the appointor to indemnify the appointee against liabilities arising from the invalidity of the appointment. Equally, on appointment, the appointee may reasonably require the appointor to accept the risk of any invalidity and to provide a deed of indemnity.

4-057   If the debenture is valid at the date of the appointment but potentially flawed, such as being susceptible to intervening invalidity by reason of non-registration or avoidance as a preference on a subsequent liquidation, the appointment is valid and the receiver continues entitled so as to act until the happening of the invalidating event.[20]

(b) Title to the debenture

4-058   An assignee of the debenture can only make an appointment pursuant thereto once the assignment has been completed.[21]

(c) Enforceability of charge and validity of the form of the appointment

4-059   The conditions for appointment of a receiver must have been satisfied and the appointment properly made.[22] An administrative receiver cannot be appointed if an administrator has been appointed by the court under section 8 of the Insolvency Act 1986.[23]

(d) Scope of the charge and existence of prior charges

4-060   Checks ought to be made to ascertain the precise scope of the property covered by the charges and the nature of the charges themselves. It will be important to identify whether a charge is a fixed or a floating charge. In relation to certain assets (such as book debts and other receivables) this may be far from simple.[24] It should also be established whether there are prior charges in favour of other parties over any of the assets covered by the charge. These will not prevent the appointment of a receiver, but the existence of a prior charge may affect the commercial viability of the

---

[19] In *Rolled Steel Products (Holdings) Ltd v. British Steel Corporation* [1986] Ch. 246, the appointor and receiver had actual notice of the invalidity of the debenture under which the receiver was appointed; as such they were accountable to the plaintiff company as constructive trustees. It was not argued, given the facts, that a receiver should be liable only if he had actual knowledge. It is submitted that constructive knowledge is sufficient to found liability, but the law as to what constitutes constructive knowledge is unclear: see, *e.g.* the cases discussed above in para. 3–114, including *Re Montague's Settlement* [1987] Ch. 264; *Agip (Africa) Ltd v. Jackson* [1991] Ch. 547; *Cowan de Groot Properties Ltd v. Eagle Trust plc* [1991] B.C.L.C. 1045; *Eagle Trust plc v. SBC Securities Ltd* [1992] 4 All E.R. 488; *Houghton v. Fayers* [2000] 1 B.C.L.C. 511 and *BCCI v. Akindele* (unreported, CA, June 14, 2000).

[20] *Burston Finance v. Speirway* [1974] 1 W.L.R. 1648 at 1657, *per* Walton J., and see paras. 11–05 and 11–09.

[21] *Harris & Lewin Pty Ltd v. Harris v. Lewin (Agents)* [1975] A.C.L.C. 28,279 and consider *Lever Finance v. Needlemans Trustee* [1956] Ch. 375.

[22] See above paras. 4–033–4–050.

[23] See s. 11(3)(b) of the Insolvency Act 1986. Note that the prohibition on appointment only arises on the making of the order and not on presentation of the petition (s. 10(2)(b)).

[24] See, *e.g.* above, Chap. 3.

receivership. Prior charges may have the right to appoint a superior receiver who will be able to call for control of the charged assets and the existence of other claims having priority to moneys realised from charged assets will have to be taken into account when dealing with charged property.

9. NOTICE OF APPOINTMENT

(a) To the Registrar of Companies

A person who appoints a receiver (including an administrative receiver) **4–061** or manager of a company's property under the powers contained in an instrument, or obtains am order for the appointment of a receiver or manager by the court, is under a statutory duty to give notice of the fact to the Registrar of Companies within seven days of the appointment or order. This fact is then entered on the register of charges of the company.[25] Where a person appointed as a receiver and manager under an instrument ceases to act, he is obliged to give notice to the Registrar, who will enter notice of this fact on the register of charges.[26] [27] In the case of an administrative receiver who vacates office (otherwise than by death), such notice must be given within 14 days after his vacation of office.[27]

(b) To creditors, the public and the company

After the receiver has been appointed, every invoice, order for goods or **4–062** business letter, being documents upon which the company's name appears, must contain a statement that the receiver has been appointed.[28]

On appointment, an administrative receiver is also duty bound: **4–063**

(a) forthwith to send to the company and to advertise in the prescribed manner a notice of his appointment; and

(b) within 28 days after his appointment, unless the court otherwise directs, to send a notice to all creditors of the company so far as he is aware of their addresses.[29]

The duty does not extend to an administrative receiver appointed to act with an existing administrative receiver, nor does it extend to an administrative receiver appointed in place of an administrative receiver dying or ceasing to act, save to the extent that the predecessor has failed fully to comply with the duty.[30]

---

[25] Companies Act 1985, s. 405(1).
[26] Companies Act 1985, s. 405(2).
[27] Insolvency Act 1986, s. 45(4).
[28] Insolvency Act 1986, s. 39(1).
[29] *ibid.*, s. 46(1). The content of this notice is prescribed by the Insolvency Rules 1986, r.3.2.
[30] Insolvency Act 1986, s. 46(2).

If the company is being wound up, the same duty exists, though the liquidator and administrative receiver may be the same person.[31]

4-064 There is no duty on the debenture-holder to give prior notice of the appointment to the company.[32]

[31] *ibid.*, s. 43(3).
[32] *Byblos Bank SAL v. Rushingdale Ltd* (1986) 2 B.C.C. 99,509, C.A.

CHAPTER 5

THE ADMINISTRATIVE RECEIVER AS AN "OFFICE-HOLDER"

1. INTRODUCTION

The Insolvency Act 1985 (now consolidated in the Insolvency Act 1986) **5–001** created the concept of the "office-holder", a novel status carrying special statutory privileges and responsibilities, which was conferred upon administrative receivers, liquidators (including provisional liquidators) and administrators.[1] A person holding any of these offices (unless an official receiver) is required to be qualified to act as an insolvency practitioner in relation to the company.[2] The imposition of this qualification on, and the attribution of the status of "office-holder" to, the administrative receiver involves both a recognition of the expertise required and the enhancement of the role of such a receiver and manager of a company's undertaking. The administrative receiver is no mere agent for the realisation of assets for the benefit of the debenture-holder: in the interest of the creditors generally,[3] and indeed the public, he is given powers and responsibilities designed to secure the beneficial management of the company's undertaking and the due investigation of the company's affairs, to which he will usually be a stranger.

It is important to distinguish, however, between the statutory concept **5–002** of an "office-holder", and the quite different concept of an "officer of the court". Officers of the court[4] are appointed by the court and are subject to its general supervisory jurisdiction.[5] In accordance with the rule in *ex p. James*,[6] officers of the court are obliged not only to act lawfully, but fairly and honourably. Interference with their functions may be a contempt.[7] In contrast, administrative receivers may be given directions by the court in relation to matters arising in the receivership,[8] but they are not subject to the general control of the court, they are not susceptible to the rule in *ex p. James*, and they are not protected by the principles of contempt of court.[9]

---

[1] Insolvency Act 1986, s. 233(1).
[2] *ibid.*, s. 230(1).
[3] See Hoffmann J. in *Re Aveling Barford Ltd* [1989] 1 W.L.R. 360 at 365.
[4] Such as court appointed receivers (Chap. 22), administrators (Chap. 23), provisional liquidators and liquidators in a compulsory liquidation (Chap. 2).
[5] See, *e.g. Re Atlantic Computer Systems plc* [1992] Ch. 505.
[6] (1874) 9 Ch. App 609.
[7] *Re Mead* (1875) LR 20 Eq 282. See below, para. 22–022.
[8] Pursuant to an application under s. 35 of the Insolvency Act 1986. The list of persons who can apply to the court under s. 35 is limited, and it is an interesting and unresolved question whether there is a general right in other interested parties to apply to the court for directions to be given to a receiver appointed out of court.
[9] *Re Hill* [1896] 1 Ch. 947 at 954; *Re Magic Aust Pty Ltd* (1992) 10 A.C.L.C. 929.

2. SUPPLIES BY UTILITIES

5–003 Prior to the current insolvency legislation, public utilities (like any other creditor-supplier) could require the payment of all arrears as a condition of continued or resumed supply to the company in receivership or liquidation, and thus, by the exercise of their monopoly position in the market, obtain a preference in respect of their unsecured debts over the debts due to preferential creditors and, indeed, a debenture-holder.[10] But unlike any other creditor-supplier, public utilities could not refuse supplies to a new occupier of property. A mortgagee of a company in difficulties therefore had a choice. He could appoint a receiver as agent of the company, in which case the company continued in occupation and payment or security could be demanded by the utility. Or the mortgagee could take possession as a new occupier, in which case payment or security could not be demanded.[11] If, as was usually the case, the mortgagee decided to appoint a receiver, there was an advantage in a receiver hiving down the company's business to a subsidiary which, as a new occupier, could require supplies without any responsibility for past arrears.[12]

5–004 This continues to be the position where a company property is the subject of a receivership other than an administrative receivership though, in practice, such receivers are not so often concerned with the continuation of the company's business, and are therefore less vulnerable to the withdrawal of supplies. The position is now different in the case of an administrative receiver. Section 233 of the Insolvency Act 1986 provides that, where a request is made by or with the concurrence of an office-holder (*i.e.* including an administrative receiver) for supplies of gas, electricity, water or telecommunication services, the utility[13] may not, as a condition of supply, require the payment of charges for supplies provided prior to the "effective date".

5–005 Where an administrative receiver is the only office-holder in relation to a particular company, the "effective date" is the date on which he was appointed or the date on which the first of his predecessors in office was

---

[10] The courts recognised no restriction on the right of a creditor to insist upon a collateral advantage, or a condition of continuing supplies, if the creditor possessed the legal right to cut off supplies: *Husey v. London Electricity Supply* [1902] 1 Ch. 411 at 421 (court appointed receiver). See also *Wellworth Cash & Carry (North Shields) Ltd v. North Eastern Electricity Board* (1986) 2 B.C.C. 265, where the threatened use of the Electricity Board's power to cut off electricity needed by a voluntary liquidator to keep food frozen, unless the pre-liquidation debt to the Board was paid in full, was "deplored". Nevertheless, the Board was held to be entitled to exercise such power. Creditors other than utilities can still withhold supplies unless pre-receivership debts are paid in full, and this does not amount to an abuse of a dominant position within Art. 86 of the EEC Treaty: *Leyland DAF Ltd v. Automotive Products Plc* [1993] B.C.C. 385, CA.

[11] *North American Trust Co. v. Consumer Gas Co.* (1997) 147 D.L.R. (4th) 645.

[12] For hive-downs, see below Chap. 9. *cf.* the technique available to liquidator appointed by the court to seek an order vesting the property in the liquidator himself, who thereby becomes a new occupier: *Re Fir View Furniture Co. Ltd, The Times*, February 8, 1971, *per* Brightman J., and see the Insolvency Act 1986, s. 145(1).

[13] See Insolvency Act 1986, s. 233(5) for a description of the relevant utilities whose services are covered by the section.

appointed.[14] Questions arise as to the effective date where there are two dates potentially available (*e.g.* in the case of a concurrent administrative receivership and liquidation). Is the effective date that of the appointment of the administrative receiver or the date of the liquidation? And, where there are concurrent office-holders, is it relevant which of the office-holders requests or concurs in the request for supplies? It is suggested that the effective date is that relating to the appointment of the office-holder in question, save that, where a composition or scheme is approved after the date of his appointment, the effective date is the date of such approval.

The legitimate interests of the supplier in getting paid are protected, **5–006** in that the utility may make it a condition of giving a supply that the office-holder personally guarantees the payment of any new charges.[15] To this extent, a hive-down still carries the advantage that no guarantee by the administrative receiver can be required. But a hive-down is unlikely to be worthwhile if undertaken simply for this reason and in practice a receiver will always see to it that the post-hive-down debts of the subsidiary are paid, if only to avoid the risk of facing an allegation of fraudulent trading by himself or wrongful trading by the subsidiary's directors.

3. DELIVERY AND SEIZURE OF PROPERTY

Under section 234 of the Insolvency Act 1986 an administrative receiver, **5–007** as an office-holder,[16] can apply to the court for an order that any person[17] who has in his possession any property, books, papers or records to which the company appears to be entitled should give those items up to the administrative receiver. No specific sanctions are prescribed in the Act to deal with non-compliance. The administrative receiver has a lien on the property or proceeds of sale for expenses incurred in connection with the seizure or disposal.

The section applies both to items actually belonging to the company **5–008** and also to those the subject-matter of a dispute as to ownership.[18] The court can, in proceedings under this section, decide questions of title.[19]

---

[14] *ibid.*, s. 233(4)(b).

[15] *ibid.*, s. 233(2)(a).

[16] See Insolvency Rules 1986, Pt. 7, on the detailed procedure for an application by an office holder.

[17] This may include a liquidator appointed prior to an administrative receiver: *Re First Express Ltd* [1991] B.C.C. 782.

[18] See *Re London Iron & Steel Co. Ltd* [1990] B.C.L.C. 372 where the court held that it had power to deal with an application under s. 234 for an order that property be handed over to an administrative receiver even though there was a dispute as to its ownership which could have been the subject of separate legal proceedings. It now appears that the courts are readily prepared to address questions of disputed ownership on an application under s. 234: see *Euro Commercial Leasing Ltd v. Cartwright & Lewis* [1995] B.C.C. 830 (a solicitors' lien); *Re Cosslett (Contractors) Ltd* [1998] Ch. 495 (plant on a construction site). The court has no power to determine ownership where the question of ownership falls to be determined by a foreign court: *Re Leyland DAF Ltd* [1994] B.C.C. 166.

[19] *ibid.*

The court would be unlikely to make an order under this provision in favour of an administrative receiver unless the items involved fall within the property charged,[20] are needed to support the debenture-holder's title or are otherwise required to carry out the administrative receiver's duties and functions.

5–009   Where an administrative receiver has reasonable grounds for believing that he is entitled to seize or dispose of any property and does so, he now has special statutory protection as an office-holder under section 234(4) of the Insolvency Act 1986. If it turns out that the property seized or disposed of did not belong to the company, the administrative receiver will not be liable to any person in respect of any loss or damage resulting from the seizure or disposal except in so far as it is caused by his negligence. This applies whether or not the administrative receiver has acted following a court order under section 234(2). The protection afforded by these provisions is limited to tangible property although the administrative receiver may have recourse to other defences in any action for wrongful interference with contractual relations.[21]

5–010   Applications under section 234 should normally be made on notice, and an application without notice can only be justified if two conditions are met:

> (i) notice to the respondent would be likely to cause injustice to the applicant as a result of delay or because of action that would be taken before the hearing; and
> (ii) any damage that the respondent might suffer can be compensated by a cross-undertaking or the risk of loss to the respondent which cannot be compensated is clearly outweighed by the risk of injustice to the applicant.[22]

Section 234 only allows an office-holder to gain possession of an item in specie. It does not form the statutory basis for an action in conversion by the office-holder.[23]

4. CO-OPERATION FROM DIRECTORS, ETC.

5–011 Under section 235(2) of the Insolvency Act 1986, an office-holder (including an administrative receiver) may require, without a court order, that directors and certain others attend upon him and/or give him such information about the company as he may reasonably require. The

---

[20] See *Re First Express Ltd*, [1991] B.C.C. 782.
[21] See *Welsh Development Agency v. Export Finance Co. Ltd* [1992] B.C.C. 270, CA at 287–288 where the Court rejected the receivers' defence to an action for wrongful interference on the basis that subss. 234(3) and (4) were inapplicable to choses in action but held that the receivers' conduct as agents of the company was immune on the basis of the rule in *Said v. Butt* [1920] 2 K.B. 497. The Court of Appeal concluded that the references to seizure meant that ss. 234(3) and 234(4) only applied to tangibles.
[22] See *Re First Express Ltd* [1991] B.C.C. 782 at 785E.
[23] *Smith (administrator of Cosslett (Contractors) Ltd) v. Bridgend County Borough Council* [2000] 1 B.C.L.C. 775 at 787b, CA.

persons subject to the requirements of this provision include not only all present and past officers of the company, but also certain promoters, and certain persons "in the employment of" the company.[24] The term "employment" is given an expanded definition by section 235(3)(c), so as to include "employment under a contract for services". This will accordingly include professional advisers to the company.

Section 235 does not provide any guidance as to how a court should **5–012** determine the reasonableness of any requirement by the administrative receiver. By analogy with cases decided under section 236 (see below) it is suggested that what may reasonably be required must involve a consideration of what is required for the efficient conduct of the receivership. The test is what is "reasonably required" not what is "needed", and the onus of showing that a requirement is a reasonable one will be on the office-holder. In most cases the views of the administrative receiver will be entitled to a good deal of weight.[25]

Failure to heed the office-holder's request without reasonable excuse **5–013** is a criminal offence punishable by the imposition of a fine.[26] A failure to respond can also be the subject of an application to the court to compel compliance,[27] or can be a ground for an application under section 236 (below). As an administrative receiver is not an officer of the court subject to the general control of the court, there would not appear to be any obvious mechanism for the recipient of a request under section 235 to seek an order that an unreasonable request be withdrawn, short of commencing an action for a declaration.[28] The office-holder's unreasonable conduct in making a request will be a defence to any application to enforce the request or to a criminal charge.[29]

A person who is subject to a request under section 235 would have no **5–014** defence to an application to enforce compliance or to criminal liability under the section if he refused to respond to questions simply because he feared that he might incriminate himself by his answers. This is because section 235 implicitly abrogates the privilege against self-incrimination.[30] Such criminal liability for non-disclosure would not itself

---

[24] Insolvency Act 1986, s. 235(3), (4).

[25] In the context of s. 236 of the Insolvency Act 1986, see, *e.g. Sasea Finance Ltd v. KPMG* [1998] B.C.C. 216 at 220F and *Re Atlantic Computers plc* [1998] B.C.C. 200 at 209D, *per* Robert Walker J. The further proceedings in the *Sasea Finance* case at [1998] 1 B.C.L.C. 559, indicate the limits to the possible use of s. 236 for tactical purposes in litigation.

[26] Insolvency Act 1986, ss. 235(5) and 430 and Sched. 10.

[27] See Insolvency Rules 1986, r. 7.20 and *Re Wallace Smith Trust Co. Ltd* [1992] B.C.C. 707.

[28] It is thought that the note in Sealy and Milman, *The Annotated Guide to the Insolvency Legislation* (5th ed.), p. 271, to the effect that an unreasonable request under s. 235 could be subjected to the general power of the court to control an office-holder, is too wide. It does not distinguish between office-holders who are also officers of the court, and therefore subject to its general supervisory jurisdiction, and other office-holders, such as administrative receivers, who are not officers of the court nor subject to that supervisory jurisdiction. See above, para. 5–02.

[29] See Insolvency Act 1986, s. 235(5) where liability depends on failure to meet the office-holder's request "without reasonable excuse".

[30] *Bishopsgate Investment Ltd v. Maxwell* [1993] Ch. 1

infringe the European Convention on Human Rights,[31] but the later use of information obtained might do so.[32]

5–015 As an office holder, the administrative receiver of a company has a duty to report to the Secretary of State on the conduct of the company's directors if the company has become insolvent.[33] The Secretary of State also has powers to compel disclosure of information acquired by an office-holder.[34] Consequently, the administrative receiver can disclose to the Secretary of State information or documents obtained under section 235, so that, for example, the Secretary of State can determine whether disqualification proceedings should be brought against the directors concerned. This is so even if the office holder has given an assurance that information or documents will only be used for the office-holder's own, limited, purposes.[35] So while an administrative receiver may, in his discretion, give undertakings of confidentiality in respect of information obtained or to be obtained by him under section 235, he cannot be required to give such undertakings,[36] and he cannot give an assurance that information will be withheld from anyone to whom he must report the information, or anyone who can by law require the information of him.[37]

5–016 The positive duty of co-operation in section 235 is underpinned by the more extensive inquisitorial powers outlined below.

5. EXAMINATION ON OATH OF DIRECTORS, ETC.

5–017 Section 236 of the Insolvency Act 1986 confers on an office-holder "an extraordinary power to assist him in obtaining information about the company's affairs",[38] a power also described as "drastic and far-reaching".[39] Under the section, an administrative receiver may, as an office-holder, seek an order from the court for the attendance of any officer of the company, any person known or suspected of having any property of the company or supposed to be indebted to it, or any person the court thinks capable of giving information concerning the promotion, formation, business, dealings, affairs or property of the company. Also under the section, such a person may be ordered to submit an affidavit

---

[31] See *Fayed v. UK* (1994) 18 E.H.R.R. 93 and *Saunders v. U.K.* [1997] B.C.C. 872 on investigations under Part XIV of the Companies Act 1985.

[32] *ibid.*

[33] Company Directors Disqualification Act 1986, s. 7(3).

[34] *ibid.*, s. 7(4).

[35] See *Re Polly Peck International plc* [1994] B.C.C. 15. The case concerned an administrator, rather than an administrative receiver, but the reasoning is equally applicable to an administrative receiver, being based on the duties and responsibilities of office-holders in general under the Company Directors Disqualification Act 1986.

[36] *Re Barlow Clowes Gilt Managers Ltd* [1992] Ch. 208; *McIsaac, Petitioners; Joint Liquidators of First Tokyo Index Trust Ltd* [1994] B.C.C. 410.

[37] In *Re Arrows Ltd* (No. 4) [1995] 2 A.C. 75 at 102–3, *per* Lord Browne-Wilkinson.

[38] In *Re Castle New Homes Ltd* [1979] 1 W.L.R. 1075 at 1080G, *per* Slade J, referring to s. 268 of the Companies Act 1948, one of the statutory predecessors to s. 236 of the Insolvency Act 1986. See also *Joint Administrators of British & Commonwealth Holdings plc v. Spicer & Oppenheim* [1993] A.C. 426 at 439D, *per* Lord Slynn.

[39] *Re Rolls Razor Ltd* (No. 2) [1970] Ch. 576 at 583D, *per* Megarry J., addressing s. 268 of the Companies Act 1948.

to the court containing an account of his dealings with the company or to produce any books, papers or records in his possession or under his control relating to the company or to its promotion. An order for production of documents may be made even if the person in possession of the documents holds a valid lien[40] although any order for production will be without prejudice to the lien. A person summoned under this procedure can also be examined in private on oath, either orally or by interrogatories.[41]

Section 237(3) of the Insolvency Act 1986 provides that the court may **5-018** order a person to be examined in any part of the United Kingdom where he may be for the time being, or in any place outside England and Wales. In a few cases, an examination overseas may be more convenient than requiring the proposed examinee to attend in England and Wales, with travelling and hotel expenses and the possible need for an interpreter.[42]

Where a person summoned to appear fails to do so without reason- **5-019** able excuse or where there are reasonable grounds for believing that he is about to, or has, absconded with a view to avoiding an appearance before the court, the court may issue a warrant for that person's arrest and for the seizure of any books, papers, records, money or goods in that person's possession.[43] Express provision is made in the Insolvency Rules

---

[40] *Re Aveling Barford Ltd* [1989] 1 W.L.R. 360 at 364–365: according to Hoffmann J. a lien was irrelevant in an action by the administrative receiver for production as between himself and the solicitor since the lien could not affect third parties and s. 236 had conferred third party status on an administrative receiver ("a solicitor's lien is simply a right to retain his clients' documents as against the client and persons representing him" *per* Lord Lindley M.R. in *Re Hawkes* [1898] 2 Ch. 1 at 7). Although administrative receivers, unlike other office-holders, cannot rely on s. 246 of the Insolvency Act 1986 to render the lien unenforceable, the availability of an order for possession effectively renders the solicitor's lien substantially worthless.

[41] Insolvency Act, s. 237(4). Insolvency Rules 1986, r. 9.4, set down the procedure for hearings. In particular, a full transcript must be provided and approved by the person giving evidence. *cf.* Insolvency Act 1986, s. 133, which involves a public examination of officers or others before the court.

[42] Insolvency Rules 1986, r.12.12, deals with the mode of service on any person who is not in England and Wales. The court's jurisdiction in relation to persons residing abroad is discussed below in Chap. 25. In *McIsaac, Petitioners; Joint Liquidators of First Tokyo Index Trust Ltd* [1994] B.C.C. 410, the Court of Session (Outer House) rejected a submission than an order under s. 236 for oral examination and the production of documents could not be made against a person resident in New York. In addition, it is clear that the court has jurisdiction to make an order under s. 236 for the production of documents relating to an overseas company which is being wound up in England, even though the documents are held abroad by a third party. However, in the exercise of its discretion under the section, the court will be mindful of (i) the possibility that disclosure might expose the respondent, or its officers or employees, to liability under foreign law, (ii) the need to respect the sovereignty of other jurisdictions, and (iii) whether the order is likely to be effective. See *Re Mid East Trading Ltd* [1997] 3 All E.R. 481, Ch.D., affirmed [1998] 1 All E.R. 577, CA.

[43] Insolvency Act 1986, s. 236(4) and (5). The court may even, in a serious case, seek to restrain a person from leaving the jurisdiction under the powers in the Supreme Court Act 1981, until he has complied with his obligations: *Re Oriental Credit Ltd* [1988] Ch. 204 and *Morris v. Murjani* [1996] 1 W.L.R. 848, CA. In an appropriate case, for example, where a prospective examinee had previously failed to co-operate with the liquidators of the company concerned, the court may require security from the examinee as a condition that he be allowed to leave the country, even though he is not a British national: see *Re BCCI (No. 7)* [1994] 1 B.C.L.C. 455.

1986 for the tender of conduct money to a proposed examinee[44] and it may presumably be a reasonable excuse for non-appearance that no conduct money has been tendered.

5–020 Where it appears to the court from any evidence obtained under this provision that "any person" has in his possession any property of the company or is indebted to the company, the court may order delivery up of the property or payment of the sum involved to the administrative receiver as office-holder.[45] This part of this provision appears to have been derived from section 25 of the Bankruptcy Act 1914. In practice, such summary orders are rare and should only be made against the examinee himself on the basis of a clear admission.[46] The court should not use this provision to determine title to an asset without giving a hearing to anyone making an adverse claim to that asset. To do otherwise might constitute a breach of Article 6 of the European Convention on Human Rights (the right to a fair trial), which the courts must now uphold under sections 3 and 6 of the Human Rights Act 1998. Even when faced with an application for interim relief, the 1998 Act means that the court must take account of Article 1 of the First Protocol to the Convention (the right to peaceful enjoyment of possessions, subject to due process of law).

5–021 The court's powers under section 236 of the Insolvency Act 1986 are very wide, and even bind the Crown, so that information may be obtained under the section from government officials.[47] Nevertheless the powers are limited by other statutory obligations of confidentiality and non-disclosure. So, in *Re Galileo Group Ltd*,[48] Lightman J. held that the court's jurisdiction to order disclosure under section 236 of the Insolvency Act 1986 was implicitly limited by section 82 of the Banking Act 1987, which requires that information received for the (regulatory) purposes of the Banking Act be kept confidential, unless the relevant consents to disclosure are obtained. He therefore held that the court could not order disclosure of documents containing information within the scope of section 82, and that while the court had jurisdiction to order disclosure of redacted copies of the documents from which the confidential information had been excised,[49] it was inappropriate to exercise that jurisdiction in the circumstances, given that (i) making such an order might undermine the protection afforded by section 82 and thereby prejudice the free flow of information to the Bank of England, which was vital for the performance of the function which it then had as regulator of the banking system; (ii) framing and performing such an

---

[44] Insolvency Rules 1986, r. 9.6(4).
[45] Insolvency Act 1986, ss. 237(1) and (2).
[46] See *Re A Debtor (No. 26 of 1982)* (1983) 126 S.J. 783; *The Times*, October 25, 1983.
[47] *Soden v. Burns* [1996] 3 All E.R. 967.
[48] [1999] Ch. 100.
[49] In this case, any redaction would have been undertaken by the recipient of information, because of its duties in relation to the information. Note also *Soden v. Burns* [1996] 3 All E.R. 967, 986b–c, *per* Robert Walker J., where, in the absence of such duties, any redaction was to be undertaken at the behest of the examinee in question, rather than by the recipient of the information.

order might well be very difficult; (iii) there was a risk that failure to remove all embargoed material might constitute a criminal offence; and (iv) there was a risk that that the redacted document might prove misleading.

6. THE APPROACH OF THE COURTS TO MAKING ORDERS UNDER SECTION 236

The position under section 236 was explained by Buckley J in *Re Rolls* **5–022** *Razor Ltd*[50] in a passage subsequently approved by the Court of Appeal in *Re Esal (Commodities) Ltd*[51] and by the House of Lords in the leading case of *British & Commonwealth Holdings plc v. Spicer & Oppenheim*[52]:

> "The powers conferred by section [236] are powers directed to enabling the court to help a liquidator to discover the truth of the circumstances connected with the affairs of the company, information of trading, dealings, and so forth, in order that the liquidator may be able, as effectively as possible, and, I think, with as little expense as possible to complete his function as liquidator, to put the affairs of the company in order and to carry out the liquidation in all its various aspects, including, of course, the getting in of any assets of the company available in the liquidation."

In the same case the House of Lords rejected a suggestion that had **5–023** arisen in earlier cases that the powers of the court under section 236 might be limited to assisting the office-holder to reconstitute the state of knowledge of the company.[53]

> "The wording of the section contains no express limitation to documents which can be said to be part of a process of reconstituting the company's state of knowledge. The words are quite general . . . nor do I see any support in earlier judgments which may have been cited to us relating to the predecessors of section 236 or to comparable sections for such a limitation to 'reconstituting the company's knowledge' ".[54]

Before making any order under section 236, the office-holder will need to **5–024** prove to the satisfaction of the court that the information he seeks under the proposed order is in fact reasonably required.[55] In the usual case his views will be given great weight, and he is under no duty to make out the

---

[50] [1968] 3 All E.R. 698 at 700.
[51] (1988) 4 B.C.C. 475 at 480.
[52] [1993] A.C. 426.
[53] See, e.g. *In re Rolls Razor Ltd* (No. 2) [1970] Ch. 576, 591–2, *per* Megarry J. and *Cloverbay Ltd v. BCCI* [1991] Ch. 90, 102, *per* Browne-Wilkinson V.-C.
[54] *Per* Lord Slynn [1993] A.C. 426 at 437B-D.
[55] The test is one of "reasonable requirement", not "absolute need": see *Re Atlantic Computers plc* [1998] B.C.C. 200, and *Joint Liquidators of Sasea Finance Ltd v. KPMG* [1998] B.C.C. 216.

requirement in such detail as would be expected in, for example, an application for specific disclosure in the context of ongoing litigation.[56]

5–025   When considering the exercise of its discretion under section 236, the court may also be interested in the steps taken by the administrative receiver before applying to the court. Unless there are factors negativing this (for instance, cases of great urgency), an administrative receiver ought in most cases to seek co-operation under section 235 of the Insolvency Act 1986 where a proposed examinee comes within that section, and in other cases may be well advised to submit a questionnaire seeking written answers. Although under the old bankruptcy and winding-up provisions information was often sought first by means of a questionnaire, it is entirely a matter for the court's discretion whether the trustee or liquidator is required to submit a questionnaire before being granted an order for an affidavit or an examination on oath.[57] In practice, persons of whom misconduct is suspected, usually directors or other insiders, will often not be allowed the advance notice of inquiries that a questionnaire would give, whereas parties who have no likely motive for concealing information will often only be requested to answer a questionnaire, and may only be examined if the answers to the questionnaire prove unsatisfactory.[58]

5–026   As section 236(2) confers a general discretion on the court,[59] any question concerning the exercise of that discretion will involve the court in a balancing exercise.[60] On the one hand, the court will wish to help the office-holder discharge his functions efficiently, expeditiously, and in the interest of creditors, recognising that the office-holder is usually a stranger to the relevant events. On the other, the courts have long been aware of the potential for oppression in use of such powers,[61] and have sought to limit that potential through their approach to the exercise of discretion under the section.

[56] In relation to the matters stated in this paragraph, see In *Re John T. Rhodes Ltd* [1987] B.C.L.C. 77 at 79h, *per* Hoffmann J.; Insolvency Rules 1986, r. 9.2(1), and *Joint Liquidators of Sasea Finance Ltd v. KPMG* [1998] B.C.C. 216.

[57] *Re Norton Warburg Holdings Ltd* [1983] B.C.L.C. 235 and *Re Embassy Art Products* [1988] B.C.L.C. 1.

[58] See *Re Norton Warburg Holdings Ltd* [1983] B.C.L.C. 235 (detailed written questions were required since the examinees had indicated that they would provide all reasonable assistance) and *Re Embassy Art Products* [1988] B.C.L.C. 1 (where no prior notice of questioning was required). *cf. Re Rolls Razor (No. 2)* [1970] Ch. 576 (no need for prior questioning where suspicious circumstances existed) and *House of Spring Gardens Ltd v. Waite* [1985] J.P.L. 173 (cross-examination in proceedings for a freezing injunction as to assets without prior notification of area of questioning).

[59] *British & Commonwealth Holdings plc v. Spicer and Oppenheim* [1993] A.C. 426 at 437A–440A, *per* Lord Slynn. See also Lord Woolf's judgment in the Court of Appeal in the same case, [1992] Ch. 342 at 392–3.

[60] The need for a balancing exercise is repeated in numerous cases: see, *e.g. Cloverbay v. BCCI* [1991] Ch. 90; *British & Commonwealth Holdings plc v. Spicer and Oppenheim* [1993] A.C. 426; *Re BCCI (No. 7)* [1994] 1 B.C.L.C. 455; *Re Bishopsgate Investment Management Ltd* (No. 2) [1994] B.C.C. 732; *Re Maxwell Communications Corporation plc* [1994] B.C.C. 741; *Re BCCI (No. 12)* [1997] 1 B.C.L.C. 526; *Re Atlantic Computers plc* [1998] B.C.C. 200; *Joint Liquidators of Sasea Finance Ltd v. KPMG* [1998] B.C.C. 216.

[61] Such powers date back to s. 115 of the Companies Act 1862: see, *e.g. Re North Australia Territory Co.* (1890) 45 Ch.D. 87 at 93, *per* Bowen LJ; and *Re Castle New Homes Ltd* [1979] 1 W.L.R. 1075 at 1089G, *per* Slade J.

In each case, the court will take into account several factors when **5–027** exercising its discretion in relation to what is an extraordinary power. For example, the case for making an order against an officer of the company will usually be stronger than against a third party because of the fiduciary duties and the statutory duty under section 235(2)(a) owed by the former. Similarly, the court will take into account the width of the order sought and the amount of work involved in complying with the order.[62]

Although in many cases the reasonable requirements of the office- **5–028** holder will not extend beyond that contained in the company's records and the knowledge of its officers, in some cases the interest of creditors will be substantial (particularly in the case of some of the spectacular corporate failures of the 1990's) and the reasonable requirements of the office-holder will be treated as extending to information which the company itself may never have actually possessed.[63] The production of such documents will be ordered where this will enable the office-holder to perform his functions properly.[64]

7. SECTION 236 AND PENDING LITIGATION

One particularly important aspect of the balancing exercise the court **5–029** undertakes when faced with an application under section 236 is ensuring that the section "is not to be used for giving a litigant (just because he is an office-holder) special advantages in ordinary litigation".[65] Such an unfair advantage is regarded as one of the main forms of oppression to which an order under section 236 may give rise.[66] The court will have regard both to the reasonable requirements of the officer-holder to carry out his task, and the need to avoid making an order which is unnecess-ary, unreasonable or oppressive to the person who is the subject of the order, because it would give the office-holder an unfair advantage over him in litigation.

Under the pre-1986 winding-up provisions, these restrictions usually **5–030** meant that, where a liquidator had either begun or made a firm decision to begin proceedings against the proposed examinee, it would be rare for

---

[62] See [1993] A.C. 426 at 440H–441A *per* Lord Slynn: whilst recognising that the order placed an extensive and inconvenient burden on the auditors and may lay them open to further claims, he stated that these were only factors in the balancing exercise. The auditors' argument that such an order would result in a flood of similar applications was dismissed. In any event, it was not disputed that the examinee was entitled to an order for the costs of compliance.

[63] See *Re Brook, Martin & Co. (Nominees) Ltd* [1993] B.C.L.C. 328.

[64] See *per* Woolf L.J. in the Court of Appeal in *British & Commonwealth*, above, at 390: "the reason for the existence of the powers was to assist office holders to achieve the relevant administrative purposes identified in s. 8(3) of the Act".

[65] *Re Atlantic Computers plc* [1998] B.C.C. 200 at 208F–209A, *per* Robert Walker J., citing In *Re North Australian Territory Co.* (1890) 45 Ch.D. 87; In *Re Bletchley Boat Co. Ltd* [1974] 1 W.L.R. 630; In *Re Castle New Homes Ltd* [1979] 1 W.L.R. 1075 and *Re Esal (Commodities) Ltd* [1990] B.C.C. 708. See also *Cloverbay Ltd v. BCCI* [1991] Ch. 90 at 102E, *per* Browne-Wilkinson V.-C.

[66] *Re BCCI (No. 12)* [1997] 1 B.C.L.C. 526.

him to obtain an order for examination.[67] This approach was known as the "Rubicon Test": "a rule of thumb under which relief under section 236 would be withheld if office-holders had already commenced proceedings against, or definitely decided (mentally crossed the Rubicon) to proceed against the proposed witness [*i.e.* examinee]".[68] An order might have been granted, however, if the examination avoided questions connected with the proceedings.[69]

5–031 Subsequently, in proceedings brought under the current legislation, the Court of Appeal has recognised that a firm decision by an office-holder to bring an action against the person to be examined is not a bar to the grant of an order, although it may be an important factor to take into account on the question of discretion.[70] Nevertheless, recent cases have indicated that the old "Rubicon Test" had at least a "germ of truth" in it,[71] and the courts remain unlikely to make an order under section 236 if the office-holder of the company in question would thereby gain an unfair advantage in litigation.[72] Consequently, when litigation by, or involving, the office-holder is on foot, or imminent, the courts are very unwilling to make any order under section 236 against another party to that litigation, or against witnesses in the action, which might give the office-holder such an unfair advantage,[73] though orders have been made against a background of pending actions involving the office-holder.[74]

5–032 So, for example, in *Joint Liquidators of Sasea Finance Ltd v. KPMG*,[75] the liquidators made an application under section 236 against the former auditors of the company, seeking disclosure of documents. By the time

---

[67] *Re Castle New Homes Ltd* [1979] 1 W.L.R. 1075, *per* Slade J.

[68] *Re Atlantic Computers plc* [1998] B.C.C. 200 at 208E, *per* Robert Walker J.

[69] *Re Franks, ex p. Gittins.* [1892] 1 Q.B. 646, *per* Vaughan Williams J.

[70] *Cloverbay v. BCCI* [1991] Ch. 90, CA; *Re John T. Rhodes Ltd* [1987] B.C.L.C. 77. Browne-Wilkinson V.-C. in *Cloverbay* specifically noted that the subjective nature of the office-holder's precise intentions was an inappropriate basis for determining whether an order should be available. The Court consequently recommended a more "case-by-case", empirical approach to making orders under s. 236.

[71] *Re Bishopsgate Investment Management (No. 2)* [1994] B.C.C. 732 at 739E, *per* Hoffmann J; *Re BCCI (No. 12)* [1997] 1 B.C.L.C. 526 at 538–9, *per* Robert Walker J.; *Re Atlantic Computers plc* [1998] B.C.C. 200 at 208F, *per* Robert Walker J.

[72] *Re Atlantic Computers plc* [1998] B.C.C. 200 at 208F–209A, *per* Robert Walker J., citing In *Re North Australian Territory Co.* (1890) 45 Ch.D. 87; In *Re Bletchley Boat Co. Ltd* [1974] 1 W.L.R. 630; In *Re Castle New Homes Ltd* [1979] 1 W.L.R. 1075 and *Re Esal (Commodities) Ltd* [1990] B.C.C. 708. See also *Cloverbay Ltd v. BCCI* [1991] Ch. 90 at 102E, *per* Browne-Wilkinson V.-C.

[73] See *Re J.N. Taylor Finance Pty Ltd* [1998] B.P.I.R. 347 at 369F–370C, *per* Evans-Lombe J. This was a case on s. 426 of the Insolvency Act 1986 (assistance to foreign insolvency courts) which looked at the authorities on s. 236 for the purpose of deciding whether to make an order under s. 426 in aid of the Supreme Court of South Australia, which, under Part 5.9 of the Australian Corporations Law, had directed the oral examination of various people concerned in the collapse of the company and a related entity. The case was overruled by the Court of Appeal in *Re Southern Equities Corporation Ltd* [2000] B.C.C. 123, on the basis that the cases concerning s. 236 should not be used to determine whether a foreign investigative procedure (such as the Australian procedure under Part 5.9 of the Corporations Law) is so oppressive that an order in aid of that procedure under s. 426 should be refused. The Court of Appeal did not address the English approach to s. 236.

[74] *Soden v. Burns* [1996] 3 All E.R. 967. See below, para. 5–038.

[75] [1998] B.C.C. 216.

of their application, the liquidators had issued a "protective writ" against the auditors, to stop limitation periods running, alleging professional negligence. Robert Walker J. held that, although there was some prejudice to KPMG in granting the liquidators' application, because it might give information to the liquidators earlier than otherwise, the balance weighed in favour of making the order sought, as there was considerable public interest in ascertaining the truth about a very substantial corporate collapse. Of significance to the court in making its decision were the facts that the litigation was still at a very early stage, and that only negligence, and not fraud or dishonesty, had been alleged against KPMG. The fact that the examination could render the evidence of the examinee open to scrutiny at an earlier point in time than would be the case in normal litigation was a factor, but not an over-riding factor, to be taken into account in determining whether or not the order would be oppressive.

When a further application was made in the same proceedings,[76] by **5–033** which the office-holders sought an order that the respondents answer interrogatories, Scott V.-C. refused the application. He deplored the tactic of issuing a protective writ and then seeking to use section 236. He also indicated that trying to use section 236 to extract explanations or justifications for known facts in the context of pending litigation, rather than to discover facts, was an unacceptable tactic, and any such application would be refused.

If the office-holder has the benefit of extensive disclosure of docu- **5–034** ments in connection with an action already commenced, the court may decline to grant an order under section 236. On the other hand, the mere fact that proceedings had already been successfully taken against a person involved with the company will not of itself make an examination oppressive, vexatious or unfair.[77] Nor does the principle against being sued twice about the same matter apply in these circumstances since the grant of an order does not necessarily mean that the office-holder will be commencing further proceedings.[78]

8. OTHER FORMS OF PROTECTION FROM OPPRESSION UNDER SECTION 236

As well as giving a proposed examinee protection from oppression by **5–035** carefully considering whether an order under the section should be made at all, a court may also choose the particular type of order it makes with a view to minimising any prejudice. The courts regard an order for oral examination as the most potentially oppressive order they can make under section 236. An order to swear an affidavit deposing to the affairs of the company in question is less likely to be oppressive,[79] and least

---

[76] *Re Sasea Finance Ltd* (in liq) [1998] 1 B.C.L.C. 559.
[77] *Re John T. Rhodes Ltd* [1987] B.C.L.C. 77.
[78] *ibid.*
[79] *Soden v. Burns* [1996] 3 All E.R. 967 at 985e, *per* Robert Walker J.

likely to be oppressive is an order for the production of documents relating to the dealings or affairs of the company.[80] Consequently, a court may be more willing to make an order for the production of documents than for oral examination.[81] Furthermore, the court has jurisdiction to order disclosure of redacted documents, where ordering disclosure of the unedited document would be unlawful or undesirable.[82] The court may also direct the staged disclosure of documents, where the bulk of the documents to be disclosed is very great, in order to minimise the risk of oppression and prejudice by disruption, stress or expense. When considering such factors, the court will have regard to the respondent's resources, as well as the requirements of the office-holder.[83]

5–036   Further, where the court is considering an application under section 236 for an order directing disclosure of evidence previously given by some third party to the person who is the subject of the proposed order, either the court can refuse to make the order without first hearing objections from the third party, or it can impose a condition that the third party be notified of the order and given the opportunity to object to disclosure within a specified time.

5–037   So, in *Morris v. Director of the Serious Fraud Office*,[84] Nicholls V.-C. indicated that, save in exceptional cases, an office-holder was not entitled to use section 236 to obtain documents from the Serious Fraud Office, which the SFO had obtained from a third party, without giving the third party (in that case, a firm of accountants) an opportunity to object to the production of those documents on the basis that such production would be oppressive.

5–038   In *Soden v. Burns*,[85] inspectors had been appointed by the Department of Trade and Industry under section 432 of the Companies Act 1985 to investigate the collapse of Atlantic Computers plc, and they had received evidence from third parties. The administrators of Atlantic applied under section 236 for disclosure of the transcripts of that evidence, which they admitted they might use in pending civil litigation. The court ordered disclosure of the transcripts, but not of documents mentioned in them, on condition that each witness who had given evidence was notified of such disclosure, and was given the opportunity to apply to set aside the order in so far as it affected him. The court also considered what might be done about citations in a transcript, which were attributed or attributable to some other person than the person giving evidence. If the citations were important, the person cited should be asked for his views about disclosure. If the citations were less important, they might be obliterated, or certified unimportant by counsel for the DTI Inspectors.

---

[80] *Cloverbay Ltd v. BCCI* [1991] Ch. 90 at 103C, *per* Browne-Wilkinson V.-C.; *Re British & Commonwealth Holdings plc* [1992] B.C.C. 165 at 185, *per* Ralph Gibson L.J.
[81] See *Re J.N. Taylor Finance Pty Ltd* [1998] BPIR 347, and the comments on that case in footnote 73 above.
[82] *Re Galileo Group Ltd* [1999] Ch. 100.
[83] *Re BCCI (No. 12)* [1997] 1 B.C.L.C. 526.
[84] [1993] Ch. 372.
[85] *Soden v. Burns* [1996] 3 All E.R. 967.

9. THE PARTICULAR POSITION OF AN ADMINISTRATIVE RECEIVER

The present section 236 of the Insolvency Act 1986 is largely based upon **5–039** similar powers formerly only applying in the case of bankruptcy[86] and winding-up.[87] In argument on the exercise of the court's discretion, reference is frequently made to authorities dealing with those earlier provisions. It is questionable whether applications by administrative receivers under section 236 should be treated in exactly the same way as similar applications in relation to a company by its liquidators.[88]

Though an administrative receiver is an office-holder under the **5–040** current insolvency legislation, with all that implies,[89] the fact remains that an administrative receiver acts principally for the benefit of the debenture-holder who appointed him, whereas a liquidator or an administrator acts for the benefit of all the creditors of a company, or at least a broad class of them. In winding-up cases under the statutory forerunners of section 236, a party other than a liquidator who sought an examination of this kind had to show that it would be for the general benefit of the winding-up, rather than for the personal advantage of the applicant.[90] Equally, in the old bankruptcy cases, the applicant was said to be required to show some probable benefit to the creditors.[91] Yet an administrative receiver may well wish to use section 236 for the particular benefit of his appointor, for example, by using the section to obtain information which is then to be disclosed to his appointor. This issue arises frequently, and is often compounded by the fact that (at least in the early days of the receivership) the same firm of solicitors will often act for both the administrative receiver and the debenture-holder who appointed him.[92]

Before the concept of the administrative receiver was created, and the **5–041** powers under section 236 were conferred on him as an office-holder, it was said that a debenture-holder was entitled, as against the receiver appointed by him, to be put in possession of all information concerning the receivership which was available to the receiver.[93] It is doubtful

---

[86] Bankruptcy Act 1914, s. 25.

[87] Companies Act 1985, s. 561.

[88] Or now, by its administrators.

[89] See above, para. 5–01.

[90] *Re Imperial Continental Water Corp* (1886) 33 Ch.D. 314, CA and *Re Embassy Art Products Ltd* [1988] B.C.L.C. 1.

[91] *ex p. Nicholson, Re Willson* (1880) 14 Ch.D. 243.

[92] Even if the debenture-holder is content that it should not receive confidential information, the examinee may not be happy that an assurance to this effect from the solicitor is workable in practice. Moreover, if information disclosed in the examination is obtained by the debenture-holder from another source, it may be difficult for the solicitor to disprove the suspicions that will inevitably arise. It is not a satisfactory solution to try to erect a "Chinese wall" by designating one partner in a firm to deal with the s. 236 application by the administrative receiver, and designating another partner to advise the debenture holder: see *Re A Firm of Solicitors* [1992] Q.B. 959; *Re a Firm of Solicitors* [1997] Ch. 1; and *Prince Jefri Bolkiah v. KPMG* [1999] 2 A.C. 222.

[93] See *per* Fox L.J. in *Gomba Holdings UK Ltd v. Minories Finance Ltd* (1989) 5 B.C.C. 27 at 29F.

whether this statement is directly applicable to information obtained by an administrative receiver as an office-holder using his powers under sections 235 or 236. While the relationship between an administrative receiver and the debenture-holder who appointed him is clearly a close one, it is suggested that the overriding principle is that disclosure of information obtained by an administrative receiver under sections 235 or 236 to a debenture-holder will only be permissible where such disclosure will assist the beneficial conduct of the receivership.[94]

5–042　In certain cases the administrative receiver might claim that the receivership would be assisted by his disclosing such information to the debenture-holder, either for the purposes of securing additional funding for the conduct of litigation by the company in receivership against the directors of the company or its professional advisers, or in order to facilitate the making of a direct claim by the debenture-holder against such persons,[95] in the hope that such a claim might reduce the claim of the debenture-holder against the company, with a possible knock-on effect for the benefit of unsecured creditors. These issues have been raised in two decisions, one in England and one in Scotland, with differing results.

5–043　Chronologically, the first case is the decision of Harman J. in *Re a Company (No. 005374 of 1993)*.[96] In that case, administrative receivers sought leave to disclose to their appointor bank, information obtained under section 236 which appeared to show that a director of the company had misappropriated a VAT refund in breach of his duties to the company. Harman J. held that he had a discretion to grant leave on two grounds: first, if the disclosure was "for the purposes of the office which the office-holders hold" or second, if disclosure is "otherwise justified by the balance of considerations of how justice is properly to be attained". He permitted disclosure, but it is not clear on which ground. Harman J. held that the claims that the bank might bring were "closely analogous to the claims by the company and might lead to the company being relieved of liability" and that "there appear to be dealings here of such a nature that, in my view, justice can only properly be achieved if the information is made available to the bank which lent the money."

5–044　Harman J. clearly based his reasoning on the earlier decision of Millett J. in *Re Esal (Commodities) Ltd (No. 2)*,[97] that being the only case referred to in his judgment. In Esal, the company concerned was in liquidation, and a member of the committee of inspection had applied for access to information gathered by the company's liquidator under

---

[94] See by analogy to liquidations, *per* Millett J. in *Re Barlow Clowes Gilt Managers* [1992] Ch. 208 at 217G and *per* Dillon L.J. in *Re Headington Investments Ltd* [1993] Ch. 452 at 494G–495B.

[95] The position often arises that the lender believes that it may have its own claims against the directors of the company in fraud or misrepresentation arising out of the statements made to obtain the loan to the company. Or the administrative receiver may obtain information which suggests that, if the lender knew of these facts, it could bring such a claim.

[96] [1993] B.C.C. 734.

[97] [1990] B.C.C. 708.

section 236. The applicant wished to obtain the documents for use in a fraudulent trading action which he had already brought against the company's bank. Millett J. held that, save in exceptional circumstances, access to the information sought should be allowed by the court only if the use proposed to be made is within the purpose of the statutory procedure, that is to say, that the use proposed to be made of the material is to assist the beneficial winding up of the company.[98] In the circumstances, therefore, disclosure could not be said to be for the purposes of the beneficial winding-up of the company. In spite of this, Millett J. held that this was an exceptional case which justified the grant of leave. He gave as his reasons the fact that the third party's claim was "closely related to the liquidation"; that the third party's allegations, if true, disclosed a major banking scandal that ought not to be hushed up; that the material was already to some extent in the public domain and would increasingly come into the public domain in the course of the litigation; and that the third party's counsel said that he could plead his case without the documents but in such a way that he could get them on discovery.

It is suggested that Harman J.'s reasons do not stand close scrutiny. It **5–045** is far from clear what the bank's claim against the director would be, and even more difficult to see how advancement of any such claim could assist the beneficial realisation of the bank's security. Further, Millett J. did not hold that there was an overriding discretion to order disclosure when the judge's view of the interests of justice require it. Millett J. had commented that "the proper administration of justice would be better served by the grant of leave than by its refusal", but only in the context of permitting advance disclosure of documents which would in any event come into the third party's hands on discovery. He did this as a practical matter to prevent repeated applications to amend and arguments as to whether what was pleaded had come from the documents (which had already been seen by the third party in his capacity as a member of the committee of inspection).

A different and more restrictive approach than that of Harman J. was **5–046** taken by Lord Cameron of Lochbroom in a Scottish case arising out of the Maxwell saga, *Re First Tokyo Index Trust Ltd.*[99] In that case, the liquidators of a company applied for leave to disclose documents obtained under section 236 to a bank. Rather unusually, the company had no creditors of any significance. Instead the bank had become the sole shareholder of the company as a consequence of enforcing a charge over the shares from the company's parent to secure a loan from the bank on which the parent had defaulted. The bank had then appointed the liquidators. In this sense the case had close parallels with the

---

[98] Note, however, that these grounds for disclosure are too narrow according to Lord Browne-Wilkinson in the later case of In *Re Arrows Ltd (No. 4)* [1995] 2 A.C. 75 at 102E–G, because an office-holder can lawfully make disclosure to public authorities to whom he is obliged or permitted to give information.

[99] Court of Session, September 30, 1993, reported only in *The Times* Law Report, December 1, 1993.

situation which arises in receiverships in which the party principally interested in the outcome of the insolvency was the bank which appointed the office-holder. Over a period of a year or more, the bank had spent very substantial sums of money funding an inquiry by the liquidators of the company into the circumstances surrounding the disposal of the assets of the company. Apparently it had been intended that the company's assets should have been pledged to secure the loan from the bank, but the assets were in fact sold elsewhere and the proceeds used to support other Maxwell companies.

5-047   The liquidators made it clear to the court that the company intended to commence proceedings against certain of the persons who had given the information under section 236 and who had been the custodians of the company's assets. The bank also indicated that it was considering commencing its own proceedings against the same persons, but on different and distinct grounds from those of the company, such as misrepresentation. The liquidators, supported by the bank, sought orders permitting wholesale disclosure of all of the information obtained to the bank on two grounds:

> (a) that in the particular circumstances where the bank was the only party having a substantial interest in the liquidation of the company, the "purposes of the liquidation" extended to attempting to obtain redress for the bank;
> (b) that as the bank would be funding the litigation by the company, disclosure was necessary to demonstrate to the bank that the proceedings would be likely to be successful and to keep it informed of progress.

5-048   Lord Cameron rejected these arguments. He held that the crucial point in the case which distinguished it from the *Esal* case was that the claim of the bank would proceed on separate and distinct grounds to the claim of the company, and there was in any event no such claim yet pleaded by the bank. In contrast, in *Esal* the information had been obtained to found a fraudulent trading claim by the liquidators, which was precisely the same claim which the third party had also brought and had been able to formulate. Lord Cameron applied the *dictum* of Dillon L.J. in the case of *Re Headington Investments Ltd*,[1]

> "Cases where persons other than prosecution or regulatory author-ities seek disclosure or inspection of transcripts may raise a variety of different considerations. In some cases, disclosure will clearly be justified because, to adopt the words of Millett J. in *Re Barlow Clowes Gilt Managers Ltd*, 'the use proposed to be made of the material is to assist the beneficial winding up of the company;' . . .
> But the mere fact that the transcript is wanted for use in proceedings, whether civil or criminal, is not enough. The process of

[1] [1993] Ch. 452 at 494G–495B: see also *per* Megarry J. in *Re Spiraflite Ltd* [1979] 1 W.L.R. 1096 at 1100.

private examination does not leave the Court with a pool of information to be made available to any third party who may want to go fishing to see what he can find that might be helpful in civil or criminal proceedings, *e.g.* as material for cross-examination if a witness gives evidence in such proceedings which might be thought inconsistent with what he had said on examination under section 236 of the Act of 1986, or as material to anticipate discovery."

On the facts, Lord Cameron was also not impressed by the argument **5–049** that the bank needed to have access in order to determine whether to continue funding the litigation by the company. The bank had already spent considerable sums and had undertaken to support the commencement of proceedings. Given that the bank presumably had confidence in the solicitors and counsel employed by the liquidators, at that stage the bank did not need access to further information. In other cases, however, where an appointing bank is not already committed to providing support for litigation in the receivership, it is suggested that the court might be prepared to permit limited disclosure, subject to suitable undertakings being given to ensure confidentiality was preserved, in order to enable the receivers to persuade the appointor to provide such funding.

10. SELF-INCRIMINATING INFORMATION

The importance attached to ensuring that the office-holder can perform **5–050** his functions in an effective and expeditious manner has meant that persons subject to duties under section 235, whether obliged to provide information under that section or under section 236, cannot, as a matter of English domestic law, invoke the privilege against self-incrimination.[2] The courts have recognised that the task of the office-holder would be incapable of proper performance if the examinee could invoke such a privilege.

The abrogation of the privilege against self-incrimination in **5–051** inquisitorial proceedings, such as those under section 236, is compatible with the European Convention on Human Rights. Article 6 of the Convention provides in part that,

"In the determination of his civil rights and obligations or of any criminal charge against him, everyone is entitled to a fair and public hearing within a reasonable time by an independent and impartial tribunal established by law."

[2] See In *Re Arrows Ltd* (No. 4) [1995] 2 A.C. 75; *Bishopsgate Investment Management Ltd v. Maxwell* [1993] Ch. 1, CA. In the latter case, Stuart-Smith L.J. at 46 noted that Insolvency Rules 1986, r. 9.4(7) permits written records taken under s. 236 to be used as evidence against a respondent of any statement made by him in the course of the examination: *cf. Re Keypak Homecare Ltd* [1990] B.C.L.C. 440 which related to the position under the old winding-up provisions. Note also *Re Arrows (No. 2)* [1992] B.C.C. 446; *Re A.E. Farr* [1992] B.C.C. 150 and *Re Jeffrey Levitt* [1992] B.C.C. 137.

Article 6 does not appear to apply to an investigation under section 236, since in essence it is not a determination of civil or criminal rights.[3] This is so notwithstanding that there is in section 237(1) a summary but separate power to order delivery up of the company's property on the basis of evidence obtained under section 236.

5–052   This distinction is demonstrated by *Fayed v. U.K.*[4] and *Saunders v. U.K.*[5] Both cases concerned a challenge to the activities of Department of Trade and Industry inspectors who had been appointed under Part XIV of the Companies Act 1985 to examine the affairs of various companies, and in their reports had made adverse findings against respectively Mr Fayed and Mr Saunders. The activities of the inspectors were held not to fall within the scope of Article 6, being investigations rather than adjudications: the reports themselves did not determine any legal right or obligation so as to fall within Article 6.

5–053   In *Saunders v. U.K.*, the European Court of Human Rights also held that self-incriminating information lawfully obtained from a person under compulsion or threat of compulsion could not, under Article 6, be used against him in his trial on criminal charges. As a result of the incorporation of the Human Rights Convention into domestic law by the Human Rights Act 1998, such material would therefore have to be excluded from evidence in any criminal trial. While the *Saunders* case concerned information obtained by Department of Trade and Industry inspectors, appointed under Part XIV of the Companies Act 1985, there is no reason why the case should not apply equally to information obtained by the use, or threatened use, of section 236, or under section 235, which is itself backed by criminal sanctions.

5–054   The Human Rights Act 1998 will, however, probably have less impact on the use in subsequent civil proceedings, for example by the administrative receiver, of information obtained under these sections, or by threat of an application for an order under section 236.

5–055   In *Official Receiver v. Stern*,[6] the Court of Appeal held that proceedings under the Company Directors Disqualification Act 1986 were not criminal proceedings, and it was not in breach of the respondents' rights to a fair trial under the European Convention for the Official Receiver to use against them information he had received pursuant to section 235 of the Insolvency Act 1986.

5–056   The relevant factors relied on by the Court in coming to this conclusion were (i) disqualification proceedings are not criminal proceedings, but are regulatory proceedings primarily for the protection of the public, even though the proceedings often involve serious allegations and almost always carry stigma for a person disqualified; (ii) there are various degrees of coercion involved in the different investigative

---

[3] Other articles of the European Convention on Human Rights will affect the conduct of examinations under s. 236 of the Insolvency Act 1986. See below, paras 5–064—5–066.

[4] (1994) 18 E.H.R.R. 93.

[5] [1997] B.C.C. 872.

[6] [2000] U.K.H.R.R. 332, affirming the decision of Scott V.-C., unreported, December 20, 1999.

procedures available in corporate insolvency, which may therefore give rise to different degrees of prejudice if the information obtained is sought to be used in disqualification proceedings; and (iii) it is generally best for questions of fairness to be decided by the trial judge rather than in advance.

It is likely that ordinary civil proceedings instituted by an administra- **5–057** tive receiver, for example, for breach of duty against a director, will be even less likely to incline a trial judge to exclude material obtained by compulsion under section 235 or 236, because such proceedings do not carry the "stigma" of disqualification.

In the context of civil litigation, the right to a fair hearing under **5–058** Article 6 of the European Convention also requires compliance with the principle of "equality of arms".[7] "As regards litigation involving opposing private interests,[8] 'equality of arms' implies that each party must be afforded a reasonable opportunity to present his case— including his evidence—under conditions which do not place him at a substantial disadvantage *vis-à-vis* his opponent".[9] The English courts already strive to ensure that no unacceptable "inequality of arms" results from an order under section 236 by means of the limitations on the section examined above, such as the limitations on when an order will be made, or what type of order might be made. If anything more need be done in the context of civil litigation to protect "equality of arms", it is likely that it will be achieved through the exclusion of prejudicial evidence at trial.[10]

It seems that an examinee can, save possibly in exceptional circum- **5–059** stances,[11] still refuse to provide the requested information if it is protected by legal professional privilege,[12] though no privilege can be asserted by solicitors in respect of documents in their possession but which belonged to the company itself.[13]

---

[7] *Neumeister v. Austria*, Judgment of 27 June, 1968, A 8, (1968) 1 E.H.R.R. 91; *X v. Federal Republic of Germany* (1963) 6 Y.B. 520 at 574.

[8] This is how the English courts clearly understand litigation by a liquidator for the benefit of the company and those "interested" in its assets: see *Cloverbay Ltd v. BCCI* [1991] Ch. 90 at 108D, *per* Nourse L.J.

[9] *Dombo Beheer v. Netherlands*, Judgment of 27 October, 1993, A 274-A at para. 33, (1993) 18 E.H.R.R. 213 at 229–30. See also *Feldbrugge v. Netherlands,* Judgment of May 29, 1986, A 99 at para. 44, (1986) 8 E.H.R.R. 425, 436–7, and *Van de Hurk v. Netherlands,* Judgment of April 19, 1994, A 288, (1994)18 E.H.R.R. 481.

[10] The civil courts now have a discretion under CPR, r. 32.1 to exclude evidence where its prejudicial effect outweighs its probative value: *Grobbelaar v. Sun Newspapers Ltd* (*The Times*, August 12, 1999, CA). The preferred practice of the courts in both criminal and regulatory cases is to leave the question of fairness to the trial judge (see respectively In *Re Arrows Ltd (No. 4)* [1995] 2 A.C. 75 and *Official Receiver v. Stern*, unreported, February 2, 2000, affirming the decision of Scott V.-C., also unreported, December 20, 1999). It therefore seems likely that this practice would be followed in the context of civil litigation.

[11] See *dicta* of Vinelott J. in *Re Brook Martin & Co. (Nominees) Ltd* [1993] B.C.L.C. 328 at 336–7.

[12] See the Australian decision of *Re Compass Australia Pty Ltd* (1992) 10 A.C.L.C. 1380 and *Re Highgrade Traders Ltd* [1984] B.C.L.C. 151, CA.

[13] *Re Brook Martin & Co. (Nominees) Ltd* [1993] B.C.L.C. 328.

11. PROCEDURE

5–060 The detailed procedures relating to court applications are set out in Insolvency Rules 1986, rr. 9.1 to 9.6. The application is made by the office-holder in question.[14] An order granted to that office-holder ceases to have effect if he ceases to hold office.[15]

5–061 Rule 9.2(4) provides that the application may be made without notice. Such an application used to be the common way of seeking an order under section 236. That approach has now been rejected, and an application on notice is the normal procedure.[16] Where a person is to be ordered to disclose confidential information or documents belonging to a third party, the general rule is that the third party must be joined.[17] In making an application for an examination on oath, the applicant must disclose all material facts to the court. This appears to apply as much to an application on notice as to an application without notice.[18]

5–062 Rule 9.2(1) provides that a statement supporting the application shall be prepared by the office-holder. The statement is, in principle, confidential.[19] Formerly, these reports were not filed and were not disclosed to the examinee, so as to allow the office-holder to explain his position fully to the court without putting the proposed examinee on notice of facts which could be used to the detriment of the insolvency administration.[20] In *Re British & Commonwealth Holdings plc*,[21] the Court of Appeal indicated that office-holder reports will now be available to the proposed examinee, or to the person whose documents are sought to be inspected, if such disclosure is necessary to enable the court fairly to dispose of an application to resist or set aside an order under section 236. This might well be the case where it is not clear from the affidavits what the case is that the proposed examinee, or person whose documents are sought, has to meet. If such a need arises, it shifts the burden onto the office-holder to prove that the material needs to be kept confidential.[22] Best practice should be to separate any confidential information in respect of which disclosure is to be resisted from the rest of the report and to place it in one or more confidential annexes.[23]

5–063 Section 236 of the Insolvency Act 1986 confers powers on the court, although in practice an examination under the section is conducted by,

---

[14] *Re Maxwell Communications Corporation plc* [1994] B.C.C. 741.

[15] *Re Kingscroft Insurance Co. Ltd* [1994] B.C.C. 343. Since the examination is by the court, it is questionable whether this result should follow.

[16] *Re Maxwell Communications Corporation plc* [1994] B.C.C. 741 at 747 and 752, *per* Vinelott J.; *Re PFTZM Ltd* [1995] 2 B.C.L.C. 354; *Re Murjani (a bankrupt)* [1996] 1 B.C.L.C. 272 at 284–285 (a case under s. 366 of the Insolvency Act 1986.

[17] *Re Murjani (a bankrupt)* [1996] 1 B.C.L.C. 272 at 285–286.

[18] *John T. Rhodes (No. 2)* (1987) 3 B.C.C. 588 at 593.

[19] *Re Aveling Barford Ltd* [1989] 1 W.L.R. 360.

[20] See *Re Gold Co.* (1879) 12 Ch.D. 77.

[21] [1992] B.C.C. 165. See also *Re British & Commonwealth Holdings plc (No. 2)* [1992] B.C.C. 172, CA, [1992] B.C.C. 977, HL and *Re Bishopsgate Investment Management Ltd (No. 2)* [1994] B.C.C. 732.

[22] See, *e.g. Re Murjani (a bankrupt)* [1996] 1 B.C.L.C. 272 at 282–284.

[23] See, *e.g. Re Bishopsgate Investment Management Ltd (No. 2)*, [1994] B.C.C. 732.

or on the instructions of, the applicant officeholder. In such circumstances, only he, or solicitor or counsel instructed by him, may put questions to an examinee, subject to one exception. That exception is the rare case where there are two office-holders in respect of a company, and an order for examination has been made on the application of one of them. In such a case, the other office-holder might, with leave of the court and if the applicant did not object, attend and question the examinee, but only through the applicant.[24]

When conducting an examination under section 236, the office-holder **5–064** will be a "public authority", subject to the provisions of the Human Rights Act 1998. This is because he will be a "person certain of whose functions are functions of a public nature" (s. 6(3)(b) of the 1998 Act), and he will not fall within the exception to that definition (s. 6(5)) which provides that "[i]n relation to a particular act, a person is not a public authority by virtue only of subsection (3)(b) if the nature of the act is private". An examination under section 236, which takes place under threat of coercion, and is undertaken by a court, or by an office-holder as its nominee, is undoubtedly a "public" act.[25]

In consequence, an administrative receiver or other office holder **5–065** conducting an examination under section 236 must not infringe any of the rights guaranteed by the European Convention on Human Rights and imported into English law by the 1998 Act. For present purposes, the right most likely to be of importance is the right to respect for private and family life (Article 8 of the Convention).[26] Nevertheless, action necessary in the interests of the economic well-being of the country, or the protection of the rights of others, does not infringe this right (Article 8(2)). Any intrusion into an individual's privacy or family life will therefore have to be justified by reference to the office-holder's need for information to protect national economic interests, or the rights of others. Furthermore, the principle of proportionality means that a more serious intrusion will require a more compelling justification.[27]

If an office-holder proposes to take steps which would violate rights **5–066** guaranteed by the Convention, or in fact has taken such steps, he will be open to an action under section 8 of the 1998 Act for an injunction, damages or other remedy.

Any transcript obtained following an examination is not available for **5–067** inspection, without a court order, by any person other than the office-holder who made the original application or any person who could have made a similar application.[28] Similarly, the court may give directions as

---

[24] *Re Maxwell Communications Corporation plc* [1994] B.C.C. 741.

[25] For further consideration of what is a "public authority", and the principles by which the question is resolved, see Grosz, Beatson & Duffy, *Human Rights: The 1998 Act and the European Convention* (Sweet & Maxwell, 2000), paras 4–02—4–24.

[26] An office-holder's request under s. 236 that an individual produce a very large quantity of documentation might possibly infringe the individual's rights under Art. 4 (prohibition of forced labour) at least if the request does not provide for appropriate recompense.

[27] *ibid.* paras. 5–12—5–15.

[28] Insolvency Rules 1986, r. 9.5(2).

to the custody and inspection of any documents obtained under this procedure.[29]

5–068 As indicated above, an administrative receiver will generally only be entitled to use any information or documents obtained under the procedure for the purposes of the receivership, and he should seek leave of the court if he proposes to use any of them for any other purpose.[30] An administrative receiver is also subject to an implied, qualified duty of confidentiality in respect of information obtained under section 236.[31] The duty does not prevent him from using information obtained by means of section 236 in the performance of his tasks,[32] and he can disclose it to State bodies when required or authorised to do so.[33] The court can also relieve him of this duty of confidentiality.[34]

5–069 The administrative receiver may, in his discretion, give undertakings of confidentiality in respect of information obtained or to be obtained by him under section 236, or under the threat of the section, though such undertakings cannot be required of him.[35] He cannot give an assurance that information will be withheld from anyone to whom he must report the information, or anyone who can by law require the information of him.[36] Third parties who are concerned that the administrative receiver may breach any previous assurances about confidentiality or legal professional privilege may seek an order of the court restraining disclosure,[37] although this may not be forthcoming in the context of criminal investigations.[38]

5–070 There is no public interest immunity to prevent the disclosure of transcripts of evidence made under section 236 to prosecuting or regulatory authorities.[39] Furthermore, the person who might be the object of the possible criminal or regulatory proceedings cannot compel concurrent disclosure to himself.[40]

---

[29] *ibid.*, r. 9.5(4).

[30] See *Re Esal Commodities Ltd (No. 1)* [1989] B.C.L.C. 59, CA.; *Re Esal (Commodities) Ltd (No. 2)* [1990] B.C.C. 708 and *Re Acli Metals (London) Ltd* [1989] B.C.L.C. 749 for instances of disclosure permitted in circumstances not directly related to the office-holder's duties. In relation to disclosure by an administrative receiver to his appointor, see above, paras 5–041 to 5–049.

[31] See In *Re Arrows Ltd* (No. 4) [1995] 2 A.C. 75 at 102–3, *per* Lord Browne-Wilkinson, indicating that the limits on disclosure indicated by Millett J. in *Re Esal (Commodities) Ltd (No. 2)* [1990] B.C.C. 708 and In *Re Barlow Clowes Gilt Managers Ltd* [1992] Ch. 208 are too tightly drawn, as they would apparently (and incorrectly) preclude the office-holder from disclosing information obtained by him under s. 236 to persons to whom he may, or must, by law divulge that information. See also *Re a Company (No. 005374 of 1993)* [1993] B.C.C. 734 and *Soden v. Burns* [1996] 3 All E.R. 967.

[32] The tasks of an office-holder include taking and defending proceedings: *Soden v. Burns* [1996] 3 All E.R. 967 at 991a, *per* Robert Walker J.

[33] In *Re Arrows Ltd* (No. 4) [1995] 2 A.C. 75 at 102–3, *per* Lord Browne-Wilkinson.

[34] *Re a Company (No. 005374 of 1993)* [1993] B.C.C. 734.

[35] *Re Barlow Clowes Gilt Managers Ltd* [1992] Ch. 208; *McIsaac, Petitioners; Joint Liquidators of First Tokyo Index Trust Ltd* [1994] B.C.C. 410.

[36] *In re Arrows Ltd* (No. 4) [1995] 2 A.C. 75 at 102–3, *per* Lord Browne-Wilkinson.

[37] See *Re Barlow Clowes Gilt Managers Ltd* [1992] Ch. 208 and *Dubai Bank Ltd v. Galadari* [1989] 5 B.C.C. 722.

[38] In *Re Arrows Ltd* (No. 4) [1995] 2 A.C. 75.

[39] *Re Headington Investments Ltd* [1993] Ch. 452.

[40] *ibid.*

The court has a discretion to award any person attending on examina- **5–071** tion any other costs incurred by him (save for the costs of a solicitor and/ or counsel employed to attend any examination).[41] In practice, it is unlikely that an examinee will be able to obtain an order for costs.[42] In certain circumstances, an order for costs may be made against the examinee.[43]

[41] Insolvency Rules 1986, r. 9.4(5).

[42] But see *Morris and Others v. Bank of America National Trust and Savings Association* (unreported, Robert Walker J., February 6, 1997), discussing *Re Aveling Barford* [1988] 3 All E.R. 1019 (Hoffmann J.) and the apparently contrary decision of Vinelott J. in *Re Cloverbay Ltd* [1989] B.C.L.C. 724.

[43] Insolvency Rules 1986, r. 9.6(1) and (2).

CHAPTER 6

TAKING CONTROL

6–001 The appointment by a debenture-holder of a receiver takes the management of the company's property out of the hands of its directors and places them in the hands of the receiver.[1] The complete change of control from the board of directors to the receiver needs to be effected, in many cases, with great speed.

> "Professional receivers plan the take-over with military precision. On the day a big company goes into receivership there are suddenly accountants everywhere. The receiver himself usually moves into the managing director's office, the finance director is given a thorough grilling, teams burrow through the company's books, and men are posted at all entrances to make sure that in the confusion nobody makes off with anything of conceivable value."[2]

6–002 In exercising his powers of management the primary duty of the receiver is to try to bring about a situation in which the secured debt and interest is paid.[3] Subject to that primary duty he owes a duty to manage the property with due diligence.[4] Taking control is usually a necessary step in the process of realisation. The Insolvency Act 1986 provides that in the absence of an inconsistent provision in the debenture the powers conferred upon an administrative receiver in the debenture shall be deemed to include: "Power to take possession of, collect and get in the property of the company and, for that purpose, to take such proceedings as may seem to him expedient."[5] The reference to "the property of the company" is limited to the property over which the administrative receiver is or, but for the appointment of another receiver over part of the property, would be receiver or manager.[6]

6–003 In addition, the debenture under which the receiver is appointed will invariably give him a power to take control or possession of the company's assets charged by the debenture. It is now a common form provision in debentures that all of a company's assets are to be charged.

---

[1] *Re Joshua Shaw & Sons* (1989) 5 B.C.C. 188 at 190, and see above, paras 2–017 *et seq.* For a statement of the more far reaching effect of the appointment of a receiver by the court, see *Moss Steamship Company Ltd v. Whinney* [1912] A.C. 254 at 263, *per* Lord Atkinson, and see below, para 22–006. For the effect of the appointment of a receiver upon the powers of the directors see further above, para. 2–022 to 2–025.

[2] Stephen Aris, *Going Bust* (1985), p. 86.

[3] *Ford v. Transtec Automotive (Campsie) Ltd* (unreported Jacob J., March 31, 2000).

[4] *Medforth v. Blake* [2000] Ch. 86 at 102F–G.

[5] s. 42 and Sched. 1, para. 1.

[6] Insolvency Act 1986, s. 42(2)(b). By contrast, an administrator's powers are exercisable in respect of all the property of the company: Insolvency Act 1986, s. 14.

Where, however, the debenture charges only certain of the assets, the receivers may in practice be prevented from getting at the charged assets without dealing in some way with the uncharged assets. The Court of Appeal in *Rushingdale Ltd SA v. Byblos Bank SAL*,[7] in such a case, applied a liberal interpretation to the customary sweeping-up power conferred by debentures on receivers to "do all such acts and things as may be considered to be incidental or conducive to any of the matters or powers aforesaid" and invoked this power so interpreted to support the view that it was arguable that the receiver could enter the company's uncharged leasehold property to take possession of and realise charged chattels.

Care must be taken not to seize property which is not the property of **6–004** the company. Whilst an administrative receiver is granted statutory exemption from liability to third parties for any loss or damage caused to tangible property belonging to them, that exemption applies only if at the date of seizure he believes and has reasonable grounds to believe that he is entitled to do so and he is not negligent.[8]

Practical difficulties can arise where the management of the company **6–005** are hostile to the appointment of receivers. Taking control will invariably involve taking possession of premises. It is a criminal offence to use or threaten violence to secure entry to premises where the person using violence or making the threat knows there is a person on the premises opposed to his entry.[9] The existence of an interest in the premises or a right to possession or occupation is not usually a defence.[10] The violence in question can be against person or property so that breaking into property in those circumstances would suffice.[11] Accordingly, where the appointment is "hostile" particular care must be taken in gaining entry and an application to court for possession may be required. For these reasons it is common for secured lenders to seek an invitation from directors to appoint receivers. The request also assists to negative the prospects of argument about the validity of the demand. Indeed, if the company is insolvent and receivership offers the best prospect of minimising the loss to the general body of creditors, the directors may have a duty to request appointment.[12]

Where it is necessary to take control of assets in order properly to **6–006** safeguard them, or to ensure their beneficial realisation, the receiver will have not only a power but a duty to take control of the assets. For example, where the charged property included a reversion upon a lease, the receiver's immediate duty was to examine the lease and (if appropriate) serve notice exercising rights of rent review.[13]

As part of the process of safeguarding the assets, the receiver will want **6–007** to ensure that charged assets are properly insured. The Insolvency Act

---

[7] (1986) 2 B.C.C. 99,509.
[8] Insolvency Act 1986, s. 234(3), (4). See above, para. 5–009.
[9] Criminal Law Act 1977, s. 6(1).
[10] *ibid.*, s. 6(2).
[11] *ibid.*, s. 6(4).
[12] Insolvency Act 1986, s. 214(3).
[13] *Knight v. Lawrence* (1991) B.C.C. 411 at 418. See further below, Chap. 7.

1986[14] gives administrative receivers the express power to obtain and maintain insurance in respect of the business and property of the company. Non-administrative receivers must look for the power to insure in their debentures. Since it is often difficult to check quickly upon the extent and adequacy of cover effected by the company, professional receivers tend to subscribe to schemes which give them blanket cover, which they can use until the company's position is clarified. In so far as repairs may be required, the Insolvency Act 1986[15] authorises an administrative receiver to carry out any works necessary for the realisation "of the property of the company".

6–008   Taking control will sometimes involve the taking of legal proceedings and the statutorily implied powers include the ability to take proceedings in the name of the company[16] and to employ solicitors and counsel.[17] The company's assets are not vested in the receiver and therefore he cannot sue in his own name.[18]

6–009   In *Wheeler v. Warren*[19] the company had contracted to sell property prior to the receivership. The receiver sued upon the contract in the name of the company. It was held that the power to get in the company's property authorised the claim for specific performance of the contract since that would get in the purchase price, an asset of the company. There was an alternative claim for rescission of the contract. The claim for rescission was the mode of getting in the company's property if specific performance was not granted, for an order for rescission would recover the entire beneficial interest in the property, which had prima facie passed on exchange of contracts to the purchaser.

6–010   The Act further authorises the administrative receiver to claim in various types of insolvencies.[20] It is not expressly stated in the case of this power (unlike the case of power to commence proceedings) that the claim has to be made in the name of the company, but that would appear to be the proper course, since the debt will be owed to the company.

6–011   Property which ceases to be the property of a company prior to the receivership will, in the ordinary case, fall outside the scope of the charge and receivership. The receiver's powers to challenge the circumstances in which the property was transferred, with a view to recovering the property for the benefit of the receivership, are in general limited to cases in which the company itself could take proceedings to recover the property. So, for example, a receiver may be able to institute proceedings in the name of the company to recover assets which have been

---

[14] Insolvency Act 1986, Sched. 1, para. 7.
[15] *ibid.*, Sched. 1, para. 12.
[16] *ibid.*, paras. 1 and 5.
[17] *ibid.*, para. 4.
[18] See *Levermore v. Levermore* [1979] 1 W.L.R. 1277; *Robertson v. Oskar* (1983–4) 8 A.C.L.R. 570; *Lochab Brothers v. Kenya Furfural* (1985) L.R.C. (Comm.) 737, CA, Kenya.
[19] [1928] Ch. 840, CA.
[20] Insolvency Act 1986, Sched. 1, para. 20.

transferred in breach of the directors' fiduciary duties to the company, or for damages or compensation in lieu.[21]

It has also been held in *Merton v. Hammond Suddards*[22] that a receiver **6–012** may be able to apply for a declaration as to the voidness of a disposal of the company's property after the presentation of a winding up petition as a result of the operation of section 127 of the Insolvency Act 1986, and that this was so even though the floating charge pursuant to which the receiver had been appointed had not crystallised at the time of the disposal. The moneys recovered were held to fall within the scope of the crystallised floating charge. The decision was reached on the basis that section 127 contains no express restriction upon the persons entitled to invoke it,[23] and that it is not designed simply to benefit unsecured creditors. The result is somewhat surprising, because so far as the holder of the uncrystallised floating charge was concerned, at the time of the disposal of the property the company remained free to deal with the property transferred in the ordinary course of its business.[24]

In contrast, causes of action which are vested by statute solely in the **6–013** liquidator or administrator of a company, such as the right to apply to the court for relief under s. 213 (fraudulent trading), s. 214 (wrongful trading), s. 238 (transactions at an undervalue) or s. 239 (preferences) of the Insolvency Act 1986, are not exercisable by the receiver and any monetary recoveries pursuant to those sections will not fall within the charge under which the receiver was appointed.[25] But recoveries *in specie* by a liquidator or administrator pursuant to sections 238 or 239 (transactions at an undervalue and preferences) would probably fall within the scope of a charge over the company's property.[26] If so, the liquidator would be entitled to decline to pursue such relief unless he obtained an agreement from the receiver to give up his claims to such assets, or unless the recovery of such assets would otherwise provide a tangible benefit for unsecured creditors.[27]

Section 423 of the Insolvency Act 1986 provides that where a debtor **6–014** has entered into a transaction with any other person at an undervalue and the transaction was entered into for the purpose of putting assets

---

[21] In view of the limits on the receiver's statutory powers of action under the Insolvency Act 1986 as explained below, it may be of some assistance if he is able to frame a claim on behalf of the company on the basis of the principles set out by Dillon L.J. in *West Mercia Safetywear Limited v. Dodd* (1988) 4 B.C.C. 30, CA: see below Chapter 11.

[22] [1996] 2 B.C.L.C. 470. This point was not dealt with in the subsequent appeal *sub nom. Mond v. Hammond Suddards* [2000] Ch. 40, CA.

[23] See also *Re Argentum Reductions (U.K.) Limited* [1975] 1 W.L.R. 186.

[24] It may be that such a result would be justified in the interest of unsecured creditors if the recovery of the property resulted in a surplus or greater surplus becoming available for distribution to unsecured creditors than would otherwise be the case.

[25] See *e.g. Re M.C. Bacon Limited* [1991] Ch. 127 at 137; *Re Ayala Holdings Limited (No. 2)* [1996] 1 B.C.L.C. 467; *Re Oasis Merchandising Services Limited* [1998] Ch. 170, CA.; and *Re Exchange Travel (Holdings) Limited (No. 3), Katz v. McNally* [1997] 2 B.C.L.C. 579, CA.

[26] See *e.g. N.A. Kratzmann Pty Ltd. v. Tucker (No. 2)* (1968) 123 C.L.R. 295 (High Court of Australia); *Ross v. Taylor* [1985] S.L.T. 387; *Bank of New Zealand v. Essington* (1990) 5 A.C.S.R. 86 at 89–90 (Supreme Court of New South Wales).

[27] *Ex parte Cooper, In Re Zucco* (1875) L.R. 10 Ch. App. 510 at 511–512, CA. See further Chapter 11 below.

beyond the reach of or otherwise prejudicing a person who is making or may at some time make a claim against the debtor, then application may be made to the court for an order restoring the position to that which it would have been if the transaction had not been entered into and protecting the interests of the persons on whose behalf the application is treated as made. If the debtor is a company in liquidation or the subject of an administration order, the liquidator or administrator may apply, as, with leave, may any other person who is or may be prejudiced (referred to as the "victim" of the transaction). If the debtor is a company which is not in liquidation or administration any "victim" of the transaction may apply. This jurisdiction will not be available to a receiver, because he will not have suffered prejudice so as to qualify as a victim of the transaction, but it might provide a debenture-holder, who could qualify as a victim, with the means of seeking to bring back within the scope of his charge, assets of which the company was denuded prior to the receivership.

CHAPTER 7

DUTIES AND LIABILITIES OF A RECEIVER AND OF HIS APPOINTOR

In a work on receivers, it is appropriate to consider the duties and **7–001**
liabilities both of the receiver and of the debenture-holder who appoints
the receiver, for there is a mutual interest on the part of each of the
receiver and his appointor that the other shall not be unnecessarily
exposed to claims. For this purpose it is essential that each should know
the extent of the other's duties and liabilities to third parties. The
similarity (though not identity) of their duties and liabilities to third
parties suggests that they should be considered together in Part I of this
Chapter. In Part II there will be a consideration of the duties and
liabilities of the receiver and his appointor *inter se*.

PART I—DUTIES AND LIABILITIES OF DEBENTURE-HOLDER AND RECEIVER TO THIRD PARTIES

1. PRELIMINARY

It is of the essence of a security that the chargor gives the chargee rights **7–002**
and powers over the chargor's property, and agrees to the chargee using
those rights and powers in his own interests to achieve repayment of the
debt which he is owed.[1] But recognising that a mortgage is merely a
security for the payment of a debt or performance of an obligation, and
with the intention of ensuring that the mortgagee or receiver acts fairly,
equity affords certain protections to the mortgagor and any other
persons who are interested in the equity of redemption.[2] What equity's
"core value" of fairness requires will naturally vary depending on the
circumstances and the particular relationship between the parties.[3]
Invariably equity will require a mortgagee[4] or receiver to act in good
faith and to use the powers conferred upon him for proper purposes. In
appropriate circumstances equity may also impose upon a mortgagee or
receiver a duty to exercise due diligence or a duty to take reasonable
care. Such duties may be owed to the mortgagor and to others interested

[1] See, *e.g. per* Lord Hoffmann in Re *BCCI S.A. (No. 8)* [1998] A.C. 214 at 226, HL.
Cited at para. 3–001 above.
[2] *Burgess v. Auger* [1998] 2 B.C.L.C. 478 and *Medforth v. Blake* [2000] Ch. 86 at 102A–B.
[3] *Parker Tweedale v. Dunbar Bank Plc* [1991] Ch. 12; *Downsview Nominees Ltd v. First
City Corp* [1993] A.C. 295, PC; *Medforth v. Blake* [2000] Ch. 86.
[4] The duties are the same in case of a legal and an equitable mortgagee: *Leech v.
National Bank of New Zealand* [1996] 3 N.Z.L.R. 707.

in the equity of redemption,[5] including any guarantor of the secured indebtedness.[6] In the event of breach of these duties, equity may require the mortgagee or receiver to make good (or provide compensation for) any consequent loss in value of the equity of redemption and in particular to give credit for that loss in the taking of accounts between the mortgagee and the mortgagor.

7–003   The relatively strict duties of a mortgagee "in possession", and the basic duties of a receiver or of a mortgagee who is not in possession, namely to act in good faith and for proper purposes, are long established. But there has been an acute conflict in the authorities as to whether a receiver or a mortgagee who is not in possession are under any further duties such as a general duty of care or even a general duty to act fairly to the mortgagor and others interested in the equity of redemption.

7–004   It is proposed to consider first the duty of a mortgagee and receiver to act in good faith and for proper purposes; secondly the duties of the mortgagee if he takes possession; and thirdly to consider how far there may be other duties imposed upon a mortgagee not in possession or upon a receiver, such as a general duty of care or a duty to act fairly.

2. DUTY TO ACT IN GOOD FAITH AND FOR PROPER PURPOSES

7–005   A mortgagee and a receiver both owe a duty in exercising their powers to do so in good faith for the purpose of preserving, exploiting[7] and realising the assets comprised in the security and obtaining repayment of the sum secured.[8] A want of good faith or the exercise of powers for an improper purpose will suffice to establish a breach of duty.[9]

7–006   A mortgagee is at all times free to consult his own interest alone whether and if so when to enforce his security or exercise any of the powers conferred on him as mortgagee. His decision to exercise or refrain from exercising such powers is not constrained by reason of the fact that the exercise or non-exercise of the powers will occasion damage

---

[5] e.g. subsequent mortgagees, but not beneficiaries under trusts of the mortgaged property: *Parker Tweedale v. Dunbar Bank plc* [1991] Ch. 12.

[6] *ENT Pty Ltd v. McVeigh* (1996) 6 Tas.R. 202. The liability to guarantors is based on the ground of their interest in the equity of redemption, and not on the existence of any common law duty of care as held in *Standard Chartered Bank v. Walker* [1982] 1 W.L.R. 1410, CA and *American Express v. Hurley* [1985] 3 All E.R. 564. It is because general creditors, contributories, officers, employees and members of the debtor company are not so interested that no duty is owed to them: see *Burgess v. Auger* [1998] 2 B.C.L.C. 478. See also below, para 19–01.

[7] This extends to exploiting a "ransom strip" or exploiting the dependence of customers who have no contractual right to the on-going supply of products and no alternative source for the products produced by the charged business by demanding a high price for that land or for those products: see *Ford AG-Werke AG v. Transtec Automative (Campsie) Ltd* March 31, 2000, Jacob J.

[8] *Bank of New Zealand v. Essington* (1991) 9 A.C.L.C. 1039; *Medforth v. Blake* [2000] Ch. 86 at 102G.

[9] *Downsview Nominees Ltd v. First City Corp* [1993] A.C. 295 at 317; *Yorkshire Bank plc v. Hall* [1999] 1 W.L.R. 1713 at 1728E; *Medforth v. Blake* [2000] Ch. 86 at 102A–B.

or loss to the mortgagor. Provided the mortgagee acts in good faith, he is entitled to subordinate any conflicting interest of the mortgagor (as well as those of creditors and third parties[10]) to what he genuinely perceives to be his own interest in securing repayment.

Provided he acts in good faith, when deciding whether and if so how **7–007** to exercise powers vested in him, a receiver is likewise entitled and indeed obliged to give priority to the interests of the mortgagee in securing repayment.

Breach of the duty of good faith involves something more than **7–008** negligence or even gross negligence: it requires some dishonesty, or improper motive, some element of bad faith, to be established. Reckless indifference to the rights or interests of others or shutting one's eyes deliberately to the consequences of one's actions may suffice to establish dishonesty or bad faith.[11] In judging whether the mortgagee or receiver were acting in good faith in deciding how best to serve the interests of the mortgagee, it would be inappropriate to apply any "Wednesbury" type test of reasonableness, but if the decision lay outside the range which the court thought might be arrived at by a reasonable commercial man, this might provide some evidence that the decision was not taken in good faith.

The use of powers for improper purposes will extend to the exercise of **7–009** powers for the purposes of the advancement of the interests of the debenture-holder other than as mortgagee (*e.g.* as a competitor of the mortgagor) or (whether by pressure or otherwise) to obtain a collateral advantage unprovided for by the debenture (*e.g.* to inhibit proceedings by the mortgagor against the debenture-holder or anyone else).[12]

So, for example, a first debenture-holder and receiver appointed by it **7–010** were held liable for breach of duty where the receiver was appointed and the receivership conducted for the purpose of disrupting an existing receivership under a second debenture and preventing enforcement of the second debenture. Damages were awarded reflecting the loss occasioned by such appointment and receivership.[13]

3. MORTGAGEE IN POSSESSION

In the absence of an agreement or statutory provision to the contrary, a **7–011** mortgagee is entitled to possession for the purpose of protecting or

---

[10] *The Grosvenor (Mayfair) Estate v. Edward Erdman Property Investment Ltd,* May 3, 1996, Lightman J.

[11] *Medforth v. Blake* [2000] Ch. 86 at 103D. On the meaning of dishonesty in commercial matters see *Royal Brunei Airlines v. Tan* [1995] 2 A.C. 378 at 389–391. See also the comments of Lord Hoffmann on the dangers inherent in the concept of the "hypothetical decent honest man" in *Aktieselskabet Dansk Skibsfinansiering v. Brothers,* Court of Final Appeal of Hong Kong (unreported, March 9, 2000). On the difficulties inherent in seeking to apply the *Wednesbury* test to the review of commercial decisions by liquidators, see *Re Edennote Ltd* [1996] 2 B.C.L.C. 389 at 394g–h.

[12] *Speed Seal Ltd v. Paddington* [1986] 1 All E.R. 91 and see *also Quennell v. Maltby* [1979] 1 W.L.R. 318, CA.

[13] *Downsview Nominees Ltd v. First City Corp.* [1993] A.C. 295, PC.

enforcing his security as soon as the mortgage is granted, whether or not the mortgagor is in default[14] and whether or not the mortgagor has a cross-claim against the mortgagee.[15] This is to be contrasted with the right to appoint a receiver, which only arises when the conditions for making such an appointment specified in the mortgage are satisfied. The appointment of a receiver as agent of the mortgagor and taking possession are alternative remedies: such an appointment cannot remain in force once the mortgagee takes possession, whereupon the receiver becomes the agent of the mortgagee.[16] The intention to take possession is not sufficient to constitute a mortgagee in possession: the intention of the mortgagee must be accompanied by an unequivocal act of taking possession. Thus, for example, the collection of rents is not conclusive of this issue.[17]

7–012 By taking possession the mortgagee becomes the manager of the charged property.[18] The authorities establish that a mortgagee in possession is accountable to the mortgagor for his possession and management[19] of the charged property on the basis of "wilful default".

> "If a mortgagee takes possession of the mortgaged property, he is liable to account for rent on the basis of wilful default; he must keep the mortgaged premises in repair; he is liable for waste. Those duties are imposed to ensure that a mortgagee is diligent in discharging his mortgage and returning the property to the mortgagor."[20]

7–013 The precise content of the liability for "wilful default" has not been clearly defined.[21] Although "wilful default" has often been said to be a "strict" liability,[22] in fact the majority of cases appear to have treated "wilful default" as synonymous with a failure on the part of the mortgagee to exercise "due diligence".[23] So it has been said that the mortgagee must account not only for all he receives but also for all he ought to have received had he managed the property with due diligence.[24] But other than indicating that liability will attach even though

[14] The most recent authority is *Ropaigealach v. Barclays Bank plc* [2000] Q.B. 263.
[15] *TSB Bank plc v. Platts* [1998] 2 B.C.L.C. 1 at 10, CA.
[16] *North American Trust Company v. Consumer Gas Company* (1997) 147 D.L.R. (4th) 645.
[17] *North American Trust Co. v. Consumer Gas Co.* (1997) 147 D.L.R. (4th) 645, citing *Noyes v. Pollock* (1886) 32 Ch.D. 53.
[18] *Kendle v. Melsom* [1998] 193 C.L.R. 46 at 64, H Ct of Australia.
[19] Where a mortgagee exercises his power of sale, different considerations have traditionally been applied (see below).
[20] *Downsview Nominees Ltd v. First City Corp* [1993] A.C. at 315A, *per* Lord Templeman.
[21] See the discussion by Stannard (1979) Conv. 345 and the summary by Frisby (2000) 63 M.L.R. 413 at 418–419.
[22] See, *e.g. per* Robert Walker L.J. in *Yorkshire Bank plc v. Hall* [1999] 1 W.L.R. 1713 at 1728E–F and Megarry & Wade, *The Law of Real Property*, (6th ed.) (Charles Harpum), para. 19–069.
[23] *Per* Turner L.J. in *Sherwin v. Shakspear* (1854) 5 De G.M. & G. 517 at 537.
[24] See, *e.g.* the discussion in Megarry & Wade (*op. cit.*) and *Medforth v. Blake* [2000] Ch. 86 at 92G.

the default of the mortgagee is not "wilful" in the sense of being deliberate, the "due diligence" formulation is of itself no help in indicating the precise level of "diligence" (*i.e.* care) which will be regarded as "due". Some older authorities tended to indicate that more than mere negligence (*i.e.* a failure to take reasonable care) might be required,[25] but recent authorities have tended to assimilate the "due diligence" standard with a duty to take reasonable care.[26] So it has been said that the duty requires the mortgagee in possession to be active in protecting and exploiting the security, maximising the return but without taking any undue risks.[27]

4. OTHER DUTIES

The question arises whether and (if so) in what circumstances the **7–014** general duty of the mortgagee or receiver to act in good faith and for proper purposes is supplemented by other duties, such as a duty to exercise powers with reasonable care or a duty to act fairly.

Three general principles can be stated. First, as mentioned above, the **7–015** powers conferred on a mortgagee are conferred on him for his own benefit: he is not a trustee of them for the mortgagor: and accordingly the mortgagee can act in his own interests in making any decision as to whether or not, and if so, when to exercise his powers.[28] Secondly, a receiver can also give priority to the interests of his appointor in deciding whether, and if so when and how he should exercise the powers vested in him. But unlike a mortgagee a receiver, once appointed, cannot simply remain passive: he has a duty to preserve and protect the charged assets.[29] And thirdly, it has long been established that if a mortgagee or a receiver decides to exercise a *power of sale*, he will generally owe a duty of care to the mortgagor in respect of the *manner* in which he does so.[30]

At common law no duty of care on the exercise of a power of sale was **7–016** recognised because in the view of the common law the mortgagee was in form and substance the legal owner exercising the power of sale of his own property for his own benefit.[31] Equity, however, intervened to protect the equity of redemption and prevent redemption being evaded by anything other than a bona fide sale at arms' length. The Court of

[25] See, *e.g. Hughes v. Williams* (1806) 12 Ves. 493 and *Brandon v. Brandon* (1862) 19 W.R. 287

[26] See, *e.g. Palk v. Mortgage Services Funding plc* [1993] Ch. 330 at 338 and *Medforth v. Blake* [2000] Ch. 86. See also *Leech v. National Bank of New Zealand* [1995] 2 N.Z.L.R. 30.

[27] *Per* Nicholls V.-C. in *Palk v. Mortgage Services Funding plc* [1993] Ch. 330 at 338A. See also *Hughes v. Williams* (1806) 12 Ves. 493.

[28] *China and South Sea Bank Ltd v. Tan Soon Gin* [1990] 1 A.C. 536

[29] See below, para. 7–030.

[30] See, e.g. *Cuckmere Brick v. Mutual Finance Ltd* [1971] Ch. 949; *Downsview Nominees Ltd v. First City Corp* [1993] A.C. 297 at 315; *Yorkshire Bank plc v. Hall* [1999] 1 W.L.R. 1713 at 1728E–F; and *Medforth v. Blake* [2000] Ch. 86 at 98H–99A.

[31] *Gilligan & Nugent v. National Bank Ltd* [1901] 2 I.R. 513. For the perpetuation of this approach in precluding a claim for loss of title deeds, see *Browning v. Handiland's Group* (1976) 35 P.C.C.R. 345. For the analogous application in case of resale by a vendor on default by a purchaser, see *Sullivan v. Darkin* [1986] N.Z.L.R. 214.

Chancery went further and recognised a duty of care on sale on the part of the mortgagee in the case of *Wolff v. Vanderzee*[32] and the existence of this duty was affirmed by the Privy Council in *McHugh v. Union Bank of Canada*.[33]

7–017   This equitable duty of care has on occasion been equated with and expressed in terms of the tort of negligence,[34] but this has been said to be wrong.[35] Nor should contractual duties be implied.[36] Whether expressed as a common law duty or as a duty in equity, the ambit of the duty is the same,[37] and as with the common law duty, the equitable duty of care may be modified, and accordingly enlarged or reduced, by contract.[38] A breach of the duty may give rise to a claim to equitable set off against any sums claimed by the mortgagee under the mortgage.[39] The limitation period is the same for a breach of a common law duty of care and an equitable duty of care.[40]

7–018   The more contentious issue is whether there should be any general duty of care or fairness owed by a mortgagee or receiver in circumstances *other* than when a power of sale is exercised.

(a) A general duty of care?

7–019   In 1955, in an extemporary judgment, the Court of Appeal in *Re B. Johnson Ltd*[41] overlooked the earlier authorities relating to the duty arising in the exercise of a power of sale and held that the only duty of a

---

[32] 10 L.T. (N.S.) 353 at 354. See also *Tomlin v. Luce* (1888) 51 Ch.D. 573; (1889) 43 Ch.D. 191 and *Nash v. Eads* (1880) 25 Sol.J. 95, CA.

[33] [1913] A.C. 299 at 311 "It is well settled law that it is the duty of a mortgagee when realizing the mortgaged property by sale to behave in conducting such realization as a reasonable man would behave in the realization of his own property, so that the mortgagor may receive credit for the fair value of the property sold". See also *Movitex v. Bulfield* [1988] B.C.L.C. 105.

[34] See cases cited in the second sentence above n.5, and see the reference to the bounds set by common law and equity alike on the extent to which a mortgagee can ignore the mortgagor's interests in *Palk v. Mortgage Services Funding plc* [1993] Ch. 330 at 337F.

[35] *Downsview Nominees Ltd v. First City Corp* [1993] 2 A.C. 295 at 315. It can be no objection that the breach of an equitable duty gives rise to a claim in damages: see, *e.g. Bristol and West Building Society v. Mothew* [1998] Ch. 1, CA. But there have been suggestions that the imposition of such a duty of care has no foundation in traditional equitable principles in the absence of a fiduciary relationship: see the comment by Sealy in [2000] Camb. L.J. 31 at 33. In *Medforth v. Blake* at [2000] Ch. 102E, Scott V.-C. demonstrated obvious irritation at such debate over the precise source of the duty of care "I do not, for my part, think it matters one jot whether the duty is expressed as a common law duty or a duty in equity. The result is the same". But it is suggested that the issue may well be of some significance given the limited application of the Unfair Contract Terms Act 1977, which only applies to *common law* duties of care: see below, para. 7–054.

[36] *Yorkshire Bank plc v. Hall* [1999] 1 W.L.R. 1713 at 1728D; [1999] 1 All E.R. 879 at 893.

[37] *Medforth v. Blake* [2000] Ch. 86 at 102D–E.

[38] But it should be noted that the potential application of the Unfair Contract Terms Act 1977 may be different: see below para. 7–054.

[39] *TSB Bank plc v. Platts* [1998] 2 B.C.L.C. 1, and see below, Chap. 16. A breach of contractual duty owed by a creditor to a guarantor, if repudiatory, may operate to discharge the guarantor from all liability, but a breach of the equitable duty (and in particular the duty on sale to obtain the best price reasonably obtainable) does not have this effect: *Stott v. Skipton BS* [2000] 1 All E.R. (Comm) 257.

[40] *Raja v. Lloyd's TSB Bank plc, The Times,* May 16, 2000.

[41] [1955] Ch. 634 at 651, *per* Sir R. Evershed M.R. and at 662, *per* Jenkins L.J.

receiver and manager was to act in good faith and in accordance with the powers given to him under the debenture, but that in no circumstances did he owe to the mortgagor a duty of care. In 1971 the equitable duty of care on a sale was revived by the Court of Appeal in *Cuckmere Brick v. Mutual Finance*[42] and was later reinforced by the decision of the Privy Council in 1983 in the case of *Tse Kwong Lam v. Wong Chit Sen*.[43] The like duty on the part of a receiver was recognised by the Court of Appeal in 1982 in the case of *Standard Chartered Bank v. Walker*.[44]

In *Downsview Nominees Ltd v. First City Corporation Ltd*[45] ("*Downsview*") the Privy Council affirmed that a mortgagee who was not in possession or a receiver and manager appointed by him who decided to exercise a power of sale owed a duty to take reasonable care to obtain the best price reasonably obtainable, but held that neither a mortgagee nor a receiver owed a general duty of care in any other circumstances. In *Yorkshire Bank plc v. Hall*[46] ("*Yorkshire Bank*"), Robert Walker L.J. also rejected a suggestion that a general equitable duty of care should be imposed upon a mortgagee simply because in the circumstances there was no conflict between his interests and those of the mortgagor, stating that such a principle would "be fraught with uncertainty and difficulty" and that he could "find no warrant for it in the authorities".[47]   **7–020**

The view expressed in *Downsview*, circumscribing so narrowly the circumstances in which a mortgagee who was not in possession or receiver might owe a duty of care was the subject of detailed criticism in the second edition of this work and has now been rejected by the Court of Appeal in *Medforth v. Blake*[48] ("*Medforth*").   **7–021**

In *Medforth*, Scott V.-C. did not differ from Robert Walker L.J.'s views in the *Yorkshire Bank* case, but indicated clearly that he regarded the views expressed by Lord Templeman in *Downsview* as being too narrow. Scott V.-C. found that it "does not seem to me to make commercial sense nor, more importantly, to correspond with the principles expressed in the bulk of the authorities" that a duty of care should be owed when a power of sale was exercised, but not when a power to manage a business was being exercised. Scott V.-C. also founded himself heavily upon what was conceded to be the duty of a mortgagee in possession to exercise due diligence in the management of the charged property.   **7–022**

Scott V.-C. expressed the view that equity should be flexible in adjusting the duties owed according to the "requirements of the time"   **7–023**

---

[42] [1971] Ch. 949. *Re B. Johnson* was not cited or referred to in *Re Cuckmere Brick*. In *American Express International Banking Corp v. Hurley* [1985] 3 All E.R. 564, Mann J. held that the law was as stated in *Cuckmere Brick* and not *Re B. Johnson*.

[43] [1983] 1 W.L.R. 1349.

[44] [1982] 1 W.L.R. 1410 followed in *American Express International Banking Corp v. Hurley,* [1985] 3 All E.R. 564 and *Bishop v. Bonham* [1988] 1 W.L.R. 742 at 750; and in *Ireland in McGowan v. Gannas* [1983] I.L.R.M. 516.

[45] [1993] 2 A.C. 295.

[46] [1999] 1 W.L.R. 1713

[47] *ibid.*, at 1729A–C

[48] [2000] Ch. 86.

and that the extent and scope of any duty additional to a duty of good faith would depend upon the particular facts of the particular case.[49] He then held that subject to what he acknowledged was a receiver's primary duty to bring about a situation in which interest on the secured debt can be paid and the debt itself repaid, a receiver who exercises his powers to manage charged property owes a duty to the mortgagor and to those interested in the equity of redemption to do so with due diligence.[50]

7–024   Although the decision in *Medforth* has not commanded universal support, and might be criticised for the methods by which Scott V.-C. sought to distinguish some of the contrary authorities, it has generally been welcomed as bringing the law into line with good commercial practice.[51] As Scott V.-C. acknowledged, receivers must be free to put the interests of the debenture-holder first in making any decision in good faith as to the course which the receivership will take. But subject to that overriding requirement, there will usually be no good reason why, in implementing their decisions in relation both to management and disposal of charged assets, receivers should not be required to use reasonable skill and care and be answerable to the mortgagor if they do not.[52]

7–025   It is suggested that the approach to the imposition of equitable duties in *Medforth* will necessarily require in each case an examination of whether there is any conflict between the interests of the mortgagee and the mortgagor. If there is such conflict, then the receiver will not be liable to the mortgagor if he chooses to put the interests of the mortgagee first, in accordance with his principal duty.

7–026   Where the interests of the mortgagee and mortgagor are not in conflict, then it is suggested that as a matter of principle the courts should be ready to impose a duty of care upon a mortgagee or receiver in the absence of some relevant countervailing consideration. In other words, the existence of a coincidence of interests is a strong pointer to the existence of a duty of care, but it will not invariably bring such a duty into existence.

7–027   Where the interests of the mortgagee and mortgagor are not in conflict, a further pointer to the existence or absence of a duty of care may also be whether the exercise of the power in question involves the incurring of risks or liabilities or the expenditure (or foregoing) of money which would otherwise be available for the potential repayment of the mortgage.

7–028   An example of the existence of a conflict between the interests of chargor and chargee so as to exclude a duty of care is to be seen in the

---

[49] *Medforth* at 102B–D

[50] *Medforth* at 102F–H.

[51] For a contrary view from Australia, to the effect that *Medforth* is not only inconsistent with *Downsview* but also "shows a limited understanding of the historical genesis of receiverships" see O'Donovan, *Company Receivers and Administrators* (2nd ed.), para. 11–260, referring, *inter alia* to *Expo International Pty Ltd v. Chant* [1979] 2 N.S.W.L.R. 820.

[52] See the comment by Frisby in (2000) 63 M.L.R. 413 at 420–421 to the effect that what is being targeted is careless behaviour rather than a deliberate course of conduct that will benefit the mortgagee to the detriment of the mortgagor. Properly analysed and applied, *Medforth* does not overturn the balance of power between mortgagee and mortgagor.

exercise of the contractual power of appointment of a receiver. The very appointment of a receiver involves an inherent conflict of interest, involving as it does the replacement as managers of the mortgagor's property of the directors by the appointee of the debenture-holder's choice. In such a situation, in the absence of some qualification in the debenture, the debenture-holder is entitled to look only to his own interests. So long as he acts in good faith, if he considers that the appointment will serve his best interests, he is under no duty to refrain from doing so because such an appointment will frustrate advanced negotiations to refinance the company or will cause loss to the company or its unsecured creditors.[53]

But whilst a mortgagee may owe no duty of care in making the **7–029** decision whether and if so when to appoint, if the power to appoint a receiver is exercised, it is the interest of both mortgagee and mortgagor that care should be taken to ensure that a competent and qualified person is appointed. Hence a duty of care may be owed to ensure the appointment of a competent professional.[54]

As indicated above, a mortgagee has no duty at any time to exercise **7–030** his powers as a mortgagee, to take possession or to appoint a receiver and preserve the security[55] or its value[56] or to realise or exploit his security, *e.g.* by selling securities before they become valueless.[57] The mortgagee is free to exercise the rights and remedies available to him "simultaneously or contemporaneously or successively or not at all".[58] But once the decision has been taken by the mortgagee to exercise his power to appoint a receiver, then provided that action would not damage the interests of the debenture-holder,[59] the receiver has no right to remain passive if this would damage the interests of the company as mortgagor. The receiver has the power to manage independent of the power to sell[60] and provided that the debenture-holder is not prejudiced, the receiver must be active in the protection and preservation of the charged property over which he has been appointed. Accordingly the receiver of a reversion upon a lease may be liable at the instance of the mortgagor and the mortgagee for the respective loss occasioned to them by failure to inspect the lease and trigger a rent review clause in due time.[61] But the receiver is not obliged to carry on the company's business

---

[53] *Re Potters Oils Ltd (No. 2)* [1986] 1 W.L.R. 201.

[54] *Shamji v. Johnson Matthey Bankers Ltd* [1991] B.C.L.C. 36 at 42. The requirement that an administrative receiver has to be qualified insolvency practitioner to be eligible for appointment under the Insolvency Act 1986 suggests that this duty will usually be satisfied by the appointment of such a person.

[55] *AIB Finance v. Debtors* [1998] 2 B.C.L.C. 665.

[56] *Yorkshire Bank plc v. Hall* [1999] 1 W.L.R. 1713.

[57] *China Sea Bank Ltd v. Tan Soon Gin (alias George Tan)* [1990] 1 A.C. 536.

[58] *ibid.* 545 quoted with approval by Callinan J. in the High Court of Australia and in *Pan Foods v. ANZ Bank* (2000) 170 A.L.T.R. 579 at 592.

[59] The debenture-holder may, of course, be required to give his consent as holder of security to disposals by the receiver of charged assets.

[60] *Medforth v. Blake* [2000] Ch. 86 at 103A.

[61] *Knight v. Lawrence* [1991] B.C.C. 411, cited with approval in *Medforth v. Blake* [2000] Ch. 86 at 99F.

either at the expense of the debenture-holder or at the mortgaged premises.[62]

7-031   A mortgagee is not a trustee of his power of sale and accordingly can be under no duty to the mortgagor to exercise that power.[63] A receiver is likewise under no general duty to exercise a power of sale,[64] but may be obliged to do so if a failure to do so would cause loss to the mortgagee and mortgagor (*e.g.* by the goods in question perishing).

7-032   Having determined to exercise a power of sale, subject to one qualification, the mortgagee and receiver are entitled to choose their own time for that sale.[65] This means that they are not obliged to defer a sale until an expected rise in the market is realised[66] or until after the company has had the opportunity to redeem the mortgage,[67] or (it is suggested) until after making an application for planning permission or until after the outcome of such an application is known. The one qualification is that apart from cases where there is a need for an urgent sale (*e.g.* where the goods are perishable) they must fairly and properly expose the property to the market or sell at a price which is based upon such exposure.[68] It has been suggested that elementary common sense and fairness may require them to avoid selling at the worst possible moment for the mortgagor,[69] but this suggestion cannot stand with the priority to be accorded to the mortgagee's interests in obtaining repayment.

7-033   Where there is a market for the asset in question, the duty to take reasonable care to obtain the best price reasonably obtainable[70] will usually require a sale to be made at the current market value.[71] The

---

[62] *Medforth v. Blake* [2000] Ch. 86 at 102G-H; *Expo International Pty Ltd v. Chant* [1979] 2 N.S.W.L.R. 820 at 841–842. See further, paras 8–020 to 8–027 below.

[63] *Bishop v. Bonham* [1988] 1 W.L.R. 742 at 749 citing *Cuckmere Brick v. Mutual Finance* [1971] Ch. 949 at 965–6.

[64] *Routestone Ltd v. Minories Finance Ltd* [1997] B.C.C. 180 at 187G.

[65] *Cuckmere Brick v. Mutual Finance* [1971] Ch. 949 at 965G–966A; *Reliance Permanent Building Society v. Harwood-Stamper* [1944] Ch. 362 at 372; *and Bank of Cyprus (London) Ltd v. Gill* [1980] 2 Lloyd's Rep. 51. Compare the analogous duty of a vendor, who sues for damages for breach of contract, to mitigate damages, a duty which does not extend to nursing the land as a speculative builder and to sell it off gradually: see *Keck v. Faber Jellett and Keeble* (1915) 60 Sol.J. 378.

[66] *Cuckmere Brick v. Mutual Finance* [1971] Ch. 949; *South Sea Bank Ltd v. Tan Soon Gin (alias George Tan)* [1990] 1 A.C. 536. See also *Henry Roach (Petroleum) Pty Ltd v. Credit House (Vic) Pty Ltd* [1976] V.R. 309 at 313 and *Pendlebury v. Colonial Mutual Life Assurance Society Ltd* (1912) 13 C.L.R. 676 at 701.

[67] *Routestone Ltd v. Minories Finance Ltd* [1997] B.C.C. 180.

[68] *Predeth v. Castle Phillips Finance Co. Ltd* [1986] 2 E.G.L.R. 144 at 148D, *per* Ralph Gibson LJ.

[69] *Per* Lord Denning M.R. in *Standard Chartered Bank v. Walker* [1982] 1 W.L.R. 1410, CA. This may be particularly important where there are drastic seasonal fluctuations in price, as in some agricultural situations. In *McGowan v. Gannas* [1983] I.L.R.M. 516 Carrol J. posed, but left unanswered, the question whether a receiver, who knows that the market is very bad, is entitled to go ahead and sell at a bargain price.

[70] *Cuckmere Brick v. Mutual Finance* [1971] Ch. 949.

[71] *China and South Seas Bank Ltd v. Tan Soon Gin (alias George Tan)* [1990] 1 A.C. 536 at 545, cited with approval in *Palk v. Mortgage Services Funding plc* [1993] Ch. 330 at 337. See further s. 420A(1) of the Australian Corporations Law and s. 345B of the New Zealand Companies Act 1955 which reflect the distinction between market value and the

mortgagee or receiver are accordingly obliged to make reasonable and proper arrangements to expose the property to the market and to achieve the sale itself. This duty may be broken, for example, if advertisements for the property are placed too late, or in an obscure newspaper, or omit the fact that the property has the benefit of a valuable planning permission, or if inquiries from interested parties are not responded to in an appropriate manner.[72] Likewise the duty may be broken if the receiver or mortgagee selects an inappropriate method of sale by private treaty rather than some form of public auction or following a public tender process.

In *Palk v. Mortgage Services Funding plc*[73] ("*Palk*") the Court of **7–034** Appeal left open the question whether a mortgagee can, instead of selling, lease the property in such a way that the accruing interest exceeds the rent and substantially increases the burden on the mortgagor. It is suggested that, as was evident on the facts of that case, the interests of mortgagor and mortgagee in such a case may well be in conflict. The mortgagor would wish there to be an order for sale of his house in order to stop interest accruing on most of the mortgage debt, but the mortgagee might not wish the house to be sold until the property market improved. If such a conflict exists, it is suggested that a decision not to sell could only constitute a breach of duty by the mortgagee if it is so improvident as to be indicative of a lack of good faith on his part. But where a mortgagee intends to act in such a way that the refusal to sell exposes the mortgagor to a risk of loss disproportionate to any gain to the mortgagee, the court may, in its discretion, order the sale of the property at the suit of the mortgagor pursuant to section 91(2) of the Law of Property Act 1925 (which expressly applies to actions for foreclosure, redemption or for sale). This is not the same as imposing an independent duty upon the mortgagee which would give rise to a reduction in the secured debt or in an obligation to pay compensation in equity.

(b) A general duty of fairness?

In the Court of Appeal in *Palk*, Nicholls V.-C. made a number of **7–035** observations, obiter, as to the duties which a mortgagee owes to a mortgagor. He stated that,

> ". . . in the exercise of his rights over his security the mortgagee must act fairly towards the mortgagor. His interest in the property has priority over the interest of the mortgagor, and he is entitled to proceed on that footing. He can protect his own interest, but he is

---

best price reasonably obtainable. For an illustration of circumstances in which the market was not tested, but where the best price reasonably obtainable was secured, see *Re Blastclean Services Ltd* (1985) 2 N.Z.C.L.C. 99,282.

[72] See, e.g. *American Express International Banking Corp v. Hurley* [1985] 3 All E.R. 564; *Commercial and General Acceptance Ltd v. Nixon* (1981) 152 C.L.R. 491; *Davy v. Nathan Securities Ltd* (1989) 4 N.Z.C.L.C. 65,321.

[73] [1993] Ch. 330

not entitled to conduct himself in a way which unfairly prejudices the mortgagor. If he takes possession, he might prefer to do nothing and bide his time, waiting indefinitely for an improvement in the market, with the property empty meanwhile. That he cannot do. He is accountable for his actual receipts from the property. He is also accountable to the mortgagor for what he would have received but for his default. So he must take reasonable care of the property. Similarly if he sells the property; he cannot sell hastily at a knock-down price sufficient to pay off his debt. The mortgagor also has an interest in the property and is under a personal liability for the shortfall. The mortgagee must keep that in mind. He must exercise reasonable care to sell only at the proper market value . . . ."

7–036 Nicholls V.-C. then expressed the view, again *obiter*, that the mortgagee's duties in and about the exercise of his powers of letting and sale should not be confined to the duty to obtain a proper market rent or a proper market price, and concluded that,

> "quite apart from section 91(2) there is a legal framework which imposes some constraints of fairness on a mortgagee who is exercising his remedies over his security."

7–037 Reference can also be made to similar comments by Scott V.-C. in his judgment in *Medforth*. Scott V.-C. did not refer to the decision in *Palk*, albeit that it was cited to the Court of Appeal, but he did make a passing reference to the fact that the equitable duties which were imposed upon a mortgagee were "introduced in order to ensure that a mortgagee dealt fairly and equitably with the mortgagor".

7–038 It is suggested that when read in context, the remarks of Nicholls V.-C. in *Palk* and Scott V.-C. in *Medforth* were not intended to establish a free-standing duty upon a mortgagee to act fairly to a mortgagor in all circumstances, or a new basis upon which a mortgagor could seek to challenge the conduct of a mortgagee or receiver on the grounds of "unfair prejudice" to his interests. Were there to be such a free-standing duty to act fairly, it would subsume (and render redundant) the established free-standing duties to act in good faith and to act with due care. The remarks in *Palk* and *Medforth* are to be understood as setting out the core aim of Equity of achieving a fair balance between the interests of the mortgagor and mortgagee. Equity achieves this result (1) by imposing the free-standing duty to act in good faith, (2) (where to do so does not interfere with the right of the mortgagee to have regard exclusively to his own interests) by imposing the free-standing duty to act with due care and regard for the interests of the mortgagor, and (3) by requiring the court to take into account the question of fairness when any question arises as to the exercise of a discretion *e.g.* whether to order a sale of mortgaged property at the instance of the mortgagor against the wishes of the mortgagee.

5. THE CONTENT OF THE DUTY OF CARE

A mortgagee or receiver is only to be adjudged negligent if he has acted **7–039** as no mortgagee or receiver of ordinary competence acting with ordinary care and (where appropriate) on competent advice would act. In deciding whether he has fallen short of his duty, the facts must be looked at broadly and he will not be adjudged to be in default unless he is plainly on the wrong side of the line. Thus, if two or more alternative courses of action are available, there is no negligence if the course taken might have commended itself to a competent mortgagee or receiver, even though subsequent events show that it was in fact the "wrong" course.[74] No allowance will be made for lack of experience or expertise on the part of the mortgagee or receiver.[75] But the failure to seek expert advice may in certain circumstances constitute negligence.[76] Thus, the sale of sound and lighting equipment for use at concerts of popular music, being of a specialist nature, has been held to require specialist advice from a person knowledgeable about the popular music industry.[77] Equally, in the case of a sale of land it is likely to be appropriate for a mortgagee or receiver to obtain and pay due regard to expert professional advice.

What is the position if proper care is taken to select and instruct such **7–040** an expert, the advice of such expert is obtained and quite reasonably accepted and acted on, but such advice is subsequently found to be both wrong and negligent? Is the mortgagee or receiver liable to the mortgagor despite the absence of any personal fault? Who should bear the risk of such negligence?

The question whether the mortgagee is liable in these circumstances **7–041** was considered by the members of the Court of Appeal in the case of *Cuckmere Brick*, but only decided by Cross L.J. who in his judgment said as follows:

> "[Counsel for the mortgagee] further submitted that even if we should be of opinion that a mortgagee was liable to account to the mortgagor for loss occasioned by his own negligence in the exercise of his power of sale, it was not right that he should be liable for the negligence of an agent reasonably employed by him . . . I do not accept the submission. In support of it, counsel pointed out that a trustee is not liable for the default of an agent whom it is reasonable for him to employ. But the position of a mortgagee is quite different from that of a trustee. A trustee has not, qua trustee, any interest in

---

[74] Consider *Maynard v. West Midland RHA* [1984] 1 W.L.R. 634 at 638.

[75] See *Clark & Lindsell on Torts* (17th ed.) Chap. 11.

[76] "It may well be right that in most cases for a liquidator to sell an asset of the company without a proper valuation would amount to negligence, but I do not think that that is something which can be laid down as a general rule": *per* Nourse L.J. in *Pitman v. Top Business Systems* [1984] B.C.L.C. 593 at 597d–597e.

[77] *American Express Banking Corp v. Hurley* [1985] 3 All E.R. 564 where the judge held the receiver negligent in failing (1) to obtain such advice and (2) to advertise the sale in publications concerning the popular music industry.

the trust property,[78] and if an agent employed by him is negligent his right of action against the agent is an asset of the trust. A mortgagee, on the other hand, is not a trustee and if he sues the agent for negligence any damages which he can recover belong to him.[79] Of course in many cases the mortgagee may suffer no damage himself by reason of the agent's negligence because the purchase price, though less than it should have been, exceeds what is owing to the mortgagee. In such circumstances it may be that nowadays the law would allow the mortgagor to recover damages directly from the agent although not in contractual relations with him; but that was certainly not so 100 years ago when *Wolff v. Vanderzee*[80] was decided. In those days the only way to achieve justice between the parties was to say that the mortgagee was liable to the mortgagor for any damage which the latter suffered by the agent's negligence and to leave the mortgagee to recover such damages, and also any damage which he has suffered himself, from the agent. I do not think that we can say that the mortgagee used to be liable to the mortgagor for the negligence of his agent, but that that liability disappeared at some unspecified moment of time when the law had developed enough to allow the mortgagor to sue the agent himself.

In my judgment, therefore, if either the [defendant mortgagees] or [the agents] were guilty of negligence in connection with the sale, the defendants are liable to compensate the plaintiffs [mortgagors] for any damage they have suffered by reason of that negligence."[81]

7–042   The other members of the Court found it unnecessary to decide the question, because in the court below the mortgagees had conceded that they were liable for any negligence of their agents. But Salmon L.J.[82] did say that the argument against liability "certainly could not be squared with Cotton L.J.'s judgment in *Tomlin v. Luce*" and Cairns L.J.[83] stated that, if the point were open to the defendants, "I should need more argument to satisfy me that Kekewich J. and Cotton L.J. [in *Tomlin v. Luce*][84] were wrong".

[78] *i.e.* beneficial interest. A trustee has of course his right to a lien.
[79] Whilst the mortgagee cannot claim more than his own loss (see *per* Aickin J. in *Commercial and General Acceptance Ltd v. Nixon* (1981) 152 C.L.R. 491, his loss includes any liability to the mortgagor, and accordingly the imposition of a strict liability on the mortgagee ensures that there is recovered the full difference between the price obtained and the price that should have been obtained.
[80] (1869) 20 L.T. 350. In that case, Stuart V.-C. held that a mortgagee was accountable to the mortgagor for the loss in purchase price occasioned by the auctioneer describing the property as let at £150 per annum when in fact it was let at £182.
[81] At 973.
[82] At 969.
[83] At 980.
[84] Kekewich J. at (1888) 41 Ch.D. 573 held that a first mortgagee was liable to account for the loss occasioned to the second mortgagee by the auctioneer misdescribing the roads on the property as completely kerbed, which led to the allowance of compensation to the purchaser. His judgment was challenged, not on liability, but quantum. The challenge was

The approach adopted by Cross L.J. creates a form of strict liability on **7–043** the mortgagee. His duty of care to sell at the best price reasonably obtainable is not delegable in the sense that he can avoid or perform his duty merely by appointing a reputable agent to conduct the sale, but extends to ensuring that reasonable care is taken by any agent or professional adviser employed by him in the sale. The extension of his duty may be an accident of history, but it promotes justice for the mortgagor who is thereby saved from the invidious, and often difficult, task of apportioning blame between the mortgagee and his agents and can also claim credit for any loss when settling accounts with the mortgagee.[85] Moreover, the mortgagee can be assumed to be better placed to know the facts relating to a claim against the agent,[86] is frequently in a better financial position to pursue the claim, and ultimately it must be remembered that it was the mortgagee who chose the agent who was later negligent.[87] Once the special rule applicable to mortgagees is accepted, there is no sufficient reason to distinguish the position of the mortgagee and the receiver,[88] and it would therefore appear that a receiver is subject to a like strict liability in respect of disposals.[89] After *Medforth* it remains to be seen whether similarly strict principles will be applied to the negligence of agents in situations other than disposals of the charged property.

---

successful, but the Court of Appeal proceeded on the basis that the finding of liability was correct: (1889) 43 Ch.D. 191. The judgment of the Court of Appeal was referred to with apparent approval in *Downsview* at 312 and *Medforth* at 934D–E as deciding that a mortgagee is liable for the loss occasioned by a misstatement by his appointed auctioneer. The judgment of Kekewich J. drew a distinction between errors in matters of detail (for which a mortgagee was not liable) and serious blunders (for which he was liable), but it is suggested that the proper distinction is between errors that amount to negligence and errors that do not: see *per* Gibbs C.J. in *Commercial & General Acceptance Ltd v. Nixon* (1981) 152 C.L.R. 491 at 497 and *per* Aickin J. at 511.

[85] This is the approach adopted in relation to an equivalent statutory duty in *Commercial & General Acceptances Ltd v. Nixon* (1981) 152 C.L.R. 491.

[86] "For a mortgagor to sue an agent in circumstances where there has been no prior relationship between them and he cannot know the instructions that were given by the mortgagee could be an exercise fraught with difficulty": *per* Wilson J. in *Commercial & General Acceptances Ltd v. Nixon,* (1981) 152 C.L.R. 491 at 520 and see *per* Mason J. at 505.

[87] This factor was adverted to as relevant to the question whether the duty was "delegable" or not by Lord Radcliffe in *Riverstone Meat v. Lancashire Shipping* [1961] A.C. 807 at 863. For a consideration of the scope of delegable and non-delegable duties in tort, *e.g. Street on Tort*, (10th ed.), pp. 250–2. The alternative would be to liken the liability of the mortgagee to that of a solicitor who does not abdicate all responsibility by acting on the advice of counsel, but is normally protected if he does: *Davy-Chiesman v. Davy-Chiesman* [1984] Fam. 48. A similar strict duty is imposed by statute on building societies (see *Reliance Permanent BS v. Harwood-Stamper* [1944] 1 Ch. 362 at 372) and on all mortgagees in Queensland: see *Commercial & General Acceptances Ltd v. Nixon* (1981) 152 C.L.R. 491, above. Consider also *Austin Securities Ltd v. Northgate* [1969] 1 W.L.R. 529 (liquidator cannot shelter behind mistakes of solicitor).

[88] The receiver may readily be assumed to be protected by an insurance policy covering such a claim, as to the potential relevance of which see *Smith v. Bush* [1990] 1 A.C. 831 at 858–859.

[89] *Medforth* at [2000] Ch. 99F citing *Tomlin v. Luce* (1889) 43 Ch.D. 191.

6. THE SELF-DEALING AND FAIR-DEALING RULES

7–044 These two rules impose constraints upon sales (and other dealings) by a mortgagee and receiver. Mortgagees and receivers both owe fiduciary duties.[90] A trustee (a term which includes a trustee for debenture-holders[91]) is subject to a very strict "self-dealing" rule to the effect that he will not be allowed to enter into a transaction in which he has a personal interest which may conflict with his duty unless he has the informed consent of all of the beneficiaries or the leave of the court.[92] A receiver is subject to a like duty and is accordingly disqualified from purchasing charged property from the mortgagee[93] and (in the case of a receiver appointed by trustees for debenture-holders) from purchasing debentures from debenture-holders without the leave of the court. Mortgagees are, however, subject to less severe restrictions[94]:

(a) a strict but very limited "self-dealing" rule whereby a mortgagee may not sell to himself or to a trustee for himself; and

(b) a "fair dealing" rule whereby a conflict of interest makes a sale voidable (or the subject of a claim to damages) unless it can be shown (the onus being on the mortgagee or purchaser) that the sale was at full market value.

It is considered that where a receiver sells as agent of the mortgagor to a company in which the mortgagee has an interest: (1) the self-dealing rule does not apply, since there are two real parties to the transaction; and (2) the fair dealing rule is applicable on the basis that the receivership sale involves the exercise of the mortgagee's remedies. To be absolutely safe in such a case, the mortgagee can seek a sale by the court.

7–045   The case of *Tse Kwong Lam v. Wong Chit Sen*[95] is illuminating as to the application of these rules and the nature and extent of the duties of a mortgagee and the remedies available to a mortgagor. The mortgagee sold the mortgaged property at auction at an undervalue to a company of which he was a director and shareholder and of which the remaining directors and shareholders were his wife and children. The mortgagor sought to set aside the sale and in the alternative claimed damages. The Privy Council held that:

(a) whilst a mortgagee cannot validly sell to himself, or a trustee for himself, a sale to a company in which he is interested is not necessarily invalid; but in view of the conflict of interest and duty involved, the ordinary rules regarding burden of proof are

---

[90] *Watts v. Midland Bank* [1986] B.C.L.C. 15 at 23.

[91] *Re Magadi Soda Co.* (1925) 95 L.J.R. (Ch.) 217.

[92] *Tito v. Waddell (No. 2)* [1977] Ch. 106; *Re Thompson's Settlement* [1986] Ch. 99; *Snell on Equity* (30th ed.), para 11–68.

[93] *Nugent v. Nugent* [1908] 1 Ch. 546 (purchase from mortgagee).

[94] *Farrar v. Farrar's Ltd* (1888) 40 Ch.D. 395, CA; *Tse Kwong Lam v. Wong Chit Sen* [1983] 1 W.L.R. 1394, PC; *Movitex v. Bulfield* [1988] B.C.L.C. 104.

[95] [1983] 1 W.L.R. 1349.

reversed, and in order to sustain the transaction and avoid a claim in damages the mortgagee and his company must affirmatively prove that reasonable care was taken to obtain the best price;

(b) the mortgagee had failed in his duty to take all reasonable steps to obtain the best price reasonably obtainable;

(c) the mortgagee was not excused from this duty or the consequences of his breach by a provision in the mortgage excluding liability for selling without first complying with the requirements as to the existence of default by the mortgagor or giving prior notice to the mortgagor;

(d) the ordinary remedy for the breach in such a case (where the purchaser was related in this way to the mortgagee) was an order setting aside the sale;

(e) such remedy was precluded by the delay of the mortgagor in seeking such a remedy, since the purchaser had meanwhile incurred substantial expenditure on the property and the grant of such a remedy would be inequitable; and

(f) damages should be awarded representing the difference between the true market value at the date of the auction and the price in fact paid.

Lord Templeman stated the law relating to the relevant duties thus: **7–046**

"The mortgagee and the company seeking to uphold the transaction must show that the sale was in good faith and that the mortgagee took reasonable precautions to obtain the best price reasonably obtainable at the time. The mortgagee is not, however, bound to postpone the sale in the hope of obtaining a better price or to adopt a piecemeal method of sale which could only be carried out over a substantial period or at some risk of loss."[96]

7. EXCLUSION OR LIMITATION OF LIABILITY

The question arises how far (if at all) it is possible to exclude or limit a **7–047** duty or liability of the mortgagee or receiver. As seen above, the duty or liability will ordinarily be owed to the mortgagor and to all persons interested in the equity of redemption including any guarantor. Although seeking and obtaining the informed consent of each member of the class affected will no doubt preclude subsequent challenge, in most cases it is unlikely to be possible to obtain such unanimous consent. It is a sensible precaution (where practicable) to give members notice of a proposed transaction, and thus afford an opportunity to them to make representations, but a failure to object prior to the transaction does not preclude any challenge to the transaction after it has been completed. Accordingly

[96] [1983] 1 W.L.R. 1349 at 1355.

it will in most cases be necessary to look at whether provisions in the mortgage or guarantee are effective to limit the duty or liability of the mortgagee or receiver.

(a) Privity of contract

7–048 A mortgage or guarantee may contain express provisions limiting the duty or liability of the mortgagee.[97] When considering whether and if so to what extent the mortgage or guarantee may limit the duty or liability of the receiver, who is not a party to the contract, it is necessary to have regard to the position both at common law and under statute.

7–049   At common law, whilst the mortgagee may obtain protection for himself, the established principles of privity of contract[98] continue to preclude the conferment of any direct exemption on third parties, *e.g.* any prospective receiver.[99] They equally preclude the recognition by English law of any doctrine of vicarious immunity, *i.e.* that an agent performing a contract for his principal is entitled to any immunity from liability which the contract confers on the principal.[100] But the law of contract recognises four possible indirect methods of securing the protection of the receiver which may be reflected in a provision in the mortgage or guarantee:

(a) the mortgagee expressly contracting as agent for any such receiver (an agency which may be previously authorised or subsequently ratified) may exact from the mortgagor or guarantor a term limiting the duty or liability of the receiver[1];

(b) the mortgagor or guarantor may agree with the mortgagee not to sue the receiver (which agreement the mortgagee can enforce for the benefit of the receiver)[2];

(c) (in a case where the mortgagee assumes an obligation to indemnify the receiver) the mortgagor or guarantor may agree to pay over all the proceeds of a claim against the receiver to the mortgagee; or

---

[97] *Bishop v. Bonham* [1988] 1 W.L.R. 742 at 752. An exemption clause in a mortgage exempting a mortgagee from liability for a receiver's default will not bind a guarantor under a separate instrument: *McManus v. Royal Bank* (1983) 47 C.B.R. (N.S.) 252 at 257.

[98] Which may not survive in their current form if reviewed by the House of Lords and Privy Council: see *The Mahkutai* [1996] A.C. 650 at 664–5.

[99] For a consideration of this topic, see E. Macdonald, *Exemption Clauses and Unfair Terms* (1999), pp.229–248.

[100] *Scruttons v. Midland Silicones* [1962] A.C. 446. A contract may confer immunity against claims in tort by third parties in exceptional circumstances: *Leigh & Sillivan Ltd v. Aliakmon Shipping Co. Ltd* [1985] Q.B. 350 at 397 approved in *White v. Jones* [1995] 2 A.C. 207 at 239, *per* Steyn L.J.; *Southern Water Authority v. Carey* [1985] 2 All E.R. 1077; *Norwich City Council v. Harvey* [1989] 1 W.L.R. 828 at 837.

[1] See *Anson's Law of Contract*, (27th ed.), pp. 442–4 In *Expo International Ply. Ltd v. Chant* [1979] 2 N.S.W.L.R. 820 Needham J. held that such a provision was ineffective if the identity of the receiver was unknown at the date of the mortgage. Consider, however, *Port Jackson Stevedoring Ply. Ltd v. Salmond & Spraggon (Australia) Pty Ltd* [1981] 1 W.L.R. 138.

[2] *Snelling v. John G. Snelling Ltd* [1973] 1 Q.B. 87. See also *The Elbe Maru* [1978] 1 Lloyd's Rep. 206; *The Chevalier Roze* [1983] 2 Lloyd's Rep. 438 at 443 (need for real possibility of prejudice to mortgagor or guarantor).

(d) the mortgage or guarantee may contain a provision expressly authorising the mortgagee acting as agent for the mortgagor or guarantor to agree with the receiver as a term of his appointment that, in consideration of his acceptance of the appointment, the duty or liability of the receiver to the mortgagor or guarantor shall be restricted.

English common law has now been fundamentally changed by the **7–050** Contracts (Rights of Third Parties) Act, which came into force on the November 11, 1999 and applies to contracts which are entered into at least six months after that date (*i.e.* after May 11, 2000) or (if entered into earlier) which expressly provide for the application of the Act. Section 1 of the Act provides that a person not a party to a contract (a "third party") may in his own right enforce a term of the contract if the contract expressly provides that he may or (unless on a proper construction of the contract it appears that the parties did not intend the term to be enforceable by the third party) the term purports to confer a benefit on him.[3] The third party must be expressly identified in the contract by name, as a member of a class or as answering a particular description, but need not be in existence when the contract is entered into. Accordingly protection can be conferred both on the mortgagee and any receiver if and when appointed by the mortgagee.

(b) Construction of exemption clause

Once it is clear that an exemption provision on which the mortgagee or **7–051** receiver is entitled to rely has been included in the instrument, the next question is whether, as a matter of construction, the provision covers the breach of duty.[4] If the language of the agreement reasonably admits of two constructions, one giving a wider and the other a narrower scope for application of the exemption clause, the *contra proferentem* rule will be applied and the construction adopted giving the narrower scope. In other words, the exemption clause will only be effective if the words are clear and fairly susceptible of one meaning only.[5]

Hence a clause exempting a mortgagee from responsibility for loss **7–052** occasioned to the mortgagor on exercise of the power of sale will not exonerate a mortgagee from liability for negligence to the mortgagor; an exclusion of liability for negligence must be expressly conferred.[6] A clause giving protection against liability for sales made before the power of sale has become exercisable will not extend to claims in respect of a

---

[3] For a full consideration of the provisions of the 1999 Act see *Chitty on Contracts* (28th ed.) Chap. 19 or Treitel, *The Law of Contract* (10th ed.), p.600.

[4] For the general principles governing the construction of exemption clauses, see *Chitty on Contracts* (28th ed.), Vol. 1 paras 14.005–14.056.

[5] The same strict construction is applicable to indemnity clauses: *Canada Steamship Lines v. R.* [1952] A.C. 192 at 208.

[6] *Bishop v. Bonham* [1988] 1 W.L.R. 842 at 852 (power to sell without liability for loss howsoever arising only authorised sale within limits of duty of care imposed by the general law and, accordingly, did not exempt from liability for loss arising from failure to take care to obtain proper price).

failure to exercise due care to obtain the best price obtainable.[7] And a provision that the receiver shall be deemed the agent of the mortgagor who shall be solely responsible for his defaults will not exclude liability of the mortgagee for defaults of the receiver occasioned by the directions of the mortgagee.[8]

7–053   The *contra proferentem* rule applies both to clauses excluding liability and to clauses limiting the amount of damages recoverable (albeit less strictly in the latter case).[9] However, it is not permissible to adopt a strained construction to prevent a party in default relying on either type of clause, and such a clause may afford protection if sufficiently widely drawn, even in the case of a fundamental breach of contract.[10]

(c) Unfair Contract Terms Act 1977

7–054   The Unfair Contract Terms Act 1977 imposes two limitations on the ability to exclude or restrict liability by means of contract terms. First, it limits the extent to which civil liability for "negligence" can be avoided by means of contract terms. "Negligence" is defined as the breach of any obligation, arising from the express or implied terms of the contract or from any common law duty to take reasonable care or exercise reasonable skill. Secondly, it limits the extent to which a person who has contracted on his written standard terms of business can exclude or restrict liability for breach of contract or render a contractual performance substantially different from that which was reasonably expected of him.

7–055   At the date of the second edition of this work, the earlier view that mortgagees and receivers owed common law duties of care was in the process of being displaced by recognition of the duties as equitable. The opinion was expressed that for this reason the Act had no application, but as a matter of caution, in case this view proved wrong, there was some detailed consideration of the 1977 Act. The displacement of the earlier view is now complete[11] and it is now abundantly clear that the duties are equitable and do not arise at common law or from the express or implied terms of any contract.[12] Accordingly it would seem clear that the 1977 Act has no application to such clauses.[13]

[7] *American International Banking Corp v. Hurley* [1985] 1 All E.R. 564; *Bishop v. Bonham,* [1988] 1 W.L.R. 842.

[8] *Tse Kwong Lam v. Wong Chit Sen* [1983] 1 W.L.R. 1349 at 1360.

[9] *Standard Chartered Bank v. Walker* [1982] 1 W.L.R. 1410. But this distinction is open to question: see E. Macdonald, *Exemption Clauses and Unfair Terms* (1999), pp. 48–50.

[10] *Ailsa Craig Fishing v. Malvern Fishing* [1983] 1 W.L.R. 964, HL; *George Mitchell (Chesterhall) Ltd v. Finney Lock Seeds Ltd* [1983] 2 A.C. 803.

[11] See above, para. 7–017.

[12] See, *e.g. per* Robert Walker L.J. in *Yorkshire Bank plc v. Hall* [1999] 1 W.L.R. 1713 at 1728D–E.

[13] Likewise it has been held that a provision in trust deeds entitling trustees to charge remuneration is not contractual (see In *Re Duke of Norfolk's Settlement Trusts* [1982] 1 Ch. 61 at 77A; and that there is no statutory restriction on the breadth of exoneration clauses contained in trust deeds (see *Armitage v. Nurse* [1998] Ch. 241 and Mr Justice Lightman, "The Chancery Approach to Trustees' Liability" (1999) Vol. 5, 1 Journal of Pensions Management, 11–17). In her article at [2000] 63 M.L.R. 413, Frisby expresses a view that the courts might be persuaded to deal with the matter by a "de facto application of UCTA principles". It is suggested that this is unlikely given the approach adopted in relation to exoneration clauses and express trustees.

8. WRONGFUL INTERFERENCE WITH CONTRACT

Knowingly to procure or induce a party to break his contract to the **7–056** damage of the other contracting party without reasonable justification or excuse is a tort.[14] The tort covers dealings with the contract-breaker which the third party knows to be inconsistent with the contract. The question raised is how far this tort has application to actions of a receiver or a debenture-holder in repudiating contracts of the company.[15] The relevant principles would appear to be as follows:

(a) Notwithstanding the grant of the charge or the appointment of the receiver, in the ordinary case the contract continues in force between the parties to the contract and the other party is free to bring proceedings against the company to protect or enforce the contract by way of injunction[16] or order for specific performance of the company's obligation, *e.g.* to buy[17] or to sell.[18] Any order so made is binding on the company and the receiver to the extent that he acts as agent of the company, but unless the contract or obligation bound the chargee this order made enforcing the contract or obligation does not prejudice the rights of the chargee in respect of the enforcement of his security;

(b) If a person is granted a charge on property which he knows to be subject to a contractual obligation, he can be restrained from exercising his rights under the charge in such a way as to interfere with the performance of that contractual obligation.[19] The essential feature is the attachment of the contractual obligation to a specific asset or specific assets as opposed to the mere imposition of a requirement to fulfil an obligation (*e.g.* to make a payment or set up a fund out of the general funds of the company).[20]

---

[14] For this tort generally, see *Clarke & Lindsell on Torts* (17th ed.), Chap. 23 and *Law Debenture & Trust Corp v. Ural Caspian Oil Corp Ltd* [1995] Ch. 152.

[15] See *Re Botibol* [1947] 1 All E.R. 26 at 28 and *Airline Airspares v. Handley Page* [1970] Ch. 193. For an account of the Chap. of accidents which explain the decision in Airline Airspares, see Mr Justice Lightman, "The Challenges Ahead" [1996] J.B.L. 113 at 114.

[16] *Ash & Newman Ltd v. Creative Devices Research Ltd* [1991] B.C.L.C. 403 (protecting right of pre-emption).

[17] *Amec Properties v. Planning Research* [1992] 13 E.G. 109.

[18] *Freevale v. Metrostore Holding Ltd* [1984] Ch. 199.

[19] *Swiss Bank v. Lloyd's Bank* [1979] Ch. 548 at 571–572. See, however, *MacJordan Construction Ltd v. Brookmount Erostin Ltd* [1992] B.C.L.C. 350, CA: see also *Astor Chemical v. Synthetic Technology* and *Hill & Partners v. FNFC* [1989] B.C.L.C. 89, CA.

[20] Scott L.J. suggests in *MacJordan v. Brookmount Erostin Ltd* [1992] B.C.L.C. 350, CA that if the grant of a floating charge will not interfere, but the grant of a fixed charge will, the relief may not be available against the grantee of a floating charge who thereafter crystallises his floating charge. This suggestion cannot be correct: the result must be the same whether the grant of the fixed charge is a one-or two-stage exercise. See also the discussion of the limits of the tort in *Law Debenture & Trust Corp v. Ural Caspian Oil Corp Ltd* [1995] Ch. 152.

(c) In the absence of such knowledge, the chargee and the receiver are free (*vis-à-vis* the third parties) to cause the company to repudiate or ignore its outstanding contractual obligations to third parties as long as the chargee's title is equal to or superior to the third party's rights,[21] though this course may give rise to a claim in respect of the loss occasioned by the company if involving an unnecessary and unreasonable exercise of the chargee's powers.[22]

(d) The receiver as agent for the company is equally free of liability to third parties for causing the company to breach its contracts with them,[23] for no person can be liable for the tort of interference with contractual relations if he acts as agent for one of the contracting parties.[24] A receiver appointed by the court may not enjoy this exemption from liability since he is not the agent of the company.[25]

(e) Neither the receiver nor the debenture-holder can interfere with the existing equitable rights of third parties over property of the company having priority to the charge.[26] The reason for this is that the charge attaches only to property in which the company has a beneficial interest and to the extent of that beneficial interest.[27] A threat of such action may be restrained by injunction, and it has been suggested that such action if implemented

[21] *Hill & Partners v. FNFC* [1989] B.C.L.C. 89, CA.; *Astor Chemical Ltd v. Synthetic Technology Ltd* [1990] B.C.C. 97; *The Kalingrad* [1997] 2 Lloyd's Rep 35 at 39.

[22] *Airline Airspares v. Handley Page* [1970] Ch. 193. The receiver has the power to repudiate pre-receivership contracts with impunity unless the power is exercised dishonestly or recklessly: *Re Diesel's Components Pty Ltd* [1985] 9 A.C.L.R. 825 at 828, *per* McPherson J.

[23] *Lathia v. Dronsfield* [1987] B.C.L.C. 321, so long as he acts in good faith and within the scope of his authority.

[24] *Welsh Development Agency v. Export Finance* [1990] B.C.C. 270, CA. The Court of Appeal based the immunity of the receiver on English, Australian and New Zealand authority dealing with directors acting as agents of a company: *Said v. Butt* [1920] 2 K.B. 497; *Scammell v. Hurley* [1929] 1 K.B. 419; *Thomson v. Deakin* [1952] Ch. 646 at 680- 81; *O'Brien v. Dawson* (1942) 66 C.L.R. 18, *per* Starke J. at 32 and *per* McTiernan J. at 34, HCt. of Australia; *Rutherford v. Poole* [1953] V.L.R. 130 at 135–136, CA., Vic; *Official Assignee v. Dowling* [1964] N.Z.L.R. 578 at 580–581, Sup. Ct.N.Z.). The Court of Appeal in *Welsh Development Agency* laid to rest doubts as to the application of such agency principles to the "unusual" agency of a receiver which had been expressed by Peter Gibson J. in *Telemetrix plc v. Modern Engineers* [1985] 1 B.C.C. 99, 417 at 420. In *Einhorn v. West Mount Investments Ltd* (1969) 6 D.L.R. (3rd) 71, affd. 11 D.L.R. (3rd) 509; 73 W.W.R. 161 it was held that directors who prevented a company from performing its contract by diverting its assets to an associated company might be liable for the tort. It is unclear whether the basis of this decision was that *Said v. Butt*, above, was wrong or that the immunity of agents did not extend to directors who are in reality the masters rather than the agents of the company or that the special facts akin to sharp practice justified piercing the corporate veil. But directors are surely agents for the purpose: see *Northern Counties v. Jackson & Steeple* [1974] 1 W.L.R. 1133 at 1144. See also *Mancetter Developments v. Garmanson* [1986] Q.B. 1212 at 1223, *per* Kerr L.J. and *De Jetley Marks v. Greenwood* [1936] 1 All E.R. 863 at 872 (liability of directors in conspiracy).

[25] *Telemetrix plc v. Modern Engineers* [1985] 1 B.C.C. 99, 417 explaining *Re Botibol,* [1947] 1 All E.R. 26. This may also be the position of a receiver whose agency for the company has ceased on winding-up and who thereafter acts as principal.

[26] *Freevale v. Metrostore* [1984] Ch. 199.

[27] *Sharp v. Woodwich BS* [1998] B.C.C. 115, HL.

may constitute a tort and accordingly give rise to a claim in damages.[28] But this can only be so where the debenture-holder or receiver acted with notice of the existence of the trust.[28a]

9. TRESPASS AND BREACH OF WARRANTY

The debenture-holder and his receiver will be liable to the company in **7–057** tort for damages for the acts of the receiver in interfering with the possession of the company or dealing with its property, if the receiver is invalidly or improperly appointed.[29] The receiver will also ordinarily be liable to third parties if in the course of his receivership he takes possession of or deals with property that does not belong to the company.[30] But section 234(3) and (4) of the Insolvency Act 1986 confers upon an administrative receiver exemption from such liability if, at the date of seizure or disposal, he believes and has reasonable grounds for believing that he is entitled to seize or dispose of the property and is not negligent. The provision only applies to physical property which can be seized and does not apply, for example, to book debts.[31]

Liability may also arise for breach of warranty of authority where the **7–058** receiver in his dealings with a third party has purported to act as agent for the company when such agency never arose (because the receiver was never validly appointed) or has terminated (because of supervening liquidation or the appointment of a receiver by the court).[32]

10. LIABILITY FOR OTHER TORTS

A director is not liable for torts committed by the company merely **7–059** because it is his acts which are sufficient to make the company liable in tort: the mere carrying out of the duties of a director do not render a director liable. It is necessary that either he himself (and not the company through his agency) committed the tort; or that he assumed personal responsibility (not merely responsibility on behalf of his company) to the claimant for the acts constituting the tort; or that he ordered or procured the commission of tortious acts by the company.[33]

---

[28] *Telemetrix plc v. Modern Engineers* [1985] 1 B.C.C. 99, 417 where Peter Gibson J. granted injunctions restraining a receiver from assigning to third parties options over land already agreed by the company to be assigned to the plaintiffs after threats by the receiver to assign to the third party.

[28a] *Competitive Insurance Company v. Davies Investments Ltd* [1975] 1 W.L.R. 1240.

[29] *Ford & Carter Ltd v. Midland Bank Ltd* [1979] 129 N.L.J. 543; *Pollnow v. Garden Mews-St. Leonards Pty Ltd* (1985) 9 A.C.L.R. 82. Section 232 of the Insolvency Act 1986 is unlikely to protect an administrative receiver in this context: see above, Chap. 3.

[30] See *Re Goldburg (No. 2)* [1912] 1 K.B. 606. The third party has the option of treating the receiver as his agent in order to obtain an account of profits in relation to the receiver's dealings with the third party's property: see *Re Simms* [1934] Ch. 1, CA.

[31] *Welsh Development Agency v. Exfinco* [1992] B.C.C. 270, CA.

[32] *Starkey v. Bank of England* [1903] A.C. 114.

[33] *Williams v. Natural Life Ltd* [1998] 1 W.L.R. 830, HL; *Standard Chartered Bank v. Pakistan National Shipping Corp. (No. 2)* [2000] 1 Lloyd's Rep. 218 at 230–236, CA. See valuable discussion in the article "Directors Tortious Liability" by R. Grantham and C. Rickett in (1999) 62 M.L.R. 133.

In each case, the degree of participation of the director in question must be examined and, in cases of torts containing a mental element, the state of mind and knowledge of the director must also be investigated. Accordingly a director may be liable for a breach of copyright[34] or the tort of waste[35] where the act in question was carried out on his instructions. A director will only be liable in negligence for the negligent advice given by the company if he assumed personal responsibility for that advice and the claimant relied on that assumption of responsibility.[36]

7–060   The same considerations apply in the case of claims to hold a receiver liable for torts committed by the company during his receivership. If the conduct of the receiver falls within one of the three categories above, and he has so acted at the instance of the debenture-holder, the debenture-holder will be equally liable.

11. BREACH OF STATUTORY DUTY

7–061 Various statutory duties are imposed specifically on the debenture-holder and the receiver. Thus the receiver is under a duty to pay preferential creditors out of certain assets coming to his hands in priority to the debenture-holder,[37] and is personally liable to the preferential creditors if he fails to do so.[38] If in breach of this duty the receiver pays the debenture-holder, the debenture-holder comes under a statutory duty to pay the preferential creditors.[39] Other statutory duties are imposed on the company, and though a receiver is not ordinarily liable for breach of these,[40] he may be if he deliberately puts the company into breach. Any available discretion on his part ought normally to be exercised to avoid a breach which constitutes a criminal offence (*e.g.* non payment of VAT).[41] Certain statutory duties are imposed on the party fulfilling a particular description, *e.g.* the occupier of property, and if the receiver assumes the role, then he will fall subject to the statutory duty and be liable for breach.[42]

---

[34] *Evans v. Spritebrand* [1985] 1 W.L.R. 317 at 323–324, *per* Slade LJ.

[35] *Mancetter Developments v. Garmanson* [1986] 1 All E.R. 449 at 452a; [1986] Q.B. 1212 at 1217A; *per* Dillon L.J.

[36] *Williams v. Natural Health Foods Ltd* [1998] 1 W.L.R. 830, HL.

[37] See *Standard Chartered Bank v. Walker* [1982] 1 W.L.R. 1410; *American Express International Banking Corp v. Hurley* [1985] 1 All E.R. 564.

[38] *IRC v. Goldblatt* [1972] Ch. 498; *Re H&K Medway Ltd* [1997] 1 B.C.L.C. 545. See further below, Chap. 21.

[39] *Woods v. Winskill* [1913] 2 Ch. 303; *Westminster Corporation v. Haste* [1950] 1 Ch. 442 (the period of limitation for this statutory liability runs from the date when the receiver has sufficient sums to pay the preferential creditors); *IRC v. Goldblatt* [1972] Ch. 498.

[40] *e.g.* the duty of an owner to maintain means of escape in case of fire in good condition: *Solomons v. Gertzenstein* [1954] 2 Q.B. 243.

[41] *Re John Willment (Ashford) Ltd* [1980] 1 W.L.R. 73 at 78A-78B; and see *Sargent v. CCE* [1995] 1 W.L.R. 821.

[42] *Meigh v. Wickenden* [1942] 2 K.B. 160, a case exemplifying "the peculiar results produced by the Factories Acts": *per* Danckwerts L.J. in *Lawson v. Hosemaster* [1966] 2 All E.R. 944 at 951. *cf. Liverpool Corp Hope* [1938] 1 K.B. 751 (no liability for non-payment of rates).

12. THE HUMAN RIGHTS ACT 1998

Section 6 of the Human Rights Act 1998[43] makes it unlawful for a **7–062** "public authority" to act in a way which is incompatible with a Convention right unless precluded from acting differently by one or more provisions of, or made under, primary legislation. "Public authority" for this purpose includes any person certain of whose functions are functions of a public nature: his act are "acts of a public authority" if the nature of the acts are not private. A "victim" of an act of a public authority committed after October 2, 2000 made unlawful by section 6 may bring proceedings against the public authority [44] claiming any relief that is just and appropriate, and this includes damages where this is necessary to afford just satisfaction.[45] The victim may also rely on a Convention right in any legal proceedings.[46]

An Officer of the Court[47] is clearly a "public authority" for this **7–063** purpose, and it is thought that a receiver might also be a public authority in so far as he exercises certain functions as an office-holder, *e.g.* the investigatory powers under section 235 and 236 of the 1986 Act.[48] The term "victim" requires more than that the person in question is interested in the compliance by the "public authority" with the Convention right: in the ordinary case he must be directly affected by or threatened with non-compliance, though in some cases substantial indirect effect may be sufficient.[49] Depending on the facts and circumstances, a company director, officer, creditor or shareholder may qualify as a victim.

13. FRAUDULENT AND WRONGFUL TRADING

A receiver is subject to the law of fraudulent trading[50] in respect of the **7–064** period prior to liquidation when he trades as agent for the company and may be held liable on a subsequent liquidation.[51] He will only be held liable if his personal conduct can be categorised as dishonest.[52] A receiver is not exposed to liability for wrongful trading in respect of the company of which he is the receiver, for he is not a director of the company; but if there is a hiving-down, a receiver may be at risk in

---

[43] For a full consideration of this Act see Lester & Pannick, *Human Rights Law and Practice* (1999), Grosz Beatson and Duffy, *Human Rights — the 1998 Act and the European Convention* and Harris, O'Boyle, Warbick, *Law of the European Convention of Human Rights,* (2nd ed., 2000).

[44] Section 7 of the 1998 Act.

[45] Section 8 of the 1998 Act.

[46] Section 7(1)(b) of the 1998 Act.

[47] Such as a provisional liquidator, a liquidator in a winding-up by the court and an administrator.

[48] See above, Chap. 4 and paras 5–020, 5–051 to 5–058 and 5–064 to 5–066.

[49] See, *e.g. Marckx v. Belgium* (1979) 2 E.H.R.R. 330, para 27.

[50] See above, para. 2–03.

[51] *Powdrill v. Watson* [1995] 2 A.C. 394 at 408.

[52] *Re Soban BV* [1996] 1 B.C.L.C. 446; *Aktieselskabet Dansk Skibsfinansiering v. Brothers* [2000] 1 H.K.L.R.D. 568, Court of Final Appeal of Hong Kong, March 9, 2000.

respect of the subsidiary if he is a director of the subsidiary or the directors of the subsidiary act on his instructions.[53]

14. LIABILITY OF DEBENTURE-HOLDER FOR ACTS OF RECEIVER

7–065 In the case where the receiver is acting as agent of the debenture-holder, the debenture-holder will be liable for the acts of the receiver as his agent in accordance with ordinary agency principles. If a receiver is appointed to act as agent for the mortgagor, the exercise of the power of appointment does not of itself render the appointor liable for the receiver's acts or omissions.[54] Accordingly the mortgagee is not liable if such a receiver sells at an undervalue.[55] But even if the receiver is appointed and acts as agent of the mortgagor, the mortgagee will be liable and responsible for the receiver's acts and defaults if the mortgagee gives directions to or puts pressure on the receiver or so interferes with the conduct of the receivership as to prevent the exercise of independent judgment by the receiver.[56] In this case, any provision in the debenture excluding liability of the receiver will be of no avail to the mortgagee, for the mortgagee will be held liable personally in respect of the impugned acts as his own acts, and not merely vicariously in respect of a liability of the receiver.

7–066 The debenture-holder has no duty to supervise the receiver and, save perhaps in the case of actual knowledge or suspicion of misconduct, has no obligation to intervene in the receivership.[57]

15. LIABILITY OF RECEIVER IN CONTRACT

7–067 A receiver will be personally liable under contracts entered into by him except in so far as the contract otherwise provides and under contracts of employment adopted by him.[58] The statutory liability of the receiver is not analogous to the contractual liability of a guarantor, and is not discharged by conduct which would discharge the liability of a surety, *e.g.* the giving of time to the company.[59]

---

[53] See above, para. 2–04. For an analysis of the concept of a shadow director, see *Secretary of State v. Deverell* [2000] 2 W.L.R. 907, CA, a case on the Company Directors Disqualification Act.

[54] The legal position is on all fours with that of a shareholder who exercises a power to appoint a director unless he interferes with company's affairs by giving instructions to the appointee. No liability attaches if the mortgagee merely acquiesces or with full knowledge has the opportunity to intervene: active intervention is required: *National Bank of Greece v. Pinios* [1990] 1 A.C. 637 at 648–649, *per* Lloyd L.J.

[55] *Commonwealth Bank of Australia v. Muirhead* [1997] 1 Qd R567.

[56] *Medforth v. Blake* [2000] Ch. 86 at 95B.

[57] *National Bank of Greece v. Pinios* [1990] 1 A.C. 637 at 661–662, *per* Nicholls L.J.; *Downsview Nominees Ltd v. First City Corp* [1993] A.C. 295 at 317D-E; *Medforth v. Blake* [2000] Ch. 86 at 94C.

[58] See below, Chap. 8.

[59] See *British Airways Board v. Parish* [1979] 2 Lloyd's Rep. 361.

16. LIABILITY TO ACCOUNT AND PROVIDE INFORMATION

(a) During the receivership

A non-administrative receiver is, during the receivership, under a **7–068** statutory duty under section 38 of the Insolvency Act 1986 to send accounts of receipts and payments to the Registrar of Companies. An administrative receiver has a duty under section 48 of the Insolvency Act 1986 to send a report to the Registrar of Companies and all creditors and (unless the court otherwise directs) to lay a copy of his report before a meeting of the company's unsecured creditors. Both types of receiver are also under an equitable duty to the company, enforceable in the name of the company by the directors, to supply information required by the directors to enable them to perform their duties, *e.g.* to file accounts and to enable the company to redeem, if it bona fide intends to do so,[60] but the equitable duty stops short of requiring the receiver to supply any information which in his judgment would be prejudicial to the debenture-holder for him to supply.[61]

(b) End of receivership

At the close of the receivership, the receiver is under a general duty to **7–069** account.[62]

17. LIABILITY AS CONSTRUCTIVE TRUSTEE

If the directors of a company grant a debenture in breach of their **7–070** fiduciary duties to the company and the grantee appoints a receiver, the grantee and the receiver may in certain circumstances become liable as constructive trustees in respect of all assets which come into their hands.[63] The current test appears to be whether the debenture—holder or receiver respectively had knowledge of such facts as would make it unconscionable for him to retain the assets received.[64]

PART II—DUTIES AND LIABILITIES OF DEBENTURE-HOLDER AND RECEIVER TO EACH OTHER

1. LIABILITY OF RECEIVER TO APPOINTOR

(a) Contract

The offer and acceptance of the appointment as receiver constitutes a **7–071** contract between the appointor and the appointee. The terms of the

---

[60] *Downsview Nominees Ltd v. First City Corp* [1993] A.C. 295.

[61] *Gomba Holdings (U.K.) Ltd v. Homan* [1986] F.T.L.R. 126, *per* Hoffmann J. To like effect see *Irish Oil v. Donnelly* (unreported, Costello J., March 27, 1983). For an administrative receiver's position, see s. 48 of the Insolvency Act 1986.

[62] *Smiths Ltd v. Middleton* [1979] 3 All E.R. 842. The receiver is a fiduciary: see above, paras 7–044 to 7–074.

[63] See *Rolled Steel Products (Holdings) Ltd v. British Steel Corp* [1986] Ch. 246 and above, Chap. 3.

[64] *BCCI v. Akindele* (unreported, CA, June 14, 2000). See also above, Chap. 3.

contract may be fully set out in a written agreement which fully regulates the relationship between the parties and defines the duties and liabilities of the receiver. There may be no written document beyond the appointment itself.

7–072   In the absence of any indication to the contrary, there will be implied an obligation on the part of the receiver to act with all reasonable skill and care.[65] This obligation subsists whether the receiver acts as agent for the mortgagor or agent for the mortgagee or in a personal capacity.[66] Any carelessness by the receiver will constitute a breach of contract entitling the appointor to sue for damages. The measure of damages will be the full loss occasioned and not be limited to the sum required to pay off the mortgage: but if the appointor is liable to the mortgagor for the negligence of the receiver, the mortgagor will be entitled to an indemnity against this liability also. The limitation period will run from the date of the careless act or omission. In any case where the receiver is acting as agent for the appointor, and the appointor is held liable for the default of the receiver (in the absence of any express exclusion in the contract of agency), he will be entitled under an implied term of the contract of agency to an indemnity from the receiver.[67]

(b) Tort

7–073   A co-extensive duty and liability to the contractual duty of skill and care may exist under the tort of negligence.[68] In this case, the limitation period will run from the date of damage sustained by the appointor. This will ordinarily, but not necessarily, be the same date as the act of negligence.[69]

(c) Fiduciary duty

7–074   A receiver, whether he acts as agent for the company, as agent for the debenture-holder or as principal, owes to his appointor fiduciary duties in relation to the realisation of the charged assets, although he is not a full trustee of the charged assets.[70] He is duty bound to keep the debenture-holder fully informed about the receivership.[71]

---

[65] This passage was cited with approval by the New Zealand CA in *R.A. Price Securities v. Henderson* [1989] 2 N.Z.L.R. 257 at 261 which held that a receiver's primary duty is to recover the sums due under the debenture, a duty which the receiver was held to have overlooked in his concern to continue trading. A nominee director owes a like duty to the person nominating him: *Kuwait Asia Bank v. National Mutual Life Nominees* [1991] 1 A.C. at 221–222.

[66] Invariably the receiver will be appointed or (in the case of an administrative receiver) be deemed to be appointed as agent of the mortgagor until liquidation.

[67] *American Express International Banking Corp v. Hurley* [1985] 1 All E.R. 564 at 471g–471h.

[68] *National Bank of Greece v. Pinios* [1990] 1 A.C. 637 at 650, 662.

[69] See the discussion in UBAF v. European American Banking Corp [1984] 2 All E.R. 226, referring to *Forster v. Outred* [1982] 1 W.L.R. 86; and *Pirelli General Cable Works v. Oscar Faber & Partners* [1983] 2 A.C. 1, H.L.

[70] *Visbord v. F.C.T.* (1943) 68 C.L.R. 354; *In re Magadi Soda Co.* (1925) 94 L.J.R. (Ch.) 217.

[71] *Gomba Holdings v. Minories Finance* (1987) 3 B.C.C. 643 at 644–645; *Re Magadi Soda* (1925) 94 L.J. Ch. 217. But see paras 5–041 to 5–049 in respect of information obtained under ss. 235 and 236 of the Insolvency Act 1986.

2. LIABILITY OF APPOINTOR TO RECEIVER

A contract collateral to the appointment may expressly confer rights on **7–075** the receiver in respect of (for example) remuneration or an indemnity. The indemnity will not extend to losses or liabilities incurred as a consequence of the receiver's own negligence or default unless the appointor consented to such a breach of duty[72] nor will it extend to conduct of the receiver which he knows constitutes a tort.[73] In default of an express provision regulating the position, the court will readily infer a warranty on the part of the appointor of his authority to make the appointment. Section 34 of the Insolvency Act 1986, in addition, confers on the court a discretionary jurisdiction to order the appointor or person on whose behalf the appointment is made to indemnify a person appointed receiver or manager against any liability arising solely by reason of the invalidity of the appointment.[74] Further, the appointor may be liable to indemnify the receiver in respect of any liability to the company or third parties incurred by the receiver in acting pursuant to the instructions of his appointor.[75]

PART III—WAIVER AND RELEASE

Rights of and against a receiver and his appointor may be waived or **7–076** released. Whilst the equitable doctrine of waiver (or acquiescence) requires knowledge of the right which is being waived (or the wrong which is being acquiesced in) the effect of a release made for consideration is entirely a matter of construction of the release and does not depend on knowledge of the claim in question.[76] Equity may preclude reliance on a release if such reliance is unconscionable.[77]

---

[72] *R. A. Price Securities Ltd v. Henderson* [1989] 2 N.Z.L.R. 257 (such implication may more readily be made where the receiver acts in accordance with the directions of the appointor.)

[73] *W. Cory v. Lambton* (1916) 86 L.J.K.B. 401.

[74] See above, para. 3–148.

[75] *Per* Evershed M.R. in *Re B. Johnson & Co. (Builders) Ltd* [1955] Ch. 634 at 647–648 cited in *R. A. Price Securities Ltd v. Henderson* [1989] 2 N.Z.L.R. 257.

[76] *Village Cay Marina Ltd v. Acland* [1998] 2 B.C.L.C. 327 at 334, PC *per* Lord Hoffmann.

[77] *Naeem v. BCCI S.A.* [2000] 3 All E.R. 51 CA. This issue was not raised or investigated at first instance: see [1999] 2 All E.R. 1005.

CHAPTER 8

CONTINUATION OF TRADING

8–001 The primary purpose and advantage of a floating charge over the undertaking as distinct from a fixed charge over specific assets is that the creditor is afforded as part of his security the right on crystallisation (1) to continue the company's business and to do so through an individual (the receiver) who in the eyes of the law (until winding up) acts as agent for the company; and (2) to sell either the undertaking and business so continued as a going concern or simply to sell the assets charged. The matters to be considered here are the duties and powers of the creditor and of the receiver so appointed in respect of the conduct of business and sale.

1. POWERS TO TRADE

(a) Legal considerations

8–002 Debentures have for many years included provisions expressly conferring upon the receiver the power to carry on the company's business and the right to do so as agent of the company. These provisions are designed to enable the mortgagee to enjoy the advantage of his nominee, the receiver, displacing the mortgagor from control of the mortgaged property and from receipt of the income derived from it whilst at the same time avoiding assuming the liabilities of a mortgagee in possession.[1] In the case of an administrative receiver, the Insolvency Act 1986 deems the power to carry on the company's business and right to do so as agent of the company to be conferred on the receiver in the absence of some inconsistent provision in the debenture.[2] In any case where the power and right are conferred, in the absence of some clearly indicated intention to the contrary, the receiver will be deemed to be exercising the power to trade (and accordingly to enter into contracts) as agent of the company unless and until the company goes into liquidation.[3] Liquidation does not terminate the right to carry on the company's business, but the receiver cannot thereafter carry on business as agent of the company. Exceptionally, if authorised by the debenture-holder, the receiver may carry on business as agent for the debenture-holder, or (if

---

[1] *Medforth v. Blake* [2000] Ch. 86 at 93–4.

[2] Section 42(1) and Sched. 1, para. 14. In the case of non-administrative receivers, the law continues to be that such receiver has no power to carry on business unless the power is conferred by the debenture: *Bompas v. King* [1886] 33 Ch.D. 279. If a receiver is given power both to trade and to borrow, he is authorised to purchase on credit terms: *Ross v. Taylor* [1985] S.L.T. 387.

[3] Insolvency Act 1986, s. 44(1)(a) (administrative receivers) and *Thomas v. Todd* [1926] 2 K.B. 511.

the circumstances so require) he will carry on business as principal. On liquidation, only one of the last two courses is available and the latter is the usual.

The purpose of appointing the receiver to be agent of the company is **8–003** "simply in order to free the debenture-holders who appointed him from responsibility for his acts".[4] The powers of management of the directors are suspended and the receiver has complete control of the company's affairs. The relative positions of the receiver and the directors appear clearly from the judgment of Brightman J. in *Re Emmadart*[5]:

> ". . . the appointment of a receiver for debenture-holders suspends the powers of the directors over the assets in respect of which the receiver has been appointed so far as it is requisite to enable the receiver to discharge his functions[6] . . . The authority of a receiver is not however, co-terminous with the authority of the board of directors. The powers of the receiver stem from (i) the powers contained in the memorandum and articles of association of the company to create mortgages and charges, coupled with (ii) the particular powers which have been conferred on a duly appointed receiver pursuant to the due exercise of the company's borrowing powers."[7]

Prior to the Insolvency Act 1986, one limitation was recognised on the **8–004** powers which could be conferred on a receiver. A receiver appears to have been limited in the scope of his activities as agent of the company by the powers contained in the company's memorandum and articles.[8] There is nothing in the Act which would appear to remove this limitation on the powers of the administrative receiver.[9] However, a person dealing with an administrative receiver in good faith and for value is no longer concerned to inquire whether the receiver is acting within his powers,[10] and accordingly is not prejudiced if the transaction is *ultra vires*. The sole effect of the transaction being *ultra vires* will be to expose the receiver to liability to his appointor or the company if damage results. The apparent limitation on powers of the receiver as agent of the company, however, should not apply to the debenture-holder when exercising his powers as

---

[4] *Per* Cross J. in *Lawson v. Hosemaster* [1965] 1 W.L.R. 1399 at 1410; [1965] 3 All E.R. 401 at 410; reversed [1966] 1 W.L.R. 1300; [1966] 2 All E.R. 944.

[5] [1979] Ch. 540.

[6] At 544, citing *Lawson v. Hosemaster*, above and *Newhart Developments Ltd v. Co-operative Commercial Bank Ltd* [1978] Q.B. 814. The power extends to control over the rights and powers of the company at least in so far as they have commercial value or significance: *Independent Pension Trustee Ltd v. Capital LAW Construction Co. Ltd*, *The Times* Scots Law Report, November 1, 1996.

[7] At 547. See also above, para. 2–022.

[8] *Lawson v. Hosemaster* [1966] 1 W.L.R. 1300 at 1315; [1966] 2 All E.R. 944 at 951. See also above Chap. 3.

[9] Section 42(1) reads into a debenture the powers specified in Sched. 1 unless inconsistent with its provisions: it does not deal with the question whether the powers purportedly conferred on the receiver are *ultra vires*.

[10] Insolvency Act 1986, s. 42(3). "Good faith" means a belief that everything is being rightly and properly done: see *Mogridge v. Clapp* [1892] 3 Ch. 382.

mortgagee or to the receiver when exercising, as agent of the mortgagee
or as principal, powers delegated to him by the mortgagee.[11] One further
limitation may exist where the receiver proposes to enter into a
transaction for which statute requires the consent of the shareholders.[12]

(i) New contracts

8–005　A receiver (administrative[13] or non-administrative[14]) may if so authorised prior to any liquidation enter into contracts in the name and on
behalf of the company, and if he does so and stipulates that he will not
be personally liable, then the company alone will be liable and the
receiver will not be. The stipulation need not be express: it may be
implied.[15]

(ii) Prior contracts

8–006　In the case of contracts made prior to his appointment, the receiver
generally has a free choice whether and for how long the company
should give effect to them. He may decide that the contract shall
continue in force so long as the company fulfils its obligations thereunder, or at any time may decide to repudiate and bring the contract to
an end. If and when the receiver decides that the company shall
repudiate the contract, the other party is left with his remedy in damages
against the company and a claim as an unsecured creditor and has no
claim against the receiver or his appointor, notwithstanding the
receiver's interim adoption of the contracts in the course of managing
the company's business. This does not offend against basic conceptions
of justice and fairness. The liability has been undertaken by the company
at the inception of the contract and the benefit accrues to the company
even when the receiver is in office. The other contracting party (like
other creditors) must look to the company for payment. During the
receivership the other contracting party is in no way inhibited from
exercising his contractual rights and remedies.[16]

8–007　To this general rule there are two exceptions. First, the receiver
cannot effect the discharge of contracts entered into by the company
which are binding on the appointing debenture-holder and are specifically enforceable, *e.g.* for the sale or lease of property.[17] Secondly, if the

---

[11] In the case of companies incorporated under the Companies Acts the purpose of the
ultra vires rule is to protect creditors and shareholders against misapplication of funds by
the directors: *Trevor v. Whitworth* [1887] 12 App.Cas. 409 at 414–415. A mortgagee of the
undertaking can be subject to no restriction beyond those imposed by the debenture and
by equitable duties with regard to the realisation of the mortgaged property (discussed
above in Chap. 7).

[12] *Demite Ltd v. Protec Health Ltd* [1998] B.C.C. 638: see below, paras. 9–19 and 9–20.

[13] Insolvency Act 1986, s. 44(1)(b).

[14] *ibid.*, s. 37.

[15] *Hill Samuel & Co. Ltd v. Laing* (1988) 4 B.C.C. 9 at 20–21 Ct. of Session not following
the *dictum* of Cross J. to the contrary at first instance in *Lawson v. Hosemaster* [1965] 1
W.L.R. 1399 at 1410–1411.

[16] *Re Atlantic Computer Systems plc* [1992] Ch. 505 at 526–527, CA.

[17] See above, Chap. 7. See also *Cater-King Pty Ltd v. Westpac Banking Corporation* [1989]
7 A.C.L.C. 993.

receiver has adopted any contract of employment in the course of carrying out his functions, though his freedom of action in respect of a repudiation of the contract is unchanged, he is personally liable on the contract to the other contracting party.[18] The receiver should also bear in mind that his treatment of employees can give rise to liabilities which will pass onto a purchaser of the business and therefore have an impact on the price which may be obtained.[19]

(iii) Ratified contracts

A receiver can ratify a contract purportedly made on behalf of the **8–008** company by an agent of the company without authority before or after the date of the receivership, and indeed, if the contract is advantageous, the receiver may be in default of his duty if he refuses to do so.[20] Further, a contract made during an earlier receivership may be ratified by a later receiver or (when all or any receiverships are discharged) by the company itself. The only bar to such ratification is an earlier disclaimer of the contract by a prior receiver or the acquisition of rights by third parties in respect of any property in question between the date of the purported contract and ratification.[21] Such ratification does not operate to impose any personal liability on any earlier receiver during whose receivership the purported contract was made or the later receiver who ratified it.[22] The ratification does not constitute "the entering into" of a contract for the purposes of section 44(1)(b) of the Insolvency Act 1986 so as to require the receiver when ratifying to disclaim personal liability.[23] Nor does ratification of a contract of employment necessarily involve adoption of the contract by the receiver within the meaning of the section if the ratification takes place within 14 days of the appointment of the receiver.[24]

(iv) Indemnity as to contracts

If the receiver trades in his own name, then he must either rely on his **8–009** statutory right to an indemnity out of the assets of the company[25] or his contractual indemnity (if any) from his debenture-holders. Though paragraph 32 of the Statement issued by the Council of the Institute of Chartered Accountants in England and Wales in November 1983 entitled "Guidance for Members in Practice-Professional Liability of

---

[18] In the case of administrative receivers under the Insolvency Act 1986, s. 44(1)(b), and in the case of other receivers under s. 37(1)(a) of the Insolvency Act 1986. For discussion of extent of liability, see below, Chap. 19.

[19] See below, para. 9–47.

[20] *Lawson v. Hosemaster* [1966] 1 W.L.R. 1300 at 1314.

[21] *ibid.* at 1316.

[22] *ibid.* at 1316.

[23] This is implicit in *Lawson v. Hosemaster* [1966] 1 W.L.R. 1300. The alternative view would preclude any ratification without assuming personal liability. For such ratification would involve either the unilateral imposition of a new term by the receiver (*i.e.* his exemption from personal liability) or (if the other party agreed to this term) the making by the parties of a new contract between the parties incorporating this term.

[24] Insolvency Act 1986, ss. 37(2) and 44(2).

[25] *ibid.*, ss. 37(1)(b) and 44(1)(c).

Accountants and Auditors" advises that a member appointed to manage a business should endeavour to obtain a full indemnity from his appointor,[26] many appointors are clearing banks and they are generally reluctant to give indemnities at the time of appointment.

(b) Commercial considerations

8–010   In the short term, excellent reasons for carrying on trading may include:

(a) enabling work in progress to be completed so as to realise a higher sale price or to guard against set-offs in respect of book debts (except in so far as there are effective retentions of title, the receiver will obtain stock and work in progress without payment[27] and will often easily be able to make a profit); and

(b) enabling the receiver to make inquiries and make better informed decisions as to future trading.

8–011   To justify trading on in the long term there must be a prospect of:

(a) trading out, *i.e.* into a position of solvency; or, more frequently,

(b) selling the business as a going concern at a sum substantially greater than the break-up value of the assets.

8–012   For any trading to be feasible, the receiver must have access to:

(a) employees able and willing to carry on the work;

(b) unencumbered supplies of any materials required;

(c) finance, normally only obtainable from trading cash flow or loans from the appointing debenture-holder;

(d) an available market for the finished product.

8–013   The receiver is under a duty not to diminish the assets available to preferential creditors and he must have this in mind when considering the assets available for trade. In the (perhaps rare) case where the company has at the commencement of the receivership a fund of money available to discharge liabilities to preferential creditors, the receiver should not count on using these funds, for their loss may expose him to personal liability to the preferential creditors who have first call on such funds.[28] However, by analogy to the position in winding up, it may be possible to ask the court for directions to enable the receiver to use these funds without risk, joining the preferential creditors as parties if they

---

[26] A solicitor who fails to advise the receiver to obtain an indemnity may be liable in negligence: *R. A. Price Securities Ltd v. Henderson* [1989] 2 N.Z.L.R. 257, NZCA.

[27] The receiver should bear in mind that the conversion of floating charge assets such as stock into fixed charge assets such as book debts during the receivership does not remove them from the pool of assets available to pay preferential creditors: Technical Release 14, para 14 (June 1999). For an analysis of receivership trading on floating charge assets see Anderson (1994) The Company Lawyer Vol. 15(7) 195.

[28] *Westminster Corporation v. Haste* [1950] Ch. 442 and see below, Chap. 21.

refuse to consent.[29] In principle, the same duty applies where the company has unrealised assets such as stock or work in progress. The preferential creditors have first call on their realisable value. But their value if the receiver decides not to trade is likely to be very low indeed, and trading may be essential if any beneficial realisation is to be achieved. If the receiver decides that he should prudently trade on, he will inevitably use such assets, and this method of realisation should not ordinarily expose the receiver to liability if the initial decision can reasonably be justified in the interests of the preferential creditors, even if in fact (notwithstanding the exercise of all reasonable diligence and expertise) the endeavour fails to produce additional funds for them.

In case of doubt as to the wisdom of trading on, a receiver is probably **8–014** safer in simply realising assets than in attempting to trade on, since he can have no duty to trade on if the results are speculative. The receiver is not required by law to take into account, or indeed entitled, at the expense of the debenture-holder or company, to promote, the interests of employees in any decision which he makes, such as continuing business so as to mitigate the hardship of unemployment. The duty to take into account the interests of employees is imposed on directors by section 309 of the Companies Act 1985. The duty does not, however, extend to receivers and accordingly cannot justify or legitimise any action taken by a receiver which is not otherwise justifiable on purely commercial grounds.[30]

Concern for his public image and humanitarian considerations may **8–015** impel the appointor to require the receiver to trade on, but the receiver should not be bound by these considerations. In any event, before acceding to any such requirement of the appointor the receiver should seek an indemnity for his own protection.[31]

In order to equip himself to make a decision whether to trade on, the **8–016** receiver will first obtain valuations on the alternative "going concern" and "break-up" bases and expert advice as to the prospects, methods and time-scales for such sales. The receiver must then exercise his judgment as to whether the anticipated benefits justify the risks and greatly increased costs of trading on.

In reaching a decision, the receiver will evaluate the following factors **8–017** and information:

(a) financial information as to past and current trading sales and profit forecasts and the marketability of the product or service;
(b) inventory and valuation of stock and work-in-progress;
(c) assessment of retention of title claims;
(d) value and usefulness of intellectual property;

---

[29] Insolvency Act 1986, s. 35.

[30] There may be such commercial grounds if a going concern transfer is contemplated, as failure to consult employees properly may give rise to liabilities which pass to the purchaser and so depress the price which he is prepared to pay.

[31] The appointor should also be careful that he does not seek to direct the actions of the receiver so that the receiver does not become the appointor's agent: see above, para. 8–11.

    (e) position as to debtors;

    (f) investments in subsidiary and associated companies and any interdependence with them;

    (g) the attitude of preferential and secured creditors towards trading on and the risk that secured creditors will enforce their securities so as to frustrate continued trading;

    (h) rights of occupation of premises and possible relocation;

    (i) availability of customers and suppliers and any alternative sources of supply and customers;

    (j) availability and capability of the workforce and co-operation of any trade unions involved;

    (k) availability and reliability of plant and machinery;

    (l) control over overheads in relation to planned production;

    (m) (on rare occasions) availability of European Union, United Kingdom and local authority grants;

    (n) ability of management;

    (o) product liability and insurance for same;

    (p) taxation consequences (though these generally affect the company and any liquidator rather than the receiver and his appointor);

    (q) prospects and consequences of liquidation.

8–018 Before considering whether to trade, the receiver should have in mind the distinct duties he owes in respect of his decision whether or not to continue to trade and (if he decides to trade) in respect of the manner of trading. A decision whether or not to continue trading and if so for how long does not require the consent of the company or the debenture-holder, but a cautious receiver will, if practicable, consult both. As receiver in respect of such a decision, he owes a duty of care to the debenture-holder,[32] and whilst he owes a duty of care to the company not to trade if this course is calculated neither to enable repayment of the secured debt and interest thereon nor to promote or safeguard the value of the equity of redemption, he owes to the company no duty to trade, however damaging this course may be to the company.[33] The consent of the debenture-holder and the company will preclude subsequent complaint by them. Even if such consent is not forthcoming, for the receiver to show that he elicited and gave due consideration to their views or objections before acting goes a long way to displacing any charge of negligence. As a matter of practice, a receiver is unlikely ever to ignore the debenture-holder's wishes, for this would (in the case of a non-administrative receiver) ordinarily lead to his removal and (in the case of either type of receiver) lead to a refusal of any indemnity. But the debenture-holder and the receiver must take care that no directions are given by the debenture-holder and that the decision is genuinely that of the receiver alone, for otherwise the receiver may be held to be acting

---

[32] *R. A. Price Securities Ltd v. Henderson* [1989] 2 N.Z.L.R. 257, NZCA.
[33] See below, paras 8–020 *et seq.*

as agent of the debenture-holder[34] and if the decision leads to loss to the company and is challenged as negligent, the debenture-holder may become liable to the company or lose rights against guarantors.[35] The receiver has a right to apply to the court for directions on the question of whether to continue trading,[36] but the court will not ordinarily decide questions involving commercial judgment which are the responsibility of the receiver.[37]

If the receiver does decide to carry on trading, he is under a duty to **8–019** take reasonable steps in order to do so profitably and accordingly (for example) obtain available discounts.[38] And if the mortgagee instructs the receiver to carry on the business in a manner that is in breach of the receiver's duty to the mortgagor, the mortgagee will likewise incur liability to the mortgagor.[39]

2. DUTY TO TRADE

The law is clear in recognising a duty on the part of a receiver appointed **8–020** by the court (where this is practicable) to preserve the goodwill of the company's business and for this purpose to carry on its business and (where necessary for this purpose) pay debts incurred in the course of its business even if this course is not in the interests of the holder of the crystallised floating charge. This duty arises from the special role of the court-appointed receiver who has the responsibility of holding the scales evenly between the company and the chargee and must not sacrifice the interests of the one to the other.[40]

The position of the receiver appointed out of the court is quite **8–021** different. He has a primary duty to deal with or realise the security in the best interests of the chargee and in particular to try to bring about a situation in which interest on the secured debt can be paid and the debt itself repaid.[41] He has only a secondary duty to the company to exercise care to prevent avoidable loss. Such a receiver will only be required to protect the interests of the company where means are available and may be given effect consistently with the performance of his primary duty.

The question accordingly arises whether this secondary duty to the **8–022** company can in any circumstances require the receiver to continue the company's business and preserve its goodwill, e.g. by fulfilling outstanding contracts.

---

[34] *American Express v. Hurley* [1985] 3 All E.R. 564.
[35] *Standard Chartered Bank v. Walker* [1982] 1 W.L.R. 1410, CA.
[36] Insolvency Act 1986, s. 35.
[37] *MTI Trading Systems Ltd v. Winter* [1998] B.C.C. 591 at 595; *Re Osmosis Group Ltd* [2000] B.C.C. 428 (administrator).
[38] *Medforth v. Blake* [2000] Ch. 86 at 93.
[39] *ibid.* at 95.
[40] For the position of such receivers, see below, Chap. 22. They are rarely appointed in practice because of the availability and advantages of an appointment out of court.
[41] *Medforth v. Blake* [2000] Ch. 86 at 102.

8–023   The authorities in this field prior to the *Downsview* case[42] are not particularly helpful either because they fail to have regard to the differing roles of the two types of receiver or because they were decided before the law recognised that a mortgagee and receiver owed to the mortgagor a duty not merely to be honest but to be careful.

8–024   Thus, in *R. v. Board of Trade*,[43] where the Divisional Court equated the two receiverships for the purpose of determining whether their management could be the subject of an investigation of the affairs of the company under sections 164 and 165 of the Companies Act 1948 (now sections 431 and 432 of the Companies Act 1985), Phillimore J.[44] *obiter*, and in the form of a rhetorical question, suggested that there was in each case a like duty to preserve goodwill, without noting the distinct roles of the receivers. Winn J. did not expressly advert to the question, but cited the *dictum* of Buckley L.J. in *Re Newdigate Colliery Ltd*[45] which distinguished the role and duty of the court-appointed receiver to preserve goodwill from that of a receiver appointed by a debenture-holder who is not, and referred to *Re B. Johnson*[46] which held that the receiver appointed out of court had no such duty. It may therefore be thought (by implication at least) that Winn J. disagreed with Phillimore J.; Lord Parker C.J. enthusiastically (but confusingly) agreed with both judgments.

8–025   In *Airlines Airspares v. Handley Page*[47] the question arose whether a receiver appointed by debenture-holders can hive down the undertaking to a newly-formed subsidiary in anticipation of the sale of such subsidiary, notwithstanding that such action must put it out of the power of the company to fulfil an outstanding contract with the plaintiff. The cases on the duty of court-appointed receivers to protect the company's goodwill were cited and relied on, but the distinction was not drawn between the two types of receiver, nor was *Re B. Johnson* cited. Graham J. upheld the right of the receiver to proceed with his hive-down,[48] stating as the relevant principal that a receiver can repudiate a contract if the repudiation will not adversely affect the realisation of the assets or seriously affect the trading prospects of the company in question, if it is able to trade in the future. This formulation and its application is difficult to fault as a statement of the principles applicable to court-appointed receivers, but overstates the restrictions on the powers of a receiver appointed out of court.

8–026   On the other side, there is the decision in *Re B. Johnson*[49] where the Court of Appeal (in unreserved judgments) laid down in emphatic terms the absence of the duty on the part of a receiver appointed by

---

[42] [1993] A.C. 295.
[43] [1965] 1 Q.B. 603.
[44] At 613.
[45] [1912] 1 Ch. 468 at 478.
[46] [1955] Ch. 634, as to which see above, Chap. 7.
[47] [1970] Ch. 193.
[48] As to hive-downs see below Chap. 9.
[49] [1965] 1 W.L.R. 1399 at 1410–1411 (but compare the approach of Danckwerts L.J. in the Court of Appeal at [1966] 1 W.L.R. 1300 at 1314.

debenture-holders to carry on business. Unfortunately the court equally emphatically laid down the absence of any duty of care on the part of the debenture-holder or receiver, holding that the duty is limited to acting honestly, a view repeated as late as 1965 by Cross J. in *Lawson v. Hosemaster*[50] and affirmed, with limited qualifications, by the Privy Council in *Downsview v. First City Corporation.*[51] The difficulty is that these two holdings, if not mutually dependent, are at least mutually supportive, and the second proposition was subsequently decisively rejected by the Court of Appeal in *Cuckmere Brick v. Mutual Finance*[52] and *Standard Chartered Bank v. Walker*[53] and by the Privy Council in *Tse Kwong Lam v. Wong Chit Sen.*[54] The fate of the second proposition must indicate that there are doubts as to the validity of the first, doubts which can only have increased with the rejection of *Downsview* by the Court of Appeal in *Medforth v. Blake.*[55]

The Court of Appeal in *Medforth v. Blake* held that in exercising his **8–027** powers of management, (subject to his primary duty to try to secure payment of the sum due to secured creditors) a receiver owes a duty to manage the secured property with due diligence; that due diligence does not oblige him to continue to carry on a business on the mortgaged property previously carried on by the mortgagor; but that if he does carry on business, due diligence requires reasonable steps to be taken in order to do so profitably.

Accordingly in the present state of the law in the absence of a specific **8–028** provision to the contrary in the debenture it would seem that there can be imposed on the mortgagee and receiver no duty to trade. It is suggested that there is much to be said for imposing such a duty if:

    (a) the company has the necessary funds (as the court will not require the debenture-holder or receiver to dip in his own pockets[56] or to risk a charge of fraudulent trading);

    (b) this course is necessary to secure a beneficial realisation of the company's undertaking as a going concern;

    (c) a sale as a going concern in the short term is likely; and

    (d) a cesser of business would lead only to a disadvantageous sale for a reduced break-up value.

---

[50] [1966] 2 All E.R. 944 at 951.

[51] [1993] A.C. 295, PC.

[52] [1971] Ch. 949, applied by the Court of Appeal in *Bishop v. Bonham* [1988] 1 W.L.R. 742. See also *Parker-Tweedale v. Dunbar Bank plc* [1991] Ch. 12; [1990] 3 W.L.R. 767, CA.

[53] [1982] 1 W.L.R. 1410; [1982] 3 All E.R. 838; *see also American Express v. Hurley* [1985] 3 All E.R. 564; *Knight v. Lawrence* (1991) B.C.C. 411.

[54] [1983] 1 W.L.R. 1349.

[55] [2000] Ch. 86, CA.

[56] *Re B. Johnson* [1965] Ch. 634 at 662.

CHAPTER 9

DISPOSALS AND REORGANISATIONS

9–001 Receivers are appointed primarily to effect the recovery as far as possible of the debt owed by the company to the debenture-holder. It may be possible to achieve this through the collection of rents from the company's properties or the collection of book debts arising from or made good by continued trading. Most commonly however, disposal of the company's assets is required.

9–002   Sales of company's assets involve a degree of tension between the duty of the receiver in equity to take reasonable care to obtain a proper price[1] and the legitimate objective of the receiver to sell on terms which require him to retain only the minimum prudent level of reserves against potential liabilities (in particular under the sale contract) before making any distribution to his appointor. This objective results in receivership sale contracts being drafted so as to provide the maximum permissible exclusion of warranties and liabilities, in contrast with the position in a solvent business sale where the terms typically provide considerable protection for the purchaser. At first sight, the receivership form of contract would appear to conflict with the obligation to obtain a proper price. However, the conflict may be more apparent than real since the vendor company will invariably be insolvent. This will mean that any warranties, which it might have given, will be of little commercial value to the purchaser. In practice therefore it will usually be difficult to demonstrate that the absence of warranties has depressed the price.

1. SALE AS A GOING CONCERN

9–003 Sale of the business and assets of the company as a going concern will, where it is possible, tend to fetch a higher price than the sale of assets on break-up basis. There are a number of reasons for this: the costs of removal and transportation of the assets are avoided; the utilisation of the assets in the business can proceed without interruption; the continuity of the business activity (although not of the corporate structure) makes it more likely that the goodwill of the company can be maintained; skills and knowledge of the company's employees can be preserved; and, commonly, such a transaction will qualify as a going concern transfer for VAT purposes avoiding the need for the purchaser to pay VAT.[2]

---

[1] *Downsview Nominees Ltd v. First City Corporation* [1993] A.C. 295, PC and see above, paras 7–015 to 7–017; *Re B. Johnson & Co. (Builders) Ltd* [1955] Ch. 634; *Cuckmere Brick Co. v. Mutual Finance Ltd* [1971] Ch. 949.

[2] VAT (Special Provisions) Order 1995, (S.I. No. 1286), art. 5.

A sale as a going concern frequently means a transfer of employees' **9–004** contracts under the Transfer of Undertakings (Protection of Employment) Regulations 1981 ("TUPE"). This accords with the "rescue culture" said to underlie the 1986 Act and is clearly socially desirable. There is little support for it as an end in itself in the receivership regime, which is not in the main a collective process.[3] The transfer of employees' rights to the purchaser of a business means the purchaser assumes a series of contingent liabilities and is likely to take account of that fact by offering a lower price. In circumstances where the contingent liabilities for employees on a going concern sale are very considerable, this may have the effect of depressing the price below that which could be achieved on a break up sale. There is no authority in the legislation which permits a receiver to achieve the socially desirable object of preserving jobs by taking a lower price than could otherwise be achieved.[4] Accordingly it is purely fortuitous that in most circumstances going concern values of assets are sufficient to offset the depressive affect of TUPE transfers.

In normal circumstances a going concern sale will only be achievable, **9–005** if at all, some time after the receiver's appointment and the receiver will therefore continue the company's business to keep its goodwill alive in the hope of achieving such a sale.[5] In a limited number of circumstances the continuation of the company's business after receivership will not be a practical possibility. This may be so for a variety of reasons. The value of the business may be dependant upon a number of key people who may be likely to leave during the period of uncertainty that invariably follows a receiver's appointment. The business may involve complex ongoing contracts and there may be real fears that the customer will choose to exercise termination rights in those contracts if receivers are appointed without a successor to the business immediately being in place. In those circumstances it is not uncommon for the details of a going concern sale to be negotiated on receivership terms prior to the receiver's appointment so that the receiver is an a position to effect the sale immediately after appointment. This minimises disruption and uncertainty and preserves value. Such a sale is commonly known as "prepackaged".

Whenever contemplating a sale the receiver must be mindful of his **9–006** duty to take reasonable care to obtain a proper price. This will usually mean that he will seek expert advice on the value of the company's

---

[3] Sections 40 and 42 to 49 of the 1986 Act are collective in approach.

[4] The criticisms of the receivers' failure to consult employees in *Kerry Foods Ltd v. Creber* [2000] I.R.L.R. 10, EAT resulted in a protective award which was payable by the purchaser of the business not by the vendor company. Even if the liability for the award had not transferred (because the dismissals were for an economic, technical or organisational reason) the case does not suggest that the award would have ranked other than as an unsecured claim in the liquidation of the vendor. But, now that it has been established that liability for failure to consult can fall on the purchaser, the prospect of purchasers seeking price reductions to offset the liability may provide commercial justification for receivers fulfilling consultation obligations.

[5] He must take reasonable steps in doing so to try to run the business profitably *Medforth v. Blake* [2000] Ch. 86, CA.

assets.[6] In a traditional business this may involve valuations of land and plant and machinery. In other businesses it may extend to valuations of income streams, intellectual property or permissions granted by public authorities. Valuations serve two purposes; they give the receiver an idea of the values he might expect to achieve and, if a sale at that level can be negotiated, they protect the receiver from claims that he has not achieved a proper price.

9–007   In many cases initial valuations will have been obtained prior to the receivers appointment as part of an Independent Business Review (which in general now replaces the former Investigating Accountants Report) which is often commissioned jointly by the company and its lenders prior to the receivership appointment so as to assess the options available when the company's difficulties become apparent.

9–008   If a "pre-packaged" sale is effected the receiver will not have been able to expose the business to the market (although the company may previously have done so) and accordingly it will be important not only that he can justify the need for an immediate sale but that also he can justify the price achieved by reference to expert valuation advice and such pre-receivership marketing that may have occurred.

9–009   In the normal circumstance where a going concern sale is looked for the receiver will prepare a sales pack describing the assets and business for sale to prospective purchasers. He will also generally advertise the business for sale. Care should be taken to ensure that the advertisements appear in publications most likely to come to the attention of prospective purchasers for the particular business and that wherever possible sufficient time is allowed to enable prospective purchasers to make enquiries and negotiate a sale.[7] There will be cases where time is short, for instance, where the company is incurring substantial trading losses or where uncertainty is likely to lead to a very immediate fall off of new business. In these circumstances the comprehensiveness of the receiver's sales pack assumes an increased importance since the purchaser will have very limited time for due diligence. The absence of warranties makes purchaser due diligence particularly important in receivership sales. The sales pack should include a description of the nature of the business, giving details of its structure and organisation and referring, where appropriate, to brochures and advertising materials. In addition, the document ought to include lists of assets (tangible and intangible) which have been offered for sale. In giving information to potential purchasers, the receiver will almost invariably be dependant upon using information and figures produced by the company's directors and employees. As such the receiver should (where possible) quote specific sources and always expressly disclaim personal responsibility of liability of himself, his staff or agents.

9–010   Where the sale document offers for sale any shares in the company (*e.g.* if there has been a "hive-down" of part of the assets and business

---

[6] See above, para. 7–039
[7] *Standard Chartered Bank v. Walker* [1982] 1 W.L.R. 1410. See also para. 7–033 above.

of the company in receivership into a subsidiary which is then offered for sale) the receiver must take care to comply with the restriction on issue of "investment advertisements" under the Financial Services Act 1986.[8]

Any marketing process will inevitably lead to the disclosure to **9–011** prospective purchasers of commercially sensitive or confidential information to a greater or lesser extent. A receiver should naturally exercise care and discretion in deciding what confidential information concerning the affairs of the company to make available to the prospective purchasers. Often the persons who might be most interested in acquiring the business and assets will be trade competitors of the company in receivership. Also the amount of information that a potential purchaser will wish to know will increase, as he becomes more serious in his intentions to acquire the business from the receiver.

It had been held in Australia that a receiver acting bona-fide will not **9–012** be restrained from disclosing confidential information relating to business contracts to a proposed purchaser, even though there was a risk that the proposed purchaser would use the information to harm the company.[9] Notwithstanding this, the receiver should take care to reveal confidential information on strict undertakings as to preservation of that confidentiality so as to minimise the risk inherent in revealing details which could damage the company's business in the event that no sale is concluded. He may wish to take a layered disclosure approach, releasing material of particular sensitivity only to those potential purchasers who have demonstrated their financial qualifications and commitment to buying the business during the initial negotiation process.

A receiver should bear in mind that the availability of contractually **9–013** enforceable confidentiality undertakings from unsuccessful bidders for the business may be important to the successful purchaser who will wish to prevent misuse of confidential information which had been disclosed during the sale process.

Care should be taken during the negotiation process to be reasonable **9–014** in any assertions regarding the possibility of rival offers. Over zealousness can result in damages for fraudulent misrepresentation.[10] Exclusion

---

[8] Broadly speaking, unless the advertisement is of a type falling within a number of exemptions contained in s. 58 of the Act and various statutory instruments made thereunder, no person other than an authorised person shall issue or cause to be issued an investment advertisement in the United Kingdom unless its contents have been approved by an authorised person: see s. 57 of the Financial Services Act 1986. A detailed exposition of this topic lies outside the scope of this book and reference should be made to Lomnicka & Powell, *Encyclopaedia of Financial Services Law* (Sweet & Maxwell). Paragraph 5 of the Financial Services Act 1986 (Investment Advertisements) (Exemptions) (No. 2) Order 1988 (S.I. 1988 No. 716) which provides that s. 57 of the Financial Services Act 1986 shall not apply to an investment advertisement if the invitation is made or the invitation given by or on behalf of a body corporate for the purposes of or with a view to the disposal of shares in a body corporate consisting of shares carrying 75 *per* cent, or more of the voting rights exercisable in general meetings of the company. This might well exempt many sales of subsidiaries from the requirements of s. 57.

[9] *Re Neon Signs (Australia) Ltd* [1965] V.R. 125.

[10] *Smith New Court Securities v. Scrimgeour Vickers (Asset Management) Ltd* [1997] A.C. 254, HL.

clauses will not protect the company or, to the extent of his responsibility for the fraudulent misrepresentations, the receiver from liability.

9–015   Legal advice should be taken in drawing up the contracts and dealing with the other legal formalities of the sale. In the sale of a solvent business the usual practice is for the purchaser's solicitors to prepare the first draft sale contract. In a receivership sale it is the receiver's solicitors who prepare the draft. This is probably the practical consequence of the receiver's need so far as possible to exclude warranties and liability in the sale documentation.

2. THE SALE CONTRACT

9–016 The receiver will wish to ensure that the sale which is achieved creates the minimum practical exposure to risk and liability on his part and on the part of his appointing lender. The content of the draft sale contract will reflect these concerns. The extent to which the receiver can achieve his object will depend on the commercial strength of his position in the case. Nonetheless the core aim of minimising liabilities to achieve a clear fund for distribution to the secured lender will usually be adhered to.

(a) The parties

9–017 The company in receivership should be the vendor. The assets of the company do not vest in the receiver. It should be made clear that the receiver is acting only as agent of the company and that personal liability of the receiver is excluded.[11] The receiver will also be a party in his own right to take the benefit of the exclusions, limitations and indemnities in his favour which the contract will contain. The Contracts (Rights of Third Parties) Act 1999 will, unless excluded by a sale contract made on or after May 11, 2000, have the effect of allowing a receiver to sue on the benefit of exclusions and indemnities in his favour even if he is not a party.[12] There are many circumstances in which a receiver will not necessarily wish to give other third parties rights to sue under a receivership sale contract. It is also not yet clear how the Act will work in practice. It is, therefore, likely that the effect of the Act will be excluded in most sale contracts for the immediate future and the receivers will continue to be parties.

9–018   The purchaser will often be a new company incorporated or activated for the purpose of acquiring the business. Although receivers avoid deferred consideration wherever possible, there will usually be contractual obligations imposed upon the purchaser in favour of the receiver and the company in receivership under the sale contract. The financial standing of the purchaser should, therefore, always be considered and where appropriate, a suitable guarantor of its obligations should be found. This will often be a parent company. If an appropriate guarantor

---

[11] The receiver will be personally liable in the absence of an exclusion (s. 44(1)(b) of the 1986 Act).

[12] See further above, para. 7–050.

cannot be provided, the receiver should seek to bolster the purchaser's obligations by some form of cash cover in the agreement. His ability to do this will, of course, depend on the extent of his bargaining position. His need to do so will depend on his commercial judgment of the potential value of the purchaser's post contractual obligations.

It is often the case that a director of the vendor company or its **9–019** holding company will be the purchaser or, more commonly, that the purchaser will be a company associated with such a director within the meaning of section 320 of the Companies Act 1985. It was held in *Demite Limited v. Protec Health Ltd*[13] that when, in those circumstances, the receiver was selling as agent of the company (and therefore the vendor was the company) and the transaction was a substantial property transaction, it was subject to section 320 of that Act. The sale was therefore voidable by the vendor company, in that case acting by its provisional liquidator. The difficulty arises because the statutory predecessor of section 320 pre-dates the reforms contained in the Insolvency Act 1986 and goes back to a period when a receiver could have been a director or someone connected with a director and acting in league with him. The point seems to have been overlooked when the Insolvency Act 1986 was passed: the exemption for liquidators should have been broadened to include other office-holders, including administrative receivers.

A resolution of the vendor company (and, where the director is a **9–020** director of the holding company, of that company) affirming the transaction will authorise it. However, practical difficulties may arise in obtaining such a resolution. If a majority of members in favour of the transaction cannot be secured the receiver may have to request that the debenture-holder join in the sale to exercise its own power of sale.[14] Alternatively, the receiver could apply to the court for a sale by the court, with conduct given to the receiver.

Even where the requisite majority of members is available timing will **9–021** be an issue if an opposing minority refuse to consent to the meeting to verify the transaction being held at short notice.[15] In such a case it may be appropriate for the receiver to arrange at point of sale for the meeting of members to be called to ratify the sale, and to take irrevocable powers of attorney[16] from the consenting members to vote their shares when the meeting is held.

---

[13] [1998] B.C.C. 638 The decision appears to be at odds with the decision in *Re ELS Ltd* [1995] Ch. 11 to the effect that following crystallisation of the floating change assets were no longer subject to distraint for rates as crystallisation had effected an assignment of the goods in question to the debenture holder so that they were no longer the company's assets. For a critique of the decision see Rajani, *Insolvency Law and Practice* Vol. 14, No. 5, 1998, p. 275.

[14] If registered land is involved this will not be effective unless the debenture is registered. It was also suggested in *Demite* that directions of the court could be sought. It is difficult to see how these could override the provisions of s. 320 of the Companies Act 1985.

[15] See s. 369 Companies Act 1985, s. 369.

[16] Powers of Attorney Act 1971, s. 4(1).

(b) Recitals

9–022 The recitals in the sale contract will usually be brief. The appointment of the receiver will usually be recited and referenced to the debentures or other security documents under which he is appointed. A receiver will usually wish to avoid warranting the validity of his appointment.[17]

9–023   Recitals will also often set out the position that the purchaser is proceeding relying on his own investigation of the assets and in the knowledge that he bears the full risk of title to the assets not passing to him and that that is a reasonable risk since the company is in receivership. The purpose of such a recital is to bolster the case for enforceability of the wide exclusions which will be in the body of the contract.

(c) Definitions

9–024   In general, the aim will be to limit clearly the definitions of those assets being disposed of. This may be by reference to description and by reference to schedules or location. The assets should also be defined as those of the vendor so as to avoid any suggestion that third party assets are being sold. Conversely, where the definitions relate to areas where the purchaser is to assume liabilities (such as employees) or provide indemnities (such as third party stock or third party assets held in the business), the receiver will wish to have as wide a definition as possible to take account of the fact that his knowledge of the business may be incomplete.

9–025   In a going concern sale, the framework for the definition of the assets sold will usually be a definition of the business to which they relate. In circumstances where different businesses are operated under the same corporate structure and there are several disposals, care will be needed to ensure that there is no overlap, particularly in the area of shared facilities and access to records of the business.

(d) The sale and title

9–026 The usual formula is for the company to sell whatever right, title and interest (if any) it may have in a list of assets of the business (as defined). The primary purpose of this formulation is to ensure that the purchaser cannot sue if the title is defective or absent.[18] The formulation also has the effect of providing the vendor and receiver with a degree of protection against an action for conversion if it should prove any of the assets "sold" did not belong to the vendor company.[19]

9–027   The assets sold will vary according to the purchaser's requirements but will commonly include the business equipment, the stock (including any interest of the vendor in retention of title stock) and work in progress,

---

[17] Validity of the appointment is dealt with in Chap. 4.

[18] But see *Nottingham Patent Tile and Brick Co. v Butler* [1885] 15 Q.B. 261 and *Faruqui v. English Real Estates Ltd* [1979] 1 W.L.R. 963 in relation to property sales which suggest that the formulation will not protect the vendor if the defects are known to the vendor but not disclosed at the time of the sale.

[19] *Port v. Auger* [1994] 1 W.L.R. 862 at 872

the company's contracts, intellectual property, the goodwill and the business premises. For the avoidance of doubt, there will generally be a provision stating that no assets other than those listed are being sold and (without limitation to that provision) specifically listing assets which are not included in the sale. Some of these items are those which the company has a duty to retain, such as its records and statutory books. Others will be items which the receivers may find it difficult to value correctly at the point of the sale such as potential damages claims against third parties, rights to refunds of taxes (such as VAT) and the rights that the vendor may have in respect of the company's pension fund. The vendor will also wish to make it clear that he is not disposing of assets used in the business which belong to third parties such as leased equipment or third parties tooling held in the business. Finally, there will be assets such as cash in bank or book debts which will not realise any greater value if sold to the purchaser than if collected by the vendor. Even if book debts are not sold, there may be provisions in the contract for the purchaser's assistance in collection.

(e) The price

The sale contract will apportion the price between the assets sold. Where **9–028** land is included in the sale, this will be important for stamp duty purposes. In the case of other assets, the apportionment is more likely to be relevant to the division between fixed and floating charge realisations, although the extent to which plant and machinery are fixtures and are therefore, part of the land, is relevant for stamp duty purposes. The purchaser will have its own views on how it would like the assets apportioned. This should not stop the receiver taking valuation advice relating to the apportionment of the price to ensure that he is not exposed to criticism in particular from preferential creditors or a liquidator.[20]

(f) Payment and completion

Wherever possible a receiver will look for immediate payment. If for any **9–029** reason consideration has to be deferred, he will usually look for adequate assurance of payment either by a guarantee deposit or through taking debenture security. Occasionally, there may be assets the worth of which neither the purchaser nor the receiver is certain but which can only be realised in the process of running the business. These might include some new process or product. In those situations, if the receiver feels he is unable to achieve a price from the purchaser at the point of sale which adequately reflects the potential for future income, he may look for additional consideration based on future earnings.

Where the sale clearly falls within HM Customs and Excise criteria for **9–030** transfer as a going concern,[21] the sale will usually be completed without

---

[20] See Statement of Insolvency Practice, June 14, 1999, para. 3.6 for best practice recommendations on this point.
[21] (Special Provisions) Order 1995 (S.I. No. 1286), art. 5.

payment of VAT. But there will always be a clause requiring the purchaser to pay VAT should it later prove that VAT was, in fact, due on the sale. Particular care needs to be taken with regard to property. The grant of a fee simple in a new or unfinished commercial building or civil engineering work is standard rated for VAT purposes. "New" basically means that the building or engineering work is up to three years old. Alternatively in the case of "old" buildings it is also possible that an election has been made in the past to waive the exemption (also known as the option to tax) under Schedule 10, paragraph 2 to the Value Added Tax Act 1994. This has the effect of making all future dealings relating to the building by the party who exercised it taxable at the standard rate. The receiver should make enquiries to ascertain the age of the building and any alterations and also whether the company has opted to tax.

9-031 In both these situations VAT will be chargeable on the sale of the property unless the conditions for a transfer as a going concern are met. These conditions require the purchaser to use the property for the same purpose as it was used by the vendor and if the vendor had opted to tax the property the purchaser will do likewise.

9-032 The requirements for a going concern transfer relating to property must be in place before contracts are exchanged. The receiver should therefore ensure that he has details of the purchaser's VAT registration and any application to opt together with HM Customs and Excise's acknowledgement before exchange.

9-033 Where the sale is of only a limited part of the company's assets more akin to a break up sale, payment of VAT will usually be provided for in the consideration. In hybrid cases where there is perceived to be a significant risk that VAT may be payable, or where there are concerns that the purchaser's covenant to pay VAT that is due may not be substantial, a VAT deposit may be taken to abide Customs and Excise determination on the point.

(g) Property and risk

9-034 The receiver will generally wish to pass risk to the purchaser immediately the purchaser takes over the business and will wish to retain title until he has been paid in full. This is particularly so if there is an element of deferred consideration. The practical enforcement of such a title retention will depend upon the particular assets over which title is retained. In practice, it will be more effective against fixed plant than stock or work in progress.

(h) Third party assets

9-035 Invariably a business will hold some third party assets. There has been an increasing trend in recent years towards asset based financing. The receiver will not purport to sell these items. The vendor company's obligation will generally be limited to an obligation to assign the benefit of contracts where that is permissible and a limited obligation to assist with the novation of contracts where it is not. The purchaser will often wish to take possession of these assets and to use them in the business. From the receiver's point of view, this may either be a practical necessity, because the assets are essential in the business, or may be desirable because the value of outstanding payments due on the contracts may be less than their value to the purchaser. The purchaser may therefore be prepared to enhance his price for the business for the chance of acquiring them.

If negotiations with the third party owners can be concluded before **9–036** the sale, there will be little difficulty. However, not infrequently, the sale will precede completion of discussions with the finance companies.[22] The receiver will not be protected by section 234(3) of the Insolvency Act in relation to the disposal of property which he knows not to be the property of the company. Excluding those items from the sale is one line of defence against a claim from the true owner. By including them in the sale the company will have given up possession and will thereby have disabled itself from complying with any demand that the owner might make for return of the equipment. There is, also, a risk of a claim by the owner for damages for conversion.[23] To protect the company and the receiver[24] from such claims, the sale contract will generally include an obligation on the purchaser to redeliver third party equipment on demand from the owner and indemnities in favour of the company and the receiver for any loss suffered by them as a result of the purchaser's failure so to do.

(i) Third party stock

Third party stock is similar to other third party assets with the important **9–037** practical difference that generally speaking it has been supplied to the company for consumption or resale. The owner is therefore generally more interested in being paid the invoice price for the goods rather than recovering them. It is now established that an undertaking from a receiver to pay the invoice price of goods, if it should prove that the retention of title claim is good, will prevent the supplier obtaining an injunction against their sale.[25]

The purchaser will usually wish to be able to dispose of or consume **9–038** the stock in the course of business. The purchaser may also be concerned to ensure that the receiver does not antagonise the suppliers of the business in the process of seeking proof of their retention of title claims. The purchaser may also feel himself in a better commercial position to negotiate a favourable settlement of retention of title claims as he may

---

[22] See *Transag Haulage v. Leyland Daf Finance plc* [1994] 2BCLC 88; *On Demand Information plc v. Michael Gerson (Finance) plc* [1999] 2 All E.R. 811 affirmed on appeal, July 31, 2000, unreported, CA and *Alf Vaughan & Co. Ltd v. Royscot Trust Plc* [1999] 1 All E.R. (Comm) 856 for the importance of the receiver obtaining relief against forfeiture before sale if he proposes to pass title to the purchaser. Relief against forfeiture is not available after sale.

[23] *Martindale v. Smith* (1841) 1 Q.B. 389.

[24] See *Clerk and Lindsell on Torts* (17th Ed.), p. 640 and *Re Samuel (No. 2)* [1945] Ch. 408 for the liability of agents assisting in wrongful disposals.

[25] *Lipe Ltd v. Leyland Daf Ltd* [1993] B.C.C. 385.

be offering further business to the suppliers in question. It is therefore not unusual for the purchaser to agree to acquire all the stock, including the stock subject to third party rights, at a price discounted to take into account likely payments required for third party suppliers.

9–039   Where there is considerable uncertainty about the number of retention of title claims or their validity, there may be a retention from the purchase price to meet the claims. Unless the receiver is very confident about the level of retention of title claims that will have to be met, he will be unlikely to agree that the vendor company will bear a risk of them without some limitation as to the quantum of liability and the time within which the claims must be made. To take on any open-ended liability would be inconsistent with his aim of providing clear funds for distribution to the debenture-holder.

9–040   In any event, since the stock subject to third party claims may not be the property of the company, unless the receiver agrees to take on the responsibility of the claims, the sale contract will provide that the purchaser must deliver up the stock on demand or indemnify the vendor and the receiver company for damages. There may also be provision for the purchaser to conduct defence of the claims in the name of the company subject to indemnities for costs in the company's favour.

(j) Intellectual property

9–041 Intellectual property is a field in which third party rights abound. It can be both a problem and an opportunity for a receiver. The company may own valuable intellectual property rights which should be identified, protected and realised. It is likely to be prudent for the receiver to take advice concerning this. On the other hand, the company's assets may be severely devalued because of the absence or termination of intellectual property rights. The company's business may be reliant on the use of computer software under licences which may be terminable on receivership or a company may have costly equipment for the production of products which can only be sold if the licence to manufacture and sell is maintained. Without those rights, the equipment may be valuable only as scrap. The owners of these rights will often be in a position of considerable commercial strength. Relief against forfeiture is not available for as (except perhaps in the area of commissioned works) the rights of the company as licensee can probably not be classified as either proprietary or possessory.[26]

9–042   Aside from the trading issues, the receiver has the difficulty in simply identifying third party intellectual property much of which does not have to be registered anywhere. For that reason, any sale of intellectual property will usually exclude intellectual property of third parties and will be subject to any third party consent that may be required. The receiver will usually also wish to impose upon the purchaser an

---

[26] See *Sport International Bussum BV v. Inter-Footwear* [1984] 1 W.L.R. 776 and *On Demand Information plc v. Michael Gerson Plc* [1999] 2 All E.R. 811 at 821, affirmed on appeal, July 31, 2000, unreported, for this requirement.

obligation not to use the intellectual property without obtaining consent and will always look for an indemnity for any damage that might be suffered through unauthorised use.

(k) Apportionment of pre-payments and liabilities

As with any other business sale, there should be a clear point in time **9–043** from which the purchaser assumes obligations for the ongoing liabilities of the business. As the company is likely to be insolvent it is common for the sale contract to provide that as to past liabilities not assumed by the purchaser the company remains responsible for them but is under no obligation to the purchaser to discharge them. The receiver will usually try to resist giving credit for pre-payments, particularly those made before his appointment, unless they are clearly represented in the value which the purchaser is paying for the business.

(l) Records

The company will have to hand over to the purchaser VAT records **9–044** unless HM Customs and Excise agree otherwise.[27] Where the records are handed over the receiver will wish to retain access to them both to account for VAT for the receivership trading and to pursue any claim that there may be for VAT refunds.

The receiver will wish to retain for the liquidator the statutory books **9–045** of the company and the ownership of the general company books and records.[28] The receiver will also have a practical need to consult these documents for the collection of book debts and for dealing with preferential creditors. The receiver will, however, usually wish to avoid the trouble and expense of removal and storage of the records.[29] Fortunately, the purchaser will generally require access to the records for the purposes of the ongoing business. The sale contract will, therefore, frequently provide that ownership of the records is retained by the company and that the company may allow the purchaser possession of them. Such a clause should also provide that the purchaser must hold the records for six years and must allow the receivers and any liquidator access to them and deliver them up at their request. There are frequently also conditions requiring the provision of office facilities for receivership staff.

(m) Employees

This subject is dealt with in detail in Chapter 19. The framing of the **9–046** contract in respect of employees will depend upon whether the receiver has dismissed employees before embarking on the sale process or whether the employees remain in the business at the point of sale.

---

[27] See Value Added Tax Act 1994, s.49 and Sched. 11, para. 6.

[28] See *Engely v. South Metropolitan Browning and Bottling Company* [1892] 1 Ch. 442 for a case where the court compelled a court appointed receiver to deliver records to a liquidator against suitable undertakings.

[29] Such an approach may not now constitute best practice (Statement of Insolvency Practice, August 1, 1997 para. 16).

Whatever the factual situation, the provisions of regulation 5 of the Transfer of Undertakings (Protection of Employment) Regulations 1981 as interpreted by the House of Lords in *Litster v. Forth Dry Dock & Engineering Co. Ltd*[30] are so wide that it is unlikely that the receiver will be prepared to permit the company to give any indemnity to the purchaser against the prospect that dismissed employees may transfer.[31]

9–047   The contract may take one of two forms. The contract will either state that the employees have been dismissed or state that they are transferring; but in either case the receiver will wish to make it clear that the purchaser will have no recourse should it prove that employees other than those expected to transfer do, in fact, transfer. Indeed in relation to those employees who are expected to transfer the receiver will wish to impose an express obligation upon the purchaser to employ them so as to guard against voluntary and unfair dismissal claims if for any reason they do not transfer by operation of law. If commercial pressure force him to do so, the receiver may be prepared to provide a retention out of the purchase monies to be applied towards claims from "unexpected" transferring employees made within the defined period. The receiver will expect the purchaser to be concerned as to the manner in which the company's obligations to consult employees about the transfer have been carried out. Any liability for failure to consult transferring employees will fall upon the purchaser.[32] It should be noted that pension arrangements relating to employees do not normally transfer. The purchaser will have to make separate arrangements for future pension entitlements of the employees.[33]

(n) Contracts

9–048 The receiver will wish to provide that the purchaser takes the benefit and burden of existing contracts for supplies to and by the company. There will be provisions for the vendor to provide limited assistance with novation. In addition, there will be provision for assignment of those contracts capable of assignment together with an indemnity in favour of the company and the receiver in relation to the burden of the contracts. There may also be a specific provision for the purchaser to deal with warranty claims. The obligation for the purchaser to perform contracts and to deal with warranty claims can be important to minimise practical and legal resistance to the receiver's collection of pre-sale book debts. Also, while the receiver is not liable for pre-receivership contracts which

---

[30] [1990] 1 A.C. 546.

[31] The receiver should bear in mind that even when dismissing employees for an economic technical or other reason the manner of dismissal itself may none the less be unfair. If so the liability for damages for unfair dismissal will not transfer but will remain with the company in receivership: *Kerry Foods Ltd v. Creber* [2000] I.R.L.R. 10, EAT.

[32] *Kerry Foods Ltd v. Creber.*

[33] Transfer of Undertakings (Protection of Employment) Regulations 1981 (S.I. No. 1794), reg. 7. Personal pension plans, however are sometimes provided as part of the employment contract and the employees obligation to make contributions may therefore transfer. For a detailed consideration see below, Chap. 19.

have been continued during the trading period or post receivership contracts where he has excluded liability, he will wish so far as possible to ensure that he has provided for the liabilities incurred during the receivership trading period both as a matter of professional reputation and to avoid any suggestion of fraudulent trading.[34] In practice too, the receiver may have been commercially obliged to give to important suppliers undertakings to procure the company's fulfilment of its payment obligations during the receivership period and he will wish to ensure that these are adequately covered either by the price paid by the purchaser or by collateral indemnities in the contract.

(o) Book debts
The receiver may wish to obtain the purchaser's assistance with the **9–049** collection of book debts. If, as is frequently the case, the purchaser will change its name following the sale or trade under a name similar to that previously used by the vendor, there is a risk of confusion amongst the creditors of the business. Accordingly, it is sensible to provide a trust and accounting obligation on the purchaser in respect of payments received by it for pre-sale book debts. It may also be wise to provide that, where customers do not make it clear to which debts particular payments relate, those payments should be appropriated to the earliest outstanding book debts due from the customer in respect of the business. This will be particularly important in those circumstances where the purchaser is acting as the vendor's agent in the collection of book debts.

(p) Goodwill
The sale of the goodwill will carry with it the right to use the trade **9–050** names of the company. The receiver will not be able to agree to change the vendor's name unless he also controls the vendor's holding company. It should also be made clear that the right to use the company name is made available to the purchaser only in so far as the vendor is able lawfully to do so. The receiver will wish to retain the right to use the vendor's name in relation to the completion of the statutory requirements in the receivership.

Where the purchaser wishes to retain the director of the vendor **9–051** company in a managerial position or where the purchaser is a management buy-out team and the purchaser wishes to trade under the same or a similar name as the vendor, the purchaser will have to have regard to Sections 216 and 217 of the Insolvency Act 1986 and the need to seek leave of the court unless the circumstances fall within the three cases prescribed in the Insolvency Rules.[35] These provisions are dealt with in more detail below, but it should be remembered that, where two or more businesses operated by the company in receivership are sold separately, none of the purchasers is likely to be a purchaser of substantially the

---

[34] See above, para. 2–020.
[35] Insolvency Rules 1986, rr. 4.228–4.230.

whole of the business and this will limit the purchaser's avenues for excluding the operation of section 216 without leave of the court.[36]

(q) Exclusions

9–052 The receiver will wish to exclude in respect of himself and the company all warranties as to title, description and fitness for purpose. He will also wish to obtain the purchaser's acknowledgement that the purchaser is relying on his own enquiries and specialist advice and not on any representations of the vendor, the receiver or his staff or agent. The purchaser will be asked to acknowledge that this is reasonable on the grounds that the company is in receivership and the receiver does not have full knowledge of its affairs. It is important to bolster the reasonableness of the exclusions in the light of the provisions in sections 2(2) and 11(1) of the Unfair Contract Terms Act 1977.

9–053 In addition to the general exclusions there should be included a specific statement that the receiver is not personally liable on the sale contract whether under Section 44(1) of the Insolvency Act or otherwise, that he contracts as agent of the company[37] and that he is party to the contract in his own name only for the purpose of taking the benefit of the exclusions, indemnities and other rights in his favour which the contract contains.

(c) Properties

9–054 Conditions relating to the sale of land whether leasehold or freehold are generally very detailed. It is common practice to provide for them in a separate schedule. Care should be taken to ensure that the definitions in the contract are compatible with the definitions in any standard sale conditions subject to which the property is sold, albeit with appropriate modifications for an insolvency sale. The property should be sold without full or limited title guarantee. Generally, the terms of the contract will exclude the right of the purchaser to raise requisitions as to title. It is generally convenient for the completion of the property sale to occur at the same time as the completion of the sale of the business.

9–055 Where landlord's consent is required for the assignment of leaseholds, it should if possible be obtained prior to the sale. If this cannot be done and the purchaser goes into occupation on completion of the business sale, it will invariably be a breach of the terms of the lease and the purchaser should indemnify the vendor for any damage suffered. Unless the property is let at below current market rent, the landlord is likely in practice to be happier to have a solvent assignee rather than an insolvent tenant.

9–056 Difficulties can arise where the purchaser wishes to occupy the company's premises on a short term basis only following the sale. This may be to complete existing contracts or to allow time for the removal of plant and machinery. Occasionally, the purchaser's occupation will be under a

---

[36] Insolvency Rules 1986, r. 4.228.
[37] Assuming there is no liquidation: see Chap. 11.

licence. If the purchaser has exclusive occupation the licence may be construed as a tenancy.[38] If there is a tenancy at will, there should be no difficulty in obtaining possession as such a tenancy is outside the Landlord and Tenant Act 1954, Part II.[39] Often a purchaser will require a definite period of occupation. Where a tenancy of business premises is for a period exceeding six months, the tenant will have security of tenure under the Part II of the Landlord and Tenant Act 1954 unless an order has first been obtained to exclude the tenancy from the protection provided by that Act.[40] It is not always sufficient merely to provide that the tenancy should be for six months or less. Section 43(3)(b) of the Landlord and Tenant Act 1954 provides that, where the tenant carries on the same business as the previous occupier, the tenant will have security if his period of occupation aggregated with that of the previous occupier exceeds 12 months. It will frequently be the case that the purchaser will be conducting the same business from the premises of that previously carried on by the vendor. It is often assumed that the problem of aggregation of the periods of occupation only arises when the vendor company was in occupation of the premises as a tenant and the purchaser will become a successor to that lease. In fact, section 43(3)(b) of the Landlord and Tenant Act 1954 appears to address the continuity of the business and not the continuity of the tenancy. Accordingly, previous occupation by the vendor as a free-holder would seem to be sufficient to trigger security provided there is continuity in the business carried on.[41]

It is therefore frequently the case that occupation by the purchaser of **9–057** the premises even for only a short period will require the parties to contract out of the Landlord and Tenant Act. A joint application by the Landlord and Tenant is required. The order must be obtained and the excluded tenancy entered into prior to the purchaser taking occupation. In practice the application for the court order to contract out of security of tenure is usually made very shortly before the sale is to be concluded and, (subject to court lists), can be dealt with swiftly and without attendance. But on occasion there is delay where only a short period of occupation is required by the purchaser, but the aggregation of occupation referred to above will result in security of tenure if not excluded. Court officials may wrongly suppose that tenancies for six months or less cannot be contracted out of the Act. A practical way of minimising the risk of this happening is to provide the contractual tenancy period of more than six months with a provision in the body of the agreement for the vendor to break the tenancy after the period actually required by the purchaser.[42]

---

[38] *Street v. Mountford* [1985] A.C. 809. The Landlord & Tenant Act 1954, Pt. II applies to tenancies at no rent; see *Woodfall on Landlord and Tenant* Vol. 2, para. 22–023.

[39] This is so whether the tenancy at will arises by operation of law or by express agreement. *Wheeler v. Mercer* [1957] A.C. 416 and *Manfield and Sons v. Botchin* [1970] 2 Q.B. 612.

[40] Landlord and Tenant Act 1954, Pt. II, s. 43(3).

[41] This point was argued in *Cricket Ltd v. Shaftesbury plc* [1999] 3 All E.R. 283 at 287 but expressly left open by Neuberger J.

[42] The inclusion of a break clause does not prevent the tenancy from being for a term certain: *Scholl Manufacturing Co. v Clifton (Slim-Line)* [1967] Ch. 41, CA.

3. HIVE-DOWN

(a) The concept

9–058 A "hive-down" is the transfer of certain assets of the business of the company in receivership to a new wholly-owned subsidiary controlled by the receiver, but leaving behind the liabilities. Without the dead weight of the accumulated debts of the parent, the subsidiary may prove both profitable and marketable.[43] Hiving-down has advantages for the receiver in that the business can be conducted through the subsidiary, thereby avoiding personal contractual liability.[44]

9–059 The principal advantages relate to the preservation and realisation of the business itself[45]: hiving-down is often an important ingredient in preparing the business for an advantageous sale to a purchaser. The benefits of this course of action include the following:

(a) the receiver can choose the assets which are profitable or otherwise desirable to transfer;

(b) the more saleable assets can be combined with the carry-forward of capital allowances and trading losses for use against future profits for tax purposes. The right to relief in respect of trading losses is not a chose in action, still less is it assignable by the company in receivership. It is only by means of a hive-down of substantially the whole of the business of the company to a subsidiary that such losses will be capable of transfer to the subsidiary to be set against future profits. Under section 343 of the Income and Corporation Taxes Act 1988 (as amended), provided that the transfer is achieved at a time when the transferee is a subsidiary of the transferor, the transferee can take over the past trading losses of the transferor as if it had always carried on the trade.[46] The hive-down should be effected prior to the execution of any agreement for sale if the tax losses are to be utilised in this way. It may be too late to hive-down after an agreement is signed, since the beneficial interest in the shares in the subsidiary will have already passed to the purchaser[47];

---

[43] Hiving-down prior to receivership may be difficult because it may open up the directors to challenges by a subsequent liquidator.

[44] But the receiver may take on the responsibilities of being a director or shadow director of the subsidiary — responsibilities which could extend, for example, to personal liability for wrongful trading of the subsidiary if the business does not prosper. See above, para. 2–020.

[45] Minimising the risk of distress for rates, VAT and taxes is no longer an advantage following the decision in *Re ELS Ltd* [1995] Ch. 11 to the effect that crystallisation of the floating charge takes floating charge assets beyond such distress

[46] The amount of losses carried forward is reduced by the difference between "relevant liabilities" (liabilities of the transferor prior to hive-down which were not transferred) and "relevant assets" (the value of any assets of the transferor prior to hive-down which were not transferred and the value of the consideration paid by the transferee for the transfer). In practice, the restriction of the losses means that this is no longer the primary reason for hiving down a business.

[47] See *IRC v. Ufitec Group Ltd* [1977] 3 All E.R. 924; *Wood Preservation Ltd v. Prior* [1969] 1 W.L.R. 1077 and *J. Sainsbury v. O'Connor (H.M.I.T)* [1991] 1 W.L.R. 963.

(c) the subsidiary will be "clean" in the sense of not being saddled with the old company's debts or any disadvantageous credit standing with suppliers[48];

(d) it ought to be easier to establish the profitability of the business of the subsidiary;

(e) trading can continue without interruption even if the parent company is wound up;

(f) Customs and Excise will not allow a receiver to obtain a repayment of VAT where there are pre-receivership liabilities in respect of VAT. In the case of a business which generates repayments, a hive-down solves this problem in relation to prospective repayments because the subsidiary will be able to obtain separate VAT registration and will be able to claim refunds on its own account, thereby avoiding any claim of Crown set-off;

(g) Section 233 of the Insolvency Act 1986 provides that an administrative receiver can require gas, electricity and telecommunication services to be provided so long as he personally guarantees payment for supplies after the date of his appointment: the supplier cannot as a condition of supply make it a condition that pre-receivership bills are paid.[49] A subsidiary will be a new customer and will be entitled to such supplies without payment of its parent's debts. Accordingly, whilst a hive-down is not necessary to secure continued supplies without paying off arrears, it does have the advantage that the receiver can thereby secure such supplies without being required to give a personal guarantee.

(b) Legality

By virtue of section 42(1) and paragraphs 15 and 16 of Schedule 1 to the **9–060** Insolvency Act 1986, and unless the powers are inconsistent with any provisions of the debenture, an administrative receiver will have the power to establish subsidiaries of the company and to transfer to any such subsidiaries of the company the whole or any part of the business and property of the company. This power may be exercised for the purpose of a hive-down. The hive-down cannot prejudice third party property rights. Legal and equitable interests in the company's property must be respected and will not be prejudiced.[50] But purely contractual obligations may be converted into mere monetary claims in damages against the company. Prior to the Insolvency Act 1986, the legality of hive-downs had been challenged as involving the wholesale repudiation of contractual obligations by the company. Objection was taken on the

---

[48] The hive-down may not solve all the problems in this regard: supplies may be cut off before the hive-down is effected.

[49] Other suppliers continue to be entitled to insist on payment of all sums outstanding as a condition of any supply: see above, paras. 5–003 to 5–006.

[50] *Freevale v. Metrostore Holdings* [1984] Ch. 199 and *Telemetrix v. Modern Engineers of Bristol (Holdings) plc* [1985] B.C.L.C. 213.

basis that the company was divesting itself of its undertaking, thereby making it impossible to fulfil contractual duties. The challenge failed in the case of hive-downs by receivers appointed by debenture-holders on the ground that the receiver is entitled (whilst the company is not) to repudiate outstanding contracts of the company. This was thought necessary to achieve a beneficial realisation for the debenture-holder.[51] There may be a difference depending upon whether the receiver is acting as agent for the company or as principal, since if acting as agent for a contracting party he may be exempt from a claim in tort for interfering with the contractual relations between the company and the third parties, but may not be exempt if he is acting as principal.[52] If there is such a distinction, then the receiver appointed out of court will be exposed once winding-up has commenced, since his agency thereupon terminates.[53] Where a mortgagee acquires his rights without notice of the rights of another party under a subsisting contract, the tort of wrongful interference with contract cannot preclude the mortgagee from enforcing his rights or remedies on the basis of his superior title.[54] If no complaint can be made against the mortgagee in such a case, surely none can be made against the receiver whether acting as agent of the mortgagee or as principal in right of the mortgagee. A receiver appointed by the court is always potentially exposed, since he never acts as agent for the company. He should seek the directions of the court before proceeding with a hive-down and the order will afford him protection.

(c) Method

9–061 The hive-down company will ideally be a newly-formed company or possibly a subsidiary which has never traded. The receiver should take care to ensure that suitable directors are appointed, usually the receiver himself and/or members of his staff. The hive-down company may now have only one issued share,[55] held by the company in receivership. The receiver should also ensure that the subsidiary keeps statutory books and proper books of account and that the requirements of Part VII of the Companies Act 1985 are complied with, *e.g.* as to auditors and accounts; that all proper insurances are taken out; and that separate VAT registration is taken up.

---

[51] *Airline Airspares v. Handley Page* [1970] Ch. 193. "The lemon may, so to speak, be squeezed dry": *per* McPherson J. in *Re Diesel's & Components Pty Ltd* (1985) 9 A.C.L.R. 825 at 828.

[52] Consider *Re Botibol* [1947] 1 All E.R. 26 at 28; *Telemetrix v. Modern Engineers* [1985] B.C.L.C. 213 and *Welsh Development Agency v. Export Finance Co.* [1992] B.C.C. 270.

[53] *Gosling v. Gaskell and Grocott* [1897] A.C. 575.

[54] See *Edwin Hill & Partners v. First National Finance Corp* [1989] B.C.L.C. 89, CA; *Swiss Bank Corp v. Lloyd's Bank* [1979] Ch. 548 at 571–572: the reversal on appeal ([1982] A.C. 548) does not affect the authority of the judgment on this point. See also above, Chap. 7.

[55] Note that, since July 15, 1992, it is possible to have a subsidiary which has only one share: see the Companies (Single Member Private Ltd Companies) Regulations 1992 (S.I. No. 1699) which implement the Twelfth E.C. Company Law Directive (Directive 89/667: [1989] O.J. L395/40) of December 21, 1989.

The assets transferred will usually consist of plant, machinery, office **9–062** furniture, equipment, vehicles, stock, work-in-progress and goodwill (including the right to use any trading name as the successor to the business carried out by the company in receivership) and the benefit of trading contracts. Initially, any interest in land (freehold or leasehold), trade marks, patents, licences, copyrights, rights in designs, cash and book-debts are left in the parent. There is usually no advantage in incurring expense in transferring the land[56] and intellectual property rights in the initial hive-down when it is not known for certain that the subsidiary company will either be able to trade successfully or that a buyer will be found. In due course, these assets can be sold to the subsidiary or to a purchaser together with the shares of the subsidiary. The liabilities of the parent company are of course left with the parent company.

It is important that the price for the assets to be hived-down is fixed so **9–063** as to equate to the price attributed to those assets when the subsidiary company is sold, thus giving rise to no profit or loss on the transaction. This is achieved by providing in the hive-down contract for the transfer of the trading assets to the subsidiary for a consideration to be certified either by an independent valuer or by the receiver's firm. The purchase price is left outstanding on inter-company loan. When the subsidiary is sold to a purchaser, either a supplementary agreement is made between the company in receivership and its subsidiary, removing the requirement for the valuer's certificate and inserting a figure for the price which equates to the price at which the hived-down assets have been valued for the purposes of the sale of the subsidiary; or a certificate will be issued at the appropriate price. The purchaser of the shares of the subsidiary will agree to discharge the inter-company loan so that, on completion, the company in receivership will receive the purchase price for the assets sold.[57]

(d) Employees

The usual practice before the Insolvency Act 1986 was that employees **9–064** were left with the parent and their services subcontracted to the hive-down subsidiary. The parent would invoice the subsidiary for the labour and pay the employees itself to avoid any suggestion that contracts of employment had been novated. The idea, of course, was to leave liabilities in respect of contracts of employment with the parent as far as

[56] There may be a positive disadvantage in transferring land and other assets subject to corporation tax on chargeable gains. Where the transfer to a third party will give rise to a chargeable gain, this will arise in the hive-down company, by virtue of ss. 178 and 179 of the Taxation of Chargeable Gains Act 1992, but a direct sale of the property to the hive-down company following a sale of the shares in the hive-down company to a third party will result in the liability being an unsecured claim in the subsequent liquidation of the transferor of the shares: see below, Chap. 13.

[57] The price paid by the purchaser for the shares will be equal to the net value of the subsidiary after taking account of the inter-company loan. Note that the potential charge under s.179 of the Taxation of Chargeable Gains Act 1992 will be relevant and a purchaser would normally expect to be indemnified against it or reduce the price offered to take account of it.

possible and enhance the value to a purchaser of the hive-down company or business. Following the Insolvency Act 1986, the basic practice is still the same in that employees are generally retained in the parent company and not re-hired by the hive-down subsidiary. The legal position has, however, been affected by the provisions of section 44 of the Insolvency Act 1986[58] and by the interpretation placed by the House of Lords on the Transfer of Undertakings (Protection of Employment) Regulations 1981.

9–065 Potential liability under section 44(1) of the Insolvency Act 1986 is discussed in detail in Chapter 19.

9–066 The Transfer of Undertakings (Protection of Employment) Regulations 1981 provide that, where there is a transfer from one person to another of an undertaking in the nature of a commercial business, contracts of employment shall not be terminated by the transfer but shall have effect after the transfer as if originally made between the employee and the transferee.[59] In effect, there is an automatic transfer of all of the transferor's rights, powers, duties and liabilities under or in connection with employment contracts (except in respect of an occupational pension scheme) to the transferee of the undertaking. There is a special exception in the case of a receivership hive-down or a hive-down in the course of a voluntary liquidation, to the effect that the transfer shall, for the purposes of the Regulations, be deemed not to have been effected until immediately before the transferee company ceases to be a wholly-owned subsidiary of the transferor company.[60] This means that the liabilities of the hive-down company will be suspended until its shares are sold to a third party. The practice of dismissing employees a short time before hive-down in an attempt to avoid the ultimate operation of regulation 5 and thus to obtain a higher price for the sale of the subsidiary has largely been rendered ineffective by the decision of the House of Lords in *Litster v. Forth Dry Dock & Engineering Co. Ltd*[61] Accordingly, the receiver will have to deal with the potential purchaser of the hive-down business on the basis that the liabilities relating to the existing employees will be transferred with the hive-down company. This position has been further endorsed by the decision *Re Maxwell Fleet Management Ltd (No. 2)*.[62]

4. PROHIBITIONS ON RE-USE OF COMPANY NAMES

9–067 When a business is sold, either as a going concern or as part of a hive-down, it may often be the case that a purchaser will wish to retain any goodwill attaching to the name of the old company or its products and for

---

[58] Now amended by the Insolvency Act 1994 as a consequence of the decision of the Court of Appeal in *Re Paramount Airways (No. 3)* [1994] 2 All E.R. 513.

[59] reg. 5.

[60] reg. 4.

[61] [1990] 1 A.C. 546. See further below, Chap. 19. See also *Longden v. Ferrari* [1994] B.C.C. 250.

[62] [2000] 2 B.C.L.C. 155.

that purpose may wish to acquire the rights to use the old company's name in its business. It is also frequently the case that the purchaser wishes to employ a director of the old company in a managerial position in the new business because he has a particular expertise and will be able to ensure a degree of continuity during the period of transition. Management buy-outs from receivers will almost invariably exhibit these features. In such cases, it will be important to have regard to the provisions of sections 216 and 217 of the Insolvency Act 1986 which provide for restrictions on the re-use of the name of an insolvent company.[63]

Section 216 of the 1986 Act applies to a person where a company has **9–068** gone into insolvent liquidation and the person was a director or shadow director of the company at any time in the 12 months before liquidation. In such cases, except with the leave of the court[64] or in certain prescribed circumstances, for a period of five years the ex-director cannot be a director of or in any way be concerned in the promotion, formation or management of any other company which is known by the same name as the company in liquidation or which is known by a name which is so similar as to suggest an association with that company.[65] Contravention of the section is an offence and will result in both the director of the old company and any other person who acts on his instructions knowing him to be in breach of section 216 being personally liable with the new company for any debts which it incurs during the period of prohibition.[66]

These provisions contain a number of traps for the unwary, par- **9–069** ticularly if the old company goes into liquidation sooner than might have been contemplated at the time of purchase of the business from the receiver. In order to mitigate the potential effects of these sections in appropriate cases, and to provide a means by which a director can avoid the need to make a formal application to the court for leave at a later stage, the Insolvency Rules 1986 provide for three "excepted cases" in which the prohibitions will not operate.[67]

The first excepted case applies, *inter alia*, where a company acquires **9–070** the whole or substantially the whole of the business of the insolvent company under arrangements made with its administrative receiver.[68] If,

---

[63] The section was introduced to deal with the prevalence of the "phoenix company" syndrome. The Cork Committee had noted (at para. 1813): ". . . there is widespread dissatisfaction at the ease with which a person trading through the medium of one or more companies with limited liability can allow such a company to become insolvent, form a new company, and then carry on trading much as before, leaving behind him a trail of unpaid creditors, and often repeating the process several times. The dissatisfaction is greatest where the director of an insolvent company has set up business again using a similar name for the new company and trades with assets purchased at a discount from the liquidator of the old company."

[64] The court will only grant leave with reference to the use of the name by specified companies and not generally: see *Re Lightning Electrical Contractors* [1996] B.C.C. 950.

[65] References to the name by which a company is known are to the name of the company itself or any name under which it carries on business.

[66] See *Thorne v. Silverleaf* [1994] B.C.C. 109.

[67] See rr. 4.228–4.230 of the Insolvency Rules 1986.

[68] In *Re Bonus Breaks Ltd* [1991] B.C.C. 546 at 547D–547F, Morritt J. expressed some surprise (*obiter*) at the view reported to be widely held in the insolvency profession that this "first excepted case" only applied where there was a sale both of assets and liabilities

within 28 days of completion of the arrangements[69] the purchasing company gives a notice in the statutory form to all the creditors of the insolvent company of whose address it is aware, then any director of the old company named in the notice will be permitted to be a director of or concerned in the management, etc. of the purchaser company.[70] It is suggested, that if the purchaser of a business from a receiver wishes to use what might become a prohibited name and also wishes to engage a director of the old company, it would be prudent for him to give a notice under the rules in respect of that director. Similarly, if the receiver wishes to employ a director of the old company to manage a similarly-named subsidiary into which the business of the parent company has been hived down, he should consider issuing such a notice.

9–071   The second excepted case provides temporary but automatic protection for up to six weeks pending determination of a formal application to the court for leave to act, provided that the application is issued "not later than" seven days from the date on which the company went into insolvent liquidation. The time-limits prescribed in this case seem to have little or no logic to them. In many cases where liquidation follows receivership, directors of the old company may not have been kept regularly informed of the state of the old company and may not learn of its liquidation until several weeks after it has occurred. In these cases, notwithstanding that the rules provide for the application to be made "not later than" seven days after liquidation, the court may be persuaded to exercise its discretion to extend this time limit so that the application for leave is treated as having been made in time and the automatic six-week protection period will begin to run (albeit without prejudice to any acts which have been done in the interim).[71] Additionally, the period of protection of six weeks bears little resemblance to the period which it may take for an application for leave to be heard and determined if the court decides to call for a report from the liquidator of the company.[72] Although there does not appear to be the jurisdiction to extend the six-week period referred to in the Insolvency Rules, in such cases the court

by an insolvency practitioner. The learned judge thought it clearly arguable that the statutory notice could have been given where there was a sale of the whole or substantially the whole of the business without the purchaser taking on any of the liabilities of the old company. It is thought that this interpretation is commercially sound and in line with the scheme of the Insolvency Rules. It should be noted that this exception is unlikely to apply where there are separate sales of businesses operated on a divisional basis by one corporate entity.

[69] This somewhat vague phrase is not defined. It is thought that it would include the completion of the hive-down transfer even though the price would not have been paid at that time.

[70] Curiously there does not appear to be any mechanism for the creditors of the old company to do anything in response to the receipt of such a notice. If the notice is correctly given in accordance with the Rules, permission to act follows automatically.

[71] *Re Evans Hunt Scott Ltd* (unreported, Mummery J., June 24, 1991) in which reference was made to the factors relevant to the exercise of the discretion to extend time by analogy to the principles applied in the case of *Re Virgo Systems Ltd* (1989) 5 B.C.C. 833. Mummery J. also observed in argument that the correct rule under which to extend the time limits was r. 4.3 of the Insolvency Rules 1986, not r. 12.9 and RSC, Ord. 3 which applied only to questions of computation of time.

[72] Under r. 4.227 of the Insolvency Rules 1986.

may be prepared to make an "interim order" permitting the director to continue acting pending final determination of his application.[73]

The third excepted case provides simply that leave is not required **9–072** where the new company has been known by the prohibited name for 12 months before the old company went into liquidation and it has not been dormant during that period.

If advantage cannot be taken of the first or third "excepted cases", an **9–073** application to the court for leave to act will have to be made. On such an application, the court will be concerned to examine the reasons for the demise of the previous company and the responsibility of the director for that demise, the circumstances surrounding the sale of the business (and in particular the fairness of the price paid), together with the role which the director is to have in the management of the new company.[74]

5. SALE OF PROPERTY SUBJECT TO A SECURITY

Although a mortgagee exercising a power of sale can transfer charged **9–074** property free of interests postponed to his charge,[75] in the ordinary case a receiver who acts as agent for the company in receivership cannot transfer a better title to property than could be transferred by the company itself. Section 43(1) of the Insolvency Act 1986 gives the court jurisdiction on an application by the administrative receiver to authorise him to dispose of property, which is subject to a charge having priority over the charge of his appointor, free of such charge. It must be a condition of any such order that the net proceeds of sale, and (where those proceeds are less than such amount as may be determined by the court to be the net amount that would be realised on a sale of the property in the open market by a willing seller) such sum as may be required to make good any deficiency, shall be applied towards discharging the security. If there is more than one security, the condition must require application of the net proceeds and further sum (if any) towards discharging these securities in the order of their priorities.[76] The jurisdiction of the court can only be exercised if the court is satisfied that the disposal (with or without other assets) would be likely to promote a more advantageous realisation of the company's assets than would otherwise be effected and if the property in question is property of which

---

[73] See, *e.g. Re Oasis Marketing Ltd*, (unreported, Warner J., June 18, 1988).

[74] See *Re Oasis Marketing Ltd* (unreported, Warner J., June 18, 1988); Harp, *Insolvency Intelligence* (November 1988); and *Re Bonus Breaks Ltd* [1991] B.C.C. 546.

[75] See, *e.g. Duke v. Robson* [1973] 1 W.L.R. 267 and ss. 2(1) and 104(1) of the Law of Property Act 1925.

[76] Insolvency Act 1986, s. 43(4). Curiously, the Act does not make express provision for what is to happen if a sale has to be made at a time when there is doubt about the validity of any charge or if an application has been made to set aside a charge or if there is a dispute as to priorities between chargees. In *Re Newman Shopfitters (Cleveland) Ltd* [1991] B.C.L.C. 407 the court held, in relation to the similar power to order sale in administrations (s. 15(2) of the 1986 Act) that there was no power within the section to order that the proceeds be retained pending the outcome of a dispute as to the validity of the security. If an application to challenge the security was already on foot such an order might be sought as interim relief in that action.

the administrative receiver is or, but for the appointment of some other personal receiver of part of the company's property, would be the receiver and manager.[77] A copy of the order must be sent by the administrative receiver to the Registrar of Companies within 14 days under penalty of a fine.[78]

6. RECONSTRUCTIONS AND SCHEMES

9–075 As an alternative to a sale of the business, it may be possible for a scheme of arrangement to be promoted and sanctioned under sections 425–427 of the Companies Act 1985. There is also the possibility of a company voluntary arrangement under Part I of the 1986 Act.[79] The terms of section 425 of the Companies Act 1985 would not appear to allow a receiver to make the application to the court for sanction of the scheme in his own name and he would have to apply in the name of the company. He would also have to be satisfied that the promotion of the scheme was in the interests of the receivership and fell within his powers under the debenture, including those imported by section 42 of and Schedule 1 to the Insolvency Act 1986. As a practical matter it will be essential for the receiver to hold informal consultative meetings with members and creditors, who will be able to indicate informally whether they will vote in favour of the proposals.

7. FORCED SALE OF ASSETS

9–076 Where the business cannot be sold as a going concern or hived-down, and no scheme is possible, the receiver will have to sell on a "break-up" or "gone concern" basis. In the case of freehold or leasehold interests in land, he should employ reputable agents. In the case of plant, machinery and vehicles, he should consult reputable valuers and auctioneers specialising in the type of articles in question. In the case of intellectual property, the receiver will need the advice of patent agents and other specialists. In all cases, a record should be kept of attempts to sell. The question of a receiver's duties and potential liabilities on sale are dealt with in detail in Chapter 7.

9–077 In the absence of a going concern sale the cash flow impact of the requirement for the purchaser to pay VAT on the assets may have a further depressive effort on the price.

8. SALES AT VALUATION

9–078 A regular feature of many receiverships (as of many liquidations) is the sale of certain assets "at a valuation", *i.e.* not at a price expressly agreed between the parties but at a price to be fixed by a third party valuer. This

[77] *ibid.*, s. 43(7).
[78] *ibid.*, s. 43(5).
[79] See above, paras 2–013 *et seq.*

practice is particularly prevalent in the case of a sale including stock, but it also has its place and advantages when the conclusion of a contract for sale cannot sensibly or properly await the required valuation. The practice is well established and recognised.

Nonetheless there are two old authorities which affirm the proposition **9–079** that a fiduciary (a term which includes receivers and liquidators as well as trustees) cannot sell at a valuation, since this involves a delegation to the valuer of the power to fix the price, and such a delegation can only be permissible if authorised by provision in the instrument appointing him or some applicable statutory provision.[80]

It is suggested, however, that these authorities reflect thinking at a **9–080** time before valuation became more of a scientific exercise and when in both theory and practice the valuer exercised very much a personal judgment applying such subjective standards as he thought fit. In such a situation, the identity of the valuer in the case of any valuation was a matter of prime importance, for the valuation necessarily reflected his particular predispositions. It is hardly surprising that against such a background the court would not allow fiduciaries to substitute the judgment of a valuer for their own judgment as to the market or proper price. The professional qualifications of valuers, and the principles of valuation, evolved in the nineteenth century, and with them has grown the recognition of valuation as a form of science. The competent expert is expected to determine objectively the market value or at least approximate to it. With the substitution of objective standards by qualified experts for subjective standards by amateurs, the objection to the use of valuers to fix a price has gone. The fiduciary has sufficiently discharged his duty by selecting the purchaser and the formula for the valuation. The function of the valuer in working out the value gives scope for the exercise by him of professional judgment. The recognition of the developments in valuation and their implications in the law of contract may be found in the judgment of the House of Lords in *Sudbrook Trading Estate Ltd v. Eggleton*[81] Similar reasoning applies with equal force in the field of "fiduciaries" and there can be little doubt that, if the opportunity arises, the two authorities in question should be over-ruled so that the law can catch up with modern practice.[82]

9. GRANT OF LEASES

The conduct of the receivership may require the grant by the receiver of **9–081** leases of the company's property. A debenture is deemed to give an

---

[80] *Peters v. Lewes and East Grinstead Ry Co.* [1881] 18 Ch.D. 429; and *Re Earl of Wilton's Settled Estates* [1907] 1 Ch. 50. This proposition has been accepted as current law in some leading textbooks: see, *e.g. Emmett on Title* (19th ed.), para. 13.004; *Halsbury's Laws of England* (4th ed.), Vol. 42, paras. 94 and 827; *Wolstenholme and Cherry* Vol. 3, pp. 139 and 219; Lewin, *The Law of Trusts* (6th ed.), pp. 511 and 585; *Farrand, Contract and Conveyance* (4th ed.), pp. 251 and 309.

[81] [1983] 1 A.C. 444. See also *Jones v. Sherwood Computer Services plc* [1992] 1 W.L.R.277.

[82] See G. Lightman, "Sales at Valuation by Fiduciaries" [1985] Conveyancer 44.

administrative receiver the power to grant leases in the name of the company unless such power is inconsistent with any of the provisions of the debenture.[83] Leases may be granted by the debenture-holder as mortgagee but more usually they are granted by the administrative receiver in the name and on behalf of the company. The latter course, however, can only be adopted and a good title passed to the prospective lessee if there are no further charges over the property precluding the exercise of the power of lease by the company or if such chargees consent. In the case of a lease by the administrative receiver as agent of the company, there is no limitation on the nature, length or terms of the lease that might be granted so long as the company has the power to grant such a lease and is not precluded from so acting, *e.g.* by the terms of its own head-lease.

9–082   The company and the debenture-holder may by agreement (whether or not contained in the debenture) restrict or extend the statutory powers of leasing conferred on mortgagees.[84] In practice, the debenture frequently confers on the debenture-holder the unlimited powers of leasing of a beneficial owner. Subject to any such provision in the debenture, the statutory powers of leasing will be applicable. These powers are subject to limitations:

  (a) they are only exercisable after the mortgagee has taken possession (and thus rendered himself liable to account as a mortgagee in possession on the basis of wilful default[85]) or after he has appointed a receiver of the income of the property;
  (b) the lease must be made to take effect in possession not later than 12 months after its execution;
  (c) the lease must reserve the best rent reasonably obtainable without any fine being taken;
  (d) the lease must contain a condition of re-entry in the event of rent being in arrears for a period not exceeding 30 days; and
  (e) the term of lease must not exceed, in the case of agricultural and occupation leases, 50 years and, in the case of building leases, 999 years.[86]

9–083   In any case where these conditions are not satisfied, and the lease is not authorised by some express power conferred by the debenture, the lease will not bind the company after redemption unless the company

---

[83] Insolvency Act 1986, s. 42(1) and Sched. 1, para. 17.

[84] Law of Property Act 1925, s. 99(14). In any event the court has a discretion under Law of Property Act 1925 s91(2) to order a sale where the exercise of leasing powers at a rental substantially less than the ongoing interest payable on the loan would unfairly prejudice the borrower: see *Palk v. Mortgage Services Funding plc* [1993] Ch. 330. That case concerned the exercise of the power by a mortgagee but in principle it would seem to be applicable also to a receiver.

[85] See above, paras 7–012 and 7–013.

[86] Law of Property Act 1925, ss. 99(2) and 100(2).

has given its consent, which it may do informally.[87] The like consent will in such a case be required of any subsequent mortgagees, if the lease is to bind them.

If the lease is granted in the name of the company, unless expressly **9–084** authorised by the debenture, no covenant may effectively be included on the part of the company other than the usual qualified covenant for quiet enjoyment.[88] Any such express authority would, it seems, determine on winding-up. Thereafter, in any case where the acceptance of covenants by the landlord is essential to an advantageous letting, the administrative receiver may achieve this result by exercising (where not excluded by the debenture) his statutory power to establish a subsidiary,[89] granting a lease imposing no covenants on the company to the subsidiary and then causing the subsidiary to grant an underlease in whatever terms are desired. In certain cases, *e.g.* the disposal of flats in a block, the receiver may, at the same time or subsequently, divest himself of the subsidiary or its reversion on the sub-lease by a transfer to the sub-tenants.

The question arises whether the receiver or mortgagee can grant a **9–085** lease, not at a fixed rent, but at a rent to be determined by a valuer according to a formula, *e.g.* the formula laid down as an essential requirement for the grant of a valid lease by a mortgagee, namely the best rent reasonably obtainable.[90] Whilst the law cannot be said to be entirely clear, the balance of authority certainly favours an affirmative answer,[91] and this view is reinforced by considerations of convenience and accepted common practice. Indeed, if the answer were otherwise, a receiver or mortgagee could not grant leases containing rent review clauses. Since the inclusion of such clauses is essential to maintain the value of the reversion in the case of anything other than a short-term lease, the limitation on the powers of the receiver and mortgagee would operate most harshly on them, on the company, on other chargees and indeed on the ordinary creditors of the company.

---

[87] *Chapman v. Smith* [1907] 2 Ch. 97 at 102.
[88] Law of Property Act 1925, s. 8(1).
[89] See the Insolvency Act 1986, Sched. 1, para. 15.
[90] Law of Property Act 1925, s. 99(13).
[91] *Lloyd's Bank v. Marcan* [1973] 1 W.L.R. 339 and 1387 at 1391H, *per* Russell L.J.

CHAPTER 10

RECEIVERS AND BANKERS

10–001 A receiver will come across bankers in several contexts. The debenture-holder/appointor may well be a clearing bank. In that case the receiver will usually be expected to open an account at the bank and relatively few problems arise. In other situations, a receiver will almost invariably wish to open a special bank account with a clearing bank in connection with the receivership and is likely to use the same clearer as the debenture-holder. In the course of the receivership, the company's relationships with its bankers, where they are not the appointors, pose special problems of set-off and priority in the receivership administration. In looking at these situations it will be important to remember that a receiver will often be wearing two quite different hats: one simply as agent or controller of the company; the other representing in effect the rights of the appointing debenture-holder/mortgagee, which can be more extensive than those of the company itself.

1. COMPANY'S ACCOUNT

10–002 A receiver should immediately upon appointment give notice of his appointment to the company's bankers. Provided that the company's moneys at its bankers (more accurately, the bankers' debt to the company) are within the charges in respect of which the receiver is appointed, his appointment will revoke the authority of the directors to deal with such moneys. The bank, upon receiving notice, will no longer be able to rely upon the usual company mandate entitling one or more directors or officers to control the account and will have to accept the sole control of the receiver. Likewise, any cheques or bills of exchange drawn prior to the receivership but presented or payment instructions received after notice of the receivership must be dishonoured or refused.

2. BANKER'S RIGHT TO COMBINE ACCOUNTS

10–003 This right can create problems for receivers in two different contexts. First, there is the pre-existing relationship of the company with its banker under which the bank is likely to have a power to combine different accounts of the company, either by reason of an express provision in a debenture, or by reason of a letter of set-off, or simply under the general law.[1] This class of problem is dealt with in this section.

---

[1] For the right under the general law, sometimes inaccurately referred to as the operation of "the banker's lien", see Lord Denning M.R. and Buckley L.J. (dissenting) in

A second type of problem which can arise where a receiver opens a special receivership account is dealt with below under the heading "Receivership Account".

In some cases there may be an express or implied agreement to keep **10–004** the accounts in question separate, *e.g.* where one account is a current account and the other is a loan account.[2] In the *Halesowen* case[3] the House of Lords held that:

(a) whilst it was competent for the parties to determine the duration of their agreement, the courts would readily infer that it was only intended to continue in force during the active life of the company or whilst it continues as a going concern, and this period must be at an end on liquidation[4] and that alternatively upon a winding-up, such a contractual agreement could not prevail against the compulsory set-off provisions of the statute.[5]

(b) For the purpose of determining whether such an agreement survives receivership it is necessary to note the important distinctions between winding up and receivership. In particular, a receivership does not necessarily mean the end of the company as a going concern.

Both the bank and the receiver probably each have certain choices. **10–005** Where the bank in question is the appointor, few problems will arise in practice because the bank and the receiver will terminate the company's previous banking relationship and will combine accounts. The situation may be different where the bank is not the appointor. The receiver could, although it is unlikely in practice, choose to continue the company's ordinary accounts with the bank and the company's business. However, in practice he will normally close the company's ordinary accounts and open one or more special receivership accounts.[6] In this case, a receiver will instruct the company's bank to dishonour cheques presented and payment instructions received after notice of receivership, and to transfer any credit balance to the new account. Where the debenture includes a fixed charge on book debts, a receiver may be able

---

Halesowen Presswork v. National Westminster Bank [1971] 1 Q.B. 1, CA and Lord Cross (dissenting) on appeal (*sub. nom. National Westminster Bank v. Halesowen Presswork*) [1972] A.C. 785 at 814, HL. See also *Re Charge Card Services* [1987] Ch. 150 at 173–174 where an analogy was drawn between a banker's right to combine accounts and a system of running accounts in a financial agreement, and *Welsh Development Agency v. Export Finance* [1992] B.C.L.C. 148 at 167, *per* Dillon L.J., CA. where such an analogy was rejected.

[2] See *Bradford Old Bank v. Sutcliffe* [1918] 2 K.B. 833.

[3] [1972] A.C. 785.

[4] *Per* Viscount Dilhorne at 805–806, *per* Lord Cross at 811, *per* Lord Kilbrandon at 820.

[5] These do not apply to receivership set-off: see below, Chap. 16. In so far as the majority considered that there was some policy of insolvency law preventing creditors contracting out of liquidation set-off for the benefit of the other creditors, they appear to have been mistaken and the view of Lord Cross, who dissented on this point, is to be preferred.

[6] See further below, para 10–016.

successfully to argue that a bank cannot assert any right of set-off and combination because it was on notice of the existence of the charge.[7] The bank for its part could, although this is most unlikely to happen, choose to continue to keep the company as its customer, despite the receivership. Almost invariably, if it can do so under the terms of the company's facilities, it will terminate the banking relationship. It would seem, therefore, that where there has been an agreement to keep accounts separate, there may have to be a close examination of the facts in each case to see whether the banking relationship has ceased and whether the company has ceased to be a going concern.

10–006   An example of an agreement to keep accounts separate which survived the appointment of a receiver and entitled the receiver to claim a credit balance is *Direct Acceptance Corp. v. Bank of New South Wales*.[8] The company, which was controlled by the debenture-holder's nominees, agreed with the company's bankers that the existing overdraft would be frozen and a new account opened as part of an informal receivership. The possibility of a receiver being appointed was mentioned. It was expressly agreed that there would be no set-off between the old and new accounts. Nevertheless, when the company went into receivership, the bank claimed the right to combine accounts and take the credit on the new account towards the liability of the old account. The bank argued for an implied term that the accounts would be kept separate only whilst the new account remained a current account, and suggested that on the appointment of the receiver, operations on the new account "would, if not necessarily, at any rate in practice, cease".[9] On the rather special facts of that case, Macfarlan J. refused to imply any such term. Further, he held that whilst "there may be many considerations of practice" why the operation of the account should not continue after receivership, there was no rule of law preventing the operation of the new account after the appointment of a receiver.[10] The receiver was entitled to claim the credit balance on the new account.

3. COMBINATION OF ACCOUNTS AND PREFERENTIAL DEBTS

10–007 In *Re E.J. Morel (1934) Ltd*[11] the company originally had one current account, which was substantially overdrawn. This account was frozen. A new current account (account No. 2) was opened and a No. 3 account, a wages account, was also opened. The bank as a lender for the payment of wages was a preferential creditor to the extent that the sums in respect of wages paid by it, if left unpaid, would have been preferential debts in a receivership or winding up.[12] The No. 2 account was to be kept

---

[7] See below, Chap. 16.
[8] (1968) 88 W.N. (Pt. 1) (N.S.W.) 498.
[9] *ibid.* at 503.
[10] *ibid.* at 504.
[11] [1962] Ch. 21.
[12] Insolvency Act 1986, Sched. 6, para. 11.

in credit to a larger sum than the debit on the No. 3 account. Whenever a debit to the wages account was more than four months old (after which it would cease to be preferential) the amount of the debit was transferred from the No. 2 account to the No. 3 account. The intention was to ensure that the whole of the debit balance was preferential at all times and covered by a credit balance on the No. 2 account. When the company was wound up its balances were as follows:

No. 1 account: £1,839 DR.
No. 2 account: £1,544.12s.4d. CR.
No. 3 account: £1,623.11s.11d. DR.

The bank claimed to set off the credit on the No. 2 account against the **10–008** debit of the No. 1 account rather than against the No. 3 account in order to claim preferential treatment of the debt on the No. 3 account. The liquidator claimed that the No. 2 account had to be set off against the No. 3 account. It was held that the frozen No. 1 account could not be combined with the No. 2 account, and that the No. 2 and No. 3 accounts were in substance one account so that in effect only minimal sums were advanced by the bank towards wages. The No. 2 and No. 3 accounts were to be set off against each other. The case also contains a *dictum* to the effect that, even if the No. 2 account could in principle have been combined with the No. 1 account, it should in fact be combined with the No. 3 account so as to reduce the preferential claim as far as possible.

This *dictum* was disapproved by Walton J. in *Re Unit 2 Windows Ltd* [13] **10–009** in a case involving set-off against the preferential claims of the Crown. He held that, where set-off was available against both a preferential and non-preferential debt, the set-off should apply rateably over the two debts. Walton J. based this conclusion on the true construction of the special statutory provisions applicable in a bankruptcy and liquidation. These are not directly applicable in receivership, [14] but since Walton J. considered that his solution was "the only logical and sensible solution", [15] it may be expected to apply in receivership.

4. COMBINATION OF ACCOUNTS AND DEPOSITS FOR SPECIAL PURPOSES

Where a lender lends money to a debtor for the purpose of the discharge **10–010** of his debts or other liabilities, depending on the intention of the lender, either as expressed or inferred, the transaction may give rise to:

---

[13] [1985] 1 W.L.R. 1383 *cf.* the position in Scotland where there exists a law of compensation or retention: see *Turner v. Lord Advocate* [1993] B.C.L.C. 1463, especially at 1472. See also Chap. 21.

[14] See n. 5.

[15] At p. 1388.

(a) a resulting trust for the lender but subject to a power on the part of the debtor to pay the debts or liabilities;

(b) a resulting trust but subject to the right of the lender to require the debtor to apply the money in discharge of the debts and liabilities; or

(c) a trust in favour of the creditors; or

(d) a straightforward gift or loan to the debtor.[16]

Where prior to receivership the company makes a deposit of separately identifiable moneys with bankers for a special purpose of which they have notice at the time of deposit,[17] and this earmarking is effective to create a trust of the moneys, the bank will not in any event be able to set such credits off against any overdrawn balances.[18]

10–011   For this principle to apply it is not necessary that the bank should have express notice of a trust as long as it has notice of the relevant facts creating the trust. Thus, in *Quistclose Investments Ltd v. Rolls Razor Ltd*[19] a lender placed moneys in a special bank account to be used only for the payment of dividends by a company in financial trouble. The company went into liquidation and the dividend was not paid. It was held that the moneys in the account were held on trust for the lender. It followed that they could not be set off against any debit balance of the company.

10–012   The *Quistclose* case was followed in *Re Northern Developments (Holding) Ltd*,[20] where a group of lenders paid a large sum into an account in the name of the company to be paid to the creditors of a subsidiary, which was in financial trouble. The subsidiary went into receivership when just over half the fund remained in being. It was held, following the *Quistclose* case,[21] that there was a "purpose trust"[22] affecting the moneys enforceable by the lenders and by the creditors of the subsidiary.

---

[16] P. Millet Q.C., "The Quistclose Trust: Who Can Enforce It?" (1985) 101 L.Q.R. 269; Rickett, "Different Views on the Scope of the Quistclose Analysis" (1991) 107 L.Q.R. 608.

[17] *Union Bank of Australia v. Murray-Aynsley* [1898] A.C. 693, PC.

[18] *Quistclose Investments Ltd v. Rolls Razor Ltd* [1970] A.C. 567, HL.

[19] *ibid.*

[20] *Per* Megarry V.-C. (unreported, October 6, 1978).

[21] See above, n.16.

[22] A purpose trust is a trust where the trust property is earmarked for use for a particular purpose, and is not available to be used for any other purpose. "Instances in the books are legion": *per* Dillon L.J. in *Re EVTR* [1987] B.C.L.C. 646 at 651c, a case where a special purpose loan led to a constructive trust in favour of the lender. See also *Re Goldcorp Exchange* [1995] 1 A.C. 74 especially at pages 100–135. For recent examples in which express purpose trusts been found not to have been created see *Re Holiday Promotions (Europe)* [1996] 2 B.C.L.C. 618, *Re Challoner Club Ltd* (in liquidation) *The Times*, November 4, 1997, Ch.D. *Box v. Barclays Bank Plc* [1998] 5 Lloyd's Rep Bank 185 and *Re Griffin Trading Co.* [2000] B.P.I.R. 256. The Court of Appeal in *Twinsectra Ltd v. Yardley & Others* [1999] Lloyd's Rep Bank 438 in applying *Quistclose* suggested that in principle the degree of certainty with regard to the objects of a *Quistclose* type trust "need be no more than is necessary to enable the restriction on the recipient's use of the money to be identified and enforced," *per* Clarke L.J. at para 76 of the judgment. The Court of Appeal granted leave to appeal to the House of Lords. The *Twinsectra* case has recently been applied in *Barnabas Hurst-Bannister v. New Cap Reinsurance Corp Ltd* (J. Jarvis Q.C. sitting as a Deputy High Court Judge Chancery Division: unreported December 14, 1999).

A further *"Quistclose"* situation occurred in *Carreras Rothmans Ltd v.* **10–013**
Freeman Mathews Treasure Ltd[23] where moneys were paid into a special
account by the principal to enable its advertising agent, then in financial
difficulties, to pay sums owed by the agent to certain creditors. The agent
went into liquidation. It was held, following the *Quistclose* and *Northern
Developments* decisions, that the moneys were subject to a trust and that:

> ". . . the principle in all these cases is that equity fastens on the
> conscience of the person who receives from another property
> transferred for a specific purpose only and not therefore for the
> recipient's own purposes, so that such person will not be permitted
> to treat the property as his own and to use it for other than the
> stated purpose."[24]

A bank may even be bound by such a trust where it does not know all **10–014**
the facts but is put on inquiry. In *Neste Oy v. Lloyd's Bank*,[25] the bank
had a right of set-off applying to accounts of different companies in a
group, including a company referred to as "PSL". The plaintiff
shipowner regularly made payments into PSL's account to enable PSL,
as the plaintiff's agent, to discharge debts incurred by the plaintiff's
vessels. PSL did not have to keep such sums separate and Bingham J.
declined to hold that such payments were generally held on trust.
However, in relation to the final payment made by the plaintiff, at a time
when the debts covered by the payment had not been discharged by PSL
and PSL knew that it was ceasing trade and would not give value for the
payment, Bingham J. held that sum was held on constructive trust for the
plaintiff. Whilst the bank did not know all the facts at the time it
received this sum, it had been put on inquiry by being told that PSL was
to cease trading and to invite the bank to appoint a receiver. An inquiry
at that stage would have elicited the facts giving rise to the constructive
trust. As a result, the bank was not entitled to set off this final sum.
Bingham J. added: "By the time the set-off was effected the bank was
even more clearly on notice". Although this is true, it is suggested that
notice at any time after the payment was irrelevant, since a payment
without constructive notice would have given the bank a vested right to
set-off.[26] It is also doubtful that the plaintiff should have been promoted
effectively to the status of a secured creditor in respect of the final
payment, instead of being left to his right of proof.[27] There are many
cases of equal hardship to makers of deposits and prepayments where

---

[23] [1985] Ch. 207, *per* Peter Gibson J.

[24] At 222B.

[25] [1983] 2 Lloyd's Rep. 658; *[1982] Com.L.R. 185, per* Bingham J.

[26] See *Clark v. Ulster Bank Ltd* [1950] N.I. 132, where it was held that, upon receiving
notice that the customer's No. 2 account was a trust account, the bank was entitled to
combine it with the No. 1 account as at the date of receiving such notice.

[27] However, in *Kingscroft Insurance Co. v. Weavers,* [1993] 1 Lloyd's Rep. 187, *Neste Oy*
was referred to with approval but was held not to apply to the facts of that case, which
concerned bank deposits created by an underwriting agent in the names of certain of its
principals, who subsequently went into provisional liquidation.

the device of a constructive trust has not been imported to cure the absence of an express or implied trust.[28]

10–015   The recent decision of *Triffit Nurseries v. Salads Etcetera Ltd*[29] confirms that the appointment of administrative receivers appointed by a bank over the assets of a mercantile agent will not affect a change in the beneficial ownership of moneys collected in by the agent even though the agent's business ceased to be a going concern on the appointment of the receivers. Despite the receivers' appointment it was held that the agent obtained an absolute right to recover debts in respect of goods consigned to it by its principal and the debts were not converted into trust assets held on the principal's behalf.

5. RECEIVERSHIP ACCOUNTS

(a) Company accounts

10–016 A receiver will, until winding-up, normally act as agent for the company under the terms of the debenture or charge. An administrative receiver is deemed to be the agent of the company unless and until there is a winding-up.[30] When a receiver opens a receivership account he should do so ideally in the name of the company but make his position as agent clear. The account would in such a situation be entitled "Account of X. Ltd, A.B. [Administrative] Receiver".[31] It is common for separate accounts to be opened for fixed charge and floating charge realisations with all realisations that can properly be characterised as fixed charge realisations being paid into the fixed charge account. If there is any possibility that the floating charge realisations will be insufficient to pay the preferential creditors, the receiver will have to take care when making payments out of floating charge realisations or in obtaining an overdraft facility to meet the cash flow difficulties which are common at the beginning of a receivership. In case of doubt, directions can be applied for.

10–017   The determination of the receiver's agency for the company on liquidation will not affect the account, save that the receiver cannot take the account into overdraft: he cannot in this way create a fresh debt or liability of the company, without becoming personally liable, but his power to deal with any moneys standing to the credit of the account will be unaffected. In principle, if the company's account would otherwise go into overdraft, it should be redesignated the receiver's personal account, but in practice this does not always happen.

---

[28] See below, Chap. 17.

[29] [2000] B.C.C. 98; approved [2000] 1 B.C.L.C. 761, CA.

[30] Insolvency Act 1986, s. 44(1)(a).

[31] If the receiver signs cheques drawn in the company's name, it seems that the cheque will be that of the company and not the receiver: see *Bondina v. Rollaway Shower Blinds* [1986] 1 W.L.R. 517, CA, a case where a director signed a cheque under the company name and was held to have signed the company's cheque (rather than his own) on the grounds that his signature adopted the wording on the cheque relating to the company.

(b) Receiver's accounts

The alternative course, which may be insisted on by the bank, especially **10–018** if there is any chance of the account being overdrawn, is for the administrative receiver to open an account in his own name, but making the special position of the account clear, *e.g.* by entitling it "X, Administrative Receiver of Y Ltd". In this case the account can be taken into overdraft after winding up.[32]

(c) Interest mitigation

A high rate of interest may be accruing on the appointor's debt and it **10–019** may be possible to alleviate this, at least to a large extent, by opening an account for realisations with the appointor and obtaining some form of interest offset arrangement. Major banks are usually prepared to come to such arrangements, but where there is doubt as to whether floating charge realisations will be sufficient to pay preferential creditors, such realisations should be excluded from any offset arrangement.[33]

Alternatively, a receiver may come to an arrangement with the **10–020** appointor when transferring funds enabling him to claw back funds in these circumstances.[34]

In the absence of any such arrangement, or if the account is not with the debenture-holder, money should as far as possible be kept on an interest-bearing deposit.

(d) Practical steps

The receiver will want to have any credit balances (if any remain after **10–021** combination of accounts) transferred to the receivership account.[35] Notice of the appointment of the receiver will determine the authority of the directors to act on the company's behalf in relation to charged assets, which normally include sums standing to the company's credit at a bank. The bank holding the credit balance will want to see a copy of the receiver's appointment. The bank holding a credit balance may also call for a copy of the debenture or other security instrument and seek to satisfy itself as far as practicable that the receiver has been validly appointed. If such checks are not made and it subsequently turns out that the appointment was invalid, unless there is any estoppel binding the company, a bank that parts with the company's money will (it seems) be acting in breach of mandate. On the other hand there may not be any loss: either the company is likely to be able to recover its moneys from the receiver or, in so far as the receiver has paid off the company's liabilities, the bank may be afforded equitable relief.[36] The special

---

[32] A receiver who after his signature on a contractual document merely adds the words "receiver for X Ltd" is to be treated as contracting personally: *Kettle v. Dunster* (1926) 43 T.L.R. 770.

[33] Samwell, *Corporate Receiverships* (2nd ed., 1988), p. 97: see further para. 10–026 below.

[34] Stewart, *Administrative Receivers and Administration* (1987), p. 132.

[35] The receivers should also instruct the bank to reject any payments that are presented and which are drawn on the company's accounts: see generally above, para. 10–002.

[36] *Liggett v. Barclays Bank* [1928] 1 K.B. 48.

statutory protection afforded to persons dealing with an administrative receiver[37] extends only to acts beyond the administrative receiver's powers and not to a situation where he is invalidly appointed and has no power at all.

10–022   In the vast majority of cases the appointment of a receiver will be made by a clearing bank. In such a case the appointing bank will require that the receiver's account or accounts be opened at one of its branches which will normally be at the branch where the company's own account or accounts were maintained. Some clearing banks have combined their debt recovery management teams with suitable account handling facilities within its regional service centres which will enable the receiver to operate the accounts more efficiently.

10–023   If the receiver is not appointed by a clearing bank, and in the absence of other considerations, he will have a discretion as to which bank or banks he will chose at which to open his accounts. Clearly he will be likely to select one where there is no question of any pre-appointment debt being owed by the company. Where a receiver proposes to open a receivership account with a bank that is not the appointor but which is a bank that is owed money by the company, the receiver should give notice of his appointment, if he has not previously done so, prior to opening such an account. Once such a creditor bank has notice of the appointment, it will have notice of the appointor's security and of the crystallisation of any floating charges and will not be able to set off the company's pre-existing overdrawn account with it against any credits paid into the receivership account, assuming of course that such credits consist of moneys falling within the appointor's security.[38] A cautious receiver in such a situation may well obtain the specific agreement of the non-appointor bank to exclude set-off.

10–024   Prior to the the receiver's appointment the company may have used electronic systems[39] to accept customer payments by credit or debit cards. The receiver clearly may benefit from the adoption and continued use of such systems, e.g. in the case of a company with many trading outlets. In such a case there may well be an attempt by the bank to effect a set-off as between charges owing pre-appointment and credit card receipts pending at the date of appointment.[40]

10–025   The receivers should record all transactions during the period of the receivership.[41] Payments out are normally made by cheques but suitable electronic systems may also be employed for certain multiple payments, e.g. salaries.[42]

---

[37] Insolvency Act 1986, s. 42(3).

[38] See below, Chap. 16.

[39] Sometimes known as "PDQ" systems.

[40] As to the rules governing set off see generally Chap. 16.

[41] A frequently used system is the so called Turnkey IPS (Insolvency Practitioners System) which has been developed exclusively for insolvency practitioners. The need to maintain suitable records reflects the provisions of the Insolvency Rules 1986, r. 3.32 regarding an administrative receiver's abstract of receipts and payments.

[42] Use is often made of such systems as the "Autopay" or "Bacs" bank payment systems.

(e) Separate accounts

A receivership account should be kept entirely separate and moneys **10–026**
therein should not be mixed, *e.g.* with realisations from other receiverships or with the receiver's own moneys. Further, in accordance with
normal practice, separate accounts should be kept (where applicable) for
fixed and floating charge realisations, reflecting the interest of preferential creditors in the latter, but not in the former. Where there is no
floating charge, only a fixed charge account will be opened.[43]

Receivers in practice often act by members of the staff of the firms of **10–027**
accountants to which receivers belong. In the case of the operation of
the receivership bank account, the bank may, in the absence of special
agreement, refuse to accept instructions from anyone other than the
receiver himself.

(f) Personal liability

Any advances to the company in receivership but not in liquidation will **10–028**
generally involve the receiver in causing the company to make a post-
receivership contract. Unless personal liability is excluded (and the
receiver in practice is reluctant to accept such liability) a receiver will be
personally liable to repay any such advances.[44] A bank is most unlikely to
be agreeable to an exclusion of personal liability. A *modus vivendi* must
be reached. This may take the form of the receiver accepting personal
liability, but limited to receivership assets in his hands, or the appointor
himself assuming liability. Once the company has gone into liquidation,
all loans must be to the receiver personally or his appointor.[45]

Even prior to winding-up a bank may find it more convenient simply **10–029**
to lend moneys to the receiver personally, assuming that he is of high
standing and repute. This avoids any difficult problems of construction of
the powers in the debenture, at least as far as the bank is concerned.

In *Hill Samuel & Co. Ltd v. Laing*[46] the Outer House of the Court of **10–030**
Session held that a receiver who had opened an account at his
appointing bank in his own name could in principle be liable[47] for the
sums due on the account, applying the principles embodied in the
Scottish equivalent to section 44(1)(b) of the Insolvency Act 1986.[48] The

---

[43] Invariably the receivers will need an overdraft facility on any new account to facilitate
trading and to maximise realisations. In particular receivers will generally prepare a
specific request for this facility together with trading forecasts. The bank may even require
a personal guarantee or guarantees from the receivers themselves.

[44] Insolvency Act 1986, s. 37 and in the case of administrative receivers also pursuant to
the Insolvency Act 1986, s. 44(1)(b).

[45] *Robinson Printing Co. Ltd v. Chic Ltd* [1905] 2 Ch. 123.

[46] (1988) 4 B.C.C. 9.

[47] The Court held that there had to be an inquiry into the nature of the arrangement.
The receiver alleged that there was an implied term in the banking contract to the effect
that any advances were made at the bank's own risk.

[48] Companies (Floating Charges and Receivers) (Scotland) Act 1972, s. 17(2). Both
sections provide personal liability in respect of any contract entered into by a receiver
"except in so far as the contract otherwise provides". *cf. Re Boynton Ltd* [1910] Ch. 519,
where a court-appointed receiver borrowed money from a bank without any express
exclusion of personal liability. (Court-appointed receivers are personally liable on contracts

Court held that the standard wording in a debenture stipulating that the receiver was to be the agent of the company and that the company should "alone be personally liable" for the acts and defaults of a receiver only applied as between the bank and the company and did not exempt the receiver from liability under the statutory provision. Moreover, the Court held that the equivalent of section 44(1)(b) applied to contracts between the receiver and the appointing bank and rejected the argument that it applied only as between the receiver and third parties.

6. RECEIVER'S BORROWING POWERS

10–031 In every case a proposed lending bank will have to scrutinise carefully the powers given to the receiver in the debenture. In the case of an administrative receiver a power to borrow is deemed to be provided in the absence of inconsistent provisions.[49] In the case of other receivers, there may be an express power to borrow or, if the receiver is expressly made the agent of the company and he has express power to carry on the company's business, there is probably an implied power to borrow for that purpose.[50] In the rare case where the receiver is the agent of the appointor and not the agent of the company, he will again, where he has express power to carry on the business, probably be held to have implied authority to borrow.[51] The power to borrow as agent of the company must terminate on liquidation, for thereafter the receiver cannot create fresh debts or liabilities of the company.[52]

As to security, the debenture may well authorise the receiver to give security and to give it ahead of the appointor's charges. In the case of administrative receivers, there is a deemed power to give security in the absence of contrary provision[53] but (it seems) no deemed power to give such security with priority over the appointor.[54] In the case of other receivers, a power to carry on business may imply a power to give security for borrowings.[55] However, a power to give such security priority over the debenture-holder is only likely to be implied where the receiver is to be agent of the debenture-holder.[56]

7. INDEMNITY

10–032 In view of the risk of personal liability in various aspects of the receivership it is in principle desirable for a receiver to seek an

---

entered into by them unless liability is excluded). It was held that the fact that the receiver was an officer of the court administering assets under its control was a factor pointing to an implied exclusion of personal liability.

[49] Insolvency Act 1986, s. 42 and Sched. 1, para. 4.
[50] See *General Auction Estate Co. v. Smith* [1891] 3 Ch. 432.
[51] *Robinson Printing Co. Ltd v. Chic Ltd* [1905] 2 Ch. 123.
[52] See above, Chap. 4.
[53] Insolvency Act 1986, s. 42, Sched. 1, para. 3.
[54] See below, Chap. 21.
[55] See *Re Patent File Co.* [1890] 6 Ch. App. 83 at 86, 88.
[56] See *Robinson Printing Co. Ltd v. Chic Ltd* [1905] 2 Ch. 123.

indemnity in respect of such liabilities from his appointor at the time of appointment. A receiver's statutory indemnity[57] will be useless if the company has no assets. It is not the practice of clearing banks to give such indemnities, save in the case of very special situations. The receiver is expected to rely upon the appointing bank's practice of standing behind its receiver and "seeing him right" if anything goes wrong otherwise than due to his own default or negligence.[58] If a receiver is not appointed by a clearing bank, an indemnity should be obtained from the appointor covering the receiver against potential liabilities.

---

[57] s. 37(1)(b) (receivers), s. 44(1)(c) (administrative receivers).
[58] In the case of negligence in particular, the receiver will probably be insured and will be expected to look to his insurers.

CHAPTER 11

RECEIVERS AND WINDING-UP

11–001 Whilst receivership is in essence a remedy for a debenture-holder, winding-up involves the administration of the company's property for the benefit of all the company's creditors. The receiver appointed out of court is the choice of the debenture-holder, whereas the liquidator is in effect the choice of the unsecured creditors. Generally speaking, during the period of any receivership of a company in liquidation, the receiver's administration takes precedence and a liquidator has a secondary role. This is the case whether the receiver is appointed before or after the commencement of winding-up.[1] The liquidator's special responsibilities are threefold:

(a) the liquidator alone can invoke certain statutory remedies, *e.g.* in respect of preferences;
(b) the liquidator has the right and duty to scrutinise the security of the debenture-holder and conduct of the receiver;
(c) the liquidator has the right to all assets which lie outside the charge and to any surplus of assets after discharge of the secured debt.

1. CAN A RECEIVER PETITION?

11–002 A non-administrative receiver can petition in the name of the company in order to preserve or protect its assets.[2] The debenture-holder can petition if he can show that a benefit to him would accrue from the winding-up.[3] The Insolvency Act 1986, Sched. 1, para. 21, gives an administrative receiver "power to present . . . a petition for the winding

---

[1] See *Re Potters Oils Ltd* [1986] 1 W.L.R. 201 where Hoffmann J. (as he then was) affirmed the right of a debenture-holder to appoint a receiver after liquidation if it thought that its best interests would be served by such an appointment. This was so despite the fact that the receiver's remuneration would he paid out of funds otherwise available to the unsecured creditors. If the receiver is appointed after a winding-up, he requires the court's leave to take possession from the liquidator, an officer of the court, but he is entitled to leave as of right (*ibid.* at 206). The receiver, if appointed after the liquidation, is entitled to require the liquidator to transfer to him the assets of the company to enable the receiver to pay off the secured and preferential creditors: *Manley, Petitioner* [1985] S.L.T. 42.

[2] *Re Emmadart Ltd* [1979] Ch. 540 (winding-up order saved company from liability for unoccupied property rate); *Re Roinobs Ltd* (unreported, Nourse J., October 25, 1983) (group tax relief under an arrangement with the Inland Revenue became available on liquidation); and see *Bank of New Zealand v. Essington Developments Pty Ltd* (1990) 5 A.C.S.R. 86 at 88; (1991) 9 A.C.L.C. 1039 at 1041.

[3] *Re Borough of Portsmouth Tramways Co.* [1892] 2 Ch. 362. In *Re Emmadart Ltd* [1979] Ch. 540, the debenture-holder appeared as a supporting creditor on the receiver's petition. See also *Re Anvil Estates Ltd* (unreported, 1993) discussed by Pugh & Ede in (1994) 10 Insolvency Law and Practice 47.

up of the company". Although no limitation is placed upon the exercise of the power, since the administrative receiver is deemed to be the agent of the company until liquidation, it is thought that he should petition in the name of the company.[4]

Where a petition is by the receiver in the name of the company, the **11–003** company need not be served under the Insolvency Rules 1986.[5] The court may expect the directors and secretary to be made respondents and served where practicable, in case they wish to oppose, although this is not required by the 1986 Rules.[6]

Unlike a creditor, a receiver is not entitled to a winding-up order "*ex* **11–004** *debito justitiae*": the court will exercise its discretion whether to make such an order.[7]

Whether a receiver can call the requisite meetings of members and **11–005** creditors to wind-up the company voluntarily depends on whether the receiver is given such a power, explicitly or implicitly, by the terms of the debenture under which he is appointed.[8]

2. CAN A RECEIVER RESIST A PETITION?

Nothing in the 1949 Rules required a winding-up petition to be served **11–006** on a receiver and, prior to the Insolvency Act 1986, he appears to have had no *locus standi* to appear in his own right.[9] Now, however, any petitioner for a winding-up order who knows that an administrative receiver has been appointed in relation to a company must send a copy of the petition to the receiver.[10] Further, paragraph 21 of Schedule 1 to the Insolvency Act 1986 expressly empowers an administrative receiver to defend a petition. It is thought that this power should be exercised in the name of the company, and not in the receiver's own name.[11]

The mere fact that all the company's available assets are charged to **11–007** the full by the debenture cannot of itself bar a winding-up order.[12] A

---

[4] The general rule is that a receiver has no *locus standi* to sue in his own name, save in respect of rights to which he is personally entitled: *Robertson v. Oskar* (1984) 8 A.C.L.R. 570.

[5] Insolvency Rules 1986, r. 4.8.

[6] See *Re Emmadart Ltd* [1979] Ch. 540 at 548; *Re Roisnob Ltd* (unreported, Nourse J., October 25, 1983).

[7] *Re Emmadart Ltd* [1979] Ch. 540 at 547–548.

[8] See *Valorum Ltd v. Rilett* (unreported, HH Judge Boggis Q.C., December 2, 1999) where receivers purported to call a meeting of the members of the company ultimately with a view to placing the company into voluntary liquidation. The receivers argued that they had power under the debenture to call such a meeting, specifically under a clause which provided that the receivers could "do all such other things as may from time to time be considered by such receivers to be conducive to the exercise of his or their functions as receivers". The argument was rejected, since the receivers had advanced no reasons as to why they wished to call the meeting.

[9] He could, however, cause the company to appear to oppose the petition.

[10] Insolvency Rules 1986, r. 4.10 (2). The Cork Report, at para. 468, suggested that the receiver should be given notice.

[11] Compare above, n. 4. A voluntary liquidator who appears on a petition in order to assist the court does so in his own name (*Re Medisco Equipment* (1983) 1 B.C.C. 98,944) but the positions of the voluntary liquidator and the receiver are not analogous.

[12] Insolvency Act 1986, s. 125(1).

winding-up order has been made where there was a receivership in progress and the majority of creditors opposed the making of such an order.[13] However, the right of an unpaid creditor to obtain a winding-up order is a class right and, if the majority of the class consider that they have a better chance of getting paid if a winding-up order is not made, then the court may well give effect to the wishes of those opposing creditors and refuse a winding-up order.[14] Moreover, whilst it is not the usual practice of the Companies Court to grant lengthy adjournments, a very lengthy adjournment has been granted where an ongoing receivership gave rise to a reasonable prospect of a return for unsecured as well as secured creditors.[15]

11–008   The receiver's control over the company may not prevent the directors from causing the company to oppose a petition, if the receiver does not wish to reserve to himself the power to represent the company on the petition.[16]

3. INVALIDITY OF CHARGES

(a) Non-registration

11–009 In practice, all charges over any property of a company registered in England and Wales under which receivers are likely to be appointed are registrable, and unless registered within 21 days after the date of creation, are void as against a liquidator, administrator or creditor.[17] The position is the same in respect of charges on property in England and Wales created by companies incorporated outside Great Britain which,

---

[13] *Re Clandown Colliery* [1915] 1 Ch. 369. In that case, however, there were rather special circumstances in that the chairman of the company had in reality been carrying on business in the company's name and this was a state of affairs which was not reasonable or proper in the interests of innocent unsecured creditors. Furthermore, the opposing creditors gave no reason for their opposition.

[14] *Re Crigglestone Coal Co. Ltd* [1906] 2 Ch. 327 at 331–332. The opposing creditors should give notice to the petitioning creditor, file evidence and appear by counsel at the hearing if the opposition is to be effective. See also *Re Macrae* [1961] 1 W.L.R. 229, CA; *Re Swain* [1965] 1 W.L.R. 909, CA. In *Re Leigh Estates (U.K.) Ltd* [1994] B.C.C. 292, the court held that in evaluating the strength of support or opposition to a petition, secured creditors were to be treated as unsecured creditors to the extent of any deficiency, and drew an analogy between the class rights of creditors on the hearing of a winding up petition and in relation to voting on a scheme of arrangement under s. 425 of the Companies Act 1985. Where there are no assets in the estate, the court must ask itself whether it is just and equitable to wind up the company, for example to promote an investigation: *Bell Group Finance (Pty) Ltd (in liq.) v. Bell Group (U.K.) Holdings Ltd* [1996] 1 B.C.L.C. 304. Debenture-holders and receivers will not be able successfully to oppose a winding-up petition where the object of their opposition is to prevent an investigation of the validity of the debenture: *ibid.* The court will pay much more attention to the views of creditors who are wholly independent of the company: *Re Southard* [1979] 1 W.L.R. 1198, CA, *per* Buckley L.J. at 1205 and para. 11.03.

[15] *Re Northern Developments (Holdings) Ltd* (unreported, Templeman J., June 16, 1976 affirmed, on Appeal, March 1, 1977, CA).

[16] *Re Reprographic Exports (Euromart) Ltd* (1978) 122 S.J. 400; *Bank of New Zealand v. Essington Developments Pty Ltd* (1990) 5 A.C.S.R. 86; (1991) 9 A.C.L.C. 1039; and see above, para. 2–017.

[17] See above, Chap. 3. In the case of companies registered in England or Wales, registration is required of charges created over property within or outside the U.K.

at the date of creation of the charge, have an established place of business in Great Britain.[18] The effect of non-registration within the requisite period is to make the moneys secured immediately payable.[19]

(b) Floating charges

A floating charge created in favour of a person not connected with a **11–010** company is not invalidated by the subsequent liquidation of the company or the making of an administration order against it, provided that the company was solvent at the time of creation and did not become insolvent as a consequence of the transaction creating the charge.[20] But subject thereto, a floating charge created:

(a) in favour of a person connected to the company[21] within two years of the commencement of winding-up or the presentation of a petition for an administration order (the onset of insolvency); or

(b) in favour of any other person within one year of these dates; or

(c) in either case between the presentation of a petition for an administration order and the making of such an order,
    is invalid except to the extent of the aggregate of

(i) the value of the consideration for the creation of the charge that is paid or supplied to the company at the same time as or after the creation of the charge; and

(ii) the interest (if any) agreed to be payable on these amounts.[22]

For the purposes of this provision, the value of any goods or services supplied shall be the amount in money which could reasonably have been expected to be obtained for supplying the goods or services in the ordinary course of business at that time on the same terms (apart from the consideration) as those on which they were supplied to the company.[23]

The phrase "at the same time as" in section 245(2)(a) and (b) of the **11–011** 1986 Act replaces "at the time of" in section 617 of the Companies Act 1985. The old phrase was interpreted very loosely in favour of lenders where money was lent on the faith of a promise to execute a debenture but the execution was delayed by the borrower.[24] Moneys paid some considerable time before the execution of the debenture were held to be secured. Although the legislature, in altering the wording, did not intend

---

[18] *Re Oriel Ltd* [1986] 1 W.L.R. 180, and see above, Chap. 3.

[19] Companies Act 1985, s. 395(2).

[20] Insolvency Act 1986, s. 245(4).

[21] For the definition of a person connected with a company, see Insolvency Act 1986, ss. 249 and 435.

[22] Insolvency Act 1986, s. 245(1), (2).

[23] Insolvency Act 1986, s. 245(5).

[24] See *Re Columbian Fireproofing Co. Ltd* [1910] 2 Ch. 120, CA (11 days); *Re F. & E. Stanton Ltd* [1929] 2 Ch. 180 (5–54 days).

any change in the law, the Court of Appeal[25] has held that the previous decisions were (a) not binding, because they were based on different wording, and (b) erroneous. They held that moneys paid prior to execution were not secured unless the interval was *de minimis* (such as a coffee break) or unless there was a prior binding agreement which amounted to an equitable charge.[26]

11–012   Under the previous law, the courts were very indulgent to chargee banks in applying the rule in *Clayton's* case[27] and in treating withdrawals subsequent to the charge as being cash advanced after and in consideration of the charge.[28] A similar approach may be expected to be taken under section 245 of the Insolvency Act 1986.

11–013   Such cash advances must, however, benefit the company, and not *merely* be a means of substituting a secured for an unsecured debt (or a better for an existing security) to the benefit of one creditor at the expense of another.[29] Underhand conduct on the part of the chargee is not pre-requisite to the operation of section 245.[30] The new wording in s.245(2)(b) has clarified the fact that the discharge or reduction of a debt is as good as cash. It is still the case therefore that in a genuine business transaction designed to benefit the company's business, the discharge of a debt will validate a floating charge even if the result is to make a formerly unsecured creditor secured under the floating charge.[31] In each case, the court looks at the substance of what is happening.[32]

11–014   The invalidation of the floating charge only takes effect as at the date of commencement of the winding-up or presentation of the petition for the administration order, and only invalidates the security element in the floating charge. The invalidation has no retrospective effect, and accordingly any realisation of the security by the debenture-holder or the receiver prior to that date is unaffected, and any payment made prior to that date cannot be recovered under section 245 by the liquidator.[33] For this purpose, the commencement of a compulsory winding-up is the presentation of the petition to wind up.[34]

[25] *Re Shoe Lace Ltd* [1993] B.C.C. 609, affirming on different grounds the judgment of Hoffmann J. (as he then was) [1992] B.C.C. 367. See also *Re Fairway Magazines Ltd* [1993] B.C.C. 924.
[26] *Re Shoe Lace Ltd* [1993] B.C.C. 609 at 619F–619H, CA.
[27] (1816) 1 Mer. 572; (1816) 35 ER. 781.
[28] *Re Yeovil Glove Co. Ltd* [1965] Ch. 148; [1964] 2 All E.R. 849; *Re Thomas Mortimer Ltd* [1965] Ch. 186.
[29] *Re Fairway Magazines Ltd* [1992] B.C.C. 924; *Re G.T. Whyte & Co. Ltd* [1983] B.C.L.C. 311, applying *Re Matthew Ellis Ltd* [1933] Ch. 458, CA.
[30] *Re Fairway Magazines Ltd* [1993] B.C.C. 924; *Re G. T. Whyte & Co. Ltd* [1983] B.C.L.C. 311 at 317.
[31] See, under the old wording, *Re Mathew Ellis Ltd* [1933] Ch. 458, CA (loan made by chairman of company used to pay debts to firm of which he was partner in order to secure further supplies on credit and thereby to be able to continue the business). *cf. Re Destone Fabrics Ltd* [1941] Ch. 319.
[32] *Re Mathew Ellis Ltd* [1933] Ch. 458 at 474, 478, CA.
[33] *Mace Builders (Glasgow) Ltd v. Lunn* [1987] Ch. 191, CA. That was a decision on the wording prior to the Insolvency Act 1986. The section has been completely rewritten, but there does not appear to have been any intention of altering the law so as to make the invalidity retrospective.
[34] *Re Shoe Lace Ltd* [1993] B.C.C. 609, CA.

(c) Transactions at an undervalue and preferences[35]

Sections 238–241 afford to liquidators and administrators extensive **11–015** rights of recovery in respect of transactions at an undervalue or preferences. The object is to secure the distribution of an insolvent company's assets equally amongst its body of creditors.

Sections 238–241 provide that a liquidator or administrator may apply **11–016** to the court to set aside a transaction, to release or discharge (in whole or in part) any charge or security given by a company or to direct payment by a person to the office-holder of such sums as the court shall think fit in respect of benefits received if the transaction was entered into "at a relevant time" by the company (i) for no consideration or for a consideration the value of which was significantly less than the value of the consideration provided by the company, or (ii) with a creditor of the company or guarantor of any of its debts or liabilities, and has the effect (and the decision by the company to enter into it was influenced by a desire to produce the effect) of placing that person in a better position in a liquidation than he would have been in if the transaction had not been entered into.[36] A "relevant time" as defined by section 240 of the Insolvency Act 1986 is one at which the company was unable to pay its debts within the meaning of section 123 of the Insolvency Act 1986 or became so unable by reason of the transaction or preference; and if also that time was either:

(a) (in the case of a preference given to person not connected with the company[37]) within six months; or

(b) (in the case of a transaction at an undervalue or a preference given to a person so connected) within two years of the date of presentation of the petition for administration or the commencement of the winding-up; or

(c) between presentation of a petition for administration and the subsequent making of such an order.

Payments made to a holder of a valid debenture prior to the commence- **11–017** ment of the liquidation will rarely be liable to be set aside as a preference within the meaning of section 239. Under section 239(4)(b) of the 1986 Act, a hypothetical liquidation is posited, taking effect immediately after the transaction which is sought to be impugned, and the court must examine whether the debenture-holder's position is

[35] The concept of a preference presupposes knowledge on the part of the company that the company's assets are insufficient to pay all creditors: see *Re Sarflax* [1979] Ch. 592, *per* Oliver J. at 602. But a belief that creditors would all be paid eventually is insufficient to preclude a preference where it is known that all creditors cannot be paid in full at the time the preferential payment is made: *Re F.P. & C.H. Matthews Ltd* [1982] Ch. 257, CA. It is thought that the propositions expressed in these cases remain valid, notwithstanding Millett J.'s denial of the utility of cases decided before the 1986 Act in *Re MC Bacon Ltd* [1990] B.C.C. 78 at 87.

[36] Insolvency Act 1986, s. 238(4).

[37] For the definition of a connected person, see Insolvency Act 1986, ss. 249 and 435. For the purpose of ss. 239 and 241, a person is not to be treated as a connected person by reason only of his being an employee of the company.

better, by reason of the payment being made, than it would otherwise have been.[38] Normally, the debenture-holder's position would not be any better than in the hypothetical liquidation, since the debenture-holder would be entitled to payment by virtue of his charge in any event.[39] However, there are situations where the debenture-holder's position might be improved by such payments, *e.g.* if the charge is liable to challenge on any of the grounds set out in the text, or if the debenture-holder receives more than the total of any secured debt, or (in the case of a crystallised floating charge) if the result of the payment is that creditors who were preferential as at the date of the hypothetical liquidation go unpaid in whole or in part.

11–018   The grant of relief under sections 238 and 239 is discretionary.[40] Relief in respect of a transaction at an undervalue is precluded if the company entered into the transaction in good faith and in the ordinary course of its business and if, at the time it did so, there were reasonable grounds for believing that the transaction would benefit the company.[41] In any event, it is unlikely that the grant of a debenture could successfully be challenged as a transaction at an undervalue.[42] Further, the interests acquired by purchasers from the holder of a debenture potentially voidable under these provisions, or from a receiver appointed thereunder, are not open to challenge if their acquisition was in good faith, for value and without notice of the circumstances rendering the debenture open to challenge on the grounds of undervalue or preference.[43] The protection extends to any "interest in property which was acquired from a person other than the company",[44] an expression which should surely include in this context a receiver as well as the debenture-holder who appointed him, even where the receiver is acting as the "deemed agent" of the company, for in substance, if not in form, the acquisition is from the debenture-holder.

11–019   For a transaction to fall within section 238(4)(b) of the 1986 Act, the transaction must be (i) entered into by the company; (ii) for a consideration; (iii) the value of which measured in money or money's worth; (iv) is significantly less than the value; (v) also measured in money or money's worth; (vi) of the consideration provided by the company. This requires a comparison to be made between the value obtained by the company

---

[38] There can be no voidable preference unless the party in question is actually preferred: *Lewis v. Hyde* [1997] B.C.C. 976, PC.

[39] In Australia, it has been held that an essential element of any alleged preference is that it should decrease the property available for distribution in the liquidation, and hence that there can be no preference where payment is made to a debenture-holder who would have been entitled to payment within a liquidation in any event: *Wily v. St George Partnership Banking Ltd* [1999] B.P.I.R. 1030.

[40] *Re Paramount Airways Ltd (in Administration)* [1993] Ch. 223.

[41] Insolvency Act 1986, s. 238(5).

[42] See below.

[43] Insolvency Act 1986, s. 241(2), (2A), (3), (3A), (3B) and (3C). Similar protection was given under the predecessor, s. 320 of the Companies Act 1948, because s. 44(2) of the Bankruptcy Act 1914 was read into the Companies Act 1948: see *Mace Builders (Glasgow) Ltd v. Lunn* [1986] Ch. 459 Scott J. (at 469, and in [1987] Ch. 191) (Court of Appeal, *per* Lord Donaldson M.R.) at 199.

[44] Insolvency Act 1986, s. 241(2)(a).

for the transaction and the value of the consideration provided by the company. Both values must be measurable in money or money's worth and both must be considered from the company's point of view.[45]

The first issue for the court is to define the relevant "transaction" **11–020** which is sought to be impugned. "Transaction" is defined in section 436 of the 1986 Act as including a "gift, agreement or arrangement, and references to entering into a transaction shall be construed accordingly". These are wide words, which will doubtless be given a broad interpretation by the courts.[46] Difficulties can arise where two or more persons have entered into a number of different arrangements, and the question arises as to whether the dealings are to be treated as one, or more than one, transaction for the purposes of section 238. In *Phillips v. Brewin Dolphin Bell Lawrie Ltd*,[47] the Court of Appeal decided that the relevant transaction had to be identified by reference to the person with whom it was entered into and only the elements of the transaction and that person could be taken into account. The company in liquidation had sold the shares in a subsidiary (which had been incorporated for the purposes of a hive down) to X, and further agreed to sub-lease certain equipment to X's parent company, Y. The two contracts were entered into simultaneously. On an application by the liquidator of the company that the sale of the shares in the subsidiary was a transaction at an undervalue, X argued that the "transaction" for the purposes of section 238 included the sub-lease agreement, so that the consideration payable by X's parent under the sub-leases had to be taken into account. The Court of Appeal rejected this argument, since the two contracts had been entered into with different persons, *i.e.* X and its parent and had been deliberately kept separate. This result seems harsh and was probably not intended by Parliament.

The approach in that case can be contrasted with the approach of the **11–021** Court of Appeal in *Barclays Bank v. Eustice*,[48] which was not cited in the *Brewin Dolphin* case and in which the Court of Appeal agreed for the purpose of s.423 of the Insolvency Act 1986 to treat three related transactions alleged to amount to an undervalue as one transaction consisting of three parts. This was done at the invitation of the parties but was described by the Court as "realistic".

It seems that the grant of a debenture by a company will rarely if ever **11–022** fall within section 238, since the grant of security does not deplete the company's assets, and in any event is not capable of valuation in money or money's worth.[49]

---

[45] *Re MC Bacon Ltd* [1990] B.C.L.C. 324, at 340, *per* Millett J. (as he then was); approved subsequently by the Court of Appeal in *National Bank of Kuwait v. Menzies* [1995] 1 B.C.L.C. 1 at 9 and *Phillips v. Brewin Dolphin Bell Lawrie Ltd* [1999] 1 W.L.R. 2052 at 2061–2, *per* Morritt L.J.

[46] *Phillips v. Brewin Dolphin Bell Lawrie Ltd* [1999] 1 W.L.R. 2052 at 2060H *per* Morritt L.J.

[47] [1999] 1 W.L.R. 2052.

[48] [1995] 2 B.C.L.C. 630

[49] *Re MC Bacon Ltd* [1990] B.C.L.C. 324.

11–023   The meaning of "consideration" in section 238 has yet to be fully clarified by judicial decisions. The question of whether "consideration" in section 238 has its usual legal meaning has not yet been decided, but it is clear that it connotes the *"quid pro quo"* for that which it is alleged the company disposed of at an undervalue.[50] Even where, as between transferor and transferee, full consideration is apparently given, there may still be a transaction at an undervalue if the interests of a third party are prejudicially affected by the transaction. In *Agricultural Mortgage Corporation plc v. Woodward*,[51] a husband entered into a lease of his agricultural holding in favour of his wife at what was assumed to be a full market rent, the purpose of the lease being to prevent the claimant mortgagee taking vacant possession of the land. Since the loss of vacant possession reduced the value of the land from over £1 million to less than £500,000, the wife was placed in a "ransom position" *vis-à-vis* the mortgagee. Since that ransom position had not been reflected in the rent, the lease was held by the Court of Appeal to be at an undervalue. It was also argued by the mortgagee in *Woodward* that the mere detriment to the husband in reducing the value of his land by virtue of the lease could constitute "consideration", but the Court of Appeal expressly left the point open for later decision.

(d) Extortionate credit transactions

11–024 Under the 1986 Act, a liquidator or administrator may apply for relief in respect of any extortionate credit transaction entered into by the company within the period of three years before the company went into liquidation or the administration order was made.[52] The section applies to transactions which, having regard to the risk accepted by the creditor, require grossly exorbitant payments to be made (whether unconditionally or in certain contingencies) in respect of the provision of credit, or which otherwise grossly contravene ordinary principles of fair dealing. The court is given power to set aside the whole or any part of any obligation created by the transaction, vary the terms of the transaction or the terms on which any security is held or require the surrender of any security. Jurisdiction under this section is exercisable concurrently with the jurisdiction in respect of transactions at an undervalue.

(e) Commencement of winding-up

11–025 A compulsory winding-up is deemed to commence on the date of presentation of the petition on which the order is made.[53] Accordingly, the order has retrospective effect and will invalidate all charges created by the company after the date of the petition unless the court otherwise orders.[54]

---

[50] *Phillips v. Brewin Dolphin Bell Lawrie Ltd* [1999] 1 W.L.R. 2052 at 2061C.

[51] [1995] 1 B.C.L.C. 1, which was decided under s. 423 of the 1986 Act, the wording of which is, for the purpose of the point in the text, the same as s. 238.

[52] Insolvency Act 1986, s. 244.

[53] *ibid.*, s. 129.

[54] *ibid.*, s. 127. A transaction contravening s. 127 is unlikely to be validated unless it was in the ordinary course of business or for the company's benefit: see *Re T W Construction*

A voluntary winding-up commences on the date of the resolution to this effect. Receivers have been held to have standing to apply under section 127 of the 1986 Act, on the basis that the statute imposes no limitation on who might apply.[55] Property recovered as a result of a void disposition of a company's property is caught by a debenture if that debenture would have covered the property prior to the disposition. Since such dispositions are void, the character of the property disposed of does not change.[56]

4. CONSEQUENCES OF INVALIDITY OF CHARGES

Where a charge under which a receiver has been appointed is invalid, so **11–026** also is his appointment, and he is a trespasser in respect of all assets of which he takes possession.[57]

In the case of a charge void for non-registration (where the charge is **11–027** valid as against the company[58]) it seems that:

(a) a receiver may act safely until liquidation except in so far as (d) applies[59];

(b) if the sums due under the charge are repaid before either (i) liquidation or (ii) subject to (d) below, a challenge, the chargee cannot be required to repay such sums unless the repayment is voidable as a fraudulent preference[60];

(c) prior to such challenge the receiver can validly sell assets of the company[61];

(d) where the receiver or chargee with notice of the relevant facts receives moneys caught by another charge having priority, the receiver or chargee holds such moneys as constructive trustee for the other chargee.[62]

[1954] 1 W.L.R. 540; *Re Operator Control Cabs* [1970] 3 All E.R. 657; *Re Gray's Inn Construction Co.* [1980] 1 W.L.R. 711, CA; *Re S.A. & D. Wright Ltd* [1992] B.C.C. 503. In *Re Durum Ltd, Royal Bank of Scotland plc v. Bhardwaj* (unreported, Neuberger J., July 28, 2000) the court validated a sale of property to a third party solely to the extent necessary to validate the security granted by the purchaser to the funder of the transaction. The same problem does not arise in case of a voluntary liquidation (not followed by a compulsory winding-up), since the winding-up commences at the date of the resolution and there is no question of any retrospective operation: Insolvency Act 1986, s. 86.

[55] *Merton and anor. v. Hammond Suddards and anor* [1996] 2 B.C.L.C. 470. See also *Re Argentum Reductions (U.K.) Ltd* [1975] 1 W.L.R. 186 and para. 6–011 above.

[56] *Merton and anor. v. Hammond Suddards and anor* [1996] 2 B.C.L.C. 470.

[57] *Re Goldburg (No. 2)* [1912] 1 K.B. 606.

[58] *Re Monolithic Building Co.* [1915] 1 Ch. 643.

[59] *Dictum* of Walton J. in *Burston Finance Ltd v. Speirway* [1974] 1 W.L.R. 1648 at 1657E.

[60] *Re Parkes Garage* [1929] 1 Ch. 139; *Re Ehrmann Bros Ltd* [1906] 2 Ch. 697 at 708, *per* Romer L.J.; *Welsh Development Agency v. Export Finance Co. Ltd* [1990] B.C.C. 393 at 412B–412C (not reversed on this point on appeal). Likewise if the charge holder seizes the charged assets prior to the liquidation: *Mercantile Bank of India v. Chartered Bank* [1937] 1 All E.R. 231 at 241, *per* Porter J., relying on the pledge case of *Wrightson v. McArthur & Hutchisons* [1921] 2 K.B. 807; *Re Row Dal Constructions Property Ltd* [1966] V.R. 249; *N. V. Slavenburg's Bank v. Intercontinental Ltd* [1980] 1 W.L.R. 1076 at 1090–1091.

[61] *Royal Bank of Canada v. First Pioneer Investments* (1980) 106 D.L.R. (3d) 330.

[62] *Welsh Development Agency v. Export Finance Co. Ltd* [1990] B.C.C. 393 at 412. It

Where a floating charge is avoided by the special provisions relating to floating charges in a subsequent winding-up, sums repaid under the charge prior to the commencement of the winding-up do not have to be repaid.[63]

11–028   In all the above-mentioned situations, at the time of the action taken by the receiver or repayment, the security is perfectly valid against the company and has not been challenged by the parties who presently or in the future may have *locus standi* to do so.

11–029   In a case where the invalidity of the charge arises only from the invalidity of the guarantee secured by the charge, the House of Lords has held that the receiver should only be treated as a trespasser from the date that a writ is served on him claiming damages.[64]

11–030   Where a receiver has been appointed under an invalid charge, but his management of the company has incontrovertibly benefited that company, the receiver might be entitled to remuneration on a *quantum meruit* basis.[65]

5. APPOINTMENT AFTER WINDING-UP

11–031 A winding-up does not prevent the appointment of a receiver,[66] though an administration order does.[67] Where a receiver is appointed after a winding-up order, he will need the leave of the court to take possession of the charged assets, but such leave will be given as a matter of course.[68]

11–032   So far as the costs of the winding up are concerned, in relation to voluntary liquidations, section 115 of the Insolvency Act 1986 provides that "all expenses properly incurred in the winding-up, including the remuneration of the liquidator are payable out of the company's assets in priority to all other claims". In both compulsory and voluntary winding up, rule 4.218 of the Insolvency Rules 1986 lists in order of priority a number of categories of costs, charges and expenses of expenses of the liquidation which are payable "out of the assets".

Prior to the Insolvency Act 1986, it was well understood that the expression "the company's assets" in the forerunner of section 115 included assets which were the subject of a floating charge which had not crystallised at the moment of winding up.[69] Thus where a receiver was appointed after the making of a winding up order, the costs of the

---

proved unnecessary on appeal to deal with the suggestion that the charge-holder with superior rights needed to intervene positively to assert his rights to the moneys: [1992] B.C.C. 270 at 286G, *per* Dillon L.J. and at 304E–304F, *per* Staughton L.J.

[63] *Mace Builders (Glasgow) Ltd v. Lunn* [1987] Ch. 191.

[64] *Ford & Carter v. Midland Bank* (1979) 129 N.L.J. 543, HL. The receiver appeared to have been acting as such prior to that date with the company's consent.

[65] *Monks v. Poynice Pty Ltd* (1987) 8 N.S.W.L.R. 62.

[66] *Re Henry Pound Son & Hutchins* (1889) 42 Ch.D. 402; *Strong Carlyle Press* [1893] 1 Ch. 268; *Re Northern Garage Ltd* [1946] Ch. 188.

[67] See below, Chap. 23.

[68] *Re Henry Pound Son & Hutchins* (1889) 42 Ch.D. 402; *Re Potters Oils Ltd* [1986] 1 W.L.R. 201, *per* Hoffmann J. at 206.

[69] *Re Lewis Merthyr Consolidated Collieries* [1929] 1 Ch. 498, CA; *Re Griffin Hotel Company* [1941] 1 Ch. 129; *Re Barleycorn Enterprises Limited* [1970] Ch. 465, CA.

liquidator in the winding up were payable prior to the preferential creditors out of the assets subject to the floating charge. On the other hand, where the receivership preceded the making of a winding up order (even if after the date of presentation of the petition) or the passing of a resolution for the voluntary liquidation of the company, so that the floating charge had crystallised prior to liquidation, it had been held prior to the 1986 Act that the costs of the liquidator were postponed to the claims of the preferential creditors and those of the debenture holder.[70]

In *Re M.C. Bacon Limited*[71] Millett J. held that the 1986 Act had not **11–033** changed the position in relation to priorities where the floating charge had not crystallised prior to liquidation. In so doing he affirmed the continued validity of the pre-1986 decision in *Re Barleycorn Enterprises Limited*. However, in *Re Portbase Clothing Ltd*[72] it was held by Chadwick J. that the effect of changes introduced by the 1986 Act is to give priority to the costs of the liquidation over the claims of the holder of a floating charge, even if the liquidator is appointed after the crystallisation of the floating charge.[73] This represents a reversal of the pre-1986 law.

Chadwick J. noted that sections 115 and 175(2)(a) of the 1986 Act make it explicit that in a winding up, preferential debts rank after the expenses of the winding up, and that section 175(2)(b) of the 1986 Act makes it equally clear that preferential creditors in a winding up are to be given priority over the debenture holder in respect of assets subject to a "floating charge". He then observed that the altered definition of a "floating charge" in section 251 of the 1986 Act, which refers to a charge which "as created" was a floating charge, has the effect that under section 175(2)(b) preferential creditors are given priority over the assets covered by a charge which "as created" was a floating charge, even if it has crystallised prior to the liquidation. Chadwick J. then held that because of the relative priorities accorded to preferential claims and liquidation costs in sections 115 and 175, the giving of priority to preferential claims over the claims of the holders of a crystallised floating charge must necessarily also have resulted in the elevation of liquidation expenses above the claims of the holders of a charge which "as created" was a floating charge. He pointed out that the priority to be accorded to liquidation expenses over preferential creditors must have been intended to apply to the same assets out of which preferential debts are to be paid.

It should be noted that on the facts of *Portbase,* the crystallisation of the floating occurred on the company ceasing to trade, which was both prior to the resolution to wind up and the subsequent appointment of administrative receivers. Accordingly, section 40 of the Insolvency Act 1986 was not brought into play, and it is unclear from the judgment whether Chadwick J's decision would have been different had the

---

[70] *Re Christonette International Limited* [1982] 1 W.L.R. 1245.
[71] [1991] Ch. 127.
[72] [1993] Ch. 388.
[73] Not following *Re Christonette International* [1982] 1 W.L.R. 1245.

receivership (as opposed to crystallisation) preceded the winding up. In such a case it might have been argued that section 40 of the 1986 Act places express statutory obligations upon an administrative receiver to pay preferential creditors in priority to the claims of the debenture holder, but makes no express mention of any duty upon the receiver to pay liquidation expenses in priority to the claims of the debenture holder.

11–034 The decision in *Portbase* can be justified as a matter of logic applied to the statutory language. Moreover, the priority afforded to liquidation expenses can be justified as a matter of policy on the grounds that it seeks to ensure that irrespective of whether a floating charge crystallises, or a receiver is appointed, before or after liquidation begins, funds should be available to enable a liquidator to pay liquidation expenses and preferential claims in the winding up, and to wind up the affairs of the insolvent company in the interests of preferential and unsecured creditors.

Against these points, as indicated in the second edition of this work,[74] it could be argued that there is no reason to suppose that the change in the meaning of a floating charge in the Insolvency Act 1986 was either (a) intended to benefit any parties other than preferential creditors, or (b) was intended to change the meaning of "assets" in provisions dealing with the costs of winding up.[74a] It might also be argued that the decision in *Portbase* could have undesirable consequences if it led to receivers seeking to promote the interests of their appointor by selling floating charge assets in haste and making distributions as soon as possible prior to any liquidation, with the aim of ensuring that as and when a liquidator was appointed, there would be no "assets" of any description left upon which section 115 or rule 4.218 could bite in respect of liquidation expenses.[74b]

11–035   Notwithstanding the unresolved issues and doubts referred to above, *Portbase* has now apparently been accepted and applied by the Court of Appeal in *Mond v. Hammond Suddards*.[75] The case raised the question of whether the costs incurred by a liquidator in unsuccessfully challenging a receiver's rights to certain monies could be paid as costs and expenses incurred in the winding up, and if so whether they ranked in priority to the claims of the debenture holder to the floating charge assets. The charge in question had crystallised by the appointment of administrative receivers prior to the company going into liquidation. Chadwick L.J. (who gave the only reasoned judgment) held, applying

---

[74] See para. 11–10 of the second edition.

[74a] Although it might be said that Parliament must be taken to have known of the decision in *Re Barleycorn Enterprises* that the word "assets" meant the same in the equivalent of sections 175(2)(a) and section 115, so that if the meaning was changed in relation to one, it would be changed in relation to the other.

[74b] See also the discussion by *Hanson* [1993] 9 Insolvency Law & Practice 80 at p.81 and by *Doyle* [1994] 10 Insolvency Law and Practice 134 at p.140.

[75] [2000] Ch. 40 at 50E, affirming that in relation to the priority of liquidation expenses, the effect of section 251 is that it is irrelevant whether the floating charge crystallises prior to or after liquidation.

Re M.C. Bacon Limited,[76] that the liquidator's expenses were not recoverable as liquidation expenses at all.[77] However, in an earlier part of his judgment Chadwick L.J. applied the decision in *Portbase*, affirming the view that following the 1986 Act it makes no difference for the purposes of priorities whether the floating charge crystallised before or after liquidation. Given that the *Mond v. Hammond Suddards* case involved the crystallisation of the charge by the appointment of a receiver, Chadwick L.J.'s judgment must also be taken to be inconsistent with any argument based upon section 40 of the 1986 Act that Portbase is limited to cases involving crystallisation other than by the appointment of a receiver (see above).

It is notable that the correctness or applicability of *Portbase* was not challenged in argument in *Mond v. Hammond Suddards*. It may be that the opportunity for the Court of Appeal to reconsider the decision in *Portbase* will arise if and when it is called upon to resolve the manifest conflict between the decisions in *Mond v. Hammond Suddards* and *Re Exchange Travel (Holdings) Limited (No. 3), Katz v. McNally*[78] in relation to the issue of whether the costs of unsuccessful proceedings by a liquidator are automatically payable as liquidation expenses or not.[79]

6. END OF RECEIVER'S AGENCY/CONTINUATION OF POWERS

(a) Termination of agency

The winding-up order or resolution for winding-up terminates the **11–036** receiver's agency for the company.[80] The powers given by the debenture to exploit the company's undertaking and assets, however, continue unaffected, save only that they cannot be exercised so as to create any new debt or fresh liability.[81] The receiver can, therefore, carry on the business of the company,[82] get in and realise the company's assets[83] and take proceedings in the name of the company to recover assets.[84] He

---

[76] [1991] Ch. 127.

[77] In so doing, Chadwick L.J. did not deal with the contrary dicta of Phillips and Morritt L.JJ. in *Katz v. McNally* [1997] 2 B.C.L.C. 579, CA, which was not cited to the Court of Appeal in Mond: see further paras. 21–056 *et seq.* below.

[78] [1997] 2 B.C.L.C. 579, CA.

[79] As to which see the discussion in paragraphs 21–056 *et seq.* below.

[80] Insolvency Act 1986, s. 44(1) (a) (administrative receivers), *Gosling v. Gaskell* [1897] A.C. 575, HL; *Barrows v. Chief Land Registrar, The Times*, October 20, 1977, *per* Whitford J. (winding-up order); *Thomas v. Todd* [1926] 2 K.B. 511; The appointment of provisional liquidators of a company appears similarly to terminate the agency: see above, para. 2–14.

[81] Winding-up merely determines the receiver's power to pledge the company's credit: *per* Needham J. in *Mercantile Credit Ltd v. Atkins* [1985] 1 N.S.W.L.R. 670 at 679, affirmed 10 A.C.L.R. 153.

[82] *Gosling v. Gaskell* [1897] A.C. 595.

[83] *Re Henry Pound Son & Hutchins* (1889) 42 Ch.D. 402, CA.

[84] *Goughs Garage v. Pugsley* [1930] 1 K.B. 615, CA. The receiver will personally be at risk as to costs: see below, para. 11–042. The requirement on the receiver not to render the company liable for costs is analogous to the requirement placed on directors suing in the name of the company during a receivership to indemnify the company against any liability for costs: see above, Chap. 2.

may do so either as agent for the debenture-holder or as principal: "If
the receiver continues to act, he does not automatically become the
agent of the mortgagee but he may become so if the mortgagee treats
him as such."[85] For the receiver to become the agent of the debenture-
holder it will have to be shown that the relationship of principal and
agent has been constituted between them.[86] Ordinarily, the receiver
carries on the business and exercises his other surviving powers as
principal,[87] incurs personal liability[88] but claims a right of indemnity out
of any assets in his hands.[89]

11–037   As a principal, the receiver will not be bound by any restriction on the
powers of the company. Where the receiver acts as agent of the
company, the company, and hence the receiver, will be bound by
statutory and other restrictions on the company's actions.[90]

(b) Realisation and disposal of assets

11–038 The termination of the receiver's agency does not prevent the receiver
from realising the assets charged.[91]

11–039   Although section 127 of the Insolvency Act 1986 prevents valid
dispositions of the company's property after the commencement of the
winding-up, this does not apply to dispositions by a receiver of property
contained in a relevant charge.[92] Despite the winding-up, the receiver is

---

[85] Per Mann J. in American Express International Banking Corp v. Hurley [1985] 3 All
E.R. 564 at 568 (citing Re Wood [1941] Ch. 112); Edmonds v. Westland Bank Ltd [1991] 2
N.Z.L.R. 655.

[86] Royal Bank of Scotland v. O'Shea (unreported, February 3, 1998), per Morritt L.J.

[87] Gaskell v. Gosling [1896] 1 Q.B. 669 at 699, per Rigby L.J. (dissenting) whose
judgment was upheld on appeal by the House of Lords. The Cork Report, para. 461
suggested that legislation was appropriate to clarify the receiver's position after the
termination of his agency, but this was not included in the Insolvency Act 1985.

[88] Sowman v. David Samuel Trust [1978] 1 W.L.R. 22 at 26; Gaskell v. Gosling [1896] 1
Q.B. 669.

[89] Insolvency Act 1986, s. 44(1)(c) (administrative receivers); Insolvency Act 1986,
s. 37(1) (non-administrative receivers).

[90] See e.g. Demite Ltd v. Protec Health Ltd & ors. [1998] B.C.C. 638: receivers, as agents
of the company, sold the business of the company in receivership to a party connected with
a former director of the company, without obtaining the approval of the members of the
company in general meeting. The sale was held to be voidable at the election of the
company, under s. 320 of the Companies Act 1985.

[91] Gaskell v. Gosling [1897] A.C. 595, per Rigby L.J.; Sowman v. David Samuel Trust Ltd
[1978] 1 W.L.R. 22; Barrows v. Chief Land Registrar, The Times, October 20, 1977: Re
Sobam BV and anor [1996] 1 B.C.L.C. 446. Nor does it prejudice his lien securing his
entitlement to an indemnity against liabilities properly incurred prior to termination out of
the assets of the company: Hill v. Venning [1979] 4 A.C.L.R.555.

[92] Sowman v. David Samuel Trust Ltd [1978] 1 W.L.R. 22 at 30C, per Goulding J.; Re
Henry Pound Son & Hutchins (1889) 42 Ch.D. 402 at 421, per Cotton L.J.; Re Landmark
Corporation Ltd (1968) 88 W.N. (Pt. 1) (N.S.W.) 195; Re Otway Coal Co. Ltd [1953] V.L.R.
557, per O'Bryan J. at 565; Sheahan v. Carrier Air Conditioning Pty Ltd (1996) 189 C.L.R.
407, H.Ct of Australia). Re Clifton Place Garage Ltd [1970] Ch. 477, CA does not suggest
the contrary. The moneys sought (unsuccessfully) to be recovered as void dispositions in
that case were moneys of a subsidiary and were not charged under the debenture: see the
facts set out at 479–480 and Re Margart Pty Ltd [1985] B.C.L.C. 314 at 319.

entitled to continue or take legal or other action[93] in the name of the company.[94]

Despite the winding-up, the receiver may take possession of the **11–040** property subject to the charge.[95] The receiver will require the leave of the court to take possession of the company's assets if a court-appointed liquidator has possession of those assets. The need to obtain leave in such a case is based on the fact that the court-appointed liquidator in a compulsory winding-up is an officer of the court.[96] It follows that leave is also required where a provisional liquidator has possession and refuses to deliver up, but not in the case of a voluntary liquidator. Leave is given "as of right".

(c) Costs of action
The right of a receiver to take or continue proceedings in the name of **11–041** the company to preserve its assets is part of the debenture-holder's security and accordingly survives winding-up.[97]

Where, after a winding-up order or resolution to wind up, the receiver **11–042** is suing in the name of the company, he does so as a principal in the exercise of the powers granted by the debenture, so that costs may be ordered against him personally or to be payable as expenses of the receivership.[98] The costs of defending an action adopted by a receiver after the defendant company has gone into liquidation may similarly be payable by the receiver.[99]

(d) Leases
Any authority to impose on the company obligations, other than the **11–043** usual qualified covenant for quiet enjoyment, by a grant of a lease would probably be determined on a winding-up.[1]

---

[93] *Bacal Contracting Ltd v. Modern Engineering (Bristol) Ltd* [1980] 2 All E.R. 655.

[94] *Gough's Garages Ltd v. Pugsley* [1930] 1 K.B. 615 (application for new lease in exercise of statutory rights); *Newhart Ltd v. Co-op Commercial Bank* [1978] Q.B. 814. To the opposite effect, see the *dictum* of Cotton L.J. in *Re Henry Pound Son & Hutchins* (1889) 42 Ch.D. 402 at 421, although his view may simply have been based on the construction of the particular debenture in question: see the explanation of the *dictum* in *Kelaw Pty Ltd v. Catco Development Pty Ltd* (1989) 15 N.S.W.L.R. 587 at 592, *per* Brownie J.

[95] *Re Henry Pound Son & Hutchins* (1889) 42 Ch.D. 402 at 422–423; *Re Potters Oils Ltd (No. 2)* [1986] 1 W.L.R. 201 at 206A–206B, *per* Hoffmann J.; *Re Landmark Corporation Ltd* (1968) 88 W.N. (Pt. 1) (N.S.W.) 195 at 196–197, where Street J. suggests that unless the liquidator challenges the receiver's right to possession, leave need not be sought.

[96] *Re Henry Pound Son & Hutchins* (1889) 42 Ch.D. 402 at 422; *Re Potters Oils Ltd (No. 2)* [1986] 1 W.L.R. 201.

[97] *Goughs Garages Ltd v. Pugsley* [1930] 1 K.B. 615; *Newman Bros v. Allum* [1934] N.Z.L.R. 694.

[98] *Bacal Contracting Ltd v. Modern Engineering (Bristol) Ltd* [1980] 2 All E.R. 655; *S & M Hotels v. Family Housing Association* (unreported, CA, Transcript 1979/132). See also *Kelaw Pty Ltd v. Catco Developments Pty Ltd* (1989) 15 N.S.W.L.R. 587 and C. de Kerloy, "The Personal Liability of Liquidators and Administrative Receivers for the Costs of an Unsuccessful Action", Receivers, Administrators and Liquidators Quarterly (2000) Vol. 4, issue 1, 13.

[99] *Anderson v. Hyde* [1996] 2 B.C.L.C. 144 (Northern Ireland Court of Appeal)

[1] See above, para. 9–084.

[2] Insolvency Act 1986, s. 36.

7. EFFECT ON RECEIVER'S REMUNERATION

11–044 In a winding-up, the liquidator has a statutory power to apply to the court to fix the remuneration of a receiver.[2] The court has power to fix such remuneration in relation to a period prior to the application, even where the receiver has died or ceased to act prior to the application. In special circumstances, the court may require repayment of all or part of the remuneration paid for any period prior to the making of the order. The court will, however, only interfere where the remuneration can clearly be seen to be excessive.[3]

8. CUSTODY OF BOOKS AND DOCUMENTS

11–045 Despite an order or resolution to wind up, the receiver will be entitled to documents necessary to support the debenture-holder's title to assets charged.[4] A liquidator will be entitled to documents relating to the management and business of the company in so far as they are not needed to support such title.[5]

11–046 Although there is authority to the effect that a court-appointed receiver can be compelled to deliver documents to a liquidator entitled to them on receipt of an undertaking to produce them to the receiver on request,[6] there is no such authority with respect to other receivers. However, general practice supports the proposition that delivery up in return for an undertaking and subsequent production on request should occur and could be compelled in respect of non-administrative receivers.[7]

11–047 Under section 234 of the Insolvency Act 1986, an administrative receiver can apply as an "office-holder" to the court to compel "any person" to deliver to him books, papers or records "to which the company appears to be entitled". The phrase "any person" is wide enough to cover a liquidator.[8] The application should normally be made on notice.[9] Questions of disputed ownership will now normally be decided by the courts on such an application,[10] but not where this issue falls for decision by a foreign court.[11] Likewise under section 234, a liquidator can apply as an "office-holder" for delivery up of papers and documents except in so far as they are needed to support the debenture-holder's title to the charged assets, since these latter documents would not be ones to which the company (as against the debenture-holder) would "appear to be entitled".

---

[3] *Re Potters Oils Ltd* [1986] 1 W.L.R. 201. For court-appointed receivers, see below, para. 22–029.

[4] *Re Landmark Corporation Ltd* (1968) 88 W.N. (Pt. 1) (N.S.W.) 195.

[5] Kerr, *op cit.*, p. 435.

[6] *Engel v. South Metropolitan Brewing Co.* [1892] 1 Ch. 442.

[7] See Kerr, *op cit.*, p. 435.

[8] *Re First Express Ltd* [1991] B.C.C. 782.

[9] *ibid.* and see above, Chap. 5.

[10] *Re London Iron and Steel Co. Ltd* [1970] B.C.L.C. 372; and see *Re Coslett Construction Ltd* [1998] Ch. 495

[11] *Re Leyland DAF Ltd* [1994] 2 B.C.L.C. 106.

Whilst both administrative receivers and liquidators have the ability to **11–048** seek orders for the production of documents held subject to a lien under section 236 of the 1986 Act,[12] receivers do not have the additional assistance of section 246, which makes unenforceable liens over documents as against, *inter alia*, liquidators and provisional liquidators to the extent that the enforcement of the lien would deny possession of the books, papers, etc. The special assistance to liquidators does not extend to "documents which give title to property and are held as such".[13]

9. ACCOUNTS

By statute[14] a liquidator may require a receiver to render accounts of **11–049** receipts and payments and pay over any sums payable to the liquidator.

10. CALLS ON CAPITAL

As between a non-administrative receiver and a liquidator, calls after a **11–050** winding-up order or resolution can only be made by the liquidator.[15] If the liquidator fails or neglects to make a call, the non-administrative receiver can apply to the court for an order requiring the liquidator to make the call or authorising the receiver to use the liquidator's name to make the call.[16] Although the Insolvency Act 1986 gives administrative receivers an apparently unrestricted power to make calls on uncalled capital,[17] it is suggested that the power should be construed as exercisable only until a liquidation in accordance with the rules that govern other receivers. It is unlikely that the legislators intended that, after a liquidation, both the liquidator and the receiver should have concurrent powers to make calls: it is sufficient that the administrative receiver can compel the liquidator to exercise his power.

11. VOIDABLE PREFERENCE AND MISFEASANCE

Prior to the Insolvency Act 1986, where a liquidator recovered sums of **11–051** money in respect of a "fraudulent preference"[18] the recovery was held to be designed to benefit unsecured creditors and so fell outside assets charged by a debenture.[19] The position is the same under the 1986

---

[12] *Re Aveling Barford Ltd* (1988) 4 B.C.C. 548 and see above, Chap. 5.

[13] s. 246(3). The meaning (or lack of meaning) of the words "held as such" is discussed in *Re SEIL Trade Finance Ltd* [1992] B.C.C. 538.

[14] Insolvency Act 1986, ss. 38 and 41.

[15] *Fowler v. Broad's Patent Co.* [1893] 1 Ch. 724. The rationale for the rule is "that the moment you have got a liquidation, the call-making power is limited to the statutory power of making calls in a winding up", *per* Vaughan Williams J. at 730.

[16] *Fowler v. Broad's Patent Co.* [1893] 1 Ch. 724; *Re Westminster Syndicate Ltd* (1908) 99 L.T. 924; *Re South Australian Barytes Ltd* (1977) 3 A.C.L.R. 52 at 63.

[17] Insolvency Act 1986, s. 42 and Sched. 1, para. 19.

[18] Under the Companies Act 1948, s. 321, replaced by the Companies Act 1985, s. 615.

[19] *Re Yagerphone* [1935] Ch. 392; *Re MC Bacon Ltd* [1991] Ch. 127 at 137; see also *Re Quality Camera Co. Property Ltd* (1965) 83 W.N. (Pt. 1) (N.S.W.) 226; [1965] N.S.W.R. 1330.

Act.[20] If the subject-matter of the preference was not money, but specific and identifiable property, the subject of the floating charge, on its recovery this probably fell within the property charged by the debenture.[21] In any case, where the recoveries fell outside the charge, they constituted "assets of the company available for payment of general creditors". Again, it is suggested that the position is the same under the 1986 Act.

11–052   The debenture-holder or receiver has no right to bring proceedings to recover property invoking the statutory voidable preference provisions.[22] This can only be done by the liquidator, and he should not do so, if the property recovered falls within a charge, unless:

> (a) the debenture-holder agrees to give up his claim on the property recovered for the benefit of all the creditors[23]; or
>
> (b) (it is thought) the interests of the unsecured creditors require that this action be taken (*e.g.* because the recovery will produce a surplus of secured assets over secured liabilities, leaving a balance available for unsecured creditors).[24]

The same reasoning is equally applicable to recoveries by the liquidator under the Insolvency Act 1986 in respect of "transactions at an undervalue"[25] and "extortionate credit transactions".[26]

11–053   In case of such recoveries by an administrator, it is thought that the same principle applies during the period of administration or if the administration is immediately followed by a liquidation. But (in the absence of some provision in a scheme of arrangement precluding this result) if the administration order is discharged and liquidation does not immediately follow, the recovery may fall within the scope of a charge created by a debenture whether prior or subsequent to the recovery.

---

[20] *Re Oasis Merchandising Services Ltd (in liq), Ward v. Aitken* [1998] Ch. 170, CA; *Re Exchange Travel (Holdings) Limited (No. 3), Katz v. McNally* [1997] 2 B.C.L.C. 579, CA.; *Re Floor Fourteen Ltd* [1999] 2 B.C.L.C. 666.

[21] See *N.A. Kratzmann Pty Ltd v. Tucker (No. 2)* (1968) 123 C.L.R. 295, HCt of Australia); *Ross v. Taylor* [1985] S.L.T. 387; *Bank of New Zealand v. Essington Developments Pty Ltd* (1990) 5 A.C.S.R. 86 at 89–90, *per* McLelland J.

[22] Insolvency Act 1986, s. 239. It is considered that the change in the wording of the preference provisions has made no difference in this regard. In *Re MC Bacon Ltd* [1991] Ch. 127 Millett J., at 137, rejected the argument that, since s. 239(3) empowered the court to restore the position to what it would have been had the preference not been given (when the assets given in order to prefer the creditor would have been subject to the charge), the proceeds of a successful s. 239 action would belong to the debenture-holder.

[23] *Ex p. Cooper* (1875) L.R. 10 Ch. App. 510 at 511; *Willmott v. London Celluloid Co.* (1886) 34 Ch.D. 147, CA. See also *Albert Gregory Ltd v. C. Niccol Ltd* (1916) 16 SR. (N.S.W.) 214; *Couve v. J. Pierre Couve Ltd* [1933] 49 C.L.R. 486.

[24] Any recovery for the secured creditor may benefit the unsecured creditors by reducing the amount of his unsecured indebtedness, in respect of which he will compete with the unsecured creditors. On the other hand, the effect of a successful claim under s. 239 might be make the respondent an unsecured creditor in a sum similar to the reduction in the secured creditor's unsecured claim. Nevertheless, unsecured creditors might benefit where, for example, the value of property given in discharge of a debt has increased significantly since the discharge.

[25] Insolvency Act 1986, s. 238.

[26] *ibid.*, s. 244.

Recoveries by a liquidator in respect of wrongful trading claims **11–054** under section 214 of the Insolvency Act 1986 are not caught by a charge over the company's assets, since such claims are special statutory rights in liquidation designed to benefit unsecured creditors[27] and therefore the same considerations apply as in the case of voidable preference recoveries. The same applies to fraudulent trading claims under section 213.[28]

Recoveries by a liquidator for "misfeasance" (breach of duty) against **11–055** directors and others will usually fall within the property charged.[29]

Following the decision of the Court of Appeal in *West Mercia* **11–056** *Safetyware Ltd v. Dodd*,[30] it seems that many proceedings under the fraudulent trading, wrongful trading, voidable preference and undervalue provisions[31] could instead (or in the alternative) be based on misfeasance. Given the obvious advantage to the debenture-holder of the proceedings being brought in misfeasance, the receiver should ensure that the liquidator agrees in such cases to make a misfeasance claim and agrees a fair method of appropriating recoveries between different heads of claim. Failing such agreement, the receiver should consider whether he should mount concurrent proceedings in the name of the company and seek to have those heard with the liquidator's proceedings.

12. RATES

The position upon liquidation in relation to rates is dealt with in **11–057** Chapter 20.

---

[27] *Re MC Bacon Ltd* [1991] Ch. 127, *per* Millett J. at 136–138. *Re Oasis Merchandising Services Ltd, supra.* Knox J. in *Re Produce Marketing Consortium Ltd (No. 2)* [1989] B.C.L.C. 520 at 554a stated that the fruits of successful s. 214 proceedings would go to the debenture-holders, though it is not clear whether any argument was addressed on the point and no relevant cases were cited.

[28] See *Oasis Merchandising Services Ltd (supra)* at [1998] Ch. 170, CA.

[29] *Re Anglo-Austrian Printing Union* [1895] 2 Ch. 891; s. 212 of the Insolvency Act 1986. This section, (unlike the Insolvency Act 1986, ss. 214, 238–239), does not create a right or remedy but merely a special procedure for recovery. Thus, whereas the cause of action which is the subject of a misfeasance summons may exist prior to the winding-up of the company, and thus can be subject to the floating charge, rights of action under ss. 214, 239–40 exist solely by virtue of the winding-up of the company and cannot exist before such winding up. See also *Re Asiatic Electric Co. Property Ltd* (1970) 92 W.N. (N.S.W.) 361, *per* Street J. at 362; [1970] 2 N.S.W.R. 612 at 613.

[30] (1988) 4 B.C.C. 30. See also *Facia Footwear Ltd (in admin.) v. Hinchcliffe* [1998] 1 B.C.L.C. 218; *Berg Sons & Co. Ltd v. Mervyn Hampton Adams* [1993] B.C.L.C. 1045. The breach of fiduciary duty is actionable by the company, and not at the suit of any individual creditor: *Yukong Line Ltd of Korea v. Rendsburg Investments Corporation of Liberia* [1998] 2 B.C.L.C. 485. In *Knight v. Frost* [1999] 1 B.C.L.C. 364 at 382 Hart J. decided that in order for a preference to be actionable as a misfeasance, the breach of duty must have taken place within the time limits imposed in relation to voidable preferences by the 1986 Act. The mere fact that a payment would be recoverable as against the recipient under s. 239 of the 1986 Act does not necessarily mean that the directors of the company which authorised the payment are *ipso facto* liable for misfeasance: *Re Brian D. Pierson (Contractors) Ltd* [1999] B.C.C. 26, where it was held *obiter* that misfeasance would not be found where s. 239 was satisfied only on the basis of a statutory presumption as to desire.

[31] Insolvency Act 1986, ss. 213, 214, 239 and 240.

13. RECEIVER'S INDEMNITY UPON HANDING OVER ESTATE TO LIQUIDATOR

11–058 It is sometimes convenient for a receiver to hand over the estate of the company to a liquidator without fully carrying out the administration required in the receivership. In such a situation, a suitable indemnity should be taken.[32]

14. EFFECT ON CONTRACTS OF EMPLOYMENT AND OTHER CONTRACTS

11–059 As a general rule, liquidation of a company, whether voluntary or compulsory, does not itself operate to determine subsisting contracts between the company and third parties, although there is an exception in the case of contracts which by their express terms or by necessary implication cannot survive liquidation. Hence arises the need for the statutory provision for disclaimer of unprofitable contracts.[33] Special rules have developed in the case of contracts of employment.[34]

15. PUBLIC EXAMINATION OF THE RECEIVER

11–060 Where the company is being wound up by the court, the Official Receiver may, at any time before dissolution of the company, apply to the court for the public examination (amongst others) of any person who has acted as an administrator or receiver or manager, and (unless the court otherwise orders) shall make such an application if he is requested to do so by (a) one-half in value of the company's creditors or (b) three-quarters in value of the company's contributories.[35]

---

[32] Since each situation is different, legal advice should preferably be obtained in each case.

[33] Insolvency Act 1986, s. 178(3).

[34] See below, para. 19–04.

[35] Insolvency Act 1986, s. 133.

CHAPTER 12

RETENTION OF TITLE

"Unsecured creditors rank after . . . holders of floating charges and **12–001** they receive a raw deal . . ."[1] An unpaid supplier of goods in a receivership is a mere unsecured creditor for the price and the receiver can make use of the goods for the benefit of the receivership without paying him. The supplier in turn will often strive to gain priority by means of provisions in the contract of supply which attempt to retain his title to the goods or may insist that he be given a charge in respect of the goods supplied.

It has long been recognised that the owner of goods can lease them to **12–002** a company and yet retain legal title so as to gain priority over other creditors. In *McEntire v. Crossley Bros. Ltd*,[2] the suppliers hired a machine to an individual on the basis that once a number of instalments were paid title would pass. Meanwhile a plate was to remain affixed to the machine stating that the suppliers were the owners. The House of Lords held that the agreement did not constitute an unregistered charge and title did not pass to the individual's assignee in bankruptcy.

Alternatively, the supplier can attempt to retain the equitable or **12–003** beneficial interest in the goods by means of a trust which would make the company a bare trustee of the property. In that case the trusteeship will be recognised and enforced as long as the property or its proceeds are traceable and unless and until the property has been disposed of or charged to a purchaser in good faith for value without notice of the trust.[2a] Such an attempt was made in *Re Bond Worth Ltd*[3] where the sellers attempted to retain "equitable and beneficial ownership" of the goods supplied until paid for or resold, but the buyer's complete freedom to deal with the goods in the ordinary course of business was held to be inconsistent with the notion of a trust creating an absolute rather than a security interest and on its true construction the contract was found to create a registrable floating charge.[4]

---

[1] *Per* Templeman L.J. in *Borden (U.K.) Ltd v. Scottish Timber* [1981] Ch. 25, CA.

[2] [1893] A.C. 457, HL.

[2a] The receiver who has disposed of the property without notice of the trust is subject to no personal liability: see *Competitive Insurance Company v. Davies Investments Ltd* [1975] 1 W.L.R. 1240.

[3] [1980] Ch. 228.

[4] This result may be contrasted with the successful attempt to create a trust over goods supplied and their proceeds in the Australian case of *Associated Alloys Pty Ltd v. ACN 001 452 106 Pty Ltd* (2000) 171 A.L.R. 568 (High Court of Australia). As discussed below, it is doubtful whether an English court would take the same approach to the issue of the creation of a trust as the majority in the High Court of Australia. The judgment of Kirby J., who dissented on the issue of the creation of a trust, contains a brief but useful summary of the state of the law relating to retention of title clauses in England, Scotland, Ireland, New Zealand, Australia, Canada and the United States.

12–004   As a further alternative the supplier may require the company to grant a charge over the property supplied and/or other assets of the company. In this event the charge will usually only be effective against another creditor or the liquidator of the company if registered.[5]

These situations and devices are considered further below.

1. RETENTION OF LEGAL TITLE

12–005 The most frequent retention of title provision arising in the course of supply of goods on credit provides for the supplier to retain title until payment or other performance of some other obligation by the buyer.

12–006   Whether the supplier retains his legal title under the arrangement with the company depends not only on the language and form but also on the substance of the transaction. The parties' intentions and the label they have placed upon the transaction are a guide, but the real question in each case is the true nature of the substantive rights of the parties. If the substantive rights or their exercise are inconsistent with retention, then there will be no retention of title.[6]

12–007   In *Re Peachdart*[7] the seller supplied leather to the company to be made into handbags. The conditions of sale reserved title to the leather until payment was received in full. The seller argued as part of his case that throughout the process of manufacture the company remained a bailee of the goods. This contention was rejected by Vinelott J.:

> "It seems to me that the parties must have the intention that at least after a piece of leather had been appropriated to be manufactured into a handbag and work had started on it (when the leather would cease to have any significant value as raw material) the leather would cease to be the exclusive property of [the sellers] . . . and that [the sellers] would thereafter have a charge on handbags in the course of manufacture and on the distinctive products which would come into existence at the end of the process of manufacture (the value of which would be derived for the most part from [the company's] reputation and skill in design and the skill in his workforce) . . . that I accept does some violence to the language . . ."[8]

12–008   In *Chaigley Farms Ltd v. Crawford Kaye & Grayshire Ltd*,[9] the retention of title clause extended to "livestock" but the object of the contract was the supply of animals for slaughter. The buyer was held to have the authority to slaughter and thereby acquire title to the various parts of the animal.[10] Such authority continued despite receivership until specifically

---

[5] Companies Act 1985, s. 395, and see above, Chap. 3.
[6] *Welsh Development Agency v. Export Finance Co.* [1992] B.C.C. 270, CA; *Orion Finance v. Crown Financial Management* [1996] B.C.C. 621 at 625–627 *per* Millett L.J.; and see above, paras 3–014 to 3–15.
[7] [1984] Ch. 131.
[8] *ibid.* at 142.
[9] [1996] B.C.C. 957
[10] That result is queried below.

revoked. Thus, the retention of title may be defeasible if the company is given power to deal with or change the identity of the goods.

2. RETENTION OF BENEFICIAL OWNERSHIP

As with the retention of legal title, the substantive rights of the parties **12–009** will decide whether the beneficial ownership is retained. For there to be an effective retention of beneficial ownership there must be a duty imposed to segregate the goods and proceeds and keep them distinct. The court must also be satisfied that the true relationship between the parties is a fiduciary one, rather than merely that of debtor and creditor.

One of the earliest authorities in this area was the *Romalpa* case,[11] **12–010** where the relevant clause provided for retention of title until payment of everything due from the company to the seller. The company was obliged (*inter alia*) to store the goods in such a way as to identify them as the property of the seller. Although there was no provision for keeping the proceeds of resale separate, the Court of Appeal held that the proceeds could be traced by the sellers on the grounds that the various provisions of the retention of title clause replaced the normal debtor/creditor relationship of seller and buyer with a fiduciary relationship. The decision is open to question and the case has frequently been distinguished[12]; it may well have been the concession by the receiver that the company had been a bailee of the goods which was crucial in leading to this result.[13] Four more recent authorities illustrate with greater clarity the proposition stated at the beginning of this section.

In *Re Andrabell Ltd*[14] the seller supplied travel bags to the company **12–011** and reserved title until payment in full. All the bags were sold by the company in the ordinary course of business and the proceeds of sale were paid into the company's ordinary current account. The lack of any obligation to store the goods separately and the lack of any obligation to keep the proceeds of sale separate were important factors in the decision that there was no fiduciary relationship and that the seller had no interest in the proceeds of sale.

In *Re Shulman Enterprises*[15] the company was a freight forwarder with **12–012** agency contracts in the IATA common form with various carriers. This form of contract provided that moneys received by the company in respect of freight as agent for the carrier belonged to the carrier. The company had also granted a security interest over all its assets to its bankers. The company filed for bankruptcy under Chapter XI[16] and a dispute arose

---

[11] *Aluminium Industrie Vaassen B. V. v. Romalpa Aluminium Ltd* [1976] 1 W.L.R. 676, CA.

[12] See below, para. 12–013. In *Specialist Plant Services v. Braithwaite* (1987) 3 B.C.C. 119 the opposite result to that in the *Romalpa* case was achieved by the Court of Appeal despite the use of similar wording in the clause. It is considered that the *Romalpa* case could now be regarded as wrongly decided.

[13] *Re Bond Worth* [1980] Ch. 228 at 662.

[14] [1984] 3 All E.R. 407.

[15] 744 F. 2d 393 (1983).

[16] For Chap. 11 of the Bankruptcy Code (U.S.), see below, para. 23–01.

whether receivables for freight belonged to the carriers or the bank. The United States Court of Appeals for the Second Circuit held that the court was not bound by the terminology of the IATA agreement:

> ". . . where the public interests or the rights of third parties are involved, the relationship between contracting parties must be determined by its real character rather than by the form and colour that the parties have given it."

The absence of any provision requiring the company to segregate receipts of freight from its own moneys was an important factor in leading the Court to hold that, despite the language used, the relationship was simply that of debtor and creditor, and that the bankers, and not the carriers, were accordingly entitled to the receivables.

12–013 In *E. Pfeiffer Weinkellerei-Weineinkauf GmbH & Co. v. Arbuthnot Factors Ltd*[17] the claimant, Pfeiffer, supplied wine to Springfield Wine Importers Ltd, on terms that Springfield could sell on in business operations carried on in due order, and: "all claims that he gets from the sale or due to another legal reason regarding our goods, with all rights including his profit amounting to his obligations towards us, will be passed on to us".[18] Springfield sub-sold the wine to sub-purchasers on credit terms and then entered into a factoring agreement with Arbuthnot Factors Ltd in relation to the money owed by the sub-purchasers. Pfeiffer argued that the relationship between itself and Springfield was a fiduciary one, and that accordingly it was entitled to the proceeds of the sub-sales as beneficial owner. Arbuthnot Factors Ltd argued that any beneficial interest which Pfeiffer had in the proceeds was in the nature of a charge which was void for non-registration. Phillips J. distinguished the *Romalpa* decision and held that the provisions of the retention of title clause were inconsistent with a fiduciary relationship, and that the true relationship between Pfeiffer and Springfield was that of debtor and creditor with Pfeiffer having an interest by way of security in respect of the debts created by the sub-sales. Such a registrable charge was void as against Springfield's creditors for non-registration.[19]

12–014 In *Compaq Computer Ltd v. Abercorn Group Ltd*[20] Compaq Computer Ltd had supplied computer products to Abercorn Group Ltd under a dealership agreement which reserved title until payment of the price of those products and any other sums owing by Abercorn Group Ltd to Compaq Computer Ltd Abercorn Group Ltd sub-sold these goods, and assigned the proceeds of such sub-sales under an invoice discounting agreement to the second defendant, Kellock. Compaq Computer Ltd argued that Abercorn Group Ltd held the goods as bailee and agent by virtue of the dealership agreement, that Abercorn Group Ltd were under a fiduciary duty to account for these proceeds to Compaq

---

[17] (1987) 3 B.C.C. 608.
[18] See at 610, and see below, para. 12–059, for the full clause.
[19] See *per* Phillips J. at 615–616.
[20] [1991] B.C.C. 484.

Computer Ltd, and that accordingly Compaq Computer Ltd were entitled to the proceeds of sale. The defendants argued that such rights as were created over the proceeds of sale were a charge on book debts or a floating charge on Abercorn Group Ltd's undertaking or property which was accordingly void for non-registration. Mummery J. held that the true relationship between Compaq Computer Ltd and Abercorn Group Ltd was not a fiduciary relationship.[21]

3. CREATION OF CHARGE

". . . any contract which, by way of security for the payment of a **12–015** debt, confers an interest in property defeasible or destructible upon payment of such debt, or appropriates such property for the discharge of the debt, must necessarily be regarded as creating a mortgage or charge . . ."[22]

". . . I can see nothing in principle to prevent a vendor and a purchaser of specific ascertained chattels from expressly agreeing that the vendor shall have a mortgage or charge over such chattels to secure the payment of the unpaid purchase price, in addition to or in substitution for any lien which might be conferred on him by the Sale of Goods Act . . ."[23]

Where the legal property in the goods remains in or is passed back to the seller a charge will be a legal charge. If, however, the legal property has passed to the company and remains with it, the charge will be equitable.[24]

Where a seller takes a charge from the company over goods sold to it **12–016** or over the proceeds of resale of such goods, the charge will usually fall within a class requiring registration under section 395 of the Companies Act 1985.[25] A charge over the goods themselves, under which the company remains in possession of the goods, will probably come within the category of charges which if executed by an individual would be registrable as a bill of sale.[26] A charge over future proceeds of sale, unless provision is made for paying the proceeds into a special account, is likely to be registrable as a floating charge.[27]

[21] See *per* Mummery J. at 495; see below, para. 12–15 below.

[22] *Per* Slade J. in *Re Bond Worth* [1980] Ch. 228 at 248.

[23] *ibid.* at 249.

[24] See para. 3–001 above, and the *dicta* of Atkin L.J. in *National Provincial and Union Bank v. Charnley* [1924] 1 K.B. 431 at 449; of Buckley L.J. in *Swiss Bank Corp. v. Lloyds Bank Ltd* [1982] A.C. 584 at 594, CA; and of Millett J. in *Re Charge Card Services Limited* [1987] Ch. 150 at 176.

[25] *Tatung v. Galex Telesure Ltd* (1989) 5 B.C.C. 325. The reasoning of the decision was approved by Hoffmann J. in *Re Weldtech Equipment Ltd* (1991) B.C.C. 16.

[26] See Gough, *Company Charges* (2nd edn. 1996) Chap. 18.

[27] *Siebe Gorman & Co. v. Barclays Bank* [1979] 2 Lloyd's Rep. 142; *Re Armagh Shoes* [1984] B.C.L.C. 405 (Northern Ireland, *per* Hutton J.); *Re Bond Worth* [1980] Ch. 228; *Re Brightlife Ltd* [1987] Ch. 200; *Royal Trust Bank v. National Westminster Bank* [1996] B.C.C. 613, *per* Millett L.J. at 618, 619.

12–017   If such a charge requires registration but is not registered, the company itself remains bound by the charge[28] but the charge is void as against a liquidator, administrator or creditor of the company.[29]

4. LOSS OF TITLE

12–018 Even where title is successfully retained as against a company, including its receiver, title may still be lost to third parties under certain rules of law applying in favour of purchasers in good faith in the interests of commerce. The most frequently encountered of such rules are encapsulated in sections 21 and 25 of the Sale of Goods Act 1979. In the case of each section, for the retained title of the seller to be lost to a third party purchaser, there must have been a sub-sale which purportedly passed title in the property from the original buyer to the third party purchaser.[30] It is not enough if there is merely an agreement to sell, and in this respect it should be noted that a sub-sale which is itself governed by a retention of title clause is merely an agreement to sell and not a sale.[31] Title can also be lost when goods supplied are incorporated into the goods of another or made into new goods during a manufacturing process. These possibilities are examined below.

(a) Buyer in possession

12–019 Section 25 of the Sale of Goods Act 1979 provides:

> "Where a person having bought or agreed to buy goods obtains, with the consent of the seller, possession of the goods or the documents of title to the goods, the delivery or transfer by that person, or by a mercantile agent acting for him, of the goods or documents of title, under any sale, pledge, or other disposition thereof, to any person receiving the same in good faith and without notice of any lien or other right of the original seller in respect of the goods, has the same effect as if the person making the delivery or transfer were a mercantile agent in possession of the goods or documents of title with the consent of the owner."

12–020 In *Archivent Sales & Developments Ltd v. Strathclyde*[32] the sellers agreed to sell goods to the company for incorporation into a building upon which the company was working as a contractor. The sellers retained title to the goods. The goods were delivered to site and were included in an interim certificate, which was paid by the employers. The company never paid the sellers and went into receivership. The sellers sued the employers, claiming title to the goods. The sellers argued that the

---

[28] At least whilst it is a going concern: see *Re Monolithic Building Co.* [1915] 1 Ch. 643.
[29] See above, paras 3–132 *et seq.*
[30] See *Shaw v. Commissioner of Police* [1987] 1 W.L.R. 1332, CA, especially at 1337 *per* Lloyd. L.J.
[31] *Re Highway Foods International Ltd* [1995] 1 B.C.L.C. 209.
[32] (1985) 27 Build. L.R. 98.

employers were not protected by the predecessor to section 25 of the Sale of Goods Act 1979 because the buyer company had never been in possession of the goods, since they passed directly into the control of the employers and because there was no delivery by the company to the employer. The Scottish Court of Session held that the employer's control did not preclude possession on the part of the company. Moreover, delivery to the employer by the company was established by evidence that the goods had been measured by the employer's surveyor and not rejected. Accordingly, the seller had lost title to the goods and title had been acquired by the employer.

In *Four Point Garage Ltd v. Carter*[33] a customer agreed to buy a **12–021** particular make and model of car from a dealer company. The dealer bought such a car from another dealer and arranged delivery direct to the customer. The other dealer retained title to the car. The customer's dealer went into liquidation having failed to pay for the car. Simon Brown J. held, *inter alia*, that title passed to the customer under section 25 of the Sale of Goods Act 1979 since no distinction could be drawn between, on the one hand, a delivery to a buyer who then delivers to a sub-buyer and, on the other hand, a direct delivery by a seller to a sub-buyer. The direct delivery constituted constructive delivery to the buyer and constructive delivery by the buyer to the sub-buyer.

(b) Apparent authority

Section 21 of the Sale of Goods Act 1979 provides in so far as material, **12–022** that:

> ". . . where goods are sold by a person who is not their owner, and who does not sell them under the authority or with the consent of the owner, the buyer acquires no better title to the goods than the seller had, unless the owner of the goods is by his conduct precluded from denying the seller's authority to sell."

In many cases, retention of title provisions expressly or impliedly authorise a resale and therefore the sale takes place with the authority or consent of the owner.[34] Where, however, resale is not permitted or is only permitted in circumstances not observed by the company, the question arises whether the seller is estopped by his conduct from claiming title as against the third party purchaser. The answer depends on whether the seller has "invested the person dealing with them with the indicia of property"[35] so as to estop the seller from asserting his claim to title.

(c) Accessio and specificatio

A seller who has successfully reserved title can nevertheless lose it in **12–023** certain circumstances where the goods are incorporated into the goods of another or made into a new object altogether.

---

[33] [1985] 3 All E.R. 12.

[34] For implied authorisation, see *Aluminium Industrie Vaassen BV v. Romalpa Aluminium Ltd* [1976] 1 W.L.R. 676 at 689, CA; *Re Bond Worth* [1980] Ch. 228 at 246; and *Four Point Garage v. Carter* [1985] 3 All E.R. 12 at 16, *per* Simon Brown J.

[35] *Per* Lord Halsbury in *Henderson v. Williams* [1895] 1 Q.B. 521 at 525.

12–024 In order to clarify this subject it is useful to look briefly to a system of law which has developed detailed principles, *i.e.* Roman law. The basic concepts are (a) accessio, the incorporation of an accessory belonging to A into a principal object belonging to B, whereby the accessory adheres to the principal, *e.g.* a handle to a cup, and (b) specificatio , the creation of a new product by A from the materials of B or of B and C, *e.g.* where grapes and sugar are made into wine.

12–025 The first question in either Roman or English law appears to be whether there is any effective contractual provision governing the ownership of the accessory or the new product as the case may be. Thus, Robert Goff L.J. in the *Clough Mill* case[36] stated that it was open to the parties to a sale contract to agree that a new product would belong to the seller.[37] Subject to established rules relating to charges, penalties, forfeiture, etc., there appears to be no reason why the parties cannot freely contract as to ownership in such cases. Such a contract will require careful drafting. In *Specialist Plant Services Ltd v. Braithwaite Ltd*[38] goods were supplied to the defendant on terms that:

> ". . . [if] the said goods and materials or any part thereof supplied hereunder in any way whatsoever become a constituent of another article or other articles the Company shall be given the ownership of this (these) new article(s) as surety for the full payment of what the customer owes the Company. To this end the Company and the customer now agree that the ownership of the article(s) in question, whether finished or not, are to be transferred to the Company . . ."[39]

12–026 The Company applied for an injunction to prevent the receiver from selling machines into which had been incorporated parts which it had supplied. The Court of Appeal held that the retention of title clause created a charge by way of security over the machines which was void for non-registration, and accordingly there was no basis for the granting of the injunction.[40]

12–027 In the absence of agreement, the Roman law rules were in summary as follows: if the goods of A and B were mixed so that they were readily separable, no change of ownership took place,[41] unless the goods of A. could be seen as an accessory of the goods of B (*e.g.* a handle and pan where the handle is attached by a screw). In that case the identity of the accessory merged with that of the principal and A lost his ownership. There were rules providing compensation for A.[42] Where A's materials were used to make a new object, one view was that the new object

---

[36] [1985] 1 W.L.R. 111, CA.
[37] At 119H.
[38] (1987) 3 B.C.C. 119.
[39] *ibid.*, at 120.
[40] See *per* Balcombe L.J. at 123.
[41] This was "confusio": see *the discussion in Foskett v. McKeown* [2000] 2 W.L.R. 1299 HL at 1311C–D, *per* Lord Hoffmann, 1316E–1317F *per* Lord Hope (dissenting) and 1336B–1337B *per* Lord Millett.
[42] See Buckland, *Textbook of Roman Law* (3rd ed., 1966), pp. 210–211.

belonged to the owner of the materials. Another view held that it belonged to the maker. Justinian effected a compromise solution whereby the new object belonged to its maker if not reducible to its original form but otherwise remained in the ownership of the owner of the materials.[43]

In English law, by contrast, the fact that A's goods have become **12–028** accessory to B's is immaterial if separation can take place without damage to the principal item: A retains his ownership.[44] If separation would involve such damage, A's ownership is lost by accession.[45] In the case of the creation of a new object, the *Borden* case[46] shows that where the new object is not reducible to its original form, the supplier of the material loses his ownership and prima facie the buyer/maker acquires title. This suggests that in this respect English law follows the Justinianic compromise. Where the skill and labour expended on the materials becomes a major component of value, English law will tend to imply an intention for title to vest in the maker.[47]

In *Chaigley Farms Ltd v. Crawford Kaye & Grayshire Ltd*,[48] it was held **12–029** that title was lost to animals upon slaughter, apparently (or at least partly) because the meat, having been separated from the hide, bone, blood, etc. was a new object. It is respectfully doubted whether meat is a new object. The actual result in the case could perhaps be justified on the basis that the intention of the parties on the facts of that case was limited to the seller retaining title in "livestock", which term in the context did not include slaughtered animals or the parts into which such animals were to be divided, such as hide, bones, blood, meat, etc.[49]

Where materials are incorporated into real property so as to become **12–030** part of the real property, title passes by operation of law to the owner of the land irrespective of any retention of title clause.[50]

If a party wrongfully mixes goods belonging to another with his own **12–031** goods of substantially the same nature and quality (*e.g.* oil), and they cannot be separated for practical purposes, the mixture is held in common by both parties such that the innocent party is entitled to receive from the mixture a quantity equal to that of his goods which went into the mixture. If there is doubt as to either the quantity or quality of the mixture, the matter should be resolved in the innocent party's favour and he is entitled to claim damages from the wrongdoer for losses suffered, in respect of quality or otherwise, as a result of the admixture.[51]

---

[43] *ibid.*, p. 215.

[44] *Hendy Lennox (Industrial Engines) v. Grahame Puttick* [1984] 1 W.L.R. 485. The summary of what this case decides in *Chaigley Farms Ltd v. Crawford, Kaye & Grayshire Ltd* [1996] B.C.C. 957 at 961D appears to confuse the English and Roman Law tests.

[45] *Appleby v. Myers* (1867) L.R. 2 C.P. 651 at 659–660, *per* Blackburn J.

[46] [1981] Ch. 25, CA.

[47] *Re Peachdart* [1984] Ch. 131.

[48] [1996] B.C.C. 957.

[49] See *ibid.* at p.963.

[50] See further below, Chap. 18.

[51] *Indian Oil Corporation Ltd v. Greenstone Shipping SA (Panama); the Ypatianna* [1988] Q.B. 345, *per* Staughton J. See also *Mercer v. Craven Grain Storage Ltd* [1994] C.L.C. 328, HL at 329E–G (storers of grain were not entitled to question the title of depositors of the grain because the storers were only bailees). See also *the discussion in Foskett v. McKeown* [2000] 2 W.L.R. 1299, HL at 1336–1337, *per* Lord Millett.

5. INCORPORATION OF THE RETENTION OF TITLE CLAUSE INTO THE CONTRACT

12–032 In order to discover whether title has been retained, one must first determine whether the retention of title clause has been incorporated in the contract between the seller and the company.

12–033 The clearest case of incorporation arises where the company has by some duly authorised agent signed a contractual document incorporating a retention of title clause into the relevant contract or contracts of sale. The signature will be effective even if the document is not read and even if it is in "regrettably small print".[52] A misrepresentation, however, about the effect of the clause will prevent it being incorporated, even by means of a signed document.[53] Lack of authority on the part of the signatory may also be a defence, subject to the question of implied or of ostensible authority. The signatory will be held to be impliedly authorised to sign the document if it is of a kind which is within the usual scope of a person in his position with the company.[54] He will be held to have ostensible authority if he was held out by the company as having authority to sign documents of that kind.[55] Other contractual defences also apply and thus the receiver will want to ascertain the circumstances in which any such document was executed.

12–034 In the absence of any signed document the seller must prove that the company was aware or ought to have been aware of the retention of title clause.[56] Another way of putting this is that the seller must have given reasonable notice of the clause.[57] The notice will prima facie not be sufficient if it is contained in a non-contractual document[58] or in a post-contractual document.[59] Thus, one might have thought that retention of title clauses contained in such post-contractual documents as invoices and delivery notes will be ineffective. However, the seller may have an argument based on a "course of dealing". This appears to mean that if there has been a course of transactions where post-contractual notice of the clause has been given, the company may be bound even though its agent or officer has not read the clause.[60] The rationale appears to be that the post-contractual notice is reasonable notice for the purposes of incorporation in future contracts.

---

[52] *L'Estrange v. Graucob* [1934] 2 K.B. 394.

[53] *Curtis v. Chemical Cleaning Co.* [1951] 1 K.B. 805.

[54] *Hely-Hutchinson v. Brayhead* [1968] 1 Q.B. 549, CA.

[55] *Freeman & Lockyer v. Buckhurst Park Props* [1964] 2 Q.B. 480 at 503, *per* Diplock L.J.; and see the very clear exposition in *British Bank of the Middle East v. Sun Life Assurance Co. of Canada (U.K.) Ltd* [1983] 2 Lloyd's Rep. 9, HL.

[56] *Per* Scrutton L.J. in *L'Estrange v. Graucob* [1934] 2 K.B. 394 at 403.

[57] *Parker v. SE. Ry.* (1877) 2 C.P.D. 416.

[58] *Chapelton v. Barry UDC* [1940] 1 K.B. 532; *McCutcheon v. MacBrayne* [1964] 1 W.L.R. 125; *Burnett v. Westminster Bank* [1966] 1 Q.B. 742.

[59] *Olley v. Marlborough Court* [1949] 1 K.B. 532; *Chapelton v. Barry UDC* [1940] 1 K.B. 532.

[60] *Spurling v. Bradshaw* [1956] 1 W.L.R. 461; *Snow v. Woodcroft* [1985] B.C.L.C. 54; *cf. British Crane Hire v. Ipswich Plant Hire* [1975] Q.B. 303.

There may be a difference in the degree of notice required to **12–035** incorporate a clause that might be regarded as an "unusual" type of retention of title clause as opposed to a "usual" one.[61] An allegation by a receiver that a clause is an "unusual" one and therefore needs some special degree of notice to be incorporated may require to be proved by evidence. In the *Robert Horne* case[62] the "unusual" nature of the clause was conceded. In the *John Snow* case[63] Boreham J. decided the clause was "not so unusual" in the absence of evidence to show that it was unusual.

There may also be an incorporation problem where the seller and the **12–036** company have used different forms with inconsistent terms. A provision in one set of terms stating that it overrides any terms put forward by the other party does not decide this conflict.[64] The correct analysis appears to be the traditional one of offer and acceptance.[65] Where the offer incorporates one set of terms and the acceptance incorporates an inconsistent set of terms, the acceptance amounts to a counter-offer.[66] The question then is whether the counter-offer is accepted, otherwise there is no consensus at all.[67]

6. EFFECT OF DIFFERENT TYPES OF RETENTION OF TITLE CLAUSE

(a) Introduction

"There has been a spate of decisions in recent years concerning **12–037** these so-called *Romalpa* cases. But it is of great importance to bear in mind that these cases have been concerned with different clauses, very often in materially different terms . . ."[68]

The types of retention of title clause commonly in use divide up between the "simple" type of clause where only title to the goods sold is attempted to be retained and the "complex" type of clause which attempts to create rights over proceeds of resale or hire. "Simple" and "complex" clauses are often combined in a series of clauses or sub-clauses. A distinction may also have to be drawn between "fixed" retentions, where title is retained only until the particular goods in question are paid for, and "floating" retentions, which provide for title to remain in the seller until, *e.g.* all sums due from the buyer company to the seller have been discharged.

---

[61] *Robert Horne Paper Co. Ltd v. Rioprint Ltd* (unreported, Tudor Evans J., November 10, 1978); *John Snow & Co. v. Woodcroft* [1985] B.C.L.C. 54.

[62] See above.

[63] See above.

[64] *Butler Machine Tool Co. v. Ex-Cell-o-Corp.* [1979] 1 W.L.R. 401 at 402.

[65] *ibid., per* Lawton and Bridge L.JJ.

[66] *ibid.*

[67] *ibid.*

[68] *Clough Mill v. Martin* [1985] 1 W.L.R. 111, *per* Goff L.J.

(b) Simple retention of title

12–038 Section 2 of the Sale of Goods Act 1979 defines a contract for the sale of goods as one ". . . by which the seller transfers or agrees to transfer the property in goods to the buyer . . .". Section 16 provides that in the case of a sale of unascertained goods no property in the goods is transferred unless and until the goods are ascertained. Section 17 provides that in the case of specific or ascertained goods property passes when the parties intend. Such intention is to be ascertained by looking to the terms of the contract, the parties' conduct and the circumstances of the case.

12–039 Section 18 of the Sale of Goods Act 1979 sets out detailed rules for ascertaining the presumed intention of the parties in relation to the passing of property if a different intention does not appear from the agreement. Generally speaking, in such cases property passes upon delivery.

12–040 Where goods have not been paid for, the seller has certain limited statutory rights, *e.g.* a lien whilst he remains in possession, and a right of stoppage in transitu.[69] Once the seller has parted with possession and the property in the goods, he normally has no satisfactory statutory remedy if the buyer becomes insolvent and defaults, even if the buyer still has possession of the goods.

12–041 Where the buyer goes into receivership, goods supplied by an unpaid seller in which the property has passed to the buyer are caught by the usual floating charge on stock, etc. In order to avoid this, a seller can attempt to insert into the contract of sale a clause whereby property in goods sold is not to pass unless and until it has been paid for. If effectively incorporated into the contract, there is no doubt that such a clause will be valid and effective to preserve the seller's rights to the goods against a debenture-holder.[70]

(c) Floating retention

12–042 The simple retention of title clause referred to above suffers from certain drawbacks. Often it is not easy to identify whether the particular goods held by a buyer going into receivership have been paid for. It may well happen that the goods still held by the buyer have been paid for but the buyer owes money to the seller for goods which have been resold. A common solution is to provide that property in goods is not to pass until all goods supplied have been paid for. In that case, as long as the account with the buyer has never swung into balance, any goods supplied by the seller and held by the buyer when it goes into receivership will be covered by the clause.

12–043 Whilst under the Sale of Goods Act 1979 the parties to a contract are free to decide when property passes, the creation of such a floating retention appears to offend against the statutory principle that notice should be given of floating charges by registration.[71]

---

[69] See Sale of Goods Act 1979, Pt. V.
[70] *Clough Mill v. Martin* [1985] 1 W.L.R. 111, CA.
[71] See Companies Act 1985, ss. 395 and 396.

In the *Romalpa* case,[72] the contract provided that property was only to **12–044** pass once the buyer had paid all that was due to the seller. At first instance, the seller's right to recover goods held by the buyer's receiver was "admitted".[73] It was also admitted that the retention of title clause had made the buyer a bailee for the seller in respect of the goods.[74] In these circumstances, it could hardly have been argued that the floating retention amounted to a floating charge.[75]

In *Snow v. Woodcroft*,[76] the contract again provided for property to **12–045** pass only when the buyer had met all indebtedness to the seller. The concessions made in the *Romalpa* case were not repeated. Nevertheless, Boreham J. cited the *Romalpa* case as authority for the validity of a clause providing for retention of title "until the buyer has discharged the whole of his indebtedness to the seller".[77]

It can be argued from the first instance decision in *Romalpa* [78] and **12–046** from the Court of Appeal's decision in *Clough Mill v. Martin* [79] that floating retention cannot fall within section 395(1) of the Companies Act 1985 because any charge would not be "created by" the buyer company. But such an argument assumes the very thing to be proved, *i.e.* it assumes that as a matter of construction of the contract the clause can and does operate as a valid and effective floating retention of title as opposed to a transfer of title subject to a floating charge.[80] Although the Court of Appeal decision in *Clough Mill v. Martin*[81] dealt with a simple form of clause, the dicta in the case tended to suggest that a floating retention would not be construed to be a floating charge. Thus, for example, Goff L.J. specifically considered the application of the retention of title clause in that case to situations where the seller claimed title to partly-paid goods and, whilst accepting that the effect of the retention of title clause was very similar to that of a charge, he held that the clause did not create a charge.[82]

In *Armour v. Thyssen Edelstahlwerke AG*[83] a German company, **12–047** Thyssen Edelstahlwerke AG, supplied steel strips to Carron Company Ltd, a Scottish company, on terms that "all goods delivered by us remain our property (goods remaining in our ownership) until all debts owed to us including any balances existing at relevant times . . . are settled"[84] Receivers were appointed to Carron Company Ltd. The Scottish Outer

---

[72] [1976] 1 W.L.R. 676, CA.
[73] [1976] 1 W.L.R. 676 at 780D–780E.
[74] *ibid.* at 680H.
[75] See *per* Goff L.J. in *Clough Mill v. Martin* [1985] 1 W.L.R. 111 at 114H.
[76] [1985] B.C.L.C. 54.
[77] *ibid.* at 62F–62G.
[78] [1976] 1 W.L.R. 676, *per* Mocatta J.
[79] [1985] 1 W.L.R. 111 at 119D, 121, 122–124, 125.
[80] Compare the converse point made by Oliver L.J. in *Clough Mill v. Martin* [1985] 1 W.L.R. 111 at 123.
[81] [1985] 1 W.L.R. 111.
[82] *ibid.* at 120–121. See also William Goodhart Q.C.'s note on *Clough Mill* (1986) 49 M.L.R. 96.
[83] (1990) B.C.C. 925.
[84] *ibid.* at 926c.

House and, on appeal, the Inner House of the Court of Session held that the clause constituted an attempt, ineffective under the law of Scotland, to create a right of security over corporeal moveables without transfer of possession and that title to the steel strip had passed to Carron Company Ltd on delivery and thus formed part of the general assets of the company available to creditors. The House of Lords, after citing sections 17 and 19 of the Sale of Goods Act 1979, held that the parties in the contract of sale clearly expressed their intention that the property in the steel strips should not pass to Carron Company Ltd until all debts due by it to Thyssen Edelstahlwerke AG had been paid, and Lord Keith could see no grounds for refusing to give effect to that intention.[85] He commented:

> "I am, however, unable to regard a provision reserving title to the seller until payment of all debts due to him by the buyer as amounting to the creation by the buyer of a right of security in favour of the seller. Such a provision does in a sense give the seller security for the unpaid debts of the buyer. But it does so by way of a legitimate retention of title, not by virtue of any right over his own property conferred by the buyer."[86]

It therefore appears now to be settled at the highest level that a "floating retention" does not of itself constitute a floating or indeed any other charge.

12–048   If goods are sold subject to a retention of title clause and the purchaser then on-sells and delivers the goods to a sub purchaser also subject to a retention of title clause, then the original seller will retain title to the goods in the hands of the sub purchaser unless and until the sub purchaser pays the purchaser the price of the goods.[87]

(d) Claims to proceeds of sale

12–049   In practice, where the proceeds of resale have been received prior to receivership, they will often have disappeared into an overdrawn bank account. On the other hand, claims to tracing may arise where the proceeds of resale have not yet been received or where they have been kept in a traceable form.

12–050   Where the retention of title clause makes no express provision with regard to the proceeds of resale but simply reserves title to the goods, the first question that arises is whether the buyer had any right of resale prior to going into receivership. In the *Romalpa* case,[88] the Court of Appeal mentioned with apparent approval the agreement between the parties that a term was to be implied permitting resale whilst the price of the goods remained unpaid.[89] The argument turned upon whether the

[85] See *per* Lord Keith at 928f.
[86] See *per* Lord Keith at 929a.
[87] *Re Highway Foods International* [1995] B.C.C. 271.
[88] [1976] 1 W.L.R. 676.
[89] At 684C, 693B–693C, 693H; see also *Four Point Garage Ltd v. Carter* [1985] 3 All E.R. 12.

term to be implied was a right to resell on the buyer's own account or on behalf of the seller. The Court of Appeal found that the normal creditor/debtor relationship had been replaced as a result of the special provisions in the contract in that case by a fiduciary relationship, which meant that resales were made on behalf of the seller. This suggests that in the case of a simple retention provision the ordinary debtor/creditor relationship would persist and an implied term would, in so far as it permitted resale, permit it on the buyer's own account, so that the proceeds became the property of the buyer. This was precisely the effect of the decision in *Re Andrabell Ltd*[90] In that case, there was a simple form of clause and credit was given for a fixed period rather than terminating with resale. This suggested that the proceeds of sale could be dealt with as the buyer thought fit and negatived any fiduciary relationship. In the absence of such a relationship the seller had no interest in the proceeds of sale. It was also held that, in the case of a clause setting out detailed provisions for payment, a term imposing an obligation to account would not be implied since it was not necessary to give business efficacy to the agreement.

A similar position arises in the case of goods supplied for incorporation into some larger product or for manufacture into a new product. In *Hendy Lennox Industrial Engines Ltd v. Grahame Puttick Ltd*[91] a clause in a sale of engines to be incorporated into generating sets which simply reserved title and permitted retaking in the event of default was held not to give rise to a fiduciary relationship in relation to the proceeds of resale. In *Borden (U.K.) Ltd v. Scottish Timber*[92] a simple retention of title clause relating to the sale of resin to be made into chipboard was held not to give rise to a fiduciary relationship and the buyers were held entitled to use the goods for manufacture in such a way that the manufactured products became the property of the buyer. It was further held that a tracing right extending to the manufactured products would constitute a floating charge. In a receivership such a floating charge would be void unless registered.[93] **12–051**

The greatest difficulty arises where express provision is made in a complex form of clause in relation to proceeds of resales. We have already seen that in the *Romalpa* case[94] the clause was held to give rise to a fiduciary relationship and it was held that the proceeds of resale could be traced. The question arises whether a clause simply following the *Romalpa* model would today be effective. **12–052**

In the *Borden* case,[95] Bridge L.J. described that type of clause as "presumably effective". Other subsequent judicial pronouncements on the decision in the *Romalpa* case suggest that it might not today be **12–053**

[90] [1984] B.C.L.C. 522, *per* Peter Gibson J.
[91] [1984] 1 W.L.R. 485, *per* Staughton J.
[92] [1981] Ch. 25, CA.
[93] Companies Act 1985, ss. 395, 396.
[94] [1976] 1 W.L.R. 676, CA.
[95] [1981] Ch. 25, CA.

decided in the same way. In the *Bond Worth* case,[96] Slade J. regarded as "a concession of crucial importance" the admission that the retention of title clause had made the buyers bailees of the goods. In the *Borden* case,[97] Bridge L.J. regarded the "bailee" concession as a clearly distinguishing feature in the *Romalpa* case. Templeman L.J. in the *Borden* case[98] cited a comment by Roskill L.J. in the *Romalpa* case where, in refusing leave to appeal, he stated that the *Romalpa* decision "could not govern any other case". In *Clough Mill v. Martin*[99] Goff L.J. considered that the decision in the *Romalpa* case was based on the concession that title to the goods remained with the sellers and that the buyers became bailees of the foil on delivery to them.

12–054 In *Specialist Plant Services v. Braithwaite*[1] the Court of Appeal actually reached the opposite conclusion to that held in the *Romalpa* case on similar wording, but without explaining how that could be reconciled with *Romalpa*.

12–055 The *Romalpa* case has been distinguished in English cases dealing with complex clauses in a manufacturing situation. In *Re Peachdart Ltd*[2] leather was supplied for making into handbags. There was a clause in many ways similar to the one in the *Romalpa* case. The effective dispute concerned the proceeds of sale of completed and uncompleted handbags. Vinelott J. considered it a "vital difference" that the *Romalpa* case concerned the proceeds of sale of unmanufactured goods. In the case in question he found that the parties could not have intended, even assuming that the buyer became a bailee on delivery, that the buyers would remain bailees throughout the manufacturing process so that the sellers whilst unpaid could enter the buyer's premises and remove partly or completely manufactured handbags and that on a sale of a handbag the buyer would be obliged to pay the proceeds into a separate account not to be used in the course of trade. The seller also had a factual problem in that the sale records of the buyer relating to the handbags did not identify the supplier of the leather, so that the sellers could not connect any finished product to its unpaid raw materials. Thus although the clause expressly provided for a fiduciary relationship and for tracing, Vinelott J. found that the parties must have intended that at the latest when manufacturing work began on a piece of leather it would cease to be the seller's property and the seller would have a charge on handbags in the course of manufacture which would in due course shift to the proceeds of sale. This was despite an express provision that property in the leather would "remain" with the seller. In coming to this conclusion Vinelott J. appeared to be influenced by the fact that once manufacture began the leather ceased to have any significant value as raw material and the value in the finished product would derive mostly from the

[96] [1980] Ch. 228.
[97] [1981] Ch. 25, CA.
[98] *ibid.*
[99] [1985] 1 W.L.R. 111, CA.
[1] (1987) 3 B.C.C. 119.
[2] [1984] 1 Ch. 131, *per* Vinelott J.

buyer's skill and reputation. The sellers conceded in that case that a charge such as was found by Vinelott J. was void for non-registration.[3]

In *Clough Mill v. Martin*[4] the Court of Appeal was, in a case involving **12–056** a complex clause, only faced with a claim to the goods themselves. The goods had not been manufactured and a claim of this type had been conceded in *Re Peachdart Ltd*. After finding that the simple retention of title part of the clause did not amount to a registrable charge, the Court of Appeal went on to consider the situation where manufacture had taken place. The goods supplied consisted of yarn and the buyer was a manufacturer of fabrics. The fourth part of the clause provided that if any of the goods were "incorporated in or used as material for other goods . . . the property in the whole of such goods shall be and remain with the seller . . .". Goff L.J. considered the position where, after default in payment, the seller had terminated the contract of sale and resold the manufactured product over which he claimed title. He found it impossible to believe that the parties intended the seller to have the windfall of the value of the new product without having to account to the buyer for any surplus over the sum due to the seller. To avoid this there had to be a trust or a charge. An intention to create a trust was discounted on the grounds that sellers must know that other sellers reserve title and "the prospect of two lots of material, supplied by different sellers, each subject to a *Romalpa* clause which vests in the seller the legal title in a product manufactured from both lots of material, is not at all sensible".[5] Accordingly, Goff L.J. considered that this part of the clause created a charge, although he recognised that he was doing "violence to the language" of the relevant part of the clause. Oliver L.J. felt that it was not necessary to decide the point but was inclined to agree with Goff L.J.[6]

Sir John Donaldson M.R. considered, first, that where, despite **12–057** incorporation, etc., the goods remained separate and identifiable, the attempt in the clause to acquire title to other goods which had never belonged to the seller created a charge by the buyer in relation to those goods. Where the goods ceased to be identifiable and the new product belonged to the buyer, the clause would again create a charge.

With regard to the incidental question to whom such a new product **12–058** belonged, the Court of Appeal expressed no concluded view, but again the dicta are of interest. In the *Hendy Lennox* case[7] the goods had simply been incorporated in a way in which they remained easily removable

---

[3] See also *Modelboard Ltd v. Outer Box Ltd* [1992] B.C.C. 945, *per* Michael Hart Q.C. (held title to cardboard passed once processed such that the vendor's interest was by way of charge); see *Ian Chisholm Textiles Ltd v. Griffiths* [1994] B.C.C. 96 *per* David Neuberger Q.C. (held title to cloth passed once it was combined to any significant extent with goods owned by another such that the vendor's interest was by way of charge); *see Chaigley Farms Ltd v. Crawford, Kaye & Grayshire Ltd* [1996] B.C.C. 957, *per* Garland J. (held title to livestock passed once the livestock was slaughtered).
[4] [1985] 1 W.L.R. 111, CA.
[5] *ibid.* at 120E–120F.
[6] *ibid.* at 124H.
[7] [1984] 1 W.L.R. 485.

without damaging the larger entity. There was no new product and title had not passed as a result of the incorporation. In the *Borden* case the goods had undergone an irreversible process of manufacture and a new product was created. It was there held that tracing could not extend to the new product. The sellers had lost their ownership of the resin supplied by them and any interest in the new chipboard product would have been by way of charge. The chipboard itself belonged to the buyer/manufacturer. In the *Clough Mill* case,[8] Goff L.J. was of the view that it was open to the parties to agree that the new product would belong to the seller. Oliver L.J. reserved his view but seemed inclined to agree with Goff L.J. on this point. Sir John Donaldson M.R. expressed no view on the ownership of new products point. The importance of the question of ownership in this context is that if the new product belongs to the buyer, the seller's rights will not have been "retained" but must necessarily have been created by the buyer company and accordingly may constitute a registrable charge; but if the seller obtained an original title under the terms of the sale agreement, the question of the creation of a charge by the company will only arise in the windfall situation considered by Goff and Oliver L.JJ.

12–059　　Neither the *Peachdart*[9] nor the *Clough Mill*[10] decision dealt with the ordinary resale situation where a complex form of clause is employed. Cases since *Peachdart* and *Clough Mill* show a strong inclination by the English courts to distinguish *Romalpa* in resale and analogous situations where a complex form of clause has been used. In *E. Pfeiffer Weinkellerei-Weineinkauf GmbH & Co. v. Arbuthnot Factors Ltd*[11] the relevant clause stated:

> "The buyer is only allowed to dispose of the goods or to sell them in business operations carried out in due order and as long as there is no delay in payment. All claims that he gets from the sale or due to another legal reason regarding our goods, with all rights including his profit amounting to his obligations towards us, will be passed on to us. On demand the buyer is obliged to notify the assignment of the claim, to give us in writing all necessary information concerning the assertion of our claims, and to deliver up all necessary documents."[12]

12–060　Phillips J. distinguished the case from *Romalpa* by reference to the proceeds of sale provisions.[13] He noted that Springfield Wine Importers Ltd's claims were only passed on up to the amount of its outstanding obligations to Pfeiffer, which was inconsistent with the proposition that the beneficial interest in all proceeds was to be vested in Pfeiffer.[14]

---

[8] [1985] 1 W.L.R. 111, CA.
[9] [1994] 1 Ch. 131.
[10] See above, n. 95.
[11] (1987) 3 B.C.C. 608; for the facts see above, para. 12–03.
[12] See at 610.
[13] See *per* Phillips J. at 615, 1st column.
[14] See at 615, 2nd column.

Secondly, he stated that "the language used is essentially that of assignment or cession by Springfield of rights owned by Springfield", and thus he held that the clause constituted an agreement whereby Springfield assigned to Pfeiffer future choses in action which were owned by Springfield, namely, future debts owed by sub-purchasers. Thus, what was created was a charge by way of security over property of Springfield.[15]

In *Tatung (U.K.) Ltd v. Galex Telesure Ltd*,[16] a supplier of electrical **12–061** goods supplied equipment to three companies which went into receivership. The supplier argued they were entitled to the proceeds of sale or hire of such goods. With regard to proceeds, there were two relevant clauses. The first provided that:

> "The buyer shall be at liberty to sell the goods in the ordinary course of business in the name of the buyer and as principal and not as agent for the company notwithstanding the fact that title to the goods has not then passed to the buyer but the benefit of any such contract of sale and the proceeds of any such sale shall belong to the company absolutely."[17]

The second provided that:

> ". . . the buyer shall have the power to resell or otherwise deal with the goods in the ordinary course of business in the name of the buyer on condition: . . . (b) that the proceeds of resale or other dealing shall in any period preceding payment of the full price as aforesaid be held by the buyer in a separate account as trustee thereof for the company."[18]

Despite the "trustee" wording in the second formula, Phillips J. rejected **12–062** the submission that the defendant companies were fiduciaries of the goods prior to disposal and thus also rejected the submission that the plaintiffs derived an absolute equitable interest in the proceeds of the goods after their disposal. He noted that the plaintiff's interest in the proceeds of sale and hire were defeasible upon payment of the debts owed to the plaintiffs, and he held that accordingly they were interests by way of security rather than an absolute interest. He went on to state that this conclusion entirely accorded with the requirements of business efficacy having regard to the basic relationship between the plaintiffs and defendants of vendors and purchasers.[19]

In *Compaq Computer Ltd v. Abercorn Group Ltd*[20] the relevant clause **12–063** stated:

---

[15] See at 616.
[16] (1989) 5 B.C.C. 325. The reasoning of the decision was approved by Hoffmann J. in *Re Weldtech Equipment Ltd* [1991] B.C.C. 16.
[17] See at 328.
[18] *ibid.*
[19] See at 333h.
[20] (1991) B.C.C. 484. For the facts see above, para. 12–03.

"In so far as the dealer may sell or otherwise dispose of the Compaq products or receive any moneys from any third party in respect of the Compaq products, he shall strictly account to Compaq for the full proceeds thereof (or such moneys as the dealer shall receive) as the seller's bailee or agent and shall keep a separate account of all such proceeds or moneys for such purpose."[21]

Mummery J. noted that the beneficial interest of the seller in the debts was determinable on the payment of the debts, and consequently the rights and obligations of the parties were in reality and in substance characteristic of those of the parties to a charge and not of those in a trustee/beneficiary or other fiduciary relationship.[22]

A strikingly different approach to the subject has been taken in recent dicta of the High Court of Australia in *Associate Alloys Pty Ltd v. ACN*.[23] In that case, steel was supplied to be manufactured into various steel products. The retention of title clause provided for retention of title to the goods, for their custody by the buyer as "fiduciary agent and bailee" and:

"In the event that the [buyer] uses the goods/products in some manufacturing . . . process . . ., then the buyer shall hold such part of the proceeds of such manufacturing . . . as relates to the goods/products in trust for the [seller]. Such part shall be deemed to equal in dollar terms the amount owing by the [buyer] to the [seller] at the time of the receipt of such proceeds."

It is important to note that the seller's claim failed and was bound to fail at every level, because the seller failed to prove the receipt of relevant "proceeds" by the buyer. Nevertheless, the case is interesting because of its discussion of and very divergent views expressed about attempts to create a trust over proceeds of manufactured products using goods to which title had been retained.

The decision of the New South Wales Court of Appeal and the forceful dissent of Kirby J. in the High Court of Australia followed the approach of the English cases discussed above and considered that there was a registrable charge on book debts.

The majority of the High Court, however, distinguished the English cases on the following grounds:

(1) The true construction of the wording in this case was that the trust was over only the "proceeds" and not the debts from which those proceeds resulted. In coming to this conclusion, the majority recognised that it followed from their approach that the buyer could completely nullify the effect of the provision by dealing with the debts in such a way that no

---

[21] See at 491d.
[22] See at 495g.
[23] (2000) 171 ALR 568.

relevant proceeds would arise.[24] It is not at all clear whether the English courts would have come to the same conclusion on this question of construction.[25]

(2) The trust did not require an express segregation provision, since the obligation to segregate followed from the trust.[26]

(3) The provision did not create a "windfall" problem.[27]

(4) The trust was not defeasible upon payment of the debt,[28] because a term was to be implied to the effect that the constitution of a trust over proceeds pro tanto discharged the debt.[29] It is respectfully doubted whether the English courts, on the basis of the authorities discussed above, would have taken the same view. It is suggested that the more likely intention of the parties was that the proprietary trust rights would co-exist with the debt until discharge of the debt, providing security for it. Suppose for example that the proceeds held on trust were quite properly placed into a segregated account at X bank, but the bank went into liquidation, whilst the buyer remained solvent. On the view of the majority, the seller could only claim (via the trust) in the bank's insolvency. It is difficult to believe that the parties really intended to deprive the seller of his usual right to enforce the debt. The commercial sense of the transaction was that the trust of the proceeds would provide "security" for the debt.

(e) Post-receivership transactions

The receiver, whether acting as agent of the company or as principal, will **12–064** stand in the shoes of the company and exercise its rights and thus in theory should be in no better or worse position than the company itself. In practice, however, where any rights claimed by the seller would be void as against the debenture-holder who appointed the receiver on the grounds of constituting an unregistered but registrable charge, the receiver will be able to take advantage of such invalidity. Strictly speaking, the receiver's appointor should be joined in any proceedings to take the registration point.[30] But in practice costs can be saved by agreeing to waive this technical requirement.[31]

In cases where the sale contract has not been terminated and where **12–065** there is an implied right of resale, unless that right has been effectively terminated, there would appear to be no reason why a receiver should

---

[24] At p. 576.

[25] See the ongoing debate in the English cases on fixed and floating charges as to whether it is possible or sensible to distinguish proceeds from the debt which gives rise to them, discussed in Chap. 3.

[26] At p.579.

[27] Compare the discussion of the *Clough Mill* decision, above.

[28] In which case it would have amounted to a trust by way of charge: see the English cases discussed above.

[29] At pp. 582–583.

[30] See *Independent Automatic Sales Ltd v. Knowles and Foster* [1962] 1 W.L.R. 974, and see above, para. 3–132.

[31] As occurred in *Re Peachdart Ltd* [1984] 1 Ch. 131, *per* Vinelott J.

not resell the goods.[32] In such a case the receiver will hold the proceeds subject to any effective trust imposed by the sale contract which would have bound the company on any such sale by the company, but if no trust is imposed or no registered charge created over the proceeds binding on the appointing debenture-holder, the proceeds will form part of the receivership realisations. If the contract is terminated and the seller intervenes to prevent resales, it will probably be implicit in any arrangement (whether sanctioned by the court or otherwise) which enables the receiver to continue resales that the entitlement to the proceeds of resales will be determined on the basis of entitlement to the goods themselves prior to resale.[33]

12–066 Where a supplier claiming under an retention of title clause has refused to agree to resales by the receiver and has commenced proceedings which threaten to prejudice the receivership by holding up the use or resale of goods supplied, the receiver may be able to obtain relief by invoking the court's power in certain circumstances to order a sale of goods to which title is in dispute.[34] In practice a receiver will be likely to offer an undertaking to a retention of title claimant (to pay the value of the goods in the event of the claimant proving his claim) in order to prevent the claimant from successfully applying for an injunction restraining sale.[35]

7. INSOLVENCY ACT 1986

12–067 Section 43 of the Insolvency Act 1986 enables an administrative receiver to apply to the court to enable him to sell property over which he is a receiver or manager free of any prior "security". The property in question must, in the context,[36] be property of the company charged to the debenture-holder, which in turn prevents this section applying to property the subject of an effective retention of title clause. A contrary argument could perhaps be based on the definition of "security",[37] which, if read literally, seems wide enough to cover a valid retention of title clause. It is considered that since section 43 extends only to property beneficially owned by the company, an administrative receiver could not apply under this section to sell goods to which title had been validly retained. This view is perhaps supported by the distinction drawn in the equivalent provision applying to administrators[38] between, on the one hand, "property of the company subject to a security" and, on the other, goods in the possession of the company but subject to security rights

---

[32] *Chaigley Farms Ltd v. Crawford, Kaye & Grayshire Ltd* [1996] B.C.C. 957.

[33] See *Hendy Lennox v. Grahame Puttick Ltd* [1984] 1 W.L.R. 485 at 497A–497B.

[34] C.P.R. Pt 25.1(1)(c)(v), which permits a party to proceedings to apply for the sale of chattels in question in the proceedings which are of a perishable nature or "which for any other good reason it is desirable to sell quickly".

[35] *Lipe Ltd v. Leyland DAF Ltd* [1993] B.C.C. 385

[36] See Insolvency Act 1986, s. 43(7).

[37] *ibid.*, s. 248(b).

[38] *ibid.* s. 15.

involving retention of ownership, including hire-purchase agreements, chattel leases and retention of title clauses. If this view is correct, administrative receivers remain vulnerable to pressure where goods the subject of an undoubtedly valid retention of title clause need to be sold as part of the business or other property of the company charged to the debenture-holder.

CHAPTER 13

TAXATION OF COMPANIES IN ADMINISTRATION AND ADMINISTRATIVE RECEIVERSHIP[1]

1. INTRODUCTION AND OVERVIEW

13–001 Tax considerations can sometimes play a vital part in the realisation of a company's property by either an administrator or an administrative receiver.[2] The incidence of taxation may affect whether the company can trade profitably[3] or whether an administrator or receiver can achieve a beneficial sale of the company's property.

13–002   A receiver will be subject to the preferential claims of tax authorities determined in accordance with section 40 and Schedule 6 to the Insolvency Act 1986 and this can present the receiver with a problem of priority as between those claims and the rights of debenture-holders. An administrator is under no obligation to pay or satisfy preferential debts during the continuation of the administration. He will however, have to have regard to the position of creditors who would be preferential in a liquidation when it comes to considering an exit from administration.[4]

13–003   A receiver may be affected by the appointment of a liquidator to the company over whose assets he has been appointed.[5] An administrator will have to be aware that his acts may affect the tax liabilities in any liquidation after the administration has come to an end.

13–004   Where the company over which the receiver or administrator has been appointed is a member of a group, a number of significant tax implications also need to be considered when a liquidator is appointed to another company which is part of the group.

13–005   In general, both an administrator and a receiver are in similar positions: both are agents of the company over which they have been appointed. As a consequence, their actions are those of the company and it is the company which is liable for any tax. Nevertheless, there are certain situations in which questions arise as to whether an administrator or receiver can become liable to account for tax.

13–006   This chapter looks at some of the specific tax issues which an administrator or receiver needs to be aware of when carrying out his duties.

---

[1] This chapter does not attempt a comprehensive treatment of the taxation of receivership but focuses on particular problems which appear to be of legal interest. A fuller treatment of the subject may be found in A. C. R. Davis, *Tolley's Taxation in Corporate Insolvency* (3rd ed., 1996).

[2] See also Chap. 9 on disposals by receivers.

[3] Continuation of trading by a receiver is dealt with in Chap. 8.

[4] See para. 23–084.

[5] For the effect generally on receivership of liquidation, see Chap. 11.

2. APPOINTMENT

Neither an administrator nor a receiver incurs any personal liability for tax **13–007** liabilities of the company which have accrued prior to their appointment. A receiver does, however, have a duty to pay preferential debts out of assets which are subject to a floating charge (which was a floating charge "as created" regardless of whether it has since crystallised) in priority to the debenture-holder or mortgagee and these may include unpaid tax liabilities.[6] A failure to pay is actionable in tort as a breach of statutory duty.[7] The preferential debts include PAYE, payments made under the construction industry tax deduction scheme, VAT, insurance premium tax, landfill tax, car tax, excise duties, lottery duty and air passenger duty.[8] Whereas PAYE and NIC deductions made over a 12 month period prior to the relevant date are expressly made preferential, there is in addition an indirect preference for PAYE and NIC in respect of deductions from payments made to employees in respect of their preferential claims.[9]

PAYE and NIC contributions arising during an administration have **13–008** super-priority pursuant to section 19(5) and (6) in respect of both new employees and in respect of employees whose employment contracts have been adopted by the administrator.[10]

The appointment of an administrator or receiver does not end an **13–009** accounting period.[11] Where, however, the administrator or receiver takes the decision that the company should cease trading, an accounting period will end on the company so ceasing to trade.

For the purposes of Value Added Tax, it is not clear whether **13–010** receivership or administration (as opposed to liquidation) gives the Commissioners of Customs and Excise the power to bring a VAT period to an end. That power depends upon the true construction of Regulations 25(3)[12] and 30 of the Value Added Tax Regulations 1995.[13] These apply, in the words of Regulation 30,

> "Where any person . . . dies or becomes incapacitated and control of his assets passes to another person, being a personal representative, trustee in bankruptcy, receiver, liquidator, or person otherwise acting in a representative capacity . . ."

---

[6] Insolvency Act 1986, s. 40; see also Chaps 11 and 21.

[7] *IRC v. Goldblatt* [1972] Ch. 498; *Westminster v. Treby* [1936] 2 All E.R. 21; *Woods v. Winskill* [1913] 2 Ch. 303; *Westminster Corporation v. Haste* [1950] Ch. 442.

[8] Insolvency Act 1986, Sched. 6, paras 1–7.

[9] *Re FJL Realisations Ltd* (Unreported, CA, July 10, 2000).

[10] *ibid.*

[11] Income and Corporation Taxes Act 1988, s. 12.

[12] Reg. 25(3) provides that:
"... where for the purposes of this Part of these Regulations the Commissioners have made a requirement of any person pursuant to regulation 30—
(a) then the period in respect of which taxable supplies were being made by the person ... who became incapacitated shall end on the day previous to the date when ... incapacity took place; and
(b) a return made on his behalf shall be furnished in respect of that period no later than the last day of the month next following the end of that period, ..."

[13] S.I. 1995 No. 2518.

Arguably, a company that has had a receiver appointed is not one that has become "incapacitated", and the reference to a receiver can be understood as a reference to receiver of an incapacitated individual.[14] But it seems to be accepted in practice that the Commissioners do have such a power in the case of corporate receivership.[15]

13–011   A receiver has no duty to inform the Inland Revenue of his appointment other than the general duty under section 46(1)(b) of the Insolvency Act 1986 to notify creditors within 28 days of the appointment.

13–012   Where a receiver begins carrying on the business of the company over whose assets he has been appointed, he must, within 21 days of doing so, inform the Commissioners of Customs and Excise in writing of that fact and the date upon which the receivership commenced.[16]

3. LIABILITIES ARISING DURING THE APPOINTMENT

(a) Tax on capital gains

13–013 Where on the sale of property by either an administrator or administrative receiver a chargeable gain arises, it is treated as having been made by the company.[17] Accordingly, neither a mortgagee, a receiver nor an administrator (nor any liquidator) is personally liable in respect of the tax on such gain.[18]

13–014   Where, therefore, an asset is sold prior to liquidation in either receivership or administration, the liability will be an unsecured claim in any subsequent liquidation, if not previously paid by the company.

13–015   Where the asset is sold after liquidation, the position is more complicated. If there are free assets surplus to the receivership, the corporation tax liability will be payable as an expense of the liquidation.[19] Where liquidation precedes receivership, assets which are subject to a charge which was a floating charge when it was created are subject to payment of the expenses of the liquidation,[20] and one of those expenses is the payment of corporation tax.

13–016   Where receivership precedes liquidation but the sale is after liquidation, then on the basis of the decisions in *Re Portbase Clothing Limited*[21]

---

[14] *cf. Re John Willment (Ashford) Ltd* [1980] 1 W.L.R. 73 at 76H; *Sargent v. Commissioners of Customs and Excise* [1995] STC 398, CA.

[15] SPI Technical Release 2 which states (para 4.1) that: "for VAT compliance purposes, the insolvency practitioner takes responsibility for the VAT accounting of the trader from the date of the appointment."

[16] Value Added Tax Regulations 1995, reg. 9(2). The question whether (and if so in what circumstances) this applies to non-administrative receivers and the question when a receiver can be said to be carrying on the business of the company is dealt with below.

[17] Taxation of Chargeable Gains Act 1992, s. 26 and s. 60.

[18] *Re Mesco Properties Ltd* [1980] 1 W.L.R. 96 at 99B.

[19] Insolvency Rules 1986, r. 4.218(1)(p). See also, *Re Mesco Properties Ltd* [1980] 1 W.L.R. 96.

[20] ss. 175, 251 of the Insolvency Act 1986; *Re Barleycorn Enterprises Ltd* [1970] Ch. 465, CA and see Chaps 11 and 21.

[21] [1993] Ch. 388.

and *Mond v. Hammond Suddards*[22] it would seem that in spite of crystallisation by the appointment of the receiver, the assets subject to the crystallised floating charge will be available for payment of corporation tax as an expense of the winding-up.[23]

(b) Tax on income

(i) Trading income

Prior to liquidation, an administrator will, and a receiver will normally, **13–017** trade as agent of the company.[24] The trade, receipts and profits will therefore be those of the company and the company will be liable for corporation tax. Even if one viewed the administrator or receiver as the recipient of the income, the company and not the administrator or receiver would be liable. This is because the charge to tax, which would otherwise be made on the recipient of income under section 59(1) of the Income and Corporation Taxes Act 1988, is specifically disapplied by sections 6(2) and 59(4) of that Act in the case of companies.

Where the receiver causes the company to trade after his agency is **13–018** determined by liquidation, it is considered that any profits he makes will still be profits of the company and therefore the liability will remain that of the company.[25] The reason for this is that regardless of the capacity in which the receiver is acting the profits still accrue to the benefit of the company in reducing its indebtedness to the debenture-holder.[26]

An administrator's appointment will be terminated before liquidation **13–019** and so the question of an administrator trading during liquidation does not arise.

(ii) Rental income

An administrator or receiver is no more liable to tax on rental income **13–020** received than to tax on trading receipts, for the reasons already set out above. The Inland Revenue used to suggest that section 23(7) of the Income and Corporation Tax Act 1988, which dealt with rental income, applied to receivers of companies. Section 23(7) provided that where rents were received by any person on behalf of another and tax under Schedule A charged on the principal had not been paid, the Collector could by notice require the agent to pay the collector any sums from time to time received by the agent. Failure to comply with the notice carried a penalty of £300. Whatever merits this suggestion may once

---

[22] [2000] Ch. 40, CA. The cases are discussed in paras 11–032 *et seq.* above.

[23] If the decision in *Portbase* and the *dicta* in *Mond v. Hammond Suddards* are wrong, then the assets which are the subject of the crystallised floating charge will not be available for the payment of corporation tax, and the decision in *Re Christonette International Limited* [1982] 1 W.L.R. 1245 would remain good law.

[24] See Chaps 11 and 23.

[25] Income and Corporation Taxes Act 1988, s. 8(1) which makes corporation tax chargeable on a company's profits "wherever arising" and *ibid.* s. 8(2) which provides for a company to be chargeable to corporation tax on profits arising in the winding-up of the company. The old case of *IRC v. Thompson* [1936] 2 All E.R. 651 which might have been taken suggest the contrary was discussed in the first edition of this work at para. 13–03.

[26] *Gosling v. Gaskell and Grocott* [1897] A.C. 575.

have had, it is no longer relevant because section 23(7) was repealed by the Finance Act 1995. The position now is that only the company itself is liable for tax on rental income. Although the primary Schedule A charging provision, which is now to be found in the Income and Corporation Taxes Act 1988, s. 21, provides that tax is to be charged on and paid by "the person receiving or entitled to the income in respect of which the tax . . . is to be charged", this section only applies to income tax and not to corporation tax.[27] Companies cannot be charged income tax but only corporation tax[28] and the charge to corporation tax is imposed only on the company itself.

(iii) Interest

13–021 As in the case of trading and rental income, liability for tax on interest received by an administrator or receiver falls on the company.[29] Where an administrator or receiver pays any yearly interest chargeable to tax under Case III of Schedule D, there will be an obligation to deduct and account for tax at the lower rate.[30] The receiver will be the person "by or through whom" the interest is paid.[31] A failure to deduct and account will render the administrator or receiver personally liable.[32] There is an exception from the obligation to deduct tax where the interest is payable in the United Kingdom on an advance from a bank if, when the interest is paid, the person beneficially entitled to the interest is within the charge to corporation tax as respects the interest.[33]

(iv) Income after liquidation

13–022 On the basis of the decisions in *Re Portbase Clothing Limited*[34] and *Mond v. Hammond Suddards*,[35] it would seem that corporation tax on income arising after liquidation would be a "necessary disbursement" of the liquidator which would be payable as an expense ahead of the claims of preferential creditors and the holders of floating charges.[36]

(c) PAYE

13–023 The appointment of a receiver out of court does not, generally speaking, discharge employees[37] and therefore prior to winding-up employees normally remain in the employ of the company. Regulation 2(1) of the

---

[27] Income and Corporations Taxes Act s. 21(3).

[28] *ibid.*, s. 6.

[29] *ibid.*, s. 8(2).

[30] *ibid.*, ss. 349(2), 4 and 1A, currently 20 per cent.

[31] *ibid.*, s. 349(2).

[32] *ibid.*, s. 350(1). *Kerr on Receivers and Administrators* (17th ed.), Chap. 26 expresses the view that the receiver is not personally liable and that the Inland Revenue must assess the company under *ibid.*, Sched. 16, para. 4(2). It is submitted that this view is not correct.

[33] *ibid.*, s. 349(3)(a).

[34] [1993] Ch. 388.

[35] [2000] Ch. 40, CA.

[36] See *Re Mesco Properties Ltd* [1980] 1 W.L.R. 96, CA and *Re Toshoku Finance U.K. plc* [2000] 1 B.C.L.C. 683, CA. The correctness of the decision in *Portbase* and the *dicta* in *Mond v. Hammond Suddards* is discussed in paras. 11–032 *et seq.* above and paras. 21–056 *et seq.* below.

[37] See Chap. 19.

Income Tax (Employments) Regulations 1993[38] defines the employer as any person paying emoluments. A receiver acting as agent for a company could argue that it is the company that is paying emoluments through the receiver as its agent. The Inland Revenue take the view that, when a company is in receivership, it is the receiver who actually pays the emoluments and therefore it is the receiver who is under an obligation to account for, and operate, PAYE. In the particular context of PAYE, the Revenue's argument may be correct, since it must frequently be the case that (where both companies are in the same group) an employee is employed by company A but paid by company B as agent for company A and the Regulations are presumably designed to fix the paying company with the obligation of deducting and accounting for PAYE, even if it is only acting as agent for the other company.

Similar arguments could arise as to whether an administrator is **13–024** personally liable in respect of deductions of PAYE during the administration, but since in relation to new and "adopted" employees these deductions have been held to have super-priority,[39] the question is rarely likely to be raised in the future.

(d) Returns

Prior to liquidation, returns must be made by the proper officer of the **13–025** company[40] or, as a result of a 1993 amendment[41] through such other persons as may for the time being have the express, implied or apparent authority of the company to act on its behalf. It is considered that an administrative receiver will normally have sufficient authority to act on behalf of a company to be able to sign a return[42] and it is not necessary for him to seek any specific authority from the company. It should be remembered that in signing the return the receiver is declaring that the return is correct and complete to the best of his knowledge and belief.

The Inland Revenue has argued that receivers automatically become **13–026** the proper officer because they have authority to act as agent of the company. It is suggested that this view is wrong. The 1993 provisions were enacted to protect the Inland Revenue when they accepted claims from people who were not the proper officer but who appeared to have authority from the company. If the Inland Revenue's view is correct, the practical effect is that a company will have more than one proper officer and consequently each would be obliged to make a return: this cannot be correct. However, if a receiver does make a return, he will have accepted the role of proper officer.

A practical consequence of the change is that an administrative **13–027** receiver may be able to consent to the surrender of group relief and amend group relief claims made prior to his appointment[43] without the co-operation of the company secretary.

---

[38] S.I. 1993 No. 744.

[39] *Re FJL Realisations Ltd* (Unreported, CA, July 10, 2000).

[40] Taxes Management Act 1970, s. 108(1).

[41] Finance Act 1993, Sched. 14, para. 7.

[42] See Sched. 1 of the Insolvency Act 1986.

[43] It is submitted that provided the alteration is made within the two year time limit, the surrendering company can withdraw its consent unless the liability of the company to which the group relief has surrendered has become fixed.

13–028   Where the company is in liquidation, only a liquidator can make a return.[44] It is not uncommon for a liquidator to require a payment from a receiver in order to secure the liquidator's co-operation. Any such payment will be held for the benefit of the liquidation.

4. VALUE ADDED TAX

13–029 It was held in *Re John Willment (Ashford) Ltd*[45] that a receiver had a discretion whether or not to account for VAT. However, because a failure to account would cause the company to commit a criminal offence, the receiver could only properly exercise that discretion in favour of Customs and Excise.[46] The criminal sanction was removed in 1985.

13–030   An amendment to the VAT legislation in 1985[47] enabled regulations to be made for persons carrying on "a business" of a company ". . . in . . . receivership . . ." to be treated as taxable persons. Under what is now Regulation 9 of the VAT Regulations 1995,[48] Customs & Excise have the power to treat a receiver who is carrying on the business of the company as a taxable person. Regulation 9 does not use the words "the business", but the references to "his business" and "that business" suggest that the Regulation deals with "the" business of the company, not "a" business of the company. This, and the reference to the company "going into receivership", particularly alongside references to liquidation and administration orders, suggests that Regulation 9 was dealing only with administrative receivership. The appointment of an LPA receiver does not mean that the company has gone into receivership and an LPA receiver, whilst he may carry on "a" business of the company, will not be able to carry on "the" business of the company, since even if the company has at the time of his appointment no other business, it remains open to the directors to commence any other business that they can properly cause the company to carry on. This view was accepted by the Court of Appeal in *Sargent v. Commissioners of Customs and Excise*.[49]

13–031   Regulation 9 raises a number of other problems. First, is it necessary that the person in question should be carrying on business on his own account? If it is, then the right of the Commissioners will not arise in the case of a receiver who carries on the business of the mortgagor company as its agent until such agency terminates on liquidation. The judgment in the *Sargent*[50] case, where there was no liquidation, assumes that Regulation 9 covers a receiver acting as agent for the company.

[44] Taxes Management Act 1970, s. 108(1) as amended by Finance Act 1993, Sched. 14, para. 7 and s. 108(3).
[45] [1980] 1 W.L.R. 73.
[46] Brightman J. in that case left open questions relating to fraudulent trading and misrepresentation.
[47] Finance Act 1985, s. 31, amending Value Added Tax Act 1983, s. 31.
[48] S.I. 1985 No. 886.
[49] [1995] S.T.C. 398
[50] *ibid.*

Secondly, Regulation 9 empowers the Commissioners to treat a **13–032** person carrying on the business as "a" taxable person, not "the" taxable person. Therefore any liability arising prior to the commissioners notifying the receiver would appear to remain the liability of the company. The Customs form of notification[51] of claim states in the Notes on the reverse side of the form: "1. You are to be treated as the taxable person named overleaf under VAT Regulations, 1995 Regulations 9 and 30".[52] But since Regulation 9 does not appear to give Customs the power to treat the receiver as the taxable person, such a notice appears to be invalid or ineffective as a notice under Regulation 9. At first instance in the *Sargent* case[53] it was assumed that a letter purporting to treat the receiver as "the taxable person" was effective under Regulation 9.

Thirdly, the Court of Appeal held in the Sargent case that notwith- **13–033** standing that the receiver had a discretion whether to pay the VAT element to Customs & Excise, for public policy reasons that discretion could only be exercised in favour of Customs & Excise. This was so notwithstanding that the criminal sanction had been removed.

Fourthly, it is not clear how far the exercise of the Commissioners' **13–034** discretion under Regulation 9 has retrospective effect. In the *Sargent* case,[54] the letter from the Commissioners purported to treat the receiver as the taxable person "with effect from the date of his appointment". Although Regulation 11 gives the Commissioners a discretion which can be exercised from the date of appointment of the receiver, it is difficult to see how Regulation 11 can be construed as authorising the exercise of this discretion on a date subsequent to the appointment with retrospective effect. If Regulation 11 were read in that way a receiver could not safely pay over sums including a VAT element to a mortgagee until the relevant period of limitations ran out. This could not have been the intention of the legislation.

5. HIVE DOWNS[55]

The major tax advantage of hiving down the assets of an insolvent **13–035** company to a new subsidiary, *i.e.* the transfer of trading losses for the benefit of the purchaser, was substantially removed in 1986.[56] As a result of this change, where, following the transfer of the trade to the new subsidiary, the liabilities of the transferor exceeds its assets, the losses transferred to the subsidiary under section 343 of the Income and Corporation Taxes Act 1988 are to be reduced by an amount equal to the excess. This means that the practice of leaving the transferor

---

[51] VAT 157.

[52] In the *Sargent* case the Customs wrote a letter pursuant to reg. 11 purporting to treat the receiver as "the taxable person".

[53] [1995] S.T.C. 398.

[54] *ibid.*

[55] See also Chap. 9.

[56] Finance Act 1986, s. 42 and Sched. 10, para. 1(2) (effective in respect of transfers on or after March 19, 1986), now s. 343(4) of the Income and Corporation Taxes Act 1988.

company with all the liabilities (for which the creditors would ultimately get a deduction when writing off the bad debts) whilst at the same time transferring all the tax losses to the subsidiary which could set such losses against subsequent trading profits has, to a large extent, been stopped.

13–036   Where, despite the application of section 343(4) of the Income and Corporation Taxes Act 1988, there are trading losses which can be transferred to the new subsidiary, in order to carry forward the trading losses the hive down will have to take place prior to any winding-up order or resolution to wind-up the company. Once the company is in the process of being wound-up the company for tax purposes no longer owns its business beneficially but holds it on trust for its creditors.[57] In *Ayerst v. C&K Construction Ltd*[58] a company already in receivership went into liquidation. The receiver and the liquidator joined in an agreement hiving down the whole of the business to an existing subsidiary, which carried on the business thereafter. The shares in the subsidiary were sold to a third party. The subsidiary claimed to be able to carry forward losses and capital allowances. The House of Lords held that on the making of the winding-up order against the parent company it ceased in a taxation sense to be the beneficial owner of the shares in its subsidiary and therefore a necessary element for the carry forward was lacking.[59]

13–037   It is thought that the hive down does not have to take place prior to the presentation of a winding-up petition which leads to a winding-up order, in order to avoid the effect of the principle in the *Ayerst* case. Despite the retrospective effect for some purposes of section 129(2) of the Insolvency Act 1986, which deems the winding-up to commence at the time of the presentation of the petition, a company facing a petition but not yet the subject of a winding-up order, is not in the process of being wound-up for the present purposes.[60]

13–038   It is also vital to appreciate that on the sale of the hive down company it ceases to be a member of its former group. This may have adverse tax consequences if the hive down company still holds chargeable assets transferred to it within the previous six years by the former group companies, as the hive down company will be deemed to have disposed of these assets.[61] It is therefore common practice not to transfer assets with potentially large gains at the time of the hive down although this can be done, if appropriate, after the hive down company has left the group. Any resultant gain therefore arises in the vendor company which may either have trading losses or capital losses suffered in the same accounting period or unutilised capital losses brought forward from earlier years to shelter the gains.

---

[57] *Ayerst v. C&K Construction Ltd* [1976] A.C. 167, HL; *IRC v. Olive Mill Spinners Ltd* 41 T.C. 77.

[58] [1976] A.C. 167 HL.

[59] For an alternative view see P. Ridgway, "Beneficial Ownership in Liquidations (An Essay in Support of Wood Preservation)", The Corporate Tax Planning Review Vol. 2, Issue 4, 279.

[60] See *Re Christonette International Ltd* [1982] 1 W.L.R. 245.

[61] Taxation of Chargeable Gains Tax Act 1992, s. 179.

Where it will be impossible, or very difficult, to preserve trading **13–039** losses by means of a hive down as a result of the stringent requirements of section 768 of the Income and Corporation Taxes Act 1988, it will be advisable to consider other means of utilising the losses already incurred or to maximise the use of trading losses likely to be incurred in the foreseeable future.

Where it is foreseen that the company will cease to trade, thereby **13–040** bringing the company's accounting period to an end for taxation purposes, certain events such as the disposal of assets with large potential gains should be planned to take place in the same accounting period. This is because trading losses can be used to shelter profits of whatever description, including chargeable gains arising in the same accounting period or in any accounting period following wholly or partly in the three years immediately preceding the accounting period in which the loss was incurred. Any unused trading losses can only be set off against future trading income of the same trade. This is not of any practical use if the company has ceased to trade.

6. LIQUIDATOR APPOINTED TO ONE COMPANY IN A GROUP

On the appointment of a liquidator to a company which is part of a **13–041** group, the following matters should be borne in mind. As the appointment of a liquidator to a company results in the company ceasing to have beneficial ownership of its assets, including shares in its subsidiary companies, the group relationship is dissolved.[62] As a result, the benefits previously enjoyed because of the group status are no longer available. In particular this means that the company in liquidation can no longer claim or surrender group relief,[63] or have the option to pay interest or dividends gross.[64]

An important exception applies with regard to the group status in **13–042** connection with corporation tax on capital gains. The appointment of a liquidator does not result in the dissolution of the group relationship.[65] Thus, transfers of assets between group companies still take place or are deemed to take place at a price which results in neither gain or loss to the transferor company.[66] This may give considerable opportunity to carry out some tax planning even at this late stage by the transfer of assets with potential gains to another group company with capital losses before disposing of them to a third party. Any transfer of this sort should be considered in the context of the Inland Revenue's statement of

---

[62] *IRC v. Olive Mill Spinners Ltd* [1963] 1 W.L.R. 712; *Ayerst v. C&K Construction Ltd* [1976] A.C. 167, HL.
[63] Income and Corporation Taxes Act 1988, s. 402.
[64] *ibid.*, s. 247.
[65] Taxation of Chargeable Gains Act 1992, s. 170(11).
[66] *ibid.*, s. 171.

September 20, 1985, on the application of the principles established in
Furniss v. Dawson.[67]

13–043   Section 101 of the Finance Act 2000, allows companies within a group
to elect for a disposal to deemed to have been made intra group before
being sold outside the group so as to obviate the need to make a real
intra group transfer. Such an election should be beneficial to both
administrators and receivers.

[67] [1984] A.C. 474. The Inland Revenue statement may be found in the ICAEW T.R.
588.

CHAPTER 14

CONVEYANCES AND TRANSFERS

1. PRE-WINDING UP

In any case where a receiver wishes to sell and convey or transfer **14–001** property of the company, he must first consider whether the sale should be made:

(a) by the receiver as agent for the company;
(b) by the debenture-holder as mortgagee; or
(c) pursuant to an order of the court.

(a) Sales by company or debenture-holder

In the ordinary case, the desire of the debenture-holder to avoid being a **14–002** party to any transaction (as well as considerations of convenience) results in all transactions being entered into by the receiver as agent for the company whenever this is practicable, the only participation of the debenture-holder being the release of its charge on completion.

The non-administrative receiver is normally nowadays expressly given **14–003** by the debenture a power of attorney enabling him to convey or transfer on behalf of the company. Prior to the Law of Property (Miscellaneous Provisions) Act 1989, a non-administrative receiver, in order to be able to transfer or lease land by deed as agent of the mortgagor, had to be appointed by deed.[1] The one qualification was that, where the mortgagor had signed and sealed the transfer or lease, the mortgagor's agent could be authorised to deliver the deed without any authorisation under seal.[2] The Act provides in section 1(1)(c) for the abolition of any rule which "requires authority by one person to another to deliver an instrument as a deed on his behalf to be given by deed". The question raised is whether, after this legislation, authority under seal is required for an agent to sign and seal though not to deliver.[3] It is thought that the answer is in the negative: (a) the common law rule required authorisation under seal for execution of deeds, *i.e.* for the composite exercise of

---

[1] *Phoenix Properties Ltd. v. Wimpole Street Nominees Ltd* [1992] B.C.L.C. 737, *per* Mummery J., preferring the view in the first edition of this work at p. 49 to the views of *Kerr on Receivers* (17th ed.), pp. 228–9, and *Halsbury's Laws* (4th ed.), para. 804. The contrary appears to have been assumed in *Re Wood* [1941] Ch. 112 and in *Sowman v. David Samuel Trust* [1978] 1 W.L.R. 22 at 30–31.

[2] *Longman v. Viscount Chelsea* (1989) 58 P. & C.R. 189 at 198–199, *per* Nourse L.J.: it is questionable whether this is in accordance with principle.

[3] See Bowden, "Land Options and Executing Deeds after the Law of Property (Miscellaneous Provisions) Act 1989" (1990) 1 Journal of Property Finance 539; Virgo and Harpum, "Breaking the Seal: the new law on deeds" [1991] Lloyd's Maritime and Commercial Law Quarterly 209; Emmet, *Title* (20th. ed.), paras. 20.001 to 20.005; Megarry and Wade, *The Law of Real Property* (6th ed.), para. 5–038.

signing, sealing and delivering.[4] and not the first two alone; and (b) the legislation cannot reasonably have been intended to have such limited application and effect. In the case of administrative receivers, their implied power to use the company's seal and to execute deeds and other instruments in the name and on behalf of the company is in no way dependent on the form of their appointment.[5]

14–004 The Insolvency Act 1986 (in the absence of any inconsistent provision) confers on an administrative receiver power to use the company's seal and to execute deeds and other documents in the name and on behalf of the company.[6] For the non-administrative receiver, the use of the company's seal requires the co-operation of the board of directors and this can create difficulties. However, in the usual case, a non-administrative receiver is expressly authorised by the charge to convey in the name of or on behalf of the company and accordingly can make use of statutory powers of conveying by signing the name of the company in the presence of at least one witness, such execution taking effect as if the company had executed the conveyance.[7]

14–005 The administrative receiver does not require the co-operation of the directors of the company, but it may be advantageous for him to obtain the directors' co-operation and concurrence (if possible) since this may preclude a subsequent challenge to the transaction. The directors' concurrence with the transaction is particularly valuable if the directors, as often happens, are also guarantors to whom the receiver owes a duty of care in connection with the sale.[8] Receivers who as agent of the company sell the company's business (or any significant asset) to a new company controlled by one or more directors of the vendor company are required to obtain a requisite resolution of the vendor company's members.[9]

14–006 The practical limitation on the utility of a sale by the receiver in the name of the company is that, as the sale is by the company (as on any sale by the company whether in receivership or not), the sale is subject to all outstanding charges whether prior or subsequent to the charge of the debenture-holder, save to the extent that the chargees agree to release their charges on completion of the sale. To obtain the concurrence of such chargees in a sale may be impracticable. A sale by the debenture-holder will be free of all charges postponed to his charge, but subject to any prior charges.[10] Accordingly, a sale by the debenture-holder is appropriate when his charge is a first charge and there are subsequent chargees who will not concur in a sale by the receiver on behalf of the company.

---

[4] *Longman v. Viscount Chelsea* (1989) 58 P. & C.R. 189 at 195.

[5] Insolvency Act 1986, s. 42 and Sched. 1, paras. 8 and 9.

[6] *ibid.*

[7] See s. 74(3) of the Law of Property Act 1925, as amended by the Law of Property (Miscellaneous Provisions) Act 1989, Sched. 2, s. 4 (to delete the former requirement of sealing by the agent).

[8] See Chap. 7.

[9] Companies Act 1985, s. 320; *see Demite Ltd v. Protec Health Ltd* [1998] B.C.C. 638. See also Chap. 9.

[10] Law of Property Act 1925, s. 101; *Kerr on Receivers* (17th ed.), p. 370. For equivalent Australian statutory powers, see O'Donovan, *op cit.*, pp. 102, 104.

(b) Section 43: over-reaching prior charges

Section 43 of the Insolvency Act 1986 provides that an administrative **14–007** receiver may apply to the court for an order authorising him to dispose of any property of the company free from a security to which it is subject and which ranks in priority to the charge held by the appointing debenture-holder. The court may make such an order if satisfied that the disposal (with or without other assets) would be likely to promote a more advantageous realisation of the company's assets than would otherwise be effected. The court will need to be satisfied that there is a reasonable prospect that this objective will be achieved.[11] The court must as a condition of such an authorisation require that the net proceeds of sale plus any sum by which the net proceeds fall short of the net proceeds on a realisation of the property on the open market shall be applied towards discharging the sums secured by the security[12] and, if more than one charge, the sums secured by those charges or securities in the order of their priorities. It is thought that, in computing the net proceeds, credit must be given for any sum required to be paid to obtain the redemption of a security which has priority to that to which the order relates and whose holder agrees to accept redemption upon completion of the sale. An application under s.43 should, where time permits, be supported by valuation evidence, since such evidence is critical to the exercise of the court's discretion.[13]

The question arises whether the security-holder whose security is to be **14–008** over-reached can artificially raise the net market value of the charged property by making an unrealistically high offer to buy in the property at a price approaching the secured debt outstanding.[14] It may fairly be said that the open market value should reflect the premium value of the property to any particular purchaser willing to pay the price. But the

---

[11] See with regard to the meaning of this expression, *Re Harris Simons Construction Ltd* [1989] 1 W.L.R. 368; *Re Consumer & Industrial Press Ltd* (1988) 4 B.C.C. 68; *Re Manlon Trading Ltd* (1988) 4 B.C.C. 455; *Re Primlaks (U.K.) Ltd.* (1989) 5 B.C.C. 710; *Re SCL Building Services Ltd* (1989) 5 B.C.C. 746; *Re Rowbotham Baxter Ltd* [1990] B.C.C. 113; *Re Chelmsford City Football Club* (1980) Ltd. [1991] B.C.C. 133; *Re Land and Property Trust Co. plc* [1991] B.C.C. 446; *Re Arrows Ltd (No. 3)* [1992] B.C.C. 131; *Re Maxwell Communications Corporation plc* [1992] B.C.C. 372; *Re Dallhold Estates (U.K.) Pty. Ltd* [1992] B.C.C. 394; *Re Structures & Computers Ltd* [1998] B.C.C. 348; *Re Lomax Leisure Ltd* [1999] 2 B.C.L.C. 126 on the construction of similar words in s. 8 of the Insolvency Act 1986.

[12] Insolvency Act 1986, s. 43(3). This sum includes not only capital but ongoing interest and (subject to the court's over-riding discretion) costs which can be added to the security under the general law or under the terms of the instrument: see *Re ARV Aviation Ltd* (1988) 4 B.C.C. 708, dealing with similar wording in s. 15 of the Insolvency Act 1986. The court has no power to order that a receiver's costs, expenses and remuneration be paid in priority to the sums secured under prior charges (other than receivers appointed by the court); see *Choudhri v. Palta* [1994] 1 B.C.L.C. 184, CA. For circumstances in which the Court will refuse to make an order authorising disposal of property of the company free from a security to which it is subject see *Re Newman Shopfitters* [1991] B.C.L.C. 407.

[13] See *Re ARV Aviation Ltd* (1988) 4 B.C.C. 708 at 713, dealing with similar wording in s. 15 of the Insolvency Act 1986.

[14] Touche Ross & Co., *Insolvency Act 1985, The Key Issues and Implications for Companies*, point out at p. 13: "This provision will be difficult to operate if the prior chargee offers to buy in his security at a relatively high price approaching the debt outstanding".

premium value in this case does not reflect what the security-holder is willing to pay, but what he is willing to give credit for against a debt whose repayment at best is questionable. It is suggested that the court can discount such an offer as in substance an offer of such credit rather than outright payment. It may also be possible to discount such offers, whether made by the security-holder or anyone else, as ransom demands which it is the scheme and policy of the Act to preclude: the security-holder is to be justly compensated, not unjustly enriched, for the loss of a security impeding an advantageous realisation.

(c) Sales by the court

14–009 Situations arise when no sale can be achieved without an order for sale by the court. Examples include:

(a) where the validity or continued subsistence of the debenture is challenged[15];

(b) where there is a dispute as to priority between the debenture-holder and another chargee and no agreement can be reached as to sale;

(c) where the charge is not made by deed (in which case the statutory power of sale does not apply)[16];

(d) where the charge is equitable only and either:

    (i) there is no power of attorney empowering the chargee to convey; or

    (ii) no declaration of trust by the mortgagor in favour of the mortgagee authorising the mortgagee to appoint himself or his nominee trustee in place of the mortgagor[17]; or

    (iii) there has been a deposit of the deeds.

In any such case, the court has a discretionary power to make an order for sale,[18] and in the exercise of this jurisdiction may authorise the debenture-holder to proceed with and complete a conditional contract or intended sale. Incidental to the exercise of this power, the court may direct that entries which have been made by parties to the action in the Land Registry or Land Charges Registry and whose continued subsistence would preclude completion should be vacated.[19]

---

[15] *Greendon v. Mills* [1973] 223 E.G. 1957.

[16] See Law of Property Act 1925, s. 101(1)(i); Megarry & Wade, *The Law of Real Property* (6th ed., 2000), para. 19–085; *Re Hodson & Howes Contract* (1887) 35 Ch.D. 668; contrast *Re White Rose Cottage* [1965] Ch. 940 at 951, *per* Lord Denning M.R.

[17] In cases d(i) and d(ii) there is doubt whether the mortgagee can convey legal title. The position of the mortgagee in this situation may be analogous with that of one of several executors who has power to contract to sell land, but cannot complete a conveyance, without the concurrence of his co-executors or an rder of the court: Snell, *The Principles of Equity* (30th ed.), p. 358.

[18] Law of Property Act 1925, s. 91, as amended by S.I. 1991 No. 724, Art. 2(8), Sched. 1.

[19] *National Westminster Bank v. Hornsea Pottery* (unreported, May 11, 1984, CA).

(d) A Warranty by receiver[20]

On any sale, a receiver should as a general rule avoid giving a warranty. **14–010** A warranty that is given should be for limited periods only so as to avoid the need to retain funds to cover potential liability under the warranty and so delay remission of proceeds to the debenture-holder. It is suggested that:

(a) a receiver should never give a personal warranty, least of all in the case of a sale of land not including a business carried on thereat; or

(b) if he does, he should before giving any warranty ensure that he is covered by a completely satisfactory indemnity from an undoubtedly solvent debenture-holder or that there is sufficient security provided for him in some other manner, *e.g.* by bank bond, to enable him to close the receivership in due course and pay over all remaining moneys. It has been suggested that it might be useful to provide in the debenture or charge provisions to the effect that:

 (i) a purchaser of the charged assets need not inquire as to whether any default under the charge has occurred or notice required by the charge has been given;

 (ii) as regards a purchaser, a sale by the receiver should be deemed to be within the power of sale granted by the charge despite any impropriety or irregularity; and

 (iii) the company's remedy in the event of any irregularity or impropriety would be restricted to damages.[21]

It seems that this type of provision can provide protection for a purchaser[22] as long as such purchaser has no actual knowledge of an irregularity and any irregularity is not obvious, *e.g.* on the face of the documents.[23]

2. POST WINDING UP

Winding-up will not prevent the receiver disposing of assets the subject **14–011** of the charge over which he is appointed or the debenture-holder exercising powers of disposition as mortgagee.[24] The debenture-holder can execute conveyances and transfers in the name of the company if the debenture includes a power of attorney granted to the debenture-holder:

---

[20] See also Chap. 9.

[21] O'Donovan, *op cit.*

[22] *Dicker v. Augerstein* (1876) 3 Ch.D. 600 and see Chap. 7.

[23] *Selwyn v. Garfit* (1888) 38 Ch.D. 273.

[24] *Gaskell v. Gosling* [1896] 1 Q.B. 669, *per* Rigby L.J. whose judgment was upheld in the House of Lords; *Sowman v. David Samuel Trust Ltd* [1978] 1 W.L.R. 22 at 30, *per* Goulding J.; *Barrows v. Chief Land Registrar, The Times*, October 20, 1977, *per* Whitford J.

such a power survives liquidation.[25] It is more questionable whether a non-administrative receiver can execute such a conveyance or transfer in the name of the company. On balance, it is thought that the receiver does have such power, most particularly if the debenture includes a power of attorney conferred on the receiver.[26] Any doubts as to such power on the part of an administrative receiver are removed by the Insolvency Act 1986, which expressly confers such a power on administrative receivers.[27]

[25] *Sowman v. David Samuel Trust* [1978] 1 W.L.R. 22 at 30; *Barrows v. Chief Land Registrar, The Times,* October 20, 1977.

[26] See the discussion in *Sowman v. David Samuel Trust,* above and *Kerr on Receivers* (17th edn), pp. 332–333; and see the illuminating article by Peter Millett Q.C., "The Conveyancing Powers of Receivers After Liquidation" (1977) 41 Conv. (N.S.) 83. See also *Re Leslie Homes* (1984) 8 A.C.L.R. 1020 where McLelland J. held that whilst only the liquidator could affix the company's seal, the receiver could execute a contract or transfer on behalf of the company under his own hand and seal. See now n. 3 above, in relation to sealing.

[27] s. 42 and Sched. 1, paras. 2, 8 and 9.

CHAPTER 15

RECEIVERS AND LEASES

1. LEASES AS SECURITY

The receiver may be appointed in relation to a company which is the **15–001** lessee of one or more properties. At one level, the appointment of a receiver as the agent of the company does not change the relationship between the landlord and the company as tenant; the company can continue to enjoy its rights as tenant, acting through the agency of the receiver. At another level, the fact of the appointment of the receiver may give the landlord rights which it did not enjoy against the company prior to the appointment of the receiver. Further, the receiver is likely to be appointed at a time when the company is in financial difficulties and its difficulties may have led to it failing to pay the rent due under the lease or to commit other breaches of the lease. Accordingly, this chapter will consider the various landlord and tenant issues that may confront a receiver of a company tenant either as a result of the appointment of the receiver or, more generally, because of the financial position of the company at the time of the appointment.

The questions which are likely to arise
The questions which are likely to arise include the following: **15–002**

- (a) Was the grant of the charge a breach of the terms of the lease?
- (b) Was the appointment of the receiver a breach of the terms of the lease?
- (c) Is the landlord entitled to seek forfeiture of the lease by reason of the grant of the charge or the appointment of the receiver?
- (d) Is the landlord entitled to seek forfeiture of the lease by reason of non-payment of rent or other breaches of covenant?
- (e) Other questions arising in relation to a possible forfeiture.
- (f) Will the company be able to obtain relief from forfeiture?
- (g) Will the chargee be able to obtain relief from forfeiture?
- (h) Is the landlord entitled to distrain for unpaid rent?
- (i) Is the landlord entitled to intercept rent otherwise payable to the company tenant by its sub-tenants?
- (j) When should the chargee release the lease from the charge?
- (k) Questions arising in respect of assigning the lease or subletting the premises;
- (l) Does the receiver have any personal liabilities?

Although this chapter will focus on cases where the company (in relation to which the receiver is appointed) is the tenant, the chapter will also include brief remarks which are relevant where the company is a landlord.

Was the grant of the charge a breach of the terms of the lease?

15–003 In the absence of an express provision to the contrary in the lease, the lessee is free to assign, underlet, part with possession of the premises and to charge the lease.[1] It is common for commercial leases to include a covenant controlling the lessee's ability to assign, underlet, part with possession of the demised premise or charge the lease. The reference to charging the lease plainly includes the grant of a fixed charge over the lease. There is no decided case as to whether a covenant against charging a lease prohibits the grant of a floating charge in respect of the company which is the lessee. This may be because the typical charge will include both a fixed and a floating charge. Based on the analysis of the nature of a floating charge set out in Chapter 3, it is arguable that the grant of a floating charge alone in relation to the company, without there being a fixed charge of the lease, will not necessarily result in the subsequent creation of a charge of the lease and so is not contrary to the lease. However, when the floating charge crystallises, the result will be a charge over the lease; nonetheless, the floating charge may have crystallised without any specific conduct on the part of the lessee company and it may be argued by the tenant that it has not acted contrary to the terms of the lease.[2]

If the lease does not expressly prohibit "charging" the lease, but does prohibit assignment or subletting or parting with possession, it will be necessary to consider whether the grant of a charge involves any of these transactions. The grant of a charge is not an assignment of the lease or of the premises. The grant of a charge is generally considered not to involve a subletting even though the chargee has the same protection, powers and remedies as if there were a mortgage by sub-demise.[3] If the mortgage, somewhat unusually, is in the form of an actual subdemise, then such a mortgage is a subletting within the meaning of the covenant.[4] The grant of a charge does not itself involve a parting with possession.[5] The covenant may contain an absolute prohibition on some or all of those things but, more usually, the covenant will be a qualified covenant which provides that the landlord's consent is needed to the proposed transaction. The express terms of a qualified covenant are subject to statutory modifications. First, where licence is required to

---

[1] See *Woodfall on Landlord and Tenant* (Looseleaf Ed.) Vol. 1, para. 11–113.

[2] Fisher & Lightwood's *Law of Mortgages* (10th ed.), p. 259 asserts that a covenant in a lease against charging the lease is broken by the grant of a floating charge but the authority cited (*Fell v. Charity Lands Official Trustee* [1898] 2 Ch. 44) is not in point.

[3] Law of Property Act 1925, s. 87(1); and see *Gentle v. Faulkner* [1900] 2 Q.B. 267 and *Grand Junction Ltd v. Bates* [1954] 2 Q.B. 160 at 168.

[4] *Serjeant v. Nash Field & Co.* [1903] 2 K.B. 304.

[5] Fisher & Lightwood's *Law of Mortgages* (10th ed.), p. 335 suggests that as and when the chargee later enters into possession, there will not be a parting with possession by the lessee contrary to the covenant. Megarry & Wade, *The Law of Real Property* (6th ed.), p. 1180 puts forward the opposite view.

a mortgage by sub-demise, such licence is not to be unreasonably withheld.[6] Further, more generally, a covenant in a lease against assigning, under-letting, charging or parting with the possession of the demised premises or any part thereof is subject to a proviso to the effect that such consent is not to be unreasonably withheld.[7] If the landlord unreasonably withholds consent to the charge, then his consent ceases to be required and the lessee can grant the charge without such consent and without committing a breach of the lease. A prospective chargee should carefully check the terms of any lease before accepting a charge over it to ensure that the grant of the charge will not involve a breach of covenant and that all the requirements of the lease are complied with.[8] It should also check whether the subsequent taking of possession or the appointment of a receiver will trigger a right to forfeiture on the part of the landlord.

Was the appointment of the receiver a breach of the terms of the lease?
In the absence of an express provision to such effect, the appointment of **15–004** a receiver in relation to a company tenant will not place the company in breach of its lease. Furthermore, it would be unusual for a lease to contain an express provision which had that effect. But it is a separate matter whether the lease contains a forfeiture clause which permits the landlord to claim a forfeiture of the lease in the event of the appointment of a receiver in relation to the company lessee.

Is the landlord entitled to seek forfeiture of the lease by reason of the grant of the charge or the appointment of the receiver?
The standard forfeiture clause in a commercial lease will permit **15–005** forfeiture of the lease in the event of any breach by the tenant of its obligations contained in the lease. Thus, if the grant of, or the existence of, the charge involved a breach of the lease, then the landlord is entitled to seek to forfeit the lease on that account. It is commonplace for the forfeiture clause to permit forfeiture in the event of the appointment of a receiver in relation to the company tenant.

Is the landlord entitled to seek forfeiture of the lease by reason of the non-payment of rent or other breaches of covenant?
The standard form of forfeiture clause in a commercial lease will permit **15–006** forfeiture in the event of non-payment of rent or breach by the tenant of its obligations contained in the lease.

---

[6] Law of Property Act 1925, s. 86(1).

[7] Landlord and Tenant Act 1927, s. 19(1). For the case law as to what amount to reasonable grounds for refusal of consent, see the standard text books on landlord and tenant. As to the duty on the landlord to consider and respond to an application for consent and not to withhold consent unreasonably, see the Landlord and Tenant Act 1988.

[8] A grant in breach of covenant is effective, although it may render the lease liable to forfeiture: see *Old Grovebury Manor Farm v. W. Seymour (No. 2)* [1979] 1 W.L.R. 1397 (a case of assignment in breach of covenant).

Other questions arising in relation to a possible forfeiture

15–007 The first question which arises is whether the alleged breach has been committed or the alleged event which may give rise to a forfeiture has occurred. The second question is whether the right to forfeit has been waived by the landlord. This question is principally important in relation to once and for all breaches as compared with continuing breaches. The third question is whether the landlord has complied with any statutory formalities before being able to seek forfeiture. The statutory formalities usually require the tenant to be given the opportunity to remedy the breach (if the breach is remediable) so as to avoid forfeiture. The fourth question is whether the landlord has effected a forfeiture (subject to the possibility of relief from forfeiture). The last question is whether the tenant or the chargee will be able to obtain relief from forfeiture. These questions will be considered with particular reference to the factual situations most likely to occur as a result of, or at the same time as, the appointment of a receiver of the company.

Waiver

15–008 The law of waiver is an example of the general principles relating to election between inconsistent rights. A landlord is held to have waived a right to forfeit which has arisen (whether by reason of a previous breach of covenant or by reason of some other specified event entitling the landlord to forfeit) when the landlord, with knowledge of the breach or the event giving rise to the forfeiture, does some unequivocal act which recognises the continuing existence of the lease at a time after the right to forfeit has arisen. Knowledge in this context is knowledge of the facts which constitute the breach or the event entitling the landlord to forfeit rather than knowledge of the law as to whether the facts amount to a breach or not.[9] The act in question must be communicated to the tenant. The most usual act relied on is the demand for or the acceptance of rent.[10] A demand for rent will cause a waiver in law irrespective of the subjective intention of the landlord, and waiver occurs though the demand was inadvertent.[11] A demand for, or an acceptance of, rent due prior to the breach will not indicate a waiver. In the case of a once and for all breach, waiver of the right to forfeit for that breach means that the right to forfeit for that breach is forever gone; in the case of a continuing breach, waiver of the right to forfeit by recognising the existence of the lease up to a certain date, will not prevent the landlord

---

[9] *David Blackstone Ltd v. Burnetts (W. End) Ltd* [1973] 1 W.L.R. 1487. The authorities are reviewed in *Cornillie v. Saha* (1996) 72 P. & C.R. 147. This is the traditional view in the law of landlord and tenant in respect of waiver of the contractual right to forfeit. In *Peyman v. Lanjani* [1985] Ch. 457, in the context of the waiver of the equitable right to rescind, the Court of Appeal held that a party should not be taken to have elected to affirm or rescind a contract unless he has knowledge, not only of the facts, but also of the right to elect. It has been recognised that the requirements for waiver of forfeiture are less strict (and more favourable to the tenant) than is the case with the principles of election in other contexts: *Oliver Ashworth Ltd v. Ballard Ltd* [2000] Ch 12 at 30E.

[10] *Expert Clothing v. Hillgate House* [1986] Ch. 340.

[11] *Central Estates (Belgravia) Ltd v. Woolgar (No. 2)* [1972] 1 Q.B. 48.

forfeiting for a continuation of the breach after that date. If the grant of a charge is a breach of a covenant in the lease, such breach will be committed when the charge is granted and will be a once and for all breach. If the event of forfeiture is the appointment of a receiver, that event occurs when the receiver is appointed and is a once and for all event, even though the receiver's appointment continues to be effective. The distinction between once and for all breaches and continuing breaches is a completely different distinction from that between remediable and irremediable breaches.

Remedying the breach

A right of forfeiture of a lease is not enforceable, by action or otherwise, **15–009** unless and until the landlord serves on the tenant a notice specifying the particular breach complained of, requiring the tenant to remedy the breach (if the same is capable of remedy) and requiring the tenant to make compensation in money for the breach.[12] Further, the right of forfeiture is not exercisable unless the tenant fails within a reasonable time of the notice to remedy the breach (if the same is capable of remedy) and to make reasonable compensation in money, to the satisfaction of the landlord, for the breach.[13] No such notice is needed in the case of forfeiture for non-payment of rent and the landlord need not wait a reasonable time for the tenant to pay the rent after the time allowed by the forfeiture provision for payment of rent.[14] A section 146 notice is needed where the right to forfeit arises by reason of the appointment of a receiver even though such an event is not separately a breach of covenant.[15] The general test for remediability is whether the harm that has been done to the landlord by the relevant breach is, for practical purposes, capable of being retrieved within a reasonable time.[16] The Court of Appeal has held that the grant of a sub-lease in breach of a covenant against sub-letting is an irremediable breach[17] and the reasoning in this case would indicate that the grant of a charge in breach of covenant will be held irremediable. It is suggested that the appointment of a receiver which gives rise to a right to forfeit would be capable of remedy by removing the receiver.[18] Although a breach may be held

---

[12] Law of Property Act 1925, s. 146(1). Despite the apparent mandatory language, it has been held that the notice is not bad for not requiring compensation in money: *Lock v. Pearce* [1893] 2 Ch. 271.

[13] Law of Property Act 1925, s. 146(1).

[14] Law of Property Act 1925, s. 146(11). It is usual for the forfeiture provision in the lease to give the tenant some days or weeks before the right to forfeit for non payment of rent arises.

[15] See *Halliard Property v. Jack Segal* [1978] 1 W.L.R. 377 (right to forfeit in the event of insolvency of a surety).

[16] *Savva v. Hussein* [1996] 2 E.G.L.R. 65

[17] *Scala House & District Property Co. Ltd v. Forbes* [1974] Q.B. 575 and see *Expert Clothing v. Hillgate House* [1986] Ch. 340 which affirmed as the *ratio decidendi* of the *Scala* case that a breach of a covenant against assignment, sub-letting or parting with possession was irremediable, but held that a breach of a covenant to give notice of a grant of a charge was remediable.

[18] In the case of an administrative receiver, who can only be removed by the court, this would seem to be an unlikely option.

irremediable for the purposes of section 146(1) of the Law of Property Act 1925, this does not mean that the court does not have power to grant relief against forfeiture in relation to that breach.

The forfeiture

15–010 A landlord may seek to forfeit the lease by action or by peaceable re-entry. There is no requirement that the landlord obtain the leave of the court before commencing proceedings or before peaceably re-entering where the ground of forfeiture is the appointment of a receiver over the company tenant. Where the landlord brings proceedings against the tenant for possession based on a forfeiture of the lease, the landlord must state in the particulars of claim the name and address of any underlessee or mortgagee entitled to claim relief against forfeiture of whom he knows.[19] In the light of these provisions, it should be normal practice for a chargee of a lease to inform a landlord of the existence of the charge.[20]

An application for relief from forfeiture by the tenant

15–011 In the event of a forfeiture, the tenant will wish to consider applying for relief from forfeiture. It is necessary to consider separately the provisions dealing with relief from forfeiture where the ground of forfeiture is breach of covenant or other event (but not non-payment of rent) and relief from forfeiture where the ground of forfeiture is non-payment of rent. In the former case, the tenant may apply for relief from forfeiture under section 146(2) of the Law of Property Act 1925. In the latter case, the tenant may obtain automatic relief from forfeiture under section 212 of the Common Law Procedure Act 1852 (in the case of proceedings for forfeiture brought in the High Court) or under section 138 of the County Courts Act 1984 (in the case of proceedings for forfeiture brought in the county court). The automatic effect of relief from forfeiture applies where the tenant pays off the arrears of rent and costs in accordance with the time limits laid down in those statutory provisions. In addition, the tenant is entitled to apply for relief from forfeiture for non-payment of rent under sections 210 of the Common Law Procedure Act 1852 and/ or section 38 of the Supreme Court Act 1981 (in the High Court) and under section 138 of the County Courts Act 1984 (in the county court). A receiver has no *locus standi* in his own right to apply for relief from forfeiture but he will normally be able to act as agent for the company tenant and make such an application in the name of the company.[21] Where the tenant obtains automatic relief or where the court grants relief to the tenant, the lease is retrospectively revived without the need

---

[19] CPR 16 PD–002, para. 6.8, Sched. 2, C6.3(2). In the county court, the landlord must file the particulars of claim for service by the court on the mortgagee or underlessee: CPR, Sched. 2, C6.3(2). The position is less clear in the High Court. The rules of court were considered in *Rexhaven v. Nurse* (1996) 28 H.L.R. 241 and *Croydon (Unique) v. Wright* [1999] 4 All E R 257.

[20] See Megarry & Wade, *The Law of Real Property* (6th ed.), p. 830.

[21] *Goughs Garages v. Pugsley* [1930] 1 K.B. 615; the receiver's authority to act in this way will survive a subsequent liquidation.

for any further lease to be granted. The right to seek relief is an assignable chose in action and may be assigned by the company (acting through its receiver) to a purchaser of the right.[22]

An application for relief from forfeiture by the chargee
By section 87 of the Law of Property Act 1925, a chargee of a lease has **15–012** the same protection powers and remedies as if it had a sub-term less by one day than the term vested in the chargor. This enables a chargee to claim relief from forfeiture of the lease in the same way as an underlessee could claim such relief. There are two ways in which a chargee can claim relief from forfeiture. The first is by relying on the statutory powers which confer on the tenant the right to automatic relief or the right to seek relief. In a series of decisions, the Court of Appeal has held that the references to "lessee" in section 138 of the County Courts Act 1984, section 38 of the Supreme Court Act 1981 and section 146(2) of the Law of Property Act 1925 all include an "underlessee" and therefore a chargee.[23] Where the forfeiture is on a ground other than non-payment of rent, and relief is obtained by a chargee under section 146(2) of the Law of Property Act 1925, the relief is retrospective to the date of forfeiture.[24] The same applies where the forfeiture is for non-payment of rent and relief is granted in the first way described above.[25] The second way in which a chargee can seek relief from forfeiture is pursuant to section 146(4) of the Law of Property Act 1925; this provision applies whether the forfeiture is for non-payment of rent or on another ground. The chargee can apply under this provision even in those exceptional circumstances[26] where the lessee cannot seek relief.[27] The grant of relief operates by way of an order vesting the premises in the chargee as a lessee. The court has power to impose conditions on the grant of the vesting order. The court is likely to require the chargee to covenant with the landlord to perform the covenants in the forfeited lease.[28] The making of the vesting order is not retrospective so that there is likely to be a gap between the date when the former lease ended as a result of the forfeiture and the date of the vesting order.[29] During this

[22] *Howard v. Fanshawe* [1895] 2 Ch. 581.
[23] *United Dominions Trust v. Shellpoint Trustees* [1993] 4 All E.R. 310 and the cases together reported as *Escalus Properties v. Robinson* [1996] Q.B. 231, applied in *Bank of Ireland Home Mortgages v. South Lodge Developments* [1996] 1 E.G.L.R. 91.
[24] *Dendy v. Evans* [1910] 1 K B 263.
[25] Either as a result of the statutory provisions expressly so providing or as a result of *Dendy v. Evans* [1910] 1 K B 263.
[26] Law of Property Act 1924, s. 146(8), (9) and (10).
[27] Law of Property (Amendment) Act 1929, s. 1.
[28] *Gray v. Bonsall* [1904] 1 K B 601 at 608; *Official Custodian for Charities v. Parway Estates Developments* [1985] Ch151 at 164. A chargee would normally be reluctant to take on this obligation. Before the coming into force of the Landlord and Tenant (Covenants) Act 1995 on the January 1, 1996, such a covenant by an original lessee (as the chargee would be) would have endured for the remainder of the term of the lease; now the original lessee will be released from the covenant from the date of a lawful assignment: see ss. 5 and 11; but, the original lessee may be required to enter into an "authorised guarantee agreement" under s. 16 of the 1995 Act in relation to the liability of the first assignee.
[29] *Cadogan v. Dimovic* [1984] 1 W.L.R. 609

period the landlord is prima facie entitled to damages for trespass from persons in possession of the premises.[30] Whether the chargee obtains relief by way of retrospective reinstatement of the lease or by way of a vesting order, he holds the lease as substitute security subject to an equity of redemption in favour of the chargor.[31] The chargee's preference as to the mode by which relief from forfeiture is obtained will normally be, first, the grant of relief to the lessee, second, the grant of relief to the chargee under section 146(2) and third, the grant of a vesting order to the chargee. Under the first of these, the chargee avoids taking on direct liability under the covenants in the lease; under the first and second of these, relief is retrospective so that there is no gap between forfeiture and the reinstatement of the lease; under the third mode of obtaining relief, the chargee will usually have to give a direct covenant to the landlord and there will be a gap between forfeiture and the grant of the vesting order which has consequences as regards the payment of damages for trespass and the effect on derivative interests.[32]

The time for applying for relief

15–013 The tenant or the chargee is entitled to apply for relief from forfeiture under section 146(2) of the Law of Property Act 1925 while "a lessor is proceeding" to enforce its right of forfeiture. Similarly, a chargee is entitled to apply for relief under section 146(4) of the 1925 Act while a lessor is so proceeding. A landlord begins to proceed to enforce his right of forfeiture as soon as he serves a section 146 notice and an application for relief may thereupon be made.[33] Where the lessor has brought court proceedings claiming possession as a result of a forfeiture, the lessor is proceeding to enforce the right of forfeiture until the lessor executes a judgment for possession obtained in those proceedings.[34] Upon execution of the judgement, the tenant or chargee loses the right to seek relief under section 146(2) or section 146(4). In some circumstances the tenant or chargee may have proper grounds to have the judgment set aside.[35] Where the lessor has sought to enforce his right of forfeiture by peaceable re-entry without court proceedings, it has been held that the lessor does not cease to proceed to enforce his right of forfeiture on the taking of possession and the court retains jurisdiction under section 146(2) and section 146(4) to grant relief from forfeiture.[36] The time

---

[30] *Official Custodian for Charities v. Mackey* [1985] Ch. 168 and *Official Custodian for Charities v. Mackey (No. 2)* [1985] 1 W.L.R. 1308.

[31] *Chelsea Estates Investment Trust v. Marche* [1955] Ch. 328 and *Official Custodian for Charities v. Parway Estates Developments* [1985] Ch. 151 at 164.

[32] See the difficulties in *Hammersmith and Fulham LBC v. Tops Shop Centres* [1990] Ch. 237.

[33] *Pakwood Transport v. 15 Beauchamp Place* (1978) 36 P. & C.R. 112.

[34] *Rogers v. Rice* [1892] 2 Ch. 170.

[35] *Rexhaven v. Nurse* (1996) 28 H.L.R. 241; in that case the judgment was not set aside to allow a mortgagee to apply for relief from forfeiture because the mortgagee had been notified under the rules of court of the proceedings for forfeiture and had neglected to intervene and seek relief until after a judgment for possession had been executed. The judgment was set aside in *Croydon (Unique) v. Wright* [1999] 4 All E.R. 257; this case concerned forfeiture for non-payment of rent and County Courts Act 1984, s. 138.

[36] *Billson v. Residential Apartments* [1992] 1 A.C. 494.

limits for seeking relief from forfeiture for non-payment of rent differ depending on whether the landlord is enforcing the right of forfeiture in the High Court or in the county court, or by peaceable re-entry.[37]

The court's discretion to grant relief from forfeiture
The court has a wide discretion in relation to the circumstances in which, **15–014** and the terms on which, it will be prepared to grant relief from forfeiture. It is possible to state some general principles which guide the approach of the court. In the case of forfeiture for non-payment of rent, equity regarded the right of forfeiture as security for payment of the rent, with the result that if the arrears of rent were paid off and the landlord was reimbursed his costs and expenses, it was normally considered just to grant relief from forfeiture; save in exceptional cases, the court would not have regard to other breaches of covenant.[38] In the case of forfeiture on other grounds, an applicant for relief was normally required to remedy, that is undo the consequences of, the breach, make compensation for any damage caused and make it clear that the covenants would be performed in the future. In such circumstances, a court would be minded to grant relief from forfeiture. The court would consider the conduct of the tenant, the nature and gravity of the breach and the value of the property being forfeited. Different views have been expressed as to the relevance of the fact that the breach was deliberate or wilful. It has been said that wilful breaches should only exceptionally be relieved against because sound principle required that the landlord should not be forced to remain in a relationship of landlord and tenant with a person in deliberate breach of his obligations.[39] However, the more recent approach is to hold that relief from forfeiture in the case of a wilful breach is not to be confined to exceptional cases, although the court should not in exercising its discretion encourage the belief that parties to a lease can ignore their obligations and buy their way out of any consequential forfeiture.[40] Where the breach consists of doing something, *e.g.* the grant of a charge without first asking for the landlord's consent, it will be relevant to ask whether such consent could have been unreasonably withheld. The above principles will therefore

---

[37] In summary, the position is: in the High Court, following an order for possession, within six months of execution: Common Law Procedure Act 1852, s. 210; in the High Court, following peaceable re-entry, no statutory time limit but a six month limit is used as a guide; in the county court, following an order for possession, within six months after execution: County Courts Act 1984, s. 138(9A)–(9C); in the county court, following peaceable re-entry, within six months of the re-entry: County Courts Act 1984, s.139(2). If the application for relief is made by the chargee under s. 146(4) of the Law of Property Act 1925, the application must be made while "the lessor is proceeding", as to which see the main text. For a full treatment, see *Woodfall on Landlord and Tenant* (Looseleaf ed.), Vol. 1 at paras 17–178—17–195.

[38] *Gill v. Lewis* [1956] 2 Q B 1. It was suggested in *Re Naaem* [1990] 1 W.L.R. 48 that where the landlord as creditor was bound by a voluntary arrangement which restricted the landlord's ability to recover in full the arrears of rent, relief might be granted on terms that the tenant only paid off part of the arrears in accordance with the voluntary arrangement but this suggestion has since been doubted: *March Estates v. Gunmark* [1996] 2 B.C.L.C. 1.

[39] *Shiloh Spinners v. Harding* [1973] A.C. 691.

[40] *Southern Depot v. British Railways Board* [1990] 2 E.G.L.R. 39.

apply where the breach alleged is the grant of a charge of the lease in breach of covenant. Where the event which gives rise to the forfeiture is the appointment of a receiver, the court is likely to consider whether the landlord suffers any prejudice by reason of the appointment of the receiver over and above the prejudice suffered by reason of any financial weakness of the company tenant. It is unlikely that a court would refuse relief from forfeiture where the only matter complained of was the appointment of a receiver and the lease had a value which the company acting through its receiver wished to realise. As indicated above, the chargee will normally prefer that relief be granted to the tenant rather than to the chargee direct. This reluctance is matched by the consideration that it will probably be more difficult, against the wishes of the landlord, to obtain an order vesting the premises in the chargee as compared with obtaining a grant of relief to the tenant itself; this is because the court will be more cautious about forcing on the landlord the relationship of landlord and tenant with someone whom the landlord has not freely accepted. Of course, the landlord may positively prefer the making of a vesting order in favour of the chargee rather than the grant of relief to the tenant because the making of a vesting order may provide the landlord with a better covenant (that of the chargee rather than the lessee) and there may be the consequential advantages that the landlord may be able to claim damages for trespass in relation to the gap between the forfeiture of the lease and the making of the vesting order. Relief may be refused where the landlord has acted reasonably in re-letting the premises following the forfeiture.[41]

Relief against forfeiture for breach of a condition against liquidation

15–015   Although generally speaking the jurisdiction to grant relief, whether to the company tenant or to the chargee, is unlimited, in the case of breach of a condition against the winding-up of the tenant or the taking of the lease into execution, relief cannot be granted to the lessee where the lease is of:

    (a) agricultural or pastoral land;
    (b) mines or minerals;
    (c) a public house or beershop;
    (d) a furnished dwelling-house;
    (e) property with respect to which the personal qualifications of the tenant are of importance for the preservation of the value or character of the property or on the ground of neighbourhood to the landlord or any person holding under him.[42]

Further, in all other cases of a breach of this condition, the court cannot grant any relief to the tenant unless either the landlord takes

---

[41] *Silverman v. AFCO (U.K.)* [1988] 1 E.G.L.R. 51, *Fuller v. Judy Properties* [1992] 1 E.G.L.R. 75 and *Bank of Ireland Home Mortgages v. South Lodge Developments* [1996] 1 E.G.L.R. 91.
[42] Law of Property Act 1925, s. 146(9).

steps to forfeit and the tenant applies for relief, or the lease is sold within one year.[43] In default of such application or sale, relief both under statute and under the inherent jurisdiction of equity is barred.[44] The existence of a specifically enforceable contract for sale is sufficient for this purpose.[45] In the case where such a sale takes place, the court, in the exercise of its discretion whether to grant relief, considers whether the lessor is secure in respect of the future performance of the covenants of the lease, and for this purpose the standing and trustworthiness of the purchaser may be relevant. If the purchaser is of good standing and trustworthy, the court will incline to grant relief, for to refuse to do so would involve giving the value of the lease to the lessor at the expense of the lessee.[46]

But neither the statutory exclusion nor the restriction of the grant of **15–016** relief to the lessee has application to a claim for relief by a mortgagee.[47] Nor will the court impose, as a condition of the grant of relief, a requirement that the mortgagee sells the lease whether within a fixed period or at all, for "any requirement which might prejudice a mortgagee's security or interfere with his choice of remedies is at odds with the principle on which relief is granted".[48]

Is the landlord entitled to distrain for unpaid rent?

A landlord's right to distrain for rent is unaffected by the creation of or **15–017** crystallisation of a floating charge over the tenant company.[49] It may be in the interests of the receiver and debenture-holder that the subject-matter or proceeds of the distress be applied in payment of preferential creditors rather than the landlord, and in the following circumstances it may be possible to achieve this result. In a case where the lessee was in liquidation, a liquidator was held entitled to restrain distress on the ground that the company's assets were insufficient to pay preferential creditors, notwithstanding that the company's assets were charged to secure a sum far exceeding their value.[50] Kerr suggests that on his appointment, even in the absence of a liquidation, the receiver might equally apply for such relief in the name of the company or (if so authorised) of a preferential creditor.[51] Alternatively the receiver has

---

[43] *ibid.*, s. 146(10).

[44] *Official Custodian for Charities v. Parway Estates* [1985] Ch. 151.

[45] *Harry Lay v. Fox* (1963) 186 E.G. 15.

[46] *ibid.*

[47] Law of Property (Amendment) Act 1929, s. 1 amending s. 146(4) of the Law of Property Act 1925, and see *Official Custodian for Charities v. Parway Estates* [1985] Ch. 151.

[48] *Per* Nourse J. in *Official Custodian for Charities v. Mackey (No. 2)* [1985] 1 W.L.R. 1308; [1985] 2 All E.R. 1016 at 1024.

[49] *Re Roundwood Colliery Co.* [1897] 1 Ch. 373 at 393 and see *Purcell v. Queensland Public Curator* (1922) 31 C.L.R. 220. *Metropolitan Life v. Essere Print Ltd* (1990) N.Z.C.L.C. 66, 775 (Jeffries J.); [1991] 3 N.Z.L.R. 170, NZCA contrasts the common law position with the result of the New Zealand Statute Reforms in 1908, which have the effect of preventing such distress. See also below, Chap. 20.

[50] *Re South Rhondda Colliery Co.* [1928] W.N. 126. See also Insolvency Act 1986, s. 176.

[51] (17th ed.), p. 204, n. 86.

power to petition for a winding-up[52] so as to lay the basis for an application by the liquidator to restrain distress.

Release of the lease from the charge

15–018   Unlike a liquidator, a receiver has no right to disclaim a lease. But the chargee may at any time release from its charge any property and the effect is to restore the powers of the directors of the chargor to deal with the asset. This may be done because the property in question is not of any value, or not of sufficient value to merit efforts at realisation, or because it attracts liability for unoccupied property rates on the part of the receiver.[53] A decision whether or not to release frequently has to be taken in regard to leases. Care must be taken to ensure that the release of the lease from the charge does not inadvertently release a guarantor in respect of the debt which was secured by the charge.[54]

Disclaimer of the lease

15–019   A liquidator of a lessee company, notwithstanding the fact that it has charged its lease as security, may, subject to the requirements of the section, disclaim the lease as onerous property under section 178 of the Insolvency Act 1986. The effect of disclaimer is to determine, as from the date of the disclaimer, the rights, interests and liabilities of the company in or in respect of the property disclaimed; but it does not, except so far as is necessary for the purpose of releasing the company, affect the rights and liabilities of any other person.[55] A chargee may, as a "person claiming an interest in the disclaimed property" under section 181 of the Act, apply to the court for a vesting order within three months of becoming aware of the disclaimer or of receiving a copy of the liquidator's notice of disclaimer, whichever is the earlier.[56] A court cannot make a vesting order on the application of a chargee except on terms that the chargee is made subject to the same liabilities to which the company was subject at the commencement of the winding-up, alternatively subject to the same liabilities as there would have been if the chargee had taken an assignment at the commencement of the winding-up.[57]

Personal liability of receiver

15–020   The receiver is not personally liable under the covenants in the lease, or for an occupation rent in respect of the period that the company under

---

[52] See above, Chap. 11.

[53] See below, Chap. 20.

[54] The relevant principles are summarised in *Chitty on Contracts* (28th, ed.), Vol. 2, para. 44–093; see also *op. cit.* at paras. 44–095—44–096 as to the responsibility owed by a secured creditor to a surety in relation to the realisation of the security; and see also *Skipton Building Society v. Stott* [2000] 2 All E.R. 779.

[55] Insolvency Act 1986, s. 178(4). The effect of this provision was analysed in detail in *Hindcastle v. Barbara Attenborough* [1997] A.C. 70; see, in particular, at 89 where the position of a third party such as an underlessee or chargee is discussed.

[56] Insolvency Rules 1986, r. 4.194; the period may be extended pursuant to r. 4.3.

[57] Insolvency Act 1986, s. 182(1).

his receivership continues in beneficial occupation,[58] unless he agrees with the lessor to assume such liability.[59] Such agreement is on occasion a method of reconciling the interests of the lessor in securing the due performance of the covenants with the interests of the receiver in having an opportunity, without interference or legal action by the lessor, to secure a beneficial realisation to a respectable and responsible assignee. No liability will attach to the receiver and no agreement for personal liability will be inferred merely because the receiver continues, as agent of the company, to pay rent. Further, a receiver who pays rent in his own name will not be liable as tenant by estoppel unless the landlord has been induced by such payment to believe that the lease had been assigned to the receiver.[60] Although the onset of a winding-up deprives the receiver of his agency for the company, continued beneficial occupation thereafter by the receiver, whether as principal or as agent of the mortgagee, still does not render him (or the mortgagee) liable for rent: a contract to pay must be established. The distinction to be drawn is between the receipt of benefits of a subsisting contract between the landlord and the company (in which case the receiver, whether appointed by or out of court, is under no liability) and the receipt of benefits under a contract to which the receiver personally is a party (in which case he may be exposed to liability).[61]

If the receiver decides not to perform the terms of the lease, he will **15–021** render the tenant liable for breach. The receiver will not, however, be liable for the tort of inducing the tenant to breach its contract, although he may be liable if he acts in bad faith or outside his authority.[62]

Under section 109(8)(i) of the Law of Property Act 1925, which **15–022** applies in the case of statutory appointments and which is often incorporated by reference into debentures, there is an "obligation" on the part of the receiver to pay (*inter alia*) rents out of moneys coming into his hands. It has, however, been held with regard to other sums payable under section 109(8) that the prospective payee has no *locus standi* to enforce payment and that the obligation is owed to the mortgagee and mortgagor alone.[63] A failure to make such payment out of receipts may expose the receiver to liability at the instance of the mortgagor or mortgagee if such failure occasions loss to either of them.[64]

---

[58] *Hand v. Blow* [1901] 2 Ch. 721; *Re Westminster Motor Garage Co.* (1914) 84 L.J. Ch. 573; *Re British Investments Etc. Pty Ltd* [1979] A.C.L.C 31 at 100; *Rangatira Pty Ltd v. Viola Hallam Ltd* [1957] N.Z.L.R. 1188 at 1190.

[59] *Hay v. Swedish Ry.* (1892) 8 T.L.R. 775; *Consolidated Entertainments v. Taylor* [1937] 4 All ER. 432; *Central London Electricity v. Berners* [1945] 1 All E.R. 160. The agreement between lessor and receiver may limit the receiver's liability to assets in his hands as receiver.

[60] *Rangatira Pty Ltd v. Viola Hallam Ltd* [1957] N.Z.L.R. 1188; *Re British Investment Etc. Pty Ltd* [1979] A.C.L.C. 31.

[61] *Consolidated Entertainments v. Taylor* [1937] 4 All E.R. 432.

[62] *Lathia v. Dronsfield Bros Ltd* [1987] B.C.L.C. 321; *Welsh Development Agency v. Export Finance Co.* [1992] B.C.C. 270, CA (counterclaim).

[63] *Liverpool Corporation v. Hope* [1938] 1 K.B. 751; *Re John Willment (Ashford) Ltd* [1980] 1 W.L.R. 73. See below, Chap. 21.

[64] *Visbord v. Federal Commissioner of Taxation* (1943) 68 C.L.R. 354 at 385.

Personal liability of the receiver: trespass

15–023 There is an open question whether a receiver, appointed by a mortgagee of a lease, who continues to act as such and causes or permits the mortgagor to continue in occupation or to receive rent from sub-lessees during the period between the service of proceedings for forfeiture by the lessor and an order for possession in favour of the lessor, may be liable as a trespasser for mesne profits.[65] The lessor is certainly entitled to mesne profits in respect of this period during which he has been deprived of possession from the lessee and the sub-lessee. This is a type of damages for trespass.[66] If the receiver has personally authorised the trespass, in principle he may be held liable as a joint tortfeasor.[67] A distinction might be drawn between the positive act of authorising continued occupation (occasioning personal liability) and the passive act of accepting rent from sub-lessees, but this distinction is tenuous, for the receipt (even if not anticipated by a demand for payment) is equivalent to an endorsement of the continued occupation of the sub-lessees.

Head-landlord's right to rent under sub-lease

15–024 In a case where the receiver is being paid rent by sub-lessees of the company but is not causing the company to pay rent to the lessor, the lessor can serve notice[68] on the sub-lessees in any case where the lessee's rent is in arrears, requiring all future payments of rent, whether already accrued due or not, to be paid to the lessor until the lessee's arrears have been paid in full.[69] The effect of such a notice is to transfer from the company in receivership to the lessor the benefit of the obligation of the sub-lessees to pay rent until all arrears are paid off. An immediate relationship of landlord and lessee is deemed to be established between the head landlord and the sub-lessee.[70] Following service of the notice, the lessor may recover the rent payable by the sub-lessees by action or distress; moreover, he is not thereby precluded from proving in the liquidation for any balance of the arrears due from the head lessee.[71] The sub-lessee may, however, deduct any sums paid to the head lessor from the amount due to his immediate landlord.[72]

15–025   In *Rhodes v. Allied Dunbar Pension Services Ltd*; *Re Offshore Ventilation Ltd*.[73] the question arose whether a landlord who had served a

---

[65] See *Official Custodian for Charities v. Mackey (No. 2)* [1985] 1 W.L.R. 1308; [1985] 2 All E.R. 1016 where the lessors were held estopped from making such a claim by obtaining judgment for mesne profits against the lessees in a sum equivalent to the rent under the forfeited lease and satisfaction of such judgment by the receivers out of rents received from the sub-lessees.

[66] See *Woodfall on Landlord and Tenant* (Looseleaf ed.), Vol. 1, para. 19–012.

[67] See above, Chap. 7.

[68] The notice may be served by registered post, recorded delivery or personally: *Jarvis v. Hemmings* [1912] 1 Ch. 462 and Recorded Delivery Service Act 1962, s. 1.

[69] Law of Distress Amendment Act 1908, s. 6.

[70] *ibid.*, s. 3.

[71] See Woodfall, *The Law of Landlord and Tenant* (Looseleaf ed.), Vol. 1, paras 9–083—9–084.

[72] *ibid.*, para. 9–085.

[73] [1987] 1 W.L.R. 1703, Harman J.; [1989] 1 W.L.R. 800, CA.

notice under section 6 after he had had notice of the appointment of receivers under a debenture thereby gained priority over the receivers. The debenture was in a usual form, with a charge by way of legal mortgage over the lessee's interest and a fixed charge over debts, as well as a floating charge. Harman J. at first instance treated the matter as one of priority between competing assignments, namely, an equitable assignment of the right to receive the under-rents effected by the crystallisation of the floating charge and the statutory assignment of the same right effected by the service of a notice under section 6. He held that the debenture-holder had priority because the landlord had notice of the debenture-holder's assignment when the landlord gave notice.

The Court of Appeal held that on the facts there was no equitable **15–026** assignment to the debenture-holder and the question of competing assignments therefore did not arise. On the true construction of the debenture, the entitlement to the under-rents as between the debenture-holder and the company was governed by the charge by way of legal mortgage and not by the fixed charge on debts or the general floating charge; the company remained entitled to the under-rents unless and until the debenture-holder went into possession, which it had not. The appointment of receivers made no material difference to this analysis, since they were deemed to be the agents of the company and received the under-rents as such. Moreover, even if the debenture-holder had gone into possession, section 6 would still have been available to the landlord, since the debenture-holder's sub-term would have been subject to the rights conferred on the superior landlord under the Act.

The result of the Court of Appeal's decision is that, in a case involving **15–027** the common type of debenture employed in *Rhodes v. Allied Dunbar*, the lessor can obtain priority by serving notice on sub-lessees. Debenture-holders will no doubt consider re-drafting their charges so as to cover the right to under-rents expressly. In that event, the question of competing assignments will have to be considered once again.

The construction of the debenture by the Court of Appeal excluding **15–028** rentals from the scope of the fixed charge on debts has been questioned.[74]

2. GRANT AND ASSIGNMENT OF LEASES

The terms of any lease held by the company must be carefully considered **15–029** before any commitment is assumed whether to assign, sub-let or part with possession. Practically invariably, leases contain provisions regulating these matters, but the provisions vary in their content between absolute prohibitions and provisions merely requiring subsequent notification to the lessor. But the common form provision requires the prior written consent of the lessor, such consent not to be unreasonably

---

[74] Moss and Segal, "Insolvency and Leases", in 1992 Blundell Memorial Lectures, paras 11–004 and 11–008.

withheld.[75] The advantage of an assignment is, of course, that the tenant company may be able to realise any value there may be in the lease. Further, in relation to "new tenancies" that is tenancies granted on or after January 1, 1996, an assignment which is permitted by the covenants in the lease will result in the assignor being released from any liability as original tenant or under a direct covenant which would otherwise endure for the remainder of the term.[76] However, the tenant company may be required to enter into an "authorised guarantee agreement" guaranteeing to the landlord the obligations of the assignee during the period that the lease is vested in the assignee.[77] If the assignor is in receivership and its covenant is not of substantial value, the landlord may choose to dispense with the requirement of an authorised guarantee agreement. The covenant against assignment or sub-letting may sometimes contain an express proviso to the effect that the landlord's consent is not required in the case of an assignment or sub-lease to a subsidiary or associated company.[78] In a case where the lease contains such a proviso, and no other applicable restriction,[79] there is afforded to the receiver an opportunity to escape from the covenant, for he may with impunity assign or sub-let to a subsidiary or associated company (if necessary, acquired or incorporated for the purpose) and then freely dispose of the company.

3. REVERSIONS AS SECURITY

15–030 The powers of leasing of a mortgagor and of a mortgagee are considered at above, paragraphs 9–016 and 9–017. A mortgagee will be bound by a lease granted by the mortgagor before the grant of the mortgage. A mortgagee will also be bound by a lease granted by the mortgagor after the grant of the mortgage provided that the mortgagor has acted within its powers of leasing and obtained any necessary consent from the mortgagee. Where the mortgagee is bound by such a lease, the mortgagee of the reversion also takes subject to any statutory rights of the lessee (or of a sub-lessee holding under such lessee) to the grant of a

---

[75] If the lease requires the tenant to obtain the landlord's consent to the assignment or underletting but does not expressly state that such consent is not to be unreasonably withheld, a proviso to this effect is implied by statute: see Landlord and Tenant Act 1927, s. 19(1)(a) amended in respect of assignments in relation to covenants in "qualifying leases" (essentially commercial leases granted on or after January 1, 1996) by the Landlord and Tenant (Covenants) Act 1995. For the case law as to what amount to reasonable grounds for refusal of consent, see the standard text books on landlord and tenant. As to the duty of a landlord to consider and respond to an application for consent to assignment or underletting, see the Landlord and Tenant Act 1988. If the sale is by the mortgagee in exercise of its power of sale, then any licence required for such sale is not to be unreasonably withheld: Law of Property Act 1925, s. 89(1).

[76] Landlord and Tenant (Covenants) Act 1995, ss. 5 and 11.

[77] *ibid.*, s. 16.

[78] This is no longer usual; at the present time, the usual reference to associated or subsidiary companies in a covenant which controls alienation, etc. is one which only permits the tenant to share occupation with an associated or subsidiary company.

[79] *e.g.* precluding disposal of shares in any assignee of the lease.

new lease[80] or to purchase the reversion,[81] and to any like contractual rights so long as these rights are duly protected by registration or (in the case of registered land) subsist as over-riding interests.[82] .Of course, the mortgagee and any receiver may be principally concerned with the right to enjoy the benefits of the reversion and, in particular, the right to receive the rent payable under the lease. The mortgagee may benefit from these rights by taking possession of the rents or by appointing a receiver who will receive the rents as agent for the mortgagor. A problem can arise where the mortgagor has bargained with the lessee for the payment by the lessee of "rent" substantially in advance of the due dates for payment of rent under the lease. Although this will not commonly occur, it may happen for cash flow reasons (possibly with a discount given by the mortgagor to the tenant) or for tax reasons or because there is a connection between the landlord and the tenant.[83] It is necessary to analyse the effect of such an agreement as between the landlord and the tenant and then to consider the extent to which a receiver or a mortgagee is bound by it. Such an advance payment (over and above what is required by way of advance payment by the terms of the lease) is not a fulfillment of the obligation to pay rent; it is an advance to the landlord with an agreement that on the day when the rent becomes due such advance will be treated as a fulfillment of the obligation to pay rent.[84] This agreement will bind the landlord and the landlord's agent such as a receiver. Such an agreement has also been held to create an equitable interest in the property capable of binding third parties.[85] Whether such an equitable interest will bind third parties, such as the mortgagee, will depend on the sequence of events and the doctrine of notice (for unregistered conveyancing) and the principles of land registration (for registered conveyancing). The position will also be affected in the case of leases granted on or after January 1, 1996 by the Landlord and Tenant (Covenants) Act 1995. If the sequence is that the landlord grants a lease, then makes an agreement for an advance payment of rent, then mortgages the reversion, the mortgagee will in most circumstances be bound by the agreement because it will be held to

---

[80] The Landlord and Tenant Act 1954, Pt. II provides for the circumstances in which business tenants are entitled to continue and/or to renew their leases; see s. 36(4) dealing with powers of leasing and s. 67 dealing with mortgagees in possession. See also the right to extended leases or new leases for residential long lessees under the Leasehold Reform Act 1967 and the Leasehold Reform, Housing and Urban Development Act 1992, Part I, Chap. II; see, in particular, ss. 12, 13 of the 1967 Act and s. 58 of the 1993 Act.

[81] For the powers of long lessees to acquire the freehold see the Leasehold Reform Act 1967 and the Leasehold Reform, Housing and Urban Development Act 1993, Part I, Chap. II and, in particular ss. 12, 13 of the 1967 Act and s. 5 of the 1993 Act. For the operation of both the 1967 Act and the 1993 Act, see *Hague on Leasehold Enfranchisement* (3rd ed.) and, for the special provisions relating to mortgagees of the reversion, see Chaps. 13, 28, 32 and 34.

[82] See, *e.g. London and Cheshire Insurance Co. Ltd v. Laplagrene Co. Ltd* [1971] Ch. 499 and the Land Registration Act 1925 as amended by the Land Registration Act 1986.

[83] These suggestions were put forward in *Dibeek Holdings v. Notaras* [2000] A.C.T.S.C. 1.

[84] *De Nicholis v. Saunders* (1870) L.R.5 C.P. 589; *Cook v. Guerra* (1872) L.R.C.P. 132.

[85] *Green v. Rheinberg* (1911) 104 L.T. 149; *Grace Rymer Investments v. Waite* [1958] Ch. 831; *Dibeek Holdings v. Notaras* [2000] A.C.T.S.C. 1.

have constructive notice of it (unregistered land) or the equitable rights of the tenant will be an overriding interest binding the mortgagee under the subsequent mortgage (registered land).[86] The same result was reached where the sequence was that the landlord granted a mortgage, then granted a lease which was initially not binding on the mortgagee, then made an agreement with the tenant for an advance payment of rent, then obtained the consent of the mortgagee to the lease; the lease was binding on the mortgagee by reason of its consent and the equity arising out of the advance payment agreement was binding because the mortgagee had actual or constructive notice of it.[87] In the case of a lease granted on or after January 1, 1996, the agreement made by the landlord would appear to qualify as a landlord covenant.[88] and, accordingly, will be enforceable by the tenant against a mortgagee in possession of the reversion who is entitled to the rents and profits.[89] If the sequence is that the landlord grants the lease, then mortgages the reversion, then makes an agreement with the tenant for advance payment of rent, that agreement does not bind the mortgagee.[90]

---

[86] *Green v. Rheinberg* (1911) 104 L.T. 149; *Grace Rymer Investments v. Waite* [1958] Ch. 831.

[87] *Dibeek Holdings v. Notaras* [2000] A.C.T.S.C. 1.

[88] As defined in s. 28(1) of the 1995 Act; see also the definition therein of "covenant" and "collateral agreement".

[89] Landlord and Tenant (Covenants) Act 1995, s. 15(2).

[90] *De Nicholls v. Saunders* (1870) L.R. 5 C.P. 589. This is subject to any argument that the agreement between the landlord and the tenant (even after the grant of the mortgage) is a landlord covenant which will bind a mortgage who subsequently takes possession: see s. 15(2) of the Landlord and Tenant (Covenants) Act 1995.

CHAPTER 16

SET-OFF AND LIENS IN RECEIVERSHIP

PART I — SET-OFF

1. INTRODUCTION

A set-off is a monetary cross-claim which by operation of law or equity **16–001** also operates as a defence to the claim made in the action.

> ". . . it is something which provides a defence because the nature and quality of the sum so relied upon are such that it is a sum which is proper to be dealt with as diminishing the claim which is made, and against which the sum so demanded can be set off."[1]

There is an important distinction between the ordinary rules of set-off and insolvency set-off. In this context insolvency refers only to bankruptcy for individuals and liquidation for companies. It does not include receivership.[2]

The ordinary rules of set-off address questions of procedure[3] and **16–002** cash-flow.[4] They enable a defendant to require his cross-claim to be tried together with the claimant's claim. Ordinary set-off thus ensures that judgment is given simultaneously in both claims and this relieves the defendant from having to find the cash to satisfy the claimant's judgment before the defendant's cross-claim is determined.

"Insolvency" set-off is not merely procedural but affects the substan- **16–003** tive rights of the parties. It allows the defendant in effect to use his cross-claim as a form of security. It is based on English law's sense of justice, which is not shared by all legal systems.

In the case of receivership, the debenture-holder as an assignee of **16–004** claims pursuant to the charges in the debenture can obtain a significant advantage if the mortgagor has, in its contracts with others, excluded set-off.[5] Thus, where a haulier contracted on the basis that its services were to be paid for without deduction, set-off or abatement, the receiver of the haulier appointed by the debenture-holder was able to recover the sums due to the haulier for the benefit of the debenture-holder despite the existence of cross-claims.[6]

---

[1] In *Re A Bankruptcy Notice* [1934] Ch. 431, CA at 437, *per* Lord Hanworth M.R., cited by Dillon L.J. in *BICC plc v. Burndy Corp* [1985] Ch. 232, CA at 247. Any such liquidated debt or money demanded howsoever arising may be set off: *The Raven* [1908] 2 Lloyd's L.R. 266 at 272, *per* Parker J.
[2] See below, para. 16–019.
[3] *Aectra Refining Inc v. Exmar NV* [1994] 1 W.L.R. 1634, CA.
[4] *Stein v. Blake* [1996] A.C. 243 at 251, *per* Lord Hoffmann.
[5] *John Dee Group Ltd v. WMH (21) Ltd* [1998] B.C.C. 972, CA.
[6] *ibid.*

(a) Cross-claim qualification

16–005 Whether a cross-claim qualifies as a set-off is of particular importance in three sets of circumstances.

(i) Summary judgment application

16–006 If a claimant seeks summary judgment, only if the cross-claim of the defendant qualifies as set-off will the cross-claim stand as a defence entitling the defendant to leave to defend as of right. Any other cross-claim can only be relied on as grounds for invoking the court's discretionary jurisdiction to stay execution of the claimant's judgment until trial of the cross-claim.[7]

(ii) Winding-up petition

16–007 If the company has an arguable defence of set-off to the full amount claimed by the petitioner, the presentation and advertisement of a winding-up petition should be restrained.[8] The existence of a cross-claim, though substantially overlapping the petitioner's debt, is not a ground for restraining the petition, but is relevant only to the exercise of discretion whether to make the order for winding-up at the substantive hearing of the petition.[9]

(iii) Exercise of rights or remedies

16–008 A cross-claim qualifying as a set-off (but no other cross-claim) is a defence not merely to the claim to payment but also to a claim to invoke rights or remedies available upon non-payment, e.g. forfeiture of a lease for non-payment of rent,[10] distress by a landlord,[11] withdrawal of a vessel for non-payment of hire,[12] or forfeiture of interest under a joint venture,[13] or available upon default, e.g. under a mortgage which restricts the mortgagee's right to take possession or appoint a receiver on the happening of a default.[14] On an interlocutory application for an

---

[7] *Stewart Gill Ltd v. Horatio Myer & Co. Ltd* [1992] Q.B. 600.

[8] *McDonald's Restaurants Ltd v. Urbandivide Co. Ltd* [1994] 1 B.C.L.C. 306.

[9] See *Re A Company* [1992] 1 W.L.R. 351 and para. 2–037 above.

[10] *British Anzani (Felixstowe) Ltd v. International Marine Management (U.K.) Ltd* [1980] Q.B. 637. See also *Liverpool Properties v. Old Bridge* (1985) 276 E.G. 1352.

[11] *Eller v. Grovecrest* [1995] Q.B. 272, CA — the *dictum* to the contrary in *Connaught Ltd v. Indoor Leisure* [1994] 1 W.L.R. 501 at 511, *per* Neill L.J., was not cited in *Eller*.

[12] *Federal Commerce & Navigation Co. Ltd v. Molena Alpha Inc.* [1978] Q.B. 927 at 974. In *BICC v. Burndy Corp* [1985] Ch. 232, Dillon L.J. (with whom Ackner L.J. concurred) held that, in the case of an agreement by a co-owner to transfer his half interest in certain patents to his co-owner on default of payment of sums due under the agreement, it was a defence to a claim to specific performance of the obligation to transfer alleged to have been triggered by such default that there was a legal set-off of sums due under an unconnected contract. Kerr L.J. dissented on this question, holding that (at any rate if no claim to a legal set-off had previously been notified) only an equitable set-off would be sufficient for this purpose, *i.e.* a claim which impeached the claimant's title to specific performance.

[13] *Per* Dillon L.J. in *BICC plc v. Burndy Corp* [1985] Ch. 232 at 247.

[14] *Ashley Guarantee plc v. Zacaria* [1993] 1 W.L.R. 62, CA, cited with approval in *TSB Bank plc v. Platts* [1998] 2 B.C.L.C. 1,10. In the *Ashley Guarantee* case, Nourse L.J. at 66–68 on the basis of Slade L.J.'s judgment in *National Westminster Bank v. Skelton* [1993] 1 W.L.R. 72 considered that:

    (i) in the absence of any contractual or statutory constraint, the mortgagee's right to

injunction to restrain a debenture-holder from appointing a receiver or to restrain a receiver so appointed from acting, the court must adopt the *Cyanamid*[15] approach[16] unless it appears that allowing the receiver to continue to act will make the prosecution of the action by the mortgagor impracticable[17] or will be the equivalent of judgment against the mortgagor in the action.[18] In that case, the court must take into account the relative strengths of the parties' cases.[19] The court will in any event need to take into account the fact that if the debenture-holder is not allowed to enforce his security until after trial, the security may prove worthless.[20]

In drafting debentures, secured creditors may well wish to incorporate **16–009** provisions designed to exclude set-off and to provide for conclusive certificates in respect of the indebtedness to limit the scope for challenges by the mortgagor to actual or proposed appointments of receivers on grounds related to the existence or amount of the debt.

(b) Set-off at law

At common law, set-off was allowed by the Statutes of Set-Off dating from **16–010** the early eighteenth century. These allowed set-off in respect of liquidated debts and money demands between the same parties in the same right which could readily and without difficulty be ascertained at the time of pleading.[21] The debts did not have to be related and set-off was possible even if the quantum of the cross-claim was in dispute provided that the amount of the demand was clearly ascertainable.[22] Thus, no set-off could be raised against a claim in unliquidated damages.[23] And where a claimant sued in his capacity as a trustee, a defendant could not set off a debt due to him from the claimant in his personal capacity.[24] In the early nineteenth century, the common law developed the defence of abatement under which the defendant was allowed to plead, by way of defence in reduction of a claim for the price of a chattel sold with a warranty or work to be performed according to contract, that by reason of non-compliance with

possession is not defeated by a cross-claim even if liquidated, admitted and in excess of the mortgage arrears or a right to unliquidated damages giving rise to a right of setoff;
  (ii) a right to liquidated damages giving rise to a right of set-off may defeat the right to possession if equal to the arrears.

[15] [1975] A.C. 396.
[16] *Rushingdale v. Byblos Bank* (1986) 2 B.C.C. 99,509, CA.
[17] Consider *Cayne v. Global Natural Resources* [1984] 1 All E.R. 225.
[18] *Cambridge Nutrition v. BBC* [1990] 3 All E.R. 523. If a receiver is purported to be appointed prior to the grant of any relief and the issue of the validity of the appointment cannot be finally determined until trial, the grant of an injunction restraining the receiver from acting cannot resolve the uncertainty whether the floating charge has crystallised, and this uncertainty may paralyse dealings with the property by the mortgagor. This impasse may only be capable of being resolved by appointment of a receiver by the court.
[19] See, *e.g. Series 5 Software Ltd v. Clarke* [1996] 1 All E.R. 853.
[20] *Rushingdale v. Byblos Bank* (1986) 2 B.C.C. 99,509, CA.
[21] See *Stein v. Blake* [1996] A.C. 243 and *B. Hargreaves Ltd v. Action 2000 Ltd* [1993] B.C.L.C. 1111, CA.
[22] *Aectra Refining Inc v. Exmar NV* [1994] 1 W.L.R. 1634, CA.
[23] See *Halsbury's Laws of England* (4th ed.), Vol. 42, para. 421.
[24] *Rees v. Watts* (1885) 11 Ex. 410.

the warranty or non-performance of the work, the chattel was diminished in value[25] This defence, though developed independently, may be regarded as a common law version of equitable set-off, available in relation to limited categories of contract.[26]

(c) Set-off in equity

16–011   Equity allowed a wider right of set-off which was available wherever equity regarded the cross-claim as entitling the defendant to be protected in one way or another against the claimant's claim and the relationship of the claim and cross-claim or other factors rendered it unjust in the eyes of equity that the claim should be enforced without regard to the cross-claim.[27] Thus, for example, equity allowed a debt due from the beneficiary to be set off against a claim by his trustees[28] and an unliquidated demand to be set off against a debt where both claims were sufficiently closely connected as to raise an equity precluding the claimant's claim being given effect to without the claimant at the same time giving credit for the defendant's claim against him.[29] Equitable set-off was not, however, available in a case where it was unconscionable for the defendant to seek to set up the equitable defence, for example if the claimant's or defendant's claim was held, not beneficially, but on trust.[30] The remedy of equitable set-off is available in any case where the defence of abatement was available at common law,[31] but the cross-claim does not need to serve to reduce or diminish the claimant's claim to qualify as equitable set-off.[32]

(d) The current position

16–012   The equitable right of set-off has been available as a defence to claims at law since the Judicature Acts. These Acts did not change the substantive law, but only the procedure.[33]

16–013   In any case where the claimant has a monetary claim against the defendant,[34] the defence of set-off will be available to the defendant who

---

[25] *Basten v. Butter* (1806) 7 East 479; *BICC plc v. Burndy Corp* [1985] Ch. 232 at 247; and see *Halsbury, op. cit.*, para. 411.

[26] *Sim v. Rotherham Metropolitan BC* [1987] Ch. 216 at 258–259.

[27] See *Dole Dried Fruit v. Trust in Kerwood* [1990] 2 Lloyd's Rep. 309, CA.

[28] *Cochrane v. Green* (1860) 9 C.B. (N.S.) 448.

[29] *Morgan & Son Ltd v. Martin Johnson Ltd* [1949] 1 K.B. 107 (claimant's claim for storage charge for lorry: defendant's cross-claim for damages for delivery of lorry to wrong person in breach of contract or for negligent storage: held defendant had right of equitable set-off).

[30] See Meagher, Gummow and Lehane, *Equity, Doctrines and Remedies* (3rd ed.), paras 2866–2868, explaining *N. W. Robbie & Co. Ltd v. Witney Warehouse Co. Ltd* [1963] 1 W.L.R. 1324.

[31] *Sim v. Rotherham Metropolitan BC* [1987] Ch. 216 at 259. A clause excluding set-off may be drafted in insufficiently wide terms to exclude the defence of abatement: *A.C. Sim (Southern) Ltd v. Dacon* 19 Constr. L.R. 1.

[32] *Dole Dried Fruit v. Trust in Kerwood* [1990] 2 Lloyd's Rep. 309, CA.

[33] *Stumore v. Campbell* [1892] 1 Q.B. 314, CA, but compare *Federal Commerce and Navigation Co. v. Molena Alpha Inc.* [1978] Q.B. 927 at 974, *per* Lord Denning M.R.

[34] It would appear that equitable set-off is equally available if the claimant's claim is unliquidated: *TSB Bank v. Platts* [1998] 2 B.C.L.C. 1 at 10, CA; *Hanak v. Green* [1958] 2

has before the action begins[35] monetary cross-claim against the claimant which:

(a) is for a debt or liquidated demand accrued due; or
(b) is unliquidated but "so closely connected with the claimant's demand that it would be manifestly unjust to allow him to enforce payment without taking into account the cross-claim".[36]

Hobhouse J. considered the application of the second of these **16–014** grounds in *The Leon*.[37] In rejecting the hirer's claim to set-off against his liability for charterhire a claim for damages for breach of duty by the owners of the vessel in respect of the ship's bunkers, he said:

". . . equitable set-off has [not] been reduced to an exercise of discretion . . . the defence has to be granted or refused by an application of legal principle. The relevant principle is that identified by Lord Cottenham in *Rawson v. Samuel*[38]: 'The equity of the bill impeached the title to the legal demand.' What this requires is that the court or arbitrator should consider the relationship between the claim and the cross-claim. This is why not every cross-claim, even though it arises out of the same transaction, necessarily gives rise to an equitable set-off.[39] Applying the principle to cases where the plaintiff is claiming time charterhire . . . in the cases . . . where the right of the equitable set-off has been upheld, the cross-claim has involved something which could be identified as depriving the charterers of the use of the vessel or prejudicing or hindering that use."

It should be noted that, whilst as a matter of law cross-claims arising out **16–015** of the same transaction do not necessarily give rise to equitable set-off,[40] it is unusual for them not to be sufficiently connected with the claim for

---

Q.B. 9. A restriction to liquidated claims "would accord with no principle of law or logic", to use the words of Parker J. in *The Raven* [1908] 2 Lloyd's L.R. 266 at 271, rejecting the argument that a defendant could only set off connected unliquidated and not liquidated claims (whether connected or not).

[35] *Edmunds v. Lloyd's Italico* [1986] 1 W.L.R. 492, CA, where the defendant's potential cross-claim for repayment of a sum paid after the issue of the writ in satisfaction (but not accepted in satisfaction) of the claimants' claim was held not to be available as a set-off, as it arose after the action began (following *Richards v. James* (1848) 2 Exch. 471).

[36] *Per* Lord Denning M.R. in *Federal Commerce and Navigation Ltd v. Molena Alpha Inc.* [1978] Q.B. 927 at 975; *TSB Bank plc v. Platts* [1998] 2 B.C.L.C. 1 at 10, CA: see also *British Anzani (Felixstowe) Ltd v. International Marine Management (U.K.) Ltd* [1980] Q.B. 637 and *Melville v. Grapelodge* (1980) 39 P.C.R. 179.

[37] [1985] 2 Lloyd's L.R. 470 at 474–475. Hobhouse J. (at 476) instanced as possible bases for a claim to equitable set-off over-riding fraud and mutual accounts. The latter is explicable on the ground that there is an implied agreement for set-off.

[38] (1841) Cr. & Ph. 161 at 179.

[39] To like effect, see *The Aries* [1977] 1 W.L.R. 185 at 193, *per* Lord Simon and at 191, *per* Lord Wilberforce; *Newfoundland Government v. Newfoundland Railway Co.* (1888) 13 App.Cas. 199 at 212; *Federal Commerce Ltd v. Molena Alpha Inc.* [1978] 1 Q.B. 927 at 981F, per Goff L.J. and *The Raven* [1908] 2 Lloyd's L.R. 266 at 272.

[40] *Esso Petroleum v. Milton* [1997] 1 W.L.R. 938, CA (leave to appeal given to HL, *ibid.* at 1060)

this purpose. The limited scope of the exception has led judges to make statements to the effect that equitable set-off is available where the cross-claim arises out of the same contract or transaction,[41] but such a formulation, whilst in most cases a reliable guide, is not a full or completely accurate statement of the law. For example, irrespective of connection, for policy reasons, the defence of equitable set-off is denied to claims based on dishonoured bills of exchange,[42] direct debits[43] and claims for charterhire of vessels.[44]

16–016   Equitable set-off is available using an unliquidated cross-claim even against a secured liquidated claim, if there is a sufficient connection.[45] However, there is no set-off against a secured subrogation right, even where the cross-claim is liquidated and established.[46]

16–017   The state of the law regarding set-off has been criticised as unsatisfactory,[47] but a broad interpretation of the doctrine of equitable set-off or the grant of a stay of execution pending the trial of a counterclaim has generally been sufficient to safeguard a defendant's cashflow when justice requires that result, and not if the defendant does not deserve that indulgence.[48]

(e) Exclusion of the right of set-off

16–018 The right of set-off can be excluded by agreement[49] but clear and unambiguous words must be used.[50] A clause precluding set-off may be

---

[41] *e.g.* Templeman J. in *Business Computers Ltd v. Anglo-African Leasing Ltd* [1977] 1 W.L.R. 578 at 585C; Lord Denning M.R. in *The Brede* [1974] Q.B. 233 at 248F.

[42] *Brown Shipley & Co. v. Alicia Hosiery* [1966] 1 Lloyd's Rep. 668, CA; *Willment Bros Ltd v. North West Thames Regional Health Authority* [1984] Build.L.R. 51, CA.

[43] *Esso Petroleum v. Milton* [1997]1 W.L.R. 938, CA (leave to appeal to HL was given, *ibid.* at 1060 but the appeal was not pursued).

[44] *The Aries* [1977] 1 W.L.R. 185, and see historical explanation of the exception applicable in *The Brede* [1974] Q.B. 233. The exception also extends to carriage of goods by road and to cases where the claim is in respect of loss and damage or delay: see (1985) J.B.L. 68. The special protection once accorded to rent due under a lease (*Hart v. Rogers* [1916] 1 K.B. 646) is no longer so accorded (*British Anzani v. International Marine Ltd* [1980] 1 Q.B. 137).

[45] *TSB Bank plc v. Platts* [1998] 2 B.C.L.C. 1, 10, CA, distinguishing *Samuel Keller (Holdings) Ltd v. Martins Bank* [1971] 1 W.L.R. 43.

[46] *Brown v. Cork* [1985] B.C.L.C. 363, CA.

[47] *Per* Leggatt L.J. in *Axel Johnson v. MG Mineral* [1992] 1 W.L.R. 270 at 274.

[48] *Per* Staughton L.J. in *Axel Johnson v. MG Mineral* [1992] 1 W.L.R. 270 at 276; *per* Hoffmann L.J. in *Aectra Refining Inc v. Exmar NV* [1994] 1 W.L.R. 1634 at 1652, CA.

[49] *John Dee Group Ltd v. WMH (21) Ltd* [1998] B.C.C. 972, CA; *Coca Cola v. Finsat International Ltd* [1996] 2 B.C.L.C. 626; *BICC plc v. Burndy Corp* [1985] Ch. 232 at 248; *Continental illinois v. Papanicolaou* [1986] 2 Lloyd's Rep. 441. *Hongkong and Shanghai Banking Corp v. Kloeckner & Co.* [1989] 3 All E.R. 513 and see above, Chap. 10. The parties cannot, however, by agreement preclude the court from exercising its jurisdiction to grant a stay of execution of a judgment pending trial of a counterclaim, but special circumstances must be established. The court will more readily grant a stay if the judgment has been obtained summarily, and not at a trial: *Continental Illinois v. Papanicolaou* [1986] 2 Lloyd's Rep. 441, and *Schofield v. Church Army* [1986] 1 W.L.R. 1328, CA. A guarantee may impose on a guarantor an obligation to make a payment on default by the principal, and not merely to pay any deficiency brought out in the final accounting, and therefore precludes any right of set-off: *Hyundai v. Papadopoulos* [1980] 1 W.L.R. 1129; [1980] 2 All E.R. 29 at 47G.

[50] *Esso Petroleum v. Milton* [1997]1 W.L.R. 938, CA (leave to appeal to HL was given,

construed strictly.[51] It may also require justification as being reasonable under section 13(1)(b) of the Unfair Contract Terms Act 1977[52] but the exception from this requirement of clauses in "any contract so far as it relates to the creation or transfer of an interest in land"[53] extends to such clauses in a charge of land.[54]

(f) Set-off and assignees

An assignee of a debt takes subject to any pre-existing legal right of set-off.[55] Thus, where a bank was owed money by a customer, it was held to have an existing right of legal set-off, which took priority over a subsequent assignment of moneys which were in the future to become due from the bank to the customer as a result of the proposed collection by the bank of a letter of credit for the customer.[56] **16–019**

In the absence of agreement between the assignor and the debtor that any assignment shall be free of equities,[57] the assignee of a debt or claim takes subject to equities existing at the time of notice to the debtor of the assignment between the debtor and assignor[58] and accordingly the debtor is entitled to the like right of set-off to which he was entitled as against the assignor at the date of notice of the assignment.[59] There is an apparent exception to these principles. A tenant who has a claim against his lessor cannot set off that claim against a claim by a purchaser or mortgagee of his lessor's estate in respect of liabilities under the lease accruing after the sale or mortgage (*e.g.* rent) unless the tenant's claim constitutes an interest in land. A mere claim for damages, *e.g.* for breach of contract, cannot affect the purchaser or mortgagee, whether or not he had notice.[60] In accordance with these principles, a debtor is not entitled to set off against the assignee a debt which has neither accrued due at the date of notice of the assignment nor is closely connected with the **16–020**

---

ibid. at 1060 but the appeal was not pursued); *Connaught Ltd v. Indoor Leisure* [1994] 1 W.L.R. 501; *Gilbert-Ash (Northern) Ltd v. Modern Engineering (Bristol) Ltd* [1974] A.C. 689, HL.

[51] *Re Richbell Strategic Holdings Ltd* [1997] 2 B.C.L.C. 429.

[52] *Stewart Gill Ltd v. Horatio Myer & Co. Ltd* [1992] Q.B. 600; *Skipskredittforeningen v. Emperor Navigation SA* [1997] 2 B.C.L.C. 398; *Esso Petroleum v. Milton* [1997] 1 W.L.R. 938, CA (*supra*).

[53] Section 1(2) and Sched. 1.

[54] Consider *Electricity Supply Nominees Ltd v. IAF Group Ltd* (1992) 67 P. & C.R. 28 (lease).

[55] *Marathon Electrical Manufacturing Co. v Mashreqbank* [1997] 2 B.C.L.C. 460.

[56] *ibid.*

[57] *Hilger Analytical Ltd v. Rank Precision Industries Ltd* [1984] B.C.L.C. 301: a provision in debenture that it was transferable free of equities enabled transfer to take place and transferee to appoint a receiver notwithstanding a claim by company to set aside the debenture and for damages exceeding the amount secured on the ground of misrepresentation.

[58] But not subject to equities between the debenture and intermediate assignees: *The Raven* [1908] 2 Lloyd's L.R. 266.

[59] *Newfoundland Government v. Newfoundland Railway Co.* (1888) 13 App.Cas. 199, PC, explained by Lord Simon in *The Aries* [1977] 1 W.L.R. 185 at 193: "You cannot equitably take the benefit of an assignment without also assuming its burdens; both flow out of and are inseparably connected with the same transaction".

[60] *Reeves v. Pope* [1914] 2 K.B. 291 and see discussion in Wood, *English and International Set-Off*, para. 16–106.

claim, even though it arises out of a contract made before the assignment.[61]

2. RECEIVERSHIP SET-OFF

(a) General

16–021   The grant of a charge over a company's debts has been held to have a one-sided impact on the availability of set-off between the chargee on the one side and the company's other (unsecured) creditors on the other. The company acting by the receiver is entitled to the same rights of set-off as would have been available to the company if no charge had been created. Accordingly, for example, the company in receivership can set off pre-receivership debts against post-receivership rentals due under a lease.[62] But the company's other creditors' rights of set-off are restricted as set out below.

16–022   The position of a receiver in relation to set-off can be more clearly understood if at the outset a fundamental distinction is drawn between the two capacities in which the receiver may be acting. To put it another way, the first and vital question to be asked is: "Which hat is the receiver wearing?"

16–023   If the receiver is wearing his company hat, that is, acting as the company's agent, the ordinary rules of set-off apply, and the receiver will be bound by any set-off which would bind the company if there were no receiver.

16–024   If, however, the receiver is wearing his mortgagee's hat, that is, relying on his appointor's security, he will be in the same position for set-off purposes as an assignee of the company's debts[63] (this assumes, of course, that debts are charged by the debenture). The general rule that an assignee of a debt is subject only to equities existing at the date of the notice of the assignment will then apply.[64] Therefore, once notice has been given of the assignment (notice will be considered in more detail below), no new equity can be created: and a debtor is entitled to set off against the receiver only those sums which he had a vested right to set off against the company on the relevant date, i.e. that on which he was given notice of the assignment.[65]

16–025   The company is the correct claimant in the first case and the debenture-holder is the correct claimant in the second case. In neither case is the receiver personally a claimant, for in both cases he is merely

---

[61] *Business Computers Ltd v. Anglo-African Leasing Ltd* [1977] 1 W.L.R. 578.

[62] *West St. Properties Pty Ltd v. Jamison* [1974] 2 N.S.W.L.R. 435, discussed in Meagher, Gummow and Lehane, *Equity, Doctrines and Remedies* (3rd ed.), para. 2869 (there is no requirement for mutuality in the availability of set-off).

[63] *Roadshow Entertainment Pty Ltd v. CEL Home Video Pty Ltd* (unreported, NSWCA, October 10, 1997)

[64] The explanation substantially as set out here was cited with approval by Vinelott J. in *Astor Chemicals Ltd v. Synthetic Technology Ltd* [1990] B.C.C. 97 at 105H–106D.

[65] *Edward Nelson v. Faber* [1903] 2 K.B. 367 at 375.

an agent.[66] In practice, to save costs, in the second case the parties often permit the receiver suing in the name of the company to claim the more protected position of an assignee, without requiring the joinder of the debenture-holder.[67]

(b) When set-off is available

Set-off will be permitted to a debtor of the company in the following cases: **16–026**

(1) Connected claims arising out of the same transaction or series of transactions.[68] In *Handley Page Ltd v. Customs and Excise*,[69] it was agreed between Handley Page Ltd and Rockwell Ltd that Handley Page should accept two six-month bills of exchange drawn by Rockwell who would then pay an import deposit to Customs under Handley Page's name and that Handley Page would receive repayments of the deposit. Rockwell discounted the bills and paid the deposit. Before the bills became due, Handley Page went into receivership, and subsequently dishonoured the bills on presentation. Rockwell paid the bills, recovered the deposit from Customs and sought to set off the amount of the bills against its debt to the company and against its liability to account to the company for the deposit. Set-off was allowed.

This result has been explained (in the *Business Computers* case[70]) on the grounds that: **16–027**

(a) the debts were "part of the same contract, or at any rate closely related"; and

(b) Rockwell's liability on the bills dated back to the date they were discounted, *i.e.* before the receiver was appointed.[71]

(2) Liquidated claims which have accrued due before the relevant date,[72] *even where the debt is not payable until after the relevant date.*[73] In *Biggerstaff v. Rowatt's Wharf*,[74] oil merchants owed rent to the company prior to the appointment of the receiver. At the relevant date, the company was also liable to the oil merchants in respect of short delivery in a sale of oil. Set-off was allowed. **16–028**

---

[66] Compare *Cretanor Maritime Co. v. Irish Marine Management Ltd* [1978] 1 W.L.R. 966; and the position where a receiver claims that a charge is void for non-registration: *Independent Automatic Sales v. Foster* [1962] 1 W.L.R. 974, which suggests that a debenture-holder would have to be joined. See also *Re Peachdart* [1984] Ch. 131 where the parties agreed to dispense with joining the debenture holder to save costs.

[67] *Business Computers Ltd v. Anglo-African Leasing Co. Ltd* [1977] 1 W.L.R. 578.

[68] *Government of Newfoundland v. Newfoundland Railway Co.* [1888] 13 App.Cas. 199, PC; *Hanak v. Green* [1958] 2 Q.B. 9; *Sun Caddies Pty Ltd v. Polites* [1939] V.L.R. 132; *West St. Properties Pty Ltd v. Jamison* [1974] 2 N.S.W.L.R. 435.

[69] [1970] 2 Lloyd's Rep. 459.

[70] *Business Computers Ltd v. Anglo-African Leasing Co. Ltd* [1977] 1 W.L.R. 578 at 585.

[71] See also *Collins v. Jones* (1830) 10 B. & C. 777; *Re Moseley Green Coal & Coke Co. Ltd (Barretts Case No. 2)* (1864) 4 De.G. & Sm. 756; *Re Waite* [1956] 1 W.L.R. 1226 at 1232, *per* Lord Evershed M.R.

[72] See above, n. 69.

[73] *Christie v. Taunton Delmard Lane & Co.* [1893] 2 Ch. 175.

[74] [1892] 2 Ch. 93, CA.

16–029   *(3) Where a debt arises from the company by virtue of the receiver's acceptance of performance of a contract which was entered into before the date of receivership*[75] *or where a debt arises from the other party to the contract by reason of such performance.*[76] In *Rother Iron Works Ltd v. Canterbury Precision Engineers,*[77] the claimant company prior to receivership owed the defendant moneys in respect of goods sold and delivered and the company had contracted to sell goods to the defendant. The receiver delivered the goods but was met with a claim to set off. The Court of Appeal held that:

> (a) if the chose in action consisting of the rights under the contract became subject to the charge on the appointment of the receiver, the debenture-holder could not be in a better position to assert those rights than the assignor company had been; and
>
> (b) the company's claim as charged by the crystallised floating charge was always subject to the right of set-off.[78]

The receiver could, it is thought, have insisted on payment in full at the time of delivery or else have repudiated the sale contract and refused to deliver unless a new contract was made, excluding set-off. The *Rother Iron* case thus provides a trap for unwary receivers.

16–030   More generally, the trap can be avoided in relation to both pre eand post receivership contracts made by or on behalf of the company by the debenture-holder insisting that the company exclude set-off in its general contractual documentation.[79] Where a receiver on appointment finds that there is no such provision, he can, as well as threatening to cause the company not to perform any existing contract unless set-off for pre-receivership debts is excluded, seek to exclude set-off in any contract made by him on behalf of the company.[80]

(c) When set-off is not available

16–031   Set-off will not be permitted to a debtor of the company in the following cases:

(1) In respect of debts acquired by the debtor of the company from a third party after the commencement of the receivership with a view to improving his position. In *Robbie & Co. v. Witney Warehouse,*[81] the claimant company had sold goods on credit to the defendants. A receiver was then appointed by debenture-holders who held a floating charge over all the company's assets. The receiver permitted the company to continue trading, and further goods were sold on credit to the defendant.

---

[75] *George Barker (Transport) Ltd v. Eynon* [1974] 1 W.L.R. 462.
[76] *Rother Iron Works Ltd v. Canterbury Precision Engineers* [1974] Q.B. 1, CA.
[77] *ibid.*
[78] See also *Marathon Electrical Manuf Co. v Mashreqbank* [1997] 2 B.C.L.C. 460, where it was pointed out inter alia that the *Rother Iron* case is inaccurately summarised in the *Business Computers* case [1977] 1 W.L.R. 578.
[79] *John Dee Group Ltd v. WMH (21) Ltd* [1998] B.C.C. 972, CA.
[80] *ibid.* at first instance [1997] B.C.C. 518.
[81] *Robbie & Co. v. Witney Warehouse Co. Ltd* [1963] 1 W.L.R. 1324.

Before the appointment of the receiver, the claimant had owed a debt for goods sold and delivered to a subsidiary company of the defendant. After the receiver was appointed, the subsidiary assigned this debt to the defendant, who attempted to set it off against its debt to the claimant. The Court of Appeal held that:

(a) on the construction of the debenture, each debt owed by the defendants, as it arose after the appointment of the receiver, was assigned to the debenture-holder in equity; and

(b) at the time the debts were assigned in equity to the debenture-holder, by crystallisation of the floating charge, the defendants had no cross-claim and no right of set-off, and the subsidiary had no direct claim against the debenture-holders. There was, therefore, no mutuality of beneficial interest, and set-off was not allowed.

(2) In respect of debts neither accrued due as at the relevant date nor **16–032** *connected with the debt due to the company.* In *Business Computers Ltd v. Anglo-African Leasing Ltd*[82] at the relevant date the company was owed the price of two computers by the defendant. Also prior to the relevant date the company had defaulted on a payment of an instalment due under a hire-purchase transaction with the defendant involving another computer, but no sum other than the instalment had accrued due. The receiver of the company repudiated the hire-purchase agreement and the repudiation was accepted by the defendant. The defendant sold the computer and claimed to set off against the company's claim a sum of damages claimable as a result of the repudiation of the hire-purchase agreement. It was held that the defendant could not do so, since that claim had not accrued due at the relevant date (*i.e.* the date of notification of the appointment of the receiver) and was not connected with the company's claim against it.

(d) Notice

(i) Floating charges
The debenture-holder's position where debts are charged by a floating **16–033** charge is that of a holder of an incomplete assignment, which is completed by the appointment of a receiver.[83] In the case of a floating charge, the giving of notice of such appointment to the debtor of the company establishes the critical point at which rights as between the assignee and debtor are crystallised, *i.e.* the relevant date for deciding whether the debtor has an existing right of set-off.

---

[82] *Re Pinto Leite & Nephews* [1929] 1 Ch. 221 at 233; *Business Computers Ltd v. Anglo-African Leasing Co. Ltd* [1977] 1 W.L.R. 578 at 584A; *Felt and Textiles of New Zealand Ltd v. Hubrich Ltd* [1968] N.Z.L.R. 716; *Rendell v. Doors and Doors Ltd* [1975] 2 N.Z.L.R. 191; *Leichhardt Emporium Pty Ltd v. AGC* [1979] 1 N.S.W.L.R. 701.

[83] *George Barker (Transport) Ltd v. Eynon* [1974] 1 W.L.R. 462 at 467. See further above, Chap. 3.

(ii) Special problems created by a fixed charge on book or other debts

16–034 Where debts are charged by an effective fixed charge,[84] there is a completed assignment as at the date of the charge as between assignor and assignee. As between assignee and debtor, however, the assignee's title is not complete until notice is given to the debtor.

16–035 A question then arises whether registration of the charge constitutes the giving of notice of the assignment to the debtor, so as to rule out future set-offs of debts not then due or arising out of or closely connected with the same transaction. Is the date of registration the "relevant date" at which the relationship of assignee and debtor is crystallised?

16–036 The argument in favour of treating registration as notice in this context rests on the view that registration constitutes notice of a charge, even if not notice of its terms.[85] Professor Goode[86] has suggested a qualification to this view. His qualification is that notice of a charge is given by registration "only to those who could reasonably be expected to search", and this would "normally exclude a buyer in the ordinary course of business".

16–037 It is suggested that registration will not of itself constitute the giving of notice of assignment to the debtor, for the notice required to be given to the debtor is actual notice, and not merely actual notice, but notice in plain and unambiguous terms of the assignment.[87] Registration is, at most, constructive notice. Furthermore, there is no express statutory requirement when registering a charge to state whether the charge is fixed or floating. Until recently, registration would therefore not necessarily disclose on a search whether the assignment was complete or not.[88] Current practice appears to be to require an applicant for registration to disclose whether a charge is fixed or floating, and this is now noted on the register.

16–038 A debtor ought not, therefore, to be fixed with notice simply by reason of the registration of the charge. But if the debtor has in fact done a search, and it is clear from the search that there is a fixed charge on his debt, this must be notice sufficient to complete the title of the assignee and crystallise the rights as between debtor and assignee, since notice to the debtor does not have to come from the assignor or assignee.[89]

16–039 Registration of a fixed charge on book debts at the Companies Registry may constitute the giving of notice to the Crown (of which the Companies Registry is an emanation) preventing any other Crown Department, such as the Inland Revenue, from setting off subsequent liabilities of the company against prior debts to the company.

---

[84] See *Siebe Gorman v. Barclays Bank* [1979] 2 Lloyd's Rep. 142 at 160.

[85] *Wilson v. Kelland* [1910] 2 Ch. 306 at 313; *Siebe Gorman v. Barclays Bank* [1979] 2 Lloyd's Rep. 142 where it was held that registration of the charge did not amount to notice of a special provision restricting dealing with the property charged.

[86] *Goode, Legal Problems of Credit and Security* (1982), pp. 26–27.

[87] *James Talcott v. John Lewis* [1940] 3 All E.R. 592 and see *Halsbury's Laws of England* (4th ed.), Vol. 6, para. 48. See also *By Appointment (Sales) Ltd v. Harrods* (unreported, December 1, 1977, CA.); *Cowan dc Groot v. Eagle Trust* [1992] 4 All E.R. 700.

[88] For the effect of registration of a floating charge, see *Biggerstaff v. Rowatt's Wharf* [1896] 2 Ch. 93 at 101 at 103.

[89] *Lloyd v. Banks* (1868) 3 Ch.App. 488 and see *Halsbury, op. cit.*

(e) Practical lessons for receivers

It is important to bear in mind that a receiver appointed out of court **16–040** may generally cause the company to repudiate its contracts.[90] Upon appointment, a receiver should therefore take a close look at existing contracts, including any potential set-offs, and wherever possible repudiate burdensome contracts or set-off arrangements. Where the company has yet to perform works or deliver goods to a debtor of the company under a pre-receivership contract, the receiver should contact the creditor and agree to exclude any set-off before causing the company to perform.[91] The exclusion should, if possible, be under seal to prevent any arguments about consideration. But an express or implied agreement not to repudiate the contract should suffice as consideration for the agreement to exclude set-off.

It is also important to note that the special statutory rules governing **16–041** set-off in liquidation and bankruptcy do not apply in receivership.[92]

(f) Surplus in group receiverships

Some very complicated problems can arise where a debenture-holder **16–042** puts companies in a group into receivership and a surplus arises. The companies will generally have given cross-guarantees of each other's indebtedness to the debenture-holder. Often all or some of them will have gone into liquidation before the receivership is completed.

Once the existence of a surplus from the receiverships becomes **16–043** obvious, the receiver, who is bound by the equities belonging to the companies,[93] has the duty of working out rights of marshalling between the companies and of ensuring that the correct sums are paid to the correct companies. In *Re St. Clair Sampson Ltd*[94] seven companies in a group executed cross-guarantees to a bank, and each company charged its assets as security to the bank. A receiver was appointed to each company and sufficient was realised to repay the bank. The liquidator of St. Clair Sampson, which had paid substantially more than its due proportion of the total indebtedness of the group to the bank, claimed that the surplus remaining in the hands of the receiver should be distributed in such a way that each company would (so far as its assets were sufficient) have discharged its own indebtedness to the bank and an equal share of the deficiency attributable to the indebtedness to the bank of those companies which were unable to discharge that indebtedness in full. Two of the other companies in the group were owed substantial sums by St. Clair Sampson on trading account. Their joint liquidators admitted that St. Clair Sampson had claims for contribution against those companies, but claimed that, by virtue of the proviso to section 5

---

[90] *Airline Airspares Ltd v. Handley Page* [1970] Ch. 193.

[91] See discussion of the *Rother Iron Works* case, above.

[92] See, *e.g. Business Computers Ltd v. Anglo-African Leasing Co. Ltd* [1977] 1 W.L.R. 578 and *MS Fashions Ltd v. BCCI* [1993] Ch. 425, CA.

[93] *Freevale v. Metrostore* [1984] Ch. 199; *Telemetrix plc v. Modern Engineers* [1985] B.C.L.C. 213.

[94] *Sub nom. Brown v. Cork* [1985] B.C.L.C. 363.

of the Mercantile Law Amendment Act 1856,[95] these claims for contribution were secured claims only to the extent of any amount by which the contribution claim against each company exceeded the inter-company indebtedness due from St. Clair Sampson to that company. The Court of Appeal held that the inter-company indebtedness was not to be set off against the contribution claims in this way.

16–044   There are two important features of the decision for present purposes. First, a receiver holding a surplus must ensure that it is paid to the correct party. If there is doubt and no agreement between the parties potentially affected, he will need to seek directions from the court. Secondly, section 5 of the Mercantile Law Amendment Act 1856 operates by way of subrogation to the creditor's rights and entitles the creditor's full claim to be used to obtain payment. This does not permit to be raised by way of set-off a cross-claim available against the surety entitled to contribution. The reference in the proviso to "the just proportion to which . . . [an under-paying co-surety] . . . shall be justly liable" is a reference to the amount which is recoverable from the under-paying co-surety pursuant to the body of section 5, not to that amount adjusted so as to allow for other indebtedness between the parties.

16–045   The further point was made by the Court of Appeal, to the effect that where, at the commencement of the relevant winding-up the principal creditor had not been paid in full, the relevant "insolvency" rule[96] prevented any set-off. It is not however, clear why "insolvency" set-off was relevant to a subrogated secured claim, which stands outside liquidation. The actual rule of "insolvency" set-off relied on, namely the exclusion from set-off of surety claims which are still contingent at the relevant liquidation date, is outside the scope of this work but it may be remarked that the rule has become of dubious validity in the light of the reasoning in the House of Lords decision in *Stein v. Blake*.[97] Moreover, even if the rule were still applicable to liquidation, a similar result to that forbidden by the rule might be achieved by means of the principle of quasi-retainer (*Cherry v. Boultbee*[98]), which does not offend against "insolvency" principles.[99]

PART II — LIENS

16–046 Unlike most of the types of charge or mortgage entered into by a company which have to be registered, liens are a type of security which

---

[95] Set out in *Rowlatt on Principal and Surety* (5th ed., 1999), p. 274.

[96] *Re Waite* [1956] 1 W.L.R. 1226, CA.

[97] [1996] A.C. 243. That case emphasises that all contingent claims are provable and available for set-off and hindsight is used in giving a value to a claim which was contingent at the relevant liquidation date. The fact that a surety's contribution claim was merely contingent at the relevant date should not matter if by the time the matter is considered a value can be given to the contingent claim and if there is no remaining "double proof/double dividend" problem — *i.e.* the creditor has been paid in full.

[98] 4 My. & Cr. 442.

[99] *Re Melton* [1918] 1 Ch. 37, CA, *per* Scrutton L.J. at 57–61.

may not have to be registered and even in the absence of registration can sometimes take priority over registered charges.[99]

Liens are of three types: **16–047**

    (a) possessory liens which arise by operation of common law, statute or contract, and consist of a right to retain possession as security for payment of a debt against the owner or other person entitled to property[1];

    (b) equitable liens which are a form of equitable charge arising by operation of equity from the relationship of the parties, *e.g.* unpaid vendor and purchaser, and enforceable by means of an order for sale[2]; and

    (c) contractual liens giving rise to a charge.[3]

1. REGISTRATION

Section 395(1) of the Companies Act 1985 requires registration of **16–048** charges created by a company. The two conditions for triggering this section are accordingly:

    (a) that the interest brought into existence is not a mere possessory lien (which is not registrable[4]) but a charge[5]; and

    (b) that the interest is created by the company whether expressly or impliedly[6] and does not arise by operation of law.[7]

2. PRIORITIES

A lien will not have priority over a prior registered fixed charge or a **16–049** prior registered crystallised floating charge save with the express or implied consent of the debenture-holder.[8] A lien will, however, have priority over a prior uncrystallised floating charge unless the charge contains a prohibition on the creation of such liens and the grantee of

---

[99] Statutory liens may have priority over prior charges, including crystallised floating charges: see *Channel Airways v. Manchester Corp* [1974] 1 Lloyd's L.R. 456 (in which Forbes J. at 460 distinguished a receiver appointed under a debenture who could create a lien and a receiver appointed by the court who could not).

[1] Such lien is a right of self-help which arises by operation of law when a particular relationship arises: *Re Molton Finance* [1968] 1 Ch. 325 at 329, *per* Diplock L.J.

[2] See Snell, *The Principles of Equity* (13th ed.), p. 529ff.

[3] *Re Welsh Irish Ferries Ltd* [1986] Ch. 471 at 478.

[4] *Re Wallis and Simmonds (Buildings) Ltd* [1974] 1 W.L.R. 391; *Waitomo Wools v. Nelsons* [1974] N.Z.L.R. 484.

[5] *Re Wallis and Simmonds (Buildings) Ltd* [1974] 1 W.L.R. 391; *Re Welsh Irish Ferries Ltd* [1986] Ch. 471.

[6] *Re Wallis and Simmonds (Buildings) Ltd* [1974] 1 W.L.R. 391 cited with approval in *Associated Alloys Pty Ltd v. ACN 001 452 106 Pty Ltd* (2000) 171 A.L.R. 568 at 596 *per* Kirby J.

[7] *Brunton v. Electrical Engineering Co.* [1892] 1 Ch. 434 (solicitor's lien); *London & Cheshire Insurance Co. v. Laplagrene Property Co.* [1971] Ch. 499 (unpaid vendor's lien).

[8] *Brown v. Associated British Motors Ltd* [1932] N.Z.L.R. 655.

the lien has actual knowledge of such prohibition.[9] This is because the floating charge is an incomplete equitable assignment which permits the creation of such liens in the ordinary course of business.[10] In a case where there is such a prohibition and knowledge of the prohibition, a lien created by the company can only enjoy priority with the express or implied consent of the debenture-holder.[11] Constructive knowledge of the prohibition is insufficient to postpone the lien to the floating charge.[12] Knowledge of the floating charge does not constitute knowledge of any prohibition therein contained, for the floating nature of the charge implies authority to carry on the company's ordinary course of business.[13] Actual knowledge of a prohibition on the creation of charges or liens will not operate to postpone a lien arising by operation of law, for such a lien is not created by the company.[14]

3. PRACTICAL LESSONS

16–050 Certain practical lessons for receivers arise from the case of *George Baker (Transport) Ltd v. Eynon*.[15] The relevant events were:

(a) pre-receivership:

  (i) the contract for carriage made between the carrier and the company provided for a contractual lien over goods carried to secure all sums due to the carrier;

  (ii) the company came to owe money to the carrier in respect of carriage;

  (iii) the company ordered the carriage of a particular consignment of meat;

(b) post-appointment of receiver:

  (iv) the carriers collected meat and performed the carriage ordered in (a)(iii); save that

  (v) the meat was retained at the carrier's depot against payment of both this carriage and the pre-receivership carriage.

16–051 The court allowed the carriers to set up the lien against the receiver in respect of both sums. It seems from this case that a receiver is, in such a situation, put to an election either:

---

[9] *Re British Tea Table Co. (1897) Ltd* (1909) 101 L.T. 707; *George Barker (Transport) Ltd v. Eynon* [1974] 1 W.L.R. 462; [1974] 1 All E.R. 900; *Parsons v. Sovereign Bank of Canada* [1913] A.C. 161.

[10] *Business Computers Ltd v. Anglo-African Leasing Co. Ltd* [1977] 1 W.L.R. 578.

[11] *Williams v. Allsup* (1861) 10 C.B.N.S. 417; (1861) 142 E.R. 514; *Tappenden v. Artus* [1964] 2 Q.B. 185; [1963] 3 All E.R. 213; *Albermarle Supply Co. Ltd* [1928] 1 K.B. 307.

[12] See above, para. 3–060.

[13] *Brunton v. Electrical Engineering Corporation* [1891] 1 Ch. 434 (solicitor's lien for fees incurred after commencement of receivership).

[14] *ibid.*

[15] [1974] 1 W.L.R. 462; [1974] 1 All E.R. 900, followed in *Re Diesels and Components Pty Ltd* (1985) 9 A.C.L.R. 825, *per* McPherson J.

(a) to permit the carriage to go ahead and impliedly authorise the creation of a post-receivership lien as a result of the pre-receivership contract; or

(b) repudiate the contract of carriage[16] and physically prevent the carriage if necessary[17]; and

(c) either negotiate a new agreement with the carrier excluding any lien in respect of pre-receivership debts or contract with a fresh carrier.

Another point of interest arising from that case concerns the point at **16–052** which a lien arises. The general law is that a possessory lien only arises once the contracted-for services have been rendered.[18] This can however, be varied by agreement and in *George Barker v. Eynon* a term was implied allowing the liens to be asserted at a point of time prior to full performance.

---

[16] See *Airlines Airspares Ltd v. Handley Page Ltd* [1970] Ch. 193; [1970] 1 All E.R. 29.

[17] Blanchard, *The Law of Company Receiverships in Australia and New Zealand* (1982), para. 904 points out that otherwise the carrier might refuse to accept the repudiation and try to insist on performance without an order for specific performance (citing *White & Carter (Councils) Ltd v. McGregor* [1962] A.C. 413; [1961] 3 All E.R. 1128).

[18] *Wiltshire Iron Co. v. GW Railway Co.* [1871] L.R. 6 Q.B. 776.

CHAPTER 17

RECEIVERS AND UNSECURED CREDITORS: EXECUTION, DISTRESS, FREEZING INJUNCTIONS AND TRUSTS

17–001 One set of problems facing a receiver concerns the special rights of creditors other than the debenture-holder. Local authorities (in respect of rates), landlords (in respect of rents) and preferential creditors are dealt with elsewhere in this work.[1] This chapter concerns a variety of other unsecured creditors who may claim priority over the debenture-holder's charges.

1. EXECUTION CREDITORS

(a) Garnishee orders

17–002 One method of enforcement of a judgment is for an unsecured creditor to seek an order that a third party who owes money to the company should pay it directly to the creditor. Such an order does not constitute a charge on the moneys, nor does it operate as an assignment of the company's rights to the creditor.[2] A debenture-holder may therefore be able to intervene and successfully assert title provided he does so at an appropriate time. In *Robson v. Smith*,[3] Robson was the holder of a debenture containing a floating charge. The company defaulted. Robson obtained judgment and levied execution by *fieri facias*, but failed to recover the whole sum due. Trade creditors also obtained judgments and obtained a garnishee order *nisi* in respect of a sum due from a third party. The next day Robson obtained a similar order. The trade creditors obtained garnishee orders absolute and Robson obtained a similar order the next day, expressed to rank behind the orders obtained by the trade creditors. The third party paid the sums under the orders in the manner directed. Robson then launched an action against one of the trade creditors claiming the sum paid over to that creditor. Romer J. rejected this claim on the grounds that, when the third party had paid the money over, the floating charge had not crystallised: "No receiver had been appointed at the instance of a debenture-holder, nor had the plaintiff taken any step, as against the company, to enforce his security or to prevent the company from carrying on business". The evidence showed that "the company continued for some time afterward to carry on business . . .", so that crystallisation did not take place as a result of cesser of business. Whilst the charge remained floating, the debenture-

---

[1] See below, Chap. 20, for rates, above, Chap. 15, for rent and below, Chap. 21 for preferential creditors.

[2] Re *Combined Weighing and Advertising Machine Co.* (1889) 43 Ch.D. 99.

[3] [1895] 2 Ch. 118.

holder could not single out a particular debt due to the company and require it to be paid to him. Moreover, although the debenture contained a restriction on further charges, Romer J. held that this could not be material since "garnishee proceedings are only a form of execution, and do not lead to any 'charge', in the true sense, being created by the company . . ."

Robson v. Smith was followed by the Court of Appeal in *Evans v. Rival* **17–003** *Granite*.[4] The debenture-holder had demanded payment under the debenture but had taken no steps to enforce the security when another creditor obtained a garnishee order nisi in respect of a bank account. The debenture-holder contested the creditor's application but the Court made the order absolute.

The Court rejected the idea that the mere existence of a floating **17–004** charge over the debt prevented it from being taken in execution.[5] That would have been inconsistent with the company's freedom to carry on business, which had to be subject to the processes of law if the company did not pay its debts.[6] The notion that the debenture-holder could crystallise the floating charge over a single debt was also rejected,[7] and the Court held that, in order to attain priority, the floating charge had to have crystallised.

Unfortunately, the Court did not clearly indicate what events might be **17–005** sufficient to bring about such crystallisation. Vaughan Williams L.J. considered that there had to be some action by the debenture-holder to appoint a receiver to enforce his security, or some intervention by the debenture-holder to terminate the company's licence to carry on business. Fletcher Moulton L.J. stated that the charge would only crystallise when the company ceased to trade or when the debenture-holder intervened. Buckley L.J. agreed that the debenture-holder "must do something to turn his security from a floating to a fixed charge", but also alluded to the possibility that crystallisation would occur automatically on the occurrence of an event defined in the debenture.[8] An automatic crystallisation clause in a debenture may therefore be effective to defeat execution.[9]

Norton v. Yates[10] indicates that, if a receiver is appointed before **17–006** payment of moneys to the creditor pursuant to a garnishee order *nisi*, then the debenture-holder will gain priority. As has been seen, *Robson v. Smith*[11] is authority for the proposition that actual payment over will

---

[4] [1910] 2 K.B. 979, CA.

[5] *cf. Re London Pressed Hinge Co. Ltd* [1905] 1 Ch. 576 where neither *Robson v. Smith* nor *Robinson v. Burnell's Bakery* [1904] 2 K.B. 624 (below, n. 18) was cited. The case law is discussed by the Federal Court of Australia in *Wily v. St George Partnership Banking Ltd* [1999] B.P.I.R. 1030.

[6] [1910] 2 K.B. 979 at 995, *per* Fletcher Moulton L.J.

[7] This is certainly the case in the absence of an express provision for partial crystallisation. On crystallisation generally, see above, Chap. 3.

[8] See also *Davey & Co. v. Williamson* [1898] 2 Q.B. 194 and the discussion of automatic crystallisation in above, Chap. 3.

[9] See, *e.g. Gough on Company Charges* (2nd ed., 1996), p. 256.

[10] [1906] 1 K.B. 112.

[11] [1895] 2 Ch. 118.

defeat any subsequent action by the debenture-holder. But what is the significance of the making of a garnishee order absolute? *Evans v. Rival Granite*[12] might be taken to imply that such an order will itself defeat the claim of a debenture-holder, but it is suggested that this cannot be correct. A garnishee order is simply a means of execution and not a charge capable of transforming an unsecured creditor into a secured one.[13] As such, though the judgment contains confusing references to garnishee orders as "charges", the decision of Walton J. in *Cairney v. Back*[14] is probably right: the appointment of a receiver after an order absolute but before payment over was held to be sufficient to gain priority for the debenture-holder's charge.

17–007 The analysis above only applies to floating charges over debts. The now common fixed charge over book and other debts will, if valid, obviate this problem, but gives rise to another. If the creditor has actual notice that the company's debt is the subject of a fixed charge, he cannot properly obtain payment without the consent of the debenture-holder. If the creditor does not have this notice, then he can properly obtain a garnishee order and accept payment. If the company's debtor does not have actual notice of the fixed charge, he can and must pay in accordance with the garnishee order; but if he is aware of the fixed charge, then by payment to the execution creditor he obtains no discharge from his liability to pay the debenture-holder, and accordingly is at risk of having to pay twice.

(b) Writs of *fieri facias*

17–008 The writ of *fieri facias* requires a sheriff to seize and sell goods of a debtor to meet the creditor's claim. When seizure is made, the goods can be left in the physical possession of the debtor by agreement, the sheriff taking constructive possession only. None of these processes gives any charge over the goods.[15]

17–009 Despite earlier cases which appeared to give undue weight to the mere existence of a debenture,[16] it is now clear that the creditor has priority if execution is completed prior to crystallisation.[17] A debenture-holder can

---

[12] [1910] 2 K.B. 979, CA.

[13] See *Robson v. Smith* [1895] 2 Ch. 118, *per* Romer J.

[14] [1906] 2 K.B. 746.

[15] In *Peck v. Craighead* [1995] 1 B.C.L.C. 337, M.E. Mann Q.C., sitting as a Deputy Judge of the High Court, decided that a creditor who had executed under a writ of *fieri facias* was a secured creditor within the meaning of s. 258(4) of the 1986 Act, the security being "not unlike a lien". It is, however, thought that this is not correct. The contrary view is supported by *Relwood Pty Ltd v. Manning Homes Pty Ltd (No. 2)* [1992] 2 Qd. R. 197 at 200, lines 5–40, where the references to security in some of the earlier case law, including that relied on in the *Peck* case, were explained as being founded on an ambiguity of language, so that the references to security did not connote any proprietary interest in goods seized in execution.

[16] See particularly *Re Standard Manufacturing Co.* [1891] 1 Ch. 627, CA; *Re Opera Ltd* [1891] 3 Ch. 260, CA.

[17] *Palmer's Company Law*, Vol. 2, para. 13–138. The *dicta* in *Evans v. Rival Granite* were expressed to relate to priorities in cases concerning seizure by sheriffs. *cf. Lochab Brothers v. Kenya Furfural* [1985] L.R.C. (Comm.) 737 where the majority of the Court of Appeal of Kenya held that execution was completed on sale, and accordingly prior to payment of the proceeds to the execution creditor.

obtain priority if he intervenes to crystallise his security before the execution is completed by payment of moneys over to the execution creditor.

The case of *Robinson v. Burnell's Bakery*[18] illustrates an alternative **17–010** approach on somewhat unusual facts. The sheriff seized goods subject to a floating charge, but before the debenture-holder could intervene the company agreed to make periodic payments out of earnings in consideration of the suspension of the execution proceedings. A receiver was subsequently appointed and he claimed these sums from the sheriff. Channell J. found that the sheriff had made the agreement with the company as agent for the creditor, that the execution had not of itself determined the company's licence to trade and, as such, the sums paid were simply repayments of the company's debt in the ordinary course of its business.[19] The creditors were thus entitled to the moneys, for the debenture-holder had not intervened to crystallise his security in time.

The learned judge did not give any opinion as to what might have **17–011** been the case if the goods had been sold and the proceeds held or paid over by the sheriff. It is suggested that the proceeds would have the same status as the goods, *i.e.* they would be the property of the company subject to the floating charge and therefore susceptible to being taken by the debenture-holder or receiver upon crystallisation. If, however, the proceeds are actually paid over to creditors prior to, or without notice of, crystallisation, it is suggested that the creditors acquire legal title to the money free of the debenture-holder's equity.

2. CHARGING ORDERS

By virtue of the Charging Orders Act 1979 the court may, as part of the **17–012** execution of a judgment, impose a charge on the property of a debtor. In practice, this tends not to cause a problem in receiverships since a charging order will typically relate to land, and any land owned by the company will almost certainly be subject to a prior fixed charge in favour of the debenture-holder.

In the unlikely event of the charging order affecting an asset over **17–013** which there is a floating charge, the position is not at all clear. Lord Brightman indicated in *Roberts Petroleum v. Kenny*[20] that a charging order *nisi* (which is obtained *ex parte*) is a defeasible right that only becomes indefeasible on being made absolute. As such and by analogy to the other types of execution discussed above, it is suggested that, in order to secure priority, the debenture-holder would have to intervene to bring about a crystallisation of his security before the charging order is

---

[18] [1904] 2 K.B. 624.
[19] The case and this analysis were followed and applied to very similar facts by Salter J. in *Heaton & Dugard v. Cutting Bros.* [1925] 1 K.B. 655; *cf. Taunton v. Sheriff of Warwickshire* [1895] 2 Ch. 319.
[20] [1983] 2 A.C. 192, HL.

made absolute.[21] Alternatively, crystallisation pursuant to an automatic crystallisation clause could probably prevent the charging order being made absolute.

17–014   It may sometimes be possible to apply to discharge a charging order on the grounds of non-disclosure, *e.g.* in relation to creditors of whom the applicant was aware, of whom the debenture-holder might be one. Generally speaking, the court will deprive the applicant of any advantage gained by means of such non-disclosure, but the remedy is discretionary and may be refused if the court considers that such a sanction would be too severe in all the circumstances.[22]

17–015   In *Jelle Zwemstra v. Walton and Stuart*,[23] a charging order absolute had been granted at a time when the debtor was insolvent, albeit unknown to the chargee. On the application of the trustee in bankruptcy, the charging order was discharged pursuant to what is now Schedule 1, rule 50.7 of the Civil Procedure Rules. It is doubted whether that decision can be correct, given that the chargee would apparently be permitted to retain the benefit of his execution in such circumstances under section 346 of the 1986 Act (the equivalent of section 183 in a corporate context) and the apparent conflict between the decision and the *Roberts Petroleum* case. In *Banque Nationale de Paris Plc v. Montman Ltd & Others*[24] it was held that an unsecured creditor had no standing to apply to set aside a charging order absolute in similar circumstances to the *Jelle Zwemstra* case, since an unsecured creditor was not a "person interested" within the meaning of section 3(5) of the Charging Orders Act 1979 and CPR Schedule 1, rule 50.7. A secured creditor would certainly be a "person interested" for the purpose of having standing to make the application.

3. FREEZING INJUNCTIONS

17–016 A receiver may discover upon his appointment that a party claiming to be an unsecured creditor has frozen all or some of the charged assets of the company pending the resolution of that creditor's claim. This was the situation considered by the Court of Appeal in *Cretanor Maritime Co. v. Irish Marine Management Ltd*[25] There, the company had become the charterer of a vessel and subsequently had executed a debenture containing a floating charge. During a dispute with the company, the owners of the vessel obtained a freezing injunction[26] restraining the

---

[21] The case actually decided that the intervention of the statutory scheme brought into effect by a resolution to wind up the company was sufficient reason for a refusal to make a charging order absolute. The House was concerned not to elevate one unsecured creditor to secured status in the winding-up.

[22] *Zealcastle Ltd v. Galadari* (unreported, Harman J., July 28, 1986).

[23] [1997] 6 C.L. 347.

[24] Unreported, Miss H. Williamson Q.C., July 20, 1999.

[25] [1978] 1 W.L.R. 966, CA.

[26] Traditionally, the freezing injunction was known as a "Mareva" injunction, being a shorthand of the name of the case in which the type of injunciton was first reported. The

company from taking out of the jurisdiction assets which might be required to meet the owners' claim. The Court of Appeal appears to have accepted that subsequently the company impliedly bound itself by contract not to remove the moneys. A receiver was appointed over the company's assets, who applied for the release of certain sums from the injunction. It was held that a receiver who was the company's agent was bound by the injunction and could not apply for its release, but the debenture-holder was entitled to apply. The injunction did not confer any sort of lien or proprietary right over the property in question but merely safeguarded it to await an eventual execution after judgment. Upon the appointment of the receiver, the floating charge crystallised and the debenture-holder had a fixed charge over the assets of the company. This would prevail over any future execution. Although the application at first instance had been made by the receiver, the Court of Appeal was prepared to treat it as if it had been made by the debenture-holder and simply added him as party to the summons. Moreover, the debenture-holder was entitled to apply without becoming a party to the action.

The *Cretanor* case was distinguished by Harman J. in *Capital Cameras* **17–017** *Ltd v. Harold Lines Ltd*[27] where the facts were analogous. Harman J. pointed out that in the *Cretanor* case the receiver had been applying as agent of the company in a situation where the company was restrained by contract from removing the money from the jurisdiction. The receiver was therefore seeking an order for the release of moneys so that he could cause the company to breach a pre-receivership contract. He could not be allowed to do this as agent for the company.[28] In the *Capital Cameras* case, there were no contractual terms binding the company in relation to the assets subject to the freezing injunction and thus Harman J. rejected the argument of two of the defendants to the effect that the company by its administrative receivers (as opposed to the debenture holder) was the wrong party to have applied to court for variation of the injunction. He went on to point out that the appointment of authorised insolvency practitioners would probably mean that the assets were no longer in jeopardy and that the injunction could be varied to allow the receiver to deal with the assets.

Even where the release of the freezing injunction was with a view to a **17–018** breach of an agreement binding the company but not a debenture-holder, it may well be possible as a practical matter to persuade the party who has obtained a freezing injunction to agree to an application being made by the receiver alone in order to save costs.

new terminology has been introduced by the Civil Procedure Rules: see CPR Pt 25, and the accompanying Practice Direction.
[27] [1991] 1 W.L.R. 54.
[28] A receiver can as agent for the company but using the priority of the debenture-holder cause the company effectively to repudiate purely contractual agreements: see above, Chap. 7.

4. TRUSTS[29]

17–019 Property held on trust by the company will not normally fall under any of the debenture-holder's charges. Whilst this principle may be relatively easy to apply in the rare case of an express trust,[30] difficult situations can arise where persons who might otherwise be ordinary unsecured creditors claim priority by virtue of an entitlement under an implied trust.

17–020   In *Re Kayford*,[31] the company, being on the verge of liquidation, sought and obtained advice on how to safeguard customers who sent deposits with orders. A separate account was used for new deposits and the bank were told of the arrangement. Megarry J. held that the intention to create a trust was clear even though the word "trust" was not used and the subject-matter and beneficiaries were sufficiently certain. The subject-matter being personalty, no writing was needed. Payment into a separate bank account was indicative of, but not essential to, the creation of a trust.[32]

17–021   One can contrast with this the case of *Re London Wine Company (Shippers) Ltd*[33] The company sold wine for investment, and often merely "kept" wine for the client without any particular bottles being appropriated to any particular contract of sale. The buyer was sent a certificate purporting to signify his beneficial ownership of the wine purchased by him. Certain buyers suggested after the appointment of the receiver that, even if title to the wine had failed to pass under the usual rules relating to sale of goods, the company held the wine on trust for them. Oliver J. held that the trust failed for uncertainty of subject-matter, since the wine which would have been beneficially owned had not been segregated and could not be identified. The argument that the company held a specified proportion of the wine on trust, so that the buyer became an equitable tenant in common of the entire stock of wine, was also rejected.[34]

---

[29] See also above, Chap. 10, "Bankers" and below, Chap. 18, "Building Contracts".

[30] But see, for example, the difficulties encountered in *Re ILG Travel Ltd* [1995] 2 B.C.L.C. 128 and *cf.* the approach of the Court of Appeal of New South Wales in *Stephens Travel Service v. Qantas Airways* (1998) 13 N.S.W.L.R. 331.

[31] [1975] 1 W.L.R. 279.

[32] Compare *Re English and American Insurance Co. Ltd* [1994] 1 B.C.L.C. 649 (where an insurance company agreed to hold all monies relating to a particular class of its business in a segregated account, and was found to hold the account on trust for the assureds); *Re Lewis's of Leicester Ltd* [1995] 1 B.C.L.C. 428 (where trusts were held to be established in favour of concessionaires of a department store); *Re Holiday Promotions (Europe) Ltd* [1996] 2 B.C.L.C. 618 (where the alleged trust funds were deposits in respect of holidays, but where there was no segregated account and no sufficient indication of any intention to create a trust).

[33] (1976) 126 N.L.J. 977; [1986] P.C.C. 121.

[34] Similar issues arose against a similar factual background in *Re Stapylton Fletcher Ltd* [1994] 1 W.L.R. 1181, which also concerned the purchase and storage of wine. However, on the facts of *Stapylton*, when a customer contracted to purchase wine, that wine was taken from the company's general trading stock, moved to an adjacent storage unit, and stored with wine of the same character and vintage which had already been bought by other customers. Judge Paul Baker Q.C. held that this segregation from the general stocks of the company was the crucial distinction from the *London Wine Shippers* case, as it meant that the wine was ascertained for the purposes of s. 16 of the Sale of Goods Act

Re Kayford was considered by the Court of Appeal in *Re Chelsea* **17–022**
Cloisters Ltd[35] In that case an insolvency accountant supervising the
affairs of a company in serious financial trouble placed deposits from
tenants into a separate account. The intention to create a separate fund
apart from the company's property available to its creditors generally
was held to be sufficient to create a trust.

Both the *Kayford and London Wine* decisions were considered in **17–023**
relation to certainty of subject matter in *Hunter v. Moss*.[36] The *London
Wine* approach to certainty was held to apply only to tangibles and not to
intangibles, on the grounds that tangible assets, even where they appear
to be part of a homogeneous mass, are physically separate and therefore
distinguishable from others in the same mass.[37] Furthermore, certain
items in such a mass may have distinguishing characteristics, *e.g.* wine
that has gone bad through faulty storage. By contrast, intangibles such as
shares are not distinguishable from each other and need not be
separately identified in any way. There is therefore sufficient certainty of
subject-matter where a trust is declared as to a particular percentage of
the shares in a company where the trustee has more than enough shares
to form the subject-matter of the trust, even if the shares subject to the
trust are not separately identified.

Whether the decision in *Hunter v. Moss* is good law is not entirely **17–024**
clear, given in particular the decision of the Privy Council in *Re Goldcorp
Exchange Ltd*.[38] A company in receivership had dealt in gold and other
precious metals, and agreed to sell unascertained bullion to its customers
for future delivery. Each customer received an invoice or certificate
signifying his ownership. The company did not, in fact, keep sufficient
bullion to satisfy all of its customers' contracts, and there was no
appropriation of any of the bullion to any of those contracts. The
company got into financial difficulties, and receivers were appointed.
The judgment of the Board was delivered by Lord Mustill, who
explained why a contract for the sale of unascertained goods could pass
no title to any such goods. A buyer could not acquire title to goods
unless and until it is known to what goods that title relates. Notwithstanding that both parties might agree and intend that property to goods
shall pass, from "the very nature of things" property cannot pass until
the goods are ascertained.[39] This reasoning was held to apply equally to
an argument that a title in equity could be created by the sale.[40] Hence,

---

1979. The fact that the bottles were then mixed with other wine of the same character and
vintage, and thus could not be identified as belonging to any particular customer, meant
that the customer became a tenant in common of the whole bulk of the wine of that
character and vintage, along with the other customers who had bought such wine.

[35] (1980) 41 P. & C.R. 98, CA.

[36] [1993] 1 W.L.R. 934; affirmed by the Court of Appeal, [1994] 1 W.L.R. 452 with
abbreviated reasons on the point in question. As far as one can tell from the reports, the
facts did not involve insolvency.

[37] At 940.

[38] [1995] A.C. 74, PC.

[39] *ibid.*, at 89E–90G.

[40] *ibid.*, at 90G.

the reasoning in the *London Wine Shippers* case was expressly applied
and approved by the Privy Council.[41]

17–025   There is little doubt that the reasoning of the Board in *Goldcorp* sits
uneasily with the decision in *Hunter v. Moss*. Lord Mustill explains that
neither legal nor equitable title can pass until it is clear to which title,
hence which goods, the transaction is supposed to relate. That same
reasoning would also dictate that no effective declaration of trust was
made in *Hunter v. Moss*, as the parties in *Hunter v. Moss* could not
possibly know to which of the shares the trust related. The fact that all
the shares were the same could not affect the logic of the reasoning
adopted in *Goldcorp*.

17–026   The apparent tension between the two decisions was considered by
Neuberger J. in *Re Harvard Securities Ltd, Holland v. Newbury*.[42] That
case also concerned title in shares which had not been appropriated to
any contract of sale. After a thorough review of the relevant authorities
and texts, Neuberger J. concluded that *Hunter v. Moss* was binding on
him, and that, whilst "not particularly convinced by the distinction",[43] the
reasoning in *Hunter v. Moss* applied to shares and other intangibles,
whilst the reasoning in *Goldcorp* applied to chattels. It appears that,
unless and until the issue is raised before the House of Lords, this
distinction represents the law.[44]

17–027   The circumstances in which a company in receivership which had
acted as a mercantile agent might hold the proceeds of book debts on
trust for its principal were discussed by the Court of Appeal in *Triffitt
Nurseries (A Firm) v. Salads Etc. Ltd*.[45] The claimants were the producers
of salad vegetables which were sold to supermarkets and wholesale
markets by the company in receivership prior to the receivers being
appointed. The claimants accepted that prior to the receivership the
proceeds of the debts paid by the markets for the vegetables were owned
by the company, since the company had the right to mix the proceeds of
the book debts with its own monies, and to take its commission out of
those proceeds. The claimants argued that upon the appointment of
receivers and the cessation of the company's business, the proceeds of
debts still outstanding at that time and collected by the receivers were
subject to a trust in their favour, and that at the date of the receivership
the claimants had been entitled to demand payment direct from the
markets. The arguments were rejected by the Court of Appeal, on the
basis that the company's title to the book debts was not somehow limited

---

[41] *ibid.* at 100A. On this basis, there is not always a trust where specific performance of a
contract for the sale or supply of a commodity is available, for specific performance may be
available in respect of goods which are neither specific nor ascertained if there are no
alternative sources of supply: see *Chitty on Contract* 28th ed., Vol. 1, para. 28.016.

[42] [1997] 2 B.C.L.C. 369.

[43] [1997] 2 B.C.L.C. 369 at 383a.

[44] See *Re CA Pacific Finance Ltd* [2000] 1 B.C.L.C. 494 at 509 and *Re Harvard Securities
Ltd.* [1997] 2 B.C.L.C. 369, 381 where reliance is placed on the distinction and it is pointed
out that leave to appeal was refused in *Hunter v. Moss* after the report of the Privy Council
decision in *Goldcorp*.

[45] [2000] 1 B.C.L.C. 761, CA.

or defeasible, but absolute, and that the appointment of receivers and the cessation of business did not alter that fact. The only way in which the claimants might have succeeded in claiming the proceeds from the receivers was if the receivers had been guilty of sharp practice in obtaining payment, which was not suggested. A claim to the proceeds would also have succeeded if the receivers had, after their appointment, accepted further consignments and sold further produce (whenever consigned) — in which case the receivers might be deemed personally to have adopted the contracts.

In *Associated Alloys Pty Ltd v. A.C.N. 001 452 106 Pty Ltd*[46] the **17–028** majority of the High Court of Australia recognised the effectiveness of an express trust of the proceeds of sale of goods supplied under a retention of title clause. The trust expressly applied to the proceeds of sale of all products which were made using steel supplied by the sellers, the beneficial interest of the sellers being stated to be equal to the amount owing from the buyers to the sellers at the time of receipt of the proceeds. It was held that the absence of any express requirement on the buyer to keep the proceeds separate from his own assets did not affect the existence of the trust, since the trust was express and hence the obligation to keep the proceeds separate existed by necessary implication in any event.[47] The High Court of Australia was prepared to imply a term that the debt owing from the buyer to the seller at the time of receipt of the proceeds was discharged *pro tanto* on receipt by the buyer of the proceeds, so that no equity of redemption vested in the buyer. The case is discussed further in Chapter 12.

5. DISTRESS FOR TAXES

Distress is a primitive but legal form of self-help which entitles one party **17–029** to seize property of another to enforce payment of the other's liability to the seizer. Statute has provided for distress in the case of a number of taxes.[48]

There is no reported case law concerning the priority of authorities who have distrained for taxes on a "person" as opposed to taxes charged on property. The question arises: at what point in the process of distraining upon and selling goods does the distraining tax authority become entitled to keep possession of goods and sell them (or receive and keep the proceeds of sale, as the case may be), where a receiver has been appointed? The answer to this question depends upon whether distress by tax authorities is analogous to distress for rates or to execution.[49]

---

[46] (2000) 171 A.L.R. 568, High Court of Australia.

[47] See further *Stephens Travel Service International Pty Limited v. Qantas Airways* (1988) 13 N.S.W.L.R. 331 (New South Wales Court of Appeal); *Walker v. Corboy* (1990) 19 N.S.W.L.R. 382 (New South Wales Court of Appeal); and *cf. Re ILG Travel Limited* [1995] 2 B.C.L.C. 128.

[48] See *Halsbury's Laws of England* (4th ed. reissue), Vol. 13, para. 827.

[49] See also Samwell, *Corporate Receiverships* (2nd ed., 1988), p. 80.

17–030   The use of the word "distress" by Parliament would seem to suggest that distress for taxes is analogous to other forms of distress. But it is sometimes said that distress for taxes is a statutory remedy more analogous to execution than to distress for rent.[50] The importance of the distinction is that when a person distrains for rent, he takes a pledge of the goods by taking possession of the goods in question.[51] The distrainor thus takes security over the goods seized, and this security interest could take priority over the interest of a debenture-holder having a floating charge.[52] Where goods are seized by execution creditors pursuant to a writ of *fieri facias*,[53] the creditor takes no pledge of the goods seized.[54] The creditor thus has no security interest which can take priority over the security of the debenture-holders. Seizure of the goods is merely a step towards selling the goods and, thus, being paid.

17–031   In a number of cases, the courts have distinguished between distress for taxes and distress for rent.[55] However, those cases deal with rather different issues, such as whether the category of goods upon which distraint can be levied is the same in the case of statutory distress as under the common law.[56]

17–032   The law in relation to execution creditors is far from clear, and few principles emerge which could be applied by analogy.[57] Certain of the authorities in that area are treated as decisions on the priority of execution creditors as against floating charge-holders, yet the judgements in the cases do not address the issue of priorities.[58] If the right of the tax authorities to sell goods distrained upon or to keep the proceeds of sale depends on the priorities of secured creditors, little guidance is to be found on this point in the cases on execution creditors.

[50] See *Halsbury's Laws of England* (4th ed. reissue), Vol. 13, para. 827.

[51] In the case of the common law of distress for rent, by taking possession of the goods, the distrainor becomes a pledgee: see *Halsbury* (4th ed.), Vol. 13, para. 601.

[52] This is the basis upon which the Inland Revenue themselves argue that they have priority over debenture-holders in relation to goods seized prior to crystallisation of the floating charge. For an account of the position of the Inland Revenue, see *Tolley's Taxation in Corporate Insolvency* (2nd ed), Chap. 4.

[53] In fact, the person distraining under the purely common law right of distraint for rent would not take a "pledge" of the goods in the sense in which the word is normally used, as the common law gave the "pledgee" no right of sale.

[54] See above, paras 17–008 and 17–009.

[55] See *Halsbury*, Vol. 13 (4th ed.), para. 604, above, n. 4 and the cases cited there. Surprisingly, the *Herbert Berry* case (see below) is not listed.

[56] The case of *Potts v. Hickman* [1941] A.C. 212 concerns the detailed wording of s. 1 of the Landlord and Tenant Act 1709; but see the more general statements of Viscount Maugham and Lord Wright, at 235 and 241 respectively. The cases discussed in the *Hickman* case generally concerned the issue whether the limitations of the categories of goods which could be distrained upon at common law should apply to statutory distraint: see *per* Lord Wright, at 241; also *Swaffer v. Mulcahy* [1924] 1 K.B. 608; *Hutchins v. Chambers* (1758) 1 Burr. 579; *MacGregor v. Clamp* [1914] 1 K.B. 288.

[57] For a criticism of the case law in relation to execution creditors, see R.J. Calnan, "Priorities Between Execution Creditors and Floating Charges" (1982) 10 N.Z.U.L.R. 111; D.M. Hare and D. Milman, "Debenture Holders and Judgement Creditors — Problems of Priority" [1982] L.M.C.L.O. 57.

[58] *e.g.*, *Re Standard Manufacturing Co.* [1891] 1 Ch. 627; *Re Opera Ltd* [1891] 3 Ch. 286. In particular, it is implicit in the cases that a floating charge is a fixed charge coupled with a licence to deal, a view of the floating charge which was rejected by the Court of Appeal in this area in *Evans v. Rival Granite Quarries Ltd* [1910] 2 K.B. 979.

The authority which bears most closely on this issue appears to be **17–033** *Herbert Berry Ltd v. IRC*.[59] That case concerned the power of the Inland Revenue to sell goods which they had seized under their power of distraint prior to the voluntary liquidation of the debtor company. The Inland Revenue had kept constructive possession of the goods under a walking possession agreement.[60] The House of Lords decided that the Inland Revenue could sell the goods and keep the proceeds. It is implicit in the decision that the Inland Revenue had become secured creditors of the debtor company upon taking possession of the goods.[61] Unless the Inland Revenue had acquired a security interest in the goods prior to the creditors' voluntary liquidation, the goods or their proceeds would have fallen to be distributed on a *pari passu* basis. Thus, the Inland Revenue must have become pledgees of the goods upon taking possession. If this is correct, where distress for taxes is levied (that is, possession taken of the goods) but not completed by sale prior to the crystallisation of a floating charge, the debenture-holder's interest will nevertheless be postponed to the interest of the distrainor.[62]

The tax authorities levying the distraint will often be preferential **17–034** creditors. Where that is so, their status as secured or unsecured creditors will make little difference, unless the assets of the company are insufficient to pay the preferential creditors in full. If seizure of possession of the goods constitutes the relevant tax authorities a pledgee, then this might affect the *pari passu* distribution of assets amongst the preferential creditors as a whole.[63] If seizure does not make the tax authorities a pledgee, the receiver may be entitled to an injunction to protect the interests of the general body of preferential creditors by preventing completion of the distress.[64]

If the receiver or debenture-holder launches a compulsory winding-up **17–035** petition to try to combat distress that has been put in but not completed by sale, the court is unlikely to restrain the sale unless there are special reasons (such as unconscionable conduct or delay) which would render sale inequitable.[65] Compulsory winding-up may provide some relief for the other preferential creditors in that, if a winding-up order is secured within three months after the completion of the distress, the proceeds are divided rateably so that "the list of preferential creditors will have

---

[59] [1977] 1 W.L.R. 1437, HL.

[60] On the nature and effect of walking possession agreements, see *National Commercial Bank of Scotland v. Arcam Demolition and Construction Ltd* [1966] 2 Q.B. 593 at 599, CA, *per* Lord Denning M.R. *cf. Peck v. Craighead* [1995] 1 B.C.L.C. 337.

[61] *cf. Roberts Petroleum v. Bernard Kenny* [1983] 2 A.C. 192, HL: see above, para. 17–013.

[62] The issue of the priority of the distrainor was not specifically addressed in the *Herbert Berry* case. However, at least one of the judges (see Buckley L.J. in the Court of Appeal in [1977] 3 All E.R. 729 at 733, where he refers to over-riding rights) appears to acknowledge that the issue rests on priority of securities. On the other hand, the courts' affirmation of *Re Great Ship Co. Ltd* (1863) 4 De G.J. & S.63 suggests that the courts were simply unaware of any policy justification for enforcing *pari passu* distribution.

[63] At least, assuming that there is no relevant negative pledge clause in the debenture, of which the creditor has notice.

[64] *cf. Taggs Island Casino Ltd v. Richmond Upon Thames BC* [1967] R.A. 70. See also *Re ELS Ltd* [1995] Ch. 11 at 26–27.

[65] See *Re Memco Engineering Ltd* [1986] Ch. 86.

added to it the [distrainor's] claim and the creditors then on the list will be paid *pari passu* from the distress fund. Needless to say the [distrainor's] debt, as added to the list, will include the [distrainor's] claim in respect of non-preferential as well as preferential debts".[66]

17–036   Where the relevant chattels are subject to a fixed charge, even if subsequent distress for taxes were to create a pledge, this would rank behind the fixed charge.

[66] *ibid.*, at 98E–F.

CHAPTER 18

CONSTRUCTION CONTRACTS

1. FEATURES OF CONSTRUCTION CONTRACTS

Construction contracts raise issues lying at the heart of insolvency law: **18–001** the conflict between freedom of contract and the *pari passu* rule, contractual and procedural rights functioning as security, and the nature of property subject to a contingency.[1] More particularly, they have certain special features:

    (a) the industry uses many different standard forms which are often revised by the drafting bodies and amended by the parties,[2] and which tend to be lengthy and difficult to construe[3];

    (b) most of the work is carried out by sub-contractors resulting in chains of contracts under which one contract may incorporate the terms of others higher up the chain[4];

    (c) responsibility for decisions often rests with the architect or the engineer who, although appointed as the agent of the employer, owes an independent duty to both employer and contractor to act fairly[5];

    (d) the employer is given considerable "security" for performance: all payment obligations are qualified in one way or another[6] and there is extensive use of bonds and guarantees. By contrast, the contractor is afforded minimal "security" for payment[7];

---

[1] See generally, Davis, *Construction Insolvency* (2nd ed., 1999).

[2] Current forms of main contract include: for building work, JCT 1998, printed in several different versions by the Joint Contracts Tribunal; for engineering work, ICE (7th ed.) published by the Institution of Civil Engineers; for international projects, FIDIC (Test ed., 1998) in various versions from the Fédération Internationale des Ingénieurs-Conseils; for government work, GC/Works/1 (1998), published by The Stationery Office.

[3] See generally May, *Keating on Building Contracts* (6th ed., 1995).

[4] Standard forms of sub-contract include: DOM/1 and DOM/2 published by the Construction Confederation and NSC/C (formerly the Green Form of nominated sub-contract) by the JCT for use on building work, and the Blue Form by the Civil Engineering Contractors' Association for use on engineering work.

[5] *Sutcliffe v. Thakrah* [1974] A.C. 727, HL.

[6] Payment to the contractor normally depends on the issue of certificates; interim payments are on account of the contract sum and are subject to adjustment later; retention is conditional on the works being completed; all payment is subject to suspension on a termination; or to direct payments being made to sub-contractors or suppliers; or to set-off or abatement generally.

[7] "Security" for contractors is found in a minority of cases and is usually limited to a trust of part of the contract sum or a payment guarantee.

(e) plant and materials which are fixed to the land as part of the permanent works lose the quality of a chattel and become part of the land whether or not they have been paid for[8]; and

(f) aspects of construction contracts relating to payment, set-off and adjudication of disputes are now governed by statute.[9]

2. TERMINATION CLAUSES

18–002 Almost all of the standard forms include clauses allowing either party to terminate on the insolvency of the other.[10] Traditionally, the employer's power of termination has been wider than that given to the contractor,[11] and the range of events entitling either party to terminate was wider under the building than the engineering forms.[12] With the most recent editions, however, these differences have been removed[13] and all of the forms now include termination clauses with receivership and administration as insolvency events.[14] It remains essential, however, to check that the wording of the clause precisely covers the event which has happened since termination clauses are strictly construed by the court.[15] This is because they are in the nature of forfeiture clauses even though the word "forfeiture" is no longer used in connection with them.[16] The court has jurisdiction to grant a declaration of rights in respect of an insolvency termination clause in case of difficulty.[17]

18–003 In most cases, termination takes place on service of a notice, with the exception of the current editions of the JCT forms where termination is automatic on bankruptcy or liquidation and discretionary on notice in the case of administration and receivership. Some sub-contracts provide for automatic termination in the event of a termination under the main contract in order to enable the contractor to deny the sub-contractor further access to the site without being in repudiatory breach.

18–004 The standard forms do not expressly exclude the common law, which applies in addition to the express termination clause.[18] It may be possible to terminate under the contract without waiving a right to accept a

---

[8] *Sims v. London Necropolis Co.* (1885) 1 T.L.R. 584.

[9] Housing Grants, Construction and Regeneration Act 1996, considered below.

[10] The main exception is GC/Works/1 (1998).

[11] The contractor had no express power to terminate in the event of the insolvency of the employer under JCT 81 or ICE (6th ed.).

[12] For example, main and sub-contracts for engineering works allowed termination only on winding up.

[13] The employer and the contractor now have reciprocal rights to terminate for insolvency under the JCT, ICE and FIDIC forms.

[14] However, JCT forms still do not include the appointment of a receiver under a fixed charge. See Totty and Moss, *Insolvency,* Chap. H.6 for a useful table showing the relevant insolvency events included in each form.

[15] *Hill v. London Borough of Camden* (1980) 18 B.L.R. 31, CA.

[16] May, *Keating on Building Contracts,* (6th ed., 1995) at 257.

[17] *Midland Land Reclamation Ltd v. Warren Energy Ltd* [1997] C.I.L.L. 1222, Judge Peter Bowsher Q.C. (declaration not granted).

[18] In *Perar BV v. General Surety & Guarantee Co. Ltd* (1994) 66 B.L.R. 71, CA, the contract (in JCT 81 form) expressly preserved the common law in the context in the power to terminate, but not in the sub-clause conferring post-termination rights. The Court of Appeal considered that the parties must have intended to exclude the common law as far

repudiation at common law. In *LMK v. Aegon Insurance*[19] the court was asked to assume that a works contractor was already in repudiatory breach before administrative receivers were appointed to it. The works contract was not in a standard form. The management contractor relied on a termination clause entitling it to terminate "the works" for insolvency before realising that the contract was defective in that it did not entitle the contractor to recover its losses caused by the termination. It was held that, on a true construction of the works contract, the reliance on the termination clause did not prevent the contractor from accepting a repudiation at common law later and claiming damages to the full extent of its losses. It is worth noting that, as a contractual termination event, the appointment of administrative receivers cannot be a breach of contract; the only breach will be a failure to pay any sum found due to the employer after the works have been completed.[20]

As well as conferring the power to terminate, express clauses also give **18–005** the employer access to a bundle of rights which are intended to facilitate the completion of the works. These rights include:

(a) to terminate the contractor's licence and repossess the site;
(b) to engage another contractor to complete the work;
(c) to suspend all further payment to the contractor until after the completion of the works;
(d) to use the contractor's plant and materials on site for the purpose of the completion contract;
(e) to pay sub-contractors and suppliers direct and set off equivalent amounts against sums due or to become due to the contractor; and
(f) to set off the additional cost incurred in having the work completed and other losses resulting from the termination against sums otherwise due to the contractor.

3. POSSESSION OF THE SITE

An injunction restraining termination is analogous to specific perfor- **18–006** mance of the contract.[21] Specific performance will be ordered in

---

as the post-termination rights were concerned and that the sub-clause constituted a complete code. This aspect of the decision is questionable since it appears close to the 'argument from redundancy' criticised by Lord Hoffmann in *Beaufort Developments (N.I.) Ltd v. Gilbert-Ash N.I. Ltd* [1999] 1 A.C. 266 at 273, HL. Clause 27.8 of JCT 98 now expressly preserves common law rights in respect of the whole termination clause, which can no longer therefore be described as a 'complete code'.

[19] *Laing Management Ltd and Morrison-Knudson Ltd v. Aegon Insurance Co. (U.K.) Ltd* (1997) 86 B.L.R. 70, Judge Humphrey Lloyd Q.C.
[20] *Perar BV v. General Surety & Guarantee Co. Ltd* (1994) 66 B.L.R. 72 at 85, CA.
[21] *Munroe v. Wivenhoe Railway Co.* (1865) 12 L.T. 655 at 657, CA.

connection with a construction contract in appropriate cases.[22] It may be ordered against the contractor by restraining it from stopping work,[23] or, in theory at least, against the employer, by refusing to order the contractor to leave site.[24] In *Hounslow London Borough Council v. Twickenham Garden Developments Ltd*,[25] the employer served a termination notice under JCT 63 for failing to proceed regularly with the work which was disputed by the contractor. Megarry J. refused to grant an injunction ordering the contractor to leave the site, on two grounds:

    (a) the contractor's licence to occupy the site was subject to an implied condition that the employer would not revoke it during the course of the work; and

    (b) equity would not grant an injunction unless it were satisfied that the contract had been validly terminated, since otherwise it would be aiding a breach of contract.

18–007 In subsequent cases, however, injunctions have been granted removing the contractor from the site.[26] This practice has resulted in part from a change in the criteria for granting interlocutory injunctions.[27] In view of *American Cyanamid Co. v. Ethicon Ltd*[28] it is considered that an injunction would now be granted compelling a contractor to leave the site where there was a triable issue as to whether the contractor's employment had been terminated and where the contractor could be adequately compensated in damages.[29]

4. RELIEF FROM FORFEITURE

18–008 Equity has long asserted the right to grant relief against the contractual provisions providing for the forfeiture of property. In *Shiloh Spinners v. Harding*[30] Lord Wilberforce indicated that apart from cases of fraud, accident or mistake, relief from forfeiture is potentially available where a party to a transaction is given a right to terminate the contract (or the

---

[22] *Wolverhampton Corporation v. Emmons* [1901] 1 Q.B. 515, CA; *Co-Operative Insurance Society Ltd v. Argyll Stores (Holdings) Ltd* [1998] A.C. 1 at 13, HL, per Lord Hoffmann.

[23] In *Channel Tunnel Group v. Balfour Beatty Construction Ltd* [1993] A.C. 334, the House of Lords intimated that it would have considered granting an injunction restraining the builders of the Channel Tunnel from suspending work but for a jurisdictional bar.

[24] *Hounslow London Borough Council v. Twickenham Garden Developments Ltd* [1971] Ch. 233.

[25] [1971] Ch. 233.

[26] See May, *Keating on Building Contracts* (6th ed., 1995), p. 294.

[27] When the *Hounslow* case was decided, a plaintiff had to show a prima facie case when applying for an interlocutory injunction: *Fellowes v. Fisher* [1976] Q.B. 122, CA.

[28] [1975] A.C. 396, HL.

[29] *Tara Civil Engineering Ltd v. Moorfield Developments Ltd* (1989) 46 B.L.R. 72, Judge Peter Bowsher Q.C.; compare *Robert Salzer Constructions Ltd v. Elmbee Ltd* (1991) 10 A.C.L.R. 64, Sup Ct of Victoria (injunction granted restraining employer from serving a termination notice).

[30] [1973] A.C. 691, HL.

contract terminates automatically) on the happening of a particular event, and the purpose of the insertion of such right to terminate is essentially to act as security for the payment of money or the performance of some other contractual obligation which can still effectively be performed when the application for relief against forfeiture comes before the court.[31]

The *Shiloh Spinners* case concerned relief against forfeiture of a lease **18–009** of land, but it has since been affirmed that the jurisdiction can be exercised in relation to interests in personal property as well as in land.[32] But in *Scandinavian Trading Tanker v. Flota Petrolena Ecuatoriana (The Scaptrade)*[33] and subsequent cases it has been emphasised that the jurisdiction only extends to contracts which involve the forfeiture of proprietary or possessory rights.[34]

It is an unresolved question whether relief from forfeiture would be **18–010** available in relation to an ordinary building contract. Relief from forfeiture was granted in the unusual case of *Underground (Civil Engineering) Limited v. London Borough of Croydon*[35] where the employer terminated the contractor's employment and re-entered the site when only three week's work remained outstanding, but only on the ground that the contractor was to become entitled to a 125 year lease of the property within one month after practical completion. It was stated, *obiter,* that relief would not have been available in the case of an ordinary building contract in view of the absence of any proprietary or possessory right which might justify the court's intervention.[36] Although

---

[31] So, for example, relief against forfeiture cannot be granted in relation to a finance lease of a chattel after the chattel has been sold to a third party, unless the lessor and lessee agreed at the time of sale that their rights should be determined as if the property had not been sold and the proceeds of sale substituted for the property: *On Demand Information plc v. Michael Gerson (Finance) plc,* unreported, CA, July 31, 2000.

[32] See *e.g. BICC plc v. Burndy Corporation* [1985] Ch. 233, CA (relief granted in relation to ownership of patent rights); *Jobson v. Johnson* [1989] 1 W.L.R. 1026, CA (relief available in relation to contract for sale of shares); *Transag Haulage v. Leyland DAF Finance* [1994] 2 B.C.L.C. 88 (relief granted in relation to hire purchase agreements for three lorries which determined on the appointment of administrative receivers to a haulage company); and *On Demand Information plc v. Michael Gerson (Finance) plc,* unreported, CA, July 31, 2000 (relief available in relation to four finance leases of video editing equipment, but not granted due to the equipment having been sold to a third party prior to the date of the hearing).

[33] [1983] 2 A.C. 694, HL (relief not available in relation to a hiring under a time charter of a ship which gave no interest in or right of possession to the vessel but which was simply a contract for services to be rendered to the charterer by the shipowner through the shipowner's employees, namely the master and crew).

[34] See *e.g. Sport International Bussum v. Inter-Footwear* [1984] 1 W.L.R. 776, HL (relief not available in relation to a purely contractual licence to use trade marks and names). *cf. On Demand Information plc v. Michael Gerson (Finance) plc (supra),* in which Robert Walker L.J. stated that "Contractual rights which entitle the hirer to indefinite possession of chattels so long as hire payments are duly made, and which qualify and limit the owner's general property in the chattels, cannot aptly be described as purely contractual rights."

[35] [1990] E.G.C.S. 48 (Thomas Morison Q.C.). By analogy, relief may be available where the contractor also has an interest in the development project.

[36] See also *Westminster Properties Pty Ltd v. Comco Constructions Pty Ltd* (1991) 5 W.A.R. 191, CA of Western Australia (no relief for the employer against termination by the contractor).

an ordinary building contract will contain terms giving the contractor the right to "possession" of the site and a right not to be hindered or prevented in the carrying out of the building works on the site, it would no doubt be argued that unlike the indefinite possessory rights conferred on a hirer under a hire purchase agreement or on a lessee under a finance lease, which rights are the main purpose of the contract and qualify and limit the owner's general right to the property in question, the rights conferred on a contractor under a building contract are strictly limited and designed simply to enable the contractor to carry out the main purpose of the contract, which is the supply by him to the employer of building services.

5. SUSPENSION OF PAYMENT

18–011 The contractor's receivables are seriously affected by termination. Most forms include an automatic suspension of payment in that event: sums due cease to be due[37] or provisions requiring further payment cease to apply.[38] The contract thus freezes the contractor's cash flow, and therefore its ability to preserve the status quo with sub-contractors, and the prospects of the sale of the business are reduced. In addition, uncertified work in progress remains inchoate and other sums which are conditional on completion cease to be recoverable as debts as the condition becomes incapable of fulfilment. The certification process is replaced by the procedure under the termination clause under which the value of present and future receivables is credited to the contractor in the final account before the employer's cross-claims are set off. It is possible that the employer's suspension of payment is affected by the Housing Grants, Construction and Regeneration Act 1996, which is discussed below.

6. NOVATION

18–012 Administrative receivers appointed to a contractor would prefer to sell the business as a going concern to a single purchaser who negotiates novations with each individual employer.[39] Under a novation, the purchaser undertakes to the employer to be bound as if it had been a party to the contract from the inception and the employer releases the insolvent contractor from liability. The original contract is replaced by a new contract between the employer and the purchaser.[40] In practice, the

[37] GC/Works/1 (1998), cl. 57(1)(a).
[38] Under cl. 27.6.4.1 of JCT 98, the suspension does not apply to sums due for 28 days or more before termination which the employer has "unreasonably not discharged". There is as yet no case law on the criterion of reasonableness in this context.
[39] The options available to employers are set out in JCT Practice Note 24, and its Scottish equivalent, the SBCC Insolvency Practice Guide, which include forms of novation agreement. See below under 'Employees' for TUPE implications of novations.
[40] *Scarf v. Jardine* (1882) 7 App. Cas. 345, *Chatsworth Investments Ltd v. Cussins (Contractors) Ltd* [1969] 1 All E.R. 143, CA; *Westminster City Council v. Reema Construction Ltd (No. 2)* (1990) 24 Con. L.R. 26, Judge Peter Bowsher Q.C.

purchaser may pay a lump sum to the receivers on completion of the sale agreement and a percentage of receivables in existence as at termination as and when they are realised. The receivers' strategy will include the release of existing bonds and the repayment of cash deposited as security with the bondsman, new bonds being procured by the purchaser.

It is now common for funders to require contractors to enter into **18–013** direct agreements which include a promise to novate to a substituted entity if the contractor were to become entitled to terminate. Funders also require similar agreements from sub-contractors to novate to the employer on the contractor's default. There is a possibility that, in the event of a concurrent receivership and winding up, such arrangements will be held to be contrary to the policy of the statutory scheme governing distribution of assets in winding up.[41] There is a further practical point that a provision compelling novation in this way may be defective from a practical point of view unless it also provides for the novation of the architect or engineer or some other person the exercise of whose judgment is an integral part of the contract.

7. ASSIGNABILITY

Viewed as a security asset, a construction contract is vulnerable in view **18–014** of its long-term nature and the risks inherent in the construction process. As between the parties, however, the contract is not merely an asset but a relationship expressed in legal terms. As a consequence, a receiver appointed to enforce a charge over a construction contract has first to restore the relationship, by persuading the other party not to terminate or to withdraw a termination notice already served. If he cannot do so, the debenture-holder's prospects of recovering receivables will be reduced.

This "relationship" quality suggests that a construction contract is not **18–015** marketable in the same way as a debt. This is because the contract is based on reciprocal obligations and understandings, notably that in all matters where the architect has to apply his professional skill, he will act fairly in applying the terms of the contract.[42] For example, the Court of Appeal has stated:

> "When the benefit of a contract is assigned, the character of the obligation is not changed. Before the assignment, the [construction] managers were, in some respects, obliged to act on the instructions or directions of the [employer]. The assignment could not change

---

[41] *British Eagle International Air Lines Ltd v. Compagnie Nationale Air France* [1975] 1 W.L.R. 758, HL; *Carreras Rothmans Ltd v. Freeman Mathews Treasure Ltd* [1985] Ch. 207, Peter Gibson J.

[42] *Sutcliffe v. Thakrah* [1974] A.C. 727, HL; or, it might be added, that the employer would not call a demand guarantee obtained in connection with the contract without just cause.

that and render them subject to the orders of [the assignee banks].
A new agreement would be needed to achieve that."[43]

Alternatively, the contract may be expressly non-assignable or only partly
assignable.[44] All of the standard forms place restrictions on assignability.
An assignee under an assignment in breach of the contract acquires no
rights against the person in the position of debtor,[45] but the assignor will
owe a duty to the assignee to apply the benefit to its use.[46]

18–016   What is the effect of a non-assignability clause on the rights of a
creditor who has obtained a charge over the contract? A charge may not
be a breach of a provision which bars "assignments", although charges
over rights are often referred to as assignments.[47] It is thought that a
receiver appointed pursuant to a charge by a contractor over the benefit
of a contract containing a non-assignability provision would be entitled
to exercise the charge-holder's contractual rights as against the company,
such as the power to take proceedings against the employer using the
contractor's name, but the receiver may not be entitled to assert the
rights of an assignee, *e.g.* to call for payment direct or to limit the
employer's cross-claims to those crystallising before receipt of notice of
appointment.

8. DIRECT PAYMENT

18–017 Most of the work on a construction project is sub-contracted. Payment is
channelled through the contractor who is beneficially entitled (in the
absence of a trust) to all sums payable under interim certificates, even if
the contract obliges it to "pay over" sums identified by the certificate to
particular sub-contractors.[48] It is in the employer's interest that the sub-
contractors are paid since otherwise they may suspend work causing
delay and disruption to the project. The standard forms recognise the
employer's interest by allowing it to pay the sub-contractors direct, and
to be discharged from liability to the contractor to that extent, in two
situations:

---

[43] *L/M International Construction v. The Circle Ltd Partnership* (1995) 49 Con. L.R. 12 at
22, *per* Staughton L.J. Hence the use of direct or step-in agreements whereby the
contractor agrees to allow lenders to substitute a new entity in the event of the employer's
insolvency. See also *Don King (Productions) Inc. v. Warren* [1998] 2 All E.R. 608 at 634, *per*
Lightman J., affirmed [1999] 2 All E.R. 218, CA.
[44] *Yeandle v. Wynn Realisations Ltd (in administration)* (1995) 47 Con. L.R. 1, CA; *Flood
v. Shand Construction Ltd* (1996) 54 Con. L.R. 125, CA.
[45] *Helstan Securities Ltd v. Hertfordshire County Council* [1978] 3 All E.R. 262; *Linden
Gardens Ltd v. Lenesta Sludge Disposals Ltd* [1994] 1 A.C. 85, HL; *Modern Weighbridge &
Scale Services Pty Ltd v. ANR* (1996) 12 B.C.L. 224, Sup. Ct of South Australia.
[46] *Linden Gardens Ltd v. Lenesta Sludge Disposals Ltd* [1994] 1 A.C. 85 at 108, HL.
[47] See, *e.g. Business Computers Ltd v. Anglo-African Leasing Ltd* [1977] 1 W.L.R. 578.
[48] *Veitchi Co. v. Crowley Russell & Co.* [1972] S.C. 225, Court of Session (Outer House).

(a) where the architect certifies that the contractor has failed to prove payment of previous sums.[49] This power is available from the inception of the contract but is normally limited to payment to nominated sub-contractors[50];

(b) where the contractor's employment has been terminated.[51] This power can be exercised in favour of any supplier or sub-contractor and is not subject to any prior architect's certificate.

Under clause 35 of JCT 98, on the architect's certificate of non-payment **18–018** the employer becomes *obliged* to pay direct to sub-contractors, and future sums payable to the contractor are reduced accordingly. Under a direct warranty with each nominated sub-contractor, the employer undertakes to ensure that the architect operates clause 35.[52] If the employer fails to do this, the sub-contractor is entitled to recover from the employer in the absence of a certificate.[53] If, at the time for the reduction and the payment, there is in existence either a resolution or a petition to wind up the contractor, the clause ceases to have effect.[54] If the resolution or petition is discovered only after the direct payment has been made, the sub-contractor is liable to reimburse the employer for it on demand.[55] Under clause 27 of JCT 98, the power to pay direct on a termination does not arise if the event relied on is bankruptcy, liquidation "or the filing of a petition alleging insolvency" against the contractor. This expression can cover a petition for an administration order, depending on whether the petition alleges that the company is insolvent or merely that it is "likely" to become insolvent.[56] Instead of reducing the amount of a future payment, as under clause 35, the employer has power to deduct the amount of a direct payment under clause 27 from sums due or to become due to the contractor.

Whichever clause is relied on, the effect is to convert a duty to pay the **18–019** contractor into a power to pay the contractor's creditors and to set off the amount of such payments against the contractor's receivables. Direct payment clauses are therefore strictly construed.[57] The payment is usually made by the employer in its own right but under one form it is made as agent for the contractor,[58] and under another, pursuant to a

---

[49] JCT 98, cl. 35; ICE (7th ed.), cl. 59(7); FIDIC (Test ed. 1998), cl. 5.4.

[50] GC/Works/1 (1998), cl. 48(4) applies to any sub-contractor or supplier but only allows the employer to withhold payment to the contractor until the proof has been provided.

[51] JCT 98, cl. 27; GC Works/1 (1998), cl. 57. There is no additional power to pay direct on termination under the ICE or FIDIC forms.

[52] NSC/W (1998 ed.), cl. 7.1.

[53] *Construction Award No. 9 (1988)* [1995] 2 Construction Law Yearbook 103, Christopher Thomas Q.C.

[54] JCT 98, cl. 35.13.5.3.4.

[55] NSC/W (1998 ed.), cl. 7.2.

[56] Insolvency Act 1986, s. 8.

[57] *J.A. Milestone & Sons Ltd v. Yates Castle Brewery Ltd* [1938] 2 All E.R. 439.

[58] SIA (Singapore Institute of Architects) (5th ed., 1997), cl. 32.

deemed assignment by the contractor to the sub-contractor.[59] The discharge may be achieved by a right of deduction or set-off,[60] by automatic reduction,[61] by treating the payment as part of the cost of completing the works,[62] or as discharging the debt owed by the employer,[63] or by imposing on the contractor a duty to repay.[64] The efficacy of these differing approaches will depend on the proper construction of each clause.

18–020   Direct payment clauses potentially conflict with the policy underlying bankruptcy and winding up. In *Re Wilkinson, ex p. Fowler*[65] direct payments were made to suppliers after the contractor went bankrupt pursuant to a clause which applied if the engineer considered that the contractor had unreasonably delayed payment. Bigham J. held that the payments and the consequential deductions from sums otherwise due to the bankrupt were validly made. But the trustee had conceded that the clause was an authority given by the contractor which was not revoked on his bankruptcy, and relevant authority against the employer's case[66] was not cited to the court. Nevertheless, *Re Wilkinson* was followed in *Re Tout and Finch*[67] in which Wynn-Parry J. approved payments to nominated sub-contractors pursuant to a direct payment clause which took effect on the winding up of the contractor. In that case, the sub-contractors were entitled to payment in any event as equitable assignees of the contractor's right to retention under the main contract. In neither of these cases was the *pari passu* rule raised in argument. The reasoning in these cases has been adopted in Australia[68] and the Republic of Ireland.[69]

18–021   In the *British Eagle*[70] case, contractual provisions resulting in a distribution of the company's property in a manner contrary to the *pari passu* rule[71] were invalidated. Neither *Re Wilkinson* nor *Re Tout and Finch* were cited in argument in *British Eagle* and the House of Lords held that an authority given by the airlines to IATA analogous to that given by the contractor in *Re Wilkinson* was revoked on winding up. For these reasons, it is submitted that *Re Wilkinson* and *Re Tout and Finch* (as far as it concerns the direct payment clause) should no longer be

---

[59] *HM Attorney General v. McMillan & Lockwood Ltd* [1991] 1 N.Z.L.R. 53, New Zealand CA.

[60] *e.g.* JCT 98, cl. 27.

[61] *e.g.* JCT 98, cl. 35.

[62] SIA (Singapore Institute of Architects) (5th ed., 1997), cl. 32.

[63] *AN Bail Co. v. Gingras* [1982] 2 S.C.R. 475, Sup. Ct of Canada.

[64] FIDIC (Test ed., 1998), cl. 5.4.

[65] [1905] 2 K.B. 713.

[66] *Re Holt, ex p. Gray* (1888) 15 L.J.Q.B. 5.

[67] [1954] 1 W.L.R. 178.

[68] *Re C.G. Monkhouse Properties Ltd* (1968) S.R. (N.S.W.) 429, Sup. Ct of New South Wales; *Gericevich Contracting Pty Ltd v. Sabemo (W.A.) Pty Ltd* [1984] 9 A.C.L.R. 452, Sup. Ct of Western Australia.

[69] *Glow Heating Ltd v. Eastern Health Board* (1992) 8 Const. L.J. 56.

[70] *British Eagle International Air Lines Ltd v. Compagnie Nationale Air France* [1975] 1 W.L.R. 758, HL.

[71] Contained in the Companies Act 1948, s. 302, the Companies Act 1985, s. 597, and now in the Insolvency Act 1986, s. 107.

followed, as has been held in Canada,[72] Singapore,[73] New Zealand,[74] Northern Ireland[75] and Hong Kong.[76]

In contrast with these winding up cases, there is no authority on the **18–022** effect of receivership or administration on direct payment clauses. If the contractor's debts were subject to a floating charge, it may be argued that the clause should be invalidated on the ground that it deprives preferential creditors of their statutory priority under section 40 of the Insolvency Act 1986. Against this, the employer might argue that the rights of preferential creditors can only attach to the proceeds of debts collected by the receiver after taking account of equities of third parties, and that its right of recourse following direct payment is such an equity,[77] alternatively that it was an inherent flaw in the charged property.

The effect of administration will depend on the wider question of the **18–023** consequences of administration orders on set-off generally.[78]

9. RETENTION OF TITLE

In addition to the retention of title problems encountered in other **18–024** industries,[79] receivers and administrators appointed to contractors will need to consider (1) whether items have become part of the land, (2) whether property has passed pursuant to another contract in the chain, and (3) the potential effect of section 25 of the Sale of Goods Act 1979 in the special context of a construction project.

(a) Chattel or fixture

Construction work involves the annexation to land of different kinds of **18–025** chattel: building materials, more significant items of plant or machinery or complex structures fabricated off site. Whether these items remain chattels or become part of the land depends on the degree and purpose of the annexation,[80] with the emphasis on the purpose.[81] If the attachment is temporary, in order that the item can be used for its own sake, it will remain a chattel.[82] But if the attachment is permanent and for the

---

[72] *AN Bail Co. v. Gingras* [1982] 2 S.C.R. 475, Sup Ct of Canada (*British Eagle* not cited).

[73] *Joo Yee Construction Pte Ltd v. Diethelm Industries Pte Ltd* [1990] 2 M.L.J. 66, HCt of Singapore.

[74] *HM Attorney-General v. McMillan & Lockwood Ltd* [1991] 1 N.Z.L.R. 53, New Zealand CA.

[75] *B. Mullan & Sons (Contractors) Ltd v. Ross* (1996) 54 Con. L.R. 161, Northern Ireland CA.

[76] *Golden Sand Marble Factory Ltd v. Easy Success Enterprises Ltd* [1999] 2 H.K.C. 356, HCt of Hong Kong.

[77] *Business Computers Ltd v. Anglo-African Leasing Ltd* [1977] 2 All E.R. 741. See above, Chap. 16.

[78] See below, Chap. 23.

[79] See above, Chap. 12.

[80] *Holland v. Hodgson* (1872) L.R. 7 C.P. 328, cited with approval in *Elitestone Ltd v. Morris* [1997] 1 W.L.R. 687, HL which distinguished between a chattel, a fixture and an object which becomes part of the land.

[81] *Berkley v. Poulett* (1976) 241 E.G. 911.

[82] *e.g. Blower and Sedens v. Workers' Compensation Board* (1983) 50 A.R. 66, affirmed 68 A.R. 156, Alberta CA (two ton crane sitting on track bolted to floor remained a chattel).

better enjoyment of the land, it will be a fixture.[83] If a piece of machinery has become part of the land, then the same applies to its component parts, even if they are individually capable of removal.[84] Similarly, a lift or an escalator is likely to be a fixture even if intended to be replaced during the life of the building. The attachment is not temporary in that they are designed to remain *in situ* until replaced, and their purpose is for the benefit of the building rather than the enjoyment of the equipment in itself.

(b) Tenant's fixtures

18–026 Where the annexation is by a tenant for the purpose of his trade, the items in question remain the property of the tenant if capable of removal "without losing their essential character"[85] or their "essential utility or value"[86] or without causing "irreparable damage"[87] to the freehold.[88] At the end of the tenancy, the tenant is entitled as against the landlord to sever and remove such items, restoring them to the character of chattels.[89] It does not matter whether the chattels originally affixed belonged to the tenant or were hired to him by a third party.[90]

(c) Mortgagees

18–027 Once a chattel has become a fixture, it will vest in a mortgagee of the land, whether the annexation occurs before or after the mortgage,[91] and the mortgagor loses any right to remove it.[92] Incorporation will normally override any retention of title clause in the supplier's terms and conditions.[93] If the items were supplied on terms that the supplier could enter and repossess them, *e.g.* if instalments under a hire-purchase agreement were not paid, the supplier would have an equitable interest in the nature of a right of entry which would bind and have priority over the rights of any subsequent mortgagee apart from a legal mortgagee

---

[83] *e.g. Belgrave Nominees Pty Ltd v. Barling-Scott Airconditioning (Aust.) Pty Ltd* [1984] V.R. 947, Sup. Ct of Victoria (air-conditioning plant installed on the roof of a building was a fixture).

[84] *Sheffield and South Yorkshire Permanent Benefit Society v. Harrison* (1884) 15 Q.B.D. 358, CA.

[85] *Young v. Dalgety plc* [1987] 1 E.G.L.R. 116 at 119.

[86] *Webb v. Frank Bevis* [1940] 1 All E.R. 247.

[87] *Young v. Dalgety plc* [1987] 1 E.G.L.R. 116; *Spyer v. Phillipson* [1931] 2 Ch. 183 at 209–10, CA; and see *Woodfall on Landlord and Tenant*, paras 13.141 and 146.

[88] *New Zealand Government Property Corporation v. H.M. & S. Ltd.* [1982] Q.B. 1145, CA.

[89] *Bain v. Brand* (1876) 1 App. Cas. 762 at 772; *Hobson v. Gorringe* [1897] 1 Ch. 182 at 192, CA; *New Zealand Government Property Corporation v. H.M. & S. Ltd.* [1982] Q.B. 1145.

[90] See the cases referred to in the previous note and *Re Galway Concrete Ltd* [1983] I.L.R.M. 402, Keane J. A contract to sell the right to enter and remove tenants' fixtures did not require to be evidenced in writing under s. 4 of the Statute of Frauds (see *Hallen v. Runder* (1834) 1 C.M. & R. 266; *Lee v. Gaskell* (1876) 1 Q.B.D. 700) and accordingly does not fall within the requirement of s. 2 of the Law of Property (Miscellaneous Provisions) Act 1989 that a contract for the sale of interests in land should be in writing.

[91] *Reynolds v. Ashby & Son* [1904] A.C. 466 at 473, HL, *per* Lord Lindley.

[92] *Gough v. Wood* [1894] 1 Q.B. 713 at 718, CA, *per* Lindley L.J.

[93] *Re Yorkshire Joinery Co. Ltd* (1967) 111 S.J. 701, Plowman J.

without notice of the supplier's right.[94] The rights of a prior mortgagee would not be affected unless he had granted an implied licence to the mortgagor to enter into such a contract and consented to allow the supplier to sever and remove its chattels at any time before, but not after, the mortgagee entered into possession.[95]

(d) Precautions for contractors

A contractor should consider the means available to protect his right of **18–028** entry and removal as against any pre-existing and later created mortgages. As regards the former, he should investigate whether any such mortgages exist and, if they do, obtain the agreement of such mortgagees to the priority of his right of removal over their rights. As regards the latter, he should protect his equitable interest (in case of registered land) by registration of a caution and (in case of unregistered land) if no registration is possible,[96] by affixation of a notice of his rights on the equipment in question.

(e) Passing of title up the chain

The general rule is that title to materials supplied under a building **18–029** contract will pass to the landowner on incorporation.[97] Where the contract provides for payment under interim certificates, there is authority that title to unfixed materials will pass to the employer on the issue of the relevant certificate.[98] It is thought more likely that title to unfixed materials will be held to pass to the employer on payment only if the main contract clearly evinces such an intention.[99] This is the assumption behind the inter-locking provisions of the standard forms of main and sub-contract under which title passes to the employer on payment of the contractor[1] and the sub-contractor agrees not to deny that the employer has become the owner of its materials in that event even if the sub-contractor has not been paid for them.[2]

(f) Section 25 of the Sale of Goods Act 1979

Under this section, a person who has bought or agreed to buy goods and **18–030** who obtains possession of them with the seller's consent can transfer title by delivering or transferring the goods under a sale, pledge or other

---

[94] *Re Morrison, Jones & Taylor Ltd* [1914] 1 Ch. 50 at 58, CA. It is suggested that an alternative (and preferable) analysis would be that the hirer had a legal interest, namely a "licence coupled with an interest": compare *Hounslow LBC v. Twickenham Garden Developments Ltd* [1971] Ch. 233 at 254, and Megarry and Wade, *The Law of Real Property* (6th ed., 2000), paras 14–328, 17–005.

[95] *Gough v. Wood* [1894] 1 Q.B. 713 at 720; *Ellis v. Glover & Hobson Ltd* [1908] 1 K.B. 388 at 397, C.A.

[96] See Megarry and Wade, above, n. 92.

[97] *Tripp v. Armitage* (1839) 4 M. & W. 687 at 698.

[98] *Banbury Railway Co. v. Daniel* (1884) 54 L.J. Ch. 265.

[99] *Egan v. State Transport Authority* (1982) 31 S.A.S.R. 481 at 537, 542, Sup. Ct of South Australia, not following *Banbury Railway Co. v. Daniel* (1884) 54 L.J. Ch. 265; compare *Allco Steel Corporation Ltd v. Australian Capital Development Corporation Pty Ltd* (1997) 14(4) B.L.M. 1, New South Wales, CA.

[1] See, *e.g.* JCT 98, cl. 16.1.

[2] See, *e.g.* DOM/1, cl. 21.4.5.

disposition to any third person who receives the goods in good faith and without notice of any right of the original seller in respect of them. Section 25 has been invoked in the construction industry in cases of contractor insolvency. If the employer can show that it had paid for unfixed goods before the insolvency which had been supplied to the contractor under a contract for the sale of goods and that it had no notice of any retention of title clause, it can rely on the section as a defence to a claim by the unpaid supplier.[3] If materials are supplied under a sub-contract for goods and services, however, the employer has no defence.[4] Receivers appointed to the contractor may be able to prevent the owner repossessing its goods by offering a personal undertaking that, should the claim prove to be valid, they would either return the goods or pay their invoice values.[5]

10. PLANT AND EQUIPMENT

18–031 On the contractor's insolvency, it may be important for the employer to be able to use the contractor's plant and equipment for the completion contract, especially if it was manufactured specifically for the project. To this end, the employer often reserves various rights with effect from the execution of the contract, the delivery of the plant to site or the termination of the contractor's employment.

18–032   The employer may reserve a right to seize, use and/or sell the plant on termination. If a right to sell is not in aid of a pre-existing proprietary right, it may be capable of challenge. For example, in *Re Cosslett (Contractors) Ltd*[6] it was held that a power of sale in the ICE (5th ed.) termination clause was a floating charge over plant and equipment which was not binding on an administrator of the contractor for want of registration under section 395 of the Companies Act 1985. The powers to take possession of and use the plant in order to complete the works were not in the nature of a charge and remained binding. The employer later sold the plant to the completion contractor. After crediting its value, the employer had a net cross-claim exceeding £2 million. The administrator issued proceedings in his own name claiming damages in

---

[3] *Archivent Sales & Developments Ltd v. Strathclyde General Council* (1984) 27 B.L.R. 98, Court of Session (Outer House). The case proceeded on the assumption that payment under cl. 14 of JCT 63 was a "disposition" under s. 25. See also *Thomas Graham & Sons Ltd v. Glenrothes Development Corp* [1967] S.C. 284; *Four Point Garage Ltd v. Carter* [1985] 3 All E.R. 12; *W. Hanson (Harrow) Ltd v. Rapid Civil Engineering Ltd* (1987) 38 B.L.R. 106, Judge John Davies Q.C.; *Modern Structural (Scotland) Plastics v. Tayloroof* (unreported, December 3, 1990, Edinburgh Sheriff Court).

[4] *Dawber Williamson Roofing Ltd v. Humberside County Council* (1979) 14 B.L.R. 70, Mais J. (a case on Sale of Goods Act 1893, s. 25); *Sauter Automation Ltd v. Goodman (Mechanical Services) Ltd* (1986) 34 B.L.R. 81, Mervyn Davies J.; *compare Remm Construction (S.A.) Pty Ltd v. Allco Newsteel Pty Ltd* (1990) 53 S.A.S.R. 471.

[5] *Lipe Ltd v. Leyland DAF Ltd* [1993] B.C.C. 385, C.A., discussed in Chap. 12 above; see also *Mayflower Foods Ltd v. Barnard Brothers Ltd* (1997) 14(1) B.L.M. 1, Judge Hegarty Q.C.; *Alucraft Pty Ltd v. Costain Australia Ltd* (1991) 7 B.C.L. 179, Sup. Ct of Victoria.

[6] [1997] 4 All E.R. 115, reversing Jonathan Parker J. who had construed the contract as imposing a fixed, equitable charge on the plant; see also *Young v. Matthew Hall Mechanical & Electrical Engineers Pty Ltd* (1988) 13 A.C.L.R. 399, Sup. Ct of Western Australia.

conversion and succeeded at first instance[7] but lost on appeal.[8] It was held by the Court of Appeal that:

(a) the administrator's power to recover the company's property under section 234 of the Insolvency Act 1986 could only be exercised in respect of property in the hands of a third party at the time of the application. It could not be shown that the employer had disposed of the plant in order to deprive the administrator of his right under section 234;

(b) although the floating charge was invalid against the administrator, the termination clause, and in particular the power of sale and the right of set-off of the cost to complete, remained valid against the company.

It followed that the employer was entitled to set off its cross-claim against, among other things, the proceeds of sale of the plant. The problem of non-registration could have been avoided by providing for a transfer of ownership on delivery to site,[9] in which case the contract would not be registrable as an instrument which if executed by an individual would be registrable as a bill of sale.[10]

11. COPYRIGHT

Copyright subsists in plans, drawings, computer software and a building **18–033** itself.[11] It is most frequently asserted by architects and engineers, design and build contractors and specialist sub-contractors. A client who commissions design work becomes the owner of the work on payment but is not entitled to copy it without the designer's consent. In practice, a licence to copy is usually implied, limited to the purpose for which the work was originally procured.[12] The major difficulty occurs where the client (usually the employer, but it could be another person in the contract chain) becomes insolvent before the work has been completed, leaving the designer unpaid. To what extent can the designer use its copyright as leverage to obtain payment of its unsecured debt? In an Australian case, an architect sued a mortgagee who had gone into possession on the winding up of the employer. The court held that the employer's implied licence had passed to the mortgagee and was irrevocable, having been granted in return for the right to recover the

---

[7] *Smith v. Bridgend Borough Council* (unreported, September 8, 1998), in which Judge Toulmin Q.C. awarded the administrator an interim payment of £389,000.

[8] *Smith v. Bridgend Borough Council* [2000] 1 B.C.L.C. 775, CA.

[9] *Bennett & White (Calgary) Ltd v. Municipal District of Sugar City (No. 5)* [1951] A.C. 786, PC.

[10] *Reeves v. Barlow* (1884) 12 Q.B.D. 436, CA.

[11] Copyright Designs and Patents Act 1988, ss. 1, 3 and 4; *Meikle v. Maufe* [1941] 3 All E.R. 144, Uthwatt J.

[12] *Blair v. Osborne and Tomkins* [1971] 2 Q.B. 78, CA.; *Stovin-Bradford v. Volpoint Properties Ltd* [1971] Ch. 1007, CA; *Robin Ray v. Classic FM plc* [1998] F.S.R. 622 at 640–644, Lightman J.

debt by the ordinary litigation process. Copyright could not be used to 'render valueless what might be an enormous past investment in the building'.[13] Similarly, in *Hunter v. Fitzroy Robinson & Partners*[14] Oliver J. refused an application by an architect to prevent another firm using his designs after the employer went into receivership. The receivers had purported to assign the copyright licence to the purchaser on the sale of the building.

18–034 An injunction has, however, been granted to a contractor in a case where a design and build contract was terminated under an express term before work had actually commenced on site.[15] In another Australian case, a firm of engineers recovered damages for infringement of copyright on the ground that a licence granted in their retainer was expressly non-assignable, and that no licence would, in the circumstances, be implied from conduct.[16] Standard forms of engagement now contain such a restriction[17] and also confer rights in the event of non-payment, either to suspend the licence[18] or to revoke it.[19]

12. EMPLOYEES

18–035 Whether a person is an employee is an important question for many reasons.[20] There is no single test for people working in the construction industry and much depends on the facts.[21] For example, in *Ferguson v. John Dawson & Partners (Contractors) Ltd*[22] the claimant was taken on by the defendant's site agent, who informed him that "there were no cards, we were purely working as a lump labour force".[23] The case concerned a claim for damages for breach of statutory duty in respect of inujries sustained at work. One of the questions that arose was whether the claimant was an employee since such a duty was owed to an employee but not to a self-employed person. The Court of Appeal noted that working on the "lump" meant that deductions would not be made for tax or national insurance; it was a device which was convenient for both parties, "but which in reality did not affect the relationship of the parties or the performance of the substance of the contract between them".[24] The claimant's situation could be summed up by saying that he

---

[13] *Ng v. Clyde Securities Ltd* [1976] 1 N.S.W.L.R. 443 at 446, *per* Wootten J., HCt of New South Wales.

[14] (1977) 10 B.L.R. 84.

[15] *High Mark v. Patco Malaysia* (1984) 28 B.L.R. 129, HCt of Malaya.

[16] *Mateffy Perl Nagy Pty Ltd v. Devefi Pty Ltd* [1992] I.P.R. 505, Fed. Ct of Australia.

[17] SFA/99, cl. 4.1 (no assignment without consent); however ACE (2nd ed., 1998), cl. 3.4 provides that consent to assignment will not be unreasonably delayed or withheld, which may not be sufficient to prevent a transfer in an insolvency context.

[18] SFA/99, cl. 6.2.

[19] ACE (2nd ed., 1998), cl. 7.1.

[20] *e.g.* when considering preferential debts falling within categories 1 and 5, Sched. 6 of the Insolvency Act 1986, the TUPE Regulations and the Construction Industry Tax Deduction Scheme.

[21] See Ryley and Goodwyn, *Employment Law for the Construction Industry* (2000).

[22] [1976] 1 W.L.R. 1213, CA.

[23] *ibid.*, at 1217.

[24] *ibid.*, at 1219, CA, *per* Megaw L.J.

did as he was told and was paid an hourly wage for so doing, thus making him an employee.[25]

The Transfer of Undertakings (Protection of Employment) Regu- **18–036** lations 1981[26] may apply where a purchaser novates contracts previously carried on by an insolvent contractor. In *Rolfe v. Amey Construction Ltd*[27] administrative receivers appointed to Farr plc sold to Amey the right to seek novations of 37 of Farr's ongoing contracts. A few employers refused to co-operate with Amey who eventually obtained novations of 33 contracts. Some of Farr's employees were not taken on by Amey and applied to the Secretary of State for Employment for redundancy payments, but they were refused on the ground that there had been a relevant transfer under the Regulations under which Amey had assumed liability for the employees who had been made redundant. On Amey refusing to meet the payments, the employees applied to an industrial tribunal which upheld their claim. Amey's acquisition amounted to a relevant transfer of Farr's construction business since:

(a) part of the consideration paid by Amey was for goodwill which was defined as including all intellectual property rights relating to the novated contracts;

(b) Amey had obtained almost all of Farr's ongoing contracts, and would have novated more of them had the employers agreed;

(c) disruption was kept to a minimum through Amey paying key sub-contractors direct;

(d) before entering into the agreement with the receivers, Amey had offered employment to key site and head office staff;

(e) Amey took over part of Farr's premises and some plant and equipment and site accommodation under a separate agreement.

Under the Construction Industry Scheme, which came into effect on **18–037** August 1, 1999,[28] 714 certificates, which entitled a registered sub-contractor to be paid gross of tax, were replaced by forms CIS5 and CIS6. Since the Scheme came into force, there has been a considerable increase in the number of employees in the industry.

13. CONSTRUCTION BONDS AND GUARANTEES

Construction contracts are often supported by surety bonds and demand **18–038** guarantees.[29] The issuers of such documents can play an important role in a restructuring of a contractor. Receivers are generally keen to obtain

---

[25] See also *Lee Ting Sang v. Chung Chi-Keung* [1990] I.C.R. 409, PC; *Lane v. Shire Roofing Co. (Oxford) Ltd* [1995] I.R.L.R. 493, CA; *Bolwell v. Redcliffe Homes Ltd* [1999] P.I.Q.R. 243, CA; *Costain Building & Engineering Ltd v. Smith* [2000] I.C.R. 215, EAT.

[26] See below, Chap. 19.

[27] Unreported, November 13, 1992.

[28] Income and Corporation Taxes Act 1988, ss. 559–567, as amended by Finance Act 1995, Sched. 25; Income Tax (Sub-Contractors in the Construction Industry) Regulations 1975, as amended.

[29] Moss and Marks, *Rowlatt on Principal and Surety* (5th ed.,1999), Chap. 17.

the release of any security given to guarantors in support of the company's counter-indemnity.

18-039   The issuer of a surety bond agrees to pay the employer a fixed amount on condition that if the contractor performs the construction contract the promise to pay is void and the issuer is released from the bond. As the bond is conditioned on the contractor's performance it takes effect as a guarantee.[30] Difficulties arise in practice if the bond also includes wording entitling the employer to payment on demand,[31] or requires notice of potential claims to be given within a short period after the relevant breach[32] or that proceedings be issued within a short time after completion.[33] A demand guarantee is a primary obligation[34] and is usually issued in the form of a bank undertaking to pay up to a fixed sum on receipt of a demand accompanied by such documents as may be specified in the guarantee.[35] The draftsman sometimes uses language more appropriate to a secondary obligation, resulting in a difficult issue of construction.[36] But the most common issue with a demand guarantee remains that of "unfair calling".

18-040   If the employer's demand only has to be accompanied by a statement that the contractor is in breach of contract, there is a risk it will be based on a false statement, especially if the bank has agreed to accept such a statement as conclusive.[37] The court considers that the contractor takes the risk of the bond being called in that situation and will not grant an injunction restraining the bank from paying in the absence of clear and manifest fraud by the employer of which the bank has notice.[38] This is known as "the fraud exception" as it displaces the ordinary criteria for an interlocutory injunction and is based on the policy of not undermining international trade by interfering with unconditional or documentary banking obligations. The contractor's remedy is to bring proceedings against the employer under the contract[39] but until the works have been completed and the final account agreed[40] it may not be clear whether

---

[30] *Trafalgar House Construction (Regions) Ltd v. General Surety & Guarantee Co. Ltd* [1996] A.C. 199, HL.

[31] *Harmon Contract (U.K.) Ltd v. Cigna Insurance Co. of Europe SA NV* (unreported, April 16, 1992), Judge James Fox-Andrews Q.C.; *TBV Power Ltd v. Elm Energy and Recycling (U.K.) Ltd* (unreported, November 21, 1995), Judge James Fox-Andrews Q.C.

[32] *Oval (717) Ltd v. Aegon Insurance Co. (U.K.) Ltd* (1997) 85 B.L.R. 97, Mr Recorder Colin Reese Q.C.

[33] *Clydebank v. Fidelity & Deposit Company of Maryland* [1916] S.C. 69; *De Vere Hotels Ltd v. Aegon Insurance Co. (U.K.) Ltd* [1998] C.I.L.L. 1346, Judge Esyr Lewis Q.C.

[34] The use of the word "guarantee" in this context is widespread among banks but inaccurate.

[35] The JCT has agreed forms of demand bond for use with JCT 98 with the British Bankers Association securing the earning of an advance payment, the delivery of off-site materials and the repayment of retention.

[36] See, *e.g. Esal (Commodities) Ltd v. Oriental Credit Ltd* [1985] 2 Lloyd's Rep. 546, CA.

[37] *Bache & Co. (London) Ltd v. Banque Vernes et Commerciale de Paris SA* [1973] 2 Lloyd's Rep. 437, CA.

[38] *Edward Owen Engineering Ltd v. Barclays Bank International Ltd* [1978] 1 Q.B. 159, CA.

[39] See, *e.g. ENS Ltd v. Derwent Cogeneration Ltd* (1998) 62 Con. L.R. 141, Judge Richard Havery Q.C.

[40] *Cargill International SA v. Bangladesh Sugar and Food Industries Corp* [1996] 4 All E.R. 563, affirmed [1998] 2 All E.R. 406, CA suggests that a term may normally be implied that the bond proceeds will be brought into account at the final account stage.

there is a cause of action. In the meantime, the contractor suffers loss of cash flow (as the bank will have recovered its payment to the employer from the contractor under its counter-indemnity) and assumes the risk of the employer's insolvency before repayment. Nevertheless, the court is willing to intervene to prevent injustice in appropriate cases. These may include circumstances where:

(a) the bond requires service of a prior notice on the contractor which has not in fact been served. A statement that the notice was properly served may be treated as fraudulent and an injunction granted against the bank under the fraud exception[41];

(b) if the evidence of fraud is powerful but not quite sufficient the court may order summary judgment against the bank but grant a stay of execution to allow the contractor to litigate the underlying dispute[42];

(c) the bond gives rise to serious questions of construction as to its obligation and a wrongful call could harm the contractor's commercial reputation or its future bonding capacity[43];

(d) relief is sought against the employer restraining it from making the demand, relying on terms in the underlying contract which place restrictions on the employer's right of recourse against the bond[44];

(e) there is a genuine issue to be tried whether the bond has expired according to its terms[45] or whether, by certifying under the bond, the engineer is threatening to interfere with the underlying contract.[46]

14. RETENTION TRUSTS[47]

Retention is a conditional debt defeasible by set-off. It is conditional on **18–041** the issue of certificates of practical completion (when half is released) and of making good defects (when the balance becomes due); it is defeasible by rights of recourse conferred by the contract or available at common law. Retention is withheld under both main and sub-contracts and has traditionally been regarded as security for performance.[48] The

[41] *Kvaerner John Brown Ltd v. Midland Bank plc* [1998] C.L.C. 446, Cresswell J.

[42] *Balfour Beatty Civil Engineering v. Technical and General Guarantee Co. Ltd* (1999) 68 Con. L.R. 180, CA.

[43] *Hawker Siddeley Power Engineering Ltd v. Peterborough Power Ltd* (unreported, Judge Peter Bowsher Q.C., May 9, 1994); see also *ADI Ltd and Bains Harding Ltd v. State Electricity Commission of Victoria* (1997) 13 B.C.L. 337, Sup. Ct of Victoria.

[44] e.g. *Reed Construction Services Pty Ltd v. Kheng Seng (Australia) Pty Ltd* (1999) 15 B.C.L. 158, Sup. Ct of New South Wales.

[45] *Gibraltar Homes Ltd v. Agroman (Gibraltar) Ltd* (unreported, Gibraltar, CA, No. 15 of 1996, Sir Brian Neill).

[46] *Press Construction Ltd v. Penspen Ltd and Barclays Bank plc* (unreported, Michael Kershaw Q.C., April 16, 1996).

[47] Moss, "Retention Trusts" (1992) 5 Insolvency Intelligence 25.

[48] *Calvert v. London Dock* (1838) 2 Keen's Rep. 638.

conditional nature of retention means that payment may be deferred for a long time. The JCT forms provide the contractor, or the sub-contractors as the case may be, with security for payment of retention in the form of a contractual trust.[49] There are four particular areas to consider: constitution, sub-trusts, recourse and registrability.

(a) Constitution

18–042 Clause 30.5 of JCT 98 provides that:

"1. the Employer's interest in the Retention is fiduciary as trustee for the Contractor and for any Nominated Sub-Contractor (but without obligation to invest);

. . .

3. The Employer shall . . . if the Contractor or any Nominated Sub-Contractor so requests, at the date of payment under each Interim Certificate place the Retention in a separate banking account . . ."

Construed together, the two parts of this clause impose a duty on the employer to create a trust on request. Once a request has been made, the court will grant specific performance by a mandatory injunction ordering the employer to pay an amount equivalent to the retention into a designated trust account.[50] The same applies if the express duty to fund the retention contained in clause 30.5.3 is deleted but clause 30.5.1 remains.[51]

18–043 The account represents the identifiable property necessary to constitute the trust. If administrative receivers[52] or a liquidator[53] were appointed in relation to the employer before this could be done, specific performance would not be granted and the contractor would be an ordinary unsecured creditor in respect of its retention. The position on the appointment of administrators is at yet untested.

18–044 A request can be made at any time during the contract[54] but not, it seems, after termination of the contractor's employment.[55] Interlocutory injunctions have been granted on the eve of the employer's formal insolvency[56] but doubt has been cast on this practice by Scott L.J.:

---

[49] JCT main contracts which incorporate a retention trust are: Standard Form of Building Contract (JCT 63, 80, 98), Standard Form With Contractor's Design (JCT 81, 98), Intermediate Form (IFC 84, 98), Fixed Fee Form (JCT 67), Management Contract (JCT 87, 98). The trust is stepped down into the conditions of nominated sub-contract (NSC/C) and works contract (WC/2) but not to named sub-contracts (NAM/C) or domestic sub-contractors (DOM/1 and DOM/2).

[50] *Rayack Construction Ltd v. Lampeter Meat Co. Ltd* (1979) 12 B.L.R. 30, Vinelott J. (a case on JCT 63).

[51] *Wates Construction (London) Ltd v. Franthom Property Ltd* (1991) 53 B.L.R. 23, CA.

[52] *MacJordan Construction Ltd v. Brookmount Erostin Ltd* (1991) 56 B.L.R. 1, [1992] B.C.L.C. 350, CA.

[53] *Re Jartay Developments Ltd* (1982) 22 B.L.R. 134, Nourse J.

[54] *J.F. Finnegan Ltd v. Ford Sellar Morris Developments Ltd (No. 1)* (1991) 53 B.L.R. 38.

[55] *Balfour Beatty Ltd v. Britannia Life Ltd* [1997] S.L.T. 10, Court of Session (Outer House).

[56] *J.F. Finnegan Ltd v. Ford Sellar Morris Developments Ltd (No. 2)* (1991) 27 Con. L.R. 41, Judge Esyr Lewis Q.C.; compare *GPT Realisations Ltd v. Panatown Ltd* (1992) 61 B.L.R. 88, Judge Peter Bowsher Q.C., in which an injunction sought by administrative receivers appointed to a contractor was refused in part on grounds of lateness.

"It is at this point that I should mention the doubts I feel regarding the specific enforceability of an obligation to set aside a retention fund. In a case where the employer is insolvent when the application for a mandatory order is made, the mandatory order would, assuming it were complied with, give preference to the contractor as against other unsecured creditors. I do not see any reason why the court should do such a thing . . .".[57]

This *dictum* of Scott L.J. appears to be in conflict with generally **18–045** applicable insolvency principles as set out in *Roberts Petroleum v. Bernard Kenny Ltd*.[58] That case concerned the discretion of the court to make absolute a charging order nisi so as to create security in favour of a judgment creditor of an insolvent debtor. In dealing with the race between the judgment creditor for security and the shareholders acting to protect the general body of creditors, Lord Brightman stated:

". . . Roberts applied to the District Registrar for a charging order in the hope of obtaining an advantage over other unsecured creditors; . . . the shareholders of Kenny, on professional advice, put the company into voluntary liquidation at short notice in the hope of depriving Roberts of that advantage. Neither step nor counter step casts any discredit on those involved. There is nothing in the nature of sharp practice on either side, nor has this been suggested in your Lordships' House. A person who has the misfortune to have given credit to a company which runs into financial difficulties has every right to seek to secure himself. And such company or its other creditors have every right to hasten liquidation in order to thwart such a purpose".[59]

If the approach put forward by Lord Brightman is the correct one, then it **18–046** would seem to be perfectly acceptable for a contractor or sub-contractor to apply for a mandatory order to set up a trust retention fund notwithstanding the obvious insolvency of the employer. It is equally open to a debenture-holder to appoint a receiver to protect his security or for shareholders, as in *Roberts Petroleum v. Bernard Kenny Ltd*, to seek to protect the general body of creditors by causing the company to go into liquidation. None of these approaches is discreditable. It would not seem to be right for the court to refuse relief merely because the employer or contractor against whom proceedings are brought is insolvent when other concerned parties have adequate remedies.

(b) Sub-contract trusts

Nominated sub-contracts place an obligation on the contractor to set **18–047** aside a fund if it attempts to grant a fixed charge or a mortgage over the retention or fails to pay it to the sub-contractor when it falls due, but this

---

[57] *MacJordan Construction Ltd v. Brookmount Erostin Ltd* [1992] B.C.L.C. 350 at 359; (1991) 56 B.L.R. 1 at 15, CA.
[58] [1983] 2 A.C. 192, HL.
[59] *ibid.*, at 206.

right is rarely, if ever, invoked.[60] Instead, the trust wording has been construed as an equitable assignment to the sub-contractor of its proportion of the retention withheld under the main contract.[61] The cases have concerned applications in the winding up of the contractor for directions whether the employer could set off against the sub-contractors' retention,[62] or the liquidator should account to them on receipt of payment from the employer[63] or, it seems, for retention already collected by him.[64]

(c) Rights of recourse

18–048 Clause 30.1.1.2 of JCT 98 provides:

> "Notwithstanding the fiduciary interest of the Employer in the Retention . . . the Employer is entitled to exercise any right under this Contract of withholding and/or deduction from monies due or to become due to the Contractor against any amount so due under an Interim Certificate".

This provision reflects the function of retention as a security for performance and enables the employer to make withdrawals from the trust account without being in breach of trust. This may explain why the account is opened in the employer's sole name.[65] If a right of set-off exceeding the retention arose before the contractor's request that it be funded, the court would not grant an injunction.[66] In this connection, the employer has been described as an active, self-interested trustee[67] rather than a beneficiary of the trust.[68]

18–049   There is a tension between the right of retention as performance security and the retention trust as payment security. At first sight the employer is entitled to recourse against the whole retention, including that attributable to work carried out by sub-contractors, even if the sub-contractors are not in breach. Although hard on the sub-contractors, this is the logical outcome of privity of contract. The imposition of a trust as security for payment ought not to affect the overriding purpose of retention as security for performance. However, the court has overridden the employer's rights of recourse by allowing sub-contractors to recover retention in this situation. In *Re Arthur Sanders*, Nourse J. stated that:

---

[60] BEC/FASS Green Form, clause 11(h) for use with JCT 63; NSC/4, cl. 21.9.1 for use with JCT 80; NSC/C, cl. 4.22 for use with JCT 98.

[61] *Re Tout and Finch Ltd* [1954] 1 All E.R. 127; see also *Nam Fang Electrical v. City Developments Ltd* [1997] 1 S.L.R. 585, HCt of Singapore.

[62] *Re Arthur Sanders Ltd* (1981) 17 B.L.R. 125.

[63] *Re Tout and Finch Ltd* [1954] 1 All E.R. 127.

[64] *Harry Bibby & Co. Ltd v. Neill Construction Ltd* [1973] E.G.D. 52, 225 E.G. 2297, CA.

[65] *Zhong You (China) Design Co. v. Fuyuan Landmark (Shenzhen) Ltd* [1996] 2 H.K.C. 342, HCt of Hong Kong.

[66] *Henry Boot Building Ltd v. The Croydon Hotel & Leisure Co. Ltd* (1985) 36 B.L.R. 41, CA.

[67] Hayton, "The Significance of Equity in Construction Contracts" [1994] 1 Construction Law Yearbook 19.

[68] *Wates Construction (London) Ltd v. Franthom Property Ltd* (1991) 53 B.L.R. 23 at 30, CA.

"... the position as between employer, contractor and sub-contractor under the present RIBA Conditions [JCT 63] and the FASS Sub-contract [the Green Form] is that the employer holds a due proportion of the retentions on trust for the contractor as trustee for the Sub-contractor".[69]

Nourse J. concluded (at 140) that the sub-contractor's proportion of **18–050** retention could never be a "sum due" to the contractor since it could only be received by the contractor as trustee. His analysis was approved by the Court of Appeal in *P.C. Harrington Contractors Ltd v. Co. Partnership Developments Ltd*[70] which concerned the JCT management contract. In that case, a retention trust had been set up before administrative receivers were appointed to the management contractor. The architect certified that the cost to complete the works exceeded the balance of the retention account which was withdrawn by the employer. A works contractor successfully claimed its proportion of retention direct from the employer on the ground, among other things, that the employer's right of recourse extended only to retention withheld against the management contractor's fee.

It is submitted that the analysis of Nourse J. in *Re Arthur Sanders* and **18–051** of the Court of Appeal in *Harrington v. Co. Partnership* fails to take adequate cognisance of the employer's right of recourse.[71] In *Rafidain Bank v. Saipem SpA*,[72] it was suggested that a construction trust be construed in two stages: first, as a matter of contract as if there were no trust, and only then to see whether the imposition of a trust made a difference. It is possible that, had the Court of Appeal in *Harrington v. Co. Partnership* adopted this approach, it might have concluded that the employer's right of recourse was an inherent limitation in the chose in action forming the subject matter of the trust.[73]

A further issue concerns the effect of termination of the contractor's **18–052** employment on the trust. The case of *Balfour Beatty v. Britannia Life*[74] concerned facts almost identical to those in *Harrington v. Co. Partnership* with the exception that the trust account had not been set up before administrative receivers were appointed to the contractor. The Court of Session took a different view on the construction of the management and works contracts, and, in particular, held that the payment regime in the termination clause superseded the other provisions in the contract.

[69] *Re Arthur Sanders Ltd* (1981) 17 B.L.R. 125 at 138.
[70] (1998) 88 B.L.R. 44, CA.
[71] The reasoning in *Re Arthur Sanders* was not followed for this reason in *Hsin Chong Construction Co. Ltd v. Yaton Realty Co. Ltd* (1986) 40 B.L.R. 119, HCt of Hong Kong, or in *Balfour Beatty Ltd v. Britannia Life Ltd* [1997] S.L.T. 10, Court of Session (Outer House).
[72] Unreported, March 2, 1994, CA.
[73] Compare *KBH Construction Pty Ltd v. Lidco Aluminium Products Pty Ltd* (1991) 7 B.C.L. 183 ("one of the terms of the trust qualifying the builder's obligations as trustee and limiting the sub-contractor's beneficial entitlement", *per* Giles J. at 191, Sup. Ct of New South Wales).
[74] [1997] S.L.T. 10, Court of Session (Outer House).

"At best the rights of management contractors against employers remain contingent until the final payment provisions of the contract come into effect. A trust of a contingent sum cannot survive an event that evacuates the contingency, or leaves it incapable of fulfilment. The net effect is that upon determination of the contract any trust which did subsist in favour of the works contractors terminates and is of no continuing substance. . . . in that event the protection of the employer's interests is paramount."[75]

18–053 The contingency was the certificate of making good defects which had not been issued before the termination.[76] Alternatively, the court might have held that the termination clause was one of the terms of the trust. Until the works could be completed and the final account of the completion contractor agreed, it would not be known whether the employer was net debtor or creditor of the contractor, and the trust should therefore continue as protection for the contractor and the works contractors in the meantime. The position is different where the project has been satisfactorily completed and neither employer nor contractor claims any right of recourse against retention. In that case, the contractor becomes a bare trustee and the sub-contractors have a direct right against the employer.[77] Similarly, a contractor might have a right against a funder if the terms as to retention in the finance agreement and the main contract were back to back.[78]

(d) Registrability

18–054 Retention as such is simply a deduction sanctioned by the contract. Although it operates as an informal security, it is not a mortgage or charge over the property of the debtor in the contractual relationship and therefore there is no registration requirement. The JCT forms are silent as to the purpose of the retention trust, although clearly it functions as security for payment. Industry practice is not to treat the trust as registrable even if could be described as a charge. There is no English authority on the point.[79] However, in a case concerning a retention trust set up under an Australian standard form,[80] the court

---

[75] [1997] S.L.T. 10, *per* Lord Penrose.

[76] The same situation as in *Harrington*, but in that case the Court of Appeal appears to have waived the conditionality of retention on the ground that the trust gave the works contractor a vested interest in the fund, and restricted the effect of the termination clause to retention withheld against the contractor's fee.

[77] *Sanders v. Vautier* (1841) 4 Beav. 115. This appears to be the basis of the cases considered at (b) above.

[78] Hayton, "The Significance of Equity in Construction Contracts" [1994] 1 Construction Law Yearbook 19 at 21. Such a claim failed in *Re Jartay Developments Ltd* (1982) 22 B.L.R. 134 because the terms were different, but the facts were unusual.

[79] In *Lovell Construction Ltd v. Independent Estates plc* [1994] 1 B.C.L.C. 31, it was left undecided whether, had the trust of the contract sum been a charge, it would have been registrable as a charge over a book debt. An argument that it was an unregistered floating charge was abandoned as the employer could not use the account in the ordinary course of business: see *Wates Construction (London) Ltd v. Franthom Property Ltd* (1991) 53 B.L.R. 23, CA.

[80] *Re Old Inns Ltd* (1994) 13 A.C.S.R. 141, Sup. Ct of New South Wales.

assumed without argument that the account took effect as a charge but concluded that it was not a charge over a book debt, relying on English authorities,[81] and was not registrable.

15. CONSTRUCTION TRUSTS AND ESCROWS

The trust is also used as the means of protecting interim payments **18–055** against the risk of employer insolvency. In *Lovell Construction Ltd v. Independent Estates plc*,[82] the main contract was in the JCT 1980 form but the parties had a side agreement whereby the employer agreed a schedule of monthly payments on account of the contract sum. The employer agreed to deposit in a trust account one month in advance the amount specified in the schedule in respect of the following month's work. The agreement stated that it was to facilitate payment under the contract and nominated the parties' solicitors as trustees of the account, the terms of the trust being that payment should be made on presentation of the architect's certificates issued under the contract. Fixed charge receivers were appointed to the development and the employer went into liquidation. The liquidator argued that the side letter was a charge over book debts which was not binding on him for want of registration under section 395 of the Companies Act 1985. The court rejected the claim, holding that the machinery laid down by the agreement was the means of payment rather than security for payment, and therefore no charge was created.

By contrast, in *Bouygues SA v. Shanghai Links*[83] the entire contract **18–056** sum of U.S. \$33 million was set aside but, on the contract being terminated before completion, the contractor failed in an application for an injunction restraining the depositor from making withdrawals from the account. It was held that, on its true construction, the escrow account was to pay interim instalments of the contract price but did not extend to payment of damages or sums falling due after a termination.

Problems with trust and escrow accounts concern the conditions for **18–057** payment out, *e.g.* on an insolvency termination if the architect ceases to act[84] or where international sanctions or a change in local law prevent the issue of the necessary certificate[85] or where a receiver appointed to an employer decides to "mothball" the project.[86] Finally, the *Quistclose* case[87] has been applied in the industry for the following purposes: to pay

---

[81] *Re Brightlife Ltd* [1987] Ch. 200, and subsequent cases discussed in above, Chap. 3.

[82] [1994] 1 B.C.L.C. 31, Judge Fox-Andrews Q.C.. A trust similar to that employed in the *Lovell* case, but with a secondary trust in favour of the first line of sub-contractors on the contractor's formal insolvency, was proposed by Sir Michael Latham in his industry review, *Constructing the Team* (1994), but was not enacted in the Housing Grants, Construction and Regeneration Act 1996. Two standard forms provide for a trust of the contract sum: SEACC which integrates the trust, and The Engineering and Construction Contract which includes a trust as an optional clause.

[83] [1998] 2 H.K.L.R.D. 479, HCt of Hong Kong.

[84] *Lovell Construction Ltd v. Independent Estates plc* [1994] 1 B.C.L.C. 31.

[85] *Rafidain Bank v. Saipem SpA* (unreported, March 2, 1994, CA).

[86] Hayton, "The Significance of Equity in Construction Contracts" [1994] 1 Construction Law Yearbook 19 at 29.

[87] *Barclays Bank Ltd v. Quistclose Investments Ltd* [1970] A.C. 567, HL. See above, Chap. 10.

an arbitrator's fees so as to enable a contractor to take up an award,[88] to pay a sub-sub-contractor direct on the impending insolvency of the sub-contractor,[89] and for payment of retention by the employer.[90]

16. HOUSING GRANTS, CONSTRUCTION AND REGENERATION ACT 1996

18–058 A "construction contract" which falls within the definition in the Housing Grants, Construction and Regeneration Act 1996[91] has to contain specific terms as to adjudication, payment and set-off. In default, the terms of the Scheme for Construction Contracts[92] will be implied.[93] Certain agreements for the development and financing of projects are excluded from the Act[94] which applies to contracts entered into on or after May 1, 1998. Most of the standard forms now include their own procedure. Bespoke forms often incorporate one of the available sets of adjudication rules. The main features of statutory adjudication are:

(a) the adjudicator has to reach a decision within 28 days, which can be extended by 14 days with the consent of the referring party or longer if both parties agree[95];

(b) the adjudicator's decision is binding until the dispute is finally determined by litigation or arbitration[96];

(c) the parties are jointly and severally liable for the adjudicator's fees and expenses[97] but it is unclear whether an adjudicator has power to make an order for costs, and security for costs, without the parties' consent.[98]

18–059 Adjudication is a "proceeding" for the purposes of section 11(3) of the Insolvency Act 1986 and cannot be brought against a company in

---

[88] *Re McKeown* [1974] N.I.L.R. 226, HCt of Northern Ireland.

[89] *Analogy Pty Ltd v. Bell Basic Industries Ltd* (1996) 12 B.C.L. 291, Sup. Ct of Western Australia.

[90] *Re Old Inns Ltd* (1994) 13 A.C.S.R. 141, Sup. Ct of New South Wales.

[91] Housing Grants, Construction and Regeneration Act 1996, ss. 104–107. The definition is complex but will probably include most commercial construction contracts. Contracts which are oral, for supply only, or for residential occupiers are excluded, as are contracts for the construction and demolition of plant and equipment for power generation, water treatment, mineral extraction, pharmaceuticals, oil and gas.

[92] The Scheme for Construction Contracts (England and Wales) Regulations 1998 (S.I. 1998 No. 649).

[93] Housing Grants, Construction and Regeneration Act 1996, s. 114.

[94] The Construction Contracts (England and Wales) Exclusion Order 1998 (S.I. 1998 No. 648).

[95] Housing Grants, Construction and Regeneration Act 1996, s. 108(2); Scheme for Construction Contracts, para. 19(1).

[96] Housing Grants, Construction and Regeneration Act 1996, s. 108(3).

[97] Scheme for Construction Contracts, para. 25.

[98] In *Northern Developments (Cumbria) Ltd v. J. & J. Nichol* [2000] B.L.R. 158 at 167, Judge Peter Bowsher Q.C. held that an adjudicator appointed under the Scheme had no power to make an order for costs, not following *John Cothliff Ltd v. Allen Build (North West) Ltd* [1999] C.I.L.L. 1546, Judge Marshall Evans Q.C. (under appeal). The available adjudication rules are either silent on the issue or state that the parties will bear their own costs.

administration without the consent of the administrator or leave of the court.[99] A receiver might continue an adjudication begun before his appointment, serve a notice of adjudication or take enforcement proceedings in respect of an adjudicator's decision by applying for summary judgment.[1]

The use of "pay when paid" clauses is now restricted to cases where **18–060** the non-payment is due to specific insolvency events affecting the paying party, including an administration order, the appointment of an administrative receiver or a receiver or manager of its property, and a winding up order or resolution.[2]

Set-off and abatement in connection with construction contracts is **18–061** also regulated by the Act which overlays certain procedural conditions to the valid exercise of contractual and common law rights.[3] Non-compliance results in the loss of such rights against the payment concerned but not against future sums provided the conditions are satisfied in relation to them. It is currently an open question whether the suspension of payment on termination is a "withholding" requiring a notice under the Act[4] to be enforceable. If so, a receiver could recover book debts notwithstanding the termination of the contractor's employment.[5]

17. ARBITRATION

Under the Arbitration Act 1996, proceedings issued in court under a **18–062** contract containing an arbitration clause are now subject to a mandatory stay for arbitration.[6] An administrative receiver will have the power, unless specifically excluded in the debenture under which he is appointed, to "refer to arbitration any question affecting the company".[7] In the short term having to go to arbitration may be an immediate disadvantage to a receiver of the contractor because invariably as claimant he will have to make an initial payment on account to the arbitrator and in addition will have to bear half of the interim accounts that the arbitrator submits. Arbitrators may ask for a substantial payment on account of fees to be incurred at the hearing and will not

---

[99] A. Straume (U.K.) Ltd v. Bradlor Developments Ltd [1999] C.I.L.L. 1520, Judge Behrens (leave refused).

[1] See, e.g. Bouygues (U.K.) Ltd v. Dahl-Jensen U.K. Ltd [2000] B.L.R. 49, Dyson J. affirmed, The Times, August 17, 2000, CA. Enforcement proceedings are excluded from the arbitration clause in the JCT and ICE forms for this reason.

[2] Housing Grants, Construction and Regeneration Act 1996, s. 113.

[3] ibid., ss. 110–111.

[4] ibid, s. 111.

[5] In KNS Industrial Services (Birmingham) Ltd v. Sindall Ltd (unreported, July 17, 2000, Humphrey LLoyd J.) it was doubted whether a notice was required in respect of suspension of payment under DOM/1 (para. 2.5). See Davis, "Adjudication and Insolvency" (2000) 11(4) Construction Law 22.

[6] Arbitration Act 1996, s. 9. The case of Northern Regional Health Authority v. Derek Crouch Construction Co. Ltd [1984] Q.B. 644, CA. which decided that the court had no jurisdiction to open up and review an architect's certificate was overruled in Beaufort Developments (N.I.) Ltd v. Gilbert-Ash N.I. Ltd [1999] 1 A.C. 266, H.L.

[7] Insolvency Act 1986, s. 42, and Sched. 1, para. 6.

release their awards until all their fees have been discharged. Such arbitrations may tend to involve receivers in a greater drain on financial resources than may occur in a case brought to court.

18. PAYMENT IN COURT

18–063 It sometimes happens that a receiver finds on his appointment over the property of a contractor that one asset of the company is a sum paid into court as an offer of settlement. Such a payment cannot be taken out without the court's permission.[8] The question then arises as to whether the court will give leave for that sum to be recovered by the receiver acting in the name of the contractor. In the Court of Appeal case of *Peal Furniture Ltd v. Adrian Share (Interiors) Ltd*[9] leave to withdraw the money in court was given to the receiver. A differently constituted Court of Appeal in a liquidation case, *W.A. Sherratt Ltd v. John Bromley (Church Stretton) Ltd*[10] subsequently held that the *Peal Furniture* case was decided *per incuriam*. The Court of Appeal in *Sherratt* held that a payment into court fell within a line of bankruptcy cases which decided that the other parties to the litigation became a potentially secured creditor to the extent of the payment in.[11] In so far as the opposing party recovered judgment he would be a secured creditor in a supervening bankruptcy up to the amount in court. In the *Sherratt* case the Court of Appeal thus held that, in view of the fact that a payment constituted a potential security, the subsequent winding up was not a sufficient reason to allow a liquidator of the company to withdraw the sums in court.

18–064 By inference, the appointment of a receiver would not be a sufficient reason to give leave to withdraw such sums since the payment into court will constitute a potential security ranking ahead of the debenture-holder's charge.[12] An order for payment to one of the parties' solicitors to be held by them 'to the order of the court' confers the same level of protection as a payment into court.[13]

---

[8] CPR Part 36.6(5) replacing RSC Ord. 22, without, it seems, affecting the relevance of the cases discussed below.

[9] [1977] 1 W.L.R. 464, CA.

[10] [1985] 1 Q.B. 1038, CA.

[11] *Re Gordon* [1897] 2 Q.B. 516; *Re Ford* [1900] 2 Q.B. 211; *Dessau v. Rowley* [1916] W.N. 238; *Re A Debtor* (1932) 101 L.J. Ch. 372.

[12] *Toprak Enerji Sanayi AS v. Sale Tilney Technology plc* [1994] 3 All E.R. 483 at 503, *per* Judge Diamond Q.C.

[13] *Re Mordant, Mordant v. Halls* [1996] 1 F.L.R. 334, Sir Donald Nicholls V.-C.; see also *Choski Tube Co. Ltd v. Corrotherm Industries Ltd* (unreported, June 24, 1998, CA).

CHAPTER 19

RECEIVERS AND EMPLOYEES

One of the most important resources of a business over which a receiver **19–001** is appointed is likely to be the employees. The relationship of the company with its labour force imports a host of problems from labour law, some of which create a danger of personal liability for receivers.[1] The greatest danger of personal liability arises from changes set out in the Insolvency Act 1985 and consolidated in the Insolvency Act 1986.

There is some authority that a receiver owes a general duty of care to employees of the company to act reasonably in taking decisions which affect them[2] but this is inconsistent with the established principles governing the ambit of duties owed by receivers.[3]

1. CONTRACTS OF EMPLOYMENT

(a) Survival of existing employment contracts

(i) Pre-liquidation

Court-appointed receivers. The general rule is that the appointment by **19–002** the court of a receiver of the undertaking of a company does not affect existing contracts of the company but, as an exception to this rule, it does operate as a dismissal of the company's employees.[4] The theory is that the appointment effects a change in the personality of the employer from the company to the receiver, because the court-appointed receiver cannot contract as agent for the company, and any such change must operate as a dismissal. The contrast is with the appointment by the court of the receiver of a company[5] (as opposed to its undertaking): such an appointment will not terminate contracts of employment, because such a receiver is constituted the managing agent of the company in place of its directors, and there is accordingly no change in the personality of the

---

[1] For a fuller treatment of these aspects of employment law see Sweet & Maxwell's *Encyclopaedia of Employment Law*; Grunfeld, *The Law of Redundancy*, Sweet & Maxwell, 1990; J. Bowers, *Bowers on Employment Law* (5th ed., Blackstone Press, 2000); D. Pollard, *Corporate Insolvency; Employment and Pension Rights* (2nd ed., Butterworths, 2000).

[2] *Larsen v. Henderson* [1990] I.R.L.R. 514. This is a Scottish decision the authority of which is undercut by the fact that the decisions which it purports to follow do not on analysis support the proposition.

[3] See *Burgess v. Auger* [1998] 2 B.C.L.C. 478 and above, Chap. 7.

[4] *Reid v. Explosives Co.* (1887) 19 Q.B.D. 264; *Re Foster Clark Ltd's Indenture Trusts* [1966] 1 All E.R. 43 at 49; *Nicoll v. Cutts* [1985] B.C.L.C. 322. *cf.* the *dicta* of the Privy Council in *Parsons v. Sovereign Bank of Canada* [1913] A.C. 160 at 167 and 171 (a case concerning a contract for the supply of goods); *South Western of Venezuela (Barqisiment) Railway Co.* [1902] 1 Ch. 701 and *Sipad Holding DDPO v. Popovic* (1996) 12 A.C.L.C. 307 at 309. See further para. 22–019 below.

[5] See below, paras 22–006 *et seq.*

employer. There is no logical reason why the appointment of a receiver of the undertaking of a company should have this impact on contracts of employment and not on other continuing contracts which survive the court order. The likely explanation (as for similar principles applicable in case of compulsory liquidation[6]) is a tenderness towards employees.

19–003   *Receivers of undertaking appointed by debenture-holders.* The rare case of an appointment by debenture-holders of a receiver to act as agent for the debenture-holders or as principal has the same effect as a court appointment in substituting the receiver for the company as the employer and therefore terminating contracts of employment. Such an appointment will only occur in practice in the rare case where the debenture does not provide that the receiver shall be agent for the company[7] and the receiver is not an administrative receiver.[8]

19–004   The usual case of an appointment of a receiver to act as agent for the company does not affect the personality of the employer, and accordingly contracts of employment,[9] for services and of agency[10] are unaffected, unless they expressly or impliedly provide to the contrary or could no longer be performed consistently with the appointment and role of receiver, such as the managing director of the company who may no longer have any substantial functions to perform.[11]

19–005   *Administrators.* The appointment of an administrator operates as the appointment of a managing agent of the company and accordingly does not terminate contracts of employment.[12] In this respect it is similar to the appointment of a receiver out of court.

(ii) Post-liquidation

19–006   *Compulsory liquidation.* The generally accepted principle is that a compulsory liquidation operates as from the date of publication of the order as a dismissal of all the company's employees. For the principle to

---

[6] See below, para. 19–006.

[7] See, *e.g. Re Vimbos* [1900] 1 Ch. 470; *Robinson Printing Co. v. Chic Ltd* [1905] 2 Ch. 123.

[8] Under s. 44(1)(a) of the Insolvency Act 1986, an administrative receiver is deemed to be an agent of the company until liquidation. There is no express qualification that the deeming provision is subject to provisions to the contrary in the debenture, but it is thought that such a qualification should be implied. Nonetheless, it is difficult to conceive why a debenture should ever contain a provision to the contrary.

[9] *Re Foster Clark Ltd's Indenture Trusts* [1966] 1 W.L.R. 125; *Re Mack Truck's (Britain) Ltd* [1967] 1 W.L.R. 780; *Griffiths v. Social Services Secretary* [1974] Q.B. 468; [1973] 3 All E.R. 1184; *Deaway Ltd v. Calverley* [1973] I.C.R. 546; *James Miller Holdings v. Graham* [1978] A.C.L.C. 30 at 187.

[10] *Re Peek Winch & Tool Ltd* [1979] C.A.T. 190, CA; and see *Reigate Union Manufacturing* [1918] 1 K.B. 592 and 606, CA, *per* Scruton L.J.

[11] In *Re Mack Trucks (Britain) Ltd* [1967] 1 All E.R. 977 at 982, Pennycuick J. instanced as a contract whose terms are inconsistent with the appointment "of a new managing agent" a contract for employment of a manager. By contrast, in *Griffiths v. Social Services Secretary* [1974] Q.B. 468, the appointment of a receiver and manager was held not to effect dismissal of the managing director, because his contract of employment placed him strictly under the control of the board of directors and the receiver would have limited involvement in the running of the company's business.

[12] See below, para. 23–025.

apply it is unnecessary that the company is insolvent: the position is the same if liquidation is on a creditors or contributory's petition. The principle is based on the premise that the order for winding up automatically terminates the company's business.[13] The premise, whatever its validity in practice in the nineteenth century when the principle was established, is unsustainable, most particularly in today's rescue culture when closure on the making of the order is far from inevitable. An alternative explanation or justification for the principle is that it affords (as an act of tenderness to employees) special treatment of contracts of employment designed to crystallise their position at the earliest possible moment and enable them immediately to seek employment elsewhere free of all fetters to a doomed company.[14] It is however, doubtful if this alternative basis can justify a rule of law so out of line with other accepted principles of law. But the principle must be treated as established law until reviewed by an appellate court. Accordingly, if a compulsory liquidation follows the appointment of an administrative receiver, the contracts of employment which survive the receivership will immediately be terminated.

Voluntary liquidation. A voluntary liquidation does not necessarily **19–007** result in the dismissal of a company's employees. There was some early authority that the position in the case of a voluntary liquidation was the same in the case of a compulsory winding-up.[15] But it is now reasonably clear that voluntary liquidation only operates as notice of dismissal if it involves the positive step of termination of the employee's employment by the company.[16] For this purpose, it is necessary to have regard to the facts of the particular case, and relevant factors include whether the company is solvent[17] or insolvent[18]; whether the company has previously intimated to the relevant employee that his employment is likely to terminate on liquidation[19]; whether the liquidation involves the immediate cessation of the company's business; whether the employee's continuation in office is inconsistent with the role of the liquidator, *e.g.* the case of the managing director[20]; and whether a receiver has been appointed who has not adopted the contract of employment. In a doubtful case, an employee may seek clarification of the liquidator's intentions, and so prompt the service of a notice of dismissal. Frequently

---

[13] *Re English Joint Stock Bank, ex p. Harding* (1867) L.R. 3 Eq. 341; *Re General Rolling Stock Co. Chapman's Case* (1866) 1 Eq. 346; *Fox Bros. v. Bryant* [1979] I.C.R. 64. It is thought that a winding-up order is effective to dismiss employees, even though the order is wrongly made and subsequently discharged on appeal, and that the discharge of the order on appeal does not effect a reinstatement.

[14] McPherson, *The Law of Company Liquidation* (3rd ed.), p. 174, n. 29.

[15] *Re Imperial Wine Co; Shirreff's Case* (1872) 14 Eq. 417.

[16] *Midland Counties Bank v. Attwood* [1905] 1 Ch. 357; *Gerard v. Worth of Paris* [1936] 2 All E.R. 905, CA; *Fox Bros. v. Bryant* [1979] I.C.R. 64. See McPherson, *The Law of Compulsory Liquidation* (3rd ed.), p. 174–175.

[17] *Gerard v. Worth of Paris* [1936] 2 All E.R. 905.

[18] *Fowler v. Commercial Timber Co.* [1930] 2 K.B. 1; *Reigate v. Union Manufacturing Co.* [1918] 1 K.B. 592.

[19] *ibid.*

[20] *Fowler v. Commercial Timber Co.* [1930] 2 K.B. 1 at 16.

the passing of a resolution for winding up has the effect that the company in fact ceases to trade.

(b) Dismissal

19–008 Where the appointment of the receiver brings about a dismissal, the dismissal is in law the act of the company, and not of the receiver. In the case of contracts which survive the receivership, the receiver has the option to continue them or to treat them as discharged. In the latter case, the company is in law again treated as having dismissed the employee. Whether the dismissal is effected by the appointment of the receiver or by the receiver as agent of the company, the employee may have a claim in breach of contract against the company and will have the rights afforded by statute in the case of dismissal by an insolvent employer.[21]

19–009 Where an employee's contract is terminated, the employee and the trustees of his occupational pension schemes (if any) have rights to certain payments from the Secretary of State for Trade and Industry, who becomes subrogated to the employee's and trustees' rights against the company.[22] Thus, subject to a statutory limit (at present £230 per week), the employee can claim up to eight weeks' arrears of pay, sums in lieu of notice, holiday pay and a redundancy payment or the basic award (but not compensatory award) in respect of unfair dismissal.[23]

(c) Continuance and adoption

(i) Prior to the Insolvency Act 1986

19–010 Prior to the Insolvency Act 1986, it was clearly established that if the receiver, as agent for the company, continued the employment of the company's employees, the company was alone liable for salary accrued due after as well as before the date of the receivership and for any damages or other award made on the subsequent dismissal of such employees.

19–011 In *Nicoll v. Cutts*,[24] the employee, prior to receivership, had been the only working director and had been in charge of the day-to-day running of the business. Before the receivership the employee was hospitalised as a result of a road accident. The receiver did not immediately cause the company to dismiss the employee, but discussed the company's business with him as though he were an employee and obtained his assistance

---

[21] Employment Rights Act 1996, ss. 182–190.

[22] This does not apply where the receiver is appointed over the book debts only: *Secretary of State for Employment v. Stone* [1994] I.C.R. 761.

[23] For the detailed provisions see the Employment Rights Act 1996, s. 183(3). The relevant forms and booklets can be obtained by the receiver from the Job Centre. It should be noted that the payment must be at the rate of at least the national minimum wage which is currently for most purposes £3.60 an hour pursuant to the National Minimum Wage Act 1998. Failure to pay the minimum wage is a criminal offence and under s.32 directors and other officers may commit an offence if the employer company does so and the same is with their consent, connivance or neglect.

[24] [1985] B.C.L.C. 322, CA, considered in *Re Atlantic Computer Systems plc* [1992] Ch. 505, CA and in *Powdrill v. Watson* [1995] 2 A.C. 395 at 440–441, HL.

from his bed in hospital. Three weeks after his appointment the receiver terminated the employee's contract of service by one month's notice, and sold the business of the company as a going concern. The employee claimed from the receiver the amount of his salary in respect of the period after the date of the receiver's appointment. His claim to prove for this sum in the subsequent liquidation of the company would have been worthless in view of the company's insolvency. The employee argued:

> "that it makes no sense that an employee, whose service contract is continued by the bank's receiver in order to assist in realising the company's assets to the best advantage, should, *qua* payment of his remuneration for the period of that continuation of his service contract, get nothing (save from the State's Redundancy Fund[25]) and be postponed to the bank getting payment in full."[26]

Nevertheless the Court of Appeal was unable to find any legal basis for the employee's claim because: **19–012**

(a) section 369(2) of the Companies Act 1948 (subsequently section 492(3) of the Companies Act 1985) did not assist since it only made the receiver personally liable for contracts entered into by him, , *i.e.* after the commencement of the receivership, whereas the employee was employed under a pre-existing contract[27];

(b) the receiver was not obliged to pay to the employee the sum claimed as part of the costs and expenses of the receivership; that concept only covered sums actually paid by the receiver or sums which he was liable to pay.

The receiver had a discretion whether or not to pay, and such discretion was to be exercised taking into consideration whether the interests of the debenture-holder and the company in the beneficial realisation of the charged assets were served by making the payment.[28] The receiver had properly exercised his discretion not to pay the employee.

(ii) From the Insolvency Act 1986 to the Insolvency Act 1994
The decision in *Nicoll v. Cutts* prompted Parliament to enact sections **19–013** 44(1)(b) and (2) of the Insolvency Act 1986.[29] Sections 44(1)(b) and (2) provides that:

> "[The administrative receiver] is personally liable on any contract entered into by him in the carrying out of his functions (except in so

---

[25] Now the National Insurance Fund.

[26] [1985] B.C.L.C. 322, CA, *per* Dillon L.J. at 324.

[27] See also above, Chap. 8.

[28] *cf.* the similar approach to an *ex gratia* payment by the liquidator in *Re Banque des Marchands de Moscou (No. 2)* [1953] 1 W.L.R. 172.

[29] See *Re Atlantic Computer Systems plc.* [1992] Ch. 505, CA and *Powdrill v. Watson* [1995] 2 A.C. 395 at 441.

far as the contract otherwise provides) and on any contract of employment adopted by him in the carrying out of those functions ... [but] the administrative receiver is not to be taken to have adopted a contract of employment by reason of anything done or omitted to be done within 14 days after his appointment."

A similar amendment was enacted to impose the same liability to employees on receivers of companies who are not administrative receivers.[30] An analogous provision was introduced by section 19 in respect of administrators but instead of imposing personal liability on the administrator, it instead confers entitlement on the employees to priority payment.

19–014 The statute raised three particular problems: (1) it left unclear the legal significance of the 14 day period; (2) it contained no definition of the term "adopt" and accordingly left open the question whether a receiver or administrator adopted a contract only if he became a party to it by way of novation or whether it was sufficient that he treated it as continuing in force; and (3) what was the extent of a receiver's liability "on" an adopted contract of employment. These questions were resolved by the House of Lords in the combined appeals in *Powdrill v. Watson* and *In re Leyland Daf ("Powdrill")*.[31]

19–015 *The 14-day period.* The House of Lords held that the proviso to the sections is designed to give the receiver or administrator 14 days in which to decide upon their attitude to outstanding contracts of employment. Their freedom of choice is not to be limited by any interim arrangements they make in respect of the 14-day decision period. If the receiver or administrator makes a final decision to adopt the contract before the 14-day period has expired, his decision is not binding unless and until continued after the 14 days. He may however within the 14-day period contract to adopt after expiration of the 14-day period or to assume immediately the obligations imposed by adoption, and such a contract will have full legal effect.

19–016 *Meaning of adoption in sections 19 and 44.* In *Powdrill*, the House of Lords held that the concept of "adoption" in sections 19 and 44 does not mean "novate", for the legislation was clearly intended to alter, and not confirm, the legal position established in *Nicoll v. Cutts*. The legislation was directed at curing the mischief of a receiver or administrator making use of an employee's services without full payment. The House of Lords held that the concept of "adoption" in sections 19 and 44 connotes some conduct by a receiver or administrator which amounts to an election to treat a contract of employment as giving rise to a separate liability in the receivership or administration. It was further held that if a receiver or administrator caused the company to continue the employment for more than 14 days after his appointment, this would inevitably be conduct

---

[30] Insolvency Act 1986, s. 37(1).
[31] [1995] 2 A.C. 395.

amounting to such an election, and the contract of employment would have been "adopted" for the purpose of sections 19 and 44. The House of Lords indicated that it was not possible to pick and choose between different liabilities under the contract, so that if a contract of employment is adopted, it is adopted as a whole.[32] It is implicit in the decision that conduct by a receiver or administrator amounting to an adoption of the contract of employment will be treated as such, irrespective of any purported notification to the employee that the contract of employment is not being adopted.[33]

The extent of an administrative receiver's liability under an adopted **19–017** *contract.* At first instance in *Re Leyland Daf,* Lightman J. held that if an administrative receiver adopted a contract of employment, the literal wording of section 44 meant that the administrative receiver would be personally liable for all liabilities whenever incurred of whatever kind under the adopted contract.[34] The House of Lords noted that this would have resulted in an administrative receiver becoming personally liable for "imponderable" past and future liabilities and would have made the task of the administrative receiver in considering whether to continue to employ staff to trade the business of a company almost impossible. Because these results were considered to be inimical to the rescue culture which the 1986 Act was designed to promote, the House of Lords adopted what it acknowledged to be a "forced construction" of section 44, holding that the liability of an administrative receiver on any adopted contract must be subject to the same temporal restriction as applies to contracts adopted by an administrator under section 19, namely that it is restricted to liabilities incurred under the adopted contract while he was receiver.[35]

(iii) After the Insolvency Act 1994

Administrative receivers and administrators. Alerted to the potential **19–018** impact of sections 19 and 44 of the 1986 Act upon administrative receivers and administrators by the decision of the Court of Appeal in *Powdrill,*[36] Parliament acted swiftly and without waiting for the decision of the House of Lords, by passing the Insolvency Act 1994 to limit the scope of these sections. The 1994 Act amended the provisions of section 19 and 44 in so far as they applied to contracts of employment adopted on or after March 15, 1994. The technique used by Parliament was to amend the 1986 Act so as to restrict the scope of liabilities which would attract priority under section 19(5) in the case of administrations, and

---

[32] [1995] 2 A.C. 394 at 448–450 *per* Lord Browne–Wilkinson.

[33] The House of Lords in effect overruled the unreported decision of Harman J. in *Re Specialised Mouldings Limited,* February 13, 1987, and affirmed the decision of the Court of Appeal that standard-form letters to employees purporting to avoid adoption would be of no effect if the contract was in fact continued for more than 14 days after appointment: see *Powdrill v. Watson* [1994] 2 B.C.L.C. 118 at 141c–d, CA.

[34] [1995] 2 A.C. 394 at 413–415.

[35] For a comment on the case, see Mr. Justice Lightman, "The Challenges Ahead" [1996] J.B.L. 113 at 121–122. See also *Lindop v. Stuart Noble & Sons Ltd* [1999] B.C.C. 616 (Ct of Session).

[36] [1994] 2 B.C.L.C. 118, CA.

for which an administrative receiver would be personally liable under section 44, to so-called "qualifying liabilities". Such "qualifying liabilities" are liabilities for wages, salary or contributions to an Occupational Pension Scheme in respect of services rendered after adoption of a contract of employment. In addition, in the case of administrative receivers, section 44(2B) of the 1986 Act (as amended) provides that where an administrative receiver is personally liable in respect of a qualifying liability for services rendered partly before and partly after the adoption of the contract, his liability shall only extend to so much of the sum as is payable in respect of the services rendered after the adoption of the contract. In the case of administrators, section 19(8) of the 1986 Act (as amended) provides that so much of any qualifying liability as represents payment in respect of services rendered before the adoption of the contract shall be disregarded.[37]

19-019 The most important consequence of the amendments made in 1994 is to prevent the administrative receiver from being personally liable to an employee who is dismissed without notice in a receivership for sums which would have been payable under his adopted contract of employment in lieu of notice, or for damages for wrongful dismissal. Equally, such sums will not qualify for priority payment from the assets of a company in the case of an administration. The 1994 Act is also entirely consistent with the decision of Evans-Lombe J. at first instance in *Powdrill*[38] that statutory compensation for unfair dismissal does not qualify for priority in an administration or result in personal liability for an administrative receiver, because such liabilities are not liabilities "under" or "on" a contract of employment.[39]

19-020 Notwithstanding the changes introduced by the 1994 Act, difficult issues may still arise over when a particular liability is incurred for the purposes of sections 19 and 44 and whether it amounts to a qualifying liability.[40] So, for example, in *Re a Company (No. 005174 of 1999)*[41] Neuberger J. held that for the purposes of section 19(9) of the 1986 Act (as amended), which deems wages or salary payable in respect of a period of holiday to be wages or salary in respect of services rendered during the period by reference to which the holiday entitlement arose, the effect of the

---

[37] In the House of Lords in *Powdrill v. Watson* [1995] 2 A.C. 394 at 446–447, Lord Browne-Wilkinson reached a similar result in respect of the unamended 1986 Act by applying the Apportionment Act 1870 to liabilities for wages.

[38] [1994] 2 B.C.L.C. 118 at 132e.

[39] See also *Albion Automotive Ltd v. Shaw* (EAT 523/94 unreported).

[40] Difficult issues of limitation may also arise. In *Re Maxwell Fleet and Facilities Management Ltd* [1999] 2 B.C.L.C. 721 it was held that in an administration where contracts of employment had been adopted prior to the changes introduced by the 1994 Act, the employees' contractual claims for wrongful dismissal under their adopted contracts accrued when they were dismissed. This would also be the case in an administrative receivership in relation to the administrative receiver's personal liability for breach of contract. It was further held that in an administration, a separate statutory obligation to pay employee's claims arises under s.19(5) of the 1986 Act on the discharge of the administration order, which attracts a 6 year limitation period. The enforcement of the statutory charge created by s.19(5) is subject to a separate limitation period of 12 years under s.20 of the Limitation Act 1980.

[41] [2000] 1 W.L.R. 502.

adopted contract of employment for a number of teachers was that they accrued holiday entitlement for the period after the relevant term worked. As a result their holiday pay for the summer holidays after the summer term ended was a qualifying liability. Neuberger J. indicated that the proper approach to the question of whether a particular liability falls within the definition of qualifying liabilities is to look primarily at the terms of the contract of employment, taking into account all surrounding circumstances known or reasonably capable of being known to the parties at the time, but also looking at the nature of the liability and the factual circumstances in which it falls to be paid."[42]

Non-Administrative Receivers. Non-administration receivers are in the **19–021** worst possible position in relation to adoption. They are not covered by the changes introduced by the 1994 Act, although no convincing reason has been given for their exclusion. Such receivers will only be safe from personal liability if they cause the company to dismiss all employees whom they are able to cause it to dismiss within the initial 14 day period. Thereafter, and subject to the validity of "contracting out" (see below), they may be forced to seek to negotiate new contracts with such employees as they wish to employ to run the business, but on terms which exclude their personal liability. The debenture may authorise the receiver to pay such employees as a cost of the receivership in priority to the other creditors of the company.

Contracting Out. Whilst the decision in *Powdrill* has settled that it is **19–022** not possible to "contract out" of adoption itself, the Insolvency Act 1986 left open the question of whether, following adoption, it is possible for an employee and a receiver to "contract out" of the employee's personal claims against the receiver. It is also an open question as to whether it is permissible for a receiver to dismiss employees during the initial 14 day period and then to re-engage them on new contracts of employment incorporating the same terms as the old, but expressly excluding any personal liability on his part. Following the changes in the 1994 Act, these issues are now only likely to arise in relation to non-administrative receiverships, because it is unlikely that there would be any practical incentive for employees and administrative receivers to contract out of liability for the limited "qualifying liabilities". The issue is essentially one of policy, and at first instance in both *Powdrill*[43] and *Leyland Daf*[44] it was accepted that there are no public policy reasons to prevent such agreements between receivers and employees.[45] The policy of the original statute, now confirmed by the amendments introduced by the 1994 Act, is to prevent receivers encouraging expectations of payment for work, and then disappointing them. Absent any questions of sham or duress, an agreed variation of an adopted contract or a dismissal and re-

---

[42] [2000] 1 W.L.R. 502 at 508.

[43] [1994] 2 B.C.L.C. 118 at 129f–130b (Evans-Lombe J.).

[44] [1995] 2 A.C. 394 at 411D-F (Lightman J.).

[45] The point was raised in argument in relation to administrators in *Powdrill* in the Court of Appeal, but the Court of Appeal did not consider it necessary to determine the issue: see [1994] 2 B.C.L.C. 118 at 141. The point did not arise in the House of Lords.

engagement on terms excluding personal liability, are not of themselves objectionable. Indeed they may operate to the benefit of the employee if the only alternative is dismissal. As discussed below, any such agreement must be clear and unequivocal to be effective, and a unilateral statement by the receivers coupled with a failure to object on the part of the employee will not be sufficient.[46]

(d) Re-employment and new employees

19–023 The receiver, as agent for the company, has power to enter into new contracts of employment, re-employing former employees and employing new employees. As indicated above, where a contract is adopted, the receiver incurs personal liability on it, and the same is true of new contracts entered into after his appointment unless he takes avoiding action. If the receiver is to avoid personal liability under such contracts, he must ensure that the contracts contain express provisions to this effect.[47] Therefore, as noted above, a receiver can by dismissing and subsequently re-employing them, avoid incurring personal liability by retaining the existing workforce and thereby adopting their contracts of employment.

19–024 If the receiver requires employees under existing contracts to agree to new terms, depending upon the significance of the new term this may amount to:

> (a) a variation of the old contract of employment which will have been adopted so that the receiver will be personally liable; or
> (b) a new contract, under which the receiver will be personally liable.

If the receiver seeks to impose a new term to which the employee does not agree, and the variation is sufficiently serious to be a repudiatory breach, the employee may treat this conduct as constructive dismissal by the company.[48]

19–025 Once a compulsory liquidation supervenes, all existing contracts of employment come to an end, as does the receiver's agency for the company. This will also ordinarily (though not necessarily) happen once a voluntary liquidation supervenes. Thereafter the receiver can only employ either as principal or (where so authorised and so stated in the contract) as agent for his appointor. If he employs as principal, he will be personally liable under the contract, but entitled to an indemnity out of the charged assets.

19–026 Where there has been a dismissal and re-employment by the receiver in whatsoever capacity, there will be no common law right to damages for wrongful dismissal if in every respect the employment remains the same, since the employee will have suffered no loss by reason of the

---

[46] See *e.g.* the approach of Evans-Lombe J. to the wording of the relevant letter in *Powdrill*: [1994] 2 B.C.L.C. 118 at 130.

[47] The receiver was held personally liable because this provision was omitted in *Re Mack Trucks (Britain) Ltd* [1967] 1 W.L.R. 780.

[48] See in particular *Western Excavating Ltd v. Sharp* [1978] Q.B. 761 and *Hogg v. Dover College* [1990] I.C.R. 39.

dismissal. Likewise, there will not be any entitlement to a redundancy payment, since re-engagement on the same terms of employment by the receiver, whether as agent of the company or not, will lead the employee to being regarded as not having been dismissed.[49] Accrued statutory continuity rights are transferred to this new employment.

(e) Consultation with trades unions or elected representatives over redundancies

Upon commencement of the receivership, the receiver should notify the **19–027** employees immediately of the position. If he considers that 20 or more redundancies are necessary and there are one or more union recognised by the company, he must confer with officials of any such trade unions as soon as possible after the proposal to dismiss has been made and (in the absence of a recognised union), with elected representatives of the workforce.[50] There are minimum periods for consultation: where 100 or more are to be made redundant at one establishment[51] within a period of 90 days or less, at least 90 days must be allowed for consultation before the first of those dismissals takes effect. At least 30 days must be given where between 20 and 99 employees are to be made redundant.

Where no union is recognised the employer must consult with **19–028** employee representatives who have already been appointed or elected by the affected employees for other purposes (*e.g.* a works council) or if this has not occurred, the employer must arrange for an election by affected employees.[52] The employer may choose whether to consult an already appointed works council or alternatively arrange for a special election procedure to take effect, but if the union is recognised that is the sole channel for consultation.

At the commencement of the consultation, the employer must disclose **19–029** in writing to the union or elected representatives the following information[53]: the reason for the loss of jobs; the number, although not necessarily the names of those to be dismissed; the total number of workers employed and the proposed method of selection. This consultation must take place "with a view to reaching agreement".[54]

The mere fact of the insolvency of the company on the appointment **19–030** of the receiver does not in itself relieve the company of its obligations with regard to consulting unions or elected representatives about proposed redundancies so as to absolve the employer from liability.[55]

---

[49] Employment Rights Act 1996, ss. 138, 145.

[50] The phrase "an employer proposing to dismiss as redundant" includes cases where the employer is in administration and the administrator proposes the dismissals: *Re Hartlebury Printers Ltd* [1992] I.C.R. 559 at 569h.

[51] "Establishment" has a technical meaning: see *Barratt Developments Ltd v. UCATT* [1978] I.C.R. 319; *Green & Son (Castings) Ltd v. ASTMS and AUEW* [1984] I.R.L.R. 135.

[52] Trade Union and Labour Relations (Consolidation) Act 1992, s. 188(1B)(b)(ii).

[53] *ibid.*, s. 188(4).

[54] *ibid.*, s. 188(6).

[55] *Clarks of Hove Ltd v. Bakers' Union* [1978] I.C.R. 1076, CA. See also *Angus Jowett & Co. Ltd v. NUTGW* [1985] I.C.R. 646, EAT; *APAC v. Kirvin Ltd* [1978] I.R.L.R. 318; *Hamish Armour v. ASTMS* [1979] I.R.L.R. 24; *USDAW v. Leancut Bacon Ltd* [1981] I.R.L.R. 295; *Re Hartlebury Printers Ltd* [1992] I.C.R. 559 at 570e; *GMB v. Rankin & Harrison* [1992] I.R.L.R. 514.

Rather, there must be "special circumstances" for this liability to be avoided and ". . . to be special the event must be something out of the ordinary, something uncommon . . ." A "sudden disaster" would qualify as being "special".[56]

19–031 A breach of the consultation procedures may enable a recognised trade union or elected representatives (as relevant) to claim a protective award from an employment tribunal. That award is a sum which is "just and equitable in all the circumstances having regard to the employer's default" subject to a maximum of 90 days' pay.[57]

19–032 A receiver may also possibly be subject to criminal liability if he fails to notify the Secretary of State for Trade and Industry of impending redundancies.[58]

2. TRANSFER OF THE UNDERTAKING[59]

(a) The general principle

19–033 At common law the transfer of the business of the company would in almost all cases terminate contracts of employment.[60] The position was radically altered by The Transfer of Undertakings (Protection of Employment) Regulations 1981[61] which was introduced to put into effect the EU Acquired Rights Directive.[62]

> "The general scheme of the Regulations is directly contrary to the pre-existing law. The general rule is that on the transfer of a business the employees of that business are transferred with it, *i.e.* the employees' contract of employment . . . undergoes a statutory novation"[63]

(b) What is a transferred undertaking?

19–034 The Regulations apply to transfers of an "undertaking". This term is not precisely defined but includes "any trade or business". Tribunals must consider the substance and not the form in deciding whether there is an

---

[56] *Clarks of Hove v. Bakers' Union* [1978] I.C.R. 1076, CA at 1085, *per* Geoffrey Lane L.J.

[57] Trade Union and Labour Relations (Consolidation) Act 1992, ss. 189 and 190.

[58] Trade Union and Labour Relations (Consolidation) Act 1992, s. 194(3). The liability is extended to "any director manager secretary or other similar officer of the body corporate, or any person who was purporting to act in such capacity": these latter words may possibly "catch" the receiver. *cf. Re B Johnson & Co (Builders) Ltd* [1955] Ch. 634.

[59] See generally P. Elias Q.C. and J. Bowers, *Transfer of Undertakings: The Legal Pitfalls* (5th ed., Longmans, 1994); J. Bowers Q.C. *et al.*, *Transfer of Undertakings Encyclopaedia* (Sweet & Maxwell, 2000).

[60] *Brace v. Calder* [1895] 2 Q.B. 253: *Re Foster Clark Ltd's Indenture Trusts* [1966] 1 W.L.R. 125; [1966] 1 All E.R. 43.

[61] S.I. 1981 No. 1794) ("Transfer Regulations"). The Regulations are intended to implement E.C. Directive 77/187: [1977] O.J. L61/26 (the so-called "Acquired Rights Directive") as amended.

[62] EC Directive 77/187 as now amended by Directive 98/50. The Acquired Rights Directive is compulsorily applicable to insolvency proceedings whose object is to effect a corporate rescue to keep the business intact but not to proceedings the purpose of which is to liquidate the assets of the transferor. This is because Art. 1(1) limits its scope to transfers made "as a result of a legal transfer or merger" (*Abels v. Bedrijfsvereniging* [1985] E.C.R. 469; *d'Urso v. Ercole Marelliu Elettromeccanica Generale* [1992] IRLR 136; *Jules Dethier Equipement SA v. Jules Dassy* [1998] I.R.L.R. 266).

[63] *Premier Motors v. Total Oil* [1984] I.C.R. 58.

undertaking and whether there has been a transfer of that undertaking.[64] A transfer "may take place whether or not any property is transferred to the transferee by the transferor". The Regulations also apply to the transfer of part of an undertaking and the question in such a case is whether the part transferred is a self-contained, separate and severable part of the whole and whether there is an economic entity which retains its identity after transfer.[65] The factors to be taken into account in determining this question derive from the European Court of Justice case of *Spijkers*[66] and include whether assets or staff were transferred and whether the undertaking was carried on in the same or a similar way. The factor of whether the majority of staff are transferred is one amongst many to be considered.[67]

(c) The consequences of a transfer of undertaking

There is a general provision that a relevant transfer shall not in itself **19–035** terminate employment contracts.[68] Quite the contrary, contracts of employment will have effect "as if originally made" between the employee and the transferee of the business. The transferee takes over all "rights, powers, duties and liabilities of or in connection with any such contract" of employment.[69] However, occupational pensions and criminal liabilities[70] are expressly excluded from the liabilities transferred.

As a result of the Regulations, the employees of the company[71] will **19–036** generally become the employees of the transferee of the business. This is so even where the transferee makes it clear from the start that he has no intention of keeping the employees so transferred.[72] Where there is a substantial change in an employee's working conditions to his detriment,

---

[64] Transfer Regulations, reg. 2(2). There have been several decisions of the European Court of Justice on the proper construction of the Directive and in particular the meaning of undertaking, *e.g. Landsorganisationen i Danmark v. Ny Molle Kro* [1987] I.R.L.R. 37; *Berg & Busschers v. Besselsen* [1989] I.R.L.R. 447. In *Allen v. Amalgamated Construction Co. Ltd* [2000] IRLR 119, the ECJ reiterated that the central question was whether there was a transfer of an economic entity even though the transfer was between two companies in the same group with the same ownership, the same management and operate from the same premises. In certain sectors in which the activity is based essentially on manpower, a group of workers engaged in a joint activity on a permanent basis may itself constitute an economic entity. That entity is capable of maintaining its identity after it has been transferred where the new employer does not merely pursue the activity but also takes over a major part in numbers and skills of the employees specifically assigned by the predecessor to the task.

[65] *ECM (Vehicle Delivery Service) Ltd v. Cox* [1999] I.R.L.R. 559.

[66] [1986] E.C.R. 1119.

[67] See also *Betts v. Brintel* [1997] I.R.L.R. 361; *Whitewater Leisure Management Ltd v. Barnes* [2000] I.R.L.R. 456.

[68] Transfer Regulations, reg. 5(1). The definition of employee in the Regulations is unusually wide, applying to anyone who works for another in any capacity except an independent contractor under a contract for services; it does not include a partner: *Cowell v. Quilter Goodison Co. Ltd and Q.C. Management Services Ltd* [1989] I.R.L.R. 392, CA.

[69] Transfer Regulations, reg. 5(2).

[70] This does not include, however, "any provisions . . . which do not relate to benefits for old age, invalidity or survivors", added by the Trade Union Reform and Employment Rights Act 1993, s. 33.

[71] Or in some cases the employees of the debenture-holder or the receiver.

[72] *Premier Motors v. Total Oil* [1984] I.C.R. 58 at 62, E.A.T.

the employee has a right to terminate his contract of employment without notice. The mere fact that there is a new employer is not a "substantial change" unless the employee shows that in all the circumstances the change of employers is a "significant change" to the employee's detriment.[73]

(d) Application of the Regulations only to those employed "immediately before the transfer"

19–037 Regulation 5(3) provides that Regulations only apply in respect of those employed "immediately before the transfer".[74] This is often highly material in the context of the receivership. Authoritative guidance on the meaning of those words was given by the House of Lords in *Litster v. Forth Dry Dock & Engineering Co. Ltd*.[75] Their Lordships decided that in order that the manifest purpose of the Regulations might be achieved and effect be given to the clear (but inadequately expressed) intention of Parliament, certain words must be read in by necessary implication. This principle justified not taking a narrow approach to the phrase "a person employed immediately before the transfer". To do so would render the Regulations "capable of ready evasion through the transferee arranging with the transferor for the latter to dismiss its employees a short time before the transfer becomes operative", said Lord Keith. Lord Oliver[76] thought that it was necessary to remember in this regard that the purpose of the Directive and the Regulations was to "safeguard" the rights of employees on transfer and that there was a mandatory obligation to "provide remedies which are effective and not merely symbolic to which the Regulations are intended to give effect. The remedies . . . in the case of an insolvent transferor are largely illusory unless they can be exerted against the transferee as the Directive contemplates". It was thus the duty of the court to give to regulation 5 a construction which accords with the decisions of the European Court of Justice on the corresponding provisions of the Directive. Regulation 5(3) had to be construed on the "footing that it applies to a person employed immediately before the transfer or who would have been so employed if he had not been unfairly dismissed before transfer for a reason connected with the transfer".[77]

19–038   Lord Oliver stated that the sequence of events in the transfer in question could not be rationally explained otherwise than on the basis that the dismissal of the workforce was engineered to prevent any

---

[73] Transfer Regulations, reg. 5(5) as amended by the Trade Union Reform and Employment Rights Act 1993, s. 33. See *University of Oxford v. Humphreys* [2000] I.R.L.R. 183.

[74] See, *e.g.* differing conclusions in *Apex Leisure Hire v. Barratt* [1985] I.R.L.R. 452; *Secretary of State for Employment v. Anchor Hotel* [1985] I.C.R. 724; *Secretary of State for Employment v. Spence* [1987] Q.B. 179 and, subsequent to *Litster* (see below), see *Brook Lane Finance Co. Ltd v. Bradley* [1988] I.C.R. 423. The European Court of Justice considered the matter in *P. Bork International A/S v. Foreningen afArbejdsledere i Danmark* [1989] I.R.L.R. 41.

[75] [1990] 1 A.C. 546.

[76] At 576G.

[77] *Per* Lord Templeman at p. 554H.

liability attaching to Forth Estuary Engineering Ltd (the solvent trans-feree). On the other hand:

> "Where, before the actual transfer takes place, the employment of an employee is terminated for a reason unconnected with the transfer, I agree that the question of whether he was employed 'immediately' before the transfer cannot sensibly be made to depend on the temporal proximity between the two events, except possibly in a case where they are so closely connected in point of time, that it is, for practical purposes, impossible realistically to say that they are not precisely contemporaneous."[78]

There may be complex and uncertain situations where a transferor negotiates with several purchasers in order to gain the best price, and the actual transferee is not identifiable until the day of contract and completion. In such a situation it has been much debated whether the *Litster* principle applies before the specific transferee has been identified, so that anyone dismissed before that time would not be employed immediately before the transfer.[79] It is the better view that transfer takes place at the moment of completion rather than on exchange of contracts.

While the *Litster* approach may make sense in a solvent situation, it **19–039** may not make sense in a receivership or administration. In the latter type of case the aim of selling the business as a going concern and saving as many jobs as can be saved often requires the shedding of some staff prior to sale. Purchasers often will not or cannot accept all the existing employees. The effect of *Litster* in such situations may be to prevent one or more sales that may have saved some jobs or may be to encourage the shedding of employees at a stage when it is not clear how many employees would be accepted by a purchaser.

(e) The voidable transfer

Another problem which arises from time to time is that the transfer of **19–040** the business is itself voidable, *e.g.* because the directors acted in breach of their duties and the transferee had notice of such breach (particularly where the transferee is controlled by these directors or persons connected with them). In the event that the transfer is avoided, *e.g.* as a result of action taken by a receiver of the transferor, the position of the employees appears to be in doubt. The Regulations make no specific provision for the reversing of contracts of employment to the transferor in such cases. Logic suggests that, in cases where employees' contracts follow the business, the avoidance of a transfer of the business should revest the contracts in the transferor, and this conclusion has been reached by the European Court of Justice as the proper construction of the relevant Directive.[80]

---

[78] At 575D.
[79] *Harrison Bowden Ltd v. Bowden* [1994] I.C.R. 186; *Ibex Trading Co. v Walton* [1994] I.R.L.R. 564; *Morris v. John Grose Ltd* [1998] I.C.R. 655.
[80] *Berg & Busschers v. Besselsen* [1989] I.R.L.R. 447.

(f) Transfers and unfair dismissal

19–041 If either before or after a relevant transfer an employee is dismissed and if the principal reason for the dismissal is the transfer or a reason connected with it, the employee is treated as having been dismissed unfairly,[81] unless the principal reason for the dismissal is "an economic, technical or organisational reason entailing changes in the workforce of either the transferor or the transferee . . .".[82] In that case, the employer is treated as having demonstrated some other potentially fair reason for dismissal within section 98(1)(b) of the Employment Rights Act 1996. The question still remains in such a case of economic, technical or organisational reason whether the dismissal was in fact fair for the purposes of section 98(4) of the 1996 Act.[83] It is important to note that any such reason must entail "a change in the workforce". A desire by the new employers to whom the business had been transferred to put all their employees on the same footing by reducing the pay of employees taken over did not entail "a change in the workforce" so that an employee who had his pay reduced had been automatically unfairly dismissed.[84] On the other hand, it has been decided that the dismissal of the entire workforce by a receiver prior to a transfer necessarily entailed "a change in the workforce".[85] The cases are by no means easy to reconcile on this point.[86]

19–042 To qualify as an economic reason, the reason for dismissal must be connected with the conduct or running of the business itself and not merely a desire to achieve a better price for the entity transferred.[87] Where the reason does qualify and the employee is held to have been fairly dismissed because of a change in the workforce, he may still be entitled to a redundancy payment.[88]

(g) Information and consultation over transfers

19–043 The "employer" has a duty to give advance warning of a relevant transfer and (amongst other things) of its "legal economic and social implications . . . for the affected employees . . ." to representatives of

---

[81] Transfer Regulations, reg. 8(1).

[82] Transfer Regulations, reg. 8(2). This does not apply to an overseas employee, that is one who ordinarily works outside the United Kingdom: reg. 13(1).

[83] *Berriman v. Delabole Slate Ltd* [1985] I.C.R. 546, CA; *McGrath v. Rank Leisure Ltd* [1985] I.C.R. 527; *Crawford v. Swinton Insurance Brokers Ltd* [1990] I.C.R. 85; *Whitehouse v. Chas A Blatchford & Sons Ltd* [1999] I.R.L.R. 492; *Kerry Foods Ltd v. Creber* [2000] I.R.L.R. 10.

[84] See above, n. 53.

[85] *Anderson v. Dalkeith Engineering* [1985] I.C.R. 66, E.A.T.

[86] "Workforce" means the workforce as an entity separate from the individuals who make up that workforce. The issue under the Transfer Regulations is whether the reason for dismissal involved a change in that workforce. There could be such a change even if the same people were retained but were given different jobs by the transferee: *Crawford v. Swinton Insurance Ltd* [1990] I.C.R. 85; *Porter and Nanayakkara v. Queens Medical Centre* [1993] I.R.L.R. 486.

[87] *Wendelboe v. L.J. Music Aps* [1985] E.C.R. 457; *Gateway Hotels Ltd v. Stewart* [1988] I.R.L.R. 287; *Wheeler v. Patel & J. Golding Group of Companies* [1987] I.R.L.R. 211.

[88] *Meickle v. McPhail* [1983] I.R.L.R. 351; *Canning v. Niaz* [1983] I.R.L.R. 431 (no claim possible); *Gorictree Ltd v. Jenkinson* [1985] I.C.R. 51 and *Anderson v. Dalkeith* [1985] I.C.R. 66 (claim possible).

any recognised independent trade union.[89] Where measures are to be taken which will affect employees, there must be consultation with the recognised union(s) if unions are recognised "with a view to seeking their agreement".[90] In the absence of a recognised union the employer must inform and consult (if necessary) with employee representatives already appointed or elected by the affected employees for another purpose or arrange for such representatives to be appointed by way of the procedure laid down in the Regulations.[91]

Failure to comply with this duty can lead to an award of compensa- **19–044** tion being made against the "employer" of up to 13 weeks' pay,[92] unless the "employer" shows

"(a) that there were special circumstances which rendered it not reasonably practical for him to perform the duty; and
 (b) that he took all such steps towards its performance as were reasonably practicable in those circumstances".[93]

Such an award of compensation may well rank as a preferential debt and thus affect the receivership.[94] Liability in a transfer situation passes to the transferee.[95]

(h) Hive-downs

Special rules apply to hive-down and employment rights. By regulation 4 **19–045** of the Regulations the transfer is not deemed to take place until either the subsidiary ceases to be wholly owned by the holding company (whether by share or asset sale and whether by transfer of all or by a majority of the shares) or the business of the subsidiary is transferred. The transfer then comes out of a form of suspended animation. In general it should be therefore possible for the vendor to terminate contracts long before the ultimate sale to the third party so that the latter has no liabilities to employees.[96]

---

[89] Transfer Regulations, reg. 10. The original restriction to recognised unions was in breach of the Acquired Rights Directive according to the European Court of Justice in *Commission of the European Communities v. U.K,* [1994] I.C.R. 664. See *Institute of Professional Civil Servants v. Secretary of State for Defence* [1987] I.R.L.R. 373, Ch.D.

[90] reg. 10(5) inserted by the Trade Union Reform and Employment Rights Act 1993, s. 33.

[91] As amended by the Collective Redundancies and Transfer of Undertakings (Protection of Employment) (Amendment) Regulations 1999 (S.I. 1999 No. 1925).

[92] As amended by the Collective Redundancies and Transfer of Undertakings (Protection of Employment) (Amendment) Regulations 1999 (S.I. 1999 No. 1925), formerly four weeks.

[93] Transfer Regulations, reg. 10. As to what might constitute "special circumstances" in such a case. *cf. Bakers' Union v. Clarks of Hove Ltd* [1978] I.R.L.R. 366; *Armour v. ASTMS* [1979] I.R.L.R. 24; *APAC v. Kirvin Ltd* [1978] I.R.L.R. 318; *USDA W v. Leancut Bacon Ltd* [1981] I.R.L.R. 295; *GMB v. Rankin and Harrison, The In House Lawyer* (all decided on the basis of similar wording in the Employment Protection Act 1975).

[94] Insolvency Act 1986, Sched. 6, paras (9)(b) and 13(2)(e) and see below, Chap. 21. The maximum is only two weeks' pay and it may be set off against a protective award for failure to consult about redundancies or damages for breach of contract: reg. 11(7).

[95] *Kerry Foods Ltd v. Creber* [2000] I.R.L.R. 10. *Cf. Angus Jowett v. NUTGW* [1985] I.C.R. 646.

[96] It is likely that reg 4 will be abolished when a reformed TUPE is drafted.

19–046   It is not possible for the parties to contract out of those parts of the Regulations which deal with the duty to inform and consult trade unions, the transfer of the contract of employment and unfair dismissal.[97]

19–047   In *Re Maxwell Fleet and Facilities Management Ltd (in Administration) (No. 2)*[98] the court had to consider the effect of a purported hive down of the assets and business of MFFM to Fleet Distribution and Management Limited ("FDML"). Joint administrators were appointed to MFFM and a complicated transaction was structured which involved essentially the following steps:

(a) two subscriber shares in an off the shelf company Dancequote were transferred to the Administrators;

(b) FDML's purchase of the assets and business of MFFM would follow the hive-down of such assets and business into a subsidiary company

By the first agreement between MFFM, the administrators and Dancequote, MFFM sold to Dancequote MFFM's business as a going concern and Dancequote agreed "not to take into its employ" any employees whose names were set out in a schedule. By a deed of assignment MFFM assigned its interest in its business premises to Dancequote. By a second agreement, Dancequote agreed to sell to FDML the business of Dancequote as a going concern. The only difference between the first and second agreement was that there was no exclusion relating to the employees in the second agreement.

19–048   Dancequote had no trading activities of any sort. Mr David Mackie Q.C. (sitting as a Deputy High Court Judge) decided that these transactions were "not part of an orthodox hive down by which the viable parts of a business are segregated from the remainder and placed by the Administrator in the position where they may continue to flourish and/or to be sold"[99] Rather, the intermediary Dancequote was "introduced . . . for one purpose only, achieving the mutual wish of the contracting parties to transfer the business to FDML stripped of the liability to employees". The judge saw "no warrant for construing Regulation 4 differently from the remainder" of the Regulations[1] Regulation 4 must be interpreted in accordance with the overall purpose of the Regulations derived from the Acquired Rights Directive. The reality of the transaction was "the sale of a business on one day complicated by a mutual desire to avoid what would otherwise be the effect of the Regulations. In substance it was a single transfer . . . and it [regulation 4] should be construed to defeat an ingenious device, designed to deprive employees of protection which would otherwise be available to them".

[97] Transfer Regulations, reg. 12.
[98] [2000] 2 B.C.L.C. 155.
[99] [2000] 2 B.C.L.C. at 165g.
[1] [2000] 2 B.C.L.C. at 166b.

CHAPTER 20

RECEIVERS AND RATES

1. NATURE OF RATES[1]

Rates fall into two categories: occupied property rates and unoccupied **20–001** property rates. Both are a direct levy by way of taxation made in relation to land within a local government area as a means of defraying local government expenses, and both constitute a personal charge, in the former case on the occupier of the property, and in the latter case on the owner of the property.[2]

In the case of occupied property rates, in case of default in payment, **20–002** an action for payment did not lie prior to 1989: the only available remedies were either (so long as the defaulter remained in occupation) distress on the defaulter's goods on the property, or (in the case of an individual) bankruptcy proceedings[3] or (in the case of a company) a winding-up petition.[4] As a result of the Non-Domestic Rating (Collection and Enforcement) (Local Lists) Regulations 1989,[5] however, the local authority can now for the first time sue[6] or it can elect to seek a liability order from a magistrates' court[7] and then distrain[8] or seek a winding-up order.[9]

From 1897[10] to 1986 rates were a preferential debt payable (*pari passu* **20–003** with other preferential debts) out of assets in the hands of a receiver subject to a floating charge in priority to the claims of the debenture-holders. As a result of the recommendations of the Cork Committee on Insolvency,[11] rates are, under the provisions of the Insolvency Act 1986, no longer preferential in either a receivership or liquidation. In this chapter the potential personal liability of receivers for the payment of rates is considered, together with the local authorities rights to distrain on the property of the company.[12]

---

[1] For a general account, see *Ryde on Rating and the Council Tax.*
[2] See below and *Ryde, op cit.,* Div. B, Chap. 3.
[3] *Re McGreavy* [1950] Ch. 269.
[4] *Re North Bucks Furniture Ltd* [1939] Ch. 690.
[5] (S.I. 1989 No. 1058), made pursuant to the Local Government Finance Act 1988 and in force from July 21, 1989. The text can be found in *Ryde, op cit.,* Div. J, para. [933].
[6] reg. 20.
[7] reg. 12.
[8] reg. 14.
[9] reg. 18.
[10] Preferential Payments in Bankruptcy Amendment Act 1897.
[11] (1982) Cmnd. 8558, para. 1427.
[12] See also *Ryde on Rating and the Council Tax,* Div. G, Chap. 2, "Insolvency", by Moss and Pascoe.

2. OCCUPIED PROPERTY RATES

20–004 There are four necessary ingredients for rateable occupation[13]:

(a) there must be actual occupation, in the sense of some actual use or enjoyment, however, slight;

(b) the occupation must be exclusive in the sense that a person using it may prevent others using it in the same way;

(c) the occupation must be beneficial in the sense of being of some value or benefit to the occupier; and

(d) the occupation must have some degree of permanence, and not be entirely transient or intermittent.

Rateable occupation is a question of fact, namely whether the required occupation exists, and does not depend upon legal title.[14]

(a) Liability of the receiver pre-liquidation

20–005 After a great deal of uncertainty and confusion in the authorities,[15] the occasion for clarifying English law arose in the case of *Ratford and Hayward v. Northavon RDC.*[16] In that case, receivers and managers were appointed under a debenture which included the usual "deemed agency" clause. The receivers decided to carry on the company's business and by letter they notified the rating authority of this decision. Thereafter they managed the business and from time to time had representatives at the company's premises, which they subsequently caused the company to sell. The justices granted the rating authority a distress warrant against the receivers as rateable occupiers.

20–006 At first instance, Kennedy J. held that the letter to the rating authority was prima facie evidence that the receivers were in rateable occupation, and that the burden was on them to show that there was no change in rateable occupation. He further held that it was open to the justices (even if the burden of proof was on the rating authority to prove a change of rateable occupation) to find that on the above facts the receivers were the rateable occupiers.

20–007 The Court of Appeal reversed his decision. Slade L.J. held that:

(a) a receiver may be in rateable occupation and the deemed agency clause will not necessarily prevent him from being in occupation for rating purposes;

(b) by reason of the provisions of section 97(1) of the General Rate Act 1967, on the application by the rating authority for a distress warrant against the receivers, since the receivers were possible rateable occupiers, the onus of proof at least in the

---

[13] *Ryde, op cit.*, Div. B.

[14] *Per* Lord Herschell in *Assessment Committee v. Halkyn Drainage* [1894] A.C. 177 at 125.

[15] The old cases are dealt with in detail in the first edition of this work.

[16] [1987] Q.B. 357.

first instance was upon the receivers to show that no change of rateable occupation had taken place;

(c) the receivers had prima facie discharged this burden by showing that they had been appointed on terms which, though empowering them to do so, did not oblige them to take possession and provided that, in carrying out their activities, they should be deemed to be the agents of the company;

(d) the onus then shifted to the rating authority to show that the receivers had dispossessed the company or, to put it another way, to show that the quality of any possession of the premises which the receivers might have enjoyed was not that of mere agents;

(e) the facts showing that the receivers managed and controlled the company's business and assets and had a presence at the company's premises were quite consistent with the company remaining in legal possession and rateable occupation; and

(f) accordingly, the rating authority had failed to discharge the onus which had shifted to them and therefore the receivers were not to be held to be the rateable occupiers.

Slade L.J. concluded as follows:

"Save for those cases such as *Richards*,[17] where the terms of the receiver's appointment have effected or required dispossession of the company, I think that no case has been cited to us in which a receiver has ever been held to be in occupation of occupied premises. The reason, I infer, is not far to seek. Any occupation of the relevant premises enjoyed by a receiver will normally be enjoyed by him in his capacity as agent for some other party. Though it is possible for him to take independent possession of the premises as principal, such cases I suspect may be comparatively rare."[18]

(b) Liability of the receiver post-liquidation

Difficult and largely unexplored questions arise as to the identity of the **20–008** person liable for rates where the receiver continues to use the company's premises after liquidation. The general principle is clear that, on liquidation, the receiver's agency for the company determines, as does his right and power to create liabilities on the part of the company. As noted above, a critical factor in the Court of Appeal's reasoning in *Ratford* was that the receiver occupied the property as agent of the company. Once that agency determines on liquidation it might accordingly be thought that the main obstacle in the way of imposing liability on the receiver, who continues beneficial occupation after liquidation, would be removed. This is indeed a powerful argument, and would result in the receiver or (if he so acts as agent for the debenture-holder) the

---

[17] *Richards v. Kidderminster Oversears* [1896] Ch. 212.
[18] [1987] Q.B. at 379E–F.

debenture-holder being held to be rateable occupier rather than the company and accordingly liable for rates. On the other hand, the receiver's position as agent was not identified as the only factor in Ratford: it is in each case necessary to show that the receiver had in fact dispossessed the company. Where nothing in fact has changed (other than the loss of the receiver's deemed agency) upon the liquidation of the company, it might be difficult to conclude that the receiver had in fact dispossessed the company sufficient to constitute him (or the debenture-holder) the rateable occupier. It may be, therefore, that the receiver could foist on the liquidator, as part of the cost of the liquidation, liability for rates for any period prior to realisation.[19]

3. UNOCCUPIED PROPERTY RATES[20]

20–009 Rates may be levied in respect of unoccupied properties. Where this is done, the special feature is that the rate is levied on the "owner" of the property,[21] a term defined as meaning the person entitled to possession.[22]

(a) Liability of the receiver pre-liquidation

20–010 The potential liability upon a receiver in respect of rates, where the company over whose assets he is appointed receiver is the owner of unoccupied property, was considered in detail by Arden J. in *Brown v. City of London*.[23] Receivers, who were appointed by the debenture-holder in November 1993, secured the relevant properties, oversaw repairs required by former tenants, employed various professional advisors in connection with the properties, and agreed to sell the properties. The properties were sold in March 1995 by the debenture-holder pursuant to powers in the debenture. The local authority sought recovery of unoccupied property rates for the period between November 1993 and March 1995, either through imposing personal liability on the receivers, or through a direction of the court that the receivers pay the rates out of the assets of the company.

20–011 Arden J. rejected the local authority's claim. In order to impose personal liability on the receivers, the local authority needed to establish that the receivers were "the owner", that is, the persons entitled to possession of, the property. The Judge held that even as in accordance with *Ratford* the possession of an agent is to be attributed to his principal,[24] so also the entitlement of an agent to possession must likewise be attributed to his principal. Accordingly, since the receivers were appointed on terms that they were agents of the company, the

---

[19] Compare *Re Mesco Properties Ltd* [1980] 1 W.L.R. 96.
[20] See generally *Ryde on Rating and the Council Tax*, Div. B, Chap. 3, and Div. G, Chap. 2.
[21] Local Government Finance Act 1988, s. 45(1)(a).
[22] s. 65(1).
[23] [1999] 1 W.L.R. 1070, also reported *sub nom. Re Sobam* B.V.; [1996] 1 B.C.L.C. 446.
[24] Above, para. 20–005.

receivers were not "entitled to possession" of the property and were accordingly not liable themselves to pay the rates.

The Judge considered that the earlier case of *Banister v. Islington* **20–012** *LBC*, [25] in which the Divisional Court had imposed personal liability in respect of unoccupied property rates on a receiver appointed out of court as agent of the company, was to be regarded, because of its special facts, as an exception to the general principle to be derived from *Ratford*. In the *Banister* case the receiver had originally been in possession of the property for the purpose of managing the business, and had not disputed that as such he had been in rateable occupation. The Divisional Court held that upon voluntarily giving up possession the receiver remained the person entitled to possession.

In view of the *Ratford* decision, it is unlikely that the special facts **20–013** which occurred in *Banister* would occur again: a receiver such as that in the Banister case will almost certainly not be found to have been in rateable occupation on similar facts. In the absence of such a finding it will be the company that will have remained in rateable occupation so that when the company ceases occupation it will be the company and not the receiver that remains entitled to possession.[26] In the event that there is a risk of liability on facts similar to *Banister v. Islington LBC*, it is considered that this liability could be avoided by the debenture-holder's releasing the unoccupied properties from his charge. Another possible solution is for the receiver[27] or debenture-holder to petition for the winding-up of the company, creating a situation which is dealt with below.

In rejecting the local authority's claim in *Brown v. City of London*, **20–014** Arden J. also rejected the following three additional arguments: (i) that the receivers should be directed to pay the rates as an expense of the receivership; (ii) that the receivers were required to pay the rates by reason of the incorporation into the debenture of section 109(8) of the Law of Property Act 1925[28]; and (iii) that the receivers should be directed to pay the rates because otherwise they might incur liability for fraudulent trading.

In rejecting the argument that the receivers should be required to pay **20–015** the rates as an expense of the receivership,[29] Arden J. held that there was no distinction to be drawn between an ongoing liability for rates and an ongoing liability for rent. In *Re Atlantic Computer Systems plc*[30] the Court of Appeal had taken the view that the liability for rent under an existing lease would not be held to be payable as an expense of the receivership.

---

[25] (1972) 71 L.G.R. 239, Div. Ct.

[26] See *Ryde, op cit.*, Div. G, Chap. 2, "Insolvency" by Moss and Pascoe.

[27] See above, Chap. 11.

[28] This sub-section provides for the receiver to apply moneys received by him in discharge of rents, taxes, rates and outgoings whatever affecting the mortgaged property. It was incorporated into the debenture by cl. 14.06(c) thereof: see [1996] 1 B.C.L.C. 446 at 450. See further below, para. 20–019 below.

[29] See [1996] 1 W.L.R. 1070 at 1085–1086.

[30] [1992] Ch. 505 at 524.

20-016   In support of the argument based on section 109(8) of the Law of
Property Act 1925, Counsel for the local authority had relied upon the
Court of Appeal decision in *Sargent v. Customs & Excise Comrs*[31] to the
effect that a receiver, as the holder of a discretion, could not exercise
that discretion against paying VAT collected from tenants to the VAT
authorities. Arden J. distinguished the *Sargent* decision on the grounds
that, whereas it might be said that a tenant paying VAT to the receiver
did so in the expectation that it would be paid on to the VAT
authorities, the receivers in the *Sobam* case had not received any funds
from third parties.[32] Moreover, it was not possible to quantify, even in
approximate terms, the value of the benefit which the companies and the
debenture-holders received from the council in respect of the rates
payable by the companies.[33]

20-017   Finally, the contention that the receivers might be found liable for
fraudulent trading was rejected on the basis that the receivers' decision
to postpone the sale of the properties was done in performance of their
duties to the bank, that the council's claim was an unsecured one to
which only assets of the company not required to pay the bank were
applicable, that the receivers' decision did not deprive the council of any
its rights to have recourse against those assets, and that it did not
prejudice the council.[34]

(b) Liability of the receiver post-liquidation

20-018   The Non-Domestic Rating (Unoccupied Property) Regulations 1989[35]
exclude from liability, in respect of unoccupied property rates, any non-
domestic hereditament where the "owner" is a company in compulsory
or voluntary winding-up.[36] The exemption seems to assume that there is
only one "owner" in such a situation.[37] Following *Brown v. City of
London*,[38] provided that the receiver has acted prior to liquidation only
as agent of the company and has not personally gone into rateable
occupation, and provided that the debenture-holder has not gone into
possession as mortgagee, it is suggested that the "owner" is the former
rateable occupier, the company. If that is correct, then the property is
exempt from unoccupied property rates.[39]

20-019   Since the object of unoccupied property rates appears to be to
encourage the beneficial use of land, and given that the exemption in the
case of liquidation appears to be a recognition that non-use in such a

---

[31] [1995] 1 W.L.R. 821.
[32] See also *In re Grey Marlin Ltd* [2000] 1 W.L.R. 370 at p. 375.
[33] [1996] 1 W.L.R. 1070 at 1084.
[34] [1996] 1 W.L.R. 1070 at 1086–1088.
[35] (S.I. 1989 No. 2261), made pursuant to the Local Government Finance Act 1988.
[36] reg. 2(2)(1).
[37] Local Government Finance Act 1988, s. 50 allows the Secretary of State to make
regulations "to deal with any case where (apart from the regulations) there would be more
than one owner . . . at a particular time". No relevant regulation appears to have been
made in relation to unoccupied properties.
[38] See the discussion above.
[39] This point was expressly left open in the *Brown* case, and in the earlier decision of *Re
Leigh Estates (U.K.) Ltd* [1994] B.C.C. 292.

situation is probably unavoidable, it is a pity that the exemption does not cover receivership and administration orders, where non-use is also likely to be unavoidable.

4. DISTRESS ON GOODS OF THE COMPANY

If a company makes a default in payment of rates, whether before or **20–020** after the commencement of the receivership, the question arises whether its goods are vulnerable to distress. That in turn depends on whether goods subject to a crystallised floating charge are goods of the company within regulation 14 of the Non-Domestic Rating (Collection and Enforcement) (Local Lists) Regulations 1989 and therefore amenable to distress.

It is well established that property subject to a crystallised floating **20–021** charge does not belong to a debtor company. The only difficulty lies in the Court of Appeal decision in the *Marriage, Neave* case.[40]

In *Re Marriage, Neave & Co.*, the right to distrain for rates also **20–022** depended upon whether such goods were "goods of the debtor". Lindley L.J. pointed out that the rates in question "can only be distrained for upon the goods of the person assessed".[41]

The point argued and dealt with in the judgments was whether the **20–023** debenture deed in that case transferred the goods in question to the trustees so as to make them no longer the property of the company. Unfortunately, the terms of the relevant deeds are not fully set out in the report but there appears to have been:

(a) a demise to trustees by a trust deed[42]; and
(b) a debenture with conveyance of property of the company generally, with the express exception of chattels which could be charged without the registration of a bill of sale, the security to constitute a floating charge.[43]

Some further clues to the wording can be gained from the facts relating to the same company and the same documents set out in *Paterson v. Gas Light and Coke Co.*[44] Counsel for the churchwardens and overseers submitted in opening in the *Marriage, Neave* case that:

(a) the goods were "not covered by the debenture trust deed and they therefore belong to the company . . ."[45]
(b) "A debenture charging the goods of the company is merely an equitable charge by way of a floating security, the goods

---

[40] *Re Marriage, Neave & Co.* [1896] 2 Ch. 663, CA.
[41] At 672.
[42] At 664.
[43] At 664.
[44] [1896] 2 Ch. 476 at 476–477.
[45] At 668.

remaining the property of the company subject to that charge."[46]

In reply, they were asked to deal only with the construction of the debenture deed.[47]

20–024　　Counsel for the debenture-holders submitted that:

(a) the goods were not the goods of the company on the grounds that the goods "are assigned to the trustees of the debenture deed"[48]; they also argued that there was no exclusion of the goods from such assignment[49];

(b) "the effect of the debentures themselves is that the goods belong to the debenture-holders subject only to the company's equity of redemption."[50]

There is no record of any argument to the effect that, whilst goods subject to a floating charge remained the goods of the company prior to crystallisation, they ceased to be goods of the company after crystallisation. Nor do the judgments deal with this point.

20–025　Lindley L.J. held that the debenture deed did include the chattels but only had the effect of creating "an equitable charge" on the goods. The goods therefore belonged to the company subject to such a charge.[51]

20–026　　Lopes L.J. agreed and stated that the goods were excepted from the trust deed, could not therefore be said to belong to the debenture-holders and belonged to the company subject to the equitable charge.[52]

20–027　　Rigby L.J. distinguished the judgment of North J. in *Richards v. Overseas of Kidderminster*[53] (where it had been held that distress for rates was not available) on the grounds that in that case "there was an actual assignment of the goods to other persons, and that assignment was relied upon".[54]

20–028　　None of the judgments refers to the fact that the proposed distress would have taken place after the crystallisation of the floating charge resulting from both liquidation and receivership affecting the company.[55] None of the judgments considers the point that such crystallisation resulted in a completed assignment of the chattels in favour of the debenture-holders.[56]

---

[46] At 668.
[47] At 670.
[48] At 669.
[49] At 669–670.
[50] At 670.
[51] At 673.
[52] At 675.
[53] [1896] 2 Ch. 212.
[54] At 678.
[55] At 665.
[56] *George Barker v. Eynon* [1974] 1 W.L.R. 462 at 467, *per* Edmund Davies L.J., citing *Biggerstaff v. Rowatt's Wharf Ltd* [1896] 2 Ch. 93; *N. W. Robbie & Co. Ltd v. Witney Warehouse Ltd* [1963] 1 W.L.R. 1324. Both Lindley and Lopes L.JJ. gave judgments both in Marriage, Neave (28, July 30, 1896) and the *Biggerstaff* (April 14, 15, 1896) cases. In the

Accordingly, what *Marriage, Neave* actually deals with and decides in **20–029** terms of arguments put forward and considered is that the creation of a floating charge over assets of a company does not make them cease to be the goods of the company for the purposes of distress for rates. The facts themselves deal with a post-crystallisation situation, but such a situation and its legal effects are not considered.

In *Re Roundwood Colliery*[57] the Court of Appeal held, in the context **20–030** of a contractual right to distrain (given to a landlord) in respect of goods belonging to the company but off the demised premises, that goods over which a floating charge had not crystallised when distress was put in still belonged to the company and were available for distraint. This was not affected by crystallisation taking place after distress was put in but before it was enforced. On the other hand, it seems clear from *Re Roundwood Colliery* that, had crystallisation occurred prior to distress being put in, "as between the landlord and the debenture-holders, these goods had become the property of the latter before the landlord seized them".[58] It is not absolutely clear why the crystallisation point had not occurred to Lindley L.J. when in the previous year he gave his judgment in *Marriage, Neave*. The explanation may be that the arguments of counsel in *Re Roundwood Colliery* in the Court of Appeal in 1897 (although not at first instance in 1896) appear to have referred to the significance of crystallisation on the appointment of a receiver.[59] The arguments also refer to *Marriage, Neave*, but the case is not picked up in the judgments. The different approaches to crystallisation in the two cases may therefore simply be the result of the point being argued in *Re Roundwood Colliery* but not in *Marriage, Neave*.[60]

In coming to their conclusion in *Marriage, Neave* two members of the **20–031** Court of Appeal were influenced by the consideration that distress was the only remedy for recovering rates, since the bringing of an action to recover rates was then impossible.[61] Rates can now be recovered by action.[62]

At a time when rates could not be sued for but when they were still **20–032** preferential, and it was thought that a local authority had a prima facie right to distrain for rates despite the crystallisation of a floating charge

Biggerstaff case, it was held that a debtor of the company in receivership could set off a cross-claim despite notice of a floating charge covering the debt due to the company. Lindley L.J. and Lopes L.J. based their decisions on the fact that the company could carry on its business as if the debenture did not exist (at 101 and 103). Only Kay L.J. pointed out that the assignment created by the floating charge did not become complete until the receiver was appointed. *Biggerstaff* was not cited in *Marriage, Neave*.

[57] [1897] 1 Ch. 373.
[58] *Per* Lindley L.J. at 393.
[59] See at 387–388.
[60] The approach in *Re Roundwood Colliery* has been followed in New Zealand in *Metropolitan Life v. Essere Print Ltd* (1990) N.Z.C.L.C. 66,775 at 66,779, *per* Jeffries J., a case concerning a New Zealand statute dealing with distress for rent. *Marriage, Neave* was not cited. Jeffries J's decision was affirmed by the New Zealand Court of Appeal ([1991] 3 N.Z.L.R. 170) without *Re Roundwood Colliery* being mentioned in the judgments.
[61] *Per* Lindley L.J. at 674; *per* Lopes L.J. at 676.
[62] Non-Domestic Rating (Collection and Enforcement) (Local Lists) Regulation 1989 (S.I. 1989 No. 1058), reg. 20.

over the relevant goods, the receiver was able to obtain an injunction to prevent distress on the basis that rates were preferential and that any such distress might give the local authority an unfair preference over the other preferential creditors.[63] As a result of their preferential status, local authorities in practice tended to agree to rely on their preferential status and did not attempt to distrain in respect of pre-receivership liabilities for rates.[64] There was therefore no need to apply for an injunction to restrain distress. Under the Insolvency Act 1986, rates are no longer preferential,[65] so that it is not clear whether, if distress were in principle to be available, a receiver could any longer apply to restrain distress. It certainly seems arguable that a receiver should be able to protect the preferential creditors to whom he owes statutory duties from loss of priority to a claim for rates, which the legislature has demoted to having an unsecured non-preferential status.[66] Even if the local authority were to be held to have priority over the debenture-holder, the legislature appears to have demoted the local authority below the remaining preferential creditors, who should therefore in principle have priority over rates.

20–033   The authorities and arguments referred to above were considered by Ferris J. in *Re ELS Ltd, Ramsbottom and Another v. Luton Borough Council and Another*.[67] He held that: (a) the *Marriage, Neave* decision applied ". . . only to a mere charge which does not operate by way of assignment and which . . . confers no power, without the assistance of the court, to appoint a receiver, take possession or sell"; (b) if *Marriage, Neave* could not be confined in this way, the later Court of Appeal decisions in *Biggerstaff v. Rowatt's Wharf*,[68] *Re Roundwood Colliery*[69] and *Robbie v. Witney Warehouse*[70] were inconsistent with it and he was entitled to follow them in preference to *Marriage, Neave*. He therefore held that the local authorities in that case could not distrain in respect of assets over which a floating charge had crystallised by means of the appointment of receivers. The alternative argument based on the priority rights of preferential creditors[71] was left open.

20–034   The right of distress (were it applicable) could only be exercised in respect of the goods of the company on the rated property. Once the receiver has sold the goods, any right to distrain would be lost and there is no right to the proceeds.[72] If tenants of the company's property pay

---

[63] *Taggs Island Casino v. Richmond BC* [1967] R.A. 70. Failure to give effect to preferential creditors' rights gave rise to a cause of action against the receiver: *Westminster City Council v. Treby* [1936] 2 All E.R. 21; *Woods v. Winskill* [1913] 2 Ch. 303; *Westminster v. Haste* [1950] Ch. 442.

[64] Samwell, *Corporate Receiverships* (2nd ed., 1988), p. 81.

[65] Insolvency Act 1986, s. 175 and Sched. 6.

[66] See *Ryde on Rating and the Council Tax*, Div. G, Chap. 2, "Insolvency" by Moss and Pascoe, para. 272.

[67] [1995] Ch. 11.

[68] [1896] 2 Ch. 93 (in fact a slightly earlier case: see above, n. 45).

[69] [1897] 1 Ch. 373.

[70] [1963] 1 W.L.R. 1324.

[71] See above.

[72] *Re British Fullers Earth Co. Ltd* (1901) 17 T.L.R. 232.

the receiver rents inclusive of rates, the amount of the rates so paid is not recoverable by the rating authority from the receiver.[73]

5. PAYMENT OUT OF ASSETS

Section 109(8) of the Law of Property Act 1925, which is frequently **20–035** incorporated into or repeated in debentures with certain extensions and modifications, provides, *inter alia*, for the payment of rates out of moneys received by the receiver.[74] However, this does not give the local authority any right to enforce payment.[75] Where section 109(8) itself applies, the rationale appears to be that the local authority is not one of the class for whose benefit the statutory duty was created.

Where the provisions merely apply as a matter of contract, the local **20–036** authority has no contractual relationship with the receiver, or for that matter with the debenture-holder or the company. In relation to contracts entered into after May 11, 2000, the question arises whether the terms of the contract provide the local authority with a remedy pursuant to the Contracts (Rights of Third Parties) Act 1999. The answer is probably in the negative for it is to be inferred that there is no intention to confer a benefit on the local authority. No doubt in many or even most cases the application of the Act will be excluded by the express terms of the debenture.

The receiver may, however, be liable to the company as mortgagor if **20–037** the company suffers loss from a failure to pay rates.[76]

6. EXCLUSION FROM POSSESSION

Where a company in receivership is the subject of a "sit-in" or "work-in" **20–038** by the workforce, the company may cease to be the rateable occupier and there may come a point where the workforce becomes such instead. In *Re Briant Colour Printing Co. Ltd*,[77] a voluntary liquidator dismissed all the employees, who promptly occupied the company's factory as part of a "work-in", excluding the liquidator. Although the company (acting by the liquidator) took possession proceedings and obtained an appropriate order, it never became necessary to enforce it because a purchaser

---

[73] *Re Mayfair and General Property Trust Ltd* [1945] 2 All E.R. 523.; *Liverpool Corporation v. Hope* [1938] 1 K.B. 751.

[74] See also above, para. 20–014.

[75] *Liverpool Corporation v. Hope* [1938] 1 K.B. 751, CA: see also *Re John Wilment (Ashford) Ltd* [1980] 1 W.L.R. 73 and below, Chap. 21.

[76] *Visbord v. Federal Taxation Commissioner* (1943) 68 C.L.R. 354 at 385–386. See also *Re Kentish Homes Ltd* [1993] B.C.C. 212. In *Re Toshoku Finance UK plc* [2000] 1 B.C.L.C. 683, the Court of Appeal overruled *Re Kentish Homes Ltd* to hold that, if the liquidator has sufficient assets and no question of priority between post-liquidation debts arises, the liquidator *must* pay a tax liability imposed on the company in liquidation. See further above, Chap. 13. Where a liquidator does so, there is likely to be a corresponding increase in the risk of the liquidator making a claim over against the receiver, in reliance on s. 109(8).

[77] [1977] 1 W.L.R. 942.

was found who was acceptable to the workforce. The local authority sought a declaration that the rates during the relevant period should be paid as an expense of the winding-up. The Court of Appeal upheld Slade J.'s judgment that the company was not in rateable occupation whilst the liquidator was excluded and expressed the view that, if the company was not in rateable occupation, the workforce was. In this context, it should be remembered that a person can be in rateable occupation without the consent of the owner of the property.[78]

---

[78] *Assessment Committee of Holywell Union v. Halkyn Drainage Co.* [1894] A.C. 117 at 125, *per* Lord Herschell.

CHAPTER 21

REMOVAL, RESIGNATION, TERMINATION AND DISCHARGE

1. REMOVAL

(a) Removal by debenture-holder

A receiver appointed by a debenture-holder (other than an administra- **21–001** tive receiver) can be removed by his appointor unless there is a stipulation to the contrary in the debenture or in his appointment. Notice of removal is only effective on receipt by the receiver.[1]

An administrative receiver can only be removed by a Court Order **21–002** made under section 45 of the Insolvency Act 1986. This reflects the enhanced status of qualified administrative receivers[2] and is designed to prevent attempts to interfere with their performance of their statutory duties.[3]

(b) Removal by the court

The Insolvency Act 1986 gives no guidance to a court acting on an **21–003** application for removal of an administrative receiver under section 45. It is, however, likely that the court would apply the same case-law principles that continue to be applicable to the removal of other receivers under the court's inherent jurisdiction. These principles indicate that the application to remove a receiver may be made by a person with a sufficient interest to make it.[4] This includes the company, another debenture-holder, the receiver himself[5] or his appointor.[6] An application can also be made by a partner in the receiver's firm, where that firm has day-to-day conduct of the receivership.[7] The applicant must show sufficient cause for removal. The court will not lightly intervene.[8]

---

[1] *Windsor Refrigerator Co. Ltd v. Branch Nominees Ltd* [1961] Ch. 375 at 398, *per* Donovan L.J. For general information on the question of removal, see S. A. Frieze, "Removing An Office Holder"; Insolvency Intelligence, Vol. 10, Issue 6, p. 43, June 1997.

[2] See above, Chap. 5.

[3] For such an attempt, see *IRC v. Goldblatt* [1972] Ch. 498 where the particular strategem proved unsuccessful.

[4] See *Deloitte & Touche A.G. v. Johnson* [1999] 1 W.L.R. 1605, PC for principles governing the removal of liquidators under Cayman law, s. 106 of the Companies Law (1995 rev.). The Privy Council held that as well as standing in a technical sense, an applicant normally needed to have a real interest in the matter. Thus, where removal was sought on the basis of a conflict of interest, a creditor may well have a real interest, but a potential debtor will not. A creditor for a very small sum who will not be materially affected may have technical standing but no real interest: see *Walker Morris v. Khalastchi* (unreported, July 17, 2000, Nicholas Strauss Q.C. sitting as a Deputy High Court Judge).

[5] An application by an administrative receiver is rarely likely to be justified in view of the statutory right to resign: see *infra*.

[6] *Strong v. Carlyle Press* [1893] 1 Ch. 268, CA.

[7] *Re A & C Supplies Ltd* [1998] 1 B.C.L.C. 603; [1998] B.C.C. 708.

[8] *Re Neon Signs (Australasia) Ltd* [1965] V.R. 125.

21–004 In the ordinary case, the debenture-holder will be left to appoint a replacement,[8a] but in an appropriate case the court may be persuaded to replace the administrative receiver with a receiver appointed by the court.[9] Where an administrative receiver is removed by the court, he must comply with the notice requirements under the Insolvency Act 1986 and the Companies Act 1985.

(c) Displacement

21–005 Where a receiver is appointed in respect of a second or subsequent charge, this does not prevent prior chargees from making their own appointments. For the sake of convenience the prior chargee might appoint the same person. If he appoints someone else, that receiver will take precedence. Where the displaced receiver under the second or subsequent charge has been appointed by the court, a receiver appointed by the prior chargee will need to seek the leave of the court to get possession of the charged assets, unless the order making the appointment states that the order is made "without prejudice to the rights of prior encumbrancers".[10]

(d) Ceasing to be qualified

21–006 An administrative receiver automatically vacates office if he ceases to be qualified to act as an insolvency practitioner in relation to the company in question.[11] Under rule 3.35 of the Insolvency Rules 1986, the receiver must give the same notices as if he had resigned and rule 3.33 were relevant.

(e) The making of an administration order

21–007 An administrative receiver must also vacate office where an administration order is made.[12] The administrative receiver is not obliged to give notice to the company.[13] An administrative receiver who vacates office on an administrator being appointed is relieved of any duty which he might have to pay preferential creditors.[14]

(f) Death

21–008 When an administrative receiver dies, his appointor must give notice to the Registrar of Companies, to the company (or any liquidator of the company) and to any creditors' committee. This notice must be given as soon as the appointor becomes aware of the death of the administrative receiver.[15]

[8a] The court has not power to appoint a replacement administrative receivers: see *Re A & C Supplies* [1998] 1 B.C.L.C. 603 at 609f.

[9] See below, Chap. 22.

[10] *Re Metropolitan Amalgamated Estates* [1912] 2 Ch. 497; *Underhay v. Read* (1887) 20 Q.B.D. 209. See below, Chap. 22.

[11] Insolvency Act 1986, s. 45(2).

[12] *ibid.*, s. 11(1)(b).

[13] *ibid.*, r.3.35 as amended by the Insolvency (Amendment) Rules 1987 (S.I. 1987 No. 1919), Sched., para 33.

[14] Insolvency Act, s. 11(5). It is unclear whether any distributions already made to preferential creditors on account will stand. It would seem likely that they will stand, although there is no authority on this point.

[15] Insolvency Rules 1986, r. 3.34.

2. RESIGNATION

Non-administrative receivers are unable to resign unless this is specifi- **21–009** cally provided for in the debenture, in the appointment, or unless the debenture-holder consents. Administrative receivers are permitted to resign "by giving notice . . . in the prescribed manner to such persons as may be prescribed" by rules made pursuant to section 45(1) of the Insolvency Act 1986. The relevant rule is rule 3.33 of the Insolvency Rules 1986. Where he resigns, the administrative receiver must give at least seven days' notice to his appointor, the company, and any creditors' committee. Where the company is in liquidation, the notice should be given to the liquidator. The notice must state the date on which the resignation is to take effect. Notice must also be given to the Registrar of Companies.

It is difficult to see why the position of all receivers was not equated by **21–010** the Insolvency Act. The position of non-administrative receivers remains a peculiar one. Whilst unable to resign, they are unlikely to be compelled by a court to carry out any duties involving personal discretion or judgment, for this would be analogous to ordering specific performance of a contract for personal services.[16] The court is likely, despite any objection by the appointor, on application by the receiver to order his removal (if appropriate) on terms that the receiver meets out of his own pocket any additional costs and expenses and any losses occasioned to the appointor. In any ordinary case, such compensation should be an adequate remedy for the appointor. The court may order the receiver to comply with statutory provisions requiring the filing of documents or similar non-discretionary tasks, exercising a jurisdiction in this respect analogous to that exercised over liquidators.

3. INDEMNITY AND CHARGES

When removed from office, a non-administrative receiver can retain sums **21–011** payable to preferential creditors for the purpose of discharging his personal liability to pay such preferential creditors.[17] Since those sums are payable out of assets coming into his hands[18] it seems to follow that a non-administrative receiver who vacates his position is entitled to retain and realise assets subject to a floating charge in order to pay preferential creditors. In the usual case where a non-administrative receiver is made agent of the company in respect of the period until any liquidation, he can claim an implied right of indemnity against the assets in receivership for his costs, expenses, remuneration and all sums for which he is personally liable.[19] There is also a specific statutory indemnity out of the assets where he becomes personally liable on a post-receivership contract made by him.[20]

---

[16] See *Hill v. Parsons* [1972] 1 Ch. 305.
[17] *IRC v. Goldblatt* [1972] Ch. 498.
[18] Insolvency Act 1986, s. 40.
[19] See *Hill v. Venning* [1979] 4 A.C.L.R. 555.
[20] Insolvency Act 1986, s. 37(1).

21–012   Under the Insolvency Act 1986, all administrative receivers (in respect of the period prior to any liquidation) are deemed to be agents of the company and have a specific statutory indemnity with regard to personal liability incurred upon post receivership contracts and any contract of employment they have "adopted".[21] As agents they also have an implied right of indemnity out of the assets in respect of their costs, expenses, remuneration and any other sums for which they are personally liable, such as an undertaking to pay any sums due to a retention of title claimant.[22] Neither indemnity extends to losses or liabilities incurred in consequence of his own negligence or default.[23]

21–013   The 1986 Act further provides that where at any time an administrative receiver, receiver or manager vacates office:

(a) his remuneration and any expenses properly incurred by him, and

(b) any indemnity to which he is entitled out of the assets of the company,

shall be charged on and paid out of any property of the company which is in his custody or under his control at that time in priority to any security held by the person by or on whose behalf he was appointed.[24]

21–014   The practical problem no doubt sought to be resolved by the creation of a charge is that a receiver's lien for his remuneration, etc. is ordinarily lost if the receiver hands over moneys or other assets in his hands immediately upon vacating office. The new provision appears to provide a secured right of payment out of the assets in respect of remuneration, expenses and rights of indemnity without any need to retain the assets to ensure payment. In practice, it is questionable whether the charge created by this provision will ever persuade a receiver who vacates office to part with assets over which he has a lien in situations where he would not already have been willing to hand them over in return for an appropriate undertaking. The reason is that the charge created by this provision would seem to be unprotected as against bona fide purchasers without notice of the charged assets.

4. DUTY TO CEASE ACTING

21–015 Once a receiver has in his hands sufficient moneys to discharge all the debts of the company which he is bound to discharge, all possible claims

---

[21] Insolvency Act 1986, s. 44(1)(b). On the meaning of "adoption" in relation to s. 44(1)(b), see above, Chap. 19.

[22] *Lipe Ltd v. Leyland Daf* [1993] B.C.C. 385, CA. Retention of title claims generally are dealt with above in Chap. 12.

[23] *R.A. Price v. Henderson* [1989] N.Z.L.R. 257 at 262, NZCA.

[24] Insolvency Act 1986, ss. 45(3) (administrative receivers) and s. 37(4) (other receivers and managers). *Cf.* the parallel provisions for administrators in s. 19 and the case-law thereon: *Re Sheridan Securities Ltd* (1988) 4 B.C.C. 200; *Powdrill v. Watson* [1995] 2 A.C. 394, HL and see below, Chap. 23.

which could be made against him and in respect of which he is entitled to an indemnity, his own remuneration, and all moneys secured by the charges under which he was appointed, it will be his duty to cease acting,[25] in the absence of any provision to the contrary in the charge under which he has been appointed. Receivers who pay off their debenture-holders, thereby ceasing to be receivers, who do not reserve further funds for costs cannot continue to act as receivers in order to raise further funds to pay themselves.[26] The duty to cease acting does not come into force so long as there remains a contingent liability secured by the debenture.[27]

Whilst the duty can easily be stated in principle, it can cause great **21–016** difficulty in practice. This is particularly so where the company is not in liquidation and yet is insolvent. The dilemma in such cases has been illustrated by a receiver recalling[28] the detailed background of the case of *Re G.L. Saunders Ltd*[29] In that case the receiver was appointed over fixed and floating charge assets. There was a large claim by preferential creditors in the receivership, far larger than the extent of the floating charge realisations available to them. Within a few months enough had been realised from fixed charge realisations to repay the debenture-holder, but the company was not yet in liquidation. By this time ". . . the receivership had reached a stage where the receiver could have concluded his work and handed the assets back to the company". The receiver does not explain whether by this stage he had also realised all the floating charge assets, as appears to be required by what is now section 40 of the Insolvency Act 1986.[30] The receiver appeared to regard the existence of the duty to make such realisations as being in doubt. In the event, the receiver balked at the prospect of handing the insolvent company's assets to the directors and adopted the "common practice" of leaving a small amount of the debenture-holder's debt unpaid. The receiver preferred this as "the correct moral and ethical approach". Whilst that may well be so, this approach cannot absolve a receiver of his legal duty to terminate the receivership and hand the assets back to the company, whether or not there is a liquidator.

---

[25] *Rottenberg v. Monjack* [1992] B.C.C. 688; Kerr, *The Law and Practice as to Receivers* (17th ed.), p. 437. Kerr suggests that the receiver's duty is to cease acting "forthwith", but presumably this means "with all due expedition", and not literally forthwith. The receiver will have tasks to perform, *e.g.* making distributions and closing bank accounts before he can be expected to file notice of ceasing to act. See also in relation to the duty to accept redemption, *Downsview v. First City Corp* [1993] A.C. 295, PC discussed in Chap. 7 above.

[26] *Rottenberg v. Monjack* [1992] B.C.C. 688.

[27] See *Re Rudd & Son Ltd* (1986) 2 B.C.C. 98, 955, CA and *cf. Banner Lane Realisations Ltd v. Berisford* [1997] 1 B.C.L.C. 380, CA where future debts secured by a debenture included contingent debts. In accordance with the same principle, a guarantor who pays a sum demanded by the secured creditor as being payable at the date of demand has no right to subrogation to the security if the creditor or the receiver incurs further liabilities secured by the charge between the dates of demand and payment: *Austin v. Royal* (1998–1999) 47 N.S.W.L.R. 27, New South Wales Court of Appeal.

[28] "Fixed Charge Surplus. The Argument is Over" by Hatton and Cooke in [1985] 1 Insolvency Law and Practice 137.

[29] [1986] 1 W.L.R. 215.

[30] Then the Companies Act 1948, s. 94 and subsequently s. 196 of the Companies Act 1985.

21–017   One possible answer to the dilemma for an administrative receiver may lie in the express power to present a winding-up petition conferred on him by the Insolvency Act 1986[31] in the absence of any provision to the contrary in the debenture. The objection might be raised that the administrative receiver has no *locus standi* to present such a petition where it is not necessary to protect the assets subject to the debenture-holder's charge.[32] Where the company is clearly insolvent and no voluntary arrangement with creditors is in force, it is suggested that the court may accept that it is proper for an administrative receiver to look to the interest of the general body of unsecured creditors. This is particularly so when it is considered that an administrative receiver shares with liquidators and administrators the special status of "office holder".[33]

21–018   The receiver cannot put the company into voluntary liquidation, as he has no power to convene a meeting of the company in order to pass a winding-up resolution.[34]

21–019   Where the receiver remains in office when the company is placed in liquidation, he may wish to postpone the dissolution of the company when liquidation has been concluded. If he has sufficient reason for delaying dissolution, he can make an application to the court to defer dissolution.[35]

21–020   Where the administrative receiver vacates office at the end of his receivership, he must give notice to any liquidator who has been appointed, as well as to members of any creditors' committee in the receivership.[36] All receivers must give notice to the Registrar of Companies of ceasing to act, and that fact is to be noted on the Register of Charges.[37] Section 45(4) of the Insolvency Act 1986 imposes an additional requirement on an administrative receiver to give notice to the Registrar of Companies. This can be done by endorsement on the notice given under the Companies Act 1985.[38]

5. DISTRIBUTION OF REALISATIONS

21–021 The specific provisions of each charge or debenture must be considered, but generally the debenture will adopt, often with modifications, the scheme of sections 109(8) and 109(6) of the Law of Property Act 1925. The order of payment set out below is one which reflects common

---

[31] s. 42 and para. 21 of Sched. 1: see above, para. 2–017.
[32] Prior to the Insolvency Act 1985, in order to petition, a receiver needed to show some benefit to the charged assets: see *Re Emmadart* [1979] Ch. 540.
[33] See above, Chap. 5.
[34] *Valorem Ltd v. Rilett* (Unreported, December 2, 1999) (HH Judge Boggis Q.C.).
[35] Under the Insolvency Act 1986, s. 201 (voluntary liquidation) or s. 205 (compulsory liquidation).
[36] Insolvency Rules, r.3.35(1).
[37] Companies Act 1985, s. 405(2).
[38] Insolvency Rules, r.3.35(2).

provisions in debentures. The receiver owes a duty both to the company[39] and to the debenture-holder[40] to make payments in the order stipulated, and the company and debenture-holder may at any time agree to a variation in the order,[41] but no duty is owed to third parties to make payment to them in accordance with stipulated or varied order for payment.[42]

(a) Fixed charge realisations[43]

(i) Costs of realisation

Were the Law of Property Act 1925, s. 109(8) to be followed unvaried in **21–022** the charge or debenture, the receiver's costs charges and expenses would be subsumed, together with his remuneration, under the lower heading of receiver's "commission". However, it is commonly provided that the receiver should have his costs, charges and expenses separately.[44] It is obviously beneficial for the debenture-holder and receiver alike to provide that this sum should be paid as a first charge on realisations.

In the case of a winding-up, a creditor can in some circumstances **21–023** apply to the court for an order for the payment of a sum as part of the "costs of the winding up". A notable example occurs in the case of an application by a landlord for the payment of rent as part of the costs of the winding-up where the liquidator has retained possession of leased premises for the benefit of the winding-up.[45] However, the concept "costs of the receivership" cannot be used by a creditor to found any analogous application in the case of a receiver appointed out of court.[46]

The receiver may discharge or agree with a creditor to discharge as **21–024** part of the costs of the receivership, a debt and liability of the company incurred prior to (as well as after) the commencement of the receivership if its discharge is required in the interests of the receivership, *e.g.* in order to preserve valuable goodwill and secure continued supplies.[47] But the receiver cannot properly discharge any such liability and afford the

---

[39] *Yourell v. Hibernian Bank Ltd* [1918] A.C. 372, at 387; *Visbord v. FCT* (1943) 68 C.L.R. 354; *Re Kentish Homes Ltd* [1993] B.C.C. 212 at 219G–221E (overruled on other grounds in *Re Toshoku Finance UK plc* [2000] 1 B.C.L.C. 683, CA).

[40] *Leicester Permanent Building Society v. Butt* [1943] Ch. 308.

[41] *Yourell v. Hibernian Bank Ltd* [1918] A.C. 372.

[42] *Leicester Permanent Building Society v. Butt* [1943] Ch. 308; *Yourell v. Hibernian Bank Ltd* [1918] A.C. 372; *Liverpool Corporation v. Hope* [1938] 1 K.B. 751 (no duty to rating authority to pay rates); and see the VAT cases dealt with in Chap. 13 above.

[43] This heading deals with assets caught by a charge which was always a fixed charge and not with assets subject to a crystallised floating charge: those assets are dealt with under the heading of "floating charge realisations".

[44] See *Marshall v. Cottingham* [1982] Ch. 82.

[45] *e.g. Re ABC Coupler Engineering (No. 3)* [1970] 1 W.L.R. 702. There is a discussion of cases and the underlying principles in *Re Atlantic Computer Systems plc* [1992] Ch. 505, CA, a case concerning administration orders.

[46] *Nicoll v. Cutts* [1985] B.C.L.C. 322, CA; *Re Atlantic Computer Systems Plc* [1992] Ch. 505, CA. The actual decision in *Nicoll v. Cutts* relating to employment contracts (as opposed to the general receivership principle) was in part reversed by statute: see the detailed discussion in Chap. 19 above.

[47] *Nicoll v. Cutts* [1985] B.C.L.C. 322 at 326, CA; *Leyland Daf Ltd v. Automotive Products plc* [1993] B.C.C. 385.

creditor such a preference over all other creditors (secured and unsecured) unless this course is commercially justified. A "moral" claim to such priority does not afford a basis of itself to such payment, though the receiver may take into account the consequence to the receivership of a failure to satisfy such a claim.[48]

(ii) ". . . all rents, taxes, rates and outgoings whatever affecting the mortgaged property"[49]

21–025 The receiver has a discretion as between himself and the debenture-holder,[50] but generally speaking is under no obligation[51] to creditors, to make these payments or to agree with a creditor to do so. Obviously the receiver will wish to make payments where he has incurred personal liability.[52] He will also wish to make payments where the only liability is that of the company alone, but where the creditor will otherwise withhold services or supplies or where otherwise there will be jeopardy to the company's goodwill required for the continuation of the company's business or its beneficial realisation.[53] Three limitations on the free exercise of this discretion do exist:

> (a) Circumstances may arise where the receiver can only properly exercise his discretion in favour of payment. In *Re John Willment (Ashford) Ltd* [54] the receiver had caused the company to trade and receive VAT payments in respect of supplies subject to VAT. The question put to Brightman J. was whether the receiver could use the sums of VAT received by the company to repay the debenture-holder, despite the company's obligation to pay a like sum of VAT to the Customs and Excise. Brightman J. took a dim view of this suggestion. He held that causing the company not to pay would constitute causing the company to commit a criminal offence, and in the circumstances the discretion could only properly be exercised in favour of making the payment.[55]

---

[48] A fiduciary cannot be charitable or satisfy merely moral claims at the expense of the beneficiaries unless either duly authorised or such action is justified in the interests of the beneficiaries. *Cf. Buttle v. Saunders* [1950] 2 All E.R. 193.

[49] Law of Property Act 1925, s. 109(8)(i). It is thought that there may be a considerable overlap between (a) and (b).

[50] *Re John Willment (Ashford) Ltd* [1980] 1 W.L.R. 73 at 77 and see above, Chap. 13.

[51] *Liverpool Corporation v. Hope* [1938] 1 K.B. 751. Creditors who have no right themselves to compel payment cannot achieve their goal indirectly via a liquidator's right to enforce payment on behalf of the company as mortgagor: *Re Kentish Homes Ltd* [1993] B.C.C. 212 at 221F–222B. Overruled on other grounds in *Re Toshoku Finance UK plc*, [2000] 1 B.C.L.C. 683, CA.

[52] See above, Chap. 8. In such a case, the creditor of the receiver is entitled by way of subrogation to the receiver's right of indemnity out of the receivership assets: *Re British Power Traction Ltd* [1910] 2 Ch. 470.

[53] For statutory restrictions on the withholding of supplies see above, Chap. 5 and above, Chap. 8. For a recent case on withholding supplies by a receiver see *Re Transtec Automotive (Campsie) Ltd* (unreported, Jacob J., March 31, 2000).

[54] [1980] 1 W.L.R. 73: and [1980] 1 W.L.R. 73: and see also *Sargent v. Commissioners of Customs and Excise* [1995] 1 W.L.R. 821; *Re Grey Marlin Ltd* [2000] 1 W.L.R. 370.

[55] A non-payment of VAT is no longer a criminal offence and the current position in relation to VAT is discussed in detail in Chap. 13 above.

The Willment case was distinguished by Vinelott J. in *Re Liverpool Commercial Vehicles Ltd*,[56] where VAT had been received in the form of a credit arising out of the repossession of goods by a supplier and no actual moneys had been paid to the receivers. The receivers were not obliged to pay to the Customs and Excise a sum equal to that credited.

(b) Since any payment operates to "prefer" the payee to the debenture-holder, subsequent chargees and other creditors, the receiver must first satisfy himself that the making of the payment is in the interest of the receivership and not merely that the making of the payment is just.

(c) The receiver must consider whether non-payment of the sums authorised to be paid under this heading might cause loss to the company as mortgagor or the debenture-holder. For the company or debenture-holder may be able to claim that the receiver owes them a duty to make payment[57] and may be able to claim damages from the receiver, if non-payment leads to loss. Unless there is a surplus for the mortgagor, it is unlikely that it would be able to show any loss.[58] In the case of the debenture-holder, non-payment is usually to his benefit. There is also a theoretical possibility of the mortgagor obtaining an injunction to compel payment, but it is difficult to see in what circumstances it would be right to grant such an injunction[59]

(iii) The receiver's remuneration included in the heading of the "commission" under the Law of Property Act 1925, s. 109(8)(iii) or an equivalent provision in the debenture

Under the Law of Property Act 1925, s. 109(6) unless varied, the **21–026** receiver's "commission" includes the receiver's remuneration, costs, charges and expenses. The amount actually payable is that specified in the receiver's appointment up to a rate of five per cent of all money received but if none is specified, the maximum rate of five per cent prevails. Frequently the debenture varies section 109 by providing that the remuneration is to be such reasonable remuneration as is agreed between the receiver and debenture-holder.[60] This type of clause gives more flexibility, since it is often difficult to predict how much work the receivership will require. Whilst the five per cent rate may be reasonable in the case of receivers of income, for whom section 109(6) was originally meant, it can produce odd results in the case of receipt of realisations. While there may be an easy realisation of several million

---

[56] [1984] B.C.L.C. 587 at 592. For the detailed facts see para. 21–043 below.

[57] *Visbord v. F.C.T.* [1943] 68 C.L.R. 354.

[58] See, *e.g. Re Kentish Homes Ltd* [1993] B.C.C. 212 at 221C (overruled on other grounds in *Toshoku Finance, The Times*, March 29, 2000). Unless and until there is such a surplus, it may also be the case, depending on the terms of the debenture, that the right to receive damages is charged to the debenture holder.

[59] See *Re John Willment (Ashford) Ltd* [1980] 1 W.L.R. 73.

[60] If the debenture does not expressly limit the remuneration that can be agreed to a reasonable sum, such a limitation, it is suggested, can readily be implied.

pounds, it may require lengthy and difficult legal proceedings to make a relatively small recovery. It might be fairer to provide for the easy, lucrative work to be charged on a time basis and the difficult unrewarding work to be charged on the Official Receiver's scale in liquidations. A proper alternative in a very substantial case would be to agree a time basis throughout. Such variations can be found in practice.

21–027   Whatever basis underlies the remuneration which is claimed, receivers appointed by the court should bear in mind their duties as fiduciaries to justify the fees which they incur in protecting, getting in and realising the assets of the estate.[61]

(iv) Interest due to the debenture-holder under the Law of Property Act 1925, s. 109(8)(iv) or a similar provision in the debenture

21–028   This is a straight-forward head of payment.

(v) The capital due to the debenture-holder under the Law of Property Act 1925, s. 109(8)(v) or a similar provision in the debenture

21–029   Again, this is a straight-forward calculation.

(vi) Residue

21–030   Any "residue" goes to the company, being the person "who is otherwise entitled to the mortgaged property" under the proviso to the Law of Property Act 1925, s. 109(8) or a similar provision in the debenture, assuming that there are no subsequent chargees. It makes no difference from a legal point of view whether the company is in liquidation or not.

Sometimes it will be clear at a relatively early stage in the receivership that there will be funds available after paying the charge-holder in full. In such a case, the administrative receiver and the charge-holder may be prepared to transfer surplus funds to the liquidator, or to release certain assets from the charge in order for the liquidator to be able to deal with those assets. Liquidators are often asked to undertake to return funds or assets to the administrative receiver if the receiver is subsequently notified of preferential claims or claims against him as receiver, of which he was not previously aware. Such an undertaking is usually limited to the funds or assets transferred to the liquidator by the administrative receiver which remain in the hands of the liquidator. A liquidator may, in these circumstances, be prepared to agree to give the administrative receiver prior notice of any proposed distribution to creditors. Undertakings of this type should only be sought and given where the administrative receiver has not yet discharged all his own obligations. Where he has done so, he has a duty to vacate office. It would therefore not be appropriate for him to seek an indemnity or undertaking from the liquidator before transferring any surplus assets or funds to him.

---

[61] See *Mirror Group Newspapers plc v. Maxwell* [1998] B.C.C. 324; [1998] 1 B.C.L.C. 638 (Ferris J.); [1999] B.C.C. 684 (Chief Taxing Master Hurst). See also article by Mr Justice Lightman, "Officeholders Charges — Cost Control and Transparency" in (1998) 11 *Insolvency Intelligence* 1.

Where a receiver is appointed under fixed and floating charges and **21–031**
the debenture-holder has been paid in full, there will be a surplus of
fixed charge realisations. On the other hand, preferential creditors may
remain unsatisfied, *e.g.* if there is a deficiency of floating charge assets to
satisfy their claims. The receiver may wish to satisfy the claims of
preferential creditors but it has been established that the fixed charge
surplus should normally be paid to the company and not to the
preferential creditors.

In *Re Lewis Merthyr Consolidated Collieries*[62] the Court of Appeal held **21–032**
that the priority given to preferential creditors in respect of realisations
of assets subject to a floating charge[63] applied only to assets caught by
the floating charge, even where the receiver was also appointed under a
fixed charge.

In *Re G.L. Saunders Ltd*,[64] the receiver had been appointed under **21–033**
fixed and floating charges. There were huge debts to preferential
creditors which more than exhausted the floating charge realisations. On
the other hand the fixed charge realisations were sufficient to pay the
debenture-holder in full and leave a large surplus. By the time the
receiver issued his summons for directions the company was in liquidation. The question posed by the receiver was whether he should pay the
surplus of fixed charge realisations to the liquidator or to the preferential
creditors. There were important differences in the consequences of each
course. A direct payment to preferential creditors would have left the
liquidator without any moneys to pay his costs of the winding-up or his
remuneration. Moreover, because the liquidation had begun well after
the commencement of the receivership, the amounts treated as preferential in the liquidation were different (and in fact much less) than the
sums which would be treated as preferential in the receivership. These
consequences were however, regarded as irrelevant to the legal result,
which was that, following the *Lewis Merthyr* case,[65] the surplus on fixed
charged realisations had to be paid to the liquidator and not to the
preferential creditors. On the basis of (a) the wording of the particular
debenture and (b) the effective discharge of the debenture (since the
debenture-holder had been paid in full), a surplus of fixed charged
realisations did not fall within the floating charge so as to bring the
preferential creditors' rights into play.

**(b) Floating charge realisations (including crystallised floating
charges)**

The usual order of payments out of sums realised from assets subject to **21–034**
a charge which as created was a floating charge is similar to that referred
to in respect of fixed charge realisations, save for:

(i) the special priority of preferential creditors, and

---

[62] [1929] 1 Ch. 498.
[63] Now Insolvency Act 1986, s. 40.
[64] [1986] 1 W.L.R. 215.
[65] [1929] 1 Ch. 498.

(ii) in the event of a winding-up, the special priority of the costs and expenses of the winding-up.

(i) Preferential creditors

21–035   *Rights to priority.* Section 40(1) of the Insolvency Act 1986 provides that, where the receiver is appointed on behalf of the holders of any debentures of the company[66] secured by "a charge which, as created, was a floating charge" and the company is not at the time of appointment[67] being wound-up, preferential creditors are to be paid in priority to the debenture-holders out of assets coming into the hands of the receiver. Preferential creditors have priority over the holders of all floating charges, not just those pursuant to which a receiver had been appointed.[68] It was held by the Court of Appeal in the *Lewis Merthyr* case[69] that the reference to assets coming into the hands of the receiver only applied to assets subject to a floating charge and not assets subject to a fixed charge.[70] In *Re G.L. Saunders Ltd*[71] it was held that the fixed charge surplus arising after the debenture-holder had been paid in full did not fall within the floating charge.

21–036   Before the Insolvency Act 1986 the rights of preferential creditors could be defeated by a crystallisation of the floating charge prior to the appointment of a receiver, so that the charge was no longer a floating charge by the material date.[72] The effectiveness of a provision in a debenture whereby the debenture-holder could crystallise the floating charge prior to the appointment of a receiver by giving notice to the company was accepted by Nourse J. in *Re Woodroffes Musical Instruments Ltd*[73] In that case he also accepted the argument that a cesser of business crystallised a floating charge over the company's assets.[74] Subsequently, Hoffmann J. held in *Re Brightlife Ltd*[75] that crystallisation by notice prior to winding up defeated the rights of preferential creditors.

---

[66] The word "company" as used in s. 40 does not include an entity incorporated under the Industrial and Provident Societies Acts: *Re Devon and Somerset Farmers Ltd* [1993] B.C.C. 410. *Cf.* the approach to the meaning of "company" in the context of administrative receivership in *Re International Bulk Commodities Ltd* [1993] Ch. 77 and see the discussion in relation to foreign incorporated companies in below, Chap. 23.

[67] For the policy reasons underlying the different treatment of fixed and floating charges in this context, see *Re Portbase Clothing Ltd* [1993] Ch. 388.

[68] *Re H & K Medway Ltd* [1997] 2 All E.R. 321. See also Insolvency Act 1986, s. 40(2); Companies Act 1985, s. 196.

[69] See above, n. 48.

[70] See also *Re Portbase Clothing Ltd* [1993] Ch. 388 at 20E–F; *cf. Re MC Bacon Ltd (No. 2)* [1990] B.C.C. 430.

[71] [1986] 1 W.L.R. 215. See para. 21–033 above.

[72] *Stein v. Saywell* (1969) 121 C.L.R. 529 (although this case has been reversed by statute in most states of its native Australia) and see *Re Christonette International Ltd* [1982] 1 W.L.R. 1245 (Vinelott J.), *Re Woodroffes Musical Instruments Ltd* [1986] Ch. 366; *Re Brightlife Ltd* [1987] Ch. 200.

[73] [1986] Ch. 366.

[74] See also *William Gaskell Group Ltd v. Highley* [1993] B.C.C. 200 at 208.

[75] [1987] Ch. 200.

The effect of the Insolvency Act 1986 was to ensure that crystallisation **21–037** of a floating charge at any time between its creation and the appointment of a receiver or a liquidation[76] no longer defeated the special rights of preferential creditors.[77]

If a receiver ignores the preferential creditors' rights to payment out **21–038** of assets in his hands, he is personally liable for breach of statutory duty to pay damages in the sums he should have paid to them.[78] Nor do the courts take kindly to attempts to evade liability to pay preferential creditors. Thus, where debenture-holders removed the receiver and obtained payment of floating charge realisations without the deduction of sums due to preferential creditors, both the receiver and debenture-holder were held liable to the preferential creditors.[79] It is unclear whether notice of the claims made by the preferential creditors is a prerequisite to a debenture-holder's liabilities. In *IRC v. Goldblatt*,[80] Goff J. held that a debenture-holder would hold monies on constructive trust for a preferential creditor where the monies were received with notice of a statutory duty under which they should have been paid in settlement of a prior claim. Whether notice is in fact necessary for such a claim has been questioned on the basis that such a claim would be for restitutionary damages arising on breach of statutory duty.[81]

As a result of section 45 of the Insolvency Act 1986 a debenture- **21–039** holder can no longer remove an administrative receiver directly, but the latter has a right to resign. If he does so, he must be sure to discharge any sums payable to preferential creditors before handing any assets or any sum to any subsequent receiver or to the debenture-holder, if the risk of personal liability to the preferential creditor is to be obviated.

Where a receiver resigns and is replaced by a second receiver, the first **21–040** must pay or provide for the preferential debts of which he had notice, before accounting to the second receiver.[82] In practice, however, the second receiver or the first receiver's appointor will usually grant the first receiver an indemnity.

(ii) Categories of preferential claims[83]

PAYE.[84] PAYE deductions which have been made or should have **21–041** been made in the 12 months before the relevant date.

Deductions in the same period in respect of payments to sub- **21–042** contractors in the construction industry under section 559 of the Income and Corporation Taxes Act 1988.

---

[76] Now Insolvency Act 1986, s. 40(1) (receiver); s. 175(2)(b) and s. 251 (liquidation).
[77] See *Re Portbase Clothing Ltd* [1993] Ch. 338; *Mond v. Hammond Suddards* [2000] Ch. 40, CA.
[78] *Woods v. Winskill* [1913] 2 Ch. 303; *Westminster v. Treby* [1936] 2 All E.R. 21; *Westminster Corp v. Haste* [1950] Ch. 442; *IRC v. Goldblatt* [1972] Ch. 498.
[79] *IRC v. Goldblatt* [1972] Ch. 498.
[80] *ibid.*
[81] See the discussion by Professor Goode in (1981) Journal of Business Law 476 and *Totty and Moss on Insolvency*, H2.11.
[82] *IRC v. Goldblatt* [1972] 1 Ch. 498, *per* Goff J. at 505C.
[83] Insolvency Act 1986, s. 175 and Sched. 6.
[84] See also above, Chap. 13.

21–043   *VAT.*[85] VAT is preferential where it is referable to the six month period before the relevant date. In *Re Liverpool Commercial Vehicles Ltd*[86] the question arose as to whether a credit containing VAT issued to the company in receivership created a preferential debt. The company had purchased vehicles from a supplier under terms which included a retention of title clause. At the time of supply the invoices contained VAT, which was treated by the supplier as output tax and by the company as input tax. The company took the benefit of the input tax by setting it off against output tax. After joint receivers were appointed, the suppliers demanded and obtained the return of the vehicles. The supplier gave the company a credit note for the purchase price including VAT. Vinelott J. held that, even if the return of the vehicles was liable to VAT (the point being left open), the VAT could not be preferential since it was not referable to the applicable period prior to the receivership (then 12 months). Counsel for the Customs and Excise had argued that the original supply subject to the retention of title was a conditional supply and the company had, until it paid for the vehicles, only a contingent right to credit for the VAT as input tax. Once the supplier repossessed the goods, the credit was retrospectively invalidated and the output tax against which it had been set became payable. Such output tax was within the relevant period so as to make the claim preferential. This argument was rejected by Vinelott J. as being "wholly at variance with the structure of the legislation".[87]

21–044   *Car tax.* Car tax which became due on the 12 month period before the relevant date. This tax represents the difference between the standard rate of VAT and the pre-VAT 25 per cent purchase tax on cars. It appears to be an anomalous accident of the passage of the Insolvency Act 1985 through Parliament that, whilst the preferential period for VAT has been reduced to six months, the preferential period for car tax remains at 12 months.

21–045   *Betting duty.* General Betting Duty, gaming licence duty and bingo duty payable during the 12 month period before the relevant date.

21–046   *National insurance.* Class 1 and Class 2 contributions under the Social Security Act 1975 which became due in the 12 month period before the relevant date.

21–047   *Pension contributions.* Pension contributions to occupational pension schemes and state scheme premiums under Schedule 3 to the Social Security Pensions Act 1975.

21–048   *Remuneration of employees.*

(a) Sums due to employees or former employees by way of remuneration (including sums deductible by way of PAYE and

---

[85] See also above, Chap. 13.
[86] [1984] B.C.L.C. 587, Vinelott J.
[87] [1984] B.C.L.C. 587 at 591g–h.

NIC[87a] in respect of the whole or part of a four month period before the relevant date up to a limit to be set by the Secretary of State. This category includes remuneration ordered under a protective award.[88]

(b) Accrued holiday remuneration (including sums deductible by way of PAYE and NIC) in respect of any period prior to the relevant date due to a person dismissed before, on or after the relevant date.

(c) Sums advanced and applied for the payment of debts which would otherwise have been preferential under (a) or (b).

Levies on Coal and Steel Production. Sums due at the relevant date in **21–049** respect of certain ECSC levies and in respect of certain surcharges.

The relevant date. As a result of section 40 of the Insolvency Act **21–050** 1986, where a receiver is appointed on behalf of holders of debentures secured by a charge which "as created" was a floating charge, and if at the date of such appointment there has been no resolution to wind up the company and no winding-up order has been made,[89] the "relevant date" for preferential payments, which have to be paid prior to the debenture-holder's claims, is the date of appointment of a receiver under the relevant floating charge. In practice the floating charge will often cover all or substantially the whole of the company's assets and the receiver will be an administrative receiver, but the preferential creditor's priority and the "relevant date" apply irrespective of this.

Where a winding-up resolution has been passed or a winding-up order **21–051** made prior to the appointment of a receiver, the following rules apply[90]:

(a) where a winding-up order followed "immediately" upon the discharge of an administration order, the "relevant date" is that of the making of the administration order.

(b) in other cases, where there is a resolution to wind up the company, that is the "relevant date"; where there is no such resolution, it is the date of the winding-up order or the date of any earlier appointment of a provisional liquidator.

Where a winding-up follows a receivership, the preferential creditors may well be different because of the different relevant dates in each case.[91]

(iii) Set-off against preferential claims

Frequently a creditor who has both preferential and non-preferential **21–052** claims against a company also owes it money. One situation where this occurs is where the company has money at its bankers and those bankers

---

[87a] *Re FJL Realisations Ltd,* (unreported, Court of Appeal, July 10, 2000). See also Chap 13 above.

[88] See above, Chap. 19.

[89] "In the course of being wound up" in the section does not apply merely where a petition has been presented: *Re Christonette International Ltd* [1982] 1 W.L.R. 1245 and *cf.* Insolvency Act 1986, s. 247(2).

[90] Insolvency Act 1986, s. 387.

[91] This was assumed in *G.L. Saunders Ltd* [1986] 1 W.L.R. 215.

have advanced moneys both for non-preferential purposes and also for wages or a wages account.[92] Another such situation is where the Crown as the Revenue or Department of Health and Social Security has a preferential claim but in the shape of the Customs and Excise owes the company monies by way of a refund of VAT.

21–053   The problem of set-off which arises was stated by Walton J. in the winding-up case of *Re Unit 2 Windows Ltd*[93]:

> "If . . . there is a creditor who, but for a set-off of £Z, would have claims against the company of £X which would be preferential, and £Y which would be non-preferential, then, on the assumption that Z is less than X + Y, how . . . are the two claims of the creditor, the preferential and the non-preferential to be calculated?"

Three possible solutions are mentioned by Walton J.:

(a) £Z could first be set off against the non-preferential claim of £Y and any balance against the preferential claim of £X. This solution would benefit the preferential creditor concerned;

(b) £Z could be spread rateably as between £X and £Y;

(c) £Z could first be set off against preferential claims. This would favour other preferential creditors (if there are insufficient funds to pay them in full) and/or the debenture-holder.

Walton J. opted for solution (b) on the construction of the special statutory provisions applicable to set-offs in winding up. These do not apply in receivership[94] and therefore *Re Unit 2 Windows Ltd* is not directly applicable. However, in construing the statutory provisions Walton J. opted for a result which he considered to be "the only logical and sensible solution".[95] On that basis, this solution should apply to receivership situations in the absence of a contrary agreement.

21–054   Where the preferential creditor is the Crown in respect of taxes, duties or penalties, there is a special feature in that the company cannot set off in cases other than winding-up[96] without the leave of the court.[97] Whereas leave to set-off will normally be refused where the company is solvent, since the provision is a relic of the old rule excluding set off based on Crown prerogative, one would expect the court to permit set off in the case of an insolvent receivership. The point is that set-off between solvent parties is based on a desire to prevent cross-actions, whereas in insolvency, where cross-actions against the insolvent estate would be futile, the desire is to do substantial justice between the

---

[92] As in *Re E.J. Morel (1934) Ltd* [1962] Ch. 21.

[93] [1985] 1 W.L.R. 1383 at 1385. *Cf.* the position in Scotland: *Turner, Petitioner* [1993] B.C.C. 299, Court of Session.

[94] *Business Computers Ltd v. Anglo African Leasing Ltd* [1972] 1 W.L.R. 578. Nor do they apply in Scotland: see *Turner, Petitioner* [1993] B.C.C. 299, Court of Session.

[95] [1985] 1 W.L.R. 1383 at 1388H.

[96] *Re Cushla Ltd* [1979] 3 All E.R. 415, Vinelott J.

[97] Crown Proceedings Act 1947, s. 35(2) and RSC, Ord. 77, r. 6.

parties.[98] In the case of any insolvent receivership, substantial justice appears to require that set-off be allowed against a Crown preferential debt.

(iv) Remuneration and preferential creditors
Generally speaking, debentures provide for payment of remuneration **21–055** out of charged assets without distinguishing between assets subject to fixed and floating charges. This raises the question whether a receiver could properly favour the debenture-holder by taking his remuneration out of the floating charge assets. It is considered that remuneration should be taken rateably from each class of asset, but the point is not free from doubt.[99] A further question is whether the receiver and debenture-holder can by agreement prejudice the preferential creditors in this way. The courts would presumably see such an agreement as a breach of the receiver's duty to pay preferential creditors and thus void.[1] Likewise, a provision in a debenture providing for remuneration to be paid, *e.g.* only out of assets subject to a floating charge may be void as contravening the policy of the statutory provisions. On the other hand it may be that different rates of remuneration can be provided for fixed and floating charge realisations either in the debenture or, if the debenture permits, by agreement, if and in so far as these different rates genuinely attempt to reflect lesser or greater difficulties or likely difficulties in the realisations concerned.

(v) Costs and expenses of winding up
The question of the priority to be accorded to the costs and expenses of **21–056** winding up has been discussed in Chapter 11. In short, on the basis of the decisions in *Re Portbase Clothing Limited*[2] and *Mond v. Hammond Suddards,*[3] irrespective of whether a receiver is appointed or the floating charge crystallises prior to or after the making of a winding up order or the passing of a resolution for voluntary winding up, the costs and expenses of the liquidation will rank ahead of the claims of the preferential creditors and of the claims of the holder of the (crystallised) floating charge.[4]

The question of whether a liquidator should be able to treat costs **21–057** incurred by him in unsuccessful litigation against a receiver as expenses of the winding up has prompted a number of recent inconsistent decisions. In *Re M.C. Bacon Limited*[5] Millett J. decided that costs

[98] *Forster v. Wilson* (1843) 12 M & W 191 at 203–204, *per* Parke B; *Stein v. Blake* [1994] A.C. 243 at 251, HL and see above, Chap. 16.

[99] The solution suggested appears to be fair and just. *Cf.* the solution adopted by Walton J. to the set-off problem discussed above. Another possible analogy would be to regard the receiver as a first chargee (for his remuneration) over two assets (the fixed and floating charge assets) and the debenture holder and preferential creditors as second chargees in each case: see *Flint v. Howard* [1893] 2 Ch. 54 at 72 following *Barnes v. Ralston* 1 Y. & C. Cl. 401.

[1] *IRC v. Goldblatt* [1972] Ch. 498.
[2] [1993] Ch. 388.
[3] [2000] Ch. 40, CA.
[4] See paras 11–032 *et seq.* above.
[5] [1991] Ch. 127.

incurred by a liquidator in attempting unsuccessfully to avoid the debenture holder's charge as a preference and in pursuing an action for wrongful trading could not be an expense of the winding up under section 175(2)(a) of the 1986 Act, nor an expense properly incurred in the winding up under section 115 of the 1986 Act. Millett J. held that section 115 was merely a section dealing with priorities and not conferring substantive rights to expenses in the liquidation. Hence the liquidator had no automatic statutory right of recoupment of expenses in relation to the unsuccessful litigation. Millett J. further commented that it would be wholly unjust were the liquidator to be allowed his costs of unsuccessful proceedings against the debenture holder out of floating charge assets in priority to the claims of the debenture holder even though that charge had not crystallised at the commencement of the liquidation.

21–058   Millett J.'s analysis was doubted and rejected, *obiter,* by Morritt and Phillips L.JJ. in *Re Exchange Travel (Holdings) Limited (No.3), Katz v. McNally.*[6] Phillips L.J. indicated that section 115 of the 1986 Act was not merely a priority section (as Millett J. had held in *Re M.C. Bacon*) but created the right and obligation to pay liquidation expenses which was not cut down by the words of rule 4.218 of the Insolvency Rules 1986. Phillips L.J. indicated that the apparent conflict identified by Millett J. between the expression "expenses properly incurred in the winding up" in section 115 and the expression "any necessary disbursements by the liquidator" in rule 4.218(1)(m) was to be resolved by interpreting the latter in light of the former. Accordingly "necessary" disbursements in rule 4.218(1)(m) was to be interpreted to mean disbursements rendered necessary by the proper performance of the liquidator's duties, rather that unnecessary disbursements not properly incurred.

21–059   The consequence of the Court of Appeal's view would be that if a liquidator incurred expenses in unsuccessful proceedings to challenge the validity of a debenture, then provided that he had acted properly in so doing, (*i.e.* he had brought the proceedings on reasonable grounds), then his costs of so doing would rank ahead both of the preferential creditors and (assuming *Re Portbase Clothing* to have been correctly decided) ahead of the claims of the debenture holder himself in respect of floating charge assets. It is to be noted that the Court of Appeal expressly indicated that they had not heard full argument on the point and it does not appear that they were referred to, or had in mind, the effect of the decision in Portbase.

21–060   The same point arose more recently in two cases argued on the same day. In *Re Floor Fourteen Limited*[7] David Donaldson Q.C. (sitting as a Deputy High Court Judge) was faced with an opposed application for directions from a liquidator who wished to use retained funds to pursue claims against the former directors of the company who claimed that the liquidator could have no automatic entitlement to use such monies for

[6] [1997] 2 B.C.L.C. 579, CA.
[7] [1999] 2 B.C.L.C. 666.

his costs, but did not contend that the proceedings were inappropriate. The Deputy Judge preferred and applied the reasoning in *Katz v. McNally* and did not follow *Re M.C. Bacon,* and gave the directions sought.

In contrast, in *Mond v. Hammond Suddards*[8] the Court of Appeal **21–061** expressly followed and adopted the approach of Millett J. in *Re M.C. Bacon Limited*. Chadwick L.J. (who gave the only reasoned judgment) expressly indicated that section 115 was merely a section dealing with priorities and indicated that Parliament could not have intended to give the liquidator an automatic right to recover the costs of unsuccessful litigation. It is, however, to be noted that whilst Chadwick L.J. clearly had in mind and referred to his own decision in *Portbase,* the Court of Appeal in *Mond v. Hammond Suddards* was apparently not referred in argument to the decision in Katz v. McNally and that authority was not mentioned in the judgments.

In these circumstances it is manifest that the entire issue of the scope **21–062** of liquidation expenses in relation to unsuccessful litigation requires clarification in a fully reasoned decision of the Court of Appeal. It may well be that this will also provide the occasion upon which the Court can be persuaded to revisit the decision in *Portbase.*

(c) Where the debenture-holder is missing

Generally speaking debenture-holders are banks or other lending institu- **21–063** tions. In a number of cases, however, they are private appointors. Where such private appointors are humans, they may disappear (as humans sometimes do). This leaves the receiver with the problem that he has moneys which ought to be paid to the missing debenture-holder. He can await the appearance of the debenture-holder, but the more practical alternative may be to pay any moneys into court under section 63 of the Trustee Act 1925.[9] Although as between the mortgagor and mortgagee moneys in a receiver's hands are regarded as belonging to the mortgagor until actual payment to the mortgagee (and accordingly the mortgagor is at risk if they are lost or misappropriated by the receiver[10]) nonetheless as between receiver and the mortgagee the receiver holds any moneys as trustee for the debenture-holder (and then as to any surplus as trustee for the mortgagor).[11]

---

[8] [2000] Ch. 40, CA.

[9] For the procedure, see CPR, Sched. 1, RSC, Ord. 92, r. 2.

[10] *White v. Metcalf* [1903] 2 Ch. 567 at 571.

[11] *Bacal Contracting Ltd v. Modern Engineering (Bristol) Ltd* [1980] 2 All E.R. 655 at 659g–h. The essentials of any trusteeship are clearly satisfied: (1) the receiver owes fiduciary duties; and (2) he is under a duty to keep the debenture-holder's moneys separate from his own (*Henry v. Hammond* [1913] 2 K.B. 515). See also *Smiths Ltd v. Middleton* [1979] 3 All E.R. 842. In *Visbord v. FCT* (1943) 68 C.L.R. 354, HCt of Australia), Starke J. referred to the receiver's duty to pay the surplus to the mortgagee as a mandate and "not . . . a trust" (at 376) whereas Williams J. referred to the receiver as holding realisations "in a fiduciary capacity on behalf of the mortgagee and the mortgagor . . ." (at 387).

(d) Duties on redemption

21–064 The receiver and mortgagee are duty bound on redemption to return the charged assets to the company or other person with a prior right to the equity of redemption (*e.g.* a second mortgagee).[12] Where an administrative receiver ceases to act, the administrative receiver must hand to the company (or its liquidator) all the records in his possession which belong to the company.

21–065   In relation to documents, three different categories may exist:

(a) documents generated pursuant to the duty to manage the business and sell assets — these must be delivered up to the person entitled to the return of the assets;

(b) documents generated for the purpose of providing advice or information about the receivership to the mortgagee—these belong to the mortgagee;

(c) documents generated for the purpose of enabling the receiver to discharge his professional duties (save for those which fall within (i) or (ii) above) belong to the receiver.[13]

The receiver has a duty to maintain sufficient accounting information to enable the directors to discharge their statutory duties to publish accounts.[14] Regulation 10A of the Insolvency Regulations 1986 requires a receiver to keep records for six years or to hand them to a successor as "the responsible insolvency practitioner". An abstract of receipts and payments must be filed within two months of ceasing to act, unless the court extends this time limit.[15]

---

[12] *Downsview v. First City Corp* [1993] A.C. 295, PC.
[13] *Gomba Holdings v. Minories Finance* (1987) 3 B.C.C. 644, Hoffmann J., affd. [1989] 1 All E.R. 261, CA.
[14] *Smith Ltd v. Middleton* [1979] 3 All E.R. 942.
[15] Insolvency Rules 1986, r. 3.32.

CHAPTER 22

RECEIVERS APPOINTED BY THE COURT

1. INTRODUCTION

Under a succession of statutes since 1873, culminating in the Supreme **22–001** Court Act 1981,[1] the High Court has had jurisdiction to appoint a receiver at any stage in proceedings in all cases in which it appears to the court to be just and convenient to do so.[2] The jurisdiction is discretionary and accordingly as a matter of principle ought not to be fettered by rules.[3]

There are however, a very limited number of rules of law and an **22–002** abundance of rules of practice to which the court will have regard in deciding any application for the appointment of receiver. The distinction between these rules is that rules of law bind in every case and are (unless later held to be wrongly stated or reversed by statute) immutable. On the other hand, rules of practice are merely guidelines of varying weight (often merely expressions of common sense) which may give way in the particular circumstances of a particular case and which are subject to evolution and review in changing times and social conditions.

The risk of confusion arising from the conversion of rules of practice **22–003** into rules of law is inherent in a system of precedent and must constantly be guarded against. An example lies in the rule that orders should not be made calculated to compel a party to perform a contract for personal services. This is a rule of practice, not of law, and the approach to this rule has changed since the nineteenth century when it was strictly applied. Today the rule has been relaxed where justice so requires.

> "Much has happened since the late 1890s. In those days the court regularly ordered a husband or wife to return to the matrimonial bed,[4] but declined to order Desdemona to attend at Covent Garden twice weekly and to sing the Willow Song before being docilely strangled on her matrimonial couch; the court eagerly made orders in the one case and delicately refused to make them in the other. An injunction is a flexible weapon . . . in general it is true that the

---

[1] s. 37(1). An arbitration agreement may confer on the arbitrator a power to appoint a receiver, but such a provision is rarely found. The alternative is for the court to appoint a receiver in aid of the arbitration proceedings under s. 12(6)(h) of the Arbitration Act 1950; see Mustill and Boyd, *Commercial Arbitration* (2nd ed., 1989), p. 331.

[2] For an application for the appointment of a receiver of a company rejected as unjust and inconvenient, see *William & Humbert v. W & H Trade Marks* [1986] A.C. 368 at 429–430.

[3] *Kirklees Metropolitan BC v. Wickes Building Supplies* [1993] A.C. 227 at 271B.

[4] The reference is to decrees for restitution of conjugal rights.

411

court will not grant injunctions forcing people to live together, or to be friends together, or to play together, or possibly even to sing together. I say the court would not: I can conceive of exceptional cases in the 20th century when the court might."[5]

The principal rule of law in this area is that the jurisdiction to appoint a receiver, like the jurisdiction to grant an injunction, can only be exercised in aid of some legal or equitable right.[6] This usually, although not invariably, takes the shape of a cause of action.[7] Accordingly, the court cannot at the instance of a secured creditor appoint a receiver and manager of the security and other property with a view to the combined and advantageous sale of the charged and uncharged property together, for the creditor has no interest in or right in respect of the uncharged property.[8] There is a further rule of law that the court must not appoint a receiver and manager of a body on which Parliament has expressly conferred powers, duties and responsibilities, for it would be wrong for the court by such appointment to assume such powers, duties or responsibilities.[9] Subject only to these limitations, the court has an unlimited power to appoint a receiver if it is just and convenient to do so.[10]

22–004   The rules of practice relating to the appointment of a receiver are essentially the same as those governing the grant of an injunction. Thus a receiver will not be appointed unless the appointment secures some legitimate advantage for the applicant. No appointment will be made if, for example, the property is valueless or incapable of beneficial realisation.[11]

---

[5] *Per* Templeman L.J. in *Transatlantic Records v. Bulitown* (unreported, February 28, 1980, CA). See also the analagous comments of Lord Hoffmann on the grant of orders for specfic performance in *Co-operative Insurance v. Argyll Stores Ltd* [1998] A.C. 1, HL.

[6] *Siskina v. Distos Compania* [1979] A.C. 210; *E.D. & F Man (Sugar) v. Evalend Shipping* [1989] 2 Lloyd's Rep 192; *Mercedes Benz AG v. Leiduck* [1996] 1 A.C. 284; *Morris v. Murjani* [1996] 1 W.L.R. 848, CA. In Australia, see *Bond Brewing Holdings Ltd v. National Australia Bank Ltd* (1990) 1 A.C.S.R. 445, Full Court of the Sup. Ct of Victoria.

[7] *Channel Group v. Balfour Beatty Ltd.* [1993] A.C. 334 at 362B–D, applied in *Mercantile Group (Europe) AG. v. Aiyela* [1994] Q.B. 366.

[8] *Britannia Building Society v. Crammer* [1997] B.P.I.R. 596.

[9] *Gardner v. London Chatham & Dover Railways* (1861) 2 Ch.App.Cas. 201 and *Parker v. Camden London BC* [1986] 1 Ch. 162 (no receiver can be appointed of houses owned by local authorities in respect of which the local authority is charged with the duty of maintenance under s. 111 of the Housing Act 1957). See also *Maclaine Watson & Co. Ltd. v. International Tin Council* [1988] 1 at 17C *per* Millett J.; approved [1989] Ch. 253 at 271, CA, declining to appoint a receiver to an organisation established by treaty between sovereign states.

[10] *Derby v. Weldon* [1990] Ch. 65 at 76–77, *per* Lord Donaldson M.R., citing Jessel M.R. to like effect in *Beddow v. Beddow* [1878] 9 Ch. D. 89 at 93. See also *Parker v. Camden London BC* [1986] Ch. 162 at 173 and 176, *Bourne v. Colodense* [1985] ICR 291; *Maclaine Watson & Co. Ltd. v. International Tin Council* [1988] Ch. 1 at 17C *per* Millett J.; approved [1989] Ch. 253 at 271, CA. See also the examination of the development of the law by Colman J. in *Soinco v. Novokuznetsk Aluminium Plant* [1997] 3 All E.R. 523, holding that there was no longer any basis for refusing to appoint a receiver by way of equitable execution simply because such an appointment would not have been made by the Court of Chancery prior to 1873.

[11] *J. Walls v. Legge* [1923] 2 K.B. 240.

The court will not, save in extraordinary circumstances, appoint a **22–005** receiver on an application without notice[12] but it will not shrink from doing so where it is appropriate.[13] Where the appointment of a receiver is sought as an interim or protective measure, a cross-undertaking in damages will ordinarily be required of the applicant in favour of the other party to the litigation, whether the order is made with or without notice.[14] The same may not be true where the receiver is appointed by way of equitable execution.[15]

2. TYPES OF COURT RECEIVERSHIP

The court may appoint several different types of receivers in respect of a **22–006** company. It may appoint a receiver and manager of a company's business and undertaking. In this case the powers of the directors to conduct its business and dispose of its assets are in abeyance for the duration of the receivership.[16]

The court may also appoint a receiver or receiver and manager of the **22–007** company itself in cases where the company is incapable of managing its own affairs by reason of the absence of a properly constituted board, or deadlock on the board of directors.[17] The same approach may also be adopted where there is dissension on the board following misconduct or an irretrievable breakdown between the shareholders in a "quasi-partnership" and a petition has been presented for the winding up of the company or under section 459 of the Companies Act 1985 claiming that the affairs of the company have been or are being conducted in a manner which is unfairly prejudicial to the interests of the members or some of them.[18] The appointment will, however, only be made as a temporary measure pending the resolution of the difficulties which prevent the board from exercising control of the company's affairs or

---

[12] *Re Connolly Bros* [1911] 1 Ch. 731 at 742; *National Australia Bank v. Bond Brewing* [1991] 1 V.L.R. 386 ("only the most pressing need can warrant such an invasion without notice"). For an example of such an appointment see *Clarke v. Heathfield* [1985] I.C.R. 203.

[13] *Don King Productions v. Warren* [2000] B.C.C. 263.

[14] *National Australia Bank Ltd. v. Bond Brewing Holdings Ltd* (1990) 1 A.C.S.R. 722, HCt of Australia.

[15] *Allied Irish Bank v. Ashford Hotels Ltd* [1998] B.C.C. 440 at 446–7. If a receiver is appointed under the provisions of the Criminal Justice Act 1988, it appears that the usual practice is not to require an undertaking to be given: In *re Andrews* [1999] 1 W.L.R. 1236 at 1246D. No remedy is available other than under the cross-undertaking in damages if it turns out that the appointment should not have been made: *Pollnow v. Garden Mews-St. Leonard Pty. Ltd* (1985) 9 A.C.L.R. 82.

[16] *Moss Steamship Company Ltd v. Whinney* [1912] A.C. 254 at 263.

[17] See *Stanfield v. Gibbon* [1925] W.N. 11. For an interesting case in which the court appointed its own receivers in order to overcome the practical difficulties created by the appointments out of court by different lenders of two receivers over the same property with equal priority, see *Bass Breweries v. Delaney* [1994] B.C.C. 851.

[18] *Wilton Davis v. Kirk* [1997] B.C.C. 770; *Re Worldhams Park Golf Course Ltd* [1998] 1 B.C.L.C. 554. See also *Duffy v. Super Centre Development Corp* [1967] 1 N.S.W.R. 382, *Wayland v, Nidamon Pty* (1986) 11 A.C.L.R. 209 and compare *Verhelst v. Going Places Travel Centre Pty* (1980) A.C.L.C. 34,138.

which make it inappropriate that they should do so.[19] Thus in the case of litigation relating to a "quasi-partnership" company, a receiver and manager may be appointed pending the dismissal of the petition, the making of a winding up order, or the making of an order under section 461 of the Companies Act 1985 regulating the management of the company or directing one party to sell his shares to the other.[20]

22–008   The court may also appoint a receiver or a receiver and manager of a company or specified assets at the instance of a person who claims that he owns assets which have been improperly transferred to the company,[21] or at the instance of a shareholder[22] or creditor[23] if assets are in jeopardy because of the risk of misappropriation or dissipation by those in control of its affairs[24] or because of breach or evasion of a freezing injunction.[25] Although the court may be more reluctant to appoint a receiver in a case in which sufficient protection against dissipation can be given to the applicant by the grant of an injunction,[26] and is most unlikely to appoint a receiver simply to provide a regime for the proper administration of the affairs of a company in financial difficulties where the company objects to

[19] See *Stanfield v. Gibbon* [1925] W.N. 11. Such a receiver is entitled to make all reasonable requests for information from any party to the dispute to enable him to carry on the business, and those requests should be complied with: *Parsons v. Mather & Platt* (unreported, December 9, 1976, Court of Appeal transcript 392A, p. 6).

[20] See *Re A Company* [1987] B.C.L.C. 133. The appointment may extend to the company's wholly owned subsidiaries: *Wilton Davis v. Kirk* [1997] B.C.C. 770. The court has jurisdiction under s. 461 of the Companies Act 1985 to direct that the party whose conduct occasioned the appointment should bear the receiver's costs and expenses: *Re Worldhams Golf Course* [1998] 1 B.C.L.C. 554.

[21] *BCCI SA v. BRS Kumar* [1994] 1 B.C.L.C. 211.

[22] *e.g.* on the presentation of a petition to wind up or under s. 459 or on the institution of a derivative action.

[23] Including a claimant in an action against the company.

[24] See *Krishna v. Chandra* [1928] A.I.R. 49 at 50, *per* Lord Sumner. The purpose of a freezing injunction — and, it is suggested, the appointment of a receiver at the behest of a claimant — is not to rewrite the established principles of insolvency law by giving the claimant some form of security which he does not enjoy, or indirectly to achieve a similar result by interfering with the payment of other debts by a company in the ordinary course of business: see *The Angel Bell* [1981] Q.B. 65 and *K/S A/S Admiral Shipping v. Portlink Ferries* [1984] 2 Lloyd's Reports 166, CA. See also *Normid Housing Association v. Ralph & Mansell* [1989] 1 Lloyd's Rep. 265 at 275. For examples of the appointment of receivers to ensure that disputed property was properly managed pending trial, see *Hart v. Emelkirk* [1983] 1 W.L.R. 1289 and *Daiches v. Bluelake Investments* (1986) 51 P. & C.R. 51.

[25] *International Credit and Investment Co. (Overseas) Ltd v. Adham* [1998] B.C.C. 134. To avoid the irrevocable damage which the appointment may cause the court may impose a protective regime under the supervision of an independent accountant: *Don King Productions v. Warren* [2000] B.C.C. 263.

[26] In *National Australia Bank Ltd v. Bond Brewing Holdings Ltd* the Supreme Court of Victoria held at (1990) 1 A.C.S.R. 445, reversing the judgment of Beach J. at (1990) 1 A.C.S.R. 405, that whilst there was no principle that a court could only be appointed at the behest of someone asserting a proprietary interest in the property concerned, the applicant nevertheless had to show both that he was seeking to protect some legal or equitable right and that no other adequate remedy was available to protect that right. In this latter respect the law in Australia may be more restrictive than the approach in England as set out in *Derby v. Weldon (No. 3)* [1990] Ch. 65. See also *Global Funds Management (NSW) Ltd v. Burns Philp Trustee Company* (1990) 3 A.C.S.R. 183.

the appointment,[27] the overriding issue will be whether the appointment is right and just in the particular circumstances of the case.[28]

The Court may appoint a receiver by way of equitable execution over **22–009** any asset of the company, including future debts[29] and causes of action of the company against the company's directors for breach of duty.[30] The original basis for such appointment was to act as a substitute where execution at law would be ineffective to enable a judgment creditor to obtain payment of his judgment debt,[31] but the appointment may now be made whenever it is just and convenient to do so.[32]

The effect of such an appointment may be both negative and positive. **22–010** Negatively the appointment operates as an injunction restraining the company from dealing with the asset in question. Positively the order may authorise the receiver to realise or otherwise bring to account the asset in question, and (in the case of a cause of action) to sue in the name of the company. The order will operate to create a charge in favour of the judgment creditor if, but only if, the receiver is directed by the order to hold the asset for or pay its proceeds or other realisation to the judgment creditor.[33] The effect of the appointment may be nullified by the making of a winding up order or the appointment of a provisional liquidator prior to completion of the execution.[34]

The court may appoint a receiver *ad litem* of a company in receiver- **22–011** ship for the limited purpose of determining whether the company has a cause of action against the debenture-holder and/or the receiver and if appropriate to prosecute such actions.[35]

The court may, on the application of a secured creditor, appoint a **22–012** receiver and manager of the company's undertaking to protect the interests of the creditor.[36] The court has jurisdiction to make such an appointment irrespective of whether the secured creditor has himself

---

[27] In *National Australia Bank Ltd v. Bond Brewing Holdings Ltd* the Supreme Court of Victoria held that where a company resisted the appointment, a receiver would not be appointed simply in order to provide a regime for the administration of a financially embarrassed company: see (1990) 1 A.C.S.R. 445. Refusing an application for special leave to appeal, the High Court of Australia was willing to assume that circumstances could exist in which a receiver could be appointed in respect of a company not expressly alleged to be insolvent at the instance of an unsecured creditor, but upheld the decision of the Supreme Court of Victoria on the facts: see (1990) 1 A.C.S.R. 722.

[28] *Derby v. Weldon (No. 3)* [1990] Ch. 65 at 77B–E.

[29] *Soinco SACI v. Novokuznetsk Aluminium Plant* [1997] 3 All E.R. 523.

[30] See *Levermore v. Levermore* [1979] 1 W.L.R. 1277.

[31] See, *e.g.* *Re Shephard* (1889) 43 Ch.D. 131.

[32] *Soinco SACI v. Novokuznetsk Aluminium Plant* [1997] 3 All E.R. 523.

[33] *Re Potts* [1893] 1 Q.B. 648; *Re Pearce* [1919] 1 K.B. 354.

[34] *Croshaw v. Lyndhurst Ship Co.* [1897] 2 Ch. 154 at 162–3.

[35] *Swisstex Finance Pty. Ltd. v. Lamb* (1985) 10 A.C.L.R. 135.

[36] The order for the appointment of a receiver may be made on the application of a subsequent incumbrancer if the prior incumbrancer has neither taken possession nor appointed a receiver: *Re Metropolitan Amalgamated Estates* [1912] 2 Ch. 497. The appointment by the court of a receiver at the instigation of a creditor other than the debenture-holder will not automatically crystallise a floating charge unless the debenture specifically so provides: consider *Bayhold Financial Corp. Ltd. v. Clarkson Co. Ltd* (1991) 10 C.B.R. (3d) 159, Sup. Ct. of Nova Scotia, Appellate Division.

power to make such an appointment out of court,[37] but it is rare for such a secured creditor to want an appointment by the court. As a practical matter, the only occasion when it is likely that a secured creditor will apply for such an order will be when the debenture does not in the particular circumstances authorise such an appointment out of court.[38] In such a case, the court has jurisdiction to make an appointment.[39]

22–013   In the exercise of this jurisdiction, the court will in the ordinary case respect the right of the company to carry on its business without interference by the creditor until the occurrence of an event which under the terms of the debenture gives the creditor a right to intervene. But notwithstanding the absence of a provision to this effect in the debenture, the court may, in the exercise of its discretion, make such an appointment if:

> (a) the security is in jeopardy[40];
> (b) the company is in default of payment of either principal or interest;[41] or
> (c) the company ceases to be a going concern.[42]

The ground of "jeopardy" should not be given a narrow meaning, and the filing of a creditor's winding up petition has been held to justify the appointment of a receiver by the court.[43] But a mere lack of present assets equal to the debenture-holder's eventual debt is not sufficient if the company is not in financial difficulties and there is no evidence (a) that the charged assets are at risk of being seized or (b) that the company will be unable to pay the sums due to the debenture-holder at the end of the day.[44]

22–014   The appointment may be limited to the assets in jeopardy, and not extend to assets free from risk because, for example, they are the subject of a fixed charge.[45] The court may also appoint a receiver and manager of a company's undertaking on the application of the creditor or the

---

[37] *Britannia Building Society v. Crammar* [1997] BPIR 596 citing *Tillett v. Nixon* (1883) 23 Ch.D. 238.

[38] See also the unusual facts of *Bass Breweries v. Delaney* [1994] B.C.C. 851 where one of two rival secured creditors sought the appointment of court receivers to act independently in circumstances in which two rival debenture-holders with equal priority had both appointed receivers pursuant to the powers in their charges.

[39] *McMahon v. North Kent Ironworks* [1891] 2 Ch. 148. Though the circumstances for such an order must be rare, the court may appoint a receiver notwithstanding that the debenture-holder has already done so: *Re "Slogger" Automatic Feeder Co. Ltd* [1915] 1 Ch. 478 and see para. 22–023.

[40] *Re Victoria Steamboats* [1897] 1 Ch. 158; *New York Taxi Cab Co. Ltd* [1913] 1 Ch. 1; *Re Tilt Cove Copper Co. Ltd* [1913] 2 Ch. 588. In the absence of a provision entitling him to do so, a debenture-holder has no right to appoint a receiver on the ground that his security is in jeopardy: he has merely an "equity" to apply to the court for such an appointment on this ground: *Cryne v. Barclays Bank* [1987] B.C.L.C. 548.

[41] *Re Crompton* [1914] 1 Ch. 954.

[42] *Hubbuck v. Helms* (1887) 56 L.T. 232; *Hodson v. Tea Co.* [1880] 14 Ch.D. 859.

[43] *Re Victoria Steamboats* [1897] 1 Ch. 158.

[44] *Re New York Taxi Cab Co. Ltd* [1913] 1 Ch. 1 as explained in *Re Tilt Cove Copper Co. Ltd* [1913] 2 Ch. 588. The *Tilt Cove* case itself concerned a proposal to give all the company's assets to the shareholders, and a receiver was appointed at the behest of the debenture holders.

[45] *Gregson v. Taplin* (1915) 112 L.T. 985.

company in a case where the validity of the creditor's debenture or appointment of a receiver is in dispute.

The court will only appoint a receiver and manager of a business if the **22–015** charge includes the goodwill of the business or the preservation of the security requires that the business is continued. The appointment will only be made so as to give an opportunity for a beneficial realisation of the security by a sale of the business as a going concern or pending resolution of a dispute as to the entitlement to the business.[46] The business may be carried on in England or abroad.[47]

In a case where a beneficial realisation requires the sale, or inclusion **22–016** in a sale, of an asset, and there is a dispute between the debenture-holder and company as to whether the asset is charged or whether the debenture is valid, notwithstanding that the company objects to the sale, the court may order such sale, making in the order appropriate provision for safeguarding the proceeds (or any part thereof) to await the resolution of the dispute.[48] An application for such an order may be made by a court-appointed receiver or by a receiver appointed out of court. The order may include any appropriate consequential order for vacating entries (*e.g.* estate contracts or cautions) at the Land Charges Registry and the Land Registry.[49] If the company owns an asset which is not charged, though the beneficial realisation of its charged asset requires that this asset is also included in the sale, the court cannot order a sale of the uncharged asset against the wishes of the company. If the company persists in its objection to the inclusion of the asset in the sale, the receiver can only seek to put the company into liquidation and hope for greater co-operation in the sale from the liquidator than received from the directors.

Instead of applying for the appointment of a receiver by the court, any **22–017** creditor (secured or otherwise) may pursue the alternative remedy of presenting a winding-up petition and applying immediately thereafter for the appointment of a provisional liquidator.[50] A creditor has the right by such means to protect the company's assets so that they are available for equal distribution amongst all the creditors.[51] The availability of this alternative remedy may be relevant on an application for the appointment of a receiver and manager, for it may afford a more convenient and satisfactory method of realising the company's assets and protecting its creditors.

---

[46] *Halsbury's Laws of England* (4th ed.), Reissue Vol. 39(2), paras 482–3. The court may authorise the manager to borrow money on security having priority to any existing debenture if the money is required to preserve the assets and goodwill, though even in this case the security will be postponed to the receiver's right to an indemnity unless contrary provision is made: *Greenwood v. Algeciras Railway* [1894] 2 Ch. 205.

[47] *Re Huinal Copper* [1910] W.N. 218.

[48] CPR 1998 Pt 25.1(1)(c)(v). See also ss. 114(3)(c) and 166(3)(b) of the Insolvency Act 1986 and *Arab Bank plc v. Mercantile Holdings Ltd.* [1994] 2 All E.R. 74.

[49] *Hornsea Potteries v. Destian* (unreported, CA, May 11, 1984).

[50] See paras 2.012 and 2.013, above. This remedy was successfully invoked by the debenture-holder in *Re Capital Expansion and Development Corporation Ltd*, *The Times*, November 30, 1992, when precluded by an injunction granted without notice from enforcing its security.

[51] *Re Dry Docks Corporation of London* [1888] 39 Ch.D. 306 at 314.

3. PROCEDURE ON APPLICATION FOR APPOINTMENT

22–018 An application for the appointment of a receiver made in existing proceedings must be made in accordance with CPR 1998 Part 23 and the Practice Direction supplementing that Part.[52] The court will ordinarily appoint the nominee of a mortgagee if the nominee is qualified and otherwise unobjectionable. As a matter of law, the appointee does not have to be qualified to act as an insolvency practitioner in relation to the company, for the provisions of Part XIII of the Insolvency Act 1986 do not apply to any receiver of a company other than an administrative receiver. But no doubt in practice the courts will require that its appointees and officers have identical qualifications. The court has a discretion whether to order that the receiver provides security.[53] If the order does require security the appointment will be conditional and ineffective until the receiver provides the requisite security, unless the court gives liberty to act forthwith. This it may do if the applicant is willing and able to give an undertaking to be responsible for the receiver's acts and defaults.

4. CHOICE BETWEEN APPOINTMENT IN AND OUT OF COURT

(a) Disadvantages
22–019 The appointment of a receiver or receiver and manager by the court has substantial disadvantages for the mortgagee.

    (a) There is first of all the expense and trouble of the application to the court and any delay which may occur until the order is made (ordinarily after a hearing on notice) and drawn up, and any security required by the order is provided by the receiver.

    (b) The selection of the receiver or receiver and manager is in the hands of the court which may have regard to the wishes of the company. In practice, the court gives effect to any proper choice of the mortgagee, but the appointee must be seen to be independent,[54] in stark contrast with an appointee under a debenture.

    (c) Unlike the appointee out of court,[55] a court-appointed receiver or receiver and manager is no-one's agent and certainly not an

---

[52] CPR 1998 1/RSC/30, r.1/1.

[53] CPR 1998 1/RSC/30, r.2. The security shall be by guarantee unless the court otherwise directs: *ibid.*

[54] *Halsbury's Laws of England* (4th ed.), Vol. 39, para. 845–851. The position may be different in the case of a receiver appointed by way of equitable execution: *Fuggle v. Bland* (1883) 11 Q.B.D. 711, *Cummins v. Perkins* [1899] 1 Ch. 16.

[55] *Griffiths v. Secretary of State* [1974] Q.B. 468 at 485–486.

agent of the company.[56] It has traditionally[57] been thought that the appointment of a receiver and manager by the court operates to terminate the employment of the company's employees.[58] Hence, if their employment is continued, it is under a new contract with the receiver. The termination of the employees' contracts of employment with the company gives rise to rights to damages against the company.[59] The need to avoid this result may be a legitimate ground upon which the company may seek to oppose the appointment of the receiver. The appointment does not affect the directors' tenure of office or right to remuneration.[60]

(d) The court-appointed receiver is personally liable under contracts entered into by him, though he expressly contracts as receiver and manager.[61] He is, however, entitled to an indemnity out of the assets of the company to the extent that they are sufficient.[62]

(e) The court-appointed receiver has to go through the procedures (and incur the costs) of applications to the court for authority if any proposed action lies outside the ambit of any existing order[63] and in any event in respect of submitting his accounts, fixing his remuneration[64] and obtaining his discharge.

(f) The court-appointed receiver is considered to be appointed for the benefit, not of the debenture-holder alone, but of all persons interested in the assets of the company. Accordingly, unlike the receiver appointed out of court who acts for the primary benefit of the debenture-holder who appointed him, the court appointed receiver is under a duty to hold the scales evenly between the company and the debenture-holder. Thus Buckley L.J. said in *Re Newdigate Colliery Ltd*[65]:

[56] *Channel Airways v. Manchester Corp.* [1974] 1 Lloyd's Rep. 456.

[57] For an alternative view that the appointment of a receiver by the court need not invariably result in the termination of employment contracts, see O'Donovan, *Company Receivers and Administrators*, para. 20.670, citing *International Harvester Export. v. International Harvester Australia* (1982) 7 A.C.L.R. 391 and *Sipad Holding DDPO v. Popovic* (1996) 12 A.C.L.C. 307 at 309.

[58] See, *e.g. Reid v. Explosives Co. Ltd* (1887) 19 Q.B.D. 264 and see para. 19–002, above.

[59] *Measures v. Measures* [1910] 2 Ch. 248, *Re Mack Trucks (Britain) Ltd* [1967] 1 W.L.R. 780.

[60] *Re South Western of Venezuela Railway* [1902] 1 Ch. 701.

[61] *Re Burt, Boulton and Hayward v. Bull* [1895] 1 Q.B. 276. He does not incur personal liability if he merely causes the company to carry out contracts already made prior to his appointment: *Parsons v. Sovereign Bank of Canada* [1913] A.C. 160.

[62] *Boehm v. Goodall* [1911] 1 Ch. 155.

[63] If the receiver enters into a contract which is conditional upon obtaining the approval of the court, the court will require to be satisfied before it gives such approval that the entry into the contract is in the interests of the company and its creditors, not as at the date of the contract, but as at the date that approval is given: *Yap Yoke Luan v. Ong Wee Tok* [1984] 1 M.L.J. 23.

[64] His remuneration must be fixed by the court before he is entitled to appropriate to his own use funds of the receivership: *Cape v. Redarb Pty Ltd* (1992) 10 A.C.L.C. 333, Fed. Ct. of Australia.

[65] [1912] 1 Ch. 468 at 478. His role has been described as that of a caretaker: *Paterson v. Gaslight & Coke Co.* [1896] 2 Ch. 476.

"It has been truly said that in the case of a legal mortgage the legal mortgagee can take possession if he chooses of the mortgaged property, and being in possession can say 'I have nothing to do with the mortgagor's contracts. I shall deal with this property as seems to me most to my advantage ...' This appellant is not in that position. He is an equitable mortgagee who has obtained an order of the court under which its officer takes possession of assets in which the mortgagee and mortgagor are both interested, with the duty and responsibility of dealing with them fairly in the interest of both parties."

Accordingly, the court-appointed receiver has a continuing duty to preserve the goodwill of the company's business for the benefit of all persons interested, and (though he is not personally bound by or liable under existing contracts)[66] he should not disregard existing contracts and cease carrying on the business merely because this course would accelerate repayment to the debenture-holder.[67] The receiver appointed out of court is under no such continuing duty.[68] The duty does not extend to requiring him to carry out a contract if to do so would necessitate borrowing money ranking in priority to the debenture and the contract would prove unprofitable.[69]

(g) The court-appointed receiver is neither an administrative receiver nor an office-holder for the purposes of the Insolvency Act 1986, for the definition requires that the appointment be made by or on behalf of the debenture-holder.[70] Most significantly, the court-appointed receiver is not vested with the rights and privileges conferred on office-holders by sections 233–237 and 246(1) of the Insolvency Act[71] and in particular the various powers of investigation and the right to continued supplies from utilities.[72]

(h) In a case where the company denies the existence of the debt or the existence or validity of the security, the court may order that the receiver release to the company sufficient funds to challenge the right of the claimant to the order.[73]

[66] *e.g.* to pay interest payable during the receivership on mortgages made prior to the receivership order: see *Bayhold Financial Corp. Ltd. v. Clarkson Co. Ltd* (1991) 10 C.B.R. (3d) 159, Sup. Ct. of Nova Scotia, Appellate Division).

[67] *Re Newdigate Colliery Ltd* and *Parsons v. Sovereign Bank of Canada* [1913] A.C. 161. He may close the company's business without the prior approval of the court if the business has no, or ceases to have any, goodwill: *Bayhold Financial Corp. Ltd. v. Clarkson Co. Ltd* (1991) 10 C.B.R. (3d) 159, Sup. Ct of Nova Scotia, Appellate Divisions.

[68] He may, however, be expected to wish to preserve goodwill by completing rather than repudiating contracts: *Ashby Warner v. Simmons* [1936] 2 All E.R. 697 at 709.

[69] *Re Thames Ironworks* (1902) 106 L.T. 674.

[70] Insolvency Act 1986, ss. 29(2)(a) and 251.

[71] See Chap. 5.

[72] Insolvency Act 1986, s. 233 and see Chap. 5.

[73] See *Royal Bank of Canada v. West-Can Resource* (1990) 3 C.B.R. (3d) 55 and *Royal Bank of Canada v. Tower Aircraft* (1991) 3 C.B.R. (3d) 60.

(b) Advantages

The appointment by the court has, potentially, certain advantages over **22–020** the appointment out of court.

> (a) Where the validity of the debenture or right to appoint a receiver is disputed, the court may appoint a receiver and authorise him to enter into transactions (such as sales) binding on the mortgagee and the company irrespective of the outcome of the dispute.[74]
>
> (b) The court-appointed receiver may be authorised by the court to borrow money on security having priority to any existing debenture if the money is required to preserve the assets and goodwill (though the security will be postponed to the receiver's right to an indemnity unless contrary provisions are made).[75]
>
> (c) Foreign courts may on occasion (but not invariably) be more ready to recognise and give effect to the status and power of the court-appointed receiver on grounds of comity.[76]

5. THE RECEIVER AS AN OFFICER OF THE COURT

The court-appointed receiver, unlike the receiver appointed out of court, **22–021** is an officer of the court. His status has a number of consequences for third parties. Thus, in the case of a court-appointed receiver (but not a receiver appointed out of court):

> (a) a landlord cannot distrain[77] and the receiver cannot be sued[78] without leave of the court.[79] The rightfulness of a claim by or against the receiver will be determined on an application to the court in the proceedings in which the receiver is appointed[80];
>
> (b) a payment by the receiver in the course of his duties is not open to challenge on a subsequent liquidation as a preference since it is to be treated as a payment authorised by the court[81];
>
> (c) the receiver as an officer of the court is subject to the obligation, not merely to act lawfully, but also in accordance

---

[74] See n. 41, above. Likewise the court may appoint a receiver to resolve conflicts between mortgagees whose charges rank equally: see *Bass Breweries Ltd v. Delaney* [1994] B.C.C. 851.

[75] *Greenwood v. Algeciras Railways* [1894] 2 Ch. 205. If he borrows in excess of any limit set, he may be denied an indemnity out of the assets of the company: *Bayhold Financial Corp. Ltd. v. Clarkson Co. Ltd* (1991) 10 C.B.R. (3d) 159, Sup. Ct of Nova Scotia, Appellate Divisions.

[76] *cf.* paras 25–032 *et seq.*

[77] *Sutton v. Rees* (1869) 9 Jur N.S. 456.

[78] *L.P. Arthur (Insurance) Ltd. v. Sisson* [1966] 1 W.L.R. 1384. See also *Re Magic Aust Pty Ltd* (1992) 10 A.C.L.C. 929 (court appointed liquidator).

[79] *Hand v. Blow* [1901] 2 Ch. 721, 735.

[80] *I.R.C. v. Hoogstraten* [1985] Q.B. 1077 at 1093.

[81] *International Harvester Export Co. v. International Harvester Australia Co.* [1983] V.R. 539 at 549.

with principles of justice and honest dealing.[82] This obligation extends to payment of the costs of proceedings which he has brought or defended on behalf of the company.[83]

22–022 The status of the court-appointed receiver as an officer of the court has consequences in the field of contempt. Interference with the performance of his duty or his possession of property may constitute a contempt of court.[84] Receivers appointed out of court are not similarly protected.[85] Likewise, breach of duty by the court-appointed receiver may constitute a contempt.[86] A third party with a claim against the property over which the receiver ha been appointed should apply to the court for leave to enforce his rights. The court will then adjudicate upon the rival claims, seeking to do justice between those interested.[87]

6. INTER-RELATIONSHIP OF APPOINTMENTS BY COURT AND OUT OF COURT

22–023 The court may make an appointment of a receiver during a subsisting receivership out of court.[88] The effect of such an order is to displace the debenture-holder's receiver[89] and terminate his authority to act as agent of the company.[90] If an appointment is made by the court on the application of a second or subsequent mortgagee, the prior mortgagee may subsequently appoint a receiver, but such receiver cannot exercise his powers as such without the prior leave of the court[91] unless the court order making the appointment states that the order is made "without prejudice to the rights of prior incumbrancers".[92]

7. POWERS, DUTIES AND LIABILITIES

22–024 In general, the powers of a receiver appointed by the court are governed by the terms of the order appointing him. The receiver appointed by way

---

[82] Re Tyler [1907] 1 K.B. 865; ex p. James (1874) 9 Ch. App. 609. For the analagous position of the administrator as an officer of the court, see para. 23–041, below.

[83] Re London Metallurgical Company [1895] Ch. 758; Re Wenborn [1905] 1 Ch. 413; Smith v. UIC Insurance Company Ltd, H.H. Judge Dean Q.C., January 19, 1999.

[84] See, e.g. Re Mead (1875) L.R. 20 Eq. 282 (ousting from possession); and Searle v. Choat [1884] 25 Ch.D. 723 (suing receiver). Until a receiver has taken steps to obtain control of assets situated abroad in accordance with local law, it may not be a contempt for a creditor who is not a party to the litigation in which the receiver was appointed to attempt to seize those assets first: see Re Maudslay, Sons and Field [1900] 1 Ch. 602. For a study of a court-appointed receiver's status in the context of the N.U.M. strike, see G. Lightman, "A Trade Union in Chains" (1987) C.L.P. 25.

[85] See Re Hill [1896] 1 Ch. 947 at 954; Re Magic Aust Pty Ltd (1992) 10 A.C.L.C. 929 ("improper pressure").

[86] Re Gent (1888) 40 Ch.D. 190.

[87] See, e.g. Randfield v. Randfield (1860) 1 Dr. & Sm. 310, Re Maidstone Palace of Varieties Ltd [1909] 2 Ch. 283, L.P. Arthur (Insurance) Ltd v. Sisson [1966] 1 W.L.R. 1384.

[88] Re Slogger Automatic Feeder Co. Ltd [1915] 1 Ch. 478.

[89] Re Maskelyne British Typewriters [1898] 1 Ch. 133.

[90] Hand v. Blow [1901] 2 Ch. 721 at 732.

[91] Re Metropolitan Estates [1912] 2 Ch. 497.

[92] Underhay v. Read [1887] 20 Q.B.D. 209.

of equitable execution will generally have very limited powers of management (if any), whereas other court-appointed receivers and managers, such as those appointed pending resolution of litigation to determine who should manage the company, may have far-reaching powers of management.

In general a receiver appointed by the court ought not to bring **22–025** proceedings in the action in which he was appointed, but should adopt a neutral position.[93] The court appointed receiver has no right, without the leave of the court, to bring proceedings in the name of the company.[94] If he wishes to institute proceedings to recover or protect property over which he is appointed, the receiver should generally seek the assistance of a party to the action who should make such an application, with the receiver having power to do so in default or in cases of urgency.[95]

A receiver appointed by the court is under the same fiduciary duties[96] **22–026** and duties of care[97] as the receiver appointed out of court. So, for example, a court appointed receiver must act in good faith and must not compete with the company, or seek to profit from his position.[98] If he wishes to purchase, whether himself or through a company, any of the property over which he is appointed, he can only do so with the leave of the court.[99] The court appointed receiver must take reasonable care to obtain the best price reasonably obtainable for any property which he sells.[1]

As an officer of the court the receiver appointed by the court has one **22–027** important privilege in relation to his conduct of the receivership. The court has power, on his release or discharge, to protect the receiver from liability for acts done in the course of his duties, but will only do so after investigation or making provisions for the investigation of claims of which the court has notice.

8. DISCHARGE

The court may discharge the receiver if it is just to do so, *e.g.* if the **22–028** original appointment should never have been made or if default,

---

[93] *Comyn v. Smith* (1823) 1 Hog 81.

[94] *Viola v. Anglo-American Cold Storage Co.* [1912] 2 Ch. 305 and *Re Scottish Properties Ltd* (1977) 2 A.C.L.R. 264.

[95] *Parker v. Dunn* (1845) 8 Beav. 498, *Re Sacker* (1888) 22 Q.B.D. 179.

[96] *Re Magadi Soda Company Ltd.* (1925) 41 T.L.R. 297; *Mirror Group Newspapers plc v. Maxwell* [1998] B.C.C. 324 at 333 (a fiduciary duty of protecting, getting in, realising and ultimately passing on to others assets and property).

[97] *IRC v. Hoogstraten* [1985] Q.B. 1077. In *Clarke v. Heathfield* [1985] I.C.R. 203, Dillon L.J. said: "The question of indemnity to sequestrators appointed by the court was considered by this court in the case of *IRC v. Hoogstraten*: the position of a court appointed receiver cannot be significantly different". The receiver is not immune from suit by the person on whose application he was appointed: *L.P. Arthur (Insurance) Ltd v. Sisson* [1966] 1 W.L.R. 1384. See also *Procopi v. Maschakis* (1969) 211 E.G. 31 (receiver is not invariably bound to accept offer of highest bidder, *e.g.* if tardy and vacillating).

[98] *Re Gent* (1892) 40 WR 267; *Re Newdigate Colliery Ltd* [1912] 1 Ch. 468 and *Duffy v. Super Centre Development Ltd* [1967] 1 N.S.W.R. 382.

[99] *Re Magadi Soda Co. Ltd* (1925) 41 T.L.R. 297, *Nugent v. Nugent* [1908] 1 Ch. 546.

[1] *Telsen Electric v. JJ. Eastick* [1936] 3 All E.R. 266, *AIDC v. Co-operative Farmers* (1978) 2 A.C.L.R. 543, *Cape v. Redbarb (No. 2)* (1992) 10 A.C.L.C. 1272 at 1282.

misconduct or other ground for unfitness is shown. If the company goes into liquidation, the court may direct that the liquidator replace the receiver if the assets of the company are at least sufficient to pay the secured creditors and no conflict of interest is likely to arise between the secured and other creditors.[2] Such a replacement cannot be made by the court in case of a receiver appointed out of court.[3]

9. REMUNERATION, LIEN AND INDEMNITY

22–029 A receiver appointed by the court has an entitlement to remuneration irrespective of whether the order for his appointment was rightly made and whether the receivership proved beneficial. The remuneration must be authorised by the court, which may direct that such remuneration shall be fixed by reference to such scales or rates of professional charges as it thinks fit, or that it shall be assessed on the standard basis by a costs judge or a district judge.[4] The receiver must justify the reasonableness and prudence of the tasks undertaken for which remuneration is sought, in the same way as he must justify the reasonableness and prudence of incurring disbursements for which he seeks allowance and reimbursement.[5]

22–030   The receiver may insist, as a condition of accepting appointment, that the person seeking his appointment or someone else be personally responsible for his remuneration and indemnify him. In default of some such agreement, the receiver can only look to the assets the subject of the receivership.[6] He has a lien over all the assets over which he is appointed: the lien is not limited to those over which he has assumed control and it survives his discharge, for the lien is independent of possession or a continuing right to possession.[7] The court has no jurisdiction to order a party to pay the remuneration and expenses of the receiver as part of the costs "of and incidental to the proceedings".[8]

10. RECEIVERSHIP AND FOREIGN INSOLVENCY PROCEEDINGS

22–031 The Court of Appeal has held that a receiver will not be appointed by way of equitable execution of a foreign judgment.[9] That decision was on the basis that the foreign judgment was not recognised as a judgment by

---

[2] *Strong v. Carlyle Press* [1893] 1 Ch. 268.
[3] *Re Joshua Stubbs* [1891] 1 Ch. 475.
[4] RSC, Ord. 30, r.3, to be found in CPR Sched. 1.
[5] *Mirror Group Newspapers plc v. Maxwell* [1998] 1 B.C.L.C. 638: (the taxation is reported [1999] B.C.C. 694); B.C.C. 324; and see Mr Justice Lightman "Officeholders Charges — Cost Control and Transparency" (1998) 11 *Insolvency Intelligence* 1.
[6] *Alliance & Leicester BS v. Edgeshop* [1995] 2 B.C.L.C. 506 at 507G.
[7] *Mellor v. Mellor* [1992] 1 W.L.R. 517.
[8] In *re Andrews* [1999] 1 W.L.R. 1236 (but they may fall within the ambit of the cross-undertaking in damages given by the party on whose application the receiver is appointed).
[9] *Perry v. Zissis* [1977] 1 Lloyd's Rep. 607.

English law and therefore no receiver could be appointed to enforce it by way of equitable execution.

The willingness of the courts to assist and co-operate in the case of **22–032** foreign liquidations, administrations and receiverships is considered in Chapter 26. It is sufficient to say that the assistance may include the appointment of a receiver of the company in question or of some or all of its assets.

CHAPTER 23

ADMINISTRATORS UNDER AN ADMINISTRATION ORDER

23–001 A number of legal systems[1] have adopted legislation designed to achieve the rehabilitation of a company which has fallen on hard times, but which, if afforded a form of moratorium,[2] or an opportunity to enter into a scheme of arrangement with its creditors, has a reasonable prospect of recovery.[3] A familiar characteristic is that the court is given jurisdiction to appoint an officer to manage the affairs of the company[4] and to regulate or restrict the exercise by creditors of the company of their rights and remedies, as a temporary measure whilst the necessary steps are taken to safeguard its future. The Insolvency Act 1986 introduced a version of this jurisdiction into English law in the form of administration orders.[5] The essential nature of administration was summarised by Nicholls L.J. giving the judgment of the Court of Appeal in *Re Atlantic Computer Systems plc*[6] where he said:

> ". . . an administration is intended to be only an interim and temporary regime. There is to be a breathing space while the company, under new management in the person of the administrator, seeks to achieve one or more of the purposes set out in section 8(3). There is a moratorium on the enforcement of debts and rights,

---

[1] *e.g.* Australia and South Africa. In the United States in the form of Chap. XI of the Bankruptcy Code, there is a fully developed sophisticated system for corporate "reorganisation". Under the Companies Act of Singapore, s. 227B(10), there is conferred on the court an overriding jurisdiction to make a judicial management order (the equivalent of an administration order) "if it considers the public interest so requires" and to appoint an interim judicial manager. As to this legislation, see *Re Cosmotron Electrics (Singapore) Pte Ltd* [1989] 2 M.L.J. 11.

[2] Although for convenience references are made in this chapter to a "moratorium", strictly speaking there is no moratorium (a legal authorisation to a debtor to postpone payment for a certain time), since the debts and liabilities remain payable, but only a quasi- moratorium affecting remedies for non-payment. The difference may have conflict of laws implications: see para. 25–021.

[3] Important questions can arise as to whether such procedures result in unfair competition or involve State aid. See further *Ecotrade Srl v. Altiforni e Ferriere di Servola SpA (AFS) (C200/97)* [1999] 2 C.M.L.R. 804.

[4] This is not the case in the United States under Chap. XI where (unless the court otherwise orders) the existing management remains in control. An intermediate course is taken in Ireland under the Companies (Amendment) Act 1990 and Companies Act 1990. Under the Australian procedure contained in Part 5.3A of the Corporations Law, an administrator is appointed but the court is not necessarily involved, although it has a supervisory role.

[5] A voluntary moratorium is normally only practicable in the case of a small company with a lot of goodwill and largely local creditors. The Insolvency Bill 2000 includes provisions for a short moratorium (modelled on that in administration) to be available to small companies wishing to enter into a company voluntary arrangement, without the need to apply for an administration order.

[6] [1992] Ch. 505 at 528, CA. See also *Re Bradwin Ltd's Petition* [1997] N.I.L.R. 394.

---

proprietary and otherwise, against the company, so as to give the administrator time to formulate proposals and lay them before the creditors, and then implement any proposals approved by the creditors. In some cases winding-up will follow, in others it will not."

Section 8 of the 1986 Act empowers the court to make an administration order, that is to say, an order that during the period for which the order is in force the affairs, business and property of the company[7] shall be managed by a person (to be known as "the administrator") appointed for the purpose by the court.[8] Section 9(1) provides that an application to the court for an administration order shall be by petition which will usually be presented by the company,[9] the directors[10] or one or more creditors[11] or a combination of them but may be presented by other parties in a number of special situations.[12] The two pre-conditions to the making of the order are that:

(a) the court is satisfied that the company is or is likely to become unable to pay its debts[13]; and

---

[7] Under the Insolvent Partnerships Order 1994 (S.I. 1994 No. 2421) the court now has jurisdiction to make an administration order in respect of an insolvent partnership, but partnership insolvency is outside the scope of this book. See further *Re Kyrris (No. 2)* [1998] B.P.I.R. 111; *Re H.S. Smith & Sons, The Times,* January 6, 1999.

[8] The person appointed administrator must be qualified to act as an insolvency practitioner: see above, Chap. 4. If an unqualified person is appointed, the appointment will be valid, but the court should replace him: consider *Garden Mews-St. Leonards Pty Ltd v. Butler Poliway Pty Ltd* (1985) 9 A.C.L.R. 117. See further below, para. 23–045.

[9] In *Re Kentish Homes Group* (unreported, July 31, 1989), Harman J. followed *Re Emmadart Ltd* [1979] Ch. 540 and held that companies are not entitled to present petitions pursuant only to resolutions of their directors. See also *Re Chelmsford City Football Club (1980) Ltd* [1991] B.C.C. 133 and *Re Land and Property Trust Co. plc.* [1991] B.C.C. 446 (on appeal [1993] B.C.C. 462).

[10] Either all the directors have to join in the petition, or, since all directors are bound by a properly passed board resolution, one director can present a petition on behalf of all the directors (including any who voted against the resolution) — *Re Equiticorp International plc* [1989] 1 W.L.R. 1010; see further *Re Instrumentation Electrical Services Ltd* (1988) 4 B.C.C. 301; *Re Business Properties Ltd* (1988) 4 B.C.C. 684 and (particularly as regards the sufficiency of directors' interests) *Re Land and Property Trust Co. plc* [1991] B.C.C. 446.

[11] A claimant for money had and received may be a creditor although he has also a claim to trace the same money against the company as constructive trustee: *Re Prime Metals Trading Ltd* [1984] B.C.L.C. 543. As to cross-undertakings in damages, see *Re Gallidoro Trawlers Ltd* [1991] B.C.C. 691.

[12] See s. 7(4) (see also r.2.1(4)) (supervisors of corporate voluntary arrangements); s. 9(1) and the Banks (Administration Proceedings) Order 1989 (S.I. 1989 No. 1276) (Financial Services Authority); s. 9(1) and Magistrates' Courts Act 1980, s. 87A (magistrates' clerks); Financial Services Act 1986, s. 74 (recognised organisations and bodies or the Secretary of State); Building Societies Act 1986, Sched. 15A, para. 11 (Building Societies Commission).

[13] As defined by s. 123 of the Insolvency Act 1986. Under the definition, a company is to be deemed to be insolvent if the value of its assets is less than the amount of its liabilities, taking into account its prospective and contingent liabilities, as to which see *Stonegate Securities Ltd v. Gregory* [1980] Ch. 576; *Re A Company* [1986] B.C.L.C. 261 and *Byblos Bank v. Al-Khudhairy* [1987] B.C.L.C. 232 CA. Consider also *Xonics Photochemical Inc. v. Mitsui* 841 F. 2d. 198 (7th Cir., 1988); *Covey v. Commercial National Bank of Peoria CCH Bankr Dec 74,530* (7th Cir., Ct. of App. 1992). It is possible for the court to make an order where a company is asset solvent but cash insolvent, but this will be unusual — *Re Business Properties Ltd* (1988) 4 B.C.C. 684. See also *Re Imperial Motors (U.K.) Ltd* (1989) 5 B.C.C. 214.

(b) the court considers that the making of such an order would be likely to achieve[14] the purpose of securing any one or more of the following:

(i) the survival of the company, and the whole or any part of its undertaking, as a going concern[15];

(ii) the approval under Part 1 of the 1986 Act of a composition in satisfaction of the company's debts or a scheme of arrangement of its affairs;

(iii) the sanctioning under section 425 of the Companies Act 1985 of a compromise or arrangement between the company and any such person as is mentioned in that section; or

(iv) a more advantageous realisation of the company's assets than would be effected on a winding-up.

The order is required to specify the purpose or purposes for whose achievement it is made.

23–002   Four limitations on the jurisdiction exist:

(a) Though interim orders may be made,[16] an interim administrator cannot be appointed.[17]

(b) An administrator cannot be appointed if a chargee under a floating charge has appointed an administrative receiver[18] unless the court is satisfied either that the appointor has consented[19] or that, if the administration order were made, the charge or security by virtue of which the receiver was appointed would be liable to be released or discharged under sections 238 to 240[20] or would be avoided under section 245 of the Act.[21] For the bar to exist, there must be a valid appointment of a receiver under a

---

[14] See below, para. 23–016.

[15] The interim or temporary nature of administration implies some limitation on this purpose. In *Re Bradwin Ltd's Petition* [1997] N.I.L.R. 394, the High Court in Northern Ireland held that a proposal by the company to let out its premises and to repay its creditors out of the resultant income stream over a period of time, would go outside the statutory purpose.

[16] s. 9(4) and (5); see also *Re Gallidoro Trawlers Ltd* [1991] B.C.C. 691.

[17] s. 13(1); *Re A Company (No. 00175 of 1987)* (1987) 3 B.C.C. 124; *Re Gallidoro Trawlers Ltd* [1991] B.C.C. 691. In Scotland it has been held that there is power to appoint an interim administrator: *Air Ecosse Ltd v. Civil Aviation Authority* (1987) 3 B.C.C. 492; *Re Avenel Hotel Ltd* (unreported, March 1987). See also *Scottish Exhibition Centre Ltd, Noters* [1993] B.C.C. 529; *Scottish Exhibition Centre Ltd v. Mirestop* [1994] B.C.C. 845; *Secretary of State for Trade and Industry v. Palmer* [1994] B.C.C. 990.

[18] s. 9(3). In *Re A Company (No. 00175 of 1987)* (1987) 3 B.C.C. 124, it was held that there is no power to adjourn to allow time for repayment because s. 9(3) is mandatory.

[19] If the appointor is minded to consent, it is advantageous to do so at the earliest possible moment since the timing of the consent determines when the pre-hearing moratorium commences and accordingly the company's assets are safeguarded to satisfy his (and other creditors') claims.

[20] As a transaction at an undervalue or a preference, see above, Chap. 11.

[21] As a floating charge created with a fixed period prior to the date of the administration order, see above, Chap. 11.

valid floating charge.[22] If the validity of the appointment or charge is challenged, then the validity must be determined before the administration order can be made[23] but not before the petition for such order can be issued or interim relief granted.

(c) The jurisdiction is not exercisable in respect of a company after it has gone into liquidation[24] or where the company is an insurance company within the meaning of the Insurance Companies Act 1982.[25]

(d) The order does not affect the legal relationship between the company and other persons. Contracts may, and frequently do, identify administration as an event of default which either terminates the counterparty's obligations automatically or gives rise to a power of termination. Such provisions take effect accordingly to their own terms. In the absence of any such provisions, the making of an administration order is unlikely to be regarded as an anticipatory breach.[26] The general rule is also that, subject to any provisions to the contrary in the relevant agreement, contracts continue to bind companies in administration and that administrators do not enjoy the same freedom as receivers to disregard contracts.[27] The moratorium

---

[22] In *Re Croftbell Ltd* [1990] B.C.C. 781, a submission was made that a debenture should be disregarded for the purposes of s. 9 on the ground that it was merely artificial and aimed at circumventing the purposes of Part II. The submission failed.

[23] The fact that the appointment of an administrative receiver has the effect of barring an administration order may be a relevant factor, in a case where the validity of the floating charge or the appointment is challenged, for the court on the basis of balance of convenience more readily to grant interim injunctions restraining the holder making such an appointment or ordering his appointment to be discharged.

[24] As to the effect of rescission of a winding-up order, see *Re SN Group plc* [1993] B.C.C. 808.

[25] s. 8(4). Specific exemption may also result from other legislation, *e.g.* Water Industry Act 1991 and Railways Act 1993 (but note that "administration" procedures under those Acts apply some of the provisions of Part II of the 1986 Act in modified form). Banks and licensed institutions were also excluded when the legislation first took effect. The provisions of Part II of the Act now apply to authorised institutions and former authorised institutions as modified by the Banks (Administration Proceedings) Order 1989 (S.I. 1989 No. 1276). Foreign registered banks remain excluded by the terms of the Order. Administration (with modifications) is available in respect of building societies under the Building Societies Act 1986, s. 90A. The provisions of Part II of the Act are modified in their application to insolvency in the financial markets by the Companies Act 1989, s. 175, the Financial Markets and Insolvency Regulations 1991 (S.I. 1991 No. 880) and the Financial Markets and Insolvency (Money Market) Regulations 1995 (S.I. 1995 No. 2049). Other instances of special requirements or modifications may be encountered under other legislation applicable to specific sectors, *e.g.* the Housing Act 1996. All these matters are outside the scope of this chapter and are not taken into account in the remainder of the text.

[26] *Smith v. DFC of T* (1997) 15 A.C.L.C. 3 (a case on the effect in Australia of the equivalent provisions in Australian law); see also *Triffit Nurseries v. Salads Etcetera Ltd*, [2000] 1 B.C.L.C. 761, CA.

[27] *Astor Chemical Ltd v. Synthetic Technology Ltd* [1990] B.C.C. 97 (see further *British and Commonwealth Holdings plc v. Barclays Bank plc* [1998] 1 W.L.R. 1 where the Court of Appeal upheld a decision that administrators were bound by the terms of an agreement which bound the company by virtue of an order under the Companies Act 1985, s.425). An administrator has no power of disclaimer such as that available to a liquidator.

is procedural and is not intended to destroy the proprietary or substantive rights of creditors.[28] Administrators will not ordinarily be permitted to take the benefits of the company's contracts without meeting its obligations.[29] However, this area of law is not fully developed. In *Re P. & C. and R. & T. (Stockport) Ltd*[30] it was held that joint venturers could not insist on their contractual rights under a joint venture agreement in order to control the actions of administrators of the company which was the joint venture vehicle. The question was whether one joint venturer could decline to transfer a lease to the joint venture company in administration pursuant to the provisions of the joint venture agreement on the ground that the company in administration could no longer discharge its own contractual obligations to that party under the same agreement. It was held that the company in administration could compel perfection of its proprietary interest in the lease regardless of its inability to comply with its own general obligations under the agreement.[31]

1. SCOPE OF THE MORATORIUM

23–003 In a simple case the moratorium will commence with the presentation of a petition for an administration order. However, the moratorium does not commence on the presentation of the petition if there is already an administrative receiver of the company in office and the person by or on whose behalf that receiver was appointed has not consented to an administration order being made. In that case section 10(3) provides that the moratorium shall not begin unless and until the appointor consents. Once the moratorium has commenced it will apply by virtue of section 10 until an order is made or the petition is dismissed. If an order is made the moratorium is continued under section 11 for as long as the order is in force.

23–004   The principal features of the moratorium under section 11 of the Insolvency Act 1986 are that:

    (a) no resolution may be passed or order made for the winding up of the company;

    (b) no administrative receiver of the company may be appointed;

---

[28] *Re Sibec Developments Ltd* [1992] 1 W.L.R. 1253. In *Re Mirror Group (Holdings) Ltd* [1992] B.C.C. 972 the court held that it had jurisdiction to direct administrators to assign the benefit of contractual rights to an interested third party but declined to do so in the absence of an application for such directions by the administrators. In the same case Nicholls V.-C. commented that the company — which was in the course of a s. 8(3)(d) administration — could not be subjected to an injunction compelling it to find money.

[29] *Re Japan Leasing (Europe) plc* [1999] B.P.I.R. 911.

[30] [1991] B.C.C. 98.

[31] Consider also *Re Olympia & York Canary Wharf Ltd (No. 2)* [1993] B.C.C. 159.

(c) no other steps may be taken to enforce any security over the company's property,[32] or to repossess goods in the company's possession under any hire-purchase agreement,[33] except with the consent of the administrator or the leave of the court and subject (where the court gives leave) to such terms as the court may impose;

(d) no other proceedings[34] and no execution or other legal process may be commenced or continued, and no distress may be levied, against the company or its property except with the consent of the administrator or the leave of the court and subject (where the court gives leave) to such terms as it may impose.

The moratorium under section 10(1) (*i.e.* the moratorium where there is an administration petition pending) applies only (1), (3) and (4) above. There being no administrator capable of giving consent before an administration order is made, the only dispensation is by leave of the court. No leave is required for the presentation of a winding-up petition,[35] for the appointment of an administrative receiver or the carrying out by an administrative receiver of any of his functions.[36]

Where an administration order has been made, an LPA receiver must **23–005** vacate office if required to do so by the administrator. Any administrative receiver automatically vacates office and any pending winding-up petition is dismissed.[37] The prohibition on "proceedings" leaves open (subject to obtaining the necessary leave[38]) the possibility of presenting

---

[32] See, *e.g. Re Meesan Investment Ltd* (1988) 4 B.C.C. 788; *Royal Trust Bank v. Buchler* [1989] B.C.L.C. 130. It has been held that a mortgagee of land who takes possession is not enforcing his security: he is merely exercising his legal rights to possession incident to his rights as estate owner and his action is for recovery of possession see, *e.g. West Penwith RDC v. Gunnell* [1968] 1 W.L.R. 1153 and *Esso v. Alstonbridge* [1975] 1 W.L.R. 1474 at 1481. But this technical approach can have no application in the present statutory context in which the statutory purpose requires the freezing of all secured creditors' rights, the foremost of which must be the right to possession. Compare *Redditch BS v. Roberts* [1940] Ch. 415 at 420.

[33] For these purposes "hire purchase agreement" includes conditional sale agreements, chattel leasing agreements and retention of title agreements. These terms are all defined by the Insolvency Act 1986. Section 436 applies the Consumer Credit Act 1974 definitions of "conditional sale agreement" and "hire purchase agreement". Section 251 provides definitions of "chattel leasing agreement" and "retention of title agreement".

[34] This term includes interpleader proceedings *(Eastern Holdings Establishment of Vaduz v. Singer & Friedlander Ltd* [1967] 1 W.L.R. 1017) and a counterclaim exceeding the company's claim *(Langley Constructions (Brixham) Ltd v. Wells* [1969] 1 W.L.R. 503) but not the simple defence to an application made by the company in administration *(Pasdale Pty. Ltd v. Concrete Constructions* (1996) 14 A.C.L.C. 354). In *Simoon Pty. Ltd v. Renbay Systems Pty. Ltd* (1995) 13 A.C.L.C. 1792, the Supreme Court of New South Wales left open the question of whether leave was required, under the Australian procedure, to make an application for security for costs.

[35] s. 10(2). See further *Re A Company (No. 001992 of 1988)* (1988) 4 B.C.C. 451; *Re Manlon Trading Ltd* (1988) 4 B.C.C. 455; *Re A Company (No. 001448 of 1989)* (1989) 5 B.C.C. 706.

[36] s. 10(2). But see *Re A Company (No. 00175 of 1987)* (1987) 3 B.C.C. 124.

[37] s. 11(1) and (2); see also s. 11(4) and (5).

[38] Under s. 11(3)(d). On any such application the prospective effect of s.127 of the Insolvency Act 1986 would require careful consideration.

petitions to wind up or for relief under sections 459–461 of the Companies Act 1985,[39] though no order can be made for winding-up save after (even if immediate upon) the discharge of the administration order. A petition[40] in respect of prejudicial conduct by the administrator does not require leave.

23–006   The moratorium provides protection for the company, for its property and for its possessory rights in respect of certain categories of third party goods in its possession.[41] The overall scope of the moratorium has not yet been judicially explained, but there have been a series of decisions on section 11 which elucidate particular aspects:

(a) The restriction on enforcement of security over "the company's property" extends to the enforcement of security rights over special assets leased to it.[42]

(b) The restriction on repossession of leased goods in the "possession" of the company extends to repossession by the owner of goods held by third parties under sub-leases created by the company in their favour.[43]

(c) Forfeiture of leases by peaceable re-entry does not constitute security enforcement.[44]

(d) "Proceedings" and "other legal process" do not cover non-judicial actions, , e.g. service of contractual notices to terminate rights or crystallise liabilities.[45]

(e) The exercise of contractual rights of set-off does not amount to either the enforcement of security or the initiation of proceedings.[46]

(f) Statutory rights of detention constitute security.[47]

---

[39] Administration is not a suitable procedure to resolve deadlock where the company has a surplus of assets and a winding-up is needed to distribute the assets (an administrator cannot normally distribute assets to members), *Re Business Properties Ltd* (1988) 4 B.C.C. 684 at 686.

[40] s. 27. On the scope of the moratorium under the Australian procedure, consider *J & B Records v. Brashs Pty Ltd* (1994) 12 A.C.L.C. 534.

[41] See above, para. 23–004.

[42] *Bristol Airport plc v. Powdrill* [1990] Ch. 744; *sub nom. Re Paramount Airways Ltd* [1990] B.C.C. 130.

[43] *Re Atlantic Computer Systems plc* [1992] Ch. 505, CA.

[44] *Razzaq v. Pala* [1997] 1 W.L.R. 1336; *Clarence Café Ltd v. Comchester Properties Ltd* [1999] L. & T.R. 303; *Re Lomax Leisure Ltd* [1999] 3 W.L.R. 652; refusing to follow *Exchange Travel Agency Ltd v. Triton Property Trust plc* [1991] B.C.C. 341; see also *Re Olympia & York Canary Wharf Ltd* [1993] B.C.C. 154.

[45] *Bristol Airport plc v. Powdrill* [1990] Ch. 744; *Re Olympia & York Canary Wharf Ltd* [1993] B.C.C. 154; *Scottish Exhibition Centre Ltd v. Mirestop* [1994] B.C.C. 845; in the *Olympia & York* case the question of whether a demand or notice falls within s. 11(3)(c) was left open. For decisions on what amounts to enforcement in other contexts, see *Re John Jones, ex p. The National Provincial Bank* [1932] 1 Ch. 548; *400 Lonsdale Nominees Pty. Ltd v. Southern Cross Airlines Holdings Ltd (in liquidation)* (1993) 11 A.C.L.C. 744 and *Re Scandees Danish Home Ice Cream Pty. Ltd* (1995) 13 A.C.L.C. 605.

[46] *Electro Magnetic (S) Ltd v. Development Bank of Singapore Ltd* [1994] 1 S.L.R. 734 — a decision on the equivalent provisions of the judicial management procedure in Singapore.

[47] *Bristol Airport plc v. Powdrill* [1990] Ch. 744.

(g) Leave to pursue a claim for a remedial constructive trust will be refused because such claims are inimical to the statutory scheme for the distribution of assets in insolvency.[48]

(h) "Proceedings" governed by section 11(3)(d) are not confined to actions brought by creditors.[49]

(i) The moratorium applies to criminal proceedings.[50]

(j) An application for extension of time under section 404 of the Companies Act 1985 to register a charge does not constitute "proceedings . . . against the company or its property".[51]

(k) Adjudication of a dispute under a building contract pursuant to s108 Housing Grants Construction and Regeneration Act 1996, being a form of arbitration albeit one where the arbitrator has a discretion as to procedure and the full rules of natural justice do not apply, is nonetheless "other proceedings" for the purposes of section 11(3)(d).[52]

(l) Retention of property by a lien holder in the face of a call for delivery by the administrator constitutes enforcement of security.[53]

(m) The application by solicitors of client account money in satisfaction of outstanding bills is the enforcement of security but, even on the assumption that the original lien is destroyed by the payment out and that any repayment is property of the company, a fresh general lien arises on restitution of the money.[54]

(n) Goods are in the possession of a company "under" an agreement for the purposes of the moratorium notwithstanding that the company's rights under the agreement have been terminated prior to presentation of an administration petition and the owner has been wrongly prevented from repossessing.[55]

(o) An application to an industrial tribunal alleging unfair selection for redundancy and seeking reinstatement constitutes "proceedings". An application made without prior consent or leave is not however, a nullity.[56]

---

[48] *Re Polly Peck International plc (No. 5)* [1998] 2 B.C.L.C. 185, CA.

[49] *Biosource Technologies Inc v. Axis Genetics plc* [2000] 1 B.C.L.C. 286. In *Air Ecosse Ltd v. Civil Aviation Authority* (1987) 3 B.C.C. 492, the Court of Session held that s11(3)(d) did not apply to actions by regulatory authorities. In the light of the more recent English decisions it is thought that *Air Ecosse* would not be followed by the English courts. See also *Bristol Airport plc v. Powdrill* [1990] Ch. 744.

[50] *Re Rhondda Waste Disposal Co. Ltd, The Times,* March 2, 2000, CA.

[51] *Re Barrow Borough Transport Ltd* [1990] Ch. 227.

[52] *A. Straume (U.K.) Ltd v. Bradlor Developments Ltd* [2000] B.C.C. 333.

[53] *Bristol Airport plc v. Powdrill* [1990] Ch. 744; see further *Re Sabre International Products Ltd* [1991] B.C.C. 694.

[54] *Euro Commercial Leasing Ltd v. Cartwright & Lewis* [1995] 1 B.C.L.C. 618.

[55] *Re David Meek Access Ltd & Anor.* [1993] B.C.C. 175 (leave to repossess was given).

[56] *Carr v. British International Helicopters Ltd* [1993] B.C.C. 855; *Re Paramount Airways Ltd (No. 3)* [1993] B.C.C. 662, on appeal *sub nom. Powdrill v. Watson* [1995] 2 A.C. 394, HL. In *Re AGB Research plc* [1994] N.P.C. 56 it was held that landlords, who had asserted their right of re-entry by giving possession to another party, could not rely on s. 11(3) to deny forfeiture.

    (p) The moratorium does not prevent time running for the purposes of the Limitation Act 1980.[57]

    (q) Where the appointment of administrative receivers follows the presentation of an administration petition, section 10(3) does not apply and the moratorium operates, in effect, for the benefit of the administrative receivers pending dismissal of the petition, *e.g.* to prevent landlord's distress.[58]

The order does not protect directors or sureties.[59]

2. PETITION

(a) Petition and affidavit

23–007 Administration proceedings commence with the presentation of a petition.[60] Before a petition can be filed, an affidavit in support must be prepared and sworn.[61] The "staying" power of the petition is of such force that it could be used as a potent instrument of abuse, and accordingly the inherent power of the court to strike out proceedings including such petitions may be a necessary, if cautiously exercised, antidote.[62] Once presented, a petition cannot be withdrawn without the leave of the court.[63] This should be borne in mind in the context of any proposal to pay off a petitioning creditor and should act as a further deterrent against frivolous and vexatious petitions.

(b) Independent report

23–008 Rule 2.2 provides that an independent report on the company's affairs may be prepared with a view to its being exhibited to the affidavit in support. The rules impose no absolute requirement that such a report be prepared, but rule 2.3 provides that the affidavit must state whether such a report been prepared and, if not, give an explanation why not. In the early years of administration the court emphasised the importance of independent reports on a number of occasions[64] and, in practice,

---

[57] *Re Maxwell Fleet and Facilities Management Ltd* [2000] 1 All E.R. 464.

[58] *Re Nuthall Lighting Ltd* (unreported, Ferris J. November 3, 1998) where leave to levy distress was refused. It is questionable whether the refusal of leave in such circumstances is consistent with the purposes of the moratorium.

[59] As to the analogous position of a creditor proceeding against a surety after a winding-up order or a scheme of arrangement, see *Commercial Banking Co. of Sydney Ltd v. Galy* [1978] 2 N.S.W.L.R. 271.

[60] See generally rr. 2.1–2.5 and Forms 2.1 and 2.2.

[61] *Re West Park Golf & Country Club* [1997] 1 B.C.L.C. 20.

[62] Consider *Re A Company (No. 002567 of 1982)* [1983] 1 W.L.R. 927 and *Bryanston Finance v. de Vries (No. 2)* [1976] Ch. 63; *Re Genesis Technologies International (S) Pty. Ltd* [1994] 3 S.L.R. 390 (High Court of Singapore); *Re West Park Golf & Country Club* [1997] 1 B.C.L.C. 20 (a partnership administration case).

[63] s. 9(2)(b). See also *Re Business Properties Ltd* (1988) 4 B.C.C. 684.

[64] *Re Newport County Association Football Club* (1987) 3 B.C.C. 635; *Re W.F. Fearman Ltd* (1988) 4 B.C.C. 139; *Re Manlon Trading Ltd* (1988) 4 B.C.C. 455; *Re Primlaks (U.K.) Ltd* (1989) 5 B.C.C. 710; *Re Rowbotham Baxter Ltd* [1990] B.C.C. 113; *Re Shearing & Loader Ltd* [1991] B.C.C. 232.

independent reports became increasingly complex documents.[65] The correct approach to both the provision of a rule 2.2 report and its content is now covered by a Practice Statement.[66]

Where an independent report is provided it may be made by the **23–009** person proposed as administrator and this will often be the most convenient course. The person preparing the report must sufficiently acquaint himself with the company's affairs[67] and the report must identify the section 8 purposes which, in the opinion of the person preparing it, may be achieved for the company by an administration order being made.[68] The views of experienced impartial insolvency practitioners set out in a fairly detailed report will carry weight with the court.[69] *Re Sharps of Truro Ltd*[70] is authority for the proposition that the usual requirement for full disclosure on an application without notice is particularly important in administration where only the administrator can apply for discharge. However, in *Re MTI Trading Systems Ltd*[71] it was held that the ordinary consequences of non-disclosure do not necessarily apply since creditors' interests should not be jeopardised by a failure of disclosure by the applicant if the case otherwise has merit.

Rule 2.2 reports may be used by the Secretary of State in subsequent **23–010** director disqualification proceedings. Where a company acting by its directors has invited the court to act on a report on the hearing of a petition, the principle that no-one may approbate and reprobate with regard to a document will apply.[72]

(c) Service and abridgement of time

Section 9 provides that notice of a petition must be given forthwith to **23–011** any person who has appointed, or is or may be entitled to appoint, an administrative receiver.[73] Section 9 also includes provisions for rules to include a requirement that notice be given to other persons and detailed provisions dealing with filing and service of the petition are contained in rules 2.5-2.8.[74] The petition must be served on:

---

[65] For the significance of financial information, see *Re SCL Building Services Ltd* (1989) 5 B.C.C. 746; *Re Dallhold Estates (U.K.) Pty Ltd* [1992] B.C.C. 394.

[66] *Practice Statement (Administration Orders: Reports)* [1994] 1 W.L.R. 160 set out in the Appendices to this work.

[67] *Re Tajik Air Ltd* [1996] 1 B.C.L.C. 317; *Re Sharps of Truro Ltd* [1990] B.C.C. 94.

[68] r. 2.2. In *Re Maxwell Communications Corporation plc* [1992] B.C.C. 372 rival independent reports were presented.

[69] *Re Structures & Computers Ltd* [1998] 1 B.C.L.C. 292.

[70] [1990] B.C.C. 94. As to non-disclosure, see also *Astor Chemical Ltd v. Synthetic Technology Ltd* [1990] B.C.C. 97. But note *Cornhill Insurance plc v. Cornhill Financial Services Ltd* [1992] B.C.C. 818 on both non-disclosure and the power to rescind on application by a creditor: see below, para. 23–031. It is suggested that the power of an aggrieved creditor to seek rescission provides, in effect, the same remedy as an application to discharge by the administrator. The distinction is procedural.

[71] [1997] B.C.C. 703, on refusal of leave to appeal [1998] B.C.C. 400, CA.

[72] *Re Circle Holidays International plc* [1994] B.C.C. 226. See also *Re Synthetic Technology Ltd* [1993] B.C.C. 549.

[73] See further *Re Croftbell Ltd* [1990] B.C.C. 781.

[74] See also Form 2.3.

(a) any person who has appointed, or is or may be entitled to appoint, an administrative receiver[75];

(b) if an administrative receiver has been appointed, on him;

(c) if there is a pending winding-up petition, on the petitioner and the provisional liquidator (if any);

(d) the person proposed as administrator;

(e) if the petition is presented by creditors of the company, on the company.

Notice of the petition must be given to persons charged with an execution or other legal process, or who have distrained against the company or its property.

23–012   The question whether or not the court may dispense with service caused some initial difficulty. In *Re Vosper Ship Repairers Ltd*,[76] it was held that the court could dispense with service if a person entitled to appoint an administrative receiver consented. Doubts were expressed about the power to dispense with service in *Re Valarette Ltd*.[77] In *Re Cavco Floors Ltd*,[78] Harman J. made an administration order in reliance on a solicitors' undertaking to present a petition, having been given evidence that the debenture-holder consented to abridgment and to the proposed order. The judgment states that the requirement for service on the proposed administrator can be waived. In *Re Chancery plc*,[79] Harman J. again dispensed with service but in the special circumstances of an administration petition in respect of an authorised institution under the Banking Act, presented by the bank's directors with the Bank of England having been notified and having agreed to short notice. In *Re Shearing & Loader Ltd*,[80] an administration order was made on an undertaking to present a petition forthwith. However, in *Cornhill Financial Services Ltd v. Cornhill Insurance plc*[81] Dillon L.J. expressly approved earlier criticism by Harman J. of the practice of obtaining administration orders on such undertakings. Despite the criticism of this practice, it is considered that in special cases administration orders can and should continue to be made on undertakings.

23–013   Abridgment of time is a related question. Rule 2.7 provides that a petition should be served not less than five days before the date fixed for

---

[75] It is not clear whether these words cover a debenture-holder whose power to appoint is subject to pre-conditions (e.g. service of demand). The point, on which there were submissions but no decision was made in *Re Brixham Pottery Ltd* (unreported, February 4, 1988; see further Anderson, "Administration: Rights of Secured Creditors" (1990) 6 I.L. & P. 130), will not arise in the case of debentures created before December 29, 1986 because of the provisions of Sched. 11, para. I of the Act. A well-drawn debenture created subsequently will include express provision for the power to appoint to arise on presentation of an administration petition.

[76] Unreported, February 17, 1987.

[77] Unreported, October 15, 1987. (J. Chadwick, Q.C.).

[78] [1990] B.C.C. 589.

[79] [1991] B.C.C. 171.

[80] [1991] B.C.C. 232; see also *Re Rowbotham Baxter Ltd* [1990] B.C.C. 113.

[81] [1992] B.C.C. 818.

the hearing. In *Re A Company (No. 00175 of 1987)*,[82] it was held that there was nothing in the Act which could be read as impliedly restricting the power of the court to abridge time under rule 12.9. Vinelott J. found it difficult to conceive of circumstances in which an order would be made without giving a debenture-holder time to decide whether or not to appoint an administrative receiver. Conversely, the court may be requested to adjourn a petition but, save in the most exceptional circumstances, it is not appropriate to adjourn or stand over a petition for a substantial period.[83]

(d) Interim orders

The presentation of a petition gives rise to the power of the court on **23–014** hearing the petition (a term presumably wide enough to include hearings of applications prior to the first formal hearing of the petition) to make interim orders "or any other order that it thinks fit".[84] Wider language it is scarcely possible to conceive. But without prejudice to the generality of this language it is provided that interim orders may restrict the exercise of any powers by the directors or of the company (whether by reference to the consent of the court or of a person qualified to act as an insolvency practitioner in relation to the company or otherwise).[85] It is suggested that in fact the Act does build in certain limitations on this apparently unlimited jurisdiction, and in particular it cannot be exercised to prevent persons exercising rights recognised as subsisting irrespective of the presentation of the petition. Thus, the section cannot be used as a basis of jurisdiction to restrain presentation of a petition to wind up[86] or the appointment of an administrative receiver or the exercise by such receiver of his powers (unless the charge under which he is appointed is open to challenge under sections 238 to 240 or 245).[87] Nor can new positive obligations be foisted on creditors, *e.g.* to supply or lend money to the company, as opposed to the imposition of restrictions on the exercise of existing rights.[88] Subject to such built-in limitations, the court can impose on the company and its creditors any scheme for protecting and preserving its assets and its future as the circumstances require.

---

[82] 1987) 3 B.C.C. 124; see also *Re Gailidoro Trawlers Ltd* [1991] B.C.C. 691.

[83] *Re Chelmsford City Football Club (1980) Ltd* [1991] B.C.C. 133; *Re Kyrris (No. 1)* [1998] B.P.I.R. 103.

[84] s. 9(4). As an alternative the court has power to make an administration order for a limited period: *Re Scrummys Ltd* (unreported, 1987; see further Homan, *Administrations under the Insolvency Act 1986* (1989) I.C.A.E.W. Research Board Research Paper); *Re Newport County Association Football Club Ltd* (1987) 3 B.C.C. 635.

[85] s. 9(5); see further above, para. 23–002 and above, nn. 16 and 17.

[86] In *Re W.F. Fearman Ltd* (1988) 4 B.C.C. 139 the court refused to use its s. 9(4) power to appoint a provisional liquidator but made an appointment under a pending winding-up petition instead.

[87] See above, para. 23–002.

[88] With the statutory exception under s. 233 of supplies of utilities, as to which see above, para. 5–003.

(e) Hearing

23–015 Any of the following may appear or be represented on the hearing of the petition[89]:

(a) the petitioner;

(b) the company;

(c) any person who has appointed an administrative receiver, or is or may be entitled to do so;

(d) the administrative receiver, if one has been appointed;

(e) any person who has presented a winding-up petition;

(f) the proposed administrator;

(g) with the leave of the court, any other person who appears to have an interest justifying his appearance.

Although questions of the petitioner's status normally need to be resolved before the final order is made, liquidation principles do not apply since it would frustrate the purpose of the legislation if any such issue necessarily had to be decided before an order could be made.[90] Although there is no provision for contributories' petitions,[91] the interests of shareholders and management in not having the business of the company taken out of their hands and sold to a third party were taken into account in *Re Imperial Motors (U.K.) Ltd.*[92] In *Re Chelmsford City Football Club (1980) Ltd*[93] the court applied the classic winding-up test[94] and held that, since the company was plainly insolvent, shareholders had no interests sufficient to justify them being heard.[95] Although the opposition of creditors who obtain leave is relevant to a consideration of whether there is any real prospect[96] of the intended purposes of an administration order being achieved, the court will not simply count heads.[97] The interests of secured creditors are relevant but less persuasive than the interests of other creditors.[98] Although the

---

[89] r. 2.9. See also r. 7.53 (right of attendance). The petition will be listed to be heard by a judge in public in accordance with para. 5.1(5) of the Practice Direction on Insolvency Proceedings. In an appropriate case the court may be persuaded to sit in private: see the terms of para. 5.1(5) of the Practice Direction on Insolvency Proceedings and Part 39.2 of the CPR. See also *Re Chancery plc* [1991] B.C.C. 171.

[90] *Re MTI Trading Systems Ltd* [1997] B.C.C. 703, on refusal of leave to appeal [1998] B.C.C. 400, CA.

[91] *Re Land and Property Trust Co. plc* [1991] B.C.C. 446.

[92] (1989) 5 B.C.C. 214.

[93] [1991] B.C.C. 133.

[94] *Re Rica Gold Washing Co.* (1879) 11 Ch.D. 36.

[95] The members were also creditors and were given leave to be heard in the latter capacity. In *Re K&H Options Ltd* (unreported, February 17, 2000), the possibility that future realisations would result in a balance sheet surplus was held to give members a tangible interest in the outcome and leave was given under r. 2.9(1)(g).

[96] See below, para. 23–016.

[97] *Re Land and Property Trust Co. plc* [1991] B.C.C. 446; *Re Rowbotham Baxter Ltd* [1990] B.C.C. 113; *Re Arrows Ltd (No. 3)* [1992] B.C.C. 131. See also *Re Genesis Technologies International (S) Pty Ltd* [1994] 3 S.L.R. 390, HCt of Singapore; *Re Structures & Computers Ltd* [1998] 1 B.C.L.C. 292.

[98] *Re Consumer & Industrial Press Ltd* (1988) 4 B.C.C. 68; *Re Imperial Motors (U.K.) Ltd* (1989) 5 B.C.C. 214 (a case where the petitioner was a secured creditor).

proposed administrators are nominated by the petitioner in the petition, the court may find itself required to consider an alternative nomination. Where that issue arises (and subject to conflict of interest considerations), the court is likely to favour the appointment of prospective administrators who are already familiar with the company's business. Such knowledge may derive, for example, from preparation of a rule 2.2 report or from acting as investigating accountants.[99] In *Re Structures & Computers Ltd*[1] the court made an administration order notwithstanding the opposition of a major creditor which also applied for its nominee to be appointed as an additional administrator. Although the application failed, the proposal was regarded by the court as reasonable and it was left open to the creditor to pursue a further application at a later date.

The court must be satisfied that making an order would be likely to **23–016** achieve one or more of the statutory purposes.[2] The test is whether there is a "real prospect" (as opposed to a mere hope or possibility) that one or more of the statutory purposes may be achieved.[3] Opposition to a creditor's petition by the company or its members on the ground that management could achieve the relevant purpose more cheaply is unlikely to be persuasive.[4]

(f) Costs

If an administration order is made, the costs of the petitioner, and any **23–017** other person appearing whose costs are allowed by the court, are payable as an expense of the administration.[5] In an exceptional case, such costs can include the costs of a party who has unsuccessfully opposed the order being made.[6] The petition costs are not protected by the statutory charges under section 19(4) and (5),[7] but will ordinarily rank ahead of those charges.[8] Directors are personally at risk in respect of the costs of an administration petition. In *Re W.F. Fearman Ltd (No. 2)*[9] it was held that directors should bear costs which they had incurred in respect of an administration petition notwithstanding rule 2.4(3) which provides that

[99] *Re Maxwell Communications Corporation plc* [1992] B.C.C. 372; *Re Strand Libraries Ltd* (unreported, May 20, 1996).
[1] [1998] 1 B.C.L.C. 292.
[2] s. 8(1)(b).
[3] *Re Harris Simons Construction Ltd* [1989] 1 W.L.R. 368; see also *Re Consumer & Industrial Press Ltd* (1988) 4 B.C.C. 68 *Re Manlon Trading Ltd* (1988) 4 B.C.C. 455; *Re Primlaks (U.K.) Ltd* (1989) 5 B.C.C. 710; *Re SCL Building Services Ltd* (1989) 5 B.C.C. 746; *Re Rowbotham Baxter Ltd* [1990] B.C.C. 113; *Re Chelmsford City Football Club (1980) Ltd* [1991] B.C.C. 133; *Re Land and Property Trust Co. plc* [1991] B.C.C. 446; *Re Arrows Ltd (No. 3)* [1992] B.C.C. 131; *Re Maxwell Communications Corporation plc* [1992] B.C.C. 372; *Re Dallhold Estates (U.K.) Pty. Ltd* [1992] B.C.C. 394.
[4] See further *Re K&H Options Ltd* (unreported, Neuberger J. February 17, 2000). See also *Re Greek Taverna* [1999] B.C.C. 153.
[5] r. 2.9. See also *Re Shearing & Loader Ltd* [1991] B.C.C. 232 and *Re Dallhold Estates (U.K.) Pty. Ltd* [1992] B.C.C. 394. For a case where no administration order was made, see *Re Business Properties Ltd* (1988) 4 B.C.C. 684.
[6] *Re Structures & Computers Ltd* [1998] 1 B.C.L.C. 292.
[7] See below, para. 23–044.
[8] *Re A Company (No. 005174 of 1999)* [2000] I.C.R. 263.
[9] (1988) 4 B.C.C. 141.

an administration petition presented by directors shall be treated as a petition of the company from and after presentation. However, in *Re Gosscott (Groundworks) Ltd*[10] where the court also had to deal with the costs of a failed administration petition (presented in good faith) and an unopposed winding-up order, it was ordered that the company's costs on the administration petition be paid as costs in the winding-up. In *Re Land and Property Trust Co. plc*[11] directors who persisted with an unrealistic company petition were ordered to pay the costs of opposing creditors personally. The order was subsequently discharged on appeal, but expressly affirmed the jurisdiction to award costs against directors. In *Re Tajik Air Ltd*[12] it was held that the test is whether reason and justice require the directors to pay the costs and that this will usually mean that it must be established that they have caused costs to be incurred for an improper purpose, *e.g.* if their aim was to achieve a private advantage at the expense of creditors.

(g) Notice and advertisement

23–018 If the court makes an administration order,[13] the administrator must advertise the order and give notice forthwith to specified persons.[14]

3. EFFECT OF ADMINISTRATION ORDER

(a) Power of administrator

23–019 The administrator is empowered to do all such things as are necessary for the management of the affairs, business and property of the company;[15] he is given (without prejudice to the generality of the foregoing) the same statutory powers as are conferred on an administrative receiver;[16] and he is given certain powers not conferred on administrative receivers, *e.g.* to appoint and remove directors,[17] to call meetings of members and creditors[18] and to deal with charged property as though it was uncharged.[19] In the exercise of his powers he is to be deemed to be acting as agent of the company.[20] A person dealing with him in good faith and for value is not concerned to inquire whether the administrator is acting within his powers.[21]

---

[10] (1988) 4 B.C.C. 372.
[11] [1991] B.C.C. 446; on appeal [1993] B.C.C. 462 (see also [1991] 1 W.L.R. 601).
[12] [1996] 1 B.C.L.C. 317.
[13] Form 2.4
[14] r. 2.10. See also Forms 2.4A, 2.5 (as to which see further "Dear Insolvency Practitioner", Issue No. 50, June 2000), 2.6, 2.7 and below, para. 23–053.
[15] s. 14(1)(a).
[16] s. 14(1). See further below, para. 23–064.
[17] s. 14(2)(a).
[18] s. 14(2)(b).
[19] See below, paras 23–066 to 23–068.
[20] s. 14(5); see further *Re Hartlebury Printers Ltd* [1992] I.C.R. 559.
[21] s. 14(6).

(b) Directors, officers and employees

The order has an immediate effect on the directors and officers, but no **23–020** such direct effect on employees.

(i) Directors

All powers of the company and its officers which could be exercised in **23–021** such a way as to interfere with the exercise by the administrator of his powers cease to be exercisable except with the consent of the administrator, which may be given either generally or in relation to particular cases.[22] The statutory language suggests that the criterion for the survival of any power in the directors is not whether the particular exercise of a particular power would interfere, but whether any exercise of the particular power could interfere. If this is correct, it is difficult to conceive that any power will survive in the directors, in the absence of some consent given by the administrator. But it is also difficult to believe that the Act intended to preclude the directors from applying to the court in the name of the company for the discharge of the administrator or of the administration order, or indeed from proceeding with an appeal against the making of the administration order merely because the administrator is given statutory power to bring or defend proceedings in the name of the company.[23] The question may be rendered academic, for the administrator is expressly given power to appoint or remove any director[24] and theoretically this could be exercised immediately to change the composition of the board and preclude any appeal or application to the court. The court might be expected to interfere to prevent this course being taken unless the appeal was an abuse of process.

(ii) Statement of affairs and co-operation

On the making of the administration order, the administrator must **23–022** forthwith require the preparation of a statement of affairs (which is in a prescribed form), verified by affidavit and submitted to the administrator within 21 days or such extended period as the administrator or the court may allow.[25] This statement of affairs must show as at the date of the administration order:

    (a) particulars of the company's assets, debts and liabilities;
    (b) the names and addresses of its creditors;
    (c) the securities held by them respectively;
    (d) the dates when the securities were respectively given; and
    (e) such further or other information as may be prescribed.[26]

---

[22] s. 14(4). See further below, para. 2–011.

[23] Compare the position of directors of a company after the making of a winding-up order or appointment of a provisional liquidator: see *Re Union Accident Insurance Co.* [1972] 1 W.L.R. 640. See further above, para. 2–047.

[24] s. 14(2)(a).

[25] s. 22(4). See generally rr. 2.11–2.15 and Forms 2.8 and 2.9. There is no provision for filing this statement of affairs at Companies House, unlike a receivership statement of affairs.

[26] s. 22(2).

23–023 The administrator may require to make and submit such a statement[27] (and subsequently release from such an obligation[28]) some or all of the following:

> (a) existing or past officers of the company;
> (b) persons who took part in the company's formation at any time within one year before the date of the administration order;
> (c) persons employed under contracts of service or for services at the date of the order, or within one year before that date, who in the administrator's opinion are capable of giving (some of) the information required;
> (d) officers or employees under contracts of service or for services (whether present or within the past year) of a company which is or was within that year an officer of the company.

23–024 Each of the foregoing is under a general duty to co-operate with the administrator and in particular to give such information concerning the company and its promotion, formation, business, dealings, affairs or property as the administrator may at any time reasonably require, and to attend on the administrator at such time as the administrator may reasonably require.[29] Failure without reasonable excuse to comply with this obligation exposes the person concerned on conviction to a fine.[30]

(iii) Contracts of employment

23–025 The whole scheme of the statute militates in favour of the view that the order does not operate as a dismissal of the company's employees.[31] This is to avoid the draconian consequences of a winding-up order (which does operate as such a dismissal[32]) and to give the administrator an opportunity to save the company or its undertaking in whole or in part. Automatic and immediate wholesale dismissal of employees would in many cases prove a mortal wound. The appointment by the court of an administrator, like the appointment out of court of an administrative receiver (but unlike the appointment of a receiver by the court[33]) leaves the contractual relations between company and employees in this respect unaffected.[34]

---

[27] s. 22(3); see also r. 2.11 and Form 2.8.

[28] s. 22(5); see also r. 2.14.

[29] s. 235(2). For enforcement of this duty see *Re A.E. Farr Ltd* [1992] B.C.C. 150; *Re Wallace Smith Trust Co. Ltd* [1992] B.C.C. 707; *cf.* the duty of co-operation with a receiver appointed by the court (see above, Chap. 22) and with an administrative receiver (see above, Chap. 5).

[30] s. 235(5).

[31] This appears to have been assumed in *Re Hartlebury Printers Ltd* [1992] I.C.R. 559 where it was held that the Employment Protection Act 1975, s. 99, applied to an employer company in administration and that administration was not *per se* a special circumstance.

[32] See *MacDowalls Case* (1886) 32 Ch.D. 366 and see above, Chap. 19.

[33] See *Fox Bros. v. Bryant* [1979] I.C.R. 64 and see above Chaps 19 and 22.

[34] Industrial tribunal applications arising out of dismissals by an administrator require leave or consent under s. 11(3) whilst an administration order is in force. Such leave will usually be given: *Carr v. British International Helicopters Ltd* [1993] B.C.C. 855. See also *Re Paramount Airways Ltd (No. 3)* [1993] B.C.C. 662; on appeal *sub nom. Powdrill v. Watson* [1995] 2 A.C. 394, HL.

The Act contains relatively few provisions dealing specifically with **23–026** employees. The administrator has power to employ and dismiss employees.[35] Section 19 (as amended by the Insolvency Act 1994[36]) applies a statutory charge to the property of the company when a person ceases to be the administrator. The charge covers "qualifying liabilities" incurred while the administrator was in office under contracts of employment entered into or adopted[37] by the administrator, or any predecessor of his in carrying out the functions of an administrator. "Qualifying liabilities" are liabilities under contracts of employment to pay wages, salary or contributions to occupational pension schemes in respect of services rendered after adoption. The term includes wages or salary payable in respect of periods of holiday or sickness after adoption. Sums payable in lieu of holiday are only "qualifying liabilities" to the extent that the period by reference to which the entitlement arose was after adoption. Employees are amongst those who may be required to give a statement of affairs under section 22 and to co-operate with the administrator under section 235.[38]

The financial position of a company in administration will often **23–027** necessitate some immediate or early redundancies and it may not be practicable to observe either notice periods or consultation procedures.[39] An administrator who adopts a contract of employment does not undertake a personal liability even if he causes the employer company to incur liability for wrongful dismissal.[40] This does not mean that administrators can properly disregard the normal incidents of employment law and practice.[41] In this respect there are two constraints. First, administrators (to a much greater extent than administrative receivers) must always take into account liabilities which their actions cause the company to incur and which may rank *pari passu* with pre-administration liabilities in a subsequent liquidation or even take priority under section 19. Secondly, the standards of conduct expected from administrators as officers of the court include a duty to act fairly and honourably.[42] It is questionable whether devices to defeat employees' contractual or statutory rights are consistent with that duty.[43]

---

[35] s. 14 and Sched. 1, para. 11.

[36] The amendments apply to contracts of employment adopted on or after March 15, 1994: Insolvency Act 1994, s. 1(7).

[37] As to the meaning of "adoption", see *Powdrill v. Watson* [1995] 2 A.C. 394, HL and generally Chap. 19 above. In *Re Maxwell Communication Corporation plc & Ors* (unreported, July 14, 1995), administrators obtained procedural directions regulating the manner in which *Paramount* claims were to be brought in court proceedings. The directions made provision for a questionnaire to be completed by claimants before claims were pursued and restricted the use of statutory demands (as to the statutory charge, see below, paras 23–069 to 23–070).

[38] See above, para. 23–023.

[39] As to which see above, Chap. 19.

[40] *Gregory v. Wallace* [1998] I.R.L.R. 387.

[41] *Ibex Trading Co. Ltd v. Walton* [1994] I.C.R. 907.

[42] See below, para. 23–040.

[43] Consider *Re Maxwell Fleet and Facilities Management Ltd (No 2)*, [2000] 2 B.C.L.C. 155.

(c) Unsecured creditors

23–028 Creditors hold a key position in administration. The procedure is only available in respect of companies which are or are likely to become unable to pay their debts[44] and creditors (either alone or in conjunction with others) are amongst the classes of persons entitled to petition for the making of an administration order.[45]

23–029   Creditors have rights under rule 7.53 of the Insolvency Rules 1986 to attend, at their own expense, in court or in chambers at any stage of the proceedings. Attendance may be in person or by the creditor's solicitor. If so requested in writing by a creditor (who pays the costs and keeps the court informed of his address), the court must give him notice of any step in the proceedings. If the exercise of such rights gives rise to expense to be borne out of the assets of the company[46] which would not otherwise have arisen and ought not to be so borne, the court may direct that the costs be paid by the creditor (whose rights remain in abeyance until payment). The court may appoint one or more persons to represent the creditors (or any class of them), to have the rights conferred by rule 7.53, instead of the rights being exercisable by creditors individually. If two or more persons are so appointed, they must (if at all) instruct the same solicitor.

23–030   Creditors are amongst those who have the right to inspect the court file under rule 7.31.[47] Creditors also have rights to require the administrator to provide them with a list of the company's creditors and the amount of their respective debts unless a statement of the company's affairs has been filed in court.[48]

23–031   The legislation does not require creditors, other than those who have appointed an administrative receiver or who may have power so to do, to receive notice of an administration petition or be served with it.[49] Further, creditors are not entitled to appear or be represented on the hearing of the petition as of right but may appear or be represented with the leave of the court.[50] In *Cornhill Insurance plc v. Cornhill Financial Services Ltd* [51] it was held that the court has jurisdiction under rule 7.47 to rescind an administration order on the application of a disaffected creditor.

23–032   Following the making of an administration order, individual creditors are unlikely to be concerned with the routine court aspects of the procedure, but if a vacancy occurs, the creditors form part of the residual class of persons entitled to apply for the vacancy to be filled under section 13(3). Creditors may also apply to the court for an order protecting their

---

[44] s. 8(1).

[45] s. 9(1).

[46] See further r. 13.8.

[47] See further *Astor Chemical Ltd v. Synthetic Technology Ltd* [1990] B.C.C. 97.

[48] r. 12.17 see further rr. 7.31 and 13.11.

[49] r.2.9.

[50] *ibid.* See further *Re Rowbotham Baxter Ltd* [1990] B.C.C. 113 and *Re Chelmsford City Football Club (1980) Ltd* [1991] B.C.C. 133.

[51] [1992] B.C.C. 818. See also *Re MTI Trading Systems Ltd* [1997] B.C.C. 703, on refusal of leave to appeal [1998] B.C.C. 400, CA, a case involving doubts about the status of the petitioner and allegations of non-disclosure.

interests under section 27[52] and a group of creditors may challenge the administrator's remuneration under rule 2.50. At various stages during the course of the administration the creditors are entitled to receive progress reports.[53] Creditors' meetings are necessary to consider the administrator's proposals and substantial revisions (all of which require creditors' approval before implementation) and may also be held for other reasons. Creditors amounting to one-tenth in value may also require the administrator to summon a creditors' meeting.[54] The mandatory meeting of creditors to approve the administrator's proposals may also establish a committee of creditors to safeguard its interests.

(d) Secured creditors

Security is defined by section 248 as meaning "any mortgage, charge, lien **23–033** or other security" unless the context otherwise requires.[55] Secured creditors are creditors for all purposes in administration and all the provisions of the Act and the Rules apply to secured creditors except that they have restricted voting rights at creditors' meetings.[56] The special provisions of administration which affect all secured creditors are as follows:

(a) The moratorium provisions regarding the enforcement of securities over the company's property.

(b) The possibility that after an administration order has been made any receiver of part of the company's property may be required to vacate office by the administrator.

(c) The power of the court to authorise the disposal of fixed charge security under section 15.

(d) The ability of the administrator to deal with floating charge security in exercise of his powers under section 15.

There are additional provisions relevant to those secured creditors able to appoint administrative receivers.

As has been discussed in Chapter 3, a charge created by a company **23–034** requiring registration under sections 395 and 396 of the Companies Act 1985 will be void against an administrator of the company if it is not duly registered. The effect of these provisions was considered in *Orion Finance Ltd. v. Crown Financial Management Ltd*[57] where the issue arose in an unusual way. A company which subsequently went into administration (and thereafter liquidation) had executed an assignment of rent payable to it under chattel leases. The assignee brought proceedings against the lessee for payment of rent. It was held that the assignment was an assignment by way of charge which was void for want of

[52] See below, paras 23–071 and 23–074.
[53] r. 2.30.
[54] s. 17(3). See also r. 2.21 and s. 18(2).
[55] Note also s. 246 See also *Bristol Airport plc v. Powdrill* [1990] Ch. 744 at 760; *sub nom. Re Paramount Airways Ltd* [1990] B.C.C. 130 at 149, CA.
[56] r. 2.24.
[57] [1994] B.C.C. 897 (Vinelott J.), affirmed on appeal, [1996] B.C.C. 621 at 631, CA.

registration against the administrators and liquidators of the original lessor company. The further question which then arose was whether section 395 had the additional effect of relieving the lessee from any obligation to pay the assignee. It was held that, where a charge on a debt is void against an administrator of the creditor company for want of registration, this will also be a complete defence to a claim by the chargee against the debtor. It mattered not that notice of the assignment had been given to the debtor prior to the administration, directing it to pay the assignee. Avoidance of the charge under section 395 was thus treated as depriving it of all effect as regards not only the assignor company (in administration) and the assignee, but also as regards the chattel lessee.

This result can be contrasted with the decision in *Smith (administrator of Cosslett (Contractors) Ltd) v. Bridgend County Borough Council*.[58] In that case, the defendant council had a contractual right to retain and use certain plant and equipment which a company in administration had used for building works upon the council's land. The right of retention continued to be valid against the company notwithstanding the administration and therefore prevented the administrator from using his powers under section 234 of the Insolvency Act to recover the plant and equipment whilst it was being used by a replacement contractor which the defendant council had employed to complete the works. The defendant council also had a contractual right to sell the plant and equipment and to apply the proceeds in reduction of its claims against the contractor. The council purported to exercise this right when it engaged the replacement contractor by agreeing that it could remove and keep the plant and equipment when it finished the works. An earlier decision of the Court of Appeal held that whilst the council's contractual right of retention and use was a good defence to a claim for delivery up by the administrator under section 234, its right of sale was an unregistered charge.[59] In *Smith v. Bridgend* it was accepted that this power of sale was void against the administrator, and that if the administrator had found the council in possession of the plant and equipment at the end of the works, he would have had an unanswerable claim for possession under section 234. But the Court of Appeal held that the administrator was not entitled to damages in conversion against the council for loss of the opportunity to assert this claim.

The precise basis for the decision of the Court of Appeal is difficult to discern, but it appears to have rested upon two propositions: first, that, as between the company and the chargee, the charge remained good notwithstanding the appointment of the administrator; and secondly, that as the administrator was essentially the agent of the company in administration, which could not have made a claim in conversion, the "statutory serendipity" of section 395 which rendered the power of sale void as against the administrator should not give him a better right to

---

[58] [2000] 1 B.C.L.C. 775, CA.
[59] *Re Cosslett (Contractors) Limited* [1998] Ch. 495.

damages of loss of his reversionary interest in the plant and equipment than the company would have had.

The first proposition has been discussed in Chapter 3.[60] As to the second proposition, it can be remarked that it seems to place too little weight upon the policy which underlies the application of section 395 to administrations. The manifest objective of section 395 in the case of administrations is to permit the administrator to recover and deal with property subject to an unregistered charge for the benefit of the creditors of the company as a whole.

It would be regrettable if the decision in *Smith v. Bridgend* on the scope of the tort of conversion encouraged chargees to dispose of charged property speedily so as to defeat claims to possession by an administrator under section 234. Chargees contemplating such a course ought to consider the effect of section 11 of the 1986 Act which prohibits the enforcement of any security over the company's property without the consent of the administrator or the leave of the court. The argument that the exercise of its power of sale by the council amounted to the enforcement of its security contrary to section 11 does not appear to have been raised in argument or to have been dealt with in the judgments in *Smith v. Bridgend*.[60a]

Application for an extension of time under section 404 can be made **23–035** without leave but is very unlikely to succeed if it is clear that administration will be followed by insolvent liquidation.[61]

---

[60] In support of the first proposition, the Court of Appeal relied on *Re Monolithic Building Company* [1915] 1 Ch. 643 which was said to be authority that non-registration does not render a charge void against a grantor company in liquidation as opposed to its liquidator. But on closer analysis it is apparent that the judgments in *Monolithic* only confirm that a charge remains valid against a company whilst it is a going concern prior to the appointment of a liquidator. The case concerned an action by a chargee to enforce her security and raised the question of the validity of the charge and of priorities between the chargor company and the successive chargees. The company was not in liquidation and the Court of Appeal was not called upon to consider the effect of section 395 in a liquidation, still less whether there was any distinction to be drawn so far as section 395 was concerned between a liquidator and the company in liquidation. The dictum of Phillimore L.J. at [1915] 1 Ch. 667 that section 395 "leaves the security to stand as against the company while it is a going concern. It does not make the security binding on the liquidator as successor of the company." did not consider whether the security was binding upon the company after it had ceased to be a going concern and a liquidator had been appointed. Moreover, Phillimore L.J. was mistaken in his reference to the liquidator being the "successor" to the company: unlike a trustee in bankruptcy, the property of a company does not vest in a liquidator in a winding up. The case which does stand as authority for the proposition that an unregistered charge will not be void as against the company in liquidation, *Independent Automatic Sales Ltd v. Knowles and Foster* [1962] 1 W.L.R. 974, was not referred to in the judgment in *Smith v. Bridgend*.

[60a] It is also to be noted that in *Smith v. Bridgend* there was no claim by the administrator for an account along the lines of the claim which the liquidator was permitted to bring in *Independent Automatic Sales Ltd* (see Chapter 3 above). Nor was there any claim in restitution by the administrator on the basis that the council had obtained a benefit from exercise of a power of sale which was void as against him, over property to which he would have had an unanswerable claim to possession. These arguments, together with the point on section 11 remain open for consideration in future cases.

[61] *Re Barrow Borough Transport Ltd* [1990] Ch. 227.

23–036   The most profound significance of administration for a secured creditor lies in the need to obtain leave of the court to enforce the security unless the administrator consents. The onus is on the secured creditor seeking leave to enforce but it is not necessary to make any criticism of the administrator in order to obtain leave. An application for leave must be approached by balancing the interests of secured and unsecured creditors.[62] The Court of Appeal issued detailed guidelines on when leave to enforce security should be granted in *Re Atlantic Computer Systems plc*.[63] The following is a summary:

(a) The applicant for leave must make out his case.

(b) The moratorium is to assist achievement of the purposes of the administration. If leave will not interfere it should normally be given.

(c) In other cases there must be a balancing exercise.

(d) Great weight should normally be given to proprietary rights.

(e) It is normally enough for the applicant to demonstrate significant loss.[64]

(f) In assessing prospective losses to either side the court will have regard to the full circumstances.

(g) The degree of probability of loss will be taken into account.

(h) Conduct will be relevant.

(i) The factors applicable to the grant of leave also apply to the question of appropriate conditions to attach to a grant.

(j) The same factors will be relevant to the question of the appropriate conditions to attach to a refusal.

(k) In security cases the adequacy of the security is an important factor.

(l) The court will not usually deal with questions of validity of security. It will normally only need to be satisfied that the applicant has a seriously arguable case.[65]

(e) Shareholders

23–037   Administration is a creditor-controlled procedure. Once an administration order is made, the role of shareholders is marginal. The administrator has power to call a meeting of members.[66] Members share the right of creditors to apply to the court for relief under section 27 (protection of interests of creditors and members),[67] to inspect the court file and to exercise rights of attendance.[68]

---

[62] *Re Meesan Investment Ltd* (1988) 4 B.C.C. 788; *sub nom. Royal Trust Bank v. Buchler* [1989] B.C.L.C. 130.

[63] [1992] Ch. 505. See also *Bristol Airport plc v. Powdrill* [1990] Ch. 744; *sub nom. Re Paramount Airways Ltd* [1990] B.C.C. 130, CA. If an order for leave to detain property is made under s. 11(3)(c) without notice, it is desirable that leave should only be granted for a limited period: *Re Air Europe Ltd* (*The Independent*, May 6, 1991).

[64] In *Re David Meek Access Ltd & Anor* [1993] B.C.C. 175 the court preferred to consider loss by reference to depreciation in capital value rather than unpaid hire-purchase instalments.

[65] Consider also *Scottish Exhibition Centre Ltd, Noters* [1993] B.C.C. 529.

[66] s. 14(2). "Member" has an extended meaning under s. 250. As to the conduct of meetings of members, see r. 2.31.

[67] See below, paras 23–071 and 23–074.

[68] See above, paras 23–029 to 23–030.

4. ORIGINAL AND SUBSEQUENT APPOINTMENTS OF ADMINISTRATOR

The administrator is appointed by the court (the original appointment **23–038** being made by the administration order itself). Section 231 provides that, if more than one person is appointed, the order shall declare whether the administrators must act jointly or may act severally. In an exceptional case where the court has appointed an additional administrator to deal with matters where the other administrators have (or might be seen to have) a conflict of interest, the court may give supplementary directions delineating different areas of responsibility to be performed by one or more of the administrators to the exclusion of the others.[69] Any vacancy may be filled by the court whether occurring "by death, resignation or otherwise."[70] "Otherwise" includes removal by the court, either on application by the administrator or a creditor or shareholder, or of its own motion. The court also has an inherent power to make a temporary additional appointment where an administrator is not performing his functions.[71] Section 19(2) provides that an administrator shall vacate office, if he ceases to be qualified to act as an insolvency practitioner in relation to the company[72] or if the administration order is discharged. He may also resign by giving notice of his resignation to the court in the "prescribed circumstances".[73] Rule 2.53 provides that an administrator may give notice[74] of his resignation on the grounds of:

(a) ill health;
(b) intention to cease to be in practice as an insolvency practitioner;
(c) conflict of interest, or change of personal circumstances, precluding or making impractical further discharge of his duties; or
(d) with the leave of the court, other circumstances.

Section 13(3) provides that an application may be made to fill a vacancy in the office of administrator by the continuing administrator of the company or (in default of such administrator) by the committee of creditors appointed under section 26[75] or (in default of both) by the company or the directors or by any creditor or creditors of the company.[76]

---

[69] *Re Polly Peck International plc* (unreported, October 25, 1990). *Re Ionica plc* (unreported, October 29, 1998, Rattee J.).
[70] s. 13. As to the procedure on the death of an administrator, see r. 2.54.
[71] *Clements v. Udall, The Times*, July 7, 2000.
[72] Consider *Re A.J. Adams (Builders) Ltd* [1991] B.C.C. 62.
[73] s. 19(1).
[74] Forms 2.16 and 2.17.
[75] See below, paras 23–047 and 23–051.
[76] See further r. 2.55.

5. STATUS OF ADMINISTRATOR

23–039 The administrator[77] enjoys a number of distinct capacities.

(a) Officer of court

23–040 The administrator (like the liquidator appointed on a compulsory liquidation[78] and a court-appointed receiver) is an officer of the court.[79] This status involves special privileges and responsibilities. Thus he is protected by the law of contempt[80] against any interference with the performance of his duties and he has a right of access to the court for directions.[81] On the other hand, in his dealings he must act fairly and honourably,[82] and generally, whilst not being generous at the creditors' expense, he should if occasion requires temper the insistence on his strict legal and equitable rights with a respect for moral justice and honest dealings.[83] It has been assumed that the administrator owes a duty of care to the company,[84] and that his status as an officer of the court in no way affords any immunity from liability for negligence or entitles him to be judged by any lower standard than the ordinary standard of care.[85] In *Barclays Mercantile v. Sibec Developments Ltd*[86] it was held that where an owner is wrongfully prevented from exercising proprietary rights during the moratorium, the court has power to order the administrator to pay compensation in the administration proceedings without the need for the owner to bring an action in conversion. The mere fact that a wrong commercial decision is taken does not, of itself, mean that the administrator's conduct is open to challenge.[87]

---

[77] The appointment is personal but in *Re Cellermet Ltd* (unreported, 1987; see further Phillips, "Administration Orders — The First Few Months" (1987) 8 Co. Law 273) the court permitted an administrator to give a power of attorney to a colleague but indicated that a s. 18 variation order to make the appointment joint might be more appropriate.

[78] A liquidator in a voluntary liquidation is not an officer of the court: *Re TH Knitwear (Wholesale)* [1988] Ch. 275.

[79] *Re Atlantic Computer Systems plc* [1992] Ch. 505. For the court appointed receiver, see above, para. 22–011.

[80] See further *Bristol Airport plc v. Powdrill* [1990] Ch. 744; *sub nom. Re Paramount Airways Ltd* [1990] B.C.C. 130, CA; *Re Sabre International Products Ltd* [1991] B.C.C. 694.

[81] The court will, however, usually rely on the administrator's commercial judgment and will not expect such decisions to be referred to it. See further *MTI Trading Systems Ltd v. Winter* [1998] B.C.C. 591.

[82] *Re Japan Leasing (Europe) plc* [1999] B.P.I.R. 911. The administrator must respond promptly to requests for leave to enforce security and should not use the moratorium as a bargaining counter. It is also helpful for the administrator to give reasons for any refusal of leave if the reasons are not obvious: *Re Atlantic Computer Systems plc* [1992] Ch. 505 at 529. However, he has no duty to advise a creditor claiming security as to how to protect his position: *Re Sabre International Products Ltd* [1991] B.C.C. 694.

[83] This is the rule in *ex p. James* (1874) 9 Ch.App 609; see also *Re Wyvern Developments Ltd* [1974] 1 W.L.R. 1097; *Re Clark, ex p. Texaco* [1975] 1 W.L.R. 559. See also *Powdrill v. Watson* [1994] I.C.R. 395, CA, on appeal [1995] 2 A.C. 394, HL.

[84] In *Re Charnley Davies Ltd* [1990] B.C.C. 605 it was common ground that an administrator has a duty to the company to take reasonable steps to obtain a proper price for its assets. The duty extends to the timing of the sale: *ibid.* at 618.

[85] This common law liability in tort is distinguishable from the equitable duties of a receiver identified in *Downsview Nominees Ltd v. First City Corporation Ltd* [1993] A.C. 295, PC which is discussed in detail in above, Chap. 7. In administration, in contrast to receivership, there is no paramount duty to an appointing mortgagee with which a duty of care would be inconsistent.

[86] [1992] 1 W.L.R. 1253.

[87] *MTI Trading Systems v. Winter* [1998] B.C.C. 591.

(b) Officer of company

Again like the court-appointed liquidator, but unlike the receiver **23–041** appointed by a debenture-holder, he is an officer of the company, for like the liquidator, and unlike the receiver, he is the governing body of the company managing its affairs as well as its business and property.[88] As an officer of the company, the administrator is on a subsequent liquidation subject to misfeasance proceedings. If in the course of the winding-up it appears that the administrator has misapplied or retained, or become accountable for, any money or other property of the company, or been guilty of misfeasance or breach of any fiduciary or other duty in relation to the company in connection with the carrying out of his duties as an administrator, relief may be granted against him under section 212. The application to the court may be made by the official receiver, the liquidator, a creditor or a contributory (though, in the case of the contributory, leave of the court is required for the application, but it is unnecessary that he should benefit from any order made on the application).[89] The relief may take the form of an order for:

(a) repayment, restoration or an account for the money or property or any part of it, with interest at such rate as the court thinks just; or

(b) contribution to the company's assets by way of compensation of such sum as the court thinks just.[90]

The grant to an administrator of his release does not preclude such an application, but in this case the leave of the court is required.[91]

(c) Agent of company

In exercising his powers the administrator is to be deemed to be acting **23–042** as agent of the company[92] and is not personally liable on any contract entered into or adopted by him[93] in the carrying out of his functions except in so far as the contract otherwise provides. In these respects, his position is like that of a liquidator, and unlike that of a court-appointed receiver.[94] On the other hand, there is a special provision for debts and liabilities incurred by an administrator to be charged on the assets when an administrator vacates office.[95]

(d) Fiduciary

The administrator (like a liquidator) owes to the company (but not **23–043** individual creditors)[96] the duties of a fiduciary to exercise good faith and

---

[88] *Re Home Treat Ltd* [1991] B.C.C. 165. See also ss. 8(2) and 17(2).

[89] s. 212(5).

[90] s. 212(3).

[91] ss. 20(3) and 212(4).

[92] s. 14(5). See further *Re Hartlebury Printers Ltd* [1992] I.C.R. 559.

[93] *Gregory v. Wallace* [1998] I.R.L.R. 387.

[94] Consider *Stead Hazel v. Cooper* [1933] 1 K.B. 840 at 843.

[95] s. 19 as amended by the Insolvency Act 1994. This provision extends to adoption of employment contracts and to acts of a predecessor administrator.

[96] See *Knowles v. Scott* [1891] 1 Ch. 717 at 722–723.

the professional skill and care of an insolvency practitioner. The rule against a fiduciary allowing any conflict to arise between his duty and his interest is strictly to be enforced. Without the court's prior sanction, to be sought on an application made at his own cost, the administrator cannot purchase any asset nor can he make for himself any profit, even if the profit will otherwise be made by some third party and the loss of opportunity occasions no financial loss to the company. If an administrator who is a solicitor employs his own firm, or any partner in it, to act on behalf of the company, profit costs may only be paid if they are authorised by the creditors' committee, the creditors or the court. It must be an open question whether the administrator is entitled to protection as a trustee under sections 30 and 61 of the Trustee Act 1925 but as an officer of the company he is entitled to invoke section 727 of the Companies Act 1985 and seek relief from liability if he acted honestly and reasonably and ought fairly to be excused.[1]

23–044   Just as a trustee must hold the balance fairly between beneficiaries interested in capital and income, or a court-appointed receiver must hold the balance between the interested parties, so must the administrator hold the balance fairly between different creditors and different classes of creditors, and no undue preferential treatment must be afforded to one over the other.[2]

(e) Office-holder

23–045   As an office-holder, an administrator is vested with the special powers and privileges conferred by sections 230-241 and 244-246, powers and privileges shared (in the case of sections 230–237[3]) with liquidators and administrative receivers and (in the case of sections 238–241 and 244–246[4]) with liquidators alone. These provisions enable the administrator:

(a) in a summary fashion, with the assistance (where required) of the court, to obtain information regarding the company's assets and dealings and to recover its property;

(b) to challenge certain prior transactions of the company; and

(c) to secure the continued supply of gas, electricity, water and telecommunication services to the company without first providing for arrears accrued prior to the date of the administration order, albeit the supplier can insist on a personal guarantee from the administrator in respect of charges for supplies made thereafter.[5]

---

[97] *Re R. Gertzenstein Ltd* [1937] Ch. 115. As to fixing of the administrator's remuneration under the Rules, see generally rr. 2.47–2.50; *Re Charnley Davies Business Services Ltd* (1987) 3 B.C.C. 408; *Re Sheridan Securities Ltd* (1988) 4 B.C.C. 200; *Re Brooke Marine Ltd* [1988] B.C.L.C. 546; also *Mirror Group Newspapers plc v. Maxwell* [1998] B.C.C. 324 and [1999] B.C.C. 684.

[98] r. 2.47.

[99] Consider *Re Windsor Steam* [1928] Ch. 609; [1929] 1 Ch. 151 in relation to liquidators.

[1] *Re Home Treat Ltd* [1991] B.C.C. 165.

[2] Consider *Re Atlantic Computer Systems plc* [1992] Ch. 505 at 542.

[3] See above, Chap. 5.

[4] See above, Chap. 11.

[5] s. 233.

These provisions also validate his acts as administrator notwithstanding any defects in his appointment or qualifications[6] and confer exemption upon him against claims by third parties from liability for loss or damage occasioned by his seizure or disposal of tangible property which does not belong to the company.[7]

Further, section 246 renders unenforceable certain liens as against the **23–046** administrator. It leaves unaffected liens on documents which give a title to property and are held as such. In *Re SEIL Trade Finance Ltd*[8] a solicitor's general lien was upheld against an office-holder who sought delivery of various documents including share certificates (which are only prima facie evidence of title). It was held that documents are "held as such" where held subject to a lien thereby rendering those words in the legislation practically meaningless. But in every other case, a lien or other right to retain possession of the books, papers or other records of the company is unenforceable to the extent that enforcement would deny possession of any books, papers or other records to the administrator. It is suggested that this provision does not extinguish the lien, but merely puts it in abeyance so long as the administrator continues in office, and that upon discharge of the administration order (unless replaced by a liquidation in which case the liquidator has a like right to override the lien or possessory right) the books, papers and records ought to be handed back so as to revive the lien or other right.[9]

6. CREDITORS' COMMITTEE

The administrator is required within three months of the making of the **23–047** administration order (or such longer period as the court may allow) to summon a meeting of the company's creditors to decide whether to approve the administrator's proposals.[10] At this meeting, if (and only if) the meeting approves (with or without modifications) such proposals, the creditors may establish a creditors' committee.[11] Such a committee (if established) may at any time require the administrator to attend before it and furnish it with such information relating to the carrying out by him of his functions as it may reasonably require.[12]

In respect of this committee, a number of questions require consideration:

---

[6] s. 232, as to which provision, see above, para. 4–052.

[7] s. 234(3), (4). The conditions for such exemption are that, at the date of the seizure or disposal, he believes and has reasonable grounds to believe that he is entitled to seize or dispose of the property and any loss or damage is not occasioned by his negligence. As to s. 234 generally, see further *Re London Iron & Steel Co. Ltd* [1990] B.C.C. 159; *Welsh Development Agency v. Export Finance Co. Ltd* [1992] B.C.C. 270, CA and *Smith v. Bridgend County Borough Council* [2000] 1 B.C.L.C. 775, CA.

[8] [1992] B.C.C. 538.

[9] Consider *Re Jet Corp. of Australia* (1985) 9 A.C.L.R. 641. See further above, para. 23–033.

[10] s. 23.

[11] s. 26.

[12] s. 26(2). See further r. 2.44.

(a) Establishment and membership

23–048 The question of establishment of the committee can only arise if and after the meeting has approved the administrator's proposals. At this stage of the meeting, it must be incumbent on the administrator to give the meeting the opportunity to appoint the committee, inform them of the choice available and put, or allow a creditor to put, the proposals for such an establishment to the vote. The meeting will then decide as a matter of principle whether to establish the committee, and if so the number of members and subject to the provisions of the Rules its composition. Rule 2.32 provides that the committee must consist of at least three and not more than five creditors.[13] They are chosen by selecting the requisite number of creditors attracting the greatest number of votes by value on a single ballot.[14]

(b) Fiduciary role

23–049 The committee fulfils an analogous role to that of the liquidation committee in an insolvent liquidation.[15] Committee members are fiduciaries. Although rule 2.46 permits dealings between the company and a committee member provided that any resultant transactions are in good faith and for value, rule 2.46 will not be construed as excluding general fiduciary responsibilities.[16] The court may, on the application of any interested person, set aside any transaction which appears to breach the requirements of rule 2.46 and give such consequential directions as it thinks fit to compensate the company for any resultant loss. In recognition of the fiduciary duties of a committee member, no committee member will be entitled to receive any payment out of the company's assets otherwise than strictly in accordance with the Rules. The only express provisions permitting payment concern payment of travelling expenses.[17] Any documents or confidential information which come to members of the committee as such can only be used in the interests of creditors as a whole and not for a member's private interest without the leave of the court.[18]

(c) Proceedings of creditors' committee

23–050 The administrator must call a first meeting of the creditors' committee within three months of its first establishment. Subject thereto, meetings occur at the instance of the administrator, the committee or any of its

---

[13] See further *Re W. & A. Glaser Ltd* [1994] B.C.C. 199.

[14] *Re Polly Peck International plc* [1991] B.C.C. 503. As to the formalities of establishment, see rr. 2.33, 2.37–2.41 and Forms 2.13 and 2.14.

[15] The statutory language creating the "creditors' committee" in the case of an administrative receivership (s. 49) and in the case of an administration are similarly phrased, except that in the case of an administration the committee are given power to apply to the court to fill a vacancy (s. 13(3)(b)). But the role of the committee in the case of administration is parallel to that of a liquidation committee rather than that of a committee in a receivership, for in the case of an administration the administrator (like the liquidator in the case of a liquidation) is responsible to all creditors, unlike the administrative receiver who is primarily responsible to the debenture-holder.

[16] *Re Bulmer, ex p. Greaves* [1937] Ch. 499; *Re Geiger* [1915] 1 K.B. 439; *Dowling v. Lord Advocate* [1963] S.L.T. 146.

[17] r. 2.45.

[18] *Plant v. Plant* [1998] 1 B.C.L.C. 38 (IVA creditors' committee); *Re Esal (Commodities) Ltd (No. 2)* [1990] B.C.C. 708 (liquidation committee).

members.[19] Procedure is governed by the Rules.[20] The acts of the committee are valid notwithstanding any defect in the appointment, election or qualifications of any member (or member's representative) or in the formalities of its establishment.[21]

(d) Functions of committee
The Act and the Rules contain various provisions dealing with the **23–051** functions of the committee:

(a) The committee shall assist the administrator in discharging his functions and act in relation to him in such manner as may be agreed from time to time.[22]

(b) On giving not less than seven days' notice in writing signed by a majority of the committee members or their respective representatives, the committee may require the administrator to attend before it and give information relating to the carrying out of his functions. Any such requirement must be to attend before the committee at a reasonable time and the committee is only entitled to such information as it may reasonably require.[23]

(c) Where a vacancy in the office of an administrator occurs in a case where there is no continuing administrator of the company, then the power to apply to the court for an order appointing a new administrator under section 13(2) devolves on the committee.[24]

(d) The committee must review the adequacy of the administrator's security from time to time.[25]

(e) Once a creditors' committee is set up, the primary responsibility for determining the administrator's remuneration falls on it and the committee also has the right to be heard on any application to the court by the administrator for an order increasing his remuneration.[26]

(f) The committee may be called upon to settle any disagreement between joint administrators over the apportionment of remuneration and to authorise payment of profit costs to a solicitor administrator's firm (or any partner in it).[27]

(g) The members of the committee are entitled to receive the administrator's abstracts of receipts and payments.[28]

(h) The committee may require taxation of costs, charges and expenses to be paid out of the company's assets.[29]

[19] r. 2.34.
[20] rr. 2.35, 2.36 and 2.42–2.44.
[21] r. 2.46A.
[22] r. 2.34.
[23] s. 26(2) and r. 2.44. Consider also *Re W. & A. Glaser Ltd* [1994] B.C.C. 199.
[24] s. 13(3)(b).
[25] r. 12.8.
[26] rr. 2.47 and 2.49.
[27] r. 2.47.
[28] r. 2.52 and Form 2.15.
[29] r. 7.34.

(i) The committee receives notice of the administrator's resignation if there is no continuing administrator.[30]

Generally, the administrator should have regard to any express wishes of the committee but can take the matter to a creditors' meeting if he disagrees.[31]

7. DUTIES OF ADMINISTRATOR

23–052 On the making of the administration order, the administrator is under various immediate duties:

(a) Formal notification of appointment
23–053 Section 21 requires an administrator (under penalty for failure without reasonable excuse of liability to a fine) on the making of the administration order:

(a) within 14 days to send an office copy of the order to the registrar of companies;
(b) forthwith to send to the company (and to publish in the prescribed manner) a notice of the order; and
(c) within 28 days unless the court otherwise directs to send such a notice to all creditors of the company (so far as he is aware of their addresses).[32]

(b) Notification of order
23–054 Every invoice, order for goods and business letter on or in which the company's name appears issued by or on behalf of the administrator or the company must contain the administrator's name and a statement that the affairs, business and property of the company are being managed by the administrator.[33] If default is made the company is liable to a fine irrespective of fault, and the administrator and any officer of the company are also liable to a fine if without reasonable excuse they authorise or permit the default.[34] Such a default may, it is thought, also expose them to personal liability for any loss occasioned to the person dealing with the company in ignorance of the administration order, for the duty is designed for the protection of persons dealing with the company. Since the powers of the directors during the subsistence of an administration order are only exercisable by them with the consent of the administrator,[35] the directors will not be held to be authorising or permitting the prohibited course to be followed if they merely take no

---

[30] r. 2.53; see also above, para. 23–038.
[31] *Re Consolidated Diesel Engine Manufacturers Ltd* [1915] 1 Ch. 192.
[32] See also supplementary requirements under r. 2.10 and Forms 2.5 and 2.6.
[33] s. 12(1).
[34] s. 12(2). Despite illegality, failure to comply with s. 12 will not deprive the document in question of effect: *Moon Workshops v. Wallace & Phillips* [1950] C.L.Y. 736.
[35] s. 14(4).

action to prevent it, since they do not permit what they have no power to prevent.[36] They will only be liable if they are responsible for the document in question.

(c) Custody and control of assets

The administrator is under a duty to take into his custody or under his **23–055** control all the property to which the company is or appears to be entitled.[37] The duty is analogous to that of a trustee on his appointment to lose no time in placing the trust property in a state of security.[38] The duty will not preclude the exercise of ordinary judgment whether the taking control of any particular asset will cost more than the asset is worth. If in doubt in this respect, the administrator may seek the direction of the court. The administrator may apply to the court for orders for the restoration to the company of assets disposed of at an undervalue[39] or as a voidable preference.[40] In such proceedings the administrator is personally a party and security for costs will not ordinarily be appropriate. However, where the administrator exercises his agency power to bring proceedings in the name of the company, security can be ordered.[41] Since, however, a successful defendant could claim a special priority over the assets, this may be a factor in the exercise of the court's discretion in refusing an order for security.[42]

(d) Administrator's proposals

Section 23 provides that within three months of an administration **23–056** order being made, unless the court allows a longer period,[43] the administrator must send to the registrar of companies[44] and to all

---

[36] See *Sefton v. Tophams* [1967] 1 A.C. 50.

[37] s. 17. Note also s. 234 and *Welsh Development Agency v. Export Finance Co. Ltd* [1992] B.C.C. 270; *Smith v. Bridgend County Borough Council* [2000] 1 B.C.L.C. 775, CA.

[38] See *Snell's Equity* (30th ed., 2000), para. 11–04.

[39] s. 238 (transactions at an undervalue) and s. 423 (transactions defrauding creditors).

[40] s. 239.

[41] Companies Act 1985, s.726. See further *Re Dynaspan (U.K.) Ltd* [1995] B.C.C. 778; *West's Process Engineering Pty. Ltd v. Westralian Sands Ltd* (1998) 16 A.C.L.C. 1020; *Timbertown Community Enterprises Ltd v. Holiday Coast Credit Union Ltd* (1997) 15 A.C.L.C. 1679.

[42] *Smith v. UIC Insurance Co. Ltd* (unreported, H.H. Judge Dean Q.C. sitting as a deputy judge of the Commercial Court, January 19, 1999 — a case concerning a provisional liquidator). See further: Moss, "Losing can Damage your Wealth: The Estate Costs Rule" (2000) 13 *Insolvency Intelligence* 49).

[43] The company has *locus standi* to apply for an extension but the application should normally be made by the administrator: *Re Newport County Association Football Club Ltd* (1987) 3 B.C.C. 635. See also *Re NS Distribution Ltd* [1990] B.C.L.C. 169. In *Re Charnley Davies Business Services Ltd* (1987) 3 B.C.C. 408 the court discharged administration orders without s. 23 meetings taking place because there were no proposals for s. 8 purposes which could sensibly be considered following disposals of the assets. Consider also *Mann v. Abruzzi Sports Club Ltd* (1994) 12 A.C.L.C. 137 (extension of time under the equivalent Australian procedure).The High Court in Northern Ireland held in *Re McFarland Harvey Ltd* [1999] 4 BNIL 57 that any application for extension must be justified by the administrator against the background of a underlying intention that administration should not be an open-ended procedure. Again in Northern Ireland, it has been held that it is not appropriate to extend time to hold a meeting where the purposes of the order have already failed but that an extension can be coupled with a variation of the purposes: *Re V McGeown Wholesale Wines and Spirits Ltd* [1997] N.I.J.B. 190.

[44] Form 2.21.

creditors[45] a statement of his proposals for achieving the purpose or purposes for which the administration order was made. A copy of the statement must also be sent to all members[46] or, alternatively, the administrator must publish[47] a notice giving an address from which members can obtain copies free of charge. Within the same period the administrator must lay a copy of his statement before a meeting of the company's creditors convened for that purpose on not less than 14 days' notice.[48] Rule 2.16 provides that a statement by the administrator giving certain supplementary information shall be annexed to the proposals sent to the registrar of companies and laid before the creditors' meeting. Notice of the creditors' meeting must be given to all creditors of the company who are identified in the statement of affairs, or are known to the administrator and have claims against the company at the date of the administration order. Notice must also be given by advertisement in the newspaper in which the administration order was advertised unless the court otherwise directs.[49] A creditor may vote by proxy provided that the proxy is lodged before the vote is taken, even if not presented prior to the start of the meeting.[50] At the same time the Rules provide that the administrator shall send out notice to attend the meeting in Form 2.10 to any directors or officers (past or present) whose presence he considers to be required.[51]

23–057   If at the meeting there is not the requisite majority for approval of the administrator's proposals (with modifications, if any) the chairman may, and shall if a resolution is passed to that effect, adjourn the meeting for not more than 14 days.[52] The final outcome of the meeting summoned under section 23 (with details of the proposals and any modifications considered) must be reported to the court by the administrator.[53] If the administrator reports that the meeting has refused to approve the proposals (with or without modifications), the court has an unfettered discretion to discharge the administration order or to make such other order (including an interim order) as it thinks fit.[54]

23–058   If the administrator subsequently proposes to make any substantial revisions to proposals which have been approved by a creditors' meeting then he must first distribute details of his proposed revisions to creditors' and members and obtain creditors' approval in the same way as applied

---

[45] "so far as he is aware of their addresses".

[46] also "so far as he is aware of their addresses".

[47] See further r. 2.17.

[48] In *Re Harris Bus Company Ltd* (unreported, December 16, 1999, but see (2000) 16 I.L. & P. 61), it was held that the court has no power to abridge this period but can nonetheless direct under s. 17 that a creditors' meeting be held on short notice.

[49] The court has jurisdiction under r. 2.18(2) to waive the advertisement requirement retrospectively: *Re Richmond FC Ltd* (unreported, July 26, 1999).

[50] *Re Phillip Alexander Securities & Futures Ltd* [1998] B.P.I.R. 383.

[51] r. 2.18.

[52] r. 2.18.

[53] s. 24(4) and r. 2.29. See also Form 2.23. If the proposals are approved then no hearing will normally be required in respect of the report: *Re Van Kit Ltd* (unreported, 1987; see further Phillips, "Administration Orders — The First Few Months" (1987) 8 Co. Law 273).

[54] s. 24(5).

to his original proposals.[55] As with the original proposals the administrator must consent to any modifications. Whether or not revisions to proposals warrant consideration by a creditors' meeting is a matter for the decision of the administrator on whether the revisions "appear to him substantial".[56] Although the courts will not readily interfere with the administrator's decision on this point, no administrator can expect the courts to stand by idly if he purports to hold a view which the court believes he could not reasonably have reached.[57]

In *Re Smallman Construction Ltd*[58] the court held that it had a **23–059** residual jurisdiction to give directions, even after a creditors' meeting approving proposals, in order to overcome a lacuna in the original proposals where it was impractical to convene a section 25 meeting. Subsequently, in *Re Dana (U.K.) Ltd*,[59] the court suggested that administrators should anticipate the need to take decisions, which are not consistent with approved proposals, more speedily than the section 25 procedure permits and should incorporate some appropriate mechanism in their original proposals.

Sections 24 and 25 contain express requirements that the meeting to **23–060** approve proposals or (as the case may be) substantial revisions shall be conducted in accordance with the Rules.[60] A creditor is entitled to cast its votes as to £X in one way and £Y the other way, provided that the aggregate does not exceed the total debt eligible for voting.[61] Within 14 days of the conclusion of a meeting summoned under either section 23 or section 25 the administrator is required to send notice in Form 2.12 of the result of the meeting (including, where appropriate, details of the proposals as approved) to every creditor who received notice of the meeting under the rules and to any other creditors of whom he has since become aware.[62]

(e) Discharge or variation of order

The administrator may at any time apply to the court for the administra- **23–061** tion order to be discharged or to be varied so as to specify an additional purpose.[63] He is under a duty to make such an application if:

> (a) it appears to him that the purpose or each of the purposes specified in the order either has been achieved or is incapable of achievement; or

[55] s. 25; see further r. 2.17 and Form 2.22.
[56] s. 25(1).
[57] A possible criterion for what is a substantial revision is whether any reasonable creditor would have changed his decision on the original proposals if the revision had appeared in the original proposals. *cf. Re Minster Assets plc* [1985] B.C.L.C. 200. Note *R. v. Monopolies and Mergers Commission* and, *ex p. South Yorkshire Transport Ltd* [1993] 1 W.L.R. 23 for a consideration of the possible range of meaning of "substantial" in another context.
[58] (1989) 4 B.C.C. 784. Note also *Re FMS Financial Management Ltd* (1989) 5 B.C.C. 191.
[59] [1999] 2 B.C.L.C. 239.
[60] See generally rr. 2.18–2.20 and rr. 2.22–2.30 and Forms 2.11 and 2.12.
[61] *Re Polly Peck International plc* [1991] B.C.C. 503.
[62] r. 2.30 Note also ss. 24(4) and 25(6) and Form 2.23.
[63] s. 18(1).

(b) he is required to do so by a meeting of the company's creditors summoned for the purpose.[64]

On such application, the court may discharge or vary the administration order and make such other order as it thinks fit.[65]

23–062 Where a person ceases to be an administrator, section 20(1) provides that he shall have his "release" with effect from such time as the court may determine, except in the case of death when the release takes effect from the time when notice is given to the court. Where an administrator has given notice of his intention to seek his release, the court will grant the release immediately if the creditors' committee has approved the application and there is no objection from other creditors.[66] It would be wrong for the court to exercise this power without investigating or making provision for investigation of claims of which the court has notice.[67] A person who has had his "release" is discharged from all liability in respect of his acts or omissions in the administration and otherwise in relation to his conduct as administrator, but is not immune from misfeasance proceedings under section 212.[68]

23–063 The existence of a pending section 27 claim was accepted as a reason for postponing discharge of an administration order in *Re Charnley Davies Business Services Ltd*[69] In *Barclays Mercantile v. Sibec Developments Ltd*[70] administrators had applied for and obtained the discharge of the administration order upon terms that release would follow on the expiration of a specified period. During that period creditors wishing to pursue claims against the administrators successfully applied for and obtained postponement of the administrators' release. In *Re Sheridan Securities Ltd*[71] the administrator applied for the order to be discharged and for his release but a creditor appeared and applied for the release to be postponed in order that there could be an investigation of the administrator's activities, including the fact that he had apparently pursued purposes other than those specified in the order. The court discharged the administration order but postponed the administrator's release for two months with liberty to the official receiver or liquidator to apply for further postponement. A similar situation arose in *Re Exchange Travel (Holdings) Ltd*[72] where the administrators' release was delayed for three months in order to allow time for creditors with complaints against the administrators to take whatever steps they

---

[64] s. 18(2). See also above, para. 23–032. Administrators should apply promptly. The High Court in Northern Ireland expressed concern in *Re Allpoint Graphic Services Ltd* [1997] N.I.J.B. 271 where an application for discharge was made approximately four years after the realisation of the company's assets.

[65] s. 18(3). Note also s. 18(4) and Forms 2.19 and 2.20.

[66] *Re Chaumet Ltd.* (unreported, February 29, 1988).

[67] *IRC v. Hoogstraten* [1985] Q.B. 1077, CA, and the cases discussed in the next para. of the text. Contrast *Re Olympia & York Canary Wharf Holdings Ltd* [1993] B.C.C. 866.

[68] s. 20(2). See further above, para. 23–041.

[69] (1987) 3 B.C.C. 408.

[70] [1992] 1 W.L.R. 1253.

[71] (1988) 4 B.C.C. 200, followed in *Re Allpoint Graphic Services Ltd* [1997] N.I.J.B. 271.

[72] [1992] B.C.C. 954.

thought necessary, but a majority of the creditors successfully resisted the suggestion that an investigation should be funded out of the company's assets.

8. MANAGEMENT BY ADMINISTRATOR

The administrator is empowered to do all such things as may be **23–064** necessary for the management of the affairs, business and property of the company, and in addition is given all the powers specified in Schedule 1 to the Insolvency Act 1986.[73] Although an administrator acting as agent of the company is bound by its memorandum of association,[74] the powers given are of the widest scope which include all the powers of the directors prior to the administration order being made,[75] and a person dealing with an administrator in good faith and for value is not concerned to inquire whether the administrator is acting within his powers.[76] The practical limitations on the powers are few:

(a) Compliance with approved proposals

From the date of his appointment until the date of any approval of his **23–065** proposals by a meeting of creditors under section 24, the administrator must manage in accordance with any directions given by the court.[77] If the circumstances relied upon in support of the administration petition change substantially following the making of the order, an application to the court may be appropriate.[78] A question arises as to how far the administrator can properly exercise his powers of disposal in a way that will pre-empt the decision of the creditors at their meeting.[79] This is one of a number of areas where judicial thinking has developed since the introduction of administration. There is no appellate authority and the first instance decisions are not consistent. However, the judgment of Neuberger J. in *Re T&D Industries plc*[80] examined the issues and the authorities in some detail. The position (at first instance) now appears to be settled on the basis that the administrator's full schedule 1 powers are exercisable with effect from the making of the order and leave is not a necessary precondition of effecting disposals, *i.e.* there is no issue of *vires*.[81] Neuberger J. added seven points by way of guidance for future cases which can be summarised as follows:

---

[73] s. 14(1). See further *Smith v. Bridgend County Borough Council* [2000] 1 B.C.L.C. 775, CA.

[74] *Re Home Treat Ltd* [1991] B.C.C. 165, but see above, para. 23–042.

[75] *Denny v. Yeldon* [1995] 3 All E.R. 624; *Polly Peck International plc v. Henry* [1999] 1 B.C.L.C. 407 — both are cases dealing with the exercise of powers in relation to pension schemes.

[76] s. 14(6); consider also the Companies Act 1985, ss. 35 and 35B.

[77] s. 17(2)(a). The administrator must throughout have regard to the purposes for which the order was made; see further *Re Sheridan Securities Ltd* (1988) 4 B.C.C. 200.

[78] See further *Re CE King Ltd* (unreported, April 29, 1999).

[79] For background, see Anderson, "Administration: Creditor Control of Asset Disposals" (1989) 2 *Insolvency Intelligence* 49.

[80] [2000] 1 All E.R. 333.

[81] See further *Re Charnley Davies Ltd* (unreported, January 21, 1987); *Re Charnley Davies Ltd (No. 2)* [1990] B.C.L.C. 760; *Re Montin Ltd* [1999] 1 B.C.L.C. 663; *Re Osmosis Group Ltd* [1999] 2 B.C.L.C. 329.

(a) It is desirable for administrators to put their proposals to creditors as soon as possible.[82]

(b) Administrators are responsible for their decisions and the court is not a bomb shelter from the consequences.[83]

(c) If a section 24 meeting is not practicable before decisions have to be made, administrators should consider whether informal consultations are feasible.[84]

(d) Occasionally directions under section 14(3) will be appropriate, for example where a point of principle is at stake or there is a dispute.

(e) It would be a very unusual case in which the court could give real assistance on a commercial decision without a hearing at which interested parties had an opportunity to be heard.

(f) In an appropriate case, the court could order (under section 17(3)(b)) a creditors' meeting on short notice.[85]

(g) Administrators should take into account whether their decisions on disposals will render the creditors meeting redundant.[86]

From the date of such approval the administrator must manage in accordance with such proposals as from time to time revised whether by him or a predecessor of his,[87] and must exercise his powers accordingly.[88] In practice, proposals are often in such general terms that matters are largely left to the commercial judgment of the administrator. The proposals may include a provison that the administrators negotiations are to be kept confidential. The court will not readily go behind such confidentiality on the application of an aggrieved creditor.[89]

(b) Sale of property free from charges

23–066 The administrator can dispose of, or otherwise exercise his powers in relation to, any property of the company which is the subject of a floating charge as though it was not the subject of a floating charge.[90] When any such disposal takes place, the holder of the security has the same rights in respect of any property of the company which directly or indirectly represents the property disposed of as he would have had in

---

[82] See further *Re Consumer and Industrial Press Ltd (No. 2)* (1988) 4 B.C.C. 72.

[83] See further *Re NS Distribution Ltd* [1990] B.C.L.C. 169; *Re Dana (U.K.) Ltd* [1999] 2 B.C.L.C. 239; *Re Montin Ltd* [1999] 1 B.C.L.C. 663; *Re Osmosis Group Ltd* [1999] 2 B.C.L.C. 329.

[84] See further *Re Charnley Davis Ltd* (1988) 4 B.C.C. 152; *Re Dana (U.K.) Ltd* [1999] 2 B.C.L.C. 239.

[85] See further *Re Harris Bus Company Ltd* (unreported, December 16, 1999, but see (2000) 16 I.L. & P. 61).

[86] See further *Re Charnley Davies Business Services Ltd* (1987) 3 B.C.C. 408; *Re Consumer and Industrial Press Ltd (No. 2)* (1988) 4 B.C.L.C. 72; *Re NS Distribution Ltd* [1999] 1 B.C.L.C. 169; *Re Montin Ltd* [1999] 1 B.C.L.C. 663; *Re PD Fuels Ltd* [1999] B.C.C. 450.

[87] s. 17(2)(b).

[88] See also above, paras 23–056 to 23–060.

[89] *MTI Trading Systems Ltd v. Winter* [1998] B.C.C. 591.

[90] s. 15(1) and (3).

respect of the property disposed of.[91] Although the concept of an administrator dealing with floating charge security is simple, its practical application may be complicated. It may not be easy to determine whether property has been consumed entirely or whether new property represents it. These potential problems have not yet been tested in the courts. The conversion of property into cash and the use of such cash in ordinary trading activities could pose particular difficulties. The courts might well have to adopt the principles of the equitable remedy of tracing in order to resolve such difficulties.

The administrator can, but only with the authority of a court, sell **23–067** property which is subject to any other security (including fixed charges of debts) free from such security and sell goods in the possession of the company under a hire purchase agreement (a term including for this purpose conditional sale agreements, chattel leasing agreements and retention of title agreements[92]) as if all rights of the owner under the agreement were vested in the company.[93] The court may give such authority if satisfied that the sale (with or without other assets) would be likely to promote the purpose or one or more of the purposes specified in the administration order.[94] It must, however, be a condition of any such order that the net proceeds of the disposal plus (where those proceeds are less than such amount as the court determines to be the net amount realisable on an open market sale[95]) such sums as are required to make good the deficiency are applied towards discharging the sums secured by the security or payable under the hire purchase agreement,[96] or if there is more than one security the sums secured by those securities in order of priority.[97] Accordingly, the proceeds of sale of the subject of fixed charges and hire-purchase agreements can only be utilised to run the company's business to the extent of any equity remaining in the company after discharge of the sums payable to the secured creditor or owner.

---

[91] s. 15(4).

[92] s. 15(2).For definitions, see further above, para. 23–004.

[93] s. 15(2) and (3). Note again the Companies Act 1989, s. 175: see above, para. 23–002. Where a mortgagee agrees to sale and to the release of an ostensibly valid security there is no scope for a s. 15 order: *Re Newman Shopfitters (Cleveland) Ltd* [1991] B.C.L.C. 407. If the validity of the security is challenged in proceedings, then the administrator can seek interim relief in respect of the proceeds of sale pending judgment.

[94] s. 15(2). An administrator is unlikely in a normal case to obtain an order under s. 15 until he has had his proposals approved at a creditors' meeting: *Re Consumer & Industrial Press Ltd (No. 2)* (1988) 4 B.C.C. 72. The existence of a bona fide dispute as to value between the secured creditor and the administrator will call into operation the court's discretion but is not a prerequisite of jurisdiction: *Re ARV Aviation Ltd* (1988) 4 B.C.C. 708.

[95] For consideration of the effect of an unrealistically high offer of purchase on the open market price in the context of the parallel power conferred on administrative receivers, see above, Chaps 9 and 14.

[96] s. 15(5). For the purposes of determining "the sum secured by the security" it is necessary to take into account not only the capital sum secured but also all interest properly payable and any costs which the security-holder is entitled to add to the security in accordance with general law and the terms of the security instrument: *Re ARV Aviation Ltd* (1988) 4 B.C.C. 708.

[97] s. 15(6) Consider the alternative jurisdiction of the court under Law of Property Act 1925, s. 91; see further *Palk v. Mortgage Services Ltd* [1993] Ch. 330, CA.

23–068   Procedure is dealt with in rule 2.51 which provides that the court shall fix a venue for the hearing of the application and that the administrator shall give notice of the venue to the secured creditor. In *Re Discounter Catalogue Showrooms Ltd*, a section 15 order relating to retention of title goods was made without notice being given to the claimants. This is unlikely in any but the most exceptional circumstances.[1] There is no scope for anything in the nature of an interim section 15 order. However, it is possible for section 15 applications to be dealt with by a two-stage process, *i.e.* first, an order for sale and, secondly, an inquiry to ascertain what sum (if any) would be required to make good any deficiency. It is desirable for administrators seeking section 15 orders to put in valuation advice but the jurisdiction exists whether or not such advice is provided.[2]

(c) Administration expenses

23–069   Under section 19(4), where a person ceases to be administrator, his remuneration and any expenses[3] properly incurred by him are a charge on the property of the company which is in his custody or control at the time when he ceases to hold office and are to be paid out of such property in priority to any charge which was, as created, a floating charge. The established jurisdiction of the court to allow a liquidator's remuneration and expenses to be paid out of trust assets in an appropriate case, applies also to administrators.[4] Subsection (5)[5] provides that any sums payable in respect of debts or liabilities incurred, whilst administrator, under contracts entered into or adopted by him in the carrying out of his functions (or by a predecessor in the carrying out of the predecessor's functions)[6] shall be similarly charged on and paid out of company property in priority to the subsection (4) charge.[7] Under subsection (6)[8] a charge enjoying the same priority applies to "qualifying liabilities" in respect of contracts of employment which have been adopted.[9] Sums payable in respect of liabilities incurred under contracts of employment have been held to include, for the purposes of section

---

[98] Note also s. 15(7) and Form 2.18.

[99] Unreported, 1987; see further Phillips, "Administration Orders — The First Few Months" (1987) 8 Co. Law 273.

[1] See further r. 7.4(6).

[2] *Re ARV Aviation Ltd* (1988) 4 B.C.C. 708.

[3] The meaning of "expenses" in this context remains very unclear. In *Re A Company (No. 005174 of 1999)* [2000] I.C.R. 263; [2000] 1 W.L.R. 502, it was held to refer to expenses falling outside s. 19(5) and equated with minor disbursements.

[4] *Tom Wise Ltd v. Fillimore* [1999] B.C.C. 129; *Re Berkeley Applegate (Investment Consultants) Ltd* [1989] 1 Ch. 32. But see also *Polly Peck International plc v. Henry* [1999] 1 B.C.L.C. 407.

[5] As amended by the Insolvency Act 1994, s. 1(3).

[6] This includes legal fees incurred by the administrator: *Re A Company (No. 005174 of 1999)* [2000] I.C.R. 263; [2000] 1 W.L.R. 502.

[7] The administrator should ensure that there will be sufficient assets in the estate when he vacates office for such debts and liabilities to be met.

[8] See further above, para. 23–026.

[9] The administrator is not to be taken to have adopted a contract of employment for these purposes by reason of anything done or omitted within 14 days of appointment; s. 19 see further above, Chap. 19.

19(5) and (6), PAYE and employees' (primary) NIC but not employers' (secondary) NIC.[10] In *Re Maxwell Fleet and Facilities Management Ltd*,[11] section 19(5) was held to create a discrete statutory obligation to pay with a fresh limitation period applicable to both that obligation and the enforcement of the charge despite the fact that the underlying contractual obligation was statute-barred.

Obviously, the administrator must discharge his personal liabilities but **23–070** the Act is silent as to the proper treatment of liabilities incurred by the company through the exercise of the administrator's powers as its agent.[12] There are various references in the Rules[13] to payment as an "expense of the administration" and rule 2.22(4) envisages possible payments of pre-administration debts.[14] In *Re Atlantic Computer Systems plc*[15] the Court of Appeal rejected the analogy with liquidation expenses in favour of a flexible approach under which the court has a wide discretion. It follows that periodic liabilities arising out of pre-administration contracts where assets continue to be used or services continue to be received necessitate a section 11 application to the court by the creditor where the administrator refuses to pay. In the absence of such an application, payment is a matter for the administrator's proposals or for directions given by the court. In *Re Japan Leasing (Europe) plc*[16] the court held that administrators should account for money received by the company as agent after the administration order was made. The principal ground for the decision was that the money was held on trust, but that conclusion was supported by holding that the obligation to account would, in any event, have constituted an expense of the administration.

9. SAFEGUARDS FOR CREDITORS AND MEMBERS

During the period of the administration order, the affairs of the **23–071** company are in the hands of the administrator. He is under an obligation to summon meetings of creditors:

    (a) to approve his proposals[17] and substantial revisions[18] but only with such modifications to the proposals as the administrator consents to;

    (b) if requested to do so in accordance with the rules by one-tenth in value of the company's creditors, or

---

[10] *Re FJL Realisations Ltd*, *The Times*, March 21, 2000, CA.

[11] [2000] 1 All E.R. 464.

[12] In the ordinary way such liabilities are paid as they arise: *Powdrill v. Watson* [1994] I.C.R. 395, CA, on appeal [1995] 2 A.C. 394, HL.

[13] See rr. 2.9, 2.21, 2.45, 2.49 and 2.50 (see also r. 12.8).

[14] Contrast *Re Manlon Trading Ltd* (1988) 4 B.C.C. 455 where a suggestion to the effect that an administrator would make an apparently unjustified payment to a creditor who had presented a winding-up petition was described as "wholly improper".

[15] [1992] Ch. 505, CA.

[16] [1999] B.P.I.R. 911.

[17] ss. 23 and 24.

[18] s. 25.

(c) if directed to do so by the court.[19]

He is under no obligation to call any meeting of the members unless required to do so by the court.[20]

If the administrator is unsympathetic to their concerns, a creditor has three principal remedies through the courts:

(a) he may apply for the administrator's removal under section 19(1);
(b) he may (with the leave of the court) petition for a winding-up order; or
(c) he may petition under section 27.[21]

A member's remedies are likely to be limited to (1) and (3). He is unlikely to have the necessary standing to petition for winding-up, since in most cases no order will be made on his petition unless he can show that there is a probability of surplus assets available for a return to members.[22] Because of the retrospective effect of an order made on a petition, it appears unlikely that leave would be given to a member or a creditor to petition, let alone that the court would make a winding-up order on any petition other than on a petition presented by administrators as agents of the company.[23]

23–072   Under section 27, at any time when an administration order is in force, a creditor or member may apply to the court by petition for an order on the ground:

(a) that the company's affairs, business and property are being or have been managed by the administrator in a manner which is or was unfairly prejudicial to the interests of its creditors or members generally or of some part of its creditors or members (including at least himself); or
(b) that any actual or proposed act or omission of the administrator is or would be so prejudicial.[24]

---

[19] s. 17(3); see further rr. 2.19 and 2.21; *Re Harris Bus Company Ltd* (unreported, December 16, 1999), but see (2000) 16 I.L. & P. 61).

[20] For example, under s. 27(4)(c).

[21] An application for recission of the administration order under r. 7.47 (as in *Cornhill Insurance plc v. Cornhill Financial Services Ltd* [1992] B.C.C. 818) is unlikely to be appropriate after the administration has been in force for a significant period.

[22] *Re W.R. Wilicocks & Co. Ltd* [1973] Ch. 163.

[23] See above, para. 23–082.

[24] The jurisdiction is not appropriate for a challenge to the making of the order: see the first instance judgment of H.H. Judge Micklem in *Cornhill Insurance plc v. Cornhill Financial Services Ltd* [1992] B.C.C. 818 at 827 (see also the comment of Dillon L.J. at 858 in the Court of Appeal). The court may apply by analogy the principle adopted in exercise of its jurisdiction over liquidators that it will not interfere with the proposed exercise by the liquidator of his powers unless he is shown to be acting fraudulently, in bad faith or in such a way as no reasonable liquidator could act: an allegation of negligence (*e.g.* a proposed sale without a proper valuation) will not be sufficient: *Pitman v. Top Business Systems* [1984] B.C.L.C. 593 following *Leon v. York-O-Matic Ltd* [1966] 1 W.L.R. 1450. See also *Re Edennote Ltd* [1996] 2 B.C.L.C. 389, CA and *Re Charnley Davies Ltd* [1990] B.C.C. 605.

The concept "unfair prejudice" is transplanted from sections 459–461 of the Companies Act 1985. The prejudice to the petitioner must be to his interests as creditor or member.[25]

On the hearing of the petition, the court may make such order as it **23–073** thinks fit for giving relief in respect of the matters complained of, or adjourn the hearing conditionally or unconditionally, or make an interim order or any other order it thinks fit. The court may in particular:

(a) regulate the future management by the administrator of the company's affairs, business and property;

(b) require the administrator to refrain from doing or continuing an act complained of by the petitioner or to do an act which the petitioner has complained he has omitted to do;

(c) require the summoning of a meeting of creditors or members for the purpose of considering such matters as the court may direct;

(d) discharge the administration order and make such consequential provision as it thinks fit.

But no order shall prejudice or prevent:

(a) the implementation of any composition or scheme approved under section 4 of the Insolvency Act 1986 or any compromise or arrangement sanctioned under section 425 of the Companies Act 1985; or

(b) (where the application for the order was made more than 28 days after the approval of any proposals or revised proposals) the implementation of those proposals or revised proposals.[26]

Ostensibly, the language of the section is sufficiently wide to enable the court to make a winding-up order, and indeed, if the administration order is to be discharged, this may be in many cases the inevitable order. However, the administrator will probably be required to present a winding-up petition.[27]

The threat to administrators posed by section 27 remains largely **23–074** unexplored. In *Re Charnley Davies Ltd*[28] the court refused to order the trial of preliminary issues in a section 27 case because, in part, it was dealing with new legislation. By the time the case came for trial, it had become a simple action for professional negligence. It was then held that although such negligence, if established, would amount to misconduct, it would neither constitute nor evidence unfairly prejudicial management. Such allegations fall outside the scope of section 27.[29] An administrator

---

[25] *Re A Company (No. 004475 of 1982)* [1983] Ch. 178. As to the meaning of "unfairness," in section 459, see *O'Neill v. Phillips* [1999] 1 W.L.R. 1092, HL.

[26] s. 27(3)

[27] Consider *Re Brooke Marine Ltd* [1988] B.C.L.C. 546.

[28] (1989) 4 B.C.C. 152.

[29] [1990] B.C.C. 605 (the allegations of negligence failed).

is at personal risk in respect of the costs of applications by disaffected creditors under sections 11 and 27.[30] *Re Atlantic Computer Systems plc* suggests that section 11 and section 27 issues will normally be distinct and that section 27 should not and need not be used where the remedy being sought is really leave under section 11.[31] Similarly, section 27 should also not be used where the Rules provide a specific procedure to challenge a particular form of decision, *e.g.* on admission to vote at a creditors' meeting.[32]

10. FOREIGN COMPANIES AND EXTRA-TERRITORIAL EFFECT[33]

23–075   Initial assumptions were that an administration order could only be made in respect of a company incorporated in England or Scotland[34] but the point was left open in *Re International Bulk Commodities Ltd*.[35] In *Re Dallhold Estates (U.K.) Pty. Ltd*[36] the court made an order in respect of a foreign registered company following a request for an order in aid made under section 426 of the Insolvency Act 1986. Whether or not an administration order can be made in respect of a foreign registered company in the absence of such a request is yet to be resolved by the courts.[37]

23–076   A company subject to an administration order may have creditors and assets abroad, and another unanswered question is whether the prohibitions on the commencement of proceedings and seizure of property are limited to such activity in the United Kingdom or extend world-wide.[38] In *Re Bank of Credit and Commerce International* SA Browne-Wilkinson V.-C. commented[39] unfavourably on the lack of an international convention regulating international insolvency. The risk is that the efficacy of insolvency procedures will be undermined by creditors pursuing assets in different jurisdictions.[40]

[30] *Re Charnley Davies Ltd* (1988) 4 B.C.C. 152; *Re Atlantic Computer Systems plc* [1992] Ch. 505; *Barclays Mercantile v. Sibec Developments Ltd* [1992] 1 W.L.R. 1253
[31] [1990] B.C.C. 439; *on appeal* [1992] Ch. 505.
[32] *MTI Trading Systems Ltd v. Winter* [1998] B.C.C. 591.
[33] This subject is considered in detail in para. 25–015 above.
[34] The proposition was not in dispute in *Felixstowe Dock & Railway Co. v. United States Lines Inc.* [1989] Q.B. 360.
[35] [1993] Ch. 77 as to which see also *Re Devon and Somerset Farmers Ltd* [1994] Ch. 57.
[36] [1992] B.C.C. 394. In *Re Bank of Credit and Commerce International SA & Anor* [1993] B.C.C. 787, Rattee J. referred to the liquidator in *Dallhold* as having been "correctly advised" that an administration order could not be made under s. 8 in respect of a company incorporated abroad.
[37] See further: Moss, "Administration Orders for Foreign Companies" (1993) 6 Insolvency Intelligence 19; Moss, "Administration Orders for Foreign Companies Revisited" (1994) 7 Insolvency Intelligence 33; *Moss*, "Insurance Company Insolvency — a Step in the Right Direction" (1999) 12 *Insolvency Intelligence* 51.
[38] See the discussion in Chap. 25.
[39] [1992] B.C.C. 83 at 89.
[40] In *Felixstowe Dock & Railway Co. Ltd* [1989] Q.B. 360 the court refused to set aside Mareva injunctions obtained by English and European trade creditors in the English courts preventing a company subject to proceedings under Chap. 11, U.S. Bankruptcy Code from removing assets from the jurisdiction. This result may have been influenced by the judge's perception that the U.S. proceedings discriminated (on the facts of that particular case) against English and European creditors. See further Chaps 25 and 26 on cross-frontier co-operation in insolvency proceedings.

An alternative and more constructive approach may lie in the co- **23–077** operation of courts in different jurisdictions permitting concurrent insolvency procedures.[41]

11. SCHEME OF ARRANGEMENT

Section 425 of the Companies Act 1985 as amended by Schedule 6, **23–078** paragraph 11 to the Insolvency Act 1985 reads as follows:

> "(1) Where a compromise or arrangement is proposed between a company and its creditors . . . the court may on the application of the . . . administrator, order a meeting of the creditors . . . to be summoned in such manner as the court directs.
>
> (2) If a majority in number representing three-fourths in value of the creditors . . . present and voting either in person or by proxy at the meeting, agree to any compromise or arrangement, the compromise or arrangement, if sanctioned by the court, is binding on all creditors . . . ."

A scheme of arrangement was proposed by administrators in *Re British & Commonwealth Holdings plc (No. 3)*[42] to enable them to make an interim distribution. The administrators successfully argued that the rights of subordinated creditors would be unaffected by the scheme and obtained directions enabling them to apply to the court for a meeting of creditors on the footing that the trustee for the subordinated creditors would have no right to be given notice or to vote.

12. LIQUIDATION AND OTHER EXIT ROUTES

The administration procedure is designed to relieve the company from **23–079** pressure whilst one or other of the statutory purposes is pursued. It is a means to an end, not an end in itself. In particular, it is not a procedure for general distribution to creditors whether according to the statutory scheme applicable in liquidation or otherwise. In *Re St Ives Windings Ltd*[43] Harman J. expressed a provisional view that the court had no power to sanction an administrator making distributions where appointed for the purposes specified in section 8(3)(a) and (d). However, in another case of an administration order made for the dual purposes of survival of the company and more advantageous realisation of assets, it was held that an administrator has power, if the assets are

---

[41] Consider *Re Bank of Credit and Commerce International SA* [1992] B.C.C. 83; *Re Maxwell Communications Corporation plc* [1992] B.C.C. 372 and *Re Maxwell Communications Corporation plc (No. 2)* [1992] B.C.C. 757.

[42] [1992] 1 W.L.R. 672: see also *Re Maxwell Communications Corporation plc* [1993] 1 W.L.R. 1402. As to schemes generally, see Chap. 2 above.

[43] (1987) 3 B.C.C. 634. See also *Re Barrow Borough Transport Ltd* [1990] Ch. 227 at 234–235 and *Re Bradwin Ltd's Petition* [1997] N.I.L.R. 394.

sufficient, to pay off pre-administration creditors in full.[44] In a further case which involved an insolvent bank, a payment on account to depositors was sanctioned in order to preserve the goodwill of the business.[45] More recently the court sanctioned payment in full to creditors who would have been preferential in a compulsory liquidation and a payment to unsecured creditors on a *pari passu* basis.[46] The special circumstances in the latter case were that the administrators were in possession of substantial funds available for distribution but liquidation would have ended the possibility of a further significant sum becoming available from a pension scheme surplus. On the existing state of the authorities (all decided at first instance) the position appears to be that administrators' powers under paragraph 13 of Schedule 1 are wide enough to permit distributions to be made to creditors but that it will only be appropriate for them to exercise such powers in exceptional circumstances where, for example, liquidation or a voluntary arrangement is either impractical or will have consequences which are injurious to creditors' interests, or where there are sufficient funds to pay all classes of creditors in full. Administrators lack the powers of a liquidator to determine provable debts and should not make general distributions to creditors without obtaining directions under section 14(3).

23–080   Section 18(2) requires an administrator to apply for discharge if it appears either that the purposes for which the order was made have been achieved, or that they are incapable of achievement.[47] In an ordinary case, apart from those situations where the company and all or part of its business have survived, there will then be four possible routes[48] for the distribution of funds in the hands of the administrators and for doing anything else necessary to resolve the affairs of the company:

(a) compulsory liquidation
(b) creditors' voluntary liquidation
(c) voluntary arrangement under Part I of the Insolvency Act 1986, or
(d) scheme of arrangement under section 425 of the Companies Act 1985.

This area demonstrates particular lack of foresight on the part of the draftsmen of the Act.[49] The only provisions of the legislation which address post-discharge procedures expressly deal with compulsory liquidation. However, even in those cases for which the statutory scheme of

---

[44] *Re John Slack Ltd.* (unreported, July 2, 1990).
[45] *Re Mount Banking plc* (unreported, January 25, 1993).
[46] *Re WBSL Realisations 1992 Ltd* [1995] 2 B.C.L.C. 576.
[47] Note r. 2.16(2).
[48] It may be necessary to seek a variation of the order under s. 18(1): *Re St Ives Windings Ltd* (1987) 3 B.C.C. 634.
[49] The drafting of Part II of the Act is lamentable (or "mediocre", *per* Neuberger J. in *Re T&D Industries plc* [2000] 1 All E.R. 333). This is only one of a number of areas, *e.g.* the scope of the moratorium, adoption of contracts of employment and administration expenses, where the deficiencies of the legislation have been exposed by litigation.

distribution applicable to liquidation is entirely appropriate, there are practical objections. The fees payable and the restrictions upon investment in compulsory liquidation mean that a creditors' voluntary liquidation would usually be more in the interest of creditors where substantial assets are involved. A further complication arises in cases where funds are available for interim distribution to creditors. No winding-up resolution or order can be passed or made whilst the administration order is in force.[50] If the administration is to continue, any interim distribution has to be made under a voluntary arrangement or a scheme of arrangement.[51] In practice, none of the available exit routes is free from difficulties.

Although an administrator can propose a voluntary arrangement **23–081** under Part I, some aspects of the procedure may make it unacceptable for some creditors. In a voluntary arrangement proposed by an administrator, the votes of creditors are calculated according to the amount of the creditor's debt as at the date of the administration order.[52] Creditors are not entitled to vote in respect of unliquidated or unascertained claims except where the chairman agrees an estimated minimum value for voting purposes.[53] Further, the "relevant date" for calculating preferential debts is also the date of the administration order.[54] Where there are significant post-administration order liabilities which have not been and do not have to be paid, these provisions could cause serious injustice to those creditors and may mean that there are an additional class of creditors of the company who are not bound by the arrangement.[55] Whilst the powers of the court in respect of a scheme of arrangement under section 425 of the Companies Act 1985 are so extensive that many difficulties can be overcome, the procedure may be thought too cumbersome and expensive for ordinary cases. The preferred route for final distributions will often be one or other form of liquidation particularly because of the liquidator's statutory powers to wind up the company's affairs[56] and because of the mechanism of proof of debt to enable him to determine the ranking of claims in the liquidation.

In choosing between compulsory and voluntary liquidation, there are **23–082** three provisions which must be borne in mind:

    (a) A creditors' voluntary liquidation is deemed to have commenced at the time of the passing of the winding-up resolution. Unless the company is already in voluntary liquidation, a compulsory liquidation is deemed to commence at the time of

---

[50] s. 11(3)(a).
[51] See, *e.g. Re British & Commonwealth Holdings plc (No. 3)* [1992] 1 W.L.R. 672.
[52] r.1.17(2).
[53] r. 1.17(3), *Doorbar v. Alltime Securities Ltd* [1995] B.C.C. 1149.
[54] s. 387(2).
[55] On the practical use of voluntary arrangements and the power of dissenting parties to interfere, consider also *Re Olympia & York Canary Wharf Holdings Ltd* [1993] B.C.C. 866.
[56] *e.g.* disclaimer, ss. 178–182.

the presentation of the winding-up petition.[57] The legislation provides no express automatic dispensation from the effects of section 127 which provides for the avoidance of property dispositions after the commencement of winding-up. This is a point to be considered in relation to the timing of any winding-up petition designed to secure that administration is followed by compulsory liquidation.

(b) Section 387 of the Insolvency Act 1986 provides that the "relevant date" for calculation of preferential debts is to be the date of the administration order in those cases where a winding-up order is made immediately upon the discharge of the administration order. In the case of a voluntary liquidation, the "relevant date" is that of the passing of the winding-up resolution. It follows that choice between the two forms of insolvent liquidation procedure could materially affect the rights of preferential or potentially preferential creditors.

(c) The third area for consideration relates to preferences and transactions at an undervalue. Here, too, the legislation employs the concept of liquidation occurring "immediately upon the discharge of an administration order".[58] The significance of this lies in determination of the antecedent period within which it must be established that a preference or transaction at an undervalue occurred, if it is to be attacked. In this case, however, the legislation makes no distinction in terms between compulsory and voluntary liquidation. It follows that either form of liquidation is capable of occurring immediately upon the discharge of an administration order but, in practice, this may be more difficult to achieve with a creditors' voluntary liquidation.

23–083   Compulsory liquidation requires a winding-up petition. Rule 4.7(7) provides that an administrator's petition shall be expressed to be the petition of the company by its administrator and shall contain an application under section 18 requesting discharge of the administration order. These provisions result from amendments to the Rules made following the decision in *Re Brooke Marine Ltd*[59] where it was held that the court had no jurisdiction to make a winding-up order on an application for discharge of the administration order. Although section 140(1) provides that the court may appoint the administrator to be liquidator,[60] rule 4.7(10) provides that an administrator seeking

---

[57] ss. 86 and 129.

[58] s. 240(3).

[59] [1988] B.C.L.C. 546; see also *Re Charnley Davies Business Services Ltd* (1987) 3 B.C.C. 408.

[60] In *Re Exchange Travel (Holdings) Ltd* [1992] B.C.C. 954 it was held that s. 140 gives the court no power to appoint as liquidator anyone other than a former administrator (see also "Administrator's appointment as liquidator" (1989) 2 Insolvency Intelligence 71). As to the choice of liquidator, see further *Re Charnley Davies Business Services Ltd* (1987) 3 B.C.C. 408.

appointment as liquidator in such circumstances must file in court a report which states the date on which he notified creditors of the company of his intention to seek appointment as liquidator and details of any response from creditors.

A creditors' voluntary liquidation will often be preferable in terms of **23–084** both convenience and cost. However, the mechanics of putting the company into voluntary liquidation, whilst at the same time protecting the claims of creditors who would be preferential if discharge were followed by a compulsory winding-up order (but would not be preferential if followed by a voluntary liquidation[61]) and ensuring that the onset of insolvency in the voluntary liquidation coincides with discharge of the administration order, have caused considerable difficulty. There is, as yet, no appellate authority on this point but the position established under recent first instance decisions is:

(a) A resolution for voluntary winding up cannot be passed conditionally upon another event. Section 86 provides a statutory presumption, that voluntary liquidation commences when the resolution is passed, which cannot be changed by the parties.[62]

(b) The court can make an order for discharge of the administration order conditional upon the passing of a winding-up resolution.[63]

(c) The order for discharge may be coupled with directions that the order shall not be drawn up until documents authenticating the commencement of voluntary liquidation have been lodged at court and with undertakings to bring the matter back if the resolution is not passed as anticipated.[64]

(d) The court can direct administrators to pay the creditors who would be preferential creditors in a compulsory liquidation.[65] This approach would not be suitable in a case where there was any scope for uncertainty either about the maximum aggregate

---

[61] Such potentially preferential creditors have no vested rights (except to complain under s. 27).

[62] *Re Norditrack (U.K.) Ltd* [2000] 1 W.L.R. 343; *Re West Cumberland Iron and Steel Co.* (1889) 40 Ch.D.361; *Re Mark One (Oxford Street) plc* [1999] 1 W.L.R. 1445 not followed on this point. *Norditrack* disapproved a practice which began in the early administration cases; see further *Re Parameters Ltd* (unreported, May 9, 1988); *Re Equiticorp International plc (No. 2)* (unreported, April 25, 1989; *Re Wheeler & Partners Ltd* (unreported, February 1990.) The practice had been expressly approved in *Re Dino Music Ltd* [2000] B.C.C. 696.

[63] *Re Powerstore Ltd* [1997] 1 W.L.R. 1280; *Re Roofstore Ltd* (unreported, September 11, 1997). This practice also began in the early administration cases, see further *Re Scotlane Ltd* (unreported, July 31, 1987); note also a reference to a winding-up resolution passed on the date of the discharge order (as contemplated in the order) in *Re Atlantic Medical Ltd* [1992] B.C.C. 653.

[64] *Re Norditrack (U.K.) Ltd* [2000] 1 W.L.R. 343; *Re Powerstore Ltd* [1997] 1 W.L.R. 1280.

[65] ss. 14(3) and 18(3). *Re Mark One (Oxford Street) plc* [1999] 1 W.L.R. 1445, not following *Re Powerstore Ltd* on this point. See further *Re WBSL Realisations 1992 Ltd* [1995] 2 B.C.L.C. 576.

of preferential debts or the sufficiency of residual funds to pay claims secured under section 19.[66]

(e) The court can also direct (either in conjunction with or as an alternative to directions to pay creditors direct) that funds be paid into a trust for such creditors.[67] This is a convenient solution where the amount of the claims is in dispute or has not been resolved.

---

[66] Another possibility is for the unsecured creditors to waive their claims to the extent necessary to fund payment to preferential creditors: see *Re Parameters Ltd* (unreported, May 9, 1988), *Re Scotlane Ltd* (unreported, July 31, 1987) and *Re Roofstore Ltd* (unreported, September 11, 1997). This seems an unduly cumbersome route to follow in the light of the jurisdiction to give directions.

[67] *Re Mark One (Oxford Street) plc* [1999] 1 W.L.R. 1445.

CHAPTER 24

PENSIONS

1. INTRODUCTION[1]

In recent years, pensions have become a significant practical problem for **24–001** receivers and other insolvency practitioners. The reasons include both the importance of pensions in the financial affairs of employers and employees and changes in legislation.

The establishment of funded pension schemes under trust was moti- **24–002** vated by the desire to obtain exempt approval from the Inland Revenue. A consequence of the trust structure is that scheme assets will be separate from those of the employer.

While the funds of the scheme are immunised from the insolvency of **24–003** the employer, there are nonetheless in practice six main areas of concern for receivers:

    (a) whether the insolvency of the company affects the status of the scheme;
    (b) whether contributions to the scheme should be continued;
    (c) whether funds can be recovered from the pension fund for the benefit of the creditors;
    (d) whether the scheme has a claim against the company;
    (e) whether an independent trustee should be appointed;
    (f) whether pension obligations affect the chances of selling the business.

Before examining each of these areas in turn, it is necessary to discuss the powers and duties of receivers in relation to pension matters.

2. POWERS AND DUTIES ON APPOINTMENT

(a) Introduction: the role of employer and trustees before insolvency
This is relevant in insolvency because that event affects the destination **24–004** of pension scheme powers. In practice in the day-to-day management of pension arrangements, there is a considerable interplay between the employer and the pension fund trustees. The employer and the trustees will each have been assigned various powers, duties and discretions under the pension scheme trust deed and rules. For example, the trustees may have the power to increase pensions, but only with the consent of the employer. The employer's powers, such as whether to

---

[1] For detailed treatment of the position prior to insolvency, see Ellison, *Pensions Law and Practice* (Longmans, looseleaf).

consent to such increases or to pay contributions, are nowadays characterised as being either fiduciary in nature or not as a matter of construction of the trust deed and rules.[2] When construed as being fiduciary, such powers cannot be exercised solely in the employer's commercial interests.[3] Even where such powers are not fiduciary, the employer will be constrained to exercise them in accordance with his "implied obligation of good faith" towards the members, although that duty does allow the employer to take his own financial interests into account.[4]

(b) Employer's powers and responsibilities

24–005 The assets of pension schemes are not ordinarily caught by any charge over the employer's assets. A charge over future property does, however, catch a surplus which may be payable to an employer when its pension scheme is wound up. The receiver is, however, not in a position to use the employer's powers under the pension scheme to recover that surplus because:

(a) those powers are not properly caught by the security under which the receiver is appointed; and

(b) where an employer's powers under a pension scheme are construed as being fiduciary, they will not be exercisable by a receiver or liquidator of the company in any event, because of the conflict of duties to creditors on the one hand and to members of the pension scheme on the other.[5]

On receivership, therefore, it may be that such powers in relation to pension schemes continue to be exercisable by the directors until liquidation.[6] Upon liquidation the question will arise as to whether the liquidator can or should exercise such powers.

(c) Receiver's obligations

24–006 A receiver may:

(a) be required by law to appoint an independent trustee;[6a]

(b) consider whether he should cause the employing company to stop paying contributions; and

---

[2] Any power formerly vested in the employer to pay surpluses to itself must now be exercised by the trustee: Pensions Act 1995, s. 37(2) ("PA95").

[3] See, *e.g. Mettoy Pension Trustees Ltd. v. Evans* [1990] 1 W.L.R. 1587.

[4] *Imperial Group Pension Trust Ltd. v. Imperial Tobacco Ltd* [1991] 1 W.L.R. 589; *National Grid plc v Laws* [1997] P.L.R. 157, Robert Walker J.; [1999] P.L.R. 37, CA. The obligation was invoked by Lord Millett in *Air Jamaica Ltd v. Charlton* [1999] 1 W.L.R. 1399 at 1411, HL to strike down a purported exercise of the company's power to amend the scheme in complete disregard of the members' interests.

[5] *Mettoy Pension Trustees Ltd v. Evans* [1990] 1 W.L.R. 1587 at 1616 *per* Warner J.; *Re William Makin & Sons Ltd* [1993] B.C.C. 453 at 458–9, *per* Vinelott J.; but see below for the position relating to the appointment of trustees.

[6] See above, para. 2–022.

[6a] See below, paras 24–037 *et seq.*

(c) consider what steps (if any) he can take to recover surplus assets (if any) of the scheme.

(d) Receiver's power as trustee

Where a company is trustee of a pension scheme, a receiver as such can **24–007** neither occupy the company's position nor exercise the company's power as trustee of the scheme.[7] Moreover, on receivership an independent trustee must usually be appointed.[8] Even if the circumstances otherwise permitted the receiver to be appointed trustee or exercise the fiduciary powers of the employer, the conflict of interest arising would effectively paralyse the exercise by him of his powers under the scheme, *e.g.* to press for a return of surplus.[9]

(e) Independent trustees

Notwithstanding the inability of the receiver to exercise the powers **24–008** vested in the employer, the receiver may exercise the company's power to appoint trustees of the scheme, as such power is not fiduciary in the strict sense and, provided the power is exercised in good faith for the benefit of the members, there would be no conflict of interest.[10]

The above applies only to receivers appointed before 1990, when the law requiring an independent trustee to be appointed was enacted.[10a] Where the independent trustee has to act, the question whether powers do or do not vest in the receiver (or liquidator) are largely academic. This is because the independent trustee is, generally speaking, given sole use of such powers.

3. CONTINUING THE SCHEME

An immediate consideration on appointment is whether to continue the **24–009** pension arrangements in place. There may be a variety of arrangements to consider, including:

(a) contributions to a final-salary scheme;
(b) contributions to a money-purchase scheme;
(c) contributions to a personal pension arrangement;
(d) continued unfunded benefit liabilities; and

---

[7] *Buckley v Hudson Forge Ltd* [1999] P.L.R. 151; *cf. Polly Peck International plc v. Henry* [1999] P.L.R. 135, where the administrator of a company which was trustee of its pension scheme was refused permission to appoint a professional independent trustee, on the basis that the administrator was obliged so to act, being necessary to do so in the management of the company's affairs.

[8] See below, para. 24–037.

[9] See the cases in n. 5 above. If the employing company is wound up and dissolved before the scheme is terminated, any surplus falls to the Crown as *bona vacantia: Jones v. Williams* [1989] P.L.R. 21.

[10] *Simpson Curtis Pension Trustees Ltd v. Readson* [1994] P.L.R. 289; see also *Denny v. Yeldon* [1995] 3 All E.R. 624 (administrators); *Independent Pension Trustee Ltd. v. LAW Construction Co. Ltd* [1996] O.P.L.R. 259; *The Times*, November 1, 1996, Outer House of Court of Session.

[10a] See below, para. 24–037.

(e) life cover.

(a) Contractual obligations

24–010 It is now generally accepted that pension arrangements are contractual, being regarded as "deferred pay".[11] Any change to the pension arrangements may therefore be regarded by employees as breach of contract which may constitute grounds for claiming wrongful dismissal. A receiver can normally cause a company effectively to repudiate contractual obligations where the other party to the contract has no contractual or proprietary rights binding the receiver's appointor.[12]

24–011 If the receiver does change the basis of contributions he is under a duty to advise employees and trustees of any change in the circumstances just as he is under a duty to warn employees that he is to terminate the pension scheme, so that they may consider making alternative arrangements.[13]

24–012 If the receiver, whether or not an administrative receiver, adopts one or more contracts of employment and thereby makes himself personally liable for breaches of them occurring during his tenure of office[14] this may involve him in personal liability in respect of any terms of such contract relating to the payment of pension contributions. Provided the receiver does not adopt the contracts of employment, any liability for breach will fall to be dealt with as an unsecured non-preferential claim.

24–013 The position in cases of adoptions on or after March 15, 1994 is governed by the Insolvency Act 1994, which provides that the adoption, and the receiver's personal liability, extends only to "qualifying liabilities" arising from services rendered wholly or partly after the adoption of the contract: these include contributions to an occupational pension scheme.[15]

(b) Termination of employer contributions

24–014 The receiver may well consider it in the best interests of the company and to accord with his own objectives to cause the company to cease the actual payment of contributions. This may save money, ease cash-flow, and allow some surplus to be recovered; but where the scheme is in deficit, this may trigger a statutory claim against the company by the trustees.[15a]

24–015 Whether or not a receiver can cause the employing company to exercise its power under the trust deed to terminate the liability to pay contributions, he is unlikely to be constrained from terminating the

---

[11] *Barber v. Guardian Royal Exchange Group* [1991] Q.B. 344; *National Grid plc v. Laws* [1997] P.L.R. 157; *Air Jamaica Ltd. v. Charlton* [1999] 1 W.L.R. 1399 at 1407, HL, *per* Lord Millett.

[12] *Astor Chemical v. Synthetic Technology Ltd* [1990] B.C.C. 97 at 103F–106C and see above, Chap. 8.

[13] *Larsen's Executrix v. Henderson* [1990] I.R.L.R. 512.

[14] Insolvency Act 1986, s. 37(1)(a) (non-administrative receivers); *ibid.*, s. 44(1)(b) (administrative receivers). For full consideration of these provisions and the provisions of the Insolvency Act 1994, see above, paras 19.013 to 19–019.

[15a] Insolvency Act 1986, s. 44(2A), as amended by the Insolvency Act 1994, s.2.

[15] See below, para. 24–030.

payment of those contributions; since the trustees will not be in a better position than any other unsecured creditors, the obligation to contribute to a pension scheme is unlikely to bind the receiver's appointor.

The effect on the scheme of the termination of the employer **24–016** contributions depends upon the governing provisions of the particular scheme: some schemes provide for the automatic winding-up of the scheme on the cessation of contributions; others provide for winding up to commence on the appointment of the receiver or (more commonly) the liquidator; others leave the timing of the winding-up of the scheme to the discretion of the trustees.[16]

(c) Money-purchase or final-salary

In a money-purchase (or contribution-related) scheme, or where there are **24–017** group personal pensions, or where there are insured benefits, there is a clear argument to the effect that the cessation of the employer's contributions constitutes a breach of the contract of employment. The position is much less clear cut where the scheme is salary-related, since the employer's promise is one of benefits, not contributions, and the employer could argue, on actuarial advice, that funding could be suspended or ended without prejudice to the accrual of pension rights. In some contracts of employment, the employer will have reserved the right to terminate the pension scheme, but prior notice will probably be needed.[16a]

(d) Contracted-out schemes

In many cases the employer will have made the pension scheme a **24–018** "contracted-out" one; in other words the scheme will have agreed to undertake to make provision for "guaranteed minimum pensions", which are the equivalent of the additional state pension, the State Earnings Related Pension Scheme (SERPS). In exchange for this undertaking, the National Insurance contributions are reduced. If contributions to the scheme are suspended or discontinued, the scheme may lose its contracting-out certificate, and the employer will have to pay the higher National Insurance contributions. Any contribution savings intended by terminating contributions may therefore be limited.

4. RECOVERING FUNDS FROM THE SCHEME

(a) Introduction

A receiver will be concerned to see that any funds available to the **24–019** company from the scheme are recovered. There are two main areas:

---

[16] The trustees also have power, if not under the rules of the scheme then under PA95, s. 38, to defer the winding up and to continue the scheme as a "closed" scheme, *i.e.* one which does not allow the admission of new members. This can be a useful device where, for example, there is an obligation on the trustees on winding up to secure the benefits by the purchase of annuities, which may not make economic sense in a period of poor annuity rates; it also allows the trustees and company to exercise the power to amend schemes, which might otherwise terminate on the winding up: see the unreported decisions of Re *Bacal* (Foster J.) and *Re Edward Jones Benevolent Fund Ltd* (John Chadwick Q.C.). However, the exercise by the company of its amendment power will be subject to the constraints imposed by the "implied obligation of good faith": see above, n.4.

[16a] See above, para. 24–011.

    (a) any surplus funds in the pension scheme not required for benefits; and

    (b) moneys paid wrongly to the pension fund by the company.

(b) Surpluses

24–020 Any significant surplus in a pension scheme will certainly attract the attention of a receiver since it will be a future asset of the company caught by the charge in respect of which he is acting: but recovering such surplus is fraught with difficulties.

24–021   First, a surplus will only usually emerge when a scheme is wound up and will depend upon there being money left in the scheme after all other liabilities have been secured. The winding-up of the scheme may not commence during the receivership and, even if it does, it may take some time for other liabilities to be dealt with. Surplus can be paid back to an employer not only on a winding-up of a scheme, but also (if there is an express provision to this effect) from a continuing scheme, although section 37 of PA95 imposes several statutory preconditions to such repayment.

24–022   Secondly, recovering the surplus may be contrary to the provisions of the pension scheme trust deed, and changing the provisions of the deed may prove difficult, even though an application to the Occupational Pensions Regulatory Authority may be made to do so.[17] Such prohibitions are now increasingly uncommon, since it is an Inland Revenue requirement that surpluses should be capable of being returned.

24–023   Thirdly, section 76(3)(c) of PA95[18] requires any surplus under a pension scheme to be used for the improvement of certain benefits in priority to any refund to employers.[19]

24–024   Fourthly, of every £100 surplus available for return, £40 must be deducted by the trustees for tax.[20]

24–025   Fifthly, trustees have a discretion on a winding-up to improve benefits using surplus.[21]

(c) Wrongful payments

24–026 Payments can from time to time be wrongfully made to a pension fund by a company. The usual cases are:

    (a) payments made *ultra vires*, *i.e.* the company did not have power to make contributions. While there is inherent power to make

---

[17] PA95, s. 69(3)(a).

[18] There is also a requirement for the return of surplus from an ongoing scheme: PA95, s.37(4)(d).

[19] The forerunner of s. 76–s. 58A of the Social Security Pensions Act 1975 — was held to apply even where the practitioner was appointed before the coming into force of that Act, or where the company became insolvent before that Act: *Thrells Ltd v. Lomas* [1993] 1 W.L.R. 456.

[20] See Income and Corporation Taxes Act 1988, s. 601.

[21] See PA95, s. 73: other discretions are often to be found in the trust deeds and rules, which will in any event govern the position in respect of those schemes to which s. 73 does not apply.

contributions for employees, there needs to be specific power in the articles to make contributions for directors[22]; and

(b) payments made when the company knew it was insolvent.

Re Horsley & Weight Ltd[23] is an example of an unsuccessful challenge by a liquidator. The memorandum contained an express object permitting pensions for, amongst others, directors. This was held to be capable of being an independent object in its own right. It did not have to be shown that the pension benefited the company.

Where it is possible to make a claim in respect of a wrongful payment **24–027** it can probably be brought by the receiver, since the right to make any recovery and any moneys recovered will probably be charged by the security under which the receiver is appointed.

5. CLAIMS AGAINST THE COMPANY

(a) Introduction
The trustees of the pension scheme may as a result of the receivership **24–028** maintain a variety of claims against the company. The main ones are:

(a) where a deficit crystallises on the winding up of the scheme;
(b) where the company has not paid the contributions due to the scheme, in which case the trustees will be preferential creditors in respect of certain unpaid contributions.

(b) Deficits in the scheme
If there is a deficit in the scheme, or where contributions have been **24–029** stopped otherwise than as permitted by the trust deed, the trustees may be able to make a claim against the company for the deficit or contributions under the provisions of the deed.

In any event, if there is a deficit in a pension scheme (other than a **24–030** money-purchase scheme) and either the scheme is wound up or the employer is in liquidation (but not if it is merely in receivership), the trustees have, as from June 29, 1992, a statutory claim against the employer.[24] This claim is non-preferential and unsecured.[25]

The amount of the claim is determined by the scheme's actuary. There **24–031** are guidelines on the basis of the calculation published jointly by the Institute and Faculty of Actuaries in the form of a mandatory guidance note known as GN 19, which have to be used.[26]

---

[22] See, *e.g. Normandy v. Ind Coope & Co Ltd* [1908] 1 Ch. 84.

[23] [1982] Ch. 442. See also *Re Rolled Steel Products Ltd* [1986] Ch. 246, CA and s. 238 of the Insolvency Act 1986.

[24] PA95, s. 75; the provision was introduced by the Social Security Act 1990.

[25] PA95, s. 75(8)(a).

[26] The crystallisation of the debt seems to be assessable over the period between (a) the commencement of the winding-up of the scheme (or July 1, 1992 for a centralised scheme which was already in winding up on that date) and (b) the commencement of the liquidation of the employer (or the last of them if more than one). Crystallisation seems to

24–032   Where the scheme covers employees of a group of companies, the deficit is apportioned amongst the several employers.[27]

24–033   The receiver will need to bear in mind that the appointment of a liquidator may trigger a claim against the company by a scheme which is in deficit.

(c) Unpaid contributions

24–034   The scheme may be owed by the company contributions payable by the employer and employee but unremitted to the scheme. Some of these debts to the scheme may be preferential debts,[28] which must be discharged by a receiver before any debt secured by a charge which, as created, was a floating charge[29]; other pension obligations are not preferential.[30]

(d) Loans from the scheme by the company

24–035   The scheme may also be owed loans made to the company from its pension fund, although these are likely to be less common than before; changes in the taxation rules, and in the investment regulations, have severely restricted scope for such loans.

(e) Unfunded arrangements

24–036   An increasing number of pension arrangements are unfunded; this means that the company has made pension promises in relation to which no funded scheme has been established. These unfunded arrangements have arisen following the Finance Act 1989 which restricts the provision

---

apply only once except in relation to a scheme which is not being wound up, in which case a debt is crystallised on each occasion after July 1, 1990 when an employer in a centralised scheme goes into liquidation. It also seems that a partial winding-up (*e.g.* where a substantial number of employees are transferred from the scheme, perhaps on the sale of part of the business) does not trigger a claim for any deficit.

[27] A company which participated in a scheme some years previously and has ceased to do so (*e.g.* because it has been sold) is not thought to be liable for a deficit which subsequently emerges, even though there may be pensioners and former employees in the scheme who were employed only by that company.

[28] Insolvency Act 1986, Sched. 6, para. 8 and Sched. 4 of the Pension Schemes Act 1993 (modified in minor respects by s. 137 and Sched. 5, para. 85 of the PA95); sums owed by and deducted from employees' earnings are preferential if:

(a) they were deducted from earnings paid during the four months up to the date of the administrative receiver's appointment or otherwise payable during that period (Sched. 4, para. 1 of the Pension Schemes Act 1993 formerly Social Security Pensions Act 1975, Sched. 3, para. 1);

(b) in relation to contracted-out salary-related schemes, they were employer's contributions payable in the 12 months up to the date of the administrative receiver's appointment;

(c) in relation to contracted-out money-purchase schemes, they are sums owed on account of an employers' minimum payments falling to be made in the 12 months up to the date of the administrative receiver's appointment;

(d) in relation to state scheme premiums, they are payable to the DSS in respect of the reinstatement to SERPS of an employee formerly in contracted-out employment.

[29] Insolvency Act 1986, s. 40.

[30] For a guide to recovery of contributions, see Department of Employment, *Insolvency of Employers: Safeguard of Occupational Pension Scheme Contributions* (1992) (IL2).

of benefits under approved schemes for those who join them (broadly speaking) after May 31, 1989. Such contractual promises also rank as unsecured and non-preferential debts following the appointment of a liquidator or administrative receiver.

6. DUTY TO APPOINT INDEPENDENT TRUSTEE

(a) Introduction

Since November 12, 1990, an administrative receiver has had a statutory **24–037** duty, in most cases, immediately on appointment, to satisfy himself that there is an independent trustee of any pension fund relating to a company to which he is appointed, and if not satisfied, to appoint one or secure the appointment of one.[31] The legislation gives effect to a recommendation of the Occupational Pensions Board following complaints of failures by insolvency practitioners properly to manage affiliated pension schemes[32] and several cases where practitioners were obliged to seek guidance from the courts in the light of their conflicts of interest.[33]

There is no need to make the appointment by deed, though it is **24–038** conventional to do so, since that will operate automatically to vest in the trustees certain trust property under section 40 of the Trustee Act 1925.

A receiver who is under such a duty is likewise under a duty to provide **24–039** the independent trustee with information about the scheme: this obligation is subject to the insolvency practitioner being able to recover the expenses of doing so as an expense of the insolvency or to the trustees of the scheme undertaking to meet them.[34]

(b) Schemes to which the duty does not apply

The receiver's duty does not apply to all schemes. Excluded schemes **24–040** include[35]:

(a) schemes of which each member is a trustee;
(b) schemes providing only money purchase benefits[36];
(c) schemes where the only benefits provided are death benefits and under the provisions of which no member has accrued rights;

---

[31] PA95, s. 23: the requirement was first introduced by Sched. 4, para. 1 of the Social Security Act 1990: under the previous legislation, there was no time limit as to when the receiver was to fulfil his duty: the receiver is now obliged to do so as soon as is reasonably practicable: PA95, s. 23(2). There is also provision for a time period in which the duty must be fulfilled to be prescribed, but to date no such period has been prescribed.

[32] Department of Social Security, *Protecting Pensions: Safeguarding Benefits in a Changing Environment*, Report by the Occupational Pensions Board, Cm. 573 (HMSO, February 1989), Chap. 10.

[33] *e.g. Mettoy Pension Trustees Ltd v. Evans* [1990] 1 W.L.R. 1587; *Icarus (Hertford) Ltd v. Driscoll* [1990] P.L.R. 1.

[34] PA95, s. 26.

[35] Occupational Pension Schemes (Independent Trustee) Regulations 1997 (S.I. 1997 No. 252), reg. 5 ("the Independent Trustee Regs").

[36] And also schemes which would only provide such benefits but for the fact that they provide for guaranteed minimum pensions.

> (d) schemes under which all the benefits are to be provided by
> insurance or annuity contracts specifically allocated to the
> provision of benefits for and in respect of members.

Under the previous legislation, the independent trustee provisions
applied only if the pension scheme concerned was established by trust
deed. Schemes set up by company resolution, for example, were therefore excluded. The current provisions apply where the scheme is a "trust
scheme",[37] which is defined as "an occupational pension scheme established under a trust[38]: this wider definition encompasses schemes set up
other than by deed, where the provisions nevertheless create a trust.

24-041   The provisions apply with modified effect to centralised, paid up and
partnership schemes.[39]

(c) Multi-employer schemes

24-042   Some schemes cover more than one employer, especially where there
are several companies within a group. Where the receiver is appointed
only in respect of one of the companies which is a member of the group
which participates in the scheme, and the company is either a trustee or
has the power to appoint a trustee, an independent trustee may need to
be appointed.[40]

(d) Independent trustee

24-043 There is no positive definition of independent, but persons who are
considered not to be independent include:

> (a) anyone who has an interest in the assets of the employer of the
> scheme (other than as a trustee)[41];
> (b) anyone connected or associated with the receiver;
> (c) anyone connected or associated with the employer;
> (d) anyone who has supplied services to the trustees, managers or
> employer in relation to the scheme in the three years before
> the insolvency practitioner started to act; and
> (e) anyone otherwise connected or associated with anyone inter-
> ested in the assets of the employer or of the scheme (such as
> bankers or shareholders) or with anyone who has supplied
> services as in (iv) above.

For so long as the statutory requirement for him to act applies,
the independent trustee is given sole power to exercise (a) trustee

---

[37] PA95, s. 22(1).

[38] *ibid.*, s. 124(1).

[39] Independent Trustee Regs, regs 3, 4 and 6.

[40] The provisions (Pension Schemes Act 1993, s. 119) apply to a centralised scheme
where an administrative receiver starts to act in relation to "an employer of persons in the
description or category of employment to which the scheme relates" and (a) the employer
concerned has power to appoint or remove any trustee of the scheme, or (b) the employer
concerned is a trustee of the scheme: Independent Trustee Regs, reg. 3.

[41] PA95, s. 23(3); Independent Trustee Regs, reg. 2.

discretions and (b) employer powers held as trustee of the power.[42] His function is principally to protect the interests of the members of the scheme, although an employer is considered to be a contingent beneficiary under a pension scheme. If the receiver does intend to recover surplus assets from the scheme, the independent trustee is likely to have sole power to allow this.[43] The receiver's role may well be confined to the making of representations about the position of the company and its creditors.[44]

The requirement for an independent trustee may cease once the **24–044** business has been sold on, or the insolvency practitioner vacates office, but once appointed the independent trustee remains until he is removed or retires. During an insolvency an independent trustee (whether statutorily appointed or not) cannot be removed by virtue only of a provision in the scheme.[45]

Finding a suitable independent trustee can be difficult; some candi- **24–045** dates are appropriate for very large funds only, as the fees can be considerable[46]; some have knowledge of pensions or of trust law, but not of both. The Association of Corporate Trustees maintains a list of members, and some pensions solicitors operate a trust company subsidiary for these purposes.

If an insolvency practitioner fails to comply with his obligations in **24–046** relation to the appointment of an independent trustee, he can be ordered to do so by the court on application by a member of the scheme in question.[47]

(e) Ceasing to be independent

It was initially thought that the requirement for a trustee to be **24–047** independent and that persons associated or connected with him should not have provided services to the trustees, etc. applied once and for all at the time of appointment.[48] This would have enabled independent trustees who were professionals to employ colleagues who had had no prior connection with the pension scheme. However in *Clark v. Hicks*[49] Mervyn Davies J. held that an independent trustee who used the services of a partner or an assistant in his firm in relation to the scheme ceased to be independent. It is suggested that this is an extreme result neither

---

[42] PA95, s. 25(2).

[43] As the employer's power to deal with surplus on a winding up has been held to be fiduciary, the employer is a trustee of the power: *Mettoy Pension Trustees Ltd v. Evans* [1990] 1 W.L.R. 1587.

[44] As to factors thought to be relevant, see *Thrells Ltd v. Lomas* [1993] 1 W.L.R. 456; *Air Jamaica Ltd v. Charlton* [1999] 1 W.L.R. 1399, HL.

[45] PA95, s. 25(3).

[46] Independent trustees are entitled to be paid out of the scheme's resources their reasonable fees and expenses, payable in priority to all other claims falling to be met out of the scheme's resources: PA95, s. 25(6).

[47] PA95, s. 24.

[48] D.J. Clark, "Pension Schemes: A Problem for Independent Trustees" (1993) 6 Insolvency Intelligence issue 2.

[49] [1992] O.P.L.R 185.

envisaged nor required by the legislation or its purpose.[50] There is a rival view that this was precisely the result the legislation intended to achieve.

24–048   Where an independent trustee loses his independence, he ceases to be a trustee by operation of law (unless there would be no trustees remaining).[51] The independent trustee is also under a duty to inform the insolvency practitioner of his loss of independence.[52]

7. SELLING THE BUSINESS

24–049   There are two main pensions repercussions of a receiver selling part or all of the business:

    (a) the act of sale may precipitate a winding-up of the pension scheme, crystallising debts against the company, and possibly giving rise to discretions to grant benefit enhancements or to make transfer payments to other schemes, which in either case could result in the disappearance of all or most of the surplus; and

    (b) the pensions exemption in the Transfer of Undertaking Regulations applies.[53]

The receiver should consider these matters when negotiating the price with the purchaser of the insolvent company's business.

---

[50] Mervyn Davies J. took the view that:

    (i) if Mr Clarke had been a sole practitioner and had provided services himself or through an assistant he would have remained independent; and
    (ii) Mr Clarke should "be regarded" as having ceased to be independent when his colleagues submitted their bills: *ibid.*, at 189.

[51] PA95, s. 25(4), (5).

[52] *ibid.*

[53] The Transfer of Undertaking Regulations (Protection of Employment) Regulations 1981 (S.I. 1981 No. 1794), reg. 7; this exemption has survived several legal challenges to its validity: *Walden Engineering v. Warrener* [1993] I.R.L.R. 420, EAT; *Perry v. Intec Colleges Ltd* [1993] I.R.L.R. 65, Ct of Sess.; *Adams v Lancashire CC* [1997] I.R.L.R. 436, CA.

CHAPTER 25

CONFLICT OF LAWS

This chapter attempts to identify and discuss various problems which **25–001** may arise in relation to receivership or administration in situations involving a foreign element.[1] Very broadly speaking, a relevant foreign element may be involved where a company is incorporated outside the United Kingdom or where a company incorporated in the United Kingdom is possessed of assets situated outside the United Kingdom, though these situations should not be regarded as exhaustive of those which may arise.

1. VALIDITY OF FLOATING CHARGE[2]

A floating charge has both a contractual and proprietary character.[3] It **25–002** originates in a contract entered into between the company and the ultimate debenture-holder but on crystallisation of the charge there is an immediate creation of a fixed charge over the assets of the company with the consequence that unsecured creditors are unable to enforce any rights against the property covered by the charge.[4] As a matter of English law, the charge may extend to movable property (tangible or intangible) and immovable property, whether situated in England or abroad.[5]

(a) Capacity[6]

The initial question which may arise is whether a company has capacity **25–003** to create a charge of this nature and in the context of a situation with a foreign element present, what law will govern the company's capacity to create the charge. There is no direct English authority on this question, but it has been persuasively argued that the proper approach is to consider whether the company has power to grant a mortgage over its assets under the law of the place of its incorporation,[7] the latter law

---

[1] For general discussion see Picarda, *The Law Relating to Receivers, Managers and Administrators* (2nd ed., 1990), Chap. 40; *Kerr on Receivers* (17th ed., 1989), Chap. 23; Dicey and Morris, *The Conflict of Laws* (13th ed., 2000), pp. 1151–1160; Anton, *Private International Law* (2nd ed., 1991), pp. 716–722; Gough, *Company Charges* (2nd ed., 1996), Chap. 23; Collins (1978) 27 I.C.L.Q. 691 reprinted in *Essays in International Litigation and the Conflict of Laws* (1994), p. 433.

[2] For a most valuable discussion in relation to receivers, see Collins, *op. cit.*

[3] See above, Chap. 3.

[4] See above, Chap. 3.

[5] See below, paras 25–005, 25–027.

[6] See above, paras 3–093 *et seq.*

[7] Collins (1978) 27 I.C.L.Q. 691 at 695–699.

generally being the law which determines the capacity of a company.[8] In other words, it matters not that the company has no capacity under the law of the place of its incorporation to create a floating charge as such: it is enough that the company has, under the law of its place of incorporation, the capacity to give a mortgage over its assets.[9]

(b) Authority of corporate representatives

25–004 Whether directors or others purporting to represent the company have authority to execute a charge will be determined by the law of the place of incorporation since it is that law which determines who are the company's officials authorised to act on its behalf.[10]

(c) Governing law

25–005 Assuming the company has capacity, and those executing the charge have the necessary authority, according to the foregoing principles, it may then be necessary to determine the law which governs the contractual aspects of the charge. Although the proprietary effects of the charge may ultimately depend on the *lex situs* of any assets alleged to fall within its terms,[11] the contractual aspects of the charge are governed by the law applicable to the contract, in this case a contract of mortgage.[12] Accordingly, where the parties have, as is common, chosen a law to govern the contract, that choice of law will normally be treated as effective by an English court.[13] In the absence of such a choice of law,

---

[8] See Dicey and Morris, *The Conflict of Laws* (13th ed., 2000), pp. 1110–1112. This rule is unaffected by the implementation of the Rome Convention on the Law Applicable to Contractual Obligations [1980] O.J. L266/1 in the Contracts (Applicable Law) Act 1990, since questions concerning the legal capacity of a company are excluded from the scope of the uniform rules contained in the Convention: see Rome Convention (Contracts (Applicable Law) Act 1990, Sched. I, Art. 1(2)(e).

[9] See *Re International Bulk Commodities Ltd* [1993] Ch. 77. *cf. Carse v. Copppen*, 1951 S.C. 233, decided when floating charges were not recognised under Scots law. Such recognition was first permitted in the Companies (Floating Charges and Receivers) (Scotland) Act 1972. See now Companies Act 1985, ss. 462–467, as amended by Companies Act 1989, s. 140 and Insolvency Act 1986, ss. 50–71.

[10] *Banco de Bilbao v. Sancha and Rey* [1938] 2 K.B. 176, CA; *Carl Zeiss Stiftung v. Rayner & Keeler Ltd (No. 2)* [1967] 1 A.C. 853 HL 919, 939, 972. See also *Bank of Ethiopia v. National Bank of Egypt and Liguori* [1937] Ch. 513; *Damon Compania Naviera SA v. Hapag-Lloyd International SA* [1985] 1 W.L.R. 435, C.A. The law of the place of incorporation also determines whether directors have been validly appointed: *Sierra Leone Telecommunications Co. Ltd v. Barclays Bank plc* [1998] 2 All E.R. 821. And see Foreign Companies (Execution of Documents) Regulations 1994, below para. 25–007. The question of whether an organ may bind a company or body corporate or unincorporate to a third party is excluded from the scope of the Rome Convention by Art. 1(2)(f).

[11] See below, paras 25–055—25–060.

[12] *Re Anchor Line (Henderson Bros) Ltd* [1937] Ch. 483.

[13] This was true under common law choice of law rules, which applied to contracts entered into on or before April 1, 1991: see , *e.g. Vita Food Products Inc. v. Unus Shipping Co. Ltd* [1939] A.C. 277, PC; Dicey and Morris, *The Conflict of Laws* (11th ed. 1987), pp. 1115–1182. It is equally true under the Rome Convention which applies to contracts entered into after April 1, 1991: see Art. 3(1): see Dicey and Morris, *The Conflict of Laws,* (13th ed., 2000) pp. 1216–1234. If the submission in the text is correct and a floating charge is a species of mortgage, then the rules of the Convention should apply to determine the applicable law. It is possible, however, that a floating charge may be construed as a "question governed by the law of companies" and thus excluded from the

the contract will be governed by the law of the country with which it is most closely connected.[14] Applying the latter principle, where an English company creates a charge over all of its undertaking and assets in the English form, the applicable law is almost certain to be English law.[15] The law applicable to the charge will determine (capacity apart) the validity and effect of the charge in its contractual respects and will also govern matters of construction.[16] The importance of distinguishing between the contractual and proprietary effects of a charge may be seen in the principle that if the contract creating the mortgage (charge) is subject to English law, an English court may enforce it in personam even if the charge is not recognised as effective by the *lex situs*.[17]

(d) Role of English law

Where a contract allegedly creating a charge is governed by a foreign **25–006** applicable law, it will, nonetheless, for the purposes of English proceedings, be for English law to determine whether a charge[18] requiring registration[19] in England has in fact been created through it will be necessary for the court to look to the terms of the contract and their effect under the foreign governing law to ascertain whether the elements which constitute a charge in English law are in fact present.[20] A contract governed by a foreign law may, for the purpose of English proceedings, accordingly give rise to a charge even if the contract would not have that effect under the foreign law because that law did not, say, recognise such a form of security.[21]

(e) Formalities

The Companies Act 1985 contains provisions concerning the manner in **25–007** which documents are to be executed by a company incorporated in

Convention by virtue of Art. 1(2)(e). If this construction is eventually adopted, there is not likely to be any practical difference since the common law and the Convention are very similar in relation to the power to choose the governing law.

[14] This is the formulation contained in Art. 4(1) of the Rome Convention which provides rebuttable presumptions as to what the most closely connected law will be: see Art. 4(2) and (3): see Dicey and Morris, pp. 1234–1242. If applicable (see above, n. 13), the Rome Convention will determine the law governing contracts entered into after April 1, 1991. The common law rules were very similar in effect: see Dicey and Morris, pp. 1190–1197.

[15] *Re Anchor Line (Henderson Bros) Ltd* [1937] Ch. 483.

[16] *ibid.* For the Rome Convention (n.8, above), if applicable, see Art. 10(1) subject to Contracts (Applicable Law) Act 1990, s. 2(2).

[17] *British South Africa Co. v. De Beers Consolidated Gold Mines Ltd* [1910] 2 Ch. 502; [1912] A.C. 52; *Re Smith* [1916] 2 Ch. 206; *Re Anchor Line (Henderson Bros.) Ltd* [1937] Ch. 483.

[18] *Re Interview Ltd* [1975] I.R. 382 at 395–396; *Kruppstahl AG v. Quittmann Products Ltd* [1982] I.L.R.M. 551 at 560. As to whether the charge will extend to property located abroad, see below, paras 25–056—25–060.

[19] *Re Weldtech Equipment Ltd* [1991] B.C.C. 16; *Re Interview Ltd* [1975] I.R. 382; *Kruppstahl AG v. Quittmann Products Ltd* [1982] I.L.R.M. 551.

[20] *Re Weldtech Equipment Ltd* [1991] B.C.C. 16. *Cf. Hammer and Sohne v. H.W.T. Realisations Ltd*, 1985 S.L.T. 21; *Kruppstahl AG v. Quittmann Products Ltd* [1982] I.L.R.M. 551 at 559.

[21] See *Benjamin's Sale of Goods* (5th ed., 1997), para. 25–121; *Gough, Company Charges* (2nd ed., 1996), pp. 634–635.

Great Britain,[22] which provisions have been applied, with necessary adaptations and modifications, to companies incorporated outside Great Britain.[23] As adapted and modified, section 36 of the 1985 Act establishes that a company incorporated outside Great Britain may make a contract[24] in any manner permitted by the laws of the territory in which it is incorporated[25] or, where a contract is made on behalf of such a company, it may be so made by any person who, in accordance with the law of the territory in which the company is incorporated, is acting under the authority (express or implied) of that company.[26] As adapted and modified, section 36A(2) of the 1985 Act enables a document to be executed in any manner permitted by the laws of the territory in which the company is incorporated.[27] A document which is signed by a person or persons who, in accordance with the laws of the territory in which the company is incorporated, is or are acting under the authority (express or implied) of the company and which is expressed (in whatever form of words) to be executed by the company, has the same effect, in relation to that company, as it would have in relation to a company incorporated in England if executed under the common seal of a company so incorporated.[28] In favour of a purchaser (which includes a mortgagee) a document shall be deemed to be duly executed by a company incorporated outside Great Britain if it purports to be signed by a person or persons who, in accordance with the laws of the territory in which the company is incorporated, is or are acting under the authority (express or implied) of that company.[29] As a consequence of these provisions a debenture may be regarded as duly executed by a foreign company if the execution conforms to the requirements of the law of the country in which the company is incorporated.

2. EXTRATERRITORIAL APPLICATION OF INSOLVENCY ACT 1986

25–008 The receivership or administration of a company in England will be conducted in accordance with English law and particularly the provisions of the Insolvency Act 1986.[30] Difficulties may arise in

---

[22] Companies Act 1985, ss. 36, 36A, 36C, and for Scotland, s. 36B. See above, Chap. 3.

[23] Foreign Companies (Execution of Documents) Regulations 1994, S.I. 1994 No. 950, as amended by S.I. 1995 No. 1729, made under Companies Act 1989, s. 130(b). See *Azov Shipping Co. v. Baltic Shipping Co.* [1999] 2 Lloyd's Rep. 159. For Scotland, see Companies Act 1985, s. 36B, inserted by Requirements of Writing (Scotland) Act 1995, Sched. 4, para. 51, as amended by the foregoing Regulations.

[24] The same considerations apply to the execution of a debenture: see above, Chap. 3.

[25] Foreign Companies (Execution of Documents) Regulations 1994 (S.I. 1994 No. 950), regs. 2, 3, 4(1)(a).

[26] *ibid.*, regs. 2, 3, 4(1)(b).

[27] *ibid.*, regs. 2, 3, 5(a).

[28] Companies Act 1985, s. 36A(2), as adapted and modified by regs. 2, 3 and 5(b).

[29] Companies Act 1985, s. 36A(2), as adapted and modified by regs. 2, 3 and 5(c).

[30] See *Re Bank of Credit and Commerce International SA (No. 10)* [1997] Ch. 213, holding that the English court has no power to disapply English rule on set-off in liquidation (Insolvency Rules, 1986, r. 4.90) or any other substantive rule forming part of

determining the territorial reach of relevant provisions of the Act where the receiver or administrator seeks to exercise powers under the Act against persons resident abroad or where there are creditors abroad or the company has assets which are situated abroad. Ultimately, of course, the territorial reach of any particular provision depends on the intention of Parliament but, as is so often the case, the intention of Parliament is seldom explicit so that it is necessary to interpret the relevant provisions.

Section 238 of the Insolvency Act 1986 enables an administrator[31] to **25–009** apply for an order setting aside a transaction entered into by the company with "any person" at an undervalue.[32] In *Re Paramount Airways Ltd*[33] it was held that the section applies, in relation to the administration of an English company, to any person whether that person is resident in England or not. In principle, therefore, there would seem to be no territorial limitation on the operation of this provision. In practice, however, there are two ways in which this wide jurisdiction may be limited. First, section 238(3) provides that where such an application is made, the court shall make such order as it thinks fit for the purpose of restoring the position to what it would have been if the company had not entered into the transaction: this discretion is sufficiently wide to enable the court to make no order at all in an appropriate case. Where a foreign element is involved, the court has to be satisfied that the party against whom the order is to be made is sufficiently connected with England for it to be just and proper to make the order.

Whether such a connection is established will depend on all the **25–010** circumstances of the case. Regard will be had to the residence and place of business of the party concerned, that party's connection with the company, the purpose of the transaction which is being attacked, the nature and locality of the property involved, the circumstances in which the party became involved in the transaction or received a benefit from it or acquired the property in question, whether the party acted in good faith, and whether under any relevant foreign law the party acquired a title free of any other claims to it. These factors will have to be balanced in the light of the facts of the case. But overall the court will seek to ensure that it does not act oppressively or vexatiously in operating the very wide jurisdiction it possesses.

A second limitation may also be imposed at an earlier stage in the **25–011** inquiry, for proceedings under section 238 may not be brought against a person outside the English jurisdiction unless the court grants permission for the proceedings to be served on that person abroad pursuant to the Insolvency Rules 1986.[34] In deciding whether it is a suitable case for

---

the statutory insolvency scheme contained in the Insolvency Act 1986 and the Insolvency Rules 1986. The correctness of that decision where a foreign element is involved has been questioned by Moss and Segal, *Cross-Border Issues of Insolvency of Banks* (1996, ed. Oditah), Chap 6. Rule 4.90 does not apply in receivership see *e.g. M.S. Fashions Ltd v. BCCI* [1993] Ch. 425, CA.

[31] Or a liquidator, but not a receiver: s. 238(1).
[32] See above, Chap. 11.
[33] [1993] Ch. 223, CA.
[34] Insolvency Rules 1986, r. 12.12.

permission to be granted, the court will have special regard to the strength or weakness of the plaintiff's claim that the defendant has an appropriate connection with the English jurisdiction as described above.[35]

25–012   It would seem that the above principles established in relation to section 238 of the 1986 Act apply with equal force in cases where it is alleged that a company has given a preference to any person in contravention of section 239[36] of the 1986 Act.[37] It would also seem to apply to orders in relation to extortionate credit transactions entered into by any person with the company which fall foul of section 244 of the Insolvency Act 1986 and to the provisions concerning the avoidance of certain floating charges contained in section 245.[38] It has, additionally, been held that the powers of the court to set aside a transaction defrauding creditors at the suit of a victim of the transaction,[39] extend to a foreign company and exist in respect of a transaction governed by foreign law, even a transaction relating to foreign land.[40] In such a case it may be enough that the defendant is subject to the jurisdiction of the English court without it being necessary for any further connection with England to exist.[41]

25–013   In *Re Seagull Manufacturing Co. Ltd*[42] it was held that the court had jurisdiction under section 133 of the Insolvency Act 1986 to order the public examination of a director of an English company in compulsory liquidation regarding the promotion, formation or management of the company or as to the conduct of its business or affairs, or his conduct or dealings in relation to the company, irrespective of the nationality of the director or whether he is resident or present in England. This jurisdiction was said to extend to any person within the class of persons referred to in the section,[43] although the court has a discretion as to the manner and place of such service which can extend to ordering service out of the jurisdiction.[44]

25–014   It may well be that a similar approach to that taken in *Re Seagull Manufacturing Co. Ltd* will be applied with regard to the powers which

---

[35] [1993] Ch. 223 at 240–241, CA.

[36] An application may be made by a liquidator or administrator but not by an administrative receiver: ss. 238(1), 239(1).

[37] *Re Paramount Airways Ltd* [1993] Ch. 223 at 233, 236–238, CA.

[38] Again applications may be made under these sections by an administrator or liquidator but not by an administrative receiver: ss. 238, 244(2), 245(1).

[39] Insolvency Act 1986, ss. 423–425. An application may also be made by a liquidator or administrator but not by an administrative receiver: *ibid.*, s. 424(1)(a).

[40] *Jyske Bank (Gibraltar) Ltd v. Spjeldnaes* [1999] 2 B.C.L.C. 101.

[41] *ibid.* And see *Re Howard Holdings Inc.* [1998] B.C.C. 549 (application of Insolvency Act 1986, s. 214 in liquidation of foreign company); *Re Seagull Manufacturing Co. (No. 2)* [1994] Ch. 91 (application of Company Directors' Disqualification Act 1986 to director irrespective of whether director a British subject or resident in England).

[42] [1993] Ch. 345, CA, distinguishing *Re Tucker (R.C.) (A Bankrupt), ex p. Tucker (K.R.)* [1990] Ch. 148, CA.

[43] See s. 133(1).

[44] Insolvency Rules 1986, r. 12.12. And see *Re Busytoday Ltd* [1992] 1 W.L.R. 683.

an administrative receiver or administrator under section 234 of the Insolvency Act 1986 has in relation to obtaining possession of the company's property, books, papers or records. Likewise, a similar approach may also be taken to section 235 of the Insolvency Act 1986, which deals with the duty of officers and certain other persons connected with the company to co-operate with, amongst others, an administrative receiver or administrator.

Section 236 of the Insolvency Act 1986 empowers the court, on an **25–015** application by, *inter alia*, an administrative receiver or administrator to order the examination on oath of an officer of the company, a person known or suspected to have in his possession any property of the company or supposed to be indebted to the company or a person thought to be capable of giving information concerning the promotion, formation, business dealings, affairs or property of the company.[45] The section also permits the making of an order requiring such persons to produce any books, papers or other records in his possession or under his control which relate to the company.[46] As to the former power, it has been held that the jurisdiction exists to enable the court to summon a person subject to the section irrespective of whether the relevant person is resident in the jurisdiction or has been personally served in the jurisdiction.[47] As to the latter power, it has been held that the court may make an order requiring production of documents which are located abroad.[48] The making of such an order (as making an order for examination[49]) lies within the discretion of the court.[50] To obtain, for example, an order for production of documents it will be necessary for the office-holder to demonstrate that he reasonably requires to see the documents[51] in order to carry out his statutory functions and that production of them does not impose an

---

[45] s. 236(2).

[46] s. 236(3).

[47] *McIsaac & Anor, Petitioners* [1994] B.C.C. 410. In the 2nd edition of this work, paras 25–006—25–007, attention was drawn to the difficulty in reaching this conclusion presented by *Re Tucker (R.C.) (A Bankrupt), ex p. Tucker (K.R.)* [1990] Ch. 148, CA, concerned with the interpretation of s. 25 of the Bankruptcy Act 1914. *McIsaac & Anor, Petitioners* suggests that these difficulties will be ignored, that the Tucker case will be regarded as limited to the interpretation of the legislative provision involved in that case, and that the modern trend of decisions indicates an intention to give s. 236 of the 1986 Act extraterritorial effect: see *Re Seagull Manufacturing Co. Ltd* [1993] Ch. 345, CA; *Re Paramount Airways Ltd* [1993] Ch. 223, CA; *Re Mid East Trading Ltd* [1998] 1 All E.R. 577, CA. In *McIsaac & Anor, Petitioners* it was said, however, that, where necessary, it might be possible to enforce orders made under s. 236(2) against persons outside the jurisdiction in the country where they were resident, pursuant to Insolvency Act 1986, s. 426 (see below, paras 25–066—25–075). This is clearly incorrect. Section 426 deals with the obligations of a U.K. court to render assistance to a foreign court which is designated by the Secretary of State for that purpose. The section has no concern with the obligation of a foreign court to render assistance to a U.K. court. Further, the relevant documents were situated in New York and the court was clearly wrong in assuming that the United States was a relevant country for the purposes of Insolvency Act 1986, s. 426(11) since it has not been designated as such by the Secretary of State: see Smart (1996) 41 J. Law Soc. Scotland 141.

[48] *Re Mid East Trading Ltd* [1998] 1 All E.R., 577, CA.

[49] *McIsaac & Anor, Petitioners* [1994] B.C.C. 410. See also *Re Seagull Manufacturing Co. Ltd* [1993] Ch. 345, CA; *Re Paramount Airways Ltd* [1993] Ch. 223, CA.

[50] *Re Mid East Trading Ltd* [1998] 1 All E.R. 577, CA. See above, Chap. 5.

[51] The documents must be documents which relate to the company in respect of which the application is made: *ibid.*, at 585–590.

unnecessary or unreasonable burden on the person required to produce them.[52]

25–016   Where the powers referred to above are applied as against persons outside the jurisdiction of the English court, it will be necessary to obtain the permission of the court for service in the relevant country.[53] Where an order is made under section 236 of the 1986 Act against a person who is present in England, the court may restrain that person from leaving the jurisdiction or require that he give security as a condition of leaving the country.[54]

25–017   After the making of an administration order and between the presentation of the petition and the making of the order there are statutory restrictions on proceedings and on enforcement of security by creditors.[55] Where a company has assets abroad or creditors abroad, the question arises as to whether these prohibitions are limited to activities in the United Kingdom or whether they extend worldwide.

25–018   A similar question has been raised by the provisions of section 130(2) of the Insolvency Act 1986 which prohibits the commencement of proceedings against a company without the leave of the court after a winding-up order has been made or provisional liquidator appointed. In *Re Vocalion (Foreign) Ltd*,[56] it was held that the application of the predecessor of this section as a matter of construction should be limited to proceedings in the United Kingdom. More recently, the Court of Appeal has cited that case with approval in relation to section 130(2), although there was no argument to the contrary.[57] On the other hand, in Scotland it has been held that the section applies to proceedings in foreign courts and that an injunction will be granted enforcing the prohibition against anyone within the jurisdiction.[58] The significance of this divergence in the context of a winding-up is reduced by the recognition and assertion of an equitable jurisdiction by the English courts to restrain persons subject to the jurisdiction from commencing or continuing proceedings calculated to defeat the right on the winding-up of all unsecured creditors[59] (who are in the nature of *cestuis que* trust

---

[52] See *British and Commonwealth Holdings plc v. Spicer & Oppenheimer* [1993] A.C. 426; *Re Bank of Credit and Commerce International SA (No. 12)* [1997] 1 B.C.L.C. 526. The court may take account of the risk that the relevant person might be exposed to liability under the law of the country where the documents are situated: *Re Mid-East Trading Ltd* [1998] 1 All E.R. 577, 590–593; see *MacKinnon v. Donaldson, Lufkin & Jenrette Securities Corp* [1986] Ch. 482. See above, Chap. 5.

[53] Insolvency Rules 1986, r. 12.12. See *Re Seagull Manufacturing Co. Ltd* [1993] Ch. 345, CA; *Re Paramount Airways* [1993] Ch. 223, CA.

[54] *Re Oriental Credit Ltd* [1988] Ch. 204; *Re Bank of Credit and Commerce International SA (No. 7)* [1994] 1 B.C.L.C. 455. See also *Morris v. Murjani* [1996] 1 W.L.R. 848, CA. Such an order may also be made in respect of applications under Insolvency Act 1986, ss. 133, 238–239, 244–245, 423–425.

[55] Sections 10 and 11 of the Insolvency Act 1986; and see above, Chap. 23.

[56] [1932] 2 Ch. 196; and see *Re Dynamics Corporation of America* [1972] 3 All E.R. 1046.

[57] *Mitchell v. Carter, Re Buckingham International plc* [1997] 1 B.C.L.C. 673.

[58] See *California Redwood Co. Ltd v. Walker* (1886) 13 R. 816 and *Redwood Co. Ltd v. Merchant Banking Co. of London* (1886) 13 R. 1202.

[59] Secured creditors will readily be given leave to commence proceedings against the company. To the extent that they rest on their security, they are outside the statutory

with beneficial interests extending to all the company's property under the statutory scheme[60]) to the administration and distribution of the company's assets on the basis of equality and payment *pari passu*.[61]

It is suggested that the approach of giving the administration order **25–019** statutory stay provisions of the Insolvency Act 1986 extra-territorial effect is preferable. In particular, there would appear to be no scope for exercise of the equitable jurisdiction, since there is, in the case of an administration order, no vested right on the part of unsecured creditors.[62] Administration is a collective procedure in the interests of all creditors, and one of its purposes may be a "more advantageous realisation of the company's assets than would be effected on a winding-up",[63] but no trust arises and the company does not cease to be beneficial owner of its assets, nor do the creditors acquire any beneficial interests therein. The alternative construction to the effect that the administration order statutory stay has no extra-territorial effect must be conducive to an unseemly scramble by creditors for foreign assets, a course which (if generally available) must undermine the efficacy of the legislation as a means of giving a breathing space to companies.

It is of course true that it might be unfair for English creditors who **25–020** are subject to the jurisdiction of the court to be restrained from exercising rights abroad when foreign creditors not subject to such jurisdiction are not so restrained. Such potential unfairness can be remedied by the power of the court (and, in certain situations, the administrator) to grant permission to proceed.

If the statutory stay imposed by the Insolvency Act 1986 amounted to **25–021** a moratorium[64] on debts and liabilities, on established principles of conflict of laws, it could only be expected to be given effect to abroad where English or Scots law is the law applicable to the transaction giving rise to the liability.[65] That is because a moratorium properly, so-called, discharges or modifies the relevant obligation and only the law applicable to the obligation is regarded in the conflict of laws as being able to

---

scheme and in any proceedings against the company they are enforcing rights, not against the company, but to their own property: *per* Brightman L.J. in *Re Aro Co. Ltd* [1980] Ch. 196 at 203, CA.

[60] *R. v. Registrar of Companies, ex p. Central Bank of India* [1986] 1 All E.R. 105 at 112 *per* Dillon L.J., CA; *Victoria Housing Estates Ltd v. Ashpurton Estates Ltd* [1983] Ch. 110 at 123, *per* Lord Brightman, CA.

[61] *Re Vocalion (Foreign) Ltd* [1932] 2 Ch. 196, *Mitchell v. Carter, Re Buckingham International plc* [1997] 1 B.C.L.C. 673; *Mitchell v. Carter, Re Buckingham International plc (No.2)* [1998] 2 B.C.L.C. 369, CA and see *Re Calgary & Edmonton Land Co.* [1975] 1 W.L.R 355 and consider *British Airways v. Laker Airways* [1985] A.C. 58.

[62] Note that there might be an argument in the case of an administration order which is bound to result in a liquidation, that unsecured creditors have sufficient in the way of prospective rights to enable an injunction to be granted to prevent proceedings abroad.

[63] Insolvency Act 1986, s. 8(3)(d).

[64] For the use of the term "moratorium" in this context, see above, Chap. 23.

[65] *National Bank of Greece and Athens SA v. Metliss* [1958] A.C. 509; *Adams v. National Bank of Greece SA* [1961] A.C. 255. See also *New Zealand Loan and Mercantile Agency v. Morrison* [1898] A.C. 349 (Companies Act Scheme).

discharge or modify the obligation.[66] But as has been seen in Chapter 23, sections 10 and 11 of the Insolvency Act 1986 do not discharge or modify obligations but only restrain remedies for their enforcement. Such a stay of remedies, given that it does not discriminate against foreign creditors, may be enforced by foreign courts even where the liability whose enforcement is stayed is governed by a foreign law.[67] A foreign court may also be expected to recognise the administrator as the governing body of the company entitled to act on its behalf, since this is a matter for the law of the place of incorporation.[68]

25–022   Moreover, the English court may grant an injunction against a creditor who is subject to the jurisdiction of the court to prevent him from commencing or continuing proceedings or doing any act outside the United Kingdom prohibited by the Act.[69] Further, if the creditor subject to the jurisdiction obtains satisfaction by means forbidden by the law, he may be required to disgorge his receipts to the administrator.[70] Any creditor not subject to the jurisdiction who has obtained satisfaction abroad in this way may be expected to be required, as a condition of being heard in the administration proceedings or obtaining any benefit under any scheme or of obtaining any acceptance of his proof in a subsequent liquidation, to pay over all sums so received.[71]

3. RECOGNITION OF RECEIVERS: INTRA-UNITED KINGDOM PROVISIONS

25–023   The law relating to the recognition in England of receivers appointed under the law of another part of the United Kingdom is governed by explicit statutory provisions. Thus, a receiver appointed under the law of Scotland or Northern Ireland in respect of the property of a corporation having created a charge which, as created, was a floating charge, may exercise his powers in England.[72] The recognition of these receivers' powers is, however, subject to the qualification that their exercise should not be inconsistent with English law.[73] Accordingly, although, for example, a Scottish receiver should be entitled, prima facie, to exercise the same powers over English assets as he possesses in relation to Scottish assets, English law will remain in ultimate control.

---

[66] See cases cited above, n. 65.

[67] *e.g.* in the United States under s. 304 of the Bankruptcy Code (U.S.).

[68] *Carl Zeiss Stiftung v. Rayner and Keeler Ltd* [1967] 1 A.C. 853 at 919 and 972 and 588. See below, para. 25–058.

[69] *Cf. Re Central Sugar Factories of Brazil* [1894] Ch. 369; *Re Vocalion (Foreign) Ltd* [1932] Ch. 196. And see *Mitchell v. Carter* [1997] 1 B.C.L.C. 673, Blackburne J. and CA; *Mitchell v. Buckingham International plc (No. 2)* [1998] 2 B.C.L.C. 369, Harman J. and CA. See below, paras 25–064 *et seq.*

[70] *Re Oriental Island Steam Co.* (1874) 9 Ch. App. 557; *Mitchell v. Carter* [1997] 1 B.C.L.C. 673 at 687, *per* Millett L.J.

[71] *ibid.*

[72] For receivers appointed under the law of Scotland, see Insolvency Act 1986, s. 72; for receivers appointed under the law of Northern Ireland, see Administration of Justice Act 1977, s. 7.

[73] The qualification is established in each of the above sections.

A charge created by a Scottish company over property located in **25–024** England does not require registration in England,[74] though the charge must be registered in Scotland to the extent that such registration is required by Scots law.[75]

The sections enabling the power of a receiver appointed under the law **25–025** of Scotland or Northern Ireland to be recognised in England[76] also have the wider effect of establishing the mutual recognition of receivers appointed under the law of England, Scotland and Northern Ireland as the case may be. Accordingly, an English receiver may exercise his powers in Scotland though the exercise of such powers must be consistent with Scots law.[77] Any charge created by an English company over property located in Scotland does not require registration in Scotland,[78] but such a charge must be registered in England in the usual way.[79]

Section 426 of the Insolvency Act 1986 provides for mutual judicial **25–026** assistance between courts within the various parts of the United Kingdom and for such assistance between those courts and the courts of any relevant country or territory.[80] Such assistance may be provided in relation to insolvency law, the definition of which extends to the provisions of the Insolvency Act 1986 which deal with English and Scottish receiverships and also to the provisions of the relevant Northern Irish legislation.[81] The nature of the assistance to be provided lies within the discretion of the court whose assistance is requested,[82] but it would seem that this provision may have the effect of increasing the mutual recognition of receivers' powers within the United Kingdom. Tending in the same direction is the requirement in the Insolvency Act 1986 which

[74] Companies Act 1985, s. 409.

[75] Companies Act 1985, ss. 410–424, which will be replaced by ss. 395–410 (inserted by Companies Act 1989, ss. 92–100) when those sections enter into force.

[76] See above, n. 72.

[77] In *Gordon Anderson (Plant) Ltd v. Campsie Construction Ltd and Anglo-Scottish Plant Ltd*, 1977 S.L.T. 7, a majority of the Court of Session held that the then equivalent to s. 72 of the Insolvency Act 1986 (Companies (Floating Charges and Receivers) (Scotland)) Act 1972, s. 15(4), repealed by Administration of Justice Act 1977, s. 7) had the effect of giving an English receiver the same security over Scottish assets that a Scottish receiver would obtain. See too, *Norfolk House plc (in receivership) v. Repsol Petroleum Ltd*, 1992 S.L.T. 235.

[78] Companies Act 1985, s. 424.

[79] Companies Act 1985, ss. 395–408.

[80] Insolvency Act 1986, s. 426(4). As to the meaning of "relevant country of territory", see below, para. 25–068.

[81] Insolvency Act 1986, s. 426(4), (10)(a), (b), which will be amended by the Insolvency Bill 2000, Sched. 4, Pt II, para. 16(3) and (c) if those provisions are enacted in their current form. The English court may also exercise its own general powers, beyond those of "insolvency law" in providing assistance in particular cases: *Hughes v. Hannover Ruckversicherungs-Aktiengesellschaft* [1997] 1 B.C.L.C. 497, CA. See below, para. 25–070.

[82] Insolvency Act 1986, s. 426(5). A request is authority to the requesting court to apply its own law of receivership or the comparable corresponding law of the requesting court: *ibid.* In exercising its discretion under s. 426(5) the court shall have regard, in particular, to its rules of private international law. See below, para. 25–073.

imposes a mutual obligation on United Kingdom courts to recognise each other's orders made in the exercise of jurisdiction in relation to insolvency law,[83] the definition of which includes the law concerning receivers.[84] Such recognition could thus extend to receivers appointed by the courts of the various parts of the United Kingdom. The mutual duty of recognition, in this context, is subject to the important qualification that a court is not bound to recognise the order of a court in another part of the United Kingdom to the extent that such order affects property situated within the jurisdiction of the court which is asked to recognise it.[85]

4. RECOGNITION OF RECEIVERS: FOREIGN APPOINTMENT OUT OF COURT

25–027 The position of a foreign receiver appointed otherwise than by court order and the extent to which such a receiver's powers will be recognised in England has never been directly considered in a reported English decision. In *Cretanor Maritime Co. Ltd v. Irish Marine Management Ltd*[86] a company incorporated in the Republic of Ireland created a floating charge over its assets in favour of a bank. The company had assets in England but had been restrained, by means of a Mareva injunction,[87] from dealing with them. Subsequently the charge crystallised and a receiver was appointed who sought to have the injunction discharged. It was held that the receiver, as agent of the company according to Irish law, was bound by the injunction in the same way as the company would have been had no receiver been appointed. It may be deduced, by implication, from this result that, had no injunction been granted, the receiver could have exercised in England whatever rights were available to him under Irish law. Accordingly, it is submitted that where a receiver is appointed under a law other than the law of a part of the United Kingdom in respect of the property of a corporation and in consequence of the corporation having created a charge (which as created was a floating charge), he may exercise his powers in England if the exercise of those powers is authorised by the law of the country in which the company is incorporated.[88] This view accords with principle. A receiver

---

[83] Insolvency Act 1986, s. 426(1) and (2).

[84] Insolvency Act 1986, s. 426(1), (2), (10)(a), (b) and (c) which will be amended by the Insolvency Bill 2000, Sched. 4, Pt. II, para. 16(3) if those provisions are enacted in their current form.

[85] Insolvency Act 1986, s. 426(1) and (2).

[86] [1978] 1 W.L.R. 966, CA.

[87] Now "freezing injunction": C.P.R, Pt. 25.1(1)(f). See above, Chap. 17.

[88] Dicey and Morris, *The Conflict of Laws* (13th ed. 2000), Rule 159 and pp. 1152–1155. See also *Re C.A. Kennedy Co. Ltd and Stibbe-Monk Ltd* (1976) 74 D.L.R. (3d) 87; Collins (1978) 27 I.C.L.Q. 611 at 707–710 reprinted in *Essays in International Litigation and the Conflict of Laws* (1994), p. 433. The same principle governs recognition of the powers of a liquidator appointed under foreign law. See Dicey and Morris, Rule 158 and pp. 1141–1143. As to appointments of office-holders analogous to administrators, see *Felixstowe Dock and Railway Co. v. U.S. Lines Inc.* [1989] Q.B. 360 and below, paras 25–049—25–053.

appointed pursuant to a charge normally acts, prior to liquidation, as agent of the corporation which created the charge. On general principle, the law of the place of incorporation determines who is entitled to act on behalf of the corporation.[89] After liquidation a receiver is no longer agent but retains his power to act in the corporation's name to dispose of the corporation's assets. It is suggested even in this case that it is the law of the place of incorporation which determines who has the power to act in the name of the corporation to dispose of its assets.

If the foregoing submissions are accepted, then a receiver's authority **25–028** will be recognised in England to the extent that his powers are consistent with English law.[90] It follows from this that where his authority is so recognised, then priority as between him and any other claimants will be governed by English law,[91] despite the fact that English creditors might be prejudiced in the sense that, were the receiver's authority not recognised, those creditors would have prior claims.[92]

The foregoing submissions assume, of course, that the charge has been **25–029** validly created and that it extends to the property being claimed by the receiver in accordance with the principles discussed earlier in this chapter.[93]

The obligation to register charges[94] extends to charges on property in **25–030** England which are created and to charges on property in England which is acquired by a company incorporated outside Great Britain which has an established place of business in England.[95] For the English registration provisions to apply, the company must have an established place of business in England at the time of the creation of the charge,[96] but charges created prior to the establishment of a place of business in England do not require registration.[97] The registration provisions contained in Part XII, Chapter 1 of the Companies Act 1985 apply whether or not the company has registered in accordance with the requirements of Part XXIII of that Act.[98]

A foreign receiver appointed out of court may be in a position to **25–031** invoke the provisions of the Insolvency Act 1986 which enable the English court, on the request of a court in any relevant country or territory, to provide assistance in matters relating to the receivership. This power is discussed separately below.[99]

[89] *Banco de Bilbao v. Sancha and Rey* [1938] 2 K.B. 176, CA.
[90] *Cf.* Administration of Justice Act 1977, s. 7; Insolvency Act 1986, s. 72; above, para. 25–023. See also *Re B* [1990–91] C.I.L.R. (Notes) 7 (Grand Court, Cayman Islands).
[91] *Re CA Kennedy Co. Ltd and Stibbe-Monk Ltd* (1976) 74 D.L.R. (3d) 87 at 92–93; see also *Re McKenzie Grant & Co.* (1899) 1 W.A.L.R. 116; Picarda, *Law Relating to Receivers Managers and Administrators* (2nd ed. 1990), pp. 497–498.
[92] See *Re CA Kennedy Co. Ltd and Stibbe-Monk Ltd* (1976) 74 D.L.R. (3d) 87 at 95–96.
[93] See above, paras 25–002—25–007.
[94] See Companies Act 1985, Part XII, Chap. 1. For further discussion, see above, Chap. 3.
[95] Companies Act 1985, s. 409.
[96] *Re Oriel Ltd* [1986] 1 W.L.R. 180, CA.
[97] *ibid.*
[98] *N. V. Slavenburg's Bank v. Intercontinental Natural Resources Ltd* [1980] 1 W.L.R. 1076. See above, Chap. 3.
[99] See below, paras 25–066 to 25–075. Other less formal methods of assistance may also be available.

5. RECOGNITION OF RECEIVERS: APPOINTMENT BY FOREIGN COURT[1]

25–032 The circumstances in which a receiver appointed by a foreign court may secure recognition of his powers in relation to English assets in England has not been authoritatively settled in the reported cases.[2] However, it is clear that the principles are different to those which apply to determine the recognition of a receiver pursuant to a private appointment under foreign law.[3] This difference arises because, in principle, when recognition of a receiver appointed by a foreign court is involved, the English court must satisfy itself that the foreign court was jurisdictionally competent to make the appointment according to the relevant principles of English private international law. Consequently, it becomes necessary to determine when English law will regard a foreign court as possessing such competence.[4] Where such competence is established and there are no applicable general principles of conflict of laws precluding recognition, comity requires recognition to be afforded.[5] In the case of a private appointment, the validity of the appointment must be strictly proved and comity has no place.[6]

25–033 As a general principle, the foreign court will be regarded as jurisdictionally competent if there is a "sufficient connection between the company in respect of which the receiver is appointed ('the defendant') and the jurisdiction in which the foreign receiver was appointed to justify recognition of the foreign court's order".[7] While this much may be accepted, it is not possible to state with complete certainty the circumstances in which such sufficient connection may exist.[8] At the outset,

---

[1] See also Chap. 22.

[2] See *Houlditch v. Marquis of Donegal* (1834) 8 Bli. N.S. 301; *Re Maudslay, Sons and Field* [1900] 1 Ch. 602; *Macaulay v. Guarantee Trust Co. of New York* (1927) 44 T.L.R. 99; *Re Kooperman* [1928] W.N. 101; *Schemmer v. Property Resources Ltd* [1975] Ch. 273; *Perry v. Zissis* [1977] 1 Lloyd's Rep. 607, CA; *Derby & Co. v. Weldon (No. 6)* [1990] 1 W.L.R. 1139, CA; *International Credit and Investment Co. (Overseas) Ltd v. Adham* [1994] 1 B.C.L.C. 66, affd. [1999] I.L.Pr. 302, CA; *Larkins v. NUM* [1985] I.R. 670; *Thorne Ernst and Whinney Inc. v. Sulpetro Ltd* (1987) 47 D.L.R. (4th) 315; *Canadian Imperial Bank of Commerce v. Idanell Korner Ranch Ltd* [1990] 6 W.W.R. 612; *Re Young* [1955] St.R.Qd. 254; *White v. Verkouille* [1990] 2 Qd.R. 191; *Canadian Arab Financial Corporation v. Player* [1984] C.I.L.R. 63, Cayman Islands CA.

[3] See *Re B* [1990–91] C.I.L.R. (Notes) 7, Grand Court, Cayman islands.

[4] For discussion see Dicey and Morris, pp. 1154–1155.

[5] *Canadian Arab Financial Corporation v. Player* [1984] C.I.L.R. 63, Cayman Islands, CA.

[6] See above, n. 6. See also *Gwembe Valley Development Co. v. Koshiy, The Times*, February 8, 2000.

[7] *Schemmer v. Property Resources Ltd* [1975] Ch. 273 at 287: see *too, International Credit and Investment Co. (Overseas) Ltd v. Adham* [1994] 1 B.C.L.C. 66, 70–71, affd. [1999] I.L.Pr. 302, CA; *White v. Verkouille* [1990] 2 Qd.R. 191.

[8] See the cautious and tentative exposition by Goulding J. in *Schemmer v. Property Resources Ltd* [1975] Ch. 273.

recognition will be accorded to an appointment made by a court in the country in which the company is incorporated.[9]

Secondly, it is likely that an appointment will be recognised if the defendant submitted to the jurisdiction of the court which appointed the receiver,[10] though in this context submission by a subsidiary of the defendant is likely to be regarded as insufficient to justify recognition.[11] It is also possible that the English court will recognise the order of a foreign court if the appointment is made by a court of a country other than that in which the company is incorporated, if the appointment is recognised by the courts of the country in which the company is incorporated.[12] **25–034**

A sufficient connection, for these purposes, ought to include factual connection between the company and the relevant jurisdiction where the appointment is made. Accordingly it is, in principle, possible to support the view that an appointment made by a court in a country where the central management and control of the company is exercised should be entitled to recognition.[13] The claim to recognition on this ground will, perhaps, be stronger if there is no, or little, likelihood of any intervention by the courts of the place of incorporation.[14] A strong factual link justifying recognition may also be thought to exist where the appointment is made by a court in a country where the company carries on business.[15] The strength of this link may be particularly compelling if that is the only country where business is carried on.[16] **25–035**

It seems to be established, on the other hand, that "reciprocity" by itself will not be regarded as a ground of recognition, *i.e.* that it will be insufficient to justify recognition merely to show that the appointment made by the foreign court was made in circumstances where, *mutatis* **25–036**

---

[9] *International Credit and Investment Co. (Overseas) Ltd v. Adham* [1994] 1 B.C.L.C. 66, affd. [1999] I.L.Pr. 302, CA, explicitly recognising an appointment made by the courts of the country in which the company was incorporated; *Schemmer v. Property Resources Ltd* [1975] Ch. 273. And see *North Australian Terrritory Co. Ltd v. Goldsborough Mort & Co. Ltd* (1889) 61 L.T. 716; *Macaulay v. Guarantee Trust Co. of New York* (1927) 44 T.L.R. 99; *Larkins v. NUM* [1985] I.R. 671, at 689–693. The conclusion is reinforced by the analogy with the recognition of the authority of a liquidator appointed under the law of the place of incorporation; see Dicey and Morris, Rule 158 and pp. 1141–1142.

[10] *Schemmer v. Property Resources Ltd* [1975] Ch. 273 at 287; *International Credit and Investment Co. (Overseas) Ltd v. Adham* [1994] 1 B.C.L.C. 66, 70–71; *White v. Verkouille* [1990] 2 Qd.R. 191. And see *Thorne Ernst & Whinney Inc. v. Sulpetro Ltd* (1987) 47 D.L.R. (4th) 315; *Canadian Imperial Bank of Commerce v. Idanell Korner Rauch Ltd* (1990) 6 W.W.R. 620.

[11] *Schemmer v. Property Resources Ltd* [1975] Ch. 273.

[12] *ibid.*, at 287. See also *Smart, Cross-Border Insolvency* (2nd ed. 1998), p. 167; *Macaulay v. Guarantee Trust Co. of New York* (1927) 44 T.L.R. 99.

[13] *Schemmer v. Property Resources Ltd* [1975] Ch. 273; *cf.* the definition of domicile for the purposes of the 1968 Brussels Convention on Jurisdiction and the Enforcement of Judgments in Civil and Commercial Matters [1978] O.J. L304/77 as amended (which does not apply in matters of receivership) in Civil Jurisdiction and Judgments Act 1982, ss. 41 *et seq.* For the text of an unofficial consolidated version of the Brussels Convention, as amended in 1982, 1989 and 1996 see [1998] O.J. C27/1.

[14] See Dicey and Morris, pp. 1142–1143, 1154–1155; *Re Azoff-Don Commercial Bank* [1954] Ch. 315.

[15] *Schemmer v. Property Resources Ltd* [1975] Ch. 273.

[16] *Cf.* for a tenuous analogy, *Re Harrods (Buenos Aires) Ltd* [1992] Ch. 72, CA.

mutandis, an English court would have had jurisdiction to appoint a receiver.[17]

25–037   Assuming that an English court regards the appointment as made in circumstances where the foreign court possesses the necessary jurisdictional competence, the appointment may nevertheless fail to gain recognition if it does not accord with what one might refer to as general principles of the conflict of laws. Thus, for example, in *Schemmer v. Property Resources Ltd*,[18] a receiver had been appointed in the United States, pursuant to the Securities Exchange Act 1934, to take possession of certain assets of a Bahamian company which were situated, amongst other places in England. It was held that the American statute was a penal law unenforceable in the English courts, so that any appointment made pursuant to it could not be recognised because it stemmed from a law bearing this penal character.[19]

25–038   The principle in the *Schemmer* case has been followed and extended in Hong Kong in *NanusAsia Co. Inc v. Standard Chartered Bank*,[20] where it was held that a receiver appointed by the U.S. Court in an insider trading case would not be recognised. The receiver had been careful to seek only disgorgement of profits in the interests of the victims and had not sought to enforce any penal relief available under U.S. law. Even without the penal element, recognition was denied on the basis that the receiver was appointed under public law provisions. The issue arose in the context of a trial of the issue whether the bank holding the ill-gotten proceeds had a defence to a claim by the wrongdoer's company to payment over of the monies. The bank was held entitled to hold onto these funds on the grounds that they might be held on constructive trust for the victims. This was held not to be an indirect enforcement of U.S. public law.

25–039   In *Larkins v. NUM*,[21] the English court had appointed sequestrators over the property of the National Union of Mineworkers in relation to the union's failure to comply with the orders of the court during the miners' strike in 1984. The sequestration order empowered the sequestrators to take proceedings in the Republic of Ireland to recover union funds on deposit there with a bank. Subsequently, the English court appointed, on an interlocutory basis, a receiver of the union who was given authority to bring proceedings in any jurisdiction to recover assets of the union. The Irish High Court held that the claim by the sequestrators could not be maintained since sequestration was a penal process in which it was sought to establish the authority of the court by punishing recalcitrant litigants for contempt. As far as the claim by the receiver was concerned, the Irish court made no order since the

---

[17] *Schemmer v. Property Resources Ltd* [1975] Ch. 273 at 287; *Derby & Co. Ltd v. Weldon (No. 6)* [1990] 1 W.L.R. 1139 at 1150, CA. See also *Re Trepca Mines Ltd* [1960] 1 W.L.R. 1273, CA; *Société Co-operative Sidmetal v. Titan International Ltd* [1966] 1 Q.B. 828; *Felixstowe Dock and Railway Co. v. U.S. Lines Inc.* [1989] Q.B. 360 at 374–375.
[18] [1975] Ch. 273.
[19] See, generally, Dicey and Morris, pp. 92 *et seq.*
[20] [1988] H.K.C. 377
[21] [1985] I.R. 671.

appointment was of an interlocutory character. The court did seem prepared to recognise that a claim by a receiver not appointed on an interlocutory basis could, in principle, be maintained since there were independent grounds for the appointment and the receivership was not an indirect method of enforcing the sequestration such that it amounted to an indirect method of enforcing a foreign penal law.[22]

Where the foreign receiver gains recognition, he may be permitted to **25–040** sue for the recovery of the assets in his own name.[23] Here the receiver's power receives direct recognition, though, as an alternative, the English court may create an English receivership to act as auxiliary to the principal receivership.[24] Whichever solution is adopted, the receiver may collect English property and give a good discharge for it.[25] In an appropriate case, the foreign appointee may be required to give security for costs.[26]

A receiver appointed by a foreign court may be able to take advantage of the provisions of the Insolvency Act 1986 which relate to judicial assistance. This matter is discussed below.[27]

6. ADMINISTRATIVE RECEIVERS

In the present context, the question for consideration is whether the **25–041** status of administrative receiver is confined to a person appointed in relation to a company registered under the Companies Act 1985 or whether it also exists in relation to a person appointed as a receiver or manager of a foreign (unregistered) company. In *Re International Bulk Commodities Ltd*,[28] it was held that a receiver appointed in relation to a foreign company can be an administrative receiver for the purposes of the 1986 Act and is therefore able to exercise the powers under that Act which are available to such a person. By virtue of section 251 of the Insolvency Act 1986, the relevant definition of a company, for these purposes, is to be found in section 735 of the Companies Act 1985 so that unless the contrary intention appeared, company meant a company registered under the Companies Act 1985. Mummery J. held, however, that a contrary intention could be deduced from the construction of the provisions of the Insolvency Act 1986 relating to administrative receivers

[22] This could be questionable if the receiver was under an obligation to account for any sums to the sequestrators, a point not decided in the case.

[23] See *Macaulay v. Guarantee Trust Co. of New York* (1927) 44 T.L.R. 99.

[24] *Schemmer v. Property Resources Ltd* [1975] Ch. 273 at 287; *Re Young* [1955] St. R. Qd. 254.

[25] *ibid.*; see also *Lepage v. San Paulo Copper Estates Ltd* [1917] W.N. 216.

[26] See Picarda, p. 501.

[27] See below, paras 25–066 to 25–075.

[28] The correctness of this decision was doubted in *Re Devon and Somerset Farmers Ltd* [1994] Ch. 57, but it was ultimately distinguished on the basis that it was a decision which was authority on the powers of receivers of *foreign* companies appointed under debentures so that, in consequence, it did not extend to an *English* unregistered company. For discussion, see Dicey and Morris, pp. 1157–1158; Smart, *Cross-Border Insolvency* (2nd ed., 1998) pp. 130–136; Moss (1993) 6 Insolvency Intelligence 19; (1994) 7 Insolvency Intelligence 33.

and from the Act as a whole: Parliament intended that "company" should not be confined to one registered under the 1985 Act but should include any company liable to be wound up under the provisions of Part V of the Insolvency Act 1986.[29] Since a foreign company could be wound up under these provisions, a receiver of it could be an administrative receiver.

25-042   The debenture in that case was secured by a floating charge in the English form.[30] This leaves open the effect of an appointment made under a debenture governed by a foreign law. It is suggested, however, that if:

(a) such an appointment creates a floating charge recognised by English law; and

(b) a receiver is appointed whose appointment is recognised by English law; and

(c) the receiver meets the relevant English statutory criteria,

the receiver will be regarded as an administrative receiver. It is probable that a foreign appointee's powers would be limited to those which are not inconsistent with English law.[31] More general limitations may be placed on the appointee's powers by general principles of the conflict of laws, *e.g.* a foreign appointee may be precluded from exercising powers in England which are conferred by a foreign law if these powers are penal in the English sense.[32]

25-043   No reason of principle seems to prevent the provisions concerning mutual recognition as between England and Scotland in section 72 of the Insolvency Act 1986 being extended to administrative receivers despite the fact that they are not explicitly mentioned in that section.[33] This conclusion seems to follow because a receiver for the purposes of section 72 includes a manager and a receiver and manager[34] and an administrative receiver, as far as the English provisions of the 1986 Act are concerned, must initially be one of these in addition to satisfying the other criteria established by the Act,[35] and, in relation to the Scottish provisions, an administrative receiver must initially be a receiver who also satisfies the additional requirements of the Act.[36] If this submission is accepted, the administrative receiver can only exercise his powers in the other jurisdiction to the extent that those powers are not inconsistent with the law applicable there.[37]

---

[29] As to the winding up of foreign companies, see Dicey and Morris, of pp. 1116–1149; Smart, *Cross-Border Insolvency* (2nd ed. 1998); Fletcher, *Insolvency in Private International Law* (1999), Chap. 3.

[30] *Re International Bulk Commodities Ltd* [1993] Ch. 77 at 86.

[31] *Cf.* Insolvency Act 1986, s. 72(1).

[32] *Cf. Schemmer v. Property Resources Ltd* [1975] Ch. 273, above, para. 25–037; Insolvency Act 1986, ss. 28, 50.

[33] *Cf. ibid.*, ss. 37(1), 38(1) which explicitly exclude administrative receivers.

[34] *ibid.*, s. 72(2).

[35] *ibid.*, s. 29(2).

[36] *ibid.*, ss. 51, 251.

[37] *ibid.*, s. 72(1).

7. ADMINISTRATION[38]

An important feature of the Insolvency Act 1986 is the creation of the **25–044** office of administrator to achieve one or more of the statutory purposes set out in section 8(3).[39] At least two questions may arise in the context of private international law. The first is whether an English court has power to make an administration order in respect of a foreign company. The second is the extent to which officers analogous to administrators, appointed under a foreign law, are entitled to have their status recognised in England and to exercise there the powers conferred upon them by the relevant foreign law.[40]

(a) Powers of English court

In at least two judgments at first instance it has been assumed that an **25–045** English court has no power to make an administration order in respect of a foreign company[41] and one of these decisions has been referred to, in that respect, without approval, disapproval, discussion or hearing argument on the point, by the Court of Appeal in a case in which the point was not in issue.[42] A more cautious and open view on the question has also been expressed at first instance in a case in which the point did not expressly arise for decision.[43] In view of this inconclusive state of authority, it is fair to treat the question as an arguable one and to consider the question on the merits.[44]

In *Re Dallhold Estates (U.K.) Pty. Ltd*,[45] it was held that an English **25–046** court could, on the request of a court of a designated country,[46] make an administration order in relation to a foreign company but it was said also, in this case, that the court did not have original jurisdiction to make such an order.[47] The expressed reason was that section 8 of the Insolvency Act 1986 enables the court to make an administration order in respect of a "company" which is defined for those purposes by section 735 of the Companies Act 1985[48] as a company formed and registered under that Act or any of its predecessors.

---

[38] For discussion of administration, see above, Chap. 23.

[39] Whether a person has *authority* to apply for an administration order in respect of an English company may depend on a foreign law, *e.g.* where the English company is owned by a foreign company and an officer of the foreign company acting on the latter's behalf see ks to procure an administration order in the name of the English company, the ofiicer's authority so to act may depend on the law of the country in whch the foreign company is incorporated. But whether that person has *locus standi* so to apply depends upon Insolvency Act 1986, s. 9: see *Re MTI Trading Systems Ltd* [1997] B.C.C. 703.

[40] Picarda, pp. 501–502; Dicey and Morris, pp. 1143–1144, 1149, 1158–1159.

[41] *Felixstowe Dock and Railway Co. v. U.S. Lines Inc.* [1989] Q.B. 360, 367; *Re Dallhold Estates (U.K.) Pty Ltd* [1992] B.C.L.C. 621. See to the same effect Picarda, p. 501.

[42] *Hughes v. Hannover Ruckversicherungs-Aktiengesellschaft* [1997] 1 B.C.L.C. 407 at 511, CA, referring to *Re Dallhold Estates (U.K.) Pty Ltd*, above.

[43] *Re International Bulk Commodities Ltd* [1993] Ch. 77.

[44] See also Gabriel Moss Q.C. "Administration Orders for Foreign Companies" (1993) 6 Insolvency Intelligence 19; (1994) 7 Insolvency Intelligence 33; Dicey and Morris, pp. 1158–1159; Smart, *Cross-Border Insolvency* (2nd ed., 1998), pp. 130–136.

[45] [1992] B.C.L.C. 621. See below, para. 25–074.

[46] Insolvency Act 1986, s. 426(5), (11), see below, para. 25–068.

[47] [1992] B.C.L.C. 621 at 624.

[48] s. 735(1)(a) and (b) applied to the Insolvency Act 1986 by the Insolvency Act 1986, s. 251.

It was seen in the context of discussion of administrative receivers[49] that it had been emphasised in *Re International Bulk Commodities Ltd*[50] that the definitions in section 735 apply unless the contrary intention appears. And there it was held that a receiver appointed in respect of a foreign company could be an administrative receiver since the provisions of the Insolvency Act 1986, which deal with the latter, could be construed as yielding such a contrary intention. Can a similar argument be mounted in relation to the making of an administration order?

Supporting a negative conclusion would be an argument to the effect that, since an administrator is solely a creature of English legislation, the administration procedure should apply only to companies created by that country's legislation. Here there is a contrast with the position of an administrative receiver since the latter's status originates in a contract and the English legislation merely ascribes particular powers to him.[51] It is, however, difficult to accept this argument with complete confidence because it tends to bypass the proper question which should be posed. That question is whether or not Parliament intended the power to appoint an administrator to exist in respect of foreign companies and the answer to that question must be deduced from the proper construction of the relevant statutory provisions.[52]

If one considers the purposes for the achievement of which an administration order can be made, it might be thought that an intention to extend such an order to foreign companies is indicated. For example, an order can be made to secure the survival of the company and the whole or any part of the undertaking as a going concern.[53] If we assume that the English court is presented with a problem concerning a company incorporated in Liberia which carries on all its business in England and the survival of the company could be secured by the making of the order, why should such an order not be capable of being made? There is little doubt that the English court does have jurisdiction to wind up the company, at least if there are creditors here who will receive a benefit if the company is wound up, since by doing business here the company will be regarded as having a sufficient connection with England for winding-up jurisdiction to be properly exercised.[54] Since one of the grounds on which an administration order may be made is to achieve a more advantageous realisation of the company's assets than would be effected on a winding-up, it is hard to see what reason of policy there may be for denying jurisdiction to make the administration order. The opposite conclusion would mean that the company may be killed but not cured, a proposition that does not accord with common sense.

---

[49] See above, paras 25–041 to 25–043.
[50] [1993] Ch. 77.
[51] *Re International Bulk Commodities Ltd* [1993] Ch. 77 at 85–86.
[52] *ibid.* at 84–85.
[53] Insolvency Act 1986, s. 8(3), see above, Chap. 23.
[54] See, *e.g. Re A Company (No. 00359 of 1987)* [1988] Ch. 210; *Re A Company (No. 003102 of 1991), ex p. Nyckeln Finance Co. Ltd* [1991] B.C.L.C. 539; *Re Paramount Airways Ltd* [1993] Ch. 223.

The foregoing conclusion is, perhaps, reinforced when one considers **25–047** that, according to *Re Dallhold Estates (U.K.) Pty Ltd*,[55] the English court has "indirect" jurisdiction to make the order on a request by a court of a designated country.[56] While one can accept that a court can do indirectly that which it has power to do directly, the proposition that the court may do indirectly what it cannot do directly is much more difficult to support even when, as in this case, that conclusion is expressed as the proper interpretation of relevant provisions of an English statute.[57]

If the above views are accepted, it is possible to argue (though **25–048** admittedly, in the light of the authorities, with some hesitation) that the definition of company in section 735 of the Companies Act 1985 does not apply since the provisions of the Insolvency Act 1986 which relate to administration orders reveal a contrary intention, *viz.* that such orders may be made in respect of a foreign unregistered company. Whether such an order will be made will depend on whether it is appropriate in the circumstances of the particular case.[58]

(b) Recognition of foreign appointment

Procedures of the same general nature as the administration procedure exist **25–049** in the insolvency laws of other countries. Particularly well-known in this respect is the procedure established by Chapter 11 of the United States Bankruptcy Code.[59] In *Felixstowe Dock and Railway Co. v. U.S. Lines Inc.*,[60] a U.S. corporation carrying on business worldwide, and which was registered in England under the Companies Act 1985,[61] was undergoing re-organisation in the United States pursuant to Chapter 11. In the United States, Chapter 11 proceedings involve an automatic stay restraining all persons, including those located outside the United States, from commencing or continuing proceedings against the corporation. The claimants, two English companies and a Dutch company, reacted to this by seeking and obtaining, in England, Mareva injunctions[62] against the company to prevent it removing its assets from the jurisdiction. The U.S. corporation applied to have the Mareva injunction set aside so as to permit the English assets to be transferred to the United States, and administered as part of the Chapter 11 scheme. This application was refused.

---

[55] [1992] B.C.L.C. 621.
[56] Insolvency Act 1986, s. 426(5), (11).
[57] *ibid.*
[58] See above, Chap. 23.
[59] Chap. 11 procedure is described in *Felixstowe Dock and Railway Co. v. U.S. Lines Inc.* [1989] Q.B. 360 at 366–370; Boshkoff in Fletcher (ed.), *Cross-Border Insolvency: Comparative Dimensions* (1990), pp. 60–64.
[60] [1989] Q.B. 360. For comment on this case see Ziegel in Lian *et al.* (eds.), *Current Developments in International Banking and Corporate Financial Operations* (1989), p. 313; Westbrook in Clarke (ed.), *Current Issues in Insolvency Law* (1991), p. 27; Morse in Rajak (ed.), *Insolvency Law: Theory and Practice* (1993), pp. 217–220; Dicey and Morris, *The Conflict of Laws* (13th ed. 2000), pp. 1143–1144; Smart, *Cross-Border Insolvency* (2nd ed., 1998), pp. 177–178; Fletcher, *Insolvency in Private International Law* (1999), pp. 181–185.
[61] s. 691.
[62] Now "freezing" injunctions: CPR, Pt. 25 1(1)(f). See above, Chap. 13.

25–050   According to Hirst J., "the court would in principle always wish to co-operate in every proper way with an order like the present [United States] one made by a court in a friendly jurisdiction".[63] He was urged to accept a proposition to the effect that since an English court possessed jurisdiction over an English company in similar circumstances, it should concede to the American court a jurisdiction which it claimed for itself—the so-called principle of comity or reciprocity.[64] Hirst J. was not, however, prepared to discharge the injunction by reference to this principle.[65] Discharge of the injunction would, in his view, have caused substantial prejudice to the claimants: the re-organisation of the company envisaged in the Chapter 11 proceedings involved its discontinuing activities in the European market and in such circumstances, had the assets been repatriated to the United States, the claimants could have derived no real benefit since the assets would have been used to keep the company alive and as a going concern to pursue activities in the United States only. Hirst J. further doubted whether, in a converse set of circumstances, a United States court would have released assets situated in the United States with a view to their being repatriated to England for utilisation in an English administration procedure.[66] It may be, however, that the critical point which led Hirst J. to maintain the injunction was what he regarded as the discriminatory nature of the Chapter 11 proceedings in that case, *i.e.* the benefiting of American creditors at the expense of European creditors.[67]

25–051   In the light of the decision in *Felixstowe Dock and Railway Co. v. U.S. Lines Inc.*,[68] the grounds on which recognition may be accorded to an appointment under a foreign law of a person analogous to an administrator, or to a procedure analogous to an administration procedure (in

---

[63] [1989] Q.B. 360 at 376. See also *Barclays Bank plc v. Homan* (1993) B.C.L.C. 680, Hoffmann J. and CA; *Hughes v. Hannover Ruckversicherungs-Aktiengesellschaft* [1997] 1 B.C.L.C. 497, 520, CA.

[64] See *Travers v. Holley* [1953] P. 246, CA; *Re Trepca Mines* [1960] 1 W.L.R. 1273, CA; *Société Co-operative Sidematal v. Titan International Ltd* [1966] 1 Q.B. 828; *Schemmer v. Property Resources Ltd* [1975] Ch. 273.

[65] It is generally said that this principle is relevant only in the context of decrees of a foreign court affecting matrimonial status (see *Travers v. Holley*, above) where it is now no longer relevant as a result of statute: see Family Law Act 1986. The principle was rejected in the context of liquidation in *Re Trepca Mines*, above.

[66] *Felixstowe Dock and Railway Co. v. U.S. Lines Inc.* [1989] Q.B. 360 at 389, *per* Hirst J. But see, for the opposite view, Westbrook, above.

[67] [1989] Q.B. 360 at 386, where Hirst J. makes it clear that he might have lifted the English Mareva injunction had the U.S. proceedings been "ordinary winding-up proceedings under which U.S. L.'s assets would be collected together and distributed totally and rateably amongst all their creditors", and see also at 388F. *cf. Banque Indosuez S.A. v. Ferromet Resources Inc.* [1993] B.C.L.C. 112 where it appeared that the claims of the bank could be sufficiently protected in Chap. 11 proceedings in Texas, thereby justifying the lifting of injunctions obtained in England. See also *Barclays Bank plc v. Homan* [1993] B.C.L.C. 680, Hoffmann J. and CA; *Grupo Torras S.A. v. Sheikh Fahad Mohammed Al Sabah* [1996] 1 Lloyd's Rep. 7, 11, CA; *Mithras Management Ltd v. New Visions Entertainment Corp.* (1992) 90 D.L.R. (4th) 726; *Fournier v. The Ship "Margaret Z"* [1997] 1 N.Z.L.R. 629. Note that an English administration which discriminated against U.S. creditors would probably not be enforced in the U.S.: s. 304(c)(1) of the Bankruptcy Code (U.S.).

[68] [1989] Q.B. 360.

those cases where section 426 of the Insolvency Act 1986 does not apply), remain unclear. Outside section 426, reciprocity, in the specific sense of recognition in England of a foreign jurisdiction claimed on the same or similar basis as is claimed in English law, will probably not be sufficient.[69] It is conceivable that the law might develop on the basis of an analogy with the recognition of foreign liquidations, though it must be recognised that the law on the latter topic is undeveloped,[70] and that the analogy is by no means exact. Pursuing the analogy recognition might be accorded, in principle, to a company rescue scheme instigated in the country where the company is incorporated provided there is no discrimination against English creditors.[71] Also by analogy with winding-up, an English court might regard the courts of the place of incorporation as having principal control but nevertheless conduct an ancillary winding-up of the company in relation to its English assets in accordance with English law, while at the same time working in harmony with the foreign court at the place of incorporation.[72] Subject to this, it is also conceivable that an English court will accord recognition to a rescue procedure taking place in a country other than the country of incorporation but which is nevertheless recognised in the latter country.[73] This might be particularly likely if virtually all of the business of the company is carried on in the former country.[74] A case for recognition may also be made if the procedure is instigated in a country where the company's central management and control is exercised, particularly if the company is incorporated elsewhere for reasons of legal or commercial convenience[75] and there is no likelihood of any action being taken, in relation to the company, in the country where it is incorporated.[76] Lastly, the case for recognition is relatively strong where the company itself petitions for an order analogous to an administration order in a country other than that in which it is incorporated since in such a case it can clearly be said that the company has submitted to the jurisdiction of the courts of that country.[77]

The principal restraint on the development of recognition rules in this, **25–052** as in other areas of cross-border insolvency law, is, perhaps, a desire to avoid discrimination against English creditors which might occur if the rescue procedure is accorded full recognition and assets are repatriated to the country where that procedure is being administered.[78] But if that

---

[69] See para. 25–050, above.

[70] See Dicey and Morris, pp. 1141–1144; Smart, *Cross-Border Insolvency* (2nd ed., 1998), Chaps 6, 7, 8, 12, 14; Fletcher, *The Law of Insolvency* (2nd ed., 1996), pp. 758–765; Fletcher, *Insolvency in Private International Law* (1999), pp. 165–185 and Chap. 4.

[71] *Cf. Felixstowe Dock and Railway Co. v. U.S. Lines Inc.* [1989] Q.B. 360.

[72] *ibid.* See too *Banque Indosuez SA v. Ferromet Resources Inc.* [1993] B.C.L.C. 112.

[73] Smart, p. 167 *cf. Armitage v. Att.-Gen.* [1906] P. 135.

[74] See, *e.g.* Smart, pp. 177–178.

[75] *Cf. Re A Company (No. 00359 of 1987)* [1988] Ch. 210.

[76] See *Re Vocalion (Foreign) Ltd* [1932] 2 Ch. 196; *Re Azoff-Don Commercial Bank* [1954] Ch. 315; *Re Latreefers Inc., The Times,* March 15, 2000, CA.

[77] Smart, pp. 177–178. See also *Re International Power Industries Inc.* [1985] B.C.L.C. 128; *Barclays Bank plc v. Homan* [1993] B.C.L.C. 680, Hoffmann J. and CA.

[78] *Felixstowe Dock and Railway Co. v. U.S. Lines Inc.* [1989] Q.B. 360.

obstacle can be overcome, there is no policy reason why recognition should be denied, in principle, as opposed to being ruled out in the circumstances of a particular case.[79] Where recognition is accorded on whatever ground, the power which it is sought, under foreign law, to exercise in England must be consistent with English law.[80]

25–053   If the foreign rescue procedure originates in a country which is a designated country for the purposes of section 426 of the Insolvency Act 1986, the English court may offer assistance to the foreign court or appointee to the extent permitted by that section.[81] This question is discussed below.[82]

8. ENGLISH RECEIVERS AND ADMINISTRATORS ACTING ABROAD

25–054 A receiver, whether holding office by virtue of a private appointment or by way of appointment by the court, or an administrator may seek to exercise his powers in a jurisdiction outside the United Kingdom. This section attempts to identify the difficulties which such appointees may face, largely by way of reference to receivers,[83] though some difficulties of the same or similar nature will also be faced by administrators.

25–055   In principle, a receiver appointed under English law in relation to the property of an English company which is situated in a foreign country and in consequence of the company having created a charge which, as created, is a floating charge will be free to exercise his powers in the foreign country only to the extent that the foreign country recognises the charge as valid and effective and regards the receiver as having the power so to act.[84]

25–056   Initially, a distinction must be drawn between the question whether, as a matter of English law, the charge extends to property abroad and the very different question whether the charge will be recognised in the foreign jurisdiction.[85] As to the first question, it is not in doubt that an English floating charge usually covers the assets of a company both present and future, irrespective of where the assets are located, so that the charge will extend to foreign assets. Thus, in *British South Africa Co. v. De Beers Consolidated Mines Ltd*,[86] it was held that an English

---

[79] *Cf. Re Bank of Credit and Commerce International SA* [1992] B.C.L.C. 579; *Re Bank of Credit and Commerce International SA (No. 4)* [1995] 1 B.C.L.C. 362; *Re Bank of Credit and Commerce International SA (No. 10)* [1997] Ch. 213.

[80] *Cf.* Insolvency Act 1986, s. 72(1).

[81] *Re Dallhold Estates (U.K.) Pty Ltd* [1992] B.C.L.C. 621; *Re Bank of Credit and Commerce International SA* [1993] B.C.C. 787.

[82] See below, paras 25–066 *et seq.*

[83] Dicey and Morris, pp. 1155–1157; Picarda, pp. 494–495; Collins (1975) 27 I.C.L.Q. 691, 700–701, reprinted in *Essays in International Litigation and the Conflict of Laws* (1994), p. 433.

[84] Insolvency Act 1986, ss. 72(1), 426(2).

[85] See Companies Act 1985, s. 398(3) which envisages that in the case of charges registered in the United Kingdom "further proceedings may be necessary to make the charge valid or effective according to the law of the country where the property is situate". On the recognition of English floating charges in France, see Dahan, 1996 Clunet 381.

[86] [1910] 1 Ch. 353, rev'd. on other grounds; [1912] A.C. 52.

debenture which purported to create a charge over all the property and assets of an English company operated in relation to the company's land abroad as an agreement to charge the land and thus was a valid equitable security in the eyes of English law. In *Re Anchor Line (Henderson Brothers) Ltd*[87] an English shipping company owned property located in Scotland. It executed a floating charge in Scotland over all of its undertaking, property and assets in favour of a Scottish bank, which charge was registered in England. At the time, floating charges were unknown to Scots law, which would give no effect to them.[88] When the company went into liquidation and its assets were sold off, the question arose whether, in the distribution of the proceeds, effect should be given to the floating charge to the extent that the proceeds of sale represented Scottish property. The question was answered in the affirmative and in consequence those proceeds were payable to the charge-holder. In effect, therefore, in consequence of the charge being governed by English law the English court may enforce it in personam even if it is not a valid and effective charge by the *lex situs*.[89]

Whatever the effect of the charge may be as a matter of English law, **25–057** the charge may nonetheless not be recognised as valid and effective by the *lex situs* of the assets against which the receiver wishes to enforce it. The foreign jurisdiction may take exception to the charge on a number of grounds.

First, a receiver may be denied capacity to sue in the foreign **25–058** jurisdiction either because his status is not recognised as such, or because his status, as a matter of English law, is different to that which he would possess under the law of the foreign country. Thus American courts have often said that, although it is incumbent on them as a matter of comity to enforce valid foreign voluntary assignments, such comity does not extend to enforcement when such enforcement prejudices U.S. creditors.[90] Here there is a tendency in the American courts to confuse the English notion of a receiver with the notion of a court-appointed receiver in bankruptcy proceedings, which works to the disadvantage of receivers who seek to operate in the United States.[91] A less parochial attitude may operate in other foreign jurisdictions. Thus, in *Re C.A. Kennedy Co. Ltd and Stibbe-Monk Ltd*,[92] an Ontario court was faced with

[87] [1937] Ch. 483.
[88] Recognition was permitted by Companies (Floating Charges and Receivers) (Scotland) Act 1972. See now Companies Act 1985, ss. 462–467; Insolvency Act 1986, ss. 50–71.
[89] See also *Re Commonwealth Agricultural Services Engineers Ltd* [1928] S.A.S.R. 343; Collins (1978) 27 I.C.L.Q. 691, 700–701, reprinted in *Essays in International Litigation and the Conflict of Laws* (1994), p. 433.
[90] See the discussion of these cases in *Re CA Kennedy Co. Ltd and Stibbe-Monk Ltd* (1976) 74 D.L.R. (3d) 87 at 95–96. See also Restatement, Second, The Conflict of Laws, s. 406, comment (a); Collins, (1978) 27 I.C.L.Q. 691, 708–710, reprinted in *Essays in International Litigation and the Conflict of Laws* (1994) p. 433, suggesting that a more liberal attitude is displayed by an American court in *Clarkson Co. Ltd and Rapid Data Corporation v. Rockwell International* Supp. 792 (1977). cf. *Larkins v. NUM* [1985] I.R. 670, 683–684; *Derby & Co. Ltd v. Weldon (Nos. 3 and 4)* [1990] Ch. 65, 84–86, 94, 96, CA; *Derby & Co. Ltd v. Weldon (No. 6)* [1990] 1 W.L.R. 1139, 1150, CA.
[91] Collins, 708–709, p.1.
[92] (1976) 74 D.L.R. (3d) 67.

competing claims to a debt owed to a company which had given a floating charge over its assets to an English bank. The debt was claimed by a judgment creditor under a Quebec judgment debt and by the receiver appointed by the bank. The court held that the priority of these competing claims had to be determined by the *lex situs* of the debt (asset) which was the law of Ontario. Expressly rejecting the somewhat hostile American attitude, the court accorded recognition to the appointment of the English receiver. Such recognition accords with the proper analysis of the receiver's status in English law. If, for conflict of laws purposes, a receiver could be viewed as an officer of the company, as a matter of principle, his powers and capacity to act should depend on the law of the place of incorporation.[93] It is arguable that, for conflict of laws' purposes, the receiver is an officer of the company although the Court of Appeal in England has held that under English domestic law he is not.[94] Moreover, a receiver, at least prior to liquidation, is an agent of the company[95] and his agency should be recognised, *e.g.* by analogy to the general recognition of a liquidator's agency.

25–059   A second and fatal difficulty is where the charge is repugnant to the law of the place where the assets of the company, claimed by the receiver, are situated. Thus, in *Carse v. Coppen*,[96] it was conceded by the parties and accepted by the court that, since floating charges were at that time repugnant to Scots law, a Scottish court could not regard an English floating charge created by a Scottish company as affecting Scottish property. Indeed a majority of the Court of Session went further and held that the company could not create a valid charge over its English property either.[97]

25–060   A third problem presents itself where the charge is ineffective because of a failure to comply with mandatory requirements of the *lex situs*, particularly a registration requirement. Prudence demands that where charges are created over the foreign property of a company, such charges should be registered in the country or countries where the property is situated if this is required by the law of that foreign country,[98] a course which is particularly difficult if the property has moved from one country to another in the time between the creation of the charge and the attempt to enforce it in a different foreign country. In *Luckins v. Highway Motel (Caernarvon) Pty. Ltd*,[99] a company incorporated in Victoria, which carried on the business of coach tour operator, conducted tours which passed through Western Australia where debts were incurred by the company for, amongst other things, food and accommodation. The company had created a floating charge over all its assets

---

[93] See Dicey and Morris, pp. 1152–1155.

[94] See Collins, p. 707. The English Court of Appeal decision referred to is *Re. B. Johnson & Co.* [1955] Ch. 634, CA.

[95] See above, Chap. 11. After liquidation, a receiver no longer has his agency, but retains his power to dispose of its property.

[96] 1951 S.C. 233.

[97] *Cf. Re Anchor Line (Henderson Brothers) Ltd* [1937] Ch. 483. The position in Scots law relating to floating charges was subsequently changed by legislation and is now contained in the Insolvency Act 1986.

[98] See s.398(3) of the Companies Act 1985 referred to in para. 25–056 above.

[99] (1975) 133 C.L.R. 164.

wherever situated, the charge being registered in Victoria but not in Western Australia. Subsequently the charge crystallised and a receiver was appointed in Victoria. A Western Australian creditor obtained a judgment against the company in Western Australia and sought to execute that judgment through seizure of a bus belonging to the company which was then situated in Western Australia. The receiver claimed that the bus was subject to the receivership. The High Court of Australia held that, if the charge was validly created over the bus by the law of the State where it was situated at the time of such creation, the charge was in principle capable of being recognised in Western Australia.[1] But such recognition was subject to compliance with the mandatory requirements of Western Australian law. By incurring various debts in Western Australia, the company could be held to be doing business there. This being the case, there was an obligation to register the charge in accordance with Western Australian legislation. It is, of course, implicit in this conclusion that, were there no obligation to register the charge in that State, the charge would have been valid and effective over property situated there at the time when it was sought to enforce the charge.[2]

Where the charge does not gain recognition in the foreign country **25–061** where the assets are situated, a further consequence is that the English court will not, at the instance of the debenture-holders, restrain a creditor from bringing proceedings to recover a debt in a foreign country out of assets which are situated there. This much appears from *Liverpool Marine Credit Co. v. Hunter*[3] where it was held that mortgagees of a ship were not entitled in English proceedings to prevent an English unsecured creditor of the owner of the ship from arresting the ship in New Orleans since the mortgage would not be recognised under the law of Louisiana. This decision was applied in *Re Maudslay, Sons & Field*,[4] where an English company created a charge over its assets which included a sum of money owed to it by a French company. A receiver was appointed by debenture-holders. An English creditor of the company sought to attach the debt owed by the French company in France, the response to which was an action in England by the debenture-holders to restrain the creditor from so proceeding. According to French law, the debt could only be charged effectively as against the French company if the charge was registered in France and notice of it was given to the French company. No such registration or notice was effected. The court refused to make an order in favour of the debenture-holders. The fact that the receiver was appointed could not affect the position which would normally prevail and in which the creditor would be free to pursue a claim in France since, in the absence of registration and notice required by French law, the receiver had not perfected his title to the assets according to French law.

---

[1] *ibid.* at 174–175.
[2] *ibid.*
[3] (1867) L.R.4 Eq. 62; (1868) 3 Ch. App. 479.
[4] [1900] 1 Ch. 602.

25–062   Where a creditor has obtained an English judgment against the company prior to the appointment of a receiver, if the charge subsequently crystallises and a receiver is appointed, the judgment will be unenforceable against the company in England.[5] In such circumstances the creditor may seek to enforce the judgment in a foreign country where the company has assets. The courts of that country may be prepared to recognise the judgment and enforce it despite the existence of the English charge, either because that country does not recognise floating charges as such, or, if it does recognise them, because the charge has not been registered as required by that country's law.[6]

25–063   Lastly, in the case of a receiver appointed by the court, a foreign jurisdiction may decline to recognise a receiver's appointment because it is interlocutory[7] or more generally because the appointment is made pursuant to a rule of English law which is regarded by the foreign court as being penal in nature.[8]

25–064   An English receiver or administrator may seek to take legal action abroad with a view to giving greater effect to the receivership or administration of the company. In *Barclays Bank plc v. Homan*,[9] an English registered company, Maxwell Communications Corporation plc, was subject to an administration order in England. The company had repaid to Barclays Bank, shortly before the administration order was made, the sum of U.S. $30 million, payment being made to the bank's New York branch. This payment constituted a potentially voidable preference under section 239(4) of the Insolvency Act 1986, since it put the bank into a better position than it would otherwise have been in the event of the company being liquidated. According to section 239(5) of the 1986 Act, a court is not to make an order for the repayment unless the debtor company was influenced by a desire to put the creditor in a better position. The bank took the view that it might be able to rely on this defence.

The administrators brought proceedings against the bank in the United States (where there were also proceedings under Chapter 11 of the United States Bankruptcy Code and where the principal assets of the company were situated) with a view to recovering the U.S. $30 million. Section 547 of the United States Bankruptcy Code has much the same effect as section 239 of the English Insolvency Act 1986 as regards the definition of a preference but does not contain a provision equivalent to section 239(5) of the 1986 Act. Accordingly, in U.S. proceedings, the intention of the debtor company in making the payment would be irrelevant. The bank therefore

---

[5] *Norton v. Yates* [1906] 1 K.B. 112; *Davey & Co. v. Williamson & Sons* [1898] 2 Q.B. 194; and see above, Chap. 17.

[6] See the decision of the French Cour de Cassation of October 19, 1977 in (1978) Rev. Crit. DIP. 617. See also, Dahan, 1996 Clunet 381. *cf. Mitchell v. Carter* [1997] 1 B.C.L.C. 673, Blackburne J. and CA; *Mitchell v. Buckingham International plc (No. 2)* [1998] 2 B.C.L.C. 369, Harman J. and CA

[7] *Larkins v. NUM* [1985] I.R. 671. See above, para. 25–039.

[8] *ibid. cf. Schemmer v. Property Resources Ltd* [1975] Ch. 273, above, paras 25–033 to 25–038.

[9] [1993] B.C.L.C. 680, Hoffmann J. and CA. See also *Re Bank of Credit and Commerce International SA* [1994] 1 W.L.R. 709, CA.

sought, in these English proceedings, to restrain the administrators from making this claim in the United States.

The Court of Appeal held that the principles to be applied in determining whether an injunction should be granted were those generally applicable to determining the issue of whether a plaintiff should be prevented, by order, from proceeding in a foreign jurisdiction. According to these principles,[10] if the only issue was whether an English or a foreign court was the most appropriate forum for the action, the foreign court should decide it on the principle of *forum non conveniens* and the English court should not interfere. But if the English court concluded that pursuit of the action in the foreign court would be vexatious and oppressive and that England was the natural forum, it could properly grant an injunction restraining the claimant from pursuing the foreign proceedings. Whether the action abroad was vexatious or oppressive depended on the possible injustice to the defendant if the injunction was not granted and the possible injustice to the claimant if it was: in determining the outcome, the English court had to balance these factors.

The bank had argued that it would be at a disadvantage in the United States because of the absence of a provision equivalent to section 239(5) of the Insolvency Act 1986 in section 547 of the United States Bankruptcy Code, and that this rendered proceedings in the United States vexatious or oppressive. This contention was rejected. The disadvantage to the bank had to be balanced against the advantage to the English administrator in proceeding in the United States on behalf of all the company's creditors. Although United States law was different from English law, there was nothing inherently oppressive about the difference, particularly in light of the fact that United States law might be more favourable to the bank in other respects. Accordingly, the administrators were free to pursue the claim in the United States.[11]

Were a receiver to seek to bring proceedings abroad with a view to **25–065** obtaining an advantage under a foreign law, the same principles would presumably apply.

9. JUDICIAL ASSISTANCE

Reference has already been made to the duty of mutual assistance which **25–066** exists between courts within the United Kingdom in matters of insolvency law, the definition of which includes the law relating to receivers and administrators.[12] The relevant section of the Insolvency Act 1986,

---

[10] Established in *SNI Aerospatiale v. Lee Kui Jak* [1987] A.C. 871. And see *Airbus Industrie GIE v. Patel* [1999] 1 A.C. 119.

[11] Other factors relevant to the exercise of the court's discretion were that an injunction might have been wholly ineffective because the examiner on behalf of M.C.C. could have been authorised by the U.S. court to bring the preference claim and that the *forum non conveniens* point could have been raised by the bank in the U.S. Bankruptcy Court proceedings. In fact the U.S. declined to apply U.S. law.

[12] Insolvency Act 1986, s. 426(1),(4) which will be amended if the Insolvency Bill 2000 is enacted in its current form.

namely section 426, goes beyond the intra-United Kingdom dimension and needs further consideration.[13]

25–067   The key provisions of section 426 as applied to international cases are subsections (4) and (5):

> "(4) The courts having jurisdiction in relation to insolvency law in any part of the United Kingdom shall assist the courts having the corresponding jurisdiction in any other part of the United Kingdom or any relevant country or territory.
>
> (5) For the purposes of subsection (4) a request made to a court in any part of the United Kingdom or in a relevant country or territory is authority for the court to which the request is made to apply, in relation to any matters in the request, the insolvency law which is applicable by either court in relation to comparable matters falling within its jurisdiction. In exercising its discretion under this subsection a court shall have regard, in particular, to the rules of private international law."

A number of comments must be made on the scope of, and difficulties in, these subsections.

(a) Territorial scope

25–068   Although section 426(4) seems to establish an obligation to provide relevant assistance, in international cases (as opposed to intra-United Kingdom cases) the obligation only extends to a "relevant country or territory". Relevant country or territory means, for these purposes, any of the Channel Islands,[14] the Isle of Man and any country or territory designated for the purpose of the subsection by the Secretary of State. Orders have been made designating various countries.[15] The provisions, in terms, impose an obligation on English courts to provide assistance to any relevant country or territory and do not require proof of any reciprocity. It would be in accordance with the policy of the legislation that in deciding whether to designate any particular country or territory,

---

[13] For general discussion, see Dicey and Morris, pp. 1144–1151; Fletcher, *The Law of Insolvency* (2nd ed. 1996) pp. 782–789; Fletcher, *Insolvency in Private International Law* (1999), Chap. 4; Smart, *Cross-Border Insolvency* (2nd ed. 1998), Chap. 15; Woloniecki (1986) 35 I.C.L.Q. 644; Polonsky (1996) 113 S.A.L.J. 109. For further potential for international co-operation, see below, para. 25–025 and below, Chap. 26, where the European Union Regulation on Insolvency Proceedings and the UNCITRAL Model Law on Cross-Border Insolvency are discussed.

[14] The relevant provisions of s. 426 may be extended to any of the Channel Islands thus enabling courts in any jurisdiction to which the section is extended to provide assistance to English courts in matters of receivership, administration or liquidation: Insolvency Act 1986, s. 442; see S.I. 1989 No. 2409 extending s. 426(4), (5), (10) and (11) or the 1986 Act, with modifications, to Guernsey: see *Re Seagull Manufacturing Co. Ltd* [1993] Ch. 345, CA. As to Jersey, see Dessain (1998) 11 Insolvency Intelligence 25.

[15] S.I. 1986 No. 2123 designates Anguilla, Australia, The Bahamas, Bermuda, Botswana, Canada, Cayman Islands, Falkland Islands, Gibraltar, Hong Kong, Ireland, Montserrat, New Zealand, St Helena, Turks and Caicos Islands, Tuvalu and the Virgin Islands. S.I. 1996 No. 253 designates Malaysia and South Africa. S.I 1998 No. 2766 designates Brunei-Darussallam.

the Secretary of State should have regard to the probability of the English courts obtaining assistance from the courts of that country or territory in comparable matters.[16]

(b) Duty to assist arises between courts

The duty of assistance under section 426 arises only as between courts. **25–069** Accordingly, before the English court can act it must have received a request from a relevant foreign court so to act,[17] so that a foreign receiver or administrator (or liquidator for that matter) cannot approach the English court directly. It seems likely that any foreign court in which insolvency proceedings have been commenced (provided it is in a designated country or territory) may request assistance though the English court may, in its discretion, decline the assistance requested if the foreign country is not recognised by the English court as possessing, say, the authority to appoint a receiver or an administrator.[18]

(c) Meaning of "insolvency law"

Section 426(5) provides that a request from a foreign court is authority **25–070** for the English court to apply, in relation to the matters specified in the request, either English insolvency law or the insolvency law of the requesting court in relation to comparable matters.[19] For these purposes, "insolvency law" means, in relation to England and Wales, provision made by or under the Insolvency Act 1986 as well as certain provisions of the Company Directors Disqualification Act 1986.[20] The expression thus includes the English law relating to receivership and administration.[21] In relation to any relevant country or territory the expression means so much of the law of that country or territory as corresponds to the provisions referred to above.[22] In *Hughes v. Hannover Ruckversicherungs-Aktiengesellschaft*[23] it was held by the Court of Appeal

---

[16] See *Hughes v. Hannover Ruckversicherungs-Aktiengeselleschaft* [1997] 1 B.C.L.C. 497, 510–511, CA; *England v. Smith, Re Southern Equities Corp. Ltd* [2000] 2 B.C.L.C. 21, CA.

[17] It must be emphasised that s. 426 only extends to incoming request for assistance. It does not enable an English court to request assistance from a court in a relevant country or territory: *cf. McIsaac & Anor, Petitioners* [1994] B.C.C. 410 Other more generally applicable co-operative procedures may become relevant in insolvency cases; see *e.g.* Evidence (Proceedings in other Jurisdictions) Act 1975; *Re International Power Industries NV* [1985] B.C.L.C. 128.

[18] See below, para. 25–073.

[19] *Re Dallhold Estates (U.K.) Pty Ltd* [1992] B.C.L.C. 621; *Re Bank of Credit and Commerce International SA (No. 9)* [1994] 3 All E.R. 764, revd. in part, but not on this point, [1994] 1 W.L.R. 708, CA; *Re Focus Insurance Co. Ltd* [1997] 1 B.C.L.C. 219; *Re Business City Express Ltd* [1997] 2 B.C.L.C. 510; *Hughes v. Hannover Ruckversicherungs-Aktiengesellschaft* [1997] 1 B.C.L.C. 497, CA; *Re J.N. Taylor Finance Pty Ltd* [1999] 2 B.C.L.C. 256; *England v. Smith, Re Southern Equities Corp. Ltd* [2000] 2 B.C.L.C. 21 at 53, CA.

[20] Insolvency Act 1986, s. 426(10)(a) which will be amended by Insolvency Bill 2000, Sched. 4, Pt. II, para. 16(3) if it is enacted in its current form. See too, Companies Act 1985, s. 183.

[21] *Re Dallhold Estates (U.K.) Pty Ltd* [1992] B.C.L.C. 621.

[22] Insolvency Act 1986, s. 426(10)(d).

[23] [1997] 1 B.C.L.C. 497, CA.

that for the purposes of section 426(5) the above definitions of insolvency law were exhaustive.[24] The court indicated that section 426(4)
which refers to "courts having *jurisdiction in relation to insolvency law in
any part of the United Kingdom*[25] only served, in its use of the expression
"insolvency law", to identify the court on which the obligation to provide
assistance was imposed.[26] It did not indicate that the English court could
only apply insolvency law as defined for the purposes of section 426(5).[27]
As section 426(5) added to rather than restricted the power to assist
under section 426(4), the latter section enable the English court when
requested for assistance to exercise its own general jurisdiction and
powers,[28] whilst section 426(5) enabled the court to apply the insolvency
law of England and Wales, as defined in the Insolvency Act 1986[29] or so
much of the law of a relevant country or territory as corresponds to it.[30]

25–071   The reference to "insolvency law" is apt to include both substantive
and procedural insolvency law.[31] When, however, an English court is
requested to provide assistance in the form of application of relevant
principles of foreign insolvency law, issues may arise as to when a rule of
foreign insolvency law "corresponds"[32] to a relevant provision of English
insolvency law. First, it has been held by the Court of Appeal that in
discharging the obligation to provide assistance, the court should apply
any principles, practices or discretions that the court requesting the
assistance would apply in exercising its powers under the foreign law.[33]
Application of the law of the requesting court should not be circumscribed by limitations to be found in the corresponding provisions of the
insolvency law of England,[34] unless some principle of English public
policy would be infringed were the foreign law to be applied according to
its terms.[35] Secondly, it follows from the foregoing propositions that

---

[24] *ibid.*, at 516. Thus liquidators could not obtain an order to restrain proceedings
against the company under Insolvency Act 1986, s. 130(2), since that section may not be
used to restrain foreign proceedings and the same territorial limitation was imposed under
Bermudan law, the law of the requesting court: *ibid.*, at 521: see *Re Vocalion (Foreign) Ltd*
[1932] Ch. 196.

[25] Emphasis added.

[26] [1997] 1 B.C.L.C. 497, 516, CA.

[27] *ibid.*, at 516–517.

[28] *ibid.*, at 517. Thus, the court could, but did not in the instant case, restrain foreign
proceedings by invoking its general powers to issue an anti-suit injunction.

[29] Insolvency Act 1986, s. 426(10)(a).

[30] *ibid.*, s. 426(10)(d).

[31] *Re Bank of Credit and Commerce International SA (No. 9)* [1994] 3 All E.R. 764, revd.
in part, but not on this point, [1994] 1 W.L.R., 708, CA.

[32] Insolvency Act 1986 s. 426(10)(a).

[33] *Re Southern Equities Corp. Ltd, England v. Smith,* [2000] 2 B.C.L.C. 21 at 53, CA,
disapproving *Re J.N. Taylor Finance Pty Ltd* [1999] 2 B.C.L.C. 256.

[34] In *Re Southern Equities Corp. Ltd, supra.* it was held that an English court should
accede to a request from the Supreme Court of South Australia see king examination of a
person allegedly concerned with the affairs of a company under Australia Corporations
Law, s. 596B notwithstanding the fact that such an order would not be made under the
corresponding (but different) provision of Insolvency Act 1986, s. 236 because the order
would be regarded as oppressive. Contrast *Re J.N. Taylor Finance Pty Ltd* [1999] 2 B.C.L.C.
256 where such an order under the same section of the Australian Law was denied because
it would not have been granted under s. 236.

[35] *Re Southern Equities Corp. Ltd, supra.*

foreign insolvency law need not be identical to English insolvency law to correspond to it and indeed, it may be possible for an English court to exercise powers under foreign insolvency law which are not available to the court under English law. Thus, in *Re Business City Express Ltd*[36] a request for assistance was received from an Irish court in which the English court was asked to make a scheme of arrangement, entered into in Ireland after a company had gone into examinership there, binding upon English creditors. There was no provision of English law by which this could be done.[37] The court applied Irish law to the creditors without discussing the question of whether Irish law corresponded to any provision made by or under the Insolvency Act 1986. Nonetheless, it seems appropriate in the light of the policy behind section 426[38] to give the expression "corresponds" a broad interpretation. In the particular context of *Re Business City Express Ltd*,[39] it can be readily said that examinership in Irish law corresponds to English administration[40] and that the appointment of an administrator may, but will not necessarily, lead to the approval of a creditor's voluntary arrangement[41] or the sanctioning of a scheme of arrangement.[42] This should surely be enough to enable it to be said that Irish Law "corresponds" to English law. It is, of course, open to the court in any particular case to determine whether it is appropriate, in the light of the matters specified in the request, for the court to exercise its discretion to provide the assistance requested under the relevant foreign law.[43]

(d) Nature of the duty to assist

Section 426(4) requires, in terms, that the English court "shall assist" the **25–072** foreign court which issues the request for assistance. Despite the apparently mandatory tone of this language, the court is not bound to accede to the assistance requested.[44] The correct approach is to consider whether the requested assistance can properly be granted,[45] so that assistance is ultimately a matter for the discretion of the court.[46] In the

[36] [1997] 2 B.C.L.C. 510.

[37] *ibid.*, at 513.

[38] *Re Southern Equities Corp. Ltd, supra.*

[39] [1997] 2 B.C.L.C. 510.

[40] Insolvency Act 1986, Pt II.

[41] *ibid.*, Pt I.

[42] Companies Act 1985, s. 425; Insolvency Act 1986, s. 8(3)(b),(c).

[43] See below.

[44] *Re Dallhold Estates (U.K.) Pty Ltd* [1992] B.C.L.C. 621; *Re Bank of Credit and Commerce International SA (No. 9)* [1994] 3 All E.R. 764, revd. in part, but not on this point, [1994] 1 W.L.R. 708, CA; *Re Focus Insurance Co. Ltd* [1997] 1 B.C.L.C. 219; *Re Business City Express Ltd* [1997] 2 B.C.L.C. 510; *Hughes v. Hannover Ruckversicherungs-Aktiengesellschaft* [1997] 1 B.C.L.C. 497, CA; *Re J.N. Taylor Finance Pty Ltd* [1992] 2 B.C.L.C. 256; *Re Southern Equities Corp. Ltd, England v. Smith* [2000] 2 B.C.L.C. 21, CA.

[45] *Hughes v. Hannover Ruckversicherungs-Aktiengesellschaft* [1997] 1 B.C.L.C. 497, CA; *Re Southern Equities Corp. Ltd, England v. Smith* [2000] 2 B.C.L.C. 21, CA.

[46] *Re Dallhold Estates (U.K.) Pty Ltd* [1992] B.C.L.C. 621; *Re Bank of Credit and Commerce International SA (No. 9)* [1994] 3 All E.R. 764; *Re Focus Insurance Co. Ltd* [1997] 1 B.C.L.C. 219; *Re Business City Express Ltd* [1997] 2 B.C.L.C. 510; *Hughes v. Hanover Ruckversicherungs-Aktiengesellschaft* [1997] 1 B.C.L.C. 447, CA; *Re J.N. Taylor Finance Pty Ltd* [1999] 2 B.C.L.C. 256; *Re Southern Equities Corp. Ltd, England v. Smith* [2000] 2 B.C.L.C. 21, CA.

exercise of its discretion the court will inevitably lean in favour of granting the request,[47] since the philosophy of section 426 is one which favours co-operation with the foreign court.[48] Accordingly, the English court "should exercise its discretion in favour of giving the assistance requested . . . unless there is some good reason for not doing so".[49]

25–073   Where the English court has to decide whether to apply English insolvency law or that of the requesting court pursuant to section 426(5), it is specifically envisaged that the English court is exercising a discretion since the subsection stipulates that in exercising its discretion "the court shall have regard in particular to the rules of private international law". The precise scope of this requirement is not clear. The word "shall" suggests that the provision is mandatory, but the subsection does not say that the English court *must* apply English rules of private international law. The consequence is that the English court can only provide assistance if its private international law rules would otherwise enable it to do so.[50] The use of the phrase "have regard" rather indicates that the English court must, in deciding what assistance to offer, consider the English rules on private international law so as to ascertain what effect these would have in the circumstances of the case.[51] These rules, however, should not necessarily limit the powers of the court if the court nevertheless took the view that it should provide the assistance requested.[52] Interpreting section 426 in a more limited way would be inconsistent with its purpose.[53] It is therefore likely that the relevant rules of private international law will be those which are thought to be particularly significant in the context of cross-border insolvency proceedings. So, for example, if a request for assistance were to be received from a foreign court and the effect of acceding to the request would be to enforce that country's revenue laws in England, the English court might refuse to accede to the request having regard to the well-established rule of private international law that an English court will not enforce a foreign revenue law.[54] A similar view could also be taken if acting

---

[47] *Re Dallhold Estates (U.K.) Pty Ltd* [1992] B.C.L.C. 621; *Re Bank of Credit and Commerce International SA (No. 9)* [1994] 3 All E.R. 764; *Hughes v. Hannover Ruckversicherungs-Aktiengesellschaft* [1997] 1 B.C.L.C. 497, CA; *Re Southern Equities Corp. Ltd, England v. Smith* [2000] 2 B.C.L.C. 21, CA.

[48] See *Re Southern Equities Corp. Ltd, England v. Smith* [2000] 2 B.C.L.C. 21, CA.

[49] *Re Bank of Credit and Commerce International SA (No. 9)* [1994] 3 All E.R. 764 at 785.

[50] *cf. Re Dallhold Estates (U.K.) Pty Ltd* [1992] B.C.L.C. 621.

[51] *ibid.*

[52] *e.g.* if the court did not have personal jurisdiction, in relation to the relief requested. But the court may not give extraterritorial effect to any provision of English insolvency law which is territorially limited to events occurring in England: *Hughes v. Hannover Ruckversicherungs-Aktiengesellschaft* [1997] 1 B.C.L.C. 497, CA. See also *Re Southern Equities Corp. Ltd, England v. Smith* [2000] 2 B.C.L.C. 21, CA.

[53] *Hughes v. Hannover Ruckversicherungs-Aktiengesellschaft* [1997] 1 B.C.L.C. 497, CA; *Re Southern Equities Corp. Ltd, England v. Smith* [2000] 2 B.C.L.C. 21, CA. See also *Re Business City Express Ltd* [1997] 2 B.C.L.C. 510.

[54] *Re Bank of Credit and Commerce International SA (No. 9)* [1994] 3 All E.R. 764 at 783, revd., but not on this point, [1994] 1 W.L.R. 708, CA. See also *Peter Buchanan Ltd v. McVey* [1954] I.R. 89; [1955] A.C. 516n; Smart, *Cross-Border Insolvency* (2nd ed., 1998), pp. 197–206.

pursuant to the request would infringe English public policy,[55] though the English court should be particularly careful before concluding that the law of a relevant country or territory bore this stigma.[56]

(e) Particular examples

In cases where an English court has applied English law at the request of **25–074** a court in a designated country or territory, it has as mentioned above,[57] held that an administration order may be made in respect of a foreign company.[58] Secondly, the English court has been prepared to apply the provisions of the Insolvency Act 1986 concerning transactions at an undervalue[59] when requested so to act by a foreign court,[60] and it seems probable that the other provisions of the 1986 Act which are concerned with the adjustment of prior transactions will also be applied in appropriate cases.[61] Thirdly, it has been held that the provisions of the Insolvency Act 1986 concerned with fraudulent and wrongful trading[62] may be applied under section 426.[63] Fourthly, a request pursuant to section 426 may persuade the court to order examination of an officer of a company under section 236 of the 1986 Act[64] and, where appropriate, the court may also order production of documents.[65] Fifthly, the English court also has the opportunity, in consequence of a request from a court in a designated country or territory, to apply its general powers, *e.g.* to grant an injunction.[66]

Where a court in a designated country or territory requests assistance **25–075** from the English court in the form of application of the law of the designated country or territory, then, normally, the English court should accede to the request, in part, out of considerations of comity and in part because in deciding to designate a country for the purposes of section 426, the Secretary of State will have determined that that country's insolvency law broadly corresponds to the law contained in the Insolvency Act 1986.[67] This consideration had lead the Court of Appeal to make an order requiring examination of a person pursuant to section

---

[55] *Hughes v. Hannover Ruckversicherungs-Aktiengesellschaft* [1997] 1 B.C.L.C. 497 at 518, CA; *RE J.N. Taylor Finance Pty Ltd* [1999] 2 B.C.L.C. 256; *Re Southern Equities Corp. Ltd, England v. Smith* [2000] 2 B.C.L.C. 21, CA.

[56] *Hughes v. Hannover Ruckversicherungs-Aktiengesellschaft* [1997] 1 B.C.L.C. 497 at 518, CA; *Re Southern Equities Corp. Ltd, England v. Smith* [2000] 2 B.C.L.C. 21, CA.

[57] See above, para. 25–046.

[58] *Re Dallhold Estates (U.K.) Pty Ltd* [1992] B.C.L.C. 621.

[59] Insolvency Act 1986, s. 238.

[60] *Re Bank of Credit and Commerce International SA (No. 9)* 1994 3 All E.R. 764, revd., but not on this point, [1994] 1 W.L.R. 708, CA.

[61] Insolvency Act 1986, ss. 239–246, 423–424. See *Jyske Bank (Gibraltar) Ltd v. Spjeldnaes* [1999] 2 B.C.L.C. 101.

[62] Insolvency Act 1986, ss. 212–214.

[63] *Re Bank of Credit and Commerce SA (No. 9)* [1994] 3 All E.R. 764.

[64] See *Re J.N. Taylor Finance Pty Ltd* [1999] 2 B.C.L.C. 256; *Re Southern Equities Corp. Ltd, England v. Smith* [2000] 2 B.C.L.C. 21, CA.

[65] See *Bell Group Finance Pty Ltd v. Bell Group (U.K.) Holdings Ltd* [1996] 1 B.C.L.C. 304. See also *Re Mid East Trading Ltd* [1998] 1 All E.R. 577, CA.

[66] Insolvency Act 1986, s. 426(4); *Hughes v. Hannover Ruckversiche-rungs-Aktiengesellschaft* [1997] 1 B.C.L.C. 497, CA.

[67] *Re Southern Equities Corp. Ltd, England v. Smith* [2000] 2 B.C.L.C. 21, CA.

596B of the Australian Corporations Law, even though such an order would not have been made under the corresponding (but different) provisions of section 236 of the Insolvency Act 1986.[68] And section 426 has also been applied to render a foreign scheme of arrangement binding on English creditors because it would have this binding character under foreign law despite the fact that the scheme could not be made binding under English law.[69] The English court could, of course, refuse the assistance requested if the foreign law relied on constituted a foreign penal law[70] or infringes a principle of English public policy.[71]

(f) Effect of the Insolvency Bill 2000

25–076 In its current form Clause 13(1) of the Insolvency Bill 2000 provides that the Secretary of State may by regulations made with the agreement of the Lord Chancellor make provision which he considers necessary or expedient for the purpose of giving effect, with or without modification, to the "model law on cross-border insolvency", *i.e.* the model law contained in Annex I of the report of the 30th Session of UNCITRAL.[72] The provisions of the UNCITRAL model law are discussed in Chapter 26. For present purposes it is enough to note that the Bill provides that the regulations referred to above may amend any provision of section 426 of the Insolvency Act 1986.[73]

(g) Informal co-operation

25–077 The formal procedures available under section 426 of the Insolvency Act 1986 do not preclude voluntary co-operation between officers appointed under the laws of different countries where a company may be undergoing re-organisation or liquidation. Indeed such co-operation may be of great practical value in "global" insolvencies.[74]

---

[68] *ibid.*, disapproving *Re J.N. Taylor Finance Pty Ltd* [1999] 2 B.C.L.C. 256. See above, para. *cf. Re Focus Insurance Co. Ltd* [1997] 1 B.C.L.C. 219.

[69] *Re Business City Express Ltd* [1997] 2 B.C.L.C. 510.

[70] See *Re Southern Equities Corp. Ltd, England v. Smith* [2000] 2 B.C.L.C. 21, CA. *Cf. Schemmer v. Property Resources Ltd* [1975] Ch. 273; see also *Huntington v. Attrill* [1893] A.C. 150, PC.

[71] *Hughes v. Hannover Ruckversicherungs-Aktiengesellschaft* [1997] 1 B.C.L.C. 497, CA; *Re Southern Equities Corp. Ltd, England v. Smith* [2000] 2 B.C.L.C. 21, CA.

[72] Insolvency Bill 2000, cl. 13(4).

[73] *ibid.*, cl. 13(2)(c). For the purposes of cl. 13 "insolvency law" has the same meaning as in s. 426(10)(a) and (b) of the Insolvency Act 1986, which subsections will be amended if the Insolvency Bill 2000, Sched. 4, Pt. II, para. 16(3) is enacted in its current form.

[74] See *Re Bank of Credit and Commerce International SA* [1992] B.C.L.C. 570; *Re Bank of Credit and Commerce International SA (No. 3)* [1993] B.C.L.C. 106; *Re Bank of Credit and Commerce International SA (No. 10)* [1997] Ch. 213; *Re Maxwell Communications Corporation plc* [1993] 1 W.L.R. 1042; *Barclays Bank plc. v. Homan* [1993] B.C.L.C. 680, Hoffmann J. and CA, *Re Maxwell Communications Corporation plc*, 93 F. 2d 1036 (1996); Fletcher [1997] J.B.L. 471.

CHAPTER 26

INTERNATIONAL GOVERNANCE OF INSOLVENCY PROCEEDINGS—THE EUROPEAN UNION REGULATION ON INSOLVENCY PROCEEDINGS AND THE UNCITRAL MODEL LAW

PART I—THE E.U. REGULATION

1. INTRODUCTION: NATURE AND PURPOSE OF THE REGULATION

In Part I of this chapter the prospective entry into force of the European **26–001** Union Regulation on Insolvency Proceedings will be considered, with particular regard to the impact on receiverships and administration order proceedings in which there is an international dimension.[1] For those already familiar with the principal characteristics of a cross-border insolvency, and the typical problems confronting the insolvency practitioner, the European Union (formerly known as the European Community[2]) introduces a special range of issues and complexities. The fundamental principles of the Union, based upon the concept of a unified internal market, may be implicated in various ways during the course of an international insolvency. Typical problems include: the incompatibility of different national systems of insolvency law; legal and procedural obstacles to recognition of the office-holder's standing to represent the collectivised interests in the insolvent estate and to assert claims to the debtor's foreign assets; and the numerous possibilities for exploitative behaviour by creditors and debtors alike. Into this latter category fall such practices as the ring-fencing of assets for the exclusive advantage of a restricted sub-group of creditors linked to a specific country; the utilisation of so-called "bankruptcy havens" for the purpose of defeating attempts to gather and administer property on a collective basis; and the potential for creditors to experience discriminatory treatment in consequence of their location in different jurisdictions. These, and related issues, are the subject of a copious doctrinal literature reflecting a wide diversity of approaches.[3] Although a consideration of the doctrinal aspects of the subject lies outside the scope of this chapter, it should be noted that these have had an important influence on the evolving saga of the E.U. insolvency project, and that the provisions of the Regulation in its adopted form are in many cases the outcome of a

---

[1] Councl Regulation (E.C.) No. 1346/2000 of May 29, 2000 [2000] O.J. L160/1. The text of the E.U. Official Journal can also be accessed on the Internet, via the Europa Website (in the "Publications" section) at http://europa.eu.int.

[2] In this chapter, the abbreviations "E.U." and "E.C." are employed, together with the convenient form of reference to "the Union", etc.

[3] See, *e.g.* I.F. Fletcher, *Insolvency in Private International Law* (Oxford, 1999), Chap. 1.

delicate process of achieving a consensus among negotiators from 15
Member States which, between them, represent most of the possible
schools of thought about insolvency law and policy in both its domestic
and international aspects.

26–002   The doctrinal disagreements referred to above extend to such fundamental questions as the very admissibility of the principle of parallel—or
concurrent—insolvency proceedings in relation to the same debtor. Problems of fair treatment of parties in interest, especially in relation to
expectations reasonably formed in a pre-insolvency context, are encountered irrespective of the approach favoured—whether unitary or pluralist.
If the attempt is made to subject all parties to the insolvency system of a
single state, this can result in the defeat of expectations for parties whose
dealings with the debtor were based on alternative assumptions as to
governing law. On the other hand, if it is conceded that multiple
insolvency proceedings may take place to reflect the debtor's significant
connections with different legal systems, there are associated problems of
how to ensure fairness in the treatment of different groups of creditors
with a view to minimising any arbitrary discrimination between them. This
can entail a recourse to what are, in essence, basic equitable principles
including the so-called " hotchpot" principle, and the rule against double
proof by a creditor in respect of what is in reality one and the same claim.[4]

26–003   The need to address such problems was foreseen by the authors of the
original Treaty of Rome,[5] and special provision was made in Article 220
requiring the Member States to conclude conventions on a number of
matters, including:

> "—the simplification of formalities governing the reciprocal recog-
> nition and enforcement of judgments of courts and of arbitration
> awards."

The obligation imposed by Article 220(4) was interpreted as a command
to address all categories of civil and commercial legal business, including
insolvency matters. By a further leap of vision, proper regulation of the
processes of recognition and enforcement was deemed to necessitate the
imposition of a mandatory framework of rules to control the exercise of
jurisdiction by courts throughout the Member States. This resulted in the
development of the "direct" or "double" convention as the instrument of
choice. Non-insolvency matters were resolved separately, and relatively
quickly, by the Brussels Convention of September 27, 1968.[6] In contrast,
separate and protracted efforts continued until as late as May 1996 in

---

[4] On the hotchpot rule, see Fletcher, above, n. 3, pp. 86–8. With regard to the rule
against double proof see *Re Polly Peck (No. 4)* [1996] 1 B.C.L.C. 428 at 436–8.

[5] Treaty establishing the European Economic Community, signed in Rome on March
25, 1957. This entered into force on January 1, 1958 and is still in force, though much
amended, as part of the complex series of treaties which currently link 15 European states
as members of the E.U.

[6] Convention on Jurisdiction and the Recognition and Enforcement of Judgments in
Civil and Commercial Matters, September 27, 1968, as amended. For the consolidated,
current text see [1998] O.J. C27/1.

the ultimately unsuccessful attempt to establish an E.U. Bankruptcy Convention to which all 15 of the Member States would become contracting parties.[7] The work may be broadly divided between Phase I (to 1980); and Phase II (April 1990–May 1996). As a bridging event between these two phases, we may note the significance of the Council of Europe Convention on Certain International Aspects of Bankruptcy (The Istanbul Convention of June 5, 1990, which is not yet in force[8]).

The second phase of the E.U. project came tantalisingly close to **26–004** success, but was prevented from attaining the required unanimity of signatures due to the last-minute disengagement of the U.K., for reasons of international politics that were unrelated to subject matter of the Convention itself. Fortunately, after a further hiatus of three years, the fruits of so many years' collective labour were salvaged thanks to a fresh initiative by the German and Finnish republics, which successively held the presidency of the E.U. Council of Ministers during 1999. In its revived form, the project was submitted to the Council as a proposed regulation. This type of legislative act is significant in that a regulation has the force of directly applicable law in every member state according to the terms of Article 249 (previously numbered as Article 189) of the E.C. Treaty in its amended form. This eleventh-hour conversion into a standard mode of E.U. legislative instrument has the further advantage of eliminating the lengthy delay that would have been anticipated before entry into force as a convention could have occurred, pending completion of the separate domestic procedures for ratification by each of the Member States.

The Regulation on Insolvency Proceedings was adopted by the **26–005** Council on May 29, 2000.[9] To allow time for any consequential internal adjustments in the insolvency systems of the Member States a two-year postponement of its entry into force is effected by Article 46 of the Regulation. On the day thus appointed May, 31, 2002—the Regulation will enter into force without any national legislative measures being taken by the member states, and its provisions will take precedence over any inconsistent provisions of their existing domestic laws.[10] In the remainder of this chapter, the provisions of the Regulation will be examined and their effects explained.[11]

---

[7] For a more detailed account of the history of the E.U. Bankruptcy Convention project, see Fletcher, above, n. 3, Chap. 6, pp. 247–56.

[8] E.T.S., No.136. Text published (in English only) in Fletcher, above, n. 2, at Appendix III, with commentary on the Convention *ibid.*, Chap. 7.

[9] Council Regulation (E.C.) No. 1346/2000 of May 29, 2000 [2000] O.J. L160/1.

[10] One technical matter to be noted is that, because the E.U. Insolvency Regulation is based on Arts 61(c) and 67(1) of the E.C. Treaty (as amended by the Treaty of Amsterdam), its provisions do not have effect in Denmark, which secured an exemption from measures adopted on that basis. It is likely that a parallel arrangement — possibly in the form of a Convention concluded between Denmark and the other 14 member states — will be devised in order that a unitary approach to insolvency matters can be secured across the E.U. as a whole.

[11] There is currently no officially published version issued by the E.U. itself of the final text of the proposed Convention on Insolvency Proceedings (the "Convention"), on which the text of the Regulation is closely modelled. An authentic version in English of the text as opened for signature between November 23, 1995 and May 23, 1996 was placed in the

2. SCOPE AND IMPACT OF THE REGULATION ON INSOLVENCY PROCEEDINGS AS ADOPTED BY THE E.U. COUNCIL

(a) Outline

26–006 The Regulation imposes direct control over the exercise of jurisdiction to open insolvency proceedings in any of the member states. It also regulates, by means of uniform rules for choice of law, the law applicable to such proceedings and to matters closely affected by a party's insolvency (third parties' rights *in rem*; set-off; reservation of title; contracts relating to immovable property; payment systems and financial markets; contracts of employment; registrable rights in immovable property, ships or aircraft; patents and trade marks; the validity of transactions pre- and post-commencement of insolvency proceedings that have detrimental consequences for the general body of creditors; and the effects of insolvency proceedings on pending lawsuits that involve rights or assets of the debtor). All these matters are the subject of provisions in Chapter I (Arts 1–15).[12] It next deals with the recognition in the other member states of insolvency proceedings opened in any of them whose courts have jurisdiction pursuant to Article 3. This includes the vital questions of the effects of recognition, the powers of the office-holder (referred to throughout as "the liquidator"), and the formalities required to establish the liquidator's status for the purpose of acting abroad. These matters fall within Chapter II (Arts 16–26). Next, the possibility of opening secondary insolvency proceedings at the behest of various interested parties is the subject of provisions in Chapter III (Arts 27–38). There are useful, if limited, provisions in Chapter IV (Arts 39–42), concerning the rights of all creditors to receive information from the liquidator and to lodge claims in the insolvency proceedings. Lastly, Chapter V (Arts 43–46) contains transitional and final provisions dealing with entry into force, review and amendment of the Regulation, as well as its relationship to specific conventions dealing with insolvency matters to which certain of the member states are or may become parties (see Art. 44).

public domain as part of the internal processes of scrutiny and consultation within the U.K. The text is contained in a Consultative Document published in February 1996 by the Insolvency Service of the Department of Trade and Industry (U.K.). The same text was also included (as Appendix 3, containing some minor textual inaccuracies) in the 7th Report of the House of Lords Select Committee on the European Communities, published on March 26, 1996 (HL Paper 59, available from HMSO). The Consultative Document also contains (as Annex B) the original version of the Explanatory Report on the Convention, drafted in far from perfect English. A greatly improved, revised version of the Report by Professor M. Virgos and Mr E. Schmit, was produced as E.U. Council Document 6500/96, DRS 8 (CFC), Brussels,May 3, 1996, with restricted circulation. This document, which with some further revision could serve as a valuable aid to interpretation, remains unpublished and so is unavailable for wider study. Limited reference is made in this Chapter to the information contained in the Virgos-Schmit Report, but it must be emphasised that the document carries no official status at this time, and that there are presently no indications as to the possibility of an amended version being published. See also M. Virgos, *European Community Convention on Insolvency* (Kluwer, 1998).

[12] The choice of law rules of the Regulation are discussed in detail in below, paras 26–028 to 26–064.

Two further aspects of the Regulation should be noted. First, its **26–007** substantive provisions are preceded by no less than 33 paragraphs of preliminary recitals or Preambles. While such formal recitals are a standard feature of E.C./E.U. legislation, supplying the legal basis for the measure in question as well as giving an indication of the underlying motivations for its enactment, the number and prolixity of the Preambles to the Insolvency Regulation are exceptional. Their purpose is doubtless to furnish some compensation for the lack of any official *travaux préparatoires* to serve as an aid to interpretation of the Regulation.[13] Foreseeably, courts which encounter a need to apply the Regulation will have their attention drawn to any of the Preambles which appears to supply some guidance on the meaning and approach which are to be preferred. Secondly, the Regulation is supplemented by three Annexes— A, B and C—which list, with respect to each Member State concerned, the names of the insolvency proceedings under the national system of insolvency law which come within the scope of the Regulation and the official titles of the office holders in those proceedings. These lists can be amended from time to time using the procedure established by Article 45.

(b) Subject matter

The types of proceedings covered and categories of debtor to which **26–008** the Regulation applies are as specified in Article 1(1), which provides that it shall apply to: "collective insolvency proceedings which entail the partial or total divestment of a debtor and the appointment of a liquidator". A most important series of excepted cases is created by Article 1(2), which states that the Regulation shall not apply to "insolvency proceedings concerning insurance undertakings, credit institutions, investment undertakings which provide services involving the holding of funds or securities for third parties, or to collective investment undertakings". These exclusions in relation to entities operating within the financial services sector come as a result of separate E.U. initiatives, currently in progress, to introduce harmonisation in this sector by means of Directives which will include standardised provisions governing the insolvency of such enterprises.

Article 2 of the Regulation contains eight paragraphs, lettered (a) to **26–009** (h), which supply the definitions of a number of key concepts and terms that are used. The list is by no means exhaustive, however, and it is certain that many crucial matters will require judicial interpretation with the guidance, ultimately, of the European Court of Justice. Of the definitions which are supplied, mention should be made of that in paragraph (a), which states that "Insolvency proceedings" means the collective proceedings referred to in Art.1(1), as listed in Annex A to the Regulation. As already mentioned, Annex A provides, for each member state in turn, a list of the proceedings found within the law of that

---

[13] See above, n. 11, with reference the Explanatory Report previously produced in relation to the text when it was in the form of a Convention.

country which are considered to fall within the letter and spirit of Article 1(1), and thus qualify for inclusion. The proceedings are listed in the language of the country to whose system they pertain. For the U.K., these are:

- (a) winding-up by or subject to the supervision of the court;
- (b) creditors' voluntary winding-up (with confirmation by the court);
- (c) administration;
- (d) voluntary arrangements under insolvency legislation (which would cover both the Insolvency Act 1986 or the Insolvent Partnerships Order 1994); and
- (e) bankruptcy or sequestration.

It is notable that all the procedures listed above involve a role for the court either at their inception or in their confirmation at an early stage, or at least they allow the court's jurisdiction to be invoked by an interested party to ensure that the proceedings are properly conducted. The inclusion of creditors' voluntary liquidations, which are in practice the most frequently used type of liquidation procedure for insolvent companies, was only made possible through the insertion of the proviso that there be confirmation by the court. Such a step is nowhere required under the existing legislation of the U.K., but could be quite readily accomplished under the widely framed, permissive terms of section 112 of the Insolvency Act 1986 which enable the voluntary liquidator to apply to the court to determine any question arising in the winding up of a company, and empowers the court to make "such . . . order on the application as it thinks just". It would seem that a "confirmation order" might be sought under this provision whenever it transpires that the case may give rise to a need to take cross-border action of some kind. If the case is purely domestic in nature, no such steps need be taken.

26–010   The repeated references in Articles 1 and 2 to the "collective" nature of the proceedings to which the Regulation is applicable suggests one powerful reason why administrative receivership and other types of receivership (even where the court is involved in the process of appointment) have been omitted from the list of proceedings in Annex A relating to the U.K. This is also the case with the Republic of Ireland, whose insolvency law still closely resembles that of the U.K. Although receivership—especially that arising from the existence of a floating charge—plays an important role in the practical operation of the insolvency laws of both the U.K. and Ireland, the procedure is essentially a remedy designed to advance the interest of one particular type of secured creditor, with whom resides the sole initiative as to its utilisation. Hence it cannot readily be reconciled with the "collectivity" concept that infuses the Regulation. A further aspect of administrative receivership is that it commences through a direct act of appointment by the creditor without recourse to a court, thus furnishing a second rationale for its exclusion from the Regulation's sphere of application.

As a consequence, it could well be the case in the future that the non-availability to an administrative receiver of the recognition and assistance provided under the E.U. regulation to office-holders in other types of insolvency proceedings may affect the choice of procedure to be embarked upon whenever consideration is being given to the optimum way in which to attempt to rescue an ailing U.K. or Irish company which has significant assets and interests in other E.U. countries. Although receivership can, in appropriate circumstances and in the right hands, be a very swift and effective vehicle for achieving a business rescue, a receiver can encounter severe difficulties in a case where it is necessary to enlist the co-operation of foreign courts.[14] Therefore it may prove to be tactically advantageous to opt for one of the forms of rescue procedure, such as an administration order or a voluntary arrangement, that attract the automatic benefits imparted by the Regulation.

A further important technical term is defined by Article 2(c), which **26–011** states that "winding-up proceedings" means insolvency proceedings within the meaning of point (a) involving realising the assets of the debtor, including where the proceedings have been closed by a composition or other measure terminating the insolvency, or closed by reason of the insufficiency of the assets. Proceedings which come within this definition are listed in Annex B. For the U.K., they are:

(a) winding-up by or subject to the supervision of the court;
(b) creditors' voluntary winding up (with confirmation by the court); and
(c) bankruptcy/sequestration.

The above is a significantly shorter list than that contained in Annex A to indicate those proceedings which qualify as "insolvency proceedings". Inevitably, this means that a more restricted range of options is available wherever the Regulation requires that proceedings shall be "winding up proceedings"—as in the case of Articles 3(3), 16(2) and 27, relating to the opening of secondary bankruptcies.[15] The omission of administrations, and voluntary arrangements from the scope of the secondary bankruptcy process may prove detrimental to the attainment of some types of rescue strategy for businesses with cross-border operations. Although, as has been noted already, Article 45 enables the Annexes to be amended, this would require the support of a qualified majority of the Council. Potentially some broadening of the scope of operation of the concept of "winding up proceedings" could take place in the future.

---

[14] See Chap. 25.

[15] For example, the restricted range of procedures permitted in such circumstances may preclude the most commercially appropriate course from being followed where the debtor's business is not viable in the place of its centre of main interests, but has a viable branch in another State. See P. Omar, "Jurisdiction in the European Insolvency Convention" (1999) 10 International Company and Commercial Law Review 225. See below, para. 26–018, for Secondary Insolvency Proceedings.

(c) Time of entry into force: non-retrospective effect

26–012 Article 46 provides that the Regulation shall enter into force on January 1, 2002. Article 43 declares that it shall apply only to insolvency proceedings opened after its entry into force, and further states that "Acts *done by a debtor* before the entry into force of this regulation shall continue to be governed by the law which was applicable to them at the time they were done" (emphasis added). There is a potential for confusion and uncertainty here regarding which previous events qualify as "acts done by the debtor". The Explanatory Report formerly prepared in relation to the proposed convention went some way towards assisting in the task of determining issues of validity in transitional cases by stating that "the determination of the acts done by the debtor and the time at which they are done are governed by the applicable law".[16] The basic intention behind the rule is to ensure that relations to which the debtor is party remain subject to the law which governed the debtor's acts at the time of acting.[17]

(d) International jurisdiction

26–013 The Regulation is so designed as to establish a hierarchical scheme of primary and subsidiary jurisdictional competence in relation to a debtor meeting the specific, qualifying criterion, namely that the centre of the debtor's main interests is situated within the territory of a Member State. In the case of such a debtor, the opening of insolvency proceedings is precluded save in those member states on whose courts the Regulation confers jurisdiction, regardless of whether the debtor might elsewhere fulfil any locally-evolved rules for taking jurisdiction.

26–014   It must be emphasised that there is no attempt to regulate or interfere with the taking of jurisdiction under national laws in respect of any debtor whose centre of main interests lies outside the E.U. In such cases alternative grounds for exercising jurisdiction (such as a "doing of business" or a "presence of assets" test) can still be used in any E.U. state where the locally prescribed test for "minimum contacts" happens to be met, but with the important proviso that such proceedings will not qualify for recognition or enforcement in other member states by virtue of the Regulation (although they may be recognised on a case-by-case basis according to the rules of private international law of each state separately). It is suggested, with respect, that this is a welcome contrast to the treatment of civil and commercial judgments under the Brussels Convention, which has hostile propensities for defendants domiciled outside the E.U. because of the effect of its Article 4, which enables long-arm jurisdiction to be taken against them in one E.U. state with the further consequence that any resulting judgment is automatically enforceable in all the others.[18]

---

[16] Virgos-Schmit Report, above, n. 11, at para. 306.

[17] *ibid.* See also paras 303–305.

[18] For trenchant criticism of this and other xenophobic properties of the Brussels Convention, see K. Nadelmann, 67 Colum. L.Rev. 995 (1967); 5 CML Rev.409 (1966–67); 82 Harv. L.Rev. 1282 (1968). See also I.F. Fletcher, *Conflict of Laws and European Community Law* (1982), Chap. 4, pp. 117–120.

Although the Regulation makes repeated reference to "courts", it **26–015** should be noted that its provisions are not exclusively confined to cases where proceedings are commenced or conducted in the formal context of a court. Preamble (10A) specifically calls attention to the fact that insolvency proceedings do not necessarily involve the intervention of a judicial authority, and states that "The expression *court* in this Regulation should be given a broad meaning and include a person or body empowered by national law to open insolvency proceedings".

(i) Primary competence—main proceedings
Article 3(1) provides that the courts of the Member State within the **26–016** territory of which the centre of the debtor's main interests is situated shall have jurisdiction to open insolvency proceedings. It is significant that there is no comprehensive definition of "centre of main interests" ("COMI"), but there is one especially important presumption supplied by Article 3(1) itself:

> "In the case of a company or legal person, the place of the registered office shall be presumed to be the centre of its main interests *in the absence of proof to the contrary*" (emphasis added).

The presumption supplied under Article 3(1) is thus a rebuttable one, and moreover is confined to the case where the debtor is a company or legal person. Nevertheless, it offers a useful point of departure for those wishing to locate the correct forum for commencement of insolvency proceedings involving a company, and it will be incumbent upon those who seek to have the proceedings dismissed for want of jurisdiction to sustain the burden of proving that the company's centre of main interests is in another Member State. Significantly the Regulation is silent as to the nature of the requisite "proof" that must be furnished in order to rebut the presumption established by Article 3(1). Nor does it contain any provision for resolving the contrasting possibilities of either a "positive" conflict of jurisdiction between the courts of two Contracting States, each of which concludes on the evidence before it that the debtor's COMI lies within its territory; or a "negative" conflict, where the converse arises. An example of the way in which such conflicts could occur in practice is provided by the case of *BCCI SA*, where the bank's state of incorporation was Luxembourg, but the English courts quite reasonably concluded that its main operational base was in England.[19] One could imagine that, were a similar case to arise under the Regulation, courts in both Luxembourg and the U.K. could readily persuade themselves that the COMI of BCCI was located within their jurisdiction for the purposes of Article 3(1). In practice, much might depend on the timing of the first approach to the one court rather than the other, and the extent to which the court first seized took care to

---

[19] *Re B.C.C.I. SA (No. 10)* [1997] Ch. 213. This case is further discussed in para. 26–045, below.

perform the task of determining the location of the debtor's centre of main interests in a spirit of fidelity to the principle of mutual trust that is meant to infuse the working of this regulation. There is also a risk of different evidence being submitted to the different courts and the risk of different findings of fact by the respective courts.[20] In a difficult case a reference seeking the interpretative guidance of the ECJ ought to be made. But in the meantime, since a reference can only be made to the ECJ by a national court of final appeal, the urgency of the situation may necessitate the taking of some initiatives aimed at preserving assets and maintaining the value of the insolvent estate, given that the matter may take a considerable time to be resolved.

26–017   An additional indication of the intended meaning of the expression "centre of main interests" has been supplied by Recital (13) to the Regulation, which declares:

> "The 'centre of main interests' should correspond to the place where the debtor conducts the administration of his interests on a regular basis and is therefore ascertainable by third parties".

Transparency and objective ascertainability are therefore given special emphasis in the required approach to interpretation, as is the indication that regard should be paid to the position of third parties and the reasonable expectations formed in the course of their dealings with the debtor.

(ii) Subsidiary competence—secondary proceedings

26–018   Article 3(2) states that, where the centre of the debtor's main interests is situated within the territory of a Member State, the courts of another Member State have a jurisdiction to open insolvency proceedings only if the debtor possesses *an establishment* in the territory of that other Member State. Most importantly, Article 3(2) further provides that the effects of such proceedings are restricted to the local assets of the debtor. Moreover, where insolvency proceedings have already been opened at the forum of primary competence, any proceedings opened elsewhere on the basis of an establishment can only be secondary proceedings (as defined in Chapter III). Also, territorial proceedings based on the existence of an establishment can only be opened prior to main insolvency proceedings under Article 3(1) in circumstances where special preconditions within Article 3(4) are met.

26–019   The meaning to be ascribed to the term "establishment" is thus of crucial importance in controlling the exercise of jurisdiction to open territorial proceedings—and especially those which are to be classed as "secondary proceedings"—with respect to a debtor whose centre of main interests lies in a different member state. "Establishment" is defined in Article 2(h) as: "any place of operations where the debtor carries out a

---

[20] Recital (22) to the Regulation declares that "Recognition of judgments delivered by the courts of the Member States should be based on the principle of mutual trust; to that end, grounds for non-recognition should be reduced to the minimum necessary".

non-transitory economic activity with human means and goods".[21] The mere presence of assets, such as a bank account or even immovable property (of itself and without more) does not constitute an "establishment" for the purposes of the Regulation and hence does not enable local territorial proceedings to be opened. Some insight into the intentions underlying the formulation of the concept of establishment was provided by the proposed Explanatory Report to the Convention from which the present text was derived. In that document the term is described as a place of operations through which the debtor carries out "economic activities on the market (*i.e.* externally), whether the said activities are commercial, industrial or professional", to which is added the further comment that "A purely occasional place of operations cannot be classified as 'an establishment'. A certain stability is required. . . . The decisive factor is how the activity appears externally, and not the intention of the debtor."[22] To this one might observe that the novel concept of "establishment", even with the help of the definition and explanatory comments provided (or perhaps even, because of these), will in some cases prove to be elusive and controversial. It seems inescapable that the European Court of Justice will at some stage—and perhaps on several occasions—be required to provide interpretative guidance on this matter. It is suggested that the essential question that the judge of fact must seek to answer is whether the debtor maintains a "place of business" within the jurisdiction in which the opening of secondary—or territorial—proceedings is sought by a suitably qualified party.

(e) Recognition of insolvency proceedings
The basic principle of recognition is supplied by Article 16(1), whereby **26–020** any judgment opening insolvency proceedings handed down by a court of a Member State which has jurisdiction pursuant to Article 3 shall be recognised in all other Member States *from the time that it becomes effective in the State of the opening of proceedings.* Two further, vital principles are established under the next two Articles. Article 17(1) provides that the judgment opening main proceedings under Article 3(1) shall, *with no further formalities,* produce the same effects in any other Member State as under the law of the State of opening of proceedings, except where the Regulation provides otherwise and as long as no secondary proceedings are opened in the other Member State under Article 3(2). Article 18(1) provides that the liquidator appointed by a court which has jurisdiction under Article 3(1).

"may exercise *all the powers conferred on him by the law of the State of opening of proceedings in another Member State,* as long as no

---

[21] *Cf.* the somewhat altered form of words used in the equivalent definition in Art. 2(f) of the UNCITRAL Model Law, discussed below, para. 26–085. It should be noted that the English Term "goods", which appears in the English version of both texts, is potentially misleading as an intended synonym for the French legal term "*biens*" (which can refer to intangible, as well as tangible, property). It is submitted that the judicial approach to interpretation of the crucial term "establishment" should seek to arrive at an autonomous meaning that will allow uniformity of effect to be achieved between the different legal traditions.

[22] Virgos-Schmit Report (see above, n. 11), at para. 71.

secondary proceedings have been opened there nor any preservation measure to the contrary has been taken there pursuant to a
request for opening of secondary proceedings in that State"
(emphasis added).

Article 18(3) further states that the liquidator may, in particular, remove
the debtor's assets from the territory of the Member State in which they
are situated, (subject to Articles 5 and 7),[23] but in exercising his powers
he must comply with the law of the Member State within whose territory
he intends to take action.

26–021   A further advantage for the office-holder is conferred by Article 19,
whereby the liquidator's appointment shall be evidenced by a certified
copy of the original decision appointing him or any other certificate
issued by the court which has jurisdiction. Although a translation into
the official language, or one of the official languages, of the Member
State in which he intends to act may be required, no further legalisation
or other similar formality shall be required—a provision which obviates
the need for obtaining an *exequatur*[24] as a precondition to the taking of
essential action in certain civil law countries. This provision has great
practical significance, both in terms of the acceleration of the liquidator's
ability to take timely and effective steps in relation to foreign assets
(where they are located in other Contracting States), and in the potential
savings in costs in comparison to those which have hitherto had to be
incurred in order to obtain a judicial order of enforcement from a
foreign court (especially where local creditors resist the application).

(f) Secondary insolvency proceedings

26–022   Chapter III of the Regulation enables secondary proceedings to be
opened, where jurisdiction arises from the existence of an establishment
of the debtor in the Member State in question, purely by virtue of the
opening of main proceedings elsewhere under Article 3(1). There is thus
no need for independent satisfaction of the local law's test for determining the debtor's insolvency. The mere fact (if such be the case) that the
debtor's local establishment is trading normally and does not meet any
applicable test under local insolvency laws that would enable insolvency
proceedings to be opened, is for this purpose not relevant.

26–023   Secondary proceedings can only be winding-up proceedings of the
types listed in Annex B for each Member State. This may generate
obstacles to the effective implementation of main proceedings which are
aimed at rescue and rehabilitation, rather than liquidation of the
debtor's business. It may be noted that Article 33 enables the liquidator

---

[23] Arts 5 and 7 are discussed in paras 26–036 and 26–046 below.
[24] The term "exequatur" — also known as an "executive judgment", denotes a formal
judgment authorising the execution of a foreign judgment where validity has been
recognised through a special legal procedure in the recognising State. Such procedures can
effectively amount to a retrial of the case, and may include the possibility of revising both
the factual and legal determinations of the original judgment, and even the adjustment of
the amount of the award. Inevitably such procedures add to the costs of recognition and
enforcement of foreign judgments, and can give rise to substantial delay.

in the main proceedings to obtain a stay of the secondary proceedings by application to the court which opened them, but there are unclear limitations to the obligation of the court to grant the stay, which can in any event only be obtained for periods of three months at a time (albeit such orders granting stay are renewable).

According to both Article 3(2) and Article 27, secondary proceedings **26–024** are confined in their effect to assets of the debtor situated within the territory of the Member State in which they are opened. They are, however, governed by the law of the Member State in which they are opened (Article 28), which reveals their primary value, namely to enable local expectations with regard to such matters as priority of entitlement to dividend to be met, to the extent that the locally situated assets are sufficient for this purpose, or to ensure that a locally perfected security interest retains full validity and priority as conferred under the local law. Notably, Article 29 permits the opening of secondary proceedings to take place on the request of either the liquidator in the main proceedings or any other person or authority empowered to request the opening of insolvency proceedings under the law of the State in which their opening is requested.

It is obvious that situations will occur in which the question of the *situs* **26–025** of assets at a particular moment in time will be crucial to the outcome of competing claims arising under rival proceedings (primary or secondary), or under the operation of the special choice of law rules in Articles 4–15 inclusive.[25] Some definitional rules are supplied by Article 2(g) to determine the meaning of *situs* with respect to certain types of asset, but it should be noted that many types of intangible, movable property are not covered by this provision. This may give rise to divergent rulings by national courts as to the approach to be employed in determining the *situs* of property whose very "existence" may be dependent on whatever conclusion happens to be reached through the combined application of what are potentially two variable processes. The first of these processes is the particular classification method employed (which may be utilised by the courts of one country in a way which differs from the approaches followed in other jurisdictions). The second process is the choice of law rules and methodology that are used for matters of contract.[26] Although the rules of choice of law are now supposed to be harmonised for all E.U. states through the Rome Convention of June 19, 1980 on the Law

---

[25] The Regulation does not make provision to indicate what should happen where assets are wrongfully removed from a particular jurisdiction before the relevant time. It must be presumed that the liquidator will bring proceedings in the State in which they are subsequently located to bring about the repatriation of the assets to the State in which his appointment took place.

[26] For examples of the complex problems encountered by courts when trying to determine the "conceptual *situs*" of intangible property, see, *e.g. United Bank Ltd v. Cosmic International Inc.* 542 F.2d 868 (Second Circuit, 1976); *Vishipco Line v. Chase Manhattan Bank, NA,* 660 F.2d 854 (Second Circuit, 1981); *Allied Bank International v. Banco Credito Agricola De Cartago,* 757 F.2d 516 (Second Circuit, 1985); *Callejo v. Bancomer SA,* 764 F.2d 1101 (5th Circuit, 1985). *cf. Libyan Arab Foreign Bank v. Bankers Trust Co.* [1988] Ll.Rep. 259; *MacMillan Inc. v. Bishopsgate Investment Trust plc (No. 3)* [1996] 1 W.L.R. 387, CA.

Applicable to Contractual Obligations, the problems caused by conflicts of classification and methodological diversity are yet to be fully resolved. The ECJ may be able to address these issues when it becomes empowered to interpret the Rome Convention, and it will face similar challenges in its task of interpreting the Insolvency Regulation in due course (see below). Hopefully, a consistency and symmetry between the Rome Convention and the Insolvency Regulation can eventually be established through the co-ordinating jurisdiction of the ECJ. There is an onus upon national courts, however, to play a supportive role by a sensitive and sympathetic approach to decision of cases falling within their sphere of responsibility. This can best be performed by respecting the principles of mutual trust and respect that form part of the general principles on which the operation of the law of the European Union is based.

26–026   Other important principles regarding the administration of assets under the system of primary and secondary proceedings are established by Article 32, and also by Article 20. Any creditor may lodge his claim in the main proceedings and in any secondary proceedings, and the liquidators in the respective sets of proceedings are to lodge in the other proceedings claims which have already been lodged in the proceedings for which they were appointed. This reaffirms the principle of collective treatment of all creditors' claims in the insolvency of the same debtor, but may engender considerable administrative complexity in cross-accounting and record keeping. The proposition that no creditor should gain an advantage over others of co-ordinate rank, either by means of any private acts of diligence or through participation in extraterritorial insolvency proceedings, is respected and applied by Article 20. This provision effectively embodies the *hotchpot* rule whereby such recoveries must be accounted for to the liquidator in any proceedings in which the creditor seeks to participate, and the creditor can only begin to share in distributions when creditors of the same ranking or category have obtained an equivalent dividend.

26–027   If, by some chance, the liquidation of assets in the secondary proceedings results in the full satisfaction of all claims allowable under those proceedings, Article 35 specifies that any surplus assets remaining are to be transferred to the liquidator in the main proceedings. In practice, no doubt, the limited pool of assets comprising the available estate in the secondary proceeding will in most cases be exhausted when payment has been made to those creditors whose claims enjoy preferential status according to local insolvency law. Where the process of distribution reaches the level of the non-preferential claims, it should be a matter for the primary and secondary liquidators to resolve between themselves the most efficient way in which to administer the distributional process. Thus, loss of value might be avoided if the balance of funds available in the secondary estate were used to meet claims of local, non-preferential creditors by payments to them matching the proportion of dividend which the primary liquidator is able to pay to creditors of the same degree whose claims are channelled via the main administration. Of course both liquidators must act with vigilance to ensure that no creditor is able to violate the principle against double recovery, as might happen if the same claim were processed separately in the two administrations.

(g) Uniform rules on conflict of laws

One of the principal features of the Regulation is the creation of certain **26–028** uniform conflict-of-law rules for insolvency proceedings to which the Regulation applies.[27] The Regulation establishes a general rule which, subject to defined exceptions, allocates matters to the law of the state in which proceedings have been opened.[28] Consequently, the Regulation's general choice-of-law rule is one of the means by which main insolvency proceedings are given universal, E.U. wide effect—the law of the state of opening of proceedings applies and is to be given effect across the whole of the E.U.

The law of the state of opening of proceedings does not apply for all **26–029** purposes. This limitation is necessary because, in the words of Recital (22) to the Regulation, "automatic recognition of insolvency proceedings to which the law of the opening state normally applies may interfere with the rules under which transactions are carried out in other Member States. To protect legitimate expectations and the certainty of transactions in Member States other than that in which proceedings are opened, provisions should be made for a number of exceptions to the general rule".[29] By allocating particular issues to a state other than that of the state of opening, these exceptions establish limits on the extraterritorial effect of the law of the State of the opening of main proceedings and therefore enshrine a number of significant policy decisions regarding the balance to be maintained between the law of the forum and other potentially relevant and competing jurisdictions.[30]

The general rule is set out in Article 4. This provides that, save as **26–030** otherwise provided in the Regulation, the law applicable to insolvency proceedings and their effects shall be that of the Contracting State within the territory of which such proceedings are opened (the "State of the opening of proceedings").

Article 4 stipulates that the law of the State of the opening of **26–031** proceedings is to determine the conditions for the opening of those proceedings, their conduct and their closure and in particular:

---

[27] Note that one of the objectives set out in the mandate given to the Working Group, established in 1989 by the EEC Council of Ministers to draft the Convention, was to "harmonise certain conflict rules that bear on the administration of bankruptcies . . ." M. Balz, "The European Union Convention on Insolvency Proceedings" (1996) 70 Am. Bankr. L.J. 485 at 495.

[28] Art. 4.

[29] See also recitals (25)–(28) which provide explanations of the need, and justifications, for the exceptional treatment given by the Regulation to rights in rem, set-off, payment systems and financial markets and employees' claims.

[30] "The purpose of these rules is to delineate the issues which are properly governed by insolvency law from those that should be treated as non-bankruptcy issues because non-bankruptcy policies should prevail, and then to determine the law applicable to such insolvency law situations", Balz, above, n. 27 at 506.

(a) against which debtors insolvency proceedings may be brought on account of their capacity;

(b) the assets which form part of the estate and the treatment of assets acquired by or devolving on the debtor after the opening of the insolvency proceedings;

(c) the respective powers of the debtor and the liquidator;

(d) the conditions under which set-offs may be invoked;

(e) the effects of insolvency proceedings on current contracts to which the debtor is party;

(f) the effects of the insolvency proceedings on proceedings brought by individual creditors, with the exception of lawsuits pending;

(g) the claims which are to be lodged against the debtor's estate and the treatment of claims arising after the opening of insolvency proceedings;

(h) the rules governing the lodging, verification and admission of claims;

(i) the rules governing the distribution of proceeds from the realisation of assets, the ranking of claims and the rights of creditors who have obtained partial satisfaction after the opening of insolvency proceedings by virtue of a right in rem or through a set-off;

(j) the conditions for and the effects of closure of insolvency proceedings, in particular by composition;

(k) creditors' rights after the closure of insolvency proceedings;

(l) who is to bear the costs and expenses incurred in the insolvency proceedings;

(m) the rules relating to the voidness, voidability or unenforceability of legal acts detrimental to all the creditors.

Thus, the general rule allocates to the state of the opening of proceedings issues relating to the "conditions for the opening of the proceedings, their conduct and their closure" and then provides a more detailed list of issues which "in particular" are governed by such law. It would seem that this is intended to be a non-exhaustive list of matters which relate to the opening, conduct and closure of proceedings. In this way, the law of the state of the opening of proceedings determines the procedural and substantive effects of the insolvency proceedings. The substantive effects referred to are those typical of insolvency law, *i.e.* effects which are necessary for the insolvency proceedings to fulfil its aims.[31]

26–032   The ambit of Article 4 therefore appears to be wide ranging. Because the Regulation applies to and focuses on collective insolvency proceedings

---

[31] See, in relation to the equivalent provisions of the Convention (to the extent that it can be treated as having a bearing on the interpretation of the Regulation) the Virgos — Schmit Explanatory Report, above, n. 11, para. 90.

which entail the partial or total divestment of a debtor and the appointment of a liquidator,[32] the model used for the purposes of Article 4 is that of a liquidation or bankruptcy and the activities and matters identified in Article 4 are those which typically occur or arise in a liquidation or bankruptcy (*i.e.* the rights of creditors to participate in the insolvency, the effect of the insolvency on the rights of creditors to bring proceedings against the assets of the company and the powers and rights of the insolvency officeholder).

Included in the list are "creditors' rights after the closure of insolvency **26–033** proceedings" and this presumably includes the effect of a discharge in bankruptcy proceedings. It also appears to include the effect of a variation or discharge of indebtedness arising under a voluntary arrangement.[33] Voluntary arrangements can be used in a wide variety of circumstances; at one end of the spectrum are cases in which there is a realisation of assets and distribution of the proceeds to creditors in full and final settlement of creditors' claims (*i.e.* a quasi-liquidation) whilst at the other end of the spectrum are cases which involve a debt restructuring in which the debtor's liabilities are rescheduled or restructured (with a consequential discharge or variation of the debtor's liabilities perhaps in consideration for the issue of new debt and without the realisation of assets or the payment of a cash dividend to creditors). Article 4 appears to apply to both types of case with the result that the validity of the variation or discharge of indebtedness is governed by the law of the state of the opening of proceedings. In the context of a voluntary arrangement in the U.K., the rule that the discharge or variation of liabilities made and arising under it is effective in relation to all obligations of the debtor, no matter what the governing law of the debt in question, does not represent a change in the law since, as a matter of English law, a voluntary arrangement (by analogy with the law relating to the discharge of indebtedness in an English bankruptcy and a scheme of arrangement[34]) would be effective as against all creditors bound by the voluntary arrangement wherever domiciled and whatever the law governing the debt in question. To the extent that a main proceeding commenced in a state other than the U.K. makes provision for the variation or discharge of the obligations of the debtor, then the English courts will have to recognise and give effect to the discharge under the law of that state even in cases where the obligation discharged or varied is governed by English law. This would seem to overturn the basic English rule that only a variation or discharge under English law is effective to discharge

---

[32] See Art. 1(1).

[33] See Annex A which refers in the section covering the U.K., to "voluntary arrangements under insolvency legislation".

[34] See, Dicey & Morris, *The Conflict of Laws* (13th ed.), Rule 164 and in relation to schemes of arrangement, *New Zealand Loan & Mercantile Agency Company v. Morrison* [1898] A.C. 349. See also Dicey & Morri, p. 1180, n. 53. See generally Dicker and Segal, "Cross Border Insolvencies and Rescues: The English Perspective" (1999) Int. Insolv. Rev. 127.

obligations governed by English law.[35] This interpretation has been consistently applied by the English courts.[36]

26–034 The application of national insolvency law by the courts in the state of the opening of proceedings, and the automatic extension of its effects to all member states, may interfere with the rules under which transactions are carried out in these states. Therefore, to protect legitimate expectations and the certainty of transactions in States other than the one in which proceedings are opened, the Regulation provides for a number of exceptions to the general rule.[37]

These exceptions (contained in Articles 5–15 of the Regulation) can be divided into two categories:

(a) the Regulation excludes certain rights over assets located abroad from the effects of the insolvency proceedings[38]; and

(b) the Regulation ensures that certain effects of the insolvency proceedings are governed not by the law of the state of the opening of proceedings but by the law of another state.[39]

26–035 It should be noted that these provisions, when referring to the jurisdiction that displaces the state of the opening as the governing law, refer to the law of another Member State. In certain cases, however, the jurisdiction to which the Regulation will allocate a particular issue will be a state outside the E.U. Since the Regulation is limited to the intra-Community effect of insolvency proceedings, it will be left to Member States in these cases to decide what choice-of-law rules to apply.

26–036 Article 5(1) states as follows:

"The opening of insolvency proceedings shall not affect the rights in rem of creditors or third parties in respect of tangible or intangible, movable or immovable assets (both specific assets and collections of indefinite assets as a whole which change from time to time) belonging to the debtor which are situated within the territory of another Member State at the time of the opening of proceedings."[40]

---

[35] Dicey & Morris, *The Conflict of Laws* (13th ed.), Rule 170. Note that the construction argued for above seems to be supported by the views of the Chairman of the EEC Working Group which was responsible for drafting the Convention:

"[I]t has long been argued by some that the law governing the debtor's obligations *(lex contractus)* should be applied to the issue of discharge, at least cumulatively, *i.e.,* in addition to the law of the opening State. Art. 4 now clarifies that only the law of the opening State will govern." Balz, above, n. 27 at 508.

[36] See, *e.g. National Bank of Greece and Athens S.A. v. Metliss* [1958] A.C. 509 at 513–15. Query how many of the proceedings in other states included in Annex A of the Regulation allow for a variation or discharge of the indebtedness of the debtor.

[37] Art. 5–15.

[38] Art. 5–7.

[39] Art. 8–11, 14–15.

[40] See also Recital 25 to the Regulation which explains the reasons for the exceptional treatment for rights *in rem* and that "the basis, validity and extent of . . . a right *in rem* should . . . normally be determined according to the *lex situs* and not be affected by the opening of insolvency proceedings".

In order to come within Article 5 (and therefore avoid the law of the state of the opening of proceedings affecting the right *in rem* in question) it is necessary to establish (1) the existence of rights in rem in favour of creditors or other third parties and (2) the fact that the assets in question are situated within the territory of another Member State at the time of the opening of proceedings.

Article 5 does not provide a definition of rights *in rem* but states that **26–037** rights *in rem* shall "in particular mean":

(a) the right to dispose of assets or have them disposed of and to obtain satisfaction from the proceeds of or income from those assets, in particular by virtue of a lien or a mortgage;

(b) the exclusive right to have a claim met, in particular a right guaranteed by a lien in respect of the claim or by assignment of the claim by way of a guarantee;

(c) the right to demand the assets from, and/or to require restitution by, anyone having possession or use of them contrary to the wishes of the party so entitled;

(d) a right in rem to the beneficial use of assets.

The absence of a definition appears to be deliberate and to leave the **26–038** question of what constitutes a right *in rem* to the law of the State where the assets in question are located. This was certainly the case in relation to the Convention—paragraph 100 of the Explanatory Report noted that "the Convention does not intend to impose its own definition of a right *in rem* running the risk of describing as rights *in rem* legal positions which the law of the State where the assets are located does not consider to be rights *in rem* or of not encompassing rights *in rem* which do not fulfil the conditions of that definition . . . For this reason the characterisation of a right *in rem* must be sought in the national law which, according to the normal pre-insolvency conflict of law rules, governs rights *in rem* (in general the *lex rei sitae* at the relevant time)". Recital (25) to the Regulation suggests that it is intended that this approach should apply to the Regulation also. Recital (25) explains that the "basis, validity and content of . . . a right *in rem* should . . . normally be determined according to the *lex situs*". Whether this approach is the correct one in the context of the Regulation, and the meaning to be given to and status of the Article 5(2) examples of rights *in rem*, must await a ruling in due course by the ECJ.

In many cases the issue whether a particular right constitutes a right *in* **26–039** *rem* will, as a matter of English law, be uncontroversial. There will be cases where it will become necessary carefully to examine the ambit of the reference to "rights *in rem*" to see whether particular types of right or remedy under English law can be said to be rights *in rem* for this purpose.[41] Considerable concern had been expressed in this context as to

---

[41] Consider, for instance, restitutionary proprietary remedies and rights under a constructive trust. See the distinction made between rights *in rem* and rights *ad rem* in R.

whether the floating charge would satisfy the requirements of a right *in rem*. The uncertainties have been removed by the inclusion in the Regulation of the words "(both specific assets and collections of indefinite assets as a whole which change from time to time)", which words were not incorporated into the Convention but were added to ensure that the floating charge was adequately covered.

26–040   The question also arises as to whether Article 5 applies only to rights *in rem* in existence at the date of the commencement of the relevant insolvency proceedings or to rights *in rem* created thereafter. The Explanatory Report in relation to the Convention suggested that if a right *in rem* is created after the commencement of insolvency proceedings it is not covered or protected by Article 5.[42]

26–041   It should also be noted that rights *in rem* are not immune from the effect of proceedings to which the Regulation relates. If the law of the State where the assets are located imposes a stay on the enforcement of security following the commencement of a local insolvency proceeding, the liquidator in the main proceeding or any other person empowered to do so may request secondary insolvency proceedings to be opened in that State if the debtor has an establishment there.[43] The secondary proceedings are conducted according to local law and affect the rights of secured creditors with assets in that jurisdiction in the same way as in purely domestic proceedings.

26–042   Under the general rule applicable by virtue of Article 4, insolvency set-off is subject to the law of the state of the opening of the insolvency proceedings. If insolvency proceedings are opened, it therefore falls to the law of the state of the opening of proceedings to govern the availability of set off and the conditions under which set-off can be exercised against a claim of the debtor.

26–043   Article 6 of the Regulation, provides additional protection for certain rights of set-off. It states that: "The opening of insolvency proceedings shall not affect the right of creditors to demand the set-off of their claims against the claims of the debtor, where such a set-off is permitted by the law applicable to the insolvent debtor's claim". Accordingly, rights of set off permitted by and arising in accordance with the law applicable to the insolvent debtor's claim are protected and cannot be diminished or otherwise affected by reason of the commencement of main proceedings—Article 6 therefore provides a safe harbour for such rights of set-off. The reference to the "law applicable to the insolvent debtor's claim" needs to be considered in light of the nature of the debtor's

---

Goode, Property and Unjust Enrichment, in *Essays on the Law of Restitution* (Andrew Burrows, ed., 1991), pp. 215, 217 and see, generally, W. Swadling's chapter, "Property" in *Lessons of the Swaps Litigation* (Birks and Rose, ed., 2000).

[42] Explanatory Report, para. 103.

[43] See Arts 3(2) and 29. Note that the Working Group established to draft the Convention debated at length whether security holders with foreign situated collateral should be subjected to the insolvency law of the State in which the collateral is located, at least in cases where the law of the opening State provides for some effect of insolvency on the rights of secured creditors. But such an approach was thought to be too complex. See Balz, above, n. 27, at 509.

claim. In the case of a contractual cross claim by the debtor (against the creditor's claim), presumably the proper law of that cross claim is the applicable law.[44] Such an approach has the considerable merits of simplicity and predictability—creditors will be able, at least in straightforward situations which do not involve an insolvent debtor which has a multiplicity of claims, to establish easily the law governing the availability of set-off in the event of their counterparty's insolvency and to draft documentation to ensure that set-off will be available under that law.[45]

The position is far from clear where the insolvent debtor's claim is **26–044** non-contractual, *e.g.* a claim in tort; what then is the law applicable to the insolvent debtor's claim (presumably it is necessary to apply the relevant choice of law rules such as that applied in England pursuant to the Private International Law (Miscellaneous Provisions) Act 1995) and whose choice of law rules decide the applicable law in a case involving a foreign element?

It is interesting to compare the approach laid down by the Regulation **26–045** with the current position under English law. An English court recently considered a case in which a Luxembourg bank was simultaneously subject to insolvency proceedings in Luxembourg and a winding-up in England.[46] Because the bank was incorporated in Luxembourg, the winding-up in England was to be treated as ancillary to the Luxembourg proceedings[47]; a question arose as to what law should govern rights of set-off in the English proceedings. This was a particularly serious practical problem because rights of set-off are very limited under Luxembourg law. The English court held that the English rules applied so that insolvency set-off was available and, indeed, was mandatory and self-executing.[48] If the Regulation had been in effect, the result would have been the same. English law, as the law of the state of the opening of proceedings—whether the proceedings were main or territorial

---

[44] This seems to be the case irrespective of the nature of the set off relied on by the creditor because Art. 6 is directed to the law applicable to the claim and not the law applicable to or governing the availability of the asserted right of set-off. In England, where a person seeks to establish a set-off in a cross-border context, it is necessary to consider the nature of the right of set-off relied upon in order to establish the applicable choice of law rule and therefore the law governing the availability of a set-off. See *e.g. Meyer v. Dresser* (1864) 16 C.B. (N5) 646 at 665, 666; *Maspons y Hermano v. Mildred Goyeneche & Co.* (1882) 9 Q.B.C. 530; Derham, *Set-Off* (2nd ed.), p. 135 and Wood, *English and International Set-Off*, para. 23–026. The nature and type of set-off seem to be irrelevant for the purpose of Article 6 which simply focusses on the cross-claim which forms the basis of the creditor's set-off and the law relating to it, rather than the type of set-off relied upon and the law applicable to the question of whether set-off is available.

[45] See Recital (26) to the Regulation.

[46] See *Re* Bank of Credit & Commerce Int'l SA (No. 10) [1997] Ch. 213. Admittedly a credit institution would not be subject to the Regulation, see E.U. Insolvency Regulation, Art. 1(2), but the principles enunciated by the English court are not limited to credit institutions.

[47] See *Re Bank of Credit & Commerce Int'l SA (No. 10)* [1997] Ch. 213 at 238–246. The proceeding was limited to assets in the U.K., although the English court questioned the jurisdictional basis for ancillary liquidations. Interestingly, since it was arguable that management of the Bank was conducted in and from London, (see page 224), under the Regulation the English proceeding might have been the main proceeding.

[48] See *ibid.* at 246–248.

proceedings—would govern the availability of set-off rights although any rights of set off permitted by the law applicable to BCCI's claim against the creditor would have been protected and unaffected by the winding up (so that the creditor could rely on such rights if it chose to do so). It is worth noting that, if the bank did not have an establishment in England, it could not under the Regulation be wound up in England and creditors would therefore have lost their English rights of set-off and would be limited to their rights under Luxembourg law, subject, of course, to the operation of Article 6. If BCCI's claims were governed by English law then rights of set-off permitted under English law would be protected; but it is open to question whether whether this is a reference to liquidation set-off under English law (which presumably it is not where the debtor is not in liquidation in England) or to pre-insolvency set-off under English law (which presumably it is in such circumstances).

26–046   Under Article 7, where a buyer becomes insolvent, the insolvency proceedings will not affect the rights of a seller based on a reservation of title clause if at the time of the opening of the insolvency proceedings, the asset claimed is situated within the territory of a Member State other than the State in which the proceedings are opened.[49] Thus the making of an administration order in main proceedings in England will not give rise to a stay on the seller's right to repossess goods in the company's possession[50] where those goods are located in another Member State at the time of the making of the administration order.

26–047   On the other hand, where the seller becomes insolvent after delivery of an asset to a buyer, the seller will not have grounds to rescind or terminate the sale.[51] The buyer, therefore, will not be prevented from acquiring title where at the time of the opening of proceedings the purchased asset is located within the territory of a Member State other than the state of the opening of proceedings.

26–048   Article 8 stipulates that: "The effects of insolvency proceedings on a contract conferring the right to acquire or make use of immovable property shall be governed solely by the law of the Member State within the territory of which the immovable property is situated".

26–049   Article 9 states: "[T]he rights and obligations of parties to a payment or settlement system or to a financial market shall be governed solely by the law of the Member State applicable to that system or market".

26–050   The intention of Article 9 is for the effects of an insolvency proceeding in another Member State on transactions subject to a payment or settlement system or financial market to be the same as

---

[49] See Art. 7(1). This provision presumably does not prevent the English law provisions making a charge over goods (arising out of a purported reservation of title clause) void for non registration following the liquidation of the buyer merely because the goods were located in another Member State when the winding up order is made.

[50] Insolvency Act 1986, s. 11.

[51] See Art. 7(2).

those arising in proceedings under national law.[52] This approach is designed to preserve the integrity of settlement systems and financial markets and to prevent damaging market disruptions following an insolvency of a market participant. This means that the impact of Part VII of the Companies Act 1989 on the operation of U.K. settlement systems and markets will not be affected by an insolvency proceeding in another Member State.[53]

Article 10 provides: "The effects of insolvency proceedings on employ- **26–051** ment contracts and relationships shall be governed solely by the law of the Member State applicable to the contract of employment".[54]

Article 11 provides: "The effects of insolvency proceedings on the **26–052** rights of the debtor in immovable property, a ship or an aircraft subject to registration in a public register shall be determined by the law of the Member State under the authority of which the register is kept".

Article 12 states: "For the purposes of this Regulation a Community **26–053** patent, a Community trade mark or any other similar right established by Community law may be included only in the proceedings referred to in Article 3(1) [main proceedings]."

Article 13 states: **26–054**

"Article 4(2)(m) shall not apply where the person who benefited from a legal act detrimental to all the creditors provides proof that:

— the said act is subject to the law of a Member State other than that of the state of the opening of proceedings; and
— that law does not allow any means of challenging that act in the relevant case."

As with the exercise of rights of set-off, the Regulation provides a two-tiered approach for dealing with the law governing the avoidance of pre-insolvency transactions. In general, the law of the Member State where the proceedings are opened governs, subject to the availability of a safe harbour protection.

The basic rule of the Regulation is that under Article 4, the law of the **26–055** state of the opening of proceedings governs any possible voidness, voidability, or unenforceability of acts that may be detrimental to all the creditors' interests. This same law determines the conditions to be met, the manner in which the nullity and voidability function, and the legal consequences of nullity and voidability.

Article 13 provides an exception to the law of the state of opening of **26–056** proceedings. The defence must be pursued by, and the burden of proof is on, the party who relies on it. The aim of Article 13 is to uphold the legitimate expectations of creditors or third parties regarding the validity

---

[52] See generally Recital (27) to the Regulation.
[53] See also The Financial Markets and Insolvency (Settlement Finality) Regulations 1999 which implement Directive 98/26/E.C. on settlement finality in payment and securities settlement systems and which modify the law of insolvency in various respects.
[54] See Recital (28) to the Regulation which explains the purpose of Art. 10.

of an act or transaction undertaken in accordance with the normally applicable national law.[55]

26–057   In order for the defence to be available it is necessary for the party relying on it first to establish that the impugned act or transaction is "subject to"[56] the law of a Member State other than the state where the proceedings are opened. Second, the party must establish that the law of that other state does not allow a challenge by "any means" and "in the relevant case". "Any means" appears to connote that the act or transaction in question cannot be challenged using either rules applicable on an insolvency or other general rules of the applicable national law.[57] "In the relevant case" means that the act or transaction should not be capable of being challenged in the actual circumstances of the case.

26–058   The approach adopted by the Regulation for these purposes can be compared with the current approach of the English court to the question of what law governs the application of avoidance provisions in cases with a foreign element.

26–059   An illustration of the English approach can be found in *In re Paramount Airways Ltd (No. 2)*.[58] In that case, administrators made a claim for repayment of sums paid by an insolvent English company from its English bank account to Hambros Bank, Jersey (Hambros Jersey); the sum was to be credited to an account in the name of a Jersey company administration agent. The payment was made on the instructions of a person who was both a director and chairman of the English company. The money was ultimately paid to an account in Hambros Jersey; the account was held by a Panamanian company allegedly owned and controlled by that person.[59] The payment received by the Panamanian company was used to reduce its overdraft with Hambros Jersey. The administrators of the English company alleged that the payments to the Panamanian company were transactions at an undervalue[60] made at a time when the English company was insolvent.[61] The claim against Hambros Jersey was based on the fact that it received a benefit from the repayment of the overdraft of the Panamanian company other than in good faith, for value, and without notice of the relevant circumstances. The question was whether an order could be made against a defendant (*i.e.* Hambros Jersey) out of the jurisdiction (Jersey).

26–060   The Court of Appeal held that the statutory avoidance provisions[62] allow a claim to be made against "any person". As a matter of jurisdiction, such provisions were not subject to any territorial limitation, but, even where the court had jurisdiction to set aside a transaction, it retained a discretion under the applicable statutory provisions as to the

---

[55] See Explanatory Report, para. 138.
[56] Query the meaning of "subject to" here? In the case of a contract presumably it means the governing law of the contract.
[57] See Explanatory Report, para. 137.
[58] [1993] Ch. 223, CA.
[59] *ibid.*
[60] Insolvency Act, 1986, s. 238.
[61] In *Re Paramount Airways Ltd (No. 2)* [1993] Ch. 223 at 231.
[62] Insolvency Act, 1986, s. 423.

order it would make. Where a foreign element was involved, the English court would have to be satisfied, with respect to the relief sought against him, that the defendant was sufficiently connected with England for the order to be just and proper. When considering "sufficient connection" the court would regard a number of factors, including

> "residence and place of business of the defendant, his connection with the insolvent, the nature and purpose of the transaction being impugned, the nature and locality of the property involved, the circumstances in which the defendant became involved in the transaction or received a benefit from it or acquired the property in question, whether the defendant acted in good faith, *whether under any relevant foreign law the defendant acquired an unimpeachable title free from any claims even if the insolvent had been adjudged bankrupt or wound up locally.* The importance to be attached to these factors will vary from case to case."[63]

If the administration proceedings in this case had been subject to the Regulation (as the main proceedings) then, in order for the court to establish the availability of the Article 13 defence, it would have been necessary for the English court to determine what law the payment was "subject to". This may be a narrower test than the "sufficient connection" test that the English courts currently apply unless the "subject to" test allows the court to consider something other than the law which technically governs the effectiveness or validity of the payment or other act in question. In this context it will be necessary to clarify how to identify the law to which a payment is subject where the parties to the payment are not in a contractual relationship; it seems as though the nature of the cause of action on which the claim to recovery is based is not relevant; Article 13 directs attention to the law governing the act or transaction to be challenged and not the law to which that act or transaction is subject.

Article 14 of the Regulation concerns acts of disposal that take place **26–061** after the opening of the insolvency proceedings. Protection is provided to purchasers who acquire an asset for consideration (*i.e.* not gratuitously). The assets protected are immovable assets; ships or aircrafts subject to registration in a public register; and "securities whose existence pre-supposes registration in a register laid down by law".

The validity of any such disposal is to be governed by the law of the **26–062** state where the immovable asset is situated or under the authority of which the register is kept. Once again, this provision is designed to ensure the integrity of transactions by providing the same level of protection for bona fide purchasers for value in proceedings in another contracting state as would arise in domestic proceedings.

Under Article 15, "the effects of insolvency proceedings on a lawsuit **26–063** pending concerning an asset or a right of which the debtor has been

---

[63] In *Re Paramount Airways Ltd (No. 2)* [1993] Ch. 223 at 240 (emphasis added).

divested are to be governed solely by the law of the Member State in which that law suit is pending". The effect of the commencement of the relevant insolvency proceedings on enforcement action begun by individual creditors (prior to the opening of the proceedings) is governed by the law of the state of the opening[64] so that the collective insolvency proceedings may stay or prevent any individual enforcement action brought by creditors against the debtor's assets.

(h) Creditors' right to lodge claims

26–064 Chapter IV of the Regulation (Arts 39–42) contains a limited, but useful, set of provisions aimed at improving the position of creditors in an international insolvency case. When creditors are obliged to participate in foreign-based proceedings, disadvantages can be experienced either as a consequence of explicit provisions of the local law (direct discrimination), or as a product of more subtle—even logistical and informational—factors (indirect discrimination). Both kinds of discrimination receive some corrective attention.

26–065   Very significantly, Article 39 declares:

> "Any creditor who has his habitual residence, domicile or registered office in a Member State other than the State of the opening of proceedings, *including the tax authorities and social security authorities of Member States*, shall have the right to lodge claims in the insolvency proceedings in writing" (emphasis added).

In terms of the traditional principles embodied in the law of the U.K., for example, this overrides, for the benefit of the tax and social security authorities of other E.U. Member States, the effect of the rule in *Government of India v. Taylor*.[65] The wording of this provision makes it clear that the benefits hereby conferred under the Regulation are reserved for the exclusive advantage of E.U.-based creditors. The treatment of creditors from outside the frontiers of the Union is unregulated, and so falls to be governed by the laws and practices of the state of opening of the proceedings in question.

26–066   There are further provisions in Articles 40–42 whereby the liquidator is under a duty immediately to inform all known creditors who have their habitual residence, domicile or registered office in the other Member States. This must be done as soon as insolvency proceedings are opened. The notification is to bear the heading "Invitation to lodge claim. Time limits to be observed" in all the 12 official languages of the institutions of the E.U. (Arts 40, 42(1)), but the notice itself need only be in the official language, or one of the official languages, of the state of the opening of proceedings. Conversely, creditors are permitted to lodge their claim in the official language of the Member State of their habitual

---

[64] Art. 4(2)(f). Note that this states that the law of the State in which proceedings are opened governs the effects of insolvency proceedings on proceedings brought by individual creditors *with the exception of law suits pending*. (emphasis added).

[65] [1955] A.C. 491, HL.

residence, domicile or registered office, but may be required (at the liquidator's discretion) to provide a translation into an official language of the State of the opening of proceedings (Art. 42(2)).

It will be observed that the qualifying criteria for eligibility to benefit **26–067** from the provisions of Chapter IV in favour of creditors from other Member States are based upon the "functional" factors of habitual residence, domicile, or the location of the registered office (in the case of a company). It is noteworthy that there is no reference in the provisions of Chapter IV to the factor of nationality. It is therefore of no consequence whether a creditor (or a debtor) is a national of any of the Member States, for the purposes of the Regulation's operation, nor with regard to the enjoyment of any rights or privileges arising thereunder. Equally of significance is the corollary to this, namely that it is not a matter of relevance, for the purpose of determining standing to invoke or take benefit from provisions of the Regulation, that the party in question happens to be a citizen of a state that is not a member of the E.U. What matters is simply whether that party currently has the requisite "functional" connection with one of the Member States, by meeting one (at least) of the three stated criteria.

(i) Interpretation by the Court of Justice

By virtue of Article 234 (formerly numbered as 177)[66] of the Treaty **26–068** establishing the European Community the European Court of Justice has jurisdiction to give preliminary rulings concerning the validity and interpretation of acts of the institutions of the Community. In principle therefore the Regulation on Insolvency Proceedings, as an act of the Council, falls within the scope of Article 234. As a measure adopted pursuant to the powers conferred under Title IV of the E.C. Treaty (and in particular, based on Articles 61(c) and 67(1)), the jurisdiction of the ECJ to deliver interpretative rulings at the request of a national court is subject to special conditions and restrictions imposed by Article 68 (formerly Article 73p). Article 68(1) permits such a reference to be made only where a question on the interpretation of the Regulation is raised in a case pending before a court or tribunal of a Member State against whose decisions there is no judicial remedy under national law. Thus, only an appellate court of last resort (according to the nature and status of the proceedings in question) is eligible to make a request to the Court of Justice. The terms of Article 68(1) have the effect of making it obligatory for a national court which meets this qualifying condition to request a ruling if it considers that a decision on the question of interpretation is necessary to enable it to give judgment.

The inevitable delay, and added cost, of pursuing an appeal to the **26–069** highest level within the national legal system are likely to furnish a severe constraint upon utilisation of the facility to seek an interpretative

---

[66] The E.C. Treaty was considerably amended by the Treaty of Amsterdam of 1997, which entered into force for the U.K. on May 1, 1999. Art. 12 of the Amsterdam Treaty effected a wholesale renumbering of the Articles of the E.C. Treaty, as indicated in the text.

ruling from the ECJ in cases where, by definition, insolvency is a factor. This may retard the process of obtaining clarification on a number of matters of considerable practical importance. On the other hand, the fact that access to the ECJ has been thus restricted seems defensible in as much as it has deprived parties of a possible tactical weapon during the course of insolvency-related litigation in which the time element is especially critical, and where the ability to seek to persuade a court of first instance to refer a question to the ECJ could be potentially damaging to the collective interest of those involved.

26–070   Article 68(3) provides a further facility for the obtaining of interpretative rulings from the ECJ at the instance of the Council, the Commission or a Member State. This may well provide the most appropriate means of clarifying any points of meaning which are identified as giving rise to generalised difficulties in the operation of the Regulation, since the reference could be submitted in abstract terms, divorced from any "live" proceedings. It is also expressly provided by Article 68(3) that the ruling given by the Court of Justice in response to such a request shall not apply to judgments of courts or tribunals of the Member States which have become *res judicata*. Thus, any such ruling would have only a prospective effect, in relation to pending or subsequent cases.

(j) Final observations

26–071 It is clear that, even in advance of its formal entry into force, the E.U. Regulation and its implications must be carefully considered by all parties who engage in commercial dealings with a counterparty having substantial links (amounting at least to the maintenance of a place of business) within any state which is a member of the E.U. The possibility that either primary or secondary insolvency proceedings (or in certain circumstances, proceedings of both kinds) may be opened in relation to the counterparty in one or more of the member states must be taken into account when assessing the risks arising from any transaction, particularly where it is intended to give rise to a credit-based relationship extending over a considerable period of time. In any debtor-creditor relationship which has cross-border aspects, it is vital for the creditor to be able to anticipate in which jurisdiction the debtor may be amenable to undergo insolvency proceedings, and also to know what assets would then be comprised in those proceedings and what law or laws would be applied to determine the rights and interests of the various parties affected. Therefore, it may be prudent to engineer the agreement in such a way that it is incumbent upon the E.U.-based party to make full and proper disclosure of material facts bearing upon that party's amenability to the insolvency jurisdiction of courts that are subject to the E.U. Convention. A further disclosure requirement may need to be incorporated to cover the contingency that developments in the debtor's *modus operandi* subsequent to the commencement of the agreement may have the effect that they alter or extend the jurisdictional "catchment" that obtained at the time the agreement was concluded. Indeed, lenders may deem it advisable to make provision for it to be a default event on the part of the debtor to do anything which could bring about a change in its jurisdictional circumstances without giving the creditor advance notification (and obtaining authorisation to proceed).

Similar considerations apply to any act of the debtor that produces a **26–072** change in the location of key assets—especially those affected by real security—where this could materially alter the potential outcome for a party in interest by bringing into play any provision of the Regulation that could trigger the application of a different system of law from the one which hitherto may have been reasonably anticipated by that party. Even though the Regulation will not enter into force until 2002, it is important to keep in mind that there will be long-term agreements whose lifespan could extend into the period when the Regulation will apply to any insolvency proceedings which open in an E.U. State in relation to one of the parties concerned. Although Article 43 ensures that "acts" *of the debtor* done before entry into force of the Regulation shall continue to be governed by the law which was applicable to them originally, it is not easy to calculate the precise extent of the protection thus afforded to the interests of the other party to the "act" in question. This is particularly the case if the act involved an asset whose *situs* has subsequently been relocated to another State, under whose law further "acts" have taken place in favour of other parties whose claims or security rights might take precedence according to the law of the place where the asset is presently to be found.[67]

PART II—THE UNCITRAL MODEL LAW ON CROSS-BORDER INSOLVENCY

In May 1997 the United Nations Commission on International Trade **26–073** Law ("UNCITRAL") adopted a Model Law on Cross-Border Insolvency ("the Model Law").[68] Subsequently, a *Guide to Enactment of the Model Law on Cross-Border Insolvency* was issued by UNCITRAL as an authoritative resource for use by states which wish to enact the Model Law, or are considering whether to do so. The *Guide to Enactment* will also serve as an aid to interpretation of the Model Law's provisions as and when enacted.[69] Provision is included in the Insolvency Bill 2000 for the Model Law to be given effect in the United kingdom by regulations made by statutory instrument.[70] The enabling provision allows for implementation with or without modification, and it further allows for amendment of any provision of section 426 of the Insolvency Act 1986.

---

[67] There are plentiful examples in the *Maxwell* Saga of multiple, successive pledges, etc. of the same asset in favour of parties in divers jurisdictions, resulting in horrendous complexities for the lawyers and accountants to wrangle over, with an enormous net loss of value to the creditors involved in the battle. Such practices are by no means unique to the *Maxwell* case, although the scale of the misappropriations in that case was exceptional.

[68] UNCITRAL 30th Session, May 12–30, 1997: Official Records of the General Assembly of the United Nations, 52nd Session, Supplement No. 17 (A152/17), Part II, paras 12–225. The text of the Model Law as adopted is included in that document as Annex I (pp. 68–78).

[69] U.N. General Assembly, Document AICN.9/442 (December 19, 1997).

[70] Insolvency Bill 2000 (HL), cl. 13

The following summary explains the scope of the Model Law, and its potential impact on cross-border cases of receiverships and administrations.

1. STRUCTURE

26–074 The Model Law consists of 32 Articles, each of which is drafted as a "model provision" suitable for enactment into the existing laws of any state minded to do so. A state which takes the step of enacting any of the Model Law's provisions (not necessarily all, or any prescribed proportion of them) is referred to as an "Enacting State". An Enacting State is thus left free to enact as much, or as little, of the Model Law as it is prepared to accept at any given time, and is also left to decide on the appropriate form and means of transposing those provisions into its domestic law. As enacted in this way, the provisions become enforceable exclusively within the Enacting State: no rules of direct jurisdiction are involved, and there are no rules of choice of law. The grounds on which jurisdiction is exercisable are important because the nature of the recognition to be accorded to a foreign proceeding, and hence the quality of assistance and relief that the foreign representative may request, are determined by the circumstances under which jurisdiction was exercised in the commencement of the original proceedings.

26–075 The key principle of the Model Law is that it is not predicated upon reciprocity between states. Once a state has enacted any of the Model Law's provisions, these are available to be invoked in any case to which, objectively speaking, they are applicable. There is no condition or requirement to the effect that the foreign representative must have been appointed under the law of a state which is itself an Enacting State. There may be scope for this factor to be taken into account by the court of an Enacting State when exercising any discretion it may have regarding the provision of relief and assistance to a foreign representative.

2. SCOPE OF APPLICATION OF THE MODEL LAW

26–076 Reference is made throughout the Model Law to "foreign proceeding", a term which is defined by Article 2(a) as:

> "a collective judicial or administrative proceeding in a foreign State, including an interim proceeding, pursuant to a law relating to insolvency in which proceeding the assets and affairs of the debtor are subject to control or supervision by a foreign court for the purpose of reorganisation or liquidation."

This definition clearly precludes the application of the Model Law's provisions to cases of administrative receivership as constituted under Part III of the Insolvency Act 1986, or the equivalents under Scottish law or under the laws of other common law countries which have adopted floating charge receivership. Conversely, administration orders under Part II of the Insolvency Act 1986 should qualify, since they are "collective" and "judicial" in character. Arguably, voluntary arrangements under Part I or Part VIII of the Insolvency Act 1986 could qualify, since they also are collective and the court has a close involvement even though the procedures are not initiated by a court order.[71]

With reference to the Model Law's application to Chapter 11 reorgan- **26–077** isation proceedings under the U.S. Bankruptcy Code, there is no indication that a procedure which otherwise meets the criteria of Article 2(a) is debarred from qualifying as a "foreign proceeding" by virtue of its embodiment of the "debtor-in-possession" concept. Some technical adjustments may be needed under U.S. law and practice to enable a designated individual to claim to be the "foreign representative" for the purposes of any applications made outside the U.S. The likeliest solution is by adapting the established device known as the court-appointed examiner, to produce a species of appointment matching the criteria of Article 2(d).

Article 1(2) allows every Enacting State the option of excluding the **26–078** Model Law from having application to designated categories of proceeding that are subject to a special insolvency regime under the laws of that state. Typically, this will be used in relation to banks and insurance companies, but (as seen above in the case of the U.S. treatment of consumer debtors) other species of debtor may be exempted, as the Enacting State sees fit. This could include non-traders in the case of those States which restrict the application of insolvency law to debtors engaged in trade or commerce.

The Model Law (or such parts of it as an Enacting State decides to **26–079** adopt) is enacted into domestic law like any other statute, and the courts of that state are thus required to give effect to it in the orthodox manner. In contrast to the international obligations imposed on states which become parties to a treaty or convention, there is no active requirement

---

[71] The expression "foreign proceeding", together with the associated term "foreign representative", appear to be directly inspired by the terminology used in the U.S. Bankruptcy Code 1978, notably s. 101(23) and (24) and in s. 304. Although the definitions in the Model Law are somewhat differently drafted from those in s. 101 of the U.S. Code, it may be helpful to refer to the U.S. case law as an illustrative guide to the way in which these key expressions in the UNCITRAL Model Law may be interpreted and applied by national courts. See, *e.g. Re Hopewell International Insurance Ltd* (SDNY, August 19, 1999, Brozman C.J.), and *Vesta Fire Insurance Corpn. v. Newcap Reinsurance Corpn. Ltd* (USDNY, February 7, 2000, Sweet D.J.), on which see comments by G. Moss in (1999) 12 *Insolvency Intelligence* 68–70; (2000) 13 *Insolvency Intelligence* 46–47. National courts should bear in mind however the need to uphold the international character of the Model Law (as emphasised by Art. 8), and should resist the temptation to replicate any approaches to interpretation that may be specific to one state's law. Nevertheless, the liberal approach exemplified by the two cases referred to, allowing recognition of foreign voluntary proceedings where there is *potential*, rather than direct, involvement of the foreign court, is of particular interest.

that a state must take any special step to announce or notify other states, or UNCITRAL itself, of its enactment of the Model Law's provisions. In principle, a state could elect to take no action at all with regard to those parts of its existing law which it considers are already in conformity with those provisions. In the case of the United Kingdom, while it is arguable that many of the Model Law's provisions in terms of access, recognition and assistance are currently met under the existing rules of common law (as opposed to the more restricted application of the provisions of section 426 of the Insolvency Act 1986), there are important reasons in favour of its being implemented as a clearly identifiable part of our legislation in the manner facilitated by the Insolvency Bill 2000. This would ensure that the United Kingdom's position as an Enacting State is plainly demonstrable and can be widely publicised. It would also make the law's provisions internationally accessible without the need to study the case precedents, many of which date from the eighteenth and nineteenth centuries.

(a) Access and recognition under the terms of the Model Law

26–080 A primary benefit for the practitioner is that the Model Law creates a right of immediate and direct access to the courts of the Enacting State to "put the case" for recognition, and apply for relief and assistance, in timely fashion. This can include the obtaining of interim relief pending formal granting of recognition. This can be especially valuable, given the well-known fact that, in cross-border insolvency, speed and timing are of the essence. Article 9 is therefore of fundamental importance:

> "A foreign representative is entitled to apply directly to a court in this State."

Especially noteworthy is the absence of any precondition to this right of access, such as any requirement that the foreign proceeding must first have been accorded formal recognition before the right of access can be exercised (which would give rise to circularity problems). But, in practical terms, standing to invoke the right accorded by Article 9 is dependent upon the ability to establish "foreign representative" status, as defined by Article 2(d):

> " 'Foreign representative' means a person or body, including one appointed on an interim basis, authorised in a foreign proceeding to administer the reorganisation or the liquidation of the debtor's assets or affairs or to act as a representative of the foreign proceeding".

26–081 This definition in turn leads back to the key concept of "foreign proceeding", defined in Article 2(a).[72] Furthermore, common sense dictates that the foreign representative will wish to avoid the wastage of

---

[72] See above, para. 26–075, and remarks in above, n. 65.

costs (and any potential liability) that would ensue from an attempt to invoke legal process within the Enacting State in a case where it ultimately transpires that the foreign proceeding does not meet the criteria for recognition under the Model Law. It is essential to be sure of one's ground—but the vital principle is that rapid steps can be taken to protect the debtor's assets from local acts of individual enforcement without the customary hiatus that ensues from the need to obtain an order of recognition and execution (known in civil law countries as an *exequatur*) from the local court before anything can be done under the law of that state.

Special mention should also be made of the "procedural safe conduct" **26–082** afforded to practitioners by Article 10, which establishes the concept of *limited jurisdiction* for the purpose of the making of an application to a court in an Enacting State pursuant to the Model Law. Once that threshold has been passed, the foreign representative may be subject to conditions imposed by the court (using Article 22(2)), as well as being obliged to respect the general requirements of the local law.

Article 11 confers on the foreign representative the further right to **26–083** apply to commence a proceeding under the local insolvency law of the Enacting State if the conditions for commencing such a proceeding are otherwise met. This may prove to be a valuable weapon in the practitioner's armoury, because it will "collectivise" all matters affecting the debtor's estate in the Enacting State in question, and should put a halt to local action by individual creditors directed against particular assets. Once again, the absence of any precondition referring to recognition of the foreign proceeding is noteworthy.

The practical advantages of separation of the right of direct access **26–084** from the actual process of obtaining recognition of the foreign proceeding have already been considered. Nevertheless it is axiomatic that the material benefits to be made available under the Model Law are ultimately dependent upon the foreign proceeding meeting the criteria for international recognition that have been implanted in its provisions. These are contained in Articles 15-17. Two categories of recognition are available: the foreign proceeding may qualify as a main or as a "non-main" proceeding, according to the circumstances under which it has been opened under the law of the foreign state. The defining characteristics of the two categories are indicated by the terms of the two definitions provided in Article 2(b) and (c) respectively:

> "(b) 'foreign main proceeding' means a foreign proceeding taking place in the State where the debtor has the centre of its main interests;
>
> (c) 'foreign non-main proceeding' means a foreign proceeding, other than a foreign main proceeding, taking place in a State where the debtor has an establishment within the meaning of subparagraph (f) of this article."

Two further concepts thus require to be defined: *centre of main interests* **26–085** (COMI), and *establishment*. The COMI is not defined in the Model Law, although the same expression is used in the Istanbul Convention and also in the E.U. Regulation.[73] The hope is that a "common sense" understanding will emerge without resorting to an overly prescriptive (and also static) definition whose consequence would be to tie down the courts' ability to react to evolving business practice. Article 16(3) supplies a rebuttable presumption that the debtor's registered office, or habitual residence in the case of an individual, is presumed to be the COMI. It is to be assumed that courts will regard it as incumbent upon any party who contends that the debtor's COMI is in a different state from that indicated by applying the presumption to prove that this is the case. Logically, there should be only one place which constitutes "the" centre of the debtor's main interests: use of the definite article in the texts of both Article 2(b) and Article 16(3) presupposes that it is possible to identify its whereabouts. Experience suggests that this may not always be so: even with the assistance of the presumption, courts in different states may reach different conclusions about the "true" location of the debtor's COMI.

26–086   The term *establishment* is defined in paragraph (f) of Article 2 as follows:

> "any place of operations where the debtor carries out a non-transitory economic activity with human means and goods or services."

This definition has been adapted from one already included in the E.U. Regulation (as Article 2(h)), with the addition of the final two words ("or services").[74] If reference is made to the Explanatory Report to the draft E.U. Convention (on which the Regulation is directly based), as well as to the UNCITRAL documentation, it is apparent that the intention is to exclude the possibility that the mere presence of assets belonging to the debtor can be regarded as furnishing a basis for exercising insolvency jurisdiction that will enjoy international recognition. The additional criteria that there must be "a place of operations" at which the debtor carries out a "non-transitory economic activity" whereby "human means" are combined with either "goods" or "services"—ensures that the passive presence of assets, without more, cannot be classified as an establishment. Nor can a purely temporary or occasional place of operations fulfil the terms of the definition in Article 2(f): what is required, effectively, is that the debtor shall be shown to maintain a "place of business" within the jurisdiction in question.

26–087   Under Article 15(1), the foreign representative applies to the court of the Enacting State for recognition of the foreign proceeding in which he or she has been appointed. Article 15(2)–(4) specifies the documentation required in support of the application and Article 16 sets out the presumptions concerning recognition. The grounds for the decision of

---

[73] See above, para. 26–013.
[74] See above, para. 26–018.

recognition are specified in Article 17(1). It should be noted that Article 6 furnishes a ground for refusal of recognition, or of other assistance, if this would be manifestly contrary to the public policy of the Enacting State. Courts should pay regard to the general admonition in Article 8 regarding the overall approach to interpretation, which has been designed for the purpose of promoting international co-operation and the observance of good faith.

The permissible categories of recognition—either as a foreign main, **26–088** or as a foreign non-main, proceeding are confirmed by Article 17(2). Article 17(4) (reinforced by the notification requirements in Article 18) allows the court of the Enacting State to terminate or modify recognition in the light of altered circumstances, or further information coming to the notice of the court. Article 17(3) places emphasis on speed of determination.

(i) Interim relief pending recognition

Article 19 provides for discretionary relief under the law of the **26–089** Enacting State from the time of the filing of the application for recognition until the application is determined. This is a matter for the discretion of the court concerned: a non-exhaustive list of examples of such relief is provided by Article 1 9(a)–(c) (with cross-reference to Article 21(1)).

(b) Consequences of recognition under the Model Law: relief and assistance

Article 20 applies only to cases where a foreign proceeding is recognised **26–090** as a main proceeding. The effects under Article 20 are automatic and are not dependent on the exercise of any judicial discretion. They are:

(a) a stay over the commencement or continuation of individual actions or proceedings concerning the debtor's assets, rights, obligations or liabilities (but see Article 20(3));

(b) a stay over any type of execution against the debtor's assets; and

(c) a suspension of the debtor's right to transfer, encumber or otherwise dispose of any assets.

Under Article 20(2) the Enacting State is allowed to superimpose any exceptions to the automatic stay which are found elsewhere in its domestic insolvency law, so that they also apply in relation to a foreign main proceeding. Thus, the right of a secured creditor to enforce security subsisting over the property of the debtor, or the possibility that the court may grant specific relief from the effects of the stay upon application by a creditor (*e.g.* leave granted by the court under sections 10(1)(b) or 11(3)(c) of the Insolvency Act 1986 to allow a secured creditor to enforce security following the presentation of a petition for an administration order or during the period when such an order is in force) can be accommodated. By Article 31, recognition of a foreign proceeding as a main proceeding gives rise to a rebuttable presumption of the debtor's insolvency for the purpose of commencing an insolvency proceeding under the law of the Enacting State.

26–091   Article 21 applies to all cases where a foreign proceeding is recognised, whether as a main or as a non-main proceeding. It confers a general discretionary power upon the court of the Enacting State to grant "any appropriate relief", including those specified in Article 21(a)–(g) inclusive. The forms of relief described in Article 21(a)–(c) overlap those of Article 20(1) which will take effect automatically in the case of a foreign main proceeding: they are available on a discretionary basis in the case of a non-main proceeding. The forms of relief in Article 21(d)–(g) are discretionary in all cases. Article 21(2) offers the further prospect of application by the foreign representative for the making of an order of turnover of assets by the court of the Enacting State; the court's power is discretionary, and it must also be satisfied that the interests of creditors in the Enacting State itself are adequately protected.

26–092   By Article 22(2), the court may attach conditions to any relief granted under Articles 19 or 21.

26–093   Under Article 23, recognition of a foreign proceeding enables the foreign representative to initiate the types of actions which are available under the law of the Enacting State to enable the office holder in insolvency proceedings to avoid acts detrimental to the interests of creditors generally. In the case of a foreign non-main proceeding, Article 23(3) requires that the court must be satisfied that the action relates to assets which, under the law of the Enacting State, should be administered in the foreign non-main proceeding.

26–094   By Article 24, upon recognition of a foreign proceeding the foreign representative acquires standing to intervene in any proceedings in the Enacting State in which the debtor is a party. Article 12 (which logically belongs in Chapter II of the Model Law with other provisions dealing with the consequences of recognition) allows the foreign representative to participate in a proceeding regarding the debtor under the insolvency laws of the Enacting State. According to the *Guide to Enactment*, the right of "participation" is a limited one, merely enabling the foreign representative to make petitions, requests or submissions.

(c) Cross-border co-operation between courts and office holders— co-ordination of concurrent proceedings

26–095 Chapter IV of the Model Law (Articles 25, 26 and 27) implants useful provisions in the law of the Enacting State to establish a favourable climate, supported by positive directions to the courts of that State, under whose auspices there is to be co-operation with foreign courts and foreign representatives. In practice, the essential channels of communication will be established and sustained through the principle of allowing direct communication between the courts of the respective states and between the courts of the Enacting State and any foreign representative. Although these precepts will be familiar to judges operating within the Anglo-American common law tradition, where the doctrine of comity has long been used as a basis for international co-operation and assistance, concrete statutory confirmation of the doctrine's obligatory character, and clarification of its contents, are welcome developments. This is even more true for those jurisdictions in which there is a less developed tradition of judicial activism in international matters and in particular for those in which the courts have an ingrained disposition (and in many instances are actually subject to a constitutional duty) not to purport to exercise any power that is not explicitly sanctioned by a legislative provision of some kind.

Chapter V (Articles 28–32 inclusive) complements the provisions on **26–096** co-operation by means of specific directives as to the procedures to be followed in cases where there are concurrent proceedings under the laws of different states, in the interests of securing the optimum co-ordination between them. Article 32 is worthy of note: it embodies the celebrated principle of *hotchpot*, long a familiar feature of English case law concerned with the equalisation of distribution among creditors in multi-jurisdiction insolvency. The essence of this rule is that a creditor who has already received partial satisfaction of his unsecured balance of claim against the debtor by participating in a process of distribution taking place in another jurisdiction is not allowed to participate in any other such process without fully accounting for what has already been received in respect of the claim for which proof is lodged. Then, after due allowance has been made for those amounts, the creditor is not entitled to be paid any share of the current distribution so long as the payment to the other creditors whose claims are ranked in the same class is proportionately less than the payment the creditor has already received.

(d) Creditors' rights of access and participation

Although the Model Law is mainly concerned with the foreign repre- **26–097** sentatives' rights of access to courts,[75] Chapter II (Articles 9–14) also contains some provisions which confer rights of access upon foreign creditors. Article 13 implants into the law of the Enacting State the principle that foreign creditors are to have the same rights as local creditors regarding the commencement of, and participation in, an insolvency proceeding. This broad proposition is qualified by the import-ant provision in Article 13(2), that this does not affect the ranking of claims in an insolvency proceeding under local law. This leaves open the possibility that an Enacting State may maintain in force any provisions of its laws whereby claims of foreign creditors are allocated a lower ranking than those of local creditors (as is the case under the laws of a number of Latin American states). Article 13(2) contains a proviso, amounting to a "safety net", which states that claims of foreign creditors shall not be ranked lower than the class of general, non-preferential claims according to local law. This proviso carries a further sub-proviso that allows a foreign claim to be relegated below the class of ordinary claims if its characteristics correspond to those of a special category of postponed

---

[75] See above, para. 26–079.

claims under the local law (*e.g.* in the U.K., debts due from a company to a person held responsible for wrongful or fraudulent trading: Insolvency Act 1986, s. 215(4)).

26–098   The position of foreign revenue claims and of other claims of foreign public authorities is one of the most controversial aspects of international insolvency law. The English law rule—that such claims are excluded from any distributional process in this country as a matter of public policy—currently remains intact.[76] Seemingly, Article 13 (taken in isolation) would necessitate a change to this rule, by requiring foreign fiscal and public claims to be accorded at least the same treatment as ordinary, unsecured debts. The *status quo* could be maintained using the "public policy exception" in Article 6.

26–099   Rights of foreign creditors to receive adequate notification of the successive stages of proceedings, in step with the issuance of notification to local creditors, are governed by Article 14. The principle of equality of treatment is to apply, which means that creditors' rights in actual cases will vary with the provisions of the local law of the state in which the proceedings take place. A certain minimum assurance is generated by Article 14(2), which requires foreign creditors to be notified individually, unless the court considers that under the circumstances some other form of notification would be more appropriate (*i.e.* the mere fact that notification of local creditors can be validly effected by means of public advertisement alone does not enable a similar practice to be followed in relation to foreign creditors, unless the court actively decides that this would be more appropriate). Article 14(3) deals with time limits applicable to foreign creditors in filing their claims. The logistical problems of compliance with foreign procedural requirements, within time limits that may be strictly circumscribed, are notorious. No specific time limits are laid down: what is required is that the period allowed be "reasonable". Clearly this is a matter over which there may be considerable disagreement, and no international uniformity of the lengths of such periods seems likely to emerge. The best that can be hoped for is a clear indication of the applicable period in any given case, and a timely communication of the relevant information to the creditors concerned.

(e) Final observations

26–100 The process of enactment of the Model Law is likely to be somewhat haphazard. A number of states are known to be giving active consideration to its prospective incorporation into their laws. These include some of the world's major economic and trading powers, as well as representatives of the emerging economies. Since the benefits of the Model Law are in principle to be made available by the enacting state without regard to questions of reciprocity, the potential opportunities for office holders appointed under the insolvency law of the United Kingdom should be borne in mind whenever assets of the debtor company are known to be located in any country which has already taken the step of enacting the

---

[76] *Government of India v. Taylor* [1955] A.C. 491.

Model Law. This in turn may in some cases influence the choice of procedure, particularly where it is possible to opt for either administration or administrative receivership. The fact that an administrator has the status of "foreign representative" for the purposes of the Model Law, whereas an administrative receiver does not, could enable an office holder of the former kind to take more effective, and timely, action in other relevant jurisdictions to conserve the assets than could be achieved by an administrative receiver. Moreover, it should be noted that in certain respects the European Regulation and the UNCITRAL Model Law are capable of complementing and reinforcing each other, so that an administrator should in the near future be able to enjoy significant scope for action across at least 14 of the 15 E.U. Member States, in addition to being able to claim recognition and access to the courts of all countries throughout the world where the Model Law has been incorporated into the national law.

Appendix 1—Statutes

Law of Property Act 1925

(15 & 16 Geo. 5, c. 20)

Powers incident to estate or interest of mortgagee

101.—(1) A mortgagee, where the mortgage is made by deed, shall, by virtue **A1–001** of this Act, have the following powers, to the like extent as if they had been in terms conferred by the mortgage deed, but not further (namely):—

(i) A power, when the mortgage money has become due, to sell, or to concur with any other person in selling, the mortgaged property, or any part thereof, either subject to prior charges or not, and either together or in lots, by public auction or by private contract, subject to such conditions respecting title, or evidence of title, or other matter, as the mortgagee thinks fit, with power to vary any contract for sale, and to buy in at an auction, or to rescind any contract for sale, and to re-sell, without being answerable for any loss occasioned thereby; and

(ii) A power, at any time after the date of the mortgage deed, to insure and keep insured against loss or damage by fire any building, or any effects or property of an insurable nature, whether affixed to the freehold or not, being or forming part of the property which or an estate or interest wherein is mortgaged, and the premiums paid for any such insurance shall be a charge on the mortgaged property or estate or interest, in addition to the mortgage money, and with the same priority, and with interest at the same rate, as the mortgage money; and

(iii) A power, when the mortgage money has become due, to appoint a receiver of the income of the mortgaged property, or any part thereof; or, if the mortgaged property consists of an interest in income, or of a rentcharge or an annual or other periodical sum, a receiver of that property or any part thereof; and

(iv) A power, while the mortgagee is in possession, to cut and sell timber and other trees ripe for cutting, and not planted or left standing for shelter or ornament, or to contract for any such cutting and sale, to be completed within any time not exceeding twelve months from the making of the contract.

(2) Where the mortgage deed is executed after the thirty-first day of December, nineteen hundred and eleven, the power of sale aforesaid includes the following powers as incident thereto (namely):—

(i) A power to impose or reserve or make binding, as far as the law permits, by covenant, condition, or otherwise, on the unsold part of the mortgaged property or any part thereof, or on the purchaser and any property sold, any restriction or reservation with respect to building on or other user of land, or with respect to mines and minerals, or for the purpose of the more beneficial working thereof, or with respect to any other thing:

(ii) A power to sell the mortgaged property, or any part thereof, or all or any mines and minerals apart from the surface:—

> (a) With or without a grant or reservation of rights of way, rights of water, easements, rights, and privileges for or connected with building or other purposes in relation to the property remaining in mortgage or any part thereof, or to any property sold: and
>
> (b) With or without an exception or reservation of all or any of the mines and minerals in or under the mortgaged property, and with or without a grant or reservation of powers of working, wayleaves, or rights of way, rights of water and drainage and other powers, easements, rights, and privileges for or connected with mining purposes in relation to the property remaining unsold or any part thereof, or to any property sold: and
>
> (c) With or without covenants by the purchaser to expend money on the land sold.

(3) The provisions of this Act relating to the foregoing powers, comprised either in this section, or in any other section regulating the exercise of those powers, may be varied or extended by the mortgage deed, and, as so varied or extended, shall, as far as may be, operate in the like manner and with all the like incidents, effects, and consequences, as if such variations or extensions were contained in this Act.

(4) This section applies only if and as far as a contrary intention is not expressed in the mortgage deed, and has effect subject to the terms of the mortgage deed and to the provisions therein contained.

(5) Save as otherwise provided, this section applies where the mortgage deed is executed after the thirty-first day of December, eighteen hundred and eighty-one.

(6) The power of sale conferred by this section includes such power of selling the estate in fee simple or any leasehold reversion as is conferred by the provisions of this Act relating to the realisation of mortgages.

* * * * *

Appointment, powers, remuneration and duties of receiver

A1–002   109.—(1) A mortgagee entitled to appoint a receiver under the power in that behalf conferred by this Act shall not appoint a receiver until he has become entitled to exercise the power of sale conferred by this Act, but may then, by writing under his hand, appoint such person as he thinks fit to be receiver.

(2) A receiver appointed under the powers conferred by this Act, or any enactment replaced by this Act, shall be deemed to be the agent of the mortgagor; and the mortgagor shall be solely responsible for the receiver's acts or defaults unless the mortgage deed otherwise provides.

(3) The receiver shall have power to demand and recover all the income of which he is appointed receiver, by action, distress, or otherwise, in the name either of the mortgagor or of the mortgagee, to the full extent of the estate or interest which the mortgagor could dispose of, and to give effectual receipts accordingly for the same, and to exercise any powers which may have been delegated to him by the mortgagee pursuant to this Act.

(4) A person paying money to the receiver shall not be concerned to inquire whether any case has happened to authorise the receiver to act.

(5) The receiver may be removed, and a new receiver may be appointed, from time to time by the mortgagee by writing under his hand.

(6) The receiver shall be entitled to retain out of any money received by him, for his remuneration, and in satisfaction of all costs, charges, and expenses incurred by him as receiver, a commission at such rate, not exceeding five per centum on the gross amount of all money received, as is specified in his

appointment, and if no rate is so specified, then at the rate of five per centum on that gross amount, or at such other rate as the court thinks fit to allow, on application made by him for that purpose.

(7) The receiver shall, if so directed in writing by the mortgagee, insure to the extent, if any, to which the mortgagee might have insured and keep insured against loss or damage by fire, out of the money received by him, any building, effects, or property comprised in the mortgage, whether affixed to the freehold or not, being of an insurable nature.

(8) Subject to the provisions of this Act as to the application of insurance money, the receiver shall apply all money received by him as follows, namely:—

    (i)   In discharge of all rents, taxes, rates, and outgoings whatever affecting the mortgaged property; and

   (ii) In keeping down all annual sums or other payments, and the interest on all principal sums, having priority to the mortgage in right whereof he is receiver; and

  (iii) In payment of his commission, and of the premiums on fire, life, or other insurances, if any, properly payable under the mortgage deed or under this Act, and the cost of executing necessary or proper repairs directed in writing by the mortgagee; and

  (iv) In payment of the interest accruing due in respect of any principal money due under the mortgage; and

   (v) In or towards discharge of the principal money if so directed in writing by the mortgagee;

and shall pay the residue, if any, of the money received by him to the person who, but for the possession of the receiver, would have been entitled to receive the income of which he is appointed receiver, or who is otherwise entitled to the mortgaged property.

APPENDIX 1

Unfair Contract Terms Act 1977

(C. 50)

PART I

AMENDMENT OF LAW FOR ENGLAND AND WALES AND NORTHERN IRELAND

Introductory

Scope of Part I

A1–003   **1.**—(1) For the purposes of this Part of this Act, "negligence" means the breach—

> (*a*) of any obligation, arising from the express or implied terms of a contract, to take reasonable care to exercise reasonable skill in the performance of the contract;
> (*b*) of any common law duty to take reasonable care or exercise reasonable skill (but not any stricter duty);
> (*c*) of the common duty of care imposed by the Occupiers' Liability Act 1957 or the Occupiers' Liability Act (Northern Ireland) 1957;

but liability of an occupier of premises for breach of an obligation or duty towards a person obtaining access to the premises for recreational or educational purposes, being liability for loss or damage suffered by reason of the dangerous state of the premises, is not a business liability of the occupier unless granting that person such access for the purposes concerned falls within the business purposes of the occupier.

(2) This Part of this Act is subject to Part III; and in relation to contracts, the operation of sections 2 to 4 and 7 is subject to the exceptions made by Schedule 1.

(3) In the case of both contract and tort, sections 2 to 7 apply (except where the contrary is stated in section 6(4)) only to business liability, that is liability for breach of obligations or duties arising—

> (*a*) from things done or to be done by a person in the course of a business (whether his own business or another's); or
> (*b*) from the occupation of premises used for business purposes of the occupier;

and references to liability are to be read accordingly but liability of an occupier of premises for breach of an obligation or duty towards a person obtaining access to the premises for recreational or educational purposes, being liability for loss or damage suffered by reason of the dangerous state of the premises, is not a business liability of the occupier unless granting that person such access for the purposes concerned falls within the business purposes of the occupier.

(4) In relation to any breach of duty or obligation, it is immaterial for any purpose of this Part of this Act whether the breach was inadvertent or intentional, or whether liability for it arises directly or vicariously.

Avoidance of liability for negligence, breach of contract, etc

Negligence liability

2.—(1) A person cannot by reference to any contract term or to a notice given **A1–004** to persons generally or to particular persons exclude or restrict his liability for death or personal injury resulting from negligence.

(2) In the case of other loss or damage, a person cannot so exclude or restrict his liability for negligence except in so far as the term or notice satisfies the requirement of reasonableness.

(3) Where a contract term or notice purports to exclude or restrict liability for negligence a person's agreement to or awareness of it is not of itself to be taken as indicating his voluntary acceptance of any risk.

Liability arising in contract

3.—(1) This section applies as between contracting parties where one of them **A1–005** deals as consumer or on the other's written standard terms of business.

(2) As against that party, the other cannot by reference to any contract term—

> (*a*) when himself in breach of contract, exclude or restrict any liability of his in respect of the breach; or
> (*b*) claim to be entitled—
>
>> (i) to render a contractual performance substantially different from that which was reasonably expected of him, or
>> (ii) in respect of the whole or any part of his contractual obligation, to render no performance at all.

expect in so far as (in any of the cases mentioned above in this subsection) the contract term satisfies the requirement of reasonableness.

* * * * *

Evasion by means of secondary contract

10.—A person is not bound by any contract term prejudicing or taking away **A1–006** rights of his which arise under, or in connection with the performance of, another contract, so far as those rights extend to the enforcement of another's liability which this Part of this Act prevents that other from excluding or restricting.

Explanatory provisions

The "reasonableness" test

11.—(1) In relation to a contract term, the requirement of reasonableness for **A1–007** the purposes of this Part of this Act, section 3 of the Misrepresentation Act 1967 and section 3 of the Misrepresentation Act (Northern Ireland) 1967 is that the term shall have been a fair and reasonable one to be included having regard to the circumstances which were, or ought reasonably to have been, known to or in the contemplation of the parties when the contract was made.

(2) In determining for the purposes of section 6 or 7 above whether a contract term satisfies the requirement of reasonableness, regard shall be had in particular to the matters specified in Schedule 2 to this Act; but this subsection does not prevent the court or arbitrator from holding, in accordance with any rule of law, that a term which purports to exclude or restrict any relevant liability is not a term of the contract.

(3) In relation to a notice (not being a notice having contractual effect), the requirement of reasonableness under this Act is that it should be fair and reasonable to allow reliance on it, having regard to all the circumstances obtaining when the liability arose or (but for the notice) would have arisen.

(4) Where by reference to a contract term or notice a person seeks to restrict liability to a specified sum of money, and the question arises (under this or any other Act) whether the term or notice satisfies the requirement of reasonableness, regard shall be had in particular (but without prejudice to subsection (2) above in the case of contract terms) to—

     (*a*) the resources which he could expect to be available to him for the purpose of meeting the liability should it arise; and
     (*b*) how far it was open to him to cover himself by insurance.

(5) It is for those claiming that a contract term or notice satisfies the requirement of reasonableness to show that it does.

*   *   *   *   *

Varieties of exemption clause

A1–008   **13.**—(1) To the extent that this Part of this Act prevents the exclusion or restriction of any liability it also prevents—

     (*a*) making the liability or its enforcement subject to restrictive or onerous conditions;
     (*b*) excluding or restricting any right or remedy in respect of the liability, or subjecting a person to any prejudice in consequence of his pursuing any such right or remedy;
     (*c*) excluding or restricting rules of evidence or procedure;

and (to that extent) sections 2 and 5 to 7 also prevent excluding or restricting liability by reference to terms and notices which exclude or restrict the relevant obligations or duty.

(2) But an agreement in writing to submit present or future differences to arbitration is not to be treated under this Part of this Act as excluding or restricting any liability.

Interpretation of Part I

A1–009   **14.**—In this Part of this Act—

     "business" includes a profession and the activities of any government department or local or public authority;
     "goods" has the same meaning as in [the Sale of Goods Act 1979];
     "hire-purchase agreement" has the same meaning as in the Consumer Credit Act 1974;
     "negligence" has the meaning given by section 1(1);
     "notice" includes an announcement, whether or not in writing, and any other communication or pretended communication; and
     "personal injury" includes any disease and any impairment of physical or mental condition.

*   *   *   *   *

Section 1(2)   SCHEDULE 1

SCOPE OF SECTIONS 2 TO 4 AND 7

1. Sections 2 to 4 of this Act do not extend to—   **A1–010**

    (*a*) any contract of insurance (including a contract to pay an annuity on human life);

    (*b*) any contract so far as it relates to the creation or transfer of an interest in land, or to the termination of such an interest, whether by extinction, merger, surrender, forfeiture or otherwise;

    (*c*) any contract so far as it relates to the creation or transfer of a right or interest in any patent, trade mark, copyright or design right, registered design, technical or commercial information or other intellectual property, or relates to the termination of any such right or interest;

    (*d*) any contract so far as it relates—

        (i) to the formation or dissolution of a company (which means any body corporate or unincorporated association and includes a partnership), or

        (ii) to its constitution or the rights or obligations of its corporators or members;

    (*e*) any contract so far as it relates to the creation or transfer of securities or of any right or interest in securities.

2. Section 2(1) extends to—

    (*a*) any contract of marine salvage or towage;

    (*b*) any charterparty of a ship or hovercraft; and

    (*c*) any contract for the carriage of goods by ship or hovercraft;

but subject to this sections 2 to 4 and 7 do not extend to any such contract except in favour of a person dealing as consumer.

3. Where goods are carried by ship or hovercraft in pursuance of a contract which either—

    (*a*) specifies that as the means of carriage over part of the journey to be covered, or

    (*b*) makes no provision as to the means of carriage and does not exclude that means.

then sections 2(2), 3 and 4 do not, except in favour of a person dealing as consumer, extend to the contract as it operates for and in relation to the carriage of the goods by that means.

4. Section 2(1) and (2) do not extend to a contract of employment, except in favour of the employee.

5. Section 2(1) does not affect the validity of any discharge and indemnity given by a person, on or in connection with an award to him of compensation for pneumoconiosis attributable to employment in the coal industry, in respect of any further claim arising from his contracting that disease.

Sections 11(2), 24(2)   SCHEDULE 2

"GUIDELINES" FOR APPLICATION OF REASONABLENESS TEST

The matters to which regard is to be had in particular for the purposes of **A1–011** sections 6(3), 7(3) and (4), 20 and 21 are any of the following which appear to be relevant—

(*a*) the strength of the bargaining positions of the parties relative to each other, taking into account (among other things) alternative means by which the customer's requirements could have been met;

(*b*) whether the customer received an inducement to agree to the term, or in accepting it had an opportunity of entering into a similar contract with other persons, but without having to accept a similar term;

(*c*) whether the customer knew or ought reasonably to have known of the existence and extent of the term (having regard, among other things, to any custom of the trade and any previous course of dealing between the parties);

(*d*) where the term excludes or restricts any relevant liability if some condition is not complied with, whether it was reasonable at the time of the contract to expect that compliance with that condition would be practicable;

(*e*) whether the goods were manufactured, processed or adapted to the special order of the customer.

Employment Protection (Consolidation) Act 1978

(c. 44)

PART VII

INSOLVENCY OF EMPLOYER

Priority of certain debts on insolvency

121. [Repealed by the Insolvency Act 1985 (c. 65), Sched. 10 and **A1–012**
the Bankruptcy (Scotland) Act 1985 (c. 66) s. 75(2).]

Employee's rights on insolvency of employer

122.—[Repealed by the Employment Rights Act 1996 (c.18), Sched. 3 — **A1–013**
see below, para. A1–031.]

Payment of unpaid contributions to occupational pension scheme

123.—[Repealed by the Pension Schemes Act 1993 (c.48) — see below, **A1–014**
para. A1–041.]

Complaint to industrial tribunal

124.—[Repealed by the Employment Rights Act 1966 (c.18) — see **A1–015**
below, para. A1–037.]

Transfer to Secretary of State of rights and remedies

125.—[Repealed by the Employment Rights Act 1966 (c.18) — see **A1–016**
below, para. A1–038.]

**Power of Secretary of State to obtain information in connection with
application**

126.—[Repealed by the Employment Rights Act 1966 (c.18) — see **A1–017**
below, para. A1–039.]

Interpretation of ss. 122 to 126

127.—[Repealed by the Employment Rights Act 1966 (c.18) — see **A1–018**
below, para. A1–032.]

Charging Orders Act 1979

(c. 53)

Charging orders

Charging orders

A–019   **1.**—(1) Where, under a judgment or order of the High Court or a county court, a person (the "debtor") is required to pay a sum of money to another person (the "creditor") then, for the purpose of enforcing that judgment or order, the appropriate court may make an order in accordance with the provisions of this Act imposing on any such property of the debtor as may be specified in the order a charge for securing the payment of any money due or to become due under the judgment or order.

(2) The appropriate court is—

> (*a*) in a case where the property to be charged is a fund in court, the court in which that fund is lodged;
>
> (*b*) in a case where paragraph (*a*) above does not apply and the order to be enforced is a maintenance order of the High Court, the High Court or a county court;
>
> (*c*) in a case where neither paragraph (*a*) nor paragraph (*b*) above applies and the judgment or order to be enforced is a judgment or order of the High Court for a sum exceeding £2,000, the High Court or a county court; and
>
> (*d*) in any other case, a county court.

In this section "county court limit" means the county court limit for the time being specified in an Order in Council under section 145 of the County Courts Act 1984, as the county court limit for the purposes of this section and "maintenance order" has the same meaning as in section 2(*a*) of the Attachment of Earnings Act 1971.

(3) An order under subsection (1) above is referred to in this Act as a "charging order".

(4) Where a person applies to the High Court for a charging order to enforce moie than one judgment or order, that court shall be the appropriate court in relation to the application if it would be the appropriate court, apart from this subsection, on an application relating to one or more of the judgments or orders concerned.

(5) In deciding whether to make a charging order the court shall consider all the circumstances of the case and, in particular, any evidence before it as to—

> (*a*) the personal circumstances of the debtor, and
>
> (*b*) whether any other creditor of the debtor would be likely to be unduly prejudiced by the making of the order.

Property which may be charged

A1–020   **2.**—(1) Subject to subsection (3) below, a charge may be imposed by a charging order only on—

> (*a*) any interest held by the debtor beneficially—
>
> > (i) in any asset of a kind mentioned in subsection (2) below, or
> > (ii) under any trust; or
>
> (*b*) any interest held by a person as trustee of a trust ("the trust"), if the interest is in such an asset or is an interest under another trust and—

    (i) the judgment or order in respect of which a charge is to be imposed was made against that person as trustee of the trust, or

    (ii) the whole beneficial interest under the trust is held by the debtor unencumbered and for his own benefit, or

    (iii) in a case where there are two or more debtors all of whom are liable to the creditor for the same debt, they together hold the whole beneficial interest under the trust unencumbered and for their own benefit.

(2) The assets referred to in subsection (1) above are—

(*a*) land,

(*b*) securities of any of the following kinds—

    (i) government stock,

    (ii) stock of any body (other than a building society) incorporated within England and Wales,

    (iii) stock of any body incorporated outside England and Wales or of any state or territory outside the United Kingdom, being stock registered in a register kept at any place within England and Wales,

    (iv) units of any unit trust in respect of which a register of the unit holders is kept at any place within England and Wales, or

(*c*) funds in court.

(3) In any case where a charge is imposed by a charging order on any interest in an asset of a kind mentioned in paragraph (*b*) or (*c*) of subsection (2) above, the court making the order may provide for the charge to extend to any interest or dividend payable in respect of the asset.

Provisions supplementing sections 1 and 2

3.—(1) A charging order may be made either absolutely or subject to **A1–021** conditions as to notifying the debtor or as to the time when the charge is to become enforceable, or as to other matters.

(2) The Land Charges Act 1972 and the Land Registration Act 1925 shall apply in relation to charging orders as they apply in relation to other orders or writs issued or made for the purpose of enforcing judgments.

(3) In section 49 of the Land Registration Act 1925 (protection of certain interests by notice) there is inserted at the end of subsection (1) the following paragraph—

"(*g*) charging orders (within the meaning of the Charging Orders Act 1979) which in the case of unregistered land may be protected by registration under the Land Charges Act 1972 and which notwithstanding section 59 of this Act, it may be deemed expedient to protect by notice instead of by caution."

(4) Subject to the provisions of this Act, a charge imposed by a charging order shall have the like effect and shall be enforceable in the same courts and in the same manner as an equitable charge created by the debtor by writing under his hand.

(5) The court by which a charging order was made may at any time, on the application of the debtor or of any person interested in any property to which the order relates, make an order discharging or varying the charging order.

(6) Where a charging order has been protected by an entry registered under the Land Charges Act 1972 or the Land Registration Act 1925, an order under subsection (5) above discharging the charging order may direct that the entry be cancelled.

(7) The Lord Chancellor may by order made by statutory instrument amend section 2(2) of this Act by adding to, or removing from, the kinds of asset for the time being referred to there, any asset of a kind which in his opinion ought to be so added or removed.

(8) Any order under subsection (7) above shall be subject to annulment in pursuance of a resolution of either House of Parliament.

Completion of execution

A1–022   **4.**—[Repealed by the Insolvency Act 1985 (c.65), s.235, Sched. 10, Pt. II.]

Companies Act 1985

(c. 6)

PART I

FORMATION AND REGISTRATION OF COMPANIES; JURIDICAL STATUS AND MEMBERSHIP

* * * * *

CHAPTER III

A COMPANY'S CAPACITY; FORMALITIES OF CARRYING ON BUSINESS

A company's capacity not limited by its memorandum

35.—(1) The validity of an act done by a company shall not be called into **A1–023** question on the ground of lack of capacity by reason of anything in the company's memorandum.

(2) A member of a company may bring proceedings to restrain the doing of an act which but for subsection (1) would be beyond the company's capacity; but no such proceedings shall lie in respect of an act to be done in fulfilment of a legal obligation arising from a previous act of the company.

(3) It remains the duty of the directors to observe any limitations on their powers flowing from the company's memorandum; and action by the directors which but for subsection (1) would be beyond the company's capacity may only be ratified by the company by special resolution.

A resolution ratifying such action shall not affect any liability incurred by the directors or any other person; relief from any such liability must be agreed to separately by special resolution.

(4) The operation of this section is restricted by section 30B(1) of the Charities Act 1960 and section 112(3) of the Companies Act 1989 in relation to companies which are charities; and section 322A below (invalidity of certain transactions to which directors or their associates are parties) has effect notwithstanding this section.

Power of directors to bind the company

35A.—(1) In favour of a person dealing with a company in good faith, the **A1–024** power of the board of directors to bind the company, or authorise others to do so, shall be deemed to be free of any limitation under the company's constitution.

(2) For this purpose—

  (*a*) a person "deals with" a company if he is a party to any transaction or other act to which the company is a party;
  (*b*) a person shall not be regarded as acting in bad faith by reason only of his knowing that an act is beyond the powers of the directors under the company's constitution; and
  (*c*) a person shall be presumed to have acted in good faith unless the contrary is proved.

(3) The references above to limitations on the directors' powers under the company's constitution include limitations deriving—

(*a*) from a resolution of the company in general meeting or a meeting of any class of shareholders, or

(*b*) from any agreement between the members of the company or of any class of shareholders.

(4) Subsection (1) does not affect any right of a member of the company to bring proceedings to restrain the doing of an act which is beyond the powers of the directors; but no such proceedings shall lie in respect of an act to be done in fulfilment of a legal obligation arising from a previous act of the company.

(5) Nor does that subsection affect any liability incurred by the directors, or any other person, by reason of the directors' exceeding their powers.

(6) The operation of this section is restricted by section 30B(1) of the Charities Act 1960 and section 112(3) of the Companies Act 1989 in relation to companies which are charities; and section 322A below (invalidity of certain transactions to which directors or their associates are parties) has effect notwithstanding this section.

No duty to enquire as to capacity of company or authority of directors

A1–025   **35B.** A party to a transaction withì a company is not bound to enquire as to whether it is permitted by the company's memorandum or as to any limitation on the powers of the board of directors to bind the company or authorise others to do so.

*   *   *   *   *

PART XII

REGISTRATION OF CHARGES

CHAPTER 1

REGISTRATION OF CHARGES (ENGLAND AND WALES)

Certain charges void if not registered

A1–026   **395.**—(1) Subject to the provisions of this Chapter, a charge created by a company registered in England and Wales and being a charge to which this section applies is, so far as any security on the company's property or undertaking is conferred by the charge, void against the liquidator [or administrator] and any creditor of the company, unless the prescribed particulars of the charge together with the instrument (if any) by which the charge is created or evidenced, are delivered to or received by the registrar of companies for registration in the manner required by this Chapter within 21 days after the date of the charge's creation.

(2) Subsection (1) is without prejudice to any contract or obligation for repayment of the money secured by the charge; and when a charge becomes void under this section, the money secured by it immediately becomes payable.

Charges which have to be registered

396.—(1) Section 395 applies to the following charges— A1–027

 (*a*) a charge for the purpose of securing any issue of debentures,
 (*b*) a charge on uncalled share capital of the company,
 (*c*) a charge created or evidenced by an instrument which, if executed by an individual, would require registration as a bill of sale,
 (*d*) a charge on land (wherever situated) or any interest in it, but not including a charge for any rent or other periodical sum issuing out of the land,
 (*e*) a charge on book debts of the company,
 (*f*) a floating charge on the company's undertaking or property,
 (*g*) a charge on calls made but not paid,
 (*h*) a charge on a ship or aircraft, or any share in a ship,
 (*j*) a charge on goodwill, on a patent or a licence under a patent, on a trademark or on a copyright or a licence under a copyright.

(2) Where a negotiable instrument has been given to secure the payment of any book debts of a company, the deposit of the instrument for the purpose of securing an advance to the company is not, for purposes of section 395, to be treated as a charge on those book debts.

(3) The holding of debentures entitling the holder to a charge on land is not for purposes of this section deemed to be an interest in land.

(4) In this Chapter, "charge" includes mortgage.

* * * * *

PART XXVI

INTERPRETATION

* * * * *

"Company," etc.

735.—(1) In this Act— A1–028

 (*a*) "company" means a company formed and registered under this Act, or an existing company.

(4) The definitions in this section apply unless the contrary intention appears.

"Director" and "shadow director"

741.—(1) In this Act, "director" includes any person occupying the position of director, by whatever name called.

(2) In relation to a company, "shadow director" means a person in accordance with whose directions or instructions the directors of the company are accustomed to act.

However, a person is not deemed a shadow director by reason only that the directors act on advice given by him in a professional capacity.

(3) For the purposes of the following provisions of this Act, namely—

section 309 (directors' duty to have regard to interests of employees),
section 319 (directors' long-term contracts of employment),
sections 320 and 322 (substantial property transactions involving directors),
[section 322B (contracts with sole members who are director), and]

sections 330 to 346 (general restrictions on power of companies to make loans, etc., to directors and others connected with them),

(being provisions under which shadow directors are treated as directors), a body corporate is not to be treated as a shadow director of any of its subsidiary companies by reason only that the directors of the subsidiary are accustomed to act in accordance with its directions or instructions.

Law of Property (Miscellaneous Provisions) Act 1989

(C. 34)

Deeds and their execution

1.1. (1) Any rule of law which—   **A1–029**

(*a*) restricts the substances on which a deed may be written;
(*b*) requires a seal for the valid execution of an instrument as a deed by an individual; or
(*c*) requires authority by one person to another to deliver an instrument as a deed on his behalf to be given by deed,

is abolished.

(2) An instrument shall not be a deed unless—

(*a*) it makes it clear on its face that it is intended to be a deed by the person making it or, as the case may be, by the parties to it (whether by describing itself as a deed or expressing itself to be executed or signed as a deed or otherwise); and
(*b*) it is validly executed as a deed by that person or, as the case may be, one or more of those parties.

(3) An instrument is validly executed as a deed by an individual if, and only if—

(*a*) it is signed—

(i) by him in the presence of a witness who attests the signature; or
(ii) at his direction and in his presence and the presence of two witnesses who each attest the signature; and

(*b*) it is delivered as a deed by him or a person authorised to do so on his behalf.

(4) In subsections (2) and (3) above "sign", in relation to an instrument, includes making one's mark on the instrument and "signature" is to be construed accordingly.

(5) Where a solicitor or licensed conveyancer, or an agent or employee of a solicitor or licensed conveyancer, in the course of or in connection with a transaction involving the disposition or creation of an interest in land, purports to deliver an instrument as a deed on behalf of a party to the instrument, it shall be conclusively presumed in favour of a purchaser that he is authorised so to deliver the instrument.

(6) In subsection (5) above—

"disposition" and "purchaser" have the same meanings as in the Law of Property Act 1925;
"duly certificated notary public" has the same meaning as it has in the Solicitors Act 1974, by virtue of section 87 of that Act; and
"interest in land" means any estate, interest or charge in or over land or in or over the proceeds of sale of land.

(7) Where an instrument under seal that constitutes a deed is required for the purposes of an Act passed before this section comes into force, this section shall have effect as to signing, sealing or delivery of an instrument by an individual in place of any provision of that Act as to signing, sealing or delivery.

(8) The enactments mentioned in Schedule 1 to this Act (which in consequence of this section require amendments other than those provided by

subsection (7) above) shall have effect with the amendments specified in that Schedule.

(9) Nothing in subsection (1)(*b*), (2), (3), (7) or (8) above applies in relation to deeds required or authorised to be made under—

(*a*) the seal of the county palatine of Lancaster;
(*b*) the seal of the Duchy of Lancaster; or
(*c*) the seal of the Duchy of Cornwall.

(10) The references in this section to the execution of a deed by an individual do not include execution by a corporation sole and the reference in subsection (7) above to signing, sealing, or delivery by an individual does not include signing, selling or delivery by such a corporation.

(11) Nothing in this section applies in relation to instruments delivered as deeds before this section comes into force.

* * * * *

A1–030 Section 4 SCHEDULE 2

REPEALS

Chapter	Short title	Extent of repeal
15 & 15 Geo. 5 c. 20	The Law of Property Act 1925	Section 40 Section 73. In section 74(3), the words "and in the case of a deed by affixing his own seal,".
1971 c. 27	The Powers of Attorney Act 1971	Section 1(2). In section 7, subsection (1), the words "and seal" and in subsection (2), the words "or (4)".

Employment Rights Act 1996

(C. 18)

PART XII

Employee's rights on insolvency of employer

182. If, on an application made to him in writing by an employee, the Secretary **A1–031** of State is satisfied that—

(a) the employee's employer has become insolvent,

(b) the employee's employment has been terminated, and

(c) on the appropriate date the employee was entitled to be paid the whole or part of any debt to which this Part applies,

the Secretary of State shall, subject to section 186, to pay the employee out of the National Insurance Fund the amount to which, in the opinion of the Secretary of State, the employee is entitled in respect of the debt.

Insolvency

183.—(1) An employer has become insolvent for the purposes of this Part— **A1–032**

(a) where the employer is an individual, if (but only if) subsection (2) is satisfied, and

(b) where the employer is a company, if (but only if) subsection (3) is satisfied.

(2) This subsection is satisfied in the case of an employer who is an individual—

(a) in England and Wales if—

(i) he has been adjudged bankrupt or has made a composition or arrangement with his creditors, or

(ii) he has died and his estate falls to be administered in accordance with an order under section 421 of the Insolvency Act 1986, and

(b) in Scotland if—

(i) sequestration of his estate has been awarded or he has executed a trust deed for his creditors or has entered into a composition contract, or

(ii) he has died and a judicial factor appointed under section 11A of the Judicial Factors (Scotland) Act 1889 is required by that section to divide his insolvent estate among his creditors.

(3) This subsection is satisfied in the case of an employer which is a company—

(a) if a winding up order or an administration order has been made, or a resolution for voluntary winding up has been passed, with respect to the company,

(b) if a receiver or (in England and Wales only) a manager of the company's undertaking has been duly appointed, or (in England and Wales only) possession has been taken, by or on behalf of the holders

of any debentures secured by a floating charge, of any property of the
company comprised in or subject to the charge, or

(c) if a voluntary arrangement proposed in the case of the company for the
purposes of Part I of the Insolvency Act 1986 has been approved under
that Part of that Act.

Debts to which Part applies

A1–033 184.—(1) This part applies to the following debts—

(a) any arrears of pay in respect of one or more (but not more than eight)
weeks,

(b) any amount which the employer is liable to pay the employee for the
period of notice required by section 86(1) or (2) or for any failure of
the employer to give the period of notice required by section 86(1),

(c) any holiday pay—

(i) in respect of a period or periods of holiday not exceeding six
weeks in all, and

(ii) to which the employee became entitled during the twelve
months ending with the appropriate date,

(d) any basic award of compensation for unfair dismissal, or so much of an
award under a designated dismissal procedures agreement as does not
exceed any basic award of compensation for unfair dismissal to which
the employee would be entitled but for the agreement, and

(e) any reasonable sum by way of reimbursement of the whole or part of
any fee or premium paid by an apprentice or articled clerk.

(2) For the purposes of subsection (1)(a) the following amounts shall be
treated as arrears of pay—

(a) a guarantee payment,

(b) any payment for time off under Part VI of this Act or section 169 of the
Trade Union and Labour Relations (Consolidation) Act 1992 (payment
for time off for carrying out trade union duties etc.),

(c) remuneration on suspension on medical grounds under section 64 of
this Act and remuneration on suspension on maternity grounds under
section 68 of this Act, and

(d) remuneration under a protective award under section 189 of the Trade
Union and Labour Relations (Consolidation) Act 1992.

(3) In subsection (1)(c) "holiday pay", in relation to an employee, means—

(a) pay in respect of a holiday actually taken by the employee, or

(b) any accrued holiday pay which, under the employee's contract of
employment, would in the ordinary course have become payable to him
in respect of the period of a holiday if his employment with the
employer had continued until he became entitled to a holiday.

(4) A sum shall be taken to be reasonable for the purposes of subsection (1)(e)
in a case where a trustee in bankruptcy, or (in Scotland) a permanent or interim
trustee (within the meaning of the Bankruptcy (Scotland) Act 1985), or
liquidator has been or is required to be appointed—

(a) as respects England and Wales, if it is admitted to be reasonable by the
trustee in bankruptcy or liquidator under section 348 of the Insolvency
Act 1986 (effect of bankruptcy on apprenticeships etc.), Whether as

originally enacted or as applied to the winding up of a company by rules under section 411 of that Act, and

(b) as respects Scotland, if it is accepted by the permanent or interim trustee or liquidator for the purposes of the sequestration or winding up.

The appropriate date

185. In this Part "the appropriate date"— **A1–034**

(a) in relation to arrears of pay (not being remuneration under a protective award made under section 189 of the Trade Union and Labour Relations (Consolidation) Act 1992) and to holiday pay, means the date on which the employer became insolvent,

(b) in relation to a basic award of compensation for unfair dismissal and to remuneration under a protective award so made, means whichever is the latest of—

(i) the date on which the employer became insolvent,
(ii) the date of the termination of the employee's employment, and
(iii) the date on which the award was made, and

(c) in relation to any other debt to which this Part applies, means whichever is the later of—

(i) the date on which the employer became insolvent, and
(ii) the date of the termination of the employee's employment.

Limit on amount payable under section 182

186.—(1) The total amount payable to an employee in respect of any debt to **A1–035** which this Part applies, where the amount of the debt is referable to a period of time, shall not exceed—

(a) £230 in respect of any one week, or
(b) in respect of a shorter period, an amount bearing the same proportion to £230 as that shorter period bears to a week.

Role of relevant officer

187.—(1) Where a relevant officer has been, or is required to be, appointed in **A1–036** connection with an employer's insolvency, the Secretary of State shall not make a payment under section 182 in respect of a debt until he has received a statement from the relevant officer of the amount of that debt which appears to have been owed to the employee on the appropriate date and to remain unpaid.

(2) If the Secretary of State is satisfied that he does not require a statement under subsection (1) in order to determine the amount of a debt which was owed to the employee on the appropriate date and remains unpaid, he may make a payment under section 182 in respect of the debt without having received such a statement.

(3) A relevant officer shall, on request by the Secretary of State, provide him with a statement for the purposes of subsection (1) as soon as is reasonably practicable.

(4) The following are relevant officers for the purposes of this section—

(a) a trustee in bankruptcy or a permanent or interim trustee (within the meaning of the Bankruptcy (Scotland) Act 1985),
(b) a liquidator,
(c) an administrator,
(d) a receiver or manager,

(e) a trustee under a composition or arrangement between the employer and his creditors, and

(f) a trustee under a trust deed for his creditors executed by the employer.

(5) In subsection (4)(e) "trustee" includes the supervisor of a voluntary arrangement proposed for the purposes of, and approved under, Part I or VIII of the Insolvency Act 1986.

Complaints to employment tribunals

A1–037 **188.**—(1) A person who has applied for a payment under section 182 may present a complaint to an employment tribunal.

(a) that the Secretary of State has failed to make any such payment, or

(b) that any such payment made by him is less than the amount which should have been paid.

(2) An employment tribunal shall not consider a complaint under subsection (1) unless it is presented—

(a) before the end of the period of three months beginning with the date on which the decision of the Secretary of State on the application was communicated to the applicant, or

(b) within such further period as the tribunal considers reasonable in a case where it is not reasonably practicable for the complaint to be presented before the end of that period of three months.

(3) Where an employment tribunal finds that the Secretary of State ought to make a payment under section 182, the tribunal shall—

(a) make a declaration to that effect, and

(b) declare the amount of any such payment which it finds the Secretary of State ought to make.

Transfer to Secretary of State of rights and remedies

A1–038 **189.**—(1) Where, in pursuance of section 182, the Secretary of State makes a payment to an employee in respect of a debt to which this Part applies—

(a) on the making of the payment any rights and remedies of the employee in respect of the debt (or, if the Secretary of State has paid only part of it, in respect of that part) become rights and remedies of the Secretary of State, and

(b) any decision of an employment tribunal requiring an employer to pay that debt to the employee has the effect that the debt (or the part of it which the Secretary of State has paid) is to be paid to the Secretary of State.

(2) Where a debt (or any part of a debt) in respect of which the Secretary of State has made a payment in pursuance of section 182 constitutes—

(a) a preferential debt within the meaning of the Insolvency Act 1986 for the purposes of any provision of that Act (including any such provision as applied by any order made under that Act) or any provision of the Companies Act 1985, or

(b) a preferred debt within the meaning of the Bankruptcy (Scotland) Act 1985 for the purposes of any provision of that Act (including any such provision as applied by section 11A of the Judicial Factors (Scotland) Act 1889), the rights which become rights of the Secretary of State in accordance with subsection (1) include any right arising under any such provision by reason of the status of the debt (or that part of it) as a preferential or preferred debt.

(3) In computing tbr the purposes of any provision mentioned in subsection (2)(a) or (b) the aggregate amount payable in priority to other creditors of the employer in respect of—

(a) any claim of the Secretary of State to be paid in priority to other creditors of the employer by virtue of subsection (2), and
(b) any claim by the employee to be so paid made in his own right,

any claim of the Secretary of State to be so paid by virtue of subsection (2) shall be treated as if it were a claim of the employee.

(4) But the Secretary of State shall be entitled, as against the employee, to be so paid in respect of any such claim of his (up to the full amount of the claim) before any payment is made to the employee in respect of any claim by the employee to be so paid made in his own right.

(5) Any sum recovered by the Secretary of State in exercising any right, or pursuing any remedy, which is his by virtue of this section shall be paid into the National Insurance Fund.

Power to obtain information

190.—(1) Where an application is made to the Secretary of State under section **A1–039** 182 in respect of a debt owed by an employer, the Secretary of State may require—

(a) the employer to provide him with such information as he may reasonably require for the purpose of determining whether the application is well-founded, and
(b) any person having the custody or control of any relevant records or other documents to produce for examination on behalf of the Secretary of State any such document in that person's custody or under his control which is of such a description as the Secretary of State may require.

(2) Any such requirement—

(a) shall be made by notice in writing given to the person on whom the requirement is imposed, and
(b) may be varied or revoked by a subsequent notice so given.

(3) If a person refuses or wilfully neglects to furnish any information or produce any document which he has been required to furnish or produce by a notice under this section he is guilty of an offence and liable on summary conviction to a fine not exceeding level 3 on the standard scale.

(4) If a person, in purporting to comply with a requirement of a notice under this section, knowingly or recklessly makes any false statement he is guilty of an offence and liable on summary conviction to a fine not exceeding level 5 on the standard scale.

(5) Where an offence under this section committed by a body corporate is proved—

(a) to have been committed with the consent or connivance of, or
(b) to be attributable to any neglect on the part of,

any director, manager, secretary or other similar officer of the body corporate, or any person who was purporting to act in any such capacity, he (as well as the body corporate) is guilty of the offence and liable to be proceeded against and punished accordingly.

(6) Where the affairs of a body corporate are managed by its members, subsection (5) applies in relation to the acts and defaults of a member in connection with his functions of management as if he were a director of the body corporate.

Pension Schemes Act 1993

(c. 48)

PART VII

CHAPTER II

Interpretation of Chapter II

123.—(1) For the purposes of this Chapter, an employer shall be taken to be **A1–040** insolvent if, but only if, in England and Wales—

    (a) he has been adjudged bankrupt or has made a composition or arrangement with his creditors;

    (b) he has died and his estate falls to be administered in accordance with an order under section 421 of the Insolvency Act 1986; or

    (c) where the employer is a company—

        (i) a winding-up order or an administration order is made or a resolution for voluntary winding up is passed with respect to it,

        (ii) a receiver or manager of its undertaking is duly appointed,

        (iii) possession is taken, by or on behalf of the holders of any debentures secured by a floating charge, of any property of the company comprised in or subject to the charge, or

        (iv) a voluntary arrangement proposed for the purpose of Part I of the Insolvency Act 1986 is approved under that Part.

(2) For the purposes of this Chapter, an employer shall be taken to be insolvent if, but only if, in Scotland—

    (a) sequestration of his estate is awarded or he executes a trust deed for his creditors or enters into a composition contract;

    (b) he has died and a judicial factor appointed under section 11A of the Judicial Factors (Scotland) Act 1889 is required by that section to divide his insolvent estate among his creditors; or

    (c) where the employer is a company—

        (i) a winding-up order or an administration order is made or a resolution for voluntary winding up is passed with respect to it,

        (ii) a receiver of its undertaking is duly appointed, or

        (iii) a voluntary arrangement proposed for the purpose of Part I of the Insolvency Act 1986 is approved under that Part.

(3) In this Chapter—
"contract of employment", "employee", "employer" and "employment" and other expressions which are defined in the Employment Rights Act 1996 have the same meaning as in that Act; "holiday pay" means—

    (a) pay in respect of holiday actually taken; or

    (b) any accrued holiday pay which under the employee's contract of employment would in the ordinary course have become payable to him in respect of the period of a holiday if his employment with the employer had continued until he became entitled to a holiday;

"occupational pension scheme" means any scheme or arrangement which provides or is capable of providing, in relation to employees in any description of employment, benefits, in the form of pensions or otherwise, payable to or in respect of any such employees on the termination of their employment or on their death or retirement.

(4) For the purposes of this Chapter, the definition of "personal pension scheme" in section 1 has effect with the substitution for the words "employed earners" of the word "employees".

(5) Any reference in this Chapter to the resources of a scheme is a reference to the funds out of which the benefits provided by the scheme are from time to time payable.

Duty of Secretary of State to pay unpaid contributions to schemes

A1–041 124.—(1) If, on an application made to him in writing by the persons competent to act in respect of an occupational pension scheme or a personal pension scheme, the Secretary of State is satisfied—

(a) that an employer has become insolvent; and

(b) that at the time he did so there remained unpaid relevant contributions falling to be paid by him to the scheme,

then, subject to the provisions of this section and section 125, the Secretary of State shall pay into the resources of the scheme the sum which in his opinion is payable in respect of the unpaid relevant contributions.

(2) In this section and section 125 "relevant contributions" means contributions falling to be paid by an employer to an occupational pension scheme or a personal pension scheme, either on his own account or on behalf of an employee; and for the purposes of this section a contribution shall not be treated as falling to be paid on behalf of an employee unless a sum equal to that amount has been deducted from the pay of the employee by way of a contribution from him.

(3) Subject to subsection (3A), the sum payable under this section in respect of unpaid contributions of an employer on his own account to an occupational pension scheme or a personal pension scheme shall be the least of the following amounts—

(a) the balance of relevant contributions remaining unpaid on the date when he became insolvent and payable by the employer on his own account to the scheme in respect of the 12 months immediately preceding that date;

(b) the amount certified by an actuary to be necessary for the purpose of meeting the liability of the scheme on dissolution to pay the benefits provided by the scheme to or in respect of the employees of the employer;

(c) an amount equal to 10 per cent, of the total amount of remuneration paid or payable to those employees in respect of the 12 months immediately preceding the date on which the employer became insolvent.

(3A) Where the scheme in question is a money purchase scheme, the sum payable under this section by virtue of subsection (3) shall be the lesser of the amounts mentioned in paragraph (a) and (c) of that subsection.

(4) For the purposes of subsection (3)(c), "remuneration" includes holiday pay, statutory sick pay, statutory maternity pay under Part V of the Social Security Act 1986 or Part XII of the Social Security Contributions and Benefits Act 1992, and any payment such as is referred to in section 184(2) of the Employment Rights Act 1996.

(5) Any sum payable under this section in respect of unpaid contributions on behalf of an employee shall not exceed the amount deducted from the pay of the employee in respect of the employee's contributions to the scheme during the 12 months immediately preceding the date on which the employer became insolvent.

Certification of amounts payable under section 124 by insolvency officers

125.—(1) This section applies where one of the officers mentioned in subsection **A1–042**
(2) ("the relevant officer") has been or is required to be appointed in connection
with an employer's insolvency.
 (2) The officers referred to in subsection (1) are—

 (a) a trustee in bankruptcy;
 (b) a liquidator;
 (c) an administrator;
 (d) a receiver or manager; or
 (e) a trustee under a composition or arrangement between the employer
      and his creditors or under a trust deed for his creditors executed by the
      employer;

and in this subsection "trustee", in relation to a composition or arrangement,
includes the supervisor of a voluntary arrangement proposed for the purposes of
and approved under Part I or VIII of the Insolvency Act 1986.
 (3) Subject to subsection (5), where this section applies the Secretary of State
shall not make any payment under section 124 in respect of unpaid relevant
contributions until he has received a statement from the relevant officer of the
amount of relevant contributions which appear to have been unpaid on the date
on which the employer became insolvent and to remain unpaid; and the relevant
officer shall on request by the Secretary of State provide him as soon as
reasonably practicable with such a statement.
 (4) Subject to subsection (5), an amount shall be taken to be payable, paid or
deducted as mentioned in subsection (3)(a) or (c) or (5) of section 124 only if it
is so certified by the relevant officer.
 (5) If the Secretary of State is satisfied—

 (a) that he does not require a statement under subsection (3) in order to
      determine the amount of relevant contributions that was unpaid on the
      date on which the employer became insolvent and remains unpaid, or
 (b) that he does not require a certificate under subsection (4) in order to
      determine the amounts payable, paid or deducted as mentioned in
      subsection (3)(a) or (c) or (5) of section 124,

he may make a payment under that section in respect of the contributions in
question without having received such a statement or, as the case may be, such a
certificate.

Complaint to industrial tribunal

126.—(1) Any persons who are competent to act in respect of an occupational **A1–043**
pension scheme or a personal pension scheme and who have applied for a
payment to be made under section 124 into the resources of the scheme may
present a complaint to an employment tribunal, that—

 (a) the Secretary of State has failed to make any such payment; or
 (b) any such payment made by him is less than the amount which should
      have been paid.

 (2) Such a complaint must be presented within the period of three months
beginning with the date on which the decision of the Secretary of State on that
application was communicated to the persons presenting it or, if that is not
reasonably practicable, within such further period as is reasonable.
 (3) Where an employment tribunal finds that the Secretary of State ought to
make a payment under section 124, it shall make a declaration to that effect and
shall also declare the amount of any such payment which it finds that the
Secretary of State ought to make.

Transfer to Secretary of State of rights and remedies

A1–044 127.—(1) Where in pursuance of section 124 the Secretary of State makes any payment into the resources of an occupational pension scheme or a personal pension scheme in respect of any contributions to the scheme, any rights and remedies in respect of those contributions belonging to the persons competent to act in respect of the scheme shall, on the making of the payment, become rights and remedies of the Secretary of State.

(2) Where the Secretary of State makes any such payment as is mentioned in subsection (1) and the sum (or any part of the sum) falling to be paid by the employer on account of the contributions in respect of which the payment is made constitutes—

> (a) a preferential debt within the meaning of the Insolvency Act 1986 for the purposes of any provision of that Act (including any such provision as applied by an order made under that Act) or any provision of the Companies Act 1985; or
>
> (b) a preferred debt within the meaning of the Bankruptcy (Scotland) Act 1985 for the purposes of any provision of that Act (including any such provision as applied by section 11A of the Judicial Factors (Scotland) Act 1889),

then, without prejudice to the generality of subsection (1), there shall be included among the rights and remedies which become rights and remedies of the Secretary of State in accordance with that subsection any right arising under any such provision by reason of the status of that sum (or that part of it) as a preferential or preferred debt.

(3) In computing for the purposes of any provision referred to in subsection (2)(a) or (b) the aggregate amount payable in priority to other creditors of the employer in respect of—

> (a) any claim of the Secretary of State to be so paid by virtue of subsection (2); and
>
> (b) any claim by the persons competent to act in respect of the scheme,

any claim falling within paragraph (a) shall be treated as if it were a claim of those persons; but the Secretary of State shall be entitled, as against those persons, to be so paid in respect of any such claim of his (up to the full amount of the claim) before any payment is made to them in respect of any claim falling within paragraph (b).

Appendix 2—Statutory Instruments

Transfer of Undertakings (Protection of Employment) Regulations 1981

(S.I. 1981 No. 1794)

A draft of these Regulations has been approved by resolution of each House of **A2–001**
Parliament in pursuance of paragraph 2(2) of Schedule 2 to the European
Communities Act 1972. They are dated December 14, 1981, and made by the
Secretary of State, being a Minister designated for the purposes of section 2(2) of
that Act in relation to rights and obligations relating to employers and employees
on the transfer or merger of undertakings, businesses or parts of businesses, in
exercise of the powers conferred by that section.

Citation, commencement and extent

1.—(1) These Regulations may be cited as the Transfer of Undertakings **A2–002**
(Protection of Employment) Regulations 1981.

(2) These Regulations, except Regulations 4 to 9 and 14, shall come into
operation on February 1, 1982 and Regulations 4 to 9 and 14 shall come into
operation on May 1, 1982.

(3) These Regulations, except Regulations 11(10) and 13(3) and (4), extend to
Northern Ireland.

Interpretation

2.—(1) In these Regulations—   **A2–003**

"collective agreements," "employers' association," and "trade union" have
the same meanings respectively as in the 1974 Act or, in Northern
Ireland, the 1976 Order;

"collective bargaining" has the same meaning as it has in the 1975 Act or, in
Northern Ireland, the 1976 Order;

"contract of employment" means any agreement between an employee and
his employer determining the terms and conditions of his employment;

"employee" means any individual who works for another person whether
under a contract of service or apprenticeship or otherwise but does not
include anyone who provides services under a contract for services and
references to a person's employer shall be construed accordingly;

"the 1974 Act," "the 1975 Act," "the 1978 Act" and "the 1976 Order" mean,
respectively, the Trade Union and Labour Relations Act 1974, the Employment Protection Act 1975, the Employment Protection (Consolidation) Act
1978 and the Industrial Relations (Northern Ireland) Order 1976;

"recognised," in relation to a trade union, means recognised to any extent
by an employer, or two or more associated employers (within the
meaning of the 1978 Act, or, in Northern Ireland, the 1976 Order), for
the purpose of collective bargaining;

"relevant transfer" means a transfer to which these Regulations apply and
"transferor" and "transferee" shall be construed accordingly; and

"undertaking" includes any trade or business.

(2) References in these Regulations to the transfer of part of an undertaking are references to a transfer of a part which is being transferred as a business and, accordingly, do not include references to a transfer of a ship without more.

(3) For the purposes of these Regulations the representative of a trade union recognised by an employer is an official or other person authorised to carry on collective bargaining with that employer by that union.

A relevant transfer

A2–004   **3.**—(1) Subject to the provisions of these Regulations, these Regulations apply to a transfer from one person to another of an undertaking situated immediately before the transfer in the United Kingdom or a part of one which is so situated.

(2) Subject as aforesaid, these Regulations so apply whether the transfer is effected by sale or by some other disposition or by operation of law.

(3) Subject as aforesaid, these Regulations so apply notwithstanding—

(*a*) that the transfer is governed or effected by the law of a country or territory outside the United Kingdom;

(*b*) that persons employed in the undertaking or part transferred ordinarily work outside the United Kingdom;

(*c*) that the employment of any of those persons is governed by any such law.

(4) It is hereby declared that a transfer of an undertaking or part of one

(a) may be effected by a series of two or more transactions; and

(b) may take place whether or not any property is transferred to the transferee by the transferor.

(5) Where, in consequence (whether directly or indirectly) of the transfer of an undertaking or part of one which was situated immediately before the transfer in the United Kingdom, a ship within the meaning of the Merchant Shipping Act 1894 registered in the United Kingdom ceases to be so registered, these Regulations shall not affect the right conferred by section 5 of the Merchant Shipping Act 1970 (right of seamen to be discharged when ship ceases to be registered in the United Kingdom) on a seaman employed in the ship.

Transfers by receivers and liquidators

A2–005   **4.**—(1) Where the receiver of the property or part of the property of a company or, in the case of a creditors' voluntary winding up, the liquidator of a company or the administrator of a company appointed under Part II of the Insolvency Act 1986 transfers the company's undertaking, or part of the company's undertaking (the "relevant undertaking") to a wholly owned subsidiary of the company, the transfer shall for the purposes of these Regulations be deemed not to have been effected until immediately before—

(*a*) the transferee company ceases (otherwise than by reason of its being wound up) to be a wholly owned subsidiary of the transferor company; or

(*b*) the relevant undertaking is transferred by the transferee company to another person;

whichever first occurs, and, for the purposes of these Regulations, the transfer of the relevant undertaking shall be taken to have been effected immediately before that date by one transaction only.

(2) In this Regulation—

"creditors' voluntary winding up" has the same meaning as in the Companies Act 1948 or, in Northern Ireland, the Companies Act (Northern Ireland) 1960; and

"wholly owned subsidiary" has the same meaning as it has for the purposes of section 150 of the Companies Act 1948 and section 144 of the Companies Act (Northern Ireland) 1960.

Effect of relevant transfer on contracts of employment, etc.

5.—(1) A relevant transfer shall not operate so as to terminate the contract of **A2–006** employment of any person employed by the transferor in the undertaking or part transferred but any such contract which would otherwise have been terminated by the transfer shall have effect after the transfer as if originally made between the person so employed and the transferee.

(2) Without prejudice to paragraph (1) above, on the completion of a relevant transfer—

(*a*) all the transferor's rights, powers, duties and liabilities under or in connection with any such contract, shall be transferred by virtue of this Regulation to the transferee; and

(*b*) anything done before the transfer is completed by or in relation to the transferor in respect of that contract or a person employed in that undertaking or part shall be deemed to have been done by or in relation to the transferee.

(3) Any reference in paragraph (1) or (2) above to a person employed in an undertaking or part of one transferred by a relevant transfer is a reference to a person so employed immediately before the transfer, including, where the transfer is effected by a series of two or more transactions, a person so employed immediately before any of those transactions.

(4) Paragraph (2) above shall not transfer or otherwise affect the liabilities of any person to be prosecuted for, convicted of and sentenced for any offence.

(4A) Paragraphs (1) and (2) above shall not operate to transfer his contract of employment and the rights, powers, duties and liabilities under or in connection with it if the employee informs the transferor or the transferee that he objects to becoming employed by the transferee.

(4B) Where an employee so objects the transfer of the undertaking or part in which he is employed shall operate so as to terminate his contract of employment with the transferor but he shall not be treated, for any purpose, as having been dismissed by the transferor.

(5) Paragraphs (1) and (4A) above is without prejudice to any right of an employee arising apart from these Regulations to terminate his contract of employment without notice if a substantial change is made in his working conditions to his detriment; but no such right shall arise by reason only that, under that paragraph, the identity of his employer changes unless the employee shows that, in all the circumstances, the change is a significant change and is to his detriment.

Effect of relevant transfer on collective agreements

6. Where at the time of a relevant transfer there exists a collective agreement **A2–007** made by or on behalf of the transferor with a trade union recognised by the transferor in respect of any employee whose contract of employment is preserved by Regulation 5(1) above, then,—

(*a*) without prejudice to section 18 of the 1974 Act or Article 63 of the 1976 Order (collective agreements presumed to be unenforceable in specified circumstances) that agreement, in its application in relation to the employee, shall, after the transfer, have effect as if made by or on behalf of the transferee with that trade union., and accordingly anything done under or in connection with it, in its application as aforesaid, by or in relation to the transferor before the transfer, shall, after the transfer, be deemed to have been done by or in relation to the transferee and

(*b*) any order made in respect of that agreement, in its application in relation to the employee, shall, after the transfer, have effect as if the transferee were a party to the agreement.

Exclusion of occupational pensions schemes

A2–008   **7.** Regulations 5 and 6 above shall not apply—

(*a*) to so much of a contract of employment or collective agreement as relates to an occupational pension scheme within the meaning of the Social Security Pensions Act 1975 or the Social Security Pensions (Northern Ireland) Order 1975; or

(*b*) to any rights, powers, duties or liabilities under or in connection with any such contract or subsisting by virtue of any such agreement and relating to such a scheme or otherwise arising in connection with that person's employment and relating to such a scheme.

Dismissal of employee because of relevant transfer

A2–009   **8.**—(1) Where either before or after a relevant transfer, any employee of the transferor or transferee is dismissed, that employee shall be treated for the purposes of Part V of the 1978 Act and Articles 20 to 41 of the 1976 Order (unfair dismissal) as unfairly dismissed if the transfer or a reason connected with it is the reason or principal reason for his dismissal.

(2) Where an economic, technical or organisational reason entailing changes in the workforce of either the transferor or the transferee before or after a relevant transfer is the reason or principal reason for dismissing an employee—

(*a*) paragraph (1) above shall not apply to his dismissal; but

(*b*) without prejudice to the application of section 57(3) of the 1978 Act or Article 22(10) of the 1976 Order (test of fair dismissal), the dismissal shall for the purposes of section 57(1)(*b*) of that Act and Article 22(1)(*b*) of that Order (substantial reason for dismissal) be regarded as having been for a substantial reason of a kind such as to justify the dismissal of an employee holding the position which that employee held.

(3) The provisions of this Regulation apply whether or not the employee in question is employed in the undertaking or part of the undertaking transferred or to be transferred.

(4) Paragraph (1) above shall not apply in relation to the dismissal of any employee which was required by reason of the application of section 5 of the Aliens Restriction (Amendment) Act 1919 to his employment.

(5) Paragraph (1) above shall not apply in relation to a dismissal of an employee if—

(a) the application of section 54 of the 1978 Act to the dismissal of the employee is excluded by or under any provision of Part V or sections 141 to 149 of the 1978 Act or of section 237 or 238 of the Trade Union and Labour Relations (Consolidation) Act 1992; or

(b) the application of Article 20 of the 1976 Order to the dismissal of the employee is excluded by or under any provision of Part III or Article 76 of that Order.

Effect of relevant transfer on trade union recognition

9.—(1) This Regulation applies where after a relevant transfer the undertak- **A2–010** ing or part of the undertaking transferred maintains an identity distinct from the remainder of the transferee's undertaking.

(2) Where before such a transfer an independent trade union is recognised to any extent by the transferor in respect of employees of any description who in consequence of the transfer become employees of the transferee, then, after the transfer—

    (*a*) the union shall be deemed to have been recognised by the transferee to the same extent in respect of employees of that description so employed; and

    (*b*) any agreement for recognition may be varied or rescinded accordingly.

Duty to inform and consult representatives

10.—(1) In this Regulation and Regulation 11 below references to affected **A2–011** employees, in relation to a relevant transfer, are to any employees of the transferor or the transferee (whether or not employed in the undertaking or the part of the undertaking to be transferred) who may be affected by the transfer or may be affected by measures taken in connection with it; and references to the employer shall be construed accordingly.

(2) Long enough before a relevant transfer to enable the employer of any affected employees to consult all the persons who are appropriate representatives of any of those affected employees, the employer shall inform those representatives of—

    (a) the fact that the relevant transfer is to take place, when, approximately, it is to take place and the reasons for it; and

    (b) the legal, economic and social implications of the transfer for the affected employees; and

    (c) the measures which he envisages he will, in connection with the transfer, take in relation to those employees or, if he envisages that no measures will be so taken, that fact; and

    (d) if the employer is the transferor, the measures which the transferee envisages he will, in connection with the transfer, take in relation to such of those employees as, by virtue of Regulation 5 above, become employees of the transferee after the transfer or, if he envisages that no measures will be so taken, that fact.

(2A) For the purposes of this Regulation the appropriate representatives of any employees are—

    (a) if the employees are of a description in respect of which an independent trade union is recognised by their employer, representatives of the trade union, or

    (b) in any other case, whichever of the following employee representatives the employer chooses:—

        (i) employee representatives appointed or elected by the affected employees otherwise than for the purposes of this Regulation, who (having regard to the purposes for and the method by which they were appointed or elected) have authority from those employees to receive information and to be consulted about the transfer on their behalf;

        (ii) employee representatives elected by them, for the purposes of this Regulation, in an election satisfying the requirements of Regulation 10A(1).

(3) The transferee shall give the transferor such information at such a time as will enable the transferor to perform the duty imposed on him by virtue of paragraph (2)(d) above.

(4) The information which is to be given to the appropriate representatives shall be given to each of them by being delivered to them, or sent by post to an address notified by them to the employer, or (in the case of representatives of a trade union) sent by post to the union at the address of its head or main office.

(5) Where an employer of any affected employees envisages that he will, in connection with the transfer, be taking measures in relation to any such employees he shall consult all the persons who are appropriate representatives of any of the affected employees in relation to whom he envisages taking measures with a view to seeking their agreement to measures to be taken.

(6) In the course of those consultations the employer shall—

    (a) consider any representations made by the appropriate representatives; and

    (b) reply to those representations and, if he rejects any of those representations, state his reasons.

(6A) The employer shall allow the appropriate representatives access to the affected employees and shall afford to those representatives such accommodation and other facilities as may be appropriate.

(7) If in any case there are special circumstances which render it not reasonably practicable for an employer to perform a duty imposed on him by any of paragraphs (2) to (6), he shall take all such steps towards performing that duty as are reasonably practicable in the circumstances.

(8) Where—

    (a) the employer has invited any of the affected employees to elect employee representatives, and

    (b) the invitation was issued long enough before the time when the employer is required to give information under paragraph (2) above to allow them to elect representatives by that time,

the employer shall be treated as complying with the requirements of this Regulation in relation to those employees if he complies with those requirements as soon as is reasonably practicable after the election of the representatives.

(8A) If, after the employer has invited affected employees to elect representatives, they fail to do so within a reasonable time, he shall give to each affected employee the information set out in paragraph (2).

[**10A.**—(1) The requirements for the election of employee representatives under Regulation 10(2A) are that—

    (a) the employer shall make such arrangements as are reasonably practical to ensure that the election is fair;

    (b) the employer shall determine the number of representatives to be elected so that there are sufficient representatives to represent the interests of all the affected employees having regard to the number and classes of those employees;

    (c) the employer shall determine whether the affected employees should be represented either by representatives of all the affected employees or by representatives of particular classes of those employees;

    (d) before the election the employer shall determine the term of office as employee representatives so that it is of sufficient length to enable information to be given and consultations under Regulation 10 to be completed;

    (e) the candidates for election as employee representatives are affected employees on the date of the election;

    (f) no affected employee is unreasonably excluded from standing for election;

(g) all affected employees on the date of the election are entitled to vote for employee representatives;

(h) the employees entitled to vote may vote for as many candidates as there are representatives to be elected to represent them or, if there are to be representatives for particular classes of employees, may vote for as many candidates as there are representatives to be elected to represent their particular class of employee;

    (i) the election is conducted so as to secure that—

    (ii) so far as is reasonably practicable, those voting do so in secret, and

    (iii) the votes given at the election are accurately counted.

(2) Where, after an election of employee representatives satisfying the requirements of paragraph (1) has been held, one of those elected ceases to act as an employee representative and any of those employees are no longer represented, those employees shall elect another representative by an election satisfying the requirements of paragraph (1)(a), (e), (f) and (i).

Failure to inform or consult

11.—(1) A complaint that an employer has failed to inform or consult a **A2–012** representative of a trade union in accordance with Regulation 10 above may be presented to an industrial tribunal by that union.

(2) If on a complaint under paragraph (1) above a question arises whether or not it was reasonably practicable for an employer to perform a particular duty or what steps he took towards performing it, it shall be for him to show—

(a) that there were special circumstances which rendered it not reasonably practicable for him to perform the duty; and

(b) that he took all such steps towards its performance as were reasonably practicable in those circumstances.

(2A) If on a complaint under paragraph (1) a question arises as to whether or not any employee representative was an appropriate representative for the purposes of Regulation 10, it shall be for the employer to show that the employee representative had the necessary authority to represent the affected employees.

(2B) On a complaint under sub-paragraph (1)(a) it shall be for the employer to show that the requirements in Regulation 10A have been satisfied.

(3) On any such complaint against a transferor that he had failed to perform the duty imposed upon him by virtue of paragraph (2)(d) or, so far as relating thereto, paragraph (7) of Regulation 10 above, he may not show that it was not reasonably practicable for him to perform the duty in question for the reason that the transferee had failed to give him the requisite information at the requisite time in accordance with Regulation 10(3) above unless he gives the transferee notice of his intention to show that fact; and the giving of the notice shall make the transferee a party to the proceedings.

(4) Where the tribunal finds a complaint under paragraph (1) above well-founded it shall make a declaration to that effect and may—

(a) order the employer to pay appropriate compensation to such descriptions of affected employees as may be specified in the award; or

(b) if the complaint is that the transferor did not perform the duty mentioned in paragraph (3) above and the transferor (after giving due notice) shows the facts so mentioned, order the transferee to pay appropriate compensation to such descriptions of affected employees as may be specified in the award.

(5) An employee may present a complaint to an industrial tribunal on the ground that he is an employee of a description to which an order under

paragraph (4) above relates and that the transferor or the transferee has failed, wholly or in part, to pay him compensation in pursuance of the order.

(6) Where the tribunal finds a complaint under paragraph (5) above well-founded it shall order the employer to pay the complainant the amount of compensation which it finds is due to him.

(7) Where an employer, in failing to perform a duty under Regulation 10 above, also fails to comply with the requirements of section 99 of the 1975 Act or Article 49 of the 1976 Order (duty of employer to consult trade union representatives on redundancy)—

> (a) any compensation awarded to an employee under this Regulation shall go to reduce the amount of remuneration payable to him under a protective award subsequently made under Part IV of that Act or Part IV of that Order and shall also go towards discharging any liability of the employer under, or in respect of a breach of, the contract of employment in respect of a period falling within the protected period under that award; and
>
> (b) conversely any remuneration so payable and any payment made to the employee by the employer under, or by way of damages for breach of, that contract in respect of a period falling within the protected period shall go to reduce the amount of any compensation which may be subsequently awarded under this Regulation;

but this paragraph shall be without prejudice to section 102(3) of that Act and Article 52(3) of that Order (avoidance of duplication of contractual payments and remuneration under protective awards).

(8) An industrial tribunal shall not consider a complaint under paragraph (1) or (5) above unless it is presented to the tribunal before the end of the period of three months beginning with—

> (a) the date on which the relevant transfer is completed, in the case of a complaint under paragraph (1);
>
> (b) the date of the tribunal's order under paragraph (4) above, in the case of a complaint under paragraph (5);

or within such further period as the tribunal consider reasonable in a case where it is satisfied that it was not reasonably practicable for the complaint to be presented before the end of the period of three months.

(9) Section 129 of the 1978 Act (complaint to be sole remedy for breach of relevant rights) and section 133 of that Act (functions of conciliation officer) and Articles 58(2) and 62 of the 1976 Order (which make corresponding provision for Northern Ireland) shall apply to the rights conferred by this Regulation and to proceedings under this Regulation as they apply to the rights conferred by that Act or that Order and the industrial tribunal proceedings mentioned therein.

(10) An appeal shall lie and shall lie only to the Employment Appeal Tribunal on a question of law arising from any decision of, or arising in any proceedings before, an industrial tribunal under or by virtue of these Regulations and section 13(1) of the Tribunals and Inquiries Act 1971 (appeal from certain tribunals to the High Court) shalt not apply in relation to any such proceedings.

(11) In this Regulation "appropriate compensation" means such sum not exceeding two weeks' pay for the employee in question as the tribunal considers just and equitable having regard to the seriousness of the failure of the employer to comply with his duty.

(12) Schedule 14 to the 1978 Act or, in Northern Ireland, Schedule 2 to the 1975 Order shall apply for calculating the amount of a week's pay for any employee for the purposes of paragraph (11) above and, for the purposes of that calculation, the calculation date shall be—

> (a) in the case of an employee who is dismissed by reason of redundancy (within the meaning of section 81 of the 1978 Act or, in Northern

Ireland, section 11 of the Contracts of Employment and Redundancy Payments Act (Northern Ireland) 1965) the date which is the calculation date for the purposes of any entitlement of his to a redundancy payment (within the meaning of that section) or which would be that calculation date if he were so entitled;

(b) in the case of an employee who is dismissed for any other reason, the effective date of termination (within the meaning of section 55 of the 1978 Act or, in Northern Ireland, Article 21 of the 1976 Order) of his contract of employment;

(c) in any other case, the date of the transfer in question.

Construction of references to employee representatives

11A. For the purposes of Regulations 10 and 11 above persons are employee representatives if—

(a) they have been elected by employees for the specific purpose of being given information and consulted by their employer under Regulation 10 above; or

(b) having been elected or appointed by employees otherwise than for that specific purpose, it is appropriate (having regard to the purposes for which they were elected) for their employer to inform and consult them under that Regulation,

and (in either case) they are employed by the employer at the time when they are elected or appointed.

Restriction on contracting out

12. Any provision of any agreement (whether a contract of employment or **A2–013** not) shall be void in so far as it purports to exclude or limit the operation of Regulation 5, 8 or 10 above or to preclude any person from presenting a complaint to an employment tribunal under Regulation 11 above.

Exclusion of employment abroad or as a dock worker

13.—(1) Regulation 8, 10 and 11 of these Regulations do not apply to **A2–014** employment where under his contract of employment the employee ordinarily works outside the United Kingdom.

(2) For the purposes of this Regulation a person employed to work on board a ship registered in the United Kingdom shall, unless—

(a) the employment is wholly outside the United Kingdom, or

(b) he is not ordinarily resident in the United Kingdom,

be regarded as a person who under his contract ordinarily works in the United Kingdom.

(3) [*Repealed by the Dock Work Act* 1989 (*c.* 13), *s.* 7(2).]

(4) [*Repealed by the Dock Work Act* 1989 (*c.* 13), *s.* 7(2).]

Consequential amendments

14.—(1) In section 4(4) of the 1978 Act (written statement to be given to em **A2–015** loyee on change of his employer), in paragraph (b), the reference to paragraph 17 of Schedule 13 to that Act (continuity of employment where change of employer) shall include a reference to these Regulations.

(2) In section 4(6A) of the Contracts of Employment and Redundancy Payments Act (Northern Ireland) 1965, in paragraph (b), the reference to paragraph 10 of Schedule 1 to that Act shall include a reference to these Regulations.

The Civil Procedure Rules 1998

(S.I. 1998 No. 3132)

PART 25

INTERIM REMEDIES

Orders for interim remedies

A2–016　**25.1**—(1) The court may grant the following interim remedies—

(*a*)　an interim injunction;

(*b*)　an interim declaration;

(*c*)　an order—

(i)　for the detention, custody or preservation of relevant property;

(ii)　for the inspection of relevant property;

(iii)　for the taking of a sample of relevant property;

(iv)　for the carrying out of an experiment on or with relevant property;

(v)　for the sale of relevant property which is of a perishable nature or which for any other good reason it is desirable to sell quickly; and

(iv)　for the payment of income from relevant property until a claim is decided;

(*d*)　an order authorising a person to enter any land or building in the possession of a party to the proceedings for the purposes of carrying out an order under sub-paragraph (c);

(*e*)　an order under section 4 of the Torts (Interference with Goods) Act 1977 to deliver up goods;

(*f*)　an order (referred to as a 'freezing injunction')—

(i)　restraining a party from removing from the jurisdiction assets located there; or

(ii)　restraining a party from dealing with any assets whether located within the jurisdiction or not;

(*g*)　an order directing a party to provide information about the location of relevant property or assets or to provide information about relevant property or assets which are or may be the subject of an application for a freezing injunction;

(*h*)　an order (referred to as a 'search order') under section 7 of the Civil Procedure Act 1997 (order requiring a party to admit another party to premises for the purpose of preserving evidence etc.);

(*i*)　an order under section 33 of the Supreme Court Act 1981 or section 52 of the County Courts Act 1984 (order for disclosure of documents or inspection of property before a claim has been made);

(*j*)　an order under section 34 of the Supreme Court Act 1981 or section 53 of the County Courts Act 1984 (order in certain proceedings for disclosure of documents or inspection of property against a non-party);

(*k*)　an order (referred to as an order for interim payment) under rule 25.6 for payment by a defendant on account of any damages, debt or other sum (except costs) which the court may hold the defendant liable to pay;

(*l*) an order for a specified fund to be paid into court or otherwise secured, where there is a dispute over a party's right to the fund;

(*m*) an order permitting a party seeking to recover personal property to pay money into court pending the outcome of the proceedings and directing that, if he does so, the property shall be given up to him; and

(*n*) an order directing a party to prepare and file accounts relating to the dispute. (Rule 34.2 provides for the court to issue a witness summons requiring a witness to produce documents to the court at the hearing or on such date as the court may direct)

(2) In paragraph (1)(*c*) and (*g*), 'relevant property' means property (including land) which is the subject of a claim or as to which any question may arise on a claim.

(3) The fact that a particular kind of interim remedy is not listed in paragraph (1) does not affect any power that the court may have to grant that remedy.

(4) The court may grant an interim remedy whether or not there has been a claim for a final remedy of that kind.

PART 40

JUDGMENTS, ORDERS, SALE OF LAND, ETC

II. Sale of land etc. and Conveyancing Counsel

Scope of this Section

40.15—(1) This Section—   **A2–017**

(a) deals with the court's power to order the sale, mortgage, partition or exchange of land; and

(b) contains provisions about conveyancing counsel.

(Section 131 of the Supreme Court Act 1981 provides for the appointment of the conveyancing counsel of the Supreme Court.)

(2) In this Section "land" includes any interest in, or right over, land.

Power to order sale etc.

40.16 In any proceedings relating to land, the court may order the land, or **A2–018** part of it, to be—

(a) sold;
(b) mortgaged;
(c) exchanged; or
(d) partitioned.

Power to order delivery up of possession etc.

40.17 Where the court has made an order under rule 40.16, it may order any **A2–019** party to deliver up to the purchaser or any other person—

(a) possession of the land;
(b) receipt of rents or profits relating to it; or
(c) both.

Reference to conveyancing counsel

A2–020   **40.18**—(1) The court may direct conveyancing counsel to investigate and prepare a report on the title of any land or to draft any document.

(2) The court may take the report on title into account when it decides the issue in question.

(Provisions dealing with the fees payable to conveyancing counsel are set out in the practice direction relating to Part 44).

Party may object to report

A2–021   **40.19**—(1) Any party to the proceedings may object to the report on title prepared by conveyancing counsel.

(2) Where there is an objection, the issue will be referred to a judge for determination.

(Part 23 contains general rules about making an application.)

*   *   *   *   *

SCHEDULE 1

RSC ORDER 30

RECEIVERS

Order to apply to High Court and County Court

A2–022   **A1.** This order applies to proceedings both in the High Court and the county court.

Application for receiver and injunction

A2–023   **1.**—(1) An application for the appointment of a receiver made in existing proceedings must be made in accordance with CPR Part 23 and the practice direction supplementing that Part.

(2) An application for an inuunction ancillary or incidental to an order appointing a receiver may be joined with the application for such order.

(3) The relevant practice direction will apply to an application for the immediate grant of such an injunction.

Giving of security by receiver

A2–024   **2.**—(1) A judgment or order directing the appointment of a receiver may include such directions as the court thinks fit as to the giving of security by the person appointed.

(2) Where by virtue of any judgment or order appointing a person named therein to be receiver a person is required to give security in accordance with this rule he must give security approved by the court duly to account for what he receives as receiver and to deal with it as the court directs.

(3) Unless the court otherwise directs, the security shall be by guarantee.

(4) The guarantee must be filed in the office or registry of the court in which the claim is proceeding and it shall be kept as of record until duly vacated.

Remuneration of receiver

A2–025   **3.**—(1) A person appointed receiver shall be allowed such proper remuneration, if any, as may be authorised by the court.

(2) The court may direct that such remuneration shall be—

    (*a*) fixed by reference to such scales or rates of professional charges as it thinks fit; or (*b*) assessed by a costs judge or a district judge.

(3) Where remuneration is assessed by a costs judge or district judge following a direction under paragraph 2(b), CPR rules 44.4(1) and (2) and 44.5(1) will apply as though the remuneration were costs directed to be assessed on the standard basis.

(4) An appeal shall lie from the assessment in accordance with section 8 of CPR Part 47 (CPR rules 47.21 to 47.27).

Service of order and notice

4. A copy of the judgment or order appointing a receiver shall be served by **A2–026** the party having conduct of the proceedings on the receiver and all other parties to the proceedings in which the receiver has been appointed.

Receiver's accounts

5.—(1) A receiver shall submit such accounts to such parties at such intervals **A2–027** or on such dates as the court may direct.

(2) Any party to whom a receiver is required to submit accounts may, on giving reasonable notice to the receiver, inspect, either personally or by an agent, the books and other papers relating to such accounts.

(3) Any party who is dissatisfied with the accounts of the receiver may give notice specifying the item or items to which objection is taken and requiring the receiver within not less than 14 days to file his accounts with the court and a copy of such notice shall be filed in the office or registry of the court dealing with the proceedings.

(4) Following an examination by or on behalf of the court of an item or items in an account to which objection is taken the result of such examination must be certified by a Master, the Admiralty Registrar, a district judge of the Family Division or a district judge, as the case may be, and an order may thereupon be made as to the incidence of any costs or expenses incurred.

Payment into court by receiver

6. The court may fix the amounts and frequency of payments into court to be **A2–028** made by a receiver.

Default by receiver

7.—(1) Where a receiver fails to attend for the examination of any account of **A2–029** his, or fails to submit any account, provide access to any books or papers or do any other thing which he is required to submit, provide or do, he and any or all of the parties to the cause or matter in which he was appointed may be required to attend the court to show cause for the failure, and the court may give such directions as it thinks proper including, if necessary, directions for the discharge of the receiver and the appointment of another and the payment of costs.

(2) Without prejudice to paragraph (1) where a receiver fails to attend for the examination of any account of his or fails to submit any account or fails to pay into court on the date fixed by the court any sum required to be so paid, the court may disallow any remuneration claimed by the receiver and may, where he has failed to pay any such sum into court, charge him with interest at the rate currently payable in respect of judgment debts in the High Court on that sum while in his possession as receiver.

Directions to receivers

8. A receiver may at any time request the court to give him directions and **A2–030** such request shall state in writing the matters with regard to which directions are required.

RSC ORDERS 51

RECEIVERS: EQUITABLE EXECUTION

Appointment of receiver by way of equitable execution

A2–031   **1.** Where an application is made for the appointment of a receiver by way of equitable execution, the court in determining whether it is just or convenient that the appointment should be made shall have regard to the amount claimed by the judgment creditor, to the amount likely to be obtained by the receiver and to the probable costs of his appointment and may direct an inquiry on any of these matters or any other matter before making the appointment.

Masters etc. may appoint receiver

A2–032   **2.** A Master and the Admiralty Registrar and a district judge of the Family Division shall have power to make an order for the appointment of a receiver by way of equitale execution and to grant an injunction if, and only so far as, the injunction is ancillary or incidental to such an order.

Application of rules as to appointment of receiver, etc.

A2–033   **3.** An application for the appointment of a receiver by way of equitable execution may be made in accordance with Order 30, rule 1 and rules, 2 to 6 of that order shall apply in relation to a receiver appointed by way of equitable execution as they apply in relation to a receiver appointed for any other purpose.

Appendix 3—Practice Statement

Practice Statement (Administration Orders Reports)

[Chancery Division]

1994 Jan. 17   Sir Donald Nicholls V.-C.

Practice Chancery Division—Insolvency—Application for administration order— **A3–001**
Independent report in support—Disproportionate investigation and expense to be
avoided—No report necessary in some straightforward cases—Insolvency Rules 1986
(S.I. 1986 No. 1925), r.2.2.

Sir Donald Nicholls, at the sitting of the court, handed down the following
practice statement. Administration orders under Part 2 of the Insolvency Act
1986 are intended primarily to facilitate the rescue and rehabilitation of insolvent
but potentially viable business. It is of the greatest importance that this aim
should not be frustrated by expense, and that the costs of obtaining an
administration order should not operate as a disincentive or put the process out
of the reach of smaller companies.

Rule 2.2. of the Insolvency Rules 1986 provides that an application for an
administration order may be supported by a report by an independent person to
the effect that the appointment of an administrator for the company is expedient.
It is the experience of the court that the contents of the rule 2.2 report are some
times unnecessarily elaborate and detailed. Because a report of this character is
thought to be necessary, the preliminary investigation will often have been
unduly protracted and extensive and, hence, expensive.

The extent of the necessary investigation and the amount of material to be
provided to the court must be a matter for the judgment of the person who
prepares the report and will vary from case to case. However, in the normal case,
what the court needs is a concise assessment of the company's situation and of
the prospects of an administration order achieving one or more of the statutory
purposes. The latter will normally include an explanation of the availability of
any finance required during the administration.

Every endeavour should be made to avoid disproportionate investigation and
expense. In some cases a brief investigation and report will be all that is required.
Where the court has insufficient material on which to base its decision, but the
proposed administrator is in court, he may offer to supplement the material by
giving oral evidence. In such a case he should subsequently provide a supplemen-
tal report covering the matters on which oral evidence was given so that this can
be placed on the court file.

In suitable cases the court may appoint an administrator but require him to
report back to the court within a short period so that the court can consider
whether to allow the administration to continue or to discharge the order. In
some cases the court may require the administrator to hold a meeting of
creditors before reporting back to the court, both within a relatively short period.

It is the experience of the judges who sit in the Companies Court that, in
general, a rule 2.2. report is valuable as a safeguard in assisting the court to see

whether the application has a sound basis. However, there may be straightforward cases in which such a report is not necessary because it would provide little assistance. Practitioners are reminded that the Rules do not require that a rule 2.2. report must be provided in every case.

This statement is made after consultation with the other judges of the Chancery Division.

C.R.S.

APPENDIX 4

COUNCIL REGULATION (E.C.) No. 1346/2000
of May 29, 2000
on insolvency proceedings

THE COUNCIL OF THE EUROPEAN UNION,   **A4–001**

Having regard to the Treaty establishing the European Community, and in particular Articles 61(c) and 67(1) thereof,

Having regard to the initiative of the Federal Republic of Germany and the Republic of Finland.

Having regard to the opinion of the European Parliament,[1]

Having regard to the opinion of the Economic and Social Committee,[2]

Whereas:

(1) The European Union has set out the aim of establishing an area of freedom, security and justice.

(2) The proper functioning of the internal market requires that cross-border insolvency proceedings should operate efficiently and effectively and this Regulation needs to be adopted in order to achieve this objective which comes within the scope of judicial co-operation in civil matters within the meaning of Article 65 of the Treaty.

(3) The activities of undertakings have more and more cross-border effects and are therefore increasingly being regulated by Community law. While the insolvency of such undertakings also affects the proper functioning of the internal market, there is a need for a Community act requiring co-ordination of the measures to be taken regarding an insolvent debtor's assets.

(4) It is necessary for the proper functioning of the internal market to avoid incentives for the parties to transfer assets or judicial proceedings from one Member State to another, seeking to obtain a more favourable legal position (forum shopping).

(5) These objectives cannot be achieved to a sufficient degree at national level and action at Community level is therefore justified.

(6) In accordance with the principle of proportionality this Regulation should be confined to provisions governing jurisdiction for opening insolvency proceedings and judgments which are delivered directly on the basis of the insolvency proceedings and are closely connected with such proceedings. In addition, this Regulation should contain provisions regarding the recognition of those judgments and the applicable law which also satisfy that principle.

(7) Insolvency proceedings relating to the winding-up of insolvent companies or other legal persons, judicial arrangements, compositions and analogous proceedings are excluded from the scope of the 1968 Brussels Convention on Jurisdiction and Enforcement of Judgments in Civil and Commercial Matters,[3] as amended by the Conventions on Accession to this Convention.[4]

---

[1] Opinion delivered on March 2, 2000 (not yet published in the Official Journal).

[2] Opinion delivered on January 26, 2000 (not yet published in the Official Journal).

[3] [1972] O.J. L299/32.

[4] [1975] O.J. L204/28; [1982] O.J. L388/1; [1978] O.J. L304/1; [1997] O.J. C15/1.

(8) In order to achieve the aim of improving the efficiency and effectiveness of insolvency proceedings having cross-border effects, it is necessary, and appropriate, that the provisions on jurisdiction, recognition and applicable law in this area should be contained in a Community law measure which is binding and directly applicable in Member States.

(9) This Regulation should apply to insolvency proceedings, whether the debtor is a natural person or a legal person, a trader or an individual. The insolvency proceedings to which this Regulation applies are listed in the Annexes. Insolvency proceedings concerning insurance undertakings, credit institutions, investment undertakings holding funds or securities for third parties and collective investment undertakings should be excluded from the scope of this Regulation. Such undertakings should not be covered by this Regulation since they are subject to special arrangements and, to some extent, the national supervisory authorities have extremely wide-ranging powers of intervention.

(10) Insolvency proceedings do not necessarily involve the intervention of a judicial authority; the expression "court" in this Regulation should be given a broad meaning and include a person or body empowered by national law to open insolvency proceedings. In order for this Regulation to apply, proceedings (comprising acts and formalities set down in law) should not only have to comply with the provisions of this Regulation, but they should also be officially recognised and legally effective in the Member State in which the insolvency proceedings are opened and should be collective insolvency proceedings which entail the partial or total divestment of the debtor and the appointment of a liquidator.

(11) This Regulation acknowledges the fact that as a result of widely differing substantive laws it is not practical to introduce insolvency proceedings with universal scope in the entire Community. The application without exception of the law of the State of opening of proceedings would, against this background, frequently lead to difficulties. This applies, for example, to the widely differing laws on security interests to be found in the Community. Furthermore, the preferential rights enjoyed by some creditors in the insolvency proceedings are, in some cases, completely different. This Regulation should take account of this in two different ways. On the one hand, provision should be made for special rules on applicable law in the case of particularly significant rights and legal relationships (*e.g.* rights *in rem* and contracts of employment). On the other hand, national proceedings covering only assets situated in the State of opening should also be allowed alongside main insolvency proceedings with universal scope.

(12) This Regulation enables the main insolvency proceedings to be opened in the Member State where the debtor has the centre of his main interests. These proceedings have universal scope and aim at encompassing all the debtor's assets. To protect the diversity of interests, this Regulation permits secondary proceedings to be opened to run in parallel with the main proceedings. Secondary proceedings may be opened in the Member State where the debtor has an establishment. The effects of secondary proceedings are limited to the assets located in that State. Mandatory rules of co-ordination with the main proceedings satisfy the need for unity in the Community.

(13) The "centre of main interests" should correspond to the place where the debtor conducts the administration of his interests on a regular basis and is therefore ascertainable by third parties.

(14) This Regulation applies only to proceedings where the centre of the debtor's main interests is located in the Community.

(15) The rules of jurisdiction set out in this Regulation establish only international jurisdiction, that is to say, they designate the Member State the courts of which may open insolvency proceedings. Territorial jurisdiction within that Member State must be established by the national law of the Member State concerned.

(16) The court having jurisdiction to open the main insolvency proceedings should be enabled to order provisional and protective measures from the time of the request to open proceedings. Preservation measures both prior to and after the commencement of the insolvency proceedings are very important to guarantee the effectiveness of the insolvency proceedings. In that connection this Regulation should afford different possibilities. On the one hand, the court competent for the main insolvency proceedings should be able also to order provisional protective measures covering assets situated in the territory of other Member States. On the other hand, a liquidator temporarily appointed prior to the opening of the main insolvency proceedings should be able, in the Member States in which an establishment belonging to the debtor is to be found, to apply for the preservation measures which are possible under the law of those States.

(17) Prior to the opening of the main insolvency proceedings, the right to request the opening of insolvency proceedings in the Member State where the debtor has an establishment should be limited to local creditors and creditors of the local establishment or to cases where main proceedings cannot be opened under the law of the Member State where the debtor has the centre of his main interest. The reason for this restriction is that cases where territorial insolvency proceedings are requested before the main insolvency proceedings are intended to be limited to what is absolutely necessary. If the main insolvency proceedings are opened, the territorial proceedings become secondary.

(18) Following the opening of the main insolvency proceedings, the right to request the opening of insolvency proceedings in a Member State where the debtor has an establishment is not restricted by this Regulation. The liquidator in the main proceedings or any other person empowered under the national law of that Member State may request the opening of secondary insolvency proceedings.

(19) Secondary insolvency proceedings may serve different purposes, besides the protection of local interests. Cases may arise where the estate of the debtor is too complex to administer as a unit or where differences in the legal systems concerned are so great that difficulties may arise from the extension of effects deriving from the law of the State of the opening to the other States where the assets are located. For this reason the liquidator in the main proceedings may request the opening of secondary proceedings when the efficient administration of the estate so requires.

(20) Main insolvency proceedings and secondary proceedings can, however, contribute to the effective realisation of the total assets only if all the concurrent proceedings pending are co-ordinated. The main condition here is that the various liquidators must co-operate closely, in particular by exchanging a sufficient amount of information. In order to ensure the dominant role of the main insolvency proceedings, the liquidator in such proceedings should be given several possibilities for intervening in secondary insolvency proceedings which are pending at the same time. For example, he should be able to propose a restructuring plan or composition or apply for realisation of the assets in the secondary insolvency proceedings to be suspended.

(21) Every creditor, who has his habitual residence, domicile or registered office in the Community, should have the right to lodge his claims in each of the insolvency proceedings pending in the Community relating to the debtor's assets. This should also apply to tax authorities and social insurance institutions. However, in order to ensure equal treatment of creditors, the distribution of proceeds must be co-ordinated. Every creditor should be able to keep what he has received in the course of insolvency proceedings but should be entitled only to participate in the distribution of total assets in other proceedings if creditors with the same standing have obtained the same proportion of their claims.

(22) This Regulation should provide for immediate recognition of judgments concerning the opening, conduct and closure of insolvency proceedings which come within its scope and of judgments handed down in direct connection with

such insolvency proceedings. Automatic recognition should therefore mean that the effects attributed to the proceedings by the law of the State in which the proceedings were opened extend to all other Member States. Recognition of judgments delivered by the courts of the Member States should be based on the principle of mutual trust. To that end, grounds for non-recognition should be reduced to the minimum necessary. This is also the basis on which any dispute should be resolved where the courts of two Member States both claim competence to open the main insolvency proceedings. The decision of the first court to open proceedings should be recognised in the other Member States without those Member States having the power to scrutinise the court's decision.

(23) This Regulation should set out, for the matters covered by it, uniform rules on conflict of laws which replace, within their scope of application, national rules of private international law. Unless otherwise stated, the law of the Member State of the opening of the proceedings should be applicable (*lex concursus*). This rule on conflict of laws should be valid both for the main proceedings and for local proceedings; the *lex concursus* determines all the effects of the insolvency proceedings, both procedural and substantive, on the persons and legal relations concerned. It governs all the conditions for the opening, conduct and closure of the insolvency proceedings.

(24) Automatic recognition of, insolvency proceedings to which the law of the opening State normally applies may interfere with the rules under which transactions are carried out in other Member States. To protect legitimate expectations and the certainty of transactions in Member States other than that in which proceedings are opened, provisions should be made for a number of exceptions to the general rule.

(25) There is a particular need for a special reference diverging from the law of the opening State in the case of rights *in rem*, since these are of considerable importance for the granting of credit. The basis, validity and extent of such a right *in rem* should therefore normally be determined according to the *lex situs* and not be affected by the opening of insolvency proceedings. The proprietor of the right *in rem* should therefore be able to continue to assert his right to segregation or separate settlement of the collateral security. Where assets are subject to rights *in rem* under the *lex situs* in one Member State but the main proceedings are being carried out in another Member State, the liquidator in the main proceedings should be able to request the opening of secondary proceedings in the jurisdiction where the rights *in rem* arise if the debtor has an establishment there. If a secondary proceeding is not opened, the surplus on sale of the asset covered by rights *in rem* must be paid to the liquidator in the main proceedings.

(26) If a set-off is not permitted under the law of the opening State, a creditor should nevertheless be entitled to the set-off if it is possible under the law applicable to the claim of the insolvent debtor. In this way, set-off will acquire a kind of guarantee function based on legal provisions on which the creditor concerned can rely at the time when the claim arises.

(27) There is also a need for special protection in the case of payment systems and financial markets. This applies for example to the position-closing agreements and netting agreements to be found in such systems as well as to the sale of securities and to the guarantees provided for such transactions as governed in particular by Directive 98/26/EC of the European Parliament and of the Council of May 19, 1998 on settlement, finality in payment and securities settlement systems.[5] For such transactions, the only law which is material should thus be that applicable to the system or market concerned. This provision is intended to prevent the possibility of mechanisms for the payment and settlement of transactions provided for in the payment and set-off systems or on the regulated financial markets of the Member States being altered in the case of insolvency of

[5] [1998] O.J. L166/45.

a business partner. Directive 98/26/EC contains special provisions which should take precedence over the general rules in this Regulation.

(28) In order to protect employees and jobs, the effects of insolvency proceedings on the continuation or termination of employment and on the rights and obligations of all parties to such employment must be determined by the law applicable to the agreement in accordance with the general rules on conflict of law. Any other insolvency-law questions, such as whether the employees' claims are protected by preferential rights and what status such preferential rights may have, should be determined by the law of the opening State.

(29) For business considerations, the main content of the decision opening the proceedings should be published in the other Member States at the request of the liquidator. If there is an establishment in the Member State concerned, there may be a requirement that publication is compulsory. In neither case, however, should publication be a prior condition for recognition of the foreign proceedings.

(30) It may be the case that some of the persons concerned are not in fact aware that proceedings have been opened and act in good faith in a way that conflicts with the new situation. In order to protect such persons who make a payment to the debtor because they are unaware that foreign proceedings have been opened when they should in fact have made the payment to the foreign liquidator, it should be provided that such a payment is to have a debt-discharging effect.

(31) This Regulation should include Annexes relating to the organisation of insolvency proceedings. As these Annexes relate exclusively to the legislation of Member States, there are specific and substantiated reasons for the Council to reserve the right to amend these Annexes in order to take account of any amendments to the domestic law of the Member States.

(32) The United Kingdom and Ireland, in accordance with Article 3 of the Protocol on the position of the United Kingdom and Ireland annexed to the Treaty on European Union and the Treaty establishing the European Community, have given notice of their wish to take part in the adoption and application of this Regulation.

(33) Denmark, in accordance with Articles 1 and 2 of the Protocol on the position of Denmark annexed to the Treaty on European Union and the Treaty establishing the European Community, is not participating in the adoption of this Regulation, and is therefore not bound by it nor subject to its application,

HAS ADOPTED THIS REGULATION:

CHAPTER I

GENERAL PROVISIONS

Article 1

Scope

1. This Regulation shall apply to collective insolvency proceedings which **A4–002** entail the partial or total divestment of a debtor and the appointment of a liquidator.

2. This Regulation shall not apply to insolvency proceedings concerning insurance undertakings, credit institutions, investment undertakings which provide services involving the holding of funds or securities for third parties, or to collective investment undertakings.

Article 2

Definitions

A4–003 For the purposes of this Regulation:

    (a) 'insolvency proceedings' shall mean the collective proceedings referred to in Article 1(1). These proceedings are listed in Annex A;

    (b) 'liquidator' shall mean any person or body whose function is to administer or liquidate assets of which the debtor has been divested or to supervise the administration of this affairs. Those persons and bodies are listed in Annex C;

    (c) 'winding-up proceedings' shall mean insolvency proceedings within the meaning of point (a) involving realising the assets of the debtor, including where the proceedings have been closed by a composition or other measure terminating the insolvency, or closed by reason of the insufficiency of the assets. Those proceedings are listed in Annex B;

    (d) 'court' shall mean the judicial body or any other competent body of a Member State empowered to open insolvency proceedings or to take decisions in the course of such proceedings;

    (e) 'judgment' in relation to the opening of insolvency proceedings or the appointment of a liquidator shall include the decision of any court empowered to open such proceedings or to appoint a liquidator;

    (f) 'the time of the opening of proceedings' shall mean the time at which the judgment opening proceedings becomes effective, whether it is a final judgment or not;

    (g) 'the Member State in which assets are situated' shall mean, in the case of:

        — tangible property, the Member State within the terrority of which the property is situated,

        — property and rights ownership of or entitlement to which must be entered in a public register, the Member State under the authority of which the register is kept,

        — claims, the Member State within the territory of which the third party required to meet them has the centre of his main interests, as determined in Article 3(1);

    (h) 'establishment' shall mean any place of operations where the debtor carries out a non-transitory economic activity with human means and goods.

Article 3

International jurisdiction

A4–004 1. The courts of the Member State within the territory of which the centre of a debtor's main interests is situated shall have jurisdiction to open insolvency proceedings. In the case of a company or legal person, the place of the registered office shall be presumed to be the centre of its main interests in the absence of proof to the contrary.

2. Where the centre of a debtor's main interests is situated within the territory of a Member State, the courts of another Member State shall have jursidiction to open insolvency proceedings against that debtor only if he possesses an establishment within the territory of that other Member State. The effects of those proceedings shall be restricted to the assets of the debtor situated in the territory of the latter Member State.

3. Where insolvency proceedings have been opened under paragraph 1, any proceedings opened subsequently under paragraph 2 shall be secondary proceedings. These latter proceedings must be winding-up proceedings.

4. Territorial insolvency proceedings referred to in paragraph 2 may be opened prior to the opening of main insolvency proceedings in accordance with paragraph 1 only:

  (a) where insolvency proceedings under paragraph 1 cannot be opened because of the conditions laid down by the law of the Member State within the territory of which the centre of the debtor's main interests is situated; or
  (b) where the opening of territorial insolvency proceedings is requested by a creditor who has in domicile, habitual residence or registered office in the Member State within the territory of which the establishment is situated, or whose claim arises from the operation of that establishment.

Article 4

Law applicable

1. Save as otherwise provided in this Regulation, the law applicable to **A4–005** insolvency proceedings and their effects shall be that of the Member State within the territory of which such proceedings are opened, hereafter to as the 'state of the opening of proceedings'.

2. The law of the State of the opening of proceedings shall determine the conditions for the opening of those proceedings, their conduct and their closure. It shall determine in particular:

  (a) against which debtors insolvency proceedings may be brought on account of their capacity;
  (b) the assets which form part of the estate and the treatment of assets acquired by or devolving on the debtor after the opening of the insolvency proceedings;
  (c) the respective powers of the debtor and the liquidator;
  (d) the conditions under which set-offs may be invoked;
  (e) the effects of insolvency proceedings on current contracts to which the debtor is party;
  (f) the effects of the insolvency proceedings on proceedings brought by individual creditors, with the exception of lawsuits pending;
  (g) the claims which are to be lodged against the debtor's estate and the treatment of claims arising after the opening of insolvency proceedings;
  (h) the rules governing the lodging, verification and admission of claims;
  (i) the rules governing the distribution of proceeds from the realisation of assets, the ranking of claims and the rights of creditors who have obtained partial satisfaction after the opening of insolvency proceedings by virtue of a right *in rem* or through a set-off;
  (j) the condition for and the effects of closure of insolvency proceedings, in particular by comparison;
  (k) creditors' rights after the closure of insolvency proceedings;
  (l) who is to bear the costs and expenses incurred in the insolvency proceedings;
  (m) the rules relating to the voidness, voidability or unenforceability of legal acts detrimental to all the creditors.

Article 5

Third parties' rights *in rem*

A4–006   1. The opening of insolvency proceedings shall not affect the rights *in rem* of creditors or third parties in respect of tangible or intangible, moveable or immoveable assets — both specific assets and collections of indefinite assets as a whole which change from time to time — belonging to the debtor which are situated within the territory of another Member State at the time of the opening of proceedings.

2. The rights referred to in paragraph 1 shall in particular mean:

(a) the right to dispose of assets or have them disposed of and to obtain satisfaction from the proceeds of or income from those assets, in particular by virtue of a lien or a mortgage;

(b) the exclusive right to have a claim met, in particular a right guaranteed by a lien in respect of the claim or by assignment of the claim by way of a guarantee;

(c) the right to demand the assets from, and/or to require restitution by, anyone having possession or use of them contrary to the wishes of the party so entitled;

(d) a right *in rem* to the beneficial use of assets.

3. The right, recorded in a public register and enforceable against third parties, under which a right *in rem* within the meaning of paragraph 1 may be obtained, shall be considered a right *in rem*.

4. Paragraph 1 shall not preclude actions for voidness, voidability ou unenforceability as referred to in Article 4(2)(m).

Article 6

Set-off

A4–007   5. The opening of insolvency proceedings shall not affect the right of creditors to demand the set-off of their claims against the claims of the debtor, where such a set-off is permitted by the law applicable to the insolvent debtor's claim.

2. Paragraph 1 shall not preclude actions for voidness, voidability or unforceability as referred to in Article 4(2)(m).

Article 7

Reservation of title

A4–008   1. The opening of insolvency proceedings against the purchaser of an asset shall not affect the seller's rights based on a reservation of title where at the time of the opening of proceedings the asset is situated within the territory of a Member State other than the State of opening of proceedings.

2. The opening of insolvency proceedings against the seller of an asset, after delivery of the asset, shall not consitute grounds for rescinding or terminating the sale and shall not prevent the purchaser from acquiring title where at the time of the opening of proceedings the asset sold is situated within the territory of a Member State other than the State of the opening of proceedings.

3. Paragraphs 1 and 2 shall not preclude actions for voidness, voidability or unenforceability as referred to in Article 4(2)(m).

Article 8

Contracts relating to immoveable property

The effects of insolvency proceedings on a contract conferring the right to **A4–009** acquire or make use of immoveable property shall be governed solely by the law of the Member State within the territory of which the immoveable property is situated.

Article 9

Payment systems and financial markets

1. Without prejudice to Article 5, the effects of insolvency proceedings on the **A4–010** rights and obligations of the parties to a payment or settlement system or to a financial market shall be governed solely by the law of the Member State applicable to that system or market.

2. Paragraph 1 shall not preclude any action for voidness, voidability or unenforceability which may be taken to set aside payments or transactions under the law applicable to the relevant payment system or financial market.

Article 10

Contracts of employment

The effects of insolvency proceedings on employment contract and relationships **A4–011** shall be governed solely by the law of the Member State applicable to the contract of employment.

Article 11

Effects on rights subject to registration

The effects of insolvency proceedings on the rights of the debtor in immove- **A4–012** able property, a ship or on aircraft subject to registration in a public register shall be determined by the law of the Member State under the authority of which the register is kept.

Article 12

Community patents and trade marks

For the purposes of this Regulation, a Community patent, a Community trade **A4–013** mark or any other similar right established by Community law may be included only in the proceedings referred to in Article 3(1).

Article 13

Detrimental acts

Article 4(2)(m) shall not apply where the person who benefited from an act **A4–014** detrimental to all the creditors provides proof that:

— the said act is subject to the law of a Member State other than that of the State of the opening of proceedings, and

— that law does not allow any means of challenging that act in the relevant case.

Article 14

Protection of third-party purchasers

A4–015 Where, by act concluded after the opening of insolvency proceedings, the debtor disposes, for consideration, of:

— an immoveable asset, or

— a ship or an aircraft subject to registration in a public register, or

— securities whose existence presupposes registration in a register laid down by law,

the validity of that act shall be governed by the law of the State within the territory of which the immoveable asset is situated or under the authority of which the register is kept.

Article 15

Effects of insolvency proceedings on lawsuits pending

A4–016 The effects of insolvency proceedings on a lawsuit pending concerning an asset or a right of which the debtor has been divested shall be governed solely by the law of the Member State in which that lawsuit is pending.

CHAPTER II

RECOGNITION OF INSOLVENCY PROCEEDINGS

Article 16

Principle

A4–017 1. Any judgment opening insolvency proceedings handed down by a court of a Member State which has jurisdiction pursuant to Article 3 shall be recognised in all the other Member States from the time that it becomes effective in the State of the opening of proceedings.

This rule shall also apply where, on account of his capacity, insolvency proceedings cannot be brought against the debtor in other Member States.

2. Recognition of the proceedings referred to in Article 3(1) shall not preclude the opening of the proceedings referred to in Article 3(2) by a court in another Member State. The latter proceedings shall be secondary insolvency proceedings within the meaning of Chapter III.

Article 17

Effects of recognition

A4–018 1. The judgment opening the proceedings referred to in Article 3(1) shall, with no further formalities, produce the same effects in any other Member State as under this law of the State of the opening of proceedings, unless this Regulation provides otherwise and as long as no proceedings referred to in Article 3(2) are opened in that other Member State.

2. The effects of the proceedings referred to in Article 3(2) may not be challenged in other Member States. Any restriction of the creditors' rights, in particular a stay or discharge, shall produce effects *vis-à-vis* assets situated within the territory of another Member State only in the case of those creditors who have given their consent.

Article 18

Powers of the liquidator

1. The liquidator appointed by a court which has jurisdiction pursuant to **A4–019** Article 3(1) may exercise all the powers conferred on him by the law of the State of the opening of proceedings in another Member State, as long as no other insolvency proceedings have been opened there nor any preservation measure to the contrary has been taken there further to a request for the opening of insolvency proceedings in that State. He may in particular remove that debtor's assets from the territory of the Member State in which they are situated, subject to Articles 5 and 7.

2. The liquidator appointed by a court which has jurisdiction pursuant to Article 3(2) may in any other Member State claim through the courts or out of court that moveable property was removed from the territory of the State of the opening of proceedings to the territory of that other Member State after the opening of the insolvency proceedings. He may also bring any action to set aside which is in the interests of the creditors.

3. In exercising his powers, the liquidator shall comply with the law of the Member State within the territory of which he intends to take action, in particular with regard to procedures for the realisation of assets. Those powers may not include coercive measures or the right to rule on legal proceedings or disputes.

Article 19

Proof of the liquidator's appointment

The liquidator's appointment shall be evidenced by a certified copy of the **A4–020** original decision appointing him or by any other certificate issued by the court which has jurisdiction.

A translation into the official language or one of the official languages of the Member State within the territory of which he intends to act may be required. No legislation or other similar formality shall be required.

Article 20

Return and imputation

1. A creditor who, after the opening of the proceedings referred to in Article **A4–021** 3(1) obtains by any means, in particular through enforcement, total or partial satisfaction of his claim on the assets belonging to the debtor situated within the territory of another Member State, shall return what he has obtained to the liquidator, subject to Articles 5 and 7.

2. In order to ensure equal treatment of creditors a creditor who has, in the course of insolvency proceedings, obtained a dividend on his claim shall share in

distributions made in other proceedings only where creditors of the same ranking or category have, in those other proceedings, obtained an equivalent dividend.

Article 21

Publication

A4–022   1. The liquidator may request that notice of the judgment opening insolvency proceedings and, where appropriate, the decision appointing him, be published in any other Member State in accordance with the publication procedures provided for in that State. Such publication shall also specify the liquidator appointed and whether the jurisdiction rule applied is that pursuant to Article 3(1) or Article 3(2).

2. However, any Member State within the territory of which the debtor has an establishment may require mandatory publication. In such cases, the liquidator or any authority empowered to that effect in the Member State where the proceedings referred to in Article 3(1) are opened shall take all necessary measures to ensure such publication.

Article 22

Registration in a public register

A4–023   1. The liquidator may request that the judgment opening the proceedings referred to in Article 3(1) be registered in the land register, the trade register and any other public register kept in the other Member States.

2. However, any Member State may require mandatory registration. In such cases, the liquidator or any authority empowered to that effect in the Member State where the proceedings referred to in Article 3(1) have been opened shall take all necessary measures to ensure such registration.

Article 23

Costs

A4–024 The costs of the publication and registration provided for in Articles 21 and 22 shall be regarded as costs and expenses incurred in the proceedings.

Article 24

Honouring of an obligation to a debtor

A4–025   1. Where an obligation has been honoured in a Member State for the benefit of a debtor who is subject to insolvency proceedings opened in another Member State, when it should have been honoured for the benefit of the liquidator in those proceedings, the person honouring the obligation shall be deemed to have discharged it if he was unaware of the opening of proceedings.

2. Where such an obligation is honoured before the publication provided for in Article 21 has been effected, the person honouring the obligation shall be presumed, in the absence of proof to the contrary, to have been unaware of the opening of insolvency proceedings; where the obligation is honoured after such publication has been effected, the person honouring the obligation shall be presumed, in the absence of proof to the contrary, to have been aware of the opening of proceedings.

Article 25

Recognition and enforceability of other judgments

1. Judgments handed down by a court whose judgment concerning the **A4–026** opening of proceedings is recognised in accordance with Article 16 and which concern the course and closure of insolvency proceedings, and composition approved by that court shall also be recognised with no further formalities. Such judgments shall be enforced in accordance with Articles 31 to 51, with the exception of Articles 34(2), of the Brussels Convention on Jurisdiction and the Enforcement of Judgments in Civil and Commercial Matters, as amended by the Convention of Accession to this Convention.

The first subparagraph shall also apply to judgments deriving directly from the insolvency proceedings and which are closely linked with them, even if they were handed down by another court.

The first subparagraph shall also apply to judgments relating to preservation measures taken after the request for the opening of insolvency proceedings.

2. The recognition and enforcement of judgments other than those referred to in paragraph 1 shall be governed by the Convention referred to in paragraph 1, provided that the Convention is applicable.

3. The Member States shall not be obliged to recognise or enforce a judgment referred to in paragraph 1 which might result in a limitation of personal freedom or postal secrecy.

Article 26[6]

Public policy

Any Member State may refuse to recognise insolvency proceedings opened in **A4–027** another Member State or to enforce a judgment handed down in the context of such proceedings where the effects of such recognition or enforcement would be manifestly contrary to that State's public policy, in particular its fundamental principles or the constitutional rights and liberties of the individual.

CHAPTER III

SECONDARY INSOLVENCY PROCEEDINGS

Article 27

Opening of proceedings

The opening of the proceedings referred to in Article 3(1) by a court of a **A4–028** Member State and which is recognised in another Member State (main proceedings) shall permit the opening in that other Member State, a court of which has jurisdiction pursuant to Article 3(2), of secondary insolvency proceedings without the debtor's insolvency being examined in that other State. These latter proceedings must be among the proceedings listed in Annex B. Their effects shall be restricted to the assets of the debtor situated within the territory of that other Member State.

---

[6] Note the Declaration by Portugal concerning the application of Arts 26 and 37 [2000] C183/1.

Article 28

Applicable law

A4–029 Save as otherwise provided in this Regulation, the law applicable to secondary proceedings shall be that of the Member State within the territory of which the secondary proceedings are opened.

Article 29

Right to request the opening of proceedings

A4–030 The opening of secondary proceedings may be requested by:

(a) the liquidator in the main proceedings;
(b) any other person or authority empowered to request the opening of insolvency proceedings under the law of the Member State within the territory of which the opening of secondary proceedings is requested.

Article 30

Advance payment of costs and expenses

A4–031 Where the law of the Member State in which the opening of secondary proceedings is requested requires that the debtor's assets be sufficient to cover in whole or in part the costs and expenses of the proceedings, the court may, when it receives such a request, require the applicant to make an advance payment of costs or to provide appropriate security.

Article 31

Duty to co-operate and communicate information

A4–032 1. Subject to the rules restricting the communication of information, the liquidator in the main proceedings and the liquidators in the secondary proceedings shall be duty bound to communicate information to each other. They shall immediately communicate any information which may be relevant to the other proceedings, in particular the progress made in lodging and verifying claims and all measures aimed at terminating the proceedings.

2. Subject to the rules applicable to each of the proceedings, the liquidator in the main proceedings and the liquidators in the secondary proceedings shall be duty bound to co-operate with each other.

3. The liquidator in the secondary proceedings shall give the liquidator in the main proceedings an early opportunity of submitting proposals on the liquidation or use of the assets in the secondary proceedings.

Article 32

Exercise of creditors' rights

A4–033 1. Any creditor may lodge his claim in the main proceedings and in any secondary proceedings.

2. The liquidators in the main and any secondary proceedings shall lodge in other proceedings claims which have already been lodged in the proceedings for

which they were appointed, provided that the interests of creditors in the latter proceedings are served thereby, subject to the right of creditors to oppose that or to withdraw the lodgement of their claims where the law applicable so provides.

3. The liquidator in the main or secondary proceedings shall be empowered to participate in other proceedings on the same basis as a creditor, in particular by attending creditors' meetings.

Article 33

Stay of liquidation

1. The court, which opened the secondary proceedings, shall stay the process **A4–034** of liquidation in whole or in part on receipt of a request from the liquidator in the main proceedings, provided that in that event it may require the liquidator in the main proceedings to take any suitable measure to guarantee the interests of the creditors in the secondary proceedings and of individual classes of creditors. Such a request from the liquidator may be rejected only if it is manifestly of no interest to the creditors in the main proceedings. Such a stay of the process of liquidation may be ordered for up to three months. It may be continued or renewed for similar periods.

2. The court referred to in paragraph 1 shall terminate the stay of the process of liquidation:

— at the request of the liquidator in the main proceedings,
— of its own motion, at the request of a creditor or at the request of the liquidator in the secondary proceedings if that measure no longer appears justified, in particular, by the interests of creditors in the main proceedings or in the secondary proceedings.

Article 34

Measures ending secondary insolvency proceedings

1. Where the law applicable to secondary proceedings allows for such pro- **A4–035** ceedings to be closed without liquidation by a rescue plan, a composition or a comparable measure, the liquidator in the main proceedings shall be empowered to propose such a measure himself.

Closure of the secondary proceedings by a measure referred to in the first subparagraph shall not become final without the consent of the liquidator in the main proceedings; failing his agreement, however, it may become final if the financial interests of the creditors in the main proceedings are not affected by the measure proposed.

2. Any restriction of creditors' rights arising from a measure referred to in paragraph 1 which is proposed in secondary proceedings, such as a stay of payment or discharge of debt, may not have effect in respect of the debtor's assets not covered by those proceedings without the consent of all the creditors having an interest.

3. During a stay of the process of liquidation ordered pursuant to Article 33, only the liquidator in the main proceedings or the debtor, with the former's consent, may propose measures laid down in paragraph 1 of this Article in the secondary proceedings; no other proposal for such a measure shall be put to the vote or approved.

Article 35

Assets remaining in the secondary proceedings

If by the liquidation of assets in the secondary proceedings it is possible to meet **A4–036** all claims allowed under those proceedings, the liquidator appointed in those proceedings shall immediately transfer any assets remaining to the liquidator in the main proceedings.

Article 36

Subsequent opening of the main proceedings

A4–037 Where the proceedings referred to in Article 3(1) are opened following the opening of the proceedings referred to in Article 3(2) in another Member State, Articles 31 to 35 shall apply to those opened first, in so far as the progress of those proceedings so permits.

Article 37[7]

Conversion of earlier proceedings

A4–038 The liquidator in the main proceedings may request that proceedings listed in Annex A previously opened in another Member State be converted into winding-up proceedings if this proves to be in the interests of the creditors in the main proceedings.

The court with jurisdiction under Article 3(2) shall order conversion into one of the proceedings listed in Annex B.

Article 38

Preservation mesures

A4–039 Where the court of a Member State which has jurisdiction pursuant to Article 3(1) appoints a temporary administrator in order to ensure the preservation of the debtor's assets, that temporary administrator shall be empowered to request any measures to secure and preserve any of the debtor's assets situated in another Member State, provided for under the law of that State, for the period between the request for the opening of insolvency proceedings and the judgment opening the proceedings.

CHAPTER IV

PROVISION OF INFORMATION FOR CREDITORS AND LODGEMENT OF THEIR CLAIMS

Article 39

Right to lodge claims

A4–040 Any creditor who has his habitual residence, domicile or registered office in a Member State other than the State of the opening of proceedings, including the tax authorities and social security authorities of Member States, shall have the right to lodge claims in the insolvency proceedings in writing.

---

[7] Note the Declaration by Portugal concerning the application of Arts 26 and 37 [2000] C183/1.

Article 40

Duty to inform creditors

1. As soon as insolvency proceedings are opened in a Member State, the court **A4–041** of that State having jurisdiction or the liquidator appointed by it shall immediately inform known creditors who have their habitual residences, domiciles or registered offices in the other Member States.

2. That information, provided by an individual notice, shall in particular include time limits, the penalties laid down in regard to those time limits, the body or authority empowered to accept the lodgement of claims and the other measures laid down. Such notice shall also indicate whether creditors whose claims are preferential or secured *in rem* need lodge their claims.

Article 41

Content of the lodgement of a claim

A creditor shall send copies of supporting documents, if any, and shall indicate **A4–042** the nature of the claim, the date on which it arose and its amount, as well as whether he alleges preference, security *in rem* or a reservation of title in respect of the claim and what assets are covered by the guarantee he is invoking.

Article 42

Languages

1. The information provided for in Article 40 shall be provided in the official **A4–043** language or one of the official languages of the State of the opening of proceedings. For that purpose a form shall be used bearing the heading "Invitation to lodge a claim. Time limited to be observed" in all the official languages of the institutions of the European Union.

2. Any creditor who has his habitual residence, domicile or registered office in a Member State other than the State of the opening of proceedings may lodge his claim in the official language or one of the official languages of that other State. In that event, however, the lodgement of his claim shall bear the heading "Lodgement of claim" in the official language or one of the official languages of the Stae of the opening of proceedings. In addition, he may be required to provide a translation into the official language or one of the official languages of the State of the opening of proceedings.

CHAPTER V

TRANSITIONAL AND FINAL PROVISIONS

Article 43

Applicability in time

The provisions of this Regulation shall apply only to insolvency proceedings **A4–044** opened after its entry into force. Acts done by a debtor before the entry into force of this Regulation shall continue to be governed by the law which was applicable to them at the time they were done.

Article 44

Relationship to Conventions

A4–045   1. After its entry into force, this Regulation replaces, in respect of the matters referred to therein, in the relations between Member States, the Conventions concluded between two or more Member States, in particular:

   (a) the Convention between Belgium and France on Jurisdiction and the Validity and Enforcement of Judgments, Arbitration Awards and Authentic Instruments, signed at Paris on July 8, 1899;
   (b) the Convention between Belgium and Austria on Bankruptcy, Winding-up, Arrangements, Compositions and Suspension of Payments (with Additional Protocol of June 13, 1973), signed at Brussels on July 16, 1969;
   (c) the Convention between Belgium and the Netherlands on Territorial Jurisdiction, Bankruptcy and the Validity and Enforcement of Judgments, Arbitration Awards and Authentic Instruments, signed at Brussels on March 28, 1925;
   (d) the Treaty between Germany and Austria on Bankruptcy, Winding-up Arrangements and Compositions, signed at Vienna on May 25, 1979;
   (e) the Convention between France and Austria on Jurisdiction, Recognition and Enforcement of Judgments on Bankruptcy, signed at Vienna on February 27, 1979;
   (f) the Convention between France and Italy on the Enforcement of Judgments in Civil and Commercial Matters, signed at Rome on June 3, 1930;
   (g) the Convention between Italy and Austria on Bankruptcy, Winding-up, Arrangements and Compositions, signed at Rome on July 12, 1977;
   (h) the Convention between the Kingdom of the Netherlands and the Federal Republic of Germany on the Mutual Recognition and Enforcement of Judgments and other Enforceable Instruments in Civil and Commercial Matters, signed at The Hague on August 30, 1962;
   (i) the Convention between the United Kingdom and the Kingdom of Belgium providing for the Reciprocal Enforcement of Judgments in Civil and Commercial Matters, with Protocol, signed at Brussels on May 2, 1934;
   (j) the Convention between Denmark, Finland, Norway, Sweden and Iceland on Bankruptcy, signed at Copenhagen on November 7, 1933;
   (k) the European Convention on Certain International Aspects of Bankruptcy, signed at Istanbul on June 5, 1990.

2. The Conventions referred to in paragraph 1 shall continue to have effect with regard to proceedings opened before the entry into force of this Regulation.
3. This Regulation shall not apply:

   (a) in any Member State, to the extent that it is irreconcilable with the obligations arising in relation to bankruptcy from a convention concluded by that State with one or more third countries before the entry into force of this Regulation;
   (b) in the United Kingdom of Great Britain and Northern Ireland, to the extent that is irreconcilable with the obligations arising in relation to bankruptcy and the winding-up of insolvent companies from any arrangements with the Commonwealth existing at the time this Regulation enters into force.

Article 45

Amendment of the Annexes

The Council, acting by qualified majority on the initiatives of one of its members **A4–046**
or on a proposal from the Commission, may amend the Annexes.

Article 46

Reports

No later than June 1, 2012, and every five years thereafter, the Commission shall **A4–047**
present to the European Parliament, the Council and the Economic and Social
Committee a report on the application of this Regulation. The report shall be
accompanied if need be by a proposal for adaptation of this Regulation.

Article 47

Entry into force

This Regulation shall enter into force on May 31, 2002.   **A4–048**

This Regulation shall be binding in its entirety and directly applicable in the
Member States in accordance with the Treaty establishing the European
Community.

Done at Brussels, May 29, 2000.

ANNEX A

Insolvency proceedings referred to in Article 2(a)

A4–049 BELGIË—BELGIQUE

— Het faillissement/La faillite
— Het gerechtelijk akkoord/Le concordat judiciaire
— De collectieve schuldenregeling/Le règlement collectif de dettes

DEUTSCHLAND

— Das Konkursverfahren
— Das gerichtliche Vergleichsverfahren
— Das Gesamtvollstreckungsverfahren
— Das Insolvenzverfahren

ΕΛΛΑΣ

— Πτώχενοη
— Η ειδική εκκαθάριοη
— Η προσωρινή διαχείριοη εταιρίαs. Η διοίκηοη και η διαχείριοη των πιστών
— Η υπαγωγή επιχείρηοηs υπό επίτροπο με οκοπό τη σύναψη σνμβιβασμού με τουs πιστωτέs

ESPAÑA

— Concurso de acreedores
— Quiebra
— Suspensión de pagos

FRANCE

— Liquidation judiciaire
— Redressement judiciare avec nomination d'un administrateur

IRELAND

— Compulsory winding up by the court
— Bankruptcy
— The administration in bankruptcy of the estate of persons dying insolvent
— Winding-up in bankruptcy of partnerships
— Creditors' voluntary winding up (with confirmation of a Court)
— Arrangements under the control of the court which involves the vesting of all or part of the property of the debtor in the Official Assignee for realisation and distribution
— Company examinership

ITALIA

— Fallimento
— Concordato preventivo
— Liquidazione coatta amministrativa
— Amministrazione straordinaria
— Amministrazione controllata

LUXEMBOURG

— Faillite
— Gestion contrôlée
— Concordat préventif de faillite (par abandon d'actif)
— Régime spécial de liquidation du notariat

NEDERLAND

— Het faillissement
— De surséance van betaling
— De schuldsaneringsregeling natuurlijke personen

ÖSTERREICH

— Das Konkursverfahren
— Das Ausgleichsverfahren

PORTUGAL

— O processo de falência
— Os processos especiais de recuperação de empresa, ou seja:
— A concordata
— A reconstituição empresarial
— A reestruturação financeira
— A gestão controlada

SUOMI—FINLAND

— Konkurssi/konkurs
— Yrityssaneeraus/företagssanering

SVERIGE

— Konkurs
— Företagsrekonstruktion

UNITED KINGDOM

— Winding up by or subject to the supervision of the court
— Creditors' voluntary winding up (with confirmation by the court)
— Administration
— Voluntary arrangements under insolvency legislation
— Bankruptcy or sequestration

ANNEX B

Winding up proceedings referred to in Article 2(c)

BELGIË—BELGIQUE

— Het faillissement/La faillite

DEUTSCHLAND

— Das Konkursverfahren
— Das Gesamtvollstreckungsverfahren
— Das Insolvenzverfahren

ΕΛΛΑΣ

— Πτώχευοη
— Η ειδική εκκαθάριοη

ESPAÑA

— Concurso de acreedores
— Quiebra
— Suspensión de pagos basada en la insolvencia definitiva

FRANCE

— Liquidation judiciaire

IRELAND

— Compulsory winding up
— Bankruptcy
— The administration in bankruptcy of the estate of persons dying insolvent
— Winding up in bankruptcy of partnerships
— Creditors' voluntary winding up (with confirmation of a court)
— Arrangements under the control of the court which involve the vesting of all or part of the property of the debtor in the Official Assignee for realisation and distribution

ITALIA **A4–50**

— Fallimento
— Liquidazione coatta amministrativa

LUXEMBOURG

— Faillite
— Régime spécial de liquidation du notariat

NEDERLAND

— Het faillissement
— De schuldsaneringsregeling natuurlijke personen

ÖSTERREICH

— Das Konkursverfahren

PORTUGAL

— O processo de falência

SUOMI—FINLAND

— Konkurssi/konkurs

SVERIGE

— Konkurs

UNITED KINGDOM

— Winding up by or subject to the supervision of the court
— Creditors' voluntary winding up (with confirmation by the court)
— Bankruptcy or sequestration

ANNEX C

Liquidators referred to in Article 2(b)

A4–051 BELGIË—BELGIQUE

— De curator/Le curateur
— De commissaris inzake opschorting/Le commissaire au sursis
— De schuldbemiddelaar/Le médiateur de dettes

DEUTSCHLAND

— Konkursverwalter
— Vergleichsverwalter
— Sachwalter (nach der Vergleichsordnung)
— Verwalter
— Insolvenzverwalter
— Sachwalter (nach der Insolvenzordnung)
— Treuhänder
— Vorläufiger Insolvenzverwalter

ΕΛΛΑΣ

— Ο σύνδικο
— Ο προσωριὀς διαχειριστής. Η διοικούσα επιτροπή των πιστωτών
— Ο ειδικός εκκαθαραριοτής
— Ο επίτροπος

ESPAÑA

— Depositario-administrador
— Interventor o Interventores
— Síndicos
— Comisario

FRANCE

— Représentant des créanciers
— Mandataire liquidateur
— Administrateur judiciaire
— Commissaire à l'exécution de plan

IRELAND

— Liquidator
— Official Assignee
— Trustee in bankruptcy
— Provisional Liquidator
— Examiner

ITALIA

— Curatore
— Commissario

LUXEMBOURG

— Le curateur
— Le commissaire
— Le liquidateur
— Le conseil de gérance de la section d'assainissement du notariat

NEDERLAND

— De curator in het faillissement
— De bewindvoerder in de surséance van betaling
— De bewindvoerder in de schuldsangeringsregeling natuurlijke personen

ÖSTERREICH

— Masseverwalter
— Ausgleichsverwalter
— Sachwalter
— Truehänder
— Besondere Verwalter
— Vorläufiger Verwalter
— Konkursgericht

PORTUGAL

— Gestor judicial
— Liquidatário judicial
— Comissão de credores

SUOMI—FINLAND

— Pesänhoitaja/boförvaltare
— Selvittäjä/utredare

SVERIGE

— Förvaltare
— God man
— Rekonstruktör

UNITED KINGDOM

— Liquidator
— Supervisor of a voluntary arrangement
— Administrator
— Official Receiver
— Trustee
— Judicial factor

APPENDIX 5 — UNCITRAL MODEL LAW ON CROSS-BORDER INSOLVENCY

PREAMBLE

The purpose of this Law is to provide effective mechanisms for dealing with cases of cross-border insolvency so as to promote the objectives of:

(*a*) Co-operation between the courts and other competent authorities of this State and foreign States involved in cases of cross-border insolvency;

(*b*) Greater legal certainty for trade and investment;

(*c*) Fair and efficient administration of cross-border insolvencies that protects the interests of all creditors and other interested persons, including the debtor;

(*d*) Protection and maximization of the value of the debtor's assets; and

(*e*) Facilitation of the rescue of financially troubled businesses, thereby protecting investment and preserving employment.

CHAPTER I

GENERAL PROVISIONS

Article 1. Scope of application

1. This Law applies where: **A5–001**

(*a*) Assistance is sought in this State by a foreign court or a foreign representative in connection with a foreign proceeding; or

(*b*) Assistance is sought in a foreign State in connection with a proceeding under *[identify laws of the enacting State relating to insolvency];* or

(*c*) A foreign proceeding and a proceeding under *[identify laws of the enacting State relating to insolvency]* in respect of the same debtor are taking place concurrently; or

(*d*) Creditors or other interested persons in a foreign State have an interest in requesting the commencement of, or participating in, a proceeding under *[identify laws of the enacting State relating to insolvency];*

2. This Law does not apply to a proceeding concerning *[designate any types of entities, such as banks or insurance companies, that are subject to a special insolvency regime in this State and that this State wishes to exclude from this Law].*

Article 2. Definitions

For the purposes of this Law: **A5–002**

(*a*) "Foreign proceeding" means a collective judicial or administrative proceeding in a foreign State, including an interim proceeding, pursuant to a law relating to insolvency in which proceeding the assets and affairs of the debtor are subject to control or supervision by a foreign court, for the purpose of reorganization or liquidation;

(*b*) "Foreign main proceeding" means a foreign proceeding taking place in the State where the debtor has the centre of its main interests;

(*c*) "Foreign non-main proceeding" means a foreign proceeding, other than a foreign main proceeding, taking place in a State where the debtor has an establishment within the meaning of subparagraph (*f*) of this article;

(*d*) "Foreign representative" means a person or body, including one appointed on an interim basis, authorized in a foreign proceeding to administer the reorganization or the liquidation of the debtor's assets or affairs or to act as a representative of the foreign proceeding;

(*e*) "Foreign court" means a judicial or other authority competent to control or supervise a foreign proceeding;

(*f*) "Establishment" means any place of operations where the debtor carries out a non-transitory economic activity with human means and goods or services.

Article 3. International obligations of this State

A5–003 To the extent that this Law conflicts with an obligation of this State arising out of any treaty or other form of agreement to which it is a party with one or more other States, the requirements of the treaty or agreement prevail.

Article 4. Competent court or authority

A5–004 The functions referred to in this Law relating to recognition of foreign proceedings and cooperation with foreign courts shall be performed by *[specify the court, courts, authority or authorities competent to perform those functions in the enacting State]*.

Article 5. Authorization of *[insert the title of the person or body administering reorganization or liquidation under the law of the enacting State]* to act in a foreign State

A5–005 A *[insert the title of the person or body administering a reorganization or liquidation under the law of the enacting State]* is authorized to act in a foreign State on behalf of a proceeding under *[identify laws of the enacting State relating to insolvency]*, as permitted by the applicable foreign law.

Article 6. Public policy exception

A5–006 Nothing in this Law prevents the court from refusing to take an action governed by this Law if the action would be manifestly contrary to the public policy of this State.

Article 7. Additional assistance under other laws

A5–007 Nothing in this Law limits the power of a court or a *[insert the title of the person or body administering a reorganization or liquidation under the law of the enacting State]* to provide additional assistance to a foreign representative under other laws of this State.

Article 8. Interpretation

A5–008 In the interpretation of this Law, regard is to be had to its international origin and to the need to promote uniformity in its application and the observance of good faith.

CHAPTER II

ACCESS OF FOREIGN REPRESENTATIVES AND CREDITORS TO COURTS IN THIS
STATE

Article 9. Right of direct access

A foreign representative is entitled to apply directly to a court in this State.   **A5–009**

Article 10. Limited jurisdiction

The sole fact that an application pursuant to this Law is made to a court in this **A5–010** State by a foreign representative does not subject the foreign representative or the foreign assets and affairs of the debtor to the jurisdiction of the courts of this State for any purpose other than the application.

Article 11. Application by a foreign representative to commence a proceeding under *[identify laws of the enacting State relating to insolvency]*

A foreign representative is entitled to apply to commence a proceeding under **A5–011** *[identify laws of the enacting State relating to insolvency]* if the conditions for commencing such a proceeding are otherwise met.

Article 12. Participation of a foreign representative in a proceeding under *[identify laws of the enacting State relating to insolvency]*

Upon recognition of a foreign proceeding, the foreign representative is entitled **A5–012** to participate in a proceeding regarding the debtor under *[identify laws of the enacting State relating to insolvency]*.

Article 13. Access of foreign creditors to a proceeding under *[identify laws of the enacting State relating to insolvency]*

1. Subject to paragraph 2 of this article, foreign creditors have the same rights **A5–013** regarding the commencement of, and participation in, a proceeding under *[identify laws of the enacting State relating to insolvency]* as creditors in this State.
    2. Paragraph 1 of this article does not affect the ranking of claims in a proceeding under *[identify laws of the enacting State relating to insolvency]*, except that the claims of foreign creditors shall not be ranked lower than *[identify the class of general non-preference claims, while providing that a foreign claim is to be ranked lower than the general non-preference claims if an equivalent local claim (e.g. claim for a penalty or deferred-payment claim) has a rank lower than the general non-preference claims]*.

Article 14. Notification to foreign creditors of a proceeding under *[identify laws of the enacting State relating to insolvency]*

1. Whenever under *[identify laws of the enacting State relating to insolvency]* **A5–014** notification is to be given to creditors in this State, such notification shall also be given to the known creditors that do not have addresses in this State. The court may order that appropriate steps be taken with a view to notifying any creditor whose address is not yet known.
    2. Such notification shall be made to the foreign creditors individually, unless the court considers that, under the circumstances, some other form of notification would be more appropriate. No letters rogatory or other, similar formality is required.
    3. When a notification of commencement of a proceeding is to be given to foreign creditors, the notification shall:

(a) Indicate a reasonable time period for filing claims and specify the place for their filing;

(b) Indicate whether secured creditors need to file their secured claims; and

(c) Contain any other information required to be included in such a notification to creditors pursuant to the law of this State and the orders of the court.

CHAPTER III

RECOGNITION OF A FOREIGN PROCEEDING AND RELIEF

Article 15. Application for recognition of a foreign proceeding

A5–015 1. A foreign representative may apply to the court for recognition of the foreign proceeding in which the foreign representative has been appointed.

2. An application for recognition shall be accompanied by:

(a) A certified copy of the decision commencing the foreign proceeding and appointing the foreign representative; or

(b) A certificate from the foreign court affirming the existence of the foreign proceeding and of the appointment of the foreign representative; or

(c) In the absence of evidence referred to in subparagraphs (a) and (b), any other evidence acceptable to the court of the existence of the foreign proceeding and of the appointment of the foreign representative.

3. An application for recognition shall also be accompanied by a statement identifying all foreign proceedings in respect of the debtor that are known to the foreign representative.

4. The court may require a translation of documents supplied in support of the application for recognition into an official language of this State.

Article 16. Presumptions concerning recognition

A5–016 1. If the decision or certificate referred to in paragraph 2 of article 15 indicates that the foreign proceeding is a proceeding within the meaning of subparagraph (a) of article 2 and that the foreign representative is a person or body within the meaning of subparagraph (d) of article 2, the court is entitled to so presume.

2. The court is entitled to presume that documents submitted in support of the application for recognition are authentic, whether or not they have been legalized.

3. In the absence of proof to the contrary, the debtor's registered office, or habitual residence in the case of an individual, is presumed to be the centre of the debtor's main interests.

Article 17. Decision to recognize a foreign proceeding

A5–017 1. Subject to article 6, a foreign proceeding shall be recognized if:

(a) The foreign proceeding is a proceeding within the meaning of subparagraph (a) of article 2;

(b) The foreign representative applying for recognition is a person or body within the meaning of subparagraph (d) of article 2;

(c) The application meets the requirements of paragraph 2 of article 15; and (*d*) The application has been submitted to the court referred to in article 4.

2. The foreign proceeding shall be recognized:

(*a*) As a foreign main proceeding if it is taking place in the State where the debtor has the centre of its main interests; or

(*b*) As a foreign non-main proceeding if the debtor has an establishment within the meaning of subparagraph (*f*) of article 2 in the foreign State.

3. An application for recognition of a foreign proceeding shall be decided upon at the earliest possible time.

4. The provisions of articles 15, 16, 17 and 18 do not prevent modification or termination of recognition if it is shown that the grounds for granting it were fully or partially lacking or have ceased to exist.

Article 18. Subsequent information

From the time of filing the application for recognition of the foreign proceeding, **A5–018** the foreign representative shall inform the court promptly of:

(*a*) Any substantial change in the status of the recognized foreign proceeding or the status of the foreign representative's appointment; and

(*b*) Any other foreign proceeding regarding the same debtor that becomes known to the foreign representative.

Article 19. Relief that may be granted upon application for recognition of a foreign proceeding

1. From the time of filing an application for recognition until the application is **A5–019** decided upon, the court may, at the request of the foreign representative, where relief is urgently needed to protect the assets of the debtor or the interests of the creditors, grant relief of a provisional nature, including:

(*a*) Staying execution against the debtor's assets;

(*b*) Entrusting the administration or realization of all or part of the debtor's assets located in this State to the foreign representative or another person designated by the court, in order to protect and preserve the value of assets that, by their nature or because of other circumstances, are perishable, susceptible to devaluation or otherwise in jeopardy;

(*c*) Any relief mentioned in paragraph 1(*c*), (*d*) and (*g*) of article 21.

2. *[Insert provisions (or refer to provisions in force in the enacting State) relating to notice.]*

3. Unless extended under paragraph 1 (*f*) of article 21, the relief granted under this article terminates when the application for recognition is decided upon.

4. The court may refuse to grant relief under this article if such relief would interfere with the administration of a foreign main proceeding.

Article 20. Effects of recognition of a foreign main proceeding

1. Upon recognition of a foreign proceeding that is a foreign main proceeding, **A5–020**

(*a*) Commencement or continuation of individual actions or individual proceedings concerning the debtor's assets, rights, obligations or liabilities is stayed;

(*b*) Execution against the debtor's assets is stayed; and

(*c*) The right to transfer, encumber or otherwise dispose of any assets of the debtor is suspended.

2. The scope, and the modification or termination, of the stay and suspension referred to in paragraph 1 of this article are subject to *[refer to any provisions of law of the enacting State relating to insolvency that apply to exceptions, limitations, modifications or termination in respect of the stay and suspension referred to in paragraph 1 of this article].*

3. Paragraph 1(*a*) of this article does not affect the right to commence individual actions or proceedings to the extent necessary to preserve a claim against the debtor.

4. Paragraph 1 of this article does not affect the right to request the commencement of a proceeding under *[identify laws of the enacting State relating to insolvency]* or the right to file claims in such a proceeding.

Article 21. Relief that may be granted upon recognition of a foreign proceeding

A5–021   1. Upon recognition of a foreign proceeding, whether main or non-main, where necessary to protect the assets of the debtor or the interests of the creditors, the court may, at the request of the foreign representative, grant any appropriate relief, including:

> (*a*) Staying the commencement or continuation of individual actions or individual proceedings concerning the debtor's assets, rights, obligations or liabilities, to the extent they have not been stayed under paragraph 1(*a*) of article 20;
>
> (*b*) Staying execution against the debtor's assets to the extent it has not been stayed under paragraph 1(*b*) of article 20;
>
> (*c*) Suspending the right to transfer, encumber or otherwise dispose of any assets of the debtor to the extent this right has not been suspended under paragraph 1(*c*) of article 20;
>
> (*d*) Providing for the examination of witnesses, the taking of evidence or the delivery of information concerning the debtor's assets, affairs, rights, obligations or liabilities;
>
> (*e*) Entrusting the administration or realization of all or part of the debtor's assets located in this State to the foreign representative or another person designated by the court;
>
> (*f*) Extending relief granted under paragraph 1 of article 19;
>
> (*g*) Granting any additional relief that may be available to *[insert the title of a person or body administering a reorganization or liquidation under the law of the enacting State]* under the laws of this State.

2. Upon recognition of a foreign proceeding, whether main or non-main, the court may, at the request of the foreign representative, entrust the distribution of all or part of the debtor's assets located in this State to the foreign representative or another person designated by the court, provided that the court is satisfied that the interests of creditors in this State are adequately protected.

3. In granting relief under this article to a representative of a foreign non-main proceeding, the court must be satisfied that the relief relates to assets that, under the law of this State, should be administered in the foreign non-main proceeding or concerns information required in that proceeding.

Article 22. Protection of creditors and other interested persons

A5–022   1. In granting or denying relief under article 19 or 21, or in modifying or terminating relief under paragraph 3 of this article, the court must be satisfied that the interests of the creditors and other interested persons, including the debtor, are adequately protected.

2. The court may subject relief granted under article 19 or 21 to conditions it considers appropriate.

3. The court may, at the request of the foreign representative or a person affected by relief granted under article 19 or 21, or at its own motion, modify or terminate such relief.

Article 23. Actions to avoid acts detrimental to creditors

1. Upon recognition of a foreign proceeding, the foreign representative has **A5–023** standing to initiate *[refer to the types of actions to avoid or otherwise render ineffective acts detrimental to creditors that are available in this State to a person or body administering a reorganization or liquidation]*.

2. When the foreign proceeding is a foreign non-main proceeding, the court must be satisfied that the action relates to assets that, under the law of this State, should be administered in the foreign non-main proceeding.

Article 24. Intervention by a foreign representative in proceedings in this State

Upon recognition of a foreign proceeding, the foreign representative may, **A5–024** provided the requirements of the law of this State are met, intervene in any proceedings in which the debtor is a party.

CHAPTER IV

CO-OPERATION WITH FOREIGN COURTS AND FOREIGN REPRESENTATIVES

Article 25. Cooperation and direct communication between a court of this State and foreign courts or foreign representatives

1. In matters referred to in article 1, the court shall cooperate to the maximum **A5–025** extent possible with foreign courts or foreign representatives, either directly or through a *[insert the title of a person or body administering a reorganization or liquidation under the law of the enacting State]*.

2. The court is entitled to communicate directly with, or to request information or assistance directly from, foreign courts or foreign representatives.

Article 26. Co-operation and direct communication between the *[insert the title of a person or body administering a reorganization or liquidation under the law of the enacting State]* and foreign courts or foreign representatives

1. In matters referred to in article 1, a *[insert the title of a person or body* **A5–026** *administering a reorganization or liquidation under the law of the enacting State]* shall, in the exercise of its functions and subject to the supervision of the court, cooperate to the maximum extent possible with foreign courts or foreign representatives.

2. The *[insert the title of a person or body administering a reorganization or liquidation under the law of the enacting State]* is entitled, in the exercise of its functions and subject to the supervision of the court, to communicate directly with foreign courts or foreign representatives.

Article 27. Forms of co-operation

Co-operation referred to in articles 25 and 26 may be implemented by any **A5–027** appropriate means, including:

(*a*) Appointment of a person or body to act at the direction of the court;

(*b*) Communication of information by any means considered appropriate by the court;

(*c*) Co-ordination of the administration and supervision of the debtor's assets and affairs;

(*d*) Approval or implementation by courts of agreements concerning the coordination of proceedings;

(*e*) Co-ordination of concurrent proceedings regarding the same debtor;

(*f*) *[The enacting State may wish to list additional forms or examples of co-operation].*

CHAPTER V

CONCURRENT PROCEEDINGS

Article 28. Commencement of a proceeding under *[identify laws of the enacting State relating to insolvency]* **after recognition of a foreign main proceeding**

A5–028 After recognition of a foreign main proceeding, a proceeding under *[identify laws of the enacting State relating to insolvency]* may be commenced only if the debtor has assets in this State; the effects of that proceeding shall be restricted to the assets of the debtor that are located in this State and, to the extent necessary to implement cooperation and coordination under articles 25, 26 and 27, to other assets of the debtor that, under the law of this State, should be administered in that proceeding.

Article 29. Co-ordination of a proceeding under *[identify laws of the enacting State relating to insolvency]* **and a foreign proceeding**

A5–029 Where a foreign proceeding and a proceeding under *[identify laws of the enacting State relating to insolvency]* are taking place concurrently regarding the same debtor, the court shall seek co-operation and coordination under articles 25, 26 and 27, and the following shall apply:

(*a*) When the proceeding in this State is taking place at the time the application for recognition of the foreign proceeding is filed,

　(i) Any relief granted under article 19 or 21 must be consistent with the proceeding in this State; and

　(ii) If the foreign proceeding is recognized in this State as a foreign main proceeding, article 20 does not apply;

(*b*) When the proceeding in this State commences after recognition, or after the filing of the application for recognition, of the foreign proceeding,

　(i) Any relief in effect under article 19 or 21 shall be reviewed by the court and shall be modified or terminated if inconsistent with the proceeding in this State; and

　(ii) If the foreign proceeding is a foreign main proceeding, the stay and suspension referred to in paragraph 1 of article 20 shall be modified or terminated pursuant to paragraph 2 of article 20 if inconsistent with the proceeding in this State;

(*c*) In granting, extending or modifying relief granted to a representative of a foreign non-main proceeding, the court must be satisfied that the relief relates to assets that, under the law of this State, should be administered in the foreign non-main proceeding or concerns information required in that proceeding.

Article 30. Coordination of more than one foreign proceeding

In matters referred to in article 1, in respect of more than one foreign **A5–030**
proceeding regarding the same debtor, the court shall seek cooperation and
coordination under articles 25, 26 and 27, and the following shall apply:

(a) Any relief granted under article 19 or 21 to a representative of a
foreign non-main proceeding after recognition of a foreign main
proceeding must be consistent with the foreign main proceeding;

(b) If a foreign main proceeding is recognized after recognition, or after
the filing of an application for recognition, of a foreign non-main
proceeding, any relief in effect under article 19 or 21 shall be reviewed
by the court and shall be modified or terminated if inconsistent with the
foreign main proceeding;

(c) If, after recognition of a foreign non-main proceeding, another foreign
non-main proceeding is recognized, the court shall grant, modify or
terminate relief for the purpose of facilitating coordination of the
proceedings.

**Article 31. Presumption of insolvency based on recognition of a foreign main
proceeding**

In the absence of evidence to the contrary, recognition of a foreign main **A5–031**
proceeding is, for the purpose of commencing a proceeding under *[identify laws
of the enacting State relating to insolvency]*, proof that the debtor is insolvent.

Article 32. Rule of payment in concurrent proceedings

Without prejudice to secured claims or rights *in rem*, a creditor who has received **A5–032**
part payment in respect of its claim in a proceeding pursuant to a law relating to
insolvency in a foreign State may not receive a payment for the same claim in a
proceeding under *[identify laws of the enacting State relating to insolvency]*
regarding the same debtor, so long as the payment to the other creditors of the
same class is proportionately less than the payment the creditor has already
received.

INDEX

639